S0-AAE-194

POCKET
Webster's
Thesaurus

William Collins' dream of knowledge for all began with the publication of his first book in 1819. A self-educated mill worker, he not only enriched millions of lives, but also founded a flourishing publishing house. Today, staying true to this spirit, Collins books are packed with inspiration, innovation, and practical expertise. They place you at the centre of a world of possibility and give you exactly what you need to explore it.

Language is the key to this exploration, and at the heart of Collins Dictionaries is language as it is really used. New words, phrases, and meanings spring up every day, and all of them are captured and analysed by the Collins Word Web. Constantly updated, and with over 2.5 billion entries, this living language resource is unique to our dictionaries.

Words are tools for life. And a Collins Dictionary makes them work for you.

Collins. Do more

POCKET
Webster's
Thesaurus

Collins

Second Edition 2007

© HarperCollins Publishers 2002, 2007

HarperCollins Publishers
Westerhill Road
Bishopbriggs
Glasgow
G64 2QT

HarperCollins Publishers Inc
10 East 53rd Street, New York, NY 10022

www.harpercollins.com

Collins and HarperResource are
imprints of HarperCollins Publishers

ISBN 978-0-06-114204-8

Library of Congress Cataloging-in-
Publication Data has been applied for

HarperCollins books may be purchased
for educational, business, or sales
promotional use. For information,
please write to:
Special Markets Department,
HarperCollins Publishers Inc, 10 East
53rd Street, New York, NY 10022

www.harpercollins.com

Designed by Mark Thomson

Typeset by Wordcraft Ltd, Glasgow

Printed and bound in Italy by
Rotolito Lombarda S.P.A.

Acknowledgements
We would like to thank those
authors and publishers who kindly
gave permission for copyright
material to be used in the Collins
Word Web. We would also like to
thank Times Newspapers Ltd for
providing valuable data.

CONTENTS

vi
Editorial Staff

vii
About the Type

viii
Foreword

ix-x
Using this Thesaurus

xi
Abbreviations Used in this Thesaurus

1-628
Collins Thesaurus A-Z

This thesaurus is typeset in CollinsFedra, a special version of the Fedra family of types designed by Peter Bil'ak. CollinsFedra has been customized especially for Collins dictionaries; it includes both sans serif and serif versions, in several different weights. Its relatively large x-height and open 'eye', and its basis in the tradition of humanist letterforms, make CollinsFedra both familiar and easy to read at small sizes. It has been designed to use the minimum space without sacrificing legibility, as well as including a number of characters and signs that are specific to dictionary typography. Its companion phonetic type is the first of its kind to be drawn according to the same principles as the regular typeface, rather than assembled from rotated and reflected characters from other types.

Peter Bil'ak (b. 1973, Slovakia) is a graphic and type designer living in the Netherlands. He is the author of two books, *Illegibility* and *Transparency*. As well as the Fedra family, he has designed several other typefaces including Eureka. His typotheque.com website has become a focal point for research and debate around contemporary type design.

FOREWORD

The American edition of the Collins Pocket Thesaurus, which was first published in 1990, has proved to be an immensely popular language resource. It allows you to look up a word and find a useful selection of alternatives that can replace it. It is, therefore, tremendously helpful when you are trying to find different ways of expressing yourself, as well as being an invaluable aid for crosswords and puzzles.

Collins thesauruses are designed to give the user as much help as possible in finding the right word for any occasion. Because the Pocket Thesaurus has its main entry words arranged in A-Z form, you can go straight to the word you want without having to resort to an index, just as if you were looking it up in a dictionary. In this new edition, the number of main entry words has been increased, giving you an even greater chance of finding the word you want. At the same time, the list of alternative words (synonyms) for each main entry has been reviewed so that the most helpful alternatives are included in each case. The new edition also takes account of recent changes in the language, with terms like blog, high-maintenance, alpha male, cutting edge, and supersize being found among the synonyms.

This new edition further demonstrates Collins' commitment to helping the user. As part of an innovative design, key synonyms have been put in capital letters and placed first in each list. This layout enables you to see at once which sense of the word is being referred to, which is particularly helpful when a main entry word has a number of different senses. It also gives you an idea of which synonym is the closest alternative to the word you have looked up.

These innovations mean that the American edition of the Collins Pocket Thesaurus continues to provide the user with a treasury of useful words arranged in the most helpful format possible.

USING THIS THESAURUS

Main Entry Words   printed in large bold type, eg

abbey

All main entry words, including abbreviations and combining forms, in one alphabetical sequence, eg

abject
ablaze
able

Variant spellings   shown in full, eg

amok, amuck

Parts of Speech   shown in their full form in italics, eg

ablaze *adjective*

When a word can be used as more than one part of speech, the change of part of speech is shown after a black arrow, eg

mock *verb* 1 LAUGH AT, deride, jeer ...
▶ *adjective* 3 IMITATION ...

Parts of speech may be combined for some words, eg

bat *noun* or *verb* HIT, bang, smack ...

Sense Numbers   shown in bold type, eg

mock *verb* **1** LAUGH AT, deride, jeer ...

Key Synonyms   shown in small capitals, eg

mock ... LAUGH AT

Cross References   shown in small capitals and bold type, eg

amuck *see* AMOK

Synonyms   separated by commas, eg

mock *verb* **1** LAUGH AT, deride, jeer, make fun of, poke fun at, ridicule, scoff ...

Phrases and Idioms included in entry, eg

amok, amuck *adverb* as in **run amok**

ABBREVIATIONS USED IN THIS THESAURUS

Brit	British
US	United States

abandon *verb* 1 LEAVE, desert, forsake, strand
2 GIVE UP, relinquish, surrender, yield
▶ *noun* 3 WILDNESS, recklessness

abandonment *noun* LEAVING, dereliction, desertion, forsaking

abashed *adjective* EMBARRASSED, ashamed, chagrined, disconcerted, dismayed, humiliated, mortified, shamefaced, taken aback

abate *verb* DECREASE, decline, diminish, dwindle, fade, lessen, let up, moderate, relax, slacken, subside, weaken

abbey *noun* MONASTERY, convent, friary, nunnery, priory

abbreviate *verb* SHORTEN, abridge, compress, condense, contract, cut, reduce, summarize

abbreviation *noun* SHORTENING, abridgment, contraction, reduction, summary, synopsis

abdicate *verb* GIVE UP, abandon, quit, relinquish, renounce, resign, step down (*informal*)

abdication *noun* GIVING UP, abandonment, quitting, renunciation, resignation, retirement, surrender

abduct *verb* KIDNAP, carry off, seize, snatch (*slang*)

abduction *noun* KIDNAPING, carrying off, seizure

aberration *noun* ODDITY, abnormality, anomaly, defect, irregularity, lapse, peculiarity, quirk

abet *verb* HELP, aid, assist, connive at, support

abeyance *noun* ▷▷ **in abeyance** SHELVED, hanging fire, on ice (*informal*), pending, suspended

abhor *verb* HATE, abominate, detest, loathe, shrink from, shudder at

abhorrent *adjective* HATEFUL, abominable, disgusting, distasteful, hated, horrid, loathsome, offensive, repulsive, scuzzy (*slang*)

abide *verb* TOLERATE, accept, bear, endure, put up with, stand, suffer

abide by *verb* OBEY, agree to, comply with, conform to, follow, observe, submit to

abiding *adjective* EVERLASTING, continuing, enduring, lasting, permanent, persistent, unchanging

ability *noun* SKILL, aptitude, capability, competence, expertise, proficiency, talent

abject *adjective* 1 MISERABLE, deplorable, forlorn, hopeless, pitiable, wretched
2 SERVILE, cringing, degraded, fawning, grovelling, submissive

ablaze *adjective* ON FIRE, aflame, alight, blazing, burning, fiery, flaming, ignited, lighted

able *adjective* CAPABLE, accomplished, competent, efficient, proficient, qualified, skillful

able-bodied *adjective* STRONG, fit, healthy, robust, sound, sturdy

abnormal *adjective* UNUSUAL, atypical, exceptional, extraordinary, irregular, odd, peculiar, strange, uncommon

abnormality *noun* ODDITY, deformity, exception, irregularity, peculiarity, singularity, strangeness

abode *noun* HOME, domicile, dwelling, habitat, habitation, house, lodging, pad (*slang, dated*), quarters, residence

abolish *verb* DO AWAY WITH, annul, cancel, destroy, eliminate, end, eradicate, put an end to, quash, rescind, revoke, stamp out

abolition *noun* ENDING, cancellation, destruction, elimination, end, extermination, termination, wiping out

abominable *adjective* TERRIBLE, despicable, detestable, disgusting, hateful, horrible, horrid, lousy (*slang*), repulsive, revolting, scuzzy (*slang*), vile

abort *verb* 1 TERMINATE (*a pregnancy*), miscarry
2 STOP, arrest, ax (*informal*), call off, check, end, fail, halt, terminate

abortion *noun* TERMINATION, deliberate miscarriage, miscarriage

abortive *adjective* FAILED, fruitless, futile, ineffectual, miscarried, unsuccessful, useless, vain

abound *verb* BE PLENTIFUL, flourish, proliferate, swarm, swell, teem, thrive

abounding *adjective* PLENTIFUL, abundant, bountiful, copious, full, profuse, prolific, rich

about *preposition* 1 REGARDING, as regards, concerning, dealing with, on, referring to, relating to
2 NEAR, adjacent to, beside, circa (*used with dates*), close to, nearby
▶ *adverb* 3 NEARLY, almost, approaching, approximately, around, close to, more or less, roughly

above *preposition* OVER, beyond, exceeding, higher than, on top of, upon

above board *adjective* HONEST, fair, genuine, legitimate, square, straight

abrasion *noun* (*medical*) GRAZE, chafe, scrape, scratch, scuff, surface injury

abrasive *adjective* 1 UNPLEASANT, caustic, cutting, galling, grating, irritating, rough, sharp
2 ROUGH, chafing, grating, scraping, scratchy

abreast *adjective* 1 ALONGSIDE, beside, side by side
2 ▷▷ **abreast of** INFORMED ABOUT, acquainted with, *au courant* with, *au fait* with, conversant with, familiar with, in the picture about, in touch with, keeping one's finger on the pulse of, knowledgeable about, up to date with, up to speed with

abridge *verb* SHORTEN, abbreviate, condense, cut, decrease, reduce, summarize

abroad *adverb* OVERSEAS, in foreign lands, out of the country

abrupt *adjective* 1 SUDDEN, precipitate, quick, surprising, unexpected
2 CURT, brusque, gruff, impatient, rude, short, terse

abscond *verb* FLEE, clear out, disappear, escape, make off, run off, steal away

absence *noun* 1 NONATTENDANCE, absenteeism, truancy

2 LACK, deficiency, need, omission, unavailability, want

absent *adjective* **1** MISSING, away, elsewhere, gone, nonexistent, out, unavailable
2 ABSENT-MINDED, blank, distracted, inattentive, oblivious, preoccupied, vacant, vague
▸ *verb* **3** ▷▷ **absent oneself** STAY AWAY, keep away, play truant, withdraw

absent-minded *adjective* VAGUE, distracted, dreaming, forgetful, inattentive, preoccupied, unaware

absolute *adjective* **1** TOTAL, complete, outright, perfect, pure, sheer, thorough, utter
2 SUPREME, full, sovereign, unbounded, unconditional, unlimited, unrestricted

absolutely *adverb* TOTALLY, completely, entirely, fully, one hundred per cent, perfectly, utterly, wholly

absolution *noun* FORGIVENESS, deliverance, exculpation, exoneration, mercy, pardon, release

absolve *verb* FORGIVE, deliver, exculpate, excuse, let off, pardon, release, set free

absorb *verb* **1** SOAK UP, consume, digest, imbibe, incorporate, receive, suck up, take in
2 PREOCCUPY, captivate, engage, engross, fascinate, rivet

absorbed *adjective* **1** PREOCCUPIED, captivated, engrossed, fascinated, immersed, involved, lost, rapt, riveted, wrapped up
2 DIGESTED, assimilated, incorporated, received, soaked up

absorbent *adjective* PERMEABLE, porous, receptive, spongy

absorbing *adjective* FASCINATING, captivating, engrossing, gripping, interesting, intriguing, riveting, spellbinding

absorption *noun* **1** SOAKING UP, assimilation, consumption, digestion, incorporation, sucking up
2 CONCENTRATION, fascination, immersion, intentness, involvement, preoccupation

abstain *verb* REFRAIN, avoid, decline, deny (oneself), desist, fast, forbear, forgo, give up, keep from

abstemious *adjective* SELF-DENYING, ascetic, austere, frugal, moderate, sober, temperate

abstention *noun* REFUSAL, abstaining, abstinence, avoidance, forbearance, refraining, self-control, self-denial, self-restraint

abstinence *noun* SELF-DENIAL, abstemiousness, avoidance, forbearance, moderation, self-restraint, soberness, teetotalism, temperance

abstinent *adjective* SELF-DENYING, abstaining, abstemious, forbearing, moderate, self-controlled, sober, temperate

abstract *adjective* **1** THEORETICAL, abstruse, general, hypothetical, indefinite, notional, recondite
▸ *noun* **2** SUMMARY, abridgment, digest, epitome, outline, précis, résumé, synopsis
▸ *verb* **3** SUMMARIZE, abbreviate, abridge, condense, digest, epitomize, outline, précis, shorten
4 REMOVE, detach, extract, isolate, separate, take away, take out, withdraw

abstraction *noun* **1** IDEA, concept, formula, generalization, hypothesis, notion, theorem, theory, thought

2 ABSENT-MINDEDNESS, absence, dreaminess, inattention, pensiveness, preoccupation, remoteness, woolgathering

abstruse *adjective* OBSCURE, arcane, complex, deep, enigmatic, esoteric, recondite, unfathomable, vague

absurd *adjective* RIDICULOUS, crazy (*informal*), farcical, foolish, idiotic, illogical, inane, incongruous, irrational, ludicrous, nonsensical, preposterous, senseless, silly, stupid, unreasonable

absurdity *noun* RIDICULOUSNESS, farce, folly, foolishness, incongruity, joke, nonsense, silliness, stupidity

abundance *noun* PLENTY, affluence, bounty, copiousness, exuberance, fullness, profusion

abundant *adjective* PLENTIFUL, ample, bountiful, copious, exuberant, filled, full, luxuriant, profuse, rich, teeming

abuse *noun* **1** ILL-TREATMENT, damage, exploitation, harm, hurt, injury, maltreatment, manhandling

2 INSULTS, blame, castigation, censure, defamation, derision, disparagement, invective, reproach, scolding, vilification

3 MISUSE, misapplication

▶ *verb* **4** ILL-TREAT, damage, exploit, harm, hurt, injure, maltreat, misuse, take advantage of

5 INSULT, castigate, curse, defame, disparage, malign, scold, vilify

abusive *adjective* **1** INSULTING, censorious, defamatory, disparaging, libelous, offensive, reproachful, rude, scathing

2 HARMFUL, brutal, cruel,

destructive, hurtful, injurious, rough

abysmal *adjective* TERRIBLE, appalling, awful, bad, dire, dreadful

abyss *noun* PIT, chasm, crevasse, fissure, gorge, gulf, void

academic *adjective* **1** SCHOLARLY, bookish, erudite, highbrow, learned, literary, studious

2 HYPOTHETICAL, abstract, conjectural, impractical, notional, speculative, theoretical

▶ *noun* **3** SCHOLAR, academician, don, fellow, lecturer, master, professor, tutor

accede *verb* **1** AGREE, accept, acquiesce, admit, assent, comply, concede, concur, consent, endorse, grant

2 INHERIT, assume, attain, come to, enter upon, succeed, succeed (*as heir*)

accelerate *verb* SPEED UP, advance, expedite, further, hasten, hurry, quicken

acceleration *noun* SPEEDING UP, hastening, hurrying, quickening, stepping up (*informal*)

accent *noun* **1** PRONUNCIATION, articulation, brogue, enunciation, inflection, intonation, modulation, tone

2 EMPHASIS, beat, cadence, force, pitch, rhythm, stress, timbre

▶ *verb* **3** EMPHASIZE, accentuate, stress, underline, underscore

accentuate *verb* EMPHASIZE, accent, draw attention to, foreground, highlight, stress, underline, underscore

accept *verb* **1** RECEIVE, acquire, gain, get, obtain, secure, take

2 AGREE TO, admit, approve, believe, concur with, consent to, cooperate with, recognize

acceptable *adjective*
SATISFACTORY, adequate,
admissible, all right, fair,
moderate, passable, tolerable

acceptance *noun* 1 ACCEPTING,
acquiring, gaining, getting,
obtaining, receipt, securing,
taking
2 AGREEMENT, acknowledgment,
acquiescence, admission,
adoption, approval, assent,
concurrence, consent,
cooperation, recognition

accepted *adjective* AGREED,
acknowledged, approved,
common, conventional,
customary, established, normal,
recognized, traditional

access *noun* ENTRANCE,
admission, admittance, approach,
entry, passage, path, road

accessibility *noun* 1 HANDINESS,
availability, nearness, possibility,
readiness
2 APPROACHABILITY, affability,
cordiality, friendliness,
informality
3 OPENNESS, susceptibility

accessible *adjective* 1 HANDY,
achievable, at hand, attainable,
available, near, nearby,
obtainable, reachable
2 APPROACHABLE, affable,
available, cordial, friendly,
informal
3 OPEN, exposed, liable,
susceptible, vulnerable, wide-
open

accessory *noun* 1 ADDITION,
accompaniment, adjunct,
adornment, appendage,
attachment, decoration, extra,
supplement, trimming
2 ACCOMPLICE, abettor, assistant,
associate (*in crime*), colleague,
confederate, helper, partner

accident *noun* 1 MISFORTUNE,
calamity, collision, crash, disaster,
misadventure, mishap
2 CHANCE, fate, fluke, fortuity,
fortune, hazard, luck

accidental *adjective*
UNINTENTIONAL, casual,
chance, fortuitous, haphazard,
inadvertent, incidental, random,
unexpected, unforeseen,
unlooked-for, unplanned

accidentally *adverb*
UNINTENTIONALLY, by accident, by
chance, fortuitously, haphazardly,
inadvertently, incidentally,
randomly, unwittingly

acclaim *verb* 1 PRAISE, applaud,
approve, celebrate, cheer, clap,
commend, exalt, hail, honor,
salute
▶ *noun* 2 PRAISE, acclamation,
applause, approval, celebration,
commendation, honor, kudos

acclamation *noun* PRAISE,
acclaim, adulation, approval,
ovation, plaudit, tribute

acclimatization *noun*
ADAPTATION, adjustment,
habituation, inurement,
naturalization

acclimatize *verb* ADAPT,
accommodate, accustom, adjust,
get used to, habituate, inure,
naturalize

accolade *noun* PRAISE,
acclaim, applause, approval,
commendation, compliment,
ovation, recognition, tribute

accommodate *verb* 1 HOUSE,
cater for, entertain, lodge, put
up, shelter
2 HELP, aid, assist, oblige, serve
3 ADAPT, adjust, comply, conform,
fit, harmonize, modify, reconcile,
settle

accommodating *adjective*

HELPFUL, considerate, cooperative, friendly, hospitable, kind, obliging, polite, unselfish, willing

accommodation noun HOUSING, board, digs (Brit. informal), house, lodging(s), quarters, shelter

accompaniment noun
1 SUPPLEMENT, accessory, companion, complement
2 BACKING MUSIC, backing

accompany verb 1 GO WITH, attend, chaperon, conduct, convoy, escort, hold (someone's) hand
2 OCCUR WITH, belong to, come with, follow, go together with, supplement

accompanying adjective ADDITIONAL, associated, attached, attendant, complementary, related, supplementary

accomplice noun HELPER, abettor, accessory, ally, assistant, associate, collaborator, colleague, henchman, partner

accomplish verb DO, achieve, attain, bring about, carry out, complete, effect, execute, finish, fulfill, manage, perform, produce

accomplished adjective SKILLED, expert, gifted, masterly, polished, practiced, proficient, talented

accomplishment noun
1 COMPLETION, bringing about, carrying out, conclusion, execution, finishing, fulfillment, performance
2 ACHIEVEMENT, act, coup, deed, exploit, feat, stroke, triumph

accord noun 1 AGREEMENT, conformity, correspondence, harmony, rapport, sympathy, unison
▸ verb 2 FIT, agree, conform, correspond, harmonize, match, suit, tally

accordingly adverb
1 APPROPRIATELY, correspondingly, fitly, properly, suitably
2 CONSEQUENTLY, as a result, ergo, hence, in consequence, so, therefore, thus

according to adverb 1 AS STATED BY, as believed by, as maintained by, in the light of, on the authority of, on the report of
2 IN KEEPING WITH, after, after the manner of, consistent with, in accordance with, in compliance with, in line with, in the manner of

accost verb APPROACH, buttonhole, confront, greet, hail

account noun 1 DESCRIPTION, explanation, narrative, report, statement, story, tale, version
2 (commerce) STATEMENT, balance, bill, books, charge, invoice, reckoning, register, score, tally
3 IMPORTANCE, consequence, honor, note, significance, standing, value, worth
▸ verb 4 CONSIDER, count, estimate, judge, rate, reckon, regard, think, value

accountability noun RESPONSIBILITY, answerability, chargeability, culpability, liability

accountable adjective RESPONSIBLE, amenable, answerable, charged with, liable, obligated, obliged

accountant noun AUDITOR, bean counter (informal), book-keeper

account for verb EXPLAIN, answer for, clarify, clear up, elucidate, illuminate, justify, rationalize

accredited adjective AUTHORIZED, appointed, certified, empowered, endorsed, guaranteed, licensed, official, recognized

accrue verb INCREASE, accumulate,

amass, arise, be added, build up, collect, enlarge, flow, follow, grow

accumulate *verb* COLLECT, accrue, amass, build up, gather, hoard, increase, pile up, store

accumulation *noun* COLLECTION, build-up, gathering, heap, hoard, increase, mass, pile, stack, stock, stockpile, store

accuracy *noun* EXACTNESS, accurateness, authenticity, carefulness, closeness, correctness, fidelity, precision, strictness, truthfulness, veracity

accurate *adjective* EXACT, authentic, close, correct, faithful, precise, scrupulous, spot-on (*Brit. informal*), strict, true, unerring

accurately *adverb* EXACTLY, authentically, closely, correctly, faithfully, precisely, scrupulously, strictly, to the letter, truly, unerringly

accursed *adjective* 1 CURSED, bewitched, condemned, damned, doomed, hopeless, ill-fated, ill-omened, jinxed, unfortunate, unlucky, wretched
2 HATEFUL, abominable, despicable, detestable, execrable, hellish, horrible, lousy (*slang*), scuzzy (*slang*)

accusation *noun* CHARGE, allegation, complaint, denunciation, incrimination, indictment, recrimination

accuse *verb* CHARGE, blame, censure, denounce, impeach, impute, incriminate, indict

accustom *verb* ADAPT, acclimatize, acquaint, discipline, exercise, familiarize, train

accustomed *adjective* 1 USUAL, common, conventional, customary, established, everyday, expected, habitual, normal, ordinary, regular, traditional
2 USED, acclimatized, acquainted, adapted, familiar, familiarized, given to, in the habit of, trained

ace *noun* 1 (*cards, dice, etc.*) ONE, single point
2 (*informal*) EXPERT, champion, dab hand (*Brit. informal*), master, star, virtuoso, wizard (*informal*)
▶ *adjective* 3 (*informal*) EXCELLENT, awesome (*slang*), brilliant, fine, great, outstanding, superb

ache *verb* 1 HURT, pain, pound, smart, suffer, throb, twinge
▶ *noun* 2 PAIN, hurt, pang, pounding, soreness, suffering, throbbing

achieve *verb* ATTAIN, accomplish, acquire, bring about, carry out, complete, do, execute, fulfill, gain, get, obtain, perform

achievement *noun* ACCOMPLISHMENT, act, deed, effort, exploit, feat, feather in one's cap, stroke

acid *adjective* 1 SOUR, acerbic, acrid, pungent, tart, vinegary
2 SHARP, biting, bitter, caustic, cutting, harsh, trenchant, vitriolic

acidity *noun* 1 SOURNESS, acerbity, pungency, tartness
2 SHARPNESS, bitterness, harshness

acknowledge *verb* 1 ACCEPT, admit, allow, concede, confess, declare, grant, own, profess, recognize, yield
2 GREET, address, hail, notice, recognize, salute
3 REPLY TO, answer, notice, react to, recognize, respond to, return

acknowledged *adjective* ACCEPTED, accredited, approved, confessed, declared, professed, recognized, returned

acknowledgment *noun*
1 ACCEPTANCE, admission, allowing, confession, declaration, profession, realization, yielding
2 GREETING, addressing, hail, hailing, notice, recognition, salutation, salute
3 APPRECIATION, answer, credit, gratitude, kudos, reaction, recognition, reply, response, return, thanks

acquaint *verb* TELL, disclose, divulge, enlighten, familiarize, inform, let (someone) know, notify, reveal

acquaintance *noun* 1 ASSOCIATE, colleague, contact
2 KNOWLEDGE, awareness, experience, familiarity, fellowship, relationship, understanding

acquainted with *adjective* FAMILIAR WITH, alive to, apprised of, *au fait* with, aware of, conscious of, experienced in, informed of, knowledgeable about, versed in

acquiesce *verb* AGREE, accede, accept, allow, approve, assent, comply, concur, conform, consent, give in, go along with, submit, yield

acquiescence *noun* AGREEMENT, acceptance, approval, assent, compliance, conformity, consent, giving in, obedience, submission, yielding

acquire *verb* GET, amass, attain, buy, collect, earn, gain, gather, obtain, receive, secure, win

acquisition *noun* 1 POSSESSION, buy, gain, prize, property, purchase
2 ACQUIRING, attainment, gaining, procurement

acquisitive *adjective* GREEDY, avaricious, avid, covetous, grabbing, grasping, predatory, rapacious

acquit *verb* 1 CLEAR, discharge, free, liberate, release, vindicate
2 BEHAVE, bear, comport, conduct, perform

acquittal *noun* CLEARANCE, absolution, deliverance, discharge, exoneration, liberation, release, relief, vindication

acrid *adjective* PUNGENT, bitter, caustic, harsh, sharp, vitriolic

acrimonious *adjective* BITTER, caustic, irascible, petulant, rancorous, spiteful, splenetic, testy

acrimony *noun* BITTERNESS, harshness, ill will, irascibility, rancor, virulence

act *noun* 1 DEED, accomplishment, achievement, action, exploit, feat, performance, undertaking
2 LAW, bill, decree, edict, enactment, measure, ordinance, resolution, statute
3 PERFORMANCE, routine, show, sketch, turn
4 PRETENSE, affectation, attitude, front, performance, pose, posture, show
▶ *verb* 5 DO, carry out, enact, execute, function, operate, perform, take effect, work
6 PERFORM, act out, impersonate, mimic, play, play *or* take the part of, portray, represent

act for *verb* STAND IN FOR, cover for, deputize for, fill in for, replace, represent, substitute for, take the place of

acting *noun* 1 PERFORMANCE, characterization, impersonation, performing, playing, portrayal, stagecraft, theater
▶ *adjective* 2 TEMPORARY, interim,

pro tem, provisional, substitute, surrogate

action noun 1 DEED, accomplishment, achievement, act, exploit, feat, performance
2 LAWSUIT, case, litigation, proceeding, prosecution, suit
3 ENERGY, activity, force, liveliness, spirit, vigor, vim, vitality
4 MOVEMENT, activity, functioning, motion, operation, process, working
5 BATTLE, clash, combat, conflict, contest, encounter, engagement, fight, skirmish, sortie

activate verb START, arouse, energize, galvanize, initiate, mobilize, move, rouse, set in motion, stir

active adjective 1 BUSY, bustling, hard-working, involved, occupied, on the go (informal), on the move, strenuous
2 ENERGETIC, alert, animated, industrious, lively, quick, sprightly, spry, vigorous
3 IN OPERATION, acting, at work, effectual, in action, in force, operative, working

activist noun MILITANT, organizer, partisan

activity noun 1 ACTION, animation, bustle, exercise, exertion, hustle, labor, motion, movement
2 PURSUIT, hobby, interest, pastime, project, scheme

actor noun PERFORMER, actress, luvvie (informal), player, Thespian

actress noun PERFORMER, actor, leading lady, player, starlet, Thespian

actual adjective DEFINITE, concrete, factual, physical, positive, real, substantial, tangible

actually adverb REALLY, as a matter of fact, indeed, in fact, in point of fact, in reality, in truth, literally, truly

act up verb (informal) MAKE A FUSS, have a fit, horse around, misbehave, raise Cain, raise hell

acumen noun JUDGMENT, astuteness, cleverness, ingenuity, insight, intelligence, perspicacity, shrewdness

acute adjective 1 SERIOUS, critical, crucial, dangerous, grave, important, severe, urgent
2 SHARP, excruciating, fierce, intense, piercing, powerful, severe, shooting, violent
3 PERCEPTIVE, astute, clever, insightful, keen, observant, sensitive, sharp, smart

acuteness noun 1 SERIOUSNESS, gravity, importance, severity, urgency
2 PERCEPTIVENESS, astuteness, cleverness, discrimination, insight, perspicacity, sharpness

adamant adjective DETERMINED, firm, fixed, obdurate, resolute, stubborn, unbending, uncompromising

adapt verb ADJUST, acclimatize, accommodate, alter, change, conform, convert, modify, remodel, tailor

adaptability noun FLEXIBILITY, changeability, resilience, versatility

adaptable adjective FLEXIBLE, adjustable, changeable, compliant, easy-going, plastic, pliant, resilient, versatile

adaptation noun
1 ACCLIMATIZATION, familiarization, naturalization
2 CONVERSION, adjustment, alteration, change, modification,

transformation, variation, version

add *verb* 1 COUNT UP, add up, compute, reckon, total, tot up
2 INCLUDE, adjoin, affix, append, attach, augment, supplement

addendum *noun* ADDITION, appendage, appendix, attachment, extension, extra, postscript, supplement

addict *noun* 1 JUNKIE (*informal*), fiend (*informal*), freak (*informal*)
2 FAN, adherent, buff (*informal*), devotee, enthusiast, follower, nut (*slang*)

addicted *adjective* HOOKED (*slang*), absorbed, accustomed, dedicated, dependent, devoted, habituated

addiction *noun* DEPENDENCE, craving, enslavement, habit, obsession

addition *noun* 1 INCLUSION, adding, amplification, attachment, augmentation, enlargement, extension, increasing
2 EXTRA, addendum, additive, appendage, appendix, extension, gain, increase, increment, supplement
3 COUNTING UP, adding up, computation, totalling, totting up
4 ▷▷ **in addition (to)** AS WELL (AS), additionally, also, besides, into the bargain, moreover, over and above, to boot, too

additional *adjective* EXTRA, added, fresh, further, new, other, spare, supplementary

address *noun* 1 LOCATION, abode, dwelling, home, house, residence, situation, whereabouts
2 SPEECH, discourse, dissertation, lecture, oration, sermon, talk
▶ *verb* 3 SPEAK TO, approach, greet, hail, talk to
4 ▷▷ **address (oneself) to**

CONCENTRATE ON, apply (oneself) to, attend to, devote (oneself) to, engage in, focus on, take care of

add up *verb* COUNT UP, add, compute, count, reckon, total, tot up

adept *adjective* 1 SKILLFUL, able, accomplished, adroit, expert, practiced, proficient, skilled, versed
▶ *noun* 2 EXPERT, dab hand (*Brit. informal*), genius, hotshot (*informal*), master

adequacy *noun* SUFFICIENCY, capability, competence, fairness, suitability, tolerability

adequate *adjective* ENOUGH, competent, fair, satisfactory, sufficient, tolerable, up to scratch (*informal*)

adhere *verb* STICK, attach, cleave, cling, fasten, fix, glue, hold fast, paste

adherent *noun* SUPPORTER, admirer, devotee, disciple, fan, follower, upholder

adhesive *adjective* 1 STICKY, clinging, cohesive, gluey, glutinous, tenacious
▶ *noun* 2 GLUE, cement, gum, paste

adieu *noun* GOOD-BYE, farewell, leave-taking, parting, valediction

adjacent *adjective* NEXT, adjoining, beside, bordering, cheek by jowl, close, near, neighboring, next door, touching

adjoin *verb* CONNECT, border, join, link, touch

adjoining *adjective* CONNECTING, abutting, adjacent, bordering, neighboring, next door, touching

adjourn *verb* POSTPONE, defer, delay, discontinue, interrupt, put off, suspend

adjournment *noun* POSTPONEMENT, delay,

discontinuation, interruption, putting off, recess, suspension

adjudicate verb JUDGE, adjudge, arbitrate, decide, determine, mediate, referee, settle, umpire

adjudication noun JUDGMENT, arbitration, conclusion, decision, finding, pronouncement, ruling, settlement, verdict

adjust verb ALTER, accustom, adapt, make conform, modify

adjustable adjective ALTERABLE, adaptable, flexible, malleable, modifiable, movable

adjustment noun 1 ALTERATION, adaptation, modification, redress, regulation, tuning
2 ACCLIMATIZATION, orientation, settling in

ad-lib verb IMPROVISE, busk, extemporize, make up, speak off the cuff, wing it (informal)

administer verb 1 MANAGE, conduct, control, direct, govern, handle, oversee, run, supervise
2 GIVE, apply, dispense, impose, mete out, perform, provide

administration noun MANAGEMENT, application, conduct, control, direction, government, running, supervision

administrative adjective MANAGERIAL, directorial, executive, governmental, organizational, regulatory, supervisory

administrator noun MANAGER, bureaucrat, executive, official, organizer, supervisor

admirable adjective EXCELLENT, commendable, exquisite, fine, laudable, praiseworthy, wonderful, worthy

admiration noun REGARD, amazement, appreciation,

approval, esteem, praise, respect, wonder

admire verb 1 RESPECT, appreciate, approve, esteem, look up to, praise, prize, think highly of, value
2 MARVEL AT, appreciate, delight in, take pleasure in, wonder at

admirer noun 1 SUITOR, beau, boyfriend, lover, sweetheart, wooer
2 FAN, devotee, disciple, enthusiast, follower, partisan, supporter

admissible adjective PERMISSIBLE, acceptable, allowable, passable, tolerable

admission noun 1 ENTRANCE, acceptance, access, admittance, entrée, entry, initiation, introduction
2 CONFESSION, acknowledgment, allowance, declaration, disclosure, divulgence, revelation

admit verb 1 CONFESS, acknowledge, declare, disclose, divulge, fess up (informal), own, reveal
2 ALLOW, agree, grant, let, permit, recognize
3 LET IN, accept, allow, give access, initiate, introduce, receive, take in

admonish verb REPRIMAND, berate, chide, rebuke, scold, slap on the wrist, tell off (informal)

adolescence noun 1 YOUTH, boyhood, girlhood, minority, teens
2 YOUTHFULNESS, childishness, immaturity

adolescent adjective 1 YOUNG, boyish, girlish, immature, juvenile, puerile, teenage, youthful
▶ noun 2 YOUTH, juvenile, minor, teenager, youngster

adopt *verb* 1 FOSTER, take in
2 CHOOSE, assume, espouse,
follow, maintain, take up
adoption *noun* 1 FOSTERING,
adopting, taking in
2 CHOICE, appropriation,
assumption, embracing,
endorsement, espousal, selection,
taking up
adorable *adjective* LOVABLE,
appealing, attractive, charming,
cute, dear, delightful, fetching,
pleasing
adore *verb* LOVE, admire, cherish,
dote on, esteem, exalt, glorify,
honor, idolize, put on a pedestal
(*informal*), revere, worship
adoring *adjective* LOVING,
admiring, affectionate, devoted,
doting, fond
adorn *verb* DECORATE, array,
embellish, festoon
adornment *noun* DECORATION,
accessory, embellishment,
festoon, frill, frippery, ornament,
supplement, trimming
adrift *adjective* 1 DRIFTING, afloat,
unanchored, unmoored
2 AIMLESS, directionless, goalless,
purposeless
► *adverb* 3 WRONG, amiss, astray,
off course
adroit *adjective* SKILLFUL, adept,
clever, deft, dexterous, expert,
masterful, neat, proficient, skilled
adulation *noun* WORSHIP,
fawning, fulsome praise, servile
flattery, sycophancy
adult *noun* 1 GROWN-UP, grown
or grown-up person (man *or*
woman), person of mature age
► *adjective* 2 FULLY GROWN, full
grown, fully developed, grown-up,
mature, of age, ripe
advance *verb* 1 PROGRESS, come
forward, go on, hasten, make

inroads, proceed, speed
2 BENEFIT, further, improve,
prosper
3 SUGGEST, offer, present, proffer,
put forward, submit
4 LEND, pay beforehand, supply
on credit
► *noun* 5 PROGRESS, advancement,
development, forward movement,
headway, inroads, onward
movement
6 IMPROVEMENT, breakthrough,
gain, growth, progress,
promotion, step
7 LOAN, credit, deposit, down
payment, prepayment, retainer
8 ▷▷ **advances** OVERTURES,
approach, approaches, moves,
proposals, proposition
► *adjective* 9 PRIOR, beforehand,
early, forward, in front
10 ▷▷ **in advance** BEFOREHAND,
ahead, earlier, previously
advanced *adjective* FOREMOST,
ahead, avant-garde, cutting
edge, forward, higher, leading,
precocious, progressive
advancement *noun* PROMOTION,
betterment, gain, improvement,
preferment, progress, rise
advantage *noun* BENEFIT,
ascendancy, dominance, good,
help, lead, precedence, profit,
superiority, sway
advantageous *adjective*
1 BENEFICIAL, convenient,
expedient, helpful, of service,
profitable, useful, valuable,
worthwhile
2 SUPERIOR, dominant,
dominating, favorable, win-win
(*informal*)
adventure *noun* ESCAPADE,
enterprise, experience,
exploit, incident, occurrence,
undertaking, venture

adventurer noun 1 MERCENARY, charlatan, fortune-hunter, gambler, opportunist, rogue, speculator
2 HERO, daredevil, heroine, knight-errant, traveler, voyager

adventurous adjective DARING, bold, daredevil, enterprising, intrepid, reckless

adversary noun OPPONENT, antagonist, competitor, contestant, enemy, foe, rival

adverse adjective UNFAVORABLE, contrary, detrimental, hostile, inopportune, negative, opposing

adversity noun HARDSHIP, affliction, bad luck, disaster, distress, hard times, misfortune, reverse, trouble

advertise verb PUBLICIZE, announce, inform, make known, notify, plug (informal), promote, tout

advertisement noun NOTICE, advert (Brit. informal), ad (informal), announcement, blurb, circular, commercial, plug (informal), poster

advice noun GUIDANCE, counsel, help, opinion, recommendation, suggestion

advisability noun WISDOM, appropriateness, aptness, desirability, expediency, fitness, propriety, prudence, suitability

advisable adjective WISE, appropriate, desirable, expedient, fitting, politic, prudent, recommended, seemly, sensible

advise verb 1 RECOMMEND, admonish, caution, commend, counsel, prescribe, suggest, urge
2 NOTIFY, acquaint, apprise, inform, make known, report, tell, warn

adviser noun GUIDE, aide, confidant or (fem.) confidante,
consultant, counselor, helper, mentor, right-hand man

advisory adjective ADVISING, consultative, counseling, helping, recommending

advocate verb 1 RECOMMEND, advise, argue for, campaign for, champion, commend, encourage, promote, propose, support, uphold
▶ noun 2 SUPPORTER, campaigner, champion, counselor, defender, promoter, proponent, spokesman, upholder
3 (law) LAWYER, attorney, barrister, counsel, solicitor

affable adjective FRIENDLY, amiable, amicable, approachable, congenial, cordial, courteous, genial, pleasant, sociable, urbane

affair noun 1 EVENT, activity, business, episode, happening, incident, matter, occurrence
2 RELATIONSHIP, amour, intrigue, liaison, romance

affect[1] verb 1 INFLUENCE, act on, alter, bear upon, change, concern, impinge upon, relate to
2 MOVE, disturb, overcome, perturb, stir, touch, upset

affect[2] verb PUT ON, adopt, aspire to, assume, contrive, feign, imitate, pretend, simulate

affectation noun PRETENSE, act, artificiality, assumed manners, façade, insincerity, pose, pretentiousness, show

affected adjective PRETENDED, artificial, contrived, feigned, insincere, mannered, phoney or phony (informal), put-on, unnatural

affecting adjective MOVING, pathetic, pitiful, poignant, sad, touching

affection noun FONDNESS,

attachment, care, feeling, goodwill, kindness, liking, love, tenderness, warmth

affectionate *adjective* FOND, attached, caring, devoted, doting, friendly, kind, loving, tender, warm-hearted

affiliate *verb* JOIN, ally, amalgamate, associate, band together, combine, incorporate, link, unite

affinity *noun* 1 ATTRACTION, fondness, inclination, leaning, liking, partiality, rapport, sympathy
2 SIMILARITY, analogy, closeness, connection, correspondence, kinship, likeness, relationship, resemblance

affirm *verb* DECLARE, assert, certify, confirm, maintain, pronounce, state, swear, testify

affirmation *noun* DECLARATION, assertion, certification, confirmation, oath, pronouncement, statement, testimony

affirmative *adjective* AGREEING, approving, assenting, concurring, confirming, consenting, corroborative, favorable, positive

afflict *verb* TORMENT, distress, grieve, harass, hurt, oppress, pain, plague, trouble

affliction *noun* SUFFERING, adversity, curse, disease, hardship, misfortune, ordeal, plague, scourge, torment, trial, trouble, woe

affluence *noun* WEALTH, abundance, fortune, opulence, plenty, prosperity, riches

affluent *adjective* WEALTHY, loaded (*slang*), moneyed, opulent, prosperous, rich, well-heeled (*informal*), well-off, well-to-do

afford *verb* 1 *as in* **can afford** SPARE, bear, manage, stand, sustain
2 GIVE, offer, produce, provide, render, supply, yield

affordable *adjective* INEXPENSIVE, cheap, economical, low-cost, moderate, modest, reasonable

affront *noun* 1 INSULT, offense, outrage, provocation, slap in the face (*informal*), slight, slur
▶ *verb* 2 OFFEND, anger, annoy, displease, insult, outrage, provoke, slight

aflame *adjective* BURNING, ablaze, alight, blazing, fiery, flaming, lit, on fire

afoot *adverb* GOING ON, abroad, brewing, current, happening, in preparation, in progress, on the go (*informal*), up (*informal*)

afraid *adjective* 1 SCARED, apprehensive, cowardly, faint-hearted, fearful, frightened, nervous, wired (*slang*)
2 SORRY, regretful, unhappy

afresh *adverb* AGAIN, anew, newly, once again, once more, over again

after *adverb* FOLLOWING, afterwards, behind, below, later, subsequently, succeeding, thereafter

aftermath *noun* EFFECTS, aftereffects, consequences, end result, outcome, results, sequel, upshot, wake

again *adverb* 1 ONCE MORE, afresh, anew, another time
2 ALSO, besides, furthermore, in addition, moreover

against *preposition* 1 BESIDE, abutting, facing, in contact with, on, opposite to, touching, upon
2 OPPOSED TO, anti (*informal*), averse to, hostile to, in defiance of, in opposition to, resisting, versus
3 IN PREPARATION FOR, in

anticipation of, in expectation of, in provision for

age noun 1 TIME, date, day(s), duration, epoch, era, generation, lifetime, period, span
2 OLD AGE, advancing years, decline (of life), majority, maturity, senescence, senility, seniority
▶ verb 3 GROW OLD, decline, deteriorate, mature, mellow, ripen

aged adjective OLD, ancient, antiquated, antique, elderly, getting on, gray

agency noun 1 BUSINESS, bureau, department, office, organization
2 (old-fashioned) MEDIUM, activity, means, mechanism

agenda noun LIST, calendar, diary, plan, program, schedule, timetable

agent noun 1 REPRESENTATIVE, envoy, go-between, negotiator, rep (informal), surrogate
2 WORKER, author, doer, mover, operator, performer
3 FORCE, agency, cause, instrument, means, power, vehicle

aggravate verb 1 MAKE WORSE, exacerbate, exaggerate, increase, inflame, intensify, magnify, worsen
2 (informal) ANNOY, bother, get on one's nerves (informal), irritate, nettle, provoke

aggravation noun 1 WORSENING, exacerbation, exaggeration, heightening, increase, inflaming, intensification, magnification
2 (informal) ANNOYANCE, exasperation, gall, grief (informal), hassle (informal), irritation, provocation

aggregate noun 1 TOTAL, accumulation, amount, body, bulk, collection, combination, mass, pile, sum, whole
▶ adjective 2 TOTAL, accumulated, collected, combined, composite, cumulative, mixed
▶ verb 3 COMBINE, accumulate, amass, assemble, collect, heap, mix, pile

aggression noun 1 HOSTILITY, antagonism, belligerence, destructiveness, pugnacity
2 ATTACK, assault, injury, invasion, offensive, onslaught, raid

aggressive adjective 1 HOSTILE, belligerent, destructive, offensive, pugnacious, quarrelsome
2 FORCEFUL, assertive, bold, dynamic, energetic, enterprising, militant, pushy (informal), vigorous

aggressor noun ATTACKER, assailant, assaulter, invader

aggrieved adjective HURT, afflicted, distressed, disturbed, harmed, injured, unhappy, wronged

aghast adjective HORRIFIED, amazed, appalled, astonished, astounded, awestruck, confounded, shocked, startled, stunned

agile adjective 1 NIMBLE, active, brisk, lithe, quick, sprightly, spry, supple, swift
2 ACUTE, alert, bright (informal), clever, lively, quick-witted, sharp

agility noun NIMBLENESS, litheness, liveliness, quickness, suppleness, swiftness

agitate verb 1 UPSET, disconcert, distract, excite, fluster, perturb, trouble, unnerve, worry
2 STIR, beat, convulse, disturb, rouse, shake, toss

agitation noun 1 TURMOIL, clamor, commotion, confusion, disturbance, excitement, ferment,

trouble, upheaval
2 TURBULENCE, convulsion, disturbance, shaking, stirring, tossing

agitator noun TROUBLEMAKER, agent provocateur, firebrand, instigator, rabble-rouser, revolutionary, stirrer (informal)

agog adjective EAGER, avid, curious, enthralled, enthusiastic, excited, expectant, impatient, in suspense, wired (slang)

agonize verb SUFFER, be distressed, be in agony, be in anguish, go through the mill, labor, strain, struggle, worry

agony noun SUFFERING, anguish, distress, misery, pain, throes, torment, torture

agree verb 1 CONSENT, assent, be of the same opinion, comply, concur, see eye to eye
2 GET ON (TOGETHER), coincide, conform, correspond, match, tally

agreeable adjective 1 PLEASANT, delightful, enjoyable, gratifying, likable or likeable, pleasing, satisfying, to one's taste
2 CONSENTING, amenable, approving, complying, concurring, in accord, onside (informal), sympathetic, well-disposed, willing

agreement noun 1 ASSENT, agreeing, compliance, concord, concurrence, consent, harmony, union, unison
2 CORRESPONDENCE, compatibility, conformity, congruity, consistency, similarity
3 CONTRACT, arrangement, bargain, covenant, deal (informal), pact, settlement, treaty, understanding

agricultural adjective FARMING, agrarian, country, rural, rustic

agriculture noun FARMING, cultivation, culture, husbandry, tillage

aground adverb BEACHED, ashore, foundered, grounded, high and dry, on the rocks, stranded, stuck

ahead adverb IN FRONT, at an advantage, at the head, before, cutting edge, in advance, in the lead, leading, to the fore, winning

aid noun 1 HELP, assistance, benefit, encouragement, favor, promotion, relief, service, support
▶ verb 2 HELP, assist, encourage, favor, promote, serve, subsidize, support, sustain

aide noun ASSISTANT, attendant, helper, right-hand man, second, supporter

ailing adjective ILL, indisposed, infirm, poorly, sick, under the weather (informal), unwell, weak

ailment noun ILLNESS, affliction, complaint, disease, disorder, infirmity, malady, sickness

aim verb 1 INTEND, attempt, endeavor, mean, plan, point, propose, seek, set one's sights on, strive, try
▶ noun 2 INTENTION, ambition, aspiration, desire, goal, objective, plan, purpose, target

aimless adjective PURPOSELESS, directionless, pointless, random, stray

air noun 1 ATMOSPHERE, heavens, sky
2 WIND, breeze, draft, zephyr
3 MANNER, appearance, atmosphere, aura, demeanor, impression, look, mood
4 TUNE, aria, lay, melody, song
▶ verb 5 PUBLICIZE, circulate, display, exhibit, express, give vent to, make known, make public, reveal, voice

6 VENTILATE, aerate, expose, freshen

airborne adjective FLYING, floating, gliding, hovering, in flight, in the air, on the wing

airing noun 1 VENTILATION, aeration, drying, freshening
2 EXPOSURE, circulation, display, dissemination, expression, publicity, utterance, vent

airless adjective STUFFY, close, heavy, muggy, oppressive, stifling, suffocating, sultry

airs plural noun AFFECTATION, arrogance, haughtiness, hauteur, pomposity, pretensions, superciliousness, swank (informal)

airy adjective 1 WELL-VENTILATED, fresh, light, open, spacious, uncluttered
2 LIGHT-HEARTED, blithe, cheerful, high-spirited, jaunty, lively, sprightly

aisle noun PASSAGEWAY, alley, corridor, gangway, lane, passage, path

alacrity noun EAGERNESS, alertness, enthusiasm, promptness, quickness, readiness, speed, willingness, zeal

alarm noun 1 FEAR, anxiety, apprehension, consternation, fright, nervousness, panic, scare, trepidation
2 DANGER SIGNAL, alarm bell, alert, bell, distress signal, hooter, siren, warning
▸ verb 3 FRIGHTEN, daunt, dismay, distress, give (someone) a turn, give (someone) a fright (informal), panic, scare, startle, unnerve

alarming adjective FRIGHTENING, daunting, distressing, disturbing, scaring, shocking, startling, unnerving

alcoholic noun 1 DRUNKARD, dipsomaniac, drinker, drunk, inebriate, tippler, toper, wino (informal)
▸ adjective 2 INTOXICATING, brewed, distilled, fermented, hard, strong

alcove noun RECESS, bay, compartment, corner, cubbyhole, cubicle, niche, nook

alert adjective 1 WATCHFUL, attentive, awake, circumspect, heedful, observant, on guard, on one's toes, on the lookout, vigilant, wide-awake
▸ noun 2 WARNING, alarm, signal, siren
▸ verb 3 WARN, alarm, forewarn, inform, notify, signal

alertness noun WATCHFULNESS, attentiveness, heedfulness, liveliness, vigilance

alias adverb 1 ALSO KNOWN AS, also called, otherwise, otherwise known as
▸ noun 2 PSEUDONYM, assumed name, nom de guerre, nom de plume, pen name, stage name

alibi noun EXCUSE, defense, explanation, justification, plea, pretext, reason

alien adjective 1 FOREIGN, exotic, incongruous, strange, unfamiliar
▸ noun 2 FOREIGNER, newcomer, outsider, stranger

alienate verb SET AGAINST, disaffect, estrange, make unfriendly, shut out, turn away

alienation noun SETTING AGAINST, disaffection, estrangement, remoteness, separation, turning away

alight¹ verb 1 GET OFF, descend, disembark, dismount, get down
2 LAND, come down, come to rest, descend, light, perch, settle, touch down

alight² adjective 1 ON FIRE, ablaze,

aflame, blazing, burning, fiery, flaming, lighted, lit
2 LIT UP, bright, brilliant, illuminated, shining

align *verb* **1** ALLY, affiliate, agree, associate, cooperate, join, side, sympathize
2 LINE UP, even up, order, range, regulate, straighten

alignment *noun* **1** ALLIANCE, affiliation, agreement, association, cooperation, sympathy, union
2 LINING UP, adjustment, arrangement, evening up, order, straightening up

alike *adjective* **1** SIMILAR, akin, analogous, corresponding, identical, of a piece, parallel, resembling, the same
▶ *adverb* **2** SIMILARLY, analogously, correspondingly, equally, evenly, identically, uniformly

alive *adjective* **1** LIVING, animate, breathing, in the land of the living (*informal*), subsisting
2 IN EXISTENCE, active, existing, extant, functioning, in force, operative
3 LIVELY, active, alert, animated, energetic, full of life, vital, vivacious

all *adjective* **1** THE WHOLE OF, every bit of, the complete, the entire, the sum of, the totality of, the total of
2 EVERY, each, each and every, every one of, every single
3 COMPLETE, entire, full, greatest, perfect, total, utter
▶ *adverb* **4** COMPLETELY, altogether, entirely, fully, totally, utterly, wholly
▶ *noun* **5** WHOLE AMOUNT, aggregate, entirety, everything, sum total, total, totality, utmost

allegation *noun* CLAIM, accusation, affirmation, assertion, charge, declaration, statement

allege *verb* CLAIM, affirm, assert, charge, declare, maintain, state

alleged *adjective* **1** STATED, affirmed, asserted, declared, described, designated
2 SUPPOSED, doubtful, dubious, ostensible, professed, purported, so-called, unproved

allegiance *noun* LOYALTY, constancy, devotion, faithfulness, fidelity, obedience

allegorical *adjective* SYMBOLIC, emblematic, figurative, symbolizing

allegory *noun* SYMBOL, fable, myth, parable, story, symbolism, tale

allergic *adjective* SENSITIVE, affected by, hypersensitive, susceptible

allergy *noun* SENSITIVITY, antipathy, hypersensitivity, susceptibility

alleviate *verb* EASE, allay, lessen, lighten, moderate, reduce, relieve, soothe

alley *noun* PASSAGE, alleyway, backstreet, lane, passageway, pathway, walk

alliance *noun* UNION, affiliation, agreement, association, coalition, combination, confederation, connection, federation, league, marriage, pact, partnership, treaty

allied *adjective* UNITED, affiliated, associated, combined, connected, in league, linked, related

allocate *verb* ASSIGN, allot, allow, apportion, budget, designate, earmark, mete, set aside, share out

allocation *noun* ASSIGNMENT, allotment, allowance, lot, portion, quota, ration, share

allot *verb* ASSIGN, allocate, apportion, budget, designate, earmark, mete, set aside, share out

allotment *noun* 1 PLOT, kitchen garden, patch, tract
2 ASSIGNMENT, allocation, allowance, grant, portion, quota, ration, share, stint

all-out *adjective* TOTAL, complete, exhaustive, full, full-scale, maximum, thoroughgoing, undivided, unremitting, unrestrained

allow *verb* 1 PERMIT, approve, authorize, enable, endure, let, sanction, stand, suffer, tolerate
2 GIVE, allocate, allot, assign, grant, provide, set aside, spare
3 ACKNOWLEDGE, admit, concede, confess, grant, own

allowable *adjective* PERMISSIBLE, acceptable, admissible, all right, appropriate, suitable, tolerable

allowance *noun* 1 PORTION, allocation, amount, grant, lot, quota, ration, share, stint
2 CONCESSION, deduction, discount, rebate, reduction

allow for *verb* TAKE INTO ACCOUNT, consider, make allowances for, make concessions for, make provision for, plan for, provide for, take into consideration

alloy *noun* 1 MIXTURE, admixture, amalgam, blend, combination, composite, compound, hybrid
▶ *verb* 2 MIX, amalgamate, blend, combine, compound, fuse

all right *adjective* 1 SATISFACTORY, acceptable, adequate, average, fair, O.K. or okay (*informal*), standard, up to scratch (*informal*)
2 O.K. or OKAY (*informal*), healthy, safe, sound, unharmed, uninjured, well, whole

allude *verb* REFER, hint, imply, intimate, mention, suggest, touch upon

allure *noun* 1 ATTRACTIVENESS, appeal, attraction, charm, enchantment, enticement, glamour, lure, persuasion, seductiveness, temptation
▶ *verb* 2 ATTRACT, captivate, charm, enchant, entice, lure, persuade, seduce, tempt, win over

alluring *adjective* ATTRACTIVE, beguiling, captivating, come-hither, fetching, glamorous, seductive, tempting

allusion *noun* REFERENCE, casual remark, hint, implication, innuendo, insinuation, intimation, mention, suggestion

ally *noun* 1 PARTNER, accomplice, associate, collaborator, colleague, friend, helper, homeboy (*slang*), homegirl (*slang*)
▶ *verb* 2 UNITE, associate, collaborate, combine, join, join forces, unify

almighty *adjective* 1 ALL-POWERFUL, absolute, invincible, omnipotent, supreme, unlimited
2 (*informal*) GREAT, enormous, excessive, intense, loud, severe, terrible

almost *adverb* NEARLY, about, approximately, close to, just about, not quite, on the brink of, practically, virtually

alone *adjective* BY ONESELF, apart, detached, isolated, lonely, only, on one's tod (*slang*), separate, single, solitary, unaccompanied

aloof *adjective* DISTANT, detached, haughty, remote, standoffish, supercilious, unapproachable, unfriendly

aloud *adverb* OUT LOUD, audibly, clearly, distinctly, intelligibly, plainly

already *adverb* BEFORE NOW, at present, before, by now, by then, even now, heretofore, just now, previously

also *adverb* TOO, additionally, and, as well, besides, further, furthermore, in addition, into the bargain, moreover, to boot

alter *verb* CHANGE, adapt, adjust, amend, convert, modify, reform, revise, transform, turn, vary

alteration *noun* CHANGE, adaptation, adjustment, amendment, conversion, difference, modification, reformation, revision, transformation, variation

alternate *verb* 1 CHANGE, act reciprocally, fluctuate, interchange, oscillate, rotate, substitute, take turns
▶ *adjective* 2 EVERY OTHER, alternating, every second, interchanging, rotating

alternative *noun* 1 CHOICE, option, other (*of two*), preference, recourse, selection, substitute
▶ *adjective* 2 DIFFERENT, alternate, another, other, second, substitute

alternatively *adverb* OR, as an alternative, if not, instead, on the other hand, otherwise

although *conjunction* THOUGH, albeit, despite the fact that, even if, even though, notwithstanding, while

altogether *adverb* 1 COMPLETELY, absolutely, fully, perfectly, quite, thoroughly, totally, utterly, wholly 2 ON THE WHOLE, all in all, all things considered, as a whole, collectively, generally, in general 3 IN TOTAL, all told, everything included, in all, in sum, taken together

altruistic *adjective* SELFLESS, benevolent, charitable, generous, humanitarian, philanthropic, public-spirited, self-sacrificing, unselfish

always *adverb* CONTINUALLY, consistently, constantly, eternally, evermore, every time, forever, invariably, perpetually, repeatedly, twenty-four-seven (*slang*), without exception

amalgamate *verb* COMBINE, ally, blend, fuse, incorporate, integrate, merge, mingle, unite

amalgamation *noun* COMBINATION, blend, coalition, compound, fusion, joining, merger, mixture, union

amass *verb* COLLECT, accumulate, assemble, compile, gather, hoard, pile up

amateur *noun* NONPROFESSIONAL, dabbler, dilettante, layman

amateurish *adjective* UNPROFESSIONAL, amateur, bungling, clumsy, crude, inexpert, unaccomplished

amaze *verb* ASTONISH, alarm, astound, bewilder, dumbfound, shock, stagger, startle, stun, surprise

amazement *noun* ASTONISHMENT, admiration, bewilderment, confusion, perplexity, shock, surprise, wonder

amazing *adjective* ASTONISHING, astounding, breathtaking, eye-opening, overwhelming, staggering, startling, stunning, surprising

ambassador *noun* REPRESENTATIVE, agent, consul, deputy, diplomat, envoy, legate,

minister
ambiguity noun VAGUENESS,
doubt, dubiousness, equivocation,
obscurity, uncertainty
ambiguous adjective UNCLEAR,
dubious, enigmatic, equivocal,
inconclusive, indefinite,
indeterminate, obscure, vague
ambition noun 1 ENTERPRISE,
aspiration, desire, drive,
eagerness, longing, striving,
yearning, zeal
2 GOAL, aim, aspiration, desire,
dream, hope, intent, objective,
purpose, wish
ambitious adjective ENTERPRISING,
aspiring, avid, eager, hopeful,
intent, purposeful, striving,
zealous
ambivalent adjective UNDECIDED,
contradictory, doubtful, equivocal,
in two minds, uncertain,
wavering
amble verb STROLL, dawdle,
meander, mosey (informal), ramble,
saunter, walk, wander
ambush noun 1 TRAP, lying in
wait, waylaying
▶ verb 2 TRAP, attack, bushwhack
(U.S.), ensnare, surprise, waylay
amenable adjective RECEPTIVE,
able to be influenced, acquiescent,
agreeable, open, persuadable,
responsive, susceptible
amend verb CHANGE, alter, correct,
fix, improve, mend, modify,
reform, remedy, repair, revise
amendment noun 1 CHANGE,
alteration, correction,
emendation, improvement,
modification, reform, remedy,
repair, revision
2 ALTERATION, addendum,
addition, attachment,
clarification
amends plural noun as in **make**

amends for COMPENSATION,
atonement, recompense,
redress, reparation, restitution,
satisfaction
amenity noun FACILITY,
advantage, comfort, convenience,
service
amiable adjective PLEASANT,
affable, agreeable, charming,
congenial, engaging, friendly,
genial, likable or likeable, lovable
amicable adjective FRIENDLY,
amiable, civil, cordial, courteous,
harmonious, neighborly,
peaceful, sociable
amid, amidst preposition IN THE
MIDDLE OF, among, amongst,
in the midst of, in the thick of,
surrounded by
amiss adverb 1 WRONGLY,
erroneously, improperly,
inappropriately, incorrectly,
mistakenly, unsuitably
2 as in **take (something) amiss**
AS AN INSULT, as offensive, out of
turn, wrongly
▶ adjective 3 WRONG, awry, faulty,
incorrect, mistaken, untoward
ammunition noun MUNITIONS,
armaments, explosives, powder,
rounds, shells, shot
amnesty noun GENERAL PARDON,
absolution, dispensation,
forgiveness, immunity, remission
(of penalty), reprieve
amok, amuck adverb as in
run amok MADLY, berserk,
destructively, ferociously, in a
frenzy, murderously, savagely,
uncontrollably, violently, wildly
among, amongst preposition
1 IN THE MIDST OF, amid, amidst,
in the middle of, in the thick of,
surrounded by, together with,
with
2 IN THE GROUP OF, in the class of,

in the company of, in the number of, out of

3 TO EACH OF, between

amorous adjective LOVING, erotic, impassioned, in love, lustful, passionate, tender

amount noun QUANTITY, expanse, extent, magnitude, mass, measure, number, supply, volume

amount to verb ADD UP TO, become, come to, develop into, equal, mean, total

ample adjective PLENTY, abundant, bountiful, copious, expansive, extensive, full, generous, lavish, plentiful, profuse

amplify verb 1 EXPLAIN, develop, elaborate, enlarge, expand, flesh out, go into detail

2 INCREASE, enlarge, expand, extend, heighten, intensify, magnify, strengthen, widen

amply adverb FULLY, abundantly, completely, copiously, generously, profusely, richly

amputate verb CUT OFF, curtail, lop, remove, separate, sever, truncate

amuck SEE **AMOK**

amuse verb ENTERTAIN, charm, cheer, delight, interest, please, tickle

amusement noun

1 ENTERTAINMENT, cheer, enjoyment, fun, merriment, mirth, pleasure

2 ENTERTAINMENT, diversion, game, hobby, joke, pastime, recreation, sport

amusing adjective FUNNY, comical, droll, enjoyable, entertaining, humorous, interesting, witty

analogy noun SIMILARITY, comparison, correlation, correspondence, likeness, parallel, relation, resemblance

analysis noun EXAMINATION, breakdown, dissection, inquiry, investigation, perusal, scrutiny, sifting, test

analytic, analytical adjective RATIONAL, inquiring, inquisitive, investigative, logical, organized, problem-solving, systematic

analyze verb 1 EXAMINE, evaluate, investigate, research, test, work over

2 BREAK DOWN, dissect, divide, resolve, separate, think through

anarchic adjective LAWLESS, chaotic, disorganized, rebellious, riotous, ungoverned

anarchist noun REVOLUTIONARY, insurgent, nihilist, rebel, terrorist

anarchy noun LAWLESSNESS, chaos, confusion, disorder, disorganization, revolution, riot

anatomy noun 1 EXAMINATION, analysis, dissection, division, inquiry, investigation, study

2 STRUCTURE, build, composition, frame, framework, make-up

ancestor noun FOREFATHER, forebear, forerunner, precursor, predecessor

ancient adjective OLD, aged, antique, archaic, old-fashioned, primeval, primordial, timeworn

ancillary adjective SUPPLEMENTARY, additional, auxiliary, extra, secondary, subordinate, subsidiary, supporting

and conjunction ALSO, along with, as well as, furthermore, in addition to, including, moreover, plus, together with

anecdote noun STORY, reminiscence, short story, sketch, tale, urban legend, yarn

anemic adjective PALE, ashen, colorless, feeble, pallid, sickly, wan, weak

anesthetic noun 1 PAINKILLER,
analgesic, anodyne, narcotic,
opiate, sedative, soporific
▶ adjective 2 PAIN-KILLING,
analgesic, anodyne, deadening,
dulling, numbing, sedative,
soporific

angel noun 1 DIVINE MESSENGER,
archangel, cherub, seraph
2 (informal) DEAR, beauty, darling,
gem, jewel, paragon, saint,
treasure

angelic adjective 1 PURE, adorable,
beautiful, entrancing, lovely,
saintly, virtuous
2 HEAVENLY, celestial, cherubic,
ethereal, seraphic

anger noun 1 RAGE, annoyance,
displeasure, exasperation, fury,
ire, outrage, resentment, temper,
wrath
▶ verb 2 MADDEN, annoy, displease,
enrage, exasperate, gall, incense,
infuriate, outrage, rile, vex

angle¹ noun 1 INTERSECTION,
bend, corner, crook, edge, elbow,
nook, point
2 POINT OF VIEW, approach, aspect,
outlook, perspective, position,
side, slant, standpoint, viewpoint

angle² verb FISH, cast

angry adjective FURIOUS, annoyed,
cross, displeased, enraged,
exasperated, incensed, infuriated,
irate, mad, outraged, resentful

angst noun ANXIETY,
apprehension, unease, worry

anguish noun SUFFERING, agony,
distress, grief, heartache, misery,
pain, sorrow, torment, woe

animal noun 1 CREATURE, beast,
brute
2 (applied to a person) BRUTE,
barbarian, beast, monster, savage,
wild man

▶ adjective 3 PHYSICAL, bestial,
bodily, brutish, carnal, gross,
sensual

animate verb 1 ENLIVEN, energize,
excite, fire, inspire, invigorate,
kindle, move, stimulate
▶ adjective 2 LIVING, alive, alive and
kicking, breathing, live, moving

animated adjective LIVELY,
ebullient, energetic, enthusiastic,
excited, passionate, spirited,
vivacious, wired (slang)

animation noun LIVELINESS,
ebullience, energy, enthusiasm,
excitement, fervor, passion, spirit,
verve, vivacity, zest

animosity noun HOSTILITY,
acrimony, antipathy, bitterness,
enmity, hatred, ill will,
malevolence, malice, rancor,
resentment

annals plural noun RECORDS,
accounts, archives, chronicles,
history

annex verb 1 SEIZE, acquire,
appropriate, conquer, occupy,
take over
2 JOIN, add, adjoin, attach,
connect, fasten

annihilate verb DESTROY, abolish,
decimate, eradicate, exterminate,
extinguish, obliterate, wipe out

announce verb MAKE KNOWN,
advertise, broadcast, declare,
disclose, proclaim, report,
reveal, tell

announcement noun
STATEMENT, advertisement,
broadcast, bulletin, communiqué,
declaration, proclamation, report,
revelation

announcer noun PRESENTER,
broadcaster, commentator,
master of ceremonies, newscaster,
newsreader, reporter

annoy verb IRRITATE, anger,

bother, displease, disturb, exasperate, get on one's nerves (*informal*), hassle (*informal*), madden, molest, pester, plague, trouble, vex

annoyance *noun* 1 IRRITATION, anger, bother, hassle (*informal*), nuisance, trouble 2 NUISANCE, bore, bother, drag (*informal*), pain (*informal*)

annoying *adjective* IRRITATING, disturbing, exasperating, maddening, troublesome

annual *adjective* YEARLY, once a year, yearlong

annually *adverb* YEARLY, by the year, once a year, per annum, per year

annul *verb* INVALIDATE, abolish, cancel, declare *or* render null and void, negate, nullify, repeal, retract

anoint *verb* CONSECRATE, bless, hallow, sanctify

anomalous *adjective* UNUSUAL, abnormal, eccentric, exceptional, incongruous, inconsistent, irregular, odd, peculiar

anomaly *noun* IRREGULARITY, abnormality, eccentricity, exception, incongruity, inconsistency, oddity, peculiarity

anonymous *adjective* UNNAMED, incognito, nameless, unacknowledged, uncredited, unidentified, unknown, unsigned

answer *verb* 1 REPLY, explain, react, resolve, respond, retort, return, solve
▶ *noun* 2 REPLY, comeback, defense, explanation, reaction, rejoinder, response, retort, return, riposte, solution

answerable *adjective* (usually with *for* or *to*) RESPONSIBLE, accountable, amenable, chargeable, liable, subject, to blame

answer for *verb* BE RESPONSIBLE FOR, be accountable for, be answerable for, be chargeable for, be liable for, be to blame for

antagonism *noun* HOSTILITY, antipathy, conflict, discord, dissension, friction, opposition, rivalry

antagonist *noun* OPPONENT, adversary, competitor, contender, enemy, foe, rival

antagonistic *adjective* HOSTILE, at odds, at variance, conflicting, incompatible, in dispute, opposed, unfriendly

antagonize *verb* ANNOY, anger, get on one's nerves (*informal*), hassle (*informal*), irritate, offend

anthem *noun* 1 HYMN, canticle, carol, chant, chorale, psalm 2 SONG OF PRAISE, paean

anthology *noun* COLLECTION, compendium, compilation, miscellany, selection, treasury

anticipate *verb* EXPECT, await, foresee, foretell, hope for, look forward to, predict, prepare for

anticipation *noun* EXPECTATION, expectancy, foresight, forethought, premonition, prescience

anticlimax *noun* DISAPPOINTMENT, bathos, comedown (*informal*), letdown

antics *plural noun* CLOWNING, escapades, horseplay, mischief, playfulness, pranks, tomfoolery, tricks

antidote *noun* CURE, countermeasure, remedy

antipathy *noun* HOSTILITY, aversion, bad blood, dislike, enmity, hatred, ill will

antiquated *adjective* OBSOLETE,

antique, archaic, dated, old-fashioned, out-of-date, passé

antique noun 1 PERIOD PIECE, bygone, heirloom, relic
▶ adjective 2 VINTAGE, antiquarian, classic, olden
3 OLD-FASHIONED, archaic, obsolete, outdated

antiquity noun 1 OLD AGE, age, ancientness, elderliness, oldness
2 DISTANT PAST, ancient times, olden days, time immemorial

antiseptic adjective 1 HYGIENIC, clean, germ-free, pure, sanitary, sterile, uncontaminated
▶ noun 2 DISINFECTANT, germicide, purifier

antisocial adjective 1 UNSOCIABLE, alienated, misanthropic, reserved, retiring, uncommunicative, unfriendly, withdrawn
2 DISRUPTIVE, antagonistic, belligerent, disorderly, hostile, menacing, rebellious, uncooperative

antithesis noun OPPOSITE, contrary, contrast, converse, inverse, reverse

anxiety noun UNEASINESS, angst, apprehension, concern, foreboding, misgiving, nervousness, tension, trepidation, worry

anxious adjective 1 UNEASY, apprehensive, concerned, fearful, in suspense, nervous, on tenterhooks, tense, troubled, wired (slang), worried
2 EAGER, desirous, impatient, intent, itching, keen, yearning

apart adverb 1 TO PIECES, asunder, in bits, in pieces, to bits
2 SEPARATE, alone, aside, away, by oneself, isolated, to one side
3 ▷▷ **apart from** EXCEPT FOR, aside from, besides, but, excluding, not counting, other than, save

apartment noun ROOM, accommodation, flat, living quarters, penthouse, quarters, rooms, suite

apathetic adjective UNINTERESTED, cool, indifferent, passive, phlegmatic, unconcerned

apathy noun LACK OF INTEREST, coolness, indifference, inertia, nonchalance, passivity, torpor, unconcern

apex noun HIGHEST POINT, crest, crown, culmination, peak, pinnacle, point, summit, top

apiece adverb EACH, for each, from each, individually, respectively, separately, to each

aplomb noun SELF-POSSESSION, calmness, composure, confidence, level-headedness, poise, sang-froid, self-assurance, self-confidence

apocryphal adjective DUBIOUS, doubtful, legendary, mythical, questionable, unauthenticated, unsubstantiated

apologetic adjective REGRETFUL, contrite, penitent, remorseful, rueful, sorry

apologize verb SAY SORRY, ask forgiveness, beg pardon, express regret

apology noun 1 DEFENSE, acknowledgment, confession, excuse, explanation, justification, plea
2 as in **an apology for** MOCKERY, caricature, excuse, imitation, travesty

apostle noun 1 EVANGELIST, herald, messenger, missionary, preacher
2 SUPPORTER, advocate, champion, pioneer, propagandist, proponent

apotheosis noun DEIFICATION, elevation, exaltation,

glorification, idealization, idolization

appall verb HORRIFY, alarm, daunt, dishearten, dismay, frighten, outrage, shock, unnerve

appalling adjective HORRIFYING, alarming, awful, daunting, dreadful, fearful, frightful, horrible, shocking, terrifying

apparatus noun 1 EQUIPMENT, appliance, contraption (informal), device, gear, machinery, mechanism, tackle, tools
2 ORGANIZATION, bureaucracy, chain of command, hierarchy, network, setup (informal), structure, system

apparent adjective 1 OBVIOUS, discernible, distinct, evident, manifest, marked, unmistakable, visible
2 SEEMING, ostensible, outward, superficial

apparently adverb IT APPEARS THAT, it seems that, on the face of it, ostensibly, outwardly, seemingly, superficially

apparition noun GHOST, chimera, phantom, specter, spirit, wraith

appeal verb 1 PLEAD, ask, beg, call upon, entreat, pray, request
2 ATTRACT, allure, charm, entice, fascinate, interest, please, tempt
▶ noun 3 PLEA, application, entreaty, petition, prayer, request, supplication
4 ATTRACTION, allure, beauty, charm, fascination

appealing adjective ATTRACTIVE, alluring, charming, desirable, engaging, winsome

appear verb 1 COME INTO VIEW, be present, come out, come to light, crop up (informal), emerge, occur, show up (informal), surface, turn up

2 LOOK (LIKE or AS IF), occur, seem, strike one as

appearance noun 1 ARRIVAL, coming, emergence, introduction, presence
2 LOOK, demeanor, expression, figure, form, looks, manner, mien (literary)
3 IMPRESSION, front, guise, illusion, image, outward show, pretense, semblance

appease verb 1 PACIFY, calm, conciliate, de-stress, mollify, placate, quiet, satisfy, soothe
2 EASE, allay, alleviate, calm, relieve, soothe

appeasement noun
1 PACIFICATION, accommodation, compromise, concession, conciliation, mollification, placation
2 EASING, alleviation, lessening, relieving, soothing

appendage noun ATTACHMENT, accessory, addition, supplement

appendix noun SUPPLEMENT, addendum, addition, adjunct, appendage, postscript

appetite noun DESIRE, craving, demand, hunger, liking, longing, passion, relish, stomach, taste, yearning

appetizing adjective DELICIOUS, appealing, inviting, mouthwatering, palatable, succulent, tasty, tempting, yummy (informal)

applaud verb CLAP, acclaim, approve, cheer, commend, compliment, encourage, extol, praise

applause noun OVATION, accolade, approval, big hand, cheers, clapping, hand, praise

appliance noun DEVICE, apparatus, gadget, implement,

instrument, machine, mechanism, tool

applicable *adjective* APPROPRIATE, apt, fitting, pertinent, relevant, suitable, useful

applicant *noun* CANDIDATE, claimant, inquirer

application *noun* 1 REQUEST, appeal, claim, inquiry, petition, requisition
2 EFFORT, commitment, dedication, diligence, hard work, industry, perseverance

apply *verb* 1 REQUEST, appeal, claim, inquire, petition, put in, requisition
2 USE, bring to bear, carry out, employ, exercise, exert, implement, practice, utilize
3 PUT ON, cover with, lay on, paint, place, smear, spread on
4 BE RELEVANT, be applicable, be appropriate, bear upon, be fitting, fit, pertain, refer, relate
5 ▷▷ **apply oneself** TRY, be diligent, buckle down (*informal*), commit oneself, concentrate, dedicate oneself, devote oneself, persevere, work hard

appoint *verb* 1 ASSIGN, choose, commission, delegate, elect, name, nominate, select
2 DECIDE, allot, arrange, assign, choose, designate, establish, fix, set
3 EQUIP, fit out, furnish, provide, supply

appointed *adjective* 1 ASSIGNED, chosen, delegated, elected, named, nominated, selected
2 DECIDED, allotted, arranged, assigned, chosen, designated, established, fixed, set
3 EQUIPPED, fitted out, furnished, provided, supplied

appointment *noun* 1 MEETING, arrangement, assignation, date, engagement, interview, rendezvous
2 SELECTION, assignment, choice, election, naming, nomination
3 JOB, assignment, office, place, position, post, situation
4 ▷▷ **appointments** FITTINGS, fixtures, furnishings, gear, outfit, paraphernalia, trappings

apportion *verb* DIVIDE, allocate, allot, assign, dispense, distribute, dole out, ration out, share

apportionment *noun* DIVISION, allocation, allotment, assignment, dispensing, distribution, doling out, rationing out, sharing

apposite *adjective* APPROPRIATE, applicable, apt, fitting, pertinent, relevant, suitable, to the point

appraisal *noun* ASSESSMENT, estimate, estimation, evaluation, judgment, opinion

appraise *verb* ASSESS, estimate, evaluate, gauge, judge, rate, review, value

appreciable *adjective* SIGNIFICANT, considerable, definite, discernible, evident, marked, noticeable, obvious, pronounced, substantial

appreciate *verb* 1 VALUE, admire, enjoy, like, prize, rate highly, respect, treasure
2 BE AWARE OF, perceive, realize, recognize, sympathize with, take account of, understand
3 BE GRATEFUL FOR, be appreciative, be indebted, be obliged, be thankful for, give thanks for
4 INCREASE, enhance, gain, grow, improve, rise

appreciation *noun* 1 GRATITUDE, acknowledgment, gratefulness, indebtedness, obligation, thankfulness, thanks

2 AWARENESS, admiration, comprehension, enjoyment, perception, realization, recognition, sensitivity, sympathy, understanding

3 INCREASE, enhancement, gain, growth, improvement, rise

appreciative adjective 1 GRATEFUL, beholden, affable, indebted, obliged, thankful

2 AWARE, admiring, enthusiastic, respectful, responsive, sensitive, sympathetic, understanding

apprehend verb 1 ARREST, capture, catch, nick (slang, chiefly Brit.), seize, take prisoner

2 UNDERSTAND, comprehend, conceive, get the picture, grasp, perceive, realize, recognize

apprehension noun 1 ANXIETY, alarm, concern, dread, fear, foreboding, suspicion, trepidation, worry

2 ARREST, capture, catching, seizure, taking

3 AWARENESS, comprehension, grasp, perception, understanding

apprehensive adjective ANXIOUS, concerned, foreboding, nervous, uneasy, wired (slang), worried

apprentice noun TRAINEE, beginner, learner, novice, probationer, pupil, student

approach verb 1 MOVE TOWARDS, come close, come near, draw near, near, reach

2 MAKE A PROPOSAL TO, appeal to, apply to, make overtures to, sound out

3 SET ABOUT, begin work on, commence, embark on, enter upon, make a start, undertake

▶ noun 4 COMING, advance, arrival, drawing near, nearing

5 (often plural) PROPOSAL, advance, appeal, application, invitation, offer, overture, proposition

6 ACCESS, avenue, entrance, passage, road, way

7 WAY, manner, means, method, style, technique

8 LIKENESS, approximation, semblance

approachable adjective

1 FRIENDLY, affable, congenial, cordial, open, sociable

2 ACCESSIBLE, attainable, reachable

appropriate adjective 1 SUITABLE, apt, befitting, fitting, pertinent, relevant, to the point, well-suited

▶ verb 2 SEIZE, commandeer, confiscate, impound, take possession of, usurp

3 STEAL, embezzle, filch, misappropriate, pilfer, pocket

4 SET ASIDE, allocate, allot, apportion, assign, devote, earmark

approval noun 1 CONSENT, agreement, assent, authorization, blessing, endorsement, permission, recommendation, sanction

2 FAVOR, acclaim, admiration, applause, appreciation, esteem, good opinion, praise, respect

approve verb 1 FAVOR, admire, commend, have a good opinion of, like, praise, regard highly, respect

2 AGREE TO, allow, assent to, authorize, consent to, endorse, pass, permit, ratify, recommend, sanction

approximate adjective 1 CLOSE, near

2 ROUGH, estimated, inexact, loose

▶ verb 3 COME CLOSE, approach, border on, come near, reach, resemble, touch, verge on

approximately *adverb* ALMOST, about, around, circa (*used with dates*), close to, in the region of, just about, more or less, nearly, roughly

approximation *noun* GUESS, conjecture, estimate, estimation, guesswork, rough calculation, rough idea

apron *noun* PINAFORE, pinny (*informal*)

apt *adjective* 1 INCLINED, disposed, given, liable, likely, of a mind, prone, ready
2 APPROPRIATE, fitting, pertinent, relevant, suitable, to the point
3 GIFTED, clever, quick, sharp, smart, talented

aptitude *noun* 1 TENDENCY, inclination, leaning, predilection, proclivity, propensity
2 GIFT, ability, capability, faculty, intelligence, proficiency, talent

arable *adjective* PRODUCTIVE, farmable, fertile, fruitful

arbiter *noun* 1 JUDGE, adjudicator, arbitrator, referee, umpire
2 AUTHORITY, controller, dictator, expert, governor, lord, master, pundit, ruler

arbitrary *adjective* RANDOM, capricious, chance, erratic, inconsistent, personal, subjective, whimsical

arbitrate *verb* SETTLE, adjudicate, decide, determine, judge, mediate, pass judgment, referee, umpire

arbitration *noun* SETTLEMENT, adjudication, decision, determination, judgment

arbitrator *noun* JUDGE, adjudicator, arbiter, referee, umpire

arc *noun* CURVE, arch, bend, bow, crescent, half-moon

arcade *noun* GALLERY, cloister, colonnade, portico

arcane *adjective* MYSTERIOUS, esoteric, hidden, occult, recondite, secret

arch[1] *noun* 1 CURVE, archway, dome, span, vault
2 CURVE, arc, bend, bow, hump, semicircle
▶ *verb* 3 CURVE, arc, bend, bow, bridge, span

arch[2] *adjective* PLAYFUL, frolicsome, mischievous, pert, roguish, saucy, sly, waggish

archaic *adjective* 1 OLD, ancient, antique, bygone, olden (*archaic*), primitive
2 OLD-FASHIONED, antiquated, behind the times, obsolete, outmoded, out of date, passé

archetypal *adjective* 1 TYPICAL, classic, ideal, model, standard
2 ORIGINAL, prototypic *or* prototypical

archetype *noun* 1 STANDARD, model, paradigm, pattern, prime example
2 ORIGINAL, prototype

architect *noun* DESIGNER, master builder, planner

architecture *noun* 1 DESIGN, building, construction, planning
2 STRUCTURE, construction, design, framework, make-up, style

archive *noun* 1 RECORD OFFICE, museum, registry, repository
2 ▷▷ **archives** RECORDS, annals, chronicles, documents, papers, rolls

arctic *adjective* (*informal*) FREEZING, chilly, cold, frigid, frozen, glacial, icy

Arctic *adjective* POLAR, far-northern, hyperborean

ardent *adjective* 1 PASSIONATE,

amorous, hot-blooded,
impassioned, intense, lusty
2 ENTHUSIASTIC, avid, eager, keen,
zealous

ardor *noun* **1** PASSION, fervor,
intensity, spirit, vehemence,
warmth
2 ENTHUSIASM, avidity, eagerness,
keenness, zeal

arduous *adjective* DIFFICULT,
exhausting, fatiguing, grueling,
laborious, onerous, punishing,
rigorous, strenuous, taxing, tiring

area *noun* **1** REGION, district,
locality, neighborhood, zone
2 PART, portion, section, sector
3 FIELD, department, domain,
province, realm, sphere, territory

arena *noun* **1** RING, amphitheater,
bowl, enclosure, field, ground,
stadium
2 SPHERE, area, domain, field,
province, realm, sector, territory

argue *verb* **1** DISCUSS, assert, claim,
debate, dispute, maintain, reason,
remonstrate
2 QUARREL, bicker, disagree,
dispute, fall out (*informal*), fight,
squabble

argument *noun* **1** QUARREL, clash,
controversy, disagreement,
dispute, feud, fight, row, squabble
2 DISCUSSION, assertion, claim,
debate, dispute, plea, questioning,
remonstration
3 REASON, argumentation, case,
defense, dialectic, ground(s),
line of reasoning, logic, polemic,
reasoning

argumentative *adjective*
QUARRELSOME, belligerent,
combative, contentious,
contrary, disputatious, litigious,
opinionated

arid *adjective* **1** DRY, barren, desert,
parched, sterile, torrid, waterless

2 BORING, dreary, dry, dull,
tedious, tiresome, uninspired,
uninteresting

arise *verb* **1** HAPPEN, begin, emerge,
ensue, follow, occur, result,
start, stem
2 (*old-fashioned*) GET UP, get to one's
feet, go up, rise, stand up, wake up

aristocracy *noun* UPPER CLASS,
elite, gentry, nobility, patricians,
peerage, ruling class

aristocrat *adjective* NOBLE, aristo
(*informal*), grandee, lady, lord,
patrician, peer, peeress

aristocratic *noun* UPPER-CLASS,
blue-blooded, elite, gentlemanly,
lordly, noble, patrician, titled

arm¹ *noun* UPPER LIMB, appendage,
limb

arm² *verb* (*especially with weapons*)
EQUIP, accouter, array, deck out,
furnish, issue with, provide,
supply

armada *noun* FLEET, flotilla, navy,
squadron

armaments *plural noun* WEAPONS,
ammunition, arms, guns,
materiel, munitions, ordnance,
weaponry

armed *adjective* CARRYING
WEAPONS, equipped, fitted out,
primed, protected

armistice *noun* TRUCE, ceasefire,
peace, suspension of hostilities

armor *noun* PROTECTION, armor
plate, covering, sheathing, shield

armored *adjective* PROTECTED,
armor-plated, bombproof,
bulletproof, ironclad, mailed,
steel-plated

arms *plural noun* **1** WEAPONS,
armaments, firearms, guns,
instruments of war, ordnance,
weaponry
2 HERALDRY, blazonry, crest,
escutcheon, insignia

army noun 1 SOLDIERS, armed force, legions, military, military force, soldiery, troops
2 VAST NUMBER, array, horde, host, multitude, pack, swarm, throng

aroma noun SCENT, bouquet, fragrance, odor, perfume, redolence, savor, smell

aromatic adjective FRAGRANT, balmy, perfumed, pungent, redolent, savory, spicy, sweet-scented, sweet-smelling

around preposition 1 SURROUNDING, about, encircling, enclosing, encompassing, on all sides of, on every side of
2 APPROXIMATELY, about, circa (used with dates), roughly
▶ adverb 3 EVERYWHERE, about, all over, here and there, in all directions, on all sides, throughout, to and fro
4 NEAR, at hand, close, close at hand, nearby, nigh (archaic or dialect)

arouse verb 1 STIMULATE, excite, incite, instigate, provoke, spur, stir up, summon up, whip up
2 AWAKEN, rouse, waken, wake up

arrange verb 1 PLAN, construct, contrive, devise, fix up, organize, prepare
2 AGREE, adjust, come to terms, compromise, determine, settle
3 PUT IN ORDER, classify, group, line up, order, organize, position, sort
4 ADAPT, instrument, orchestrate, score

arrangement noun 1 (often plural) PLAN, organization, planning, preparation, provision, schedule
2 AGREEMENT, adjustment, compact, compromise, deal, settlement, terms
3 ORDER, alignment,

classification, form, organization, structure, system
4 ADAPTATION, instrumentation, interpretation, orchestration, score, version

array noun 1 ARRANGEMENT, collection, display, exhibition, formation, line-up, parade, show, supply
2 (poetic) CLOTHING, apparel, attire, clothes, dress, finery, garments, regalia
▶ verb 3 ARRANGE, display, exhibit, group, parade, range, show
4 DRESS, adorn, attire, clothe, deck, decorate, festoon

arrest verb 1 CAPTURE, apprehend, catch, detain, nick (slang, chiefly Brit.), seize, take prisoner
2 STOP, block, delay, end, inhibit, interrupt, obstruct, slow, suppress
3 GRIP, absorb, engage, engross, fascinate, hold, intrigue, occupy
▶ noun 4 CAPTURE, bust (informal), cop (slang), detention, seizure
5 STOPPING, blockage, delay, end, hindrance, interruption, obstruction, suppression

arresting adjective STRIKING, cool (informal), engaging, impressive, noticeable, outstanding, phat (slang), remarkable, stunning, surprising

arrival noun 1 COMING, advent, appearance, arriving, entrance, happening, occurrence, taking place
2 NEWCOMER, caller, entrant, incomer, visitor

arrive verb 1 COME, appear, enter, get to, reach, show up (informal), turn up
2 (informal) SUCCEED, become famous, make good, make it (informal), make the grade (informal)

arrogance noun CONCEIT,

disdainfulness, haughtiness, high-handedness, insolence, pride, superciliousness, swagger

arrogant *adjective* CONCEITED, disdainful, haughty, high-handed, overbearing, proud, scornful, supercilious

arrow *noun* 1 DART, bolt, flight, quarrel, shaft (*archaic*)
2 POINTER, indicator

arsenal *noun* ARMORY, ammunition dump, arms depot, ordnance depot, stockpile, store, storehouse, supply

art *noun* SKILL, craft, expertise, ingenuity, mastery, virtuosity

artful *adjective* CUNNING, clever, crafty, shrewd, sly, smart, wily

article *noun* 1 PIECE, composition, discourse, essay, feature, item, paper, story, treatise
2 THING, commodity, item, object, piece, substance, unit
3 CLAUSE, item, paragraph, part, passage, point, portion, section

articulate *adjective* 1 EXPRESSIVE, clear, coherent, eloquent, fluent, lucid, well-spoken
▶ *verb* 2 EXPRESS, enunciate, pronounce, say, speak, state, talk, utter, voice

artifice *noun* 1 TRICK, contrivance, device, machination, maneuver, stratagem, subterfuge, tactic
2 CLEVERNESS, ingenuity, inventiveness, skill

artificial *adjective* 1 SYNTHETIC, man-made, manufactured, non-natural, plastic
2 FAKE, bogus, counterfeit, imitation, mock, sham, simulated
3 INSINCERE, affected, contrived, false, feigned, forced, phoney *or* phony (*informal*), unnatural

artillery *noun* BIG GUNS, battery, cannon, cannonry, gunnery, ordnance

artisan *noun* CRAFTSMAN, journeyman, mechanic, skilled workman, technician

artistic *adjective* CREATIVE, aesthetic, beautiful, cultured, elegant, refined, sophisticated, stylish, tasteful

artistry *noun* SKILL, brilliance, craftsmanship, creativity, finesse, mastery, proficiency, virtuosity

artless *adjective*
1 STRAIGHTFORWARD, frank, guileless, open, plain
2 NATURAL, homely, plain, pure, simple, unadorned, unaffected, unpretentious

as *conjunction* 1 WHEN, at the time that, during the time that, just as, while
2 IN THE WAY THAT, in the manner that, like
3 WHAT, that which
4 SINCE, because, considering that, seeing that
5 FOR INSTANCE, like, such as
▶ *preposition* 6 BEING, in the character of, in the role of, under the name of

ascend *verb* MOVE UP, climb, go up, mount, scale

ascent *noun* 1 RISE, ascending, ascension, climb, mounting, rising, scaling, upward movement
2 UPWARD SLOPE, gradient, incline, ramp, rise, rising ground

ascertain *verb* FIND OUT, confirm, determine, discover, establish, learn

ascetic *noun* 1 MONK, abstainer, hermit, nun, recluse
▶ *adjective* 2 SELF-DENYING, abstinent, austere, celibate, frugal, puritanical, self-disciplined

ascribe *verb* ATTRIBUTE, assign,

charge, credit, impute, put down, refer, set down

ashamed *adjective* EMBARRASSED, distressed, guilty, humiliated, mortified, remorseful, shamefaced, sheepish, sorry

ashen *adjective* PALE, colorless, gray, leaden, like death warmed over (*informal*), pallid, wan, white

ashore *adverb* ON LAND, aground, landwards, on dry land, on the beach, on the shore, shorewards, to the shore

aside *adverb* 1 TO ONE SIDE, apart, beside, on one side, out of the way, privately, separately, to the side
▶ *noun* 2 INTERPOLATION, parenthesis

asinine *adjective* STUPID, fatuous, foolish, idiotic, imbecilic, moronic, senseless

ask *verb* 1 INQUIRE, interrogate, query, question, quiz
2 REQUEST, appeal, beg, demand, plead, seek
3 INVITE, bid, summon

askew *adverb* 1 CROOKEDLY, aslant, awry, obliquely, off-center, to one side
▶ *adjective* 2 CROOKED, awry, cockeyed (*informal*), lopsided, oblique, off-center, skew-whiff (*Brit. informal*)

asleep *adjective* SLEEPING, dormant, dozing, fast asleep, napping, slumbering, snoozing (*informal*), sound asleep

aspect *noun* 1 FEATURE, angle, facet, side
2 POSITION, outlook, point of view, prospect, scene, situation, view
3 APPEARANCE, air, attitude, bearing, condition, demeanor, expression, look, manner

asphyxiate *verb* SUFFOCATE, choke, smother, stifle, strangle, strangulate, throttle

aspiration *noun* AIM, ambition, desire, dream, goal, hope, objective, wish

aspire *verb* AIM, desire, dream, hope, long, seek, set one's heart on, wish

aspiring *adjective* HOPEFUL, ambitious, eager, longing, wannabe (*informal*), would-be

ass *noun* 1 DONKEY, moke (*slang*)
2 FOOL, blockhead, dork (*slang*), halfwit, idiot, jackass, numbskull *or* numskull, oaf, schmuck (*slang*), twit (*informal, chiefly Brit.*)

assail *verb* ATTACK, assault, fall upon, lay into (*informal*), set upon

assailant *noun* ATTACKER, aggressor, assailer, assaulter, invader

assassin *noun* MURDERER, executioner, hatchet man (*slang*), hit man (*slang*), killer, liquidator, slayer

assassinate *verb* MURDER, eliminate (*slang*), hit (*slang*), kill, liquidate, slay, take out (*slang*)

assault *noun* 1 ATTACK, charge, invasion, offensive, onslaught
▶ *verb* 2 ATTACK, beset, fall upon, lay into (*informal*), set about, set upon, strike at

assemble *verb* 1 GATHER, amass, bring together, call together, collect, come together, congregate, meet, muster, rally
2 PUT TOGETHER, build up, connect, construct, fabricate, fit together, join, piece together, set up

assembly *noun* 1 GATHERING, collection, company, conference, congress, council, crowd, group, mass, meeting
2 PUTTING TOGETHER, building up, connecting, construction, piecing

together, setting up
assent *noun* 1 AGREEMENT,
acceptance, approval, compliance,
concurrence, consent, permission,
sanction
▶ *verb* 2 AGREE, allow, approve,
consent, grant, permit
assert *verb* 1 STATE, affirm,
declare, maintain, profess,
pronounce, swear
2 INSIST UPON, claim, defend,
press, put forward, stand up for,
stress, uphold
3 ▷▷ **assert oneself** BE FORCEFUL,
exert one's influence, make one's
presence felt, put oneself forward,
put one's foot down (*informal*)
assertion *noun* 1 STATEMENT,
claim, declaration,
pronouncement
2 INSISTENCE, maintenance,
stressing
assertive *adjective* CONFIDENT,
aggressive, domineering,
emphatic, feisty (*informal*),
forceful, insistent, positive, pushy
(*informal*), strong-willed
assess *verb* 1 JUDGE, appraise,
estimate, evaluate, rate, size up
(*informal*), value, weigh
2 EVALUATE, fix, impose, levy, rate,
tax, value
assessment *noun* 1 JUDGMENT,
appraisal, estimate, evaluation,
rating, valuation
2 EVALUATION, charge, fee, levy,
rating, toll, valuation
asset *noun* 1 BENEFIT, advantage,
aid, blessing, boon, feather in
one's cap, help, resource, service
2 ▷▷ **assets** PROPERTY, capital,
estate, funds, goods, money,
possessions, resources, wealth
assiduous *adjective* DILIGENT,
hard-working, indefatigable,
industrious, persevering,

persistent, unflagging
assign *verb* 1 SELECT, appoint,
choose, delegate, designate,
name, nominate
2 GIVE, allocate, allot, apportion,
consign, distribute, give out,
grant
3 ATTRIBUTE, accredit, ascribe,
put down
assignation *noun* 1 SECRET
MEETING, clandestine meeting,
illicit meeting, rendezvous, tryst
2 SELECTION, appointment,
assignment, choice, delegation,
designation, nomination
assignment *noun* TASK,
appointment, commission,
duty, job, mission, position, post,
responsibility
assimilate *verb* 1 LEARN, absorb,
digest, incorporate, take in
2 ADJUST, adapt, blend in, mingle
assist *verb* HELP, abet, aid,
cooperate, lend a helping hand,
serve, support
assistance *noun* HELP, aid,
backing, cooperation, helping
hand, support
assistant *noun* HELPER,
accomplice, aide, ally, colleague,
right-hand man, second,
supporter
associate *verb* 1 CONNECT, ally,
combine, identify, join, link, lump
together
2 MIX, accompany, consort,
hobnob, mingle, socialize
▶ *noun* 3 PARTNER, collaborator,
colleague, confederate, co-worker
4 FRIEND, ally, companion,
comrade, homeboy (*slang*),
homegirl (*slang*), mate (*informal*)
association *noun* 1 GROUP,
alliance, band, club, coalition,
federation, league, organization,
society

2 CONNECTION, blend, combination, joining, juxtaposition, mixture, pairing, union

assorted *adjective* VARIOUS, different, diverse, miscellaneous, mixed, motley, sundry, varied

assortment *noun* VARIETY, array, choice, collection, jumble, medley, mixture, selection

assume *verb* 1 TAKE FOR GRANTED, believe, expect, fancy, imagine, infer, presume, suppose, surmise, think

2 TAKE ON, accept, enter upon, put on, shoulder, take over

3 PUT ON, adopt, affect, feign, imitate, impersonate, mimic, pretend to, simulate

assumed *adjective* 1 FALSE, bogus, counterfeit, fake, fictitious, made-up, make-believe

2 TAKEN FOR GRANTED, accepted, expected, hypothetical, presumed, presupposed, supposed, surmised

assumption *noun* 1 PRESUMPTION, belief, conjecture, guess, hypothesis, inference, supposition, surmise

2 TAKING ON, acceptance, acquisition, adoption, entering upon, putting on, shouldering, takeover, taking up

3 TAKING, acquisition, appropriation, seizure, takeover

assurance *noun* 1 ASSERTION, declaration, guarantee, oath, pledge, promise, statement, vow, word

2 CONFIDENCE, boldness, certainty, conviction, faith, nerve, poise, self-confidence

assure *verb* 1 PROMISE, certify, confirm, declare confidently, give one's word to, guarantee, pledge, swear, vow

2 CONVINCE, comfort, embolden, encourage, hearten, persuade, reassure

3 MAKE CERTAIN, clinch, complete, confirm, ensure, guarantee, make sure, seal, secure

assured *adjective* 1 CONFIDENT, certain, poised, positive, self-assured, self-confident, sure of oneself

2 CERTAIN, beyond doubt, confirmed, ensured, fixed, guaranteed, in the bag (*slang*), secure, settled, sure

astonish *verb* AMAZE, astound, bewilder, confound, daze, dumbfound, stagger, stun, surprise

astonishing *adjective* AMAZING, astounding, bewildering, breathtaking, brilliant, sensational (*informal*), staggering, stunning, surprising

astonishment *noun* AMAZEMENT, awe, bewilderment, confusion, consternation, surprise, wonder, wonderment

astounding *adjective* AMAZING, astonishing, bewildering, breathtaking, brilliant, cool (*informal*), impressive, phat (*slang*), sensational (*informal*), staggering, stunning, surprising

astray *adjective or adverb* OFF THE RIGHT TRACK, adrift, amiss, lost, off, off course, off the mark, off the subject

astute *adjective* INTELLIGENT, canny, clever, crafty, cunning, perceptive, sagacious, sharp, shrewd, subtle

asylum *noun* 1 REFUGE, harbor, haven, preserve, retreat, safety, sanctuary, shelter

2 (*old-fashioned*) MENTAL HOSPITAL, funny farm (*slang*), hospital,

institution, madhouse (*informal*), psychiatric hospital, psychiatric ward

atheism *noun* NONBELIEF, disbelief, godlessness, heathenism, infidelity, irreligion, paganism, skepticism, unbelief

atheist *noun* NONBELIEVER, disbeliever, heathen, infidel, pagan, skeptic, unbeliever

athlete *noun* SPORTSPERSON, competitor, contestant, gymnast, player, runner, sportsman, sportswoman

athletic *adjective* FIT, active, energetic, muscular, powerful, strapping, strong, sturdy

athletics *plural noun* SPORTS, contests, exercises, gymnastics, races, track and field events

atmosphere *noun* 1 AIR, aerosphere, heavens, sky
2 FEELING, ambience, character, climate, environment, mood, spirit, surroundings, tone

atom *noun* PARTICLE, bit, dot, molecule, speck, spot, trace

atone *verb* (usually with *for*) MAKE AMENDS, compensate, do penance, make redress, make reparation, make up for, pay for, recompense, redress

atonement *noun* AMENDS, compensation, penance, recompense, redress, reparation, restitution

atrocious *adjective* 1 CRUEL, barbaric, brutal, fiendish, infernal, monstrous, savage, vicious, wicked
2 (*informal*) SHOCKING, appalling, detestable, grievous, horrible, horrifying, terrible

atrocity *noun* 1 CRUELTY, barbarity, brutality, fiendishness, horror, savagery, viciousness, wickedness

2 ACT OF CRUELTY, abomination, crime, evil, horror, outrage

attach *verb* 1 CONNECT, add, couple, fasten, fix, join, link, secure, stick, tie
2 PUT, ascribe, assign, associate, attribute, connect

attached *adjective* 1 SPOKEN FOR, accompanied, engaged, married, partnered
2 ▷▷ **attached to** FOND OF, affectionate towards, devoted to, full of regard for

attachment *noun* 1 FONDNESS, affection, affinity, attraction, liking, regard
2 ACCESSORY, accouterment, extension, extra, fitting, fixture, supplement

attack *verb* 1 ASSAULT, invade, lay into (*informal*), raid, set upon, storm, strike (at)
2 CRITICIZE, abuse, blame, censure, have a go (at) (*informal*), put down, vilify
▶ *noun* 3 ASSAULT, campaign, charge, foray, incursion, invasion, offensive, onslaught, raid, strike
4 CRITICISM, abuse, blame, censure, denigration, stick (*slang*), vilification
5 BOUT, convulsion, fit, paroxysm, seizure, spasm, stroke

attacker *noun* ASSAILANT, aggressor, assaulter, intruder, invader, raider

attain *verb* ACHIEVE, accomplish, acquire, complete, fulfill, gain, get, obtain, reach

attainment *noun* ACHIEVEMENT, accomplishment, completion, feat

attempt *verb* 1 TRY, endeavor, seek, strive, undertake, venture
▶ *noun* 2 TRY, bid, crack (*informal*), effort, go (*informal*), shot (*informal*),

stab (informal), trial

attend verb 1 BE PRESENT, appear, frequent, go to, haunt, put in an appearance, show oneself, turn up, visit

2 LOOK AFTER, care for, mind, minister to, nurse, take care of, tend

3 PAY ATTENTION, hear, heed, listen, mark, note, observe, pay heed

4 ▷▷ **attend to** APPLY ONESELF TO, concentrate on, devote oneself to, get to work on, look after, occupy oneself with, see to, take care of

attendance noun 1 PRESENCE, appearance, attending, being there

2 TURNOUT, audience, crowd, gate, house, number present

attendant noun 1 ASSISTANT, aide, companion, escort, follower, guard, helper, servant

▶ adjective 2 ACCOMPANYING, accessory, associated, concomitant, consequent, related

attention noun 1 CONCENTRATION, deliberation, heed, intentness, mind, scrutiny, thinking, thought

2 NOTICE, awareness, consciousness, consideration, observation, recognition, regard

3 CARE, concern, looking after, ministration, treatment

attentive adjective 1 INTENT, alert, awake, careful, concentrating, heedful, mindful, observant, studious, watchful

2 CONSIDERATE, courteous, helpful, kind, obliging, polite, respectful, thoughtful

attic noun LOFT, garret

attire noun CLOTHES, apparel, costume, dress, garb, garments, outfit, robes, wear

attitude noun 1 DISPOSITION, approach, frame of mind, mood, opinion, outlook, perspective, point of view, position, stance

2 POSITION, pose, posture, stance

attract verb APPEAL TO, allure, charm, draw, enchant, entice, lure, pull (informal), tempt

attraction noun APPEAL, allure, charm, enticement, fascination, lure, magnetism, pull (informal), temptation

attractive adjective APPEALING, alluring, charming, fair, fetching, good-looking, handsome, inviting, lovely, pleasant, pretty, tempting

attribute verb 1 ASCRIBE, assign, charge, credit, put down to, refer, set down to, trace to

▶ noun 2 QUALITY, aspect, character, characteristic, facet, feature, peculiarity, property, trait

attune verb ACCUSTOM, adapt, adjust, familiarize, harmonize, regulate

audacious adjective 1 DARING, bold, brave, courageous, fearless, intrepid, rash, reckless

2 CHEEKY, brazen, defiant, impertinent, impudent, insolent, presumptuous, shameless

audacity noun 1 DARING, boldness, bravery, courage, fearlessness, nerve, rashness, recklessness

2 CHEEK, chutzpah (informal), effrontery, impertinence, impudence, insolence, nerve

audible adjective CLEAR, detectable, discernible, distinct, hearable, perceptible

audience noun 1 SPECTATORS, assembly, crowd, gallery, gathering, listeners, onlookers, turnout, viewers

2 INTERVIEW, consultation, hearing, meeting, reception

aura *noun* AIR, ambience, atmosphere, feeling, mood, quality, tone

auspicious *adjective* FAVORABLE, bright, encouraging, felicitous, hopeful, promising

austere *adjective* 1 STERN, forbidding, formal, serious, severe, solemn, strict
2 ASCETIC, abstemious, puritanical, self-disciplined, sober, solemn, strait-laced, strict
3 PLAIN, bleak, harsh, homely, simple, spare, Spartan, stark

austerity *noun* 1 STERNNESS, formality, inflexibility, rigor, seriousness, severity, solemnity, stiffness, strictness
2 ASCETICISM, puritanism, self-denial, self-discipline, sobriety
3 PLAINNESS, simplicity, starkness

authentic *adjective* GENUINE, actual, authoritative, bona fide, legitimate, pure, real, true-to-life, valid

authenticity *noun* GENUINENESS, accuracy, certainty, faithfulness, legitimacy, purity, truthfulness, validity

author *noun* 1 WRITER, composer, creator
2 CREATOR, architect, designer, father, founder, inventor, originator, producer

authoritarian *adjective*
1 STRICT, autocratic, dictatorial, doctrinaire, dogmatic, severe, tyrannical
▶ *noun* 2 DISCIPLINARIAN, absolutist, autocrat, despot, dictator, tyrant

authoritative *adjective*
1 RELIABLE, accurate, authentic, definitive, dependable, trustworthy, valid
2 COMMANDING, assertive, imperious, imposing, masterly, self-assured

authority *noun* 1 POWER, command, control, direction, influence, supremacy, sway, weight
2 (usually plural) POWERS THAT BE, administration, government, management, officialdom, police, the Establishment
3 EXPERT, connoisseur, judge, master, professional, specialist

authorization *noun* PERMISSION, a blank check, approval, leave, license, permit, warrant

authorize *verb* 1 EMPOWER, accredit, commission, enable, entitle, give authority
2 PERMIT, allow, approve, give authority for, license, sanction, warrant

autocracy *noun* DICTATORSHIP, absolutism, despotism, tyranny

autocrat *noun* DICTATOR, absolutist, despot, tyrant

autocratic *adjective* DICTATORIAL, absolute, all-powerful, despotic, domineering, imperious, tyrannical

automatic *adjective*
1 MECHANICAL, automated, mechanized, push-button, self-propelling
2 INVOLUNTARY, instinctive, mechanical, natural, reflex, spontaneous, unconscious, unwilled

autonomous *adjective* SELF-RULING, free, independent, self-determining, self-governing, sovereign

autonomy *noun* INDEPENDENCE, freedom, home rule, self-determination, self-government, self-rule, sovereignty

auxiliary *adjective*

1 SUPPLEMENTARY, back-up,
emergency, fall-back, reserve,
secondary, subsidiary, substitute
2 SUPPORTING, accessory, aiding,
ancillary, assisting, helping
▶ *noun* 3 BACKUP, reserve
4 HELPER, assistant, associate,
companion, subordinate,
supporter

avail *verb* 1 BENEFIT, aid, assist,
be of advantage, be useful, help,
profit
▶ *noun* 2 BENEFIT, advantage, aid,
good, help, profit, use

availability *noun* ACCESSIBILITY,
attainability, handiness,
readiness

available *adjective* ACCESSIBLE,
at hand, at one's disposal, free,
handy, on tap, ready, to hand

avalanche *noun* 1 SNOW-SLIDE,
landslide, landslip
2 FLOOD, barrage, deluge,
inundation, torrent

avant-garde *adjective*
PROGRESSIVE, experimental,
ground-breaking, innovative,
pioneering, unconventional

avarice *noun* GREED, covetousness,
meanness, miserliness,
niggardliness, parsimony,
stinginess

avaricious *adjective* GRASPING,
covetous, greedy, mean, miserly,
niggardly, parsimonious, stingy

avenge *verb* GET REVENGE FOR,
get even for (*informal*), get one's
own back, hit back, punish, repay,
retaliate

avenue *noun* STREET, approach,
boulevard, course, drive, passage,
path, road, route, way

average *noun* 1 USUAL, mean,
medium, midpoint, norm,
normal, par, standard
2 ▷▷ **on average** USUALLY, as a

rule, for the most part, generally,
normally, typically
▶ *adjective* 3 USUAL, commonplace,
fair, general, normal, ordinary,
regular, standard, typical
4 MEAN, intermediate, median,
medium, middle
▶ *verb* 5 MAKE ON AVERAGE, balance
out to, be on average, do on
average, even out to

averse *adjective* OPPOSED,
disinclined, hostile, ill-disposed,
loath, reluctant, unwilling

aversion *noun* HATRED, animosity,
antipathy, disinclination,
dislike, hostility, revulsion,
unwillingness

avert *verb* 1 TURN AWAY, turn aside
2 WARD OFF, avoid, fend off,
forestall, frustrate, preclude,
prevent, stave off

aviator *noun* PILOT, aeronaut,
airman, flyer

avid *adjective* 1 ENTHUSIASTIC,
ardent, devoted, eager, fanatical,
intense, keen, passionate, zealous
2 INSATIABLE, grasping, greedy,
hungry, rapacious, ravenous,
thirsty, voracious

avoid *verb* 1 REFRAIN FROM, dodge,
duck (out of) (*informal*), eschew,
fight shy of, shirk
2 PREVENT, avert
3 KEEP AWAY FROM, bypass, dodge,
elude, escape, evade, shun, steer
clear of

avoidance *noun* EVASION,
dodging, eluding, escape, keeping
away, shunning, steering clear

avowed *adjective* 1 DECLARED,
open, professed, self-proclaimed,
sworn
2 CONFESSED, acknowledged,
admitted

await *verb* 1 WAIT FOR, abide,
anticipate, expect, look for, look

forward to, stay for

2 BE IN STORE FOR, attend, be in readiness for, be prepared for, be ready for, wait for

awake *adjective* 1 NOT SLEEPING, aroused, awakened, aware, conscious, wakeful, wide-awake

2 ALERT, alive, attentive, aware, heedful, observant, on the lookout, vigilant, watchful

▶ *verb* 3 WAKE UP, awaken, rouse, wake

4 ALERT, arouse, kindle, provoke, revive, stimulate, stir up

awaken *verb* 1 AWAKE, arouse, revive, rouse, wake

2 ALERT, kindle, provoke, stimulate, stir up

awakening *noun* WAKING UP, arousal, revival, rousing, stimulation, stirring up

award *verb* 1 GIVE, bestow, confer, endow, grant, hand out, present

▶ *noun* 2 PRIZE, decoration, gift, grant, trophy

aware *adjective* 1 ▷▷ **aware of** KNOWING ABOUT, acquainted with, conscious of, conversant with, familiar with, mindful of INFORMED, enlightened, in the picture, knowledgeable

awareness *noun* KNOWLEDGE, consciousness, familiarity, perception, realization, recognition, understanding

away *adverb* 1 OFF, abroad, elsewhere, from here, from home, hence

2 AT A DISTANCE, apart, far, remote

3 ASIDE, out of the way, to one side

4 CONTINUOUSLY, incessantly, interminably, relentlessly, repeatedly, uninterruptedly, unremittingly

▶ *adjective* 5 NOT PRESENT, abroad, absent, elsewhere, gone, not at home, not here, out

awe *noun* 1 WONDER, admiration, amazement, astonishment, dread, fear, horror, respect, reverence, terror

▶ *verb* 2 IMPRESS, amaze, astonish, frighten, horrify, intimidate, stun, terrify

awesome *adjective* 1 AWE-INSPIRING, amazing, astonishing, breathtaking, cool (*informal*), formidable, impressive, intimidating, phat (*slang*), stunning

2 (*informal*) FIRST-CLASS, ace (*informal*), choice, elite, excellent, first-rate, hand-picked, superior, world-class

awful *adjective* 1 TERRIBLE, abysmal, appalling, deplorable, dreadful, frightful, ghastly, horrendous

2 (*obsolete*) AWE-INSPIRING, awesome, fearsome, majestic, solemn

awfully *adverb* 1 BADLY, disgracefully, dreadfully, reprehensibly, unforgivably, unpleasantly, woefully, wretchedly

2 (*informal*) VERY, dreadfully, exceedingly, exceptionally, extremely, greatly, immensely, terribly

awkward *adjective* 1 CLUMSY, gauche, gawky, inelegant, lumbering, uncoordinated, ungainly

2 UNMANAGEABLE, clunky (*informal*), cumbersome, difficult, inconvenient, troublesome, unwieldy

3 EMBARRASSING, delicate, difficult, ill at ease, inconvenient, uncomfortable

awkwardness *noun*

1 CLUMSINESS, gawkiness, inelegance, ungainliness

2 UNWIELDINESS, difficulty, inconvenience

3 EMBARRASSMENT, delicacy, difficulty, inconvenience

ax *noun* 1 HATCHET, adz, chopper

2 ▷▷ **the ax** DISMISSAL (*informal*), the sack (*informal*), termination, the boot (*slang*), the chop (*slang*)

▶ *verb* 3 (*informal*) CUT BACK, cancel, dismiss, dispense with, eliminate, fire (*informal*), get rid of, remove, sack (*informal*)

axiom *noun* PRINCIPLE, adage, aphorism, dictum, maxim, precept, truism

axiomatic *adjective* SELF-EVIDENT, accepted, assumed, certain, given, granted, manifest, understood

axis *noun* PIVOT, axle, center line, shaft, spindle

axle *noun* SHAFT, axis, pin, pivot, rod, spindle

babble *verb* 1 GABBLE, burble, chatter, jabber, prattle, waffle (*informal, chiefly Brit.*)
2 GIBBER, gurgle
▶ *noun* 3 GABBLE, burble, drivel, gibberish, waffle (*informal, chiefly Brit.*)

baby *noun* 1 INFANT, babe, babe in arms, bairn (*Scot.*), child, newborn child
▶ *adjective* 2 SMALL, little, mini, miniature, minute, teeny-weeny, tiny, wee

babyish *adjective* CHILDISH, foolish, immature, infantile, juvenile, puerile, sissy, spoiled

back *noun* 1 REAR, end, far end, hind part, hindquarters, reverse, stern, tail end
2 ▷▷ **behind one's back** SECRETLY, covertly, deceitfully, sneakily, surreptitiously
▶ *verb* 3 MOVE BACK, back off, backtrack, go back, retire, retreat, reverse, turn tail, withdraw
4 SUPPORT, advocate, assist, champion, endorse, promote, sponsor
▶ *adjective* 5 REAR, end, hind, hindmost, posterior, tail

6 PREVIOUS, delayed, earlier, elapsed, former, overdue, past

backbiting *noun* SLANDER, bitchiness (*slang*), cattiness (*informal*), defamation, disparagement, gossip, malice, scandalmongering, spitefulness

backbone *noun* 1 (*medical*) SPINAL COLUMN, spine, vertebrae, vertebral column
2 STRENGTH OF CHARACTER, character, courage, determination, fortitude, grit, nerve, pluck, resolution

backbreaking *adjective* EXHAUSTING, arduous, crushing, grueling, hard, laborious, punishing, strenuous

back down *verb* GIVE IN, accede, admit defeat, back-pedal, concede, surrender, withdraw, yield

backer *noun* SUPPORTER, advocate, angel (*informal*), benefactor, patron, promoter, second, sponsor, subscriber

backfire *verb* FAIL, boomerang, disappoint, flop (*informal*), miscarry, rebound, recoil

background *noun* HISTORY, circumstances, culture, education, environment, grounding, tradition, upbringing

backing *noun* SUPPORT, aid, assistance, encouragement, endorsement, moral support, patronage, sponsorship

backlash *noun* REACTION, counteraction, recoil, repercussion, resistance, response, retaliation

backlog *noun* BUILD-UP, accumulation, excess, hoard, reserve, stock, supply

back out *verb* (often with *of*) WITHDRAW, abandon, cancel, excuse oneself, give up, go back

on, quit, resign, retreat, wimp
out (slang)

backslide verb RELAPSE, go astray,
go wrong, lapse, revert, slip, stray,
weaken

backslider noun RELAPSER,
apostate, deserter, recidivist,
recreant, renegade, turncoat

back up verb SUPPORT, aid, assist,
bolster, confirm, corroborate,
reinforce, second, stand by,
substantiate

backward adjective SLOW, behind,
dull, retarded, subnormal,
underdeveloped, undeveloped

backwards, backward adverb
TOWARDS THE REAR, behind, in
reverse, rearward

bacteria plural noun
MICROORGANISMS, bacilli,
bugs (slang), germs, microbes,
pathogens, viruses

bad adjective 1 INFERIOR, defective,
faulty, imperfect, inadequate,
lousy (slang), poor, substandard,
unsatisfactory

2 HARMFUL, damaging,
dangerous, deleterious,
detrimental, hurtful, ruinous,
unhealthy

3 EVIL, corrupt, criminal,
immoral, mean, sinful, wicked,
wrong

4 NAUGHTY, disobedient,
mischievous, unruly

5 ROTTEN, decayed, moldy, off,
putrid, rancid, sour, spoiled

6 UNFAVORABLE, adverse,
distressing, gloomy, grim,
troubled, unfortunate,
unpleasant

badge noun MARK, brand, device,
emblem, identification, insignia,
sign, stamp, token

badger verb PESTER, bully, goad,
harass, hound, importune, nag,

plague, torment

badinage noun WORDPLAY, banter,
mockery, pleasantry, repartee,
teasing

badly adverb 1 POORLY, carelessly,
imperfectly, inadequately,
incorrectly, ineptly, wrongly

2 UNFAVORABLY, unfortunately,
unsuccessfully

3 SEVERELY, deeply, desperately,
exceedingly, extremely, greatly,
intensely, seriously

bad-mouth verb (slang) CRITICIZE,
abuse, deride, insult, malign,
mock, slander, slate (informal)

baffle verb PUZZLE, bewilder,
confound, confuse, flummox,
mystify, nonplus, perplex, stump

bag noun 1 CONTAINER, receptacle,
sac, sack

▶ verb CATCH, acquire, capture,
kill, land, shoot, trap

baggage noun LUGGAGE,
accouterments, bags, belongings,
equipment, gear, paraphernalia,
suitcases, things

baggy adjective LOOSE, bulging,
droopy, floppy, ill-fitting, oversize,
roomy, sagging, slack

bail noun (law) SECURITY, bond,
guarantee, pledge, surety,
warranty

bail out, bale out verb 1 HELP,
aid, relieve, rescue, save
(someone's) bacon (informal)

2 ESCAPE, quit, retreat, withdraw

bait noun 1 LURE, allurement,
attraction, decoy, enticement,
incentive, inducement, snare,
temptation

▶ verb 2 TEASE, annoy, bother,
harass, hassle (informal), hound,
irritate, persecute, torment, wind
up (Brit. slang)

baked adjective DRY, arid,
desiccated, parched, scorched,

seared, sun-baked, torrid

balance noun 1 STABILITY, composure, equanimity, poise, self-control, self-possession, steadiness
2 EQUILIBRIUM, correspondence, equity, equivalence, evenness, parity, symmetry
3 REMAINDER, difference, residue, rest, surplus
▶ verb 4 STABILIZE, level, match, parallel, steady
5 COMPARE, assess, consider, deliberate, estimate, evaluate, weigh
6 (accounting) CALCULATE, compute, settle, square, tally, total

balcony noun 1 TERRACE, veranda
2 UPPER CIRCLE, gallery, gods

bald adjective 1 HAIRLESS, baldheaded, depilated
2 PLAIN, blunt, direct, forthright, straightforward, unadorned, unvarnished

balderdash noun NONSENSE, claptrap (informal), drivel, garbage (informal), gibberish, hogwash, hot air (informal), rubbish

baldness noun 1 HAIRLESSNESS, alopecia (Pathology), baldheadedness
2 PLAINNESS, austerity, bluntness, severity, simplicity

balk, baulk verb 1 RECOIL, evade, flinch, hesitate, jib, refuse, resist, shirk, shrink from
2 FOIL, check, counteract, defeat, frustrate, hinder, obstruct, prevent, thwart

ball noun SPHERE, drop, globe, globule, orb, pellet, spheroid

ballast noun COUNTERBALANCE, balance, counterweight, equilibrium, sandbag, stability, stabilizer, weight

balloon verb SWELL, billow, blow up, dilate, distend, expand, grow rapidly, inflate, puff out

ballot noun VOTE, election, poll, polling, voting

ballyhoo noun FUSS, babble, commotion, hubbub, hue and cry, hullabaloo, noise, racket, to-do

balm noun 1 OINTMENT, balsam, cream, embrocation, emollient, lotion, salve, unguent
2 COMFORT, anodyne, consolation, curative, palliative, restorative, solace

balmy adjective MILD, clement, pleasant, summery, temperate

baloney noun (informal) NONSENSE, claptrap (informal), crap (slang), drivel, garbage, hogwash, poppycock (informal), rubbish, stuff and nonsense, trash, tripe (informal)

bamboozle verb (informal) 1 CHEAT, con (informal), deceive, dupe, fool, hoodwink, swindle, trick
2 PUZZLE, baffle, befuddle, confound, confuse, mystify, perplex, stump

ban verb 1 PROHIBIT, banish, bar, block, boycott, disallow, disqualify, exclude, forbid, outlaw
▶ noun 2 PROHIBITION, boycott, disqualification, embargo, restriction, taboo

banal adjective UNORIGINAL, hackneyed, humdrum, mundane, pedestrian, stale, stereotyped, trite, unimaginative

band¹ noun 1 ENSEMBLE, combo, group, orchestra
2 GANG, body, company, group, party, posse (informal)

band² noun STRIP, belt, bond, chain, cord, ribbon, strap

bandage noun 1 DRESSING, compress, gauze, plaster
▶ verb 2 DRESS, bind, cover, swathe

bandit noun ROBBER, brigand, desperado, highwayman, marauder, outlaw, thief

bane noun PLAGUE, bête noire, curse, nuisance, pest, ruin, scourge, torment

bang noun 1 EXPLOSION, clang, clap, clash, pop, slam, thud, thump
2 BLOW, bump, cuff, knock, punch, smack, stroke, whack
▶ verb 3 HIT, belt (informal), clatter, knock, slam, strike, thump
4 EXPLODE, boom, clang, resound, thump, thunder
▶ adverb 5 HARD, abruptly, headlong, noisily, suddenly
6 STRAIGHT, precisely, slap, smack

banish verb 1 EXPEL, deport, eject, evict, exile, outlaw
2 GET RID OF, ban, cast out, discard, dismiss, oust, remove

banishment noun EXPULSION, deportation, exile, expatriation, transportation

banisters plural noun RAILING, balusters, balustrade, handrail, rail

bank¹ noun 1 STOREHOUSE, depository, repository
2 STORE, accumulation, fund, hoard, reserve, reservoir, savings, stock, stockpile
▶ verb 3 SAVE, deposit, keep

bank² noun 1 MOUND, banking, embankment, heap, mass, pile, ridge
2 SIDE, brink, edge, margin, shore
▶ verb 3 PILE, amass, heap, mass, mound, stack
4 TILT, camber, cant, heel, incline, pitch, slant, slope, tip

bank³ noun ROW, array, file, group, line, rank, sequence, series, succession

bankrupt adjective INSOLVENT, broke (informal), destitute, impoverished, in queer street, in the red, ruined, wiped out (informal)

bankruptcy noun INSOLVENCY, disaster, failure, liquidation, ruin

banner noun FLAG, colors, ensign, pennant, placard, standard, streamer

banquet noun FEAST, dinner, meal, repast, revel, treat

banter verb 1 JOKE, jest, kid (informal), rib (informal), taunt, tease
▶ noun 2 JOKING, badinage, jesting, kidding (informal), repartee, teasing, wordplay

baptism noun (christianity) CHRISTENING, immersion, purification, sprinkling

baptize verb (christianity) PURIFY, cleanse, immerse

bar noun 1 ROD, paling, palisade, pole, rail, shaft, stake, stick
2 OBSTACLE, barricade, barrier, block, deterrent, hindrance, impediment, obstruction, stop
3 PUBLIC HOUSE, boozer (Brit., Austral. & N.Z. informal), canteen, counter, inn, pub (informal), saloon, tavern, watering hole (facetious slang)
▶ verb 4 FASTEN, barricade, bolt, latch, lock, secure
5 OBSTRUCT, hinder, prevent, restrain
6 EXCLUDE, ban, black, blackball, forbid, keep out, prohibit

Bar noun ▷▷ **the Bar** (law) BARRISTERS, body of lawyers, counsel, court, judgment, tribunal

barb noun 1 DIG, affront, cut, gibe, insult, sarcasm, scoff, sneer
2 POINT, bristle, prickle, prong, quill, spike, spur, thorn

barbarian noun 1 SAVAGE, brute,

yahoo

2 LOUT, bigot, boor, philistine

barbaric adjective **1** UNCIVILIZED, primitive, rude, wild

2 BRUTAL, barbarous, coarse, crude, cruel, fierce, inhuman, savage

barbarism noun SAVAGERY, coarseness, crudity

barbarous adjective **1** UNCIVILIZED, barbarian, brutish, primitive, rough, rude, savage, uncouth, wild

2 BRUTAL, barbaric, cruel, ferocious, heartless, inhuman, monstrous, ruthless, vicious

barbed adjective **1** CUTTING, critical, hostile, hurtful, nasty, pointed, scathing, unkind

2 SPIKED, hooked, jagged, prickly, spiny, thorny

bare adjective **1** NAKED, nude, stripped, unclad, unclothed, uncovered, undressed, without a stitch on (informal)

2 PLAIN, bald, basic, sheer, simple, stark, unembellished

3 SIMPLE, austere, homely, spare, spartan, unadorned, unembellished

barefaced adjective **1** OBVIOUS, blatant, flagrant, open, transparent, unconcealed

2 SHAMELESS, audacious, bold, brash, brazen, impudent, insolent

barely adverb ONLY JUST, almost, at a push, by the skin of one's teeth, hardly, just, scarcely

barf verb (slang) VOMIT, be sick, heave, puke (slang), retch, spew, throw up (informal), toss one's cookies (slang)

▶ noun VOMIT, puke, sick

bargain noun **1** AGREEMENT, arrangement, contract, pact, pledge, promise

2 GOOD BUY, (cheap) purchase, discount, giveaway, good deal, reduction, snip (informal), steal (informal)

▶ verb **3** NEGOTIATE, agree, contract, covenant, promise, stipulate, transact

barge noun CANAL BOAT, flatboat, lighter, narrow boat

bark¹ noun or verb YAP, bay, growl, howl, snarl, woof, yelp

bark² noun COVERING, casing, cortex (Anatomy, botany), crust, husk, rind, skin

barracks plural noun CAMP, billet, encampment, garrison, quarters

barrage noun **1** TORRENT, burst, deluge, hail, mass, onslaught, plethora, stream

2 (military) BOMBARDMENT, battery, cannonade, fusillade, gunfire, salvo, shelling, volley

barren adjective **1** INFERTILE, childless, sterile

2 UNPRODUCTIVE, arid, desert, desolate, dry, empty, unfruitful, waste

barricade noun **1** BARRIER, blockade, bulwark, fence, obstruction, palisade, rampart, stockade

▶ verb **2** BAR, block, blockade, defend, fortify, obstruct, protect, shut in

barrier noun **1** BARRICADE, bar, blockade, boundary, fence, obstacle, obstruction, wall

2 HINDRANCE, difficulty, drawback, handicap, hurdle, obstacle, restriction, stumbling block

barter verb TRADE, bargain, drive a hard bargain, exchange, haggle, sell, swap, traffic

base¹ noun **1** BOTTOM, bed, foot, foundation, pedestal, rest, stand, support

2 BASIS, core, essence, heart, key, origin, root, source

3 CENTER, camp, headquarters, home, post, settlement, starting point, station

▶ verb **4** FOUND, build, construct, depend, derive, establish, ground, hinge

5 PLACE, locate, post, station

base² adjective **1** DISHONORABLE, contemptible, despicable, disreputable, evil, immoral, lousy (slang), scuzzy (slang), shameful, sordid, wicked

2 COUNTERFEIT, alloyed, debased, fake, forged, fraudulent, impure

baseless adjective UNFOUNDED, groundless, unconfirmed, uncorroborated, ungrounded, unjustified, unsubstantiated, unsupported

bash verb **1** (informal) HIT, belt (informal), smash, sock (slang), strike, wallop (informal)

▶ noun **2** (informal) ATTEMPT, crack (informal), go (informal), shot (informal), stab (informal), try

bashful adjective SHY, blushing, coy, diffident, reserved, reticent, retiring, timid

basic adjective ESSENTIAL, elementary, fundamental, key, necessary, primary, vital

basically adverb ESSENTIALLY, at heart, fundamentally, inherently, in substance, intrinsically, mostly, primarily

basics plural noun ESSENTIALS, ABCs, brass tacks (informal), fundamentals, nitty-gritty (informal), nuts and bolts (informal), principles, rudiments

basis noun FOUNDATION, base, bottom, footing, ground, groundwork, support

bask verb LIE IN, laze, loll, lounge, relax, sunbathe, swim in

bass adjective DEEP, deep-toned, low, low-pitched, resonant, sonorous

bastard noun **1** (informal, offensive) ROGUE, blackguard, miscreant, reprobate, scoundrel, villain, wretch

2 ILLEGITIMATE CHILD, love child, natural child

bastion noun STRONGHOLD, bulwark, citadel, defense, fortress, mainstay, prop, rock, support, tower of strength

bat noun or verb HIT, bang, smack, strike, swat, thump, wallop (informal), whack

batch noun GROUP, amount, assemblage, bunch, collection, crowd, lot, pack, quantity, set

bath noun **1** WASH, cleansing, douche, scrubbing, shower, soak, tub

▶ verb **2** WASH, bathe, clean, douse, scrub down, shower, soak

bathe verb **1** SWIM

2 WASH, cleanse, rinse, soak

3 COVER, flood, immerse, steep, suffuse

baton noun STICK, club, crook, mace, rod, scepter, staff, truncheon, wand

batten verb (usually with down) FASTEN, board up, clamp down, cover up, fix, nail down, secure, tighten

batter verb BEAT, buffet, clobber (slang), pelt, pound, pummel, thrash, wallop (informal)

battery noun ARTILLERY, cannon, cannonry, gun emplacements, guns

battle noun **1** FIGHT, action, attack, combat, encounter, engagement, hostilities, skirmish

2 CONFLICT, campaign, contest, crusade, dispute, struggle
▶ *verb* 3 STRUGGLE, argue, clamor, dispute, fight, lock horns, strive, war

battlefield *noun* BATTLEGROUND, combat zone, field, field of battle, front

battleship *noun* WARSHIP, gunboat, man-of-war

batty *adjective* CRAZY, absent-minded, bonkers (*informal*), daft (*informal*), dotty (*slang, chiefly Brit.*), eccentric, mad, odd, peculiar, potty (*Brit. informal*), touched

bauble *noun* TRINKET, bagatelle, gewgaw, gimcrack, knick-knack, plaything, toy, trifle

baulk *see* **BALK**

bawdy *adjective* RUDE, coarse, dirty, indecent, lascivious, lecherous, lewd, ribald, salacious, smutty

bawl *verb* 1 CRY, blubber, sob, wail, weep
2 SHOUT, bellow, call, clamor, howl, roar, yell

bay¹ *noun* INLET, bight, cove, gulf, natural harbor, sound

bay² *noun* RECESS, alcove, compartment, niche, nook, opening

bay³ *verb* HOWL, bark, clamor, cry, growl, yelp

bazaar *noun* 1 FAIR, bring-and-buy, fête, sale of work
2 MARKET, exchange, marketplace

be *verb* EXIST, be alive, breathe, inhabit, live

beach *noun* SHORE, coast, sands, seashore, seaside, water's edge

beached *adjective* STRANDED, abandoned, aground, ashore, deserted, grounded, high and dry, marooned, wrecked

beacon *noun* SIGNAL, beam, bonfire, flare, lighthouse, sign, watchtower

bead *noun* DROP, blob, bubble, dot, droplet, globule, pellet, pill

beady *adjective* BRIGHT, gleaming, glinting, glittering, sharp, shining

beak *noun* 1 BILL, mandible, neb (*archaic or dialect*), nib
2 (*slang*) NOSE, proboscis, snout

beam *noun* 1 SMILE, grin
2 RAY, gleam, glimmer, glint, glow, shaft, streak, stream
3 RAFTER, girder, joist, plank, spar, support, timber
▶ *verb* 4 SMILE, grin
5 RADIATE, glare, gleam, glitter, glow, shine
6 SEND OUT, broadcast, emit, transmit

bear *verb* 1 SUPPORT, have, hold, maintain, possess, shoulder, sustain, uphold
2 CARRY, bring, convey, hump (*Brit. slang*), move, take, transport
3 PRODUCE, beget, breed, bring forth, engender, generate, give birth to, yield
4 TOLERATE, abide, allow, brook, endure, permit, put up with (*informal*), stomach, suffer

bearable *adjective* TOLERABLE, admissible, endurable, manageable, passable, sufferable, supportable, sustainable

bearer *noun* CARRIER, agent, conveyor, messenger, porter, runner, servant

bearing *noun* 1 (usually with *on* or *upon*) RELEVANCE, application, connection, import, pertinence, reference, relation, significance
2 MANNER, air, aspect, attitude, behavior, demeanor, deportment, posture

bearings *plural noun* POSITION, aim, course, direction, location, orientation, situation, track, way, whereabouts

bear out verb SUPPORT, confirm, corroborate, endorse, justify, prove, substantiate, uphold, vindicate

beast noun 1 ANIMAL, brute, creature
2 BRUTE, barbarian, fiend, monster, ogre, sadist, savage, swine

beastly adjective UNPLEASANT, awful, disagreeable, horrid, mean, nasty, rotten

beat verb 1 HIT, bang, batter, buffet, knock, pound, strike, thrash
2 FLAP, flutter
3 THROB, palpitate, pound, pulsate, quake, thump, vibrate
4 DEFEAT, conquer, outdo, overcome, overwhelm, surpass, vanquish
▶ noun 5 THROB, palpitation, pulsation, throb
6 ROUTE, circuit, course, path, rounds, way
7 RHYTHM, accent, cadence, meter, stress, time

beaten adjective 1 STIRRED, blended, foamy, frothy, mixed, whipped, whisked
2 DEFEATED, cowed, overcome, overwhelmed, thwarted, vanquished

beat up verb (informal) ASSAULT, attack, batter, beat the living daylights out of (informal), knock about or around, pound, pulverize, thrash

beau noun 1 (chiefly U.S.) (old-fashioned) BOYFRIEND, admirer, fiancé, lover, suitor, sweetheart
2 DANDY, coxcomb, fop, gallant, ladies' man

beautiful adjective ATTRACTIVE,

charming, delightful, exquisite, fair, fine, gorgeous, handsome, lovely, pleasing

beautify verb MAKE BEAUTIFUL, adorn, decorate, embellish, festoon, garnish, glamorize, ornament

beauty noun 1 ATTRACTIVENESS, charm, comeliness, elegance, exquisiteness, glamour, grace, handsomeness, loveliness
2 BELLE, good-looker, lovely (slang), stunner (informal)

becalmed adjective STILL, motionless, settled, stranded, stuck

because conjunction SINCE, as, by reason of, in that, on account of, owing to, thanks to

beckon verb GESTURE, bid, gesticulate, motion, nod, signal, summon, wave at

become verb 1 COME TO BE, alter to, be transformed into, change into, develop into, grow into, mature into, ripen into
2 SUIT, embellish, enhance, fit, flatter, set off

becoming adjective 1 APPROPRIATE, compatible, fitting, in keeping, proper, seemly, suitable, worthy
2 FLATTERING, attractive, comely, enhancing, graceful, neat, pretty, tasteful

bed noun 1 BEDSTEAD, berth, bunk, cot, couch, divan
2 PLOT, area, border, garden, patch, row, strip
3 BOTTOM, base, foundation, groundwork

bedevil verb 1 TORMENT, afflict, distress, harass, plague, trouble, vex, worry
2 CONFUSE, confound

bedlam noun PANDEMONIUM, chaos, commotion, confusion,

furor, tumult, turmoil, uproar
bedraggled adjective MESSY, dirty, dishevelled, disordered, muddied, scuzzy (slang), unkempt, untidy
bedridden adjective CONFINED TO BED, confined, flat on one's back, incapacitated, laid up (informal)
bedrock noun 1 BOTTOM, bed, foundation, rock bottom, substratum, substructure
2 BASICS, basis, core, essentials, fundamentals, nuts and bolts (informal), roots
beefy adjective (informal) BRAWNY, bulky, hulking, muscular, stocky, strapping, sturdy, thickset
befall verb (archaic or literary) HAPPEN, chance, come to pass, fall, occur, take place, transpire (informal)
befitting adjective APPROPRIATE, apposite, becoming, fit, fitting, proper, right, seemly, suitable
before preposition 1 AHEAD OF, in advance of, in front of
2 EARLIER THAN, in advance of, prior to
3 IN THE PRESENCE OF, in front of
▶ adverb 4 PREVIOUSLY, ahead, earlier, formerly, in advance, sooner
5 IN FRONT, ahead
beforehand adverb IN ADVANCE, ahead of time, already, before, earlier, in anticipation, previously, sooner
befriend verb HELP, aid, assist, back, encourage, side with, stand by, support, welcome
beg verb 1 SCROUNGE, cadge, seek charity, solicit charity, sponge on, touch (someone) for (slang)
2 IMPLORE, beseech, entreat, petition, plead, request, solicit
beggar noun TRAMP, bag lady (chiefly U.S.), bum (informal), down-and-out, pauper, vagrant
beggarly adjective POOR, destitute, impoverished, indigent, needy, poverty-stricken
begin verb 1 START, commence, embark on, initiate, instigate, institute, prepare, set about
2 HAPPEN, appear, arise, come into being, emerge, originate, start
beginner noun NOVICE, amateur, apprentice, learner, neophyte, rookie (informal), starter, trainee, tyro
beginning noun 1 START, birth, commencement, inauguration, inception, initiation, onset, opening, origin, outset
2 SEED, fount, germ, root
begrudge verb RESENT, be jealous, be reluctant, be stingy, envy, grudge
beguile verb 1 FOOL, cheat, deceive, delude, dupe, hoodwink, mislead, take for a ride (informal), trick
2 CHARM, amuse, distract, divert, engross, entertain, occupy
beguiling adjective CHARMING, alluring, attractive, bewitching, captivating, enchanting, enthralling, intriguing
behave verb 1 ACT, function, operate, perform, run, work
2 CONDUCT ONESELF PROPERLY, act correctly, keep one's nose clean, mind one's manners
behavior noun 1 CONDUCT, actions, bearing, demeanor, deportment, manner, manners, ways
2 ACTION, functioning, operation, performance
behind preposition 1 AFTER, at the back of, at the heels of, at the rear of, following, later than
2 CAUSING, at the bottom of, initiating, instigating, responsible for

3 SUPPORTING, backing, for, in agreement, on the side of
▶ *adverb* **4** AFTER, afterwards, following, in the wake (of), next, subsequently
5 OVERDUE, behindhand, in arrears, in debt
▶ *noun* **6** (*informal*) BOTTOM, butt (*U.S. & Canad. informal*), buttocks, posterior

behold *verb* (*archaic or literary*) LOOK AT, observe, perceive, regard, survey, view, watch, witness

beholden *adjective* INDEBTED, bound, grateful, obliged, owing, under obligation

being *noun* **1** EXISTENCE, life, reality
2 NATURE, entity, essence, soul, spirit, substance
3 CREATURE, human being, individual, living thing

belated *adjective* LATE, behindhand, behind time, delayed, late in the day, overdue, tardy

belch *verb* **1** BURP (*informal*), hiccup
2 EMIT, discharge, disgorge, erupt, give off, spew forth, vent

beleaguered *adjective* **1** HARASSED, badgered, hassled (*informal*), persecuted, pestered, plagued, put upon, vexed
2 BESIEGED, assailed, beset, blockaded, hemmed in, surrounded

belief *noun* **1** TRUST, assurance, confidence, conviction, feeling, impression, judgment, notion, opinion
2 FAITH, credo, creed, doctrine, dogma, ideology, principles, tenet

believable *adjective* CREDIBLE, authentic, imaginable, likely, plausible, possible, probable, trustworthy

believe *verb* **1** ACCEPT, be certain of, be convinced of, credit, depend on, have faith in, rely on, swear by, trust
2 THINK, assume, gather, imagine, judge, presume, reckon, speculate, suppose

believer *noun* FOLLOWER, adherent, convert, devotee, disciple, supporter, upholder, zealot

belittle *verb* DISPARAGE, decry, denigrate, deprecate, deride, scoff at, scorn, sneer at

belligerent *adjective* **1** AGGRESSIVE, bellicose, combative, hostile, pugnacious, unfriendly, warlike, warring
▶ *noun* **2** FIGHTER, combatant, warring nation

bellow *noun or verb* SHOUT, bawl, clamor, cry, howl, roar, scream, shriek, yell

belly *noun* **1** STOMACH, abdomen, corporation (*informal*), gut, insides (*informal*), paunch, potbelly, tummy
▶ *verb* **2** SWELL OUT, billow, bulge, fill, spread, swell

bellyful *noun* SURFEIT, enough, excess, glut, plateful, plenty, satiety, too much

belonging *noun* RELATIONSHIP, acceptance, affinity, association, attachment, fellowship, inclusion, loyalty, rapport

belongings *plural noun* POSSESSIONS, accouterments, chattels, effects, gear, goods, paraphernalia, personal property, stuff, things

belong to *verb* **1** BE THE PROPERTY OF, be at the disposal of, be held by, be owned by
2 BE A MEMBER OF, be affiliated to, be allied to, be associated with, be

included in

beloved adjective DEAR, admired, adored, darling, loved, pet, precious, prized, treasured, worshipped

below preposition 1 LESSER, inferior, subject, subordinate
2 LESS THAN, lower than
▶ adverb 3 LOWER, beneath, down, under, underneath

belt noun 1 WAISTBAND, band, cummerbund, girdle, girth, sash
2 (geography) ZONE, area, district, layer, region, stretch, strip, tract

bemoan verb LAMENT, bewail, deplore, grieve for, mourn, regret, rue, weep for

bemused adjective PUZZLED, at sea, bewildered, confused, flummoxed, muddled, nonplussed, perplexed

bench noun 1 SEAT, form, pew, settle, stall
2 WORKTABLE, board, counter, table, trestle table, workbench
3 ▷▷ **the bench** COURT, courtroom, judges, judiciary, magistrates, tribunal

benchmark noun REFERENCE POINT, criterion, gauge, level, measure, model, norm, par, standard, yardstick

bend verb 1 CURVE, arc, arch, bow, lean, turn, twist, veer
▶ noun 2 CURVE, angle, arc, arch, bow, corner, loop, turn, twist

beneath preposition 1 UNDER, below, lower than, underneath
2 INFERIOR TO, below, less than
3 UNWORTHY OF, unbefitting
▶ adverb 4 UNDERNEATH, below, in a lower place

benefactor noun SUPPORTER, backer, donor, helper, patron, philanthropist, sponsor, well-wisher

beneficial adjective HELPFUL, advantageous, benign, favorable, profitable, useful, valuable, wholesome, win-win (informal)

beneficiary noun RECIPIENT, heir, inheritor, payee, receiver

benefit noun 1 HELP, advantage, aid, asset, assistance, favor, good, profit
▶ verb 2 HELP, aid, assist, avail, enhance, further, improve, profit

benevolent adjective KIND, altruistic, benign, caring, charitable, generous, philanthropic

benign adjective 1 KINDLY, amiable, friendly, genial, kind, obliging, sympathetic
2 (medical) HARMLESS, curable, remediable

bent adjective 1 CURVED, angled, arched, bowed, crooked, hunched, stooped, twisted
2 ▷▷ **bent on** DETERMINED TO, disposed to, fixed on, inclined to, insistent on, predisposed to, resolved on, set on
▶ noun 3 INCLINATION, ability, aptitude, leaning, penchant, preference, propensity, tendency

bequeath verb LEAVE, bestow, endow, entrust, give, grant, hand down, impart, pass on, will

bequest noun LEGACY, bestowal, endowment, estate, gift, inheritance, settlement

berate verb SCOLD, castigate, censure, chide, criticize, harangue, rebuke, reprimand, reprove, tell off (informal), upbraid

bereavement noun LOSS, affliction, death, deprivation, misfortune, tribulation

bereft adjective DEPRIVED, devoid, lacking, parted from, robbed of, wanting

berserk *adverb* CRAZY, amok,
enraged, frantic, frenzied, mad,
raging, wild

berth *noun* 1 BUNK, bed, billet,
hammock
2 (*nautical*) ANCHORAGE, dock,
harbor, haven, pier, port, quay,
wharf
▶ *verb* 3 (*nautical*) ANCHOR, dock,
drop anchor, land, moor, tie up

beseech *verb* BEG, ask, call upon,
entreat, implore, plead, pray,
solicit

beset *verb* PLAGUE, bedevil, harass,
pester, trouble

beside *preposition* 1 NEXT TO,
abreast of, adjacent to, alongside,
at the side of, close to, near,
nearby, neighboring
2 ▷▷ **beside oneself** DISTRAUGHT,
apoplectic, at the end of one's
tether, demented, desperate,
frantic, frenzied, out of one's
mind, unhinged

besides *adverb* 1 TOO, also, as well,
further, furthermore, in addition,
into the bargain, moreover,
otherwise, what's more
▶ *preposition* 2 APART FROM, barring,
excepting, excluding, in addition
to, other than, over and above,
without

besiege *verb* 1 SURROUND,
blockade, encircle, hem in, lay
siege to, shut in
2 HARASS, badger, harry, hassle
(*informal*), hound, nag, pester,
plague

besotted *adjective* INFATUATED,
doting, hypnotized, smitten,
spellbound

best *adjective* 1 FINEST, foremost,
leading, most excellent,
outstanding, pre-eminent,
principal, supreme, unsurpassed
▶ *adverb* 2 MOST HIGHLY, extremely,

greatly, most deeply, most fully
▶ *noun* 3 FINEST, cream, *crème
de la crème*, elite, flower, pick,
prime, top

bestial *adjective* BRUTAL, barbaric,
beastly, brutish, inhuman,
savage, sordid

bestow *verb* PRESENT, award,
commit, give, grant, hand out,
impart, lavish

bet *noun* 1 GAMBLE, long shot, risk,
speculation, stake, venture, wager
▶ *verb* 2 GAMBLE, chance, hazard,
risk, speculate, stake, venture,
wager

betoken *verb* INDICATE, bode,
denote, promise, represent,
signify, suggest

betray *verb* 1 BE DISLOYAL, be
treacherous, be unfaithful, break
one's promise, double-cross
(*informal*), inform on or against, sell
out (*informal*), stab in the back
2 GIVE AWAY, disclose, divulge,
expose, let slip, reveal, uncover,
unmask

betrayal *noun* 1 DISLOYALTY, back-
stabbing (*informal*), deception,
double-cross (*informal*), sell-out
(*informal*), treachery, treason,
trickery
2 GIVING AWAY, disclosure,
divulgence, revelation

better *adjective* 1 SUPERIOR,
excelling, finer, greater,
higher-quality, more desirable,
preferable, surpassing
2 WELL, cured, fully recovered, on
the mend (*informal*), recovering,
stronger
▶ *adverb* 3 IN A MORE EXCELLENT
MANNER, in a superior way, more
advantageously, more attractively,
more competently, more
effectively
4 TO A GREATER DEGREE, more

completely, more thoroughly
► *verb* **5** IMPROVE, enhance,
further, raise

between *preposition* AMIDST,
among, betwixt, in the middle
of, mid

beverage *noun* DRINK, liquid,
liquor, refreshment

bevy *noun* GROUP, band, bunch
(*informal*), collection, company,
crowd, gathering, pack, troupe

bewail *verb* LAMENT, bemoan, cry
over, deplore, grieve for, moan,
mourn, regret

beware *verb* BE CAREFUL, be
cautious, be wary, guard against,
heed, look out, mind, take heed,
watch out

bewilder *verb* CONFOUND, baffle,
bemuse, confuse, flummox,
mystify, nonplus, perplex, puzzle

bewildered *adjective* CONFUSED, at
a loss, at sea, baffled, flummoxed,
mystified, nonplussed, perplexed,
puzzled

bewitch *verb* ENCHANT, beguile,
captivate, charm, enrapture,
entrance, fascinate, hypnotize

bewitched *adjective* ENCHANTED,
charmed, entranced, fascinated,
mesmerized, spellbound, under
a spell

beyond *preposition* **1** PAST, above,
apart from, at a distance, away
from, over
2 EXCEEDING, out of reach of,
superior to, surpassing

bias *noun* **1** PREJUDICE, favoritism,
inclination, leaning, partiality,
tendency
► *verb* **2** PREJUDICE, distort,
influence, predispose, slant, sway,
twist, warp, weight

biased *adjective* PREJUDICED,
distorted, one-sided, partial,
slanted, weighted

bicker *verb* QUARREL, argue,
disagree, dispute, fight, row
(*informal*), squabble, wrangle

bid *verb* **1** OFFER, proffer, propose,
submit, tender
2 SAY, call, greet, tell, wish
3 TELL, ask, command, direct,
instruct, order, require
► *noun* **4** OFFER, advance, amount,
price, proposal, sum, tender
5 ATTEMPT, crack (*informal*), effort,
go (*informal*), stab (*informal*), try

bidding *noun* ORDER, beck and call,
command, direction, instruction,
request, summons

big *adjective* **1** LARGE, enormous,
extensive, great, huge, immense,
massive, substantial, supersize,
vast
2 IMPORTANT, eminent,
influential, leading, main,
powerful, prominent, significant
3 GROWN-UP, adult, elder, grown,
mature
4 GENEROUS, altruistic,
benevolent, gracious,
magnanimous, noble, unselfish

big cheese *noun* (*informal*)
MANAGER, alpha male, boss
(*informal*), bossman (*slang*),
foreman, head honcho (*slang*),
overseer, superintendent,
supervisor

bighead *noun* (*informal*) BOASTER,
braggart, know-all (*informal*)

bigheaded *adjective* BOASTFUL,
arrogant, cocky, conceited,
egotistic, immodest,
overconfident, swollen-headed

bigot *noun* FANATIC, racist,
sectarian, zealot

bigoted *adjective* INTOLERANT,
biased, dogmatic, narrow-
minded, opinionated, prejudiced,
sectarian

bigotry *noun* INTOLERANCE, bias,

discrimination, dogmatism, fanaticism, narrow-mindedness, prejudice, sectarianism

bill¹ noun 1 CHARGES, account, invoice, reckoning, score, statement, tally
2 PROPOSAL, measure, piece of legislation, projected law
3 ADVERTISEMENT, bulletin, circular, handbill, handout, leaflet, notice, placard, poster
4 LIST, agenda, card, catalog, inventory, listing, program, roster, schedule
▶ verb 5 CHARGE, debit, invoice
6 ADVERTISE, announce, give advance notice of, post

bill² noun BEAK, mandible, neb (archaic or dialect), nib

billet verb 1 QUARTER, accommodate, berth, station
▶ noun 2 QUARTERS, accommodation, barracks, lodging

billow noun 1 WAVE, breaker, crest, roller, surge, swell, tide
▶ verb 2 SURGE, balloon, belly, puff up, rise up, roll, swell

bind verb 1 SECURE, fasten, hitch, lash, stick, strap, tie, wrap
2 OBLIGE, compel, constrain, engage, force, necessitate, require
▶ noun (informal) 3 NUISANCE, bore, drag (informal), pain in the neck (informal)
4 DIFFICULTY, dilemma, quandary, spot (informal)

binding adjective COMPULSORY, indissoluble, irrevocable, mandatory, necessary, obligatory, unalterable

binge noun (informal) BOUT, bender (informal), feast, fling, orgy, spree

biography noun LIFE STORY, account, curriculum vitae, CV, life, memoir, profile, record

birth noun 1 CHILDBIRTH, delivery, nativity, parturition
2 ANCESTRY, background, blood, breeding, lineage, parentage, pedigree, stock

bisect verb CUT IN TWO, cross, cut across, divide in two, halve, intersect, separate, split

bit¹ noun PIECE, crumb, fragment, grain, morsel, part, scrap, speck

bit² noun CURB, brake, check, restraint, snaffle

bitch noun 1 (informal) COMPLAINT, gripe (informal), grouse, grumble, objection, protest
▶ verb 2 (informal) COMPLAIN, bemoan, gripe (informal), grouse, grumble, lament, object

bitchy adjective (informal) SPITEFUL, backbiting, catty (informal), mean, nasty, snide, vindictive

bite verb 1 CUT, chew, gnaw, nip, pierce, pinch, snap, tear, wound
▶ noun 2 WOUND, nip, pinch, prick, smarting, sting, tooth marks
3 SNACK, food, light meal, morsel, mouthful, piece, refreshment, taste

biting adjective 1 PIERCING, bitter, cutting, harsh, penetrating, sharp
2 SARCASTIC, caustic, cutting, incisive, mordant, scathing, stinging, trenchant, vitriolic

bitter adjective 1 SOUR, acid, acrid, astringent, harsh, sharp, tart, unsweetened, vinegary
2 RESENTFUL, acrimonious, begrudging, hostile, sore, sour, sullen
3 FREEZING, biting, fierce, intense, severe, stinging

bitterness noun 1 SOURNESS, acerbity, acidity, sharpness, tartness
2 RESENTMENT, acrimony, animosity, asperity, grudge,

hostility, rancor, sarcasm

bizarre *adjective* STRANGE, eccentric, extraordinary, fantastic, freakish, ludicrous, outlandish, peculiar, unusual, weird, zany

blab *verb* TELL, blurt out, disclose, divulge, give away, let slip, let the cat out of the bag, reveal, spill the beans (*informal*)

black *adjective* 1 DARK, dusky, ebony, jet, raven, sable, swarthy
2 HOPELESS, depressing, dismal, foreboding, gloomy, ominous, sad, somber
3 ANGRY, furious, hostile, menacing, resentful, sullen, threatening
4 WICKED, bad, evil, iniquitous, nefarious, villainous
▶ *verb* 5 BOYCOTT, ban, bar, blacklist

blacken *verb* 1 DARKEN, befoul, begrime, cloud, dirty, make black, smudge, soil
2 DISCREDIT, defame, denigrate, malign, slander, smear, smirch, vilify

blacklist *verb* EXCLUDE, ban, bar, boycott, debar, expel, reject, snub

black magic *noun* WITCHCRAFT, black art, diabolism, necromancy, sorcery, voodoo, wizardry

blackmail *noun* 1 THREAT, extortion, hush money (*slang*), intimidation, ransom
▶ *verb* 2 THREATEN, coerce, compel, demand, extort, hold to ransom, intimidate, squeeze

blackness *noun* DARKNESS, duskiness, gloom, murkiness, swarthiness

blackout *noun*
1 UNCONSCIOUSNESS, coma, faint, loss of consciousness, oblivion, swoon

2 NONCOMMUNICATION, censorship, radio silence, secrecy, suppression, withholding news

blame *verb* 1 HOLD RESPONSIBLE, accuse, censure, chide, condemn, criticize, find fault with, reproach
▶ *noun* 2 RESPONSIBILITY, accountability, culpability, fault, guilt, liability, onus

blameless *adjective* INNOCENT, above suspicion, clean, faultless, guiltless, immaculate, impeccable, irreproachable, perfect, unblemished, virtuous

blameworthy *adjective* REPREHENSIBLE, discreditable, disreputable, indefensible, inexcusable, iniquitous, reproachable, shameful

bland *adjective* DULL, boring, flat, humdrum, insipid, tasteless, unexciting, uninspiring, vapid

blank *adjective* 1 UNMARKED, bare, clean, clear, empty, plain, void, white
2 EXPRESSIONLESS, deadpan, empty, impassive, poker-faced (*informal*), vacant, vague
▶ *noun* 3 EMPTY SPACE, emptiness, gap, nothingness, space, vacancy, vacuum, void

blanket *noun* 1 COVER, coverlet, rug
2 COVERING, carpet, cloak, coat, layer, mantle, sheet
▶ *verb* 3 COVER, cloak, coat, conceal, hide, mask, obscure, suppress

blare *verb* SOUND OUT, blast, clamor, clang, resound, roar, scream, trumpet

blasé *adjective* INDIFFERENT, apathetic, lukewarm, nonchalant, offhand, unconcerned

blaspheme *verb* CURSE, abuse, damn, desecrate, execrate, profane, revile, swear

blasphemous *adjective*
IRREVERENT, godless, impious,
irreligious, profane, sacrilegious,
ungodly

blasphemy *noun* IRREVERENCE,
cursing, desecration, execration,
impiety, profanity, sacrilege,
swearing

blast *noun* 1 EXPLOSION, bang,
burst, crash, detonation,
discharge, eruption, outburst,
salvo, volley
2 GUST, gale, squall, storm, strong
breeze, tempest
3 BLARE, blow, clang, honk, peal,
scream, toot, wail
► *verb* 4 BLOW UP, break up, burst,
demolish, destroy, explode, put
paid to, ruin, shatter

blatant *adjective* OBVIOUS, brazen,
conspicuous, flagrant, glaring,
obtrusive, ostentatious, overt

blaze *noun* 1 FIRE, bonfire,
conflagration, flames
2 GLARE, beam, brilliance, flare,
flash, gleam, glitter, glow, light,
radiance
► *verb* 3 BURN, fire, flame
4 SHINE, beam, flare, flash, glare,
gleam, glow

bleach *verb* WHITEN, blanch, fade,
grow pale, lighten, wash out

bleak *adjective* 1 EXPOSED, bare,
barren, desolate, unsheltered,
weather-beaten, windswept
2 DISMAL, cheerless, depressing,
discouraging, dreary, gloomy,
grim, hopeless, joyless, somber

bleary *adjective* DIM, blurred,
blurry, foggy, fuzzy, hazy,
indistinct, misty, murky

bleed *verb* 1 LOSE BLOOD, flow,
gush, ooze, run, shed blood, spurt
2 DRAW *or* TAKE BLOOD, extract,
leech

3 (*informal*) EXTORT, drain, exhaust,
fleece, milk, squeeze

blemish *noun* 1 MARK, blot,
defect, disfigurement, fault,
flaw, imperfection, smudge,
stain, taint
► *verb* 2 STAIN, damage, disfigure,
impair, injure, mar, mark, spoil,
sully, taint, tarnish

blend *verb* 1 MIX, amalgamate,
combine, compound, merge,
mingle, unite
2 GO WELL, complement, fit, go
with, harmonize, suit
► *noun* 3 MIXTURE, alloy,
amalgamation, combination,
compound, concoction, mix,
synthesis, union

bless *verb* 1 SANCTIFY, anoint,
consecrate, dedicate, exalt,
hallow, ordain
2 GRANT, bestow, favor, give, grace,
provide

blessed *adjective* HOLY, adored,
beatified, divine, hallowed,
revered, sacred, sanctified

blessing *noun* 1 BENEDICTION,
benison, commendation,
consecration, dedication, grace,
invocation, thanksgiving
2 APPROVAL, backing, consent,
favor, good wishes, leave,
permission, sanction, support
3 BENEFIT, favor, gift, godsend,
good fortune, help, kindness,
service, windfall

blight *noun* 1 CURSE, affliction,
bane, contamination, corruption,
evil, plague, pollution, scourge,
woe
2 DISEASE, canker, decay, fungus,
infestation, mildew, pest,
pestilence, rot
► *verb* 3 FRUSTRATE, crush, dash,
disappoint, mar, ruin, spoil,
undo, wreck

blind adjective 1 SIGHTLESS, eyeless, unseeing, unsighted, visionless 2 UNAWARE OF, careless, heedless, ignorant, inattentive, inconsiderate, indifferent, insensitive, oblivious, unconscious of 3 UNREASONING, indiscriminate, prejudiced
▶ noun 4 COVER, camouflage, cloak, façade, feint, front, mask, masquerade, screen, smoke screen

blindly adverb 1 THOUGHTLESSLY, carelessly, heedlessly, inconsiderately, recklessly, senselessly 2 AIMLESSLY, at random, indiscriminately, instinctively

blink verb 1 WINK, bat, flutter 2 FLICKER, flash, gleam, glimmer, shine, twinkle, wink
▶ noun 3 ▷▷ **on the blink** (slang) NOT WORKING (PROPERLY), faulty, malfunctioning, out of action, out of order, playing up

bliss noun JOY, beatitude, blessedness, blissfulness, ecstasy, euphoria, felicity, gladness, happiness, heaven, nirvana, paradise, rapture

blissful adjective JOYFUL, ecstatic, elated, enraptured, euphoric, happy, heavenly (informal), rapturous

blister noun SORE, abscess, boil, carbuncle, cyst, pimple, pustule, swelling

blithe adjective HEEDLESS, careless, casual, indifferent, nonchalant, thoughtless, unconcerned, untroubled

blitz noun ATTACK, assault, blitzkrieg, bombardment, campaign, offensive, onslaught, raid, strike

blizzard noun SNOWSTORM, blast, gale, squall, storm, tempest

bloat verb PUFF UP, balloon, blow up, dilate, distend, enlarge, expand, inflate, swell

blob noun DROP, ball, bead, bubble, dab, droplet, globule, lump, mass

bloc noun GROUP, alliance, axis, coalition, faction, league, union

block noun 1 PIECE, bar, brick, chunk, hunk, ingot, lump, mass 2 OBSTRUCTION, bar, barrier, blockage, hindrance, impediment, jam, obstacle
▶ verb 3 OBSTRUCT, bung up (informal), choke, clog, close, plug, stem the flow, stop up 4 STOP, bar, check, halt, hinder, impede, obstruct, thwart

blockade noun STOPPAGE, barricade, barrier, block, hindrance, impediment, obstacle, obstruction, restriction, siege

blockage noun OBSTRUCTION, block, impediment, occlusion, stoppage

blockhead noun IDIOT, chump (informal), dork (slang), dunce, fool, nitwit, numbskull or numskull, schmuck (slang), thickhead, twit (informal, chiefly Brit.)

blond, blonde adjective FAIR, fair-haired, fair-skinned, flaxen, golden-haired, light, tow-headed

blood noun 1 LIFEBLOOD, gore, vital fluid 2 FAMILY, ancestry, birth, descent, extraction, kinship, lineage, relations

bloodcurdling adjective TERRIFYING, appalling, chilling, dreadful, fearful, frightening, hair-raising, horrendous, horrifying, scaring, spine-chilling

bloodshed noun KILLING, blood bath, blood-letting, butchery, carnage, gore, massacre, murder, slaughter, slaying

bloodthirsty adjective CRUEL,
barbarous, brutal, cut-throat,
ferocious, gory, murderous,
savage, vicious, warlike

bloody adjective 1 BLOODSTAINED,
bleeding, blood-soaked, blood-
spattered, gaping, raw
2 CRUEL, ferocious, fierce,
sanguinary, savage

bloom noun 1 FLOWER, blossom,
blossoming, bud, efflorescence,
opening (of flowers)
2 PRIME, beauty, flourishing,
freshness, glow, health, heyday,
luster, radiance, vigor
▶ verb 3 BLOSSOM, blow, bud,
burgeon, open, sprout
4 FLOURISH, develop, fare well,
grow, prosper, succeed, thrive,
wax

blossom noun 1 FLOWER, bloom,
bud, floret, flowers
▶ verb 2 FLOWER, bloom, burgeon
3 GROW, bloom, develop, flourish,
mature, progress, prosper, thrive

blot noun 1 SPOT, blotch, mark,
patch, smear, smudge, speck,
splodge
2 STAIN, blemish, defect, fault,
flaw, scar, spot, taint
▶ verb 3 STAIN, disgrace, mark,
smirch, smudge, spoil, spot, sully,
tarnish
4 SOAK UP, absorb, dry, take up
5 ▷▷ **blot out: a** OBLITERATE,
darken, destroy, eclipse, efface,
obscure, shadow **b** ERASE, cancel,
expunge

blow¹ verb 1 CARRY, buffet, drive,
fling, flutter, move, sweep, waft
2 EXHALE, breathe, pant, puff
3 PLAY, blare, mouth, pipe, sound,
toot, trumpet, vibrate

blow² noun 1 KNOCK, bang, clout
(informal), punch, smack, sock

(slang), stroke, thump, wallop
(informal), whack
2 SETBACK, bombshell, calamity,
catastrophe, disappointment,
disaster, misfortune, reverse,
shock

blow out verb 1 PUT OUT,
extinguish, snuff
2 BURST, erupt, explode, rupture,
shatter

blow up verb 1 EXPLODE, blast,
blow sky-high, bomb, burst,
detonate, rupture, shatter
2 INFLATE, bloat, distend, enlarge,
expand, fill, puff up, pump up,
swell
3 (informal) LOSE ONE'S TEMPER,
become angry, erupt, fly off the
handle (informal), hit the roof
(informal), rage, see red (informal)

bludgeon noun 1 CLUB, cosh (Brit.),
cudgel, truncheon
▶ verb 2 CLUB, beat up, cosh (Brit.),
cudgel, knock down, strike
3 BULLY, bulldoze (informal),
coerce, force, railroad (informal),
steamroller

blue adjective 1 AZURE, cerulean,
cobalt, cyan, navy, sapphire, sky-
colored, ultramarine
2 DEPRESSED, dejected,
despondent, downcast, low,
melancholy, sad, unhappy
3 SMUTTY, indecent, lewd,
obscene, risqué, X-rated (informal)

blueprint noun PLAN, design,
draft, outline, pattern, pilot
scheme, prototype, sketch

blues plural noun DEPRESSION,
doldrums, dumps (informal),
gloom, low spirits, melancholy,
unhappiness

bluff¹ verb 1 DECEIVE, con, delude,
fake, feign, mislead, pretend, pull
the wool over someone's eyes
▶ noun 2 DECEPTION, bluster,

bravado, deceit, fraud, humbug, pretense, sham, subterfuge

bluff² noun 1 PRECIPICE, bank, cliff, crag, escarpment, headland, peak, promontory, ridge
▶ adjective 2 HEARTY, blunt, blustering, genial, good-natured, open, outspoken, plain-spoken

blunder noun 1 MISTAKE, bloomer (informal), clanger (informal), faux pas, foul-up (slang), gaffe, howler (informal), indiscretion
2 ERROR, fault, inaccuracy, mistake, oversight, slip, slip-up (informal)
▶ verb 3 MAKE A MISTAKE, botch, bungle, err, foul up (slang), put one's foot in it (informal), slip up (informal)
4 STUMBLE, bumble, flounder

blunt adjective 1 DULL, dulled, edgeless, pointless, rounded, unsharpened
2 FORTHRIGHT, bluff, brusque, frank, outspoken, plain-spoken, rude, straightforward, tactless
▶ verb 3 DULL, dampen, deaden, numb, soften, take the edge off, water down, weaken

blur verb 1 MAKE INDISTINCT, cloud, darken, make hazy, make vague, mask, obscure
▶ noun 2 INDISTINCTNESS, confusion, fog, haze, obscurity

blurt out verb EXCLAIM, disclose, let the cat out of the bag, reveal, spill the beans (informal), tell all, utter suddenly

blush verb 1 TURN RED, color, flush, go red (as a beetroot), redden, turn scarlet
▶ noun 2 REDDENING, color, flush, glow, pink tinge, rosiness, rosy tint, ruddiness

bluster verb 1 ROAR, bully, domineer, hector, rant, storm

▶ noun 2 HOT AIR (informal), bluff, bombast, bravado

blustery adjective GUSTY, boisterous, inclement, squally, stormy, tempestuous, violent, wild, windy

board noun 1 PLANK, panel, piece of timber, slat, timber
2 DIRECTORS, advisers, committee, conclave, council, panel, trustees
3 MEALS, daily meals, provisions, victuals
▶ verb 4 GET ON, embark, enter, mount
5 LODGE, put up, quarter, room

boast verb 1 BRAG, blow one's own trumpet, crow, strut, swagger, talk big (slang), vaunt
2 POSSESS, be proud of, congratulate oneself on, exhibit, flatter oneself, pride oneself on, show off
▶ noun 3 BRAG, avowal

boastful adjective BRAGGING, cocky, conceited, crowing, egotistical, full of oneself, swaggering, swollen-headed, vaunting

bob verb DUCK, bounce, hop, nod, oscillate, wiggle, wobble

bode verb PORTEND, augur, be an omen of, forebode, foretell, predict, signify, threaten

bodily adjective PHYSICAL, actual, carnal, corporal, corporeal, material, substantial, tangible

body noun 1 PHYSIQUE, build, figure, form, frame, shape
2 TORSO, trunk
3 CORPSE, cadaver, carcass, dead body, remains, stiff (slang)
4 ORGANIZATION, association, band, bloc, collection, company, confederation, congress, corporation, society
5 MAIN PART, bulk, essence, mass, material, matter, substance

bog noun MARSH, fen, mire, morass, quagmire, slough, swamp, wetlands

bogey noun BUGBEAR, bête noire, bugaboo, nightmare

bogus adjective FAKE, artificial, counterfeit, false, forged, fraudulent, imitation, phoney or phony (informal), sham

bohemian adjective 1 UNCONVENTIONAL, alternative, artistic, arty (informal), left bank, nonconformist, offbeat, unorthodox
▶ noun 2 NONCONFORMIST, beatnik, dropout, hippie, iconoclast

boil[1] verb BUBBLE, effervesce, fizz, foam, froth, seethe

boil[2] noun PUSTULE, blister, carbuncle, gathering, swelling, tumor, ulcer

boisterous adjective UNRULY, disorderly, loud, noisy, riotous, rollicking, rowdy, unrestrained, vociferous, wild

bold adjective 1 FEARLESS, adventurous, audacious, brave, courageous, daring, enterprising, heroic, intrepid, valiant
2 IMPUDENT, barefaced, brazen, cheeky, confident, forward, insolent, rude, shameless

bolster verb SUPPORT, augment, boost, help, reinforce, shore up, strengthen

bolt noun 1 BAR, catch, fastener, latch, lock, sliding bar
2 PIN, peg, rivet, rod
▶ verb 3 RUN AWAY, abscond, dash, escape, flee, fly, make a break (for it), run for it
4 LOCK, bar, fasten, latch, secure
5 GOBBLE, cram, devour, gorge, gulp, guzzle, stuff, swallow whole, wolf

bomb noun 1 EXPLOSIVE, device, grenade, mine, missile, projectile, rocket, shell, torpedo
▶ verb 2 BLOW UP, attack, blow sky-high, bombard, destroy, shell, strafe, torpedo

bombard verb 1 BOMB, assault, blitz, fire upon, open fire, pound, shell, strafe
2 ATTACK, assail, beset, besiege, harass, hound, pester

bombardment noun BOMBING, assault, attack, barrage, blitz, fusillade, shelling

bombastic adjective GRANDILOQUENT, grandiose, high-flown, inflated, pompous, verbose, wordy

bona fide adjective GENUINE, actual, authentic, honest, kosher (informal), legitimate, real, true

bond noun 1 FASTENING, chain, cord, fetter, ligature, manacle, shackle, tie
2 TIE, affiliation, affinity, attachment, connection, link, relation, union
3 AGREEMENT, contract, covenant, guarantee, obligation, pledge, promise, word
▶ verb 4 HOLD TOGETHER, bind, connect, fasten, fix together, glue, paste

bondage noun SLAVERY, captivity, confinement, enslavement, imprisonment, subjugation

bonus noun EXTRA, dividend, gift, icing on the cake, plus, premium, prize, reward

bony adjective THIN, emaciated, gaunt, lean, scrawny, skin and bone, skinny

book noun 1 WORK, publication, title, tome, tract, volume
2 NOTEBOOK, album, diary, exercise book, jotter, pad

▶ *verb* 3 RESERVE, arrange for, charter, engage, make reservations, organize, program, schedule
4 NOTE, enter, list, log, mark down, put down, record, register, write down

booklet *noun* BROCHURE, leaflet, pamphlet

boom *verb* 1 BANG, blast, crash, explode, resound, reverberate, roar, roll, rumble, thunder
2 FLOURISH, develop, expand, grow, increase, intensify, prosper, strengthen, swell, thrive
▶ *noun* 3 BANG, blast, burst, clap, crash, explosion, roar, rumble, thunder
4 EXPANSION, boost, development, growth, improvement, increase, jump, upsurge, upswing, upturn

boon *noun* BENEFIT, advantage, blessing, favor, gift, godsend, manna from heaven, windfall

boorish *adjective* LOUTISH, churlish, coarse, crude, oafish, uncivilized, uncouth, vulgar

boost *noun* 1 HELP, encouragement, praise, promotion
2 RISE, addition, expansion, improvement, increase, increment, jump
▶ *verb* 3 INCREASE, add to, amplify, develop, enlarge, expand, heighten, raise
4 ADVERTISE, encourage, foster, further, hype, plug (*informal*), praise, promote

boot *verb* KICK, drive, drop-kick, knock, punt, put the boot in(to) (*slang*), shove

booty *noun* PLUNDER, gains, haul, loot, prey, spoils, swag (*slang*), takings, winnings

border *noun* 1 FRONTIER, borderline, boundary, line, march
2 EDGE, bounds, brink, limits, margin, rim, verge
▶ *verb* 3 EDGE, bind, decorate, fringe, hem, rim, trim

bore¹ *verb* DRILL, burrow, gouge out, mine, penetrate, perforate, pierce, sink, tunnel

bore² *verb* 1 TIRE, be tedious, fatigue, jade, pall on, send to sleep, wear out, weary
▶ *noun* 2 NUISANCE, anorak (*informal*), geek (*slang*), pain (*informal*)
3 PAIN (*informal*), yawn (*informal*)

bored *adjective* FED UP, listless, tired, uninterested, wearied

boredom *noun* TEDIUM, apathy, ennui, flatness, monotony, sameness, tediousness, weariness, world-weariness

boring *adjective* UNINTERESTING, dull, flat, humdrum, mind-numbing, monotonous, tedious, tiresome

borrow *verb* 1 TAKE ON LOAN, cadge, scrounge (*informal*), touch (someone) for (*slang*), use temporarily
2 STEAL, adopt, copy, obtain, plagiarize, take, usurp

bosom *noun* 1 BREAST, bust, chest
▶ *adjective* 2 INTIMATE, boon, cherished, close, confidential, dear, very dear

boss¹ *noun* (*informal*) HEAD, alpha male, chief, director, employer, gaffer (*informal, chiefly Brit.*), leader, manager, master, supervisor

boss² *noun* STUD, knob, point, protuberance, tip

boss around *verb* (*informal*) DOMINEER, bully, dominate, oppress, order, push around (*slang*)

bossy *adjective* DOMINEERING, arrogant, authoritarian,

autocratic, dictatorial, hectoring, high-handed, imperious, overbearing, tyrannical

botch verb 1 SPOIL, blunder, bungle, cock up (Brit. slang), foul up (slang), make a pig's ear of (informal), mar, mess up, screw up (informal)
▶ noun 2 MESS, blunder, bungle, cock-up (Brit. slang), failure, hash, pig's ear (informal)

bother verb 1 TROUBLE, alarm, concern, disturb, harass, hassle (informal), inconvenience, pester, plague, worry
▶ noun 2 TROUBLE, difficulty, fuss, hassle (informal), inconvenience, irritation, nuisance, problem, worry

bottleneck noun HOLD-UP, block, blockage, congestion, impediment, jam, obstacle, obstruction, snarl-up (informal, chiefly Brit.)

bottle up verb SUPPRESS, check, contain, curb, keep back, restrict, shut in, trap

bottom noun 1 LOWEST PART, base, bed, depths, floor, foot, foundation
2 UNDERSIDE, lower side, sole, underneath
3 BUTTOCKS, backside, behind (informal), posterior, rear, rump, seat, tush (slang)
▶ adjective 4 LOWEST, last

bottomless adjective UNLIMITED, boundless, deep, fathomless, immeasurable, inexhaustible, infinite, unfathomable

bounce verb 1 REBOUND, bob, bound, jump, leap, recoil, ricochet, spring
▶ noun 2 (informal) LIFE, dynamism, energy, go (informal), liveliness, vigor, vivacity, zip (informal)

3 SPRINGINESS, elasticity, give, recoil, resilience, spring

bound¹ adjective 1 TIED, cased, fastened, fixed, pinioned, secured, tied up
2 CERTAIN, destined, doomed, fated, sure
3 OBLIGED, beholden, committed, compelled, constrained, duty-bound, forced, pledged, required

bound² verb LIMIT, confine, demarcate, encircle, enclose, hem in, restrain, restrict, surround

bound³ verb or noun LEAP, bob, bounce, gambol, hurdle, jump, skip, spring, vault

boundary noun LIMITS, barrier, border, borderline, brink, edge, extremity, fringe, frontier, margin

boundless adjective UNLIMITED, endless, immense, incalculable, inexhaustible, infinite, unconfined, untold, vast

bounds plural noun BOUNDARY, border, confine, edge, extremity, limit, rim, verge

bountiful adjective (literary)
1 PLENTIFUL, abundant, ample, bounteous, copious, exuberant, lavish, luxuriant, prolific
2 GENEROUS, liberal, magnanimous, open-handed, prodigal, unstinting

bounty noun (literary)
1 GENEROSITY, benevolence, charity, kindness, largesse or largess, liberality, philanthropy
2 REWARD, bonus, gift, present

bouquet noun 1 BUNCH OF FLOWERS, buttonhole, corsage, garland, nosegay, posy, spray, wreath
2 AROMA, fragrance, perfume, redolence, savor, scent

bourgeois adjective MIDDLE-CLASS, conventional, hidebound,

materialistic, traditional
bout noun 1 PERIOD, fit, spell, stint, term, turn
2 FIGHT, boxing match, competition, contest, encounter, engagement, match, set-to, struggle
bow¹ verb 1 BEND, bob, droop, genuflect, nod, stoop
2 GIVE IN, acquiesce, comply, concede, defer, kowtow, relent, submit, succumb, surrender, yield
▶ noun 3 BENDING, bob, genuflexion, kowtow, nod, obeisance
bow² noun (nautical) PROW, beak, fore, head, stem
bowels plural noun 1 GUTS, entrails, innards (informal), insides (informal), intestines, viscera, vitals
2 DEPTHS, belly, core, deep, hold, inside, interior
bowl¹ noun BASIN, dish, vessel
bowl² verb THROW, fling, hurl, pitch
box¹ noun 1 CONTAINER, carton, case, casket, chest, pack, package, receptacle, trunk
▶ verb 2 PACK, package, wrap
box² verb FIGHT, exchange blows, spar
boxer noun FIGHTER, prizefighter, pugilist, sparring partner
boy noun LAD, fellow, junior, schoolboy, stripling, youngster, youth
boycott verb EMBARGO, ban, bar, black, exclude, outlaw, prohibit, refuse, reject
boyfriend noun SWEETHEART, admirer, beau, date, lover, man, suitor
boyish adjective YOUTHFUL, adolescent, childish, immature, juvenile, puerile, young
brace noun 1 SUPPORT, bolster,

bracket, buttress, prop, reinforcement, stay, strut, truss
▶ verb 2 SUPPORT, bolster, buttress, fortify, reinforce, steady, strengthen
bracing adjective REFRESHING, brisk, crisp, exhilarating, fresh, invigorating, stimulating
brag verb BOAST, blow one's own trumpet, bluster, crow, swagger, talk big (slang), vaunt
braggart noun BOASTER, bigmouth (slang), bragger, show-off (informal)
braid verb INTERWEAVE, entwine, interlace, intertwine, lace, plait, twine, weave
brainless adjective STUPID, foolish, idiotic, inane, mindless, senseless, thoughtless, witless
brains plural noun INTELLIGENCE, intellect, sense, understanding
brainy adjective (informal) INTELLIGENT, bright, brilliant, clever, smart
brake noun 1 CONTROL, check, constraint, curb, rein, restraint
▶ verb 2 SLOW, check, decelerate, halt, moderate, reduce speed, slacken, stop
branch noun 1 BOUGH, arm, limb, offshoot, shoot, spray, sprig
2 DIVISION, chapter, department, office, part, section, subdivision, wing
brand noun 1 LABEL, emblem, hallmark, logo, mark, marker, sign, stamp, symbol, trademark
2 KIND, cast, class, grade, make, quality, sort, species, type, variety
▶ verb 3 MARK, burn, burn in, label, scar, stamp
4 STIGMATIZE, censure, denounce, discredit, disgrace, expose, mark
brandish verb WAVE, display, exhibit, flaunt, flourish, parade,

raise, shake, swing, wield

brash *adjective* BOLD, brazen, cocky, impertinent, impudent, insolent, pushy (*informal*), rude

bravado *noun* SWAGGER, bluster, boastfulness, boasting, bombast, swashbuckling, vaunting

brave *adjective* 1 COURAGEOUS, bold, daring, fearless, heroic, intrepid, plucky, resolute, valiant
▶ *verb* 2 CONFRONT, defy, endure, face, stand up to, suffer, tackle, withstand

bravery *noun* COURAGE, boldness, daring, fearlessness, fortitude, heroism, intrepidity, mettle, pluck, spirit, valor

brawl *noun* 1 FIGHT, affray (*Law*), altercation, clash, dispute, fracas, fray, melee *or* mêlée, punch-up (*Brit. informal*), rumpus, scuffle, skirmish
▶ *verb* 2 FIGHT, scrap (*informal*), scuffle, tussle, wrestle

brawn *noun* MUSCLE, beef (*informal*), might, muscles, power, strength, vigor

brawny *adjective* MUSCULAR, beefy (*informal*), hefty (*informal*), lusty, powerful, strapping, strong, sturdy, well-built

brazen *adjective* BOLD, audacious, barefaced, brash, defiant, impudent, insolent, shameless, unabashed, unashamed

breach *noun* 1 NONOBSERVANCE, contravention, infraction, infringement, noncompliance, transgression, trespass, violation
2 CRACK, cleft, fissure, gap, opening, rift, rupture, split

bread *noun* 1 FOOD, fare, nourishment, sustenance
2 (*slang*) MONEY, cash, dough (*slang*)

breadth *noun* 1 WIDTH, broadness, latitude, span, spread, wideness
2 EXTENT, compass, expanse, range, scale, scope

break *verb* 1 SEPARATE, burst, crack, destroy, disintegrate, fracture, fragment, shatter, smash, snap, split, tear
2 DISOBEY, breach, contravene, disregard, infringe, renege on, transgress, violate
3 REVEAL, announce, disclose, divulge, impart, inform, let out, make public, proclaim, tell
4 STOP, abandon, cut, discontinue, give up, interrupt, pause, rest, suspend
5 WEAKEN, demoralize, dispirit, subdue, tame, undermine
6 (*of a record, etc.*) BEAT, better, exceed, excel, go beyond, outdo, outstrip, surpass, top
▶ *noun* 7 DIVISION, crack, fissure, fracture, gap, hole, opening, split, tear
8 REST, breather (*informal*), hiatus, interlude, intermission, interruption, interval, let-up (*informal*), lull, pause, respite
9 (*informal*) STROKE OF LUCK, advantage, chance, fortune, opening, opportunity

breakable *adjective* FRAGILE, brittle, crumbly, delicate, flimsy, frail, frangible, friable

breakdown *noun* COLLAPSE, disintegration, disruption, failure, mishap, stoppage

break down *verb* 1 COLLAPSE, come unstuck, fail, seize up, stop, stop working
2 BE OVERCOME, crack up (*informal*), go to pieces

break-in *noun* BURGLARY, breaking and entering, robbery

break off *verb* 1 DETACH, divide, part, pull off, separate, sever, snap off, splinter

2 STOP, cease, desist, discontinue, end, finish, halt, pull the plug on, suspend, terminate

break out *verb* BEGIN, appear, arise, commence, emerge, happen, occur, set in, spring up, start

breakthrough *noun* DEVELOPMENT, advance, discovery, find, invention, leap, progress, quantum leap, step forward

break up *verb* **1** SEPARATE, dissolve, divide, divorce, part, scatter, sever, split

2 STOP, adjourn, disband, dismantle, end, suspend, terminate

breast *noun* BOSOM, bust, chest, front, teat, udder

breath *noun* RESPIRATION, breathing, exhalation, gasp, gulp, inhalation, pant, wheeze

breathe *verb* **1** INHALE AND EXHALE, draw in, gasp, gulp, pant, puff, respire, wheeze

2 WHISPER, murmur, sigh

breather *noun* (*informal*) REST, break, breathing space, halt, pause, recess, respite

breathless *adjective* **1** OUT OF BREATH, gasping, gulping, panting, short-winded, spent, wheezing

2 EXCITED, eager, on tenterhooks, open-mouthed, wired (*slang*), with bated breath

breathtaking *adjective* AMAZING, astonishing, awe-inspiring, cool (*informal*), exciting, impressive, magnificent, phat (*slang*), sensational, stunning (*informal*), thrilling

breed *verb* **1** REPRODUCE, bear, bring forth, hatch, multiply, procreate, produce, propagate

2 BRING UP, cultivate, develop, nourish, nurture, raise, rear

3 PRODUCE, arouse, bring about, cause, create, generate, give rise to, stir up

▶ *noun* **4** VARIETY, pedigree, race, species, stock, strain, type

5 KIND, brand, sort, stamp, type, variety

breeding *noun* **1** UPBRINGING, ancestry, cultivation, development, lineage, nurture, raising, rearing, reproduction, training

2 REFINEMENT, conduct, courtesy, cultivation, culture, polish, sophistication, urbanity

breeze *noun* **1** LIGHT WIND, air, breath of wind, current of air, draft, gust, waft, zephyr

▶ *verb* **2** MOVE BRISKLY, flit, glide, hurry, pass, sail, sweep

breezy *adjective* **1** WINDY, airy, blowy, blustery, fresh, gusty, squally

2 CAREFREE, blithe, casual, easygoing, free and easy, jaunty, light-hearted, lively, sprightly

brevity *noun* **1** SHORTNESS, briefness, impermanence, transience, transitoriness

2 CONCISENESS, crispness, curtness, economy, pithiness, succinctness, terseness

brew *verb* **1** MAKE (*beer*), boil, ferment, infuse (*tea*), soak, steep, stew

2 DEVELOP, foment, form, gather, start, stir up

▶ *noun* **3** DRINK, beverage, blend, concoction, infusion, liquor, mixture, preparation

bribe *verb* **1** BUY OFF, corrupt, grease the palm *or* hand of (*slang*), pay off (*informal*), reward, suborn

▶ *noun* **2** INDUCEMENT, allurement,

backhander (*slang*), enticement, kickback (*U.S.*), pay-off (*informal*), sweetener (*slang*)

bribery noun BUYING OFF, corruption, inducement, palm-greasing (*slang*), payola (*informal*)

bric-a-brac noun KNICK-KNACKS, baubles, curios, ornaments, trinkets

bridal adjective MATRIMONIAL, conjugal, connubial, marital, marriage, nuptial, wedding

bridge noun 1 ARCH, flyover, overpass, span, viaduct
▶ verb 2 CONNECT, join, link, span

bridle noun 1 CURB, check, control, rein, restraint
▶ verb 2 GET ANGRY, be indignant, bristle, draw (oneself) up, get one's back up, raise one's hackles, rear up

brief adjective 1 SHORT, ephemeral, fleeting, momentary, quick, short-lived, swift, transitory
▶ noun 2 SUMMARY, abridgment, abstract, digest, epitome, outline, précis, sketch, synopsis
▶ verb 3 INFORM, advise, explain, fill in (*informal*), instruct, keep posted, prepare, prime, put (someone) in the picture (*informal*)

briefing noun INSTRUCTIONS, conference, directions, guidance, information, preparation, priming, rundown

briefly adverb SHORTLY, concisely, hastily, hurriedly, in a nutshell, in brief, momentarily, quickly

brigade noun GROUP, band, company, corps, force, organization, outfit, squad, team, troop, unit

bright adjective 1 SHINING, brilliant, dazzling, gleaming, glowing, luminous, lustrous, radiant, shimmering, vivid

2 INTELLIGENT, astute, aware, clever, inventive, quick-witted, sharp, smart, wide-awake

3 SUNNY, clear, cloudless, fair, limpid, lucid, pleasant, translucent, transparent, unclouded

brighten verb MAKE BRIGHTER, gleam, glow, illuminate, lighten, light up, shine

brightness noun 1 SHINE, brilliance, glare, incandescence, intensity, light, luminosity, radiance, vividness

2 INTELLIGENCE, acuity, cleverness, quickness, sharpness, smartness

brilliance, brilliancy noun
1 BRIGHTNESS, dazzle, intensity, luminosity, luster, radiance, sparkle, vividness

2 TALENT, cleverness, distinction, excellence, genius, greatness, inventiveness, wisdom

3 SPLENDOR, éclat, glamour, grandeur, illustriousness, magnificence

brilliant adjective 1 SHINING, bright, dazzling, glittering, intense, luminous, radiant, sparkling, vivid

2 SPLENDID, celebrated, famous, glorious, illustrious, magnificent, notable, outstanding, superb

3 INTELLIGENT, clever, expert, gifted, intellectual, inventive, masterly, penetrating, profound, talented

brim noun 1 RIM, border, brink, edge, lip, margin, skirt, verge
▶ verb 2 BE FULL, fill, fill up, hold no more, overflow, run over, spill, well over

bring verb 1 TAKE, bear, carry, conduct, convey, deliver, escort, fetch, guide, lead, transfer, transport

2 CAUSE, contribute to, create, effect, inflict, occasion, produce, result in, wreak

bring about verb CAUSE, accomplish, achieve, create, effect, generate, give rise to, make happen, produce

bring off verb ACCOMPLISH, achieve, carry off, execute, perform, pull off, succeed

bring up verb 1 REAR, breed, develop, educate, form, nurture, raise, support, teach, train
2 MENTION, allude to, broach, introduce, move, propose, put forward, raise

brink noun EDGE, border, boundary, brim, fringe, frontier, limit, lip, margin, rim, skirt, threshold, verge

brisk adjective LIVELY, active, bustling, busy, energetic, quick, sprightly, spry, vigorous

briskly adverb QUICKLY, actively, apace, efficiently, energetically, promptly, rapidly, readily, smartly

bristle noun 1 HAIR, barb, prickle, spine, stubble, thorn, whisker
▶ verb 2 STAND UP, rise, stand on end
3 BE ANGRY, bridle, flare up, rage, see red, seethe

bristly adjective HAIRY, prickly, rough, stubbly

brittle adjective FRAGILE, breakable, crisp, crumbling, crumbly, delicate, frail, frangible, friable

broach verb 1 BRING UP, introduce, mention, open up, propose, raise the subject, speak of, suggest, talk of, touch on
2 OPEN, crack, draw off, pierce, puncture, start, tap, uncork

broad adjective 1 WIDE, ample, expansive, extensive, generous, large, roomy, spacious, vast, voluminous, widespread
2 GENERAL, all-embracing, comprehensive, encyclopedic, inclusive, sweeping, wide, wide-ranging

broadcast noun 1 TRANSMISSION, program, show, telecast
▶ verb 2 TRANSMIT, air, beam, cable, put on the air, radio, relay, show, televise
3 MAKE PUBLIC, advertise, announce, circulate, proclaim, publish, report, spread

broaden verb EXPAND, develop, enlarge, extend, increase, spread, stretch, supplement, swell, widen

broad-minded adjective TOLERANT, free-thinking, indulgent, liberal, open-minded, permissive, unbiased, unbigoted, unprejudiced

broadside noun ATTACK, assault, battering, bombardment, censure, criticism, denunciation, diatribe

brochure noun BOOKLET, advertisement, circular, folder, handbill, hand-out, leaflet, mailshot, pamphlet

broke adjective (informal) PENNILESS, bankrupt, bust (informal), down and out, down on one's luck (informal), impoverished, insolvent, in the red, ruined, short, skint (Brit. slang)

broken adjective 1 SMASHED, burst, fractured, fragmented, ruptured, separated, severed, shattered
2 INTERRUPTED, discontinuous, erratic, fragmentary, incomplete, intermittent, spasmodic
3 NOT WORKING, defective, imperfect, kaput (informal), on the blink (slang), out of order
4 IMPERFECT, disjointed, halting, hesitating, stammering

brokenhearted *adjective*
HEARTBROKEN, desolate,
devastated, disconsolate, grief-
stricken, inconsolable, miserable,
sorrowful, wretched

broker *noun* DEALER, agent,
factor, go-between, intermediary,
middleman, negotiator

bronze *adjective* REDDISH-BROWN,
brownish, chestnut, copper,
rust, tan

brood *noun* 1 OFFSPRING, clutch,
family, issue, litter, progeny
▶ *verb* 2 THINK UPON, agonize,
dwell upon, mope, mull over,
muse, ponder, ruminate

brook *noun* STREAM, beck, burn,
rill, rivulet, watercourse

brother *noun* 1 SIBLING, blood
brother, kin, kinsman, relation,
relative
2 MONK, cleric, friar

brotherhood *noun* 1 FELLOWSHIP,
brotherliness, camaraderie,
companionship, comradeship,
friendliness, kinship
2 ASSOCIATION, alliance,
community, fraternity, guild,
league, order, society, union

brotherly *adjective* KIND,
affectionate, altruistic,
amicable, benevolent, cordial,
fraternal, friendly, neighborly,
philanthropic, sympathetic

browbeat *verb* BULLY, badger,
coerce, dragoon, hector,
intimidate, ride roughshod over,
threaten, tyrannize

brown *adjective* 1 BRUNETTE,
auburn, bay, bronze, chestnut,
chocolate, coffee, dun, hazel,
sunburned, tan, tanned, tawny,
umber
▶ *verb* 2 FRY, cook, grill, sauté,
seal, sear

browse *verb* 1 SKIM, dip into,

examine cursorily, flip through,
glance at, leaf through, look
round, look through, peruse,
scan, survey
2 GRAZE, chow down (*slang*), eat,
feed, nibble

bruise *verb* 1 DISCOLOR, damage,
injure, mar, mark, pound
▶ *noun* 2 DISCOLORATION, black
mark, blemish, contusion, injury,
mark, swelling

brunt *noun* FULL FORCE, burden,
force, impact, pressure, shock,
strain, stress, thrust, violence

brush¹ *noun* 1 BROOM, besom,
sweeper
2 ENCOUNTER, clash, conflict,
confrontation, skirmish, tussle
▶ *verb* 3 CLEAN, buff, paint, polish,
sweep, wash
4 TOUCH, flick, glance, graze, kiss,
scrape, stroke, sweep

brush² *noun* SHRUBS, brushwood,
bushes, copse, scrub, thicket,
undergrowth

brush off *verb* (*slang*) IGNORE,
blow off (*slang*), disdain, dismiss,
disregard, reject, repudiate, scorn,
snub, spurn

brush up *verb* REVISE, bone up
(*informal*), cram, go over, polish up,
read up, refresh one's memory,
relearn, study

brusque *adjective* CURT, abrupt,
discourteous, gruff, impolite,
sharp, short, surly, terse

brutal *adjective* 1 CRUEL,
bloodthirsty, heartless, inhuman,
ruthless, savage, uncivilized,
vicious
2 HARSH, callous, gruff, impolite,
insensitive, rough, rude, severe

brutality *noun* CRUELTY, atrocity,
barbarism, bloodthirstiness,
ferocity, inhumanity,
ruthlessness, savagery,

viciousness

brute noun 1 SAVAGE, barbarian, beast, devil, fiend, monster, sadist, swine
2 ANIMAL, beast, creature, wild animal
▶ adjective 3 MINDLESS, bodily, carnal, fleshly, instinctive, physical, senseless, unthinking

bubble noun 1 AIR BALL, bead, blister, blob, drop, droplet, globule
▶ verb 2 FOAM, boil, effervesce, fizz, froth, percolate, seethe, sparkle
3 GURGLE, babble, burble, murmur, ripple, trickle

bubbly adjective 1 LIVELY, animated, bouncy, elated, excited, happy, merry, sparky, wired (slang)
2 FROTHY, carbonated, effervescent, fizzy, foamy, sparkling

buccaneer noun PIRATE, corsair, freebooter, privateer, sea-rover

buckle noun 1 FASTENER, catch, clasp, clip, hasp
▶ verb 2 FASTEN, clasp, close, hook, secure
3 DISTORT, bend, bulge, cave in, collapse, contort, crumple, fold, twist, warp

bud noun 1 SHOOT, embryo, germ, sprout
▶ verb 2 DEVELOP, burgeon, burst forth, grow, shoot, sprout

budding adjective DEVELOPING, beginning, burgeoning, embryonic, fledgling, growing, incipient, nascent, potential, promising

budge verb MOVE, dislodge, push, shift, stir

budget noun 1 ALLOWANCE, allocation, cost, finances, funds, means, resources
▶ verb 2 PLAN, allocate, apportion, cost, estimate, ration

buff¹ adjective 1 YELLOWISH-BROWN, sandy, straw, tan, yellowish
▶ verb 2 POLISH, brush, burnish, rub, shine, smooth

buff² noun (informal) EXPERT, addict, admirer, aficionado, connoisseur, devotee, enthusiast, fan

buffer noun SAFEGUARD, bulwark, bumper, cushion, fender, intermediary, screen, shield, shock absorber

buffet¹ noun SNACK BAR, brasserie, café, cafeteria, refreshment counter, sideboard

buffet² verb BATTER, beat, bump, knock, pound, pummel, strike, thump, wallop (informal)

buffoon noun CLOWN, comedian, comic, fool, harlequin, jester, joker, wag

bug noun 1 (informal) ILLNESS, disease, infection, lurgy (informal), virus
2 FAULT, defect, error, flaw, glitch, gremlin
▶ verb 3 (informal) ANNOY, bother, disturb, get on one's nerves (informal), hassle (informal), irritate, pester, vex
4 TAP, eavesdrop, listen in, spy

bugbear noun PET HATE, bane, bête noire, bogey, dread, horror, nightmare

build verb 1 CONSTRUCT, assemble, erect, fabricate, form, make, put up, raise
▶ noun 2 PHYSIQUE, body, figure, form, frame, shape, structure

building noun STRUCTURE, domicile, dwelling, edifice, house

build-up noun INCREASE, accumulation, development, enlargement, escalation, expansion, gain, growth

bulbous adjective BULGING,

bloated, convex, rounded, swelling, swollen

bulge noun 1 SWELLING, bump, hump, lump, projection, protrusion, protuberance
2 INCREASE, boost, intensification, rise, surge
▶ verb 3 SWELL OUT, dilate, distend, expand, project, protrude, puff out, stick out

bulk noun 1 SIZE, dimensions, immensity, largeness, magnitude, substance, volume, weight
2 MAIN PART, better part, body, lion's share, majority, mass, most, nearly all, preponderance

bulky adjective LARGE, big, cumbersome, heavy, hulking, massive, substantial, unwieldy, voluminous, weighty

bulldoze verb DEMOLISH, flatten, level, raze

bullet noun PROJECTILE, ball, missile, pellet, shot, slug

bulletin noun ANNOUNCEMENT, account, communication, communiqué, dispatch, message, news flash, notification, report, statement

bully noun 1 PERSECUTOR, browbeater, bully boy, coercer, intimidator, oppressor, ruffian, tormentor, tough
▶ verb 2 PERSECUTE, browbeat, coerce, domineer, hector, intimidate, oppress, push around (slang), terrorize, tyrannize

bulwark noun 1 FORTIFICATION, bastion, buttress, defense, embankment, partition, rampart
2 DEFENSE, buffer, guard, mainstay, safeguard, security, support

bumbling adjective CLUMSY, awkward, blundering, bungling, incompetent, inefficient, inept,

maladroit, muddled

bump verb 1 KNOCK, bang, collide (with), crash, hit, slam, smash into, strike
2 JERK, bounce, jolt, rattle, shake
▶ noun 3 KNOCK, bang, blow, collision, crash, impact, jolt, thud, thump
4 LUMP, bulge, contusion, hump, nodule, protuberance, swelling

bumper adjective EXCEPTIONAL, abundant, bountiful, excellent, jumbo (informal), massive, whopping (informal)

bumpkin noun YOKEL, country bumpkin, hick (informal), hillbilly, peasant, redneck (slang), rustic

bumptious adjective COCKY, arrogant, brash, conceited, forward, full of oneself, overconfident, pushy (informal), self-assertive

bumpy adjective ROUGH, bouncy, choppy, jarring, jerky, jolting, rutted, uneven

bunch noun 1 NUMBER, assortment, batch, bundle, clump, cluster, collection, heap, lot, mass, pile
2 GROUP, band, crowd, flock, gang, gathering, party, team
▶ verb 3 GROUP, assemble, bundle, cluster, collect, huddle, mass, pack

bundle noun 1 BUNCH, assortment, batch, collection, group, heap, mass, pile, stack
▶ verb 2 (with out, off, into, etc.) PUSH, hurry, hustle, rush, shove, throw, thrust

bundle up verb WRAP UP, swathe

bungle verb MESS UP, blow (slang), blunder, botch, foul up, make a mess of, muff, ruin, spoil

bungling adjective INCOMPETENT, blundering, cack-handed (informal), clumsy, ham-fisted (*informal*), inept, maladroit

bunk, bunkum *noun* (*informal*)
NONSENSE, balderdash, baloney
(*informal*), garbage (*informal*),
hogwash, hot air (*informal*),
moonshine, poppycock (*informal*),
rubbish, stuff and nonsense,
twaddle

buoy *noun* 1 MARKER, beacon, float,
guide, signal
▶ *verb* 2 ▷▷ **buoy up** ENCOURAGE,
boost, cheer, cheer up, hearten,
keep afloat, lift, raise, support,
sustain

buoyancy *noun* 1 LIGHTNESS,
weightlessness
2 CHEERFULNESS, animation,
bounce (*informal*), good humor,
high spirits, liveliness

buoyant *adjective* 1 FLOATING,
afloat, light, weightless
2 CHEERFUL, carefree, chirpy
(*informal*), happy, jaunty, light-
hearted, upbeat (*informal*)

burden *noun* 1 LOAD,
encumbrance, weight
2 TROUBLE, affliction, millstone,
onus, responsibility, strain,
weight, worry
▶ *verb* 3 WEIGH DOWN, bother,
handicap, load, oppress, saddle
with, tax, worry

bureau *noun* 1 OFFICE, agency,
branch, department, division,
service
2 DESK, writing desk

bureaucracy *noun*
1 GOVERNMENT, administration,
authorities, civil service, corridors
of power, officials, the system
2 RED TAPE, officialdom,
regulations

bureaucrat *noun* OFFICIAL,
administrator, civil servant,
functionary, mandarin, officer,
public servant

burglar *noun* HOUSEBREAKER, cat
burglar, filcher, pilferer, robber,
sneak thief, thief

burglary *noun* BREAKING
AND ENTERING, break-in,
housebreaking, larceny, robbery,
stealing, theft, thieving

burial *noun* INTERMENT,
entombment, exequies, funeral,
obsequies

buried *adjective* 1 INTERRED,
entombed, laid to rest
2 HIDDEN, concealed, private,
sequestered, tucked away

burlesque *noun* 1 PARODY,
caricature, mockery, satire, send-
up (*Brit. informal*), spoof (*informal*),
takeoff (*informal*), travesty
▶ *verb* 2 SATIRIZE, ape, caricature,
exaggerate, imitate, lampoon,
make a monkey out of, make fun
of, mock, parody, ridicule, send up
(*Brit. informal*), spoof (*informal*), take
off (*informal*), take the piss out of
(*taboo slang*), travesty

burly *adjective* BRAWNY, beefy
(*informal*), big, bulky, hefty,
hulking, stocky, stout, sturdy,
thickset, well-built

burn *verb* 1 BE ON FIRE, be ablaze,
blaze, flame, flare, glow, go up in
flames, smoke
2 SET ON FIRE, char, ignite,
incinerate, kindle, light, parch,
scorch, sear, singe, toast
3 BE PASSIONATE, be angry, be
aroused, be inflamed, fume,
seethe, simmer, smolder

burning *adjective* 1 INTENSE,
ardent, eager, fervent,
impassioned, passionate,
vehement
2 CRUCIAL, acute, compelling,
critical, essential, important,
pressing, significant, urgent, vital
3 BLAZING, fiery, flaming,

flashing, gleaming, glowing, illuminated, scorching, smoldering

burnish verb POLISH, brighten, buff, furbish, glaze, rub up, shine, smooth

burrow noun 1 HOLE, den, lair, retreat, shelter, tunnel
▶ verb 2 DIG, delve, excavate, hollow out, scoop out, tunnel

burst verb 1 EXPLODE, blow up, break, crack, puncture, rupture, shatter, split, tear apart
2 RUSH, barge, break, break out, erupt, gush forth, run, spout
▶ noun 3 EXPLOSION, bang, blast, blowout, break, crack, discharge, rupture, split
4 RUSH, gush, gust, outbreak, outburst, outpouring, spate, spurt, surge, torrent
▶ adjective 5 RUPTURED, flat, punctured, rent, split

bury verb 1 INTER, consign to the grave, entomb, inhume, lay to rest
2 EMBED, engulf, submerge
3 HIDE, conceal, cover, enshroud, secrete, stow away

bush noun 1 SHRUB, hedge, plant, shrubbery, thicket
2 ▷▷ **the bush** THE WILD, backwoods, brush, scrub, scrubland, woodland

bushy adjective THICK, bristling, fluffy, fuzzy, luxuriant, rough, shaggy, unruly

busily adverb ACTIVELY, assiduously, briskly, diligently, energetically, industriously, purposefully, speedily, strenuously

business noun 1 TRADE, bargaining, commerce, dealings, industry, manufacturing, selling, transaction
2 ESTABLISHMENT, company,

concern, corporation, enterprise, firm, organization, venture
3 PROFESSION, career, employment, function, job, line, occupation, trade, vocation, work
4 CONCERN, affair, assignment, duty, pigeon (informal), problem, responsibility, task

businesslike adjective EFFICIENT, methodical, orderly, organized, practical, professional, systematic, thorough, well-ordered

businessman noun EXECUTIVE, capitalist, employer, entrepreneur, financier, industrialist, merchant, tradesman, tycoon

bust¹ noun BOSOM, breast, chest, front, torso

bust² (informal) verb 1 BREAK, burst, fracture, rupture
2 ARREST, catch, raid, search
▶ adjective 3 ▷▷ **go bust** GO BANKRUPT, become insolvent, be ruined, fail

bustle verb 1 HURRY, fuss, hasten, rush, scamper, scurry, scuttle
▶ noun 2 ACTIVITY, ado, commotion, excitement, flurry, fuss, hurly-burly, stir, to-do

bustling adjective BUSY, active, buzzing, crowded, full, humming, lively, swarming, teeming

busy adjective 1 OCCUPIED, active, employed, engaged, hard at work, industrious, on duty, rushed off one's feet, working
2 LIVELY, energetic, exacting, full, hectic, hustling
▶ verb 3 OCCUPY, absorb, employ, engage, engross, immerse, interest

busybody noun NOSY PARKER (informal) NOSY ROSY (U.S. informal), gossip, meddler, snooper, stirrer (informal), troublemaker

but conjunction 1 HOWEVER, further, moreover, nevertheless, on the contrary, on the other hand, still, yet
▶ preposition 2 EXCEPT, bar, barring, excepting, excluding, notwithstanding, save, with the exception of
▶ adverb 3 ONLY, just, merely, simply, singly, solely

butcher noun 1 MURDERER, destroyer, killer, slaughterer, slayer
▶ verb 2 SLAUGHTER, carve, clean, cut, cut up, dress, joint, prepare 3 KILL, assassinate, cut down, destroy, exterminate, liquidate, massacre, put to the sword, slaughter, slay

butt¹ noun 1 END, haft, handle, hilt, shaft, shank, stock 2 STUB, fag end, cigarette end, leftover, tip 3 (informal) BUTTOCKS, behind (informal), bottom, derrière (euphemistic), rump (informal), tush (slang)

butt² noun TARGET, Aunt Sally (Brit.), dupe, laughing stock, victim

butt³ verb or noun 1 (with or of the head or horns) KNOCK, bump, poke, prod, push, ram, shove, thrust 2 ▷▷ **butt in** INTERFERE, chip in (informal), cut in, interrupt, intrude, meddle, put one's oar in, stick one's nose in

butt⁴ noun CASK, barrel

buttonhole verb DETAIN, accost, bore, catch, grab, importune, take aside, waylay

buttress noun 1 SUPPORT, brace, mainstay, prop, reinforcement, stanchion, strut
▶ verb 2 SUPPORT, back up, bolster, prop up, reinforce, shore up, strengthen, sustain, uphold

buxom adjective PLUMP, ample, bosomy, busty, curvaceous, healthy, voluptuous, well-rounded

buy verb 1 PURCHASE, acquire, get, invest in, obtain, pay for, procure, shop for
▶ noun 2 PURCHASE, acquisition, bargain, deal

by preposition 1 VIA, by way of, over 2 THROUGH, through the agency of 3 NEAR, along, beside, close to, next to, past
▶ adverb 4 NEAR, at hand, close, handy, in reach 5 PAST, aside, away, to one side

bygone adjective PAST, antiquated, extinct, forgotten, former, lost, of old, olden

bypass verb GO ROUND, avoid, circumvent, depart from, detour round, deviate from, get round, give a wide berth to, pass round

bystander noun ONLOOKER, eyewitness, looker-on, observer, passer-by, spectator, viewer, watcher, witness

byword noun SAYING, adage, maxim, motto, precept, proverb, slogan

C

cab noun TAXI, hackney carriage, minicab, taxicab

cabal noun 1 CLIQUE, caucus, conclave, faction, league, party, set
2 PLOT, conspiracy, intrigue, machination, scheme

cabin noun 1 ROOM, berth, compartment, quarters
2 HUT, chalet, cottage, lodge, shack, shanty, shed

cabinet noun CUPBOARD, case, chiffonier, closet, commode, dresser, escritoire, locker

Cabinet noun COUNCIL, administration, assembly, counselors, ministry

caddish adjective UNGENTLEMANLY, despicable, ill-bred, lousy (slang), low, scuzzy (slang), unmannerly

café noun SNACK BAR, brasserie, cafeteria, coffee bar, coffee shop, lunchroom, restaurant, tearoom

cage noun ENCLOSURE, pen, pound

cagey, cagy adjective (informal) WARY, careful, cautious, chary, discreet, guarded, noncommittal, shrewd, wily

cajole verb PERSUADE, brown-nose (slang), coax, flatter, seduce, sweet-talk (informal), wheedle

cake noun 1 BLOCK, bar, cube, loaf, lump, mass, slab
▶ verb 2 ENCRUST, bake, coagulate, congeal, solidify

calamitous adjective DISASTROUS, cataclysmic, catastrophic, deadly, devastating, dire, fatal, ruinous, tragic

calamity noun DISASTER, cataclysm, catastrophe, misadventure, misfortune, mishap, ruin, tragedy, tribulation

calculate verb 1 WORK OUT, compute, count, determine, enumerate, estimate, figure, reckon
2 PLAN, aim, design, intend

calculated adjective DELIBERATE, considered, intended, intentional, planned, premeditated, purposeful

calculating adjective SCHEMING, crafty, cunning, devious, Machiavellian, manipulative, sharp, shrewd, sly

calculation noun 1 WORKING OUT, answer, computation, estimate, forecast, judgment, reckoning, result
2 PLANNING, contrivance, deliberation, discretion, foresight, forethought, precaution

caliber noun 1 WORTH, ability, capacity, distinction, merit, quality, stature, talent
2 DIAMETER, bore, gauge, measure

call verb 1 NAME, christen, describe as, designate, dub, entitle, label, style, term
2 CRY, arouse, hail, rouse, shout, yell
3 PHONE, ring up (informal, chiefly Brit.), telephone
4 SUMMON, assemble, convene, gather, muster, rally

▶ *noun* 5 CRY, hail, scream, shout, signal, whoop, yell

6 SUMMONS, appeal, command, demand, invitation, notice, order, plea, request

7 NEED, cause, excuse, grounds, justification, occasion, reason

call for *verb* 1 REQUIRE, demand, entail, involve, necessitate, need, occasion, suggest

2 FETCH, collect, pick up

calling *noun* PROFESSION, career, life's work, mission, trade, vocation

call on *verb* VISIT, drop in on, look in on, look up, see

callous *adjective* HEARTLESS, cold, hard-bitten, hard-boiled, hardened, hardhearted, insensitive, uncaring, unfeeling

callow *adjective* INEXPERIENCED, green, guileless, immature, naive, raw, unsophisticated

calm *adjective* 1 COOL, collected, composed, dispassionate, relaxed, sedate, self-possessed, unemotional

2 STILL, balmy, mild, quiet, serene, smooth, tranquil, windless

▶ *noun* 3 PEACEFULNESS, hush, peace, quiet, repose, serenity, stillness

▶ *verb* 4 QUIETEN, de-stress, hush, mollify, placate, relax, soothe

calmness *noun* 1 COOLNESS, composure, cool (*slang*), equanimity, impassivity, poise, sang-froid, self-possession

2 PEACEFULNESS, calm, hush, quiet, repose, restfulness, serenity, stillness, tranquillity

camouflage *noun* 1 DISGUISE, blind, cloak, concealment, cover, mask, masquerade, screen, subterfuge

▶ *verb* 2 DISGUISE, cloak, conceal, cover, hide, mask, obfuscate, obscure, screen, veil

camp[1] *noun* CAMP SITE, bivouac, camping ground, encampment, tents

camp[2] *adjective* (*informal*) EFFEMINATE, affected, artificial, mannered, ostentatious, posturing

campaign *noun* OPERATION, attack, crusade, drive, expedition, movement, offensive, push

canal *noun* WATERWAY, channel, conduit, duct, passage, watercourse

cancel *verb* 1 CALL OFF, abolish, abort, annul, delete, do away with, eliminate, erase, expunge, obliterate, repeal, revoke

2 ▷▷ **cancel out** MAKE UP FOR, balance out, compensate for, counterbalance, neutralize, nullify, offset

cancellation *noun* ABANDONMENT, abolition, annulment, deletion, elimination, repeal, revocation

cancer *noun* GROWTH, corruption, malignancy, pestilence, sickness, tumor

candid *adjective* HONEST, blunt, forthright, frank, open, outspoken, plain, straightforward, truthful

candidate *noun* CONTENDER, applicant, claimant, competitor, contestant, entrant, nominee, runner

candor *noun* HONESTY, directness, forthrightness, frankness, openness, outspokenness, straightforwardness, truthfulness

canker *noun* DISEASE, bane, blight, cancer, corruption, infection, rot, scourge, sore, ulcer

cannon noun GUN, big gun, field gun, mortar

canny adjective SHREWD, astute, careful, cautious, clever, judicious, prudent, wise

canon noun 1 RULE, criterion, dictate, formula, precept, principle, regulation, standard, statute, yardstick
2 LIST, catalog, roll

canopy noun AWNING, covering, shade, sunshade

cant¹ noun 1 HYPOCRISY, humbug, insincerity, lip service, pretense, pretentiousness, sanctimoniousness
2 JARGON, argot, lingo, patter, slang, vernacular

cant² verb TILT, angle, bevel, incline, rise, slant, slope

cantankerous adjective BAD-TEMPERED, choleric, contrary, disagreeable, grumpy, irascible, irritable, testy, waspish

canter noun 1 JOG, amble, dogtrot, lope
▶ verb 2 JOG, amble, lope

canvass verb 1 CAMPAIGN, electioneer, solicit, solicit votes
2 POLL, examine, inspect, investigate, scrutinize, study
▶ noun 3 POLL, examination, investigation, scrutiny, survey, tally

cap verb BEAT, better, crown, eclipse, exceed, outdo, outstrip, surpass, top, transcend

capability noun ABILITY, capacity, competence, means, potential, power, proficiency, qualification(s), wherewithal

capable adjective ABLE, accomplished, competent, efficient, gifted, proficient, qualified, talented

capacious adjective SPACIOUS, broad, commodious, expansive, extensive, roomy, sizable or sizeable, substantial, vast, voluminous, wide

capacity noun 1 SIZE, amplitude, compass, dimensions, extent, magnitude, range, room, scope, space, volume
2 ABILITY, aptitude, aptness, capability, competence, facility, genius, gift
3 FUNCTION, office, position, post, province, role, sphere

cape noun HEADLAND, head, peninsula, point, promontory

caper noun 1 ESCAPADE, antic, high jinks, jape, lark (informal), mischief, practical joke, prank, stunt
▶ verb 2 DANCE, bound, cavort, frolic, gambol, jump, skip, spring, trip

capital noun 1 MONEY, assets, cash, finances, funds, investment(s), means, principal, resources, wealth, wherewithal
▶ adjective 2 PRINCIPAL, cardinal, major, prime, vital
3 (old-fashioned) FIRST-RATE, excellent, fine, splendid, sterling, superb

capitalism noun PRIVATE ENTERPRISE, free enterprise, laissez faire or laisser faire, private ownership

capitalize on verb TAKE ADVANTAGE OF, benefit from, cash in on (informal), exploit, gain from, make the most of, profit from

capitulate verb GIVE IN, come to terms, give up, relent, submit, succumb, surrender, yield

caprice noun WHIM, fad, fancy, fickleness, impulse, inconstancy, notion, whimsy

capricious adjective

UNPREDICTABLE, changeful, erratic, fickle, fitful, impulsive, inconsistent, inconstant, mercurial, variable, wayward, whimsical

capsize verb OVERTURN, invert, keel over, tip over, turn over, turn turtle, upset

capsule noun 1 PILL, lozenge, tablet
2 (botany) POD, case, receptacle, seed case, sheath, shell, vessel

captain noun LEADER, boss (informal), chief, commander, head, master, skipper

captivate verb CHARM, allure, attract, beguile, bewitch, enchant, enrapture, enthrall, entrance, fascinate, infatuate, mesmerize

captive noun 1 PRISONER, convict, detainee, hostage, internee, prisoner of war, slave
▶ adjective 2 CONFINED, caged, enslaved, ensnared, imprisoned, incarcerated, locked up, penned, restricted, subjugated

captivity noun CONFINEMENT, bondage, custody, detention, imprisonment, incarceration, internment, slavery

capture verb 1 CATCH, apprehend, arrest, bag, collar (informal), secure, seize, take, take prisoner
▶ noun 2 CATCHING, apprehension, arrest, imprisonment, seizure, taking, taking captive, trapping

car noun 1 VEHICLE, auto (U.S.), automobile, clunker (informal), jalopy (informal), machine, motor, motorcar, wheels (informal)
2 (U.S. & Canad.) (RAILWAY) CARRIAGE, buffet car, cable car, coach, dining car, sleeping car, van

carcass noun BODY, cadaver

(Medical), corpse, dead body, framework, hulk, remains, shell, skeleton

cardinal adjective PRINCIPAL, capital, central, chief, essential, first, fundamental, key, leading, main, paramount, primary

care verb 1 BE CONCERNED, be bothered, be interested, mind
▶ noun 2 CAUTION, attention, carefulness, consideration, forethought, heed, management, pains, prudence, vigilance, watchfulness
3 PROTECTION, charge, control, custody, guardianship, keeping, management, supervision
4 WORRY, anxiety, concern, disquiet, perplexity, pressure, responsibility, stress, trouble

career noun 1 OCCUPATION, calling, employment, life's work, livelihood, pursuit, vocation
▶ verb 2 RUSH, barrel (along) (informal), bolt, dash, hurtle, race, speed, tear

care for verb 1 LOOK AFTER, attend, foster, mind, minister to, nurse, protect, provide for, tend, watch over
2 LIKE, be fond of, desire, enjoy, love, prize, take to, want

carefree adjective UNTROUBLED, blithe, breezy, cheerful, easygoing, halcyon, happy-go-lucky, light-hearted

careful adjective 1 CAUTIOUS, chary, circumspect, discreet, prudent, scrupulous, thoughtful, thrifty
2 THOROUGH, conscientious, meticulous, painstaking, particular, precise

careless adjective 1 SLAPDASH, cavalier, inaccurate, irresponsible, lackadaisical, neglectful, offhand, slipshod, sloppy (informal)

2 NEGLIGENT, absent-minded, forgetful, hasty, remiss, thoughtless, unthinking

3 NONCHALANT, artless, casual, unstudied

carelessness noun NEGLIGENCE, indiscretion, irresponsibility, laxity, neglect, omission, slackness, sloppiness (*informal*), thoughtlessness

caress verb 1 STROKE, cuddle, embrace, fondle, hug, kiss, make out (*informal*), neck (*informal*), nuzzle, pet

▶ noun 2 STROKE, cuddle, embrace, fondling, hug, kiss, pat

caretaker noun WARDEN, concierge, curator, custodian, janitor, keeper, porter, superintendent, watchman

cargo noun LOAD, baggage, consignment, contents, freight, goods, merchandise, shipment

caricature noun 1 PARODY, burlesque, cartoon, distortion, farce, lampoon, satire, send-up (*Brit. informal*), takeoff (*informal*), travesty

▶ verb 2 PARODY, burlesque, distort, lampoon, mimic, mock, ridicule, satirize, send up (*Brit. informal*), take off (*informal*)

carnage noun SLAUGHTER, blood bath, bloodshed, butchery, havoc, holocaust, massacre, mass murder, murder, shambles

carnal adjective SEXUAL, erotic, fleshly, lascivious, lewd, libidinous, lustful, sensual

carnival noun FESTIVAL, celebration, fair, fête, fiesta, gala, holiday, jamboree, jubilee, merrymaking, revelry

carol noun SONG, chorus, ditty, hymn, lay

carp verb FIND FAULT, cavil, complain, criticize, pick holes, quibble, reproach

carpenter noun JOINER, cabinet-maker, woodworker

carriage noun 1 VEHICLE, cab, coach, conveyance

2 BEARING, air, behavior, comportment, conduct, demeanor, deportment, gait, manner, posture

carry verb 1 TRANSPORT, bear, bring, conduct, convey, fetch, haul, lug, move, relay, take, transfer

2 WIN, accomplish, capture, effect, gain, secure

carry on verb 1 CONTINUE, endure, keep going, last, maintain, perpetuate, persevere, persist

2 (*informal*) MAKE A FUSS, create (*slang*), misbehave, raise Cain

carry out verb PERFORM, accomplish, achieve, carry through, effect, execute, fulfill, implement, realize

carton noun BOX, case, container, pack, package, packet

cartoon noun 1 DRAWING, caricature, comic strip, lampoon, parody, satire, sketch, takeoff (*informal*)

2 ANIMATION, animated cartoon, animated film

cartridge noun 1 SHELL, charge, round

2 CONTAINER, capsule, case, cassette, cylinder, magazine

carve verb CUT, chip, chisel, engrave, etch, hew, mold, sculpt, slice, whittle

cascade noun 1 WATERFALL, avalanche, cataract, deluge, downpour, falls, flood, fountain, outpouring, shower, torrent

▶ verb 2 FLOW, descend, fall, flood, gush, overflow, pitch, plunge, pour, spill, surge, teem, tumble

case¹ *noun* 1 INSTANCE, example, illustration, occasion, occurrence, specimen

2 SITUATION, circumstance(s), condition, context, contingency, event, position, state

3 (*law*) LAWSUIT, action, dispute, proceedings, suit, trial

case² *noun* 1 CONTAINER, box, canister, carton, casket, chest, crate, holder, receptacle, suitcase, tray

2 COVERING, capsule, casing, envelope, jacket, sheath, shell, wrapper

cash *noun* MONEY, brass (*Northern English dialect*), coinage, currency, dough (*slang*), funds, notes, ready money, silver

cashier¹ *noun* TELLER, bank clerk, banker, bursar, clerk, purser, treasurer

cashier² *verb* DISMISS, discard, discharge, drum out, expel, give the boot to (*slang*)

casket *noun* BOX, case, chest, coffer, jewel box

cast *noun* 1 ACTORS, characters, company, dramatis personae, players, troupe

2 TYPE, complexion, manner, stamp, style

▶ *verb* 3 CHOOSE, allot, appoint, assign, name, pick, select

4 GIVE OUT, bestow, deposit, diffuse, distribute, emit, radiate, scatter, shed, spread

5 FORM, found, model, mold, set, shape

6 THROW, fling, hurl, launch, pitch, sling, thrust, toss

caste *noun* CLASS, estate, grade, order, rank, social order, status, stratum

castigate *verb* REPRIMAND, berate, censure, chastise, criticize, lambast(e), rebuke, scold

cast-iron *adjective* CERTAIN, copper-bottomed, definite, established, fixed, guaranteed, settled

castle *noun* FORTRESS, chateau, citadel, keep, palace, stronghold, tower

cast-off *adjective* 1 UNWANTED, discarded, rejected, scrapped, surplus to requirements, unneeded, useless

▶ *noun* 2 REJECT, discard, failure, outcast, second

castrate *verb* NEUTER, emasculate, geld

casual *adjective* 1 CARELESS, blasé, cursory, lackadaisical, nonchalant, offhand, relaxed, unconcerned

2 OCCASIONAL, accidental, chance, incidental, irregular, random, unexpected

3 INFORMAL, non-dressy, sporty

casualty *noun* VICTIM, death, fatality, loss, sufferer, wounded

cat *noun* FELINE, kitty (*informal*), moggy (*slang*), puss (*informal*), pussy (*informal*), tabby

catacombs *plural noun* VAULT, crypt, tomb

catalog *noun* 1 LIST, directory, gazetteer, index, inventory, record, register, roll, roster, schedule

▶ *verb* 2 LIST, accession, alphabetize, classify, file, index, inventory, register, tabulate

catapult *noun* 1 SLING, slingshot (*U.S.*)

▶ *verb* 2 SHOOT, heave, hurl, pitch, plunge, propel

catastrophe *noun* DISASTER, adversity, calamity, cataclysm, fiasco, misfortune, tragedy, trouble

catcall noun JEER, boo, gibe, hiss, raspberry, whistle

catch verb 1 SEIZE, clutch, get, grab, grasp, grip, lay hold of, snatch, take
2 CAPTURE, apprehend, arrest, ensnare, entrap, snare
3 DISCOVER, catch in the act, detect, expose, find out, surprise, take unawares, unmask
4 CONTRACT, develop, get, go down with, incur, succumb to, suffer from
5 MAKE OUT, comprehend, discern, get, grasp, hear, perceive, recognize, sense, take in
▶ noun 6 FASTENER, bolt, clasp, clip, latch
7 DRAWBACK, disadvantage, fly in the ointment, hitch, snag, stumbling block, trap, trick

catching adjective INFECTIOUS, communicable, contagious, transferable, transmittable

catch on verb UNDERSTAND, comprehend, find out, get the picture, grasp, see, see through, twig (Brit. informal)

catchword noun SLOGAN, byword, motto, password, watchword

catchy adjective MEMORABLE, captivating, haunting, popular

categorical adjective ABSOLUTE, downright, emphatic, explicit, express, positive, unambiguous, unconditional, unequivocal, unqualified, unreserved

category noun CLASS, classification, department, division, grade, grouping, heading, section, sort, type

cater verb PROVIDE, furnish, outfit, purvey, supply

cattle plural noun COWS, beasts, bovines, livestock, stock

catty adjective SPITEFUL, backbiting, bitchy (informal), malevolent, malicious, rancorous, shrewish, snide, venomous

cause noun 1 ORIGIN, agent, beginning, creator, genesis, mainspring, maker, producer, root, source, spring
2 REASON, basis, grounds, incentive, inducement, justification, motivation, motive, purpose
3 AIM, belief, conviction, enterprise, ideal, movement, principle
▶ verb 4 PRODUCE, bring about, create, generate, give rise to, incite, induce, lead to, result in

caustic adjective 1 BURNING, acrid, astringent, biting, corroding, corrosive, mordant, vitriolic
2 SARCASTIC, acrimonious, cutting, pungent, scathing, stinging, trenchant, virulent, vitriolic

caution noun 1 CARE, alertness, carefulness, circumspection, deliberation, discretion, forethought, heed, prudence, vigilance, watchfulness
2 WARNING, admonition, advice, counsel, injunction
▶ verb 3 WARN, admonish, advise, tip off, urge

cautious adjective CAREFUL, cagey (informal), chary, circumspect, guarded, judicious, prudent, tentative, wary

cavalcade noun PARADE, array, march-past, procession, spectacle, train

cavalier adjective HAUGHTY, arrogant, disdainful, lofty, lordly, offhand, scornful, supercilious

cavalry noun HORSEMEN, horse, mounted troops

cave noun HOLLOW, cavern, cavity, den, grotto

cavern noun CAVE, hollow, pothole

cavernous adjective DEEP, hollow, sunken, yawning

cavity noun HOLLOW, crater, dent, gap, hole, pit

cease verb STOP, break off, conclude, discontinue, end, finish, halt, leave off, refrain, terminate

ceaseless adjective CONTINUAL, constant, endless, eternal, everlasting, incessant, interminable, never-ending, nonstop, perpetual, twenty-four-seven (slang), unremitting

cede verb SURRENDER, concede, hand over, make over, relinquish, renounce, resign, transfer, yield

celebrate verb 1 REJOICE, commemorate, drink to, gala, kill the fatted calf, observe, put the flags out, toast
2 PERFORM, bless, honor, solemnize

celebrated adjective WELL-KNOWN, acclaimed, distinguished, eminent, famous, illustrious, notable, popular, prominent, renowned

celebration noun 1 PARTY, festival, festivity, gala, jubilee, merrymaking, red-letter day, revelry
2 PERFORMANCE, anniversary, commemoration, honoring, observance, remembrance, solemnization

celebrity noun 1 PERSONALITY, big name, big shot (informal), dignitary, luminary, star, superstar, V.I.P.
2 FAME, distinction, notability, prestige, prominence, renown, reputation, repute, stardom

celestial adjective HEAVENLY, angelic, astral, divine, ethereal, spiritual, sublime, supernatural

celibacy noun CHASTITY, continence, purity, virginity

cell noun 1 ROOM, cavity, chamber, compartment, cubicle, dungeon, stall
2 UNIT, caucus, core, coterie, group, nucleus

cement noun 1 MORTAR, adhesive, glue, gum, paste, plaster, sealant
▶ verb 2 STICK TOGETHER, attach, bind, bond, combine, glue, join, plaster, seal, unite, weld

cemetery noun GRAVEYARD, burial ground, churchyard, God's acre, necropolis

censor verb CUT, blue-pencil, bowdlerize, expurgate

censorious adjective CRITICAL, captious, carping, cavilling, condemnatory, disapproving, disparaging, fault-finding, hypercritical, scathing, severe

censure noun 1 DISAPPROVAL, blame, condemnation, criticism, obloquy, rebuke, reprimand, reproach, reproof, stick (slang)
▶ verb 2 CRITICIZE, blame, castigate, condemn, denounce, rap over the knuckles, rebuke, reprimand, reproach, scold, slap on the wrist

center noun 1 MIDDLE, core, focus, heart, hub, kernel, midpoint, nucleus, pivot
▶ verb 2 FOCUS, cluster, concentrate, converge, revolve

central adjective 1 MIDDLE, inner, interior, mean, median, mid
2 MAIN, chief, essential, focal, fundamental, key, primary, principal

centralize verb UNIFY, concentrate, condense,

incorporate, rationalize, streamline

ceremonial *adjective* 1 RITUAL, formal, liturgical, ritualistic, solemn, stately
▶ *noun* 2 RITUAL, ceremony, formality, rite, solemnity

ceremonious *adjective* FORMAL, civil, courteous, deferential, dignified, punctilious, solemn, stately, stiff

ceremony *noun* 1 RITUAL, commemoration, function, observance, parade, rite, service, show, solemnities
2 FORMALITY, ceremonial, decorum, etiquette, niceties, pomp, propriety, protocol

certain *adjective* 1 SURE, assured, confident, convinced, positive, satisfied
2 KNOWN, conclusive, incontrovertible, irrefutable, true, undeniable, unequivocal
3 INEVITABLE, bound, definite, destined, fated, inescapable, sure
4 FIXED, decided, definite, established, settled

certainly *adverb* DEFINITELY, assuredly, indisputably, indubitably, surely, truly, undeniably, undoubtedly, without doubt

certainty *noun* 1 SURENESS, assurance, confidence, conviction, faith, positiveness, trust, validity
2 FACT, reality, sure thing (*informal*), truth

certificate *noun* DOCUMENT, authorization, credential(s), diploma, license, testimonial, voucher, warrant

certify *verb* CONFIRM, assure, attest, authenticate, declare, guarantee, testify, validate, verify

chafe *verb* 1 RUB, abrade, rasp,

scrape, scratch
2 BE ANNOYED, be impatient, fret, fume, rage, worry

chaff¹ *noun* WASTE, dregs, husks, refuse, remains, rubbish, trash

chaff² *verb* TEASE, mock, rib (*informal*), ridicule, scoff, taunt

chain *noun* 1 LINK, bond, coupling, fetter, manacle, shackle
2 SERIES, progression, sequence, set, string, succession, train
▶ *verb* 3 BIND, confine, enslave, fetter, handcuff, manacle, restrain, shackle, tether

chairman *noun* DIRECTOR, chairperson, chairwoman, master of ceremonies, president, speaker, spokesman

challenge *noun* 1 TEST, confrontation, provocation, question, trial, ultimatum
▶ *verb* 2 TEST, confront, defy, dispute, object to, question, tackle, throw down the gauntlet

chamber *noun* 1 ROOM, apartment, bedroom, compartment, cubicle, enclosure, hall
2 COUNCIL, assembly, legislative body, legislature

champion *noun* 1 WINNER, conqueror, hero, title holder, victor
2 DEFENDER, backer, guardian, patron, protector, upholder
▶ *verb* 3 SUPPORT, advocate, back, commend, defend, encourage, espouse, fight for, promote, uphold

chance *noun* 1 PROBABILITY, likelihood, odds, possibility, prospect
2 OPPORTUNITY, occasion, opening, time
3 LUCK, accident, coincidence, destiny, fate, fortune, providence

4 RISK, gamble, hazard, jeopardy, speculation, uncertainty
▶ *verb* 5 RISK, endanger, gamble, hazard, jeopardize, stake, try, venture, wager

chancy *adjective* (*slang*) DANGEROUS, difficult, hazardous, perilous, risky

change *noun* 1 ALTERATION, difference, innovation, metamorphosis, modification, mutation, revolution, transformation, transition
2 VARIETY, break (*informal*), departure, diversion, novelty, variation
3 EXCHANGE, conversion, interchange, substitution, swap, trade
▶ *verb* 4 ALTER, convert, modify, mutate, reform, reorganize, restyle, shift, transform, vary
5 EXCHANGE, barter, convert, interchange, replace, substitute, swap, trade

changeable *adjective* VARIABLE, erratic, fickle, inconstant, irregular, mobile, mutable, protean, shifting, unsettled, unstable, volatile, wavering

channel *noun* 1 ROUTE, approach, artery, avenue, course, means, medium, path, way
2 PASSAGE, canal, conduit, duct, furrow, groove, gutter, route, strait
▶ *verb* 3 DIRECT, conduct, convey, guide, transmit

chant *verb* 1 SING, carol, chorus, descant, intone, recite, warble
▶ *noun* 2 SONG, carol, chorus, melody, psalm

chaos *noun* DISORDER, anarchy, bedlam, confusion, disorganization, lawlessness, mayhem, pandemonium, tumult

chaotic *adjective* DISORDERED, anarchic, confused, deranged, disorganized, lawless, riotous, topsy-turvy, tumultuous, uncontrolled

chap *noun* (*informal*) FELLOW, bloke (*Brit. informal*), character, guy (*informal*), individual, man, person

chaperone *noun* 1 ESCORT, companion
▶ *verb* 2 ESCORT, accompany, attend, protect, safeguard, shepherd, watch over

chapter *noun* SECTION, clause, division, episode, part, period, phase, stage, topic

character *noun* 1 NATURE, attributes, caliber, complexion, disposition, personality, quality, temperament, type
2 REPUTATION, honor, integrity, rectitude, strength, uprightness
3 ROLE, part, persona, portrayal
4 ECCENTRIC, card (*informal*), oddball (*informal*), original
5 SYMBOL, device, figure, hieroglyph, letter, mark, rune, sign

characteristic *noun* 1 FEATURE, attribute, faculty, idiosyncrasy, mark, peculiarity, property, quality, quirk, trait
▶ *adjective* 2 TYPICAL, distinctive, distinguishing, idiosyncratic, individual, peculiar, representative, singular, special, symbolic, symptomatic

characterize *verb* IDENTIFY, brand, distinguish, indicate, mark, represent, stamp, typify

charade *noun* PRETENSE, fake, farce, pantomime, parody, travesty

charge *verb* 1 ACCUSE, arraign, blame, impeach, incriminate, indict

2 RUSH, assail, assault, attack, stampede, storm
3 FILL, load
4 COMMAND, bid, commit, demand, entrust, instruct, order, require
▶ *noun* 5 PRICE, amount, cost, expenditure, expense, outlay, payment, rate, toll
6 ACCUSATION, allegation, imputation, indictment
7 RUSH, assault, attack, onset, onslaught, sortie, stampede
8 CARE, custody, duty, office, responsibility, safekeeping, trust
9 WARD
10 INSTRUCTION, command, demand, direction, injunction, mandate, order, precept

charisma *noun* CHARM, allure, attraction, lure, magnetism, personality

charismatic *adjective* CHARMING, alluring, attractive, enticing, influential, magnetic

charitable *adjective* 1 TOLERANT, considerate, favorable, forgiving, humane, indulgent, kindly, lenient, magnanimous, sympathetic, understanding
2 GENEROUS, beneficent, benevolent, bountiful, kind, lavish, liberal, philanthropic

charity *noun* 1 DONATIONS, assistance, benefaction, contributions, endowment, fund, gift, hand-out, help, largesse *or* largess, philanthropy, relief
2 KINDNESS, altruism, benevolence, compassion, fellow feeling, generosity, goodwill, humanity, indulgence

charlatan *noun* FRAUD, cheat, con man (*informal*), fake, impostor, phoney *or* phony (*informal*), pretender, quack, sham, swindler

charm *noun* 1 ATTRACTION, allure, appeal, fascination, magnetism
2 SPELL, enchantment, magic, sorcery
3 TALISMAN, amulet, fetish, trinket
▶ *verb* 4 ATTRACT, allure, beguile, bewitch, captivate, delight, enchant, enrapture, entrance, fascinate, mesmerize, win over

charming *adjective* ATTRACTIVE, appealing, captivating, cute, delightful, fetching, likable *or* likeable, pleasing, seductive, winsome

chart *noun* 1 TABLE, blueprint, diagram, graph, map, plan, road map
▶ *verb* 2 PLOT, delineate, draft, map out, outline, shape, sketch

charter *noun* 1 DOCUMENT, contract, deed, license, permit, prerogative
▶ *verb* 2 HIRE, commission, employ, lease, rent
3 AUTHORIZE, sanction

chase *verb* 1 PURSUE, course, follow, hunt, run after, stalk, track
2 DRIVE AWAY, drive, expel, hound, put to flight
▶ *noun* 3 PURSUIT, hunt, hunting, race

chasm *noun* GULF, abyss, crater, crevasse, fissure, gap, gorge, ravine

chaste *adjective* PURE, immaculate, innocent, modest, simple, unaffected, undefiled, virtuous

chasten *verb* SUBDUE, chastise, correct, discipline, humble, humiliate, put in one's place, tame

chastise *verb* 1 SCOLD, berate, castigate, censure, correct, discipline, upbraid
2 (*old-fashioned*) BEAT, flog, lash,

lick (*informal*), punish, scourge, whip

chastity noun PURITY, celibacy, continence, innocence, maidenhood, modesty, virginity, virtue

chat noun 1 TALK, chatter, chinwag (*Brit. informal*), conversation, gossip, heart-to-heart, natter, tête-à-tête
▶ verb 2 TALK, chatter, chew the fat (*slang*), gossip, jaw (*slang*), natter

chatter noun 1 PRATTLE, babble, blather, chat, gab (*informal*), gossip, natter
▶ verb 2 PRATTLE, babble, blather, chat, chew the fat (*slang*), gab (*informal*), gossip, natter, rabbit (on) (*Brit. informal*), schmooze (*slang*)

cheap adjective 1 INEXPENSIVE, bargain, cut-price, economical, keen, low-cost, low-priced, reasonable, reduced
2 INFERIOR, common, poor, second-rate, shoddy, tatty, tawdry, two a penny, worthless
3 (*informal*) DESPICABLE, contemptible, lousy (*slang*), mean, scuzzy (*slang*)

cheapen verb DEGRADE, belittle, debase, demean, denigrate, depreciate, devalue, discredit, disparage, lower

cheat verb 1 DECEIVE, beguile, con (*informal*), defraud, double-cross (*informal*), dupe, fleece, fool, mislead, rip off (*slang*), swindle, trick
▶ noun 2 DECEIVER, charlatan, con man (*informal*), double-crosser (*informal*), shark, sharper, swindler, trickster
3 DECEPTION, deceit, fraud, rip-off (*slang*), scam (*slang*), swindle, trickery

check verb 1 EXAMINE, inquire into, inspect, investigate, look at, make sure, monitor, research, scrutinize, study, test, vet
2 STOP, delay, halt, hinder, impede, inhibit, limit, obstruct, restrain, retard
▶ noun 3 EXAMINATION, inspection, investigation, once-over (*informal*), research, scrutiny, test
4 STOPPAGE, constraint, control, curb, damper, hindrance, impediment, limitation, obstacle, obstruction, restraint

cheeky adjective IMPUDENT, audacious, disrespectful, forward, impertinent, insolent, insulting, pert, saucy

cheer verb 1 APPLAUD, acclaim, clap, hail
2 CHEER UP, brighten, buoy up, comfort, encourage, gladden, hearten, uplift
▶ noun 3 APPLAUSE, acclamation, ovation, plaudits

cheerful adjective HAPPY, buoyant, cheery, chirpy (*informal*), enthusiastic, jaunty, jolly, light-hearted, merry, optimistic, upbeat (*informal*)

cheerfulness noun HAPPINESS, buoyancy, exuberance, gaiety, geniality, good cheer, good humor, high spirits, jauntiness, light-heartedness

cheerless adjective GLOOMY, bleak, desolate, dismal, drab, dreary, forlorn, miserable, somber, woeful

cheer up verb 1 COMFORT, encourage, enliven, gladden, hearten, jolly along (*informal*)
2 TAKE HEART, buck up (*informal*), perk up, rally

cheery adjective CHEERFUL, breezy, carefree, chirpy (*informal*), genial, good-humored, happy, jovial, upbeat (*informal*)

chemist *noun* PHARMACIST, apothecary (*obsolete*), dispenser

cherish *verb* 1 CLING TO, cleave to, encourage, entertain, foster, harbor, hold dear, nurture, prize, sustain, treasure
2 CARE FOR, comfort, hold dear, love, nurse, shelter, support

chest *noun* BOX, case, casket, coffer, crate, strongbox, trunk

chew *verb* BITE, champ, chomp, crunch, gnaw, grind, masticate, munch

chewy *adjective* TOUGH, as tough as old boots, leathery

chic *adjective* STYLISH, cool (*informal*), elegant, fashionable, phat (*slang*), smart, trendy (*informal*)

chide *verb* (*old-fashioned*) SCOLD, admonish, berate, censure, criticize, lecture, rebuke, reprimand, reproach, reprove, tell off (*informal*)

chief *noun* 1 HEAD, alpha male, boss (*informal*), captain, commander, director, governor, leader, manager, master, principal, ruler
▶ *adjective* 2 PRIMARY, cutting-edge, foremost, highest, key, leading, main, predominant, pre-eminent, premier, prime, principal, supreme, uppermost

chiefly *adverb* 1 ESPECIALLY, above all, essentially, primarily, principally
2 MAINLY, in general, in the main, largely, mostly, on the whole, predominantly, usually

child *noun* YOUNGSTER, babe, baby, bairn (*Scot.*), infant, juvenile, kid (*informal*), minor, offspring, toddler, tot

childbirth *noun* CHILD-BEARING, confinement, delivery, labor, lying-in, parturition, travail

childhood *noun* YOUTH, boyhood *or* girlhood, immaturity, infancy, minority, schooldays

childish *adjective* IMMATURE, boyish *or* girlish, foolish, infantile, juvenile, puerile, young

childlike *adjective* INNOCENT, artless, guileless, ingenuous, naive, simple, trusting

chill *noun* 1 COLD, bite, coldness, coolness, crispness, frigidity, nip, rawness, sharpness
▶ *verb* 2 COOL, freeze, refrigerate
3 DISHEARTEN, dampen, deject, depress, discourage, dismay
▶ *adjective* 4 COLD, biting, bleak, chilly, freezing, frigid, raw, sharp, wintry

chilly *adjective* 1 COOL, brisk, crisp, drafty, fresh, nippy, penetrating, sharp
2 UNFRIENDLY, frigid, hostile, unresponsive, unsympathetic, unwelcoming

chime *verb or noun* RING, clang, jingle, peal, sound, tinkle, toll

china *noun* POTTERY, ceramics, crockery, porcelain, service, tableware, ware

chink *noun* OPENING, aperture, cleft, crack, cranny, crevice, fissure, gap

chip *noun* 1 SCRATCH, fragment, nick, notch, shard, shaving, sliver, wafer
▶ *verb* 2 NICK, chisel, damage, gash, whittle

chirp *verb* CHIRRUP, cheep, peep, pipe, tweet, twitter, warble

chivalrous *adjective* COURTEOUS, bold, brave, courageous, gallant, gentlemanly, honorable, valiant

chivalry *noun* COURTESY, courage,

gallantry, gentlemanliness,
knight-errantry, knighthood,
politeness

choice noun 1 OPTION, alternative,
pick, preference, say
2 SELECTION, range, variety
▶ adjective 3 BEST, elite, excellent,
exclusive, prime, rare, select

choke verb 1 STRANGLE, asphyxiate,
gag, overpower, smother, stifle,
suffocate, suppress, throttle
2 BLOCK, bar, bung, clog, congest,
constrict, obstruct, stop

choose verb PICK, adopt,
designate, elect, opt for, prefer,
select, settle upon

choosy adjective FUSSY,
discriminating, faddy, fastidious,
finicky, particular, picky (informal),
selective

chop verb CUT, cleave, fell, hack,
hew, lop, sever

chore noun TASK, burden, duty,
errand, job

chortle verb or noun CHUCKLE,
cackle, crow, guffaw

chorus noun 1 CHOIR, choristers,
ensemble, singers, vocalists
2 REFRAIN, burden, response,
strain
3 UNISON, accord, concert,
harmony

christen verb 1 BAPTIZE
2 NAME, call, designate, dub, style,
term, title

Christmas noun FESTIVE SEASON,
Noel, Xmas, Yule, Yuletide

chronicle noun 1 RECORD, blog
(informal), account, annals, diary,
history, journal, narrative,
register, story, weblog
▶ verb 2 RECORD, enter, narrate,
put on record, recount, register,
relate, report, set down, tell

chubby adjective PLUMP, buxom,
flabby, podgy, portly, rotund,
round, stout, tubby

chuckle verb LAUGH, chortle, crow,
exult, giggle, snigger, titter

chum noun (informal) FRIEND,
companion, comrade, crony,
homeboy (slang), homegirl (slang),
mate (informal), pal (informal)

chunk noun PIECE, block, dollop
(informal), hunk, lump, mass,
nugget, portion, slab

churlish adjective RUDE, brusque,
harsh, ill-tempered, impolite,
sullen, surly, uncivil

churn verb STIR UP, agitate, beat,
convulse, swirl, toss

cinema noun FILMS, big screen
(informal), flicks (slang), motion
pictures, movies, pictures

cipher noun 1 CODE, cryptograph
2 NOBODY, nonentity

circle noun 1 RING, disc, globe,
orb, sphere
2 GROUP, clique, club, company,
coterie, set, society
▶ verb 3 GO ROUND,
circumnavigate, circumscribe,
encircle, enclose, envelop, ring,
surround

circuit noun COURSE, journey, lap,
orbit, revolution, route, tour, track

circuitous adjective INDIRECT,
labyrinthine, meandering,
oblique, rambling, roundabout,
tortuous, winding

circular adjective 1 ROUND, ring-
shaped, rotund, spherical
2 ORBITAL, circuitous, cyclical
▶ noun 3 ADVERTISEMENT, notice

circulate verb 1 SPREAD, broadcast,
disseminate, distribute, issue,
make known, promulgate,
publicize, publish
2 FLOW, gyrate, radiate, revolve,
rotate

circulation noun 1 BLOODSTREAM
2 FLOW, circling, motion, rotation

3 DISTRIBUTION, currency, dissemination, spread, transmission

circumference noun BOUNDARY, border, edge, extremity, limits, outline, perimeter, periphery, rim

circumstance noun EVENT, accident, condition, contingency, happening, incident, occurrence, particular, respect, situation

circumstances plural noun SITUATION, means, position, state, state of affairs, station, status

cistern noun TANK, basin, reservoir, sink, vat

citadel noun FORTRESS, bastion, fortification, keep, stronghold, tower

cite verb QUOTE, adduce, advance, allude to, enumerate, extract, mention, name, specify

citizen noun INHABITANT, denizen, dweller, resident, subject, townsman

city noun TOWN, conurbation, metropolis, municipality

civic adjective PUBLIC, communal, local, municipal

civil adjective 1 CIVIC, domestic, municipal, political
2 POLITE, affable, courteous, obliging, refined, urbane, well-mannered

civilization noun 1 CULTURE, advancement, cultivation, development, education, enlightenment, progress, refinement, sophistication
2 SOCIETY, community, nation, people, polity

civilize verb CULTIVATE, educate, enlighten, refine, sophisticate, tame

civilized adjective CULTURED, educated, enlightened, humane, polite, sophisticated, tolerant,

urbane

claim verb 1 ASSERT, allege, challenge, insist, maintain, profess, uphold
2 DEMAND, ask, call for, insist, need, require
▶ noun 3 ASSERTION, affirmation, allegation, pretension, privilege, protestation
4 DEMAND, application, call, petition, request, requirement
5 RIGHT, title

clairvoyant noun 1 PSYCHIC, diviner, fortune-teller, visionary
▶ adjective 2 PSYCHIC, extrasensory, second-sighted, telepathic, visionary

clamber verb CLIMB, claw, scale, scrabble, scramble, shin

clammy adjective MOIST, close, damp, dank, sticky, sweaty

clamor noun NOISE, commotion, din, hubbub, outcry, racket, shouting, uproar

clamp noun 1 VICE, bracket, fastener, grip, press
▶ verb 2 FASTEN, brace, fix, make fast, secure

clan noun FAMILY, brotherhood, faction, fraternity, group, society, tribe

clandestine adjective SECRET, cloak-and-dagger, concealed, covert, furtive, private, stealthy, surreptitious, underground

clap verb APPLAUD, acclaim, cheer

clarification noun EXPLANATION, elucidation, exposition, illumination, interpretation, simplification

clarify verb EXPLAIN, clear up, elucidate, illuminate, interpret, make plain, simplify, throw or shed light on

clarity noun CLEARNESS, definition, limpidity,

lucidity, precision, simplicity, transparency

clash *verb* 1 CONFLICT, cross swords, feud, grapple, lock horns, quarrel, war, wrangle
2 CRASH, bang, clang, clank, clatter, jangle, jar, rattle
▶ *noun* 3 CONFLICT, brush, collision, confrontation, difference of opinion, disagreement, fight, showdown (*informal*)

clasp *noun* 1 FASTENING, brooch, buckle, catch, clip, fastener, grip, hook, pin
2 GRASP, embrace, grip, hold, hug
▶ *verb* 3 GRASP, clutch, embrace, grip, hold, hug, press, seize, squeeze
4 FASTEN, connect

class *noun* 1 GROUP, category, division, genre, kind, set, sort, type
▶ *verb* 2 CLASSIFY, brand, categorize, designate, grade, group, label, rank, rate

classic *adjective* 1 DEFINITIVE, archetypal, exemplary, ideal, model, quintessential, standard
2 TYPICAL, characteristic, regular, standard, time-honored, usual
3 BEST, consummate, finest, first-rate, masterly, world-class
4 LASTING, abiding, ageless, deathless, enduring, immortal, undying
▶ *noun* 5 STANDARD, exemplar, masterpiece, model, paradigm, prototype
6 comical (*informal*) HILARIOUS, hysterical, ludicrous, uproarious

classical *adjective* PURE, elegant, harmonious, refined, restrained, symmetrical, understated, well-proportioned

classification *noun*

CATEGORIZATION, analysis, arrangement, grading, sorting, taxonomy

classify *verb* CATEGORIZE, arrange, catalog, grade, pigeonhole, rank, sort, systematize, tabulate

classy *adjective* (*informal*) HIGH-CLASS, elegant, exclusive, posh (*informal, chiefly Brit.*), ritzy, stylish, superior, swanky, top-drawer, up-market

clause *noun* SECTION, article, chapter, condition, paragraph, part, passage

claw *noun* 1 NAIL, pincer, talon, tentacle
▶ *verb* 2 SCRATCH, dig, lacerate, maul, rip, scrape, tear

clean *adjective* 1 PURE, flawless, fresh, immaculate, impeccable, spotless, unblemished, unsullied
2 HYGIENIC, antiseptic, decontaminated, purified, sterile, sterilized, uncontaminated, unpolluted
3 MORAL, chaste, decent, good, honorable, innocent, pure, respectable, upright, virtuous
4 COMPLETE, conclusive, decisive, entire, final, perfect, thorough, total, unimpaired, whole
▶ *verb* 5 CLEANSE, disinfect, launder, purge, purify, rinse, sanitize, scour, scrub, wash

cleanse *verb* CLEAN, absolve, clear, purge, purify, rinse, scour, scrub, wash

cleanser *noun* DETERGENT, disinfectant, purifier, scourer, soap, solvent

clear *adjective* 1 CERTAIN, convinced, decided, definite, positive, resolved, satisfied, sure
2 OBVIOUS, apparent, blatant, comprehensible, conspicuous, distinct, evident, manifest,

palpable, plain, pronounced, recognizable, unmistakable
3 TRANSPARENT, crystalline, glassy, limpid, pellucid, see-through, translucent
4 BRIGHT, cloudless, fair, fine, light, luminous, shining, sunny, unclouded
5 UNOBSTRUCTED, empty, free, open, smooth, unhindered, unimpeded
6 UNBLEMISHED, clean, immaculate, innocent, pure, untarnished
▶ verb **7** UNBLOCK, disentangle, extricate, free, loosen, open, rid, unload
8 PASS OVER, jump, leap, miss, vault
9 BRIGHTEN, break up, lighten
10 CLEAN, cleanse, erase, purify, refine, sweep away, tidy (up), wipe
11 ABSOLVE, acquit, excuse, exonerate, justify, vindicate
12 GAIN, acquire, earn, make, reap, secure

clear-cut adjective STRAIGHTFORWARD, black-and-white, cut-and-dried (informal), definite, explicit, plain, precise, specific, unambiguous, unequivocal

clearly adverb OBVIOUSLY, beyond doubt, distinctly, evidently, markedly, openly, overtly, undeniably, undoubtedly

clergy noun PRIESTHOOD, churchmen, clergymen, clerics, holy orders, ministry, the cloth

clergyman noun MINISTER, chaplain, cleric, man of God, man of the cloth, padre, parson, pastor, priest, vicar

clever adjective INTELLIGENT, bright, gifted, ingenious, knowledgeable, quick-witted,

resourceful, shrewd, smart, talented

cleverness noun INTELLIGENCE, ability, brains, ingenuity, quick wits, resourcefulness, shrewdness, smartness

cliché noun PLATITUDE, banality, commonplace, hackneyed phrase, stereotype, truism

client noun CUSTOMER, applicant, buyer, consumer, patient, patron, shopper

clientele noun CUSTOMERS, business, clients, following, market, patronage, regulars, trade

cliff noun ROCK FACE, bluff, crag, escarpment, overhang, precipice, scar, scarp

climactic adjective CRUCIAL, critical, decisive, paramount, peak

climate noun WEATHER, temperature

climax noun CULMINATION, height, highlight, high point, peak, summit, top, zenith

climb verb ASCEND, clamber, mount, rise, scale, shin up, soar, top

climb down verb **1** DESCEND, dismount
2 BACK DOWN, eat one's words, retract, retreat

clinch verb SETTLE, conclude, confirm, decide, determine, seal, secure, set the seal on, sew up (informal)

cling verb STICK, adhere, clasp, clutch, embrace, grasp, grip, hug

clinical adjective UNEMOTIONAL, analytic, cold, detached, dispassionate, impersonal, objective, scientific

clip¹ verb **1** TRIM, crop, curtail, cut, pare, prune, shear, shorten, snip
▶ noun or verb **2** (informal) SMACK, clout (informal), cuff, knock, punch,

strike, thump, wallop (*informal*), whack

clip² verb ATTACH, fasten, fix, hold, pin, staple

clique noun GROUP, cabal, circle, coterie, faction, gang, set

cloak noun 1 CAPE, coat, mantle, wrap
▶ verb 2 COVER, camouflage, conceal, disguise, hide, mask, obscure, screen, veil

clog verb OBSTRUCT, block, congest, hinder, impede, jam

close¹ verb 1 SHUT, bar, block, lock, plug, seal, secure, stop up
2 END, cease, complete, conclude, finish, shut down, terminate, wind up
3 CONNECT, come together, couple, fuse, join, unite
▶ noun 4 END, completion, conclusion, culmination, denouement, ending, finale, finish

close² adjective 1 NEAR, adjacent, adjoining, at hand, cheek by jowl, handy, impending, nearby, neighboring, nigh
2 INTIMATE, attached, confidential, dear, devoted, familiar, inseparable, loving
3 CAREFUL, detailed, intense, minute, painstaking, rigorous, thorough
4 COMPACT, congested, crowded, dense, impenetrable, jam-packed, packed, tight
5 STIFLING, airless, heavy, humid, muggy, oppressive, stuffy, suffocating, sweltering
6 SECRETIVE, private, reticent, secret, taciturn, uncommunicative
7 MEAN, miserly, stingy

closed adjective 1 SHUT, fastened, locked, out of service, sealed

2 EXCLUSIVE, restricted
3 FINISHED, concluded, decided, ended, over, resolved, settled, terminated

cloth noun FABRIC, material, textiles

clothe verb DRESS, array, attire, cover, drape, equip, fit out, garb, robe, swathe

clothes plural noun CLOTHING, apparel, attire, costume, dress, garb, garments, gear (*informal*), outfit, wardrobe, wear

clothing noun CLOTHES, apparel, attire, costume, dress, garb, garments, gear (*informal*), outfit, wardrobe, wear

cloud noun 1 MIST, gloom, haze, murk, vapor
▶ verb 2 OBSCURE, becloud, darken, dim, eclipse, obfuscate, overshadow, shade, shadow, veil
3 CONFUSE, disorient, distort, impair, muddle, muddy the waters

cloudy adjective 1 DULL, dim, gloomy, leaden, louring or lowering, overcast, somber, sunless
2 OPAQUE, muddy, murky

clout (*informal*) noun 1 INFLUENCE, authority, power, prestige, pull, weight
▶ verb 2 HIT, clobber (*slang*), punch, sock (*slang*), strike, thump, wallop (*informal*)

clown noun 1 COMEDIAN, buffoon, comic, fool, harlequin, jester, joker, prankster
▶ verb 2 PLAY THE FOOL, act the fool, jest, mess about

club noun 1 ASSOCIATION, company, fraternity, group, guild, lodge, set, society, union
2 STICK, bat, bludgeon, cosh (*Brit.*), cudgel, truncheon

► *verb* 3 BEAT, bash, batter, bludgeon, cosh (*Brit.*), hammer, pummel, strike

clue *noun* INDICATION, evidence, hint, lead, pointer, sign, suggestion, suspicion, trace

clueless *adjective* STUPID, dim, dozy (*Brit. informal*), dull, half-witted, simple, slow, thick, unintelligent, witless

clump *noun* 1 CLUSTER, bunch, bundle, group, mass
► *verb* 2 STOMP, lumber, plod, thud, thump, tramp

clumsy *adjective* AWKWARD, bumbling, gauche, gawky, ham-fisted (*informal*), lumbering, maladroit, ponderous, uncoordinated, ungainly, unwieldy

cluster *noun* 1 GATHERING, assemblage, batch, bunch, clump, collection, group, knot
► *verb* 2 GATHER, assemble, bunch, collect, flock, group

clutch *verb* SEIZE, catch, clasp, cling to, embrace, grab, grasp, grip, snatch

clutches *plural noun* POWER, claws, control, custody, grasp, grip, hands, keeping, possession, sway

clutter *verb* 1 LITTER, scatter, strew
► *noun* 2 UNTIDINESS, confusion, disarray, disorder, hotchpotch, jumble, litter, mess, muddle

coach *noun* 1 BUS, car, carriage, charabanc, vehicle
2 INSTRUCTOR, handler, teacher, trainer, tutor
► *verb* 3 INSTRUCT, drill, exercise, prepare, train, tutor

coalesce *verb* BLEND, amalgamate, combine, fuse, incorporate, integrate, merge, mix, unite

coalition *noun* ALLIANCE, amalgamation, association, bloc, combination, confederation, conjunction, fusion, merger, union

coarse *adjective* 1 ROUGH, crude, homespun, impure, unfinished, unpolished, unprocessed, unpurified, unrefined
2 VULGAR, earthy, improper, indecent, indelicate, ribald, rude, smutty

coarseness *noun* 1 ROUGHNESS, crudity, unevenness
2 VULGARITY, bawdiness, crudity, earthiness, indelicacy, ribaldry, smut, uncouthness

coast *noun* 1 SHORE, beach, border, coastline, seaboard, seaside
► *verb* 2 CRUISE, drift, freewheel, glide, sail, taxi

coat *noun* 1 FUR, fleece, hair, hide, pelt, skin, wool
2 LAYER, coating, covering, overlay
► *verb* 3 COVER, apply, plaster, smear, spread

coax *verb* PERSUADE, allure, cajole, entice, prevail upon, sweet-talk (*informal*), talk into, wheedle

cocktail *noun* MIXTURE, blend, combination, mix

cocky *adjective* OVERCONFIDENT, arrogant, brash, cocksure, conceited, egotistical, full of oneself, swaggering, vain

code *noun* 1 CIPHER, cryptograph
2 PRINCIPLES, canon, convention, custom, ethics, etiquette, manners, maxim, regulations, rules, system

cogent *adjective* CONVINCING, compelling, effective, forceful, influential, potent, powerful, strong, weighty

cogitate *verb* THINK, consider, contemplate, deliberate, meditate, mull over, muse, ponder, reflect, ruminate

coherent *adjective* 1 CONSISTENT, logical, lucid, meaningful, orderly, organized, rational, reasoned, systematic
2 INTELLIGIBLE, articulate, comprehensible

coil *verb* 1 WIND, curl, loop, snake, spiral, twine, twist, wreathe, writhe

coin *noun* 1 MONEY, cash, change, copper, silver, specie
▶ *verb* 2 INVENT, create, fabricate, forge, make up, mint, mold, originate

coincide *verb* 1 OCCUR SIMULTANEOUSLY, be concurrent, coexist, synchronize
2 AGREE, accord, concur, correspond, harmonize, match, square, tally

coincidence *noun* 1 CHANCE, accident, fluke, happy accident, luck, stroke of luck
2 COINCIDING, concurrence, conjunction, correlation, correspondence

coincidental *adjective* CHANCE, accidental, casual, fluky (*informal*), fortuitous, unintentional, unplanned

cold *adjective* 1 CHILLY, arctic, bleak, cool, freezing, frigid, frosty, frozen, icy, wintry
2 UNFRIENDLY, aloof, distant, frigid, indifferent, reserved, standoffish
▶ *noun* 3 COLDNESS, chill, frigidity, frostiness, iciness

cold-blooded *adjective* CALLOUS, dispassionate, heartless, ruthless, steely, stony-hearted, unemotional, unfeeling

collaborate *verb* 1 WORK TOGETHER, cooperate, join forces, participate, play ball (*informal*),
team up
2 CONSPIRE, collude, cooperate, fraternize

collaboration *noun* TEAMWORK, alliance, association, cooperation, partnership

collaborator *noun* 1 CO-WORKER, associate, colleague, confederate, partner, team-mate
2 TRAITOR, fraternizer, quisling, turncoat

collapse *verb* 1 FALL DOWN, cave in, crumple, fall, fall apart at the seams, give way, subside
2 FAIL, come to nothing, fold, founder, go belly-up (*informal*)
▶ *noun* 3 FALLING DOWN, cave-in, disintegration, falling apart, ruin, subsidence
4 FAILURE, downfall, flop, slump
5 FAINT, breakdown, exhaustion, prostration

collar *verb* (*informal*) SEIZE, apprehend, arrest, capture, catch, grab, nab (*informal*), nail (*informal*)

colleague *noun* FELLOW WORKER, ally, assistant, associate, collaborator, comrade, helper, partner, team-mate, workmate

collect *verb* 1 ASSEMBLE, cluster, congregate, convene, converge, flock together, rally
2 GATHER, accumulate, amass, assemble, heap, hoard, save, stockpile

collected *adjective* CALM, composed, cool, poised, self-possessed, serene, unperturbed, unruffled

collection *noun* 1 ACCUMULATION, anthology, compilation, heap, hoard, mass, pile, set, stockpile, store
2 GROUP, assembly, assortment, cluster, company, crowd
3 CONTRIBUTION, alms, offering,

offertory

collective adjective COMBINED, aggregate, composite, corporate, cumulative, joint, shared, unified, united

collide verb 1 CRASH, clash, come into collision, meet head-on
2 CONFLICT, clash

collision noun 1 CRASH, accident, bump, impact, pile-up (*informal*), prang (*informal*), smash
2 CONFLICT, clash, confrontation, encounter, opposition, skirmish

colloquial adjective INFORMAL, conversational, demotic, everyday, familiar, idiomatic, vernacular

colony noun SETTLEMENT, community, dependency, dominion, outpost, possession, province, satellite state, territory

color noun 1 HUE, colorant, dye, paint, pigment, shade, tint
▶ verb 2 PAINT, dye, stain, tinge, tint
3 BLUSH, flush, redden

colorful adjective 1 BRIGHT, brilliant, multicolored, psychedelic, variegated
2 INTERESTING, distinctive, graphic, lively, picturesque, rich, vivid

colorless adjective 1 DRAB, achromatic, anemic, ashen, bleached, faded, wan, washed out
2 UNINTERESTING, characterless, dreary, dull, insipid, lackluster, vapid

colossal adjective HUGE, enormous, gigantic, immense, mammoth, massive, monumental, prodigious, vast

column noun 1 PILLAR, obelisk, post, shaft, support, upright
2 LINE, cavalcade, file, procession, rank, row

coma noun UNCONSCIOUSNESS, oblivion, stupor, trance

comb verb 1 UNTANGLE, arrange, dress, groom
2 SEARCH, forage, hunt, rake, ransack, rummage, scour, sift

combat noun 1 FIGHT, action, battle, conflict, contest, encounter, engagement, skirmish, struggle, war, warfare
▶ verb 2 FIGHT, defy, do battle with, oppose, resist, withstand

combatant noun FIGHTER, adversary, antagonist, enemy, opponent, soldier, warrior

combination noun 1 MIXTURE, amalgamation, blend, coalescence, composite, connection, mix
2 ASSOCIATION, alliance, coalition, confederation, consortium, federation, syndicate, union

combine verb JOIN TOGETHER, amalgamate, blend, connect, integrate, link, merge, mix, pool, unite

come verb 1 MOVE TOWARDS, advance, approach, draw near, near
2 ARRIVE, appear, enter, materialize, reach, show up (*informal*), turn up (*informal*)
3 HAPPEN, fall, occur, take place
4 RESULT, arise, emanate, emerge, flow, issue, originate
5 REACH, extend
6 BE AVAILABLE, be made, be offered, be on offer, be produced

come about verb HAPPEN, arise, befall, come to pass, occur, result, take place, transpire (*informal*)

come across verb FIND, bump into (*informal*), chance upon, discover, encounter, meet, notice, stumble upon, unearth

comeback noun 1 (*informal*) RETURN, rally, rebound, recovery,

resurgence, revival, triumph
2 RESPONSE, rejoinder, reply, retaliation, retort, riposte
come back verb RETURN, reappear, recur, re-enter
comedian noun COMIC, card (informal), clown, funny man, humorist, jester, joker, wag, wit
comedown noun 1 DECLINE, deflation, demotion, reverse
2 (informal) DISAPPOINTMENT, anticlimax, blow, humiliation, letdown
comedy noun HUMOR, farce, fun, hilarity, jesting, joking, light entertainment
comfort noun 1 LUXURY, cosiness, ease, opulence, snugness, wellbeing
2 RELIEF, compensation, consolation, help, succor, support
▶ verb 3 CONSOLE, commiserate with, hearten, reassure, soothe
comfortable adjective 1 RELAXING, agreeable, convenient, cozy, homely, homey, pleasant, restful, snug
2 HAPPY, at ease, at home, contented, gratified, relaxed, serene
3 (informal) WELL-OFF, affluent, in clover (informal), prosperous, well-to-do
comforting adjective CONSOLING, cheering, consolatory, encouraging, heart-warming, reassuring, soothing
comic adjective 1 FUNNY, amusing, comical, droll, farcical, humorous, jocular, witty
▶ noun 2 COMEDIAN, buffoon, clown, funny man, humorist, jester, wag, wit
comical adjective FUNNY, amusing, comic, droll, farcical, hilarious, humorous, priceless, side-

splitting
coming adjective 1 APPROACHING, at hand, forthcoming, imminent, impending, in store, near, nigh
▶ noun 2 ARRIVAL, advent, approach
command verb 1 ORDER, bid, charge, compel, demand, direct, require
2 HAVE AUTHORITY OVER, control, dominate, govern, handle, head, lead, manage, rule, supervise
▶ noun 3 ORDER, commandment, decree, demand, directive, instruction, requirement, ultimatum
4 AUTHORITY, charge, control, government, management, mastery, power, rule, supervision
commandeer verb SEIZE, appropriate, confiscate, requisition, sequester, sequestrate
commander noun OFFICER, alpha male, boss (informal), captain, chief, commanding officer, head, leader, ruler
commanding adjective CONTROLLING, advantageous, decisive, dominant, dominating, superior
commemorate verb REMEMBER, celebrate, honor, immortalize, pay tribute to, salute
commemoration noun REMEMBRANCE, ceremony, honoring, memorial service, tribute
commence verb BEGIN, embark on, enter upon, initiate, open, originate, start
commend verb PRAISE, acclaim, applaud, approve, compliment, extol, recommend, speak highly of
commendable adjective PRAISEWORTHY, admirable,

creditable, deserving, estimable, exemplary, laudable, meritorious, worthy

commendation noun PRAISE, acclaim, acclamation, approbation, approval, credit, encouragement, good opinion, kudos, panegyric, recommendation

comment noun 1 REMARK, observation, statement
2 NOTE, annotation, commentary, explanation, exposition, illustration
▶ verb 3 REMARK, mention, note, observe, point out, say, utter
4 ANNOTATE, elucidate, explain, interpret

commentary noun 1 NARRATION, description, voice-over
2 NOTES, analysis, critique, explanation, review, treatise

commentator noun 1 REPORTER, special correspondent, sportscaster
2 CRITIC, annotator, interpreter

commerce noun TRADE, business, dealing, exchange, traffic

commercial adjective
1 MERCANTILE, trading
2 MATERIALISTIC, mercenary, profit-making
▶ noun 3 ADVERTISEMENT, ad (informal), announcement, plug (informal)

commiserate verb SYMPATHIZE, console, feel for, pity

commission noun 1 DUTY, errand, mandate, mission, task
2 FEE, cut, percentage, rake-off (slang), royalties
3 COMMITTEE, board, commissioners, delegation, deputation, representatives
▶ verb 4 APPOINT, authorize, contract, delegate, depute,

empower, engage, nominate, order, select

commit verb 1 DO, carry out, enact, execute, perform, perpetrate
2 PUT IN CUSTODY, confine, imprison

commitment noun 1 DEDICATION, devotion, involvement, loyalty
2 RESPONSIBILITY, duty, engagement, liability, obligation, tie

common adjective 1 AVERAGE, commonplace, conventional, customary, everyday, familiar, frequent, habitual, ordinary, regular, routine, standard, stock, usual
2 POPULAR, accepted, general, prevailing, prevalent, universal, widespread
3 COLLECTIVE, communal, popular, public, social
4 VULGAR, coarse, inferior, plebeian

commonplace adjective
1 EVERYDAY, banal, common, humdrum, mundane, obvious, ordinary, run-of-the-mill, widespread
▶ noun 2 CLICHÉ, banality, platitude, truism

common sense noun GOOD SENSE, gumption (Brit. informal), horse sense, level-headedness, native intelligence, prudence, sound judgment, wit

commotion noun DISTURBANCE, disorder, excitement, furor, fuss, hue and cry, rumpus, tumult, turmoil, upheaval, uproar

communal adjective PUBLIC, collective, general, joint, shared

commune noun COMMUNITY, collective, cooperative, kibbutz

commune with verb
CONTEMPLATE, meditate on, muse

on, ponder, reflect on

communicate verb MAKE KNOWN, convey, declare, disclose, impart, inform, pass on, proclaim, transmit

communication noun 1 PASSING ON, contact, conversation, correspondence, dissemination, link, transmission

2 MESSAGE, announcement, disclosure, dispatch, information, news, report, statement, word

communicative adjective TALKATIVE, chatty, expansive, forthcoming, frank, informative, loquacious, open, outgoing, voluble

Communism noun SOCIALISM, Bolshevism, collectivism, Marxism, state socialism

Communist noun SOCIALIST, Bolshevik, collectivist, Marxist, Red (informal)

community noun SOCIETY, brotherhood, commonwealth, company, general public, people, populace, public, residents, state

commuter noun DAILY TRAVELER, straphanger (informal), suburbanite

compact[1] adjective 1 CLOSELY PACKED, compressed, condensed, dense, pressed together, solid, thick

2 BRIEF, compendious, concise, succinct, terse, to the point

▶ verb 3 PACK CLOSELY, compress, condense, cram, stuff, tamp

compact[2] noun AGREEMENT, arrangement, bargain, bond, contract, covenant, deal, pact, treaty, understanding

companion noun 1 FRIEND, accomplice, ally, associate, colleague, comrade, consort, homeboy (slang), homegirl (slang), mate (informal), partner

2 ESCORT, aide, assistant, attendant, chaperon, squire

companionship noun FELLOWSHIP, camaraderie, company, comradeship, conviviality, esprit de corps, friendship, rapport, togetherness

company noun 1 BUSINESS, association, concern, corporation, establishment, firm, house, partnership, syndicate

2 GROUP, assembly, band, collection, community, crowd, gathering, party, set

3 GUESTS, callers, party, visitors

comparable adjective 1 ON A PAR, a match for, as good as, commensurate, equal, equivalent, in a class with, on a level playing field (informal), proportionate, tantamount

2 SIMILAR, akin, alike, analogous, cognate, corresponding, cut from the same cloth, of a piece, related

comparative adjective RELATIVE, by comparison, qualified

compare verb 1 WEIGH, balance, contrast, juxtapose, set against

2 (usually with with) BE ON A PAR WITH, approach, bear comparison, be in the same class as, be the equal of, compete with, equal, hold a candle to, match

3 ▷▷ **compare to** LIKEN TO, correlate to, equate to, identify with, mention in the same breath as, parallel, resemble

comparison noun 1 CONTRAST, distinction, juxtaposition

2 SIMILARITY, analogy, comparability, correlation, likeness, resemblance

compartment noun SECTION, alcove, bay, berth, booth, carriage, cubbyhole, cubicle, locker, niche, pigeonhole

compass *noun* RANGE, area, boundary, circumference, extent, field, limit, reach, realm, scope

compassion *noun* SYMPATHY, condolence, fellow feeling, humanity, kindness, mercy, pity, sorrow, tender-heartedness, tenderness, understanding

compassionate *adjective* SYMPATHETIC, benevolent, charitable, humane, humanitarian, kind-hearted, merciful, pitying, tender-hearted, understanding

compatibility *noun* HARMONY, affinity, agreement, concord, empathy, like-mindedness, rapport, sympathy

compatible *adjective* HARMONIOUS, adaptable, congruous, consistent, in harmony, in keeping, suitable

compel *verb* FORCE, coerce, constrain, dragoon, impel, make, oblige, railroad (*informal*)

compelling *adjective*
1 FASCINATING, enchanting, enthralling, gripping, hypnotic, irresistible, mesmeric, spellbinding
2 PRESSING, binding, coercive, imperative, overriding, peremptory, unavoidable, urgent
3 CONVINCING, cogent, conclusive, forceful, irrefutable, powerful, telling, weighty

compensate *verb* 1 RECOMPENSE, atone, make amends, make good, refund, reimburse, remunerate, repay
2 CANCEL (OUT), balance, counteract, counterbalance, make up for, offset, redress

compensation *noun*
RECOMPENSE, amends, atonement, damages, reimbursement, remuneration, reparation, restitution, satisfaction

compete *verb* CONTEND, be in the running, challenge, contest, fight, strive, struggle, vie

competence *noun* ABILITY, capability, capacity, expertise, fitness, proficiency, skill, suitability

competent *adjective* ABLE, adequate, capable, fit, proficient, qualified, suitable

competition *noun* 1 RIVALRY, opposition, strife, struggle
2 CONTEST, championship, event, head-to-head, puzzle, quiz, tournament
3 OPPOSITION, challengers, field, rivals

competitive *adjective* 1 CUT-THROAT, aggressive, antagonistic, at odds, dog-eat-dog, opposing, rival
2 AMBITIOUS, combative

competitor *noun* CONTESTANT, adversary, antagonist, challenger, opponent, rival

compilation *noun* COLLECTION, accumulation, anthology, assemblage, assortment, treasury

compile *verb* PUT TOGETHER, accumulate, amass, collect, cull, garner, gather, marshal, organize

complacency *noun* SELF-SATISFACTION, contentment, satisfaction, smugness

complacent *adjective* SELF-SATISFIED, contented, pleased with oneself, resting on one's laurels, satisfied, serene, smug, unconcerned

complain *verb* FIND FAULT, bemoan, bewail, carp, deplore, groan, grouse, grumble, lament, moan, whine, whinge (*informal*)

complaint noun 1 CRITICISM, charge, grievance, gripe (informal), grouse, grumble, lament, moan, protest 2 ILLNESS, affliction, ailment, disease, disorder, malady, sickness, upset

complement noun 1 COMPLETION, companion, consummation, counterpart, finishing touch, rounding-off, supplement 2 TOTAL, aggregate, capacity, entirety, quota, totality, wholeness ▶ verb 3 COMPLETE, cap (informal), crown, round off, set off

complementary adjective COMPLETING, companion, corresponding, interdependent, interrelating, matched, reciprocal

complete adjective 1 TOTAL, absolute, consummate, outright, perfect, thorough, thoroughgoing, utter 2 FINISHED, accomplished, achieved, concluded, ended 3 ENTIRE, all, faultless, full, intact, plenary, unbroken, whole ▶ verb 4 FINISH, close, conclude, crown, end, finalize, round off, settle, wind up (informal), wrap up (informal)

completely adverb TOTALLY, absolutely, altogether, entirely, every inch, fully, hook, line and sinker, in full, lock, stock and barrel, one hundred per cent, perfectly, thoroughly, utterly, wholly

completion noun FINISHING, bitter end, close, conclusion, culmination, end, fruition, fulfillment

complex adjective 1 COMPOUND, composite, heterogeneous, manifold, multifarious, multiple 2 COMPLICATED, convoluted, elaborate, intricate, involved, labyrinthine, tangled, tortuous ▶ noun 3 STRUCTURE, aggregate, composite, network, organization, scheme, system 4 OBSESSION, fixation, fixed idea, idée fixe, phobia, preoccupation

complexion noun 1 SKIN, color, coloring, hue, pigmentation, skin tone 2 NATURE, appearance, aspect, character, guise, light, look, make-up

complexity noun COMPLICATION, elaboration, entanglement, intricacy, involvement, ramification

complicate verb MAKE DIFFICULT, confuse, entangle, involve, muddle, ravel

complicated adjective 1 DIFFICULT, involved, perplexing, problematic, puzzling, troublesome 2 INVOLVED, complex, convoluted, elaborate, intricate, labyrinthine

complication noun 1 COMPLEXITY, confusion, entanglement, intricacy, web 2 PROBLEM, difficulty, drawback, embarrassment, obstacle, snag

compliment noun 1 PRAISE, bouquet, commendation, congratulations, eulogy, flattery, honor, tribute ▶ verb 2 PRAISE, brown-nose (slang), commend, congratulate, extol, flatter, pay tribute to, salute, speak highly of

complimentary adjective 1 FLATTERING, appreciative, approving, commendatory, congratulatory, laudatory 2 FREE, courtesy, donated, gratis, gratuitous, honorary, on the house

compliments *plural noun*
GREETINGS, good wishes, regards, remembrances, respects, salutation

comply *verb* OBEY, abide by, acquiesce, adhere to, conform to, follow, observe, submit, toe the line

component *noun* 1 PART, constituent, element, ingredient, item, piece, unit
▶ *adjective* 2 CONSTITUENT, inherent, intrinsic

compose *verb* 1 PUT TOGETHER, build, comprise, constitute, construct, fashion, form, make, make up
2 CREATE, contrive, devise, invent, produce, write
3 CALM, collect, control, pacify, placate, quiet, soothe
4 ARRANGE, adjust

composed *adjective* CALM, at ease, collected, cool, level-headed, poised, relaxed, sedate, self-possessed, serene, unflappable

composition *noun* 1 CREATION, compilation, fashioning, formation, formulation, making, production, putting together
2 DESIGN, arrangement, configuration, formation, layout, make-up, organization, structure
3 ESSAY, exercise, literary work, opus, piece, treatise, work

composure *noun* CALMNESS, aplomb, equanimity, poise, sang-froid, self-assurance, self-possession, serenity

compound *noun* 1 COMBINATION, alloy, amalgam, blend, composite, fusion, medley, mixture, synthesis
▶ *verb* 2 COMBINE, amalgamate, blend, intermingle, mix, synthesize, unite

3 INTENSIFY, add to, aggravate, augment, complicate, exacerbate, heighten, magnify, worsen
▶ *adjective* 4 COMPLEX, composite, intricate, multiple

comprehend *verb* UNDERSTAND, apprehend, conceive, fathom, grasp, know, make out, perceive, see, take in

comprehensible *adjective* UNDERSTANDABLE, clear, coherent, conceivable, explicit, intelligible, plain

comprehension *noun* UNDERSTANDING, conception, discernment, grasp, intelligence, perception, realization

comprehensive *adjective* BROAD, all-embracing, all-inclusive, blanket, complete, encyclopedic, exhaustive, full, inclusive, thorough

compress *verb* SQUEEZE, abbreviate, concentrate, condense, contract, crush, press, shorten, squash

comprise *verb* 1 BE COMPOSED OF, consist of, contain, embrace, encompass, include, take in
2 MAKE UP, compose, constitute, form

compromise *noun* 1 GIVE-AND-TAKE, accommodation, adjustment, agreement, concession, settlement, trade-off
▶ *verb* 2 MEET HALFWAY, adjust, agree, concede, give and take, go fifty-fifty (*informal*), settle, strike a balance
3 DISHONOR, discredit, embarrass, expose, jeopardize, prejudice, weaken

compulsion *noun* 1 URGE, drive, necessity, need, obsession, preoccupation
2 FORCE, coercion, constraint,

demand, duress, obligation, pressure, urgency

compulsive adjective IRRESISTIBLE, compelling, driving, neurotic, obsessive, overwhelming, uncontrollable, urgent

compulsory adjective OBLIGATORY, binding, de rigueur, forced, imperative, mandatory, required, requisite

compute verb CALCULATE, add up, count, enumerate, figure out, reckon, tally, total

comrade noun COMPANION, ally, associate, colleague, co-worker, fellow, friend, homeboy (slang), homegirl (slang), partner

con (informal) noun 1 SWINDLE, deception, fraud, scam (slang), sting (informal), trick
▶ verb 2 SWINDLE, cheat, deceive, defraud, double-cross (informal), dupe, hoodwink, rip off (slang), trick

concave adjective HOLLOW, indented

conceal verb HIDE, bury, camouflage, cover, disguise, mask, obscure, screen

concede verb 1 ADMIT, accept, acknowledge, allow, confess, grant, own
2 GIVE UP, cede, hand over, relinquish, surrender, yield

conceit noun 1 SELF-IMPORTANCE, arrogance, egotism, narcissism, pride, swagger, vanity
2 (archaic) FANCY, fantasy, image, whim, whimsy

conceited adjective SELF-IMPORTANT, arrogant, bigheaded (informal), cocky, egotistical, full of oneself, immodest, narcissistic, too big for one's boots or breeches, vain

conceivable adjective IMAGINABLE, believable, credible, possible, thinkable

conceive verb 1 IMAGINE, believe, comprehend, envisage, fancy, suppose, think, understand
2 THINK UP, contrive, create, design, devise, formulate
3 BECOME PREGNANT, become impregnated

concentrate verb 1 FOCUS ONE'S ATTENTION ON, be engrossed in, put one's mind to, rack one's brains
2 FOCUS, bring to bear, center, cluster, converge
3 GATHER, accumulate, cluster, collect, congregate, huddle

concentrated adjective 1 INTENSE, all-out (informal), deep, hard, intensive
2 CONDENSED, boiled down, evaporated, reduced, rich, thickened, undiluted

concentration noun 1 SINGLE-MINDEDNESS, absorption, application, heed
2 FOCUSING, bringing to bear, centralization, centring, consolidation, convergence, intensification
3 CONVERGENCE, accumulation, aggregation, cluster, collection, horde, mass

concept noun IDEA, abstraction, conception, conceptualization, hypothesis, image, notion, theory, view

conception noun 1 IDEA, concept, design, image, notion, plan
2 IMPREGNATION, fertilization, germination, insemination

concern noun 1 WORRY, anxiety, apprehension, burden, care, disquiet, distress
2 IMPORTANCE, bearing, interest, relevance

3 BUSINESS, affair, interest, job, responsibility, task
4 BUSINESS, company, corporation, enterprise, establishment, firm, organization
▶ *verb* **5** WORRY, bother, disquiet, distress, disturb, make anxious, perturb, trouble
6 BE RELEVANT TO, affect, apply to, bear on, interest, involve, pertain to, regard, touch

concerned *adjective* **1** INVOLVED, active, implicated, interested, mixed up, privy to
2 WORRIED, anxious, bothered, distressed, disturbed, troubled, uneasy, upset

concerning *preposition* REGARDING, about, apropos of, as regards, on the subject of, re, relating to, respecting, touching, with reference to

concession *noun* **1** GRANT, adjustment, allowance, boon, compromise, indulgence, permit, privilege, sop
2 CONCEDING, acknowledgment, admission, assent, confession, surrender, yielding

conciliate *verb* PACIFY, appease, clear the air, mediate, mollify, placate, reconcile, soothe, win over

conciliation *noun* PACIFICATION, appeasement, mollification, placation, reconciliation, soothing

conciliatory *adjective* PACIFYING, appeasing, mollifying, pacific, peaceable, placatory

concise *adjective* BRIEF, compendious, condensed, laconic, pithy, short, succinct, terse

conclude *verb* **1** DECIDE, assume, deduce, gather, infer, judge, surmise, work out

2 END, cease, close, complete, finish, round off, terminate, wind up
3 ACCOMPLISH, bring about, carry out, effect, pull off

conclusion *noun* **1** DECISION, conviction, deduction, inference, judgment, opinion, verdict
2 END, bitter end, close, completion, ending, finale, finish, result, termination
3 OUTCOME, consequence, culmination, end result, result, upshot

conclusive *adjective* DECISIVE, clinching, convincing, definite, final, irrefutable, ultimate, unanswerable

concoct *verb* MAKE UP, brew, contrive, devise, formulate, hatch, invent, prepare, think up

concoction *noun* MIXTURE, blend, brew, combination, compound, creation, preparation

concrete *adjective* **1** SPECIFIC, definite, explicit
2 REAL, actual, factual, material, sensible, substantial, tangible

concur *verb* AGREE, acquiesce, assent, consent

condemn *verb* **1** DISAPPROVE, blame, censure, damn, denounce, reproach, reprove, upbraid
2 SENTENCE, convict, damn, doom, pass sentence on

condemnation *noun*
1 DISAPPROVAL, blame, censure, denunciation, reproach, reproof, stricture
2 SENTENCE, conviction, damnation, doom, judgment

condensation *noun*
1 DISTILLATION, liquefaction, precipitate, precipitation
2 ABRIDGMENT, contraction, digest, précis, synopsis

3 CONCENTRATION, compression, consolidation, crystallization, curtailment, reduction

condense verb **1** ABRIDGE, abbreviate, compress, concentrate, epitomize, shorten, summarize

2 CONCENTRATE, boil down, reduce, thicken

condensed adjective **1** ABRIDGED, compressed, concentrated, shortened, shrunken, slimmed-down, summarized

2 CONCENTRATED, boiled down, reduced, thickened

condescend verb **1** PATRONIZE, talk down to

2 LOWER ONESELF, bend, deign, humble or demean oneself, see fit, stoop

condescending adjective PATRONIZING, disdainful, lofty, lordly, snobbish, snooty (informal), supercilious, superior, toffee-nosed (slang, chiefly Brit.)

condition noun **1** STATE, circumstances, lie of the land, position, shape, situation, state of affairs

2 REQUIREMENT, limitation, prerequisite, proviso, qualification, restriction, rider, stipulation, terms

3 HEALTH, fettle, fitness, kilter, order, shape, state of health, trim

4 AILMENT, complaint, infirmity, malady, problem, weakness

▶ verb **5** ACCUSTOM, adapt, equip, prepare, ready, tone up, train, work out

conditional adjective DEPENDENT, contingent, limited, provisional, qualified, subject to, with reservations

conditions plural noun CIRCUMSTANCES, environment, milieu, situation, surroundings, way of life

condone verb OVERLOOK, excuse, forgive, let pass, look the other way, make allowance for, pardon, turn a blind eye to

conduct noun **1** BEHAVIOR, attitude, bearing, demeanor, deportment, manners, ways

2 MANAGEMENT, administration, control, direction, guidance, handling, organization, running, supervision

▶ verb **3** CARRY OUT, administer, control, direct, handle, manage, organize, preside over, run, supervise

4 BEHAVE, acquit, act, carry, comport, deport

5 ACCOMPANY, convey, escort, guide, lead, steer, usher

confederacy noun UNION, alliance, coalition, confederation, federation, league

confer verb **1** DISCUSS, consult, converse, deliberate, discourse, talk

2 GRANT, accord, award, bestow, give, hand out, present

conference noun MEETING, colloquium, congress, consultation, convention, discussion, forum, seminar, symposium

confess verb **1** ADMIT, acknowledge, come clean (informal), concede, confide, disclose, divulge, fess up (informal), own up

2 DECLARE, affirm, assert, confirm, profess, reveal

confession noun ADMISSION, acknowledgment, disclosure, exposure, revelation, unbosoming

confidant, confidante noun CLOSE FRIEND, alter ego, bosom friend, crony, familiar, intimate

confide verb 1 TELL, admit, confess, disclose, divulge, impart, reveal, whisper

2 (formal) ENTRUST, commend, commit, consign

confidence noun 1 TRUST, belief, credence, dependence, faith, reliance

2 SELF-ASSURANCE, aplomb, assurance, boldness, courage, firmness, nerve, self-possession

3 ▷▷ **in confidence** IN SECRECY, between you and me (and the gatepost), confidentially, privately

confident adjective 1 CERTAIN, convinced, counting on, positive, satisfied, secure, sure

2 SELF-ASSURED, assured, bold, dauntless, fearless, self-reliant

confidential adjective SECRET, classified, hush-hush (informal), intimate, off the record, private, privy

confidentially adverb IN SECRET, behind closed doors, between ourselves, in camera, in confidence, personally, privately, sub rosa

confine verb RESTRICT, cage, enclose, hem in, hold back, imprison, incarcerate, intern, keep, limit, shut up

confinement noun
1 IMPRISONMENT, custody, detention, incarceration, internment, porridge (slang)

2 CHILDBIRTH, childbed, labor, lying-in, parturition

confines plural noun LIMITS, boundaries, bounds, circumference, edge, precincts

confirm verb 1 PROVE, authenticate, bear out, corroborate, endorse, ratify, substantiate, validate, verify

2 STRENGTHEN, buttress, establish, fix, fortify, reinforce

confirmation noun 1 PROOF, authentication, corroboration, evidence, substantiation, testimony, validation, verification

2 SANCTION, acceptance, agreement, approval, assent, endorsement, ratification

confirmed adjective LONG-ESTABLISHED, chronic, dyed-in-the-wool, habitual, hardened, ingrained, inveterate, seasoned

confiscate verb SEIZE, appropriate, commandeer, impound, sequester, sequestrate

confiscation noun SEIZURE, appropriation, forfeiture, impounding, sequestration, takeover

conflict noun 1 OPPOSITION, antagonism, difference, disagreement, discord, dissension, friction, hostility, strife

2 BATTLE, clash, combat, contest, encounter, fight, strife, war

▶ verb 3 BE INCOMPATIBLE, be at variance, clash, collide, differ, disagree, interfere

conflicting adjective INCOMPATIBLE, antagonistic, clashing, contradictory, contrary, discordant, inconsistent, opposing, paradoxical

conform verb 1 COMPLY, adapt, adjust, fall in with, follow, obey, toe the line

2 AGREE, accord, correspond, harmonize, match, suit, tally

conformist noun TRADITIONALIST, stick-in-the-mud (informal), yes man

conformity noun COMPLIANCE, conventionality, observance, orthodoxy, traditionalism

confound *verb* BEWILDER, astound, baffle, confuse, dumbfound, flummox, mystify, nonplus, perplex

confront *verb* FACE, accost, challenge, defy, encounter, oppose, stand up to, tackle

confrontation *noun* CONFLICT, contest, encounter, fight, head-to-head, set-to (*informal*), showdown (*informal*)

confuse *verb* **1** MIX UP, disarrange, disorder, jumble, mingle, muddle, ravel
2 BEWILDER, baffle, bemuse, faze, flummox, mystify, nonplus, perplex, puzzle
3 DISCONCERT, discompose, disorient, fluster, rattle (*informal*), throw off balance, unnerve, upset

confused *adjective* **1** BEWILDERED, at sea, baffled, disorientated, flummoxed, muddled, nonplussed, perplexed, puzzled, taken aback
2 DISORDERED, chaotic, disorganized, higgledy-piggledy (*informal*), in disarray, jumbled, mixed up, topsy-turvy, untidy

confusing *adjective* BEWILDERING, baffling, contradictory, disconcerting, misleading, perplexing, puzzling, unclear

confusion *noun* **1** BEWILDERMENT, disorientation, mystification, perplexity, puzzlement
2 DISORDER, chaos, commotion, jumble, mess, muddle, shambles, turmoil, untidiness, upheaval

congenial *adjective*
1 PLEASANT, affable, agreeable, companionable, favorable, friendly, genial, kindly
2 COMPATIBLE, kindred, like-minded, sympathetic, well-suited

congenital *adjective* INBORN, immanent, inbred, inherent, innate, natural

congested *adjective*
1 OVERCROWDED, crowded, teeming
2 CLOGGED, blocked-up, crammed, jammed, overfilled, overflowing, packed, stuffed

congestion *noun*
1 OVERCROWDING, crowding
2 CLOGGING, bottleneck, jam, surfeit

congratulate *verb* COMPLIMENT, pat on the back, wish joy to

congratulations *plural noun or interjection* GOOD WISHES, best wishes, compliments, felicitations, greetings

congregate *verb* COME TOGETHER, assemble, collect, convene, converge, flock, gather, mass, meet

congregation *noun* ASSEMBLY, brethren, crowd, fellowship, flock, multitude, throng

congress *noun* MEETING, assembly, caucus, conclave, conference, convention, council, legislature, parliament

conjecture *noun* **1** GUESS, hypothesis, shot in the dark, speculation, supposition, surmise, theory
▶ *verb* **2** GUESS, hypothesize, imagine, speculate, suppose, surmise, theorize

conjugal *adjective* MARITAL, bridal, connubial, married, matrimonial, nuptial, wedded

conjure *verb* PERFORM TRICKS, juggle

conjurer, conjuror *noun* MAGICIAN, illusionist, sorcerer, wizard

conjure up *verb* BRING TO MIND, contrive, create, evoke, produce as if by magic, recall, recollect

connect *verb* LINK, affix, attach, couple, fasten, join, unite

connected *adjective* LINKED, affiliated, akin, allied, associated, combined, coupled, joined, related, united

connection *noun* 1 ASSOCIATION, affinity, bond, liaison, link, relationship, relevance, tie-in
2 LINK, alliance, association, attachment, coupling, fastening, junction, tie, union
3 CONTACT, acquaintance, ally, associate, friend, homeboy (*slang*), homegirl (*slang*), sponsor

connivance *noun* COLLUSION, abetting, complicity, conspiring, tacit consent

connive *verb* 1 CONSPIRE, collude, cook up (*informal*), intrigue, plot, scheme
2 ▷▷ **connive at** TURN A BLIND EYE TO, abet, disregard, let pass, look the other way, overlook, wink at

connoisseur *noun* EXPERT, aficionado, appreciator, authority, buff (*informal*), devotee, judge

conquer *verb* 1 DEFEAT, beat, crush, get the better of, master, overcome, overpower, overthrow, quell, subjugate, vanquish
2 SEIZE, acquire, annex, obtain, occupy, overrun, win

conqueror *noun* WINNER, conquistador, defeater, master, subjugator, vanquisher, victor

conquest *noun* 1 DEFEAT, mastery, overthrow, rout, triumph, victory
2 TAKEOVER, annexation, coup, invasion, occupation, subjugation

conscience *noun* PRINCIPLES, moral sense, scruples, sense of right and wrong, still small voice

conscientious *adjective* THOROUGH, careful, diligent,

exact, faithful, meticulous, painstaking, particular, punctilious

conscious *adjective* 1 AWARE, alert, alive to, awake, responsive, sensible, sentient
2 DELIBERATE, calculated, intentional, knowing, premeditated, self-conscious, studied, willful

consciousness *noun* AWARENESS, apprehension, knowledge, realization, recognition, sensibility

consecrate *verb* SANCTIFY, dedicate, devote, hallow, ordain, set apart, venerate

consecutive *adjective* SUCCESSIVE, in sequence, in turn, running, sequential, succeeding, uninterrupted

consensus *noun* AGREEMENT, assent, common consent, concord, general agreement, harmony, unanimity, unity

consent *noun* 1 AGREEMENT, acquiescence, approval, assent, compliance, go-ahead (*informal*), O.K. or okay (*informal*), permission, sanction
▶ *verb* 2 AGREE, acquiesce, allow, approve, assent, concur, permit

consequence *noun* 1 RESULT, effect, end result, issue, outcome, repercussion, sequel, upshot
2 IMPORTANCE, account, concern, import, moment, significance, value, weight

consequent *adjective* FOLLOWING, ensuing, resultant, resulting, subsequent, successive

consequently *adverb* AS A RESULT, accordingly, ergo, hence, subsequently, therefore, thus

conservation *noun* PROTECTION, guardianship, husbandry, maintenance, preservation, safeguarding, safekeeping, saving, upkeep

conservative *adjective*
1 TRADITIONAL, cautious, conventional, die-hard, hidebound, reactionary, sober
▶ *noun* 2 TRADITIONALIST, reactionary, stick-in-the-mud (*informal*)

conserve *verb* PROTECT, hoard, husband, keep, nurse, preserve, save, store up, take care of, use sparingly

consider *verb* 1 THINK, believe, deem, hold to be, judge, rate, regard as
2 THINK ABOUT, cogitate, contemplate, deliberate, meditate, ponder, reflect, ruminate, turn over in one's mind, weigh
3 BEAR IN MIND, keep in view, make allowance for, reckon with, remember, respect, take into account

considerable *adjective* LARGE, appreciable, goodly, great, marked, noticeable, plentiful, sizable *or* sizeable, substantial, supersize

considerably *adverb* GREATLY, appreciably, markedly, noticeably, remarkably, significantly, substantially, very much

considerate *adjective*
THOUGHTFUL, attentive, concerned, kindly, mindful, obliging, patient, tactful, unselfish

consideration *noun* 1 THOUGHT, analysis, deliberation, discussion, examination, reflection, review, scrutiny
2 FACTOR, concern, issue, point
3 THOUGHTFULNESS, concern, considerateness, kindness, respect, tact
4 PAYMENT, fee, recompense, remuneration, reward, tip

considering *preposition* TAKING INTO ACCOUNT, in the light of, in view of

consignment *noun* SHIPMENT, batch, delivery, goods

consist *verb* 1 ▷▷ **consist of** BE MADE UP OF, amount to, be composed of, comprise, contain, embody, include, incorporate, involve: **consist in** LIE IN, be expressed by, be found *or* contained in, inhere in, reside in

consistency *noun* 1 TEXTURE, compactness, density, firmness, thickness, viscosity
2 CONSTANCY, evenness, regularity, steadfastness, steadiness, uniformity

consistent *adjective*
1 UNCHANGING, constant, dependable, persistent, regular, steady, true to type, undeviating
2 AGREEING, coherent, compatible, congruous, consonant, harmonious, logical

consolation *noun* COMFORT, cheer, encouragement, help, relief, solace, succor, support

console *verb* COMFORT, calm, cheer, encourage, express sympathy for, soothe

consolidate *verb* 1 STRENGTHEN, fortify, reinforce, secure, stabilize
2 COMBINE, amalgamate, federate, fuse, join, unite

consort *verb* 1 ASSOCIATE, fraternize, go around with, hang about, around *or* out with, keep company, mix
▶ *noun* 2 SPOUSE, companion, husband, partner, wife

conspicuous *adjective* 1 OBVIOUS,

blatant, clear, evident, noticeable, patent, salient
2 NOTEWORTHY, illustrious, notable, outstanding, prominent, remarkable, salient, signal, striking

conspiracy noun PLOT, collusion, intrigue, machination, scheme, treason

conspirator noun PLOTTER, conspirer, intriguer, schemer, traitor

conspire verb 1 PLOT, contrive, intrigue, machinate, maneuver, plan, scheme
2 WORK TOGETHER, combine, concur, contribute, cooperate, tend

constant adjective 1 CONTINUOUS, ceaseless, incessant, interminable, nonstop, perpetual, sustained, twenty-four-seven (slang), unrelenting
2 UNCHANGING, even, fixed, invariable, permanent, stable, steady, uniform, unvarying
3 FAITHFUL, devoted, loyal, stalwart, staunch, true, trustworthy, trusty

constantly adverb CONTINUOUSLY, all the time, always, continually, endlessly, incessantly, interminably, invariably, nonstop, perpetually, twenty-four-seven (slang)

consternation noun DISMAY, alarm, anxiety, distress, dread, fear, trepidation

constituent noun 1 VOTER, elector
2 COMPONENT, element, factor, ingredient, part, unit
▶ adjective 3 COMPONENT, basic, elemental, essential, integral

constitute verb MAKE UP, compose, comprise, establish, form, found, set up

constitution noun 1 HEALTH, build, character, disposition, physique
2 STRUCTURE, composition, form, make-up, nature

constitutional adjective
1 STATUTORY, chartered, vested
▶ noun 2 WALK, airing, stroll, turn

constrain verb 1 FORCE, bind, coerce, compel, impel, necessitate, oblige, pressurize
2 RESTRICT, check, confine, constrict, curb, restrain, straiten

constraint noun 1 RESTRICTION, check, curb, deterrent, hindrance, limitation, rein
2 FORCE, coercion, compulsion, necessity, pressure, restraint

construct verb BUILD, assemble, compose, create, fashion, form, make, manufacture, put together, shape

construction noun 1 BUILDING, composition, creation, edifice
2 INTERPRETATION, explanation, inference, reading, rendering

constructive adjective HELPFUL, positive, practical, productive, useful, valuable

consult verb ASK, compare notes, confer, pick (someone's) brains, question, refer to, take counsel, turn to

consultant noun SPECIALIST, adviser, authority

consultation noun SEMINAR, appointment, conference, council, deliberation, dialogue, discussion, examination, hearing, interview, meeting, session

consume verb 1 EAT, chow down (slang), devour, eat up, gobble (up), put away, swallow
2 USE UP, absorb, dissipate, exhaust, expend, spend, squander, waste

3 DESTROY, annihilate, demolish, devastate, lay waste, ravage
4 (often passive) OBSESS, absorb, dominate, eat up, engross, monopolize, preoccupy

consumer noun BUYER, customer, purchaser, shopper, user

consummate verb **1** COMPLETE, accomplish, conclude, crown, end, finish, fulfill
▸ adjective **2** SKILLED, accomplished, matchless, perfect, polished, practiced, superb, supreme
3 COMPLETE, absolute, conspicuous, extreme, supreme, total, utter

consumption noun **1** USING UP, depletion, diminution, dissipation, exhaustion, expenditure, loss, waste
2 (old-fashioned) TUBERCULOSIS, T.B.

contact noun **1** COMMUNICATION, association, connection
2 TOUCH, contiguity
3 ACQUAINTANCE, connection
▸ verb **4** GET or BE IN TOUCH WITH, approach, call, communicate with, reach, speak to, write to

contagious adjective INFECTIOUS, catching, communicable, spreading, transmissible

contain verb **1** HOLD, accommodate, enclose, have capacity for, incorporate, seat
2 INCLUDE, comprehend, comprise, consist of, embody, embrace, involve
3 RESTRAIN, control, curb, hold back, hold in, keep a tight rein on, repress, stifle

container noun HOLDER, receptacle, repository, vessel

contaminate verb POLLUTE, adulterate, befoul, corrupt, defile, infect, stain, taint, tarnish

contamination noun POLLUTION, contagion, corruption, defilement, impurity, infection, poisoning, taint

contemplate verb **1** THINK ABOUT, consider, deliberate, meditate, muse over, ponder, reflect upon, ruminate (upon)
2 CONSIDER, envisage, expect, foresee, intend, plan, think of
3 LOOK AT, examine, eye up, gaze at, inspect, regard, stare at, study, survey, view

contemporary adjective
1 COEXISTING, concurrent, contemporaneous
2 MODERN, à la mode, current, newfangled, present, present-day, recent, up-to-date
▸ noun **3** PEER, fellow

contempt noun SCORN, derision, disdain, disregard, disrespect, mockery, neglect, slight

contemptible adjective DESPICABLE, detestable, ignominious, lousy (slang), measly, paltry, pitiful, scuzzy (slang), shameful, worthless

contemptuous adjective SCORNFUL, arrogant, condescending, derisive, disdainful, haughty, sneering, supercilious, withering

contend verb **1** COMPETE, clash, contest, fight, jostle, strive, struggle, vie
2 ARGUE, affirm, allege, assert, dispute, hold, maintain

content¹ noun **1** MEANING, essence, gist, significance, substance
2 AMOUNT, capacity, load, measure, size, volume

content² adjective **1** SATISFIED, agreeable, at ease, comfortable, contented, fulfilled, willing to accept

▶ *verb* **2** SATISFY, appease, humor, indulge, mollify, placate, please
▶ *noun* **3** SATISFACTION, comfort, contentment, ease, gratification, peace of mind, pleasure
contented *adjective* SATISFIED, comfortable, content, glad, gratified, happy, pleased, serene, thankful
contentious *adjective* ARGUMENTATIVE, bickering, captious, cavilling, disputatious, quarrelsome, querulous, wrangling
contentment *noun* SATISFACTION, comfort, content, ease, equanimity, fulfillment, happiness, peace, pleasure, serenity
contents *plural noun* CONSTITUENTS, elements, ingredients, load
contest *noun* **1** COMPETITION, game, match, tournament, trial
2 STRUGGLE, battle, combat, conflict, controversy, dispute, fight
▶ *verb* **3** DISPUTE, argue, call in or into question, challenge, debate, doubt, object to, oppose, question
4 COMPETE, contend, fight, strive, vie
contestant *noun* COMPETITOR, candidate, contender, entrant, participant, player
context *noun* **1** CIRCUMSTANCES, ambience, conditions, situation
2 FRAME OF REFERENCE, background, connection, framework, relation
contingency *noun* POSSIBILITY, accident, chance, emergency, event, eventuality, happening, incident
continual *adjective* CONSTANT, frequent, incessant,

interminable, recurrent, regular, repeated, twenty-four-seven (*slang*), unremitting
continually *adverb* CONSTANTLY, all the time, always, forever, incessantly, interminably, nonstop, persistently, repeatedly, twenty-four-seven (*slang*)
continuation *noun* **1** CONTINUING, perpetuation, prolongation, resumption
2 ADDITION, extension, furtherance, postscript, sequel, supplement
continue *verb* **1** REMAIN, abide, carry on, endure, last, live on, persist, stay, survive
2 KEEP ON, carry on, go on, maintain, persevere, persist in, stick at, sustain
3 RESUME, carry on, pick up where one left off, proceed, recommence, return to, take up
continuing *adjective* LASTING, enduring, in progress, ongoing, sustained
continuity *noun* SEQUENCE, cohesion, connection, flow, progression, succession
continuous *adjective* CONSTANT, extended, prolonged, twenty-four-seven (*slang*), unbroken, unceasing, undivided, uninterrupted
contraband *noun* **1** SMUGGLING, black-marketing, bootlegging, trafficking
▶ *adjective* **2** SMUGGLED, banned, bootleg, forbidden, hot (*informal*), illegal, illicit, prohibited, unlawful
contract *noun* **1** AGREEMENT, arrangement, bargain, commitment, covenant, pact, settlement
▶ *verb* **2** AGREE, bargain, come to

terms, commit oneself, covenant, negotiate, pledge
3 SHORTEN, abbreviate, curtail, diminish, dwindle, lessen, narrow, reduce, shrink, shrivel
4 CATCH, acquire, be afflicted with, develop, get, go down with, incur

contraction *noun* SHORTENING, abbreviation, compression, narrowing, reduction, shrinkage, shriveling, tightening

contradict *verb* DENY, be at variance with, belie, challenge, controvert, fly in the face of, negate, rebut

contradiction *noun* DENIAL, conflict, contravention, incongruity, inconsistency, negation, opposite

contradictory *adjective* INCONSISTENT, conflicting, contrary, incompatible, opposed, opposite, paradoxical

contraption *noun* (*informal*) DEVICE, apparatus, contrivance, gadget, instrument, mechanism

contrary *noun* **1** OPPOSITE, antithesis, converse, reverse
▶ *adjective* **2** OPPOSED, adverse, clashing, contradictory, counter, discordant, hostile, inconsistent, opposite, paradoxical
3 PERVERSE, awkward, cantankerous, difficult, disobliging, intractable, obstinate, stroppy (*Brit. slang*), unaccommodating

contrast *noun* **1** DIFFERENCE, comparison, disparity, dissimilarity, distinction, divergence, foil, opposition
▶ *verb* **2** DIFFERENTIATE, compare, differ, distinguish, oppose, set in opposition, set off

contribute *verb* **1** GIVE, add,

bestow, chip in (*informal*), donate, provide, subscribe, supply
2 ▷▷ **contribute to** BE PARTLY RESPONSIBLE FOR, be conducive to, be instrumental in, help, lead to, tend to

contribution *noun* GIFT, addition, donation, grant, input, offering, subscription

contributor *noun* GIVER, donor, patron, subscriber, supporter

contrite *adjective* SORRY, chastened, conscience-stricken, humble, penitent, regretful, remorseful, repentant, sorrowful

contrivance *noun* **1** DEVICE, apparatus, appliance, contraption, gadget, implement, instrument, invention, machine, mechanism
2 PLAN, intrigue, machination, plot, ruse, scheme, stratagem, trick

contrive *verb* **1** BRING ABOUT, arrange, effect, manage, maneuver, plan, plot, scheme, succeed
2 DEVISE, concoct, construct, create, design, fabricate, improvise, invent, manufacture

contrived *adjective* FORCED, artificial, elaborate, labored, overdone, planned, strained, unnatural

control *noun* **1** POWER, authority, charge, command, guidance, management, oversight, supervision, supremacy
2 RESTRAINT, brake, check, curb, limitation, regulation
▶ *verb* **3** HAVE POWER OVER, administer, command, direct, govern, handle, have charge of, manage, manipulate, supervise
4 RESTRAIN, check, constrain, contain, curb, hold back, limit,

repress, subdue

controls *plural noun* INSTRUMENTS, console, control panel, dash, dashboard, dials

controversial *adjective* DISPUTED, at issue, contentious, debatable, disputable, open to question, under discussion

controversy *noun* ARGUMENT, altercation, debate, dispute, quarrel, row, squabble, wrangling

convalescence *noun* RECOVERY, improvement, recuperation, rehabilitation, return to health

convalescent *adjective* RECOVERING, getting better, improving, mending, on the mend, recuperating

convene *verb* GATHER, assemble, bring together, call, come together, congregate, convoke, meet, summon

convenience *noun* 1 AVAILABILITY, accessibility, advantage, appropriateness, benefit, fitness, suitability, usefulness, utility
2 APPLIANCE, amenity, comfort, facility, help, labor-saving device

convenient *adjective* 1 USEFUL, appropriate, fit, handy, helpful, labor-saving, serviceable, suitable, timely
2 NEARBY, accessible, at hand, available, close at hand, handy, just round the corner, within reach

convention *noun* 1 CUSTOM, code, etiquette, practice, propriety, protocol, tradition, usage
2 AGREEMENT, bargain, contract, pact, protocol, treaty
3 ASSEMBLY, conference, congress, convocation, council, meeting

conventional *adjective*
1 ORDINARY, accepted, customary, normal, orthodox, regular,

standard, traditional, usual
2 UNORIGINAL, banal, hackneyed, prosaic, routine, run-of-the-mill, stereotyped

converge *verb* COME TOGETHER, coincide, combine, gather, join, meet, merge

conversation *noun* TALK, chat, conference, dialogue, discourse, discussion, gossip, tête-à-tête

converse¹ *verb* TALK, chat, chew the fat (*slang*), commune, confer, discourse, exchange views

converse² *noun* 1 OPPOSITE, antithesis, contrary, obverse, other side of the coin, reverse
▶ *adjective* 2 OPPOSITE, contrary, counter, reverse, reversed, transposed

conversion *noun* 1 CHANGE, metamorphosis, transformation
2 ADAPTATION, alteration, modification, reconstruction, remodeling, reorganization

convert *verb* 1 CHANGE, alter, transform, transpose, turn
2 ADAPT, apply, customize, modify, remodel, reorganize, restyle, revise
3 REFORM, convince, proselytize
▶ *noun* 4 NEOPHYTE, disciple, proselyte

convex *adjective* ROUNDED, bulging, gibbous, protuberant

convey *verb* 1 COMMUNICATE, disclose, impart, make known, relate, reveal, tell
2 CARRY, bear, bring, conduct, fetch, guide, move, send, transport

convict *verb* 1 FIND GUILTY, condemn, imprison, pronounce guilty, sentence
▶ *noun* 2 PRISONER, criminal, culprit, felon, jailbird, lag (*slang*), perp (*informal*)

conviction *noun* 1 BELIEF, creed, faith, opinion, persuasion, principle, tenet, view
2 CONFIDENCE, assurance, certainty, certitude, firmness, reliance

convince *verb* PERSUADE, assure, bring round, prevail upon, satisfy, sway, win over

convincing *adjective* PERSUASIVE, cogent, conclusive, credible, impressive, plausible, powerful, telling

convulse *verb* SHAKE, agitate, churn up, derange, disorder, disturb, twist, work

convulsion *noun* SPASM, contraction, cramp, fit, paroxysm, seizure

cool *adjective* 1 COLD, chilled, chilly, nippy, refreshing
2 CALM, collected, composed, relaxed, sedate, self-controlled, self-possessed, unemotional, unruffled
3 UNFRIENDLY, aloof, distant, indifferent, lukewarm, offhand, standoffish, unenthusiastic, unwelcoming
4 (*informal*) FASHIONABLE, hip, phat (*slang*), trendy (*informal*)
▶ *verb* 5 CHILL, cool off, freeze, lose heat, refrigerate
▶ *noun* 6 (*slang*) CALMNESS, composure, control, poise, self-control, self-discipline, self-possession, temper

cooperate *verb* WORK TOGETHER, collaborate, combine, conspire, coordinate, join forces, pool resources, pull together

cooperation *noun* TEAMWORK, collaboration, combined effort, esprit de corps, give-and-take, unity

cooperative *adjective* 1 HELPFUL, accommodating, obliging, onside (*informal*), responsive, supportive
2 SHARED, collective, combined, joint

coordinate *verb* BRING TOGETHER, harmonize, integrate, match, organize, synchronize, systematize

cope *verb* 1 MANAGE, carry on, get by (*informal*), hold one's own, make the grade, struggle through, survive
2 ▷▷ **cope with** DEAL WITH, contend with, grapple with, handle, struggle with, weather, wrestle with

copious *adjective* ABUNDANT, ample, bountiful, extensive, full, lavish, plentiful, profuse

copy *noun* 1 REPRODUCTION, counterfeit, duplicate, facsimile, forgery, imitation, likeness, model, replica
▶ *verb* 2 REPRODUCE, counterfeit, duplicate, replicate, transcribe
3 IMITATE, ape, emulate, follow, mimic, mirror, repeat

cord *noun* ROPE, line, string, twine

cordial *adjective* WARM, affable, agreeable, cheerful, congenial, friendly, genial, hearty, sociable

cordon *noun* 1 CHAIN, barrier, line, ring
▶ *verb* 2 ▷▷ **cordon off** SURROUND, close off, encircle, enclose, fence off, isolate, picket, separate

core *noun* CENTER, crux, essence, gist, heart, kernel, nub, nucleus, pith

corner *noun* 1 ANGLE, bend, crook, joint
2 SPACE, hideaway, hideout, nook, retreat
▶ *verb* 3 TRAP, run to earth
4 *as in* **corner the market** MONOPOLIZE, dominate, engross,

hog (slang)

corny adjective (slang) UNORIGINAL, banal, dull, hackneyed, old-fashioned, old hat, stale, stereotyped, trite

corporation noun 1 BUSINESS, association, corporate body, society
2 TOWN COUNCIL, civic authorities, council, municipal authorities

corps noun TEAM, band, company, detachment, division, regiment, squadron, troop, unit

corpse noun BODY, cadaver, carcass, remains, stiff (slang)

correct adjective 1 TRUE, accurate, exact, faultless, flawless, O.K. or okay (informal), precise, right
2 PROPER, acceptable, appropriate, fitting, kosher (informal), O.K. or okay (informal), seemly, standard
▶ verb 3 RECTIFY, adjust, amend, cure, emend, redress, reform, remedy, right
4 PUNISH, admonish, chasten, chastise, chide, discipline, rebuke, reprimand, reprove

correction noun 1 RECTIFICATION, adjustment, alteration, amendment, emendation, improvement, modification
2 PUNISHMENT, admonition, castigation, chastisement, discipline, reformation, reproof

correctly adverb RIGHTLY, accurately, perfectly, precisely, properly, right

correctness noun 1 TRUTH, accuracy, exactitude, exactness, faultlessness, fidelity, preciseness, precision, regularity
2 DECORUM, civility, good breeding, propriety, seemliness

correspond verb 1 BE CONSISTENT, accord, agree, conform, fit, harmonize, match, square, tally
2 COMMUNICATE, exchange letters, keep in touch, write

correspondence noun 1 LETTERS, communication, mail, post, writing
2 RELATION, agreement, coincidence, comparison, conformity, correlation, harmony, match, similarity

correspondent noun 1 LETTER WRITER, pen friend or pal
2 REPORTER, contributor, journalist

corresponding adjective RELATED, analogous, answering, complementary, equivalent, matching, reciprocal, similar

corridor noun PASSAGE, aisle, alley, hallway, passageway

corroborate verb SUPPORT, authenticate, back up, bear out, confirm, endorse, ratify, substantiate, validate

corrode verb EAT AWAY, consume, corrupt, erode, gnaw, oxidize, rust, wear away

corrosive adjective CORRODING, caustic, consuming, erosive, virulent, vitriolic, wasting, wearing

corrupt adjective 1 DISHONEST, bent (slang), bribable, crooked (informal), fraudulent, unprincipled, unscrupulous, venal
2 DEPRAVED, debased, degenerate, dissolute, profligate, vicious
3 DISTORTED, altered, doctored, falsified
▶ verb 4 BRIBE, buy off, entice, fix (informal), grease (someone's) palm (slang), lure, suborn
5 DEPRAVE, debauch, pervert, subvert
6 DISTORT, doctor, tamper with

corruption noun 1 DISHONESTY, bribery, extortion, fraud,

shady dealings (*informal*), unscrupulousness, venality
2 DEPRAVITY, decadence, evil, immorality, perversion, vice, wickedness
3 DISTORTION, doctoring, falsification

corset *noun* GIRDLE, belt, bodice

cosmetic *adjective* BEAUTIFYING, nonessential, superficial, surface

cosmic *adjective* UNIVERSAL, stellar

cosmopolitan *adjective*
1 SOPHISTICATED, broad-minded, catholic, open-minded, universal, urbane, well-traveled, worldly-wise
▶ *noun* **2** MAN *or* WOMAN OF THE WORLD, jet-setter, sophisticate

cost *noun* **1** PRICE, amount, charge, damage (*informal*), expense, outlay, payment, worth
2 LOSS, damage, detriment, expense, harm, hurt, injury, penalty, sacrifice, suffering
▶ *verb* **3** SELL AT, come to, command a price of, set (someone) back (*informal*)
4 LOSE, do disservice to, harm, hurt, injure

costly *adjective* **1** EXPENSIVE, dear, exorbitant, extortionate, highly-priced, steep (*informal*), stiff
2 DAMAGING, catastrophic, deleterious, disastrous, harmful, loss-making, ruinous

costs *plural noun* EXPENSES, budget, outgoings, overheads

costume *noun* OUTFIT, apparel, attire, clothing, dress, ensemble, garb, livery, uniform

cottage *noun* CABIN, chalet, hut, lodge, shack

cough *noun* **1** FROG *or* TICKLE IN ONE'S THROAT, bark, hack
▶ *verb* **2** CLEAR ONE'S THROAT, bark, hack

council *noun* GOVERNING BODY, assembly, board, cabinet, committee, conference, congress, convention, panel, parliament

counsel *noun* **1** ADVICE, direction, guidance, information, recommendation, suggestion, warning
2 LEGAL ADVISER, advocate, attorney, barrister, lawyer, solicitor
▶ *verb* **3** ADVISE, advocate, exhort, instruct, recommend, urge, warn

count *verb* **1** ADD (UP), calculate, compute, enumerate, number, reckon, tally, tot up
2 MATTER, be important, carry weight, rate, signify, tell, weigh
3 CONSIDER, deem, judge, look upon, rate, regard, think
4 TAKE INTO ACCOUNT *or* CONSIDERATION, include, number among
▶ *noun* **5** CALCULATION, computation, enumeration, numbering, poll, reckoning, sum, tally

counter *verb* **1** RETALIATE, answer, hit back, meet, oppose, parry, resist, respond, ward off
▶ *adverb* **2** OPPOSITE TO, against, at variance with, contrariwise, conversely, in defiance of, versus

counteract *verb* ACT AGAINST, foil, frustrate, negate, neutralize, offset, resist, thwart

counterbalance *verb* OFFSET, balance, compensate, make up for, set off

counterfeit *adjective* **1** FAKE, bogus, false, forged, imitation, phoney *or* phony (*informal*), sham, simulated
▶ *noun* **2** FAKE, copy, forgery, fraud, imitation, phoney *or* phony (*informal*), reproduction, sham

▶ *verb* 3 FAKE, copy, fabricate, feign, forge, imitate, impersonate, pretend, sham, simulate

countermand *verb* CANCEL, annul, override, repeal, rescind, retract, reverse, revoke

counterpart *noun* OPPOSITE NUMBER, complement, equal, fellow, match, mate, supplement, tally, twin

countless *adjective* INNUMERABLE, endless, immeasurable, incalculable, infinite, legion, limitless, myriad, numberless, uncountable, untold

count on *or* **upon** *verb* DEPEND ON, bank on, believe (in), lean on, pin one's faith on, reckon on, rely on, take for granted, take on trust, trust

country *noun* 1 NATION, commonwealth, kingdom, people, realm, state
2 TERRITORY, land, region, terrain
3 PEOPLE, citizens, community, inhabitants, nation, populace, public, society
4 COUNTRYSIDE, backwoods, farmland, green belt, outback (*Austral. & N.Z.*), provinces, sticks (*informal*)

countryside *noun* COUNTRY, farmland, green belt, outback (*Austral. & N.Z.*), outdoors, sticks (*informal*)

count up *verb* ADD, reckon up, sum, tally, total

county *noun* PROVINCE, shire

coup *noun* MASTERSTROKE, accomplishment, action, deed, exploit, feat, maneuver, stunt

couple *noun* 1 PAIR, brace, duo, two, twosome
▶ *verb* 2 LINK, connect, hitch, join, marry, pair, unite, wed, yoke

coupon *noun* SLIP, card, certificate, ticket, token, voucher

courage *noun* BRAVERY, daring, fearlessness, gallantry, heroism, mettle, nerve, pluck, resolution, valor

courageous *adjective* BRAVE, bold, daring, fearless, gallant, gritty, intrepid, lion-hearted, stouthearted, valiant

courier *noun* 1 GUIDE, representative
2 MESSENGER, bearer, carrier, envoy, runner

course *noun* 1 CLASSES, curriculum, lectures, program, schedule
2 PROGRESSION, development, flow, movement, order, progress, sequence, unfolding
3 ROUTE, direction, line, passage, path, road, track, trajectory, way
4 RACECOURSE, cinder track, circuit
5 PROCEDURE, behavior, conduct, manner, method, mode, plan, policy, program
6 PERIOD, duration, lapse, passage, passing, sweep, term, time
7 ▷▷ **of course** NATURALLY, certainly, definitely, indubitably, needless to say, obviously, undoubtedly, without a doubt
▶ *verb* 8 RUN, flow, gush, race, speed, stream, surge
9 HUNT, chase, follow, pursue, stalk

court *noun* 1 LAW COURT, bar, bench, tribunal
2 COURTYARD, cloister, piazza, plaza, quad (*informal*), quadrangle, square, yard
3 PALACE, hall, manor
4 ROYAL HOUSEHOLD, attendants, cortege, entourage, retinue, suite, train

▶ *verb* 5 WOO, date, go (out) with, run after, serenade, set one's cap at, take out, walk out with
6 CULTIVATE, brown-nose (*slang*), curry favor with, fawn upon, flatter, pander to, seek, solicit
7 INVITE, attract, bring about, incite, prompt, provoke, seek

courteous *adjective* POLITE, affable, attentive, civil, gallant, gracious, refined, respectful, urbane, well-mannered

courtesy *noun* 1 POLITENESS, affability, civility, courteousness, gallantry, good manners, graciousness, urbanity
2 FAVOR, benevolence, indulgence, kindness

courtier *noun* ATTENDANT, follower, squire

courtly *adjective* CEREMONIOUS, chivalrous, dignified, elegant, formal, gallant, polished, refined, stately, urbane

courtyard *noun* YARD, enclosure, quad, quadrangle

cove *noun* BAY, anchorage, inlet, sound

covenant *noun* 1 PROMISE, agreement, arrangement, commitment, contract, pact, pledge
▶ *verb* 2 PROMISE, agree, contract, pledge, stipulate, undertake

cover *verb* 1 CLOTHE, dress, envelop, put on, wrap
2 OVERLAY, coat, daub, encase, envelop
3 SUBMERGE, engulf, flood, overrun, wash over
4 CONCEAL, cloak, disguise, enshroud, hide, mask, obscure, shroud, veil
5 TRAVEL OVER, cross, pass through *or* over, traverse
6 PROTECT, defend, guard, shield

7 REPORT, describe, investigate, narrate, relate, tell of, write up
▶ *noun* 8 COVERING, canopy, case, coating, envelope, jacket, lid, top, wrapper
9 DISGUISE, façade, front, mask, pretext, screen, smoke screen, veil
10 PROTECTION, camouflage, concealment, defense, guard, shelter, shield
11 INSURANCE, compensation, indemnity, protection, reimbursement

covering *adjective* 1 EXPLANATORY, accompanying, descriptive, introductory
▶ *noun* 2 COVER, blanket, casing, coating, layer, wrapping

cover-up *noun* CONCEALMENT, complicity, conspiracy, front, smoke screen, whitewash (*informal*)

cover up *verb* CONCEAL, draw a veil over, hide, hush up, suppress, sweep under the carpet, whitewash (*informal*)

covet *verb* LONG FOR, aspire to, crave, desire, envy, lust after, set one's heart on, yearn for

covetous *adjective* ENVIOUS, acquisitive, avaricious, close-fisted, grasping, greedy, jealous, rapacious, yearning

coward *noun* WIMP (*informal*), chicken (*slang*), scaredy-cat (*informal*), yellow-belly (*slang*)

cowardice *noun* FAINT-HEARTEDNESS, fearfulness, spinelessness, weakness

cowardly *adjective* FAINT-HEARTED, chicken (*slang*), craven, fearful, scared, soft, spineless, timorous, weak, yellow (*informal*)

cowboy *noun* COWHAND, cattleman, drover, gaucho (*S. American*), herdsman, rancher, stockman

cower verb CRINGE, draw back, flinch, grovel, quail, shrink, tremble

coy adjective SHY, bashful, demure, modest, reserved, retiring, shrinking, timid

cozy adjective SNUG, comfortable, comfy (informal), homely, homey, intimate, sheltered, tucked up, warm

crack verb 1 BREAK, burst, cleave, fracture, snap, splinter, split
2 SNAP, burst, crash, detonate, explode, pop, ring
3 GIVE IN, break down, collapse, give way, go to pieces, lose control, succumb, yield
4 (informal) HIT, clip (informal), clout (informal), cuff, slap, smack, whack
5 SOLVE, decipher, fathom, get the answer to, work out
▶ noun 6 SNAP, burst, clap, crash, explosion, pop, report
7 BREAK, chink, cleft, cranny, crevice, fissure, fracture, gap, rift
8 (informal) BLOW, clip (informal), clout (informal), cuff, slap, smack, whack
9 (informal) JOKE, dig, funny remark, gag (informal), jibe, quip, wisecrack (informal), witticism
▶ adjective 10 (slang) FIRST-CLASS, ace, choice, elite, excellent, first-rate, hand-picked, superior, world-class

crackdown noun SUPPRESSION, clampdown, crushing, repression

cracked adjective BROKEN, chipped, damaged, defective, faulty, flawed, imperfect, split

cradle noun 1 CRIB, bassinet, cot, Moses basket
2 BIRTHPLACE, beginning, fount, fountainhead, origin, source, spring, wellspring

▶ verb 3 HOLD, lull, nestle, nurse, rock, support

craft noun 1 OCCUPATION, business, employment, handicraft, pursuit, trade, vocation, work
2 SKILL, ability, aptitude, art, artistry, expertise, ingenuity, know-how (informal), technique, workmanship
3 VESSEL, aircraft, boat, plane, ship, spacecraft

craftsman noun SKILLED WORKER, artisan, maker, master, smith, technician, wright

craftsmanship noun WORKMANSHIP, artistry, expertise, mastery, technique

crafty adjective CUNNING, artful, calculating, devious, sharp, shrewd, sly, subtle, wily

crag noun ROCK, bluff, peak, pinnacle, tor

cram verb 1 STUFF, compress, force, jam, pack in, press, shove, squeeze
2 OVEREAT, glut, gorge, satiate, stuff
3 STUDY, bone up (informal), mug up (Brit. slang), review, revise, swot

cramp¹ noun SPASM, ache, contraction, convulsion, pain, pang, stitch, twinge

cramp² verb RESTRICT, constrain, hamper, handicap, hinder, impede, inhibit, obstruct

cramped adjective CLOSED IN, confined, congested, crowded, hemmed in, overcrowded, packed, uncomfortable

cranny noun CREVICE, chink, cleft, crack, fissure, gap, hole, opening

crash noun 1 COLLISION, accident, bump, pile-up (informal), prang (informal), smash, wreck
2 SMASH, bang, boom, clang, clash, clatter, din, racket, thunder
3 COLLAPSE, debacle, depression,

downfall, failure, ruin
▶ *verb* 4 COLLIDE, bump (into),
crash-land (*an aircraft*), drive into,
have an accident, hit, plow into,
wreck
5 COLLAPSE, be ruined, fail, fold,
fold up, go belly up (*informal*), go
bust (*informal*), go to the wall,
go under
6 HURTLE, fall headlong, give way,
lurch, overbalance, plunge, topple
crass *adjective* INSENSITIVE,
boorish, gross, indelicate, oafish,
stupid, unrefined, witless
crate *noun* CONTAINER, box, case,
packing case, tea chest
crater *noun* HOLLOW, depression,
dip
crave *verb* 1 LONG FOR, desire,
hanker after, hope for, lust after,
want, yearn for
2 BEG, ask, beseech, entreat,
implore, petition, plead for, pray
for, seek, solicit, supplicate
craving *noun* LONGING, appetite,
desire, hankering, hope, hunger,
thirst, yearning, yen (*informal*)
crawl *verb* 1 CREEP, advance slowly,
inch, slither, worm one's way,
wriggle, writhe
2 GROVEL, brown-nose (*slang*),
creep, fawn, humble oneself, kiss
ass (*slang*), toady
3 BE FULL OF, be alive, be overrun
(*slang*), swarm, teem
craze *noun* FAD, enthusiasm,
fashion, infatuation, mania, rage,
trend, vogue
crazy *adjective* 1 RIDICULOUS,
absurd, foolish, idiotic, ill-
conceived, ludicrous, nonsensical,
preposterous, senseless
2 FANATICAL, devoted,
enthusiastic, infatuated, mad,
passionate, wild (*informal*)
3 INSANE, crazed, demented,

deranged, mad, nuts (*slang*), out of
one's mind, unbalanced
creak *verb* SQUEAK, grate, grind,
groan, scrape, scratch, screech
cream *noun* 1 LOTION, cosmetic,
emulsion, essence, liniment, oil,
ointment, paste, salve, unguent
2 BEST, crème de la crème, elite,
flower, pick, prime
▶ *adjective* 3 OFF-WHITE, yellowish-
white
creamy *adjective* SMOOTH, buttery,
milky, rich, soft, velvety
crease *noun* 1 LINE, corrugation,
fold, groove, ridge, wrinkle
▶ *verb* 2 WRINKLE, corrugate,
crumple, double up, fold, rumple,
screw up
create *verb* 1 MAKE, compose,
devise, formulate, invent,
originate, produce, spawn
2 CAUSE, bring about, lead to,
occasion
3 APPOINT, constitute, establish,
install, invest, make, set up
creation *noun* 1 MAKING,
conception, formation,
generation, genesis, procreation
2 SETTING UP, development,
establishment, formation,
foundation, inception,
institution, production
3 INVENTION, achievement,
brainchild (*informal*), concoction,
handiwork, magnum opus, pièce
de résistance, production
4 UNIVERSE, cosmos, nature, world
creative *adjective* IMAGINATIVE,
artistic, clever, gifted, ingenious,
inspired, inventive, original,
visionary
creativity *noun* IMAGINATION,
cleverness, ingenuity, inspiration,
inventiveness, originality
creator *noun* MAKER, architect,
author, designer, father, inventor,

originator, prime mover

creature noun 1 LIVING THING, animal, beast, being, brute 2 PERSON, human being, individual, man, mortal, soul, woman

credentials plural noun CERTIFICATION, authorization, document, license, papers, passport, reference(s), testimonial

credibility noun BELIEVABILITY, integrity, plausibility, reliability, trustworthiness

credible adjective 1 BELIEVABLE, conceivable, imaginable, likely, plausible, possible, probable, reasonable, thinkable 2 RELIABLE, dependable, honest, sincere, trustworthy, trusty

credit noun 1 PRAISE, acclaim, acknowledgment, approval, commendation, honor, kudos, recognition, tribute 2 as in **be a credit to** SOURCE OF SATISFACTION or PRIDE, feather in one's cap, honor 3 PRESTIGE, esteem, good name, influence, position, regard, reputation, repute, standing, status 4 BELIEF, confidence, credence, faith, reliance, trust 5 ▷▷ **on credit** ON ACCOUNT, by deferred payment, by installments, on hire-purchase, on the card, on (the) H.P., on the slate (informal), on tick (informal) ▶ verb 6 BELIEVE, accept, have faith in, rely on, trust 7 ▷▷ **credit with** ATTRIBUTE TO, ascribe to, assign to, impute to

creditable adjective PRAISEWORTHY, admirable, commendable, honorable, laudable, reputable, respectable, worthy

credulity noun GULLIBILITY, blind faith, credulousness, naivety

creed noun BELIEF, articles of faith, catechism, credo, doctrine, dogma, principles

creek noun 1 INLET, bay, bight, cove, firth or frith (Scot.) 2 (U.S., Canad., Austral., & N.Z.) STREAM, bayou, brook, rivulet, runnel, tributary, watercourse

creep verb 1 SNEAK, approach unnoticed, skulk, slink, steal, tiptoe 2 CRAWL, glide, slither, squirm, wriggle, writhe ▶ noun 3 (slang) BOOTLICKER BROWN-NOSER (slang), crawler (slang), scuzzbucket (slang), sneak, sycophant, toady 4 (slang) JERK, loser, lowlife, pervert, scumbag (slang), scuzzbucket (slang)

creeper noun CLIMBING PLANT, rambler, runner, trailing plant, vine (chiefly U.S.)

creeps plural noun ▷▷ **give one the creeps** (informal) DISGUST, frighten, make one's hair stand on end, make one squirm, repel, repulse, scare

creepy adjective (informal) DISTURBING, eerie, frightening, hair-raising, macabre, menacing, scary (informal), sinister

crescent noun MENISCUS, new moon, sickle

crest noun 1 TOP, apex, crown, highest point, peak, pinnacle, ridge, summit 2 TUFT, comb, crown, mane, plume 3 EMBLEM, badge, bearings, device, insignia, symbol

crestfallen adjective DISAPPOINTED, dejected, depressed, despondent, discouraged, disheartened, downcast, downhearted

crevice noun GAP, chink, cleft, crack, cranny, fissure, hole, opening, slit

crew noun 1 (SHIP'S) COMPANY, hands, (ship's) complement
2 TEAM, corps, gang, posse, squad
3 (informal) CROWD, band, bunch (informal), gang, horde, mob, pack, set

crib noun 1 (informal) TRANSLATION, key
2 CRADLE, bassinet, bed, cot
3 MANGER, rack, stall
▸ verb 4 (informal) COPY, cheat, pirate, plagiarize, purloin, steal

crime noun 1 OFFENSE, felony, misdeed, misdemeanor, transgression, trespass, unlawful act, violation
2 LAWBREAKING, corruption, illegality, misconduct, vice, wrongdoing

criminal noun 1 LAWBREAKER, convict, crook (informal), culprit, felon, offender, perp (informal), sinner, villain
▸ adjective 2 UNLAWFUL, corrupt, crooked (informal), illegal, illicit, immoral, lawless, wicked, wrong
3 DISGRACEFUL, deplorable, foolish, preposterous, ridiculous, scandalous, senseless

cringe verb 1 SHRINK, cower, draw back, flinch, recoil, shy, wince
2 GROVEL, bootlick (informal), crawl; creep, fawn, kowtow, pander to, toady

cripple verb 1 DISABLE, hamstring, incapacitate, lame, maim, paralyze, weaken
2 DAMAGE, destroy, impair, put out of action, put paid to, ruin, spoil

crippled adjective DISABLED, challenged, handicapped, incapacitated, laid up (informal), lame, paralyzed

crisis noun 1 CRITICAL POINT, climax, crunch (informal), crux, culmination, height, moment of truth, turning point
2 EMERGENCY, deep water, dire straits, meltdown (informal), panic stations (informal), plight, predicament, trouble

crisp adjective 1 CRUNCHY, brittle, crispy, crumbly, firm, fresh
2 CLEAN, neat, smart, spruce, tidy, trim, well-groomed, well-pressed
3 BRACING, brisk, fresh, invigorating, refreshing

criterion noun STANDARD, bench mark, gauge, measure, principle, rule, test, touchstone, yardstick

critic noun 1 JUDGE, analyst, authority, commentator, connoisseur, expert, pundit, reviewer
2 FAULT-FINDER, attacker, detractor, knocker (informal)

critical adjective 1 CRUCIAL, all-important, decisive, pivotal, precarious, pressing, serious, urgent, vital
2 DISPARAGING, captious, censorious, derogatory, disapproving, fault-finding, nagging, nit-picking (informal), scathing
3 ANALYTICAL, discerning, discriminating, fastidious, judicious, penetrating, perceptive

criticism noun 1 FAULT-FINDING, bad press, censure, character assassination, disapproval, disparagement, flak (informal), stick (slang)
2 ANALYSIS, appraisal, appreciation, assessment, comment, commentary, critique, evaluation, judgment

criticize verb FIND FAULT WITH, carp, censure, condemn, disapprove of, disparage, knock (informal), put down, slate (informal)

croak verb SQUAWK, caw, grunt, utter or speak huskily, wheeze

crook noun CRIMINAL, cheat, racketeer, robber, rogue, perp (informal), shark, swindler, thief, villain

crooked adjective 1 BENT, curved, deformed, distorted, hooked, irregular, misshapen, out of shape, twisted, warped, zigzag
2 AT AN ANGLE, askew, awry, lopsided, off-center, skew-whiff (Brit. informal), slanting, squint, uneven
3 DISHONEST, bent (slang), corrupt, criminal, fraudulent, illegal, shady (informal), underhand, unlawful

croon verb SING, hum, purr, warble

crop noun 1 PRODUCE, fruits, gathering, harvest, reaping, vintage, yield
▶ verb 2 CUT, clip, lop, pare, prune, shear, snip, trim
3 GRAZE, browse, nibble

crop up verb HAPPEN, appear, arise, emerge, occur, spring up, turn up

cross verb 1 GO ACROSS, bridge, cut across, extend over, move across, pass over, span, traverse
2 INTERSECT, crisscross, intertwine
3 OPPOSE, block, impede, interfere, obstruct, resist
4 INTERBREED, blend, crossbreed, cross-fertilize, cross-pollinate, hybridize, intercross, mix, mongrelize
▶ noun 5 CRUCIFIX, rood
6 CROSSROADS, crossing, intersection, junction

7 MIXTURE, amalgam, blend, combination
8 TROUBLE, affliction, burden, grief, load, misfortune, trial, tribulation, woe, worry
▶ adjective 9 ANGRY, annoyed, grumpy, ill-tempered, in a bad mood, irascible, put out, short
10 TRANSVERSE, crosswise, diagonal, intersecting, oblique

cross-examine verb QUESTION, grill (informal), interrogate, pump, quiz

cross out or off verb STRIKE OFF or OUT, blue-pencil, cancel, delete, eliminate, score off or out

crouch verb BEND DOWN, bow, duck, hunch, kneel, squat, stoop

crow verb GLOAT, blow one's own trumpet, boast, brag, exult, strut, swagger, triumph

crowd noun 1 MULTITUDE, army, horde, host, mass, mob, pack, swarm, throng
2 GROUP, bunch (informal), circle, clique, lot, set
3 AUDIENCE, attendance, gate, house, spectators
▶ verb 4 FLOCK, congregate, gather, mass, stream, surge, swarm, throng
5 SQUEEZE, bundle, congest, cram, pack, pile

crowded adjective PACKED, busy, congested, cramped, full, jam-packed, swarming, teeming

crown noun 1 CORONET, circlet, diadem, tiara
2 LAUREL WREATH, garland, honor, laurels, prize, trophy, wreath
3 HIGH POINT, apex, crest, pinnacle, summit, tip, top
▶ verb 4 HONOR, adorn, dignify, festoon
5 CAP, be the climax or culmination of, complete, finish,

perfect, put the finishing touch
to, round off, top

6 (*slang*) STRIKE, belt (*informal*),
biff (*slang*), box, cuff, hit over the
head, punch

Crown *noun* 1 MONARCHY, royalty,
sovereignty

2 MONARCH, emperor *or* empress,
king *or* queen, ruler, sovereign

crucial *adjective* 1 VITAL, essential,
high-priority, important,
momentous, pressing, urgent

2 CRITICAL, central, decisive,
pivotal

crucify *verb* EXECUTE, persecute,
torment, torture

crude *adjective* 1 PRIMITIVE, clumsy,
makeshift, rough, rough-and-
ready, rudimentary, unpolished

2 VULGAR, coarse, dirty, gross,
indecent, obscene, off-color,
scuzzy (*slang*), smutty, tasteless,
uncouth

3 UNREFINED, natural, raw,
unprocessed

crudely *adverb* VULGARLY, bluntly,
coarsely, impolitely, roughly,
rudely, tastelessly

crudity *noun* 1 ROUGHNESS,
clumsiness, crudeness

2 VULGARITY, coarseness,
impropriety, indecency,
indelicacy, obscenity, smuttiness

cruel *adjective* 1 BRUTAL, barbarous,
callous, hard-hearted, heartless,
inhumane, malevolent, sadistic,
spiteful, unkind, vicious

2 MERCILESS, pitiless, ruthless,
unrelenting

cruelly *adverb* 1 BRUTALLY,
barbarously, callously, heartlessly,
in cold blood, mercilessly,
pitilessly, sadistically, spitefully

2 BITTERLY, deeply, fearfully,
grievously, monstrously, severely

cruelty *noun* BRUTALITY,

barbarity, callousness, depravity,
fiendishness, inhumanity,
mercilessness, ruthlessness,
spitefulness

cruise *noun* 1 SAIL, boat trip, sea
trip, voyage

▶ *verb* 2 SAIL, coast, voyage

3 TRAVEL ALONG, coast, drift, keep
a steady pace

crumb *noun* BIT, fragment, grain,
morsel, scrap, shred, soupçon

crumble *verb* 1 DISINTEGRATE,
collapse, decay, degenerate,
deteriorate, fall apart, go to pieces,
go to rack and ruin, tumble down

2 CRUSH, fragment, granulate,
grind, pound, powder, pulverize

crummy *adjective* (*informal*)
1 DESPICABLE, contemptible, lousy
(*slang*), mean, scuzzy (*slang*)

2 INFERIOR, deficient, inadequate,
lousy (*slang*), of poor quality, poor,
substandard

3 UNWELL, below par, off color,
under the weather (*informal*)

crumple *verb* 1 CRUSH, crease,
rumple, screw up, scrumple,
wrinkle

2 COLLAPSE, break down, cave in,
fall, give way, go to pieces

crunch *verb* 1 CHOMP, champ,
chew noisily, grind, munch

▶ *noun* 2 (*informal*) CRITICAL POINT,
crisis, crux, emergency, moment
of truth, test

crusade *noun* CAMPAIGN, cause,
drive, movement, push

crush *verb* 1 SQUASH, break,
compress, press, pulverize,
squeeze

2 OVERCOME, conquer, overpower,
overwhelm, put down, quell,
stamp out, subdue

3 HUMILIATE, abash, mortify, put
down (*slang*), quash, shame

▶ *noun* 4 CROWD, huddle, jam

crust *noun* LAYER, coating, covering, shell, skin, surface

crusty *adjective* 1 CRISPY, hard
2 IRRITABLE, cantankerous, cross, gruff, prickly, short-tempered, testy

cry *verb* 1 WEEP, blubber, shed tears, snivel, sob
2 SHOUT, bawl, bellow, call out, exclaim, howl, roar, scream, shriek, yell
▶ *noun* 3 WEEPING, blubbering, snivelling, sob, sobbing, weep
4 SHOUT, bellow, call, exclamation, howl, roar, scream, screech, shriek, yell
5 APPEAL, plea

cub *noun* YOUNG, offspring, whelp

cuckoo *adjective* (*slang*) INSANE, bonkers (*informal*), crazy, daft (*informal*), foolish, idiotic, nuts (*slang*), out of one's mind, stupid

cuddle *verb* HUG, bill and coo, cosset, embrace, fondle, pet, snuggle

cudgel *noun* CLUB, baton, bludgeon, cosh (*Brit.*), stick, truncheon

cue *noun* SIGNAL, catchword, hint, key, prompting, reminder, sign, suggestion

cul-de-sac *noun* DEAD END, blind alley

culminate *verb* END UP, climax, close, come to a climax, come to a head, conclude, finish, wind up

culmination *noun* CLIMAX, acme, conclusion, consummation, finale, peak, pinnacle, zenith

culpable *adjective* BLAMEWORTHY, at fault, found wanting, guilty, in the wrong, to blame, wrong

culprit *noun* OFFENDER, criminal, evildoer, felon, guilty party, miscreant, perp (*informal*), transgressor, wrongdoer

cult *noun* 1 SECT, clique, faction, religion, school
2 DEVOTION, idolization, worship

cultivate *verb* 1 FARM, plant, plow, tend, till, work
2 DEVELOP, foster, improve, promote, refine
3 COURT, dance attendance upon, run after, seek out

cultivation *noun* 1 FARMING, gardening, husbandry, planting, plowing, tillage
2 DEVELOPMENT, encouragement, fostering, furtherance, nurture, patronage, promotion, support

cultural *adjective* ARTISTIC, civilizing, edifying, educational, enlightening, enriching, humane, liberal

culture *noun* 1 CIVILIZATION, customs, lifestyle, mores, society, way of life
2 REFINEMENT, education, enlightenment, good taste, sophistication, urbanity
3 FARMING, cultivation, husbandry

cultured *adjective* REFINED, educated, enlightened, highbrow, sophisticated, urbane, well-informed, well-read

culvert *noun* DRAIN, channel, conduit, gutter, watercourse

cumbersome *adjective* AWKWARD, bulky, burdensome, heavy, unmanageable, unwieldy, weighty

cunning *adjective* 1 CRAFTY, artful, devious, Machiavellian, sharp, shifty, sly, wily
2 SKILLFUL, imaginative, ingenious
▶ *noun* 3 CRAFTINESS, artfulness, deviousness, guile, slyness, trickery
4 SKILL, artifice, cleverness,

ingenuity, subtlety

cup noun 1 MUG, beaker, bowl, chalice, goblet, teacup
2 TROPHY

cupboard noun CABINET, press

curb noun 1 RESTRAINT, brake, bridle, check, control, deterrent, limitation, rein
▶ verb 2 RESTRAIN, check, control, hinder, impede, inhibit, restrict, retard, suppress

cure verb 1 MAKE BETTER, correct, ease, heal, mend, relieve, remedy, restore
2 PRESERVE, dry, pickle, salt, smoke
▶ noun 3 REMEDY, antidote, medicine, nostrum, panacea, treatment

curiosity noun 1 INQUISITIVENESS, interest, nosiness (informal), prying, snooping (informal)
2 ODDITY, freak, novelty, phenomenon, rarity, sight, spectacle, wonder

curious adjective 1 INQUIRING, inquisitive, interested, questioning, searching
2 INQUISITIVE, meddling, nosy (informal), prying
3 UNUSUAL, bizarre, extraordinary, mysterious, novel, odd, peculiar, rare, strange, unexpected

curl verb 1 TWIRL, bend, coil, curve, loop, spiral, turn, twist, wind
▶ noun 2 TWIST, coil, kink, ringlet, spiral, whorl

curly adjective CURLING, crinkly, curled, frizzy, fuzzy, wavy, winding

currency noun 1 MONEY, coinage, coins, notes
2 ACCEPTANCE, circulation, exposure, popularity, prevalence, vogue

current adjective 1 PRESENT, contemporary, cool (informal), fashionable, in fashion, in vogue, phat (slang), present-day, trendy (informal), up-to-date
2 PREVALENT, accepted, common, customary, in circulation, popular, topical, widespread
▶ noun 3 FLOW, course, draft, jet, progression, river, stream, tide, undertow
4 MOOD, atmosphere, feeling, tendency, trend, undercurrent

curse verb 1 SWEAR, blaspheme, cuss (informal), take the Lord's name in vain
2 DAMN, anathematize, excommunicate
▶ noun 3 OATH, blasphemy, expletive, obscenity, swearing, swearword
4 DENUNCIATION, anathema, ban, excommunication, hoodoo (informal), jinx
5 AFFLICTION, bane, hardship, plague, scourge, torment, trouble

cursed adjective DAMNED, accursed, bedevilled, doomed, ill-fated

curt adjective SHORT, abrupt, blunt, brief, brusque, gruff, monosyllabic, succinct, terse

curtail verb CUT SHORT, cut back, decrease, diminish, dock, lessen, reduce, shorten, truncate

curtain noun HANGING, drape (chiefly U.S.)

curve noun 1 BEND, arc, curvature, loop, trajectory, turn
▶ verb 2 BEND, arc, arch, coil, hook, spiral, swerve, turn, twist, wind

curved adjective BENT, arched, bowed, rounded, serpentine, sinuous, twisted

cushion noun 1 PILLOW, beanbag, bolster, hassock, headrest, pad
▶ verb 2 SOFTEN, dampen, deaden, muffle, stifle, suppress

custody noun 1 SAFEKEEPING, care, charge, keeping, protection, supervision
2 IMPRISONMENT, confinement, detention, incarceration

custom noun 1 TRADITION, convention, policy, practice, ritual, rule, usage
2 HABIT, practice, procedure, routine, way, wont
3 CUSTOMERS, patronage, trade

customary adjective USUAL, accepted, accustomed, common, conventional, established, normal, ordinary, routine, traditional

customer noun CLIENT, buyer, consumer, patron, purchaser, regular (informal), shopper

customs plural noun DUTY, import charges, tariff, tax, toll

cut verb 1 PENETRATE, chop, pierce, score, sever, slash, slice, slit, wound
2 DIVIDE, bisect, dissect, slice, split
3 TRIM, clip, hew, lop, mow, pare, prune, shave, snip
4 ABRIDGE, abbreviate, condense, curtail, delete, shorten
5 REDUCE, contract, cut back, decrease, diminish, lower, slash, slim (down)
6 SHAPE, carve, chisel, engrave, fashion, form, sculpt, whittle
7 HURT, insult, put down, snub, sting, wound
8 (informal) IGNORE, avoid, cold-shoulder, slight, spurn, turn one's back on
▶ noun 9 INCISION, gash, laceration, nick, slash, slit, stroke, wound
10 REDUCTION, cutback, decrease, fall, lowering, saving

11 (informal) SHARE, percentage, piece, portion, section, slice
12 STYLE, fashion, look, shape

cutback noun REDUCTION, cut, decrease, economy, lessening, retrenchment

cut down verb 1 FELL, hew, level, lop
2 REDUCE, decrease, lessen, lower

cute adjective APPEALING, attractive, charming, delightful, engaging, lovable, sweet, winning, winsome

cut in verb INTERRUPT, break in, butt in, intervene, intrude

cut off verb 1 SEPARATE, isolate, sever
2 INTERRUPT, disconnect, intercept

cut out verb STOP, cease, give up, refrain from

cutthroat adjective 1 COMPETITIVE, dog-eat-dog, fierce, relentless, ruthless, unprincipled
▶ noun 2 MURDERER, assassin, butcher, executioner, hit man (slang), killer

cutting adjective HURTFUL, acrimonious, barbed, bitter, caustic, malicious, sarcastic, scathing, vitriolic, wounding

cycle noun ERA, circle, period, phase, revolution, rotation

cynic noun SKEPTIC, doubter, misanthrope, misanthropist, pessimist, scoffer

cynical adjective SKEPTICAL, contemptuous, derisive, distrustful, misanthropic, mocking, pessimistic, scoffing, scornful, unbelieving

cynicism noun SKEPTICISM, disbelief, doubt, misanthropy, pessimism

d

dab *verb* 1 PAT, daub, stipple, tap, touch
▶ *noun* 2 SPOT, bit, drop, pat, smudge, speck
3 PAT, flick, stroke, tap, touch

dabble *verb* 1 PLAY AT, dip into, potter, tinker, trifle (with)
2 SPLASH, dip

daft *adjective* (*informal*) 1 FOOLISH, absurd, asinine, bonkers (*informal*), crackpot (*informal*), crazy, idiotic, silly, stupid, witless
2 CRAZY, bonkers (*slang*), crackers (*Brit. slang*), demented, deranged, insane, nuts (*slang*), touched, unhinged

dagger *noun* KNIFE, bayonet, dirk, stiletto

daily *adjective* 1 EVERYDAY, diurnal, quotidian
▶ *adverb* 2 EVERY DAY, day by day, once a day

dainty *adjective* DELICATE, charming, elegant, exquisite, fine, graceful, neat, petite, pretty

dam *noun* 1 BARRIER, barrage, embankment, obstruction, wall
▶ *verb* 2 BLOCK UP, barricade, hold back, obstruct, restrict

damage *verb* 1 HARM, hurt, impair, injure, ruin, spoil, weaken, wreck
▶ *noun* 2 HARM, destruction, detriment, devastation, hurt, injury, loss, suffering
3 (*informal*) COST, bill, charge, expense

damages *plural noun* (*law*) COMPENSATION, fine, reimbursement, reparation, satisfaction

damaging *adjective* HARMFUL, deleterious, detrimental, disadvantageous, hurtful, injurious, ruinous

dame *noun* NOBLEWOMAN, baroness, dowager, *grande dame*, lady, peeress

damn *verb* 1 CONDEMN, blast, censure, criticize, denounce, put down
2 SENTENCE, condemn, doom

damnation *noun* CONDEMNATION, anathema, damning, denunciation, doom

damned *adjective* 1 DOOMED, accursed, condemned, lost
2 (*slang*) DETESTABLE, confounded, hateful, infernal, loathsome

damp *adjective* 1 MOIST, clammy, dank, dewy, drizzly, humid, soggy, sopping, wet
▶ *noun* 2 MOISTURE, dampness, dankness, drizzle
▶ *verb* 3 MOISTEN, dampen, wet
4 ▷▷ **damp down** REDUCE, allay, check, curb, diminish, inhibit, pour cold water on, stifle

dampen *verb* 1 REDUCE, check, dull, lessen, moderate, restrain, stifle
2 MOISTEN, make damp, spray, wet

damper *noun* *as in* **put a damper on** DISCOURAGEMENT, cold water (*informal*), hindrance, restraint, wet blanket (*informal*)

dance *verb* 1 PRANCE, hop, jig, skip, sway, trip, whirl

▶ *noun* 2 BALL, disco, discotheque, hop (*informal, dated*), knees-up (*Brit. informal*), social

dancer *noun* BALLERINA, Terpsichorean

danger *noun* PERIL, hazard, jeopardy, menace, pitfall, risk, threat, vulnerability

dangerous *adjective* PERILOUS, breakneck, chancy (*informal*), hazardous, insecure, precarious, risky, unsafe, vulnerable

dangerously *adverb* PERILOUSLY, alarmingly, hazardously, precariously, recklessly, riskily, unsafely

dangle *verb* 1 HANG, flap, hang down, sway, swing, trail
2 WAVE, brandish, flaunt, flourish

dapper *adjective* NEAT, natty (*informal*), smart, soigné *or* soignée, spruce, spry, trim, well-groomed, well turned out

dare *verb* 1 RISK, hazard, make bold, presume, venture
2 CHALLENGE, defy, goad, provoke, taunt, throw down the gauntlet
▶ *noun* 3 CHALLENGE, provocation, taunt

daredevil *noun* 1 ADVENTURER, desperado, exhibitionist, madcap, show-off (*informal*), stunt man
▶ *adjective* 2 DARING, adventurous, audacious, bold, death-defying, madcap, reckless

daring *adjective* 1 BRAVE, adventurous, audacious, bold, daredevil, fearless, intrepid, reckless, venturesome
▶ *noun* 2 BRAVERY, audacity, boldness, bottle (*Brit. slang*), courage, fearlessness, nerve (*informal*), pluck, temerity

dark *adjective* 1 DIM, dingy, murky, shadowy, shady, sunless, unlit
2 BLACK, dark-skinned, dusky, ebony, sable, swarthy
3 GLOOMY, bleak, dismal, grim, morose, mournful, sad, somber
4 EVIL, foul, infernal, sinister, vile, wicked
5 SECRET, concealed, hidden, mysterious
▶ *noun* 6 DARKNESS, dimness, dusk, gloom, murk, obscurity, semi-darkness
7 NIGHT, evening, nightfall, night-time, twilight

darken *verb* MAKE DARK, blacken, dim, obscure, overshadow

darkness *noun* DARK, blackness, duskiness, gloom, murk, nightfall, shade, shadows

darling *noun* 1 BELOVED, dear, dearest, love, sweetheart, truelove
▶ *adjective* 2 BELOVED, adored, cherished, dear, precious, treasured

darn *verb* 1 MEND, cobble up, patch, repair, sew up, stitch
▶ *noun* 2 MEND, invisible repair, patch, reinforcement

dart *verb* DASH, fly, race, run, rush, shoot, spring, sprint, tear

dash *verb* 1 RUSH, bolt, fly, hurry, race, run, speed, sprint, tear
2 THROW, cast, fling, hurl, slam, sling
3 CRASH, break, destroy, shatter, smash, splinter
4 FRUSTRATE, blight, foil, ruin, spoil, thwart, undo
▶ *noun* 5 RUSH, dart, race, run, sortie, sprint, spurt
6 LITTLE, bit, drop, hint, pinch, *soupçon*, sprinkling, tinge, touch
7 STYLE, brio, élan, flair, flourish, panache, spirit, verve

dashing *adjective* 1 BOLD, debonair, gallant, lively, spirited, swashbuckling
2 STYLISH, elegant, flamboyant, jaunty, showy, smart, sporty

data *noun* INFORMATION, details,

facts, figures, statistics

date *noun* 1 TIME, age, epoch, era, period, stage
2 APPOINTMENT, assignation, engagement, meeting, rendezvous, tryst
3 PARTNER, escort, friend
▶ *verb* 4 PUT A DATE ON, assign a date to, fix the period of
5 BECOME OLD-FASHIONED, be dated, show one's age
6 ▷▷ **date from** *or* **date back to** COME FROM, bear a date of, belong to, exist from, originate in

dated *adjective* OLD-FASHIONED, obsolete, old hat, outdated, outmoded, out of date, passé, unfashionable

daub *verb* SMEAR, coat, cover, paint, plaster, slap on (*informal*)

daunting *adjective* INTIMIDATING, alarming, demoralizing, disconcerting, discouraging, disheartening, frightening, off-putting (*Brit. informal*), unnerving

dauntless *adjective* FEARLESS, bold, doughty, gallant, indomitable, intrepid, resolute, stouthearted, undaunted, unflinching

dawdle *verb* WASTE TIME, dally, delay, drag one's feet *or* heels, hang about, idle, loaf, loiter, trail

dawn *noun* 1 DAYBREAK, aurora (*poetic*), cockcrow, crack of dawn, daylight, morning, sunrise, sunup
2 BEGINNING, advent, birth, emergence, genesis, origin, rise, start
▶ *verb* 3 GROW LIGHT, break, brighten, lighten
4 BEGIN, appear, develop, emerge, originate, rise, unfold
5 ▷▷ **dawn on** *or* **upon** HIT, become apparent, come into one's head, come to mind, occur, register (*informal*), strike

day *noun* 1 TWENTY-FOUR HOURS, daylight, daytime
2 POINT IN TIME, date, time
3 TIME, age, epoch, era, heyday, period, zenith

daybreak *noun* DAWN, break of day, cockcrow, crack of dawn, first light, morning, sunrise, sunup

daydream *noun* 1 FANTASY, dream, fancy, imagining, pipe dream, reverie, wish
▶ *verb* 2 FANTASIZE, dream, envision, fancy, imagine, muse

daylight *noun* SUNLIGHT, light of day, sunshine

daze *verb* 1 STUN, benumb, numb, paralyze, shock, stupefy
▶ *noun* 2 SHOCK, bewilderment, confusion, distraction, stupor, trance, trancelike state

dazed *adjective* SHOCKED, bewildered, confused, disorientated, dizzy, muddled, punch-drunk, staggered, stunned

dazzle *verb* 1 IMPRESS, amaze, astonish, bowl over (*informal*), overpower, overwhelm, take one's breath away
2 BLIND, bedazzle, blur, confuse, daze
▶ *noun* 3 SPLENDOR, brilliance, glitter, magnificence, razzmatazz (*slang*), sparkle

dazzling *adjective* SPLENDID, brilliant, glittering, glorious, scintillating, sensational (*informal*), sparkling, stunning, virtuoso

dead *adjective* 1 DECEASED, defunct, departed, extinct, late, passed away, perished
2 NOT WORKING, inactive, inoperative, stagnant, unemployed, useless
3 NUMB, inert, paralyzed
4 TOTAL, absolute, complete, outright, thorough, unqualified,

utter
5 (*informal*) EXHAUSTED, dead beat
(*informal*), spent, tired, worn out
6 BORING, dull, flat, uninteresting
▶ *noun* **7** MIDDLE, depth, midst
▶ *adverb* **8** (*informal*) EXACTLY,
absolutely, completely, directly,
entirely, totally
deaden *verb* REDUCE, alleviate,
blunt, cushion, diminish, dull,
lessen, muffle, smother, stifle,
suppress, weaken
deadline *noun* TIME LIMIT, cutoff
point, limit, target date
deadlock *noun* **1** dead heat
DRAW, tie
2 IMPASSE, gridlock, stalemate,
standoff, standstill
deadlocked *adjective* **1** EVEN,
equal, level, neck and neck, on a
level playing field (*informal*)
2 GRIDLOCKED, at an impasse, at
a standstill
deadly *adjective* **1** LETHAL,
dangerous, death-dealing,
deathly, fatal, malignant, mortal
2 (*informal*) BORING, dull,
mind-numbing, monotonous,
tedious, tiresome, uninteresting,
wearisome
deadpan *adjective*
EXPRESSIONLESS, blank,
impassive, inexpressive,
inscrutable, poker-faced, straight-
faced
deaf *adjective* **1** HARD OF HEARING,
stone deaf, without hearing
2 OBLIVIOUS, indifferent,
unconcerned, unhearing,
unmoved
deafen *verb* MAKE DEAF, din,
drown out, split *or* burst the
eardrums
deafening *adjective* EAR-
PIERCING, booming, ear-splitting,
overpowering, piercing,
resounding, ringing, thunderous

deal *noun* **1** AGREEMENT,
arrangement, bargain, contract,
pact, transaction, understanding
2 AMOUNT, degree, extent, portion,
quantity, share
▶ *verb* **3** SELL, bargain, buy and
sell, do business, negotiate, stock,
trade, traffic
dealer *noun* TRADER, merchant,
purveyor, supplier, tradesman,
wholesaler
deal out *verb* DISTRIBUTE, allot,
apportion, assign, dispense, dole
out, give, mete out, share
deal with *verb* **1** HANDLE, attend
to, cope with, get to grips with,
manage, see to, take care of, treat
2 BE CONCERNED WITH, consider
dear *noun* **1** BELOVED, angel,
darling, loved one, precious,
treasure
▶ *adjective* **2** BELOVED, cherished,
close, favorite, intimate, precious,
prized, treasured
3 EXPENSIVE, at a premium, costly,
high-priced, overpriced, pricey
(*informal*)
dearly *adverb* **1** VERY MUCH,
extremely, greatly, profoundly
2 AT GREAT COST, at a high price
dearth *noun* SCARCITY, deficiency,
inadequacy, insufficiency, lack,
paucity, poverty, shortage, want
death *noun* **1** DYING, demise,
departure, end, exit, passing
2 DESTRUCTION, downfall,
extinction, finish, ruin, undoing
deathly *adjective* DEATHLIKE,
ghastly, grim, pale, pallid, wan
debacle *noun* DISASTER,
catastrophe, collapse, defeat,
fiasco, reversal, rout
debase *verb* DEGRADE, cheapen,
devalue, lower, reduce
debatable *adjective* DOUBTFUL,
arguable, controversial,
dubious, moot, problematical,

questionable, uncertain

debate noun 1 DISCUSSION, argument, contention, controversy, dispute
▶ verb 2 DISCUSS, argue, dispute, question
3 CONSIDER, deliberate, ponder, reflect, ruminate, weigh

debauchery noun DEPRAVITY, dissipation, dissoluteness, excess, indulgence, intemperance, lewdness, overindulgence

debonair adjective ELEGANT, charming, courteous, dashing, refined, smooth, suave, urbane, well-bred

debrief verb INTERROGATE, cross-examine, examine, probe, question, quiz

debris noun REMAINS, bits, detritus, fragments, rubble, ruins, waste, wreckage

debt noun 1 DEBIT, commitment, liability, obligation
2 ▷▷ **in debt** OWING, in arrears, in the red (informal), liable

debtor noun BORROWER, mortgagor

debunk verb EXPOSE, cut down to size, deflate, disparage, mock, ridicule, show up

debut noun INTRODUCTION, beginning, bow, coming out, entrance, first appearance, initiation, presentation

decadence noun DEGENERATION, corruption, decay, decline, deterioration, dissipation, dissolution

decadent adjective DEGENERATE, corrupt, decaying, declining, dissolute, immoral, self-indulgent

decapitate verb BEHEAD, execute, guillotine

decay verb 1 DECLINE, crumble, deteriorate, disintegrate, dwindle, shrivel, wane, waste away, wither
2 ROT, corrode, decompose, perish, putrefy
▶ noun 3 DECLINE, collapse, degeneration, deterioration, fading, failing, wasting, withering
4 ROT, caries, decomposition, gangrene, putrefaction

decease noun (formal) DEATH, demise, departure, dying, release

deceased adjective DEAD, defunct, departed, expired, former, late, lifeless

deceit noun DISHONESTY, back-stabbing (informal), cheating, chicanery, deception, fraud, lying, pretense, treachery, trickery

deceitful adjective DISHONEST, deceptive, down and dirty (informal), false, fraudulent, sneaky, treacherous, two-faced, untrustworthy

deceive verb DUPE (informal), cheat, con (informal), fool, hoodwink, mislead, swindle, trick

deceiver noun LIAR, cheat, con man (informal), double-dealer, fraud, impostor, swindler, trickster

decency noun RESPECTABILITY, civility, correctness, courtesy, decorum, etiquette, modesty, propriety

decent adjective 1 REASONABLE, adequate, ample, fair, passable, satisfactory, sufficient, tolerable
2 RESPECTABLE, chaste, decorous, modest, proper, pure
3 PROPER, appropriate, becoming, befitting, fitting, seemly, suitable
4 (informal) KIND, accommodating, courteous, friendly, generous, gracious, helpful, obliging, thoughtful

deception noun 1 TRICKERY, cunning, deceit, fraud, guile,

legerdemain, treachery
2 TRICK, bluff, decoy, hoax,
illusion, lie, ruse, subterfuge
deceptive *adjective* MISLEADING,
ambiguous, deceitful, dishonest,
false, fraudulent, illusory,
unreliable
decide *verb* REACH *or* COME TO A
DECISION, adjudge, adjudicate,
choose, conclude, determine,
make up one's mind, resolve
decidedly *adverb* DEFINITELY,
clearly, distinctly, downright,
positively, unequivocally,
unmistakably
decimate *verb* DEVASTATE, ravage,
wreak havoc on
decipher *verb* FIGURE OUT
(*informal*), crack, decode, deduce,
interpret, make out, read, solve
decision *noun* 1 JUDGMENT,
arbitration, conclusion, finding,
resolution, ruling, sentence,
verdict
2 DECISIVENESS, determination,
firmness, purpose, resolution,
resolve, strength of mind *or* will
decisive *adjective* 1 INFLUENTIAL,
conclusive, critical, crucial,
fateful, momentous, significant
2 RESOLUTE, decided, determined,
firm, forceful, incisive, strong-
minded, trenchant
deck *verb* DECORATE, adorn, array,
beautify, clothe, dress, embellish,
festoon
declaim *verb* 1 ORATE, harangue,
hold forth, lecture, proclaim, rant,
recite, speak
2 ▷▷ **declaim against** PROTEST
AGAINST, attack, decry, denounce,
inveigh, rail
declaration *noun* 1 STATEMENT,
acknowledgment, affirmation,
assertion, avowal, disclosure,
protestation, revelation,
testimony

2 ANNOUNCEMENT, edict,
notification, proclamation,
profession, pronouncement
declare *verb* 1 STATE, affirm,
announce, assert, claim,
maintain, proclaim, profess,
pronounce, swear, utter
2 MAKE KNOWN, confess, disclose,
reveal, show
decline *verb* 1 LESSEN, decrease,
diminish, dwindle, ebb, fade, fall
off, shrink, sink, wane
2 DETERIORATE, decay, degenerate,
droop, languish, pine, weaken,
worsen
3 REFUSE, abstain, avoid, reject,
say 'no', turn down
▶ *noun* 4 LESSENING, downturn,
drop, dwindling, falling off,
recession, slump
5 DETERIORATION, decay,
degeneration, failing, weakening,
worsening
decode *verb* DECIPHER, crack,
decrypt, interpret, solve,
unscramble, work out
decompose *verb* ROT, break up,
crumble, decay, fall apart, fester,
putrefy
decor *noun* DECORATION, color
scheme, furnishing style,
ornamentation
decorate *verb* 1 ADORN, beautify,
embellish, festoon, grace,
ornament, trim
2 RENOVATE, do up (*informal*),
color, color, furbish, paint, paper,
wallpaper
3 PIN A MEDAL ON, cite, confer an
honor on *or* upon
decoration *noun* 1 ADORNMENT,
beautification, elaboration,
embellishment, enrichment,
ornamentation, trimming
2 ORNAMENT, bauble, frill,
garnish, trimmings
3 MEDAL, award, badge, ribbon,

star

decorative *adjective*
ORNAMENTAL, beautifying, fancy,
nonfunctional, pretty

decorous *adjective* PROPER,
becoming, correct, decent,
dignified, fitting, polite, seemly,
well-behaved

decorum *noun* PROPRIETY,
decency, dignity, etiquette, good
manners, politeness, protocol,
respectability

decoy *noun* 1 LURE, bait,
enticement, inducement,
pretense, trap
▶ *verb* 2 LURE, deceive, ensnare,
entice, entrap, seduce, tempt

decrease *verb* 1 LESSEN, cut down,
decline, diminish, drop, dwindle,
lower, reduce, shrink, subside
▶ *noun* 2 LESSENING, contraction,
cutback, decline, dwindling,
falling off, loss, reduction,
subsidence

decree *noun* 1 LAW, act, command,
edict, order, proclamation, ruling,
statute
▶ *verb* 2 ORDER, command,
demand, ordain, prescribe,
proclaim, pronounce, rule

decrepit *adjective* 1 WEAK, aged,
doddering, feeble, frail, infirm
2 WORN-OUT, battered, beat-
up (*informal*), broken-down,
dilapidated, ramshackle, rickety,
run-down, tumbledown, weather-
beaten

decry *verb* CONDEMN, belittle,
criticize, denigrate, denounce,
discredit, disparage, put down,
run down

dedicate *verb* 1 DEVOTE, commit,
give over to, pledge, surrender
2 INSCRIBE, address

dedicated *adjective* DEVOTED,
committed, enthusiastic,
purposeful, single-minded,
wholehearted, zealous

dedication *noun* 1 DEVOTION,
adherence, allegiance,
commitment, faithfulness,
loyalty, single-mindedness,
wholeheartedness
2 INSCRIPTION, address, message

deduce *verb* CONCLUDE, draw,
gather, glean, infer, reason, take
to mean, understand

deduct *verb* SUBTRACT, decrease
by, knock off (*informal*), reduce by,
remove, take away, take off

deduction *noun* 1 SUBTRACTION,
decrease, diminution, discount,
reduction, withdrawal
2 CONCLUSION, assumption,
finding, inference, reasoning,
result

deed *noun* 1 ACTION, achievement,
act, exploit, fact, feat,
performance
2 (*law*) DOCUMENT, contract, title

deep *adjective* 1 WIDE, bottomless,
broad, far, profound,
unfathomable, yawning
2 MYSTERIOUS, abstract, abstruse,
arcane, esoteric, hidden, obscure,
recondite, secret
3 INTENSE, extreme, grave, great,
profound, serious (*informal*),
unqualified
4 ABSORBED, engrossed,
immersed, lost, preoccupied, rapt
5 DARK, intense, rich, strong, vivid
6 LOW, bass, booming, low-
pitched, resonant, sonorous
▶ *noun* 7 ▷▷ **the deep** (*poetic*)
OCEAN, briny (*informal*), high seas,
main, sea

deepen *verb* INTENSIFY, grow,
increase, magnify, reinforce,
strengthen

deeply *adverb* 1 THOROUGHLY,
completely, gravely, profoundly,
seriously, severely, to the core, to
the heart, to the quick

2 INTENSELY, acutely, affectingly, distressingly, feelingly, mournfully, movingly, passionately, sadly

deface verb VANDALIZE, damage, deform, disfigure, mar, mutilate, spoil, tarnish

de facto adverb **1** IN FACT, actually, in effect, in reality, really
▶ adjective **2** ACTUAL, existing, real

defame verb SLANDER, bad-mouth (*slang*), cast aspersions on, denigrate, discredit, disparage, knock (*informal*), libel, malign, smear

default noun **1** FAILURE, deficiency, dereliction, evasion, lapse, neglect, nonpayment, omission
▶ verb **2** FAIL, dodge, evade, neglect

defeat verb **1** BEAT, conquer, crush, master, overwhelm, rout, trounce, vanquish, wipe the floor with (*informal*)
2 FRUSTRATE, baffle, balk, confound, foil, get the better of, ruin, thwart
▶ noun **3** CONQUEST, beating, overthrow, pasting (*slang*), rout
4 FRUSTRATION, failure, rebuff, reverse, setback, thwarting

defeatist noun **1** PESSIMIST, prophet of doom, quitter
▶ adjective **2** PESSIMISTIC

defect noun **1** IMPERFECTION, blemish, blotch, error, failing, fault, flaw, spot, taint
▶ verb **2** DESERT, abandon, change sides, go over, rebel, revolt, walk out on (*informal*)

defection noun DESERTION, apostasy, rebellion

defective adjective FAULTY, broken, deficient, flawed, imperfect, not working, on the blink (*slang*), out of order

defector noun DESERTER, apostate, renegade, turncoat

defend verb **1** PROTECT, cover, guard, keep safe, preserve, safeguard, screen, shelter, shield
2 SUPPORT, champion, endorse, justify, speak up for, stand up for, stick up for (*informal*), uphold, vindicate

defendant noun THE ACCUSED, defense, offender, prisoner at the bar, respondent

defender noun **1** PROTECTOR, bodyguard, escort, guard
2 SUPPORTER, advocate, champion, sponsor

defense noun **1** PROTECTION, cover, guard, immunity, resistance, safeguard, security, shelter
2 SHIELD, barricade, bulwark, buttress, fortification, rampart
3 ARGUMENT, excuse, explanation, justification, plea, vindication
4 (*law*) PLEA, alibi, denial, rebuttal, testimony

defenseless adjective HELPLESS, exposed, naked, powerless, unarmed, unguarded, unprotected, vulnerable, wide open

defensive adjective ON GUARD, on the defensive, protective, uptight (*informal*), watchful

defer[1] verb POSTPONE, delay, hold over, procrastinate, put off, put on ice, shelve, suspend

defer[2] verb COMPLY, accede, bow, capitulate, give in, give way to, submit, yield

deference noun RESPECT, attention, civility, consideration, courtesy, honor, politeness, regard, reverence

deferential adjective RESPECTFUL, ingratiating, obedient, obeisant, obsequious, polite, reverential, submissive

defiance noun RESISTANCE, confrontation, contempt,

disobedience, disregard, insolence, insubordination, opposition, rebelliousness

defiant *adjective* 1 RESISTING, audacious, bold, daring, disobedient, insolent, insubordinate, mutinous, provocative, rebellious

deficiency *noun* 1 LACK, absence, dearth, deficit, scarcity, shortage
2 FAILING, defect, demerit, fault, flaw, frailty, imperfection, shortcoming, weakness

deficient *adjective* 1 LACKING, inadequate, insufficient, meager, scant, scarce, short, skimpy, wanting
2 UNSATISFACTORY, defective, faulty, flawed, impaired, imperfect, incomplete, inferior, lousy (*slang*), weak

deficit *noun* SHORTFALL, arrears, deficiency, loss, shortage

define *verb* 1 DESCRIBE, characterize, designate, explain, expound, interpret, specify, spell out
2 MARK OUT, bound, circumscribe, delineate, demarcate, limit, outline

definite *adjective* 1 CLEAR, black-and-white, cut-and-dried (*informal*), exact, fixed, marked, particular, precise, specific
2 CERTAIN, assured, decided, guaranteed, positive, settled, sure

definitely *adverb* CERTAINLY, absolutely, categorically, clearly, positively, surely, undeniably, unmistakably, unquestionably, without doubt

definition *noun* 1 EXPLANATION, clarification, elucidation, exposition, statement of meaning
2 SHARPNESS, clarity, contrast, distinctness, focus, precision

definitive *adjective* 1 FINAL,

absolute, complete, conclusive, decisive
2 AUTHORITATIVE, exhaustive, perfect, reliable, ultimate

deflate *verb* 1 COLLAPSE, empty, exhaust, flatten, puncture, shrink
2 HUMILIATE, chasten, disconcert, dispirit, humble, mortify, put down (*slang*), squash
3 (*economics*) REDUCE, depress, devalue, diminish

deflect *verb* TURN ASIDE, bend, deviate, diverge, glance off, ricochet, swerve, veer

deflection *noun* DEVIATION, bend, divergence, swerve

deform *verb* 1 DISTORT, buckle, contort, gnarl, mangle, misshape, twist, warp
2 DISFIGURE, deface, maim, mar, mutilate, ruin, spoil

deformity *noun* ABNORMALITY, defect, disfigurement, malformation

defraud *verb* CHEAT, con (*informal*), diddle (*informal*), embezzle, fleece, pilfer, rip off (*slang*), swindle, trick

deft *adjective* SKILLFUL, adept, adroit, agile, dexterous, expert, neat, nimble, proficient

defunct *adjective* 1 DEAD, deceased, departed, extinct, gone
2 OBSOLETE, bygone, expired, inoperative, invalid, nonexistent, out of commission

defy *verb* RESIST, brave, confront, disregard, flout, scorn, slight, spurn

degenerate *adjective* 1 DEPRAVED, corrupt, debauched, decadent, dissolute, immoral, low, perverted
▶ *verb* 2 WORSEN, decay, decline, decrease, deteriorate, fall off, lapse, sink, slip

degradation *noun* 1 DISGRACE, discredit, dishonor, humiliation, ignominy, mortification, shame

2 DETERIORATION, decline, degeneration, demotion, downgrading

degrade verb 1 DISGRACE, debase, demean, discredit, dishonor, humble, humiliate, shame
2 DEMOTE, downgrade, lower

degrading adjective DEMEANING, dishonorable, humiliating, infra dig (*informal*), shameful, undignified, unworthy

degree noun STAGE, grade, notch, point, rung, step, unit

deity noun GOD, divinity, goddess, godhead, idol, immortal, supreme being

dejected adjective DOWNHEARTED, crestfallen, depressed, despondent, disconsolate, disheartened, downcast, glum, miserable, sad

dejection noun LOW SPIRITS, depression, despair, despondency, doldrums, downheartedness, gloom, melancholy, sadness, sorrow, unhappiness

de jure adverb LEGALLY, by right, rightfully

delay verb 1 PUT OFF, defer, hold over, postpone, procrastinate, shelve, suspend
2 HOLD UP, bog down, detain, hinder, hold back, impede, obstruct, set back, slow up
▶ noun 3 PUTTING OFF, deferment, postponement, procrastination, suspension
4 HOLD-UP, hindrance, impediment, interruption, interval, setback, stoppage, wait

delegate noun 1 REPRESENTATIVE, agent, ambassador, commissioner, deputy, envoy, legate
▶ verb 2 ENTRUST, assign, consign, devolve, give, hand over, pass on, transfer

3 APPOINT, accredit, authorize, commission, depute, designate, empower, mandate

delegation noun 1 DEPUTATION, commission, contingent, embassy, envoys, legation, mission
2 DEVOLUTION, assignment, commissioning, committal

delete verb REMOVE, cancel, cross out, efface, erase, expunge, obliterate, rub out, strike out

deliberate adjective
1 INTENTIONAL, calculated, conscious, planned, prearranged, premeditated, purposeful, willful
2 UNHURRIED, careful, cautious, circumspect, measured, methodical, ponderous, slow, thoughtful
▶ verb 3 CONSIDER, cogitate, consult, debate, discuss, meditate, ponder, reflect, think, weigh

deliberately adverb
INTENTIONALLY, by design, calculatingly, consciously, in cold blood, knowingly, on purpose, willfully, wittingly

deliberation noun
1 CONSIDERATION, calculation, circumspection, forethought, meditation, reflection, thought
2 DISCUSSION, conference, consultation, debate

delicacy noun 1 FINENESS, accuracy, daintiness, elegance, exquisiteness, lightness, precision, subtlety
2 FRAGILITY, flimsiness, frailty, slenderness, tenderness, weakness
3 TREAT, dainty, luxury, savory, tidbit
4 FASTIDIOUSNESS, discrimination, finesse, purity, refinement, sensibility, taste
5 SENSITIVITY, sensitiveness, tact

delicate *adjective* 1 FINE, deft, elegant, exquisite, graceful, precise, skilled, subtle
2 SUBTLE, choice, dainty, delicious, fine, savory, tender, yummy (*informal*)
3 FRAGILE, flimsy, frail, slender, slight, tender, weak
4 CONSIDERATE, diplomatic, discreet, sensitive, tactful

delicately *adverb* 1 FINELY, daintily, deftly, elegantly, exquisitely, gracefully, precisely, skillfully, subtly
2 TACTFULLY, diplomatically, sensitively

delicious *adjective* DELECTABLE, appetizing, choice, dainty, mouthwatering, savory, scrumptious (*informal*), tasty, toothsome, yummy (*informal*)

delight *noun* 1 PLEASURE, ecstasy, enjoyment, gladness, glee, happiness, joy, rapture
▶ *verb* 2 PLEASE, amuse, charm, cheer, enchant, gratify, thrill
3 ▷▷ **delight in** TAKE PLEASURE IN, appreciate, enjoy, feast on, like, love, relish, revel in, savor

delighted *adjective* PLEASED, ecstatic, elated, enchanted, happy, joyous, jubilant, overjoyed, thrilled

delightful *adjective* PLEASANT, agreeable, charming, delectable, enchanting, enjoyable, pleasurable, rapturous, thrilling

delinquent *noun* CRIMINAL, culprit, lawbreaker, miscreant, offender, villain, wrongdoer

delirious *adjective* 1 MAD, crazy, demented, deranged, incoherent, insane, raving, unhinged
2 ECSTATIC, beside oneself, carried away, excited, frantic, frenzied, hysterical, wild, wired (*slang*)

delirium *noun* 1 MADNESS, derangement, hallucination, insanity, raving
2 FRENZY, ecstasy, fever, hysteria, passion

deliver *verb* 1 CARRY, bear, bring, cart, convey, distribute, transport
2 HAND OVER, commit, give up, grant, make over, relinquish, surrender, transfer, turn over, yield
3 GIVE, announce, declare, present, read, utter
4 RELEASE, emancipate, free, liberate, loose, ransom, rescue, save
5 STRIKE, administer, aim, deal, direct, give, inflict, launch

deliverance *noun* RELEASE, emancipation, escape, liberation, ransom, redemption, rescue, salvation

delivery *noun* 1 HANDING OVER, consignment, conveyance, dispatch, distribution, surrender, transfer, transmission
2 SPEECH, articulation, elocution, enunciation, intonation, utterance
3 CHILDBIRTH, confinement, labor, parturition

delude *verb* DECEIVE, beguile, dupe, fool, hoodwink, kid (*informal*), mislead, take in (*informal*), trick

deluge *noun* 1 FLOOD, cataclysm, downpour, inundation, overflowing, spate, torrent
2 RUSH, avalanche, barrage, flood, spate, torrent
▶ *verb* 3 FLOOD, douse, drench, drown, inundate, soak, submerge, swamp
4 OVERWHELM, engulf, inundate, overload, overrun, swamp

delusion *noun* MISCONCEPTION, error, fallacy, false impression, fancy, hallucination, illusion, misapprehension, mistake

deluxe *adjective* LUXURIOUS, costly, exclusive, expensive, grand, opulent, select, special, splendid, superior

delve *verb* RESEARCH, burrow, explore, ferret out, forage, investigate, look into, probe, rummage, search

demagogue *noun* AGITATOR, firebrand, rabble-rouser

demand *verb* 1 REQUEST, ask, challenge, inquire, interrogate, question
2 REQUIRE, call for, cry out for, entail, involve, necessitate, need, want
3 CLAIM, exact, expect, insist on, order
▶ *noun* 4 REQUEST, inquiry, order, question, requisition
5 NEED, call, claim, market, requirement, want

demanding *adjective* DIFFICULT, challenging, exacting, hard, high-maintenance, taxing, tough, trying, wearing

demarcation *noun* DELIMITATION, differentiation, distinction, division, separation

demean *verb* LOWER, abase, debase, degrade, descend, humble, stoop

demeanor *noun* BEHAVIOR, air, bearing, carriage, comportment, conduct, deportment, manner

demented *adjective* MAD, crazed, crazy, deranged, frenzied, insane, maniacal, unbalanced, unhinged

demise *noun* 1 FAILURE, collapse, downfall, end, fall, ruin
2 (*euphemistic*) DEATH, decease, departure

democracy *noun* SELF-GOVERNMENT, commonwealth, republic

democratic *adjective* SELF-GOVERNING, autonomous, egalitarian, popular, populist, representative

demolish *verb* 1 KNOCK DOWN, bulldoze, destroy, dismantle, flatten, level, raze, tear down
2 DEFEAT, annihilate, destroy, overthrow, overturn, undo, wreck

demolition *noun* KNOCKING DOWN, bulldozing, destruction, explosion, levelling, razing, tearing down, wrecking

demon *noun* 1 EVIL SPIRIT, devil, fiend, ghoul, goblin, malignant spirit
2 WIZARD, ace (*informal*), fiend, master

demonic, demoniac, demoniacal *adjective* 1 DEVILISH, diabolic, diabolical, fiendish, hellish, infernal, satanic
2 FRENZIED, crazed, frantic, frenetic, furious, hectic, maniacal, manic

demonstrable *adjective* PROVABLE, evident, irrefutable, obvious, palpable, self-evident, unmistakable, verifiable

demonstrate *verb* 1 PROVE, display, exhibit, indicate, manifest, show, testify to
2 SHOW HOW, describe, explain, illustrate, make clear, teach
3 MARCH, parade, picket, protest, rally

demonstration *noun* 1 MARCH, mass lobby, parade, picket, protest, rally, sit-in
2 EXPLANATION, description, exposition, presentation, test, trial
3 PROOF, confirmation, display, evidence, exhibition, expression, illustration, testimony

demoralize *verb* DISHEARTEN, deject, depress, discourage, dispirit, undermine, unnerve, weaken

demote verb DOWNGRADE, degrade, kick downstairs (slang), lower in rank, relegate

demur verb 1 OBJECT, balk, dispute, hesitate, protest, refuse, take exception, waver
▶ noun 2 as in **without demur** OBJECTION, compunction, dissent, hesitation, misgiving, protest, qualm

demure adjective SHY, diffident, modest, reserved, reticent, retiring, sedate, unassuming

den noun 1 LAIR, cave, cavern, haunt, hideout, hole, shelter
2 (chiefly U.S.) STUDY, cubbyhole, hideaway, living room, retreat, sanctuary, sanctum

denial noun 1 NEGATION, contradiction, dissent, renunciation, repudiation, retraction
2 REFUSAL, prohibition, rebuff, rejection, repulse, veto

denigrate verb DISPARAGE, bad-mouth (slang), belittle, knock (informal), malign, rubbish (informal), run down, slander, vilify

denomination noun 1 RELIGIOUS GROUP, belief, creed, persuasion, school, sect
2 UNIT, grade, size, value

denote verb INDICATE, betoken, designate, express, imply, mark, mean, show, signify

denounce verb CONDEMN, accuse, attack, censure, denunciate, revile, stigmatize, vilify

dense adjective 1 THICK, close-knit, compact, condensed, heavy, impenetrable, opaque, solid
2 STUPID, dozy (Brit. informal), dull, obtuse, slow-witted, stolid, thick

density noun TIGHTNESS, bulk, compactness, consistency, denseness, impenetrability, mass, solidity, thickness

dent noun 1 HOLLOW, chip, crater, depression, dimple, dip, impression, indentation, pit
▶ verb 2 MAKE A DENT IN, gouge, hollow, press in, push in

deny verb 1 CONTRADICT, disagree with, disprove, rebuff, rebut, refute
2 REFUSE, begrudge, disallow, forbid, reject, turn down, withhold
3 RENOUNCE, disclaim, disown, recant, repudiate, retract

depart verb 1 LEAVE, absent (oneself), disappear, exit, go, go away, quit, retire, retreat, withdraw
2 DEVIATE, differ, digress, diverge, stray, swerve, turn aside, vary, veer

department noun SECTION, branch, bureau, division, office, station, subdivision, unit

departure noun 1 LEAVING, exit, exodus, going, going away, leave-taking, removal, retirement, withdrawal
2 DIVERGENCE, deviation, digression, variation
3 SHIFT, change, difference, innovation, novelty, whole new ball game (informal)

depend verb 1 TRUST IN, bank on, count on, lean on, reckon on, rely upon, turn to
2 BE DETERMINED BY, be based on, be contingent on, be subject to, be subordinate to, hang on, hinge on, rest on, revolve around

dependable adjective RELIABLE, faithful, reputable, responsible, staunch, steady, sure, trustworthy, trusty, unfailing

dependant noun RELATIVE, child, minor, protégé, subordinate

dependent adjective 1 RELYING ON, defenseless, helpless, reliant, vulnerable, weak

2 ▷▷ **dependent on** or **upon**
DETERMINED BY, conditional on,
contingent on, depending on,
influenced by, subject to

depict verb 1 DRAW, delineate,
illustrate, outline, paint, picture,
portray, sketch

2 DESCRIBE, characterize, narrate,
outline, represent

depiction noun REPRESENTATION,
delineation, description, picture,
portrayal, sketch

deplete verb USE UP, consume,
drain, empty, exhaust, expend,
impoverish, lessen, reduce

deplorable adjective
1 REGRETTABLE, grievous,
lamentable, pitiable, sad,
unfortunate, wretched

2 DISGRACEFUL, dishonorable,
reprehensible, scandalous,
shameful

deplore verb DISAPPROVE OF,
abhor, censure, condemn,
denounce, object to, take a dim
view of

deploy verb POSITION, arrange, set
out, station, use, utilize

deployment noun POSITION,
arrangement, organization,
spread, stationing, use, utilization

deport verb 1 EXPEL, banish, exile,
expatriate, extradite, oust

2 ▷▷ **deport oneself** BEHAVE,
acquit oneself, act, bear oneself,
carry oneself, comport oneself,
conduct oneself, hold oneself

depose verb 1 REMOVE FROM
OFFICE, demote, dethrone,
dismiss, displace, oust

2 (law) TESTIFY, avouch, declare,
make a deposition

deposit verb 1 PUT, drop, lay,
locate, place

2 STORE, bank, consign, entrust,
lodge

▶ noun 3 DOWN PAYMENT,
installment, part payment,
pledge, retainer, security, stake

4 SEDIMENT, accumulation, dregs,
lees, precipitate, silt

depot noun 1 STOREHOUSE,
depository, repository, warehouse
(*Chiefly U.S. & Canad.*)

2 BUS STATION, garage, terminus

depraved adjective CORRUPT,
degenerate, dissolute, evil,
immoral, sinful, vicious, vile,
wicked

depravity noun CORRUPTION,
debauchery, evil, immorality,
sinfulness, vice, wickedness

depreciate verb 1 DEVALUE,
decrease, deflate, lessen, lose
value, lower, reduce

2 DISPARAGE, belittle, denigrate,
deride, detract, run down, scorn,
sneer at

depreciation noun
1 DEVALUATION, deflation,
depression, drop, fall, slump

2 DISPARAGEMENT, belittlement,
denigration, deprecation,
detraction

depress verb 1 SADDEN, deject,
discourage, dishearten, dispirit,
make despondent, oppress, weigh
down

2 LOWER, cheapen, depreciate,
devalue, diminish, downgrade,
lessen, reduce

3 PRESS DOWN, flatten, level,
lower, push down

depressed adjective 1 LOW-
SPIRITED, blue, dejected,
despondent, discouraged,
dispirited, downcast,
downhearted, fed up, sad,
unhappy

2 POVERTY-STRICKEN, deprived,
disadvantaged, needy, poor,
run-down

3 LOWERED, cheapened,

depreciated, devalued, weakened
4 SUNKEN, concave, hollow,
indented, recessed
depressing adjective BLEAK,
discouraging, disheartening,
dismal, dispiriting, gloomy,
harrowing, sad, saddening
depression noun 1 LOW
SPIRITS, dejection, despair,
despondency, downheartedness,
dumps (informal), gloominess,
melancholy, sadness, the blues
2 RECESSION, economic decline,
hard or bad times, inactivity,
slump, stagnation
3 HOLLOW, bowl, cavity, dent,
dimple, dip, indentation, pit,
valley
deprivation noun 1 WITHHOLDING,
denial, dispossession,
expropriation, removal,
withdrawal
2 WANT, destitution, distress,
hardship, need, privation
deprive verb WITHHOLD, bereave,
despoil, dispossess, rob, strip
deprived adjective POOR, bereft,
destitute, disadvantaged, down at
heel, in need, lacking, needy
depth noun 1 DEEPNESS, drop,
extent, measure
2 INSIGHT, astuteness,
discernment, penetration,
profoundness, profundity,
sagacity, wisdom
deputation noun DELEGATION,
commission, embassy, envoys,
legation
deputize verb STAND IN FOR, act
for, take the place of, understudy
deputy noun SUBSTITUTE, delegate,
legate, lieutenant, number two,
proxy, representative, second-in-
command, surrogate
deranged adjective MAD, crazed,
crazy, demented, distracted,
insane, irrational, unbalanced,

unhinged
derelict adjective 1 ABANDONED,
deserted, dilapidated, discarded,
forsaken, neglected, ruined
▶ noun 2 TRAMP, bag lady, down-
and-out, outcast, vagrant
deride verb MOCK, disdain,
disparage, insult, jeer, ridicule,
scoff, scorn, sneer, taunt
derisory adjective RIDICULOUS,
contemptible, insulting,
laughable, lousy (slang), ludicrous,
outrageous, preposterous
derivation noun ORIGIN,
beginning, foundation, root,
source
derive from verb COME FROM,
arise from, emanate from, flow
from, issue from, originate from,
proceed from, spring from, stem
from
derogatory adjective DISPARAGING,
belittling, defamatory, offensive,
slighting, uncomplimentary,
unfavorable, unflattering
descend verb 1 MOVE DOWN, drop,
fall, go down, plummet, plunge,
sink, subside, tumble
2 SLOPE, dip, incline, slant
3 LOWER ONESELF, degenerate,
deteriorate, stoop
4 ▷▷ **be descended** ORIGINATE, be
handed down, be passed down,
derive, issue, proceed, spring;
descend on ATTACK, arrive, invade,
raid, swoop
descent noun 1 COMING DOWN,
drop, fall, plunge, swoop
2 SLOPE, declivity, dip, drop,
incline, slant
3 ANCESTRY, extraction, family
tree, genealogy, lineage, origin,
parentage
4 DECLINE, degeneration,
deterioration
describe verb 1 RELATE, depict,
explain, express, narrate, portray,

recount, report, tell

2 TRACE, delineate, draw, mark out, outline

description noun 1 ACCOUNT, depiction, explanation, narrative, portrayal, report, representation, sketch

2 KIND, brand, category, class, order, sort, type, variety

descriptive adjective GRAPHIC, detailed, explanatory, expressive, illustrative, pictorial, picturesque, vivid

desert¹ noun WILDERNESS, solitude, waste, wasteland, wilds

desert² verb ABANDON, abscond, forsake, jilt, leave, leave stranded, maroon, quit, strand, walk out on (informal)

deserted adjective ABANDONED, derelict, desolate, empty, forsaken, neglected, unoccupied, vacant

deserter noun DEFECTOR, absconder, escapee, fugitive, renegade, runaway, traitor, truant

desertion noun ABANDONMENT, absconding, apostasy, betrayal, defection, dereliction, escape, evasion, flight, relinquishment

deserve verb MERIT, be entitled to, be worthy of, earn, justify, rate, warrant

deserved adjective WELL-EARNED, due, earned, fitting, justified, merited, proper, rightful, warranted

deserving adjective WORTHY, commendable, estimable, laudable, meritorious, praiseworthy, righteous

design verb 1 PLAN, draft, draw, outline, sketch, trace

2 CREATE, conceive, fabricate, fashion, invent, originate, think up

3 INTEND, aim, mean, plan, propose, purpose

▶ noun 4 PLAN, blueprint, draft, drawing, model, outline, scheme, sketch

5 ARRANGEMENT, construction, form, organization, pattern, shape, style

6 INTENTION, aim, end, goal, object, objective, purpose, target

designate verb 1 NAME, call, dub, entitle, label, style, term

2 APPOINT, assign, choose, delegate, depute, nominate, select

designation noun NAME, description, label, mark, title

designer noun CREATOR, architect, deviser, inventor, originator, planner

desirable adjective 1 WORTHWHILE, advantageous, advisable, beneficial, good, preferable, profitable, win-win (informal)

2 ATTRACTIVE, adorable, alluring, fetching, glamorous, seductive, sexy (informal)

desire verb 1 WANT, crave, hanker after, hope for, long for, set one's heart on, thirst for, wish for, yearn for

▶ noun 2 WISH, aspiration, craving, hankering, hope, longing, thirst, want

3 LUST, appetite, libido, passion

desist verb STOP, break off, cease, discontinue, end, forbear, leave off, pause, refrain from

desolate adjective 1 UNINHABITED, bare, barren, bleak, dreary, godforsaken, solitary, wild

2 MISERABLE, dejected, despondent, disconsolate, downcast, forlorn, gloomy, wretched

▶ verb 3 LAY WASTE, depopulate, despoil, destroy, devastate, lay low, pillage, plunder, ravage, ruin

4 DEJECT, depress, discourage,

dishearten, dismay, distress, grieve

desolation noun 1 RUIN, destruction, devastation, havoc
2 BLEAKNESS, barrenness, isolation, solitude
3 MISERY, anguish, dejection, despair, distress, gloom, sadness, woe, wretchedness

despair noun 1 DESPONDENCY, anguish, dejection, depression, desperation, gloom, hopelessness, misery, wretchedness
▶ verb 2 LOSE HOPE, give up, lose heart

despairing adjective HOPELESS, dejected, desperate, despondent, disconsolate, frantic, grief-stricken, inconsolable, miserable, wretched

despatch see **DISPATCH**

desperado noun CRIMINAL, bandit, lawbreaker, outlaw, villain

desperate adjective 1 RECKLESS, audacious, daring, frantic, furious, risky
2 GRAVE, drastic, extreme, urgent

desperately adverb 1 GRAVELY, badly, dangerously, perilously, seriously, severely
2 HOPELESSLY, appallingly, fearfully, frightfully, shockingly

desperation noun
1 RECKLESSNESS, foolhardiness, frenzy, impetuosity, madness, rashness
2 MISERY, agony, anguish, despair, hopelessness, trouble, unhappiness, worry

despicable adjective CONTEMPTIBLE, detestable, disgraceful, hateful, lousy (slang), mean, scuzzy (slang), shameful, sordid, vile, worthless, wretched

despise verb LOOK DOWN ON, abhor, detest, loathe, revile, scorn

despite preposition IN SPITE OF, against, even with, in the face of, in the teeth of, notwithstanding, regardless of, undeterred by

despondency noun DEJECTION, depression, despair, desperation, gloom, low spirits, melancholy, misery, sadness

despondent adjective DEJECTED, depressed, disconsolate, disheartened, dispirited, downhearted, glum, in despair, sad, sorrowful

despot noun TYRANT, autocrat, dictator, oppressor

despotic adjective TYRANNICAL, authoritarian, autocratic, dictatorial, domineering, imperious, oppressive

despotism noun TYRANNY, autocracy, dictatorship, oppression, totalitarianism

destination noun JOURNEY'S END, haven, resting-place, station, stop, terminus

destined adjective FATED, bound, certain, doomed, intended, meant, predestined

destiny noun FATE, doom, fortune, karma, kismet, lot, portion

destitute adjective PENNILESS, down and out, down on one's luck (informal), impoverished, indigent, insolvent, moneyless, penurious, poor, poverty-stricken

destroy verb RUIN, annihilate, crush, demolish, devastate, eradicate, shatter, wipe out, wreck

destruction noun RUIN, annihilation, demolition, devastation, eradication, extermination, havoc, slaughter, wreckage

destructive adjective DAMAGING, calamitous, catastrophic, deadly, devastating, fatal, harmful, lethal, ruinous

detach verb SEPARATE, cut off, disconnect, disengage, divide, remove, sever, tear off, unfasten

detached adjective 1 SEPARATE, disconnected, discrete, unconnected
2 UNINVOLVED, disinterested, dispassionate, impartial, impersonal, neutral, objective, reserved, unbiased

detachment noun
1 INDIFFERENCE, aloofness, coolness, nonchalance, remoteness, unconcern
2 IMPARTIALITY, fairness, neutrality, objectivity
3 (military) UNIT, body, force, party, patrol, squad, task force

detail noun 1 POINT, aspect, component, element, fact, factor, feature, particular, respect
2 FINE POINT, nicety, particular, triviality
3 (military) PARTY, assignment, body, detachment, duty, fatigue, force, squad
▶ verb 4 LIST, catalog, enumerate, itemize, recite, recount, rehearse, relate, tabulate
5 APPOINT, allocate, assign, charge, commission, delegate, send

detailed adjective COMPREHENSIVE, blow-by-blow, exhaustive, full, intricate, minute, particular, thorough

detain verb 1 DELAY, check, hinder, hold up, impede, keep back, retard, slow up (or down)
2 HOLD, arrest, confine, intern, restrain

detect verb 1 NOTICE, ascertain, identify, note, observe, perceive, recognize, spot
2 DISCOVER, find, track down, uncover, unmask

detective noun INVESTIGATOR, cop (slang), gumshoe (slang), private eye, private investigator, sleuth (informal)

detention noun IMPRISONMENT, confinement, custody, incarceration, quarantine

deter verb DISCOURAGE, dissuade, frighten, inhibit from, intimidate, prevent, put off, stop, talk out of

detergent noun CLEANER, cleanser

deteriorate verb DECLINE, degenerate, go downhill (informal), lower, slump, worsen

determination noun TENACITY, dedication, doggedness, fortitude, perseverance, persistence, resolve, single-mindedness, steadfastness, willpower

determine verb 1 SETTLE, conclude, decide, end, finish, ordain, regulate
2 FIND OUT, ascertain, detect, discover, learn, verify, work out
3 DECIDE, choose, elect, make up one's mind, resolve

determined adjective RESOLUTE, dogged, firm, intent, persevering, persistent, single-minded, steadfast, tenacious, unwavering

deterrent noun DISCOURAGEMENT, check, curb, disincentive, hindrance, impediment, obstacle, restraint

detest verb HATE, abhor, abominate, despise, dislike intensely, loathe, recoil from

detonate verb EXPLODE, blast, blow up, discharge, set off, trigger

detour noun DIVERSION, bypass, circuitous or indirect route, roundabout way

detract verb LESSEN, devaluate, diminish, lower, reduce, take away from

detriment noun DAMAGE, disadvantage, disservice, harm,

hurt, impairment, injury, loss

detrimental adjective DAMAGING,
adverse, deleterious, destructive,
disadvantageous, harmful,
prejudicial, unfavorable

devastate verb DESTROY,
demolish, lay waste, level, ravage,
raze, ruin, sack, wreck

devastating adjective
OVERWHELMING, cutting,
overpowering, savage, trenchant,
vitriolic, withering

devastation noun DESTRUCTION,
demolition, desolation, havoc,
ruin

develop verb 1 ADVANCE, evolve,
flourish, grow, mature, progress,
prosper, ripen
2 FORM, breed, establish, generate,
invent, originate
3 EXPAND, amplify, augment,
broaden, elaborate, enlarge,
unfold, work out

development noun 1 GROWTH,
advance, evolution, expansion,
improvement, increase, progress,
spread
2 EVENT, happening, incident,
occurrence, result, turn of events,
upshot

deviant adjective 1 PERVERTED,
kinky (slang), sick (informal),
twisted, warped
▶ noun 2 PERVERT, freak, misfit

deviate verb DIFFER, depart,
diverge, stray, swerve, veer,
wander

deviation noun DEPARTURE,
digression, discrepancy, disparity,
divergence, inconsistency,
irregularity, shift, variation

device noun 1 GADGET, apparatus,
appliance, contraption,
implement, instrument,
machine, tool
2 PLOY, gambit, maneuver, plan,
scheme, stratagem, trick, wile

devil noun 1 ▷▷ **the Devil** SATAN,
Beelzebub, Evil One, Lucifer,
Mephistopheles, Old Nick
(informal), Prince of Darkness
2 BRUTE, beast, demon, fiend,
monster, ogre, terror
3 SCAMP, rascal, rogue, scoundrel
4 PERSON, beggar, creature, thing,
wretch

devilish adjective FIENDISH,
atrocious, damnable, detestable,
diabolical, hellish, infernal,
satanic, wicked

devious adjective 1 SLY,
calculating, deceitful, dishonest,
double-dealing, insincere,
scheming, surreptitious,
underhand, wily
2 INDIRECT, circuitous, rambling,
roundabout

devise verb WORK OUT, conceive,
construct, contrive, design, dream
up, formulate, invent, think up

devoid adjective LACKING, bereft,
deficient, destitute, empty, free
from, wanting, without

devote verb DEDICATE, allot, apply,
assign, commit, give, pledge,
reserve, set apart

devoted adjective DEDICATED,
ardent, committed, constant,
devout, faithful, loyal, staunch,
steadfast, true

devotee noun ENTHUSIAST,
adherent, admirer, aficionado,
buff (informal), disciple, fan,
fanatic, follower, supporter

devotion noun 1 DEDICATION,
adherence, allegiance,
commitment, constancy,
faithfulness, fidelity, loyalty
2 LOVE, affection, attachment,
fondness, passion
3 DEVOUTNESS, godliness,
holiness, piety, reverence,
spirituality
4 ▷▷ **devotions** PRAYERS, church

service, divine office, religious observance

devour *verb* 1 EAT, chow down (*slang*), consume, gobble, gulp, guzzle, polish off (*informal*), swallow, wolf
2 DESTROY, annihilate, consume, ravage, waste, wipe out
3 ENJOY, read compulsively *or* voraciously, take in

devout *adjective* RELIGIOUS, godly, holy, orthodox, pious, prayerful, pure, reverent, saintly

dexterity *noun* 1 SKILL, adroitness, deftness, expertise, finesse, nimbleness, proficiency, touch
2 CLEVERNESS, ability, aptitude, ingenuity

diabolical *adjective* (*informal*) DREADFUL, abysmal, appalling, atrocious, hellish, outrageous, shocking, terrible

diagnose *verb* IDENTIFY, analyze, determine, distinguish, interpret, pinpoint, pronounce, recognize

diagnosis *noun* 1 EXAMINATION, analysis, investigation, scrutiny
2 OPINION, conclusion, interpretation, pronouncement

diagonal *adjective* SLANTING, angled, cross, crossways, crosswise, oblique

diagonally *adverb* ASLANT, at an angle, cornerwise, crosswise, obliquely

diagram *noun* PLAN, chart, drawing, figure, graph, representation, sketch

dialect *noun* LANGUAGE, brogue, idiom, jargon, patois, provincialism, speech, vernacular

dialogue *noun* CONVERSATION, communication, conference, discourse, discussion

diary *noun* JOURNAL, appointment book, blog (*informal*), chronicle, daily record, engagement book,

Filofax (*Trademark*), weblog

dictate *verb* 1 SPEAK, read out, say, utter
2 ORDER, command, decree, demand, direct, impose, lay down the law, pronounce
▶ *noun* 3 COMMAND, decree, demand, direction, edict, fiat, injunction, order
4 PRINCIPLE, code, law, rule

dictator *noun* ABSOLUTE RULER, autocrat, despot, oppressor, tyrant

dictatorial *adjective* 1 ABSOLUTE, arbitrary, autocratic, despotic, totalitarian, tyrannical, unlimited, unrestricted
2 DOMINEERING, authoritarian, bossy (*informal*), imperious, oppressive, overbearing

dictatorship *noun* ABSOLUTE RULE, absolutism, authoritarianism, autocracy, despotism, totalitarianism, tyranny

diction *noun* PRONUNCIATION, articulation, delivery, elocution, enunciation, fluency, inflection, intonation, speech

dictionary *noun* WORDBOOK, glossary, lexicon, vocabulary

die *verb* 1 PASS AWAY, breathe one's last, croak (*slang*), expire, give up the ghost, kick the bucket (*slang*), peg out (*informal*), perish, snuff it (*slang*)
2 DWINDLE, decay, decline, fade, sink, subside, wane, wilt, wither
3 STOP, break down, fade out *or* away, fail, fizzle out, halt, lose power, peter out, run down
4 ▷▷ **be dying** LONG, ache, be eager, desire, hunger, pine for, yearn

die-hard *noun* REACTIONARY, fanatic, old fogey, stick-in-the-mud (*informal*)

diet¹ *noun* 1 FOOD, fare,

nourishment, nutriment, provisions, rations, sustenance, victuals
2 REGIME, abstinence, fast, regimen
▶ *verb* 3 SLIM, abstain, eat sparingly, fast, lose weight

diet² *noun* COUNCIL, chamber, congress, convention, legislature, meeting, parliament

differ *verb* 1 BE DISSIMILAR, contradict, contrast, depart from, diverge, run counter to, stand apart, vary
2 DISAGREE, clash, contend, debate, demur, dispute, dissent, oppose, take exception, take issue

difference *noun* 1 DISSIMILARITY, alteration, change, contrast, discrepancy, disparity, diversity, variation, variety
2 DISAGREEMENT, argument, clash, conflict, contretemps, debate, dispute, quarrel
3 REMAINDER, balance, rest, result

different *adjective* 1 UNLIKE, altered, changed, contrasting, disparate, dissimilar, divergent, inconsistent, opposed
2 VARIOUS, assorted, diverse, miscellaneous, sundry, varied
3 UNUSUAL, atypical, distinctive, extraordinary, peculiar, singular, special, strange, uncommon

differentiate *verb* 1 DISTINGUISH, contrast, discriminate, make a distinction, mark off, separate, set off *or* apart, tell apart
2 MAKE DIFFERENT, adapt, alter, change, convert, modify, transform

difficult *adjective* 1 HARD, arduous, demanding, formidable, laborious, onerous, strenuous, uphill
2 PROBLEMATICAL, abstruse, baffling, complex, complicated,

intricate, involved, knotty, obscure
3 HARD TO PLEASE, demanding, fastidious, fussy, high-maintenance, perverse, refractory, unaccommodating

difficulty *noun* 1 LABORIOUSNESS, arduousness, awkwardness, hardship, strain, strenuousness, tribulation
2 PREDICAMENT, dilemma, embarrassment, hot water (*informal*), jam (*informal*), mess, plight, quandary, trouble
3 PROBLEM, complication, hindrance, hurdle, impediment, obstacle, pitfall, snag, stumbling block

diffidence *noun* SHYNESS, bashfulness, hesitancy, insecurity, modesty, reserve, self-consciousness, timidity

diffident *adjective* SHY, bashful, doubtful, hesitant, insecure, modest, reserved, self-conscious, timid, unassertive, unassuming

dig *verb* 1 EXCAVATE, burrow, delve, hollow out, mine, quarry, scoop, tunnel
2 INVESTIGATE, delve, dig down, go into, probe, research, search
3 (with *out* or *up*) FIND, discover, expose, uncover, unearth, uproot
4 POKE, drive, jab, prod, punch, thrust
▶ *noun* 5 POKE, jab, prod, punch, thrust
6 CUTTING REMARK, barb, crack (*slang*), gibe, insult, jeer, sneer, taunt, wisecrack (*informal*)

digest *verb* 1 INGEST, absorb, assimilate, dissolve, incorporate
2 TAKE IN, absorb, consider, contemplate, grasp, study, understand
▶ *noun* 3 SUMMARY, abridgment, abstract, epitome, précis, résumé,

synopsis

digestion noun INGESTION, absorption, assimilation, conversion, incorporation, transformation

dignified adjective DISTINGUISHED, formal, grave, imposing, noble, reserved, solemn, stately

dignitary noun PUBLIC FIGURE, bigwig (*informal*), high-up (*informal*), notable, personage, pillar of society, V.I.P., worthy

dignity noun 1 DECORUM, courtliness, grandeur, gravity, loftiness, majesty, nobility, solemnity, stateliness
2 HONOR, eminence, importance, rank, respectability, standing, status
3 SELF-IMPORTANCE, pride, self-esteem, self-respect

digress verb WANDER, depart, deviate, diverge, drift, get off the point or subject, go off at a tangent, ramble, stray

digression noun DEPARTURE, aside, detour, deviation, divergence, diversion, straying, wandering

dilapidated adjective RUINED, broken-down, crumbling, decrepit, in ruins, ramshackle, rickety, run-down, tumbledown

dilate verb ENLARGE, broaden, expand, puff out, stretch, swell, widen

dilatory adjective TIME-WASTING, delaying, lingering, procrastinating, slow, sluggish, tardy, tarrying

dilemma noun PREDICAMENT, difficulty, mess, plight, problem, puzzle, quandary, spot (*informal*)

dilettante noun AMATEUR, aesthete, dabbler, trifler

diligence noun APPLICATION, attention, care, industry, laboriousness, perseverance

diligent adjective HARD-WORKING, assiduous, attentive, careful, conscientious, industrious, painstaking, persistent, studious, tireless

dilute verb 1 WATER DOWN, adulterate, cut, make thinner, thin (out), weaken
2 REDUCE, attenuate, decrease, diffuse, diminish, lessen, mitigate, temper, weaken

dim adjective 1 POORLY LIT, cloudy, dark, gray, overcast, shadowy, tenebrous
2 UNCLEAR, bleary, blurred, faint, fuzzy, ill-defined, indistinct, obscured, shadowy
3 (*informal*) STUPID, dense, dozy (*Brit. informal*), dull, dumb (*informal*), obtuse, slow on the uptake (*informal*), thick
4 ▷▷ **take a dim view** DISAPPROVE, be displeased, be skeptical, look askance, reject, suspect, take exception, view with disfavor
▶ verb 5 DULL, blur, cloud, darken, fade, obscure

dimension noun (often plural) MEASUREMENT, amplitude, bulk, capacity, extent, proportions, size, volume

diminish verb 1 DECREASE, curtail, cut, lessen, lower, reduce, shrink
2 DWINDLE, decline, die out, recede, subside, wane

diminutive adjective SMALL, little, mini, miniature, minute, petite, tiny, undersized

din noun 1 NOISE, clamor, clatter, commotion, crash, pandemonium, racket, row, uproar
▶ verb 2 ▷▷ **din (something) into (someone)** INSTILL, drum into, go on at, hammer into, inculcate, instruct, teach

dine verb EAT, banquet, chow down (*slang*), feast, lunch, sup

dingy adjective DULL, dark, dim, drab, dreary, gloomy, murky, obscure, somber

dinner noun MEAL, banquet, feast, main meal, repast, spread (*informal*)

dip verb 1 PLUNGE, bathe, douse, duck, dunk, immerse
2 SLOPE, decline, descend, drop (down), fall, lower, sink, subside
▶ noun 3 PLUNGE, douche, drenching, ducking, immersion, soaking
4 BATHE, dive, plunge, swim
5 HOLLOW, basin, concavity, depression, hole, incline, slope
6 DROP, decline, fall, lowering, sag, slip, slump

dip into verb SAMPLE, browse, glance at, peruse, skim

diplomacy noun 1 STATESMANSHIP, international negotiation, statecraft
2 TACT, artfulness, craft, delicacy, discretion, finesse, savoir-faire, skill, subtlety

diplomat noun NEGOTIATOR, conciliator, go-between, mediator, moderator, politician, tactician

diplomatic adjective TACTFUL, adept, discreet, polite, politic, prudent, sensitive, subtle

dire adjective 1 DISASTROUS, awful, calamitous, catastrophic, horrible, ruinous, terrible, woeful
2 DESPERATE, critical, crucial, drastic, extreme, now or never, pressing, urgent
3 GRIM, dismal, dreadful, fearful, gloomy, ominous, portentous

direct adjective 1 STRAIGHT, nonstop, not crooked, shortest, through, unbroken, uninterrupted
2 IMMEDIATE, face-to-face, first-hand, head-on, personal
3 HONEST, candid, frank, open, plain-spoken, straight, straightforward, upfront (*informal*)
4 EXPLICIT, absolute, blunt, categorical, downright, express, plain, point-blank, unambiguous, unequivocal
▶ verb 5 CONTROL, conduct, guide, handle, lead, manage, oversee, run, supervise
6 ORDER, bid, charge, command, demand, dictate, instruct
7 GUIDE, indicate, lead, point in the direction of, point the way, show
8 ADDRESS, label, mail, route, send
9 AIM, focus, level, point, train

direction noun 1 WAY, aim, bearing, course, line, path, road, route, track
2 MANAGEMENT, administration, charge, command, control, guidance, leadership, order, supervision

directions plural noun INSTRUCTIONS, briefing, guidance, guidelines, plan, recommendation, regulations

directive noun ORDER, command, decree, edict, injunction, instruction, mandate, regulation, ruling

directly adverb 1 STRAIGHT, by the shortest route, exactly, in a beeline, precisely, unswervingly, without deviation
2 HONESTLY, openly, plainly, point-blank, straightforwardly, truthfully, unequivocally
3 AT ONCE, as soon as possible, forthwith, immediately, promptly, right away, straightaway

director noun CONTROLLER, administrator, chief, executive, governor, head, leader, manager, supervisor

dirge noun LAMENT, dead march, elegy, funeral song, requiem, threnody

dirt noun 1 FILTH, dust, grime, impurity, muck, mud
2 SOIL, clay, earth, loam
3 OBSCENITY, indecency, pornography, sleaze, smut

dirty adjective 1 FILTHY, foul, grimy, grubby, messy, mucky, muddy, polluted, scuzzy (*slang*), soiled, unclean
2 DISHONEST, crooked, fraudulent, illegal, lowdown (*slang*), scuzzy (*slang*), treacherous, unfair, unscrupulous, unsporting
3 OBSCENE, blue, indecent, pornographic, salacious, scuzzy (*slang*), sleazy, smutty, X-rated
4 *as in* **a dirty look** ANGRY, annoyed, bitter, choked, indignant, offended, resentful, scorching
▶ *verb* 5 SOIL, blacken, defile, foul, muddy, pollute, smirch, spoil, stain

disability noun 1 HANDICAP, affliction, ailment, complaint, defect, disorder, impairment, infirmity, malady
2 INCAPACITY, inability, unfitness

disable verb 1 HANDICAP, cripple, damage, enfeeble, immobilize, impair, incapacitate, paralyze
2 DISQUALIFY, invalidate, render *or* declare incapable

disabled adjective HANDICAPPED, challenged (*informal*), crippled, incapacitated, infirm, lame, paralyzed, weakened

disadvantage noun 1 HARM, damage, detriment, disservice, hurt, injury, loss, prejudice
2 DRAWBACK, downside, handicap, inconvenience, nuisance, snag, trouble

disagree verb 1 DIFFER (IN OPINION), argue, clash, cross swords, dispute, dissent, object, quarrel, take issue with
2 CONFLICT, be dissimilar, contradict, counter, differ, diverge, run counter to, vary
3 MAKE ILL, bother, discomfort, distress, hurt, nauseate, sicken, trouble, upset

disagreeable adjective 1 NASTY, disgusting, displeasing, distasteful, objectionable, obnoxious, offensive, repugnant, repulsive, scuzzy (*slang*), unpleasant
2 RUDE, bad-tempered, churlish, difficult, disobliging, irritable, surly, unpleasant

disagreement noun
1 INCOMPATIBILITY, difference, discrepancy, disparity, dissimilarity, divergence, incongruity, variance
2 ARGUMENT, altercation, clash, conflict, dispute, dissent, quarrel, row, squabble

disallow verb REJECT, disavow, dismiss, disown, rebuff, refuse, repudiate

disappear verb 1 VANISH, evanesce, fade away, pass, recede
2 CEASE, die out, dissolve, evaporate, leave no trace, melt away, pass away, perish

disappearance noun VANISHING, departure, eclipse, evanescence, evaporation, going, melting, passing

disappoint verb LET DOWN, disenchant, disgruntle, dishearten, disillusion, dismay, dissatisfy, fail

disappointed adjective LET DOWN, cast down, despondent, discouraged, disenchanted, disgruntled, dissatisfied,

downhearted, frustrated
disappointing *adjective*
UNSATISFACTORY, depressing,
disconcerting, discouraging,
inadequate, insufficient, lousy
(*slang*), sad, sorry
disappointment *noun*
1 FRUSTRATION, chagrin,
discontent, discouragement,
disenchantment,
disillusionment, dissatisfaction,
regret
2 LETDOWN, blow, calamity, choker
(*informal*), misfortune, setback
disapproval *noun* DISPLEASURE,
censure, condemnation, criticism,
denunciation, dissatisfaction,
objection, reproach
disapprove *verb* CONDEMN,
deplore, dislike, find
unacceptable, frown on, look
down one's nose at (*informal*),
object to, reject, take a dim view
of, take exception to
disarm *verb* 1 RENDER
DEFENSELESS, disable
2 WIN OVER, persuade, set at ease
3 DEMILITARIZE, deactivate,
demobilize, disband
disarmament *noun* ARMS
REDUCTION, arms limitation,
de-escalation, demilitarization,
demobilization
disarming *adjective* CHARMING,
irresistible, likable *or* likeable,
persuasive, winning
disarrange *verb* DISORDER,
confuse, disorganize, disturb,
jumble (up), mess (up), scatter,
shake (up), shuffle
disarray *noun* 1 CONFUSION,
disorder, disorganization,
disunity, indiscipline, unruliness
2 UNTIDINESS, chaos, clutter,
hotchpotch, jumble, mess,
muddle, shambles
disaster *noun* CATASTROPHE,

adversity, calamity, cataclysm,
misfortune, ruin, tragedy, trouble
disastrous *adjective* TERRIBLE,
calamitous, cataclysmic,
catastrophic, devastating, fatal,
ruinous, tragic
disbelief *noun* SKEPTICISM,
distrust, doubt, dubiety,
incredulity, mistrust, unbelief
discard *verb* GET RID OF, abandon,
cast aside, dispense with, dispose
of, drop, dump (*informal*), jettison,
reject, throw away *or* out
discharge *verb* 1 RELEASE, allow
to go, clear, free, liberate, pardon,
set free
2 DISMISS, cashier, discard, expel,
fire (*informal*), oust, remove, sack
(*informal*)
3 FIRE, detonate, explode, let loose
(*informal*), let off, set off, shoot
4 POUR FORTH, dispense, emit,
exude, give off, leak, ooze, release
5 CARRY OUT, accomplish, do,
execute, fulfill, observe, perform
6 PAY, clear, honor, meet, relieve,
satisfy, settle, square up
▶ *noun* 7 RELEASE, acquittal,
clearance, liberation, pardon
8 DISMISSAL, demobilization,
ejection
9 FIRING, blast, burst, detonation,
explosion, report, salvo, shot,
volley
10 EMISSION, excretion, ooze, pus,
secretion, seepage, suppuration
disciple *noun* FOLLOWER,
adherent, apostle, devotee, pupil,
student, supporter
disciplinarian *noun*
AUTHORITARIAN, despot, martinet,
stickler, taskmaster, tyrant
discipline *noun* 1 TRAINING,
drill, exercise, method, practice,
regimen, regulation
2 PUNISHMENT, castigation,
chastisement, correction

3 SELF-CONTROL, conduct, control, orderliness, regulation, restraint, strictness

4 FIELD OF STUDY, area, branch of knowledge, course, curriculum, speciality, subject

▶ verb 5 TRAIN, bring up, drill, educate, exercise, prepare

6 PUNISH, bring to book, castigate, chasten, chastise, correct, penalize, reprimand, reprove

disclose verb 1 MAKE KNOWN, broadcast, communicate, confess, divulge, let slip, publish, relate, reveal

2 SHOW, bring to light, expose, lay bare, reveal, uncover, unveil

disclosure noun REVELATION, acknowledgment, admission, announcement, confession, declaration, divulgence, leak, publication

discolor verb STAIN, fade, mark, soil, streak, tarnish, tinge

discomfort noun 1 PAIN, ache, hurt, irritation, malaise, soreness

2 UNEASINESS, annoyance, distress, hardship, irritation, nuisance, trouble

disconcert verb DISTURB, faze, fluster, perturb, rattle (informal), take aback, unsettle, upset, worry

disconcerting adjective DISTURBING, alarming, awkward, bewildering, confusing, distracting, embarrassing, off-putting (Brit. informal), perplexing, upsetting

disconnect verb CUT OFF, detach, disengage, divide, part, separate, sever, take apart, uncouple

disconnected adjective ILLOGICAL, confused, disjointed, incoherent, jumbled, mixed-up, rambling, unintelligible

disconsolate adjective INCONSOLABLE, crushed, dejected, desolate, forlorn, grief-stricken, heartbroken, miserable, wretched

discontent noun DISSATISFACTION, displeasure, envy, regret, restlessness, uneasiness, unhappiness

discontented adjective DISSATISFIED, disaffected, disgruntled, displeased, exasperated, fed up, unhappy, vexed

discontinue verb STOP, abandon, break off, cease, drop, end, give up, quit, suspend, terminate

discord noun 1 DISAGREEMENT, conflict, dissension, disunity, division, friction, incompatibility, strife

2 DISHARMONY, cacophony, din, dissonance, harshness, jarring, racket, tumult

discordant adjective
1 DISAGREEING, at odds, clashing, conflicting, contradictory, contrary, different, incompatible

2 INHARMONIOUS, cacophonous, dissonant, grating, harsh, jarring, shrill, strident

discount verb 1 LEAVE OUT, brush off (slang), disbelieve, disregard, ignore, overlook, pass over

2 DEDUCT, lower, mark down, reduce, take off

▶ noun 3 DEDUCTION, concession, cut, rebate, reduction

discourage verb 1 DISHEARTEN, dampen, deject, demoralize, depress, dispirit, intimidate, overawe, put a damper on

2 PUT OFF, deter, dissuade, inhibit, prevent, talk out of

discouraged adjective PUT OFF, crestfallen, deterred, disheartened, dismayed, dispirited, downcast, down in the mouth, glum

discouragement noun 1 LOSS

OF CONFIDENCE, dejection, depression, despair, despondency, disappointment, dismay, downheartedness
2 DETERRENT, damper, disincentive, hindrance, impediment, obstacle, opposition, setback

discouraging adjective
DISHEARTENING, dampening, daunting, depressing, disappointing, dispiriting, off-putting (Brit. informal), unfavorable

discourse noun **1** CONVERSATION, chat, communication, dialogue, discussion, seminar, speech, talk
2 SPEECH, dissertation, essay, homily, lecture, oration, sermon, treatise
▶ verb **3** HOLD FORTH, expatiate, speak, talk

discourteous adjective RUDE, bad-mannered, boorish, disrespectful, ill-mannered, impolite, insolent, offhand, ungentlemanly, ungracious

discourtesy noun **1** RUDENESS, bad manners, disrespectfulness, impertinence, impoliteness, incivility, insolence
2 INSULT, affront, cold shoulder, kick in the teeth (slang), rebuff, slight, snub

discover verb **1** FIND, come across, come upon, dig up, locate, turn up, uncover, unearth
2 FIND OUT, ascertain, detect, learn, notice, perceive, realize, recognize, uncover

discovery noun **1** FINDING, detection, disclosure, exploration, location, revelation, uncovering
2 BREAKTHROUGH, find, innovation, invention, secret

discredit verb **1** DISGRACE, bring into disrepute, defame, dishonor, disparage, slander, smear, vilify

2 DOUBT, challenge, deny, disbelieve, discount, dispute, distrust, mistrust, question
▶ noun **3** DISGRACE, dishonor, disrepute, ignominy, ill-repute, scandal, shame, stigma

discreditable adjective
DISGRACEFUL, dishonorable, ignominious, reprehensible, scandalous, shameful, unworthy

discreet adjective TACTFUL, careful, cautious, circumspect, considerate, diplomatic, guarded, judicious, prudent, wary

discrepancy noun DISAGREEMENT, conflict, contradiction, difference, disparity, divergence, incongruity, inconsistency, variation

discretion noun **1** TACT, carefulness, caution, consideration, diplomacy, judiciousness, prudence, wariness
2 CHOICE, inclination, pleasure, preference, volition, will

discriminate verb **1** SHOW PREJUDICE, favor, show bias, single out, treat as inferior, treat differently, victimize
2 DIFFERENTIATE, distinguish, draw a distinction, segregate, separate, tell the difference

discriminating adjective
DISCERNING, cultivated, fastidious, particular, refined, selective, tasteful

discrimination noun **1** PREJUDICE, bias, bigotry, favoritism, intolerance, unfairness
2 DISCERNMENT, judgment, perception, refinement, subtlety, taste

discuss verb TALK ABOUT, argue, confer, consider, converse, debate, deliberate, examine

discussion noun TALK, analysis, argument, conference, consultation, conversation, debate, deliberation, dialogue, discourse, exchange

disdain noun 1 CONTEMPT, arrogance, derision, haughtiness, scorn, superciliousness
▶ verb 2 SCORN, deride, disregard, look down on, reject, slight, sneer at, spurn

disdainful adjective CONTEMPTUOUS, aloof, arrogant, derisive, haughty, proud, scornful, sneering, supercilious, superior

disease noun ILLNESS, affliction, ailment, complaint, condition, disorder, infection, infirmity, malady, sickness

diseased adjective SICK, ailing, infected, rotten, sickly, unhealthy, unsound, unwell, unwholesome

disembark verb LAND, alight, arrive, get off, go ashore, step out of

disenchanted adjective DISILLUSIONED, cynical, disappointed, indifferent, jaundiced, let down, sick of, soured

disenchantment noun DISILLUSIONMENT, disappointment, disillusion, rude awakening

disengage verb RELEASE, disentangle, extricate, free, loosen, set free, unloose, untie

disentangle verb UNTANGLE, disconnect, disengage, extricate, free, loose, unravel

disfavor noun DISAPPROVAL, disapprobation, dislike, displeasure

disfigure verb DAMAGE, blemish, deface, deform, distort, mar, mutilate, scar

disgorge verb VOMIT, discharge, eject, empty, expel

disgrace noun 1 SHAME, degradation, dishonor, disrepute, ignominy, infamy, odium, opprobrium
2 STAIN, blemish, blot, reproach, scandal, slur, stigma
▶ verb 3 BRING SHAME UPON, degrade, discredit, dishonor, humiliate, shame, sully, taint

disgraceful adjective SHAMEFUL, contemptible, detestable, dishonorable, disreputable, ignominious, lousy (slang), scandalous, shocking, unworthy

disgruntled adjective DISCONTENTED, annoyed, displeased, dissatisfied, grumpy, irritated, peeved, put out, vexed

disguise verb 1 HIDE, camouflage, cloak, conceal, cover, mask, screen, shroud, veil
2 MISREPRESENT, fake, falsify
▶ noun 3 COSTUME, camouflage, cover, mask, screen, veil
4 FAÇADE, deception, dissimulation, front, pretense, semblance, trickery, veneer

disguised adjective IN DISGUISE, camouflaged, covert, fake, false, feigned, incognito, masked, undercover

disgust noun 1 LOATHING, abhorrence, aversion, dislike, distaste, hatred, nausea, repugnance, repulsion, revulsion
▶ verb 2 SICKEN, displease, nauseate, offend, put off, repel, revolt

disgusted adjective SICKENED, appalled, nauseated, offended, repulsed, scandalized

disgusting adjective SICKENING, foul, gross, loathsome, nauseating, offensive, repellent, repugnant, revolting

dish noun 1 BOWL, plate, platter, salver
2 FOOD, fare, recipe

dishearten verb DISCOURAGE,

cast down, deject, depress, deter, dismay, dispirit, put a damper on

disheveled *adjective* UNTIDY, bedraggled, disordered, messy, ruffled, rumpled, tousled, uncombed, unkempt

dishonest *adjective* DECEITFUL, bent (*slang*), cheating, corrupt, crooked (*informal*), disreputable, double-dealing, false, lying, treacherous

dishonesty *noun* DECEIT, cheating, chicanery, corruption, fraud, treachery, trickery, unscrupulousness

dishonor *verb* 1 SHAME, debase, debauch, defame, degrade, discredit, disgrace, sully
▶ *noun* 2 SHAME, discredit, disgrace, disrepute, ignominy, infamy, obloquy, reproach, scandal
3 INSULT, abuse, affront, discourtesy, indignity, offense, outrage, sacrilege, slight

dishonorable *adjective*
1 SHAMEFUL, contemptible, despicable, discreditable, disgraceful, ignominious, infamous, lousy (*slang*), scandalous, scuzzy (*slang*)
2 UNTRUSTWORTHY, blackguardly, corrupt, disreputable, shameless, treacherous, unprincipled, unscrupulous

disillusioned *adjective* DISENCHANTED, disabused, disappointed, enlightened, undeceived

disinclination *noun* RELUCTANCE, aversion, dislike, hesitance, objection, opposition, repugnance, resistance, unwillingness

disinclined *adjective* RELUCTANT, averse, hesitating, loath, not in the mood, opposed, resistant, unwilling

disinfect *verb* STERILIZE, clean, cleanse, decontaminate, deodorize, fumigate, purify, sanitize

disinfectant *noun* ANTISEPTIC, germicide, sterilizer

disinherit *verb* (*law*) CUT OFF, disown, dispossess, oust, repudiate

disintegrate *verb* BREAK UP, break apart, crumble, fall apart, go to pieces, separate, shatter, splinter

disinterest *noun* IMPARTIALITY, detachment, fairness, neutrality

disinterested *adjective* IMPARTIAL, detached, dispassionate, even-handed, impersonal, neutral, objective, unbiased, unprejudiced

disjointed *adjective* INCOHERENT, confused, disconnected, disordered, rambling

dislike *verb* 1 BE AVERSE TO, despise, detest, disapprove, hate, loathe, not be able to bear *or* abide *or* stand, object to, take a dim view of
▶ *noun* 2 AVERSION, animosity, antipathy, disapproval, disinclination, displeasure, distaste, enmity, hostility, repugnance

dislodge *verb* DISPLACE, disturb, extricate, force out, knock loose, oust, remove, uproot

disloyal *adjective* TREACHEROUS, faithless, false, subversive, traitorous, two-faced, unfaithful, untrustworthy

disloyalty *noun* TREACHERY, back-stabbing (*informal*), breach of trust, deceitfulness, double-dealing, falseness, inconstancy, infidelity, treason, unfaithfulness

dismal *adjective* GLOOMY, bleak, cheerless, dark, depressing, discouraging, dreary, forlorn, somber, wretched

dismantle verb TAKE APART, demolish, disassemble, strip, take to pieces

dismay verb 1 ALARM, appall, distress, frighten, horrify, paralyze, scare, terrify, unnerve
2 DISAPPOINT, daunt, discourage, dishearten, disillusion, dispirit, put off
▶ noun 3 ALARM, anxiety, apprehension, consternation, dread, fear, horror, trepidation
4 DISAPPOINTMENT, chagrin, discouragement, disillusionment

dismember verb CUT INTO PIECES, amputate, dissect, mutilate, sever

dismiss verb 1 SACK (informal), ax (informal), cashier, discharge, fire (informal), give notice to, give (someone) their marching orders, lay off, remove
2 LET GO, disperse, dissolve, free, release, send away
3 PUT OUT OF ONE'S MIND, banish, discard, dispel, disregard, lay aside, reject, set aside

dismissal noun THE SACK (informal), expulsion, marching orders (informal), notice, removal, the boot (slang), the push (slang)

disobedience noun DEFIANCE, indiscipline, insubordination, mutiny, noncompliance, nonobservance, recalcitrance, revolt, unruliness, waywardness

disobedient adjective DEFIANT, contrary, disorderly, insubordinate, intractable, naughty, refractory, undisciplined, unruly, wayward

disobey verb REFUSE TO OBEY, contravene, defy, disregard, flout, ignore, infringe, rebel, violate

disorder noun 1 UNTIDINESS, chaos, clutter, confusion, disarray, jumble, mess, muddle, shambles
2 DISTURBANCE, commotion, riot, turmoil, unrest, unruliness, uproar
3 ILLNESS, affliction, ailment, complaint, disease, malady, sickness

disorderly adjective 1 UNTIDY, chaotic, confused, disorganized, higgledy-piggledy (informal), jumbled, messy, shambolic (informal)
2 UNRULY, disruptive, indisciplined, lawless, riotous, rowdy, tumultuous, turbulent, ungovernable

disorganized adjective MUDDLED, chaotic, confused, disordered, haphazard, jumbled, unsystematic

disown verb DENY, cast off, disavow, disclaim, reject, renounce, repudiate

disparage verb RUN DOWN, belittle, denigrate, deprecate, deride, malign, put down, ridicule, slander, vilify

dispassionate adjective
1 UNEMOTIONAL, calm, collected, composed, cool, imperturbable, serene, unruffled
2 OBJECTIVE, detached, disinterested, fair, impartial, impersonal, neutral, unbiased, unprejudiced

dispatch, despatch verb 1 SEND, consign, dismiss, hasten
2 CARRY OUT, discharge, dispose of, finish, perform, settle
3 MURDER, assassinate, execute, kill, slaughter, slay
▶ noun 4 MESSAGE, account, bulletin, communication, communiqué, news, report, story

dispel verb DRIVE AWAY, banish, chase away, dismiss, disperse, eliminate, expel

dispense verb 1 DISTRIBUTE,

allocate, allot, apportion, assign, deal out, dole out, share
2 PREPARE, measure, mix, supply
3 ADMINISTER, apply, carry out, discharge, enforce, execute, implement, operate
4 ▷▷ **dispense with: a** DO AWAY WITH, abolish, brush aside, cancel, dispose of, get rid of **b** DO WITHOUT, abstain from, forgo, give up, relinquish

disperse verb 1 SCATTER, broadcast, diffuse, disseminate, distribute, spread, strew
2 BREAK UP, disband, dissolve, scatter, separate

dispirited adjective DISHEARTENED, crestfallen, dejected, depressed, despondent, discouraged, downcast, gloomy, glum, sad

displace verb 1 MOVE, disturb, misplace, shift, transpose
2 REPLACE, oust, succeed, supersede, supplant, take the place of

display verb 1 SHOW, demonstrate, disclose, exhibit, expose, manifest, present, reveal
2 SHOW OFF, flash (informal), flaunt, flourish, parade, vaunt
▶ noun 3 EXHIBITION, array, demonstration, presentation, revelation, show
4 SHOW, flourish, ostentation, pageant, parade, pomp, spectacle

displease verb ANNOY, anger, irk, irritate, offend, pique, put out, upset, vex

displeasure noun ANNOYANCE, anger, disapproval, dissatisfaction, distaste, indignation, irritation, resentment

disposable adjective 1 THROWAWAY, biodegradable, nonreturnable
2 AVAILABLE, consumable, expendable

disposal noun 1 THROWING AWAY, discarding, dumping (informal), ejection, jettisoning, removal, riddance, scrapping
2 ▷▷ **at one's disposal** AVAILABLE, at one's service, consumable, expendable, free for use

dispose verb ARRANGE, array, distribute, group, marshal, order, place, put

dispose of verb 1 GET RID OF, destroy, discard, dump (informal), jettison, scrap, throw out or away, unload
2 DEAL WITH, decide, determine, end, finish with, settle

disposition noun 1 CHARACTER, constitution, make-up, nature, spirit, temper, temperament
2 TENDENCY, bent, bias, habit, inclination, leaning, proclivity, propensity
3 ARRANGEMENT, classification, distribution, grouping, ordering, organization, placement

disproportion noun INEQUALITY, asymmetry, discrepancy, disparity, imbalance, lopsidedness, unevenness

disproportionate adjective UNEQUAL, excessive, inordinate, out of proportion, unbalanced, uneven, unreasonable

disprove verb PROVE FALSE, contradict, discredit, expose, give the lie to, invalidate, negate, rebut, refute

dispute noun 1 DISAGREEMENT, altercation, argument, conflict, feud, quarrel
2 ARGUMENT, contention, controversy, debate, discussion, dissension
▶ verb 3 DOUBT, challenge, contest, contradict, deny, impugn, question, rebut
4 ARGUE, clash, cross swords,

debate, quarrel, squabble

disqualification noun BAN, elimination, exclusion, ineligibility, rejection

disqualified adjective INELIGIBLE, debarred, eliminated, knocked out, out of the running

disqualify verb BAN, debar, declare ineligible, preclude, prohibit, rule out

disquiet noun 1 UNEASINESS, alarm, anxiety, concern, disturbance, foreboding, nervousness, trepidation, worry
▶ verb 2 MAKE UNEASY, bother, concern, disturb, perturb, trouble, unsettle, upset, worry

disregard verb 1 IGNORE, brush aside or away, discount, make light of, neglect, overlook, pass over, pay no heed to, turn a blind eye to
▶ noun 2 INATTENTION, contempt, disdain, disrespect, indifference, neglect, negligence, oversight

disrepair noun DILAPIDATION, collapse, decay, deterioration, ruination

disreputable adjective DISCREDITABLE, dishonorable, ignominious, infamous, louche, notorious, scandalous, shady (informal), shameful

disrepute noun DISCREDIT, disgrace, dishonor, ignominy, ill repute, infamy, obloquy, shame, unpopularity

disrespect noun CONTEMPT, cheek, impertinence, impoliteness, impudence, insolence, irreverence, lack of respect, rudeness, sauce

disrespectful adjective CONTEMPTUOUS, cheeky, discourteous, impertinent, impolite, impudent, insolent, insulting, irreverent, rude

disrupt verb 1 DISTURB, confuse, disorder, disorganize, spoil, upset 2 INTERRUPT, break up or into, interfere with, intrude, obstruct, unsettle, upset

disruption noun DISTURBANCE, interference, interruption, stoppage

disruptive adjective DISTURBING, disorderly, distracting, troublesome, unruly, unsettling, upsetting

dissatisfaction noun DISCONTENT, annoyance, chagrin, disappointment, displeasure, frustration, irritation, resentment, unhappiness

dissatisfied adjective DISCONTENTED, disappointed, disgruntled, displeased, fed up, frustrated, unhappy, unsatisfied

dissect verb 1 CUT UP or APART, anatomize, dismember, lay open 2 ANALYZE, break down, explore, inspect, investigate, research, scrutinize, study

disseminate verb SPREAD, broadcast, circulate, disperse, distribute, publicize, scatter

dissension noun DISAGREEMENT, conflict, discord, dispute, dissent, friction, quarrel, row, strife

dissent verb 1 DISAGREE, differ, object, protest, refuse, withhold assent or approval
▶ noun 2 DISAGREEMENT, discord, dissension, objection, opposition, refusal, resistance

dissenter noun OBJECTOR, dissident, nonconformist

dissertation noun THESIS, critique, discourse, disquisition, essay, exposition, treatise

disservice noun BAD TURN, harm, injury, injustice, unkindness, wrong

dissident adjective 1 DISSENTING,

disagreeing, discordant, heterodox, nonconformist
▶ *noun* 2 PROTESTER, agitator, dissenter, rebel

dissimilar *adjective* DIFFERENT, disparate, divergent, diverse, heterogeneous, unlike, unrelated, various

dissipate *verb* 1 SQUANDER, consume, deplete, expend, fritter away, run through, spend, waste
2 DISPERSE, disappear, dispel, dissolve, drive away, evaporate, scatter, vanish

dissipation *noun* 1 DISPERSAL, disappearance, disintegration, dissolution, scattering, vanishing
2 DEBAUCHERY, dissoluteness, excess, extravagance, indulgence, intemperance, prodigality, profligacy, wantonness, waste

dissociate *verb* 1 BREAK AWAY, break off, part company, quit
2 SEPARATE, detach, disconnect, distance, divorce, isolate, segregate, set apart

dissolute *adjective* IMMORAL, debauched, degenerate, depraved, dissipated, profligate, rakish, wanton, wild

dissolution *noun* 1 BREAKING UP, disintegration, division, parting, separation
2 ADJOURNMENT, discontinuation, end, finish, suspension, termination

dissolve *verb* 1 MELT, deliquesce, fuse, liquefy, soften, thaw
2 END, break up, discontinue, suspend, terminate, wind up

dissuade *verb* DETER, advise against, discourage, put off, remonstrate, talk out of, warn

distance *noun* 1 SPACE, extent, gap, interval, length, range, span, stretch
2 RESERVE, aloofness, coldness, coolness, remoteness, restraint, stiffness
3 ▷▷ **in the distance** FAR OFF, afar, far away, on the horizon, yonder
▶ *verb* 4 ▷▷ **distance oneself** SEPARATE ONESELF, be distanced from, dissociate oneself

distant *adjective* 1 FAR-OFF, abroad, far, faraway, far-flung, outlying, out-of-the-way, remote
2 APART, dispersed, distinct, scattered, separate
3 RESERVED, aloof, cool, reticent, standoffish, unapproachable, unfriendly, withdrawn

distaste *noun* DISLIKE, aversion, disgust, horror, loathing, odium, repugnance, revulsion

distasteful *adjective* UNPLEASANT, disagreeable, objectionable, offensive, repugnant, repulsive, scuzzy (*slang*), uninviting, unpalatable, unsavory

distill *verb* EXTRACT, condense, purify, refine

distinct *adjective* 1 DIFFERENT, detached, discrete, individual, separate, unconnected
2 DEFINITE, clear, decided, evident, marked, noticeable, obvious, palpable, unmistakable, well-defined

distinction *noun*
1 DIFFERENTIATION, discernment, discrimination, perception, separation
2 FEATURE, characteristic, distinctiveness, individuality, mark, particularity, peculiarity, quality
3 DIFFERENCE, contrast, differential, division, separation
4 EXCELLENCE, eminence, fame, greatness, honor, importance, merit, prominence, repute

distinctive *adjective*
CHARACTERISTIC, idiosyncratic,

individual, original, peculiar, singular, special, typical, unique

distinctly *adverb* DEFINITELY, clearly, decidedly, markedly, noticeably, obviously, patently, plainly, unmistakably

distinguish *verb* 1 DIFFERENTIATE, ascertain, decide, determine, discriminate, judge, tell apart, tell the difference
2 CHARACTERIZE, categorize, classify, mark, separate, set apart, single out
3 MAKE OUT, discern, know, perceive, pick out, recognize, see, tell

distinguished *adjective* EMINENT, acclaimed, celebrated, famed, famous, illustrious, noted, renowned, well-known

distort *verb* 1 MISREPRESENT, bias, color, falsify, pervert, slant, twist
2 DEFORM, bend, buckle, contort, disfigure, misshape, twist, warp

distortion *noun*
1 MISREPRESENTATION, bias, falsification, perversion, slant
2 DEFORMITY, bend, buckle, contortion, crookedness, malformation, twist, warp

distract *verb* 1 DIVERT, draw away, sidetrack, turn aside
2 AMUSE, beguile, engross, entertain, occupy

distracted *adjective* AGITATED, at sea, flustered, harassed, in a flap (*informal*), perplexed, puzzled, troubled

distraction *noun* 1 DIVERSION, disturbance, interference, interruption
2 ENTERTAINMENT, amusement, diversion, pastime, recreation
3 AGITATION, bewilderment, commotion, confusion, discord, disorder, disturbance

distraught *adjective* FRANTIC, agitated, beside oneself, desperate, distracted, distressed, out of one's mind, overwrought, worked-up

distress *noun* 1 WORRY, grief, heartache, misery, pain, sorrow, suffering, torment, wretchedness
2 NEED, adversity, difficulties, hardship, misfortune, poverty, privation, trouble
▶ *verb* 3 UPSET, disturb, grieve, harass, sadden, torment, trouble, worry

distressed *adjective* 1 UPSET, agitated, distracted, distraught, tormented, troubled, worried, wretched
2 POVERTY-STRICKEN, destitute, down at heel, indigent, needy, poor, straitened

distressing *adjective* UPSETTING, disturbing, harrowing, heart-breaking, painful, sad, worrying

distribute *verb* 1 HAND OUT, circulate, convey, deliver, pass round
2 SHARE, allocate, allot, apportion, deal, dispense, dole out

distribution *noun* 1 DELIVERY, dealing, handling, mailing, transportation
2 SHARING, allocation, allotment, apportionment, division
3 CLASSIFICATION, arrangement, grouping, organization, placement

district *noun* AREA, locale, locality, neighborhood, parish, quarter, region, sector, vicinity

distrust *verb* 1 SUSPECT, be suspicious of, be wary of, disbelieve, doubt, mistrust, question, smell a rat (*informal*)
▶ *noun* 2 SUSPICION, disbelief, doubt, misgiving, mistrust, question, skepticism, wariness

disturb *verb* 1 INTERRUPT, bother,

butt in on, disrupt, interfere with, intrude on, pester
2 UPSET, alarm, distress, fluster, harass, perturb, trouble, unnerve, unsettle, worry
3 MUDDLE, disarrange, disorder

disturbance noun
1 INTERRUPTION, annoyance, bother, distraction, intrusion
2 DISORDER, brawl, commotion, fracas, fray, rumpus

disturbed adjective 1 (psychiatry) UNBALANCED, disordered, maladjusted, neurotic, troubled, upset
2 WORRIED, anxious, apprehensive, bothered, concerned, nervous, troubled, uneasy, upset, wired (slang)

disturbing adjective WORRYING, alarming, disconcerting, distressing, frightening, harrowing, startling, unsettling, upsetting

disuse noun NEGLECT, abandonment, decay, idleness

ditch noun 1 CHANNEL, drain, dyke, furrow, gully, moat, trench, watercourse
▶ verb 2 (slang) GET RID OF, abandon, discard, dispose of, drop, dump (informal), jettison, scrap, throw out or overboard

dither verb 1 VACILLATE, faff about (Brit. informal), hesitate, hum and haw, shillyshally (informal), teeter, waver
▶ noun 2 FLUTTER, flap (informal), fluster, tizzy (informal)

dive verb 1 PLUNGE, descend, dip, drop, duck, nose-dive, plummet, swoop
▶ noun 2 PLUNGE, jump, leap, lunge, nose dive, spring

diverge verb 1 SEPARATE, branch, divide, fork, part, split, spread
2 DEVIATE, depart, digress,

meander, stray, turn aside, wander

diverse adjective 1 VARIOUS, assorted, manifold, miscellaneous, of every description, several, sundry, varied
2 DIFFERENT, discrete, disparate, dissimilar, distinct, divergent, separate, unlike, varying

diversify verb VARY, branch out, change, expand, have a finger in every pie, spread out

diversion noun 1 DETOUR, departure, deviation, digression
2 PASTIME, amusement, distraction, entertainment, game, recreation, relaxation, sport

diversity noun DIFFERENCE, distinctiveness, diverseness, heterogeneity, multiplicity, range, variety

divert verb 1 REDIRECT, avert, deflect, switch, turn aside
2 DISTRACT, draw or lead away from, lead astray, sidetrack
3 ENTERTAIN, amuse, beguile, delight, gratify, regale

diverting adjective ENTERTAINING, amusing, beguiling, enjoyable, fun, humorous, pleasant

divide verb 1 SEPARATE, bisect, cut (up), part, partition, segregate, split
2 SHARE, allocate, allot, deal out, dispense, distribute
3 CAUSE TO DISAGREE, break up, come between, estrange, split

dividend noun BONUS, cut (informal), divvy (informal), extra, gain, plus, portion, share, surplus

divine adjective 1 HEAVENLY, angelic, celestial, godlike, holy, spiritual, superhuman, supernatural
2 SACRED, consecrated, holy, religious, sanctified, spiritual

3 (*informal*) WONDERFUL, beautiful, excellent, glorious, marvelous, perfect, splendid, superlative
▶ *verb* 4 INFER, apprehend, deduce, discern, guess, perceive, suppose, surmise

divinity *noun* 1 THEOLOGY, religion, religious studies
2 GOD *or* GODDESS, deity, guardian spirit, spirit
3 GODLINESS, deity, divine nature, holiness, sanctity

divisible *adjective* DIVIDABLE, separable, splittable

division *noun* 1 SEPARATION, cutting up, dividing, partition, splitting up
2 SHARING, allotment, apportionment, distribution
3 PART, branch, category, class, department, group, section
4 DISAGREEMENT, difference of opinion, discord, rupture, split, variance

divorce *noun* 1 SEPARATION, annulment, dissolution, split-up
▶ *verb* 2 SEPARATE, disconnect, dissociate, dissolve (*marriage*), divide, part, sever, split up

divulge *verb* MAKE KNOWN, confess, declare, disclose, let slip, proclaim, reveal, tell

dizzy *adjective* 1 GIDDY, faint, light-headed, off balance, reeling, shaky, swimming, wobbly, woozy (*informal*)
2 CONFUSED, at sea, befuddled, bemused, bewildered, dazed, dazzled, muddled

do *verb* 1 PERFORM, accomplish, achieve, carry out, complete, execute
2 BE ADEQUATE, be sufficient, cut the mustard, pass muster, satisfy, suffice
3 GET READY, arrange, fix, look after, prepare, see to

4 SOLVE, decipher, decode, figure out, puzzle out, resolve, work out
5 CAUSE, bring about, create, effect, produce
▶ *noun* 6 (*informal, chiefly Brit. & N.Z.*) EVENT, affair, function, gathering, occasion, party

do away with *verb* 1 KILL, exterminate, murder, slay
2 GET RID OF, abolish, discard, discontinue, eliminate, put an end to, put paid to, remove

docile *adjective* SUBMISSIVE, amenable, biddable, compliant, manageable, obedient, pliant

docility *noun* SUBMISSIVENESS, compliance, manageability, meekness, obedience

dock¹ *noun* 1 WHARF, harbor, pier, quay, waterfront
▶ *verb* 2 MOOR, anchor, berth, drop anchor, land, put in, tie up
3 (*of spacecraft*) LINK UP, couple, hook up, join, rendezvous, unite

dock² *verb* 1 DEDUCT, decrease, diminish, lessen, reduce, subtract, withhold
2 CUT OFF, clip, crop, curtail, cut short, shorten

doctor *noun* 1 G.P., general practitioner, medic (*informal*), medical practitioner, physician
▶ *verb* 2 CHANGE, alter, disguise, falsify, misrepresent, pervert, tamper with
3 ADD TO, adulterate, cut, dilute, mix with, spike, water down

doctrinaire *adjective* DOGMATIC, biased, fanatical, inflexible, insistent, opinionated, rigid

doctrine *noun* TEACHING, article of faith, belief, conviction, creed, dogma, opinion, precept, principle, tenet

document *noun* 1 PAPER, certificate, record, report
▶ *verb* 2 SUPPORT, authenticate,

certify, corroborate, detail, substantiate, validate, verify

dodge *verb* 1 DUCK, dart, sidestep, swerve, turn aside

2 EVADE, avoid, elude, get out of, shirk

▶ *noun* 3 TRICK, device, ploy, ruse, scheme, stratagem, subterfuge, wheeze (*Brit. slang*)

dog *noun* 1 HOUND, canine, cur, man's best friend, pooch (*slang*)

2 ▷▷ **go to the dogs** (*informal*) GO TO RUIN, degenerate, deteriorate, go down the drain, go to pot

▶ *verb* 3 TROUBLE, follow, haunt, hound, plague, pursue, stalk, track, trail

dogged *adjective* DETERMINED, indefatigable, obstinate, persistent, resolute, steadfast, stubborn, tenacious, unflagging, unshakable

dogma *noun* DOCTRINE, belief, credo, creed, opinion, teachings

dogmatic *adjective* OPINIONATED, arrogant, assertive, doctrinaire, emphatic, obdurate, overbearing

doldrums *noun* ▷▷ **the doldrums** INACTIVITY, depression, dumps (*informal*), gloom, listlessness, malaise

dole *noun* 1 (*brit. & Austral. informal*) BENEFIT, allowance, gift, grant, handout

▶ *verb* 2 ▷▷ **dole out** GIVE OUT, allocate, allot, apportion, assign, dispense, distribute, hand out

dollop *noun* LUMP, helping, portion, scoop, serving

dolt *noun* IDIOT, ass, blockhead, chump (*informal*), clot (*Brit. informal*), dope (*informal*), dork (*slang*), dunce, fool, oaf, schmuck (*slang*)

domestic *adjective* 1 HOME, family, household, private

2 HOME-LOVING, domesticated, homely, housewifely, stay-at-home

3 DOMESTICATED, house-trained, pet, tame, trained

4 NATIVE, indigenous, internal

▶ *noun* 5 SERVANT, char (*informal*), charwoman, daily, help, maid

dominant *adjective* 1 CONTROLLING, assertive, authoritative, commanding, governing, ruling, superior, supreme

2 MAIN, chief, predominant, pre-eminent, primary, principal, prominent

dominate *verb* 1 CONTROL, direct, govern, have the whip hand over, monopolize, rule, tyrannize

2 TOWER ABOVE, loom over, overlook, stand head and shoulders above, stand over, survey

domination *noun* CONTROL, ascendancy, authority, command, influence, power, rule, superiority, supremacy

domineering *adjective* OVERBEARING, arrogant, authoritarian, bossy (*informal*), dictatorial, high-handed, imperious, oppressive, tyrannical

dominion *noun* 1 CONTROL, authority, command, jurisdiction, power, rule, sovereignty, supremacy

2 KINGDOM, country, domain, empire, realm, territory

don *verb* PUT ON, clothe oneself in, dress in, get into, pull on, slip on or into

donate *verb* GIVE, contribute, make a gift of, present, subscribe

donation *noun* CONTRIBUTION, gift, grant, hand-out, offering, present, subscription

donor *noun* GIVER, benefactor, contributor, donator,

philanthropist

doom noun 1 DESTRUCTION, catastrophe, downfall, fate, fortune, lot, ruin
▶ verb 2 CONDEMN, consign, damn, destine, sentence

doomed adjective CONDEMNED, bewitched, cursed, fated, hopeless, ill-fated, ill-omened, luckless, star-crossed

door noun OPENING, doorway, entrance, entry, exit

dope noun 1 (slang) DRUG, narcotic, opiate
2 (informal) IDIOT, dimwit (informal), doofus (slang), dork (slang), dunce, dweeb (slang), fool, nitwit (informal), numbskull or numskull, schmuck (slang), simpleton, twit (informal, chiefly Brit.)
▶ verb 3 DRUG, anesthetize, knock out, narcotize, sedate, stupefy

dork noun IDIOT (slang), doofus (slang), dope (slang), dunce, dweeb (slang), fool, geek (slang), nerd

dormant adjective INACTIVE, asleep, hibernating, inert, inoperative, latent, sleeping, slumbering, suspended

dose noun QUANTITY, dosage, draft, measure, portion, potion, prescription

dot noun 1 SPOT, fleck, jot, mark, point, speck, speckle
2 ▷▷ **on the dot** ON TIME, exactly, on the button (informal), precisely, promptly, punctually, to the minute
▶ verb 3 SPOT, dab, dabble, fleck, speckle, sprinkle, stipple, stud

dotage noun SENILITY, decrepitude, feebleness, imbecility, old age, second childhood, weakness

dote on or **upon** verb ADORE, admire, hold dear, idolize, lavish affection on, prize, treasure

doting adjective ADORING, devoted, fond, foolish, indulgent, lovesick

double adjective 1 TWICE, coupled, dual, duplicate, in pairs, paired, twin, twofold
▶ verb 2 MULTIPLY, duplicate, enlarge, grow, increase, magnify
▶ noun 3 TWIN, clone, dead ringer (slang), Doppelgänger, duplicate, lookalike, replica, spitting image (informal)
4 ▷▷ **at** or **on the double** QUICKLY, at full speed, briskly, immediately, posthaste, without delay

double-cross verb BETRAY, cheat, defraud, hoodwink, mislead, swindle, trick, two-time (informal)

doubt noun 1 UNCERTAINTY, hesitancy, hesitation, indecision, irresolution, lack of conviction, suspense
2 SUSPICION, apprehension, distrust, misgiving, mistrust, qualm, skepticism
▶ verb 3 BE UNCERTAIN, be dubious, demur, fluctuate, hesitate, scruple, vacillate, waver
4 SUSPECT, discredit, distrust, fear, lack confidence in, mistrust, query, question

doubtful adjective 1 UNLIKELY, debatable, dubious, equivocal, improbable, problematic(al), questionable, unclear
2 UNSURE, distrustful, hesitating, in two minds (informal), skeptical, suspicious, tentative, uncertain, unconvinced, wavering

doubtless adverb 1 CERTAINLY, assuredly, indisputably, of course, surely, undoubtedly, unquestionably, without doubt
2 PROBABLY, apparently, most likely, ostensibly, presumably, seemingly, supposedly

dour adjective GLOOMY, dismal, dreary, forbidding, grim, morose, sour, sullen, unfriendly

dowdy *adjective* FRUMPY, dingy, drab, dumpy (*informal*), frowzy, old-fashioned, homely (*U.S.*), shabby, unfashionable

do without *verb* MANAGE WITHOUT, abstain from, dispense with, forgo, get along without, give up, kick (*informal*)

down *adjective* 1 DEPRESSED, dejected, disheartened, downcast, low, miserable, sad, unhappy
▶ *verb* 2 (*informal*) SWALLOW, drain, drink (down), gulp, put away, toss off
▶ *noun* 3 ▷▷ **have a down on, be down on** (*informal*) BE ANTAGONISTIC *or* HOSTILE TO, bear a grudge towards, be prejudiced against, be set against, have it in for (*slang*)

down-and-out *noun* 1 TRAMP, bag lady, beggar, derelict, dosser (*Brit. slang*), pauper, vagabond, vagrant
▶ *adjective* 2 DESTITUTE, derelict, down on one's luck (*informal*), impoverished, on one's uppers (*informal*), penniless, short, without two pennies to rub together (*informal*)

downcast *adjective* DEJECTED, crestfallen, depressed, despondent, disappointed, disconsolate, discouraged, disheartened, dismayed, dispirited

downer *noun* (*informal*) MOANER, killjoy, pessimist, prophet of doom, sourpuss (*informal*), spoilsport, wet blanket (*informal*)

downfall *noun* RUIN, collapse, comeuppance (*informal*), destruction, disgrace, fall, overthrow, undoing

downgrade *verb* DEMOTE, degrade, humble, lower *or* reduce in rank, take down a peg (*informal*)

downhearted *adjective* DEJECTED, crestfallen, depressed, despondent, discouraged, disheartened, dispirited, downcast, sad, unhappy

downpour *noun* RAINSTORM, cloudburst, deluge, flood, inundation, torrential rain

downright *adjective* COMPLETE, absolute, out-and-out, outright, plain, thoroughgoing, total, undisguised, unqualified, utter

down-to-earth *adjective* SENSIBLE, matter-of-fact, no-nonsense, plain-spoken, practical, realistic, sane, unsentimental

downtrodden *adjective* OPPRESSED, exploited, helpless, subjugated, subservient, tyrannized

downward *adjective* DESCENDING, declining, earthward, heading down, sliding, slipping

doze *verb* 1 NAP, kip (*Brit. slang*), nod off (*informal*), sleep, slumber, snooze (*informal*)
▶ *noun* 2 NAP, catnap, forty winks (*informal*), kip (*Brit. slang*), shuteye (*slang*), siesta, snooze (*informal*)

drab *adjective* DULL, dingy, dismal, dreary, flat, gloomy, shabby, somber

draft¹ *noun* 1 OUTLINE, abstract, plan, rough, sketch, version
2 ORDER, bill (*of exchange*), check, postal order
▶ *verb* 3 OUTLINE, compose, design, draw, draw up, formulate, plan, sketch

draft² *noun* 1 BREEZE, current, flow, movement, puff
2 DRINK, cup, dose, potion, quantity

drag *verb* 1 PULL, draw, haul, lug, tow, trail, tug
2 ▷▷ **drag on** *or* **out** LAST, draw out, extend, keep going, lengthen,

persist, prolong, protract, spin out, stretch out

▶ *noun* 3 (*informal*) NUISANCE, annoyance, bore, bother, downer (*informal*), pain (*informal*), pest

dragoon *verb* FORCE, browbeat, bully, coerce, compel, constrain, drive, impel, intimidate, railroad (*informal*)

drain *noun* 1 PIPE, channel, conduit, culvert, ditch, duct, sewer, sink, trench
2 REDUCTION, depletion, drag, exhaustion, sap, strain, withdrawal

▶ *verb* 3 REMOVE, bleed, draw off, dry, empty, pump off *or* out, tap, withdraw
4 FLOW OUT, effuse, exude, leak, ooze, seep, trickle, well out
5 DRINK UP, finish, gulp down, quaff, swallow
6 EXHAUST, consume, deplete, dissipate, empty, sap, strain, use up

drama *noun* 1 PLAY, dramatization, show, stage show
2 THEATER, acting, dramaturgy, stagecraft
3 EXCITEMENT, crisis, histrionics, scene, spectacle, turmoil

dramatic *adjective* 1 THEATRICAL, dramaturgical, Thespian
2 POWERFUL, expressive, impressive, moving, striking, vivid
3 EXCITING, breathtaking, climactic, electrifying, melodramatic, sensational, suspenseful, tense, thrilling

dramatist *noun* PLAYWRIGHT, dramaturge, screenwriter, scriptwriter

dramatize *verb* EXAGGERATE, lay it on (thick) (*slang*), overdo, overstate, play to the gallery

drape *verb* COVER, cloak, fold, swathe, wrap

drastic *adjective* EXTREME, desperate, dire, forceful, harsh, radical, severe, strong

draw *verb* 1 SKETCH, depict, design, map out, mark out, outline, paint, portray, trace
2 PULL, drag, haul, tow, tug
3 TAKE OUT, extract, pull out
4 ATTRACT, allure, elicit, entice, evoke, induce, influence, invite, persuade
5 DEDUCE, derive, infer, make, take

▶ *noun* 6 (*informal*) ATTRACTION, enticement, lure, pull (*informal*)
7 TIE, dead heat, deadlock, gridlock, impasse, stalemate

drawback *noun* DISADVANTAGE, deficiency, difficulty, downside, flaw, handicap, hitch, snag, stumbling block

drawing *noun* PICTURE, cartoon, depiction, illustration, outline, portrayal, representation, sketch, study

drawn *adjective* TENSE, haggard, pinched, stressed, tired, worn

draw on *verb* MAKE USE OF, employ, exploit, extract, fall back on, have recourse to, rely on, take from, use

draw out *verb* EXTEND, drag out, lengthen, make longer, prolong, protract, spin out, stretch, string out

draw up *verb* 1 DRAFT, compose, formulate, frame, prepare, write out
2 HALT, bring to a stop, pull up, stop

dread *verb* 1 FEAR, cringe at, have cold feet (*informal*), quail, shrink from, shudder, tremble

▶ *noun* 2 FEAR, alarm, apprehension, dismay, fright, horror, terror, trepidation

dreadful *adjective* TERRIBLE, abysmal, appalling, atrocious, awful, fearful, frightful, hideous, horrible, shocking

dream *noun* 1 VISION, delusion, hallucination, illusion, imagination, trance
2 DAYDREAM, fantasy, pipe dream
3 AMBITION, aim, aspiration, desire, goal, hope, wish
4 DELIGHT, beauty, gem, joy, marvel, pleasure, treasure
▶ *verb* 5 HAVE DREAMS, conjure up, envisage, fancy, hallucinate, imagine, think, visualize
6 DAYDREAM, build castles in the air *or* in Spain, fantasize, stargaze

dreamer *noun* IDEALIST, daydreamer, escapist, fantasist, utopian, visionary, Walter Mitty

dreamy *adjective* 1 VAGUE, absent, abstracted, daydreaming, faraway, pensive, preoccupied, with one's head in the clouds
2 IMPRACTICAL, airy-fairy, fanciful, imaginary, quixotic, speculative

dreary *adjective* DULL, boring, drab, humdrum, monotonous, tedious, tiresome, uneventful, wearisome

dregs *plural noun* 1 SEDIMENT, deposit, dross, grounds, lees, residue, residuum, scum, waste
2 SCUM, good-for-nothings, rabble, ragtag and bobtail, riffraff

drench *verb* SOAK, drown, flood, inundate, saturate, souse, steep, swamp, wet

dress *noun* 1 FROCK, gown, outfit, robe
2 CLOTHING, apparel, attire, clothes, costume, garb, garments, togs
▶ *verb* 3 PUT ON, attire, change, clothe, don, garb, robe, slip on *or* into
4 BANDAGE, bind up, plaster, treat
5 ARRANGE, adjust, align, get

ready, prepare, straighten

dressmaker *noun* SEAMSTRESS, couturier, tailor

dribble *verb* 1 RUN, drip, drop, fall in drops, leak, ooze, seep, trickle
2 DROOL, drivel, slaver, slobber

drift *verb* 1 FLOAT, be carried along, coast, go (aimlessly), meander, stray, waft, wander
2 PILE UP, accumulate, amass, bank up, drive, gather
▶ *noun* 3 PILE, accumulation, bank, heap, mass, mound
4 MEANING, direction, gist, import, intention, purport, significance, tendency, thrust

drifter *noun* WANDERER, beachcomber, bum (*informal*), hobo (U.S.), itinerant, rolling stone, vagrant

drill *noun* 1 BORING TOOL, bit, borer, gimlet
2 TRAINING, discipline, exercise, instruction, practice, preparation, repetition
▶ *verb* 3 BORE, penetrate, perforate, pierce, puncture, sink in
4 TRAIN, coach, discipline, exercise, instruct, practice, rehearse, teach

drink *verb* 1 SWALLOW, gulp, guzzle, imbibe, quaff, sip, suck, sup
2 BOOZE (*informal*), hit the bottle (*informal*), tipple, tope
▶ *noun* 3 BEVERAGE, liquid, potion, refreshment
4 ALCOHOL, booze (*informal*), hooch *or* hootch (*informal, chiefly U.S. & Canad.*), liquor, spirits, the bottle (*informal*)
5 GLASS, cup, draft

drip *verb* 1 DROP, dribble, exude, plop, splash, sprinkle, trickle
▶ *noun* 2 DROP, dribble, leak, trickle
3 (*informal*) WEAKLING, mummy's boy, mama's boy (*informal*), namby-

pamby, softie (*informal*), weed (*informal*), wet (*Brit. informal*)

drive verb 1 OPERATE, direct, guide, handle, manage, motor, ride, steer, travel

2 GOAD, coerce, constrain, force, press, prod, prompt, spur

3 PUSH, herd, hurl, impel, propel, send, urge

4 PUSH, hammer, ram, thrust

▶ noun 5 RUN, excursion, jaunt, journey, outing, ride, spin (*informal*), trip

6 CAMPAIGN, action, appeal, crusade, effort, push (*informal*)

7 INITIATIVE, ambition, energy, enterprise, get-up-and-go (*informal*), motivation, vigor, zip (*informal*)

drivel noun 1 NONSENSE, garbage (*informal*), gibberish, hogwash, hot air (*informal*), poppycock (*informal*), rubbish, trash, twaddle, waffle (*informal, chiefly Brit.*)

▶ verb 2 BABBLE, blether, gab (*informal*), prate, ramble, waffle (*informal, chiefly Brit.*)

driving adjective FORCEFUL, compelling, dynamic, energetic, sweeping, vigorous, violent

drizzle noun 1 FINE RAIN, mist

▶ verb 2 RAIN, shower, spot or spit with rain, spray, sprinkle

droll adjective AMUSING, comical, entertaining, funny, humorous, jocular, waggish, whimsical

drone verb 1 HUM, buzz, purr, thrum, vibrate, whirr

2 ▷▷ **drone on** SPEAK MONOTONOUSLY, be boring, chant, intone, spout, talk interminably

▶ noun 3 HUM, buzz, murmuring, purr, thrum, vibration, whirring

drool verb 1 DRIBBLE, drivel, salivate, slaver, slobber, water at the mouth

2 ▷▷ **drool over** GLOAT OVER, dote

on, gush, make much of, rave about (*informal*)

droop verb SAG, bend, dangle, drop, fall down, hang (down), sink

drop verb 1 FALL, decline, descend, diminish, plummet, plunge, sink, tumble

2 DRIP, dribble, fall in drops, trickle

3 DISCONTINUE, ax (*informal*), give up, kick (*informal*), quit, relinquish

▶ noun 4 DROPLET, bead, bubble, drip, globule, pearl, tear

5 DASH, mouthful, shot (*informal*), sip, spot, swig (*informal*), tot, trace, trickle

6 DECREASE, cut, decline, deterioration, downturn, fall-off, lowering, reduction, slump

7 FALL, descent, plunge

drop off verb 1 SET DOWN, deliver, leave, let off

2 (*informal*) FALL ASLEEP, doze (off), have forty winks (*informal*), nod (off), snooze (*informal*)

3 DECREASE, decline, diminish, dwindle, fall off, lessen, slacken

drop out verb LEAVE, abandon, fall by the wayside, give up, quit, stop, withdraw

drought noun DRY SPELL, aridity, dehydration, dryness

drove noun HERD, collection, company, crowd, flock, horde, mob, multitude, swarm, throng

drown verb 1 DRENCH, deluge, engulf, flood, go under, immerse, inundate, sink, submerge, swamp

2 OVERPOWER, deaden, muffle, obliterate, overcome, overwhelm, stifle, swallow up, wipe out

drowsy adjective SLEEPY, dopey (*slang*), dozy, half asleep, heavy, lethargic, somnolent, tired, torpid

drudge noun MENIAL, dogsbody (*informal*), factotum, servant, skivvy (*chiefly Brit.*), slave, toiler, worker

drudgery *noun* MENIAL LABOR, donkey-work, fag (*informal*), grind (*informal*), hard work, labor, skivvying (*Brit.*), slog, toil

drug *noun* 1 MEDICATION, medicament, medicine, physic, poison, remedy
2 DOPE (*slang*), narcotic, opiate, stimulant
▶ *verb* 3 DOSE, administer a drug, dope (*slang*), medicate, treat
4 KNOCK OUT, anesthetize, deaden, numb, poison, stupefy

drum *verb* 1 BEAT, pulsate, rap, reverberate, tap, tattoo, throb
2 ▷▷ **drum into** DRIVE HOME, din into, hammer away, harp on, instill into, reiterate

drunk *adjective* 1 INTOXICATED, drunken, inebriated, legless (*informal*), merry (*Brit. informal*), plastered (*slang*), tipsy, under the influence (*informal*)
▶ *noun* 2 DRUNKARD, alcoholic, boozer (*informal*), inebriate, lush (*slang*), wino (*informal*)

drunkard *noun* DRINKER, alcoholic, dipsomaniac, drunk, lush (*slang*), tippler, wino (*informal*)

drunkenness *noun* INTOXICATION, alcoholism, bibulousness, dipsomania, inebriation, insobriety, intemperance

dry *adjective* 1 DEHYDRATED, arid, barren, desiccated, dried up, parched, thirsty
2 DULL, boring, dreary, monotonous, plain, tedious, tiresome, uninteresting
3 SARCASTIC, deadpan, droll, low-key, sly
▶ *verb* 4 DEHYDRATE, dehumidify, desiccate, drain, make dry, parch, sear

dry out *or* **up** *verb* BECOME DRY, harden, shrivel up, wilt, wither, wizen

dual *adjective* TWOFOLD, binary, double, duplex, duplicate, matched, paired, twin

dubious *adjective* 1 SUSPECT, fishy (*informal*), questionable, suspicious, unreliable, untrustworthy
2 UNSURE, doubtful, hesitant, skeptical, uncertain, unconvinced, undecided, wavering

duck *verb* 1 BOB, bend, bow, crouch, dodge, drop, lower, stoop
2 PLUNGE, dip, dive, douse, dunk, immerse, souse, submerge, wet
3 (*informal*) DODGE, avoid, escape, evade, shirk, shun, sidestep

dud (*informal*) *noun* 1 FAILURE, flop (*informal*), washout (*informal*)
▶ *adjective* 2 USELESS, broken, duff (*Brit. informal*), failed, inoperative, worthless

dudgeon *noun* ▷▷ **in high dudgeon** INDIGNANT, angry, choked, fuming, offended, resentful, ticked off (*informal*), vexed

due *adjective* 1 EXPECTED, scheduled
2 PAYABLE, in arrears, outstanding, owed, owing, unpaid
3 FITTING, appropriate, deserved, justified, merited, proper, rightful, suitable, well-earned
▶ *noun* 4 RIGHT(S), comeuppance (*informal*), deserts, merits, privilege
▶ *adverb* 5 DIRECTLY, dead, exactly, straight, undeviatingly

duel *noun* 1 SINGLE COMBAT, affair of honor
2 CONTEST, clash, competition, encounter, engagement, fight, head-to-head, rivalry
▶ *verb* 3 FIGHT, clash, compete, contend, contest, lock horns, rival, struggle, vie with

dues *plural noun* MEMBERSHIP FEE, charge, charges, contribution, fee, levy

dull *adjective* 1 BORING, dreary, dumpy (*informal*), flat, frowzy, homely (*U.S.*), humdrum, monotonous, plain, run-of-the-mill, tedious, uninteresting 2 STUPID, dense, dim-witted (*informal*), dozy (*Brit. informal*), slow, thick, unintelligent 3 CLOUDY, dim, dismal, gloomy, leaden, overcast 4 LIFELESS, apathetic, blank, indifferent, listless, passionless, unresponsive 5 BLUNT, blunted, unsharpened ▶ *verb* 6 RELIEVE, allay, alleviate, blunt, lessen, moderate, soften, take the edge off

duly *adverb* 1 PROPERLY, accordingly, appropriately, befittingly, correctly, decorously, deservedly, fittingly, rightfully, suitably 2 ON TIME, at the proper time, punctually

dumb *adjective* 1 MUTE, mum, silent, soundless, speechless, tongue-tied, voiceless, wordless 2 (*informal*) STUPID, asinine, dense, dim-witted (*informal*), dull, foolish, thick, unintelligent

dumbfounded *adjective* AMAZED, astonished, astounded, flabbergasted (*informal*), lost for words, nonplussed, overwhelmed, speechless, staggered, stunned

dummy *noun* 1 MODEL, figure, form, manikin, mannequin 2 COPY, counterfeit, duplicate, imitation, sham, substitute 3 (*slang*) FOOL, blockhead, dork (*slang*), dunce, idiot, nitwit (*informal*), numbskull *or* numskull, oaf, schmuck (*slang*), simpleton ▶ *adjective* 4 IMITATION, artificial,

bogus, fake, false, mock, phoney *or* phony (*informal*), sham, simulated

dump *verb* 1 DROP, deposit, fling down, let fall, throw down 2 GET RID OF, dispose of, ditch (*slang*), empty out, jettison, scrap, throw away *or* out, tip, unload ▶ *noun* 3 RUBBISH TIP, junkyard, refuse heap, rubbish heap, tip 4 (*informal*) PIGSTY, hole (*informal*), hovel, mess, slum

dumpy *adjective* (*informal*) DOWDY, frowzy, frumpish, frumpy, homely (*U.S.*), unfashionable

dunce *noun* SIMPLETON, blockhead, duffer (*informal*), dunderhead, ignoramus, moron, nincompoop, numbskull *or* numskull, thickhead

dungeon *noun* PRISON, cage, cell, oubliette, vault

duplicate *adjective* 1 IDENTICAL, corresponding, matched, matching, twin, twofold ▶ *noun* 2 COPY, carbon copy, clone, double, facsimile, photocopy, replica, reproduction ▶ *verb* 3 COPY, clone, double, repeat, replicate, reproduce

durability *noun* DURABLENESS, constancy, endurance, imperishability, permanence, persistence

durable *adjective* LONG-LASTING, dependable, enduring, hard-wearing, persistent, reliable, resistant, strong, sturdy, tough

duration *noun* LENGTH, extent, period, span, spell, stretch, term, time

duress *noun* PRESSURE, coercion, compulsion, constraint, threat

dusk *noun* TWILIGHT, dark, evening, eventide, gloaming (*Scot. or poetic*), nightfall, sundown, sunset

dusky *adjective* 1 DARK, dark-

complexioned, sable, swarthy
2 DIM, cloudy, gloomy, murky, obscure, shadowy, shady, tenebrous, twilit

dust noun **1** GRIME, grit, particles, powder
▶ verb **2** SPRINKLE, cover, dredge, powder, scatter, sift, spray, spread

dusty adjective DIRTY, grubby, scuzzy (slang), sooty, unclean, unswept

dutiful adjective CONSCIENTIOUS, devoted, obedient, respectful, reverential, submissive

duty noun **1** RESPONSIBILITY, assignment, function, job, obligation, role, task, work
2 LOYALTY, allegiance, deference, obedience, respect, reverence
3 TAX, excise, levy, tariff, toll
4 ▷▷ **on duty** AT WORK, busy, engaged, on active service

dwarf verb **1** TOWER ABOVE or OVER, diminish, dominate, overshadow
▶ adjective **2** MINIATURE, baby, bonsai, diminutive, small, tiny, undersized
▶ noun **3** MIDGET, Lilliputian, pygmy or pigmy, Tom Thumb

dweeb noun IDIOT (slang), doofus (slang), dope (slang), dunce, fool, geek, slang, nerd

dwell verb LIVE, abide, inhabit, lodge, reside

dwelling noun HOME, abode, domicile, habitation, house, lodging, pad (slang), quarters, residence

dwindle verb LESSEN, decline, decrease, die away, diminish, fade, peter out, shrink, subside, taper off, wane

dye noun **1** COLORING, color, colorant, pigment, stain, tinge, tint
▶ verb **2** COLOR, pigment, stain, tinge, tint

dying adjective EXPIRING, at death's door, failing, in extremis, moribund, not long for this world

dynamic adjective ENERGETIC, forceful, go-ahead, go-getting (informal), high-powered, lively, powerful, vital

dynasty noun EMPIRE, government, house, regime, rule, sovereignty

each *adjective* 1 EVERY
► *pronoun* 2 EVERY ONE, each and every one, each one, one and all
► *adverb* 3 APIECE, for each, individually, per capita, per head, per person, respectively, to each

eager *adjective* KEEN, agog, anxious, athirst, avid, enthusiastic, fervent, gung ho (*slang*), hungry, impatient, longing

eagerness *noun* KEENNESS, ardor, enthusiasm, fervor, hunger, impatience, thirst, yearning, zeal

ear *noun* SENSITIVITY, appreciation, discrimination, perception, taste

early *adjective* 1 PREMATURE, advanced, forward, untimely
2 PRIMITIVE, primeval, primordial, undeveloped, young
► *adverb* 3 TOO SOON, ahead of time, beforehand, in advance, in good time, prematurely

earmark *verb* SET ASIDE, allocate, designate, flag, label, mark out, reserve

earn *verb* 1 MAKE, bring in, collect, gain, get, gross, net, receive
2 DESERVE, acquire, attain, be entitled to, be worthy of, merit, rate, warrant, win

earnest *adjective* 1 SERIOUS, grave, intent, resolute, resolved, sincere, solemn, thoughtful
► *noun* 2 *as in* **in earnest**
SERIOUSNESS, sincerity, truth

earnings *plural noun* INCOME, pay, proceeds, profits, receipts, remuneration, salary, takings, wages

earth *noun* 1 WORLD, globe, orb, planet, sphere
2 SOIL, clay, dirt, ground, land, turf

earthenware *noun* CROCKERY, ceramics, pots, pottery, terracotta

earthly *adjective* 1 WORLDLY, human, material, mortal, secular, temporal
2 (*informal*) POSSIBLE, conceivable, feasible, imaginable, likely, practical

earthy *adjective* CRUDE, bawdy, coarse, raunchy (*slang*), ribald, robust, uninhibited, unsophisticated

ease *noun* 1 EASINESS, effortlessness, facility, readiness, simplicity
2 CONTENT, comfort, happiness, peace, peace of mind, quiet, serenity, tranquillity
3 REST, leisure, relaxation, repose, restfulness
► *verb* 4 RELIEVE, alleviate, calm, comfort, lessen, lighten, relax, soothe
5 MOVE CAREFULLY, edge, inch, maneuver, slide, slip

easily *adverb* WITHOUT DIFFICULTY, comfortably, effortlessly, readily, smoothly, with ease, with one hand tied behind one's back

easy *adjective* 1 NOT DIFFICULT, a piece of cake (*informal*), child's play (*informal*), effortless, no trouble, painless, plain sailing, simple, straightforward, uncomplicated, undemanding

2 CAREFREE, comfortable, cushy (*informal*), leisurely, peaceful, quiet, relaxed, serene, tranquil, untroubled

3 TOLERANT, easy-going, indulgent, lenient, mild, permissive, unoppressive

easy-going *adjective* RELAXED, carefree, casual, easy, even-tempered, happy-go-lucky, laid-back (*informal*), nonchalant, placid, tolerant, undemanding

eat *verb* **1** CONSUME, chew, devour, gobble, ingest, munch, scoff (*slang*), swallow

2 HAVE A MEAL, chow down (*slang*), dine, feed, take nourishment

3 DESTROY, corrode, decay, dissolve, erode, rot, waste away, wear away

eavesdrop *verb* LISTEN IN, earwig (*informal*), monitor, overhear, snoop (*informal*), spy

ebb *verb* **1** FLOW BACK, go out, recede, retire, retreat, subside, wane, withdraw

2 DECLINE, decrease, diminish, dwindle, fade away, fall away, flag, lessen, peter out

▶ *noun* **3** FLOWING BACK, going out, low tide, low water, retreat, subsidence, wane, withdrawal

eccentric *adjective* **1** ODD, freakish, idiosyncratic, irregular, outlandish, peculiar, quirky, strange, unconventional

▶ *noun* **2** CRANK (*informal*), character (*informal*), nonconformist, oddball (*informal*), weirdo or weirdie (*informal*)

eccentricity *noun* ODDITY, abnormality, caprice, capriciousness, foible, idiosyncrasy, irregularity, peculiarity, quirk

ecclesiastic *noun* **1** CLERGYMAN, churchman, cleric, holy man, man of the cloth, minister, parson, pastor, priest

▶ *adjective* **2** *or* **ecclesiastical** CLERICAL, divine, holy, pastoral, priestly, religious, spiritual

echo *noun* **1** REPETITION, answer, reverberation

2 COPY, imitation, mirror image, parallel, reflection, reiteration, reproduction

▶ *verb* **3** REPEAT, resound, reverberate

4 COPY, ape, imitate, mirror, parallel, recall, reflect, resemble

eclipse *noun* **1** OBSCURING, darkening, dimming, extinction, shading

▶ *verb* **2** SURPASS, exceed, excel, outdo, outshine, put in the shade (*informal*), transcend

economic *adjective* **1** FINANCIAL, commercial, industrial

2 PROFITABLE, money-making, productive, profit-making, remunerative, viable

3 (*informal*) *or* **economical** INEXPENSIVE, cheap, low-priced, modest, reasonable

economical *adjective* **1** THRIFTY, careful, frugal, prudent, scrimping, sparing

2 COST-EFFECTIVE, efficient, money-saving, sparing, time-saving

3 INEXPENSIVE, cheap, low-priced, modest, reasonable

economize *verb* CUT BACK, be economical, be frugal, draw in one's horns, retrench, save, scrimp, tighten one's belt

economy *noun* THRIFT, frugality, husbandry, parsimony, prudence, restraint

ecstasy *noun* RAPTURE, bliss,

delight, elation, euphoria, fervor,
joy, seventh heaven

ecstatic adjective RAPTUROUS,
blissful, elated, enraptured,
entranced, euphoric, in seventh
heaven, joyous, on cloud nine
(*informal*), overjoyed

eddy noun 1 SWIRL, counter-
current, counterflow, undertow,
vortex, whirlpool
▶ verb 2 SWIRL, whirl

edge noun 1 BORDER, boundary,
brink, fringe, limit, outline,
perimeter, rim, side, verge
2 SHARPNESS, bite, effectiveness,
force, incisiveness, keenness,
point
3 *as in* **have the edge on**
ADVANTAGE, ascendancy,
dominance, lead, superiority,
upper hand
4 ▷▷ **on edge** NERVOUS,
apprehensive, edgy, ill at ease,
impatient, irritable, keyed up, on
tenterhooks, tense, wired (*slang*)
▶ verb 5 BORDER, fringe, hem
6 INCH, creep, ease, sidle, steal

edgy adjective NERVOUS, anxious,
ill at ease, irritable, keyed up, on
edge, on tenterhooks, restive,
tense, wired (*slang*)

edible adjective EATABLE,
digestible, fit to eat, good,
harmless, palatable, wholesome

edict noun DECREE, act,
command, injunction, law, order,
proclamation, ruling

edifice noun BUILDING,
construction, erection, house,
structure

edify verb INSTRUCT, educate,
enlighten, guide, improve,
inform, nurture, school, teach

edit verb REVISE, adapt, condense,
correct, emend, polish, rewrite

edition noun VERSION, copy,

impression, issue, number,
printing, program (*TV, Radio*),
volume

educate verb TEACH, civilize,
develop, discipline, enlighten,
improve, inform, instruct, school,
train, tutor

educated adjective 1 TAUGHT,
coached, informed, instructed,
nurtured, schooled, tutored
2 CULTURED, civilized, cultivated,
enlightened, knowledgeable,
learned, refined, sophisticated

education noun TEACHING,
development, discipline,
enlightenment, instruction,
nurture, schooling, training,
tuition

educational adjective
INSTRUCTIVE, cultural, edifying,
educative, enlightening,
improving, informative

eerie adjective FRIGHTENING, creepy
(*informal*), ghostly, mysterious,
scary (*informal*), spooky (*informal*),
strange, uncanny, unearthly,
weird

efface verb OBLITERATE, blot out,
cancel, delete, destroy, eradicate,
erase, expunge, rub out, wipe out

effect noun 1 RESULT, conclusion,
consequence, end result, event,
outcome, upshot
2 OPERATION, action,
enforcement, execution, force,
implementation
3 IMPRESSION, essence, impact,
sense, significance, tenor
▶ verb 4 BRING ABOUT, accomplish,
achieve, complete, execute, fulfill,
perform, produce

effective adjective 1 EFFICIENT,
active, adequate, capable,
competent, productive,
serviceable, useful
2 IN OPERATION, active, current, in

effect, in force, operative
3 POWERFUL, cogent, compelling,
convincing, forceful, impressive,
persuasive, telling
effects *plural noun* BELONGINGS,
gear, goods, paraphernalia,
possessions, property, things
effeminate *adjective* WOMANLY,
camp (*informal*), feminine, sissy,
soft, tender, unmanly, weak,
womanish
effervescent *adjective* 1 BUBBLING,
carbonated, fizzy, foaming, frothy,
sparkling
2 LIVELY, animated, bubbly,
ebullient, enthusiastic,
exuberant, irrepressible, vivacious
effete *adjective* DECADENT,
dissipated, enfeebled, feeble,
ineffectual, spoiled, weak
efficacious *adjective* EFFECTIVE,
adequate, efficient, operative,
potent, powerful, productive,
successful, useful
efficiency *noun* COMPETENCE,
adeptness, capability, economy,
effectiveness, power, productivity,
proficiency
efficient *adjective* COMPETENT,
businesslike, capable, economic,
effective, organized, productive,
proficient, well-organized,
workmanlike
effigy *noun* LIKENESS, dummy,
figure, guy, icon, idol, image,
picture, portrait, representation,
statue
effluent *noun* WASTE, effluvium,
pollutant, sewage
effort *noun* 1 EXERTION,
application, elbow grease
(*facetious*), endeavor, energy, pains,
struggle, toil, trouble, work
2 ATTEMPT, endeavor, essay, go
(*informal*), shot (*informal*), stab
(*informal*), try

effortless *adjective* EASY, painless,
plain sailing, simple, smooth,
uncomplicated, undemanding
effrontery *noun* INSOLENCE,
arrogance, audacity, brazenness,
cheek (*informal*), impertinence,
impudence, nerve, presumption,
temerity
effusive *adjective* DEMONSTRATIVE,
ebullient, expansive, exuberant,
gushing, lavish, unreserved,
unrestrained
egg on *verb* ENCOURAGE, exhort,
goad, incite, prod, prompt, push,
spur, urge
egocentric *adjective* SELF-
CENTERED, egoistic, egoistical,
egotistic, egotistical, selfish
egotism, egoism *noun* SELF-
CENTEREDNESS, conceitedness,
narcissism, self-absorption,
self-esteem, self-importance, self-
interest, selfishness, vanity
egotist, egoist *noun* EGOMANIAC,
bighead (*informal*), boaster,
braggart, narcissist
egotistic, egotistical, egoistic
or **egoistical** *adjective* SELF-
CENTERED, boasting, conceited,
egocentric, full of oneself,
narcissistic, self-absorbed, self-
important, vain
egress *noun* (*formal*) EXIT,
departure, exodus, way out,
withdrawal
eject *verb* THROW OUT, banish,
drive out, evict, expel, oust,
remove, turn out
ejection *noun* EXPULSION,
banishment, deportation,
eviction, exile, removal
eke out *verb* BE SPARING WITH,
economize on, husband, stretch
out
elaborate *adjective* 1 DETAILED,
intricate, minute, painstaking,

precise, studied, thorough
2 COMPLICATED, complex, fancy, fussy, involved, ornamented, ornate
▶ verb 3 EXPAND (UPON), add detail, amplify, develop, embellish, enlarge, flesh out

elapse verb PASS, glide by, go by, lapse, roll by, slip away

elastic adjective 1 STRETCHY, plastic, pliable, pliant, resilient, rubbery, springy, supple, tensile
2 ADAPTABLE, accommodating, adjustable, compliant, flexible, supple, tolerant, variable, yielding

elated adjective JOYFUL, cock-a-hoop, delighted, ecstatic, euphoric, exhilarated, gleeful, jubilant, overjoyed

elation noun JOY, bliss, delight, ecstasy, euphoria, exhilaration, glee, high spirits, jubilation, rapture

elbow noun 1 JOINT, angle
▶ verb 2 PUSH, jostle, knock, nudge, shove

elbow room noun SCOPE, freedom, latitude, leeway, play, room, space

elder adjective 1 OLDER, first-born, senior
▶ noun 2 OLDER PERSON, senior

elect verb CHOOSE, appoint, determine, opt for, pick, prefer, select, settle on, vote

election noun VOTING, appointment, choice, judgment, preference, selection, vote

elector noun VOTER, constituent, selector

electric adjective CHARGED, dynamic, exciting, rousing, stimulating, stirring, tense, thrilling

electrify verb STARTLE, astound, excite, galvanize, invigorate, jolt, shock, stir, thrill

elegance noun STYLE, dignity, exquisiteness, grace, gracefulness, grandeur, luxury, refinement, taste

elegant adjective STYLISH, chic, delicate, exquisite, fine, graceful, handsome, polished, refined, tasteful

element noun 1 COMPONENT, constituent, factor, ingredient, part, section, subdivision, unit
2 as in **in one's element** ENVIRONMENT, domain, field, habitat, medium, milieu, sphere

elementary adjective SIMPLE, clear, easy, plain, rudimentary, straightforward, uncomplicated

elements plural noun 1 BASICS, essentials, foundations, fundamentals, nuts and bolts (informal), principles, rudiments
2 WEATHER CONDITIONS, atmospheric conditions, powers of nature

elevate verb 1 RAISE, heighten, hoist, lift, lift up, uplift
2 PROMOTE, advance, aggrandize, exalt, prefer, upgrade

elevated adjective HIGH-MINDED, dignified, exalted, grand, high-flown, inflated, lofty, noble, sublime

elevation noun 1 PROMOTION, advancement, aggrandizement, exaltation, preferment, upgrading
2 ALTITUDE, height

elicit verb 1 BRING ABOUT, bring forth, bring out, bring to light, call forth, cause, derive, evolve, give rise to
2 OBTAIN, draw out, evoke, exact, extort, extract, wrest

eligible adjective QUALIFIED, acceptable, appropriate, desirable, fit, preferable, proper, suitable, worthy

eliminate verb GET RID OF, cut out, dispose of, do away with, eradicate, exterminate, remove, stamp out, take out

elite noun BEST, aristocracy, cream, crème de la crème, flower, nobility, pick, upper class

elitist adjective SNOBBISH, exclusive, selective

elixir noun PANACEA, nostrum

elocution noun DICTION, articulation, declamation, delivery, enunciation, oratory, pronunciation, speech, speechmaking

elongate verb MAKE LONGER, draw out, extend, lengthen, prolong, protract, stretch

elope verb RUN AWAY, abscond, bolt, decamp, disappear, escape, leave, run off, slip away, steal away

eloquence noun EXPRESSIVENESS, expression, fluency, forcefulness, oratory, persuasiveness, rhetoric, way with words

eloquent adjective 1 SILVER-TONGUED, articulate, fluent, forceful, moving, persuasive, stirring, well-expressed
2 EXPRESSIVE, meaningful, suggestive, telling, vivid

elsewhere adverb IN or TO ANOTHER PLACE, abroad, away, hence (archaic), not here, somewhere else

elucidate verb CLARIFY, clear up, explain, explicate, expound, illuminate, illustrate, make plain, shed or throw light upon, spell out

elude verb 1 ESCAPE, avoid, dodge, duck (informal), evade, flee, get away from, outrun
2 BAFFLE, be beyond (someone),

confound, escape, foil, frustrate, puzzle, stump, thwart

elusive adjective 1 DIFFICULT TO CATCH, shifty, slippery, tricky
2 INDEFINABLE, fleeting, intangible, subtle, transient, transitory

emaciated adjective SKELETAL, cadaverous, gaunt, haggard, lean, pinched, scrawny, thin, undernourished, wasted

emanate verb FLOW, arise, come forth, derive, emerge, issue, originate, proceed, spring, stem

emancipate verb FREE, deliver, liberate, release, set free, unchain, unfetter

emancipation noun FREEDOM, deliverance, liberation, liberty, release

embalm verb PRESERVE, mummify

embargo noun 1 BAN, bar, boycott, interdiction, prohibition, restraint, restriction, stoppage
▶ verb 2 BAN, bar, block, boycott, prohibit, restrict, stop

embark verb 1 GO ABOARD, board ship, take ship
2 ▷▷ **embark on** or **upon** BEGIN, commence, enter, launch, plunge into, set about, set out, start, take up

embarrass verb SHAME, discomfit, disconcert, distress, fluster, humiliate, mortify, show up (informal)

embarrassed adjective ASHAMED, awkward, blushing, discomfited, disconcerted, humiliated, mortified, red-faced, self-conscious, sheepish

embarrassing adjective HUMILIATING, awkward, compromising, discomfiting, disconcerting, mortifying, sensitive, shameful, toe-curling (*informal*), uncomfortable

embarrassment *noun* 1 SHAME, awkwardness, bashfulness, distress, humiliation, mortification, self-consciousness, showing up (*informal*)
2 PREDICAMENT, bind (*informal*), difficulty, mess, pickle (*informal*), scrape (*informal*)

embellish *verb* DECORATE, adorn, beautify, elaborate, embroider, enhance, enrich, festoon, ornament

embellishment *noun* DECORATION, adornment, elaboration, embroidery, enhancement, enrichment, exaggeration, ornament, ornamentation

embezzle *verb* MISAPPROPRIATE, appropriate, filch, misuse, peculate, pilfer, purloin, rip off (*slang*), steal

embezzlement *noun* MISAPPROPRIATION, appropriation, filching, fraud, misuse, peculation, pilfering, stealing, theft

embittered *adjective* RESENTFUL, angry, bitter, disaffected, disillusioned, rancorous, soured, with a chip on one's shoulder (*informal*)

emblem *noun* SYMBOL, badge, crest, image, insignia, mark, sign, token

embodiment *noun* PERSONIFICATION, epitome, example, exemplar, expression, incarnation, representation, symbol

embody *verb* 1 PERSONIFY, exemplify, manifest, represent, stand for, symbolize, typify
2 INCORPORATE, collect, combine, comprise, contain, include

embolden *verb* ENCOURAGE, fire, inflame, invigorate, rouse, stimulate, stir, strengthen

embrace *verb* 1 HUG, clasp, cuddle, envelop, hold, seize, squeeze, take *or* hold in one's arms
2 ACCEPT, adopt, espouse, seize, take on board, take up, welcome
3 INCLUDE, comprehend, comprise, contain, cover, encompass, involve, take in
▶ *noun* 4 HUG, clasp, clinch (*slang*), cuddle, squeeze

embroil *verb* INVOLVE, enmesh, ensnare, entangle, implicate, incriminate, mire, mix up

embryo *noun* GERM, beginning, nucleus, root, rudiment

emend *verb* REVISE, amend, correct, edit, improve, rectify

emendation *noun* REVISION, amendment, correction, editing, improvement, rectification

emerge *verb* 1 COME INTO VIEW, appear, arise, come forth, emanate, issue, rise, spring up, surface
2 BECOME APPARENT, become known, come out, come out in the wash, come to light, crop up, transpire

emergence *noun* COMING, advent, appearance, arrival, development, materialization, rise

emergency *noun* CRISIS, danger, difficulty, extremity, necessity, plight, predicament, quandary, scrape (*informal*)

emigrate *verb* MOVE ABROAD, migrate, move

emigration *noun* DEPARTURE, exodus, migration

eminence *noun* PROMINENCE, distinction, esteem, fame, greatness, importance, note, prestige, renown, repute

eminent *adjective* PROMINENT, celebrated, distinguished, esteemed, famous, high-ranking, illustrious, noted, renowned, well-known

emission *noun* GIVING OFF or OUT, discharge, ejaculation, ejection, exhalation, radiation, shedding, transmission

emit *verb* GIVE OFF, cast out, discharge, eject, emanate, exude, radiate, send out, transmit

emotion *noun* FEELING, ardor, excitement, fervor, passion, sensation, sentiment, vehemence, warmth

emotional *adjective* 1 SENSITIVE, demonstrative, excitable, hot-blooded, passionate, sentimental, temperamental
2 MOVING, affecting, emotive, heart-warming, poignant, sentimental, stirring, touching

emotive *adjective* SENSITIVE, controversial, delicate, touchy

emphasis *noun* STRESS, accent, attention, force, importance, priority, prominence, significance, weight

emphasize *verb* STRESS, accentuate, dwell on, give priority to, highlight, lay stress on, play up, press home, underline

emphatic *adjective* FORCEFUL, categorical, definite, insistent, positive, pronounced, resounding, unequivocal, unmistakable, vigorous

empire *noun* KINGDOM, commonwealth, domain, realm

empirical, empiric *adjective* FIRST-HAND, experiential, experimental, observed, practical, pragmatic

employ *verb* 1 HIRE, commission, engage, enlist, retain, take on
2 KEEP BUSY, engage, fill, make use of, occupy, take up, use up
3 USE, apply, bring to bear, exercise, exert, make use of, ply, put to use, utilize
▶ *noun* 4 *as in* **in the employ of** SERVICE, employment, engagement, hire

employed *adjective* WORKING, active, busy, engaged, in a job, in employment, in work, occupied

employee *noun* WORKER, hand, job-holder, staff member, wage-earner, workman

employer *noun* BOSS (*informal*), company, firm, gaffer (*informal, chiefly Brit.*), owner, patron, proprietor

employment *noun* 1 TAKING ON, engagement, enlistment, hire, retaining
2 USE, application, exercise, exertion, utilization
3 JOB, line, occupation, profession, trade, vocation, work

emporium *noun* (*old-fashioned*) SHOP, bazaar, market, mart, store, warehouse

empower *verb* ENABLE, allow, authorize, commission, delegate, entitle, license, permit, qualify, sanction, warrant

emptiness *noun* 1 BARENESS, blankness, desolation, vacancy, vacuum, void, waste
2 PURPOSELESSNESS, banality, futility, hollowness, inanity, meaninglessness, senselessness, vanity, worthlessness
3 INSINCERITY, cheapness, hollowness, idleness

empty *adjective* 1 BARE, blank, clear, deserted, desolate, hollow, unfurnished, uninhabited, unoccupied, vacant, void
2 PURPOSELESS, banal,

fruitless, futile, hollow, inane, meaningless, senseless, vain, worthless

3 INSINCERE, cheap, hollow, idle
▶ *verb* 4 EVACUATE, clear, drain, exhaust, pour out, unload, vacate, void

empty-headed *adjective* SCATTERBRAINED, brainless, dizzy (*informal*), featherbrained, harebrained, silly, vacuous

emulate *verb* IMITATE, compete with, copy, echo, follow, mimic, rival

enable *verb* ALLOW, authorize, empower, entitle, license, permit, qualify, sanction, warrant

enact *verb* 1 ESTABLISH, authorize, command, decree, legislate, ordain, order, proclaim, sanction
2 PERFORM, act out, depict, play, play the part of, portray, represent

enamored *adjective* IN LOVE, captivated, charmed, enraptured, fond, infatuated, smitten, taken

encampment *noun* CAMP, base, bivouac, camping ground, campsite, cantonment, quarters, tents

encapsulate *verb* SUM UP, abridge, compress, condense, digest, epitomize, précis, summarize

enchant *verb* FASCINATE, beguile, bewitch, captivate, charm, delight, enrapture, enthrall, ravish, spellbind

enchanter *noun* SORCERER, conjurer, magician, magus, necromancer, warlock, witch, wizard

enchanting *adjective* FASCINATING, alluring, attractive, bewitching, captivating, charming, delightful, entrancing, lovely, pleasant

enclose *verb* 1 SURROUND, bound, encase, encircle, fence, hem in, shut in, wall in
2 SEND WITH, include, insert, put in

encompass *verb* 1 SURROUND, circle, encircle, enclose, envelop, ring
2 INCLUDE, admit, comprise, contain, cover, embrace, hold, incorporate, take in

encounter *verb* 1 MEET, bump into (*informal*), chance upon, come upon, confront, experience, face, run across
▶ *noun* 2 MEETING, brush, confrontation, rendezvous
3 BATTLE, clash, conflict, contest, head-to-head, run-in (*informal*)

encourage *verb* 1 INSPIRE, buoy up, cheer, comfort, console, embolden, hearten, reassure
2 SPUR, advocate, egg on, foster, promote, prompt, support, urge

encouragement *noun* INSPIRATION, cheer, incitement, promotion, reassurance, stimulation, stimulus, support

encouraging *adjective* PROMISING, bright, cheerful, comforting, good, heartening, hopeful, reassuring, rosy

encroach *verb* INTRUDE, impinge, infringe, invade, make inroads, overstep, trespass, usurp

encumber *verb* BURDEN, hamper, handicap, hinder, impede, inconvenience, obstruct, saddle, weigh down

end *noun* 1 EXTREMITY, boundary, edge, extent, extreme, limit, point, terminus, tip
2 FINISH, cessation, close, closure, ending, expiration, expiry, stop, termination
3 CONCLUSION, culmination, denouement, ending, finale,

resolution
4 REMNANT, butt, fragment, leftover, oddment, remainder, scrap, stub
5 DESTRUCTION, death, demise, doom, extermination, extinction, ruin
6 PURPOSE, aim, goal, intention, object, objective, point, reason
▶ *verb* **7** FINISH, cease, close, conclude, culminate, stop, terminate, wind up

endanger *verb* PUT AT RISK, compromise, imperil, jeopardize, put in danger, risk, threaten

endearing *adjective* ATTRACTIVE, captivating, charming, cute, engaging, lovable, sweet, winning

endearment *noun* LOVING WORD, sweet nothing

endeavor *verb* **1** TRY, aim, aspire, attempt, labor, make an effort, strive, struggle, take pains
▶ *noun* **2** EFFORT, attempt, enterprise, trial, try, undertaking, venture

ending *noun* FINISH, cessation, close, completion, conclusion, culmination, denouement, end, finale

endless *adjective* ETERNAL, boundless, continual, everlasting, incessant, infinite, interminable, unlimited

endorse *verb* **1** APPROVE, advocate, authorize, back, champion, promote, ratify, recommend, support
2 SIGN, countersign

endorsement *noun* **1** APPROVAL, advocacy, approbation, authorization, backing, favor, ratification, recommendation, seal of approval, support
2 SIGNATURE, countersignature

endow *verb* PROVIDE, award,

bequeath, bestow, confer, donate, finance, fund, give

endowment *noun* PROVISION, award, benefaction, bequest, donation, gift, grant, legacy

endurable *adjective* BEARABLE, acceptable, sufferable, sustainable, tolerable

endurance *noun* **1** STAYING POWER, fortitude, patience, perseverance, persistence, resolution, stamina, strength, tenacity, toleration
2 PERMANENCE, continuity, durability, duration, longevity, stability

endure *verb* **1** BEAR, cope with, experience, stand, suffer, sustain, undergo, withstand
2 LAST, continue, live on, persist, remain, stand, stay, survive

enduring *adjective* LONG-LASTING, abiding, continuing, lasting, perennial, persistent, steadfast, unfaltering, unwavering

enemy *noun* FOE, adversary, antagonist, competitor, opponent, rival, the opposition, the other side

energetic *adjective* VIGOROUS, active, animated, dynamic, forceful, indefatigable, lively, strenuous, tireless

energy *noun* VIGOR, drive, forcefulness, get-up-and-go (*informal*), liveliness, pep, stamina, verve, vitality

enforce *verb* IMPOSE, administer, apply, carry out, execute, implement, insist on, prosecute, put into effect

engage *verb* **1** PARTICIPATE, embark on, enter into, join, set about, take part, undertake
2 OCCUPY, absorb, engross, grip, involve, preoccupy
3 CAPTIVATE, arrest, catch, fix, gain

4 EMPLOY, appoint, enlist, enroll, hire, retain, take on

5 (*military*) BEGIN BATTLE WITH, assail, attack, encounter, fall on, join battle with, meet, take on

6 SET GOING, activate, apply, bring into operation, energize, switch on

engaged *adjective* **1** BETROTHED (*archaic*), affianced, pledged, promised, spoken for

2 OCCUPIED, busy, employed, in use, tied up, unavailable

engagement *noun*
1 APPOINTMENT, arrangement, commitment, date, meeting
2 BETROTHAL, troth (*archaic*)
3 BATTLE, action, combat, conflict, encounter, fight

engaging *adjective* CHARMING, agreeable, attractive, fetching (*informal*), likable or likeable, pleasing, winning, winsome

engender *verb* PRODUCE, breed, cause, create, generate, give rise to, induce, instigate, lead to

engine *noun* MACHINE, mechanism, motor

engineer *verb* BRING ABOUT, contrive, create, devise, effect, mastermind, plan, plot, scheme

engrave *verb* **1** CARVE, chisel, cut, etch, inscribe
2 FIX, embed, impress, imprint, ingrain, lodge

engraving *noun* CARVING, etching, inscription, plate, woodcut

engross *verb* ABSORB, engage, immerse, involve, occupy, preoccupy

engrossed *adjective* ABSORBED, caught up, enthralled, fascinated, gripped, immersed, lost, preoccupied, rapt, riveted

engulf *verb* IMMERSE, envelop, inundate, overrun, overwhelm, submerge, swallow up, swamp

enhance *verb* IMPROVE, add to, boost, heighten, increase, lift, reinforce, strengthen, swell

enigma *noun* MYSTERY, conundrum, problem, puzzle, riddle, teaser

enigmatic *adjective* MYSTERIOUS, ambiguous, cryptic, equivocal, inscrutable, obscure, puzzling, unfathomable

enjoy *verb* **1** TAKE PLEASURE IN or FROM, appreciate, be entertained by, be pleased with, delight in, like, relish
2 HAVE, be blessed or favored with, experience, have the benefit of, own, possess, reap the benefits of, use

enjoyable *adjective* PLEASURABLE, agreeable, delightful, entertaining, gratifying, pleasant, satisfying, to one's liking

enjoyment *noun* PLEASURE, amusement, delectation, delight, entertainment, fun, gratification, happiness, joy, relish

enlarge *verb* **1** INCREASE, add to, amplify, broaden, expand, extend, grow, magnify, swell, widen
2 ▷▷ **enlarge on** EXPAND ON, descant on, develop, elaborate on, expatiate on, give further details about

enlighten *verb* INFORM, advise, cause to understand, counsel, edify, educate, instruct, make aware, teach

enlightened *adjective* INFORMED, aware, civilized, cultivated, educated, knowledgeable, open-minded, reasonable, sophisticated

enlightenment *noun* UNDERSTANDING, awareness, comprehension, education,

insight, instruction, knowledge,
learning, wisdom
enlist verb 1 JOIN UP, enroll, enter
(into), join, muster, register, sign
up, volunteer
2 OBTAIN, engage, procure, recruit
enliven verb CHEER UP, animate,
excite, inspire, invigorate, pep up,
rouse, spark, stimulate, vitalize
enmity noun HOSTILITY, acrimony,
animosity, bad blood, bitterness,
hatred, ill will, malice
ennoble verb DIGNIFY, aggrandize,
elevate, enhance, exalt, glorify,
honor, magnify, raise
enormity noun 1 WICKEDNESS,
atrocity, depravity,
monstrousness, outrageousness,
vileness, villainy
2 ATROCITY, abomination, crime,
disgrace, evil, horror, monstrosity,
outrage
3 (informal) HUGENESS, greatness,
immensity, magnitude, vastness
enormous adjective HUGE,
colossal, gigantic, gross,
immense, mammoth, massive,
mountainous, tremendous, vast
enough adjective 1 SUFFICIENT,
abundant, adequate, ample,
plenty
▶ noun 2 SUFFICIENCY, abundance,
adequacy, ample supply, plenty,
right amount
▶ adverb 3 SUFFICIENTLY,
abundantly, adequately, amply,
reasonably, satisfactorily,
tolerably
enquire see INQUIRE
enquiry see INQUIRY
enrage verb ANGER, exasperate,
incense, inflame, infuriate,
madden
enrich verb 1 ENHANCE, augment,
develop, improve, refine,
supplement

2 MAKE RICH, make wealthy
enroll verb ENLIST, accept, admit,
join up, recruit, register, sign up
or on, take on
enrollment noun ENLISTMENT,
acceptance, admission,
engagement, matriculation,
recruitment, registration
en route adverb ON or ALONG THE
WAY, in transit, on the road
ensemble noun 1 WHOLE,
aggregate, collection, entirety, set,
sum, total, totality
2 OUTFIT, costume, get-up
(informal), suit
3 GROUP, band, cast, chorus,
company, troupe
ensign noun FLAG, banner, colors,
jack, pennant, pennon, standard,
streamer
ensue verb FOLLOW, arise, come
next, derive, flow, issue, proceed,
result, stem
ensure verb 1 MAKE CERTAIN,
certify, confirm, effect, guarantee,
make sure, secure, warrant
2 PROTECT, guard, make safe,
safeguard, secure
entail verb INVOLVE, bring about,
call for, demand, give rise to,
necessitate, occasion, require
entangle verb 1 TANGLE, catch,
embroil, enmesh, ensnare, entrap,
implicate, snag, snare, trap
2 MIX UP, complicate, confuse,
jumble, muddle, perplex, puzzle
enter verb 1 COME or GO IN or INTO,
arrive, make an entrance, pass
into, penetrate, pierce
2 JOIN, commence, embark upon,
enlist, enroll, set out on, start,
take up
3 RECORD, inscribe, list, log, note,
register, set down, take down
enterprise noun 1 FIRM, business,
company, concern, establishment,

operation

2 UNDERTAKING, adventure, effort, endeavor, operation, plan, program, project, venture

3 INITIATIVE, adventurousness, boldness, daring, drive, energy, enthusiasm, resourcefulness

enterprising *adjective*
RESOURCEFUL, adventurous, bold, daring, energetic, enthusiastic, go-ahead, intrepid, spirited

entertain *verb* 1 AMUSE, charm, cheer, delight, please, regale

2 SHOW HOSPITALITY TO, accommodate, be host to, harbor, have company, lodge, put up, treat

3 CONSIDER, conceive, contemplate, imagine, keep in mind, think about

entertaining *adjective* ENJOYABLE, amusing, cheering, diverting, funny, humorous, interesting, pleasant, pleasurable

entertainment *noun* ENJOYMENT, amusement, fun, leisure activity, pastime, pleasure, recreation, sport, treat

enthrall *verb* FASCINATE, captivate, charm, enchant, enrapture, entrance, grip, mesmerize

enthusiasm *noun* KEENNESS, eagerness, fervor, interest, passion, relish, zeal, zest

enthusiast *noun* LOVER, aficionado, buff (*informal*), devotee, fan, fanatic, follower, supporter

enthusiastic *adjective* KEEN, avid, eager, fervent, gung ho (*slang*), passionate, vigorous, wholehearted, zealous

entice *verb* ATTRACT, allure, cajole, coax, lead on, lure, persuade, seduce, tempt

entire *adjective* WHOLE, complete, full, gross, total

entirely *adverb* COMPLETELY,
absolutely, altogether, fully, in every respect, thoroughly, totally, utterly, wholly

entitle *verb* 1 GIVE THE RIGHT TO, allow, authorize, empower, enable, license, permit

2 CALL, christen, dub, label, name, term, title

entity *noun* THING, being, creature, individual, object, organism, substance

entourage *noun* RETINUE, associates, attendants, company, court, escort, followers, staff, train

entrails *plural noun* INTESTINES, bowels, guts, innards (*informal*), insides (*informal*), offal, viscera

entrance¹ *noun* 1 WAY IN, access, door, doorway, entry, gate, opening, passage

2 APPEARANCE, arrival, coming in, entry, introduction

3 ADMISSION, access, admittance, entrée, entry, permission to enter

entrance² *verb* 1 ENCHANT, bewitch, captivate, charm, delight, enrapture, enthrall, fascinate

2 MESMERIZE, hypnotize, put in a trance

entrant *noun* COMPETITOR, candidate, contestant, entry, participant, player

entreaty *noun* PLEA, appeal, earnest request, exhortation, petition, prayer, request, supplication

entrenched *adjective* FIXED, deep-rooted, deep-seated, ineradicable, ingrained, rooted, set, unshakable, well-established

entrepreneur *noun* BUSINESSMAN *or* BUSINESSWOMAN, impresario, industrialist, magnate, tycoon

entrust *verb* GIVE CUSTODY OF, assign, commit, confide, delegate, deliver, hand over, turn over

entry noun **1** WAY IN, access, door, doorway, entrance, gate, opening, passage
2 COMING IN, appearance, entering, entrance, initiation, introduction
3 ADMISSION, access, entrance, entrée, permission to enter
4 RECORD, account, item, listing, note

entwine verb TWIST, interlace, interweave, knit, plait, twine, weave, wind

enumerate verb LIST, cite, itemize, mention, name, quote, recite, recount, relate, spell out

enunciate verb **1** PRONOUNCE, articulate, enounce, say, sound, speak, utter, vocalize, voice
2 STATE, declare, proclaim, promulgate, pronounce, propound, publish

envelop verb ENCLOSE, cloak, cover, encase, encircle, engulf, shroud, surround, wrap

envelope noun WRAPPING, case, casing, cover, covering, jacket, wrapper

enviable adjective DESIRABLE, advantageous, favored, fortunate, lucky, privileged, to die for (informal), win-win (informal)

envious adjective COVETOUS, green with envy, grudging, jealous, resentful

environment noun SURROUNDINGS, atmosphere, background, conditions, habitat, medium, setting, situation

environmental adjective ECOLOGICAL, green

environmentalist noun CONSERVATIONIST, ecologist, green

environs plural noun SURROUNDING AREA, district, locality, neighborhood, outskirts, precincts, suburbs, vicinity

envisage verb **1** IMAGINE, conceive (of), conceptualize, contemplate, fancy, picture, think up, visualize
2 FORESEE, anticipate, envision, predict, see

envoy noun MESSENGER, agent, ambassador, courier, delegate, diplomat, emissary, intermediary, representative

envy noun **1** COVETOUSNESS, enviousness, jealousy, resentfulness, resentment
▶ verb **2** COVET, be envious (of), begrudge, be jealous (of), grudge, resent

ephemeral adjective BRIEF, fleeting, momentary, passing, short-lived, temporary, transient, transitory

epidemic noun SPREAD, contagion, growth, outbreak, plague, rash, upsurge, wave

epigram noun WITTICISM, aphorism, bon mot, quip

epilogue noun CONCLUSION, coda, concluding speech, postscript

episode noun **1** EVENT, adventure, affair, escapade, experience, happening, incident, matter, occurrence
2 PART, chapter, installment, passage, scene, section

epistle noun LETTER, communication, message, missive, note

epitaph noun MONUMENT, inscription

epithet noun NAME, appellation, description, designation, moniker or monicker (slang), nickname, sobriquet, tag, title

epitome noun PERSONIFICATION, archetype, embodiment, essence, quintessence, representation, type, typical example

epitomize *verb* TYPIFY, embody, exemplify, illustrate, personify, represent, symbolize

epoch *noun* ERA, age, date, period, time

equable *adjective* EVEN-TEMPERED, calm, composed, easy-going, imperturbable, level-headed, placid, serene, unflappable (*informal*)

equal *adjective* 1 IDENTICAL, alike, corresponding, equivalent, the same, uniform
2 REGULAR, symmetrical, uniform, unvarying
3 EVEN, balanced, evenly matched, fifty-fifty (*informal*), level pegging (*Brit. informal*)
4 FAIR, egalitarian, even-handed, impartial, just, on a level playing field (*informal*), unbiased
5 ▷▷ **equal to** CAPABLE OF, competent to, fit for, good enough for, ready for, strong enough, suitable for, up to
▶ *noun* 6 MATCH, counterpart, equivalent, rival, twin
▶ *verb* 7 MATCH, amount to, be tantamount to, correspond to, equate, level, parallel, tie with

equality *noun* 1 SAMENESS, balance, correspondence, equivalence, evenness, identity, likeness, similarity, uniformity
2 FAIRNESS, egalitarianism, equal opportunity, parity

equalize *verb* MAKE EQUAL, balance, equal, even up, level, match, regularize, smooth, square, standardize

equate *verb* MAKE *or* BE EQUAL, be commensurate, compare, correspond with *or* to, liken, mention in the same breath, parallel

equation *noun* EQUATING, comparison, correspondence, parallel

equilibrium *noun* STABILITY, balance, equipoise, evenness, rest, steadiness, symmetry

equip *verb* SUPPLY, arm, array, fit out, furnish, kit out, provide, stock

equipment *noun* TOOLS, accoutrements, apparatus, gear, paraphernalia, stuff, supplies, tackle

equitable *adjective* FAIR, even-handed, honest, impartial, just, proper, reasonable, unbiased

equivalence *noun* EQUALITY, correspondence, evenness, likeness, parity, sameness, similarity

equivalent *noun* 1 EQUAL, counterpart, match, opposite number, parallel, twin
▶ *adjective* 2 EQUAL, alike, commensurate, comparable, corresponding, interchangeable, of a piece, on a level playing field (*informal*), same, similar, tantamount

equivocal *adjective* AMBIGUOUS, evasive, indefinite, indeterminate, misleading, oblique, obscure, uncertain, vague

era *noun* AGE, date, day *or* days, epoch, generation, period, time

eradicate *verb* WIPE OUT, annihilate, destroy, eliminate, erase, exterminate, extinguish, obliterate, remove, root out

erase *verb* WIPE OUT, blot, cancel, delete, expunge, obliterate, remove, rub out

erect *verb* 1 BUILD, construct, put up, raise, set up
2 FOUND, create, establish, form, initiate, institute, organize, set up

▶ *adjective* 3 UPRIGHT, elevated, perpendicular, pricked-up, stiff, straight, vertical

erode *verb* WEAR DOWN *or* AWAY, abrade, consume, corrode, destroy, deteriorate, disintegrate, eat away, grind down

erosion *noun* DETERIORATION, abrasion, attrition, destruction, disintegration, eating away, grinding down, wearing down *or* away

erotic *adjective* SEXUAL, amatory, carnal, lustful, seductive, sensual, sexy (*informal*), voluptuous

err *verb* MAKE A MISTAKE, blunder, go wrong, miscalculate, misjudge, mistake, slip up (*informal*)

errand *noun* JOB, charge, commission, message, mission, task

erratic *adjective* UNPREDICTABLE, changeable, inconsistent, irregular, uneven, unreliable, unstable, variable, wayward

erroneous *adjective* INCORRECT, fallacious, false, faulty, flawed, invalid, mistaken, unsound, wrong

error *noun* MISTAKE, bloomer (*informal*), blunder, howler (*informal*), miscalculation, oversight, slip, solecism

erstwhile *adjective* FORMER, bygone, late, old, once, one-time, past, previous, sometime

erudite *adjective* LEARNED, cultivated, cultured, educated, knowledgeable, scholarly, well-educated, well-read

erupt *verb* 1 EXPLODE, belch forth, blow up, burst out, gush, pour forth, spew forth *or* out, spout, throw off
2 (*medical*) BREAK OUT, appear

eruption *noun* 1 EXPLOSION, discharge, ejection, flare-up, outbreak, outburst
2 (*medical*) INFLAMMATION, outbreak, rash

escalate *verb* INCREASE, expand, extend, grow, heighten, intensify, mount, rise

escapade *noun* ADVENTURE, antic, caper, prank, scrape (*informal*), stunt

escape *verb* 1 GET AWAY, abscond, bolt, break free *or* out, flee, fly, make one's getaway, run away *or* off, slip away
2 AVOID, dodge, duck, elude, evade, pass, shun, slip
3 LEAK, emanate, exude, flow, gush, issue, pour forth, seep
▶ *noun* 4 GETAWAY, break, break-out, flight
5 AVOIDANCE, circumvention, evasion
6 RELAXATION, distraction, diversion, pastime, recreation
7 LEAK, emanation, emission, seepage

escort *noun* 1 GUARD, bodyguard, convoy, cortege, entourage, retinue, train
2 COMPANION, attendant, beau, chaperon, guide, partner
▶ *verb* 3 ACCOMPANY, chaperon, conduct, guide, lead, partner, shepherd, usher

especial *adjective* (*formal*) EXCEPTIONAL, noteworthy, outstanding, principal, special, uncommon, unusual

especially *adverb* EXCEPTIONALLY, conspicuously, markedly, notably, outstandingly, remarkably, specially, strikingly, uncommonly, unusually

espionage *noun* SPYING, counter-intelligence, intelligence, surveillance, undercover work

espousal noun SUPPORT, adoption, advocacy, backing, championing, championship, defense, embracing, promotion, taking up

espouse verb SUPPORT, adopt, advocate, back, champion, embrace, promote, stand up for, take up, uphold

essay noun 1 COMPOSITION, article, discourse, dissertation, paper, piece, tract, treatise
▶ verb 2 (formal) ATTEMPT, aim, endeavor, try, undertake

essence noun 1 FUNDAMENTAL NATURE, being, core, heart, nature, quintessence, soul, spirit, substance
2 CONCENTRATE, distillate, extract, spirits, tincture

essential adjective 1 VITAL, crucial, important, indispensable, necessary, needed, requisite
2 FUNDAMENTAL, basic, cardinal, elementary, innate, intrinsic, main, principal
▶ noun 3 PREREQUISITE, basic, fundamental, must, necessity, rudiment, sine qua non

establish verb 1 CREATE, constitute, form, found, ground, inaugurate, institute, settle, set up
2 PROVE, authenticate, certify, confirm, corroborate, demonstrate, substantiate, verify

establishment noun 1 CREATION, formation, foundation, founding, inauguration, installation, institution, organization, setting up
2 ORGANIZATION, business, company, concern, corporation, enterprise, firm, institution, outfit (informal)
3 ▷▷ **the Establishment** THE AUTHORITIES, ruling class, the

powers that be, the system

estate noun 1 LANDS, area, domain, holdings, manor, property
2 (law) PROPERTY, assets, belongings, effects, fortune, goods, possessions, wealth

esteem noun 1 RESPECT, admiration, credit, estimation, good opinion, honor, kudos, regard, reverence, veneration
▶ verb 2 RESPECT, admire, love, prize, regard highly, revere, think highly of, treasure, value
3 CONSIDER, believe, deem, estimate, judge, reckon, regard, think, view

estimate verb 1 CALCULATE ROUGHLY, assess, evaluate, gauge, guess, judge, number, reckon, value
2 FORM AN OPINION, believe, conjecture, consider, judge, rank, rate, reckon, surmise
▶ noun 3 APPROXIMATE CALCULATION, assessment, ballpark figure (informal), guess, guesstimate (informal), judgment, valuation
4 OPINION, appraisal, assessment, belief, estimation, judgment

estimation noun OPINION, appraisal, appreciation, assessment, belief, consideration, considered opinion, judgment, view

estuary noun INLET, creek, firth, fjord, mouth

et cetera adverb 1 AND SO ON, and so forth
▶ noun 2 AND THE REST, and others, and the like, et al.

etch verb CUT, carve, eat into, engrave, impress, imprint, inscribe, stamp

etching noun PRINT, carving,

engraving, impression, imprint, inscription

eternal adjective 1 EVERLASTING, endless, immortal, infinite, never-ending, perpetual, timeless, unceasing, unending
2 PERMANENT, deathless, enduring, immutable, imperishable, indestructible, lasting, unchanging

eternity noun 1 INFINITY, ages, endlessness, immortality, perpetuity, timelessness
2 (theology) THE AFTERLIFE, heaven, paradise, the hereafter, the next world

ethical adjective MORAL, conscientious, fair, good, honorable, just, principled, proper, right, upright, virtuous

ethics plural noun MORAL CODE, conscience, morality, moral philosophy, moral values, principles, rules of conduct, standards

ethnic, ethnical adjective CULTURAL, folk, indigenous, national, native, racial, traditional

etiquette noun GOOD or PROPER BEHAVIOR, civility, courtesy, decorum, formalities, manners, politeness, propriety, protocol

euphoria noun ELATION, ecstasy, exaltation, exhilaration, intoxication, joy, jubilation, rapture

evacuate verb CLEAR, abandon, desert, forsake, leave, move out, pull out, quit, vacate, withdraw

evade verb 1 AVOID, dodge, duck, elude, escape, get away from, sidestep, steer clear of
2 AVOID ANSWERING, equivocate, fend off, fudge, hedge, parry

evaluate verb ASSESS, appraise, calculate, estimate, gauge, judge, rate, reckon, size up (informal), weigh

evaporate verb 1 DRY UP, dehydrate, desiccate, dry, vaporize
2 DISAPPEAR, dematerialize, dissolve, fade away, melt away, vanish

evasion noun 1 AVOIDANCE, dodging, escape
2 DECEPTION, equivocation, evasiveness, prevarication

evasive adjective DECEPTIVE, cagey (informal), equivocating, indirect, oblique, prevaricating, shifty, slippery

eve noun 1 NIGHT BEFORE, day before, vigil
2 BRINK, edge, point, threshold, verge

even adjective 1 LEVEL, flat, horizontal, parallel, smooth, steady, straight, true, uniform
2 REGULAR, constant, smooth, steady, unbroken, uniform, uninterrupted, unvarying, unwavering
3 EQUAL, comparable, fifty-fifty (informal), identical, level, like, matching, neck and neck, on a level playing field (informal), on a par, similar, tied
4 CALM, composed, cool, even-tempered, imperturbable, placid, unruffled, well-balanced
5 ▷▷ **get even (with)** PAY BACK, give tit for tat, reciprocate, repay, requite, retaliate

evening noun DUSK, gloaming (Scot. or poetic), twilight

event noun 1 INCIDENT, affair, business, circumstance, episode, experience, happening, occasion, occurrence
2 COMPETITION, bout, contest, game, tournament

even-tempered adjective CALM, composed, cool, imperturbable, level-headed, placid, tranquil, unexcitable, unruffled

eventful adjective EXCITING, active, busy, dramatic, full, lively, memorable, remarkable

eventual adjective FINAL, concluding, overall, ultimate

eventuality noun POSSIBILITY, case, chance, contingency, event, likelihood, probability

eventually adverb IN THE END, after all, at the end of the day, finally, one day, some time, ultimately, when all is said and done

ever adverb 1 AT ANY TIME, at all, at any period, at any point, by any chance, in any case, on any occasion
2 ALWAYS, at all times, constantly, continually, evermore, for ever, perpetually, twenty-four-seven (slang)

everlasting adjective ETERNAL, endless, immortal, indestructible, never-ending, perpetual, timeless, undying

evermore adverb FOR EVER, always, eternally, ever, to the end of time

every adjective EACH, all, each one

everybody pronoun EVERYONE, all and sundry, each one, each person, every person, one and all, the whole world

everyday adjective COMMON, customary, mundane, ordinary, routine, run-of-the-mill, stock, usual, workaday

everyone pronoun EVERYBODY, all and sundry, each one, each person, every person, one and all, the whole world

everything pronoun ALL, each thing, the lot, the whole lot

everywhere adverb TO or IN EVERY PLACE, all around, all over, far and wide or near, high and low, in every nook and cranny, the world over, ubiquitously

evict verb EXPEL, boot out (informal), eject, kick out (informal), oust, remove, throw out, turf out (informal), turn out

evidence noun 1 PROOF, confirmation, corroboration, demonstration, grounds, indication, sign, substantiation, testimony
▶ verb 2 SHOW, demonstrate, display, exhibit, indicate, prove, reveal, signify, witness

evident adjective OBVIOUS, apparent, clear, manifest, noticeable, perceptible, plain, unmistakable, visible

evidently adverb 1 OBVIOUSLY, clearly, manifestly, plainly, undoubtedly, unmistakably, without question
2 APPARENTLY, ostensibly, outwardly, seemingly, to all appearances

evil noun 1 WICKEDNESS, badness, depravity, malignity, sin, vice, villainy, wrongdoing
2 HARM, affliction, disaster, hurt, ill, injury, mischief, misfortune, suffering, woe
▶ adjective 3 WICKED, bad, depraved, immoral, malevolent, malicious, sinful, villainous
4 HARMFUL, calamitous, catastrophic, destructive, dire, disastrous, pernicious, ruinous
5 OFFENSIVE, foul, noxious, pestilential, unpleasant, vile

evoke verb RECALL, arouse, awaken, call, give rise to, induce, rekindle, stir up, summon up

evolution *noun* DEVELOPMENT, expansion, growth, increase, maturation, progress, unfolding, working out

evolve *verb* DEVELOP, expand, grow, increase, mature, progress, unfold, work out

exact *adjective* 1 ACCURATE, correct, definite, faultless, precise, right, specific, true, unerring
▶ *verb* 2 DEMAND, claim, command, compel, extort, extract, force

exacting *adjective* DEMANDING, difficult, hard, harsh, rigorous, severe, strict, stringent, taxing, tough

exactly *adverb* 1 PRECISELY, accurately, correctly, explicitly, faithfully, scrupulously, truthfully, unerringly
2 IN EVERY RESPECT, absolutely, indeed, precisely, quite, specifically, to the letter

exactness *noun* PRECISION, accuracy, correctness, exactitude, rigorousness, scrupulousness, strictness, veracity

exaggerate *verb* OVERSTATE, amplify, embellish, embroider, enlarge, overemphasize, overestimate

exaggeration *noun* OVERSTATEMENT, amplification, embellishment, enlargement, hyperbole, overemphasis, overestimation

exalt *verb* 1 PRAISE, acclaim, extol, glorify, idolize, set on a pedestal, worship
2 RAISE, advance, elevate, ennoble, honor, promote, upgrade

exaltation *noun* 1 PRAISE, acclaim, glorification, idolization, reverence, tribute, worship
2 RISE, advancement, elevation, ennoblement, promotion, upgrading

exalted *adjective* HIGH-RANKING, dignified, eminent, grand, honored, lofty, prestigious

examination *noun* 1 INSPECTION, analysis, exploration, interrogation, investigation, research, scrutiny, study, test
2 QUESTIONING, inquiry, inquisition, probe, quiz, test

examine *verb* 1 INSPECT, analyze, explore, investigate, peruse, scrutinize, study, survey
2 QUESTION, cross-examine, grill (*informal*), inquire, interrogate, quiz, test

example *noun* 1 SPECIMEN, case, illustration, instance, sample
2 MODEL, archetype, ideal, paradigm, paragon, prototype, standard
3 WARNING, caution, lesson

exasperate *verb* IRRITATE, anger, annoy, enrage, incense, inflame, infuriate, madden, pique

exasperation *noun* IRRITATION, anger, annoyance, fury, pique, provocation, rage, wrath

excavate *verb* DIG OUT, burrow, delve, dig up, mine, quarry, tunnel, uncover, unearth

exceed *verb* 1 SURPASS, beat, better, cap (*informal*), eclipse, outdo, outstrip, overtake, pass, top
2 GO OVER THE LIMIT OF, go over the top, overstep

exceedingly *adverb* EXTREMELY, enormously, exceptionally, extraordinarily, hugely, superlatively, surpassingly, unusually, very

excel *verb* 1 BE SUPERIOR, beat, eclipse, outdo, outshine, surpass, transcend
2 ▷▷ **excel in** *or* **at** BE GOOD AT,

be proficient in, be skillful at, be talented at, shine at, show talent in

excellence *noun* HIGH QUALITY, distinction, eminence, goodness, greatness, merit, pre-eminence, superiority, supremacy

excellent *adjective* OUTSTANDING, brilliant, exquisite, fine, first-class, first-rate, good, great, superb, superlative, world-class

except *preposition* 1 *or* **except for** APART FROM, barring, besides, but, excepting, excluding, omitting, other than, saving, with the exception of
▶ *verb* 2 EXCLUDE, leave out, omit, pass over

exception *noun* 1 SPECIAL CASE, anomaly, deviation, freak, inconsistency, irregularity, oddity, peculiarity
2 EXCLUSION, leaving out, omission, passing over

exceptional *adjective* 1 SPECIAL, abnormal, atypical, extraordinary, irregular, odd, peculiar, strange, unusual
2 REMARKABLE, excellent, extraordinary, marvelous, outstanding, phenomenal, prodigious, special, superior

excerpt *noun* EXTRACT, fragment, part, passage, piece, quotation, section, selection

excess *noun* 1 SURFEIT, glut, overload, superabundance, superfluity, surplus, too much
2 OVERINDULGENCE, debauchery, dissipation, dissoluteness, extravagance, intemperance, prodigality

excessive *adjective* IMMODERATE, disproportionate, exaggerated, extreme, inordinate, overmuch, superfluous, too much, undue,
unfair, unreasonable

exchange *verb* 1 INTERCHANGE, barter, change, convert into, swap, switch, trade
▶ *noun* 2 INTERCHANGE, barter, quid pro quo, reciprocity, substitution, swap, switch, tit for tat, trade

excitable *adjective* NERVOUS, emotional, highly strung, hot-headed, mercurial, quick-tempered, temperamental, volatile, wired (*slang*)

excite *verb* AROUSE, animate, galvanize, inflame, inspire, provoke, rouse, stir up, thrill

excitement *noun* AGITATION, action, activity, animation, commotion, furor, passion, thrill

exciting *adjective* STIMULATING, dramatic, electrifying, exhilarating, rousing, sensational, stirring, thrilling

exclaim *verb* CRY OUT, call out, declare, proclaim, shout, utter, yell

exclamation *noun* CRY, call, interjection, outcry, shout, utterance, yell

exclude *verb* 1 KEEP OUT, ban, bar, boycott, disallow, forbid, prohibit, refuse, shut out
2 LEAVE OUT, count out, eliminate, ignore, omit, pass over, reject, rule out, set aside

exclusion *noun* 1 BAN, bar, boycott, disqualification, embargo, prohibition, veto
2 ELIMINATION, omission, rejection

exclusive *adjective* 1 SOLE, absolute, complete, entire, full, total, undivided, whole
2 LIMITED, confined, peculiar, restricted, unique
3 SELECT, chic, cliquish, cool

(*informal*), fashionable, phat (*slang*), posh (*informal, chiefly Brit.*), restricted, snobbish, up-market

excommunicate *verb* EXPEL, anathematize, ban, banish, cast out, denounce, exclude, repudiate

excruciating *adjective* AGONIZING, harrowing, insufferable, intense, piercing, severe, unbearable, violent

exculpate *verb* ABSOLVE, acquit, clear, discharge, excuse, exonerate, pardon, vindicate

excursion *noun* TRIP, day trip, expedition, jaunt, journey, outing, pleasure trip, ramble, tour

excusable *adjective* FORGIVABLE, allowable, defensible, justifiable, pardonable, permissible, understandable, warrantable

excuse *noun* 1 JUSTIFICATION, apology, defense, explanation, grounds, mitigation, plea, reason, vindication
▶ *verb* 2 JUSTIFY, apologize for, defend, explain, mitigate, vindicate
3 FORGIVE, acquit, exculpate, exonerate, make allowances for, overlook, pardon, tolerate, turn a blind eye to
4 FREE, absolve, discharge, exempt, let off, release, relieve, spare

execute *verb* 1 PUT TO DEATH, behead, electrocute, guillotine, hang, kill, shoot
2 CARRY OUT, accomplish, administer, discharge, effect, enact, implement, perform, prosecute

execution *noun* 1 CARRYING OUT, accomplishment, administration, enactment, enforcement, implementation, operation, performance, prosecution

2 KILLING, capital punishment, hanging

executioner *noun* 1 HANGMAN, headsman
2 KILLER, assassin, exterminator, hit man (*slang*), liquidator, murderer, slayer

executive *noun* 1 ADMINISTRATOR, director, manager, official
2 ADMINISTRATION, directorate, directors, government, hierarchy, leadership, management
▶ *adjective* 3 ADMINISTRATIVE, controlling, decision-making, directing, governing, managerial

exemplary *adjective* 1 IDEAL, admirable, commendable, excellent, fine, good, model, praiseworthy
2 WARNING, cautionary

exemplify *verb* SHOW, demonstrate, display, embody, exhibit, illustrate, represent, serve as an example of

exempt *adjective* 1 IMMUNE, excepted, excused, free, not liable, released, spared
▶ *verb* 2 GRANT IMMUNITY, absolve, discharge, excuse, free, let off, release, relieve, spare

exemption *noun* IMMUNITY, absolution, discharge, dispensation, exception, exoneration, freedom, release

exercise *noun* 1 EXERTION, activity, effort, labor, toil, training, work, work-out
2 TASK, drill, lesson, practice, problem
3 USE, application, discharge, fulfillment, implementation, practice, utilization
▶ *verb* 4 PUT TO USE, apply, bring to bear, employ, exert, use, utilize
5 TRAIN, practice, work out

exert *verb* 1 USE, apply, bring to

bear, employ, exercise, make use of, utilize, wield

2 ▷▷ **exert oneself** MAKE AN EFFORT, apply oneself, do one's best, endeavor, labor, strain, strive, struggle, toil, work

exertion noun EFFORT, elbow grease (*facetious*), endeavor, exercise, industry, strain, struggle, toil

exhaust verb 1 TIRE OUT, debilitate, drain, enervate, enfeeble, fatigue, sap, weaken, wear out

2 USE UP, consume, deplete, dissipate, expend, run through, spend, squander, waste

exhausted adjective 1 WORN OUT, all in (*slang*), debilitated, done in (*informal*), drained, fatigued, knackered (*slang*), spent, tired out

2 USED UP, consumed, depleted, dissipated, expended, finished, spent, squandered, wasted

exhausting adjective TIRING, backbreaking, debilitating, grueling, laborious, punishing, sapping, strenuous, taxing

exhaustion noun 1 TIREDNESS, debilitation, fatigue, weariness

2 DEPLETION, consumption, emptying, using up

exhaustive adjective THOROUGH, all-embracing, complete, comprehensive, extensive, full-scale, in-depth, intensive

exhibit verb DISPLAY, demonstrate, express, indicate, manifest, parade, put on view, reveal, show

exhibition noun DISPLAY, demonstration, exposition, performance, presentation, representation, show, spectacle

exhilarating adjective EXCITING, breathtaking, enlivening, invigorating, stimulating, thrilling

exhort verb URGE, advise, beseech, call upon, entreat, persuade, press, spur

exhume verb DIG UP, disentomb, disinter, unearth

exigency, exigence noun NEED, constraint, demand, necessity, requirement

exile noun 1 BANISHMENT, deportation, expatriation, expulsion

2 EXPATRIATE, deportee, émigré, outcast, refugee

▶ verb 3 BANISH, deport, drive out, eject, expatriate, expel

exist verb 1 BE, be present, endure, live, occur, survive

2 SURVIVE, eke out a living, get along or by, keep one's head above water, stay alive, subsist

existence noun BEING, actuality, life, subsistence

existent adjective IN EXISTENCE, alive, existing, extant, living, present, standing, surviving

exit noun 1 WAY OUT, door, gate, outlet

2 DEPARTURE, exodus, farewell, going, good-bye, leave-taking, retreat, withdrawal

▶ verb 3 DEPART, go away, go offstage (*Theatre*), go out, leave, make tracks, retire, retreat, take one's leave, withdraw

exodus noun DEPARTURE, evacuation, exit, flight, going out, leaving, migration, retreat, withdrawal

exonerate verb CLEAR, absolve, acquit, discharge, exculpate, excuse, justify, pardon, vindicate

exorbitant adjective EXCESSIVE, extortionate, extravagant, immoderate, inordinate, outrageous, preposterous, unreasonable

exorcise verb DRIVE OUT, cast out, deliver (from), expel, purify

exotic adjective 1 UNUSUAL, colorful, fascinating, glamorous, mysterious, strange, striking, unfamiliar
2 FOREIGN, alien, external, imported, naturalized

expand verb 1 INCREASE, amplify, broaden, develop, enlarge, extend, grow, magnify, swell, widen
2 SPREAD (OUT), diffuse, stretch (out), unfold, unfurl, unravel, unroll
3 ▷▷ **expand on** GO INTO DETAIL ABOUT, amplify, develop, elaborate on, embellish, enlarge on, expatiate on, expound on, flesh out

expanse noun AREA, breadth, extent, range, space, stretch, sweep, tract

expansion noun INCREASE, amplification, development, enlargement, growth, magnification, opening out, spread

expansive adjective 1 WIDE, broad, extensive, far-reaching, voluminous, wide-ranging, widespread
2 TALKATIVE, affable, communicative, effusive, friendly, loquacious, open, outgoing, sociable, unreserved

expatriate adjective 1 EXILED, banished, emigrant, émigré
▶ noun 2 EXILE, emigrant, émigré, refugee

expect verb 1 THINK, assume, believe, imagine, presume, reckon, suppose, surmise, trust
2 LOOK FORWARD TO, anticipate, await, contemplate, envisage, hope for, predict, watch for

3 REQUIRE, call for, demand, insist on, want

expectant adjective 1 EXPECTING, anticipating, apprehensive, eager, hopeful, in suspense, ready, watchful
2 PREGNANT, expecting (informal), gravid

expectation noun 1 PROBABILITY, assumption, belief, conjecture, forecast, likelihood, presumption, supposition
2 ANTICIPATION, apprehension, expectancy, hope, promise, suspense

expediency noun SUITABILITY, advisability, benefit, convenience, pragmatism, profitability, prudence, usefulness, utility

expedient noun 1 MEANS, contrivance, device, makeshift, measure, method, resort, scheme, stopgap
▶ adjective 2 ADVANTAGEOUS, appropriate, beneficial, convenient, effective, helpful, opportune, practical, suitable, useful, win-win (informal)

expedition noun JOURNEY, excursion, mission, quest, safari, tour, trek, voyage

expel verb 1 DRIVE OUT, belch, cast out, discharge, eject, remove, spew
2 DISMISS, ban, banish, chuck out (slang), drum out, evict, exclude, exile, throw out, turf out (informal)

expend verb SPEND, consume, dissipate, exhaust, go through, pay out, use (up)

expendable adjective DISPENSABLE, inessential, nonessential, replaceable, unimportant, unnecessary

expenditure noun SPENDING, consumption, cost, expense,

outgoings, outlay, output, payment

expense *noun* COST, charge, expenditure, loss, outlay, payment, spending

expensive *adjective* DEAR, costly, exorbitant, extravagant, high-priced, lavish, overpriced, steep (*informal*), stiff

experience *noun* 1 KNOWLEDGE, contact, exposure, familiarity, involvement, participation, practice, training
2 EVENT, adventure, affair, encounter, episode, happening, incident, occurrence
► *verb* 3 UNDERGO, encounter, endure, face, feel, go through, live through, sample, taste

experienced *adjective* KNOWLEDGEABLE, accomplished, expert, practiced, seasoned, tested, tried, veteran, well-versed

experiment *noun* 1 TEST, examination, experimentation, investigation, procedure, proof, research, trial, trial run
► *verb* 2 TEST, examine, investigate, put to the test, research, sample, try, verify

experimental *adjective* TEST, exploratory, pilot, preliminary, probationary, provisional, speculative, tentative, trial, trial-and-error

expert *noun* 1 MASTER, authority, connoisseur, dab hand (*Brit. informal*), past master, professional, specialist, virtuoso
► *adjective* 2 SKILLFUL, adept, adroit, experienced, masterly, practiced, professional, proficient, qualified, virtuoso

expertise *noun* SKILL, adroitness, command, facility, judgment, know-how (*informal*), knowledge,

mastery, proficiency

expire *verb* 1 FINISH, cease, close, come to an end, conclude, end, lapse, run out, stop, terminate
2 BREATHE OUT, emit, exhale, expel
3 DIE, depart, kick the bucket (*informal*), pass away or on, perish

explain *verb* 1 MAKE CLEAR or PLAIN, clarify, clear up, define, describe, elucidate, expound, resolve, teach
2 ACCOUNT FOR, excuse, give a reason for, justify

explanation *noun* 1 REASON, account, answer, excuse, justification, motive, vindication
2 DESCRIPTION, clarification, definition, elucidation, illustration, interpretation

explanatory *adjective* DESCRIPTIVE, illustrative, interpretive

explicit *adjective* CLEAR, categorical, definite, frank, precise, specific, straightforward, unambiguous

explode *verb* 1 BLOW UP, burst, detonate, discharge, erupt, go off, set off, shatter
2 DISPROVE, debunk, discredit, give the lie to, invalidate, refute, repudiate

exploit *verb* 1 TAKE ADVANTAGE OF, abuse, manipulate, milk, misuse, play on or upon
2 MAKE THE BEST USE OF, capitalize on, cash in on (*informal*), profit by or from, use, utilize
► *noun* 3 FEAT, accomplishment, achievement, adventure, attainment, deed, escapade, stunt

exploitation *noun* MISUSE, abuse, manipulation

exploration *noun*
1 INVESTIGATION, analysis, examination, inquiry, inspection,

research, scrutiny, search
2 EXPEDITION, reconnaissance, survey, tour, travel, trip

exploratory adjective INVESTIGATIVE, experimental, fact-finding, probing, searching, trial

explore verb 1 INVESTIGATE, examine, inquire into, inspect, look into, probe, research, search
2 TRAVEL, reconnoiter, scout, survey, tour

explosion noun 1 BANG, blast, burst, clap, crack, detonation, discharge, report
2 OUTBURST, eruption, fit, outbreak

explosive adjective 1 UNSTABLE, volatile
2 VIOLENT, fiery, stormy, touchy, vehement

exponent noun 1 ADVOCATE, backer, champion, defender, promoter, proponent, supporter, upholder
2 PERFORMER, player

expose verb 1 UNCOVER, display, exhibit, present, reveal, show, unveil
2 MAKE VULNERABLE, endanger, imperil, jeopardize, lay open, leave open, subject

exposed adjective 1 UNCONCEALED, bare, on display, on show, on view, revealed, uncovered
2 UNSHELTERED, open, unprotected
3 VULNERABLE, in peril, laid bare, susceptible, wide open

exposure noun PUBLICITY, display, exhibition, presentation, revelation, showing, uncovering, unveiling

expound verb EXPLAIN, describe, elucidate, interpret, set forth, spell out, unfold

express verb 1 STATE, articulate, communicate, declare, phrase, put into words, say, utter, voice, word
2 SHOW, convey, exhibit, indicate, intimate, make known, represent, reveal, signify, stand for, symbolize
▶ adjective 3 EXPLICIT, categorical, clear, definite, distinct, plain, unambiguous
4 SPECIFIC, clear-cut, especial, particular, singular, special
5 FAST, direct, high-speed, nonstop, rapid, speedy, swift

expression noun 1 STATEMENT, announcement, communication, declaration, utterance
2 INDICATION, demonstration, exhibition, manifestation, representation, show, sign, symbol, token
3 LOOK, air, appearance, aspect, countenance, face
4 PHRASE, idiom, locution, remark, term, turn of phrase, word

expressive adjective VIVID, eloquent, moving, poignant, striking, telling

expressly adverb 1 DEFINITELY, categorically, clearly, distinctly, explicitly, in no uncertain terms, plainly, unambiguously
2 SPECIFICALLY, especially, particularly, specially

expulsion noun EJECTION, banishment, dismissal, eviction, exclusion, removal

exquisite adjective 1 BEAUTIFUL, attractive, charming, comely, lovely, pleasing, striking
2 FINE, beautiful, dainty, delicate, elegant, lovely, precious
3 INTENSE, acute, keen, sharp

extempore adverb or adjective

IMPROMPTU, ad lib, freely, improvised, offhand, off the cuff (*informal*), spontaneously, unpremeditated, unprepared

extend verb 1 MAKE LONGER, drag out, draw out, lengthen, prolong, spin out, spread out, stretch
2 LAST, carry on, continue, go on
3 WIDEN, add to, augment, broaden, enhance, enlarge, expand, increase, supplement
4 OFFER, confer, impart, present, proffer

extension noun 1 ANNEX, addition, appendage, appendix, supplement
2 LENGTHENING, broadening, development, enlargement, expansion, increase, spread, widening

extensive adjective WIDE, broad, far-flung, far-reaching, large-scale, pervasive, spacious, vast, voluminous, widespread

extent noun SIZE, amount, area, breadth, expanse, length, stretch, volume, width

extenuating adjective MITIGATING, justifying, moderating, qualifying

exterior noun 1 OUTSIDE, coating, covering, façade, face, shell, skin, surface
▶ adjective 2 OUTSIDE, external, outer, outermost, outward, surface

exterminate verb DESTROY, abolish, annihilate, eliminate, eradicate

external adjective 1 OUTER, exterior, outermost, outside, outward, surface
2 OUTSIDE, alien, extrinsic, foreign

extinct adjective DEAD, defunct, gone, lost, vanished

extinction noun DYING OUT, abolition, annihilation, destruction, eradication, extermination, obliteration, oblivion

extinguish verb 1 PUT OUT, blow out, douse, quench, smother, snuff out, stifle
2 DESTROY, annihilate, eliminate, end, eradicate, exterminate, remove, wipe out

extol verb PRAISE, acclaim, commend, eulogize, exalt, glorify, sing the praises of

extort verb FORCE, blackmail, bully, coerce, extract, squeeze

extortionate adjective EXORBITANT, excessive, extravagant, inflated, outrageous, preposterous, sky-high, unreasonable

extra adjective 1 ADDITIONAL, added, ancillary, auxiliary, further, more, supplementary
2 SURPLUS, excess, leftover, redundant, spare, superfluous, unused
▶ noun 3 ADDITION, accessory, attachment, bonus, extension, supplement
▶ adverb 4 EXCEPTIONALLY, especially, extraordinarily, extremely, particularly, remarkably, uncommonly, unusually

extract verb 1 PULL OUT, draw, pluck out, pull, remove, take out, uproot, withdraw
2 DERIVE, draw, elicit, glean, obtain
▶ noun 3 PASSAGE, citation, clipping, cutting, excerpt, quotation, selection
4 ESSENCE, concentrate, distillation, juice

extraneous adjective IRRELEVANT, beside the point, immaterial, inappropriate, off the subject, unconnected, unrelated

extraordinary adjective UNUSUAL, amazing, exceptional, fantastic, outstanding, phenomenal, remarkable, strange, uncommon

extravagance noun 1 WASTE, lavishness, overspending, prodigality, profligacy, squandering, wastefulness
2 EXCESS, exaggeration, outrageousness, preposterousness, wildness

extravagant adjective 1 WASTEFUL, lavish, prodigal, profligate, spendthrift
2 EXCESSIVE, outrageous, over the top (slang), preposterous, reckless, unreasonable

extreme adjective 1 MAXIMUM, acute, great, highest, intense, severe, supreme, ultimate, utmost
2 SEVERE, drastic, harsh, radical, rigid, strict, uncompromising
3 EXCESSIVE, fanatical, immoderate, radical
4 FARTHEST, far-off, most distant, outermost, remotest
▸ noun 5 LIMIT, boundary, edge, end, extremity, pole

extremely adverb VERY, awfully (informal), exceedingly, exceptionally, extraordinarily, severely, terribly, uncommonly, unusually

extremist noun FANATIC, die-hard, radical, zealot

extremity noun 1 LIMIT, border, boundary, edge, extreme, frontier, pinnacle, tip

2 CRISIS, adversity, dire straits, disaster, emergency, exigency, trouble
3 ▷▷ **extremities** HANDS AND FEET, fingers and toes, limbs

extricate verb FREE, disengage, disentangle, get out, release, remove, rescue, wriggle out of

extrovert adjective OUTGOING, exuberant, gregarious, sociable

exuberance noun 1 HIGH SPIRITS, cheerfulness, ebullience, enthusiasm, liveliness, spirit, vitality, vivacity, zest
2 LUXURIANCE, abundance, copiousness, lavishness, profusion

exuberant adjective 1 HIGH-SPIRITED, animated, cheerful, ebullient, energetic, enthusiastic, lively, spirited, vivacious
2 LUXURIANT, abundant, copious, lavish, plentiful, profuse

exult verb BE JOYFUL, be overjoyed, celebrate, jump for joy, rejoice

eye noun 1 EYEBALL, optic (informal)
2 APPRECIATION, discernment, discrimination, judgment, perception, recognition, taste
▸ verb 3 LOOK AT, check out (informal), contemplate, inspect, study, survey, view, watch

eyesight noun VISION, perception, sight

eyesore noun MESS, blemish, blot, disfigurement, horror, monstrosity, sight (informal)

eyewitness noun OBSERVER, bystander, onlooker, passer-by, spectator, viewer, witness

fable *noun* 1 STORY, allegory, legend, myth, parable, tale
2 FICTION, fabrication, fantasy, fish story (*informal*), invention, tall tale (*informal*), urban legend, yarn (*informal*)

fabric *noun* 1 CLOTH, material, stuff, textile, web
2 FRAMEWORK, constitution, construction, foundations, make-up, organization, structure

fabricate *verb* 1 MAKE UP, concoct, devise, fake, falsify, feign, forge, invent, trump up
2 BUILD, assemble, construct, erect, form, make, manufacture, shape

fabrication *noun* 1 FORGERY, concoction, fake, falsehood, fiction, invention, lie, myth
2 CONSTRUCTION, assembly, building, erection, manufacture, production

fabulous *adjective* 1 (*informal*) WONDERFUL, brilliant, fantastic (*informal*), marvelous, out-of-this-world (*informal*), sensational (*informal*), spectacular, superb
2 ASTOUNDING, amazing, breathtaking, inconceivable, incredible, phenomenal, unbelievable
3 LEGENDARY, apocryphal, fantastic, fictitious, imaginary, invented, made-up, mythical, unreal

façade *noun* APPEARANCE, exterior, face, front, guise, mask, pretense, semblance, show

face *noun* 1 COUNTENANCE, features, mug (*slang*), visage
2 EXPRESSION, appearance, aspect, look
3 SCOWL, frown, grimace, pout, smirk
4 FAÇADE, appearance, display, exterior, front, mask, show
5 SIDE, exterior, front, outside, surface
6 SELF-RESPECT, authority, dignity, honor, image, prestige, reputation, standing, status
▶ *verb* 7 MEET, brave, come up against, confront, deal with, encounter, experience, oppose, tackle
8 LOOK ONTO, be opposite, front onto, overlook
9 COAT, clad, cover, dress, finish

faceless *adjective* IMPERSONAL, anonymous, remote

facet *noun* ASPECT, angle, face, part, phase, plane, side, slant, surface

facetious *adjective* FUNNY, amusing, comical, droll, flippant, frivolous, humorous, jocular, playful, tongue in cheek

face up to *verb* ACCEPT, acknowledge, come to terms with, confront, cope with, deal with, meet head-on, tackle

facile *adjective* SUPERFICIAL, cursory, glib, hasty, shallow, slick

facilitate *verb* PROMOTE, expedite, forward, further, help, make easy, pave the way for, speed up

facility noun 1 SKILL, ability, adroitness, dexterity, ease, efficiency, effortlessness, fluency, proficiency
2 (often plural) EQUIPMENT, advantage, aid, amenity, appliance, convenience, means, opportunity, resource

facsimile noun COPY, carbon copy, duplicate, fax, photocopy, print, replica, reproduction, transcript

fact noun 1 EVENT, act, deed, *fait accompli*, happening, incident, occurrence, performance
2 TRUTH, certainty, reality

faction noun 1 GROUP, bloc, cabal, clique, contingent, coterie, gang, party, set, splinter group
2 DISSENSION, conflict, disagreement, discord, disunity, division, infighting, rebellion

factor noun ELEMENT, aspect, cause, component, consideration, influence, item, part

factory noun WORKS, mill, plant

factual adjective TRUE, authentic, correct, exact, genuine, precise, real, true-to-life

faculties plural noun POWERS, capabilities, intelligence, reason, senses, wits

faculty noun 1 ABILITY, aptitude, capacity, facility, power, propensity, skill
2 DEPARTMENT, school

fad noun CRAZE, fashion, mania, rage, trend, vogue, whim

fade verb 1 PALE, bleach, discolor, lose color, wash out
2 DWINDLE, decline, die away, disappear, dissolve, melt away, vanish, wane

faded adjective DISCOLORED, bleached, dull, indistinct, pale, washed out

fading adjective DECLINING, decreasing, disappearing, dying, on the decline, vanishing

fail verb 1 BE UNSUCCESSFUL, bite the dust, break down, come to grief, come unstuck, fall, fizzle out (*informal*), flop (*informal*), founder, miscarry, misfire
2 DISAPPOINT, abandon, desert, forget, forsake, let down, neglect, omit
3 GIVE OUT, conk out (*informal*), cut out, die, peter out, stop working
4 GO BANKRUPT, become insolvent, close down, fold (*informal*), go broke (*informal*), go bust (*informal*), go into receivership, go out of business, go to the wall, go under
▶ noun 5 ▷▷ **without fail** REGULARLY, conscientiously, constantly, dependably, like clockwork, punctually, religiously, twenty-four-seven (*slang*), without exception

failing noun 1 WEAKNESS, blemish, defect, deficiency, drawback, fault, flaw, imperfection, shortcoming
▶ preposition 2 IN THE ABSENCE OF, in default of, lacking

failure noun 1 DEFEAT, breakdown, collapse, downfall, fiasco, lack of success, miscarriage, overthrow
2 LOSER, black sheep, dead duck (*slang*), disappointment, dud (*informal*), flop (*informal*), nonstarter, washout (*informal*)
3 BANKRUPTCY, crash, downfall, insolvency, liquidation, ruin

faint adjective 1 DIM, distant, faded, indistinct, low, muted, soft, subdued, vague
2 SLIGHT, feeble, remote, unenthusiastic, weak
3 DIZZY, exhausted, giddy, light-headed, muzzy, weak, woozy

(informal)

▶ verb 4 PASS OUT, black out, collapse, flake out (informal), keel over (informal), lose consciousness, swoon (literary)

▶ noun 5 BLACKOUT, collapse, swoon (literary), unconsciousness

faintly adverb 1 SOFTLY, feebly, in a whisper, indistinctly, weakly
2 SLIGHTLY, a little, dimly, somewhat

fair¹ adjective 1 UNBIASED, above board, equitable, even-handed, honest, impartial, just, lawful, legitimate, proper, unprejudiced
2 LIGHT, blond, blonde, fair-haired, flaxen-haired, towheaded
3 RESPECTABLE, adequate, average, decent, moderate, O.K. or okay (informal), passable, reasonable, satisfactory, tolerable
4 BEAUTIFUL, bonny, comely, handsome, lovely, pretty
5 FINE, bright, clear, cloudless, dry, sunny, unclouded

fair² noun CARNIVAL, bazaar, festival, fête, gala, show

fairly adverb 1 MODERATELY, adequately, pretty well, quite, rather, reasonably, somewhat, tolerably
2 DESERVEDLY, equitably, honestly, impartially, justly, objectively, properly, without fear or favor
3 POSITIVELY, absolutely, really

fairness noun IMPARTIALITY, decency, disinterestedness, equitableness, equity, justice, legitimacy, rightfulness

fairy noun SPRITE, brownie, elf, imp, leprechaun, peri, pixie, Robin Goodfellow

fairy tale or **fairy story** noun
1 FOLK TALE, romance
2 LIE, cock-and-bull story (informal), fabrication, fiction,

invention, tall tale (informal), untruth

faith noun 1 CONFIDENCE, assurance, conviction, credence, credit, dependence, reliance, trust
2 RELIGION, belief, church, communion, creed, denomination, dogma, persuasion
3 ALLEGIANCE, constancy, faithfulness, fidelity, loyalty

faithful adjective 1 LOYAL, constant, dependable, devoted, reliable, staunch, steadfast, true, trusty
2 ACCURATE, close, exact, precise, strict, true

faithless adjective DISLOYAL, false, fickle, inconstant, traitorous, treacherous, unfaithful, unreliable

fake verb 1 FORGE, copy, counterfeit, fabricate, feign, pretend, put on, sham, simulate
▶ noun 2 IMPOSTOR, charlatan, copy, forgery, fraud, hoax, imitation, reproduction, sham
▶ adjective 3 ARTIFICIAL, counterfeit, false, forged, imitation, mock, phoney or phony (informal), sham

fall verb 1 DESCEND, cascade, collapse, dive, drop, plummet, plunge, sink, subside, tumble
2 DECREASE, decline, diminish, drop, dwindle, go down, lessen, slump, subside
3 BE OVERTHROWN, capitulate, pass into enemy hands, succumb, surrender
4 DIE, be killed, meet one's end, perish
5 OCCUR, befall, chance, come about, come to pass, happen, take place
6 SLOPE, fall away, incline
7 LAPSE, err, go astray, offend, sin,

transgress, trespass
▶ *noun* 8 DESCENT, dive, drop, nose dive, plummet, plunge, slip, tumble
9 DECREASE, cut, decline, dip, drop, lessening, lowering, reduction, slump
10 COLLAPSE, capitulation, defeat, destruction, downfall, overthrow, ruin
11 LAPSE, sin, transgression

fallacy *noun* ERROR, delusion, falsehood, flaw, misapprehension, misconception, mistake, untruth

fallible *adjective* IMPERFECT, erring, frail, ignorant, uncertain, weak

fall out *verb* ARGUE, clash, come to blows, differ, disagree, fight, quarrel, squabble

fallow *adjective* UNCULTIVATED, dormant, idle, inactive, resting, unplanted, unused

false *adjective* 1 INCORRECT, erroneous, faulty, inaccurate, inexact, invalid, mistaken, wrong
2 UNTRUE, lying, unreliable, unsound, untruthful
3 ARTIFICIAL, bogus, counterfeit, fake, forged, imitation, sham, simulated
4 DECEPTIVE, deceitful, fallacious, fraudulent, hypocritical, misleading, trumped up

falsehood *noun*
1 UNTRUTHFULNESS, deceit, deception, dishonesty, dissimulation, mendacity
2 LIE, fabrication, fib, fiction, story, untruth

falsify *verb* FORGE, alter, counterfeit, distort, doctor, fake, misrepresent, tamper with

falter *verb* HESITATE, stammer, stumble, stutter, totter, vacillate, waver

faltering *adjective* HESITANT, broken, irresolute, stammering, tentative, timid, uncertain, weak

fame *noun* PROMINENCE, celebrity, glory, honor, kudos, renown, reputation, repute, stardom

familiar *adjective* 1 WELL-KNOWN, accustomed, common, customary, frequent, ordinary, recognizable, routine
2 FRIENDLY, amicable, close, easy, intimate, relaxed
3 DISRESPECTFUL, bold, forward, impudent, intrusive, presumptuous

familiarity *noun* 1 ACQUAINTANCE, awareness, experience, grasp, understanding
2 FRIENDLINESS, ease, informality, intimacy, openness, sociability
3 DISRESPECT, boldness, forwardness, presumption

familiarize *verb* ACCUSTOM, habituate, instruct, inure, school, season, train

family *noun* 1 RELATIONS, folk (*informal*), household, kin, kith and kin, one's nearest and dearest, one's own flesh and blood, relatives
2 CLAN, dynasty, house, race, tribe
3 GROUP, class, genre, network, subdivision, system

famine *noun* HUNGER, dearth, scarcity, starvation

famished *adjective* STARVING, ravenous, voracious

famous *adjective* WELL-KNOWN, acclaimed, celebrated, distinguished, eminent, illustrious, legendary, noted, prominent, renowned

fan¹ *noun* 1 BLOWER, air conditioner, ventilator
▶ *verb* 2 BLOW, air-condition, cool, refresh, ventilate

fan² noun SUPPORTER, admirer, aficionado, buff (informal), devotee, enthusiast, follower, lover

fanatic noun EXTREMIST, activist, bigot, militant, zealot

fanatical adjective PASSIONATE, bigoted, extreme, fervent, frenzied, immoderate, obsessive, overenthusiastic, wild, zealous

fanciful adjective UNREAL, imaginary, mythical, romantic, visionary, whimsical, wild

fancy adjective 1 ELABORATE, baroque, decorative, embellished, extravagant, intricate, ornamental, ornate
▶ noun 2 WHIM, caprice, desire, humor, idea, impulse, inclination, notion, thought, urge
3 DELUSION, chimera, daydream, dream, fantasy, vision
▶ verb 4 SUPPOSE, believe, conjecture, imagine, reckon, think, think likely
5 WISH FOR, crave, desire, hanker after, hope for, long for, thirst for, yearn for
6 (informal) BE ATTRACTED TO, be captivated by, like, lust after, take a liking to, take to

fantasize verb DAYDREAM, dream, envision, imagine

fantastic adjective 1 (informal) EXCELLENT, awesome (slang), first-rate, marvelous, sensational (informal), superb, wonderful
2 STRANGE, fanciful, grotesque, outlandish
3 UNREALISTIC, extravagant, far-fetched, ludicrous, ridiculous, wild
4 IMPLAUSIBLE, absurd, cock-and-bull (informal), incredible, preposterous, unlikely

fantasy noun 1 IMAGINATION, creativity, fancy, invention, originality
2 DAYDREAM, dream, flight of fancy, illusion, mirage, pipe dream, reverie, vision

far adverb 1 A LONG WAY, afar, a good way, a great distance, deep, miles
2 MUCH, considerably, decidedly, extremely, greatly, incomparably, very much
▶ adjective 3 REMOTE, distant, faraway, far-flung, far-off, outlying, out-of-the-way

farce noun 1 COMEDY, buffoonery, burlesque, satire, slapstick
2 MOCKERY, joke, nonsense, parody, sham, travesty

farcical adjective LUDICROUS, absurd, comic, derisory, laughable, nonsensical, preposterous, ridiculous, risible

fare noun 1 CHARGE, price, ticket money
2 FOOD, provisions, rations, sustenance, victuals
▶ verb 3 GET ON, do, get along, make out, manage, prosper

farewell noun GOOD-BYE, adieu, departure, leave-taking, parting, sendoff (informal), valediction

far-fetched adjective UNCONVINCING, cock-and-bull (informal), fantastic, implausible, incredible, preposterous, unbelievable, unlikely, unrealistic

farm noun 1 SMALLHOLDING, croft (Scot.), farmstead, grange, homestead, plantation, ranch (chiefly North American)
▶ verb 2 CULTIVATE, plant, work

fascinate verb INTRIGUE, absorb, beguile, captivate, engross, enthrall, entrance, hold spellbound, rivet, transfix

fascinating adjective GRIPPING, alluring, captivating, compelling, engaging, engrossing, enticing, intriguing, irresistible, riveting

fascination noun ATTRACTION, allure, charm, enchantment, lure, magic, magnetism, pull

fashion noun 1 STYLE, craze, custom, fad, look, mode, rage, trend, vogue
2 METHOD, manner, mode, style, way
▶ verb 3 MAKE, construct, create, forge, form, manufacture, mold, shape

fashionable adjective POPULAR, à la mode, chic, cool (informal), in (informal), in vogue, modern, phat (slang), stylish, trendy (informal), up-to-date, with it (informal)

fast¹ adjective 1 QUICK, brisk, fleet, flying, hasty, nippy (Brit. informal), rapid, speedy, swift
2 FIXED, close, fastened, firm, immovable, secure, sound, steadfast, tight
3 DISSIPATED, dissolute, extravagant, loose, profligate, reckless, self-indulgent, wanton, wild
▶ adverb 4 QUICKLY, hastily, hurriedly, in haste, like lightning, rapidly, speedily, swiftly
5 SOUNDLY, deeply, firmly, fixedly, securely, tightly

fast² verb 1 GO HUNGRY, abstain, deny oneself, go without food
▶ noun 2 FASTING, abstinence

fasten verb FIX, affix, attach, bind, connect, join, link, secure, tie

fat adjective 1 OVERWEIGHT, corpulent, heavy, obese, plump, podgy, portly, rotund, stout, tubby
2 FATTY, adipose, greasy, oily, oleaginous
▶ noun 3 FATNESS, blubber, bulk, corpulence, flab, flesh, lard (slang), obesity, paunch, spare tire (informal)

fatal adjective 1 LETHAL, deadly, final, incurable, killing, malignant, mortal, terminal
2 RUINOUS, baleful, baneful, calamitous, catastrophic, disastrous

fatality noun DEATH, casualty, loss, mortality

fate noun 1 DESTINY, chance, divine will, fortune, kismet, nemesis, predestination, providence
2 FORTUNE, cup, horoscope, lot, portion, stars

fated adjective DESTINED, doomed, foreordained, inescapable, inevitable, predestined, preordained, sure, written

fateful adjective 1 CRUCIAL, critical, decisive, important, portentous, significant
2 DISASTROUS, deadly, destructive, fatal, lethal, ominous, ruinous

father noun 1 PARENT, dad (informal), daddy (informal), old man (informal), pa (informal), papa (old-fashioned informal), pater (old-fashioned informal, chiefly Brit.), pop (informal), sire
2 FOREFATHER, ancestor, forebear, predecessor, progenitor
3 FOUNDER, architect, author, creator, inventor, maker, originator, prime mover
4 PRIEST, padre (informal), pastor
▶ verb 5 SIRE, beget, get, procreate

fatherland noun HOMELAND, motherland, native land

fatherly adjective PATERNAL, affectionate, benevolent, benign, kindly, patriarchal, protective, supportive

fathom verb UNDERSTAND, comprehend, get to the bottom of, grasp, interpret

fatigue noun 1 TIREDNESS, heaviness, languor, lethargy,

listlessness

▶ *verb* 2 TIRE, drain, exhaust, knacker (*slang*), take it out of (*informal*), weaken, wear out, weary

fatten *verb* 1 GROW FAT, expand, gain weight, put on weight, spread, swell, thicken

2 (often with *up*) FEED UP, build up, feed, nourish, overfeed, stuff

fatty *adjective* GREASY, adipose, fat, oily, oleaginous, rich

fatuous *adjective* FOOLISH, brainless, idiotic, inane, ludicrous, mindless, moronic, silly, stupid, witless

fault *noun* 1 FLAW, blemish, defect, deficiency, failing, imperfection, shortcoming, weakness, weak point

2 MISTAKE, blunder, error, indiscretion, lapse, oversight, slip

3 RESPONSIBILITY, accountability, culpability, liability

4 ▷▷ **at fault** GUILTY, answerable, blamable, culpable, in the wrong, responsible, to blame; **find fault with** CRITICIZE, carp at, complain, pick holes in, pull to pieces, quibble, take to task; **to a fault** EXCESSIVELY, immoderately, in the extreme, overmuch, unduly

▶ *verb* 5 CRITICIZE, blame, censure, find fault with, hold (someone) responsible, impugn

faultless *adjective* FLAWLESS, correct, exemplary, foolproof, impeccable, model, perfect, unblemished

faulty *adjective* DEFECTIVE, broken, damaged, flawed, impaired, imperfect, incorrect, malfunctioning, out of order, unsound

favor *noun* 1 APPROVAL, approbation, backing, good opinion, goodwill, patronage, support

2 GOOD TURN, benefit, boon, courtesy, indulgence, kindness, service

▶ *verb* 3 SIDE WITH, indulge, reward, smile upon

4 ADVOCATE, approve, champion, commend, encourage, incline towards, prefer, support

favorable *adjective*

1 ADVANTAGEOUS, auspicious, beneficial, encouraging, helpful, opportune, promising, propitious, suitable, win-win (*informal*)

2 POSITIVE, affirmative, agreeable, approving, encouraging, enthusiastic, reassuring, sympathetic

favorably *adverb*

1 ADVANTAGEOUSLY, auspiciously, conveniently, fortunately, opportunely, profitably, to one's advantage, well

2 POSITIVELY, approvingly, enthusiastically, helpfully, with approval

favorite *adjective* 1 PREFERRED, best-loved, choice, dearest, esteemed, favored

▶ *noun* 2 DARLING, beloved, blue-eyed boy (*informal*), idol, pet, teacher's pet, the apple of one's eye

fawn¹ *verb* (often with *on* or *upon*) CURRY FAVOR, brown-nose (*slang*), crawl, creep, cringe, dance attendance, flatter, grovel, ingratiate oneself, kiss ass (*slang*), kowtow, pander to

fawn² *adjective* BEIGE, buff, grayish-brown, neutral

fawning *adjective* OBSEQUIOUS, crawling, cringing, deferential, flattering, grovelling, servile, sycophantic

fear *noun* 1 ALARM,

apprehensiveness, dread, fright, horror, panic, terror, trepidation
2 BUGBEAR, bête noire, bogey, horror, nightmare, specter
▶ *verb* 3 BE AFRAID, dread, shake in one's shoes, shudder at, take fright, tremble at
4 ▷▷ **fear for** WORRY ABOUT, be anxious about, feel concern for

fearful *adjective* 1 SCARED, afraid, alarmed, frightened, jumpy, nervous, timid, timorous, uneasy, wired (*slang*)
2 FRIGHTFUL, awful, dire, dreadful, gruesome, hair-raising, horrendous, horrific, terrible

fearfully *adverb* 1 NERVOUSLY, apprehensively, diffidently, timidly, timorously, uneasily
2 VERY, awfully, exceedingly, excessively, frightfully, terribly, tremendously

fearless *adjective* BRAVE, bold, courageous, dauntless, indomitable, intrepid, plucky, unafraid, undaunted, valiant

fearsome *adjective* TERRIFYING, awe-inspiring, daunting, formidable, frightening, horrifying, menacing, unnerving

feasible *adjective* POSSIBLE, achievable, attainable, likely, practicable, reasonable, viable, workable

feast *noun* 1 BANQUET, dinner, repast, spread (*informal*), treat
2 FESTIVAL, celebration, fête, holiday, holy day, red-letter day, saint's day
3 TREAT, delight, enjoyment, gratification, pleasure
▶ *verb* 4 EAT ONE'S FILL, gorge, gormandize, indulge, overindulge, pig out (*slang*), wine and dine

feat *noun* ACCOMPLISHMENT, achievement, act, attainment, deed, exploit, performance

feathers *plural noun* PLUMAGE, down, plumes

feature *noun* 1 ASPECT, characteristic, facet, factor, hallmark, peculiarity, property, quality, trait
2 HIGHLIGHT, attraction, main item, speciality
3 ARTICLE, column, item, piece, report, story
▶ *verb* 4 SPOTLIGHT, emphasize, foreground, give prominence to, play up, present, star

features *plural noun* FACE, countenance, lineaments, physiognomy

feckless *adjective* IRRESPONSIBLE, good-for-nothing, hopeless, incompetent, ineffectual, shiftless, worthless

federation *noun* UNION, alliance, amalgamation, association, coalition, combination, league, syndicate

fed up *adjective* DISSATISFIED, bored, brassed off (*Brit. slang*), depressed, discontented, down in the mouth, glum, sick and tired (*informal*), tired

fee *noun* CHARGE, bill, payment, remuneration, toll

feeble *adjective* 1 WEAK, debilitated, doddering, effete, frail, infirm, puny, sickly, weedy (*informal*)
2 UNCONVINCING, flimsy, inadequate, insufficient, lame, lousy (*slang*), paltry, pathetic, poor, tame, thin

feebleness *noun* WEAKNESS, effeteness, frailty, infirmity, languor, lassitude, sickliness

feed *verb* 1 CATER FOR, nourish, provide for, provision, supply, sustain, victual, wine and dine

2 (*sometimes with on*) EAT, chow down (*slang*), devour, exist on, live on, partake of
▶ *noun* 3 FOOD, fodder, pasturage, provender
4 (*informal*) MEAL, feast, nosh (*slang*), repast, spread (*informal*)

feel *verb* 1 TOUCH, caress, finger, fondle, handle, manipulate, paw, stroke
2 EXPERIENCE, be aware of, notice, observe, perceive
3 SENSE, be convinced, intuit
4 BELIEVE, consider, deem, hold, judge, think
▶ *noun* 5 TEXTURE, finish, surface, touch
6 IMPRESSION, air, ambience, atmosphere, feeling, quality, sense

feeler *noun* 1 ANTENNA, tentacle, whisker
2 APPROACH, advance, probe

feeling *noun* 1 EMOTION, ardor, fervor, intensity, passion, sentiment, warmth
2 IMPRESSION, hunch, idea, inkling, notion, presentiment, sense, suspicion
3 OPINION, inclination, instinct, point of view, view
4 SYMPATHY, compassion, concern, empathy, pity, sensibility, sensitivity, understanding
5 SENSE OF TOUCH, perception, sensation
6 ATMOSPHERE, air, ambience, aura, feel, mood, quality

fell *verb* CUT DOWN, cut, demolish, hew, knock down, level

fellow *noun* 1 MAN, bloke (*Brit. informal*), chap (*informal*), character, guy (*informal*), individual, person
2 ASSOCIATE, colleague, companion, comrade, partner, peer

fellowship *noun* 1 CAMARADERIE, brotherhood, companionship, sociability
2 SOCIETY, association, brotherhood, club, fraternity, guild, league, order

feminine *adjective* WOMANLY, delicate, gentle, ladylike, soft, tender

femme fatale *noun* SEDUCTRESS, enchantress, siren, succubus, vamp (*informal*)

fen *noun* MARSH, bog, morass, quagmire, slough, swamp

fence *noun* 1 BARRIER, barricade, defense, hedge, palisade, railings, rampart, wall
▶ *verb* 2 (*often with in or off*) ENCLOSE, bound, confine, encircle, pen, protect, surround
3 EVADE, dodge, equivocate, flannel (*Brit. informal*), parry

ferment *noun* COMMOTION, disruption, excitement, frenzy, furor, stir, tumult, turmoil, unrest, uproar

ferocious *adjective* 1 FIERCE, predatory, rapacious, ravening, savage, violent, wild
2 CRUEL, barbaric, bloodthirsty, brutal, ruthless, vicious

ferocity *noun* SAVAGERY, bloodthirstiness, brutality, cruelty, fierceness, viciousness, wildness

ferret out *verb* TRACK DOWN, dig up, discover, elicit, root out, search out, trace, unearth

ferry *noun* 1 FERRY BOAT, packet, packet boat
▶ *verb* 2 CARRY, chauffeur, convey, run, ship, shuttle, transport

fertile *adjective* RICH, abundant, fecund, fruitful, luxuriant, plentiful, productive, prolific, teeming

fertility noun FRUITFULNESS, abundance, fecundity, luxuriance, productiveness, richness

fertilizer noun COMPOST, dressing, dung, manure

fervent, fervid adjective ARDENT, devout, earnest, enthusiastic, heartfelt, impassioned, intense, vehement

fervor noun INTENSITY, ardor, enthusiasm, excitement, passion, vehemence, warmth, zeal

fester verb 1 DECAY, putrefy, suppurate, ulcerate
2 INTENSIFY, aggravate, smolder

festival noun 1 CELEBRATION, carnival, entertainment, fête, gala, jubilee
2 HOLY DAY, anniversary, commemoration, feast, fête, fiesta, holiday, red-letter day, saint's day

festive adjective CELEBRATORY, cheery, convivial, happy, jovial, joyful, joyous, jubilant, merry

festivity noun (often plural) CELEBRATION, entertainment, festival, party

festoon verb DECORATE, array, deck, drape, garland, hang, swathe, wreathe

fetch verb 1 BRING, carry, convey, deliver, get, go for, obtain, retrieve, transport
2 SELL FOR, bring in, earn, go for, make, realize, yield

fetching adjective ATTRACTIVE, alluring, captivating, charming, cute, enticing, winsome

fetish noun 1 FIXATION, mania, obsession, thing (informal)
2 TALISMAN, amulet

feud noun 1 HOSTILITY, argument, conflict, disagreement, enmity, quarrel, rivalry, row, vendetta
▶ verb 2 QUARREL, bicker, clash,

contend, dispute, fall out, row, squabble, war

fever noun EXCITEMENT, agitation, delirium, ferment, fervor, frenzy, restlessness

feverish adjective 1 HOT, febrile, fevered, flushed, inflamed, pyretic (Medical)
2 EXCITED, agitated, frantic, frenetic, frenzied, overwrought, restless, wired (slang)

few adjective NOT MANY, meager, negligible, rare, scanty, scarcely any, sparse, sporadic

fiasco noun DEBACLE, catastrophe, cock-up (Brit. slang), disaster, failure, mess, washout (informal)

fib noun LIE, fiction, story, untruth, white lie

fiber noun 1 THREAD, filament, pile, strand, texture, wisp
2 ESSENCE, nature, quality, spirit, substance
3 as in **moral fiber** RESOLUTION, stamina, strength, toughness

fickle adjective CHANGEABLE, capricious, faithless, inconstant, irresolute, temperamental, unfaithful, variable, volatile

fiction noun 1 TALE, fantasy, legend, myth, novel, romance, story, yarn (informal)
2 LIE, cock and bull story (informal), fabrication, falsehood, invention, tall tale (informal), untruth, urban legend

fictional adjective IMAGINARY, invented, legendary, made-up, nonexistent, unreal

fictitious adjective FALSE, bogus, fabricated, imaginary, invented, made-up, make-believe, mythical, untrue

fiddle verb 1 FIDGET, finger, interfere with, mess about or around, play, tamper with, tinker

2 (*informal*) CHEAT, cook the books (*informal*), diddle (*informal*), fix, swindle, wangle (*informal*)
▶ *noun* **3** VIOLIN
4 (*informal*) FRAUD, fix, racket, scam (*slang*), swindle
5 ▷▷ **fit as a fiddle** HEALTHY, blooming, hale and hearty, in fine fettle, in good form, in good shape, in rude health, in the pink, sound, strong

fiddling *adjective* TRIVIAL, futile, insignificant, pettifogging, petty, trifling

fidelity *noun* **1** LOYALTY, allegiance, constancy, dependability, devotion, faithfulness, staunchness, trustworthiness
2 ACCURACY, closeness, correspondence, exactness, faithfulness, precision, scrupulousness

fidget *verb* **1** MOVE RESTLESSLY, fiddle (*informal*), fret, squirm, twitch
▶ *noun* **2** ▷▷ **the fidgets** RESTLESSNESS, fidgetiness, jitters (*informal*), nervousness, unease, uneasiness

fidgety *adjective* RESTLESS, antsy (*slang*), impatient, jittery (*informal*), jumpy, nervous, on edge, restive, twitchy (*informal*), uneasy, wired (*slang*)

field *noun* **1** MEADOW, grassland, green, lea (*poetic*), pasture
2 COMPETITORS, applicants, candidates, competition, contestants, entrants, possibilities, runners
3 SPECIALITY, area, department, discipline, domain, line, province, territory
▶ *verb* **4** RETRIEVE, catch, pick up, return, stop
5 DEAL WITH, deflect, handle,

turn aside

fiend *noun* **1** DEMON, devil, evil spirit
2 BRUTE, barbarian, beast, ghoul, monster, ogre, savage
3 (*informal*) ENTHUSIAST, addict, fanatic, freak (*informal*), maniac

fiendish *adjective* WICKED, cruel, devilish, diabolical, hellish, infernal, malignant, monstrous, satanic, unspeakable

fierce *adjective* **1** WILD, brutal, cruel, dangerous, ferocious, fiery, menacing, savage, vicious
2 STRONG, furious, howling, inclement, powerful, raging, stormy, tempestuous, violent
3 INTENSE, cut-throat, keen, relentless, strong

fiercely *adverb* FEROCIOUSLY, furiously, passionately, savagely, tempestuously, tigerishly, tooth and nail, viciously, with no holds barred

fiery *adjective* **1** BURNING, ablaze, afire, aflame, blazing, flaming, on fire
2 EXCITABLE, fierce, hot-headed, impetuous, irascible, irritable, passionate

fight *verb* **1** BATTLE, box, clash, combat, do battle, grapple, spar, struggle, tussle, wrestle
2 OPPOSE, contest, defy, dispute, make a stand against, resist, stand up to, withstand
3 ENGAGE IN, carry on, conduct, prosecute, wage
▶ *noun* **4** CONFLICT, battle, clash, contest, dispute, duel, encounter, struggle, tussle
5 RESISTANCE, belligerence, militancy, pluck, spirit

fighter *noun* **1** SOLDIER, fighting man, man-at-arms, warrior
2 BOXER, prize fighter, pugilist

fight off verb REPEL, beat off, keep or hold at bay, repress, repulse, resist, stave off, ward off

figure noun 1 NUMBER, character, digit, numeral, symbol
2 AMOUNT, cost, price, sum, total, value
3 SHAPE, body, build, frame, physique, proportions
4 DIAGRAM, design, drawing, illustration, pattern, representation, sketch
5 CHARACTER, big name, celebrity, dignitary, personality
▶ verb 6 CALCULATE, compute, count, reckon, tally, tot up, work out
7 (usually with *in*) FEATURE, act, appear, be featured, contribute to, play a part

figurehead noun FRONT MAN, mouthpiece, puppet, titular or nominal head

figure out verb 1 CALCULATE, compute, reckon, work out
2 UNDERSTAND, comprehend, decipher, fathom, make out, see

filch verb STEAL, embezzle, misappropriate, pilfer, pinch (*informal*), take, thieve, walk off with

file¹ noun 1 FOLDER, case, data, documents, dossier, information, portfolio
2 LINE, column, queue, row
▶ verb 3 REGISTER, document, enter, pigeonhole, put in place, record
4 MARCH, parade, troop

file² verb SMOOTH, abrade, polish, rasp, rub, scrape, shape

fill verb 1 STUFF, cram, crowd, glut, pack, stock, supply, swell
2 SATURATE, charge, imbue, impregnate, pervade, suffuse
3 PLUG, block, bung, close, cork,

seal, stop
4 PERFORM, carry out, discharge, execute, fulfill, hold, occupy
▶ noun 5 ▷▷ **one's fill** SUFFICIENT, all one wants, ample, enough, plenty

filler noun PADDING, makeweight, stopgap

fill in verb 1 COMPLETE, answer, fill out (*U.S.*), fill up
2 (*informal*) INFORM, acquaint, apprise, bring up to date, give the facts or background
3 REPLACE, deputize, represent, stand in, sub, substitute, take the place of

filling noun 1 STUFFING, contents, filler, inside, insides, padding, wadding
▶ adjective 2 SATISFYING, ample, heavy, square, substantial

fill out verb COMPLETE, answer, fill in, fill up

film noun 1 MOVIE, flick (*slang*), motion picture
2 LAYER, coating, covering, dusting, membrane, skin, tissue
▶ verb 3 PHOTOGRAPH, shoot, take, video, videotape

filter noun 1 SIEVE, gauze, membrane, mesh, riddle, strainer
▶ verb 2 PURIFY, clarify, filtrate, refine, screen, sieve, sift, strain, winnow
3 TRICKLE, dribble, escape, exude, leak, ooze, penetrate, percolate, seep

filth noun 1 DIRT, excrement, grime, muck, refuse, sewage, slime, sludge, squalor
2 OBSCENITY, impurity, indecency, pornography, smut, vulgarity

filthy adjective 1 DIRTY, foul, polluted, putrid, slimy, squalid, unclean
2 MUDDY, begrimed, blackened,

grimy, grubby, scuzzy (*slang*)
3 OBSCENE, corrupt, depraved, impure, indecent, lewd, licentious, pornographic, smutty, X-rated

final *adjective* 1 LAST, closing, concluding, latest, terminal, ultimate
2 DEFINITIVE, absolute, conclusive, decided, definite, incontrovertible, irrevocable, settled

finale *noun* ENDING, climax, close, conclusion, culmination, denouement, epilogue

finalize *verb* COMPLETE, clinch, conclude, decide, settle, tie up, wind up, work out, wrap up (*informal*)

finally *adverb* 1 EVENTUALLY, at last, at length, at long last, in the end, lastly, ultimately
2 IN CONCLUSION, in summary, to conclude

finance *noun* 1 ECONOMICS, accounts, banking, business, commerce, investment, money
▶ *verb* 2 FUND, back, bankroll (*U.S.*), guarantee, pay for, subsidize, support, underwrite

finances *plural noun* RESOURCES, affairs, assets, capital, cash, funds, money, wherewithal

financial *adjective* ECONOMIC, fiscal, monetary, pecuniary

find *verb* 1 DISCOVER, come across, encounter, hit upon, locate, meet, recognize, spot, uncover
2 PERCEIVE, detect, discover, learn, note, notice, observe, realize
▶ *noun* 3 DISCOVERY, acquisition, asset, bargain, catch, good buy

find out *verb* 1 LEARN, detect, discover, note, observe, perceive, realize
2 DETECT, catch, disclose, expose,

reveal, uncover, unmask

fine¹ *adjective* 1 EXCELLENT, accomplished, exceptional, exquisite, first-rate, magnificent, masterly, outstanding, splendid, superior
2 SUNNY, balmy, bright, clear, clement, cloudless, dry, fair, pleasant
3 SATISFACTORY, acceptable, all right, convenient, good, O.K. *or* okay (*informal*), suitable
4 DELICATE, dainty, elegant, expensive, exquisite, fragile, quality
5 SUBTLE, abstruse, acute, hairsplitting, minute, nice, precise, sharp
6 SLENDER, diaphanous, flimsy, gauzy, gossamer, light, sheer, thin

fine² *noun* 1 PENALTY, damages, forfeit, punishment
▶ *verb* 2 PENALIZE, mulct, punish

finery *noun* SPLENDOR, frippery, gear (*informal*), glad rags (*informal*), ornaments, showiness, Sunday best, trappings, trinkets

finesse *noun* SKILL, adeptness, adroitness, craft, delicacy, diplomacy, discretion, savoir-faire, sophistication, subtlety, tact

finger *verb* TOUCH, feel, fiddle with (*informal*), handle, manipulate, maul, paw (*informal*), toy with

finish *verb* 1 STOP, cease, close, complete, conclude, end, round off, terminate, wind up, wrap up (*informal*)
2 CONSUME, devour, dispose of, eat, empty, exhaust, use up
3 DESTROY, bring down, defeat, dispose of, exterminate, overcome, put an end to, put paid to, rout, ruin
4 PERFECT, polish, refine
5 COAT, gild, lacquer, polish, stain,

texture, veneer, wax
▶ *noun* 6 END, cessation, close, completion, conclusion, culmination, denouement, finale, run-in
7 DEFEAT, annihilation, curtains (*informal*), death, end, end of the road, ruin
8 SURFACE, luster, patina, polish, shine, smoothness, texture

finished *adjective* 1 POLISHED, accomplished, perfected, professional, refined
2 OVER, closed, complete, done, ended, finalized, through
3 SPENT, done, drained, empty, exhausted, used up
4 RUINED, defeated, done for (*informal*), doomed, lost, through, undone, wiped out

finite *adjective* LIMITED, bounded, circumscribed, delimited, demarcated, restricted

fire *noun* 1 FLAMES, blaze, combustion, conflagration, inferno
2 BOMBARDMENT, barrage, cannonade, flak, fusillade, hail, salvo, shelling, sniping, volley
3 PASSION, ardor, eagerness, enthusiasm, excitement, fervor, intensity, sparkle, spirit, verve, vigor
▶ *verb* 4 SHOOT, detonate, discharge, explode, let off, pull the trigger, set off, shell
5 INSPIRE, animate, enliven, excite, galvanize, impassion, inflame, rouse, stir
6 DISMISS, cashier, discharge, make redundant, sack (*informal*), show the door

firebrand *noun* RABBLE-ROUSER, agitator, demagogue, incendiary, instigator, tub-thumper

fireworks *plural noun*

1 PYROTECHNICS, illuminations
2 RAGE, hysterics, row, storm, trouble, uproar

firm¹ *adjective* 1 HARD, dense, inflexible, rigid, set, solid, solidified, stiff, unyielding
2 SECURE, embedded, fast, fixed, immovable, rooted, stable, steady, tight, unshakable
3 DEFINITE, adamant, inflexible, resolute, resolved, set on, unbending, unshakable, unyielding

firm² *noun* COMPANY, association, business, concern, conglomerate, corporation, enterprise, organization, partnership

firmly *adverb* 1 SECURELY, immovably, like a rock, steadily, tightly, unflinchingly, unshakably
2 RESOLUTELY, staunchly, steadfastly, unchangeably, unwaveringly

firmness *noun* 1 HARDNESS, inelasticity, inflexibility, resistance, rigidity, solidity, stiffness
2 RESOLVE, constancy, inflexibility, resolution, staunchness, steadfastness

first *adjective* 1 FOREMOST, alpha male, chief, cutting edge, head, highest, leading, pre-eminent, prime, principal, ruling
2 EARLIEST, initial, introductory, maiden, opening, original, premier, primordial
3 ELEMENTARY, basic, cardinal, fundamental, key, primary, rudimentary
▶ *noun* 4 *as in* **from the first** START, beginning, commencement, inception, introduction, outset, starting point
▶ *adverb* 5 BEFOREHAND, at the

beginning, at the outset, firstly, initially, in the first place, to begin with, to start with

first-rate *adjective* EXCELLENT, crack (*slang*), elite, exceptional, first class, outstanding, superb, superlative, top-notch (*informal*), world-class

fishy *adjective* 1 (*informal*) SUSPICIOUS, dodgy (*Brit., Austral., & N.Z. informal*), dubious, funny (*informal*), implausible, odd, questionable, suspect, unlikely
2 FISHLIKE, piscatorial, piscatory, piscine

fissure *noun* CRACK, breach, cleft, crevice, fault, fracture, opening, rift, rupture, split

fit¹ *verb* 1 MATCH, accord, belong, conform, correspond, meet, suit, tally
2 PREPARE, arm, equip, fit out, kit out, provide
3 ADAPT, adjust, alter, arrange, customize, modify, shape, tweak (*informal*)
▶ *adjective* 4 APPROPRIATE, apt, becoming, correct, fitting, proper, right, seemly, suitable
5 HEALTHY, able-bodied, hale, in good shape, robust, strapping, trim, well

fit² *noun* 1 SEIZURE, attack, bout, convulsion, paroxysm, spasm
2 OUTBREAK, bout, burst, outburst, spell

fitful *adjective* IRREGULAR, broken, desultory, disturbed, inconstant, intermittent, spasmodic, sporadic, uneven

fitness *noun* 1 APPROPRIATENESS, aptness, competence, eligibility, propriety, readiness, suitability
2 HEALTH, good condition, good health, robustness, strength, vigor

fitting *adjective* 1 APPROPRIATE, apposite, becoming, correct, decent, proper, right, seemly, suitable
▶ *noun* 2 ACCESSORY, attachment, component, part, piece, unit

fix *verb* 1 PLACE, embed, establish, implant, install, locate, plant, position, set
2 FASTEN, attach, bind, connect, link, secure, tie
3 DECIDE, agree on, arrange, arrive at, determine, establish, set, settle, specify
4 REPAIR, correct, mend, patch up, put to rights, see to
5 FOCUS, direct
6 (*informal*) MANIPULATE, fiddle (*informal*), influence, rig
▶ *noun* 7 (*informal*) PREDICAMENT, difficulty, dilemma, embarrassment, mess, pickle (*informal*), plight, quandary

fixation *noun* PREOCCUPATION, complex, hang-up (*informal*), idée fixe, infatuation, mania, obsession, thing (*informal*)

fixed *adjective* 1 PERMANENT, established, immovable, rigid, rooted, secure, set
2 INTENT, resolute, steady, unwavering
3 AGREED, arranged, decided, definite, established, planned, resolved, settled

fix up *verb* 1 ARRANGE, agree on, fix, organize, plan, settle, sort out
2 (*often with* with) PROVIDE, arrange for, bring about, lay on

fizz *verb* BUBBLE, effervesce, fizzle, froth, hiss, sparkle, sputter

fizzy *adjective* BUBBLY, bubbling, carbonated, effervescent, gassy, sparkling

flabbergasted *adjective* ASTONISHED, amazed, astounded, dumbfounded, lost for words, overwhelmed, speechless, staggered, stunned

flabby *adjective* LIMP, baggy, drooping, flaccid, floppy, loose, pendulous, sagging

flag¹ *noun* 1 BANNER, colors, ensign, pennant, pennon, standard, streamer
▶ *verb* 2 MARK, indicate, label, note 3 (*sometimes with* down) HAIL, signal, warn, wave

flag² *verb* WEAKEN, abate, droop, fade, languish, peter out, sag, wane, weary, wilt

flagging *adjective* FADING, declining, deteriorating, faltering, waning, weakening, wilting

flagrant *adjective* OUTRAGEOUS, barefaced, blatant, brazen, glaring, heinous, scandalous, shameless

flagstone *noun* PAVING STONE, block, flag, slab

flail *verb* THRASH, beat, thresh, windmill

flair *noun* 1 ABILITY, aptitude, faculty, feel, genius, gift, knack, mastery, talent
2 STYLE, chic, dash, discernment, elegance, panache, stylishness, taste

flake *noun* 1 WAFER, layer, peeling, scale, shaving, sliver
▶ *verb* 2 BLISTER, chip, peel (off)

flake out *verb* COLLAPSE, faint, keel over, pass out

flamboyant *adjective*
1 EXTRAVAGANT, dashing, elaborate, florid, ornate, ostentatious, showy, swashbuckling, theatrical
2 COLORFUL, brilliant, dazzling, glamorous, glitzy (*slang*)

flame *noun* 1 FIRE, blaze, brightness, light
2 (*informal*) SWEETHEART, beau, boyfriend, girlfriend, heart-throb (*Brit.*), lover
▶ *verb* 3 BURN, blaze, flare, flash, glare, glow, shine

flaming *adjective* BURNING, ablaze, blazing, fiery, glowing, raging, red-hot

flank *noun* 1 SIDE, hip, loin, thigh
2 WING, side

flap *verb* 1 FLUTTER, beat, flail, shake, thrash, vibrate, wag, wave
▶ *noun* 2 FLUTTER, beating, shaking, swinging, swish, waving
3 (*informal*) PANIC, agitation, commotion, fluster, state (*informal*), sweat (*informal*), tizzy (*informal*)

flare *verb* 1 BLAZE, burn up, flicker, glare
2 WIDEN, broaden, spread out
▶ *noun* 3 FLAME, blaze, burst, flash, flicker, glare

flare up *verb* LOSE ONE'S TEMPER, blow one's top (*informal*), boil over, explode, fly off the handle (*informal*), throw a tantrum

flash *noun* 1 BLAZE, burst, dazzle, flare, flicker, gleam, shimmer, spark, streak
2 MOMENT, instant, jiffy (*informal*), second, split second, trice, twinkling of an eye
▶ *adjective* 3 (*informal*) OSTENTATIOUS, tacky (*informal*), tasteless, vulgar
▶ *verb* 4 BLAZE, flare, flicker, glare, gleam, shimmer, sparkle, twinkle
5 SPEED, dart, dash, fly, race, shoot, streak, whistle, zoom
6 SHOW, display, exhibit, expose, flaunt, flourish

flashy *adjective* SHOWY, flamboyant, garish, gaudy, glitzy (*slang*), jazzy (*informal*),

ostentatious, snazzy (*informal*)
flat¹ *adjective* 1 EVEN, horizontal,
level, levelled, low, smooth
2 DULL, boring, dead, lackluster,
lifeless, monotonous, tedious,
tiresome, uninteresting
3 ABSOLUTE, categorical,
downright, explicit, out-and-out,
positive, unequivocal, unqualified
4 PUNCTURED, blown out, burst,
collapsed, deflated, empty
▶ *adverb* 5 COMPLETELY, absolutely,
categorically, exactly, point blank,
precisely, utterly
6 ▷▷ **flat out** AT FULL SPEED, all
out, at full tilt, for all one is worth,
hell for leather (*informal*)
flat² *noun* APARTMENT, rooms
flatly *adverb* ABSOLUTELY,
categorically, completely,
positively, unhesitatingly
flatness *noun* 1 EVENNESS,
smoothness, uniformity
2 DULLNESS, monotony, tedium
flatten *verb* LEVEL, compress, even
out, iron out, raze, smooth off,
squash, trample
flatter *verb* 1 PRAISE, brown-nose
(*slang*), butter up, compliment,
pander to, soft-soap (*informal*),
sweet-talk (*informal*), wheedle
2 SUIT, become, do something
for, enhance, set off, show to
advantage
flattering *adjective* 1 BECOMING,
effective, enhancing, kind,
well-chosen
2 INGRATIATING, adulatory,
complimentary, fawning,
fulsome, laudatory
flattery *noun* OBSEQUIOUSNESS,
adulation, blandishment,
fawning, servility, soft soap
(*informal*), sweet-talk (*informal*),
sycophancy
flaunt *verb* SHOW OFF, brandish,

display, exhibit, flash about,
flourish, parade, sport (*informal*)
flavor *noun* 1 TASTE, aroma,
flavoring, piquancy, relish, savor,
seasoning, smack, tang, zest
2 QUALITY, character, essence, feel,
feeling, style, tinge, tone
▶ *verb* 3 SEASON, ginger up, imbue,
infuse, leaven, spice
flaw *noun* WEAKNESS, blemish,
chink in one's armor, defect,
failing, fault, imperfection,
weak spot
flawed *adjective* DAMAGED,
blemished, defective, erroneous,
faulty, imperfect, unsound
flawless *adjective* PERFECT,
faultless, impeccable, spotless,
unblemished, unsullied
flee *verb* RUN AWAY, bolt, depart,
escape, fly, make one's getaway,
scarper (*Brit. slang*), take flight,
take off (*informal*), take to one's
heels, turn tail
fleet *noun* NAVY, armada, flotilla,
task force
fleeting *adjective* MOMENTARY,
brief, ephemeral, passing,
short-lived, temporary, transient,
transitory
flesh *noun* 1 MEAT, brawn, fat,
tissue, weight
2 HUMAN NATURE, carnality, flesh
and blood
3 ▷▷ **one's own flesh and blood**
FAMILY, blood, kin, kinsfolk, kith
and kin, relations, relatives
flexibility *noun* ADAPTABILITY,
adjustability, elasticity, give
(*informal*), pliability, pliancy,
resilience, springiness
flexible *adjective* 1 PLIABLE, elastic,
lithe, plastic, pliant, springy,
stretchy, supple
2 ADAPTABLE, adjustable,
discretionary, open, variable

flick verb 1 STRIKE, dab, flip, hit, tap, touch
2 ▷▷ **flick through** BROWSE, flip through, glance at, skim, skip, thumb

flicker verb 1 TWINKLE, flare, flash, glimmer, gutter, shimmer, sparkle
2 FLUTTER, quiver, vibrate, waver
▶ noun 3 GLIMMER, flare, flash, gleam, spark
4 TRACE, breath, glimmer, iota, spark

flight¹ noun 1 (of air travel) JOURNEY, trip, voyage
2 AVIATION, aeronautics, flying
3 FLOCK, cloud, formation, squadron, swarm, unit

flight² noun ESCAPE, departure, exit, exodus, fleeing, getaway, retreat, running away

flimsy adjective 1 FRAGILE, delicate, frail, insubstantial, makeshift, rickety, shaky
2 THIN, gauzy, gossamer, light, sheer, transparent
3 UNCONVINCING, feeble, implausible, inadequate, lousy (slang), pathetic, poor, unsatisfactory, weak

flinch verb RECOIL, cower, cringe, draw back, quail, shirk, shrink, shy away, wince

fling verb 1 THROW, cast, catapult, heave, hurl, propel, sling, toss
▶ noun 2 BINGE (informal), bash, good time, party, rave-up (Brit. slang), spree

flip verb or noun TOSS, flick, snap, spin, throw

flippancy noun FRIVOLITY, impertinence, irreverence, levity, pertness, sauciness

flippant adjective FRIVOLOUS, cheeky, disrespectful, glib, impertinent, irreverent, offhand, superficial

flirt verb 1 LEAD ON, chat up (informal), hit on (slang), make advances, make eyes at, make sheep's eyes at, philander
2 (usually with with) TOY WITH, consider, dabble in, entertain, expose oneself to, give a thought to, play with, trifle with
▶ noun 3 TEASE, coquette, heartbreaker, hussy, philanderer

flirtatious adjective TEASING, amorous, come-hither, coquettish, coy, enticing, flirty, provocative, sportive

float verb 1 BE BUOYANT, hang, hover
2 GLIDE, bob, drift, move gently, sail, slide, slip along
3 LAUNCH, get going, promote, set up

floating adjective 1 BUOYANT, afloat, buoyed up, sailing, swimming
2 FLUCTUATING, free, movable, unattached, variable, wandering

flock noun 1 HERD, colony, drove, flight, gaggle, skein
2 CROWD, collection, company, congregation, gathering, group, herd, host, mass
▶ verb 3 GATHER, collect, congregate, converge, crowd, herd, huddle, mass, throng

flog verb BEAT, flagellate, flay, lash, scourge, thrash, trounce, whack, whip

flood noun 1 DELUGE, downpour, inundation, overflow, spate, tide, torrent
2 ABUNDANCE, flow, glut, profusion, rush, stream, torrent
▶ verb 3 IMMERSE, drown, inundate, overflow, pour over, submerge, swamp
4 ENGULF, overwhelm, surge,

swarm, sweep
5 OVERSUPPLY, choke, fill, glut, saturate

floor noun 1 TIER, level, stage, story
▶ verb 2 KNOCK DOWN, deck (slang), prostrate
3 (informal) BEWILDER, baffle, confound, defeat, disconcert, dumbfound, perplex, puzzle, stump, throw (informal)

flop verb 1 FALL, collapse, dangle, droop, drop, sag, slump
2 (informal) FAIL, come unstuck, fall flat, fold (informal), founder, go belly-up (slang), misfire
▶ noun 3 (informal) FAILURE, debacle, disaster, fiasco, nonstarter, washout (informal)

floppy adjective DROOPY, baggy, flaccid, limp, loose, pendulous, sagging, soft

floral adjective FLOWERY, flower-patterned

florid adjective 1 FLUSHED, blowsy, high-colored, rubicund, ruddy
2 FLOWERY, baroque, flamboyant, fussy, high-flown, ornate, overelaborate

flotsam noun DEBRIS, detritus, jetsam, junk, odds and ends, wreckage

flounder verb FUMBLE, grope, struggle, stumble, thrash, toss

flourish verb 1 PROSPER, bloom, blossom, boom, flower, grow, increase, succeed, thrive
2 WAVE, brandish, display, flaunt, shake, wield
▶ noun 3 WAVE, display, fanfare, parade, show
4 ORNAMENTATION, curlicue, decoration, embellishment, plume, sweep

flourishing adjective SUCCESSFUL, blooming, going places, in the pink, luxuriant, prospering,
rampant, thriving

flout verb DEFY, laugh in the face of, mock, scoff at, scorn, sneer at, spurn

flow verb 1 RUN, circulate, course, move, roll
2 POUR, cascade, flood, gush, rush, stream, surge, sweep
3 RESULT, arise, emanate, emerge, issue, proceed, spring
▶ noun 4 TIDE, course, current, drift, flood, flux, outpouring, spate, stream

flower noun 1 BLOOM, blossom, efflorescence
2 ELITE, best, cream, crème de la crème, pick
▶ verb 3 BLOSSOM, bloom, flourish, mature, open, unfold

flowery adjective ORNATE, baroque, embellished, fancy, florid, high-flown

flowing adjective 1 STREAMING, falling, gushing, rolling, rushing, smooth, sweeping
2 FLUENT, continuous, easy, smooth, unbroken, uninterrupted

fluctuate verb CHANGE, alternate, oscillate, seesaw, shift, swing, vary, veer, waver

fluency noun EASE, articulateness, assurance, command, control, facility, glibness, readiness, slickness, smoothness

fluent adjective SMOOTH, articulate, easy, effortless, flowing, natural, voluble, well-versed

fluff noun 1 FUZZ, down, nap, pile
▶ verb 2 (informal) SPOIL, bungle, make a mess of, mess up (informal), muddle

fluffy adjective SOFT, downy, feathery, fleecy, fuzzy

fluid noun 1 LIQUID, liquor, solution
▶ adjective 2 LIQUID, flowing, liquefied, melted, molten, runny,

watery

fluke noun LUCKY BREAK, accident, chance, coincidence, quirk of fate, serendipity, stroke of luck

flurry noun 1 COMMOTION, ado, bustle, disturbance, excitement, flutter, fuss, stir
2 GUST, squall

flush¹ verb 1 BLUSH, color, glow, go red, redden
2 RINSE OUT, cleanse, flood, hose down, wash out
▸ noun 3 BLUSH, color, glow, redness, rosiness

flush² adjective 1 LEVEL, even, flat, square, true
2 (informal) WEALTHY, in the money (informal), moneyed, rich, well-heeled (informal), well-off

flushed adjective BLUSHING, crimson, embarrassed, glowing, hot, red, rosy, ruddy

fluster verb 1 UPSET, agitate, bother, confuse, disturb, perturb, rattle (informal), ruffle, unnerve
▸ noun 2 TURMOIL, disturbance, dither, flap (informal), flurry, flutter, furor, state (informal)

flutter verb 1 BEAT, flap, palpitate, quiver, ripple, tremble, vibrate, waver
▸ noun 2 VIBRATION, palpitation, quiver, shiver, shudder, tremble, tremor, twitching
3 AGITATION, commotion, confusion, dither, excitement, fluster, state (informal)

fly verb 1 TAKE WING, flit, flutter, hover, sail, soar, wing
2 PILOT, control, maneuver, operate
3 DISPLAY, flap, float, flutter, show, wave
4 PASS, elapse, flit, glide, pass swiftly, roll on, run its course, slip away

5 RUSH, career, dart, dash, hurry, race, shoot, speed, sprint, tear
6 FLEE, escape, get away, run for it, skedaddle (informal), take to one's heels

flying adjective HURRIED, brief, fleeting, hasty, rushed, short-lived, transitory

foam noun 1 FROTH, bubbles, head, lather, spray, spume, suds
▸ verb 2 BUBBLE, boil, effervesce, fizz, froth, lather

focus noun 1 CENTER, focal point, heart, hub, target
▸ verb 2 CONCENTRATE, aim, center, direct, fix, pinpoint, spotlight, zoom in

foe noun ENEMY, adversary, antagonist, opponent, rival

fog noun MIST, gloom, miasma, murk, peasouper, peasoup (informal), smog

foggy adjective MISTY, cloudy, dim, hazy, indistinct, murky, smoggy, vaporous

foil¹ verb THWART, balk, counter, defeat, disappoint, frustrate, nullify, stop

foil² noun CONTRAST, antithesis, complement

foist verb IMPOSE, fob off, palm off, pass off, sneak in, unload

fold verb 1 BEND, crease, double over
2 (informal) GO BANKRUPT, collapse, crash, fail, go bust (informal), go to the wall, go under, shut down
▸ noun 3 CREASE, bend, furrow, overlap, pleat, wrinkle

folder noun FILE, binder, envelope, portfolio

folk noun PEOPLE, clan, family, kin, kindred, race, tribe

follow verb 1 COME AFTER, come next, succeed, supersede, supplant, take the place of

2 PURSUE, chase, dog, hound,
hunt, shadow, stalk, track, trail
3 ACCOMPANY, attend, escort,
tag along
4 OBEY, be guided by, conform,
heed, observe
5 UNDERSTAND, appreciate,
catch on (*informal*), comprehend,
fathom, grasp, realize, take in
6 RESULT, arise, develop, ensue,
flow, issue, proceed, spring
7 BE INTERESTED IN, cultivate, keep
abreast of, support

follower noun SUPPORTER,
adherent, apostle, devotee,
disciple, fan, pupil

following adjective 1 NEXT,
consequent, ensuing, later,
subsequent, succeeding,
successive
▶ noun 2 SUPPORTERS, clientele,
coterie, entourage, fans, retinue,
suite, train

folly noun FOOLISHNESS,
imprudence, indiscretion, lunacy,
madness, nonsense, rashness,
stupidity

fond adjective 1 LOVING, adoring,
affectionate, amorous, caring,
devoted, doting, indulgent,
tender, warm
2 FOOLISH, deluded, delusive,
empty, naive, overoptimistic, vain
3 ▷▷ **fond of** KEEN ON, addicted to,
attached to, enamored of, having
a soft spot for, hooked on, into
(*informal*), partial to

fondle verb CARESS, cuddle, dandle,
pat, pet, stroke

fondly adverb 1 LOVINGLY,
affectionately, dearly, indulgently,
possessively, tenderly, with
affection
2 FOOLISHLY, credulously, naively,
stupidly, vainly

fondness noun 1 LIKING,

attachment, fancy, love, partiality,
penchant, soft spot, taste,
weakness
2 DEVOTION, affection,
attachment, kindness, love,
tenderness

food noun NOURISHMENT, cuisine,
diet, fare, grub (*slang*), nutrition,
rations, refreshment

fool noun 1 SIMPLETON, blockhead,
dork (*slang*), dunce, halfwit, idiot,
ignoramus, imbecile (*informal*),
numbskull *or* numskull, schmuck
(*slang*), twit (*informal, chiefly Brit.*)
2 DUPE, fall guy (*informal*),
laughing stock, mug (*Brit. slang*),
stooge (*slang*), sucker (*slang*)
3 CLOWN, buffoon, harlequin,
jester
▶ verb 4 DECEIVE, beguile, con
(*informal*), delude, dupe, hoodwink,
mislead, take in, trick

foolhardy adjective RASH, hot-
headed, impetuous, imprudent,
irresponsible, reckless

foolish adjective UNWISE,
absurd, ill-judged, imprudent,
injudicious, senseless, silly

foolishly adverb UNWISELY,
idiotically, ill-advisedly,
imprudently, injudiciously,
mistakenly, stupidly

foolishness noun STUPIDITY,
absurdity, folly, imprudence,
indiscretion, irresponsibility,
silliness, weakness

foolproof adjective INFALLIBLE,
certain, guaranteed, safe,
sure-fire (*informal*), unassailable,
unbreakable

footing noun 1 BASIS, foundation,
groundwork
2 RELATIONSHIP, grade, position,
rank, standing, status

footstep noun STEP, footfall, tread

forage verb 1 SEARCH, cast about,

explore, hunt, rummage, scour, seek
► *noun* 2 (*cattle, etc.*) FODDER, feed, food, provender
foray *noun* RAID, incursion, inroad, invasion, sally, sortie, swoop
forbear *verb* REFRAIN, abstain, cease, desist, hold back, keep from, restrain oneself, stop
forbearance *noun* PATIENCE, long-suffering, moderation, resignation, restraint, self-control, temperance, tolerance
forbearing *adjective* PATIENT, forgiving, indulgent, lenient, long-suffering, merciful, moderate, tolerant
forbid *verb* PROHIBIT, ban, disallow, exclude, outlaw, preclude, rule out, veto
forbidden *adjective* PROHIBITED, banned, outlawed, out of bounds, proscribed, taboo, vetoed
forbidding *adjective* THREATENING, daunting, frightening, hostile, menacing, ominous, sinister, unfriendly
force *noun* 1 POWER, energy, impulse, might, momentum, pressure, strength, vigor
2 COMPULSION, arm-twisting (*informal*), coercion, constraint, duress, pressure, violence
3 INTENSITY, emphasis, fierceness, vehemence, vigor
4 ARMY, host, legion, patrol, regiment, squad, troop, unit
5 ▷▷ **in force: a** VALID, binding, current, effective, in operation, operative, working **b** IN GREAT NUMBERS, all together, in full strength
► *verb* 6 COMPEL, coerce, constrain, dragoon, drive, impel, make, oblige, press, pressurize
7 BREAK OPEN, blast, prise,

wrench, wrest
8 PUSH, propel, thrust
forced *adjective* 1 COMPULSORY, conscripted, enforced, involuntary, mandatory, obligatory
2 FALSE, affected, artificial, contrived, insincere, labored, stiff, strained, unnatural, wooden
forceful *adjective* POWERFUL, cogent, compelling, convincing, dynamic, effective, persuasive
forcible *adjective* 1 VIOLENT, aggressive, armed, coercive, compulsory
2 STRONG, compelling, energetic, forceful, potent, powerful, weighty
forebear *noun* ANCESTOR, father, forefather, forerunner, predecessor
foreboding *noun* DREAD, anxiety, apprehension, apprehensiveness, chill, fear, misgiving, premonition, presentiment
forecast *verb* 1 PREDICT, anticipate, augur, divine, foresee, foretell, prophesy
► *noun* 2 PREDICTION, conjecture, guess, prognosis, prophecy
forefather *noun* ANCESTOR, father, forebear, forerunner, predecessor
forefront *noun* LEAD, center, fore, foreground, front, prominence, spearhead, vanguard
foregoing *adjective* PRECEDING, above, antecedent, anterior, former, previous, prior
foreign *adjective* ALIEN, exotic, external, imported, remote, strange, unfamiliar, unknown
foreigner *noun* ALIEN, immigrant, incomer, stranger
foremost *adjective* LEADING, chief, cutting edge, highest, paramount, pre-eminent, primary, prime,

principal, supreme

forerunner noun PRECURSOR, envoy, harbinger, herald, prototype

foresee verb ANTICIPATE, envisage, forecast, foretell, predict, prophesy

foreshadow verb PREDICT, augur, forebode, indicate, portend, prefigure, presage, promise, signal

foresight noun ANTICIPATION, far-sightedness, forethought, precaution, preparedness, prescience, prudence

foretell verb PREDICT, forecast, forewarn, presage, prognosticate, prophesy

forethought noun ANTICIPATION, far-sightedness, foresight, precaution, providence, provision, prudence

forever adverb 1 EVERMORE, always, for all time, for keeps, in perpetuity, till Doomsday, till the cows come home (informal)
2 CONSTANTLY, all the time, continually, endlessly, eternally, incessantly, interminably, perpetually, twenty-four-seven (slang), unremittingly

forewarn verb CAUTION, advise, alert, apprise, give fair warning, put on guard, tip off

forfeit noun 1 PENALTY, damages, fine, forfeiture, loss, mulct
▶ verb 2 LOSE, be deprived of, be stripped of, give up, relinquish, renounce, say good-bye to, surrender

forge verb 1 CREATE, construct, devise, fashion, form, frame, make, mold, shape, work
2 FALSIFY, copy, counterfeit, fake, feign, imitate

forgery noun 1 FRAUDULENCE, coining, counterfeiting, falsification, fraudulent imitation
2 FAKE, counterfeit, falsification, imitation, phoney or phony (informal), sham

forget verb NEGLECT, leave behind, lose sight of, omit, overlook

forgetful adjective ABSENT-MINDED, careless, inattentive, neglectful, oblivious, unmindful, vague

forgive verb EXCUSE, absolve, acquit, condone, exonerate, let bygones be bygones, let off (informal), pardon

forgiveness noun PARDON, absolution, acquittal, amnesty, exoneration, mercy, remission

forgiving adjective MERCIFUL, clement, compassionate, forbearing, lenient, magnanimous, soft-hearted, tolerant

forgo verb GIVE UP, abandon, do without, relinquish, renounce, resign, surrender, waive, yield

forgotten adjective LEFT BEHIND, bygone, lost, omitted, past, past recall, unremembered

fork verb BRANCH, bifurcate, diverge, divide, part, split

forked adjective BRANCHING, angled, bifurcate(d), branched, divided, pronged, split, zigzag

forlorn adjective MISERABLE, disconsolate, down in the dumps (informal), helpless, hopeless, pathetic, pitiful, unhappy, woebegone, wretched

form noun 1 SHAPE, appearance, configuration, formation, pattern, structure
2 TYPE, kind, sort, style, variety
3 CONDITION, fettle, fitness, health, shape, trim

4 PROCEDURE, convention, custom, etiquette, protocol
5 DOCUMENT, application, paper, sheet
6 CLASS, grade, rank
▶ verb 7 MAKE, build, construct, create, fashion, forge, mold, produce, shape
8 ARRANGE, combine, draw up, organize
9 TAKE SHAPE, appear, become visible, come into being, crystallize, grow, materialize, rise
10 DEVELOP, acquire, contract, cultivate, pick up
11 CONSTITUTE, compose, comprise, make up

formal adjective 1 OFFICIAL, ceremonial, ritualistic, solemn
2 CONVENTIONAL, affected, correct, precise, stiff, unbending

formality noun 1 CONVENTION, custom, procedure, red tape, rite, ritual
2 CORRECTNESS, decorum, etiquette, protocol

format noun STYLE, appearance, arrangement, construction, form, layout, look, make-up, plan, type

formation noun 1 ESTABLISHMENT, constitution, development, forming, generation, genesis, manufacture, production
2 PATTERN, arrangement, configuration, design, grouping, structure

formative adjective DEVELOPMENTAL, influential

former adjective PREVIOUS, earlier, erstwhile, one-time, prior

formerly adverb PREVIOUSLY, at one time, before, lately, once

formidable adjective
1 INTIMIDATING, daunting, dismaying, fearful, frightful, menacing, terrifying, threatening
2 IMPRESSIVE, awesome, cool (informal), great, mighty, phat (slang), powerful, redoubtable, terrific (informal), tremendous

formula noun METHOD, blueprint, precept, principle, procedure, recipe, rule

formulate verb 1 DEFINE, detail, express, frame, give form to, set down, specify, systematize
2 DEVISE, develop, forge, invent, map out, originate, plan, work out

forsake verb 1 DESERT, abandon, disown, leave in the lurch, strand
2 GIVE UP, forgo, relinquish, renounce, set aside, surrender, yield

forsaken adjective DESERTED, abandoned, disowned, forlorn, left in the lurch, marooned, outcast, stranded

fort noun 1 FORTRESS, blockhouse, camp, castle, citadel, fortification, garrison, stronghold
2 ▷▷ **hold the fort** STAND IN, carry on, keep things on an even keel, take over the reins

forte noun SPECIALITY, gift, long suit (informal), métier, strength, strong point, talent

forth adverb FORWARD, ahead, away, onward, out, outward

forthcoming adjective
1 APPROACHING, coming, expected, future, imminent, impending, prospective, upcoming
2 ACCESSIBLE, at hand, available, in evidence, obtainable, on tap (informal), ready
3 COMMUNICATIVE, chatty, expansive, free, informative, open, sociable, talkative, unreserved

forthright adjective OUTSPOKEN, blunt, candid, direct, frank, open, plain-spoken, straightforward, upfront (*informal*)

forthwith *adverb* AT ONCE, directly, immediately, instantly, quickly, right away, straightaway, without delay

fortification *noun* 1 DEFENSE, bastion, fastness, fort, fortress, protection, stronghold
2 STRENGTHENING, reinforcement

fortify *verb* STRENGTHEN, augment, buttress, protect, reinforce, shore up, support

fortitude *noun* COURAGE, backbone, bravery, fearlessness, grit, perseverance, resolution, strength, valor

fortress *noun* CASTLE, citadel, fastness, fort, redoubt, stronghold

fortunate *adjective* 1 LUCKY, favored, in luck, jammy (*Brit. slang*), successful, well-off
2 FAVORABLE, advantageous, convenient, expedient, felicitous, fortuitous, helpful, opportune, providential, timely, win-win (*informal*)

fortunately *adverb* LUCKILY, by a happy chance, by good luck, happily, providentially

fortune *noun* 1 WEALTH, affluence, opulence, possessions, property, prosperity, riches, treasure
2 LUCK, chance, destiny, fate, kismet, providence
3 ▷▷ **fortunes** DESTINY, adventures, experiences, history, lot, success

forward *adjective* 1 LEADING, advance, first, foremost, front, head
2 PRESUMPTUOUS, bold, brash, brazen, cheeky, familiar, impertinent, impudent, pushy (*informal*)
3 WELL-DEVELOPED, advanced, precocious, premature

▶ *adverb* 4 AHEAD, forth, on, onward
▶ *verb* 5 PROMOTE, advance, assist, expedite, further, hasten, hurry
6 SEND, dispatch, post, send on

foster *verb* 1 PROMOTE, cultivate, encourage, feed, nurture, stimulate, support, uphold
2 BRING UP, mother, nurse, raise, rear, take care of

foul *adjective* 1 DIRTY, fetid, filthy, funky (*slang*), malodorous, nauseating, putrid, repulsive, scuzzy (*slang*), squalid, stinking, unclean
2 OBSCENE, abusive, blue, coarse, indecent, lewd, profane, scurrilous, vulgar
3 OFFENSIVE, abhorrent, despicable, detestable, disgraceful, lousy (*slang*), scandalous, scuzzy (*slang*), shameful, wicked
4 UNFAIR, crooked, dishonest, fraudulent, shady (*informal*), underhand, unscrupulous
▶ *verb* 5 POLLUTE, besmirch, contaminate, defile, dirty, stain, sully, taint

found *verb* ESTABLISH, constitute, create, inaugurate, institute, organize, originate, set up, start

foundation *noun* 1 GROUNDWORK, base, basis, bedrock, bottom, footing, substructure, underpinning
2 SETTING UP, endowment, establishment, inauguration, institution, organization, settlement

founder¹ *noun* INITIATOR, architect, author, beginner, father, inventor, originator

founder² *verb* 1 SINK, be lost, go down, go to the bottom, submerge
2 FAIL, break down, collapse,

come to grief, come unstuck, fall through, miscarry, misfire

3 STUMBLE, lurch, sprawl, stagger, trip

foundling noun STRAY, orphan, outcast, waif

fountain noun 1 JET, font, fount, reservoir, spout, spray, spring, well

2 SOURCE, cause, derivation, fount, fountainhead, origin, wellspring

foyer noun ENTRANCE HALL, antechamber, anteroom, lobby, reception area, vestibule

fracas noun BRAWL, affray (Law), disturbance, melee or mêlée, riot, rumpus, scuffle, skirmish

fraction noun PIECE, part, percentage, portion, section, segment, share, slice

fractious adjective IRRITABLE, captious, cross, petulant, querulous, refractory, testy, tetchy, touchy

fracture noun 1 BREAK, cleft, crack, fissure, opening, rift, rupture, split

▶ verb 2 BREAK, crack, rupture, splinter, split

fragile adjective DELICATE, breakable, brittle, dainty, fine, flimsy, frail, frangible, weak

fragment noun 1 PIECE, bit, chip, particle, portion, scrap, shred, sliver

▶ verb 2 BREAK, break up, come apart, come to pieces, crumble, disintegrate, shatter, splinter, split up

fragmentary adjective INCOMPLETE, bitty, broken, disconnected, incoherent, partial, piecemeal, scattered, scrappy, sketchy

fragrance noun SCENT, aroma, balm, bouquet, fragrancy, perfume, redolence, smell, sweet odor

fragrant adjective PERFUMED, aromatic, balmy, odorous, redolent, sweet-scented, sweet-smelling

frail adjective WEAK, delicate, feeble, flimsy, fragile, infirm, insubstantial, puny, vulnerable

frailty noun FEEBLENESS, fallibility, frailness, infirmity, susceptibility, weakness

frame noun 1 CASING, construction, framework, shell, structure

2 PHYSIQUE, anatomy, body, build, carcass

3 ▷▷ **frame of mind** MOOD, attitude, disposition, humor, outlook, state, temper

▶ verb 4 CONSTRUCT, assemble, build, make, manufacture, put together

5 DRAFT, compose, devise, draw up, formulate, map out, sketch

6 MOUNT, case, enclose, surround

framework noun STRUCTURE, foundation, frame, groundwork, plan, shell, skeleton, the bare bones

frank adjective HONEST, blunt, candid, direct, forthright, open, outspoken, plain-spoken, sincere, straightforward, truthful

frankly adverb 1 HONESTLY, candidly, in truth, to be honest

2 OPENLY, bluntly, directly, freely, plainly, without reserve

frankness noun OUTSPOKENNESS, bluntness, candor, forthrightness, openness, plain speaking, truthfulness

frantic adjective 1 FURIOUS, at the end of one's tether, berserk, beside oneself, distracted, distraught, wild

2 HECTIC, desperate, fraught

(*informal*), frenetic, frenzied
fraternity *noun* 1 CLUB,
association, brotherhood, circle,
company, guild, league, union
2 COMPANIONSHIP, brotherhood,
camaraderie, fellowship, kinship
fraternize *verb* ASSOCIATE,
consort, cooperate, hobnob, keep
company, mingle, mix, socialize
fraud *noun* 1 DECEPTION, back-
stabbing (*informal*), chicanery,
deceit, double-dealing, duplicity,
sharp practice, swindling,
treachery, trickery
2 IMPOSTOR, charlatan, fake,
fraudster, hoaxer, phoney *or*
phony (*informal*), pretender,
swindler
fraudulent *adjective* DECEITFUL,
crooked (*informal*), dishonest,
double-dealing, duplicitous,
sham, swindling, treacherous
fray *verb* WEAR THIN, chafe, rub,
wear
freak *noun* 1 ODDITY, aberration,
anomaly, malformation,
monstrosity, weirdo *or* weirdie
(*informal*)
2 ENTHUSIAST, addict, aficionado,
buff (*informal*), devotee, fan,
fanatic, fiend (*informal*), nut (*slang*)
▶ *adjective* 3 ABNORMAL,
exceptional, unparalleled,
unusual
free *adjective* 1 FOR NOTHING,
complimentary, for free (*informal*),
free of charge, gratis, gratuitous,
on the house, unpaid, without
charge
2 AT LIBERTY, at large, footloose,
independent, liberated, loose, on
the loose, unfettered
3 ALLOWED, able, clear, permitted,
unimpeded, unrestricted
4 AVAILABLE, empty, idle, spare,
unemployed, unoccupied,

unused, vacant
5 GENEROUS, lavish, liberal,
unsparing, unstinting
▶ *verb* 6 RELEASE, deliver, let out,
liberate, loose, set free, turn loose,
unchain, untie
7 EXTRICATE, cut loose, disengage,
disentangle, rescue
freedom *noun* 1 LIBERTY,
deliverance, emancipation,
independence, release
2 OPPORTUNITY, a blank check,
carte blanche, discretion, free
rein, latitude, license
free-for-all *noun* FIGHT, brawl,
dust-up (*informal*), fracas, melee *or*
mêlée, riot, row, scrimmage
freely *adverb* 1 WILLINGLY, of one's
own accord, of one's own free
will, spontaneously, voluntarily,
without prompting
2 OPENLY, candidly, frankly,
plainly, unreservedly, without
reserve
3 ABUNDANTLY, amply, copiously,
extravagantly, lavishly, liberally,
unstintingly
freeze *verb* 1 CHILL, harden, ice
over *or* up, stiffen
2 SUSPEND, fix, hold up, inhibit,
peg, stop
freezing *adjective* ICY, arctic,
biting, bitter, chill, frosty, glacial,
raw, wintry
freight *noun* 1 TRANSPORTATION,
carriage, conveyance, shipment
2 CARGO, burden, consignment,
goods, load, merchandise, payload
French *adjective* GALLIC
frenzied *adjective* FURIOUS,
distracted, feverish, frantic,
frenetic, rabid, uncontrolled, wild
frenzy *noun* FURY, derangement,
hysteria, paroxysm, passion, rage,
seizure
frequent *adjective* 1 COMMON,

customary, everyday, familiar, habitual, persistent, recurrent, repeated, usual
► *verb* 2 VISIT, attend, be found at, hang out at (*informal*), haunt, patronize

frequently *adverb* OFTEN, commonly, habitually, many times, much, not infrequently, repeatedly

fresh *adjective* 1 NEW, different, modern, novel, original, recent, up-to-date
2 ADDITIONAL, added, auxiliary, extra, further, more, other, supplementary
3 INVIGORATING, bracing, brisk, clean, cool, crisp, pure, refreshing, unpolluted
4 LIVELY, alert, energetic, keen, refreshed, sprightly, spry, vigorous
5 NATURAL, unprocessed
6 (*informal*) CHEEKY, disrespectful, familiar, forward, impudent, insolent, presumptuous

freshen *verb* REFRESH, enliven, freshen up, liven up, restore, revitalize

freshness *noun* 1 NOVELTY, inventiveness, newness, originality
2 CLEANNESS, brightness, clearness, glow, shine, sparkle, vigor, wholesomeness

fret *verb* WORRY, agonize, brood, grieve, lose sleep over, upset *or* distress oneself

fretful *adjective* IRRITABLE, crotchety, edgy, fractious, querulous, short-tempered, testy, touchy, uneasy

friction *noun* 1 RUBBING, abrasion, chafing, grating, rasping, resistance, scraping
2 HOSTILITY, animosity, bad blood,

conflict, disagreement, discord, dissension, resentment

friend *noun* 1 COMPANION, buddy (*informal*), chum (*informal*), comrade, homeboy (*slang*), homegirl (*slang*), mate (*informal*), pal (*informal*), playmate
2 SUPPORTER, ally, associate, patron, well-wisher

friendliness *noun* KINDLINESS, affability, amiability, congeniality, conviviality, geniality, neighborliness, sociability, warmth

friendly *adjective* SOCIABLE, affectionate, amicable, buddy-buddy (*informal*), close, familiar, helpful, intimate, neighborly, on good terms, pally (*informal*), sympathetic, welcoming

friendship *noun* GOODWILL, affection, amity, attachment, concord, familiarity, friendliness, harmony, intimacy

fright *noun* FEAR, alarm, consternation, dread, horror, panic, scare, shock, trepidation

frighten *verb* SCARE, alarm, intimidate, petrify, shock, startle, terrify, terrorize, unnerve

frightened *adjective* AFRAID, alarmed, petrified, scared, scared stiff, startled, terrified, terrorized, terror-stricken

frightening *adjective* TERRIFYING, alarming, fearful, fearsome, horrifying, menacing, scary (*informal*), shocking, unnerving

frightful *adjective* TERRIFYING, alarming, awful, dreadful, fearful, ghastly, horrendous, horrible, terrible, traumatic

frigid *adjective* 1 COLD, arctic, frosty, frozen, glacial, icy, wintry
2 FORBIDDING, aloof, austere, formal, unapproachable,

unfeeling, unresponsive

frills plural noun TRIMMINGS, additions, bells and whistles, embellishments, extras, frippery, fuss, ornamentation, ostentation

fringe noun 1 BORDER, edging, hem, trimming
2 EDGE, borderline, limits, margin, outskirts, perimeter, periphery
▶ adjective 3 UNOFFICIAL, unconventional, unorthodox

frisk verb 1 FROLIC, caper, cavort, gambol, jump, play, prance, skip, trip
2 SEARCH, check, inspect, run over, shake down (U.S. slang)

frisky adjective LIVELY, coltish, frolicsome, high-spirited, kittenish, playful, sportive

fritter away verb WASTE, dissipate, idle away, misspend, run through, spend like water, squander

frivolity noun FUN, flippancy, frivolousness, gaiety, levity, light-heartedness, silliness, superficiality, triviality

frivolous adjective 1 FLIPPANT, childish, foolish, idle, juvenile, puerile, silly, superficial
2 TRIVIAL, footling (informal), minor, petty, shallow, trifling, unimportant

frolic verb 1 PLAY, caper, cavort, frisk, gambol, lark, make merry, romp, sport
▶ noun 2 REVEL, antic, game, lark, romp, spree

frolicsome adjective PLAYFUL, coltish, frisky, kittenish, lively, merry, sportive

front noun 1 EXTERIOR, façade, face, foreground, frontage
2 FOREFRONT, front line, head, lead, vanguard

3 DISGUISE, blind, cover, cover-up, façade, mask, pretext, show
▶ adjective 4 FIRST, cutting edge, foremost, head, lead, leading, topmost
▶ verb 5 FACE ONTO, look over or onto, overlook

frontier noun BOUNDARY, borderline, edge, limit, perimeter, verge

frost noun HOARFROST, freeze, rime

frosty adjective 1 COLD, chilly, frozen, icy, wintry
2 UNFRIENDLY, discouraging, frigid, off-putting (Brit. informal), standoffish, unenthusiastic, unwelcoming

froth noun 1 FOAM, bubbles, effervescence, head, lather, scum, spume, suds
▶ verb 2 FIZZ, bubble over, come to a head, effervesce, foam, lather

frothy adjective FOAMY, foaming, sudsy

frown verb 1 SCOWL, glare, glower, knit one's brows, look daggers, lour or lower
2 ▷▷ **frown on** DISAPPROVE OF, discourage, dislike, look askance at, take a dim view of

frozen adjective ICY, arctic, chilled, frigid, frosted, icebound, ice-cold, ice-covered, numb

frugal adjective THRIFTY, abstemious, careful, economical, niggardly, parsimonious, prudent, sparing

fruit noun 1 PRODUCE, crop, harvest, product, yield
2 RESULT, advantage, benefit, consequence, effect, end result, outcome, profit, return, reward

fruitful adjective USEFUL, advantageous, beneficial, effective, productive, profitable, rewarding, successful, win-win (*informal*), worthwhile

fruition *noun* MATURITY, attainment, completion, fulfillment, materialization, perfection, realization, ripeness

fruitless *adjective* USELESS, futile, ineffectual, pointless, profitless, unavailing, unproductive, unprofitable, unsuccessful, vain

frustrate *verb* THWART, balk, block, check, counter, defeat, disappoint, foil, forestall, nullify, stymie

frustrated *adjective* DISAPPOINTED, discouraged, disheartened, embittered, resentful

frustration *noun* 1 OBSTRUCTION, blocking, circumvention, foiling, thwarting
2 ANNOYANCE, disappointment, dissatisfaction, grievance, irritation, resentment, vexation

fuel *noun* INCITEMENT, ammunition, provocation

fugitive *noun* 1 RUNAWAY, deserter, escapee, refugee
▶ *adjective* 2 MOMENTARY, brief, ephemeral, fleeting, passing, short-lived, temporary, transient, transitory

fulfill *verb* 1 ACHIEVE, accomplish, carry out, complete, perform, realize, satisfy
2 COMPLY WITH, answer, conform to, fill, meet, obey, observe

fulfillment *noun* ACHIEVEMENT, accomplishment, attainment, completion, consummation, implementation, realization

full *adjective* 1 SATURATED, brimming, complete, filled, loaded, replete, satiated, stocked
2 PLENTIFUL, abundant, adequate, ample, comprehensive, exhaustive, extensive, generous
3 RICH, clear, deep, distinct, loud, resonant, rounded
4 PLUMP, buxom, curvaceous, rounded, voluptuous
5 LOOSE, baggy, capacious, large, puffy, voluminous
▶ *noun* 6 ▷▷ **in full** COMPLETELY, in its entirety, in total, without exception

full-blooded *adjective* VIGOROUS, hearty, lusty, red-blooded, virile

fullness *noun* 1 PLENTY, abundance, copiousness, fill, profusion, satiety, saturation, sufficiency
2 RICHNESS, clearness, loudness, resonance, strength

full-scale *adjective* MAJOR, all-out, comprehensive, exhaustive, in-depth, sweeping, thorough, thoroughgoing, wide-ranging

fully *adverb* TOTALLY, altogether, completely, entirely, in all respects, one hundred per cent, perfectly, thoroughly, utterly, wholly

fulsome *adjective* INSINCERE, excessive, extravagant, immoderate, inordinate, sycophantic, unctuous

fumble *verb* GROPE, feel around, flounder, scrabble

fume *verb* RAGE, get hot under the collar (*informal*), rant, see red (*informal*), seethe, smolder, storm

fumes *plural noun* SMOKE, exhaust, gas, pollution, smog, vapor

fumigate *verb* DISINFECT, clean out *or* up, cleanse, purify, sanitize, sterilize

fuming *adjective* ANGRY, enraged, in a rage, incensed, on the warpath (*informal*), raging, seething, up in arms

fun *noun* 1 ENJOYMENT, amusement, entertainment, jollity, merriment, mirth,

pleasure, recreation, sport
2 ▷▷ **make fun of** MOCK, lampoon,
laugh at, parody, poke fun at,
ridicule, satirize, send up (*Brit.
informal*)
▶ *adjective* 3 ENJOYABLE, amusing,
convivial, diverting, entertaining,
lively, witty
function *noun* 1 PURPOSE,
business, duty, job, mission, *raison
d'être*, responsibility, role, task
2 RECEPTION, affair, do (*informal*),
gathering, social occasion
▶ *verb* 3 WORK, act, behave, do duty,
go, operate, perform, run
functional *adjective* 1 PRACTICAL,
hard-wearing, serviceable, useful,
utilitarian
2 WORKING, operative
fund *noun* 1 RESERVE, kitty, pool,
stock, store, supply
▶ *verb* 2 FINANCE, pay for,
subsidize, support
fundamental *adjective*
1 ESSENTIAL, basic, cardinal,
central, elementary, key,
primary, principal, rudimentary,
underlying
▶ *noun* 2 PRINCIPLE, axiom,
cornerstone, law, rudiment, rule
fundamentally *adverb*
ESSENTIALLY, at bottom, at heart,
basically, intrinsically, primarily,
radically
funds *plural noun* MONEY,
capital, cash, finance, ready
money, resources, savings, the
wherewithal
funeral *noun* BURIAL, cremation,
inhumation, interment,
obsequies
funnel *verb* CHANNEL, conduct,
convey, direct, filter, move, pass,
pour
funny *adjective* 1 HUMOROUS,
amusing, comic, comical, droll,

entertaining, hilarious, riotous,
side-splitting, witty
2 PECULIAR, curious, mysterious,
odd, queer, strange, suspicious,
unusual, weird
furious *adjective* 1 ANGRY, beside
oneself, enraged, fuming,
incensed, infuriated, livid
(*informal*), raging, up in arms
2 VIOLENT, fierce, intense,
savage, turbulent, unrestrained,
vehement
furnish *verb* 1 DECORATE, equip, fit
out, stock
2 SUPPLY, give, grant, hand out,
offer, present, provide
furniture *noun* HOUSEHOLD
GOODS, appliances, fittings,
furnishings, goods, possessions,
things (*informal*)
furor *noun* DISTURBANCE,
commotion, hullabaloo, outcry,
stir, to-do, uproar
furrow *noun* 1 GROOVE, channel,
crease, hollow, line, rut, seam,
trench, wrinkle
▶ *verb* 2 WRINKLE, corrugate,
crease, draw together, knit
further *adverb* 1 IN ADDITION,
additionally, also, besides,
furthermore, into the bargain,
moreover, to boot
▶ *adjective* 2 ADDITIONAL,
extra, fresh, more, new, other,
supplementary
▶ *verb* 3 PROMOTE, advance, assist,
encourage, forward, help, lend
support to, work for
furthermore *adverb* BESIDES,
additionally, as well, further,
in addition, into the bargain,
moreover, to boot, too
furthest *adjective* MOST DISTANT,
extreme, farthest, furthermost,
outmost, remotest, ultimate
furtive *adjective* SLY, clandestine,

conspiratorial, secretive, sneaky, stealthy, surreptitious, underhand, under-the-table

fury noun 1 ANGER, frenzy, impetuosity, madness, passion, rage, wrath
2 VIOLENCE, ferocity, fierceness, force, intensity, savagery, severity, vehemence

fuss noun 1 BOTHER, ado, commotion, excitement, hue and cry, palaver, stir, to-do
2 ARGUMENT, complaint, furor, objection, row, squabble, trouble
▶ verb 3 WORRY, fidget, flap (informal), fret, get worked up, take pains

fussy adjective 1 HARD TO PLEASE, choosy (informal), difficult, fastidious, finicky, high-maintenance, nit-picking (informal), particular, pernickety (old-fashioned, informal), picky (informal)
2 OVERELABORATE, busy, cluttered, overworked, rococo

fusty adjective STALE, airless, damp, mildewed, moldering, musty, stuffy

futile adjective USELESS, fruitless, ineffectual, unavailing, unprofitable, unsuccessful, vain, worthless

futility noun USELESSNESS, emptiness, hollowness, ineffectiveness

future noun 1 HEREAFTER, time to come
2 OUTLOOK, expectation, prospect
▶ adjective 3 FORTHCOMING, approaching, coming, fated, impending, later, subsequent, to come

fuzzy adjective 1 FLUFFY, downy, frizzy, woolly
2 INDISTINCT, bleary, blurred, distorted, ill-defined, obscure, out of focus, unclear, vague

g

gabble verb 1 PRATTLE, babble, blabber, gibber, gush, jabber, spout
▶ noun 2 GIBBERISH, babble, blabber, chatter, drivel, prattle, twaddle

gadabout noun PLEASURE-SEEKER, gallivanter, rambler, rover, wanderer

gadget noun DEVICE, appliance, contraption (informal), contrivance, gizmo (slang), instrument, invention, thing, tool

gaffe noun BLUNDER, bloomer (informal), clanger (informal), faux pas, howler, indiscretion, lapse, mistake, slip, solecism

gag[1] verb 1 SUPPRESS, curb, muffle, muzzle, quiet, silence, stifle, stop up
2 RETCH, barf (slang), heave, puke (slang), spew, throw up (informal), toss one's cookies (slang), vomit

gag[2] noun JOKE, crack (slang), funny (informal), hoax, jest, wisecrack (informal), witticism

gaiety noun 1 CHEERFULNESS, blitheness, exhilaration, glee, high spirits, jollity, light-heartedness, merriment, mirth
2 MERRYMAKING, conviviality, festivity, fun, jollification, revelry

gaily adverb 1 CHEERFULLY, blithely, gleefully, happily, joyfully, light-heartedly, merrily
2 COLORFULLY, brightly, brilliantly, flamboyantly, flashily, gaudily, showily

gain verb 1 OBTAIN, acquire, attain, capture, collect, gather, get, land, pick up, secure, win
2 REACH, arrive at, attain, come to, get to
3 ▷▷ **gain on** GET NEARER, approach, catch up with, close, narrow the gap, overtake
▶ noun 4 PROFIT, advantage, benefit, dividend, return, yield
5 INCREASE, advance, growth, improvement, progress, rise

gainful adjective PROFITABLE, advantageous, beneficial, fruitful, lucrative, productive, remunerative, rewarding, useful, win-win (informal), worthwhile

gains plural noun PROFITS, earnings, prize, proceeds, revenue, takings, winnings

gainsay verb CONTRADICT, contravene, controvert, deny, disagree with, dispute, rebut, retract

gait noun WALK, bearing, carriage, pace, step, stride, tread

gala noun FESTIVAL, carnival, celebration, festivity, fête, jamboree, pageant

gale noun 1 STORM, blast, cyclone, hurricane, squall, tempest, tornado, typhoon
2 OUTBURST, burst, eruption, explosion, fit, howl, outbreak, peal, shout, shriek

gall[1] noun 1 (informal) IMPUDENCE, brazenness, cheek (informal), chutzpah (informal), effrontery, impertinence, insolence, nerve (*informal*)

2 BITTERNESS, acrimony, animosity, bile, hostility, rancor

gall² *verb* **1** SCRAPE, abrade, chafe, irritate

2 ANNOY, exasperate, irk, irritate, provoke, rankle, vex

gallant *adjective* **1** BRAVE, bold, courageous, heroic, honorable, intrepid, manly, noble, valiant

2 CHIVALROUS, attentive, courteous, gentlemanly, gracious, noble, polite

gallantry *noun* **1** BRAVERY, boldness, courage, heroism, intrepidity, manliness, spirit, valor

2 ATTENTIVENESS, chivalry, courteousness, courtesy, gentlemanliness, graciousness, nobility, politeness

galling *adjective* ANNOYING, bitter, exasperating, irksome, irritating, provoking, vexatious

gallivant *verb* WANDER, gad about, ramble, roam, rove

gallop *verb* RUN, bolt, career, dash, hurry, race, rush, speed, sprint

galore *adverb* IN ABUNDANCE, all over the place, aplenty, everywhere, in great quantity, in great numbers, in profusion, to spare

galvanize *verb* STIMULATE, electrify, excite, inspire, invigorate, jolt, provoke, spur, stir

gamble *verb* **1** BET, game, have a flutter (*informal*), play, punt, wager

2 RISK, chance, hazard, speculate, stick one's neck out (*informal*), take a chance

▶ *noun* **3** RISK, chance, leap in the dark, lottery, speculation, uncertainty, venture

4 BET, flutter (*informal*), punt, wager

gambol *verb* **1** FROLIC, caper, cavort, frisk, hop, jump, prance, skip

▶ *noun* **2** FROLIC, caper, hop, jump, prance, skip

game¹ *noun* **1** PASTIME, amusement, distraction, diversion, entertainment, lark, recreation, sport

2 MATCH, competition, contest, event, head-to-head, meeting, tournament

3 WILD ANIMALS, prey, quarry

4 SCHEME, design, plan, plot, ploy, stratagem, tactic, trick

▶ *adjective* **5** BRAVE, courageous, gallant, gritty, intrepid, persistent, plucky, spirited

6 WILLING, desirous, eager, interested, keen, prepared, ready

gamut *noun* RANGE, area, catalog, compass, field, scale, scope, series, sweep

gang *noun* GROUP, band, clique, club, company, coterie, crowd, mob, pack, squad, team

gangling *adjective* TALL, angular, awkward, lanky, rangy, rawboned, spindly

gangster *noun* RACKETEER, crook (*informal*), hood (*slang*), hoodlum, mobster (*slang*)

gap *noun* **1** OPENING, break, chink, cleft, crack, hole, space

2 INTERVAL, breathing space, hiatus, interlude, intermission, interruption, lacuna, lull, pause, respite

3 DIFFERENCE, disagreement, disparity, divergence, inconsistency

gape *verb* **1** STARE, gawk, gawp (*Brit. slang*), goggle, wonder

2 OPEN, crack, split, yawn

gaping *adjective* WIDE, broad,

cavernous, great, open, vast, wide
open, yawning

garbage noun litter RUBBISH,
refuse, trash (*chiefly U.S.*), waste

garbled adjective JUMBLED,
confused, distorted, double-
Dutch, incomprehensible, mixed
up, unintelligible

garish adjective GAUDY, brash,
brassy, flashy, loud, showy, tacky
(*informal*), tasteless, vulgar

garland noun 1 WREATH, bays,
chaplet, crown, festoon, honors,
laurels
▶ verb 2 ADORN, crown, deck,
festoon, wreathe

garments plural noun CLOTHES,
apparel, attire, clothing, costume,
dress, garb, gear (*slang*), outfit,
uniform

garner verb COLLECT, accumulate,
amass, gather, hoard, save,
stockpile, store, stow away

garnish verb 1 DECORATE, adorn,
embellish, enhance, ornament,
set off, trim
▶ noun 2 DECORATION, adornment,
embellishment, enhancement,
ornamentation, trimming

garrison noun 1 TROOPS, armed
force, command, detachment,
unit
2 FORT, base, camp, encampment,
fortification, fortress, post,
station, stronghold
▶ verb 3 STATION, assign, position,
post, put on duty

garrulous adjective TALKATIVE,
chatty, gossiping, loquacious,
prattling, verbose, voluble

gash verb 1 CUT, gouge, lacerate,
slash, slit, split, tear, wound
▶ noun 2 CUT, gouge, incision,
laceration, slash, slit, split, tear,
wound

gasp verb 1 GULP, blow, catch one's

breath, choke, pant, puff
▶ noun 2 GULP, exclamation, pant,
puff, sharp intake of breath

gate noun BARRIER, door, entrance,
exit, gateway, opening, passage,
portal

gather verb 1 ASSEMBLE,
accumulate, amass, collect,
garner, mass, muster, stockpile
2 LEARN, assume, conclude,
deduce, hear, infer, surmise,
understand
3 PICK, cull, garner, glean, harvest,
pluck, reap, select
4 INTENSIFY, deepen, expand,
grow, heighten, increase, rise,
swell, thicken
5 FOLD, pleat, tuck

gathering noun ASSEMBLY,
company, conclave, congress,
convention, crowd, group,
meeting

gauche adjective AWKWARD,
clumsy, ill-mannered, inelegant,
tactless, unsophisticated

gaudy adjective GARISH, bright,
flashy, loud, showy, tacky
(*informal*), tasteless, vulgar

gauge verb 1 MEASURE, ascertain,
calculate, check, compute, count,
determine, weigh
2 JUDGE, adjudge, appraise, assess,
estimate, evaluate, guess, rate,
reckon, value
▶ noun 3 INDICATOR, criterion,
guide, guideline, measure, meter,
standard, test, touchstone,
yardstick

gaunt adjective EMACIATED,
angular, anorexic, bony,
cadaverous, lean, pinched,
scrawny, skeletal, skinny, spare

gawky adjective AWKWARD, clumsy,
gauche, loutish, lumbering,
maladroit, ungainly

gay adjective 1 HOMOSEXUAL, bent

(*informal*, *derogatory*), lesbian, queer (*informal*, *derogatory*)
2 CAREFREE, blithe, cheerful, jovial, light-hearted, lively, merry, sparkling
3 COLORFUL, bright, brilliant, flamboyant, flashy, rich, showy, vivid
▶ *noun* 4 HOMOSEXUAL, lesbian

gaze *verb* 1 STARE, gape, look, regard, view, watch, wonder
▶ *noun* 2 STARE, fixed look, look

gazette *noun* NEWSPAPER, journal, news-sheet, paper, periodical

gear *noun* 1 COG, cogwheel, gearwheel
2 MECHANISM, cogs, machinery, works
3 EQUIPMENT, accouterments, apparatus, instruments, paraphernalia, supplies, tackle, tools
4 CLOTHING, clothes, costume, dress, garments, outfit, togs, wear
▶ *verb* 5 EQUIP, adapt, adjust, fit

geek *noun* BORE (*slang*), anorak (*informal*), dork (*slang*), drip (*informal*), obsessive, trainspotter (*informal*), wonk (*informal*)

gelatinous *adjective* JELLY-LIKE, gluey, glutinous, gummy, sticky, viscous

gelid *adjective* COLD, arctic, chilly, freezing, frigid, frosty, frozen, glacial, ice-cold, icy

gem *noun* 1 PRECIOUS STONE, jewel, stone
2 PRIZE, jewel, masterpiece, pearl, treasure

general *adjective* 1 COMMON, accepted, broad, extensive, popular, prevalent, public, universal, widespread
2 IMPRECISE, approximate, ill-defined, indefinite, inexact, loose, unspecific, vague

3 UNIVERSAL, across-the-board, blanket, collective, comprehensive, indiscriminate, miscellaneous, sweeping, total

generally *adverb* 1 USUALLY, as a rule, by and large, customarily, normally, on the whole, ordinarily, typically
2 COMMONLY, extensively, popularly, publicly, universally, widely

generate *verb* PRODUCE, breed, cause, create, engender, give rise to, make, propagate

generation *noun* 1 PRODUCTION, creation, formation, genesis, propagation, reproduction
2 AGE GROUP, breed, crop
3 AGE, epoch, era, period, time

generic *adjective* COLLECTIVE, blanket, common, comprehensive, general, inclusive, universal, wide

generosity *noun* 1 CHARITY, beneficence, bounty, kindness, largesse *or* largess, liberality, munificence, open-handedness
2 UNSELFISHNESS, goodness, high-mindedness, magnanimity, nobleness

generous *adjective* 1 CHARITABLE, beneficent, bountiful, hospitable, kind, lavish, liberal, open-handed, unstinting
2 UNSELFISH, big-hearted, good, high-minded, lofty, magnanimous, noble
3 PLENTIFUL, abundant, ample, copious, full, lavish, liberal, rich, unstinting

genesis *noun* BEGINNING, birth, creation, formation, inception, origin, start

genial *adjective* CHEERFUL, affable, agreeable, amiable, congenial, friendly, good-natured, jovial, pleasant, warm

geniality noun CHEERFULNESS, affability, agreeableness, amiability, conviviality, cordiality, friendliness, good cheer, joviality, warmth

genius noun 1 MASTER, brainbox, expert, hotshot (informal), maestro, mastermind, savant, virtuoso, whiz (informal)
2 BRILLIANCE, ability, aptitude, bent, capacity, flair, gift, knack, talent

genre noun TYPE, category, class, group, kind, sort, species, style

genteel adjective REFINED, courteous, cultured, elegant, gentlemanly, ladylike, polite, respectable, urbane, well-mannered

gentle adjective 1 SWEET-TEMPERED, compassionate, humane, kindly, meek, mild, placid, tender
2 MODERATE, light, mild, muted, slight, soft, soothing
3 GRADUAL, easy, imperceptible, light, mild, moderate, slight, slow
4 TAME, biddable, broken, docile, manageable, placid, tractable

gentlemanly adjective POLITE, civil, courteous, gallant, genteel, honorable, refined, urbane, well-mannered

gentleness noun TENDERNESS, compassion, kindness, mildness, softness, sweetness

gentry noun NOBILITY, aristocracy, elite, upper class, upper crust (informal)

genuine adjective 1 AUTHENTIC, actual, bona fide, legitimate, real, the real McCoy, true, veritable
2 SINCERE, candid, earnest, frank, heartfelt, honest, unaffected, unfeigned

germ noun 1 MICROBE, bacterium, bug (informal), microorganism, virus
2 BEGINNING, embryo, origin, root, rudiment, seed, source, spark

germane adjective RELEVANT, apposite, appropriate, apropos, connected, fitting, material, pertinent, related, to the point or purpose

germinate verb SPROUT, bud, develop, generate, grow, originate, shoot, swell, vegetate

gesticulate verb SIGNAL, gesture, indicate, make a sign, motion, sign, wave

gesture noun 1 SIGNAL, action, gesticulation, indication, motion, sign
▶ verb 2 SIGNAL, gesticulate, indicate, motion, sign, wave

get verb 1 OBTAIN, acquire, attain, fetch, gain, land, net, pick up, procure, receive, secure, win
2 CONTRACT, catch, come down with, fall victim to, take
3 CAPTURE, grab, lay hold of, nab (informal), seize, take
4 BECOME, come to be, grow, turn
5 UNDERSTAND, catch, comprehend, fathom, follow, perceive, see, take in, work out
6 PERSUADE, convince, induce, influence, prevail upon
7 (informal) ANNOY, bug (informal), gall, irritate, upset, vex

get across verb 1 CROSS, ford, negotiate, pass over, traverse
2 COMMUNICATE, bring home to, convey, impart, make clear or understood, put over, transmit

get along verb BE FRIENDLY, agree, be compatible, click (slang), concur, hit it off (informal)

get at verb 1 GAIN ACCESS TO, acquire, attain, come to grips

with, get hold of, reach
2 IMPLY, hint, intend, lead up to, mean, suggest
3 CRITICIZE, attack, blame, find fault with, nag, pick on
getaway noun ESCAPE, break, break-out, flight
get by verb MANAGE, cope, exist, fare, get along, keep one's head above water, make both ends meet, survive
get off verb LEAVE, alight, depart, descend, disembark, dismount, escape, exit
get on verb 1 BOARD, ascend, climb, embark, mount
2 BE FRIENDLY, be compatible, concur, get along, hit it off (informal)
get over verb RECOVER FROM, come round, get better, mend, pull through, rally, revive, survive
ghastly adjective HORRIBLE, dreadful, frightful, gruesome, hideous, horrendous, loathsome, shocking, terrible, terrifying
ghost noun 1 SPIRIT, apparition, phantom, poltergeist, soul, specter, spook (informal), wraith
2 TRACE, glimmer, hint, possibility, semblance, shadow, suggestion
ghostly adjective SUPERNATURAL, eerie, ghostlike, phantom, spectral, spooky (informal), unearthly, wraithlike
ghoulish adjective MACABRE, disgusting, grisly, gruesome, morbid, sick (informal), unwholesome
giant noun 1 OGRE, colossus, monster, titan
▶ adjective 2 HUGE, colossal, enormous, gargantuan, gigantic, immense, mammoth, titanic, vast
gibberish noun NONSENSE,

babble, drivel, gobbledegook, gobbledygook (informal), mumbo jumbo, twaddle
gibe, jibe verb 1 TAUNT, jeer, make fun of, mock, poke fun at, ridicule, scoff, scorn, sneer
▶ noun 2 TAUNT, barb, crack (slang), dig, jeer, sarcasm, scoffing, sneer
giddiness noun DIZZINESS, faintness, light-headedness, vertigo
giddy adjective DIZZY, dizzying, faint, light-headed, reeling, unsteady, vertiginous
gift noun 1 DONATION, bequest, bonus, contribution, grant, hand-out, legacy, offering, present
2 TALENT, ability, capability, capacity, flair, genius, knack, power
gifted adjective TALENTED, able, accomplished, brilliant, capable, clever, expert, ingenious, masterly, skilled
gigantic adjective ENORMOUS, colossal, giant, huge, immense, mammoth, stupendous, titanic, tremendous
giggle verb or noun LAUGH, cackle, chortle, chuckle, snigger, titter, twitter
gild verb EMBELLISH, adorn, beautify, brighten, coat, dress up, embroider, enhance, ornament
gimmick noun STUNT, contrivance, device, dodge, ploy, scheme
gingerly adverb CAUTIOUSLY, carefully, charily, circumspectly, hesitantly, reluctantly, suspiciously, timidly, warily
gird verb SURROUND, encircle, enclose, encompass, enfold, hem in, ring
girdle noun 1 BELT, band, cummerbund, sash, waistband
▶ verb 2 SURROUND, bound,

encircle, enclose, encompass,
gird, ring

girl noun FEMALE CHILD, damsel
(archaic), daughter, lass, lassie
(informal), maid (archaic), maiden
(archaic), miss

girth noun CIRCUMFERENCE, bulk,
measure, size

gist noun POINT, core, essence,
force, idea, meaning, sense,
significance, substance

give verb 1 PRESENT, award,
contribute, deliver, donate, grant,
hand over or out, provide, supply
2 ANNOUNCE, communicate, issue,
notify, pronounce, transmit, utter
3 CONCEDE, grant, hand over,
relinquish, surrender, yield
4 PRODUCE, cause, engender,
make, occasion

give away verb REVEAL, betray,
disclose, divulge, expose, leak, let
out, let slip, uncover

give in verb ADMIT DEFEAT,
capitulate, collapse, concede, quit,
submit, succumb, surrender, yield

give off verb EMIT, discharge,
exude, produce, release, send out,
throw out

give out verb EMIT, discharge,
exude, produce, release, send out,
throw out

give up verb ABANDON, call it a day
or night, cease, desist, leave off,
quit, relinquish, renounce, stop,
surrender

glad adjective 1 HAPPY, contented,
delighted, gratified, joyful,
overjoyed, pleased
2 PLEASING, cheerful, cheering,
gratifying, pleasant

gladden verb PLEASE, cheer,
delight, gratify, hearten

gladly adverb HAPPILY, cheerfully,
freely, gleefully, readily, willingly,
with pleasure

gladness noun HAPPINESS,
cheerfulness, delight, gaiety, glee,
high spirits, joy, mirth, pleasure

glamorous adjective ELEGANT,
attractive, dazzling, exciting,
fascinating, glittering, glossy,
prestigious, smart

glamour noun CHARM, allure,
appeal, attraction, beauty,
enchantment, fascination,
prestige

glance verb 1 LOOK, glimpse, peek,
peep, scan, view
2 GLEAM, flash, glimmer, glint,
glisten, glitter, reflect, shimmer,
shine, twinkle
▶ noun 3 LOOK, dekko (slang),
glimpse, peek, peep, view

glare verb 1 SCOWL, frown, glower,
look daggers, lour or lower
2 DAZZLE, blaze, flame, flare
▶ noun 3 SCOWL, black look, dirty
look, frown, glower, lour or lower
4 DAZZLE, blaze, brilliance, flame,
glow

glaring adjective 1 CONSPICUOUS,
blatant, flagrant, gross, manifest,
obvious, outrageous, unconcealed
2 DAZZLING, blazing, bright,
garish, glowing

glassy adjective 1 TRANSPARENT,
clear, glossy, shiny, slippery,
smooth
2 EXPRESSIONLESS, blank, cold,
dull, empty, fixed, glazed, lifeless,
vacant

glaze verb 1 COAT, enamel, gloss,
lacquer, polish, varnish
▶ noun 2 COAT, enamel, finish,
gloss, lacquer, patina,
polish, shine, varnish

gleam noun 1 GLOW, beam, flash,
glimmer, ray, sparkle
2 TRACE, flicker, glimmer, hint,
inkling, suggestion
▶ verb 3 SHINE, flash, glimmer,

glint, glisten, glitter, glow, shimmer, sparkle

glee noun DELIGHT, elation, exhilaration, exuberance, exultation, joy, merriment, triumph

gleeful adjective DELIGHTED, cock-a-hoop, elated, exuberant, exultant, joyful, jubilant, overjoyed, triumphant

glib adjective SMOOTH, easy, fluent, insincere, plausible, quick, ready, slick, suave, voluble

glide verb SLIDE, coast, drift, float, flow, roll, run, sail, skate, slip

glimmer verb 1 FLICKER, blink, gleam, glisten, glitter, glow, shimmer, shine, sparkle, twinkle
▶ noun 2 GLEAM, blink, flicker, glow, ray, shimmer, sparkle, twinkle
3 TRACE, flicker, gleam, hint, inkling, suggestion

glimpse noun 1 LOOK, glance, peek, peep, sight, sighting
▶ verb 2 CATCH SIGHT OF, espy, sight, spot, spy, view

glint verb 1 GLEAM, flash, glimmer, glitter, shine, sparkle, twinkle
▶ noun 2 GLEAM, flash, glimmer, glitter, shine, sparkle, twinkle, twinkling

glisten verb GLEAM, flash, glance, glare, glimmer, glint, glitter, shimmer, shine, sparkle, twinkle

glitch noun PROBLEM, blip, difficulty, gremlin, hitch, interruption, malfunction, snag

glitter verb 1 SHINE, flash, glare, gleam, glimmer, glint, glisten, shimmer, sparkle, twinkle
▶ noun 2 SHINE, brightness, flash, glare, gleam, radiance, sheen, shimmer, sparkle
3 GLAMOUR, display, gaudiness, pageantry, show, showiness, splendor, tinsel

gloat verb RELISH, brag, crow, drool, exult, glory, revel in, rub it in (informal), triumph

global adjective 1 WORLDWIDE, international, planetary, universal, world
2 COMPREHENSIVE, all-inclusive, exhaustive, general, total, unlimited

globe noun SPHERE, ball, earth, orb, planet, world

globule noun DROPLET, bead, bubble, drop, particle, pearl, pellet

gloom noun 1 DARKNESS, blackness, dark, dusk, murk, obscurity, shade, shadow, twilight
2 DEPRESSION, dejection, despondency, low spirits, melancholy, sorrow, unhappiness, woe

gloomy adjective 1 DARK, black, dim, dismal, dreary, dull, gray, murky, somber
2 DEPRESSING, bad, cheerless, disheartening, dispiriting, dreary, sad, somber
3 MISERABLE, crestfallen, dejected, dispirited, downcast, downhearted, glum, melancholy, morose, pessimistic, sad

glorify verb 1 ENHANCE, aggrandize, dignify, elevate, ennoble, magnify
2 WORSHIP, adore, bless, exalt, honor, idolize, pay homage to, revere, venerate
3 PRAISE, celebrate, eulogize, extol, sing or sound the praises of

glorious adjective 1 FAMOUS, celebrated, distinguished, eminent, honored, illustrious, magnificent, majestic, renowned
2 SPLENDID, beautiful, brilliant, dazzling, gorgeous, shining, superb

3 DELIGHTFUL, excellent, fine, gorgeous, marvelous, wonderful

glory noun 1 HONOR, dignity, distinction, eminence, fame, kudos, praise, prestige, renown
2 SPLENDOR, grandeur, greatness, magnificence, majesty, nobility, pageantry, pomp
▶ verb 3 TRIUMPH, boast, exult, pride oneself, relish, revel, take delight

gloss¹ noun SHINE, brightness, gleam, luster, patina, polish, sheen, veneer

gloss² noun 1 COMMENT, annotation, commentary, elucidation, explanation, footnote, interpretation, note, translation
▶ verb 2 INTERPRET, annotate, comment, elucidate, explain, translate

glossy adjective SHINY, bright, glassy, glazed, lustrous, polished, shining, silky

glow verb 1 SHINE, brighten, burn, gleam, glimmer, redden, smolder
▶ noun 2 LIGHT, burning, gleam, glimmer, luminosity, phosphorescence
3 RADIANCE, brightness, brilliance, effulgence, splendor, vividness

glower verb 1 SCOWL, frown, give a dirty look, glare, look daggers, lour or lower
▶ noun 2 SCOWL, black look, dirty look, frown, glare, lour or lower

glowing adjective 1 BRIGHT, aglow, flaming, luminous, radiant
2 COMPLIMENTARY, adulatory, ecstatic, enthusiastic, laudatory, rave (informal), rhapsodic

glue noun 1 ADHESIVE, cement, gum, paste
▶ verb 2 STICK, affix, cement, fix, gum, paste, seal

glum adjective GLOOMY, crestfallen, dejected, doleful, low, morose, pessimistic, sullen

glut noun 1 SURFEIT, excess, oversupply, plethora, saturation, superfluity, surplus
▶ verb 2 SATURATE, choke, clog, deluge, flood, inundate, overload, oversupply

glutton noun GOURMAND, gannet (slang), pig (informal)

gluttonous adjective GREEDY, gormandizing, insatiable, piggish, ravenous, voracious

gluttony noun GREED, gormandizing, greediness, voracity

gnarled adjective TWISTED, contorted, knotted, knotty, rough, rugged, weather-beaten, wrinkled

gnaw verb BITE, chew, munch, nibble

go verb 1 MOVE, advance, journey, make for, pass, proceed, set off, travel
2 LEAVE, depart, make tracks, move out, slope off, withdraw
3 FUNCTION, move, operate, perform, run, work
4 CONTRIBUTE, lead to, serve, tend, work towards
5 HARMONIZE, agree, blend, chime, complement, correspond, fit, match, suit
6 ELAPSE, expire, flow, lapse, pass, slip away
▶ noun 7 ATTEMPT, bid, crack (informal), effort, shot (informal), try, turn
8 (informal) ENERGY, drive, force, life, spirit, verve, vigor, vitality, vivacity

goad verb 1 PROVOKE, drive, egg on, exhort, incite, prod, prompt, spur
▶ noun 2 PROVOCATION, impetus,

incentive, incitement, irritation, spur, stimulus, urge

goal *noun* AIM, ambition, end, intention, object, objective, purpose, target

gobble *verb* DEVOUR, bolt, cram, gorge, gulp, guzzle, stuff, swallow, wolf

gobbledygook *noun* NONSENSE, babble, cant, gabble, gibberish, hocus-pocus, jargon, mumbo jumbo, twaddle

go-between *noun* INTERMEDIARY, agent, broker, dealer, mediator, medium, middleman

godforsaken *adjective* DESOLATE, abandoned, bleak, deserted, dismal, dreary, forlorn, gloomy, lonely, remote, wretched

godlike *adjective* DIVINE, celestial, heavenly, superhuman, transcendent

godly *adjective* DEVOUT, god-fearing, good, holy, pious, religious, righteous, saintly

godsend *noun* BLESSING, boon, manna, stroke of luck, windfall

go for *verb* 1 FAVOR, admire, be attracted to, be fond of, choose, like, prefer
2 ATTACK, assail, assault, launch oneself at, rush upon, set about *or* upon, spring upon

golden *adjective* 1 YELLOW, blond *or* blonde, flaxen
2 SUCCESSFUL, flourishing, glorious, halcyon, happy, prosperous, rich
3 PROMISING, excellent, favorable, opportune

gone *adjective* 1 FINISHED, elapsed, ended, over, past
2 MISSING, absent, astray, away, lacking, lost, vanished

good *adjective* 1 PLEASING, acceptable, admirable, excellent, fine, first-class, first-rate, great, satisfactory, splendid, superior
2 PRAISEWORTHY, admirable, ethical, honest, honorable, moral, righteous, trustworthy, upright, virtuous, worthy
3 EXPERT, able, accomplished, adept, adroit, clever, competent, proficient, skilled, talented
4 BENEFICIAL, advantageous, convenient, favorable, fitting, helpful, profitable, suitable, useful, wholesome, win-win (*informal*)
5 KIND, altruistic, benevolent, charitable, friendly, humane, kind-hearted, kindly, merciful, obliging
6 VALID, authentic, bona fide, genuine, legitimate, proper, real, true
7 WELL-BEHAVED, dutiful, obedient, orderly, polite, well-mannered
8 FULL, adequate, ample, complete, considerable, extensive, large, substantial, sufficient
▶ *noun* 9 BENEFIT, advantage, gain, interest, profit, use, usefulness, welfare, wellbeing
10 VIRTUE, excellence, goodness, merit, morality, rectitude, right, righteousness, worth
11 ▷▷ **for good** PERMANENTLY, finally, for ever, irrevocably, once and for all

good-bye *noun* FAREWELL, adieu, leave-taking, parting

good-for-nothing *noun* 1 IDLER, black sheep, couch potato (*slang*), layabout, ne'er-do-well, skiver (*Brit. slang*), slacker (*informal*), waster, wastrel
▶ *adjective* 2 WORTHLESS, feckless, idle, irresponsible, useless

goodly *adjective* CONSIDERABLE,

ample, large, significant, sizable
or sizeable, substantial, tidy
(*informal*)

goodness *noun* 1 EXCELLENCE,
merit, quality, superiority, value,
worth

2 KINDNESS, benevolence,
friendliness, generosity, goodwill,
humaneness, kind-heartedness,
kindliness, mercy

3 VIRTUE, honesty, honor,
integrity, merit, morality,
probity, rectitude, righteousness,
uprightness

4 BENEFIT, advantage,
salubriousness, wholesomeness

goods *plural noun* 1 PROPERTY,
belongings, chattels, effects,
gear, paraphernalia, possessions,
things, trappings

2 MERCHANDISE, commodities,
stock, stuff, wares

goodwill *noun* FRIENDLINESS,
amity, benevolence, friendship,
heartiness, kindliness

go off *verb* 1 EXPLODE, blow up,
detonate, fire

2 LEAVE, decamp, depart, go away,
move out, part, quit, slope off

3 (*informal*) ROT, go bad, go stale

go out *verb* 1 LEAVE, depart, exit

2 BE EXTINGUISHED, die out,
expire, fade out

go over *verb* EXAMINE, inspect,
rehearse, reiterate, review, revise,
study, work over

gore¹ *noun* BLOOD, bloodshed,
butchery, carnage, slaughter

gore² *verb* PIERCE, impale,
transfix, wound

gorge *noun* 1 RAVINE, canyon,
chasm, cleft, defile, fissure, pass

▶ *verb* 2 OVEREAT, cram, devour,
feed, glut, gobble, gulp, guzzle,
stuff, wolf

gorgeous *adjective* 1 BEAUTIFUL,

dazzling, elegant, magnificent,
ravishing, splendid, stunning
(*informal*), sumptuous, superb

2 (*informal*) PLEASING, delightful,
enjoyable, exquisite, fine,
glorious, good, lovely

gory *adjective* BLOODTHIRSTY,
blood-soaked, bloodstained,
bloody, murderous, sanguinary

gospel *noun* 1 TRUTH, certainty,
fact, the last word

2 DOCTRINE, credo, creed, message,
news, revelation, tidings

gossip *noun* 1 IDLE TALK, blether,
chinwag (*Brit. informal*), chitchat,
hearsay, scandal, small talk,
tittle-tattle

2 BUSYBODY, chatterbox (*informal*),
chatterer, gossipmonger,
scandalmonger, tattler, telltale

▶ *verb* 3 CHAT, blether, chew the fat
(*slang*), gabble, jaw (*slang*), prate,
prattle, tattle

go through *verb* 1 SUFFER, bear,
brave, endure, experience,
tolerate, undergo, withstand

2 EXAMINE, check, explore, forage,
hunt, look, search

gouge *verb* 1 SCOOP, chisel, claw,
cut, dig (out), hollow (out)

▶ *noun* 2 GASH, cut, furrow, groove,
hollow, scoop, scratch, trench

gourmet *noun* CONNOISSEUR, *bon
vivant*, epicure, foodie (*informal*),
gastronome

govern *verb* 1 RULE, administer,
command, control, direct, guide,
handle, lead, manage, order

2 RESTRAIN, check, control, curb,
discipline, hold in check, master,
regulate, subdue, tame

government *noun* 1 RULE,
administration, authority,
governance, sovereignty,
statecraft

2 EXECUTIVE, administration,

ministry, powers-that-be, regime

governor noun LEADER, administrator, chief, commander, controller, director, executive, head, manager, ruler

gown noun DRESS, costume, frock, garb, garment, habit, robe

grab verb SNATCH, capture, catch, catch or take hold of, clutch, grasp, grip, pluck, seize, snap up

grace noun 1 ELEGANCE, attractiveness, beauty, charm, comeliness, ease, gracefulness, poise, polish, refinement, tastefulness
2 GOODWILL, benefaction, benevolence, favor, generosity, goodness, kindliness, kindness
3 MANNERS, consideration, decency, decorum, etiquette, propriety, tact
4 INDULGENCE, mercy, pardon, reprieve
5 PRAYER, benediction, blessing, thanks, thanksgiving
▶ verb 6 HONOR, adorn, decorate, dignify, embellish, enhance, enrich, favor, ornament, set off

graceful adjective ELEGANT, beautiful, charming, comely, easy, pleasing, tasteful

gracious adjective KIND, charitable, civil, considerate, cordial, courteous, friendly, polite, well-mannered

grade noun 1 LEVEL, category, class, degree, echelon, group, rank, stage
▶ verb 2 CLASSIFY, arrange, class, group, order, range, rank, rate, sort

gradient noun SLOPE, bank, declivity, grade, hill, incline, rise

gradual adjective STEADY, gentle, graduated, piecemeal, progressive, regular, slow, unhurried

gradually adverb STEADILY, by degrees, gently, little by little, progressively, slowly, step by step, unhurriedly

graduate verb 1 MARK OFF, calibrate, grade, measure out, proportion, regulate
2 CLASSIFY, arrange, grade, group, order, rank, sort

graft noun 1 SHOOT, bud, implant, scion, splice, sprout
▶ verb 2 TRANSPLANT, affix, implant, ingraft, insert, join, splice

grain noun 1 CEREALS, corn
2 SEED, grist, kernel
3 BIT, fragment, granule, modicum, morsel, particle, piece, scrap, speck, trace
4 TEXTURE, fiber, nap, pattern, surface, weave
5 as in **go against the grain** INCLINATION, character, disposition, humor, make-up, temper

grand adjective 1 IMPRESSIVE, dignified, grandiose, great, imposing, large, magnificent, regal, splendid, stately, sublime
2 EXCELLENT, cool (informal), fine, first-class, great (informal), outstanding, phat (slang), smashing (informal), splendid, wonderful

grandeur noun SPLENDOR, dignity, magnificence, majesty, nobility, pomp, stateliness, sublimity

grandiose adjective 1 PRETENTIOUS, affected, bombastic, extravagant, flamboyant, high-flown, ostentatious, pompous, showy
2 IMPOSING, grand, impressive, lofty, magnificent, majestic, monumental, stately

grant verb 1 CONSENT TO, accede to,

agree to, allow, permit
2 GIVE, allocate, allot, assign,
award, donate, hand out, present
3 ADMIT, acknowledge, concede
▶ noun 4 AWARD, allowance,
donation, endowment, gift, hand-
out, present, subsidy

granule noun GRAIN, atom, crumb,
fragment, molecule, particle,
scrap, speck

graphic adjective 1 VIVID, clear,
detailed, explicit, expressive,
lively, lucid, striking
2 PICTORIAL, diagrammatic, visual

grapple verb 1 GRIP, clutch, grab,
grasp, seize, wrestle
2 DEAL WITH, address oneself
to, confront, get to grips with,
struggle, tackle, take on

grasp verb 1 GRIP, catch, clasp,
clinch, clutch, grab, grapple, hold,
lay or take hold of, seize, snatch
2 UNDERSTAND, catch on, catch or
get the drift of, comprehend, get,
realize, see, take in
▶ noun 3 GRIP, clasp, clutches,
embrace, hold, possession, tenure
4 CONTROL, power, reach, scope
5 UNDERSTANDING, awareness,
comprehension, grip, knowledge,
mastery

grasping adjective GREEDY,
acquisitive, avaricious, covetous,
rapacious

grate verb 1 SHRED, mince,
pulverize, triturate
2 SCRAPE, creak, grind, rasp, rub,
scratch
3 ANNOY, exasperate, get on one's
nerves (informal), irritate, jar,
rankle, set one's teeth on edge

grateful adjective THANKFUL,
appreciative, beholden, indebted,
obliged

gratification noun SATISFACTION,
delight, enjoyment, fulfillment,

indulgence, pleasure, relish,
reward, thrill

gratify verb PLEASE, delight,
give pleasure, gladden, humor,
requite, satisfy

grating¹ adjective IRRITATING,
annoying, discordant,
displeasing, harsh, jarring,
offensive, raucous, strident,
unpleasant

grating² noun GRILLE, grate, grid,
gridiron, lattice, trellis

gratitude noun THANKFULNESS,
appreciation, gratefulness,
indebtedness, obligation,
recognition, thanks

gratuitous adjective 1 FREE,
complimentary, gratis,
spontaneous, unasked-for,
unpaid, unrewarded, voluntary
2 UNJUSTIFIED, baseless, causeless,
groundless, needless, superfluous,
uncalled-for, unmerited,
unnecessary, unwarranted,
wanton

gratuity noun TIP, bonus,
donation, gift, largesse or largess,
reward

grave¹ noun BURYING PLACE, crypt,
mausoleum, pit, sepulcher,
tomb, vault

grave² adjective 1 SOLEMN,
dignified, dour, earnest, serious,
sober, somber, unsmiling
2 IMPORTANT, acute, critical,
dangerous, pressing, serious,
severe, threatening, urgent

graveyard noun CEMETERY,
burial ground, charnel house,
churchyard, necropolis

gravity noun 1 IMPORTANCE,
acuteness, momentousness,
perilousness, seriousness,
severity, significance, urgency,
weightiness
2 SOLEMNITY, dignity, earnestness,

gravitas, seriousness, sobriety

gray *adjective* 1 PALE, ashen, pallid, wan

2 DISMAL, dark, depressing, dim, drab, dreary, dull, gloomy

3 CHARACTERLESS, anonymous, colorless, dull

graze¹ *verb* FEED, browse, crop, pasture

graze² *verb* 1 TOUCH, brush, glance off, rub, scrape, shave, skim

2 SCRATCH, abrade, chafe, scrape, skin

▶ *noun* 3 SCRATCH, abrasion, scrape

greasy *adjective* FATTY, oily, oleaginous, slimy, slippery

great *adjective* 1 LARGE, big, enormous, gigantic, huge, immense, prodigious, supersize, vast, voluminous

2 IMPORTANT, critical, crucial, momentous, serious, significant

3 FAMOUS, eminent, illustrious, noteworthy, outstanding, prominent, remarkable, renowned

4 (*informal*) EXCELLENT, fantastic (*informal*), fine, marvelous, superb, terrific (*informal*), tremendous (*informal*), wonderful

greatly *adverb* VERY MUCH, considerably, enormously, exceedingly, hugely, immensely, remarkably, tremendously, vastly

greatness *noun* 1 IMMENSITY, enormity, hugeness, magnitude, prodigiousness, size, vastness

2 IMPORTANCE, gravity, momentousness, seriousness, significance, urgency, weight

3 FAME, celebrity, distinction, eminence, glory, grandeur, illustriousness, kudos, note, renown

greed, greediness *noun* 1 GLUTTONY, edacity, esurience, gormandizing, hunger, voracity

2 AVARICE, acquisitiveness, avidity, covetousness, craving, desire, longing, selfishness

greedy *adjective* 1 GLUTTONOUS, gormandizing, hungry, insatiable, piggish, ravenous, voracious

2 GRASPING, acquisitive, avaricious, avid, covetous, craving, desirous, rapacious, selfish

green *adjective* 1 LEAFY, grassy, verdant

2 ECOLOGICAL, conservationist, environment-friendly, non-polluting, ozone-friendly

3 IMMATURE, gullible, inexperienced, naive, new, raw, untrained, wet behind the ears (*informal*)

4 JEALOUS, covetous, envious, grudging, resentful

▶ *noun* 5 LAWN, common, sward, turf

greet *verb* WELCOME, accost, address, compliment, hail, meet, receive, salute

greeting *noun* WELCOME, address, reception, salutation, salute

gregarious *adjective* OUTGOING, affable, companionable, convivial, cordial, friendly, sociable, social

gridlock *noun* STANDSTILL, deadlock, impasse, stalemate

grief *noun* SADNESS, anguish, distress, heartache, misery, regret, remorse, sorrow, suffering, woe

grievance *noun* COMPLAINT, ax to grind, gripe (*informal*), injury, injustice

grieve *verb* 1 MOURN, complain, deplore, lament, regret, rue, suffer, weep

2 SADDEN, afflict, distress, hurt, injure, pain, wound

grievous *adjective* 1 PAINFUL, dreadful, grave, harmful, severe
2 DEPLORABLE, atrocious, dreadful, monstrous, offensive, outrageous, shameful, shocking

grim *adjective* FORBIDDING, formidable, harsh, merciless, ruthless, severe, sinister, stern, terrible

grimace *noun* 1 SCOWL, face, frown, sneer
▶ *verb* 2 SCOWL, frown, lour *or* lower, make a face *or* faces, sneer

grime *noun* DIRT, filth, grease, grot (*slang*), smut, soot

grimy *adjective* DIRTY, filthy, foul, grubby, scuzzy (*slang*), soiled, sooty, unclean

grind *verb* 1 CRUSH, abrade, granulate, grate, mill, pound, powder, pulverize, triturate
2 SMOOTH, polish, sand, sharpen, whet
3 SCRAPE, gnash, grate
▶ *noun* 4 (*informal*) HARD WORK, chore, drudgery, labor, sweat (*informal*), toil

grip *noun* 1 CLASP, hold
2 CONTROL, clutches, domination, influence, possession, power
3 UNDERSTANDING, command, comprehension, grasp, mastery
▶ *verb* 4 GRASP, clasp, clutch, hold, seize, take hold of
5 ENGROSS, absorb, enthrall, entrance, fascinate, hold, mesmerize, rivet

gripping *adjective* FASCINATING, compelling, engrossing, enthralling, entrancing, exciting, riveting, spellbinding, thrilling

grisly *adjective* GRUESOME, appalling, awful, dreadful, ghastly, horrible, macabre, shocking, terrifying

grit *noun* 1 GRAVEL, dust, pebbles, sand
2 COURAGE, backbone, determination, fortitude, guts (*informal*), perseverance, resolution, spirit, tenacity
▶ *verb* 3 GRIND, clench, gnash, grate

gritty *adjective* 1 ROUGH, dusty, granular, gravelly, rasping, sandy
2 COURAGEOUS, brave, determined, dogged, plucky, resolute, spirited, steadfast, tenacious

groan *noun* 1 MOAN, cry, sigh, whine
2 (*informal*) COMPLAINT, gripe (*informal*), grouse, grumble, objection, protest
▶ *verb* 3 MOAN, cry, sigh, whine
4 (*informal*) COMPLAIN, bemoan, gripe (*informal*), grouse, grumble, lament, object

groggy *adjective* DIZZY, confused, dazed, faint, shaky, unsteady, weak, wobbly

groom *noun* 1 STABLEMAN, hostler *or* ostler (*archaic*), stableboy
▶ *verb* 2 SMARTEN UP, clean, preen, primp, spruce up, tidy
3 RUB DOWN, brush, clean, curry, tend
4 TRAIN, coach, drill, educate, make ready, nurture, prepare, prime, ready

groove *noun* INDENTATION, channel, cut, flute, furrow, hollow, rut, trench, trough

grope *verb* FEEL, cast about, fish, flounder, forage, fumble, scrabble, search

gross *adjective* 1 FAT, corpulent, hulking, obese, overweight
2 TOTAL, aggregate, before deductions, before tax, entire, whole
3 VULGAR, coarse, crude, indelicate, obscene, offensive

4 BLATANT, flagrant, grievous, heinous, rank, sheer, unmitigated, utter
▶ *verb* 5 EARN, bring in, make, rake in (*informal*), take

grotesque *adjective* UNNATURAL, bizarre, deformed, distorted, fantastic, freakish, outlandish, preposterous, strange

ground *noun* 1 EARTH, dry land, land, soil, terra firma, terrain, turf
2 STADIUM, arena, field, park, pitch
3 (*often plural*) LAND, estate, fields, gardens, terrain, territory
4 (*usually plural*) DREGS, deposit, lees, sediment
5 ▶▶ **grounds** REASON, basis, cause, excuse, foundation, justification, motive, occasion, pretext, rationale
▶ *verb* 6 BASE, establish, fix, found, set, settle
7 INSTRUCT, acquaint with, familiarize with, initiate, teach, train, tutor

groundless *adjective* UNJUSTIFIED, baseless, empty, idle, uncalled-for, unfounded, unwarranted

groundwork *noun* PRELIMINARIES, foundation, fundamentals, preparation, spadework, underpinnings

group *noun* 1 SET, band, bunch, cluster, collection, crowd, gang, pack, party
▶ *verb* 2 ARRANGE, bracket, class, classify, marshal, order, sort

grouse *verb* 1 COMPLAIN, bellyache (*slang*), carp, gripe (*informal*), grumble, moan, whine, whinge (*informal*)
▶ *noun* 2 COMPLAINT, grievance, gripe (*informal*), grouch (*informal*), grumble, moan, objection, protest

grove *noun* WOOD, coppice, copse, covert, plantation, spinney, thicket

grovel *verb* HUMBLE ONESELF, abase oneself, bow and scrape, brown-nose (*slang*), crawl, creep, cringe, demean oneself, fawn, kiss ass (*slang*), kowtow, toady

grow *verb* 1 INCREASE, develop, enlarge, expand, get bigger, multiply, spread, stretch, swell
2 ORIGINATE, arise, issue, spring, stem
3 IMPROVE, advance, flourish, progress, prosper, succeed, thrive
4 BECOME, come to be, get, turn
5 CULTIVATE, breed, farm, nurture, produce, propagate, raise

grown-up *adjective* 1 MATURE, adult, fully-grown, of age
▶ *noun* 2 ADULT, man, woman

growth *noun* 1 INCREASE, development, enlargement, expansion, multiplication, proliferation, stretching
2 IMPROVEMENT, advance, expansion, progress, prosperity, rise, success
3 (*medical*) TUMOR, lump

grub *noun* 1 LARVA, caterpillar, maggot
2 (*slang*) FOOD, nosh (*slang*), rations, sustenance, victuals
▶ *verb* 3 DIG UP, burrow, pull up, root (*informal*)
4 SEARCH, ferret, forage, hunt, rummage, scour, uncover, unearth

grubby *adjective* DIRTY, filthy, grimy, messy, mucky, scruffy, scuzzy (*slang*), seedy, shabby, sordid, squalid, unwashed

grudge *verb* 1 RESENT, begrudge, complain, covet, envy, mind
▶ *noun* 2 RESENTMENT, animosity, antipathy, bitterness, dislike, enmity, grievance, rancor

grueling adjective EXHAUSTING, arduous, backbreaking, demanding, laborious, punishing, severe, strenuous, taxing, tiring

gruesome adjective HORRIFIC, ghastly, grim, grisly, horrible, macabre, shocking, terrible

gruff adjective 1 SURLY, bad-tempered, brusque, churlish, grumpy, rough, rude, sullen, ungracious

2 HOARSE, croaking, guttural, harsh, husky, low, rasping, rough, throaty

grumble verb 1 COMPLAIN, bleat, carp, gripe (informal), grouch (informal), grouse, moan, whine, whinge (informal)

2 RUMBLE, growl, gurgle, murmur, mutter, roar

▶ noun 3 COMPLAINT, grievance, gripe (informal), grouch (informal), grouse, moan, objection, protest

4 RUMBLE, growl, gurgle, murmur, muttering, roar

grumpy adjective IRRITABLE, cantankerous, crotchety, ill-tempered, peevish, sulky, sullen, surly, testy

guarantee noun 1 ASSURANCE, bond, certainty, pledge, promise, security, surety, warranty, word of honor

▶ verb 2 MAKE CERTAIN, assure, certify, ensure, pledge, promise, secure, vouch for, warrant

guard verb 1 WATCH OVER, defend, mind, preserve, protect, safeguard, secure, shield

▶ noun 2 PROTECTOR, custodian, defender, lookout, picket, sentinel, sentry, warden, watch, watchman

3 PROTECTION, buffer, defense, safeguard, screen, security, shield

4 ▷▷ **off guard** UNPREPARED, napping, unready, unwary; **on guard** PREPARED, alert, cautious, circumspect, on the alert, on the lookout, ready, vigilant, wary, watchful

guarded adjective CAUTIOUS, cagey (informal), careful, circumspect, noncommittal, prudent, reserved, reticent, suspicious, wary

guardian noun KEEPER, champion, curator, custodian, defender, guard, protector, warden

guerrilla noun FREEDOM FIGHTER, partisan, underground fighter

guess verb 1 ESTIMATE, conjecture, hypothesize, predict, speculate, work out

2 SUPPOSE, believe, conjecture, fancy, imagine, judge, reckon, suspect, think

▶ noun 3 PREDICTION, conjecture, hypothesis, shot in the dark, speculation, supposition, theory

guesswork noun SPECULATION, conjecture, estimation, supposition, surmise, theory

guest noun VISITOR, boarder, caller, company, lodger, visitant

guidance noun ADVICE, counseling, direction, help, instruction, leadership, management, teaching

guide noun 1 ESCORT, adviser, conductor, counselor, leader, mentor, teacher, usher

2 MODEL, example, ideal, inspiration, paradigm, standard

3 POINTER, beacon, guiding light, landmark, lodestar, marker, sign, signpost

4 GUIDEBOOK, Baedeker, catalog, directory, handbook, instructions, key, manual

▶ verb 5 LEAD, accompany, conduct, direct, escort, shepherd,

show the way, usher
6 STEER, command, control,
direct, handle, manage, maneuver
7 SUPERVISE, advise, counsel,
influence, instruct, oversee,
superintend, teach, train

guild noun SOCIETY, association,
brotherhood, club, company,
corporation, fellowship,
fraternity, league, lodge, order,
organization, union

guile noun CUNNING, artifice,
cleverness, craft, deceit, slyness,
trickery, wiliness

guilt noun 1 CULPABILITY,
blame, guiltiness, misconduct,
responsibility, sinfulness,
wickedness, wrongdoing
2 REMORSE, contrition, guilty
conscience, regret, self-reproach,
shame, stigma

guiltless adjective INNOCENT,
blameless, clean (slang),
irreproachable, pure, sinless,
spotless, squeaky-clean,
untainted

guilty adjective 1 RESPONSIBLE, at
fault, blameworthy, culpable,
reprehensible, sinful, to blame,
wrong
2 REMORSEFUL, ashamed,
conscience-stricken, contrite,
regretful, rueful, shamefaced,
sheepish, sorry

guise noun FORM, appearance,
aspect, demeanor, disguise, mode,
pretense, semblance, shape

gulf noun 1 BAY, bight, sea inlet
2 CHASM, abyss, gap, opening, rift,
separation, split, void

gullibility noun CREDULITY,
innocence, naivety, simplicity

gullible adjective NAIVE, born
yesterday, credulous, innocent,
simple, trusting, unsuspecting,
wet behind the ears (informal)

gully noun CHANNEL, ditch, gutter,
watercourse

gulp verb 1 SWALLOW, devour,
gobble, guzzle, quaff, swig
(informal), swill, wolf
2 GASP, choke, swallow
▶ noun 3 SWALLOW, draft,
mouthful, swig (informal)

gum noun 1 GLUE, adhesive,
cement, paste, resin
▶ verb 2 STICK, affix, cement,
glue, paste

gun noun FIREARM, handgun,
piece (slang), pistol, revolver, rifle,
saturday night special (slang)

gunman noun TERRORIST, bandit,
gunslinger (slang), killer

gurgle verb 1 MURMUR, babble,
bubble, lap, plash, purl, ripple,
splash
▶ noun 2 MURMUR, babble, purl,
ripple

guru noun TEACHER, authority,
leader, master, mentor, sage,
Svengali, tutor

gush verb 1 FLOW, cascade, flood,
pour, run, rush, spout, spurt,
stream
2 ENTHUSE, babble, chatter,
effervesce, effuse, overstate, spout
▶ noun 3 STREAM, cascade, flood,
flow, jet, rush, spout, spurt,
torrent

gust noun 1 BLAST, blow, breeze,
puff, rush, squall
▶ verb 2 BLOW, blast, squall

gusto noun RELISH, delight,
enjoyment, enthusiasm, fervor,
pleasure, verve, zeal

gut noun 1 (informal) PAUNCH, belly,
potbelly, spare tire (slang)
2 ▷▷ **guts: a** INTESTINES, belly,
bowels, entrails, innards (informal),
insides (informal), stomach, viscera
b (informal) COURAGE, audacity,
backbone, bottle (Brit. slang),

daring, mettle, nerve, pluck, spirit
▶ *verb* 3 DISEMBOWEL, clean
4 RAVAGE, clean out, despoil,
empty
▶ *adjective* 5 *as in* **gut reaction**
INSTINCTIVE, basic, heartfelt,
intuitive, involuntary, natural,
spontaneous, unthinking,
visceral

gutsy *adjective* BRAVE, bold,
courageous, determined, gritty,
indomitable, plucky, resolute,
spirited

gutter *noun* DRAIN, channel,
conduit, ditch, sluice, trench,
trough

guttural *adjective* THROATY, deep,
gravelly, gruff, hoarse, husky,
rasping, rough, thick

guy *noun* (*informal*) MAN, bloke (*Brit.
informal*), chap, dude (*slang*), fellow,
lad, person

guzzle *verb* DEVOUR, bolt, cram,
drink, gobble, stuff (oneself),
swill, wolf

Gypsy, Gipsy *noun* TRAVELER,
Bohemian, nomad, rambler,
roamer, Romany, rover, wanderer

h

habit *noun* **1** MANNERISM, custom, practice, proclivity, propensity, quirk, tendency, way
2 ADDICTION, dependence

habitation *noun* **1** DWELLING, abode, domicile, home, house, living quarters, lodging, quarters, residence
2 OCCUPANCY, inhabitance, occupation, tenancy

habitual *adjective* CUSTOMARY, accustomed, familiar, normal, regular, routine, standard, traditional, usual

hack¹ *verb* CUT, chop, hew, lacerate, mangle, mutilate, slash

hack² *noun* **1** SCRIBBLER, literary hack, penny-a-liner
2 HORSE, crock, nag

hackneyed *adjective* UNORIGINAL, clichéd, commonplace, overworked, stale, stereotyped, stock, threadbare, tired, trite

hag *noun* WITCH, crone, harridan

haggard *adjective* GAUNT, careworn, drawn, emaciated, pinched, thin, wan

haggle *verb* BARGAIN, barter, beat down

hail¹ *noun* **1** BOMBARDMENT, barrage, downpour, rain, shower, storm, volley
► *verb* **2** RAIN DOWN ON, batter, beat down upon, bombard, pelt, rain, shower

hail² *verb* **1** GREET, acclaim, acknowledge, applaud, cheer, honor, salute, welcome
2 FLAG DOWN, signal to, wave down
3 ▷▷ **hail from** COME FROM, be a native of, be born in, originate in

hair *noun* LOCKS, head of hair, mane, mop, shock, tresses

hairdresser *noun* STYLIST, barber, coiffeur *or* coiffeuse

hair-raising *adjective* FRIGHTENING, alarming, bloodcurdling, horrifying, scary, shocking, spine-chilling, terrifying

hairstyle *noun* HAIRCUT, coiffure, cut, hairdo, style

hairy *adjective* **1** SHAGGY, bushy, furry, hirsute, stubbly, unshaven, woolly
2 (*slang*) DANGEROUS, difficult, hazardous, perilous, risky

halcyon *adjective* **1** PEACEFUL, calm, gentle, quiet, serene, tranquil, undisturbed
2 *as in* **halcyon days** HAPPY, carefree, flourishing, golden, palmy, prosperous

hale *adjective* HEALTHY, able-bodied, fit, flourishing, in the pink, robust, sound, strong, vigorous, well

half *noun* **1** EQUAL PART, fifty per cent, hemisphere, portion, section
► *adjective* **2** PARTIAL, halved, limited, moderate
► *adverb* **3** PARTIALLY, in part, partly

half-baked *adjective* ILL-JUDGED, ill-conceived, impractical, poorly planned, short-sighted, unformed, unthought out *or* through

half-hearted *adjective* UNENTHUSIASTIC, apathetic, indifferent, lackluster, listless, lukewarm, perfunctory, tame

halfway *adverb* 1 MIDWAY, to *or* in the middle
▶ *adjective* 2 MIDWAY, central, equidistant, intermediate, mid, middle

halfwit *noun* FOOL, airhead (*slang*), dork (*slang*), dunderhead, idiot, imbecile (*informal*), moron, numbskull *or* numskull, schmuck (*slang*), simpleton, twit (*informal, chiefly Brit.*)

hall *noun* 1 ENTRANCE HALL, corridor, entry, foyer, hallway, lobby, passage, passageway, vestibule
2 MEETING PLACE, assembly room, auditorium, chamber, concert hall

hallmark *noun* 1 SEAL, device, endorsement, mark, sign, stamp, symbol
2 INDICATION, sure sign, telltale sign

hallucination *noun* ILLUSION, apparition, delusion, dream, fantasy, figment of the imagination, mirage, vision

halo *noun* RING OF LIGHT, aura, corona, nimbus, radiance

halt *verb* 1 STOP, break off, cease, come to an end, desist, rest, stand still, wait
2 END, block, bring to an end, check, curb, cut short, nip in the bud, terminate
▶ *noun* 3 STOP, close, end, pause, standstill, stoppage

halting *adjective* FALTERING, awkward, hesitant, labored,

stammering, stumbling, stuttering

halve *verb* BISECT, cut in half, divide equally, share equally, split in two

hammer *verb* 1 HIT, bang, beat, drive, knock, strike, tap
2 (*informal*) DEFEAT, beat, drub, run rings around (*informal*), thrash, trounce, wipe the floor with (*informal*)

hamper *verb* HINDER, frustrate, hamstring, handicap, impede, interfere with, obstruct, prevent, restrict

hand *noun* 1 PALM, fist, mitt (*slang*), paw (*informal*)
2 HIRED MAN, artisan, craftsman, employee, laborer, operative, worker, workman
3 PENMANSHIP, calligraphy, handwriting, script
4 OVATION, clap, round of applause
5 ▷▷ **at** *or* **on hand** NEARBY, at one's fingertips, available, close, handy, near, ready, within reach
▶ *verb* 6 PASS, deliver, hand over

handbook *noun* GUIDEBOOK, Baedeker, guide, instruction book, manual

handcuff *verb* SHACKLE, fetter, manacle

handcuffs *plural noun* SHACKLES, cuffs (*informal*), fetters, manacles

handful *noun* FEW, small number, smattering, sprinkling

handicap *noun* 1 DISADVANTAGE, barrier, drawback, hindrance, impediment, limitation, obstacle, restriction, stumbling block
2 ADVANTAGE, head start
3 DISABILITY, defect, impairment
▶ *verb* 4 RESTRICT, burden, encumber, hamper, hamstring, hinder, hold back, impede, limit

handicraft *noun* CRAFTSMANSHIP,

art, craft, handiwork, skill, workmanship

handiwork *noun* CREATION, achievement, design, invention, product, production

handle *noun* 1 GRIP, haft, hilt, stock
▶ *verb* 2 HOLD, feel, finger, grasp, pick up, touch
3 CONTROL, direct, guide, manage, maneuver, manipulate
4 DEAL WITH, cope with, manage

hand-out *noun* 1 CHARITY, alms, dole (*Brit. & Austral. informal*)
2 LEAFLET, bulletin, circular, literature (*informal*), mailshot, press release

handsome *adjective* 1 GOOD-LOOKING, attractive, comely, dishy (*informal, chiefly Brit.*), elegant, gorgeous, personable, well-proportioned
2 LARGE, abundant, ample, considerable, generous, liberal, plentiful, sizable *or* sizeable

handwriting *noun* PENMANSHIP, calligraphy, hand, scrawl, script

handy *adjective* 1 AVAILABLE, accessible, at hand, at one's fingertips, close, convenient, nearby, on hand, within reach
2 USEFUL, convenient, easy to use, helpful, manageable, neat, practical, serviceable, user-friendly
3 SKILLFUL, adept, adroit, deft, dexterous, expert, proficient, skilled

hang *verb* 1 SUSPEND, dangle, droop
2 EXECUTE, lynch, string up (*informal*)
▶ *noun* 3 ▷▷ **get the hang of** GRASP, comprehend, understand

hang back *verb* HESITATE, be reluctant, demur, hold back, recoil

hangdog *adjective* GUILTY, cowed, cringing, defeated, downcast, furtive, shamefaced, wretched

hangover *noun* AFTEREFFECTS, crapulence, morning after (*informal*)

hang-up *noun* PREOCCUPATION, block, difficulty, inhibition, obsession, problem, thing (*informal*)

hank *noun* COIL, length, loop, piece, roll, skein

hanker *verb* (with *for* or *after*) DESIRE, crave, hunger, itch, long, lust, pine, thirst, yearn

haphazard *adjective* DISORGANIZED, aimless, casual, hit or miss (*informal*), indiscriminate, random, slapdash

happen *verb* 1 OCCUR, come about, come to pass, develop, result, take place, transpire (*informal*)
2 CHANCE, turn out

happening *noun* EVENT, affair, episode, experience, incident, occurrence, proceeding

happily *adverb* 1 WILLINGLY, freely, gladly, with pleasure
2 JOYFULLY, blithely, cheerfully, gaily, gleefully, joyously, merrily
3 LUCKILY, fortunately, opportunely, providentially

happiness *noun* JOY, bliss, cheerfulness, contentment, delight, ecstasy, elation, jubilation, pleasure, satisfaction

happy *adjective* 1 JOYFUL, blissful, cheerful, content, delighted, ecstatic, elated, glad, jubilant, merry, overjoyed, pleased, thrilled
2 FORTUNATE, advantageous, auspicious, favorable, lucky, timely, win-win (*informal*)

happy-go-lucky *adjective* CAREFREE, blithe, easy-going, light-hearted, nonchalant, unconcerned, untroubled

harangue verb 1 RANT, address, declaim, exhort, hold forth, lecture, spout (informal)
► noun 2 SPEECH, address, declamation, diatribe, exhortation, tirade

harass verb ANNOY, bother, harry, hassle (informal), hound, persecute, pester, plague, trouble, vex

harassed adjective WORRIED, careworn, distraught, hassled (informal), strained, tormented, troubled, under pressure, vexed

harassment noun TROUBLE, annoyance, bother, hassle (informal), irritation, nuisance, persecution, pestering

harbor noun 1 PORT, anchorage, haven
► verb 2 SHELTER, hide, protect, provide refuge, shield
3 MAINTAIN, cling to, entertain, foster, hold, nurse, nurture, retain

hard adjective 1 SOLID, firm, inflexible, rigid, rocklike, stiff, strong, tough, unyielding
2 STRENUOUS, arduous, backbreaking, exacting, exhausting, laborious, rigorous, tough
3 DIFFICULT, complicated, intricate, involved, knotty, perplexing, puzzling, thorny
4 UNFEELING, callous, cold, cruel, hardhearted, pitiless, stern, unkind, unsympathetic
5 PAINFUL, disagreeable, distressing, grievous, intolerable, unpleasant
► adverb 6 ENERGETICALLY, fiercely, forcefully, forcibly, heavily, intensely, powerfully, severely, sharply, strongly, vigorously, violently, with all one's might, with might and main

7 DILIGENTLY, doggedly, industriously, persistently, steadily, untiringly

hard-boiled or **hard-bitten** adjective TOUGH, cynical, hardnosed (informal), matter-of-fact, practical, realistic, unsentimental

harden verb 1 SOLIDIFY, anneal, bake, cake, freeze, set, stiffen
2 ACCUSTOM, habituate, inure, season, train

hardened adjective 1 HABITUAL, chronic, incorrigible, inveterate, shameless
2 ACCUSTOMED, habituated, inured, seasoned, toughened

hard-headed adjective SENSIBLE, level-headed, practical, pragmatic, realistic, shrewd, tough, unsentimental

hardhearted adjective UNSYMPATHETIC, callous, cold, hard, heartless, insensitive, uncaring, unfeeling

hardiness noun RESILIENCE, resolution, robustness, ruggedness, sturdiness, toughness

hardly adverb BARELY, just, only just, scarcely, with difficulty

hardship noun SUFFERING, adversity, difficulty, misfortune, need, privation, tribulation

hard up adjective POOR, broke (informal), impecunious, impoverished, on the breadline, out of pocket, penniless, short, skint (Brit. slang), strapped for cash (informal)

hardy adjective STRONG, robust, rugged, sound, stout, sturdy, tough

harm verb 1 INJURE, abuse, damage, hurt, ill-treat, maltreat, ruin, spoil, wound
► noun 2 INJURY, abuse, damage,

hurt, ill, loss, mischief,
misfortune

harmful *adjective* DESTRUCTIVE,
damaging, deleterious,
detrimental, hurtful, injurious,
noxious, pernicious

harmless *adjective* INNOCUOUS,
gentle, innocent, inoffensive,
nontoxic, safe, unobjectionable

harmonious *adjective*
1 MELODIOUS, agreeable,
concordant, consonant, dulcet,
mellifluous, musical, sweet-
sounding, tuneful
2 FRIENDLY, agreeable, amicable,
compatible, congenial, cordial,
sympathetic

harmonize *verb* BLEND, chime
with, cohere, coordinate,
correspond, match, tally, tone
in with

harmony *noun* 1 AGREEMENT,
accord, amicability, compatibility,
concord, cooperation, friendship,
peace, rapport, sympathy
2 TUNEFULNESS, euphony, melody,
tune, unison

harness *noun* 1 EQUIPMENT, gear,
tack, tackle
▶ *verb* 2 EXPLOIT, channel, control,
employ, mobilize, utilize

harrowing *adjective* DISTRESSING,
agonizing, disturbing, heart-
rending, nerve-racking, painful,
terrifying, tormenting, traumatic

harry *verb* PESTER, badger, bother,
chivvy, harass, hassle (*informal*),
molest, plague

harsh *adjective* 1 RAUCOUS,
discordant, dissonant, grating,
guttural, rasping, rough, strident
2 SEVERE, austere, cruel,
draconian, drastic, pitiless,
punitive, ruthless, stern

harshly *adverb* SEVERELY, brutally,
cruelly, roughly, sternly, strictly

harshness *noun* SEVERITY,
asperity, austerity, brutality, rigor,
roughness, sternness

harvest *noun* 1 CROP, produce,
yield
▶ *verb* 2 GATHER, mow, pick,
pluck, reap

hassle *noun* 1 ARGUMENT,
bickering, disagreement, dispute,
fight, quarrel, row, squabble
2 TROUBLE, bother, difficulty, grief
(*informal*), inconvenience, problem
▶ *verb* 3 BOTHER, annoy, badger,
bug (*informal*), harass, hound,
pester

haste *noun* 1 SPEED, alacrity,
quickness, rapidity, swiftness,
urgency, velocity
2 RUSH, hurry, hustle, impetuosity

hasten *verb* RUSH, dash, fly, hurry
(up), make haste, race, scurry,
speed

hastily *adverb* 1 SPEEDILY,
promptly, quickly, rapidly
2 HURRIEDLY, impetuously,
precipitately, rashly

hasty *adjective* 1 SPEEDY, brisk,
hurried, prompt, rapid, swift,
urgent
2 IMPETUOUS, impulsive,
precipitate, rash, thoughtless

hatch *verb* 1 INCUBATE, breed,
bring forth, brood
2 DEVISE, conceive, concoct,
contrive, cook up (*informal*), design,
dream up (*informal*), think up

hate *verb* 1 DETEST, abhor, despise,
dislike, loathe, recoil from
2 BE UNWILLING, be loath, be
reluctant, be sorry, dislike, feel
disinclined, shrink from
▶ *noun* 3 DISLIKE, animosity,
antipathy, aversion, detestation,
enmity, hatred, hostility, loathing

hateful *adjective* DESPICABLE,
abhorrent, detestable, horrible,

loathsome, lousy (*slang*),
obnoxious, odious, offensive,
repellent, repugnant, repulsive,
scuzzy (*slang*)

hatred *noun* DISLIKE, animosity,
antipathy, aversion, detestation,
enmity, hate, repugnance,
revulsion

haughty *adjective* PROUD,
arrogant, conceited,
contemptuous, disdainful,
imperious, scornful, snooty
(*informal*), stuck-up (*informal*),
supercilious

haul *verb* 1 DRAG, draw, heave, lug,
pull, tug
▶ *noun* 2 GAIN, booty, catch,
harvest, loot, spoils, takings, yield

haunt *verb* 1 PLAGUE, obsess,
possess, prey on, recur, stay with,
torment, trouble, weigh on
▶ *noun* 2 MEETING PLACE, hangout
(*informal*), rendezvous, stamping
ground

haunted *adjective* 1 POSSESSED,
cursed, eerie, ghostly, jinxed,
spooky (*informal*)
2 PREOCCUPIED, obsessed, plagued,
tormented, troubled, worried

haunting *adjective* POIGNANT,
evocative, nostalgic, persistent,
unforgettable

have *verb* 1 POSSESS, hold, keep,
obtain, own, retain
2 RECEIVE, accept, acquire, gain,
get, obtain, procure, secure, take
3 EXPERIENCE, endure, enjoy,
feel, meet with, suffer, sustain,
undergo
4 (*slang*) CHEAT, deceive, dupe,
fool, outwit, swindle, take in
(*informal*), trick
5 GIVE BIRTH TO, bear, beget, bring
forth, deliver
6 ▷▷ **have to** BE OBLIGED, be
bound, be compelled, be forced,

have got to, must, ought, should

haven *noun* SANCTUARY, asylum,
refuge, retreat, sanctum, shelter

havoc *noun* DISORDER, chaos,
confusion, disruption, mayhem,
shambles

haywire *adjective* as in **go haywire**
TOPSY-TURVY, chaotic, confused,
disordered, disorganized, mixed
up, out of order, shambolic
(*informal*)

hazard *noun* 1 DANGER, jeopardy,
peril, pitfall, risk, threat
▶ *verb* 2 JEOPARDIZE, endanger,
expose, imperil, risk, threaten
3 as in **hazard a guess** CONJECTURE,
advance, offer, presume, throw
out, venture, volunteer

hazardous *adjective* DANGEROUS,
dicey (*informal, chiefly Brit.*),
difficult, insecure, perilous,
precarious, risky, unsafe

haze *noun* MIST, cloud, fog,
obscurity, vapor

hazy *adjective* 1 MISTY, cloudy, dim,
dull, foggy, overcast
2 VAGUE, fuzzy, ill-defined,
indefinite, indistinct, muddled,
nebulous, uncertain, unclear

head *noun* 1 SKULL, crown, loaf
(*slang*), noodle (*slang*), nut (*slang*),
pate
2 LEADER, alpha male, boss
(*informal*), captain, chief,
commander, director, manager,
master, principal, supervisor
3 TOP, crest, crown, peak,
pinnacle, summit, tip
4 BRAIN, brains (*informal*), intellect,
intelligence, mind, thought,
understanding
5 ▷▷ **go to one's head** EXCITE,
intoxicate, make conceited,
puff up; **head over heels**
UNCONTROLLABLY, completely,
intensely, thoroughly, utterly,

wholeheartedly

▶ *adjective* 6 CHIEF, arch, first, leading, main, pre-eminent, premier, prime, principal, supreme

▶ *verb* 7 LEAD, be or go first, cap, crown, lead the way, precede, top 8 CONTROL, be in charge of, command, direct, govern, guide, lead, manage, run 9 MAKE FOR, aim, go to, make a beeline for, point, set off for, set out, start towards, steer, turn

headache *noun* 1 MIGRAINE, head (*informal*), neuralgia 2 PROBLEM, bane, bother, inconvenience, nuisance, trouble, vexation, worry

heading *noun* TITLE, caption, headline, name, rubric

headlong *adverb or adjective* 1 HEADFIRST, head-on 2 HASTILY, heedlessly, helter-skelter, hurriedly, pell-mell, precipitately, rashly, thoughtlessly

▶ *adjective* 3 HASTY, breakneck, dangerous, impetuous, impulsive, inconsiderate, precipitate, reckless, thoughtless

headstrong *adjective* OBSTINATE, foolhardy, heedless, impulsive, perverse, pig-headed, self-willed, stubborn, unruly, willful

headway *noun* PROGRESS, advance, improvement, progression, way

heady *adjective* 1 INEBRIATING, intoxicating, potent, strong 2 EXCITING, exhilarating, intoxicating, stimulating, thrilling

heal *verb* CURE, make well, mend, regenerate, remedy, restore, treat

health *noun* 1 WELLBEING, fitness, good condition, healthiness, robustness, soundness, strength, vigor 2 CONDITION, constitution, fettle, shape, state

healthy *adjective* 1 WELL, active, fit, hale and hearty, in fine fettle, in good shape (*informal*), in the pink, robust, strong 2 WHOLESOME, beneficial, hygienic, invigorating, nourishing, nutritious, salubrious, salutary

heap *noun* 1 PILE, accumulation, collection, hoard, lot, mass, mound, stack 2 (*often plural*) A LOT, great deal, load(s) (*informal*), lots (*informal*), mass, plenty, pot(s) (*informal*), stack(s), tons

▶ *verb* 3 PILE, accumulate, amass, collect, gather, hoard, stack 4 CONFER, assign, bestow, load, shower upon

hear *verb* 1 LISTEN TO, catch, overhear 2 LEARN, ascertain, discover, find out, gather, get wind of (*informal*), pick up 3 (*law*) TRY, examine, investigate, judge

hearing *noun* INQUIRY, industrial tribunal, investigation, review, trial

hearsay *noun* RUMOR, gossip, idle talk, report, talk, tittle-tattle, word of mouth

heart *noun* 1 NATURE, character, disposition, soul, temperament 2 BRAVERY, courage, fortitude, pluck, purpose, resolution, spirit, will 3 CENTER, core, hub, middle, nucleus, quintessence 4 ▷▷ **by heart** BY MEMORY, by rote, off pat, parrot-fashion (*informal*), pat, word for word

heartache noun SORROW, agony, anguish, despair, distress, grief, heartbreak, pain, remorse, suffering, torment, torture

heartbreak noun GRIEF, anguish, desolation, despair, misery, pain, sorrow, suffering

heartbreaking adjective TRAGIC, agonizing, distressing, harrowing, heart-rending, pitiful, poignant, sad

heartbroken adjective MISERABLE, brokenhearted, crushed, desolate, despondent, disconsolate, dispirited, heartsick

heartfelt adjective SINCERE, deep, devout, earnest, genuine, honest, profound, unfeigned, wholehearted

heartily adverb ENTHUSIASTICALLY, eagerly, earnestly, resolutely, vigorously, zealously

heartless adjective CRUEL, callous, cold, hard, hardhearted, merciless, pitiless, uncaring, unfeeling

heart-rending adjective MOVING, affecting, distressing, harrowing, heartbreaking, poignant, sad, tragic

hearty adjective 1 FRIENDLY, back-slapping, ebullient, effusive, enthusiastic, genial, jovial, warm 2 SUBSTANTIAL, ample, filling, nourishing, sizable or sizeable, solid, square

heat verb 1 WARM UP, make hot, reheat
▶ noun 2 HOTNESS, high temperature, warmth 3 INTENSITY, excitement, fervor, fury, passion, vehemence

heated adjective ANGRY, excited, fierce, frenzied, furious, impassioned, intense, passionate, stormy, vehement

heathen noun 1 UNBELIEVER, infidel, pagan
▶ adjective 2 PAGAN, godless, idolatrous, irreligious

heave verb 1 LIFT, drag (up), haul (up), hoist, pull (up), raise, tug 2 THROW, cast, fling, hurl, pitch, send, sling, toss 3 SIGH, groan, puff 4 VOMIT, barf (slang), be sick, gag, retch, spew, throw up (informal)

heaven noun 1 PARADISE, bliss, Elysium or Elysian fields (Greek myth), hereafter, life everlasting, next world, nirvana (Buddhism, Hinduism), Zion (Christianity) 2 HAPPINESS, bliss, ecstasy, paradise, rapture, seventh heaven, utopia 3 ▷▷ **the heavens** SKY, ether, firmament

heavenly adjective 1 BEAUTIFUL, blissful, delightful, divine (informal), exquisite, lovely, ravishing, sublime, wonderful 2 CELESTIAL, angelic, blessed, divine, holy, immortal

heavily adverb 1 PONDEROUSLY, awkwardly, clumsily, weightily 2 DENSELY, closely, compactly, thickly 3 CONSIDERABLY, a great deal, copiously, excessively, to excess, very much

heaviness noun WEIGHT, gravity, heftiness, ponderousness

heavy adjective 1 WEIGHTY, bulky, hefty, massive, ponderous 2 CONSIDERABLE, abundant, copious, excessive, large, profuse

heckle verb JEER, barrack (informal), boo, disrupt, interrupt, shout down, taunt

hectic adjective FRANTIC, animated, chaotic, feverish, frenetic, heated, turbulent

hedge noun 1 BARRIER, boundary, screen, windbreak
▶ verb 2 DODGE, duck, equivocate, evade, flannel (Brit. informal), prevaricate, sidestep, temporize
3 INSURE, cover, guard, protect, safeguard, shield

heed noun 1 CARE, attention, caution, mind, notice, regard, respect, thought
▶ verb 2 PAY ATTENTION TO, bear in mind, consider, follow, listen to, note, obey, observe, take notice of

heedless adjective CARELESS, foolhardy, inattentive, oblivious, thoughtless, unmindful

heel noun (slang) SWINE, bounder (old-fashioned Brit. slang), cad (Brit. informal), louse, rat, rotter (slang, chiefly Brit.), scumbag, scuzzbucket (slang), skunk

heel over verb LEAN OVER, keel over, list, tilt

hefty adjective STRONG, big, burly, hulking, massive, muscular, robust, strapping

height noun 1 ALTITUDE, elevation, highness, loftiness, stature, tallness
2 PEAK, apex, crest, crown, pinnacle, summit, top, zenith
3 CULMINATION, climax, limit, maximum, ultimate

heighten verb INTENSIFY, add to, amplify, enhance, improve, increase, magnify, sharpen, strengthen

heir noun SUCCESSOR, beneficiary, heiress (fem.), inheritor, next in line

hell noun 1 UNDERWORLD, abyss, fire and brimstone, Hades (Greek myth), hellfire, inferno, nether world
2 TORMENT, agony, anguish, misery, nightmare, ordeal, suffering, wretchedness

hellish adjective DEVILISH, damnable, diabolical, fiendish, infernal

hello interjection WELCOME, good afternoon, good evening, good morning, greetings

helm noun 1 TILLER, rudder, wheel
2 ▷▷ **at the helm** IN CHARGE, at the wheel, in command, in control, in the driving seat, in the saddle

help verb 1 AID, abet, assist, cooperate, lend a hand, succor, support
2 IMPROVE, alleviate, ameliorate, ease, facilitate, mitigate, relieve
3 REFRAIN FROM, avoid, keep from, prevent, resist
▶ noun 4 ASSISTANCE, advice, aid, cooperation, guidance, helping hand, support

helper noun ASSISTANT, adjutant, aide, ally, attendant, collaborator, helpmate, mate, partner, right-hand man, second, supporter

helpful adjective 1 USEFUL, advantageous, beneficial, constructive, practical, profitable, timely, win-win (informal)
2 COOPERATIVE, accommodating, considerate, friendly, kind, neighborly, supportive, sympathetic

helping noun PORTION, dollop (informal), piece, plateful, ration, serving

helpless adjective WEAK, challenged, disabled, impotent, incapable, infirm, paralyzed, powerless

helter-skelter adjective
1 HAPHAZARD, confused, disordered, higgledy-piggledy (informal), hit-or-miss, jumbled, muddled, random, topsy-turvy
▶ adverb 2 CARELESSLY, anyhow,

hastily, headlong, hurriedly, pell-mell, rashly, recklessly, wildly

hem noun 1 EDGE, border, fringe, margin, trimming
▶ verb 2 ▷▷ **hem in** SURROUND, beset, circumscribe, confine, enclose, restrict, shut in

hence conjunction THEREFORE, ergo, for this reason, on that account, thus

henchman noun ATTENDANT, associate, bodyguard, follower, minder (slang), right-hand man, sidekick (slang), subordinate, supporter

henpecked adjective BULLIED, browbeaten, dominated, meek, subjugated, timid

herald noun 1 MESSENGER, crier
2 FORERUNNER, harbinger, indication, omen, precursor, sign, signal, token
▶ verb 3 INDICATE, foretoken, portend, presage, promise, show, usher in

herd noun 1 MULTITUDE, collection, crowd, drove, flock, horde, mass, mob, swarm, throng
▶ verb 2 CONGREGATE, assemble, collect, flock, gather, huddle, muster, rally

hereafter adverb 1 IN FUTURE, from now on, hence, henceforth, henceforward
▶ noun 2 AFTERLIFE, life after death, next world

hereditary adjective 1 GENETIC, inborn, inbred, inheritable, transmissible
2 INHERITED, ancestral, traditional

heredity noun GENETICS, constitution, genetic make-up, inheritance

heresy noun DISSIDENCE, apostasy, heterodoxy, iconoclasm, unorthodoxy

heretic noun DISSIDENT, apostate, dissenter, nonconformist, renegade, revisionist

heretical adjective UNORTHODOX, heterodox, iconoclastic, idolatrous, impious, revisionist

heritage noun INHERITANCE, bequest, birthright, endowment, legacy, tradition

hermit noun RECLUSE, anchorite, eremite, loner (informal), monk

hero noun 1 IDOL, champion, conqueror, star, superstar, victor
2 LEADING MAN, protagonist

heroic adjective COURAGEOUS, brave, daring, fearless, gallant, intrepid, lion-hearted, valiant

heroine noun LEADING LADY, diva, prima donna, protagonist

heroism noun BRAVERY, courage, courageousness, fearlessness, gallantry, intrepidity, spirit, valor

hesitant adjective UNCERTAIN, diffident, doubtful, half-hearted, halting, irresolute, reluctant, unsure, vacillating, wavering

hesitate verb 1 WAVER, delay, dither, doubt, hum and haw, pause, vacillate, wait
2 BE RELUCTANT, balk, be unwilling, demur, hang back, scruple, shrink from, think twice

hesitation noun 1 INDECISION, delay, doubt, hesitancy, irresolution, uncertainty, vacillation
2 RELUCTANCE, misgiving(s), qualm(s), scruple(s), unwillingness

hew verb 1 CUT, ax, chop, hack, lop, split
2 CARVE, fashion, form, make, model, sculpt, sculpture, shape, smooth

heyday noun PRIME, bloom, pink,

prime of life, salad days

hiatus *noun* PAUSE, break, discontinuity, gap, interruption, interval, respite, space

hidden *adjective* CONCEALED, clandestine, covert, latent, secret, under wraps, unseen, veiled

hide¹ *verb* 1 CONCEAL, secrete, stash (*informal*)
2 GO INTO HIDING, go to ground, go underground, hole up, lie low, take cover
3 DISGUISE, camouflage, cloak, conceal, cover, mask, obscure, shroud, veil
4 SUPPRESS, draw a veil over, hush up, keep dark, keep secret, keep under one's hat, withhold

hide² *noun* SKIN, pelt

hidebound *adjective* CONVENTIONAL, narrow-minded, rigid, set in one's ways, strait-laced, ultraconservative

hideous *adjective* UGLY, ghastly, grim, grisly, grotesque, gruesome, monstrous, repulsive, revolting, scuzzy (*slang*), unsightly

hideout *noun* HIDEAWAY, den, hiding place, lair, shelter

hierarchy *noun* GRADING, pecking order, ranking

high *adjective* 1 TALL, elevated, lofty, soaring, steep, towering
2 EXTREME, excessive, extraordinary, great, intensified, sharp, strong
3 IMPORTANT, arch, chief, eminent, exalted, powerful, superior
4 (*informal*) INTOXICATED, stoned (*slang*), tripping (*informal*)
5 HIGH-PITCHED, acute, penetrating, piercing, piping, sharp, shrill, strident
▶ *adverb* 6 ALOFT, at great height, far up, way up

highbrow *noun* 1 INTELLECTUAL, aesthete, egghead (*informal*), scholar
▶ *adjective* 2 INTELLECTUAL, bookish, cultivated, cultured, sophisticated

high-flown *adjective* EXTRAVAGANT, elaborate, exaggerated, florid, grandiose, inflated, lofty, overblown, pretentious

high-handed *adjective* DICTATORIAL, despotic, domineering, imperious, oppressive, overbearing, tyrannical, willful

highlight *noun* 1 FEATURE, climax, focal point, focus, high point, high spot, peak
▶ *verb* 2 EMPHASIZE, accent, accentuate, bring to the fore, show up, spotlight, stress, underline

highly *adverb* EXTREMELY, exceptionally, greatly, immensely, tremendously, vastly, very, very much

highly strung *adjective* NERVOUS, edgy, excitable, neurotic, sensitive, stressed, temperamental, tense, twitchy (*informal*), wired (*slang*)

hijack *verb* SEIZE, commandeer, expropriate, take over

hike *noun* 1 WALK, march, ramble, tramp, trek
▶ *verb* 2 WALK, back-pack, ramble, tramp
3 ▷▷ **hike up** RAISE, hitch up, jack up, lift, pull up

hilarious *adjective* FUNNY, amusing, comical, entertaining, humorous, rollicking, side-splitting, uproarious

hilarity *noun* LAUGHTER, amusement, exhilaration, glee, high spirits, jollity, merriment, mirth

hill noun MOUNT, fell, height, hillock, hilltop, knoll, mound, tor

hillock noun MOUND, hummock, knoll

hilly adjective MOUNTAINOUS, rolling, undulating

hilt noun HANDLE, grip, haft, handgrip

hinder verb OBSTRUCT, block, check, delay, encumber, frustrate, hamper, handicap, hold up or back, impede, interrupt, stop

hindmost adjective LAST, final, furthest, furthest behind, rearmost, trailing

hindrance noun OBSTACLE, barrier, deterrent, difficulty, drawback, handicap, hitch, impediment, obstruction, restriction, snag, stumbling block

hinge verb DEPEND, be contingent, hang, pivot, rest, revolve around, turn

hint noun 1 INDICATION, allusion, clue, implication, innuendo, insinuation, intimation, suggestion
2 ADVICE, help, pointer, suggestion, tip
3 TRACE, dash, suggestion, suspicion, tinge, touch, undertone
▶ verb 4 SUGGEST, imply, indicate, insinuate, intimate

hippie noun BOHEMIAN, beatnik, dropout

hire verb 1 EMPLOY, appoint, commission, engage, sign up, take on
2 RENT, charter, engage, lease, let
▶ noun 3 RENTAL, charge, cost, fee, price, rent

hiss noun 1 SIBILATION, buzz, hissing

2 CATCALL, boo, jeer
▶ verb 3 WHISTLE, sibilate, wheeze, whirr, whiz
4 JEER, boo, deride, hoot, mock

historic adjective SIGNIFICANT, epoch-making, extraordinary, famous, ground-breaking, momentous, notable, outstanding, remarkable

historical adjective FACTUAL, actual, attested, authentic, documented, real

history noun 1 CHRONICLE, account, annals, narrative, recital, record, story
2 THE PAST, antiquity, olden days, yesterday, yesteryear

hit verb 1 STRIKE, bang, beat, clout (informal), knock, slap, smack, thump, wallop (informal), whack
2 COLLIDE WITH, bang into, bump, clash with, crash against, run into, smash into
3 REACH, accomplish, achieve, arrive at, attain, gain
4 AFFECT, damage, devastate, impact on, influence, leave a mark on, overwhelm, touch
5 ▷▷ **hit it off** (informal) GET ON (WELL), be on good terms, click (slang), get on like a house on fire (informal)
▶ noun 6 STROKE, belt (informal), blow, clout (informal), knock, rap, slap, smack, wallop (informal)
7 SUCCESS, sensation, smash (informal), triumph, winner

hit-and-miss adjective HAPHAZARD, aimless, casual, disorganized, indiscriminate, random, undirected, uneven

hitch noun 1 PROBLEM, catch, difficulty, drawback, hindrance, hold-up, impediment, obstacle, snag
▶ verb 2 FASTEN, attach, connect,

couple, harness, join, tether, tie
3 (*informal*) HITCHHIKE, thumb
a lift
4 ▷▷ **hitch up** PULL UP, jerk, tug,
yank

hitherto *adverb* PREVIOUSLY,
heretofore, so far, thus far, until
now

hit on *verb* THINK UP, arrive at,
discover, invent, light upon, strike
upon, stumble on

hoard *noun* 1 STORE,
accumulation, cache, fund,
pile, reserve, stockpile, supply,
treasure-trove
▶ *verb* 2 SAVE, accumulate, amass,
collect, gather, lay up, put by,
stash away (*informal*), stockpile,
store

hoarse *adjective* RAUCOUS, croaky,
grating, gravelly, gruff, guttural,
husky, rasping, rough, throaty

hoax *noun* 1 TRICK, con (*informal*),
deception, fraud, practical joke,
prank, spoof (*informal*), swindle
▶ *verb* 2 DECEIVE, con (*slang*), dupe,
fool, hoodwink, swindle, take in
(*informal*), trick

hobby *noun* PASTIME, diversion,
(leisure) activity, leisure pursuit,
relaxation

hobnob *verb* SOCIALIZE, associate,
consort, fraternize, hang about,
hang out (*informal*), keep company,
mingle, mix

hoist *verb* 1 RAISE, elevate, erect,
heave, lift
▶ *noun* 2 LIFT, crane, elevator,
winch

hold *verb* 1 OWN, have, keep,
maintain, occupy, possess, retain
2 GRASP, clasp, cling, clutch,
cradle, embrace, enfold, grip
3 RESTRAIN, confine, detain,
impound, imprison
4 CONSIDER, assume, believe,

deem, judge, presume, reckon,
regard, think
5 CONVENE, call, conduct, preside
over, run
6 ACCOMMODATE, contain, have a
capacity for, seat, take
▶ *noun* 7 GRIP, clasp, grasp
8 FOOTHOLD, footing, support
9 CONTROL, influence, mastery

holder *noun* 1 OWNER, bearer,
keeper, possessor, proprietor
2 CASE, container, cover

hold forth *verb* SPEAK, declaim,
discourse, go on, lecture, preach,
spiel (*informal*), spout (*informal*)

hold-up *noun* 1 DELAY, bottleneck,
hitch, setback, snag, stoppage,
traffic jam, wait
2 ROBBERY, mugging (*informal*),
stick-up (*slang*), theft

hold up *verb* 1 DELAY, detain,
hinder, retard, set back, slow
down, stop
2 SUPPORT, prop, shore up, sustain
3 ROB, mug (*informal*), waylay

hold with *verb* APPROVE OF,
agree to *or* with, be in favor
of, countenance, subscribe to,
support

hole *noun* 1 OPENING, aperture,
breach, crack, fissure, gap, orifice,
perforation, puncture, tear, vent
2 CAVITY, cave, cavern, chamber,
hollow, pit
3 BURROW, den, earth, lair, shelter
4 (*informal*) HOVEL, dive (*slang*),
dump (*informal*), slum
5 (*informal*) PREDICAMENT,
dilemma, fix (*informal*), hot water
(*informal*), jam (*informal*), mess,
scrape (*informal*), spot (*informal*),
tight spot

holiday *noun* 1 VACATION, break,
leave, recess, time off
2 FESTIVAL, celebration, feast,
fête, gala

holiness noun DIVINITY, godliness, piety, purity, righteousness, sacredness, saintliness, sanctity, spirituality

hollow adjective 1 EMPTY, unfilled, vacant, void
2 DEEP, dull, low, muted, reverberant
3 WORTHLESS, fruitless, futile, meaningless, pointless, useless, vain
▶ noun 4 CAVITY, basin, bowl, crater, depression, hole, pit, trough
5 VALLEY, dale, dell, dingle, glen
▶ verb 6 SCOOP, dig, excavate, gouge

holocaust noun GENOCIDE, annihilation, conflagration, destruction, devastation, massacre

holy adjective 1 DEVOUT, god-fearing, godly, pious, pure, religious, righteous, saintly, virtuous
2 SACRED, blessed, consecrated, hallowed, sacrosanct, sanctified, venerable

homage noun RESPECT, adoration, adulation, deference, devotion, honor, reverence, worship

home noun 1 HOUSE, abode, domicile, dwelling, habitation, pad (slang, dated), residence
2 BIRTHPLACE, home town
3 ▷▷ **at home: a** IN, available, present **b** AT EASE, comfortable, familiar, relaxed; **bring home to** MAKE CLEAR, drive home, emphasize, impress upon, press home
▶ adjective 4 DOMESTIC, familiar, internal, local, native

homeboy or **home girl** noun (slang) FRIEND, buddy (informal), chum (informal), comrade, crony,

pal (informal)

homeland noun NATIVE LAND, country of origin, fatherland, mother country, motherland

homeless adjective 1 DESTITUTE, displaced, dispossessed, down-and-out, down on one's luck (informal)
▶ noun 2 ▷▷ **the homeless** VAGRANTS, squatters

homely adjective 1 COMFORTABLE, cosy, friendly, homespun, modest, ordinary, plain, simple, welcoming
2 (U.S.) DOWDY, dumpy (informal), frowzy, frumpish, frumpy, ugly, unattractive, unfashionable

homespun adjective UNSOPHISTICATED, coarse, dumpy (informal), homely (U.S.), home-made, plain, rough

homey adjective COMFORTABLE, cozy, friendly, homespun, modest, ordinary, plain, simple, welcoming

homicidal adjective MURDEROUS, deadly, lethal, maniacal, mortal

homicide noun 1 MURDER, bloodshed, killing, manslaughter, slaying
2 MURDERER, killer, slayer

homily noun SERMON, address, discourse, lecture, preaching

homogeneity noun UNIFORMITY, consistency, correspondence, sameness, similarity

homogeneous adjective UNIFORM, akin, alike, analogous, comparable, consistent, identical, similar, unvarying

hone verb SHARPEN, edge, file, grind, point, polish, whet

honest adjective 1 TRUSTWORTHY, ethical, honorable, law-abiding, reputable, scrupulous, truthful, upright, virtuous

2 OPEN, candid, direct, forthright, frank, plain, sincere, upfront (*informal*)

honestly *adverb* 1 ETHICALLY, by fair means, cleanly, honorably, lawfully, legally
2 FRANKLY, candidly, in all sincerity, plainly, straight (out), to one's face, truthfully

honesty *noun* 1 INTEGRITY, honor, incorruptibility, morality, probity, rectitude, scrupulousness, trustworthiness, truthfulness, uprightness, virtue
2 FRANKNESS, bluntness, candor, openness, outspokenness, sincerity, straightforwardness

honor *noun* 1 GLORY, credit, dignity, distinction, fame, kudos, prestige, renown, reputation
2 TRIBUTE, accolade, commendation, homage, praise, recognition
3 FAIRNESS, decency, goodness, honesty, integrity, morality, probity, rectitude
4 PRIVILEGE, compliment, credit, pleasure
▶ *verb* 5 RESPECT, adore, appreciate, esteem, prize, value
6 FULFILL, be true to, carry out, discharge, keep, live up to, observe
7 ACCLAIM, commemorate, commend, decorate, praise
8 ACCEPT, acknowledge, pass, pay, take

honorable *adjective* RESPECTED, creditable, estimable, reputable, respectable, virtuous

honorary *adjective* NOMINAL, complimentary, in name or title only, titular, unofficial, unpaid

hoodwink *verb* DECEIVE, con (*informal*), delude, dupe, fool, mislead, swindle, trick

hook *noun* 1 FASTENER, catch, clasp, link, peg
▶ *verb* 2 FASTEN, clasp, fix, secure
3 CATCH, ensnare, entrap, snare, trap

hooked *adjective* 1 BENT, aquiline, curved, hook-shaped
2 ADDICTED, devoted, enamored, obsessed, taken, turned on (*slang*)

hooligan *noun* DELINQUENT, lager lout, ruffian, vandal, yob or yobbo (*Brit. slang*)

hooliganism *noun* DELINQUENCY, disorder, loutishness, rowdiness, vandalism, violence

hoop *noun* RING, band, circlet, girdle, loop, wheel

hoot *noun* 1 CRY, call, toot
2 CATCALL, boo, hiss, jeer
▶ *verb* 3 JEER, boo, hiss, howl down

hop *verb* 1 JUMP, bound, caper, leap, skip, spring, trip, vault
▶ *noun* 2 JUMP, bounce, bound, leap, skip, spring, step, vault

hope *verb* 1 DESIRE, aspire, cross one's fingers, long, look forward to, set one's heart on
▶ *noun* 2 DESIRE, ambition, assumption, dream, expectation, longing

hopeful *adjective* 1 OPTIMISTIC, buoyant, confident, expectant, looking forward to, sanguine
2 PROMISING, auspicious, bright, encouraging, heartening, reassuring, rosy

hopefully *adverb* OPTIMISTICALLY, confidently, expectantly

hopeless *adjective* POINTLESS, futile, impossible, no-win, unattainable, useless, vain

horde *noun* CROWD, band, drove, gang, host, mob, multitude, pack, swarm, throng

horizon *noun* SKYLINE, vista

horizontal *adjective* LEVEL, flat, parallel

horrible *adjective* 1 TERRIFYING, appalling, dreadful, frightful, ghastly, grim, grisly, gruesome, hideous, repulsive, revolting, shocking
2 UNPLEASANT, awful, cruel, disagreeable, dreadful, horrid, lousy (*slang*), mean, nasty, scuzzy (*slang*), terrible

horrid *adjective* 1 UNPLEASANT, awful, disagreeable, dreadful, horrible, terrible
2 (*informal*) UNKIND, beastly (*informal*), cruel, mean, nasty

horrific *adjective* TERRIFYING, appalling, awful, dreadful, frightful, ghastly, grisly, horrendous, horrifying, shocking

horrify *verb* 1 TERRIFY, alarm, frighten, intimidate, make one's hair stand on end, petrify, scare
2 SHOCK, appall, dismay, outrage, sicken

horror *noun* 1 TERROR, alarm, consternation, dread, fear, fright, panic
2 HATRED, aversion, detestation, disgust, loathing, odium, repugnance, revulsion

horse *noun* NAG, colt, filly, gee-gee (*slang*), mare, mount, stallion, steed (*archaic or literary*)

horseman *noun* RIDER, cavalier, cavalryman, dragoon, equestrian

horseplay *noun* BUFFOONERY, clowning, fooling around, high jinks, pranks, romping, rough-and-tumble, skylarking (*informal*)

hospitable *adjective* WELCOMING, cordial, friendly, generous, gracious, kind, liberal, sociable

hospitality *noun* WELCOME, conviviality, cordiality, friendliness, neighborliness, sociability, warmth

host¹ *noun* 1 MASTER OF CEREMONIES, entertainer, innkeeper, landlord *or* landlady, proprietor
2 PRESENTER, anchorman *or* anchorwoman, compere (*Brit.*)
▶ *verb* 3 PRESENT, compere (*Brit.*), front (*informal*), introduce

host² *noun* MULTITUDE, army, array, drove, horde, legion, myriad, swarm, throng

hostage *noun* PRISONER, captive, pawn

hostile *adjective* 1 OPPOSED, antagonistic, belligerent, contrary, ill-disposed, rancorous
2 UNFRIENDLY, adverse, inhospitable, unsympathetic, unwelcoming

hostilities *plural noun* WARFARE, conflict, fighting, war

hostility *noun* OPPOSITION, animosity, antipathy, enmity, hatred, ill will, malice, resentment, unfriendliness

hot *adjective* 1 HEATED, boiling, roasting, scalding, scorching, searing, steaming, sultry, sweltering, torrid, warm
2 SPICY, biting, peppery, piquant, pungent, sharp
3 FIERCE, fiery, intense, passionate, raging, stormy, violent
4 RECENT, fresh, just out, latest, new, up to the minute
5 POPULAR, approved, favored, in demand, in vogue, sought-after

hot air *noun* EMPTY TALK, bombast, claptrap (*informal*), guff (*slang*), verbiage, wind

hot-blooded *adjective* PASSIONATE, ardent, excitable, fiery, impulsive, spirited, temperamental, wild

hot-headed *adjective* RASH, fiery, foolhardy, hasty, hot-tempered, impetuous, quick-tempered, reckless, volatile

hot water noun (usually preceded by in) (informal) PREDICAMENT, dilemma, fix (informal), jam (informal), mess, scrape (informal), spot (informal), tight spot

hound verb HARASS, badger, goad, harry, impel, persecute, pester, provoke

house noun 1 HOME, abode, domicile, dwelling, habitation, homestead, pad (slang, dated), residence
2 FAMILY, household
3 DYNASTY, clan, tribe
4 FIRM, business, company, organization, outfit (informal)
5 ASSEMBLY, Commons, legislative body, parliament
6 ▷▷ **on the house** FREE, for nothing, gratis
▶ verb 7 ACCOMMODATE, billet, harbor, lodge, put up, quarter, take in
8 CONTAIN, cover, keep, protect, sheathe, shelter, store

household noun FAMILY, home, house

householder noun OCCUPANT, homeowner, resident, tenant

housing noun 1 ACCOMMODATION, dwellings, homes, houses
2 CASE, casing, container, cover, covering, enclosure, sheath

hovel noun HUT, cabin, den, hole, shack, shanty, shed

hover verb 1 FLOAT, drift, flutter, fly, hang
2 LINGER, hang about
3 WAVER, dither, fluctuate, oscillate, vacillate

however adverb NEVERTHELESS, after all, anyhow, but, nonetheless, notwithstanding, still, though, yet

howl noun 1 CRY, bawl, bay, clamor,

groan, roar, scream, shriek, wail
▶ verb 2 CRY, bawl, bellow, roar, scream, shriek, wail, weep, yell

hub noun CENTER, core, focal point, focus, heart, middle, nerve center

huddle verb 1 CROWD, cluster, converge, flock, gather, press, throng
2 CURL UP, crouch, hunch up
▶ noun 3 (informal) CONFERENCE, confab (informal), discussion, meeting, powwow

hue noun COLOR, dye, shade, tinge, tint, tone

hug verb 1 CLASP, cuddle, embrace, enfold, hold close, squeeze, take in one's arms
▶ noun 2 EMBRACE, bear hug, clasp, clinch (slang), squeeze

huge adjective LARGE, colossal, enormous, gigantic, immense, mammoth, massive, monumental, supersize, tremendous, vast

hulk noun 1 WRECK, frame, hull, shell, shipwreck
2 OAF, lout, lubber, lump (informal)

hull noun FRAME, body, casing, covering, framework

hum verb 1 MURMUR, buzz, drone, purr, throb, thrum, vibrate, whir
2 BE BUSY, bustle, buzz, pulsate, pulse, stir

human adjective 1 MORTAL, manlike
▶ noun 2 HUMAN BEING, creature, individual, man or woman, mortal, person, soul

humane adjective KIND, benign, compassionate, forgiving, good-natured, merciful, sympathetic, tender, understanding

humanitarian adjective
1 COMPASSIONATE, altruistic, benevolent, charitable, humane, philanthropic, public-spirited

▶ *noun* 2 PHILANTHROPIST, altruist, benefactor, Good Samaritan

humanity *noun* 1 HUMAN RACE, Homo sapiens, humankind, man, mankind, people
2 HUMAN NATURE, mortality
3 SYMPATHY, charity, compassion, fellow feeling, kind-heartedness, kindness, mercy, philanthropy

humanize *verb* CIVILIZE, educate, enlighten, improve, soften, tame

humble *adjective* 1 MODEST, meek, self-effacing, unassuming, unostentatious, unpretentious
2 LOWLY, mean, modest, obscure, ordinary, plebeian, poor, simple, undistinguished
▶ *verb* 3 HUMILIATE, chasten, crush, disgrace, put (someone) in their place, subdue, take down a peg (*informal*)

humbug *noun* 1 FRAUD, charlatan, con man (*informal*), faker, impostor, phoney *or* phony (*informal*), swindler, trickster
2 NONSENSE, baloney (*informal*), cant, claptrap (*informal*), hypocrisy, quackery, rubbish
3 KILLJOY, scrooge (*informal*), spoilsport, wet blanket (*informal*)

humdrum *adjective* DULL, banal, boring, dreary, monotonous, mundane, ordinary, tedious, tiresome, uneventful

humid *adjective* DAMP, clammy, dank, moist, muggy, steamy, sticky, sultry, wet

humidity *noun* DAMP, clamminess, dampness, dankness, moistness, moisture, mugginess, wetness

humiliate *verb* EMBARRASS, bring low, chasten, crush, degrade, humble, mortify, put down, put (someone) in their place, shame

humiliating *adjective*
EMBARRASSING, crushing, degrading, humbling, ignominious, mortifying, shaming

humiliation *noun*
EMBARRASSMENT, degradation, disgrace, dishonor, humbling, ignominy, indignity, loss of face, mortification, put-down, shame

humility *noun* MODESTY, humbleness, lowliness, meekness, submissiveness, unpretentiousness

humor *noun* 1 FUNNINESS, amusement, comedy, drollery, facetiousness, fun, jocularity, ludicrousness
2 JOKING, comedy, farce, jesting, pleasantry, wisecracks (*informal*), wit, witticisms
3 MOOD, disposition, frame of mind, spirits, temper
▶ *verb* 4 INDULGE, accommodate, flatter, go along with, gratify, mollify, pander to

humorist *noun* COMEDIAN, card (*informal*), comic, funny man, jester, joker, wag, wit

humorous *adjective* FUNNY, amusing, comic, comical, droll, entertaining, jocular, playful, waggish, witty

hump *noun* 1 LUMP, bulge, bump, mound, projection, protrusion, protuberance, swelling
▶ *verb* 2 (*slang*) CARRY, heave, hoist, lug, shoulder

hunch *noun* 1 FEELING, idea, impression, inkling, intuition, premonition, presentiment, suspicion
▶ *verb* 2 DRAW IN, arch, bend, curve

hunger *noun* 1 FAMINE, starvation
2 APPETITE, emptiness, hungriness, ravenousness
3 DESIRE, ache, appetite, craving,

itch, lust, thirst, yearning
▶ *verb* 4 WANT, ache, crave, desire, hanker, itch, long, thirst, wish, yearn
hungry *adjective* 1 EMPTY, famished, peckish (*informal, chiefly Brit.*), ravenous, starved, starving, voracious
2 EAGER, athirst, avid, covetous, craving, desirous, greedy, keen, yearning
hunk *noun* LUMP, block, chunk, mass, nugget, piece, slab, wedge
hunt *verb* 1 STALK, chase, hound, pursue, track, trail
2 SEARCH, ferret about, forage, look, scour, seek
▶ *noun* 3 SEARCH, chase, hunting, investigation, pursuit, quest
hurdle *noun* 1 FENCE, barricade, barrier
2 OBSTACLE, barrier, difficulty, handicap, hazard, hindrance, impediment, obstruction, stumbling block
hurl *verb* THROW, cast, fling, heave, launch, let fly, pitch, propel, sling, toss
hurricane *noun* STORM, cyclone, gale, tempest, tornado, twister (*U.S. informal*), typhoon
hurried *adjective* HASTY, brief, cursory, perfunctory, quick, rushed, short, speedy, swift
hurry *verb* 1 RUSH, dash, fly, get a move on (*informal*), make haste, scoot, scurry, step on it (*informal*)
▶ *noun* 2 URGENCY, flurry, haste, quickness, rush, speed
hurt *verb* 1 HARM, bruise, damage, disable, impair, injure, mar, spoil, wound
2 ACHE, be sore, be tender, burn, smart, sting, throb
3 SADDEN, annoy, distress, grieve, pain, upset, wound

▶ *noun* 4 DISTRESS, discomfort, pain, pang, soreness, suffering
▶ *adjective* 5 INJURED, bruised, cut, damaged, harmed, scarred, wounded
6 OFFENDED, aggrieved, crushed, wounded
hurtful *adjective* UNKIND, cruel, cutting, damaging, destructive, malicious, nasty, spiteful, upsetting, wounding
hurtle *verb* RUSH, charge, crash, fly, plunge, race, shoot, speed, stampede, tear
husband *noun* 1 PARTNER, better half (*humorous*), mate, spouse
▶ *verb* 2 ECONOMIZE, budget, conserve, hoard, save, store
husbandry *noun* 1 FARMING, agriculture, cultivation, tillage
2 THRIFT, economy, frugality
hush *verb* 1 QUIETEN, mute, muzzle, shush, silence
▶ *noun* 2 QUIET, calm, peace, silence, stillness, tranquillity
hush-hush *adjective* SECRET, classified, confidential, restricted, top-secret, under wraps
husky *adjective* 1 HOARSE, croaky, gruff, guttural, harsh, raucous, rough, throaty
2 MUSCULAR, burly, hefty, powerful, rugged, stocky, strapping, thickset
hustle *verb* JOSTLE, elbow, force, jog, push, shove
hut *noun* SHED, cabin, den, hovel, lean-to, shanty, shelter
hybrid *noun* CROSSBREED, amalgam, composite, compound, cross, half-breed, mixture, mongrel
hygiene *noun* CLEANLINESS, sanitation
hygienic *adjective* CLEAN, aseptic, disinfected, germ-free, healthy,

pure, sanitary, sterile

hymn *noun* ANTHEM, carol, chant, paean, psalm

hype *noun* PUBLICITY, ballyhoo (*informal*), brouhaha, plugging (*informal*), promotion, razzmatazz (*slang*)

hypnotic *adjective* MESMERIC, mesmerizing, sleep-inducing, soothing, soporific, spellbinding

hypnotize *verb* MESMERIZE, put in a trance, put to sleep

hypocrisy *noun* INSINCERITY, cant, deceitfulness, deception, duplicity, pretense

hypocrite *noun* FRAUD, charlatan, deceiver, impostor, phoney *or* phony (*informal*), pretender

hypocritical *adjective* INSINCERE, canting, deceitful, duplicitous, false, fraudulent, phoney *or* phony (*informal*), sanctimonious, two-faced

hypothesis *noun* ASSUMPTION, postulate, premise, proposition, supposition, theory, thesis

hypothetical *adjective* THEORETICAL, academic, assumed, conjectural, imaginary, putative, speculative, supposed

hysteria *noun* FRENZY, agitation, delirium, hysterics, madness, panic

hysterical *adjective* 1 FRENZIED, crazed, distracted, distraught, frantic, overwrought, raving 2 (*informal*) HILARIOUS, comical, side-splitting, uproarious

icy *adjective* 1 COLD, biting, bitter, chill, chilly, freezing, frosty, ice-cold, raw
2 SLIPPERY, glassy, slippy (*informal or dialect*)
3 UNFRIENDLY, aloof, cold, distant, frigid, frosty, unwelcoming

idea *noun* 1 THOUGHT, concept, impression, perception
2 BELIEF, conviction, notion, opinion, teaching, view
3 PLAN, aim, intention, object, objective, purpose

ideal *adjective* 1 PERFECT, archetypal, classic, complete, consummate, model, quintessential, supreme
▶ *noun* 2 MODEL, last word, paradigm, paragon, pattern, perfection, prototype, standard

idealist *noun* ROMANTIC, dreamer, Utopian, visionary

idealistic *adjective* PERFECTIONIST, impracticable, optimistic, romantic, starry-eyed, Utopian, visionary

idealize *verb* ROMANTICIZE, apotheosize, ennoble, exalt, glorify, magnify, put on a pedestal, worship

ideally *adverb* IN A PERFECT WORLD, all things being equal, if one had one's way

identical *adjective* ALIKE, duplicate, indistinguishable, interchangeable, matching, twin

identification *noun*
1 RECOGNITION, naming, pinpointing
2 EMPATHY, association, connection, fellow feeling, involvement, rapport, relationship, sympathy

identify *verb* 1 RECOGNIZE, diagnose, make out, name, pick out, pinpoint, place, point out, put one's finger on (*informal*), spot
2 ▷▷ **identify with** RELATE TO, associate with, empathize with, feel for, respond to

identity *noun* 1 EXISTENCE, individuality, personality, self
2 SAMENESS, correspondence, unity

idiocy *noun* FOOLISHNESS, asininity, fatuousness, imbecility, inanity, insanity, lunacy, senselessness

idiom *noun* 1 PHRASE, expression, turn of phrase
2 LANGUAGE, jargon, parlance, style, vernacular

idiosyncrasy *noun* PECULIARITY, characteristic, eccentricity, mannerism, oddity, quirk, trick

idiot *noun* FOOL, chump, cretin (*offensive*), dork (*slang*), dunderhead, halfwit, imbecile, moron, nincompoop, numbskull or numskull, schmuck (*slang*), simpleton, twit (*informal, chiefly Brit.*)

idiotic *adjective* FOOLISH, asinine, bonkers (*informal*), crazy, daft (*informal*), foolhardy, harebrained, insane, moronic, senseless, stupid

idle *adjective* 1 INACTIVE, redundant, unemployed, unoccupied, unused, vacant
2 LAZY, good-for-nothing, indolent, lackadaisical, shiftless, slothful, sluggish
3 USELESS, fruitless, futile, groundless, ineffective, pointless, unavailing, unsuccessful, vain, worthless
▶ *verb* 4 (often with *away*) LAZE, dally, dawdle, kill time, loaf, loiter, lounge, potter

idleness *noun* 1 INACTIVITY, inaction, leisure, time on one's hands, unemployment
2 LAZINESS, inertia, shiftlessness, sloth, sluggishness, torpor

idol *noun* 1 GRAVEN IMAGE, deity, god
2 HERO, beloved, darling, favorite, pet, pin-up (*slang*)

idolatry *noun* ADORATION, adulation, exaltation, glorification

idolize *verb* WORSHIP, adore, dote upon, exalt, glorify, hero-worship, look up to, love, revere, venerate

idyllic *adjective* IDEALIZED, charming, halcyon, heavenly, ideal, picturesque, unspoiled

if *conjunction* PROVIDED, assuming, on condition that, providing, supposing

ignite *verb* 1 CATCH FIRE, burn, burst into flames, flare up, inflame, take fire
2 SET FIRE TO, kindle, light, set alight, torch

ignominious *adjective* HUMILIATING, discreditable, disgraceful, dishonorable, indecorous, inglorious, shameful, sorry, undignified

ignominy *noun* DISGRACE, discredit, dishonor, disrepute, humiliation, infamy, obloquy, shame, stigma

ignorance *noun* UNAWARENESS, inexperience, innocence, unconsciousness, unfamiliarity

ignorant *adjective* 1 UNINFORMED, benighted, inexperienced, innocent, oblivious, unaware, unconscious, unenlightened, uninitiated, unwitting
2 UNEDUCATED, illiterate
3 INSENSITIVE, crass, half-baked (*informal*), rude

ignore *verb* OVERLOOK, blow off (*slang*), discount, disregard, neglect, pass over, reject, take no notice of, turn a blind eye to

ill *adjective* 1 UNWELL, ailing, diseased, indisposed, infirm, off-color, poorly (*informal*), sick, under the weather (*informal*), unhealthy
2 HARMFUL, bad, damaging, deleterious, detrimental, evil, foul, injurious, unfortunate
▶ *noun* 3 HARM, affliction, hardship, hurt, injury, misery, misfortune, trouble, unpleasantness, woe
▶ *adverb* 4 BADLY, inauspiciously, poorly, unfavorably, unfortunately, unluckily
5 HARDLY, barely, by no means, scantily

ill-advised *adjective* MISGUIDED, foolhardy, ill-considered, ill-judged, imprudent, incautious, injudicious, rash, reckless, thoughtless, unwise

ill-disposed *adjective* UNFRIENDLY, antagonistic, disobliging, hostile, inimical, uncooperative, unwelcoming

illegal *adjective* UNLAWFUL, banned, criminal, felonious, forbidden, illicit, outlawed, prohibited, unauthorized, unlicensed

illegality noun CRIME, felony, illegitimacy, lawlessness, wrong

illegible adjective INDECIPHERABLE, obscure, scrawled, unreadable

illegitimate adjective 1 UNLAWFUL, illegal, illicit, improper, unauthorized
2 BORN OUT OF WEDLOCK, bastard

ill-fated adjective DOOMED, hapless, ill-omened, ill-starred, luckless, star-crossed, unfortunate, unhappy, unlucky

illicit adjective 1 ILLEGAL, criminal, felonious, illegitimate, prohibited, unauthorized, unlawful, unlicensed
2 FORBIDDEN, clandestine, furtive, guilty, immoral, improper

illiterate adjective UNEDUCATED, ignorant, uncultured, untaught, untutored

ill-mannered adjective RUDE, badly behaved, boorish, churlish, discourteous, impolite, insolent, loutish, uncouth

illness noun DISEASE, affliction, ailment, disorder, infirmity, malady, sickness

illogical adjective IRRATIONAL, absurd, inconsistent, invalid, meaningless, senseless, unreasonable, unscientific, unsound

ill-treat verb ABUSE, damage, harm, injure, maltreat, mishandle, misuse, oppress

illuminate verb 1 LIGHT UP, brighten
2 EXPLAIN, clarify, clear up, elucidate, enlighten, interpret, make clear, shed light on

illuminating adjective INFORMATIVE, enlightening, explanatory, helpful, instructive, revealing

illumination noun 1 LIGHT, brightness, lighting, radiance
2 ENLIGHTENMENT, clarification, insight, revelation

illusion noun 1 FANTASY, chimera, daydream, figment of the imagination, hallucination, mirage, will-o'-the-wisp
2 MISCONCEPTION, deception, delusion, error, fallacy, misapprehension

illusory adjective UNREAL, chimerical, deceptive, delusive, fallacious, false, hallucinatory, mistaken, sham

illustrate verb DEMONSTRATE, bring home, elucidate, emphasize, explain, point up, show

illustrated adjective PICTORIAL, decorated, graphic

illustration noun 1 EXAMPLE, case, instance, specimen
2 PICTURE, decoration, figure, plate, sketch

illustrious adjective FAMOUS, celebrated, distinguished, eminent, glorious, great, notable, prominent, renowned

ill will noun HOSTILITY, animosity, bad blood, dislike, enmity, hatred, malice, rancor, resentment, venom

image noun 1 REPRESENTATION, effigy, figure, icon, idol, likeness, picture, portrait, statue
2 REPLICA, counterpart, (dead) ringer (slang), Doppelgänger, double, facsimile, spitting image (informal)
3 CONCEPT, idea, impression, mental picture, perception

imaginable adjective POSSIBLE, believable, comprehensible, conceivable, credible, likely, plausible

imaginary adjective FICTIONAL,

fictitious, hypothetical, illusory, imagined, invented, made-up, nonexistent, unreal

imagination noun 1 CREATIVITY, enterprise, ingenuity, invention, inventiveness, originality, resourcefulness, vision
2 UNREALITY, illusion, supposition

imaginative adjective CREATIVE, clever, enterprising, ingenious, inspired, inventive, original

imagine verb 1 ENVISAGE, conceive, conceptualize, conjure up, picture, plan, think of, think up, visualize
2 BELIEVE, assume, conjecture, fancy, guess (informal), infer, suppose, surmise, suspect, take it, think

imbecile noun 1 IDIOT, chump, cretin (offensive), dork (slang), fool, halfwit, moron, numbskull or numskull, schmuck (slang), thickhead, twit (informal, chiefly Brit.)
▶ adjective 2 STUPID, asinine, fatuous, feeble-minded, foolish, idiotic, moronic, thick, witless

imbibe verb 1 DRINK, consume, knock back (informal), quaff, sink (informal), swallow, swig (informal)
2 (literary) ABSORB, acquire, assimilate, gain, gather, ingest, receive, take in

imbroglio noun COMPLICATION, embarrassment, entanglement, involvement, misunderstanding, quandary

imitate verb COPY, ape, echo, emulate, follow, mimic, mirror, repeat, simulate

imitation noun 1 MIMICRY, counterfeiting, duplication, likeness, resemblance, simulation
2 REPLICA, fake, forgery, impersonation, impression, reproduction, sham, substitution
▶ adjective 3 ARTIFICIAL, dummy, ersatz, man-made, mock, phoney or phony (informal), reproduction, sham, simulated, synthetic

imitative adjective DERIVATIVE, copycat (informal), mimetic, parrot-like, second-hand, simulated, unoriginal

imitator noun IMPERSONATOR, copier, copycat (informal), impressionist, mimic, parrot

immaculate adjective 1 CLEAN, neat, spick-and-span, spotless, spruce, squeaky-clean
2 FLAWLESS, above reproach, faultless, impeccable, perfect, unblemished, unexceptionable, untarnished

immaterial adjective IRRELEVANT, extraneous, inconsequential, inessential, insignificant, of no importance, trivial, unimportant

immature adjective 1 YOUNG, adolescent, undeveloped, unformed, unripe
2 CHILDISH, callow, inexperienced, infantile, juvenile, puerile

immaturity noun 1 UNRIPENESS, greenness, imperfection, rawness, unpreparedness
2 CHILDISHNESS, callowness, inexperience, puerility

immediate adjective 1 INSTANT, instantaneous
2 NEAREST, close, direct, near, next

immediately adverb AT ONCE, directly, forthwith, instantly, now, promptly, right away, straight away, this instant, without delay

immense adjective HUGE, colossal, enormous, extensive, gigantic, great, massive, monumental, stupendous, tremendous, vast

immensity noun SIZE, bulk,

enormity, expanse, extent, greatness, hugeness, magnitude, vastness

immerse *verb* 1 PLUNGE, bathe, dip, douse, duck, dunk, sink, submerge
2 ENGROSS, absorb, busy, engage, involve, occupy, take up

immersion *noun* 1 DIPPING, dousing, ducking, dunking, plunging, submerging
2 INVOLVEMENT, absorption, concentration, preoccupation

immigrant *noun* SETTLER, incomer, newcomer

imminent *adjective* NEAR, at hand, close, coming, forthcoming, gathering, impending, in the pipeline, looming

immobile *adjective* STATIONARY, at a standstill, at rest, fixed, immovable, motionless, rigid, rooted, static, still, stock-still, unmoving

immobility *noun* STILLNESS, fixity, inertness, motionlessness, stability, steadiness

immobilize *verb* PARALYZE, bring to a standstill, cripple, disable, freeze, halt, stop, transfix

immoderate *adjective* EXCESSIVE, exaggerated, exorbitant, extravagant, extreme, inordinate, over the top (*slang*), undue, unjustified, unreasonable

immoral *adjective* WICKED, bad, corrupt, debauched, depraved, dissolute, indecent, sinful, unethical, unprincipled, wrong

immorality *noun* WICKEDNESS, corruption, debauchery, depravity, dissoluteness, sin, vice, wrong

immortal *adjective* 1 ETERNAL, deathless, enduring, everlasting, imperishable, lasting, perennial, undying

▶ *noun* 2 GOD, goddess
3 GREAT, genius, hero

immortality *noun* 1 ETERNITY, everlasting life, perpetuity
2 FAME, celebrity, glory, greatness, renown

immortalize *verb* COMMEMORATE, celebrate, exalt, glorify

immovable *adjective* 1 FIXED, firm, immutable, jammed, secure, set, stable, stationary, stuck
2 INFLEXIBLE, adamant, obdurate, resolute, steadfast, unshakable, unwavering, unyielding

immune *adjective* EXEMPT, clear, free, invulnerable, proof (against), protected, resistant, safe, unaffected

immunity *noun* 1 EXEMPTION, amnesty, freedom, indemnity, invulnerability, license, release
2 RESISTANCE, immunization, protection

immunize *verb* VACCINATE, inoculate, protect, safeguard

imp *noun* 1 DEMON, devil, sprite
2 RASCAL, brat, minx, rogue, scamp

impact *noun* 1 COLLISION, blow, bump, contact, crash, jolt, knock, smash, stroke, thump
2 EFFECT, consequences, impression, influence, repercussions, significance
▶ *verb* 3 HIT, clash, collide, crash, crush, strike

impair *verb* WORSEN, blunt, damage, decrease, diminish, harm, hinder, injure, lessen, reduce, undermine, weaken

impaired *adjective* DAMAGED, defective, faulty, flawed, imperfect, unsound

impart *verb* 1 COMMUNICATE, convey, disclose, divulge, make known, pass on, relate, reveal, tell

2 GIVE, accord, afford, bestow, confer, grant, lend, yield

impartial *adjective* NEUTRAL, detached, disinterested, equitable, even-handed, fair, just, objective, open-minded, unbiased, unprejudiced

impartiality *noun* NEUTRALITY, detachment, disinterestedness, dispassion, equity, even-handedness, fairness, objectivity, open-mindedness

impassable *adjective* BLOCKED, closed, impenetrable, obstructed

impasse *noun* DEADLOCK, dead end, gridlock, stalemate, standoff, standstill

impassioned *adjective* INTENSE, animated, fervent, fiery, heated, inspired, passionate, rousing, stirring

impatience *noun* 1 HASTE, impetuosity, intolerance, rashness
2 RESTLESSNESS, agitation, anxiety, eagerness, edginess, fretfulness, nervousness, uneasiness

impatient *adjective* 1 HASTY, demanding, hot-tempered, impetuous, intolerant
2 RESTLESS, eager, edgy, fretful, straining at the leash

impeach *verb* CHARGE, accuse, arraign, indict

impeccable *adjective* FAULTLESS, blameless, flawless, immaculate, irreproachable, perfect, unblemished, unimpeachable

impecunious *adjective* POOR, broke (*informal*), destitute, down and out, down on one's luck (*informal*), indigent, insolvent, penniless, poverty-stricken

impede *verb* HINDER, block, check, disrupt, hamper, hold up, obstruct, slow (down), thwart

impediment *noun* OBSTACLE, barrier, difficulty, encumbrance, hindrance, obstruction, snag, stumbling block

impel *verb* FORCE, compel, constrain, drive, induce, oblige, push, require

impending *adjective* LOOMING, approaching, coming, forthcoming, gathering, imminent, in the pipeline, near, upcoming

impenetrable *adjective* 1 SOLID, dense, impassable, impermeable, impervious, inviolable, thick
2 INCOMPREHENSIBLE, arcane, enigmatic, inscrutable, mysterious, obscure, unfathomable, unintelligible

imperative *adjective* URGENT, crucial, essential, pressing, vital

imperceptible *adjective* UNDETECTABLE, faint, indiscernible, microscopic, minute, slight, small, subtle, tiny

imperfect *adjective* FLAWED, damaged, defective, faulty, impaired, incomplete, limited, unfinished

imperfection *noun* FAULT, blemish, defect, deficiency, failing, flaw, frailty, shortcoming, taint, weakness

imperial *adjective* ROYAL, kingly, majestic, princely, queenly, regal, sovereign

imperil *verb* ENDANGER, expose, jeopardize, risk

impersonal *adjective* REMOTE, aloof, cold, detached, dispassionate, formal, inhuman, neutral

impersonate *verb* IMITATE, ape, do (*informal*), masquerade as, mimic, pass oneself off as, pose as (*informal*), take off (*informal*)

impersonation *noun* IMITATION, caricature, impression, mimicry, parody, takeoff (*informal*)

impertinence *noun* RUDENESS, brazenness, cheek (*informal*), disrespect, effrontery, front, impudence, insolence, nerve (*informal*), presumption

impertinent *adjective* RUDE, brazen, cheeky (*informal*), disrespectful, impolite, impudent, insolent, presumptuous

imperturbable *adjective* CALM, collected, composed, cool, nerveless, self-possessed, serene, unexcitable, unflappable (*informal*), unruffled

impervious *adjective* 1 SEALED, impassable, impenetrable, impermeable, resistant
2 UNAFFECTED, immune, invulnerable, proof against, unmoved, untouched

impetuosity *noun* HASTE, impulsiveness, precipitateness, rashness

impetuous *adjective* RASH, hasty, impulsive, precipitate, unthinking

impetus *noun* 1 INCENTIVE, catalyst, goad, impulse, motivation, push, spur, stimulus
2 FORCE, energy, momentum, power

impinge *verb* 1 ENCROACH, infringe, invade, obtrude, trespass, violate
2 AFFECT, bear upon, have a bearing on, impact, influence, relate to, touch

impious *adjective* SACRILEGIOUS, blasphemous, godless, irreligious, irreverent, profane, sinful, ungodly, unholy, wicked

impish *adjective* MISCHIEVOUS, devilish, puckish, rascally, roguish, sportive, waggish

implacable *adjective* UNYIELDING, inflexible, intractable, merciless, pitiless, unbending, uncompromising, unforgiving

implant *verb* 1 INSTILL, inculcate, infuse
2 INSERT, fix, graft

implement *verb* 1 CARRY OUT, bring about, complete, effect, enforce, execute, fulfill, perform, realize
▶ *noun* 2 TOOL, apparatus, appliance, device, gadget, instrument, utensil

implicate *verb* INCRIMINATE, associate, embroil, entangle, include, inculpate, involve

implication *noun* SUGGESTION, inference, innuendo, meaning, overtone, presumption, significance

implicit *adjective* 1 IMPLIED, inferred, latent, tacit, taken for granted, undeclared, understood, unspoken
2 ABSOLUTE, constant, firm, fixed, full, steadfast, unqualified, unreserved, wholehearted

implied *adjective* UNSPOKEN, hinted at, implicit, indirect, suggested, tacit, undeclared, unexpressed, unstated

implore *verb* BEG, beseech, entreat, importune, plead with, pray

imply *verb* 1 HINT, insinuate, intimate, signify, suggest
2 ENTAIL, indicate, involve, mean, point to, presuppose

impolite *adjective* BAD-MANNERED, discourteous, disrespectful, ill-mannered, insolent, loutish, rude, uncouth

impoliteness *noun* BAD MANNERS,

boorishness, churlishness, discourtesy, disrespect, insolence, rudeness

import verb 1 BRING IN, introduce
▶ noun 2 MEANING, drift, gist, implication, intention, sense, significance, thrust
3 IMPORTANCE, consequence, magnitude, moment, significance, substance, weight

importance noun 1 SIGNIFICANCE, concern, consequence, import, interest, moment, substance, usefulness, value, weight
2 PRESTIGE, distinction, eminence, esteem, influence, prominence, standing, status

important adjective 1 SIGNIFICANT, far-reaching, momentous, seminal, serious, substantial, urgent, weighty
2 POWERFUL, eminent, high-ranking, influential, noteworthy, pre-eminent, prominent

importunate adjective
PERSISTENT, demanding, dogged, insistent, pressing, urgent

impose verb 1 ESTABLISH, decree, fix, institute, introduce, levy, ordain
2 INFLICT, appoint, enforce, saddle (someone) with

imposing adjective IMPRESSIVE, commanding, dignified, grand, majestic, stately, striking

imposition noun 1 APPLICATION, introduction, levying
2 INTRUSION, liberty, presumption

impossibility noun
HOPELESSNESS, impracticability, inability

impossible adjective
1 UNATTAINABLE, impracticable, inconceivable, out of the question, unachievable, unobtainable, unthinkable

2 ABSURD, ludicrous, outrageous, preposterous, unreasonable

impostor noun IMPERSONATOR, charlatan, deceiver, fake, fraud, phoney or phony (informal), pretender, sham, trickster

impotence noun POWERLESSNESS, feebleness, frailty, helplessness, inability, incapacity, incompetence, ineffectiveness, paralysis, uselessness, weakness

impotent adjective POWERLESS, feeble, frail, helpless, incapable, incapacitated, incompetent, ineffective, paralyzed, weak

impoverish verb 1 BANKRUPT, beggar, break, ruin
2 DIMINISH, deplete, drain, exhaust, reduce, sap, use up, wear out

impoverished adjective
POOR, bankrupt, destitute, impecunious, needy, on one's uppers (informal), penurious, poverty-stricken

impracticable adjective
UNFEASIBLE, impossible, out of the question, unachievable, unattainable, unworkable

impractical adjective
1 UNWORKABLE, impossible, impracticable, inoperable, nonviable, unrealistic, wild
2 IDEALISTIC, romantic, starry-eyed, unrealistic

imprecise adjective INDEFINITE, equivocal, hazy, ill-defined, indeterminate, inexact, inexplicit, loose, rough, vague, woolly

impregnable adjective
INVULNERABLE, impenetrable, indestructible, invincible, secure, unassailable, unbeatable, unconquerable

impregnate verb 1 SATURATE,

infuse, permeate, soak, steep, suffuse

2 FERTILIZE, inseminate, make pregnant

impress verb 1 EXCITE, affect, inspire, make an impression, move, stir, strike, touch

2 STRESS, bring home to, emphasize, fix, inculcate, instill into

3 IMPRINT, emboss, engrave, indent, mark, print, stamp

impression noun 1 EFFECT, feeling, impact, influence, reaction

2 IDEA, belief, conviction, feeling, hunch, notion, sense, suspicion

3 MARK, dent, hollow, imprint, indentation, outline, stamp

4 IMITATION, impersonation, parody, send-up (Brit. informal), takeoff (informal)

impressionable adjective SUGGESTIBLE, gullible, ingenuous, open, receptive, responsive, sensitive, susceptible, vulnerable

impressive adjective GRAND, awesome, cool (informal), dramatic, exciting, moving, phat (slang), powerful, stirring, striking

imprint noun 1 MARK, impression, indentation, sign, stamp

▶ verb 2 FIX, engrave, etch, impress, print, stamp

imprison verb JAIL, confine, detain, incarcerate, intern, lock up, put away, send down (informal)

imprisoned adjective JAILED, behind bars, captive, confined, incarcerated, in jail, inside (slang), locked up, under lock and key

imprisonment noun CUSTODY, confinement, detention, incarceration, porridge (slang)

improbability noun DOUBT, dubiety, uncertainty, unlikelihood

improbable adjective DOUBTFUL, dubious, fanciful, far-fetched, implausible, questionable, unconvincing, unlikely, weak

impromptu adjective UNPREPARED, ad-lib, extemporaneous, improvised, offhand, off the cuff (informal), spontaneous, unrehearsed, unscripted

improper adjective 1 INDECENT, risqué, smutty, suggestive, unbecoming, unseemly, untoward, vulgar

2 UNWARRANTED, inappropriate, out of place, uncalled-for, unfit, unsuitable

impropriety noun INDECENCY, bad taste, incongruity, vulgarity

improve verb 1 ENHANCE, advance, better, correct, help, rectify, touch up, upgrade

2 PROGRESS, develop, make strides, pick up, rally, rise

improvement noun

1 ENHANCEMENT, advancement, betterment

2 PROGRESS, development, rally, recovery, upswing

improvident adjective IMPRUDENT, careless, negligent, prodigal, profligate, reckless, short-sighted, spendthrift, thoughtless, wasteful

improvisation noun

1 SPONTANEITY, ad-libbing, extemporizing, invention

2 MAKESHIFT, ad-lib, expedient

improvise verb 1 EXTEMPORIZE, ad-lib, busk, invent, play it by ear (informal), speak off the cuff (informal), wing it (informal)

2 CONCOCT, contrive, devise, throw together

imprudent adjective UNWISE, careless, foolhardy, ill-advised, ill-considered, ill-judged, injudicious, irresponsible, rash, reckless

impudence noun BOLDNESS, audacity, brazenness, cheek (*informal*), effrontery, impertinence, insolence, nerve (*informal*), presumption, shamelessness

impudent adjective BOLD, audacious, brazen, cheeky (*informal*), impertinent, insolent, pert, presumptuous, rude, shameless

impulse noun URGE, caprice, feeling, inclination, notion, whim, wish

impulsive adjective INSTINCTIVE, devil-may-care, hasty, impetuous, intuitive, passionate, precipitate, rash, spontaneous

impunity noun SECURITY, dispensation, exemption, freedom, immunity, liberty, license, permission

impure adjective 1 UNREFINED, adulterated, debased, mixed
2 CONTAMINATED, defiled, dirty, infected, polluted, tainted
3 IMMORAL, corrupt, indecent, lascivious, lewd, licentious, obscene, unchaste

impurity noun CONTAMINATION, defilement, dirtiness, infection, pollution, taint

imputation noun BLAME, accusation, aspersion, censure, insinuation, reproach, slander, slur

inability noun INCAPABILITY, disability, disqualification, impotence, inadequacy, incapacity, incompetence, ineptitude, powerlessness

inaccessible adjective OUT OF REACH, impassable, out of the way, remote, unapproachable, unattainable, unreachable

inaccuracy noun ERROR, defect, erratum, fault, lapse, mistake

inaccurate adjective INCORRECT, defective, erroneous, faulty, imprecise, mistaken, out, unreliable, unsound, wrong

inactive adjective UNUSED, dormant, idle, inoperative, unemployed, unoccupied

inactivity noun IMMOBILITY, dormancy, hibernation, inaction, passivity, unemployment

inadequacy noun 1 SHORTAGE, dearth, insufficiency, meagerness, paucity, poverty, scantiness
2 INCOMPETENCE, deficiency, inability, incapacity, ineffectiveness
3 SHORTCOMING, defect, failing, imperfection, weakness

inadequate adjective
1 INSUFFICIENT, meager, scant, sketchy, sparse
2 INCOMPETENT, deficient, faulty, found wanting, incapable, lousy (*slang*), not up to scratch (*informal*), unqualified

inadmissible adjective UNACCEPTABLE, inappropriate, irrelevant, unallowable

inadvertently adverb UNINTENTIONALLY, accidentally, by accident, by mistake, involuntarily, mistakenly, unwittingly

inadvisable adjective UNWISE, ill-advised, impolitic, imprudent, inexpedient, injudicious

inane adjective SENSELESS, empty, fatuous, frivolous, futile, idiotic, mindless, silly, stupid, vacuous

inanimate adjective LIFELESS, cold, dead, defunct, extinct, inert

inapplicable adjective IRRELEVANT,

inappropriate, unsuitable

inappropriate *adjective*
UNSUITABLE, improper,
incongruous, out of place,
unbecoming, unbefitting,
unfitting, unseemly, untimely

inarticulate *adjective* FALTERING,
halting, hesitant, poorly spoken

inattention *noun* NEGLECT,
absent-mindedness, carelessness,
daydreaming, inattentiveness,
preoccupation, thoughtlessness

inattentive *adjective*
PREOCCUPIED, careless, distracted,
dreamy, negligent, unobservant,
vague

inaudible *adjective* INDISTINCT,
low, mumbling, out of earshot,
stifled, unheard

inaugural *adjective* FIRST, initial,
introductory, maiden, opening

inaugurate *verb* 1 LAUNCH,
begin, commence, get under way,
initiate, institute, introduce, set
in motion
2 INVEST, induct, install

inauguration *noun* 1 LAUNCH,
initiation, institution, opening,
setting up
2 INVESTITURE, induction,
installation

inauspicious *adjective*
UNPROMISING, bad, discouraging,
ill-omened, ominous,
unfavorable, unfortunate,
unlucky, unpropitious

inborn *adjective* NATURAL,
congenital, hereditary, inbred,
ingrained, inherent, innate,
instinctive, intuitive, native

inbred *adjective* INNATE,
constitutional, deep-seated,
ingrained, inherent, native,
natural

incalculable *adjective* COUNTLESS,
boundless, infinite, innumerable,
limitless, numberless, untold,
vast

incantation *noun* CHANT, charm,
formula, invocation, spell

incapable *adjective*
1 INCOMPETENT, feeble,
inadequate, ineffective, inept,
inexpert, insufficient, lousy
(*slang*), unfit, unqualified, weak
2 UNABLE, helpless, impotent,
powerless

incapacitate *verb* DISABLE,
cripple, immobilize, lay up
(*informal*), paralyze, put out of
action (*informal*)

incapacitated *adjective*
INDISPOSED, *hors de combat*,
immobilized, laid up (*informal*), out
of action (*informal*), unfit

incapacity *noun* INABILITY,
impotence, inadequacy,
incapability, incompetency,
ineffectiveness, powerlessness,
unfitness, weakness

incarcerate *verb* IMPRISON,
confine, detain, impound, intern,
jail, lock up, throw in jail

incarceration *noun*
IMPRISONMENT, captivity,
confinement, detention,
internment

incarnate *adjective* PERSONIFIED,
embodied, typified

incarnation *noun* EMBODIMENT,
epitome, manifestation,
personification, type

incense¹ *verb* ANGER, enrage,
inflame, infuriate, irritate,
madden, make one's hackles rise,
rile (*informal*)

incensed *adjective* ANGRY, enraged,
fuming, furious, indignant,
infuriated, irate, maddened,
steamed up (*slang*), up in arms

incentive *noun* ENCOURAGEMENT,
bait, carrot (*informal*), enticement,

inducement, lure, motivation, spur, stimulus

inception noun BEGINNING, birth, commencement, dawn, initiation, origin, outset, start

incessant adjective ENDLESS, ceaseless, constant, continual, eternal, interminable, never-ending, nonstop, perpetual, twenty-four-seven (*slang*), unceasing, unending

incessantly adverb ENDLESSLY, ceaselessly, constantly, continually, eternally, interminably, nonstop, perpetually, persistently, twenty-four-seven (*slang*)

incident noun 1 HAPPENING, adventure, episode, event, fact, matter, occasion, occurrence
2 DISTURBANCE, clash, commotion, confrontation, contretemps, scene

incidental adjective SECONDARY, ancillary, minor, nonessential, occasional, subordinate, subsidiary

incidentally adverb PARENTHETICALLY, by the bye, by the way, in passing

incinerate verb BURN UP, carbonize, char, cremate, reduce to ashes

incipient adjective BEGINNING, commencing, developing, embryonic, inchoate, nascent, starting

incision noun CUT, gash, notch, opening, slash, slit

incisive adjective PENETRATING, acute, keen, perspicacious, piercing, trenchant

incite verb PROVOKE, encourage, foment, inflame, instigate, spur, stimulate, stir up, urge, whip up

incitement noun PROVOCATION,

agitation, encouragement, impetus, instigation, prompting, spur, stimulus

incivility noun RUDENESS, bad manners, boorishness, discourteousness, discourtesy, disrespect, ill-breeding, impoliteness

inclement adjective STORMY, foul, harsh, intemperate, rough, severe, tempestuous

inclination noun 1 TENDENCY, disposition, liking, partiality, penchant, predilection, predisposition, proclivity, proneness, propensity
2 SLOPE, angle, gradient, incline, pitch, slant, tilt

incline verb 1 PREDISPOSE, influence, persuade, prejudice, sway
2 SLOPE, lean, slant, tilt, tip, veer
▶ noun 3 SLOPE, ascent, descent, dip, grade, gradient, rise

inclined adjective DISPOSED, apt, given, liable, likely, minded, predisposed, prone, willing

include verb 1 CONTAIN, comprise, cover, embrace, encompass, incorporate, involve, subsume, take in
2 INTRODUCE, add, enter, insert

inclusion noun ADDITION, incorporation, insertion

inclusive adjective COMPREHENSIVE, across-the-board, all-embracing, blanket, general, global, sweeping, umbrella

incognito adjective IN DISGUISE, disguised, under an assumed name, unknown, unrecognized

incoherence noun UNINTELLIGIBILITY, disjointedness, inarticulateness

incoherent adjective

UNINTELLIGIBLE, confused, disjointed, disordered, inarticulate, inconsistent, jumbled, muddled, rambling, stammering, stuttering

income noun REVENUE, earnings, pay, proceeds, profits, receipts, salary, takings, wages

incoming adjective ARRIVING, approaching, entering, homeward, landing, new, returning

incomparable adjective UNEQUALED, beyond compare, inimitable, matchless, peerless, superlative, supreme, transcendent, unmatched, unparalleled, unrivaled

incompatible adjective INCONSISTENT, conflicting, contradictory, incongruous, mismatched, unsuited

incompetence noun INEPTITUDE, inability, inadequacy, incapability, incapacity, ineffectiveness, unfitness, uselessness

incompetent adjective INEPT, bungling, floundering, incapable, ineffectual, inexpert, unfit, useless

incomplete adjective UNFINISHED, deficient, fragmentary, imperfect, partial, wanting

incomprehensible adjective UNINTELLIGIBLE, baffling, beyond one's grasp, impenetrable, obscure, opaque, perplexing, puzzling, unfathomable

inconceivable adjective UNIMAGINABLE, beyond belief, incomprehensible, incredible, mind-boggling (informal), out of the question, unbelievable, unheard-of, unthinkable

inconclusive adjective INDECISIVE, ambiguous, indeterminate, open,

unconvincing, undecided, up in the air (informal), vague

incongruity noun INAPPROPRIATENESS, conflict, discrepancy, disparity, incompatibility, inconsistency, unsuitability

incongruous adjective INAPPROPRIATE, discordant, improper, incompatible, out of keeping, out of place, unbecoming, unsuitable

inconsiderable adjective INSIGNIFICANT, inconsequential, minor, negligible, slight, small, trifling, trivial, unimportant

inconsiderate adjective SELFISH, indelicate, insensitive, rude, tactless, thoughtless, unkind, unthinking

inconsistency noun
1 INCOMPATIBILITY, disagreement, discrepancy, disparity, divergence, incongruity, variance
2 UNRELIABILITY, fickleness, instability, unpredictability, unsteadiness

inconsistent adjective
1 INCOMPATIBLE, at odds, conflicting, contradictory, discordant, incongruous, irreconcilable, out of step
2 CHANGEABLE, capricious, erratic, fickle, unpredictable, unstable, unsteady, variable

inconsolable adjective HEARTBROKEN, brokenhearted, desolate, despairing

inconspicuous adjective UNOBTRUSIVE, camouflaged, hidden, insignificant, ordinary, plain, unassuming, unnoticeable, unostentatious

incontrovertible adjective INDISPUTABLE, certain, established, incontestable,

indubitable, irrefutable, positive,
sure, undeniable, unquestionable

inconvenience *noun* 1 TROUBLE,
awkwardness, bother, difficulty,
disadvantage, disruption,
disturbance, fuss, hindrance,
nuisance

▶ *verb* 2 TROUBLE, bother,
discommode, disrupt, disturb, put
out, upset

inconvenient *adjective*
TROUBLESOME, awkward,
bothersome, disadvantageous,
disturbing, inopportune,
unsuitable, untimely

incorporate *verb* INCLUDE, absorb,
assimilate, blend, combine,
integrate, merge, subsume

incorrect *adjective* FALSE,
erroneous, faulty, flawed,
inaccurate, mistaken, untrue,
wrong

incorrigible *adjective* INCURABLE,
hardened, hopeless, intractable,
inveterate, irredeemable,
unreformed

incorruptible *adjective* 1 HONEST,
above suspicion, straight,
trustworthy, upright
2 IMPERISHABLE, everlasting,
undecaying

increase *verb* 1 GROW, advance,
boost, develop, enlarge, escalate,
expand, extend, multiply, raise,
spread, swell

▶ *noun* 2 GROWTH, development,
enlargement, escalation,
expansion, extension, gain,
increment, rise, upturn

increasingly *adverb*
PROGRESSIVELY, more and more

incredible *adjective* 1 IMPLAUSIBLE,
beyond belief, far-fetched,
improbable, inconceivable,
preposterous, unbelievable,
unimaginable, unthinkable

2 (*informal*) AMAZING, astonishing,
astounding, extraordinary,
prodigious, sensational (*informal*),
wonderful

incredulity *noun* DISBELIEF,
distrust, doubt, skepticism

incredulous *adjective*
DISBELIEVING, distrustful,
doubtful, dubious, skeptical,
suspicious, unbelieving,
unconvinced

increment *noun* INCREASE,
accrual, addition, advancement,
augmentation, enlargement,
gain, step up, supplement

incriminate *verb* IMPLICATE,
accuse, blame, charge, impeach,
inculpate, involve

incumbent *adjective* OBLIGATORY,
binding, compulsory, mandatory,
necessary

incur *verb* EARN, arouse, bring
(upon oneself), draw, expose
oneself to, gain, meet with,
provoke

incurable *adjective* FATAL,
inoperable, irremediable,
terminal

indebted *adjective* GRATEFUL,
beholden, in debt, obligated,
obliged, under an obligation

indecency *noun* OBSCENITY,
immodesty, impropriety,
impurity, indelicacy, lewdness,
licentiousness, pornography,
vulgarity

indecent *adjective* 1 LEWD, crude,
dirty, filthy, immodest, improper,
impure, licentious, pornographic,
salacious, scuzzy (*slang*), X-rated
2 UNBECOMING, in bad taste,
indecorous, unseemly, vulgar

indecipherable *adjective*
ILLEGIBLE, indistinguishable,
unintelligible, unreadable

indecision *noun* HESITATION,

dithering, doubt, indecisiveness, shilly-shallying (*informal*), uncertainty, vacillation, wavering

indecisive *adjective* HESITATING, dithering, faltering, in two minds (*informal*), tentative, uncertain, undecided, vacillating, wavering

indeed *adverb* REALLY, actually, certainly, in truth, truly, undoubtedly

indefensible *adjective* UNFORGIVABLE, inexcusable, unjustifiable, unpardonable, untenable, unwarrantable, wrong

indefinable *adjective* INEXPRESSIBLE, impalpable, indescribable

indefinite *adjective* UNCLEAR, doubtful, equivocal, ill-defined, imprecise, indeterminate, inexact, uncertain, unfixed, vague

indefinitely *adverb* ENDLESSLY, ad infinitum, continually, for ever

indelible *adjective* PERMANENT, enduring, indestructible, ineradicable, ingrained, lasting

indelicate *adjective* OFFENSIVE, coarse, crude, embarrassing, immodest, off-color, risqué, rude, suggestive, tasteless, vulgar

indemnify *verb* 1 INSURE, guarantee, protect, secure, underwrite
2 COMPENSATE, reimburse, remunerate, repair, repay

indemnity *noun* 1 INSURANCE, guarantee, protection, security
2 COMPENSATION, redress, reimbursement, remuneration, reparation, restitution

independence *noun* FREEDOM, autonomy, liberty, self-reliance, self-rule, self-sufficiency, sovereignty

independent *adjective*
1 FREE, liberated, separate, unconstrained, uncontrolled
2 SELF-GOVERNING, autonomous, nonaligned, self-determining, sovereign
3 SELF-SUFFICIENT, liberated, self-contained, self-reliant, self-supporting

independently *adverb* SEPARATELY, alone, autonomously, by oneself, individually, on one's own, solo, unaided

indescribable *adjective* UNUTTERABLE, beyond description, beyond words, indefinable, inexpressible

indestructible *adjective* PERMANENT, enduring, everlasting, immortal, imperishable, incorruptible, indelible, indissoluble, lasting, unbreakable

indeterminate *adjective* UNCERTAIN, imprecise, indefinite, inexact, undefined, unfixed, unspecified, unstipulated, vague

indicate *verb* 1 SIGNIFY, betoken, denote, imply, manifest, point to, reveal, suggest
2 POINT OUT, designate, specify
3 SHOW, display, express, read, record, register

indication *noun* SIGN, clue, evidence, hint, inkling, intimation, manifestation, mark, suggestion, symptom

indicative *adjective* SUGGESTIVE, pointing to, significant, symptomatic

indicator *noun* SIGN, gauge, guide, mark, meter, pointer, signal, symbol

indict *verb* CHARGE, accuse, arraign, impeach, prosecute, summon

indictment *noun* CHARGE, accusation, allegation,

impeachment, prosecution, summons

indifference noun DISREGARD, aloofness, apathy, coldness, coolness, detachment, inattention, negligence, nonchalance, unconcern

indifferent adjective
1 UNCONCERNED, aloof, callous, cold, cool, detached, impervious, inattentive, uninterested, unmoved, unsympathetic
2 MEDIOCRE, moderate, no great shakes (informal), ordinary, passable, so-so (informal), undistinguished

indigestion noun HEARTBURN, dyspepsia, upset stomach

indignant adjective RESENTFUL, angry, disgruntled, exasperated, incensed, irate, peeved (informal), riled, scornful, ticked off (informal), up in arms (informal)

indignation noun RESENTMENT, anger, exasperation, pique, rage, scorn, umbrage

indignity noun HUMILIATION, affront, dishonor, disrespect, injury, insult, opprobrium, slight, snub

indirect adjective 1 CIRCUITOUS, long-drawn-out, meandering, oblique, rambling, roundabout, tortuous, wandering
2 INCIDENTAL, secondary, subsidiary, unintended

indiscreet adjective TACTLESS, impolitic, imprudent, incautious, injudicious, naive, rash, reckless, unwise

indiscretion noun MISTAKE, error, faux pas, folly, foolishness, gaffe, lapse, slip

indiscriminate adjective RANDOM, careless, desultory, general, uncritical, undiscriminating, unsystematic, wholesale

indispensable adjective
ESSENTIAL, crucial, imperative, key, necessary, needed, requisite, vital

indisposed adjective ILL, ailing, poorly (informal), sick, under the weather, unwell

indisposition noun ILLNESS, ailment, ill health, sickness

indisputable adjective
UNDENIABLE, beyond doubt, certain, incontestable, incontrovertible, indubitable, irrefutable, unquestionable

indistinct adjective UNCLEAR, blurred, faint, fuzzy, hazy, ill-defined, indeterminate, shadowy, undefined, vague

individual adjective 1 PERSONAL, characteristic, distinctive, exclusive, idiosyncratic, own, particular, peculiar, singular, special, specific, unique
▶ noun 2 PERSON, being, character, creature, soul, unit

individualist noun MAVERICK, freethinker, independent, loner, lone wolf, nonconformist, original

individuality noun
DISTINCTIVENESS, character, originality, personality, separateness, singularity, uniqueness

individually adverb SEPARATELY, apart, independently, one at a time, one by one, singly

indoctrinate verb TRAIN, brainwash, drill, ground, imbue, initiate, instruct, school, teach

indoctrination noun TRAINING, brainwashing, drilling, grounding, inculcation, instruction, schooling

indolent adjective LAZY, idle,

inactive, inert, languid, lethargic, listless, slothful, sluggish, workshy

indomitable *adjective* INVINCIBLE, bold, resolute, staunch, steadfast, unbeatable, unconquerable, unflinching, unyielding

indubitable *adjective* CERTAIN, incontestable, incontrovertible, indisputable, irrefutable, obvious, sure, undeniable, unquestionable

induce *verb* 1 PERSUADE, convince, encourage, incite, influence, instigate, prevail upon, prompt, talk into
2 CAUSE, bring about, effect, engender, generate, give rise to, lead to, occasion, produce

inducement *noun* INCENTIVE, attraction, bait, carrot (*informal*), encouragement, incitement, lure, reward

indulge *verb* 1 GRATIFY, feed, give way to, pander to, satisfy, yield to
2 SPOIL, cosset, give in to, go along with, humor, mollycoddle, pamper

indulgence *noun* 1 GRATIFICATION, appeasement, fulfillment, satiation, satisfaction
2 LUXURY, extravagance, favor, privilege, treat
3 TOLERANCE, forbearance, patience, understanding

indulgent *adjective* LENIENT, compliant, easy-going, forbearing, kindly, liberal, permissive, tolerant, understanding

industrialist *noun* CAPITALIST, big businessman, captain of industry, magnate, manufacturer, tycoon

industrious *adjective* HARD-WORKING, busy, conscientious, diligent, energetic, persistent, purposeful, tireless, zealous

industry *noun* 1 BUSINESS, commerce, manufacturing, production, trade
2 EFFORT, activity, application, diligence, labor, tirelessness, toil, zeal

inebriated *adjective* DRUNK, crocked (*slang*), half-cut (*informal*), intoxicated, legless (*informal*), merry (*Brit. informal*), paralytic (*informal*), plastered (*slang*), tight (*informal*), three sheets to the wind (*slang*), tipsy, under the influence (*informal*)

ineffective *adjective* USELESS, fruitless, futile, idle, impotent, inefficient, unavailing, unproductive, vain, worthless

ineffectual *adjective* WEAK, feeble, impotent, inadequate, incompetent, ineffective, inept, lousy (*slang*)

inefficiency *noun* INCOMPETENCE, carelessness, disorganization, muddle, slackness, sloppiness

inefficient *adjective* INCOMPETENT, disorganized, ineffectual, inept, wasteful, weak

ineligible *adjective* UNQUALIFIED, disqualified, ruled out, unacceptable, unfit, unsuitable

inept *adjective* INCOMPETENT, bumbling, bungling, clumsy, inexpert, maladroit

ineptitude *noun* INCOMPETENCE, clumsiness, inexpertness, unfitness

inequality *noun* DISPARITY, bias, difference, disproportion, diversity, irregularity, prejudice, unevenness

inequitable *adjective* UNFAIR, biased, discriminatory, one-sided, partial, partisan, preferential, prejudiced, unjust

inert *adjective* INACTIVE, dead,

dormant, immobile, lifeless,
motionless, static, still,
unreactive, unresponsive

inertia noun INACTIVITY, apathy,
immobility, lethargy, listlessness,
passivity, sloth, unresponsiveness

inescapable adjective
UNAVOIDABLE, certain, destined,
fated, ineluctable, inevitable,
inexorable, sure

inestimable adjective
INCALCULABLE, immeasurable,
invaluable, precious, priceless,
prodigious

inevitable adjective UNAVOIDABLE,
assured, certain, destined,
fixed, ineluctable, inescapable,
inexorable, sure

inevitably adverb UNAVOIDABLY, as
a result, automatically, certainly,
necessarily, of necessity, perforce,
surely, willy-nilly

inexcusable adjective
UNFORGIVABLE, indefensible,
outrageous, unjustifiable,
unpardonable, unwarrantable

inexorable adjective
UNRELENTING, inescapable,
relentless, remorseless,
unbending, unyielding

inexpensive adjective CHEAP,
bargain, budget, economical,
modest, reasonable

inexperience noun
UNFAMILIARITY, callowness,
greenness, ignorance, newness,
rawness

inexperienced adjective
IMMATURE, callow, green, new,
raw, unpracticed, untried,
unversed

inexpert adjective AMATEURISH,
bungling, cack-handed (informal),
clumsy, inept, maladroit,
unpracticed, unprofessional,
unskilled

inexplicable adjective
UNACCOUNTABLE, baffling,
enigmatic, incomprehensible,
insoluble, mysterious,
mystifying, strange,
unfathomable, unintelligible

inextricably adverb INSEPARABLY,
indissolubly, indistinguishably,
intricately, irretrievably, totally

infallibility noun PERFECTION,
impeccability, omniscience,
supremacy, unerringness

infallible adjective FOOLPROOF,
certain, dependable, reliable, sure,
sure-fire (informal), trustworthy,
unbeatable, unfailing

infamous adjective NOTORIOUS,
disreputable, ignominious,
ill-famed

infancy noun BEGINNINGS, cradle,
dawn, inception, origins, outset,
start

infant noun BABY, babe, bairn
(Scot.), child, minor, toddler, tot

infantile adjective CHILDISH,
babyish, immature, puerile

infatuate verb OBSESS, besot,
bewitch, captivate, enchant,
enrapture, fascinate

infatuated adjective OBSESSED,
besotted, bewitched, captivated,
carried away, enamored,
enraptured, fascinated, possessed,
smitten (informal), spellbound

infatuation noun OBSESSION,
crush (informal), fixation, madness,
passion, thing (informal)

infect verb CONTAMINATE, affect,
blight, corrupt, defile, poison,
pollute, taint

infection noun CONTAMINATION,
contagion, corruption,
defilement, poison, pollution,
virus

infectious adjective CATCHING,
communicable, contagious,

spreading, transmittable, virulent
infer verb DEDUCE, conclude, derive, gather, presume, surmise, understand
inference noun DEDUCTION, assumption, conclusion, presumption, reading, surmise
inferior adjective 1 LOWER, lesser, menial, minor, secondary, subordinate, subsidiary
▶ noun 2 UNDERLING, junior, menial, subordinate
inferiority noun 1 INADEQUACY, deficiency, imperfection, insignificance, mediocrity, shoddiness, worthlessness
2 SUBSERVIENCE, abasement, lowliness, subordination
infernal adjective DEVILISH, accursed, damnable, damned, diabolical, fiendish, hellish, satanic
infertile adjective BARREN, sterile, unfruitful, unproductive
infertility noun STERILITY, barrenness, infecundity, unproductiveness
infest verb OVERRUN, beset, invade, penetrate, permeate, ravage, swarm, throng
infested adjective OVERRUN, alive, crawling, ravaged, ridden, swarming, teeming
infiltrate verb PENETRATE, filter through, insinuate oneself, make inroads (into), percolate, permeate, pervade, sneak in (informal)
infinite adjective NEVER-ENDING, boundless, eternal, everlasting, illimitable, immeasurable, inexhaustible, limitless, measureless, unbounded
infinitesimal adjective MICROSCOPIC, insignificant, minuscule, minute, negligible,

teeny, tiny, unnoticeable
infinity noun ETERNITY, boundlessness, endlessness, immensity, vastness
infirm adjective FRAIL, ailing, debilitated, decrepit, doddering, enfeebled, failing, feeble, weak
infirmity noun FRAILTY, decrepitude, ill health, sickliness, vulnerability
inflame verb ENRAGE, anger, arouse, excite, incense, infuriate, madden, provoke, rouse, stimulate
inflamed adjective SORE, fevered, hot, infected, red, swollen
inflammable adjective FLAMMABLE, combustible, incendiary
inflammation noun SORENESS, painfulness, rash, redness, tenderness
inflammatory adjective PROVOCATIVE, explosive, fiery, intemperate, like a red rag to a bull, rabble-rousing
inflate verb EXPAND, bloat, blow up, dilate, distend, enlarge, increase, puff up or out, pump up, swell
inflated adjective EXAGGERATED, ostentatious, overblown, swollen
inflation noun EXPANSION, enlargement, escalation, extension, increase, rise, spread, swelling
inflexibility noun OBSTINACY, intransigence, obduracy
inflexible adjective 1 OBSTINATE, implacable, intractable, obdurate, resolute, set in one's ways, steadfast, stubborn, unbending, uncompromising
2 INELASTIC, hard, rigid, stiff, taut
inflict verb IMPOSE, administer, apply, deliver, levy, mete or deal

out, visit, wreak

infliction noun IMPOSITION, administration, perpetration, wreaking

influence noun 1 EFFECT, authority, control, domination, magnetism, pressure, weight 2 POWER, clout (informal), hold, importance, leverage, prestige, pull (informal)
▶ verb 3 AFFECT, control, direct, guide, manipulate, sway

influential adjective IMPORTANT, authoritative, instrumental, leading, potent, powerful, significant, telling, weighty

influx noun ARRIVAL, incursion, inrush, inundation, invasion, rush

inform verb 1 TELL, advise, communicate, enlighten, instruct, notify, teach, tip off 2 INCRIMINATE, betray, blow the whistle on (informal), denounce, grass (Brit. slang), inculpate, shop (slang, chiefly Brit.), squeal (slang)

informal adjective RELAXED, casual, colloquial, cozy, easy, familiar, homey, natural, simple, unofficial

informality noun FAMILIARITY, casualness, ease, naturalness, relaxation, simplicity

information noun FACTS, data, intelligence, knowledge, message, news, notice, report

informative adjective INSTRUCTIVE, chatty, communicative, edifying, educational, enlightening, forthcoming, illuminating, revealing

informed adjective KNOWLEDGEABLE, enlightened, erudite, expert, familiar, in the picture, learned, up to date,

versed, well-read

informer noun BETRAYER, accuser, Judas, sneak, stool pigeon

infrequent adjective OCCASIONAL, few and far between, once in a blue moon, rare, sporadic, uncommon, unusual

infringe verb BREAK, contravene, disobey, transgress, violate

infringement noun CONTRAVENTION, breach, infraction, transgression, trespass, violation

infuriate verb ENRAGE, anger, exasperate, incense, irritate, madden, provoke, rile

infuriating adjective ANNOYING, exasperating, galling, irritating, maddening, mortifying, provoking, vexatious

ingenious adjective CREATIVE, bright, brilliant, clever, crafty, inventive, original, resourceful, shrewd

ingenuity noun ORIGINALITY, cleverness, flair, genius, gift, inventiveness, resourcefulness, sharpness, shrewdness

ingenuous adjective NAIVE, artless, guileless, honest, innocent, open, plain, simple, sincere, trusting, unsophisticated

inglorious adjective DISHONORABLE, discreditable, disgraceful, disreputable, ignoble, ignominious, infamous, shameful, unheroic

ingratiate verb PANDER TO, brown-nose (slang), crawl, curry favor, fawn, flatter, grovel, insinuate oneself, kiss ass (slang), toady

ingratiating adjective SYCOPHANTIC, crawling, fawning, flattering, humble, obsequious, servile, toadying, unctuous

ingratitude *noun*
UNGRATEFULNESS, thanklessness

ingredient *noun* COMPONENT,
constituent, element, part

inhabit *verb* LIVE, abide, dwell,
occupy, populate, reside

inhabitant *noun* DWELLER,
citizen, denizen, inmate, native,
occupant, occupier, resident,
tenant

inhabited *adjective* POPULATED,
colonized, developed, occupied,
peopled, settled, tenanted

inhale *verb* BREATHE IN, draw in,
gasp, respire, suck in

inherent *adjective* INNATE,
essential, hereditary, inborn,
inbred, inbuilt, ingrained,
inherited, intrinsic, native,
natural

inherit *verb* BE LEFT, come into, fall
heir to, succeed to

inheritance *noun* LEGACY,
bequest, birthright, heritage,
patrimony

inhibit *verb* RESTRAIN, check,
constrain, curb, discourage,
frustrate, hinder, hold back or in,
impede, obstruct

inhibited *adjective* SHY,
constrained, guarded, repressed,
reserved, reticent, self-conscious,
subdued

inhibition *noun* SHYNESS, block,
hang-up (*informal*), reserve,
restraint, reticence, self-
consciousness

inhospitable *adjective*
1 UNWELCOMING, cool,
uncongenial, unfriendly,
unreceptive, unsociable,
xenophobic
2 BLEAK, barren, desolate,
forbidding, godforsaken, hostile

inhuman *adjective* CRUEL, barbaric,
brutal, cold-blooded, heartless,
merciless, pitiless, ruthless,
savage, unfeeling

inhumane *adjective* CRUEL, brutal,
heartless, pitiless, unfeeling,
unkind, unsympathetic

inhumanity *noun* CRUELTY,
atrocity, barbarism, brutality,
heartlessness, pitilessness,
ruthlessness, unkindness

inimical *adjective* HOSTILE, adverse,
antagonistic, ill-disposed,
opposed, unfavorable, unfriendly,
unwelcoming

inimitable *adjective* UNIQUE,
consummate, incomparable,
matchless, peerless, unparalleled,
unrivaled

iniquitous *adjective* WICKED,
criminal, evil, immoral,
reprehensible, sinful, unjust

iniquity *noun* WICKEDNESS,
abomination, evil, injustice,
sin, wrong

initial *adjective* FIRST, beginning,
incipient, introductory, opening,
primary

initially *adverb* AT FIRST, at or in the
beginning, first, firstly, originally,
primarily

initiate *verb* 1 BEGIN, commence,
get under way, kick off (*informal*),
launch, open, originate, set in
motion, start
2 INDUCT, indoctrinate, introduce,
invest
3 INSTRUCT, acquaint with, coach,
familiarize with, teach, train
▶ *noun* 4 NOVICE, beginner,
convert, entrant, learner,
member, probationer

initiation *noun* INTRODUCTION,
debut, enrollment, entrance,
inauguration, induction,
installation, investiture

initiative *noun* 1 FIRST STEP,
advantage, first move, lead

2 RESOURCEFULNESS, ambition, drive, dynamism, enterprise, get-up-and-go (*informal*), leadership

inject *verb* **1** VACCINATE, inoculate
2 INTRODUCE, bring in, infuse, insert, instill

injection *noun* **1** VACCINATION, inoculation, jab (*informal*), shot (*informal*)
2 INTRODUCTION, dose, infusion, insertion

injudicious *adjective* UNWISE, foolish, ill-advised, ill-judged, impolitic, imprudent, incautious, inexpedient, rash, unthinking

injunction *noun* ORDER, command, exhortation, instruction, mandate, precept, ruling

injure *verb* HURT, damage, harm, impair, ruin, spoil, undermine, wound

injured *adjective* HURT, broken, challenged, damaged, disabled, undermined, weakened, wounded

injury *noun* HARM, damage, detriment, disservice, hurt, ill, trauma (*pathology*), wound, wrong

injustice *noun* UNFAIRNESS, bias, discrimination, inequality, inequity, iniquity, oppression, partisanship, prejudice, wrong

inkling *noun* SUSPICION, clue, conception, hint, idea, indication, intimation, notion, suggestion, whisper

inland *adjective* INTERIOR, domestic, internal, upcountry

inlet *noun* BAY, bight, creek, firth *or* frith (*Scot.*), fjord, passage

inmost *or* **innermost** *adjective* DEEPEST, basic, central, essential, intimate, personal, private, secret

innate *adjective* INBORN, congenital, constitutional, essential, inbred, ingrained, inherent, instinctive, intuitive, native, natural

inner *adjective* **1** INSIDE, central, interior, internal, inward, middle
2 PRIVATE, hidden, intimate, personal, repressed, secret, unrevealed

innkeeper *noun* PUBLICAN, host *or* hostess, hotelier, landlord *or* landlady, mine host

innocence *noun* **1** GUILTLESSNESS, blamelessness, clean hands, incorruptibility, probity, purity, uprightness, virtue
2 HARMLESSNESS, innocuousness, inoffensiveness
3 INEXPERIENCE, artlessness, credulousness, gullibility, ingenuousness, naivety, simplicity, unworldliness

innocent *adjective* **1** NOT GUILTY, blameless, guiltless, honest, in the clear, uninvolved
2 HARMLESS, innocuous, inoffensive, unobjectionable, well-intentioned, well-meant
3 NAIVE, artless, childlike, credulous, gullible, ingenuous, open, simple, unworldly

innovation *noun* MODERNIZATION, alteration, change, departure, introduction, newness, novelty, variation

innuendo *noun* INSINUATION, aspersion, hint, implication, imputation, intimation, overtone, suggestion, whisper

innumerable *adjective* COUNTLESS, beyond number, incalculable, infinite, multitudinous, myriad, numberless, numerous, unnumbered, untold

inoffensive *adjective* HARMLESS, innocent, innocuous, mild, quiet, retiring, unobjectionable, unobtrusive

inoperative *adjective* OUT OF
ACTION, broken, defective,
ineffective, invalid, null and void,
out of order, out of service, useless

inopportune *adjective*
INCONVENIENT, ill-chosen,
ill-timed, inappropriate,
unfavorable, unfortunate,
unpropitious, unseasonable,
unsuitable, untimely

inordinate *adjective* EXCESSIVE,
disproportionate, extravagant,
immoderate, intemperate,
preposterous, unconscionable,
undue, unreasonable,
unwarranted

inorganic *adjective* ARTIFICIAL,
chemical, man-made

inquest *noun* INQUIRY,
inquisition, investigation, probe

inquire *verb* 1 INVESTIGATE,
examine, explore, look into, make
inquiries, probe, research
2 *or* **enquire** ASK, query, question

inquiry *noun* 1 INVESTIGATION,
examination, exploration,
inquest, interrogation, probe,
research, study, survey
2 *or* **enquiry** QUESTION, query

inquisition *noun* INVESTIGATION,
cross-examination, examination,
grilling (*informal*), inquest,
inquiry, questioning, third degree
(*informal*)

inquisitive *adjective* CURIOUS,
inquiring, nosy (*informal*), probing,
prying, questioning

insane *adjective* 1 MAD, crazed,
crazy, demented, deranged,
mentally ill, out of one's mind,
unhinged
2 STUPID, bonkers (*informal*),
daft (*informal*), foolish, idiotic,
impractical, irrational,
irresponsible, preposterous,
senseless

insanitary *adjective* UNHEALTHY,
dirty, disease-ridden, filthy,
infested, insalubrious, polluted,
scuzzy (*slang*), unclean,
unhygienic

insanity *noun* 1 MADNESS,
delirium, dementia, mental
disorder, mental illness
2 STUPIDITY, folly, irresponsibility,
lunacy, senselessness

insatiable *adjective*
UNQUENCHABLE, greedy,
intemperate, rapacious, ravenous,
voracious

inscribe *verb* CARVE, cut, engrave,
etch, impress, imprint

inscription *noun* ENGRAVING,
dedication, legend, words

inscrutable *adjective* 1 ENIGMATIC,
blank, deadpan, impenetrable,
poker-faced (*informal*)
2 MYSTERIOUS, hidden,
incomprehensible, inexplicable,
unexplainable, unfathomable,
unintelligible

insecure *adjective* 1 ANXIOUS,
afraid, uncertain, unsure
2 UNSAFE, defenseless, exposed,
unguarded, unprotected,
vulnerable, wide-open

insecurity *noun* ANXIETY, fear,
uncertainty, worry

insensible *adjective* UNAWARE,
impervious, oblivious, unaffected,
unconscious, unmindful

insensitive *adjective* UNFEELING,
callous, hardened, indifferent,
thick-skinned, tough, uncaring,
unconcerned

inseparable *adjective*
1 INDIVISIBLE, indissoluble
2 DEVOTED, bosom, close, intimate

insert *verb* ENTER, embed,
implant, introduce, place, put,
stick in

insertion *noun* INCLUSION,

addition, implant, interpolation, introduction, supplement

inside adjective 1 INNER, interior, internal, inward

2 CONFIDENTIAL, classified, exclusive, internal, private, restricted, secret

▶ adverb 3 INDOORS, under cover, within

▶ noun 4 INTERIOR, contents

5 ▷▷ **insides** (informal) STOMACH, belly, bowels, entrails, guts, innards (informal), viscera, vitals

insidious adjective STEALTHY, deceptive, sly, smooth, sneaking, subtle, surreptitious

insight noun UNDERSTANDING, awareness, comprehension, discernment, judgment, observation, penetration, perception, perspicacity, vision

insignia noun BADGE, crest, emblem, symbol

insignificance noun UNIMPORTANCE, inconsequence, irrelevance, meaninglessness, pettiness, triviality, worthlessness

insignificant adjective UNIMPORTANT, inconsequential, irrelevant, meaningless, minor, nondescript, paltry, petty, trifling, trivial

insincere adjective DECEITFUL, dishonest, disingenuous, duplicitous, false, hollow, hypocritical, lying, two-faced, untruthful

insincerity noun DECEITFULNESS, dishonesty, dissimulation, duplicity, hypocrisy, pretense, untruthfulness

insinuate verb 1 IMPLY, allude, hint, indicate, intimate, suggest

2 INGRATIATE, curry favor, get in with, worm or work one's way in

insinuation noun IMPLICATION, allusion, aspersion, hint, innuendo, slur, suggestion

insipid adjective 1 BLAND, anemic, characterless, colorless, prosaic, uninteresting, vapid, wishy-washy (informal)

2 TASTELESS, bland, flavorless, unappetizing, watery

insist verb 1 DEMAND, lay down the law, put one's foot down (informal), require

2 ASSERT, aver, claim, maintain, reiterate, repeat, swear, vow

insistence noun PERSISTENCE, emphasis, importunity, stress

insistent adjective PERSISTENT, dogged, emphatic, importunate, incessant, persevering, unrelenting, urgent

insolence noun RUDENESS, boldness, cheek (informal), disrespect, effrontery, impertinence, impudence

insolent adjective RUDE, bold, contemptuous, impertinent, impudent, insubordinate, insulting

insoluble adjective INEXPLICABLE, baffling, impenetrable, indecipherable, mysterious, unaccountable, unfathomable, unsolvable

insolvency noun BANKRUPTCY, failure, liquidation, ruin

insolvent adjective BANKRUPT, broke (informal), failed, gone bust (informal), gone to the wall, in receivership, ruined

insomnia noun SLEEPLESSNESS, wakefulness

inspect verb EXAMINE, check, go over or through, investigate, look over, scrutinize, survey, vet

inspection noun EXAMINATION, check, checkup, investigation, once-over (informal), review, scrutiny, search, survey

inspector noun EXAMINER, censor, investigator, overseer, scrutinizer, superintendent, supervisor

inspiration noun 1 INFLUENCE, muse, spur, stimulus
2 REVELATION, creativity, illumination, insight

inspire verb 1 STIMULATE, animate, encourage, enliven, galvanize, influence, spur
2 AROUSE, enkindle, excite, give rise to, produce

inspired adjective 1 BRILLIANT, cool (informal), dazzling, impressive, memorable, outstanding, phat (slang), superlative, thrilling, wonderful
2 UPLIFTED, elated, enthused, exhilarated, stimulated

inspiring adjective UPLIFTING, exciting, exhilarating, heartening, moving, rousing, stimulating, stirring

instability noun UNPREDICTABILITY, changeableness, fickleness, fluctuation, impermanence, inconstancy, insecurity, unsteadiness, variability, volatility, wavering

install verb 1 SET UP, fix, lay, lodge, place, position, put in, station
2 INDUCT, establish, inaugurate, institute, introduce, invest
3 SETTLE, ensconce, position

installation noun 1 SETTING UP, establishment, fitting, installment, placing, positioning
2 INDUCTION, inauguration, investiture
3 EQUIPMENT, machinery, plant, system

installment noun PORTION, chapter, division, episode, part, repayment, section

instance noun 1 EXAMPLE, case, illustration, occasion, occurrence, situation
▸ verb 2 QUOTE, adduce, cite, mention, name, specify

instant noun 1 SECOND, flash, jiffy (informal), moment, split second, trice, twinkling of an eye (informal)
2 JUNCTURE, moment, occasion, point, time
▸ adjective 3 IMMEDIATE, direct, instantaneous, on-the-spot, prompt, quick, split-second
4 PRECOOKED, convenience, fast, ready-mixed

instantaneous adjective IMMEDIATE, direct, instant, on-the-spot, prompt

instantaneously adverb IMMEDIATELY, at once, instantly, in the twinkling of an eye (informal), on the spot, promptly, straight away

instantly adverb IMMEDIATELY, at once, directly, instantaneously, now, right away, straight away, this minute

instead adverb 1 RATHER, alternatively, in lieu, in preference, on second thoughts, preferably
2 ▸▸ **instead of** IN PLACE OF, in lieu of, rather than

instigate verb PROVOKE, bring about, incite, influence, initiate, prompt, set off, start, stimulate, trigger

instigation noun PROMPTING, behest, bidding, encouragement, incentive, incitement, urging

instigator noun RINGLEADER, agitator, leader, motivator, prime mover, troublemaker

instill verb INTRODUCE, engender, imbue, implant, inculcate, infuse, insinuate

instinct noun INTUITION, faculty, gift, impulse, knack, predisposition, proclivity, talent, tendency

instinctive adjective INBORN, automatic, inherent, innate, intuitive, involuntary, natural, reflex, spontaneous, unpremeditated, visceral

instinctively adverb INTUITIVELY, automatically, by instinct, involuntarily, naturally, without thinking

institute noun 1 SOCIETY, academy, association, college, foundation, guild, institution, school
▶ verb 2 ESTABLISH, fix, found, initiate, introduce, launch, organize, originate, pioneer, set up, start

institution noun
1 ESTABLISHMENT, academy, college, foundation, institute, school, society
2 CUSTOM, convention, law, practice, ritual, rule, tradition

institutional adjective CONVENTIONAL, accepted, established, formal, orthodox

instruct verb 1 ORDER, bid, charge, command, direct, enjoin, tell
2 TEACH, coach, drill, educate, ground, school, train, tutor

instruction noun 1 TEACHING, coaching, education, grounding, guidance, lesson(s), schooling, training, tuition
2 ORDER, command, demand, directive, injunction, mandate, ruling

instructions plural noun ORDERS, advice, directions, guidance, information, key, recommendations, rules

instructive adjective INFORMATIVE, edifying, educational, enlightening, helpful, illuminating, revealing, useful

instructor noun TEACHER, adviser, coach, demonstrator, guide, mentor, trainer, tutor

instrument noun 1 TOOL, apparatus, appliance, contraption (informal), device, gadget, implement, mechanism
2 MEANS, agency, agent, mechanism, medium, organ, vehicle

instrumental adjective ACTIVE, contributory, helpful, influential, involved, useful

insubordinate adjective DISOBEDIENT, defiant, disorderly, mutinous, rebellious, recalcitrant, refractory, undisciplined, ungovernable, unruly

insubordination noun DISOBEDIENCE, defiance, indiscipline, insurrection, mutiny, rebellion, recalcitrance, revolt

insubstantial adjective FLIMSY, feeble, frail, poor, slight, tenuous, thin, weak

insufferable adjective UNBEARABLE, detestable, dreadful, impossible, insupportable, intolerable, unendurable

insufficient adjective INADEQUATE, deficient, incapable, lacking, scant, short

insular adjective NARROW-MINDED, blinkered, circumscribed, inward-looking, limited, narrow, parochial, petty, provincial

insulate verb ISOLATE, close off, cocoon, cushion, cut off, protect, sequester, shield

insult verb 1 OFFEND, abuse, affront, call names, put down, slander, slight, snub
▶ noun 2 ABUSE, affront, aspersion,

insolence, offense, put-down, slap
in the face (informal), slight, snub
insulting adjective OFFENSIVE,
abusive, contemptuous,
degrading, disparaging, insolent,
rude, scurrilous
insuperable adjective
INSURMOUNTABLE, impassable,
invincible, unconquerable
insupportable adjective
1 INTOLERABLE, insufferable,
unbearable, unendurable
2 UNJUSTIFIABLE, indefensible,
untenable
insurance noun PROTECTION,
assurance, cover, guarantee,
indemnity, safeguard, security,
warranty
insure verb PROTECT, assure,
cover, guarantee, indemnify,
underwrite, warrant
insurgent noun 1 REBEL,
insurrectionist, mutineer,
revolutionary, rioter
▶ adjective 2 REBELLIOUS,
disobedient, insubordinate,
mutinous, revolting,
revolutionary, riotous, seditious
insurmountable adjective
INSUPERABLE, hopeless,
impassable, impossible,
invincible, overwhelming,
unconquerable
insurrection noun REBELLION,
coup, insurgency, mutiny, revolt,
revolution, riot, uprising
intact adjective UNDAMAGED,
complete, entire, perfect,
sound, unbroken, unharmed,
unimpaired, unscathed, whole
integral adjective ESSENTIAL,
basic, component, constituent,
fundamental, indispensable,
intrinsic, necessary
integrate verb COMBINE,
amalgamate, assimilate, blend,

fuse, incorporate, join, merge,
unite
integration noun ASSIMILATION,
amalgamation, blending,
combining, fusing, incorporation,
mixing, unification
integrity noun 1 HONESTY,
goodness, honor, incorruptibility,
principle, probity, purity,
rectitude, uprightness, virtue
2 UNITY, coherence, cohesion,
completeness, soundness,
wholeness
intellect noun INTELLIGENCE,
brains (informal), judgment, mind,
reason, sense, understanding
intellectual adjective 1 SCHOLARLY,
bookish, cerebral, highbrow,
intelligent, studious, thoughtful
▶ noun 2 THINKER, academic,
egghead (informal), highbrow
intelligence noun
1 UNDERSTANDING, acumen,
brain power, brains (informal),
cleverness, comprehension,
intellect, perception, sense
2 INFORMATION, data, facts,
findings, knowledge, news,
notification, report
intelligent adjective CLEVER,
brainy (informal), bright,
enlightened, perspicacious,
quick-witted, sharp, smart, well-
informed
intelligentsia noun
INTELLECTUALS, highbrows,
literati
intelligible adjective
UNDERSTANDABLE, clear,
comprehensible, distinct, lucid,
open, plain
intemperate adjective EXCESSIVE,
extreme, immoderate, profligate,
self-indulgent, unbridled,
unrestrained, wild
intend verb PLAN, aim, have in

mind *or* view, mean, propose, purpose

intense *adjective* 1 EXTREME, acute, deep, excessive, fierce, great, powerful, profound, severe
2 PASSIONATE, ardent, fanatical, fervent, fierce, heightened, impassioned, vehement

intensify *verb* INCREASE, add to, aggravate, deepen, escalate, heighten, magnify, redouble, reinforce, sharpen, strengthen

intensity *noun* FORCE, ardor, emotion, fanaticism, fervor, fierceness, passion, strength, vehemence, vigor

intensive *adjective* CONCENTRATED, comprehensive, demanding, exhaustive, in-depth, thorough, thoroughgoing

intent *noun* 1 INTENTION, aim, design, end, goal, meaning, object, objective, plan, purpose
▶ *adjective* 2 ATTENTIVE, absorbed, determined, eager, engrossed, preoccupied, rapt, resolved, steadfast, watchful

intention *noun* PURPOSE, aim, design, end, goal, idea, object, objective, point, target

intentional *adjective* DELIBERATE, calculated, intended, meant, planned, premeditated, willful

intentionally *adverb* DELIBERATELY, designedly, on purpose, willfully

inter *verb* BURY, entomb, lay to rest

intercede *verb* MEDIATE, arbitrate, intervene, plead

intercept *verb* SEIZE, block, catch, cut off, head off, interrupt, obstruct, stop

interchange *verb* 1 SWITCH, alternate, exchange, reciprocate, swap
▶ *noun* 2 JUNCTION, intersection

interchangeable *adjective* IDENTICAL, equivalent, exchangeable, reciprocal, synonymous

intercourse *noun*
1 COMMUNICATION, commerce, contact, dealings
2 SEXUAL INTERCOURSE, carnal knowledge, coitus, copulation, sex

interest *noun* 1 CURIOSITY, attention, concern, notice, regard
2 HOBBY, activity, diversion, pastime, preoccupation, pursuit
3 ADVANTAGE, benefit, good, profit
4 STAKE, claim, investment, right, share
▶ *verb* 5 INTRIGUE, attract, catch one's eye, divert, engross, fascinate

interested *adjective* 1 CURIOUS, attracted, drawn, excited, fascinated, keen
2 INVOLVED, concerned, implicated

interesting *adjective* INTRIGUING, absorbing, appealing, attractive, compelling, engaging, engrossing, gripping, stimulating, thought-provoking

interface *noun* CONNECTION, border, boundary, frontier, link

interfere *verb* 1 INTRUDE, butt in, intervene, meddle, stick one's oar in (*informal*), tamper
2 (often with *with*) CONFLICT, clash, hamper, handicap, hinder, impede, inhibit, obstruct

interference *noun* 1 INTRUSION, intervention, meddling, prying
2 CONFLICT, clashing, collision, obstruction, opposition

interim *adjective* TEMPORARY, acting, caretaker, improvised, makeshift, provisional, stopgap

interior *noun* 1 INSIDE, center, core, heart

▶ *adjective* **2** INSIDE, inner, internal, inward
3 MENTAL, hidden, inner, intimate, personal, private, secret, spiritual

interloper *noun* TRESPASSER, gate-crasher (*informal*), intruder, meddler

interlude *noun* INTERVAL, break, breathing space, delay, hiatus, intermission, pause, respite, rest, spell, stoppage

intermediary *noun* MEDIATOR, agent, broker, go-between, middleman

intermediate *adjective* MIDDLE, halfway, in-between (*informal*), intervening, mid, midway, transitional

interment *noun* BURIAL, funeral

interminable *adjective* ENDLESS, ceaseless, everlasting, infinite, long-drawn-out, long-winded, never-ending, perpetual, protracted

intermingle *verb* MIX, blend, combine, fuse, interlace, intermix, interweave, merge

intermission *noun* INTERVAL, break, interlude, pause, recess, respite, rest, stoppage

intermittent *adjective* PERIODIC, broken, fitful, irregular, occasional, spasmodic, sporadic

intern *verb* IMPRISON, confine, detain, hold, hold in custody

internal *adjective* **1** INNER, inside, interior
2 DOMESTIC, civic, home, in-house, intramural

international *adjective* UNIVERSAL, cosmopolitan, global, intercontinental, worldwide

Internet *noun* INFORMATION SUPERHIGHWAY, cyberspace, the net (*informal*), the web (*informal*),
World Wide Web

interpose *verb* INTERRUPT, insert, interject, put one's oar in

interpret *verb* EXPLAIN, construe, decipher, decode, elucidate, make sense of, render, translate

interpretation *noun* EXPLANATION, analysis, clarification, elucidation, exposition, portrayal, rendition, translation, version

interpreter *noun* TRANSLATOR, commentator

interrogate *verb* QUESTION, cross-examine, examine, grill (*informal*), investigate, pump, quiz

interrogation *noun* QUESTIONING, cross-examination, examination, grilling (*informal*), inquiry, inquisition, third degree (*informal*)

interrupt *verb* **1** INTRUDE, barge in (*informal*), break in, butt in, disturb, heckle, interfere (with)
2 SUSPEND, break off, cut short, delay, discontinue, hold up, lay aside, stop

interruption *noun* STOPPAGE, break, disruption, disturbance, hitch, intrusion, pause, suspension

intersection *noun* JUNCTION, crossing, crossroads, interchange

interval *noun* BREAK, delay, gap, interlude, intermission, pause, respite, rest, space, spell

intervene *verb* **1** INVOLVE ONESELF, arbitrate, intercede, interfere, intrude, lend a hand, mediate, step in (*informal*), take a hand (*informal*)
2 HAPPEN, befall, come to pass, ensue, occur, take place

intervention *noun* MEDIATION, agency, interference, intrusion

interview *noun* **1** MEETING, audience, conference,

consultation, dialogue, press conference, talk
▶ *verb* 2 QUESTION, examine, interrogate, talk to
interviewer *noun* QUESTIONER, examiner, interrogator, investigator, reporter
intestines *plural noun* GUTS, bowels, entrails, innards (*informal*), insides (*informal*), viscera
intimacy *noun* FAMILIARITY, closeness, confidentiality
intimate¹ *adjective* 1 CLOSE, bosom, buddy-buddy (*informal*), confidential, dear, near, thick (*informal*)
2 PERSONAL, confidential, private, secret
3 DETAILED, deep, exhaustive, first-hand, immediate, in-depth, profound, thorough
4 SNUG, comfy (*informal*), cozy, friendly, homey, warm
▶ *noun* 5 FRIEND, close friend, confidant *or (fem.)* confidante, (constant) companion, crony, homeboy (*slang*), homegirl (*slang*), soul mate
intimate² *verb* 1 SUGGEST, hint, imply, indicate, insinuate
2 ANNOUNCE, communicate, declare, make known, state
intimately *adverb* 1 CONFIDINGLY, affectionately, confidentially, familiarly, personally, tenderly, warmly
2 IN DETAIL, fully, inside out, thoroughly, very well
intimation *noun* 1 HINT, allusion, indication, inkling, insinuation, reminder, suggestion, warning
2 ANNOUNCEMENT, communication, declaration, notice
intimidate *verb* FRIGHTEN, browbeat, bully, coerce, daunt,

overawe, scare, subdue, terrorize, threaten
intimidation *noun* BULLYING, arm-twisting (*informal*), browbeating, coercion, menaces, pressure, terrorization, threat(s)
intolerable *adjective* UNBEARABLE, excruciating, impossible, insufferable, insupportable, painful, unendurable
intolerance *noun* NARROW-MINDEDNESS, bigotry, chauvinism, discrimination, dogmatism, fanaticism, illiberality, prejudice
intolerant *adjective* NARROW-MINDED, bigoted, chauvinistic, dictatorial, dogmatic, fanatical, illiberal, prejudiced, small-minded
intone *verb* RECITE, chant
intoxicated *adjective* 1 DRUNK, drunken, inebriated, legless (*informal*), paralytic (*informal*), plastered (*slang*), tipsy, under the influence (*informal*)
2 EUPHORIC, dizzy, elated, enraptured, excited, exhilarated, high (*informal*), wired (*slang*)
intoxicating *adjective*
1 ALCOHOLIC, strong
2 EXCITING, exhilarating, heady, thrilling
intoxication *noun*
1 DRUNKENNESS, inebriation, insobriety, tipsiness
2 EXCITEMENT, delirium, elation, euphoria, exhilaration
intransigent *adjective*
UNCOMPROMISING, hardline, intractable, obdurate, obstinate, stiff-necked, stubborn, unbending, unyielding
intrepid *adjective* FEARLESS, audacious, bold, brave, courageous, daring, gallant, plucky, stouthearted, valiant

intricacy noun COMPLEXITY, complication, convolutions, elaborateness

intricate adjective COMPLICATED, complex, convoluted, elaborate, fancy, involved, labyrinthine, tangled, tortuous

intrigue verb 1 INTEREST, attract, fascinate, rivet, titillate
2 PLOT, connive, conspire, machinate, maneuver, scheme
▶ noun 3 PLOT, chicanery, collusion, conspiracy, machination, maneuver, scheme, stratagem, wile
4 AFFAIR, amour, intimacy, liaison, romance

intriguing adjective INTERESTING, beguiling, compelling, diverting, exciting, fascinating, tantalizing, titillating

intrinsic adjective INBORN, basic, built-in, congenital, constitutional, essential, fundamental, inbred, inherent, native, natural

introduce verb 1 PRESENT, acquaint, familiarize, make known
2 BRING IN, establish, found, initiate, institute, launch, pioneer, set up, start
3 BRING UP, advance, air, broach, moot, put forward, submit
4 INSERT, add, inject, put in, throw in (informal)

introduction noun 1 LAUNCH, establishment, inauguration, institution, pioneering
2 OPENING, foreword, intro (informal), lead-in, preamble, preface, prelude, prologue

introductory adjective PRELIMINARY, first, inaugural, initial, opening, preparatory

introspective adjective INWARD-LOOKING, brooding, contemplative, introverted, meditative, pensive

introverted adjective INTROSPECTIVE, inner-directed, inward-looking, self-contained, withdrawn

intrude verb INTERFERE, butt in, encroach, infringe, interrupt, meddle, push in, trespass

intruder noun TRESPASSER, gate-crasher (informal), infiltrator, interloper, invader, prowler

intrusion noun INVASION, encroachment, infringement, interference, interruption, trespass, violation

intrusive adjective INTERFERING, impertinent, importunate, meddlesome, nosy (informal), presumptuous, pushy (informal), uncalled-for, unwanted

intuition noun INSTINCT, hunch, insight, perception, presentiment, sixth sense

intuitive adjective INSTINCTIVE, innate, spontaneous, untaught

inundate verb FLOOD, drown, engulf, immerse, overflow, overrun, overwhelm, submerge, swamp

invade verb 1 ATTACK, assault, burst in, descend upon, encroach, infringe, make inroads, occupy, raid, violate
2 INFEST, overrun, permeate, pervade, swarm over

invader noun ATTACKER, aggressor, plunderer, raider, trespasser

invalid¹ adjective 1 DISABLED, ailing, bedridden, challenged, frail, ill, infirm, sick
▶ noun 2 PATIENT, convalescent, valetudinarian

invalid² adjective NULL AND VOID, fallacious, false, illogical, inoperative, irrational, unfounded, unsound, void, worthless

invalidate verb NULLIFY, annul, cancel, overthrow, undermine, undo

invaluable adjective PRECIOUS, inestimable, priceless, valuable, worth one's or its weight in gold

invariably adverb CONSISTENTLY, always, customarily, day in, day out, habitually, perpetually, regularly, unfailingly, without exception

invasion noun 1 ATTACK, assault, campaign, foray, incursion, inroad, offensive, onslaught, raid 2 INTRUSION, breach, encroachment, infraction, infringement, usurpation, violation

invective noun ABUSE, censure, denunciation, diatribe, tirade, tongue-lashing, vilification, vituperation

invent verb 1 CREATE, coin, conceive, design, devise, discover, formulate, improvise, originate, think up 2 MAKE UP, concoct, cook up (informal), fabricate, feign, forge, manufacture, trump up

invention noun 1 CREATION, brainchild (informal), contraption, contrivance, design, device, discovery, gadget, instrument 2 CREATIVITY, genius, imagination, ingenuity, inventiveness, originality, resourcefulness 3 FICTION, fabrication, falsehood, fantasy, forgery, lie, untruth, yarn

inventive adjective CREATIVE, fertile, imaginative, ingenious, innovative, inspired, original, resourceful

inventor noun CREATOR, architect, author, coiner, designer, maker, originator

inventory noun LIST, account, catalog, file, record, register, roll, roster

inverse adjective OPPOSITE, contrary, converse, reverse, reversed, transposed

invert verb OVERTURN, reverse, transpose, turn upside down, upturn

invest verb 1 SPEND, advance, devote, lay out, put in, sink 2 EMPOWER, authorize, charge, license, sanction, vest

investigate verb EXAMINE, explore, go into, inquire into, inspect, look into, probe, research, study

investigation noun EXAMINATION, exploration, inquest, inquiry, inspection, probe, review, search, study, survey

investigator noun EXAMINER, gumshoe (slang), inquirer, (private) detective, private eye (informal), researcher, sleuth

investiture noun INSTALLATION, enthronement, inauguration, induction, ordination

investment noun 1 TRANSACTION, speculation, venture 2 STAKE, ante (informal), contribution

inveterate adjective LONG-STANDING, chronic, confirmed, deep-seated, dyed-in-the-wool, entrenched, habitual, hardened, incorrigible, incurable

invidious adjective UNDESIRABLE, hateful

invigorate verb REFRESH, energize, enliven, exhilarate, fortify, galvanize, liven up, revitalize, stimulate

invincible adjective UNBEATABLE,

impregnable, indestructible, indomitable, insuperable, invulnerable, unassailable, unconquerable

inviolable adjective SACROSANCT, hallowed, holy, inalienable, sacred, unalterable

inviolate adjective INTACT, entire, pure, unbroken, undefiled, unhurt, unpolluted, unsullied, untouched, whole

invisible adjective UNSEEN, imperceptible, indiscernible

invitation noun REQUEST, call, invite (informal), summons

invite verb 1 REQUEST, ask, beg, bid, summon
2 ENCOURAGE, ask for (informal), attract, court, entice, provoke, tempt, welcome

inviting adjective TEMPTING, alluring, appealing, attractive, enticing, mouthwatering, seductive, welcoming

invocation noun APPEAL, entreaty, petition, prayer, supplication

invoke verb 1 CALL UPON, appeal to, beg, beseech, entreat, implore, petition, pray, supplicate
2 APPLY, implement, initiate, put into effect, resort to, use

involuntary adjective UNINTENTIONAL, automatic, instinctive, reflex, spontaneous, unconscious, uncontrolled, unthinking

involve verb 1 ENTAIL, imply, mean, necessitate, presuppose, require
2 CONCERN, affect, draw in, implicate, touch

involved adjective 1 COMPLICATED, complex, confusing, convoluted, elaborate, intricate, labyrinthine, tangled, tortuous
2 CONCERNED, caught (up),

implicated, mixed up in or with, participating, taking part

involvement noun CONNECTION, association, commitment, interest, participation

invulnerable adjective SAFE, impenetrable, indestructible, insusceptible, invincible, proof against, secure, unassailable

inward adjective 1 INCOMING, entering, inbound, ingoing
2 INTERNAL, inner, inside, interior
3 PRIVATE, confidential, hidden, inmost, innermost, personal, secret

inwardly adverb PRIVATELY, at heart, deep down, inside, secretly

irate adjective ANGRY, annoyed, cross, enraged, furious, incensed, indignant, infuriated, livid

irksome adjective IRRITATING, annoying, bothersome, disagreeable, exasperating, tiresome, troublesome, trying, vexing, wearisome

iron adjective 1 FERROUS, chalybeate, ferric
2 INFLEXIBLE, adamant, hard, implacable, indomitable, rigid, steely, strong, tough, unbending, unyielding

ironic, ironical adjective
1 SARCASTIC, double-edged, mocking, sardonic, satirical, with tongue in cheek, wry
2 PARADOXICAL, incongruous

iron out verb SETTLE, clear up, get rid of, put right, reconcile, resolve, smooth over, sort out, straighten out

irony noun 1 SARCASM, mockery, satire
2 PARADOX, incongruity

irrational adjective ILLOGICAL, absurd, crazy, nonsensical, preposterous, unreasonable

irrefutable *adjective* UNDENIABLE, certain, incontestable, incontrovertible, indisputable, indubitable, sure, unquestionable

irregular *adjective* 1 VARIABLE, erratic, fitful, haphazard, occasional, random, spasmodic, sporadic, unsystematic
2 UNCONVENTIONAL, abnormal, exceptional, extraordinary, peculiar, unofficial, unorthodox, unusual
3 UNEVEN, asymmetrical, bumpy, crooked, jagged, lopsided, ragged, rough

irregularity *noun* 1 UNCERTAINTY, desultoriness, disorganization, haphazardness
2 ABNORMALITY, anomaly, oddity, peculiarity, unorthodoxy
3 UNEVENNESS, asymmetry, bumpiness, jaggedness, lopsidedness, raggedness, roughness

irrelevant *adjective* UNCONNECTED, beside the point, extraneous, immaterial, impertinent, inapplicable, inappropriate, neither here nor there, unrelated

irreparable *adjective* BEYOND REPAIR, incurable, irremediable, irretrievable, irreversible

irrepressible *adjective* EBULLIENT, boisterous, buoyant, effervescent, unstoppable

irreproachable *adjective* BLAMELESS, beyond reproach, faultless, impeccable, innocent, perfect, pure, unimpeachable

irresistible *adjective* OVERWHELMING, compelling, compulsive, overpowering, urgent

irresponsible *adjective* IMMATURE, careless, reckless, scatterbrained, shiftless, thoughtless, unreliable, untrustworthy

irreverent *adjective* DISRESPECTFUL, cheeky (*informal*), flippant, iconoclastic, impertinent, impudent, mocking, tongue-in-cheek

irreversible *adjective* IRREVOCABLE, final, incurable, irreparable, unalterable

irrevocable *adjective* FIXED, fated, immutable, irreversible, predestined, predetermined, settled, unalterable

irrigate *verb* WATER, flood, inundate, moisten, wet

irritability *noun* BAD TEMPER, ill humor, impatience, irascibility, prickliness, testiness, tetchiness, touchiness

irritable *adjective* BAD-TEMPERED, cantankerous, crotchety, ill-tempered, irascible, oversensitive, prickly, testy, tetchy, touchy

irritate *verb* 1 ANNOY, anger, bother, exasperate, get on one's nerves (*informal*), infuriate, needle (*informal*), nettle, rankle with, try one's patience
2 RUB, chafe, inflame, pain

irritated *adjective* ANNOYED, angry, bothered, cross, exasperated, nettled, piqued, put out, vexed

irritating *adjective* ANNOYING, disturbing, infuriating, irksome, maddening, nagging, troublesome, trying

irritation *noun* 1 ANNOYANCE, anger, displeasure, exasperation, indignation, resentment, testiness, vexation
2 NUISANCE, drag (*informal*), irritant, pain in the neck (*informal*), thorn in one's flesh

island *noun* ISLE, ait *or* eyot (*dialect*), atoll, cay *or* key, islet

isolate *verb* SEPARATE, cut off, detach, disconnect, insulate, segregate, set apart

isolated *adjective* REMOTE, hidden, lonely, off the beaten track, outlying, out-of-the-way, secluded

isolation *noun* SEPARATION, detachment, remoteness, seclusion, segregation, solitude

issue *noun* 1 TOPIC, bone of contention, matter, point, problem, question, subject
2 OUTCOME, consequence, effect, end result, result, upshot
3 EDITION, copy, number, printing
4 CHILDREN, descendants, heirs, offspring, progeny
5 ▷▷ **take issue** DISAGREE, challenge, dispute, object, oppose, raise an objection, take exception
▶ *verb* 6 PUBLISH, announce, broadcast, circulate, deliver, distribute, give out, put out, release

isthmus *noun* STRIP, spit

itch *noun* 1 IRRITATION, itchiness, prickling, tingling
2 DESIRE, craving, hankering, hunger, longing, lust, passion, yearning, yen (*informal*)
▶ *verb* 3 PRICKLE, irritate, tickle, tingle
4 LONG, ache, crave, hanker, hunger, lust, pine, yearn

itchy *adjective* IMPATIENT, eager, edgy, fidgety, restive, restless, unsettled

item *noun* 1 DETAIL, article, component, entry, matter, particular, point, thing
2 REPORT, account, article, bulletin, dispatch, feature, note, notice, paragraph, piece

itinerant *adjective* WANDERING, migratory, nomadic, peripatetic, roaming, roving, traveling, vagrant

itinerary *noun* SCHEDULE, program, route, timetable

jab *verb or noun* POKE, dig, lunge, nudge, prod, punch, stab, tap, thrust

jabber *verb* CHATTER, babble, blether, gabble, mumble, prate, rabbit (on) (*Brit. informal*), ramble, yap (*informal*)

jacket *noun* COVERING, case, casing, coat, sheath, skin, wrapper, wrapping

jackpot *noun* PRIZE, award, bonanza, reward, winnings

jack up *verb* RAISE, elevate, hoist, lift, lift up

jaded *adjective* TIRED, exhausted, fatigued, spent, weary

jagged *adjective* UNEVEN, barbed, craggy, indented, ragged, serrated, spiked, toothed

jail *noun* 1 PRISON, nick (*Brit. slang*), penitentiary (*U.S.*), reformatory, slammer (*slang*)
▶ *verb* 2 IMPRISON, confine, detain, incarcerate, lock up, send down

jailer *noun* GUARD, keeper, warden, warder

jam *verb* 1 PACK, cram, force, press, ram, squeeze, stuff, wedge

2 CROWD, crush, throng
3 CONGEST, block, clog, obstruct, stall, stick
▶ *noun* 4 PREDICAMENT, deep water, fix (*informal*), hole (*slang*), hot water, pickle (*informal*), tight spot, trouble

jamboree *noun* FESTIVAL, carnival, celebration, festivity, fête, revelry, spree

jangle *verb* RATTLE, chime, clank, clash, clatter, jingle, vibrate

janitor *noun* CARETAKER, concierge, custodian, doorkeeper, porter

jar¹ *noun* POT, container, crock, jug, pitcher, urn, vase

jar² *verb* 1 JOLT, bump, convulse, rattle, rock, shake, vibrate
2 IRRITATE, annoy, get on one's nerves (*informal*), grate, irk, nettle, offend
▶ *noun* 3 JOLT, bump, convulsion, shock, vibration

jargon *noun* PARLANCE, argot, idiom, usage

jaundiced *adjective* 1 CYNICAL, skeptical
2 BITTER, envious, hostile, jealous, resentful, spiteful, suspicious

jaunt *noun* OUTING, airing, excursion, expedition, ramble, stroll, tour, trip

jaunty *adjective* SPRIGHTLY, buoyant, carefree, high-spirited, lively, perky, self-confident, sparky

jaw *verb* TALK, chat, chatter, chew the fat (*slang*), gossip, spout

jaws *plural noun* OPENING, entrance, mouth

jazz up *verb* ENLIVEN, animate, enhance, improve

jazzy *adjective* FLASHY, fancy, gaudy, snazzy (*informal*)

jealous *adjective* 1 ENVIOUS,

covetous, desirous, green, grudging, resentful
2 WARY, mistrustful, protective, suspicious, vigilant, watchful

jealousy noun ENVY, covetousness, mistrust, possessiveness, resentment, spite, suspicion

jeans plural noun DENIMS, Levis (Trademark)

jeer verb 1 SCOFF, barrack, deride, gibe, heckle, mock, ridicule, taunt
▶ noun 2 TAUNT, abuse, boo, catcall, derision, gibe, ridicule

jell verb 1 SOLIDIFY, congeal, harden, set, thicken
2 TAKE SHAPE, come together, crystallize, materialize

jeopardize verb ENDANGER, chance, expose, gamble, imperil, risk, stake, venture

jeopardy noun DANGER, insecurity, peril, risk, vulnerability

jerk verb or noun TUG, jolt, lurch, pull, thrust, twitch, wrench, yank

jerky adjective BUMPY, convulsive, jolting, jumpy, shaky, spasmodic, twitchy

jest noun 1 JOKE, bon mot, crack (slang), jape, pleasantry, prank, quip, wisecrack (informal), witticism
▶ verb 2 JOKE, kid (informal), mock, quip, tease

jester noun CLOWN, buffoon, fool, harlequin

jet¹ adjective BLACK, coal-black, ebony, inky, pitch-black, raven, sable

jet² noun 1 STREAM, flow, fountain, gush, spout, spray, spring
2 NOZZLE, atomizer, sprayer, sprinkler
▶ verb 3 FLY, soar, zoom

jettison verb ABANDON, discard, dump, eject, expel, scrap, throw overboard, unload

jetty noun PIER, breakwater, dock, groyne, mole, quay, wharf

jewel noun 1 GEMSTONE, ornament, rock (slang), sparkler (informal)
2 RARITY, collector's item, find, gem, humdinger (slang), pearl, treasure, wonder

jewelry noun JEWELS, finery, gems, ornaments, regalia, treasure, trinkets

jib verb REFUSE, balk, recoil, retreat, shrink, stop short

jibe see GIBE

jiffy noun (slang) INSTANT, blink of an eye (informal), flash, heartbeat (informal), second, two shakes of a lamb's tail (slang)

jig verb SKIP, bob, bounce, caper, prance, wiggle

jingle noun 1 RATTLE, clang, clink, reverberation, ringing, tinkle
2 SONG, chorus, ditty, melody, tune
▶ verb 3 RING, chime, clatter, clink, jangle, rattle, tinkle

jinx noun 1 CURSE, evil eye (informal), hex (informal), hoodoo (informal), nemesis
▶ verb 2 CURSE, bewitch, hex (informal)

jitters plural noun NERVES, anxiety, butterflies (in one's stomach) (informal), cold feet (informal), fidgets, nervousness, the shakes (informal)

jittery adjective NERVOUS, agitated, anxious, fidgety, jumpy, shaky, trembling, twitchy (informal), wired (slang)

job noun 1 TASK, assignment, chore, duty, enterprise, errand, undertaking, venture
2 OCCUPATION, business, calling, career, employment, livelihood, profession, vocation

jobless adjective UNEMPLOYED, idle, inactive, out of work, unoccupied

jocular *adjective* 1 HUMOROUS, amusing, droll, facetious, funny, joking, jovial, playful, sportive, teasing, waggish

jog *verb* 1 NUDGE, prod, push, shake, stir
2 RUN, canter, lope, trot

John Doe *noun* (*informal*) MAN IN THE STREET, average guy, average person, know-nothing (*slang*)

joie de vivre *noun* ENTHUSIASM, ebullience, enjoyment, gusto, relish, zest

join *verb* 1 CONNECT, add, append, attach, combine, couple, fasten, link, unite
2 ENROLL, enlist, enter, sign up

joint *adjective* 1 SHARED, collective, combined, communal, cooperative, joined, mutual, united
▶ *noun* 2 JUNCTION, connection, hinge, intersection, nexus, node
▶ *verb* 3 DIVIDE, carve, cut up, dissect, segment, sever

jointly *adverb* COLLECTIVELY, as one, in common, in conjunction, in league, in partnership, mutually, together

joke *noun* 1 JEST, gag (*informal*), jape, prank, pun, quip, wisecrack (*informal*), witticism
2 CLOWN, buffoon, laughing stock
▶ *verb* 3 JEST, banter, kid (*informal*), mock, play the fool, quip, taunt, tease

joker *noun* COMEDIAN, buffoon, clown, comic, humorist, jester, prankster, trickster, wag, wit

jolly *adjective* HAPPY, cheerful, chirpy (*informal*), genial, jovial, merry, playful, sprightly, upbeat (*informal*)

jolt *noun* 1 JERK, bump, jar, jog, jump, lurch, shake, start
2 SURPRISE, blow, bolt from the blue, bombshell, setback, shock
▶ *verb* 3 JERK, jar, jog, jostle, knock, push, shake, shove
4 SURPRISE, discompose, disturb, perturb, stagger, startle, stun

jostle *verb* PUSH, bump, elbow, hustle, jog, jolt, shake, shove

jot *verb* 1 NOTE DOWN, list, record, scribble
▶ *noun* 2 BIT, fraction, grain, morsel, scrap, speck

journal *noun* 1 NEWSPAPER, daily, gazette, magazine, monthly, periodical, weekly
2 DIARY, blog (*informal*), chronicle, log, record, weblog

journalist *noun* REPORTER, broadcaster, columnist, commentator, correspondent, hack, journo (*slang*), newsman *or* newswoman, pressman

journey *noun* 1 TRIP, excursion, expedition, odyssey, pilgrimage, tour, trek, voyage
▶ *verb* 2 TRAVEL, go, proceed, roam, rove, tour, traverse, trek, voyage, wander

jovial *adjective* CHEERFUL, animated, cheery, convivial, happy, jolly, merry, mirthful

joy *noun* DELIGHT, bliss, ecstasy, elation, gaiety, glee, pleasure, rapture, satisfaction

joyful *adjective* DELIGHTED, elated, enraptured, glad, gratified, happy, jubilant, merry, pleased

joyless *adjective* UNHAPPY, cheerless, depressed, dismal, dreary, gloomy, miserable, sad

joyous *adjective* JOYFUL, festive, merry, rapturous

jubilant *adjective* OVERJOYED, elated, enraptured, euphoric, exuberant, exultant, thrilled, triumphant

jubilation *noun* JOY, celebration,

ecstasy, elation, excitement, exultation, festivity, triumph

jubilee noun CELEBRATION, festival, festivity, holiday

judge noun 1 REFEREE, adjudicator, arbiter, arbitrator, moderator, umpire
2 CRITIC, arbiter, assessor, authority, connoisseur, expert
3 MAGISTRATE, beak (*Brit. slang*), justice
▸ verb 4 ARBITRATE, adjudicate, decide, mediate, referee, umpire
5 CONSIDER, appraise, assess, esteem, estimate, evaluate, rate, value

judgment noun 1 SENSE, acumen, discernment, discrimination, prudence, shrewdness, understanding, wisdom
2 VERDICT, arbitration, decision, decree, finding, ruling, sentence
3 OPINION, appraisal, assessment, belief, diagnosis, estimate, finding, valuation, view

judicial adjective LEGAL, official

judicious adjective SENSIBLE, astute, careful, discriminating, enlightened, prudent, shrewd, thoughtful, well-judged, wise

jug noun CONTAINER, carafe, crock, ewer, jar, pitcher, urn, vessel

juggle verb MANIPULATE, alter, change, maneuver, modify

juice noun LIQUID, extract, fluid, liquor, nectar, sap

juicy adjective 1 MOIST, lush, succulent
2 INTERESTING, colorful, provocative, racy, risqué, sensational, spicy (*informal*), suggestive, vivid

jumble noun 1 MUDDLE, clutter, confusion, disarray, disorder, mess, mishmash, mixture
▸ verb 2 MIX, confuse, disorder,

disorganize, mistake, muddle, shuffle

jumbo adjective GIANT, gigantic, huge, immense, large, oversized, supersize

jump verb 1 LEAP, bounce, bound, hop, hurdle, skip, spring, vault
2 RECOIL, flinch, jerk, start, wince
3 MISS, avoid, evade, omit, skip
4 INCREASE, advance, ascend, escalate, rise, surge
▸ noun 5 LEAP, bound, hop, skip, spring, vault
6 INTERRUPTION, break, gap, hiatus, lacuna, space
7 RISE, advance, increase, increment, upsurge, upturn

jumped-up adjective CONCEITED, arrogant, insolent, overbearing, pompous, presumptuous

jumpy adjective NERVOUS, agitated, anxious, apprehensive, fidgety, jittery (*informal*), on edge, restless, tense, wired (*slang*)

junction noun CONNECTION, coupling, linking, union

juncture noun MOMENT, occasion, point, time

junior adjective MINOR, inferior, lesser, lower, secondary, subordinate, younger

junk noun RUBBISH, clutter, debris, litter, odds and ends, refuse, scrap, trash, waste

jurisdiction noun 1 AUTHORITY, command, control, influence, power, rule
2 RANGE, area, bounds, compass, field, province, scope, sphere

just adverb 1 EXACTLY, absolutely, completely, entirely, perfectly, precisely
2 RECENTLY, hardly, lately, only now, scarcely
3 MERELY, by the skin of one's teeth, only, simply, solely

▶ *adjective* 4 FAIR, conscientious, equitable, fair-minded, good, honest, upright, virtuous
5 PROPER, appropriate, apt, deserved, due, fitting, justified, merited, rightful

justice *noun* 1 FAIRNESS, equity, honesty, integrity, law, legality, legitimacy, right
2 JUDGE, magistrate

justifiable *adjective* REASONABLE, acceptable, defensible, excusable, legitimate, sensible, understandable, valid, warrantable

justification *noun* 1 EXPLANATION, defense, excuse, rationalization, vindication

2 REASON, basis, grounds, warrant

justify *verb* EXPLAIN, defend, exculpate, excuse, exonerate, support, uphold, vindicate, warrant

justly *adverb* PROPERLY, correctly, equitably, fairly, lawfully

jut *verb* STICK OUT, bulge, extend, overhang, poke, project, protrude

juvenile *adjective* 1 YOUNG, babyish, callow, childish, immature, inexperienced, infantile, puerile, youthful
▶ *noun* 2 CHILD, adolescent, boy, girl, infant, minor, youth

juxtaposition *noun* PROXIMITY, adjacency, closeness, contact, nearness, propinquity, vicinity

kamikaze *adjective* SELF-DESTRUCTIVE, foolhardy, suicidal

keel over *verb* COLLAPSE, black out (*informal*), faint, pass out

keen *adjective* 1 EAGER, ardent, avid, enthusiastic, impassioned, intense, zealous
2 SHARP, cutting, incisive, razor-like
3 ASTUTE, canny, clever, perceptive, quick, shrewd, wise

keenness *noun* EAGERNESS, ardor, enthusiasm, fervor, intensity, passion, zeal, zest

keep *verb* 1 RETAIN, conserve, control, hold, maintain, possess, preserve
2 STORE, carry, deposit, hold, place, stack, stock
3 LOOK AFTER, care for, guard, maintain, manage, mind, protect, tend, watch over
4 SUPPORT, feed, maintain, provide for, subsidize, sustain
5 DETAIN, delay, hinder, hold back, keep back, obstruct, prevent, restrain
▶ *noun* 6 BOARD, food, living, maintenance
7 TOWER, castle

keeper *noun* GUARDIAN, attendant, caretaker, curator, custodian, guard, preserver, steward, warden

keeping *noun* 1 CARE, charge, custody, guardianship, possession, protection, safekeeping
2 *as in* **in keeping with** AGREEMENT, accord, balance, compliance, conformity, correspondence, harmony, observance, proportion

keepsake *noun* SOUVENIR, memento, relic, reminder, symbol, token

keep up *verb* MAINTAIN, continue, keep pace, preserve, sustain

keg *noun* BARREL, cask, drum, vat

kernel *noun* ESSENCE, core, germ, gist, nub, pith, substance

key *noun* 1 OPENER, latchkey
2 ANSWER, explanation, solution
▶ *adjective* 3 ESSENTIAL, crucial, cutting edge, decisive, fundamental, important, leading, main, major, pivotal, principal

key in *verb* TYPE, enter, input, keyboard

keynote *noun* HEART, center, core, essence, gist, substance, theme

kick *verb* 1 BOOT, punt
2 (*informal*) GIVE UP, abandon, desist from, leave off, quit, stop
▶ *noun* 3 (*informal*) THRILL, buzz (*slang*), pleasure, stimulation

kick off *verb* (*informal*) BEGIN, commence, get the show on the road, initiate, open, start

kick out *verb* DISMISS, eject, evict, expel, get rid of, remove, sack (*informal*)

kid¹ *noun* (*informal*) CHILD, baby, bairn, infant, minor, teenager, tot, youngster, youth

kid² *verb* TEASE, delude, fool, hoax, jest, joke, pretend, trick, wind up (*Brit. slang*)

kidnap *verb* ABDUCT, capture, hijack, hold to ransom, seize

kill *verb* 1 SLAY, assassinate, butcher, destroy, execute, exterminate, liquidate, massacre, murder, slaughter
2 SUPPRESS, extinguish, halt, quash, quell, scotch, smother, stifle, stop

killer *noun* ASSASSIN, butcher, cut-throat, executioner, exterminator, gunman, hit man (*slang*), murderer, slayer

killing *adjective* 1 (*informal*) TIRING, debilitating, exhausting, fatiguing, punishing
2 (*informal*) HILARIOUS, comical, ludicrous, uproarious
▶ *noun* 3 SLAUGHTER, bloodshed, carnage, extermination, homicide, manslaughter, massacre, murder, slaying
4 (*informal*) BONANZA, bomb (*slang*), cleanup (*informal*), coup, gain, profit, success, windfall

killjoy *noun* SPOILSPORT, dampener, wet blanket (*informal*)

kin *noun* FAMILY, kindred, kinsfolk, relations, relatives

kind¹ *adjective* CONSIDERATE, benign, charitable, compassionate, courteous, friendly, generous, humane, kindly, obliging, philanthropic, tender-hearted

kind² *noun* CLASS, brand, breed, family, set, sort, species, variety

kind-hearted *adjective* SYMPATHETIC, altruistic, compassionate, considerate, generous, good-natured, helpful, humane, kind, tender-hearted

kindle *verb* 1 SET FIRE TO, ignite, inflame, light
2 AROUSE, awaken, induce, inspire, provoke, rouse, stimulate, stir

kindliness *noun* KINDNESS, amiability, benevolence, charity, compassion, friendliness, gentleness, humanity, kind-heartedness

kindly *adjective* 1 GOOD-NATURED, benevolent, benign, compassionate, helpful, kind, pleasant, sympathetic, warm
▶ *adverb* 2 POLITELY, agreeably, cordially, graciously, tenderly, thoughtfully

kindness *noun* GOODWILL, benevolence, charity, compassion, generosity, humanity, kindliness, philanthropy, understanding

kindred *adjective* 1 SIMILAR, akin, corresponding, like, matching, related
▶ *noun* 2 FAMILY, kin, kinsfolk, relations, relatives

king *noun* RULER, emperor, monarch, sovereign

kingdom *noun* COUNTRY, nation, realm, state, territory

kink *noun* 1 TWIST, bend, coil, wrinkle
2 QUIRK, eccentricity, fetish, foible, idiosyncrasy, vagary, whim

kinky *adjective* 1 (*slang*) WEIRD, eccentric, odd, outlandish, peculiar, queer, quirky, strange
2 TWISTED, coiled, curled, tangled

kinship *noun* 1 RELATION, consanguinity, kin, ties of blood
2 SIMILARITY, affinity, association, connection, correspondence, relationship

kiosk *noun* BOOTH, bookstall, counter, newsstand, stall, stand

kiss *verb* 1 OSCULATE, neck (*informal*), peck (*informal*)
2 BRUSH, glance, graze, scrape,

touch
▶ *noun* 3 OSCULATION, peck
(*informal*), smacker (*slang*), smooch
(*slang*)

kit *noun* EQUIPMENT, apparatus,
gear, paraphernalia, tackle, tools

knack *noun* SKILL, ability, aptitude,
capacity, expertise, facility, gift,
propensity, talent, trick

knave *noun* ROGUE, blackguard,
bounder (*old-fashioned Brit. slang*),
rascal, rotter (*slang, chiefly Brit.*),
scoundrel, villain

knead *verb* SQUEEZE, form,
manipulate, massage, mold,
press, rub, shape, work

kneel *verb* GENUFLECT, get (down)
on one's knees, stoop

knell *noun* RINGING, chime, peal,
sound, toll

knick-knack *noun* TRINKET,
bagatelle, bauble, bric-a-brac,
plaything, trifle

knife *noun* 1 BLADE, cutter
▶ *verb* 2 CUT, lacerate, pierce, slash,
stab, wound

knit *verb* 1 JOIN, bind, fasten,
intertwine, link, tie, unite, weave
2 WRINKLE, crease, furrow, knot,
pucker

knob *noun* LUMP, bump, hump,
knot, projection, protrusion, stud

knock *verb* 1 HIT, belt (*informal*),
cuff, punch, rap, smack, strike,
thump
2 (*informal*) CRITICIZE, abuse,
belittle, censure, condemn,
denigrate, deprecate, disparage,
find fault, run down
▶ *noun* 3 BLOW, clip, clout (*informal*),
cuff, rap, slap, smack, thump
4 SETBACK, defeat, failure, rebuff,
rejection, reversal

knock down *verb* DEMOLISH,
destroy, fell, level, raze

knock off *verb* 1 STOP WORK, clock

off, clock out, finish
2 STEAL, nick (*slang, chiefly Brit.*),
pinch, rob, thieve

knockout *noun* 1 KILLER BLOW,
coup de grâce, KO or K.O. (*slang*)
2 SUCCESS, hit, sensation,
smash, smash hit, triumph,
winner

knot *noun* 1 CONNECTION, bond,
joint, ligature, loop, tie
2 CLUSTER, bunch, clump,
collection
▶ *verb* 3 TIE, bind, loop, secure,
tether

know *verb* 1 REALIZE, comprehend,
feel certain, notice, perceive,
recognize, see, understand
2 BE ACQUAINTED WITH, be familiar
with, have dealings with, have
knowledge of, recognize

know-how *noun* CAPABILITY,
ability, aptitude, expertise,
ingenuity, knack, knowledge,
savoir-faire, skill, talent

knowing *adjective* MEANINGFUL,
expressive, significant

knowingly *adverb* DELIBERATELY,
consciously, intentionally, on
purpose, purposely, willfully,
wittingly

knowledge *noun* 1 LEARNING,
education, enlightenment,
erudition, instruction,
intelligence, scholarship, wisdom
2 ACQUAINTANCE, cognizance,
familiarity, intimacy

knowledgeable *adjective* 1 WELL-
INFORMED, *au fait*, aware, clued-up
(*informal*), cognizant, conversant,
experienced, familiar, in the
know (*informal*)
2 INTELLIGENT, educated, erudite,
learned, scholarly

known *adjective* FAMOUS,
acknowledged, avowed,
celebrated, noted, recognized,

well-known
knuckle under *verb* GIVE WAY, accede, acquiesce, capitulate, cave in (*informal*), give in, submit, succumb, surrender, yield

kudos *noun* PRAISE, acclaim, applause, credit, laudation, plaudits, recognition

l

2 CORD, bootlace, shoelace, string, tie

▶ *verb* 3 FASTEN, bind, do up, thread, tie

4 MIX IN, add to, fortify, spike

lacerate *verb* TEAR, claw, cut, gash, mangle, rip, slash, wound

laceration *noun* CUT, gash, rent, rip, slash, tear, wound

lack *noun* 1 SHORTAGE, absence, dearth, deficiency, need, scarcity, want

▶ *verb* 2 NEED, be deficient in, be short of, be without, miss, require, want

lackadaisical *adjective*
1 LETHARGIC, apathetic, dull, half-hearted, indifferent, languid, listless

2 LAZY, abstracted, dreamy, idle, indolent, inert

lackey *noun* 1 HANGER-ON, brown-noser (*slang*), flatterer, minion, sycophant, toady, yes man

2 MANSERVANT, attendant, flunky, footman, valet

lackluster *adjective* FLAT, drab, dull, leaden, lifeless, muted, prosaic, uninspired, vapid

laconic *adjective* TERSE, brief, concise, curt, monosyllabic, pithy, short, succinct

lad *noun* BOY, fellow, guy (*informal*), juvenile, kid (*informal*), youngster, youth

laden *adjective* LOADED, burdened, charged, encumbered, full, weighed down

lady *noun* 1 GENTLEWOMAN, dame
2 WOMAN, female

ladylike *adjective* REFINED, elegant, genteel, modest, polite, proper, respectable, sophisticated, well-bred

lag *verb* HANG BACK, dawdle, delay, linger, loiter, straggle, tarry, trail

label *noun* 1 TAG, marker, sticker, ticket

▶ *verb* 2 MARK, stamp, tag

labor *noun* 1 WORK, industry, toil
2 WORKERS, employees, hands, laborers, workforce
3 CHILDBIRTH, delivery, parturition

▶ *verb* 4 WORK, endeavor, slave, strive, struggle, sweat (*informal*), toil

5 (usually with *under*) BE DISADVANTAGED, be a victim of, be burdened by, suffer

6 OVEREMPHASIZE, dwell on, elaborate, overdo, strain

labored *adjective* FORCED, awkward, difficult, heavy, stiff, strained

laborer *noun* WORKER, blue-collar worker, drudge, hand, manual worker, navvy (*Brit. informal*)

laborious *adjective* HARD, arduous, backbreaking, exhausting, onerous, strenuous, tiring, tough, wearisome

labyrinth *noun* MAZE, intricacy, jungle, tangle

lace *noun* 1 NETTING, filigree, openwork

laggard noun STRAGGLER, dawdler, idler, loiterer, slowcoach (*Brit. informal*), slowpoke (*informal*), sluggard, snail

laid-back adjective RELAXED, casual, easy-going, free and easy, unflappable (*informal*), unhurried

lair noun NEST, burrow, den, earth, hole

laissez faire noun NONINTERVENTION, free enterprise, free trade

lake noun POND, basin, lagoon, loch (*Scot.*), lough (*Irish*), mere, pool, reservoir, tarn

lame adjective 1 DISABLED, challenged, crippled, game, handicapped, hobbling, limping
2 UNCONVINCING, feeble, flimsy, inadequate, lousy (*slang*), pathetic, poor, thin, unsatisfactory, weak

lament verb 1 COMPLAIN, bemoan, bewail, deplore, grieve, mourn, regret, sorrow, wail, weep
▶ noun 2 COMPLAINT, lamentation, moan, wailing
3 DIRGE, elegy, requiem, threnody

lamentable adjective REGRETTABLE, deplorable, distressing, grievous, mournful, tragic, unfortunate, woeful

lampoon noun 1 SATIRE, burlesque, caricature, parody, send-up (*Brit. informal*), skit, spoof (*informal*), takeoff (*informal*)
▶ verb 2 RIDICULE, caricature, make fun of, mock, parody, satirize, send up (*Brit. informal*), take off (*informal*)

land noun 1 GROUND, dry land, earth, terra firma
2 SOIL, dirt, ground, loam
3 COUNTRYSIDE, farmland
4 PROPERTY, estate, grounds, realty
5 COUNTRY, district, nation, province, region, territory, tract
▶ verb 6 ARRIVE, alight, come to rest, disembark, dock, touch down
7 END UP, turn up, wind up
8 (*informal*) OBTAIN, acquire, gain, get, secure, win

landlord noun 1 INNKEEPER, host, hotelier
2 OWNER, freeholder, lessor, proprietor

landmark noun 1 FEATURE, monument
2 MILESTONE, turning point, watershed

landscape noun SCENERY, countryside, outlook, panorama, prospect, scene, view, vista

landslide noun 1 ROCKFALL, avalanche, landslip
▶ adjective 2 OVERWHELMING, conclusive, decisive, runaway

lane noun ROAD, alley, footpath, passageway, path, pathway, street, way

language noun 1 SPEECH, communication, discourse, expression, parlance, talk
2 TONGUE, dialect, patois, vernacular

languid adjective 1 LAZY, indifferent, lackadaisical, languorous, listless, unenthusiastic
2 LETHARGIC, dull, heavy, sluggish, torpid

languish verb 1 WEAKEN, decline, droop, fade, fail, faint, flag, wilt, wither
2 (often with *for*) PINE, desire, hanker, hunger, long, yearn
3 BE NEGLECTED, be abandoned, rot, suffer, waste away

lank adjective 1 LIMP, lifeless, straggling
2 THIN, emaciated, gaunt, lean, scrawny, skinny, slender, slim,

spare

lanky *adjective* GANGLING, angular, bony, gaunt, rangy, spare, tall

lap¹ *noun* CIRCUIT, circle, loop, orbit, tour

lap² *verb* 1 RIPPLE, gurgle, plash, purl, splash, swish, wash
2 DRINK, lick, sip, sup

lapse *noun* 1 MISTAKE, error, failing, fault, indiscretion, negligence, omission, oversight, slip
2 INTERVAL, break, breathing space, gap, intermission, interruption, lull, pause
3 DROP, decline, deterioration, fall
▶ *verb* 4 DROP, decline, degenerate, deteriorate, fall, sink, slide, slip
5 END, expire, run out, stop, terminate

lapsed *adjective* OUT OF DATE, discontinued, ended, expired, finished, invalid, run out

large *adjective* 1 BIG, considerable, enormous, gigantic, great, huge, immense, massive, monumental, sizable *or* sizeable, substantial, supersize, vast
2 ▷▷ **at large: a** FREE, at liberty, on the loose, on the run, unconfined
b IN GENERAL, as a whole, chiefly, generally, in the main, mainly
c AT LENGTH, exhaustively, greatly, in full detail

largely *adverb* MAINLY, as a rule, by and large, chiefly, generally, mostly, predominantly, primarily, principally, to a great extent

large-scale *adjective* WIDE-RANGING, broad, extensive, far-reaching, global, sweeping, vast, wholesale, wide

lark *noun* 1 PRANK, caper, escapade, fun, game, jape, mischief
▶ *verb* 2 ▷▷ **lark about** PLAY, caper, cavort, have fun, make mischief

lash¹ *noun* 1 BLOW, hit, stripe, stroke, swipe (*informal*)
▶ *verb* 2 WHIP, beat, birch, flog, scourge, thrash
3 POUND, beat, buffet, dash, drum, hammer, smack, strike
4 SCOLD, attack, blast, censure, criticize, put down, slate (*informal*), tear into (*informal*), upbraid

lash² *verb* FASTEN, bind, make fast, secure, strap, tie

lass *noun* GIRL, damsel, lassie (*informal*), maid, maiden, young woman

last¹ *adjective* 1 HINDMOST, at the end, rearmost
2 MOST RECENT, latest
3 FINAL, closing, concluding, terminal, ultimate
▶ *adverb* 4 IN THE REAR, after, behind, bringing up the rear, in *or* at the end

last² *verb* CONTINUE, abide, carry on, endure, keep on, persist, remain, stand up, survive

lasting *adjective* CONTINUING, abiding, durable, enduring, long-standing, long-term, perennial, permanent

latch *noun* 1 FASTENING, bar, bolt, catch, hasp, hook, lock
▶ *verb* 2 FASTEN, bar, bolt, make fast, secure

late *adjective* 1 OVERDUE, behind, behindhand, belated, delayed, last-minute, tardy
2 RECENT, advanced, fresh, modern, new
3 DEAD, deceased, defunct, departed, former, past
▶ *adverb* 4 BELATEDLY, at the last minute, behindhand, behind time, dilatorily, tardily

lately *adverb* RECENTLY, in recent times, just now, latterly, not long ago, of late

lateness noun DELAY, belatedness, tardiness

latent adjective HIDDEN, concealed, dormant, invisible, potential, undeveloped, unrealized

later adverb AFTERWARDS, after, by and by, in a while, in time, later on, subsequently, thereafter

lateral adjective SIDEWAYS, edgeways, flanking

latest adjective UP-TO-DATE, cool (informal), current, fashionable, modern, most recent, newest, phat (slang), up-to-the-minute

lather noun 1 FROTH, bubbles, foam, soapsuds, suds
2 (informal) FLUSTER, dither, flap (informal), fuss, state (informal), sweat, tizzy (informal)
▶ verb 3 FROTH, foam, soap

latitude noun SCOPE, elbowroom, freedom, laxity, leeway, liberty, license, play

latter adjective LAST-MENTIONED, closing, concluding, last, second

latterly adverb RECENTLY, lately, of late

lattice noun GRID, grating, grille, trellis

laudable adjective PRAISEWORTHY, admirable, commendable, creditable, excellent, meritorious, of note, worthy

laugh verb 1 CHUCKLE, be in stitches, chortle, giggle, guffaw, snigger, split one's sides, titter
▶ noun 2 CHUCKLE, chortle, giggle, guffaw, snigger, titter
3 (informal) CLOWN, card (informal), entertainer, hoot (informal), scream (informal)
4 (informal) JOKE, hoot (informal), lark, scream (informal)

laughable adjective RIDICULOUS, absurd, derisory, farcical, ludicrous, nonsensical, preposterous, risible

laughing stock noun FIGURE OF FUN, Aunt Sally (Brit.), butt, target, victim

laugh off verb DISREGARD, brush aside, dismiss, ignore, minimize, pooh-pooh, shrug off

laughter noun AMUSEMENT, glee, hilarity, merriment, mirth

launch verb 1 PROPEL, discharge, dispatch, fire, project, send off, set in motion
2 BEGIN, commence, embark upon, inaugurate, initiate, instigate, introduce, open, start

laurels plural noun GLORY, credit, distinction, fame, honor, kudos, praise, prestige, recognition, renown

lavatory noun TOILET, bathroom, cloakroom (Brit.), latrine, loo (Brit. informal), powder room, (public) convenience, washroom, water closet, W.C.

lavish adjective 1 PLENTIFUL, abundant, copious, profuse, prolific
2 GENEROUS, bountiful, free, liberal, munificent, open-handed, unstinting
3 EXTRAVAGANT, exaggerated, excessive, immoderate, prodigal, unrestrained, wasteful, wild
▶ verb 4 SPEND, deluge, dissipate, expend, heap, pour, shower, squander, waste

law noun 1 CONSTITUTION, charter, code
2 RULE, act, command, commandment, decree, edict, order, ordinance, regulation, statute
3 PRINCIPLE, axiom, canon, precept

law-abiding adjective OBEDIENT, compliant, dutiful, good, honest, honorable, lawful, orderly, peaceable

law-breaker noun CRIMINAL, convict, crook (informal), culprit, delinquent, felon, miscreant, offender, perp (informal), villain, wrongdoer

lawful adjective LEGAL, authorized, constitutional, legalized, legitimate, licit, permissible, rightful, valid, warranted

lawless adjective DISORDERLY, anarchic, chaotic, rebellious, riotous, unruly, wild

lawlessness noun ANARCHY, chaos, disorder, mob rule

lawsuit noun CASE, action, dispute, industrial tribunal, litigation, proceedings, prosecution, suit, trial

lawyer noun LEGAL ADVISER, advocate, attorney, barrister (chiefly Brit.), counsel, counselor, solicitor (chiefly Brit.)

lax adjective SLACK, careless, casual, lenient, negligent, overindulgent, remiss, slapdash, slipshod

lay¹ verb 1 PLACE, deposit, leave, plant, put, set, set down, spread
2 ARRANGE, organize, position, set out
3 PRODUCE, bear, deposit
4 PUT FORWARD, advance, bring forward, lodge, offer, present, submit
5 ATTRIBUTE, allocate, allot, ascribe, assign, impute
6 DEVISE, concoct, contrive, design, hatch, plan, plot, prepare, work out
7 BET, gamble, give odds, hazard, risk, stake, wager

lay² adjective 1 NONCLERICAL, secular
2 NONSPECIALIST, amateur, inexpert, nonprofessional

layer noun TIER, row, seam, stratum, thickness

layman noun AMATEUR, lay person, nonprofessional, outsider

layoff noun DISMISSAL, discharge, unemployment

lay off verb DISMISS, discharge, let go, make redundant, pay off

lay on verb PROVIDE, cater (for), furnish, give, purvey, supply

layout noun ARRANGEMENT, design, formation, outline, plan

lay out verb 1 ARRANGE, design, display, exhibit, plan, spread out
2 (informal) SPEND, disburse, expend, fork out (slang), invest, pay, shell out (informal)
3 (informal) KNOCK OUT, knock for six (informal), knock unconscious, KO or K.O. (slang)

laziness noun IDLENESS, inactivity, indolence, slackness, sloth, sluggishness

lazy adjective 1 IDLE, inactive, indolent, inert, slack, slothful, slow, workshy
2 LETHARGIC, drowsy, languid, languorous, sleepy, slow-moving, sluggish, somnolent, torpid

lead verb 1 GUIDE, conduct, escort, pilot, precede, show the way, steer, usher
2 PERSUADE, cause, dispose, draw, incline, induce, influence, prevail, prompt
3 COMMAND, direct, govern, head, manage, preside over, supervise
4 BE AHEAD (OF), blaze a trail, come first, exceed, excel, outdo, outstrip, surpass, transcend
5 LIVE, experience, have, pass, spend, undergo
6 RESULT IN, bring on, cause, contribute, produce
▶ noun 7 FIRST PLACE, precedence, primacy, priority, supremacy,

vanguard

8 ADVANTAGE, edge, margin, start

9 EXAMPLE, direction, guidance, leadership, model

10 CLUE, hint, indication, suggestion

11 LEADING ROLE, principal, protagonist, title role

▶ adjective 12 MAIN, chief, cutting edge, first, foremost, head, leading, premier, primary, prime, principal

leader noun PRINCIPAL, alpha male, boss (informal), captain, chief, chieftain, commander, director, guide, head, ringleader, ruler

leadership noun 1 GUIDANCE, direction, domination, management, running, superintendency

2 AUTHORITY, command, control, influence, initiative, pre-eminence, supremacy

leading adjective MAIN, chief, cutting edge, dominant, first, foremost, greatest, highest, primary, principal

lead on verb ENTICE, beguile, deceive, draw on, lure, seduce, string along (informal), tempt

lead up to verb INTRODUCE, pave the way, prepare for

leaf noun 1 FROND, blade

2 PAGE, folio, sheet

▶ verb 3 ▷▷ **leaf through** BROWSE, flip, glance, riffle, skim, thumb (through)

leaflet noun BOOKLET, brochure, circular, pamphlet

leafy adjective GREEN, bosky (literary), shaded, shady, verdant

league noun 1 ASSOCIATION, alliance, coalition, confederation, consortium, federation, fraternity, group, guild, partnership, union

2 CLASS, category, level

leak noun 1 HOLE, aperture, chink, crack, crevice, fissure, opening, puncture

2 DRIP, leakage, percolation, seepage

3 DISCLOSURE, divulgence

▶ verb 4 DRIP, escape, exude, ooze, pass, percolate, seep, spill, trickle

5 DISCLOSE, divulge, give away, let slip, make known, make public, pass on, reveal, tell

leaky adjective PUNCTURED, cracked, holey, leaking, perforated, porous, split

lean¹ verb 1 REST, be supported, prop, recline, repose

2 BEND, heel, incline, slant, slope, tilt, tip

3 TEND, be disposed to, be prone to, favor, prefer

4 ▷▷ **lean on** DEPEND ON, count on, have faith in, rely on, trust

lean² adjective 1 SLIM, angular, bony, gaunt, rangy, skinny, slender, spare, thin, wiry

2 UNPRODUCTIVE, barren, meager, poor, scanty, unfruitful

leaning noun TENDENCY, bent, bias, disposition, inclination, partiality, penchant, predilection, proclivity, propensity

leap verb 1 JUMP, bounce, bound, hop, skip, spring

▶ noun 2 JUMP, bound, spring, vault

3 INCREASE, escalation, rise, surge, upsurge, upswing

learn verb 1 MASTER, grasp, pick up

2 MEMORIZE, commit to memory, get off pat, learn by heart

3 DISCOVER, ascertain, detect, discern, find out, gather, hear, understand

learned adjective SCHOLARLY, academic, erudite, highbrow, intellectual, versed, well-informed, well-read

learner noun BEGINNER, apprentice, neophyte, novice, tyro

learning noun KNOWLEDGE, culture, education, erudition, information, lore, scholarship, study, wisdom

lease verb HIRE, charter, let, loan, rent

leash noun LEAD, rein, tether

least adjective SMALLEST, fewest, lowest, meanest, minimum, poorest, slightest, tiniest

leathery adjective TOUGH, hard, rough

leave¹ verb 1 DEPART, decamp, disappear, exit, go away, make tracks, move, pull out, quit, retire, slope off, withdraw
2 FORGET, leave behind, mislay
3 CAUSE, deposit, generate, produce, result in
4 GIVE UP, abandon, drop, relinquish, renounce, surrender
5 ENTRUST, allot, assign, cede, commit, consign, give over, refer
6 BEQUEATH, hand down, will

leave² noun 1 PERMISSION, allowance, authorization, concession, consent, dispensation, freedom, liberty, sanction
2 HOLIDAY, furlough, leave of absence, sabbatical, time off, vacation
3 PARTING, adieu, departure, farewell, good-bye, leave-taking, retirement, withdrawal

leave out verb OMIT, blow off (slang), cast aside, disregard, exclude, ignore, neglect, overlook, reject

lecherous adjective LUSTFUL, lascivious, lewd, libidinous, licentious, prurient, randy

(informal, chiefly Brit.), salacious

lecture noun 1 TALK, address, discourse, instruction, lesson, speech
2 REBUKE, dressing-down (informal), reprimand, reproof, scolding, talking-to (informal), telling off (informal)
▶ verb 3 TALK, address, discourse, expound, hold forth, speak, spout, teach
4 SCOLD, admonish, berate, castigate, censure, reprimand, reprove, tell off (informal)

ledge noun SHELF, mantle, projection, ridge, sill, step

leer noun or verb GRIN, gloat, goggle, ogle, smirk, squint, stare

lees plural noun SEDIMENT, deposit, dregs, grounds

leeway noun ROOM, elbowroom, latitude, margin, play, scope, space

left adjective 1 LEFT-HAND, larboard (nautical), port, sinistral
2 (of politics) SOCIALIST, leftist, left-wing, radical

leftover noun REMNANT, oddment, scrap

left-wing adjective SOCIALIST, communist, radical, red (informal)

leg noun 1 LIMB, lower limb, member, pin (informal), stump (informal)
2 SUPPORT, brace, prop, upright
3 STAGE, lap, part, portion, section, segment, stretch
4 ▷▷ **pull someone's leg** (informal) TEASE, fool, kid (informal), make fun of, trick, wind up (Brit. slang)

legacy noun BEQUEST, estate, gift, heirloom, inheritance

legal adjective 1 LEGITIMATE, allowed, authorized, constitutional, lawful, licit, permissible, sanctioned, valid

2 JUDICIAL, forensic, juridical

legality noun LEGITIMACY, lawfulness, rightfulness, validity

legalize verb ALLOW, approve, authorize, decriminalize, legitimate, legitimize, license, permit, sanction, validate

legation noun DELEGATION, consulate, embassy, representation

legend noun 1 MYTH, fable, fiction, folk tale, saga, story, tale
2 CELEBRITY, luminary, megastar (informal), phenomenon, prodigy
3 INSCRIPTION, caption, motto

legendary adjective 1 MYTHICAL, apocryphal, fabled, fabulous, fictitious, romantic, traditional
2 FAMOUS, celebrated, famed, illustrious, immortal, renowned, well-known

legibility noun CLARITY, neatness, readability

legible adjective CLEAR, decipherable, distinct, easy to read, neat, readable

legion noun 1 ARMY, brigade, company, division, force, troop
2 MULTITUDE, drove, horde, host, mass, myriad, number, throng

legislation noun 1 LAWMAKING, enactment, prescription, regulation
2 LAW, act, bill, charter, measure, regulation, ruling, statute

legislative adjective LAW-MAKING, judicial, law-giving

legislator noun LAWMAKER, lawgiver

legislature noun PARLIAMENT, assembly, chamber, congress, senate

legitimate adjective 1 LEGAL, authentic, authorized, genuine, kosher (informal), lawful, licit, rightful

2 REASONABLE, admissible, correct, justifiable, logical, sensible, valid, warranted, well-founded
▶ verb 3 AUTHORIZE, legalize, legitimize, permit, pronounce lawful, sanction

legitimize verb LEGALIZE, authorize, permit, sanction

leisure noun SPARE TIME, ease, freedom, free time, liberty, recreation, relaxation, rest

leisurely adjective UNHURRIED, comfortable, easy, gentle, lazy, relaxed, slow

lend verb 1 LOAN, advance
2 ADD, bestow, confer, give, grant, impart, provide, supply
3 ▷▷ **lend itself to** SUIT, be appropriate, be serviceable

length noun 1 (of linear extent) DISTANCE, extent, longitude, measure, reach, span
2 (of time) DURATION, period, space, span, stretch, term
3 PIECE, measure, portion, section, segment
4 ▷▷ **at length: a** IN DETAIL, completely, fully, in depth, thoroughly, to the full **b** FOR A LONG TIME, for ages, for hours, interminably **c** AT LAST, at long last, eventually, finally, in the end

lengthen verb EXTEND, continue, draw out, elongate, expand, increase, prolong, protract, spin out, stretch

lengthy adjective LONG, drawn-out, extended, interminable, long-drawn-out, long-winded, prolonged, protracted, tedious

leniency noun TOLERANCE, clemency, compassion, forbearance, indulgence, mercy, moderation, pity, quarter

lenient adjective TOLERANT,

compassionate, forbearing,
forgiving, indulgent, kind,
merciful, sparing

lesbian *adjective* HOMOSEXUAL,
gay, sapphic

less *adjective* 1 SMALLER, shorter
▶ *preposition* 2 MINUS, excepting,
lacking, subtracting, without

lessen *verb* REDUCE, contract,
decrease, diminish, ease, lower,
minimize, narrow, shrink

lesser *adjective* MINOR, inferior,
less important, lower, secondary

lesson *noun* 1 CLASS, coaching,
instruction, period, schooling,
teaching, tutoring
2 EXAMPLE, deterrent, message,
moral

let¹ *verb* 1 ALLOW, authorize,
entitle, give permission, give
the go-ahead, permit, sanction,
tolerate
2 LEASE, hire, rent

let² *noun* HINDRANCE, constraint,
impediment, interference,
obstacle, obstruction, prohibition,
restriction

letdown *noun* DISAPPOINTMENT,
anticlimax, blow, comedown
(*informal*), setback, washout
(*informal*)

let down *verb* DISAPPOINT,
disenchant, disillusion, dissatisfy,
fail, fall short, leave in the lurch,
leave stranded

lethal *adjective* DEADLY, dangerous,
destructive, devastating, fatal,
mortal, murderous, virulent

lethargic *adjective* SLUGGISH,
apathetic, drowsy, dull, languid,
listless, sleepy, slothful

lethargy *noun* SLUGGISHNESS,
apathy, drowsiness, inertia,
languor, lassitude, listlessness,
sleepiness, sloth

let off *verb* 1 FIRE, detonate,
discharge, explode
2 EMIT, exude, give off, leak,
release
3 EXCUSE, absolve, discharge,
exempt, exonerate, forgive,
pardon, release, spare

let on *verb* REVEAL, admit, disclose,
divulge, give away, let the cat
out of the bag (*informal*), make
known, say

let out *verb* 1 EMIT, give vent to,
produce
2 RELEASE, discharge, free, let go,
liberate

letter *noun* 1 CHARACTER, sign,
symbol
2 MESSAGE, communication,
dispatch, epistle, line, missive,
note

let-up *noun* LESSENING, break,
breathing space, interval,
lull, pause, remission, respite,
slackening

let up *verb* STOP, abate, decrease,
diminish, ease (up), moderate,
relax, slacken, subside

level *adjective* 1 HORIZONTAL, flat
2 EVEN, consistent, plain, smooth,
uniform
3 EQUAL, balanced,
commensurate, comparable,
equivalent, even, neck and neck,
on a level playing field (*informal*),
on a par, proportionate
▶ *verb* 4 FLATTEN, even off *or* out,
plane, smooth
5 EQUALIZE, balance, even up
6 RAZE, bulldoze, demolish,
destroy, devastate, flatten, knock
down, pull down, tear down
7 DIRECT, aim, focus, point, train
▶ *noun* 8 POSITION, achievement,
degree, grade, rank, stage,
standard, standing, status
9 ▷▷ **on the level** (*informal*)
HONEST, above board, fair,

genuine, square, straight

level-headed *adjective* STEADY, balanced, calm, collected, composed, cool, sensible, unflappable (*informal*)

lever *noun* 1 HANDLE, bar

▶ *verb* 2 PRISE, force

leverage *noun* INFLUENCE, authority, clout (*informal*), pull (*informal*), weight

levity *noun* LIGHT-HEARTEDNESS, facetiousness, flippancy, frivolity, silliness, skittishness, triviality

levy *verb* 1 IMPOSE, charge, collect, demand, exact

2 CONSCRIPT, call up, mobilize, muster, raise

▶ *noun* 3 IMPOSITION, assessment, collection, exaction, gathering

4 TAX, duty, excise, fee, tariff, toll

lewd *adjective* INDECENT, bawdy, lascivious, libidinous, licentious, lustful, obscene, pornographic, smutty, wanton, X-rated

lewdness *noun* INDECENCY, bawdiness, carnality, debauchery, depravity, lasciviousness, lechery, licentiousness, obscenity, pornography, wantonness

liability *noun* 1 RESPONSIBILITY, accountability, answerability, culpability

2 DEBT, debit, obligation

3 DISADVANTAGE, burden, drawback, encumbrance, handicap, hindrance, inconvenience, millstone, nuisance

liable *adjective* 1 RESPONSIBLE, accountable, answerable, obligated

2 VULNERABLE, exposed, open, subject, susceptible

3 LIKELY, apt, disposed, inclined, prone, tending

liaise *verb* LINK, communicate,

keep contact, mediate

liaison *noun* 1 COMMUNICATION, connection, contact, hook-up, interchange

2 AFFAIR, amour, entanglement, intrigue, love affair, romance

liar *noun* FALSIFIER, fabricator, fibber, perjurer

libel *noun* 1 DEFAMATION, aspersion, calumny, denigration, smear

▶ *verb* 2 DEFAME, blacken, malign, revile, slur, smear, vilify

libelous *adjective* DEFAMATORY, derogatory, false, injurious, malicious, scurrilous, untrue

liberal *adjective* 1 PROGRESSIVE, libertarian, radical, reformist

2 GENEROUS, beneficent, bountiful, charitable, kind, open-handed, open-hearted, unstinting

3 TOLERANT, broad-minded, indulgent, permissive

4 ABUNDANT, ample, bountiful, copious, handsome, lavish, munificent, plentiful, profuse, rich

liberality *noun* 1 GENEROSITY, beneficence, benevolence, bounty, charity, kindness, largesse *or* largess, munificence, philanthropy

2 TOLERATION, broad-mindedness, latitude, liberalism, libertarianism, permissiveness

liberalize *verb* RELAX, ease, loosen, moderate, modify, slacken, soften

liberate *verb* FREE, deliver, emancipate, let loose, let out, release, rescue, set free

liberation *noun* DELIVERANCE, emancipation, freedom, freeing, liberty, release

liberator *noun* DELIVERER, emancipator, freer, redeemer, rescuer, savior

libertine noun REPROBATE, debauchee, lecher, profligate, rake, roué, sensualist, voluptuary, womanizer

liberty noun 1 FREEDOM, autonomy, emancipation, immunity, independence, liberation, release, self-determination, sovereignty
2 IMPERTINENCE, impropriety, impudence, insolence, presumption
3 ▷▷ **at liberty** FREE, on the loose, unrestricted

libidinous adjective LUSTFUL, carnal, debauched, lascivious, lecherous, randy (informal, chiefly Brit.), sensual, wanton

license noun 1 CERTIFICATE, charter, permit, warrant
2 PERMISSION, authority, authorization, blank check, carte blanche, dispensation, entitlement, exemption, immunity, leave, liberty, right
3 LATITUDE, freedom, independence, leeway, liberty
4 LAXITY, excess, immoderation, indulgence, irresponsibility

license verb PERMIT, accredit, allow, authorize, certify, empower, sanction, warrant

licentious adjective PROMISCUOUS, abandoned, debauched, dissolute, immoral, lascivious, lustful, sensual, wanton

lick verb 1 TASTE, lap, tongue
2 (of flames) FLICKER, dart, flick, play over, ripple, touch
3 (slang) BEAT, defeat, master, outdo, outstrip, overcome, rout, trounce, vanquish
▶ noun 4 DAB, bit, stroke, touch
5 (informal) PACE, clip (informal), rate, speed

lie¹ verb 1 FALSIFY, dissimulate, equivocate, fabricate, fib, prevaricate, tell untruths
▶ noun 2 FALSEHOOD, deceit, fabrication, fib, fiction, invention, prevarication, untruth

lie² verb 1 RECLINE, loll, lounge, repose, rest, sprawl, stretch out
2 BE SITUATED, be, be placed, exist, remain

life noun 1 BEING, sentience, vitality
2 EXISTENCE, being, lifetime, span, time
3 BIOGRAPHY, autobiography, confessions, history, life story, memoirs, story
4 BEHAVIOR, conduct, life style, way of life
5 LIVELINESS, animation, energy, high spirits, spirit, verve, vigor, vitality, vivacity, zest

lifeless adjective 1 DEAD, deceased, defunct, extinct, inanimate
2 DULL, colorless, flat, lackluster, lethargic, listless, sluggish, wooden
3 UNCONSCIOUS, comatose, dead to the world (informal), insensible

lifelike adjective REALISTIC, authentic, exact, faithful, natural, true-to-life, vivid

lifelong adjective LONG-STANDING, enduring, lasting, long-lasting, perennial, persistent

lifetime noun EXISTENCE, career, day(s), span, time

lift verb 1 RAISE, draw up, elevate, hoist, pick up, uplift, upraise
2 REVOKE, annul, cancel, countermand, end, remove, rescind, stop, terminate
3 DISAPPEAR, be dispelled, disperse, dissipate, vanish
▶ noun 4 RIDE, drive, run
5 BOOST, encouragement, fillip, pick-me-up, shot in the arm

(*informal*)

6 ELEVATOR (*chiefly U.S.*)

light¹ *noun* 1 BRIGHTNESS, brilliance, glare, gleam, glint, glow, illumination, luminosity, radiance, shine

2 LAMP, beacon, candle, flare, lantern, taper, torch

3 ASPECT, angle, context, interpretation, point of view, slant, vantage point, viewpoint

4 MATCH, flame, lighter

▶ *adjective* 5 BRIGHT, brilliant, illuminated, luminous, lustrous, shining, well-lit

6 PALE, bleached, blond, faded, fair, pastel

▶ *verb* 7 IGNITE, inflame, kindle

8 ILLUMINATE, brighten, light up

light² *adjective* 1 INSUBSTANTIAL, airy, buoyant, flimsy, portable, slight, underweight

2 WEAK, faint, gentle, indistinct, mild, moderate, slight, soft

3 INSIGNIFICANT, inconsequential, inconsiderable, scanty, slight, small, trifling, trivial

4 NIMBLE, agile, graceful, lithe, sprightly, sylphlike

5 LIGHT-HEARTED, amusing, entertaining, frivolous, funny, humorous, witty

6 DIGESTIBLE, frugal, modest

▶ *verb* 7 SETTLE, alight, land, perch

8 ▷▷ **light on** *or* **upon** COME ACROSS, chance upon, discover, encounter, find, happen upon, hit upon, stumble on

lighten¹ *verb* BRIGHTEN, become light, illuminate, irradiate, light up

lighten² *verb* 1 EASE, allay, alleviate, ameliorate, assuage, lessen, mitigate, reduce, relieve

2 CHEER, brighten, buoy up, lift, perk up, revive

light-headed *adjective* FAINT, dizzy, giddy, hazy, vertiginous, woozy (*informal*)

light-hearted *adjective* CAREFREE, blithe, cheerful, happy-go-lucky, jolly, jovial, playful, upbeat (*informal*)

lightly *adverb* 1 GENTLY, delicately, faintly, slightly, softly

2 MODERATELY, sparingly, sparsely, thinly

3 EASILY, effortlessly, readily, simply

4 CARELESSLY, breezily, flippantly, frivolously, heedlessly, thoughtlessly

lightweight *adjective* UNIMPORTANT, inconsequential, insignificant, paltry, petty, slight, trifling, trivial, worthless

likable, likeable *adjective* ATTRACTIVE, agreeable, amiable, appealing, charming, engaging, nice, pleasant, sympathetic

like¹ *adjective* SIMILAR, akin, alike, analogous, corresponding, equivalent, identical, parallel, same

like² *verb* 1 ENJOY, be fond of, be keen on, be partial to, delight in, go for, love, relish, revel in

2 ADMIRE, appreciate, approve, cherish, esteem, hold dear, prize, take to

3 WISH, care to, choose, desire, fancy, feel inclined, prefer, want

4 (*informal*) BE ATTRACTED TO, be captivated by, be turned on by (*informal*), lust after, take a liking to, take to

likelihood *noun* PROBABILITY, chance, possibility, prospect

likely *adjective* 1 INCLINED, apt, disposed, liable, prone, tending

2 PROBABLE, anticipated, expected, odds-on, on the cards, to

be expected

3 PLAUSIBLE, believable, credible, feasible, possible, reasonable

4 PROMISING, hopeful, up-and-coming

liken verb COMPARE, equate, match, parallel, relate, set beside

likeness noun 1 RESEMBLANCE, affinity, correspondence, similarity

2 PORTRAIT, depiction, effigy, image, picture, representation

likewise adverb SIMILARLY, in like manner, in the same way

liking noun FONDNESS, affection, inclination, love, partiality, penchant, preference, soft spot, taste, weakness

limb noun 1 PART, appendage, arm, extremity, leg, member, wing

2 BRANCH, bough, offshoot, projection, spur

limelight noun PUBLICITY, attention, celebrity, fame, prominence, public eye, recognition, stardom, the spotlight

limit noun 1 BREAKING POINT, deadline, end, ultimate

2 BOUNDARY, border, edge, frontier, perimeter

► verb 3 RESTRICT, bound, check, circumscribe, confine, curb, ration, restrain

limitation noun RESTRICTION, check, condition, constraint, control, curb, qualification, reservation, restraint

limited adjective RESTRICTED, bounded, checked, circumscribed, confined, constrained, controlled, curbed, finite

limitless adjective INFINITE, boundless, countless, endless, inexhaustible, unbounded, unlimited, untold, vast

limp¹ verb 1 HOBBLE, falter, hop, shamble, shuffle

► noun 2 LAMENESS, hobble

limp² adjective FLOPPY, drooping, flabby, flaccid, pliable, slack, soft

line noun 1 STROKE, band, groove, mark, score, scratch, streak, stripe

2 WRINKLE, crease, crow's foot, furrow, mark

3 BOUNDARY, border, borderline, edge, frontier, limit

4 STRING, cable, cord, rope, thread, wire

5 TRAJECTORY, course, direction, path, route, track

6 JOB, area, business, calling, employment, field, occupation, profession, specialization, trade

7 ROW, column, file, procession, queue, rank

8 ▷▷ **in line for** DUE FOR, in the running for

► verb 9 MARK, crease, furrow, rule, score

10 BORDER, bound, edge, fringe

lineaments plural noun FEATURES, countenance, face, physiognomy

lined adjective 1 RULED, feint

2 WRINKLED, furrowed, wizened, worn

lines plural noun WORDS, part, script

line-up noun ARRANGEMENT, array, row, selection, team

linger verb 1 STAY, hang around, loiter, remain, stop, tarry, wait

2 DELAY, dally, dawdle, drag one's feet or heels, idle, take one's time

link noun 1 COMPONENT, constituent, element, member, part, piece

2 CONNECTION, affinity, association, attachment, bond, relationship, tie-up

► verb 3 FASTEN, attach, bind, connect, couple, join, tie, unite

4 ASSOCIATE, bracket, connect,

identify, relate

lip noun 1 EDGE, brim, brink, margin, rim
2 (slang) IMPUDENCE, backchat (informal), cheek (informal), effrontery, impertinence, insolence

liquid noun 1 FLUID, juice, solution
▶ adjective 2 FLUID, aqueous, flowing, melted, molten, running, runny
3 (of assets) CONVERTIBLE, negotiable

liquidate verb 1 PAY, clear, discharge, honor, pay off, settle, square
2 DISSOLVE, abolish, annul, cancel, terminate
3 KILL, destroy, dispatch, eliminate, exterminate, get rid of, murder, wipe out (informal)

liquor noun 1 ALCOHOL, booze (informal), drink, hard stuff (informal), spirits, strong drink
2 JUICE, broth, extract, liquid, stock

list¹ noun 1 REGISTER, catalog, directory, index, inventory, record, roll, series, tally
▶ verb 2 TABULATE, catalog, enter, enumerate, itemize, record, register

list² verb 1 LEAN, careen, heel over, incline, tilt, tip
▶ noun 2 TILT, cant, leaning, slant

listen verb 1 HEAR, attend, lend an ear, prick up one's ears
2 PAY ATTENTION, heed, mind, obey, observe, take notice

listless adjective LANGUID, apathetic, indifferent, indolent, lethargic, sluggish

literacy noun EDUCATION, knowledge, learning

literal adjective 1 EXACT, accurate, close, faithful, strict, verbatim, word for word
2 ACTUAL, bona fide, genuine, plain, real, simple, true, unvarnished

literally adverb STRICTLY, actually, exactly, faithfully, precisely, really, to the letter, truly, verbatim, word for word

literary adjective WELL-READ, bookish, erudite, formal, learned, scholarly

literate adjective EDUCATED, informed, knowledgeable

literature noun WRITINGS, letters, lore

lithe adjective SUPPLE, flexible, limber, lissom(e), loose-limbed, pliable

litigant noun CLAIMANT, party, plaintiff

litigate verb SUE, go to court, press charges, prosecute

litigation noun LAWSUIT, action, case, prosecution

litter noun 1 RUBBISH, debris, detritus, garbage (chiefly U.S.), muck, refuse, trash
2 BROOD, offspring, progeny, young
▶ verb 3 CLUTTER, derange, disarrange, disorder, mess up
4 SCATTER, strew

little adjective 1 SMALL, diminutive, miniature, minute, petite, short, tiny, wee
2 YOUNG, babyish, immature, infant, junior, undeveloped
▶ adverb 3 HARDLY, barely
4 RARELY, hardly ever, not often, scarcely, seldom
▶ noun 5 BIT, fragment, hint, particle, speck, spot, touch, trace

live¹ verb 1 EXIST, be, be alive, breathe
2 PERSIST, last, prevail
3 DWELL, abide, inhabit, lodge,

occupy, reside, settle
4 SURVIVE, endure, get along, make ends meet, subsist, support oneself
5 THRIVE, flourish, prosper

live² *adjective* 1 LIVING, alive, animate, breathing
2 TOPICAL, burning, controversial, current, hot, pertinent, pressing, prevalent
3 BURNING, active, alight, blazing, glowing, hot, ignited, smoldering

livelihood *noun* OCCUPATION, bread and butter (*informal*), employment, job, living, work

liveliness *noun* ENERGY, animation, boisterousness, dynamism, spirit, sprightliness, vitality, vivacity

lively *adjective* 1 VIGOROUS, active, agile, alert, brisk, energetic, keen, perky, quick, sprightly
2 ANIMATED, cheerful, chirpy (*informal*), sparky, spirited, upbeat (*informal*), vivacious
3 VIVID, bright, colorful, exciting, forceful, invigorating, refreshing, stimulating

liven up *verb* STIR, animate, brighten, buck up (*informal*), enliven, perk up, rouse

liverish *adjective* 1 SICK, bilious, queasy
2 IRRITABLE, crotchety, crusty, disagreeable, grumpy, ill-humored, irascible, splenetic, tetchy

livery *noun* COSTUME, attire, clothing, dress, garb, regalia, suit, uniform

livid *adjective* 1 (*informal*) ANGRY, beside oneself, enraged, fuming, furious, incensed, indignant, infuriated, outraged
2 DISCOLORED, black-and-blue, bruised, contused, purple

living *adjective* 1 ALIVE, active, breathing, existing
2 CURRENT, active, contemporary, extant, in use
▸ *noun* 3 EXISTENCE, being, existing, life, subsistence
4 LIFE STYLE, way of life

load *noun* 1 CARGO, consignment, freight, shipment
2 BURDEN, albatross, encumbrance, millstone, onus, trouble, weight, worry
▸ *verb* 3 FILL, cram, freight, heap, pack, pile, stack, stuff
4 BURDEN, encumber, oppress, saddle with, weigh down, worry
5 (*of firearms*) MAKE READY, charge, prime

loaded *adjective* 1 WEIGHTED, biased, distorted
2 TRICKY, artful, insidious, manipulative, prejudicial
3 (*slang*) RICH, affluent, flush (*informal*), moneyed, wealthy, well-heeled (*informal*), well off, well-to-do

loaf¹ *noun* 1 LUMP, block, cake, cube, slab
2 (*slang*) HEAD, gumption (*Brit. informal*), nous (*Brit. slang*), sense

loaf² *verb* IDLE, laze, lie around, loiter, lounge around, take it easy

loan *noun* 1 ADVANCE, credit
▸ *verb* 2 LEND, advance, let out

loath, loth *adjective* UNWILLING, averse, disinclined, opposed, reluctant

loathe *verb* HATE, abhor, abominate, despise, detest, dislike

loathing *noun* HATRED, abhorrence, antipathy, aversion, detestation, disgust, repugnance, repulsion, revulsion

loathsome *adjective* HATEFUL, abhorrent, detestable, disgusting, nauseating, obnoxious, odious, offensive, repugnant, repulsive, revolting, scuzzy (*slang*), vile

lobby *noun* 1 CORRIDOR, entrance hall, foyer, hallway, passage, porch, vestibule
2 PRESSURE GROUP
▶ *verb* 3 CAMPAIGN, influence, persuade, press, pressure, promote, push, urge

local *adjective* 1 REGIONAL, provincial
2 RESTRICTED (*chiefly U.S.*), confined, limited
▶ *noun* 3 RESIDENT, inhabitant, native

locality *noun* 1 NEIGHBORHOOD, area, district, neck of the woods (*informal*), region, vicinity
2 SITE, locale, location, place, position, scene, setting, spot

localize *verb* RESTRICT, circumscribe, confine, contain, delimit, limit

locate *verb* 1 FIND, come across, detect, discover, pin down, pinpoint, track down, unearth
2 PLACE, establish, fix, put, seat, set, settle, situate

location *noun* POSITION, locale, place, point, site, situation, spot, venue

lock¹ *noun* 1 FASTENING, bolt, clasp, padlock
▶ *verb* 2 FASTEN, bolt, close, seal, secure, shut
3 UNITE, clench, engage, entangle, entwine, join, link
4 EMBRACE, clasp, clutch, encircle, enclose, grasp, hug, press

lock² *noun* STRAND, curl, ringlet, tress, tuft

lockup *noun* PRISON, cell, jail

lock up *verb* IMPRISON, cage, confine, detain, incarcerate, jail, put behind bars, shut up

lodge *noun* 1 CABIN, chalet,

cottage, gatehouse, hut, shelter
2 SOCIETY, branch, chapter, club, group
▶ *verb* 3 STAY, board, room
4 STICK, come to rest, imbed, implant
5 REGISTER, file, put on record, submit

lodger *noun* TENANT, boarder, paying guest, resident

lodging *noun* (*often plural*) ACCOMMODATION, abode, apartments, digs (*Brit. informal*), quarters, residence, rooms, shelter

lofty *adjective* 1 HIGH, elevated, raised, soaring, towering
2 NOBLE, dignified, distinguished, elevated, exalted, grand, illustrious, renowned
3 HAUGHTY, arrogant, condescending, disdainful, patronizing, proud, supercilious

log *noun* 1 STUMP, block, chunk, trunk
2 RECORD, account, journal, logbook
▶ *verb* 3 CHOP, cut, fell, hew
4 RECORD, chart, note, register, set down

loggerheads *plural noun* ▷▷ **at loggerheads** QUARRELING, at daggers drawn, at each other's throats, at odds, feuding, in dispute, opposed

logic *noun* REASON, good sense, sense

logical *adjective* 1 RATIONAL, clear, cogent, coherent, consistent, sound, valid, well-organized
2 REASONABLE, plausible, sensible, wise

loiter *verb* LINGER, dally, dawdle, dilly-dally (*informal*), hang about *or* around, idle, loaf, skulk

loll *verb* 1 LOUNGE, loaf, recline,

relax, slouch, slump, sprawl

2 DROOP, dangle, drop, flap, flop, hang, sag

lone adjective SOLITARY, one, only, single, sole, unaccompanied

loneliness noun SOLITUDE, desolation, isolation, seclusion

lonely adjective 1 ABANDONED, destitute, forlorn, forsaken, friendless, lonesome

2 SOLITARY, alone, apart, companionless, isolated, lone, single, withdrawn

3 REMOTE, deserted, desolate, godforsaken, isolated, out-of-the-way, secluded, unfrequented, uninhabited

loner noun INDIVIDUALIST, lone wolf, maverick, outsider, recluse

lonesome adjective LONELY, companionless, desolate, dreary, forlorn, friendless, gloomy

long¹ adjective 1 ELONGATED, expanded, extended, extensive, far-reaching, lengthy, spread out, stretched

2 PROLONGED, interminable, lengthy, lingering, long-drawn-out, protracted, sustained

long² verb DESIRE, crave, hanker, itch, lust, pine, want, wish, yearn

longing noun DESIRE, ambition, aspiration, craving, hope, itch, thirst, urge, wish, yearning, yen (informal)

long-lived adjective LONG-LASTING, enduring

long shot noun OUTSIDER, dark horse

long-standing adjective ESTABLISHED, abiding, enduring, fixed, long-established, long-lasting, time-honored

long-suffering adjective UNCOMPLAINING, easy-going, forbearing, forgiving, patient,

resigned, stoical, tolerant

long-winded adjective RAMBLING, lengthy, long-drawn-out, prolix, prolonged, repetitious, tedious, tiresome, verbose, wordy

look verb 1 SEE, contemplate, examine, eye, gaze, glance, observe, scan, study, survey, view, watch

2 SEEM, appear, look like, strike one as

3 FACE, front, overlook

4 HOPE, anticipate, await, expect, reckon on

5 SEARCH, forage, hunt, seek

▶ noun 6 VIEW, examination, gaze, glance, glimpse, inspection, observation, peek, sight

7 APPEARANCE, air, aspect, bearing, countenance, demeanor, expression, manner, semblance

look after verb TAKE CARE OF, attend to, care for, guard, keep an eye on, mind, nurse, protect, supervise, take charge of, tend

look down on verb DISDAIN, contemn, despise, scorn, sneer, spurn

look forward to verb ANTICIPATE, await, expect, hope for, long for, look for, wait for

lookout noun 1 VIGIL, guard, readiness, watch

2 WATCHMAN, guard, sentinel, sentry

3 WATCHTOWER, observation post, observatory, post

4 (informal) CONCERN, business, worry

look out verb BE CAREFUL, beware, keep an eye out, pay attention, watch out

look up verb 1 RESEARCH, find, hunt for, search for, seek out, track down

2 IMPROVE, get better, perk up,

pick up, progress, shape up (*informal*)
3 VISIT, call on, drop in on (*informal*), look in on
4 ▷▷ **look up to** RESPECT, admire, defer to, esteem, honor, revere

loom *verb* APPEAR, bulk, emerge, hover, impend, menace, take shape, threaten

loop *noun* 1 CURVE, circle, coil, curl, ring, spiral, twirl, twist, whorl
▶ *verb* 2 TWIST, coil, curl, knot, roll, spiral, turn, wind round

loophole *noun* LET-OUT, escape, excuse

loose *adjective* 1 UNTIED, free, insecure, unattached, unbound, unfastened, unfettered, unrestricted
2 SLACK, easy, relaxed, sloppy
3 VAGUE, ill-defined, imprecise, inaccurate, indistinct, inexact, rambling, random
4 PROMISCUOUS, abandoned, debauched, dissipated, dissolute, fast, immoral, profligate
▶ *verb* 5 FREE, detach, disconnect, liberate, release, set free, unfasten, unleash, untie

loosen *verb* 1 UNTIE, detach, separate, undo, unloose
2 FREE, liberate, release, set free
3 ▷▷ **loosen up** RELAX, de-stress, ease up *or* off, go easy (*informal*), let up, soften

loot *noun* 1 PLUNDER, booty, goods, haul, prize, spoils, swag (*slang*)
▶ *verb* 2 PLUNDER, despoil, pillage, raid, ransack, ravage, rifle, rob, sack

lopsided *adjective* CROOKED, askew, asymmetrical, awry, cockeyed, disproportionate, skew-whiff (*Brit. informal*), squint, unbalanced, uneven, warped

lord *noun* 1 MASTER, commander,

governor, leader, liege, overlord, ruler, superior
2 NOBLEMAN, earl, noble, peer, viscount
3 ▷▷ **Our Lord** *or* **the Lord** JESUS CHRIST, Christ, God, Jehovah, the Almighty
▶ *verb* ▷▷ **lord it over** ORDER AROUND, boss around (*informal*), domineer, pull rank, put on airs, swagger

lordly *adjective* PROUD, arrogant, condescending, disdainful, domineering, haughty, high-handed, imperious, lofty, overbearing

lore *noun* TRADITIONS, beliefs, doctrine, sayings, teaching, wisdom

lose *verb* 1 MISLAY, be deprived of, drop, forget, misplace
2 FORFEIT, miss, pass up (*informal*), yield
3 BE DEFEATED, come to grief, lose out

loser *noun* 1 FAILURE, also-ran, dud (*informal*), flop (*informal*)
2 NERD, dork (*slang*), drip (*informal*), dweeb (*slang*), geek (*slang*)

loss *noun* 1 DEFEAT, failure, forfeiture, mislaying, squandering, waste
2 DAMAGE, cost, destruction, harm, hurt, injury, ruin
3 (sometimes plural) DEFICIT, debit, debt, deficiency, depletion
4 ▷▷ **at a loss** CONFUSED, at one's wits' end, baffled, bewildered, helpless, nonplussed, perplexed, puzzled, stumped

lost *adjective* 1 MISSING, disappeared, mislaid, misplaced, vanished, wayward
2 OFF-COURSE, adrift, astray, at sea, disoriented, off-track

lot *noun* 1 COLLECTION, assortment,

batch, bunch (*informal*),
consignment, crowd, group,
quantity, set
2 DESTINY, accident, chance,
doom, fate, fortune
3 ▷▷ **a lot** *or* **lots** PLENTY,
abundance, a great deal, heap(s),
load(s) (*informal*), masses (*informal*),
piles (*informal*), scores, stack(s)
loth *see* LOATH
lotion *noun* CREAM, balm,
embrocation, liniment, salve,
solution
lottery *noun* 1 RAFFLE, drawing,
sweepstakes
2 GAMBLE, chance, hazard, risk,
toss-up (*informal*)
loud *adjective* 1 NOISY, blaring,
booming, clamorous, deafening,
ear-splitting, forte (*music*),
resounding, thundering,
tumultuous, vociferous
2 GARISH, brash, flamboyant,
flashy, gaudy, glaring, lurid,
showy
loudly *adverb* NOISILY, deafeningly,
fortissimo (*music*), lustily, shrilly,
uproariously, vehemently,
vigorously, vociferously
lounge *verb* RELAX, laze, lie about,
loaf, loiter, loll, sprawl, take it easy
lousy *adjective* (*informal*) CRUMMY,
awful, crappy (*slang*), inadequate,
inferior, shabby, shoddy, terrible
lout *noun* OAF, boor, dolt, lummox
(*informal*), yob *or* yobbo (*Brit. slang*)
lovable, loveable *adjective*
ENDEARING, adorable, amiable,
charming, cute, delightful,
enchanting, likable *or* likeable,
lovely, sweet
love *verb* 1 ADORE, cherish, dote on,
hold dear, idolize, prize, treasure,
worship
2 ENJOY, appreciate, delight in,
like, relish, savor, take pleasure in

▶ *noun* 3 PASSION, adoration,
affection, ardor, attachment,
devotion, infatuation, tenderness,
warmth
4 LIKING, devotion, enjoyment,
fondness, inclination, partiality,
relish, soft spot, taste, weakness
5 BELOVED, darling, dear, dearest,
lover, sweetheart, truelove
6 ▷▷ **in love** ENAMORED, besotted,
charmed, enraptured, infatuated,
smitten
love affair *noun* ROMANCE,
affair, amour, intrigue, liaison,
relationship
lovely *adjective* 1 ATTRACTIVE,
adorable, beautiful, charming,
comely, exquisite, graceful,
handsome, pretty
2 ENJOYABLE, agreeable,
delightful, engaging, nice,
pleasant, pleasing
lover *noun* SWEETHEART, admirer,
beloved, boyfriend *or* girlfriend,
flame (*informal*), mistress, suitor
loving *adjective* AFFECTIONATE,
amorous, dear, devoted, doting,
fond, tender, warm-hearted
low[1] *adjective* 1 SMALL, little, short,
squat, stunted
2 INFERIOR, deficient, inadequate,
lousy (*slang*), poor, second-rate,
shoddy
3 COARSE, common, crude,
disreputable, rough, rude,
undignified, vulgar
4 DEJECTED, depressed,
despondent, disheartened,
downcast, down in the dumps
(*informal*), fed up, gloomy, glum,
miserable
5 ILL, debilitated, frail, stricken,
weak
6 QUIET, gentle, hushed, muffled,
muted, soft, subdued, whispered
lowdown *noun* (*informal*)

INFORMATION, gen (*Brit. informal*), info (*informal*), inside story, intelligence

lower *adjective* 1 MINOR, inferior, junior, lesser, secondary, second-class, smaller, subordinate
2 REDUCED, curtailed, decreased, diminished, lessened
▶ *verb* 3 DROP, depress, fall, let down, sink, submerge, take down
4 LESSEN, cut, decrease, diminish, minimize, prune, reduce, slash

low-key *adjective* SUBDUED, muted, quiet, restrained, toned down, understated

lowly *adjective* HUMBLE, meek, mild, modest, unassuming

low-spirited *adjective* DEPRESSED, dejected, despondent, dismal, down, down-hearted, fed up, low, miserable, sad

loyal *adjective* FAITHFUL, constant, dependable, devoted, dutiful, staunch, steadfast, true, trustworthy, trusty, unwavering

loyalty *noun* FAITHFULNESS, allegiance, constancy, dependability, devotion, fidelity, staunchness, steadfastness, trustworthiness

lubricate *verb* OIL, grease, smear

lucid *adjective* 1 CLEAR, comprehensible, explicit, intelligible, transparent
2 TRANSLUCENT, clear, crystalline, diaphanous, glassy, limpid, pellucid, transparent
3 CLEAR-HEADED, all there, *compos mentis*, in one's right mind, rational, sane

luck *noun* 1 FORTUNE, accident, chance, destiny, fate
2 GOOD FORTUNE, advantage, blessing, godsend, prosperity, serendipity, success, windfall

luckily *adverb* FORTUNATELY,

favorably, happily, opportunely, propitiously, providentially

luckless *adjective* ILL-FATED, cursed, doomed, hapless, hopeless, jinxed, unfortunate, unlucky

lucky *adjective* FORTUNATE, advantageous, blessed, charmed, favored, jammy (*Brit. slang*), serendipitous, successful, win-win (*informal*)

lucrative *adjective* PROFITABLE, advantageous, fruitful, productive, remunerative, well-paid

lucre *noun* MONEY, gain, mammon, pelf, profit, riches, spoils, wealth

ludicrous *adjective* RIDICULOUS, absurd, crazy, farcical, laughable, nonsensical, outlandish, preposterous, silly

luggage *noun* BAGGAGE, bags, cases, gear, impedimenta, paraphernalia, suitcases, things

lugubrious *adjective* GLOOMY, doleful, melancholy, mournful, sad, serious, somber, sorrowful, woebegone

lukewarm *adjective* 1 TEPID, warm
2 HALF-HEARTED, apathetic, cool, indifferent, unenthusiastic, unresponsive

lull *verb* 1 CALM, allay, pacify, quell, soothe, subdue, tranquilize
▶ *noun* 2 RESPITE, calm, hush, let-up (*informal*), pause, quiet, silence

lumber *verb* PLOD, clump, shamble, shuffle, stump, trudge, trundle, waddle

lumbering *adjective* AWKWARD, clumsy, heavy, hulking, ponderous, ungainly

luminous *adjective* BRIGHT, glowing, illuminated, luminescent, lustrous, radiant,

shining
lump noun 1 PIECE, ball, chunk, hunk, mass, nugget
2 SWELLING, bulge, bump, growth, hump, protrusion, tumor
▶ verb 3 GROUP, collect, combine, conglomerate, consolidate, mass, pool
lumpy adjective BUMPY, knobbly, uneven
lunacy noun 1 INSANITY, dementia, derangement, madness, mania, psychosis
2 FOOLISHNESS, absurdity, craziness, folly, foolhardiness, madness, stupidity
lunatic adjective 1 IRRATIONAL, bonkers (informal), crackbrained (informal), crackpot (informal), crazy, daft, deranged, insane, mad
▶ noun 2 MADMAN, maniac, nutcase (slang), psychopath
lunge noun 1 THRUST, charge, jab, pounce, spring, swing
▶ verb 2 POUNCE, charge, dive, leap, plunge, thrust
lurch verb 1 TILT, heave, heel, lean, list, pitch, rock, roll
2 STAGGER, reel, stumble, sway, totter, weave
lure verb 1 TEMPT, allure, attract, draw, ensnare, entice, invite, seduce
▶ noun 2 TEMPTATION, allurement, attraction, bait, carrot (informal), enticement, incentive, inducement
lurid adjective 1 SENSATIONAL, graphic, melodramatic, shocking, vivid
2 GLARING, intense
lurk verb HIDE, conceal oneself, lie in wait, prowl, skulk, slink, sneak
luscious adjective DELICIOUS, appetizing, juicy, mouth-watering, palatable, succulent, sweet, toothsome, yummy (informal)
lush adjective 1 ABUNDANT, dense, flourishing, green, rank, verdant
2 LUXURIOUS, elaborate, extravagant, grand, lavish, opulent, ornate, palatial, plush (informal), sumptuous
lust noun 1 LECHERY, lasciviousness, lewdness, sensuality
2 APPETITE, craving, desire, greed, longing, passion, thirst
▶ verb 3 DESIRE, covet, crave, hunger for or after, want, yearn
luster noun 1 SPARKLE, gleam, glint, glitter, gloss, glow, sheen, shimmer, shine
2 GLORY, distinction, fame, honor, kudos, prestige, renown
lusty adjective VIGOROUS, energetic, healthy, hearty, powerful, robust, strong, sturdy, virile
luxurious adjective SUMPTUOUS, comfortable, expensive, lavish, magnificent, opulent, plush (informal), rich, splendid
luxury noun 1 OPULENCE, affluence, hedonism, richness, splendor, sumptuousness
2 EXTRAVAGANCE, extra, frill, indulgence, treat
lying noun 1 DISHONESTY, deceit, mendacity, perjury, untruthfulness
▶ adjective 2 DECEITFUL, dishonest, false, mendacious, perfidious, treacherous, two-faced, untruthful
lyrical adjective ENTHUSIASTIC, effusive, impassioned, inspired, poetic, rhapsodic

macabre *adjective* GRUESOME, dreadful, eerie, frightening, ghastly, ghostly, ghoulish, grim, grisly, morbid

machiavellian *adjective* SCHEMING, astute, crafty, cunning, cynical, double-dealing, opportunist, sly, underhand, unscrupulous

machine *noun* 1 APPLIANCE, apparatus, contraption, contrivance, device, engine, instrument, mechanism, tool
2 SYSTEM, machinery, organization, setup (*informal*), structure

machinery *noun* EQUIPMENT, apparatus, gear, instruments, tackle, tools

macho *adjective* MANLY, chauvinist, masculine, virile

mad *adjective* 1 INSANE, crazy (*informal*), demented, deranged, *non compos mentis*, nuts (*slang*), of unsound mind, out of one's mind, psychotic, raving, unhinged, unstable
2 FOOLISH, absurd, asinine, bonkers (*informal*), daft (*informal*), foolhardy, irrational, nonsensical, preposterous, senseless, wild
3 ANGRY, berserk, enraged, furious, incensed, livid (*informal*), wild
4 ENTHUSIASTIC, ardent, avid, crazy (*informal*), fanatical, impassioned, infatuated, wild
5 FRENZIED, excited, frenetic, uncontrolled, unrestrained, wild, wired (*slang*)
6 ▷▷ **like mad** (*informal*) ENERGETICALLY, enthusiastically, excitedly, furiously, rapidly, speedily, violently, wildly

madden *verb* INFURIATE, annoy, derange, drive one crazy, enrage, incense, inflame, irritate, upset

madly *adverb* 1 INSANELY, crazily, deliriously, distractedly, frantically, frenziedly, hysterically
2 FOOLISHLY, absurdly, irrationally, ludicrously, senselessly, wildly
3 ENERGETICALLY, excitedly, furiously, like mad (*informal*), recklessly, speedily, wildly
4 (*informal*) PASSIONATELY, desperately, devotedly, intensely, to distraction

madman *or* **madwoman** *noun* LUNATIC, maniac, nutcase (*slang*), psycho (*slang*), psychopath

madness *noun* 1 INSANITY, aberration, craziness, delusion, dementia, derangement, distraction, lunacy, mania, mental illness, psychopathy, psychosis
2 FOOLISHNESS, absurdity, daftness (*informal*), folly, foolhardiness, idiocy, nonsense, preposterousness, wildness

maelstrom *noun* 1 WHIRLPOOL, vortex
2 TURMOIL, chaos, confusion, disorder, tumult, upheaval

maestro noun MASTER, expert, genius, virtuoso

magazine noun 1 JOURNAL, pamphlet, periodical
2 STOREHOUSE, arsenal, depot, store, warehouse

magic noun 1 SORCERY, black art, enchantment, necromancy, witchcraft, wizardry
2 CONJURING, illusion, legerdemain, prestidigitation, sleight of hand, trickery
3 CHARM, allurement, enchantment, fascination, glamour, magnetism, power
▶ adjective 4 or **magical** MIRACULOUS, bewitching, charming, enchanting, entrancing, fascinating, marvelous, spellbinding

magician noun SORCERER, conjurer, enchanter or enchantress, illusionist, necromancer, warlock, witch, wizard

magisterial adjective AUTHORITATIVE, commanding, lordly, masterful

magistrate noun JUDGE, J.P., justice, justice of the peace

magnanimity noun GENEROSITY, benevolence, big-heartedness, largesse or largess, nobility, selflessness, unselfishness

magnanimous adjective GENEROUS, big-hearted, bountiful, charitable, kind, noble, selfless, unselfish

magnate noun TYCOON, baron, captain of industry, mogul, plutocrat

magnetic adjective ATTRACTIVE, captivating, charismatic, charming, fascinating, hypnotic, irresistible, mesmerizing, seductive

magnetism noun CHARM, allure, appeal, attraction, charisma, drawing power, magic, pull, seductiveness

magnification noun INCREASE, amplification, enhancement, enlargement, expansion, heightening, intensification

magnificence noun SPLENDOR, brilliance, glory, grandeur, majesty, nobility, opulence, stateliness, sumptuousness

magnificent adjective 1 SPLENDID, cool (informal), glorious, gorgeous, imposing, impressive, majestic, regal, sublime, sumptuous
2 EXCELLENT, brilliant, fine, outstanding, phat (slang), splendid, superb

magnify verb 1 ENLARGE, amplify, blow up (informal), boost, dilate, expand, heighten, increase, intensify
2 OVERSTATE, exaggerate, inflate, overemphasize, overplay

magnitude noun 1 IMPORTANCE, consequence, greatness, moment, note, significance, weight
2 SIZE, amount, amplitude, extent, mass, quantity, volume

maid noun 1 GIRL, damsel, lass, lassie (informal), maiden, wench
2 SERVANT, housemaid, maidservant, serving-maid

maiden noun 1 GIRL, damsel, lass, lassie (informal), maid, virgin, wench
▶ adjective 2 UNMARRIED, unwed
3 FIRST, inaugural, initial, introductory

maidenly adjective MODEST, chaste, decent, decorous, demure, pure, virginal

mail noun 1 LETTERS, correspondence, junk mail, post (chiefly Brit.)

2 POSTAL SERVICE, collection, delivery, post office
▶ *verb* 3 POST, dispatch, forward, send, transmit

maim *verb* CRIPPLE, disable, hurt, injure, mutilate, wound

main *adjective* 1 CHIEF, central, essential, foremost, head, leading, pre-eminent, primary, principal
▶ *noun* 2 CONDUIT, cable, channel, duct, line, pipe
3 ▷▷ **in the main** ON THE WHOLE, for the most part, generally, in general, mainly, mostly

mainly *adverb* CHIEFLY, for the most part, in the main, largely, mostly, on the whole, predominantly, primarily, principally

mainstay *noun* PILLAR, anchor, backbone, bulwark, buttress, lynchpin, prop

mainstream *adjective* CONVENTIONAL, accepted, current, established, general, orthodox, prevailing, received

maintain *verb* 1 KEEP UP, carry on, continue, perpetuate, preserve, prolong, retain, sustain
2 SUPPORT, care for, look after, provide for, supply, take care of
3 ASSERT, avow, claim, contend, declare, insist, profess, state

maintenance *noun*
1 CONTINUATION, carrying-on, perpetuation, prolongation
2 UPKEEP, care, conservation, keeping, nurture, preservation, repairs
3 ALLOWANCE, alimony, keep, support

majestic *adjective* GRAND, grandiose, impressive, magnificent, monumental, regal, splendid, stately, sublime, superb

majesty *noun* GRANDEUR, glory, magnificence, nobility, pomp, splendor, stateliness

major *adjective* 1 MAIN, bigger, chief, greater, higher, leading, senior, supreme
2 IMPORTANT, critical, crucial, great, notable, outstanding, serious, significant

majority *noun* 1 PREPONDERANCE, best part, bulk, greater number, mass, most
2 ADULTHOOD, manhood *or* womanhood, maturity, seniority

make *verb* 1 CREATE, assemble, build, construct, fashion, form, manufacture, produce, put together, synthesize
2 PRODUCE, accomplish, bring about, cause, create, effect, generate, give rise to, lead to
3 FORCE, cause, compel, constrain, drive, impel, induce, oblige, prevail upon, require
4 AMOUNT TO, add up to, compose, constitute, form
5 PERFORM, carry out, do, effect, execute
6 EARN, clear, gain, get, net, obtain, win
7 ▷▷ **make it** (*informal*) SUCCEED, arrive (*informal*), crack it (*informal*), get on, prosper
▶ *noun* 8 BRAND, kind, model, sort, style, type, variety

make-believe *noun* FANTASY, imagination, play-acting, pretense, unreality

make for *verb* HEAD FOR, aim for, be bound for, head towards

make off *verb* 1 FLEE, bolt, clear out (*informal*), run away *or* off, take to one's heels
2 ▷▷ **make off with** STEAL, abduct, carry off, filch, kidnap, nick (*slang, chiefly Brit.*), pinch (*informal*), run away *or* off with

make out verb 1 SEE, detect, discern, discover, distinguish, perceive, recognize
2 UNDERSTAND, comprehend, decipher, fathom, follow, grasp, work out
3 WRITE OUT, complete, draw up, fill in or out
4 PRETEND, assert, claim, let on, make as if or though
5 FARE, get on, manage

maker noun MANUFACTURER, builder, constructor, producer

makeshift adjective TEMPORARY, expedient, provisional, stopgap, substitute

make-up noun 1 COSMETICS, face (informal), greasepaint (theatre), paint (informal), powder
2 STRUCTURE, arrangement, assembly, composition, configuration, constitution, construction, format, organization
3 NATURE, character, constitution, disposition, temperament

make up verb 1 FORM, compose, comprise, constitute
2 INVENT, coin, compose, concoct, construct, create, devise, dream up, formulate, frame, originate
3 COMPLETE, fill, supply
4 SETTLE, bury the hatchet, call it quits, reconcile
5 ▷▷ **make up for** COMPENSATE FOR, atone for, balance, make amends for, offset, recompense

making noun CREATION, assembly, building, composition, construction, fabrication, manufacture, production

makings plural noun BEGINNINGS, capacity, ingredients, potential

maladjusted adjective DISTURBED, alienated, neurotic, unstable

maladministration noun MISMANAGEMENT, corruption, dishonesty, incompetence, inefficiency, malpractice, misrule

maladroit adjective CLUMSY, awkward, cack-handed (informal), ham-fisted or ham-handed (informal), inept, inexpert, unskillful

malady noun DISEASE, affliction, ailment, complaint, disorder, illness, infirmity, sickness

malaise noun UNEASE, anxiety, depression, disquiet, melancholy

malcontent noun TROUBLEMAKER, agitator, mischief-maker, rebel, stirrer (informal)

male adjective MASCULINE, manly, virile

malefactor noun WRONGDOER, criminal, delinquent, evildoer, miscreant, offender, villain

malevolence noun MALICE, hate, hatred, ill will, rancor, spite, vindictiveness

malevolent adjective SPITEFUL, hostile, ill-natured, malicious, malign, vengeful, vindictive

malformation noun DEFORMITY, distortion, misshapenness

malformed adjective MISSHAPEN, abnormal, crooked, deformed, distorted, irregular, twisted

malfunction verb 1 BREAK DOWN, be on the blink (slang), fail, go wrong
▶ noun 2 FAULT, breakdown, defect, failure, flaw, glitch

malice noun ILL WILL, animosity, enmity, evil intent, hate, hatred, malevolence, spite, vindictiveness

malicious adjective SPITEFUL, ill-disposed, ill-natured, malevolent, rancorous, resentful, vengeful

malign verb 1 DISPARAGE, abuse, defame, denigrate, libel, run down, slander, smear, vilify

▶ *adjective* 2 EVIL, bad, destructive, harmful, hostile, injurious, malevolent, malignant, pernicious, wicked

malignant *adjective* 1 HARMFUL, destructive, hostile, hurtful, malevolent, malign, pernicious, spiteful
2 (*medical*) UNCONTROLLABLE, cancerous, dangerous, deadly, fatal, irremediable

malleable *adjective* 1 WORKABLE, ductile, plastic, soft, tensile
2 MANAGEABLE, adaptable, biddable, compliant, impressionable, pliable, tractable

malodorous *adjective* SMELLY, fetid, funky (*slang*), mephitic, nauseating, noisome, offensive, putrid, reeking, stinking

malpractice *noun* MISCONDUCT, abuse, dereliction, mismanagement, negligence

maltreat *verb* ABUSE, bully, harm, hurt, ill-treat, injure, mistreat

mammoth *adjective* COLOSSAL, enormous, giant, gigantic, huge, immense, massive, monumental, mountainous, prodigious

man *noun* 1 MALE, bloke (*Brit. informal*), chap (*informal*), dude (*informal*), gentleman, guy (*informal*)
2 HUMAN, human being, individual, person, soul
3 MANKIND, Homo sapiens, humanity, humankind, human race, people
4 MANSERVANT, attendant, retainer, servant, valet
▶ *verb* 5 STAFF, crew, garrison, occupy, people

manacle *noun* 1 HANDCUFF, bond, chain, fetter, iron, shackle
▶ *verb* 2 HANDCUFF, bind, chain, fetter, put in chains, shackle

manage *verb* 1 ADMINISTER, be in charge (of), command, conduct, direct, handle, run, supervise
2 SUCCEED, accomplish, arrange, contrive, effect, engineer
3 HANDLE, control, manipulate, operate, use
4 COPE, carry on, get by (*informal*), make do, muddle through, survive

manageable *adjective* DOCILE, amenable, compliant, easy, submissive

management *noun* 1 DIRECTORS, administration, board, employers, executive(s)
2 ADMINISTRATION, command, control, direction, handling, operation, running, supervision

manager *noun* SUPERVISOR, administrator, boss (*informal*), director, executive, governor, head, organizer

mandate *noun* COMMAND, commission, decree, directive, edict, instruction, order

mandatory *adjective* COMPULSORY, binding, obligatory, required, requisite

maneuver *noun* 1 STRATAGEM, dodge, intrigue, machination, ploy, ruse, scheme, subterfuge, tactic, trick
2 MOVEMENT, exercise, operation
▶ *verb* 3 MANIPULATE, contrive, engineer, machinate, pull strings, scheme, wangle (*informal*)
4 MOVE, deploy, exercise

manfully *adverb* BRAVELY, boldly, courageously, determinedly, gallantly, hard, resolutely, stoutly, valiantly

mangle *verb* CRUSH, deform, destroy, disfigure, distort, mutilate, ruin, spoil, tear, wreck

mangy *adjective* scruffy DIRTY, moth-eaten, scuzzy (*slang*), seedy, shabby, shoddy, squalid

manhandle verb ROUGH UP, knock about or around, maul, paw (informal)

manhood noun MANLINESS, masculinity, virility

mania noun 1 MADNESS, delirium, dementia, derangement, insanity, lunacy
2 OBSESSION, craze, fad (informal), fetish, fixation, passion, preoccupation, thing (informal)

maniac noun 1 MADMAN or MADWOMAN, headcase (informal), lunatic, psycho (slang), psychopath
2 FANATIC, enthusiast, fan, fiend (informal), freak (informal)

manifest adjective 1 OBVIOUS, apparent, blatant, clear, conspicuous, evident, glaring, noticeable, palpable, patent
▶ verb 2 DISPLAY, demonstrate, exhibit, expose, express, reveal, show

manifestation noun DISPLAY, demonstration, exhibition, expression, indication, mark, show, sign, symptom

manifold adjective NUMEROUS, assorted, copious, diverse, many, multifarious, multiple, varied, various

manipulate verb 1 WORK, handle, operate, use
2 INFLUENCE, control, direct, engineer, maneuver

mankind noun PEOPLE, Homo sapiens, humanity, humankind, human race, man

manliness noun VIRILITY, boldness, bravery, courage, fearlessness, masculinity, valor, vigor

manly adjective VIRILE, bold, brave, courageous, fearless, manful, masculine, strapping, strong, vigorous

man-made adjective ARTIFICIAL, ersatz, manufactured, mock, synthetic

manner noun 1 BEHAVIOR, air, aspect, bearing, conduct, demeanor
2 STYLE, custom, fashion, method, mode, way
3 TYPE, brand, category, form, kind, sort, variety

mannered adjective AFFECTED, artificial, pretentious, stilted

mannerism noun HABIT, characteristic, foible, idiosyncrasy, peculiarity, quirk, trait, trick

manners plural noun 1 BEHAVIOR, conduct, demeanor
2 POLITENESS, courtesy, decorum, etiquette, p's and q's, refinement

mansion noun RESIDENCE, hall, manor, seat, villa

mantle noun 1 CLOAK, cape, hood, shawl, wrap
2 COVERING, blanket, canopy, curtain, pall, screen, shroud, veil

manual adjective 1 HAND-OPERATED, human, physical
▶ noun 2 HANDBOOK, bible, instructions

manufacture verb 1 MAKE, assemble, build, construct, create, mass-produce, produce, put together, turn out
2 CONCOCT, cook up (informal), devise, fabricate, invent, make up, think up, trump up
▶ noun 3 MAKING, assembly, construction, creation, production

manufacturer noun MAKER, builder, constructor, creator, industrialist, producer

manure noun COMPOST, droppings, dung, excrement, fertilizer, muck, ordure

many *adjective* 1 NUMEROUS, abundant, countless, innumerable, manifold, myriad, umpteen (*informal*), various
▶ *noun* 2 A LOT, heaps (*informal*), lots (*informal*), plenty, scores

mar *verb* SPOIL, blemish, damage, detract from, disfigure, hurt, impair, ruin, scar, stain, taint, tarnish

maraud *verb* RAID, forage, loot, pillage, plunder, ransack, ravage

marauder *noun* RAIDER, bandit, brigand, buccaneer, outlaw, plunderer

march *verb* 1 WALK, file, pace, parade, stride, strut
▶ *noun* 2 WALK, routemarch, trek
3 PROGRESS, advance, development, evolution, progression

margin *noun* EDGE, border, boundary, brink, perimeter, periphery, rim, side, verge

marginal *adjective* 1 BORDERLINE, bordering, on the edge, peripheral
2 INSIGNIFICANT, minimal, minor, negligible, slight, small

marijuana *noun* CANNABIS, dope (*slang*), grass (*slang*), hemp, pot (*slang*)

marine *adjective* NAUTICAL, maritime, naval, seafaring, seagoing

mariner *noun* SAILOR, salt, sea dog, seafarer, seaman

marital *adjective* MATRIMONIAL, conjugal, connubial, nuptial

maritime *adjective* 1 NAUTICAL, marine, naval, oceanic, seafaring
2 COASTAL, littoral, seaside

mark *noun* 1 SPOT, blemish, blot, line, scar, scratch, smudge, stain, streak
2 SIGN, badge, device, emblem, flag, hallmark, label, symbol, token
3 CRITERION, measure, norm, standard, yardstick
4 TARGET, aim, goal, object, objective, purpose
▶ *verb* 5 SCAR, blemish, blot, scratch, smudge, stain, streak
6 CHARACTERIZE, brand, flag, identify, label, stamp
7 DISTINGUISH, denote, exemplify, illustrate, show
8 OBSERVE, attend, mind, note, notice, pay attention, pay heed, watch
9 GRADE, appraise, assess, correct, evaluate

marked *adjective* NOTICEABLE, blatant, clear, conspicuous, decided, distinct, obvious, patent, prominent, pronounced, striking

markedly *adverb* NOTICEABLY, clearly, considerably, conspicuously, decidedly, distinctly, obviously, strikingly

market *noun* 1 FAIR, bazaar, mart
▶ *verb* 2 SELL, retail, vend

marketable *adjective* SOUGHT AFTER, in demand, salable, wanted

marksman, markswoman *noun* SHARPSHOOTER, crack shot (*informal*), good shot

maroon *verb* ABANDON, desert, leave, leave high and dry (*informal*), strand

marriage *noun* WEDDING, match, matrimony, nuptials, wedlock

marry *verb* 1 WED, get hitched (*slang*), tie the knot (*informal*)
2 UNITE, ally, bond, join, knit, link, merge, unify, yoke

marsh *noun* SWAMP, bog, fen, morass, quagmire, slough

marshal *verb* 1 ARRANGE, align, array, deploy, draw up, group, line up, order, organize

2 CONDUCT, escort, guide, lead, shepherd, usher

marshy *adjective* SWAMPY, boggy, quaggy, waterlogged, wet

martial *adjective* MILITARY, bellicose, belligerent, warlike

martinet *noun* DISCIPLINARIAN, stickler

martyrdom *noun* PERSECUTION, ordeal, suffering

marvel *verb* 1 WONDER, be amazed, be awed, gape
 ▸ *noun* 2 WONDER, miracle, phenomenon, portent, prodigy

marvelous *adjective* 1 AMAZING, astonishing, astounding, breathtaking, brilliant, extraordinary, miraculous, phenomenal, prodigious, spectacular, stupendous
 2 EXCELLENT, fabulous (*informal*), fantastic (*informal*), great (*informal*), splendid, superb, terrific (*informal*), wonderful

masculine *adjective* MALE, manlike, manly, mannish, virile

mask *noun* 1 DISGUISE, camouflage, cover, façade, front, guise, screen, veil
 ▸ *verb* 2 DISGUISE, camouflage, cloak, conceal, cover, hide, obscure, screen, veil

masquerade *noun* 1 MASKED BALL, fancy dress party, revel
 2 PRETENSE, cloak, cover-up, deception, disguise, mask, pose, screen, subterfuge
 ▸ *verb* 3 POSE, disguise, dissemble, dissimulate, impersonate, pass oneself off, pretend (to be)

mass *noun* 1 PIECE, block, chunk, hunk, lump
 2 LOT, bunch, collection, heap, load, pile, quantity, stack
 3 SIZE, bulk, greatness, magnitude
 ▸ *adjective* 4 LARGE-SCALE, extensive, general, indiscriminate, wholesale, widespread
 ▸ *verb* 5 GATHER, accumulate, assemble, collect, congregate, rally, swarm, throng

massacre *noun* 1 SLAUGHTER, annihilation, blood bath, butchery, carnage, extermination, holocaust, murder
 ▸ *verb* 2 SLAUGHTER, butcher, cut to pieces, exterminate, kill, mow down, murder, wipe out

massage *noun* 1 RUB-DOWN, manipulation
 ▸ *verb* 2 RUB DOWN, knead, manipulate

massive *adjective* HUGE, big, colossal, enormous, gigantic, hefty, immense, mammoth, monumental, whopping (*informal*)

master *noun* 1 RULER, boss (*informal*), chief, commander, controller, director, governor, lord, manager
 2 EXPERT, ace (*informal*), doyen, genius, maestro, past master, virtuoso, wizard
 3 TEACHER, guide, guru, instructor, tutor
 ▸ *adjective* 4 MAIN, chief, foremost, leading, predominant, prime, principal
 ▸ *verb* 5 LEARN, get the hang of (*informal*), grasp
 6 OVERCOME, conquer, defeat, tame, triumph over, vanquish

masterful *adjective* 1 SKILLFUL, adroit, consummate, expert, fine, first-rate, masterly, superlative, supreme, world-class
 2 DOMINEERING, arrogant, bossy (*informal*), high-handed, imperious, overbearing, overweening

masterly *adjective* SKILLFUL,

adroit, consummate, crack (*slang*), expert, first-rate, masterful, supreme, world-class

mastermind *verb* 1 PLAN, conceive, devise, direct, manage, organize
▶ *noun* 2 ORGANIZER, architect, brain(s) (*informal*), director, engineer, manager, planner

masterpiece *noun* CLASSIC, jewel, magnum opus, *pièce de résistance, tour de force*

mastery *noun* 1 EXPERTISE, finesse, know-how (*informal*), proficiency, prowess, skill, virtuosity
2 CONTROL, ascendancy, command, domination, superiority, supremacy, upper hand, whip hand

match *noun* 1 GAME, bout, competition, contest, head-to-head, test, trial
2 EQUAL, counterpart, peer, rival
3 MARRIAGE, alliance, pairing, partnership
▶ *verb* 4 CORRESPOND, accord, agree, fit, go with, harmonize, tally
5 RIVAL, compare, compete, emulate, equal, measure up to

matching *adjective* IDENTICAL, coordinating, corresponding, equivalent, like, twin

matchless *adjective* UNEQUALED, incomparable, inimitable, superlative, supreme, unmatched, unparalleled, unrivaled, unsurpassed

mate *noun* 1 PARTNER, husband *or* wife, spouse
2 (*informal*) FRIEND, buddy (*informal*), chum (*informal*), comrade, crony, homeboy (*slang*), homegirl (*slang*), pal (*informal*)
3 COLLEAGUE, associate, companion
4 ASSISTANT, helper, subordinate
▶ *verb* 5 PAIR, breed, couple

material *noun* 1 SUBSTANCE, matter, stuff
2 INFORMATION, data, evidence, facts, notes
3 CLOTH, fabric
▶ *adjective* 4 PHYSICAL, bodily, concrete, corporeal, palpable, substantial, tangible
5 IMPORTANT, essential, meaningful, momentous, serious, significant, vital, weighty
6 RELEVANT, applicable, apposite, apropos, germane, pertinent

materialize *verb* OCCUR, appear, come about, come to pass, happen, take shape, turn up

materially *adverb* SIGNIFICANTLY, essentially, gravely, greatly, much, seriously, substantially

maternal *adjective* MOTHERLY

maternity *noun* MOTHERHOOD, motherliness

matrimonial *adjective* MARITAL, conjugal, connubial, nuptial

matrimony *noun* MARRIAGE, nuptials, wedding ceremony, wedlock

matted *adjective* TANGLED, knotted, tousled, uncombed

matter *noun* 1 SUBSTANCE, body, material, stuff
2 SITUATION, affair, business, concern, event, incident, proceeding, question, subject, topic
3 *as in* **what's the matter?** PROBLEM, complication, difficulty, distress, trouble, worry
▶ *verb* 4 BE IMPORTANT, carry weight, count, make a difference, signify

matter-of-fact *adjective* UNSENTIMENTAL, deadpan,

down-to-earth, emotionless,
mundane, plain, prosaic, sober,
unimaginative

mature adjective 1 GROWN-UP,
adult, full-grown, fully fledged,
mellow, of age, ready, ripe,
seasoned
▶ verb 2 DEVELOP, age, bloom,
blossom, come of age, grow up,
mellow, ripen

maturity noun ADULTHOOD,
experience, manhood or
womanhood, ripeness, wisdom

maudlin adjective SENTIMENTAL,
mawkish, overemotional, slushy
(informal), soppy (Brit. informal),
tearful, weepy (informal)

maul verb 1 ILL-TREAT, abuse,
manhandle, molest, paw
2 TEAR, batter, claw, lacerate,
mangle

maverick noun 1 REBEL, dissenter,
eccentric, heretic, iconoclast,
individualist, nonconformist,
protester, radical
▶ adjective 2 REBEL, dissenting,
eccentric, heretical, iconoclastic,
individualistic, nonconformist,
radical

mawkish adjective SENTIMENTAL,
emotional, maudlin, schmaltzy
(slang), slushy (informal), soppy
(Brit. informal)

maxim noun SAYING, adage,
aphorism, axiom, dictum, motto,
proverb, rule

maximum noun 1 TOP, ceiling,
height, peak, pinnacle, summit,
upper limit, utmost, zenith
▶ adjective 2 GREATEST, highest,
most, paramount, supreme,
topmost, utmost

maybe adverb PERHAPS, perchance
(archaic), possibly

mayhem noun CHAOS,
commotion, confusion,

destruction, disorder, fracas,
havoc, trouble, violence

maze noun 1 LABYRINTH
2 WEB, confusion, imbroglio,
tangle

meadow noun FIELD, grassland,
lea (poetic), pasture

meager adjective INSUBSTANTIAL,
inadequate, lousy (slang), measly,
paltry, poor, puny, scanty, slight,
small

meal noun (informal) FEAST, feed,
nosh (slang), repast, spread
(informal)

mean¹ verb 1 SIGNIFY, convey,
denote, express, imply, indicate,
represent, spell, stand for,
symbolize
2 INTEND, aim, aspire, design,
desire, plan, set out, want, wish

mean² adjective 1 MISERLY,
mercenary, niggardly,
parsimonious, penny-pinching,
stingy, tight-fisted, ungenerous
2 DESPICABLE, callous,
contemptible, hard-hearted, lousy
(slang), petty, scuzzy (slang), shabby,
shameful, sordid, vile

mean³ noun 1 AVERAGE, balance,
compromise, happy medium,
middle, midpoint, norm
▶ adjective 2 AVERAGE, middle,
standard

meander verb 1 WIND, snake,
turn, zigzag
2 WANDER, ramble, stroll
▶ noun 3 CURVE, bend, coil, loop,
turn, twist, zigzag

meaning noun SENSE,
connotation, drift, gist, message,
significance, substance

meaningful adjective SIGNIFICANT,
important, material, purposeful,
relevant, useful, valid,
worthwhile

meaningless adjective

POINTLESS, empty, futile, inane, inconsequential, insignificant, senseless, useless, vain, worthless

meanness *noun* 1 MISERLINESS, niggardliness, parsimony, selfishness, stinginess
2 PETTINESS, disgracefulness, ignobility, narrow-mindedness, shabbiness, shamefulness

means *plural noun* 1 METHOD, agency, instrument, medium, mode, process, way
2 MONEY, affluence, capital, fortune, funds, income, resources, wealth, wherewithal
3 ▷▷ **by all means** CERTAINLY, definitely, doubtlessly, of course, surely; **by no means** IN NO WAY, definitely not, not in the least, on no account

meantime, meanwhile *adverb* AT THE SAME TIME, concurrently, in the interim, simultaneously

measly *adjective* MEAGER, miserable, paltry, pathetic, pitiful, poor, puny, scanty, skimpy

measurable *adjective* QUANTIFIABLE, assessable, perceptible, significant

measure *noun* 1 QUANTITY, allotment, allowance, amount, portion, quota, ration, share
2 GAUGE, meter, rule, scale, yardstick
3 ACTION, act, deed, expedient, maneuver, means, procedure, step
4 LAW, act, bill, resolution, statute
5 RHYTHM, beat, cadence, meter, verse
▶ *verb* 6 QUANTIFY, assess, calculate, calibrate, compute, determine, evaluate, gauge, weigh

measured *adjective* 1 STEADY, dignified, even, leisurely, regular, sedate, slow, solemn, stately, unhurried
2 CONSIDERED, calculated, deliberate, reasoned, sober, studied, well-thought-out

measurement *noun* CALCULATION, assessment, calibration, computation, evaluation, mensuration, valuation

measure up to *verb* FULFILL THE EXPECTATIONS, be equal to, be suitable, come up to scratch (*informal*), fit *or* fill the bill, make the grade (*informal*)

meat *noun* FLESH

meaty *adjective* 1 BRAWNY, beefy (*informal*), burly, heavily built, heavy, muscular, solid, strapping, sturdy
2 INTERESTING, meaningful, profound, rich, significant, substantial

mechanical *adjective* 1 AUTOMATIC, automated
2 UNTHINKING, automatic, cursory, impersonal, instinctive, involuntary, perfunctory, routine, unfeeling

mechanism *noun* 1 MACHINE, apparatus, appliance, contrivance, device, instrument, tool
2 PROCESS, agency, means, method, operation, procedure, system, technique

meddle *verb* INTERFERE, butt in, intervene, intrude, pry, tamper

meddlesome *adjective* INTERFERING, intrusive, meddling, mischievous, officious, prying

mediate *verb* INTERVENE, arbitrate, conciliate, intercede, reconcile, referee, step in (*informal*), umpire

mediation *noun* ARBITRATION, conciliation, intercession, intervention, reconciliation

mediator noun NEGOTIATOR, arbiter, arbitrator, go-between, honest broker, intermediary, middleman, peacemaker, referee, umpire

medicinal adjective THERAPEUTIC, curative, healing, medical, remedial, restorative

medicine noun REMEDY, cure, drug, medicament, medication, nostrum

mediocre adjective SECOND-RATE, average, indifferent, inferior, middling, ordinary, passable, pedestrian, run-of-the-mill, so-so (informal), undistinguished

mediocrity noun INSIGNIFICANCE, indifference, inferiority, ordinariness, unimportance

meditate verb 1 REFLECT, cogitate, consider, contemplate, deliberate, muse, ponder, ruminate, think 2 PLAN, have in mind, intend, purpose, scheme

meditation noun REFLECTION, cogitation, contemplation, musing, pondering, rumination, study, thought

medium adjective 1 MIDDLE, average, fair, intermediate, mean, median, mediocre, middling, midway
▶ noun 2 MIDDLE, average, center, compromise, mean, midpoint 3 MEANS, agency, channel, instrument, mode, organ, vehicle, way 4 ENVIRONMENT, atmosphere, conditions, milieu, setting, surroundings 5 SPIRITUALIST

medley noun MIXTURE, assortment, farrago, hotchpotch, jumble, mélange, miscellany, mishmash, mixed bag (informal), potpourri

meek adjective SUBMISSIVE, acquiescent, compliant, deferential, docile, gentle, humble, mild, modest, timid, unassuming, unpretentious

meekness noun SUBMISSIVENESS, acquiescence, compliance, deference, docility, gentleness, humility, mildness, modesty, timidity

meet verb 1 ENCOUNTER, bump into, chance on, come across, confront, contact, find, happen on, run across, run into 2 CONVERGE, come together, connect, cross, intersect, join, link up, touch 3 SATISFY, answer, come up to, comply with, discharge, fulfill, match, measure up to 4 GATHER, assemble, collect, come together, congregate, convene, muster 5 EXPERIENCE, bear, encounter, endure, face, go through, suffer, undergo

meeting noun 1 ENCOUNTER, assignation, confrontation, engagement, introduction, rendezvous, tryst 2 CONFERENCE, assembly, conclave, congress, convention, gathering, get-together (informal), reunion, session

melancholy noun 1 SADNESS, dejection, depression, despondency, gloom, low spirits, misery, sorrow, unhappiness
▶ adjective 2 SAD, depressed, despondent, dispirited, downhearted, gloomy, glum, miserable, mournful, sorrowful

melee, mêlée noun FIGHT, brawl, fracas, free-for-all (informal), rumpus, scrimmage, scuffle, set-to (*informal*), skirmish, tussle

mellifluous *adjective* SWEET, dulcet, euphonious, honeyed, silvery, smooth, soft, soothing, sweet-sounding

mellow *adjective* 1 SOFT, delicate, full-flavored, mature, rich, ripe, sweet

▶ *verb* 2 MATURE, develop, improve, ripen, season, soften, sweeten

melodious *adjective* TUNEFUL, dulcet, euphonious, harmonious, melodic, musical, sweet-sounding

melodramatic *adjective* SENSATIONAL, blood-and-thunder, extravagant, histrionic, overdramatic, overemotional, theatrical

melody *noun* 1 TUNE, air, music, song, strain, theme

2 TUNEFULNESS, euphony, harmony, melodiousness, musicality

melt *verb* 1 DISSOLVE, fuse, liquefy, soften, thaw

2 (*often with away*) DISAPPEAR, disperse, dissolve, evanesce, evaporate, fade, vanish

3 SOFTEN, disarm, mollify, relax

member *noun* 1 REPRESENTATIVE, associate, fellow

2 LIMB, appendage, arm, extremity, leg, part

membership *noun* 1 MEMBERS, associates, body, fellows

2 PARTICIPATION, belonging, enrollment, fellowship

memento *noun* SOUVENIR, keepsake, memorial, relic, remembrance, reminder, token, trophy

memoir *noun* ACCOUNT, biography, essay, journal, life, monograph, narrative, record

memoirs *plural noun* AUTOBIOGRAPHY, diary, experiences, journals, life story, memories, recollections, reminiscences

memorable *adjective* NOTEWORTHY, celebrated, famous, historic, momentous, notable, remarkable, significant, striking, unforgettable

memorandum *noun* NOTE, communication, jotting, memo, message, minute, reminder

memorial *noun* 1 MONUMENT, memento, plaque, record, remembrance, souvenir

▶ *adjective* 2 COMMEMORATIVE, monumental

memorize *verb* REMEMBER, commit to memory, learn, learn by heart, learn by rote

memory *noun* 1 RECALL, recollection, remembrance, reminiscence, retention

2 COMMEMORATION, honor, remembrance

menace *noun* 1 THREAT, intimidation, warning

2 (*informal*) NUISANCE, annoyance, pest, plague, troublemaker

▶ *verb* 3 THREATEN, bully, frighten, intimidate, loom, lour *or* lower, terrorize

menacing *adjective* THREATENING, forbidding, frightening, intimidating, looming, louring *or* lowering, ominous

mend *verb* 1 REPAIR, darn, fix, patch, refit, renew, renovate, restore, retouch

2 IMPROVE, ameliorate, amend, correct, emend, rectify, reform, revise

3 HEAL, convalesce, get better, recover, recuperate

▶ *noun* 4 REPAIR, darn, patch, stitch

5 ▷▷ **on the mend** CONVALESCENT,

getting better, improving,
recovering, recuperating

mendacious *adjective* LYING,
deceitful, deceptive, dishonest,
duplicitous, fallacious, false,
fraudulent, insincere, untruthful

menial *adjective* **1** UNSKILLED,
boring, dull, humdrum, low-
status, routine
▶ *noun* **2** SERVANT, attendant,
dogsbody (*informal*), drudge,
flunky, lackey, skivvy (*chiefly Brit.*),
underling

mental *adjective* **1** INTELLECTUAL,
cerebral
2 (*informal*) INSANE, deranged,
disturbed, mad, mentally ill,
psychotic, unbalanced, unstable

mentality *noun* ATTITUDE, cast
of mind, character, disposition,
make-up, outlook, personality,
psychology

mentally *adverb* IN THE MIND,
in one's head, intellectually,
inwardly, psychologically

mention *verb* **1** REFER TO, bring
up, declare, disclose, divulge,
intimate, point out, reveal, state,
touch upon
▶ *noun* **2** ACKNOWLEDGMENT,
citation, recognition, tribute
3 REFERENCE, allusion, indication,
observation, remark

mentor *noun* GUIDE, adviser,
coach, counselor, guru, instructor,
teacher, tutor

menu *noun* BILL OF FARE, *carte du
jour*, tariff (*chiefly Brit.*)

mercantile *adjective* COMMERCIAL,
trading

mercenary *adjective* **1** GREEDY,
acquisitive, avaricious, grasping,
money-grubbing (*informal*), sordid,
venal
▶ *noun* **2** HIRELING, soldier of
fortune

merchandise *noun* GOODS,
commodities, produce, products,
stock, wares

merchant *noun* TRADESMAN,
broker, dealer, purveyor, retailer,
salesman, seller, shopkeeper,
supplier, trader, trafficker, vendor,
wholesaler

merciful *adjective* COMPASSIONATE,
clement, forgiving, generous,
gracious, humane, kind, lenient,
sparing, sympathetic, tender-
hearted

merciless *adjective* CRUEL,
barbarous, callous, hard-hearted,
harsh, heartless, pitiless,
ruthless, unforgiving

mercurial *adjective* LIVELY,
active, capricious, changeable,
impulsive, irrepressible, mobile,
quicksilver, spirited, sprightly,
unpredictable, volatile

mercy *noun* **1** COMPASSION,
clemency, forbearance,
forgiveness, grace, kindness,
leniency, pity
2 BLESSING, boon, godsend

mere *adjective* SIMPLE, bare,
common, nothing more than,
plain, pure, sheer

meretricious *adjective* TRASHY,
flashy, garish, gaudy, gimcrack,
showy, tawdry, tinsel

merge *verb* COMBINE,
amalgamate, blend, coalesce,
converge, fuse, join, meet, mingle,
mix, unite

merger *noun* UNION,
amalgamation, coalition,
combination, consolidation,
fusion, incorporation

merit *noun* **1** WORTH, advantage,
asset, excellence, goodness,
integrity, quality, strong point,
talent, value, virtue
▶ *verb* **2** DESERVE, be entitled to, be

worthy of, earn, have a right to, rate, warrant

meritorious *adjective* PRAISEWORTHY, admirable, commendable, creditable, deserving, excellent, good, laudable, virtuous, worthy

merriment *noun* FUN, amusement, festivity, glee, hilarity, jollity, joviality, laughter, mirth, revelry

merry *adjective* 1 CHEERFUL, blithe, carefree, convivial, festive, happy, jolly, joyous
2 (*Brit. informal*) TIPSY, happy, mellow, squiffy (*Brit. informal*), tiddly (*slang, chiefly Brit.*)

mesh *noun* 1 NET, netting, network, tracery, web
▶ *verb* 2 ENGAGE, combine, connect, coordinate, dovetail, harmonize, interlock, knit

mesmerize *verb* ENTRANCE, captivate, enthrall, fascinate, grip, hold spellbound, hypnotize

mess *noun* 1 DISORDER, chaos, clutter, confusion, disarray, disorganization, hotchpotch, jumble, litter, shambles, untidiness
2 DIFFICULTY, deep water, dilemma, fix (*informal*), hot water, jam (*informal*), muddle, pickle (*informal*), plight, predicament, tight spot
▶ *verb* 3 (often with *up*) DIRTY, clutter, disarrange, dishevel, muck up (*Brit. slang*), muddle, pollute, scramble
4 (often with *with*) INTERFERE, fiddle (*informal*), meddle, play, tamper, tinker

message *noun* 1 COMMUNICATION, bulletin, communiqué, dispatch, letter, memorandum, note, tidings, word

2 POINT, idea, import, meaning, moral, purport, theme

messenger *noun* COURIER, carrier, delivery boy, emissary, envoy, errand-boy, go-between, herald, runner

messy *adjective* UNTIDY, chaotic, cluttered, confused, dirty, disheveled, disordered, disorganized, muddled, scuzzy (*slang*), shambolic, sloppy (*informal*)

metamorphosis *noun* TRANSFORMATION, alteration, change, conversion, mutation, transmutation

metaphor *noun* FIGURE OF SPEECH, allegory, analogy, image, symbol, trope

metaphorical *adjective* FIGURATIVE, allegorical, emblematic, symbolic

mete *verb* DISTRIBUTE, administer, apportion, assign, deal, dispense, dole (*Brit. & Austral. informal*), portion

meteoric *adjective* SPECTACULAR, brilliant, dazzling, fast, overnight, rapid, speedy, sudden, swift

method *noun* 1 MANNER, approach, mode, modus operandi, procedure, process, routine, style, system, technique, way
2 ORDERLINESS, order, organization, pattern, planning, purpose, regularity, system

methodical *adjective* ORDERLY, businesslike, deliberate, disciplined, meticulous, organized, precise, regular, structured, systematic

meticulous *adjective* THOROUGH, exact, fastidious, fussy, painstaking, particular, precise, punctilious, scrupulous, strict

mettle *noun* COURAGE, bravery,

fortitude, gallantry, life, nerve, pluck, resolution, spirit, valor, vigor

microbe noun MICROORGANISM, bacillus, bacterium, bug (informal), germ, virus

microscopic adjective TINY, imperceptible, infinitesimal, invisible, minuscule, minute, negligible

midday noun NOON, noonday, twelve o'clock

middle adjective 1 CENTRAL, halfway, intermediate, intervening, mean, median, medium, mid
▶ noun 2 CENTER, focus, halfway point, heart, midpoint, midsection, midst

middle-class adjective BOURGEOIS, conventional, traditional

middling adjective 1 MEDIOCRE, indifferent, run-of-the-mill, so-so (informal), tolerable, unexceptional, unremarkable
2 MODERATE, adequate, all right, average, fair, medium, modest, O.K. or okay (informal), ordinary, passable, serviceable

midget noun DWARF, pygmy or pigmy, shrimp (informal), Tom Thumb

midnight noun TWELVE O'CLOCK, dead of night, middle of the night, the witching hour

midst noun ▷▷ **in the midst of** AMONG, amidst, during, in the middle of, in the thick of, surrounded by

midway adjective or adverb HALFWAY, betwixt and between, in the middle

might noun 1 POWER, energy, force, strength, vigor
2 ▷▷ **with might and main** FORCEFULLY, lustily, manfully,

mightily, vigorously

mightily adverb 1 VERY, decidedly, exceedingly, extremely, greatly, highly, hugely, intensely, much
2 POWERFULLY, energetically, forcefully, lustily, manfully, strongly, vigorously

mighty adjective POWERFUL, forceful, lusty, robust, strapping, strong, sturdy, vigorous

migrant noun 1 WANDERER, drifter, emigrant, immigrant, itinerant, nomad, rover, traveler
▶ adjective 2 TRAVELING, drifting, immigrant, itinerant, migratory, nomadic, roving, shifting, transient, vagrant, wandering

migrate verb MOVE, emigrate, journey, roam, rove, travel, trek, voyage, wander

migration noun WANDERING, emigration, journey, movement, roving, travel, trek, voyage

migratory adjective NOMADIC, itinerant, migrant, peripatetic, roving, transient

mild adjective 1 GENTLE, calm, docile, easy-going, equable, meek, peaceable, placid
2 BLAND, smooth
3 CALM, balmy, moderate, temperate, tranquil, warm

mildness noun GENTLENESS, calmness, clemency, docility, moderation, placidity, tranquillity, warmth

milieu noun SURROUNDINGS, background, element, environment, locale, location, scene, setting

militant adjective AGGRESSIVE, active, assertive, combative, vigorous

military adjective 1 WARLIKE, armed, martial, soldierly
▶ noun 2 ARMED FORCES, army,

forces, services

militate verb ▷▷ **militate against** COUNTERACT, be detrimental to, conflict with, counter, oppose, resist, tell against, weigh against

milk verb EXPLOIT, extract, pump, take advantage of

mill noun 1 FACTORY, foundry, plant, works

2 GRINDER, crusher

▶ verb 3 GRIND, crush, grate, pound, powder

4 SWARM, crowd, throng

millstone noun 1 GRINDSTONE, quernstone

2 BURDEN, affliction, albatross, encumbrance, load, weight

mime verb ACT OUT, gesture, represent, simulate

mimic verb 1 IMITATE, ape, caricature, do (informal), impersonate, parody, take off (informal)

▶ noun 2 IMITATOR, caricaturist, copycat (informal), impersonator, impressionist

mimicry noun IMITATION, burlesque, caricature, impersonation, mimicking, mockery, parody, take-off (informal)

mince verb 1 CUT, chop, crumble, grind, hash

2 as in **mince one's words** TONE DOWN, moderate, soften, spare, weaken

mincing adjective AFFECTED, camp (informal), dainty, effeminate, foppish, precious, pretentious, sissy

mind noun 1 INTELLIGENCE, brain(s) (informal), gray matter (informal), intellect, reason, sense, understanding, wits

2 MEMORY, recollection, remembrance

3 INTENTION, desire, disposition, fancy, inclination, leaning, notion, urge, wish

4 SANITY, judgment, marbles (informal), mental balance, rationality, reason, senses, wits

5 ▷▷ **make up one's mind** DECIDE, choose, determine, resolve

▶ verb 6 TAKE OFFENSE, be affronted, be bothered, care, disapprove, dislike, object, resent

7 PAY ATTENTION, heed, listen to, mark, note, obey, observe, pay heed to, take heed

8 GUARD, attend to, keep an eye on, look after, take care of, tend, watch

9 BE CAREFUL, be cautious, be on (one's) guard, be wary, take care, watch

mindful adjective AWARE, alert, alive to, careful, conscious, heedful, wary, watchful

mindless adjective STUPID, foolish, idiotic, inane, moronic, thoughtless, unthinking, witless

mine noun 1 PIT, colliery, deposit, excavation, shaft

2 SOURCE, abundance, fund, hoard, reserve, stock, store, supply, treasury, wealth

▶ verb 3 DIG UP, dig for, excavate, extract, hew, quarry, unearth

mingle verb 1 MIX, blend, combine, intermingle, interweave, join, merge, unite

2 ASSOCIATE, consort, fraternize, hang about or around, hobnob, rub shoulders (informal), socialize

miniature adjective SMALL, diminutive, little, minuscule, minute, scaled-down, tiny, toy

minimal adjective MINIMUM, least, least possible, nominal, slightest, smallest, token

minimize verb 1 REDUCE, curtail, decrease, diminish, miniaturize,

prune, shrink
2 PLAY DOWN, belittle, decry,
deprecate, discount, disparage,
make light or little of, underrate

minimum *adjective* **1** LEAST,
least possible, lowest, minimal,
slightest, smallest
▶ *noun* **2** LEAST, lowest, nadir

minion *noun* FOLLOWER, flunky,
hanger-on, henchman, hireling,
lackey, underling, yes man

minister *noun* **1** CLERGYMAN,
cleric, parson, pastor, preacher,
priest, rector, vicar
▶ *verb* **2** ATTEND, administer, cater
to, pander to, serve, take care
of, tend

ministry *noun* **1** DEPARTMENT,
bureau, council, office, quango
2 THE PRIESTHOOD, holy orders,
the church

minor *adjective* SMALL,
inconsequential, insignificant,
lesser, petty, slight, trivial,
unimportant
▶ *noun* UNDERAGE PERSON,
adolescent, child, juvenile,
teenager, youngster (*informal*),
youth

minstrel *noun* MUSICIAN, bard,
singer, songstress, troubadour

mint *verb* MAKE, cast, coin,
produce, punch, stamp, strike

minuscule *adjective* TINY,
diminutive, infinitesimal, little,
microscopic, miniature, minute

minute¹ *noun* MOMENT, flash,
instant, jiffy (*informal*), second,
tick (*Brit. informal*), trice

minute² *adjective* **1** SMALL,
diminutive, infinitesimal,
little, microscopic, miniature,
minuscule, tiny
2 PRECISE, close, critical, detailed,
exact, exhaustive, meticulous,
painstaking, punctilious

minutes *plural noun* RECORD,
memorandum, notes,
proceedings, transactions,
transcript

minutiae *plural noun* DETAILS, finer
points, ins and outs, niceties,
particulars, subtleties, trifles,
trivia

minx *noun* FLIRT, coquette, hussy

miracle *noun* WONDER, marvel,
phenomenon, prodigy

miraculous *adjective* WONDERFUL,
amazing, astonishing,
astounding, extraordinary,
incredible, phenomenal,
prodigious, unaccountable,
unbelievable

mirage *noun* ILLUSION,
hallucination, optical illusion

mire *noun* **1** SWAMP, bog, marsh,
morass, quagmire
2 MUD, dirt, muck, ooze, slime

mirror *noun* **1** LOOKING-GLASS,
glass, reflector
▶ *verb* **2** REFLECT, copy, echo,
emulate, follow

mirth *noun* MERRIMENT,
amusement, cheerfulness, fun,
gaiety, glee, hilarity, jollity,
joviality, laughter, revelry

mirthful *adjective* MERRY, blithe,
cheerful, cheery, festive, happy,
jolly, jovial, light-hearted, playful,
sportive

misadventure *noun* MISFORTUNE,
accident, bad luck, calamity,
catastrophe, debacle, disaster,
mishap, reverse, setback

misanthropic *adjective*
ANTISOCIAL, cynical, malevolent,
unfriendly

misapprehend *verb*
MISUNDERSTAND, misconstrue,
misinterpret, misread, mistake

misapprehension *noun*
MISUNDERSTANDING, delusion,

error, fallacy, misconception, misinterpretation, mistake

misappropriate verb STEAL, embezzle, misspend, misuse, peculate, pocket

misbehave verb ACT UP, be disobedient, make a fuss, make trouble, make waves

miscalculate verb MISJUDGE, blunder, err, overestimate, overrate, slip up, underestimate, underrate

miscarriage noun FAILURE, breakdown, error, mishap, perversion

miscarry verb FAIL, come to grief, fall through, go awry, go wrong, misfire

miscellaneous adjective MIXED, assorted, diverse, jumbled, motley, sundry, varied, various

miscellany noun ASSORTMENT, anthology, collection, hotchpotch, jumble, medley, mélange, mixed bag, mixture, potpourri, variety

mischance noun MISFORTUNE, accident, calamity, disaster, misadventure, mishap

mischief noun 1 TROUBLE, impishness, misbehavior, monkey business (informal), naughtiness, shenanigans (informal), waywardness
2 HARM, damage, evil, hurt, injury, misfortune, trouble

mischievous adjective 1 NAUGHTY, impish, playful, puckish, rascally, roguish, sportive, troublesome, wayward
2 MALICIOUS, damaging, destructive, evil, harmful, hurtful, spiteful, vicious, wicked

misconception noun DELUSION, error, fallacy, misapprehension, misunderstanding

misconduct noun IMMORALITY, impropriety, malpractice, mismanagement, wrongdoing

miscreant noun WRONGDOER, blackguard, criminal, rascal, reprobate, rogue, scoundrel, sinner, vagabond, villain

misdeed noun OFFENSE, crime, fault, misconduct, misdemeanor, sin, transgression, wrong

misdemeanor noun OFFENSE, fault, infringement, misdeed, peccadillo, transgression

miser noun SKINFLINT, cheapskate (informal), niggard, penny-pincher (informal), Scrooge

miserable adjective 1 UNHAPPY, dejected, depressed, despondent, disconsolate, forlorn, gloomy, sorrowful, woebegone, wretched
2 SQUALID, deplorable, lamentable, shameful, sordid, sorry, wretched

miserly adjective MEAN, avaricious, grasping, niggardly, parsimonious, penny-pinching (informal), stingy, tightfisted, ungenerous

misery noun 1 UNHAPPINESS, anguish, depression, desolation, despair, distress, gloom, grief, sorrow, suffering, torment, woe
2 (Brit. informal) MOANER, killjoy, pessimist, prophet of doom, sourpuss (informal), spoilsport, wet blanket (informal)

misfire verb FAIL, fall through, go wrong, miscarry

misfit noun NONCONFORMIST, eccentric, fish out of water (informal), oddball (informal), square peg (in a round hole) (informal)

misfortune noun 1 BAD LUCK, adversity, hard luck, ill luck, infelicity
2 MISHAP, affliction, calamity, disaster, reverse, setback, tragedy,

tribulation, trouble

misgiving noun UNEASE, anxiety, apprehension, distrust, doubt, qualm, reservation, suspicion, trepidation, uncertainty, worry

misguided adjective UNWISE, deluded, erroneous, ill-advised, imprudent, injudicious, misplaced, mistaken, unwarranted

mishandle verb MISMANAGE, botch, bungle, make a mess of, mess up (informal), muff

mishap noun ACCIDENT, calamity, misadventure, mischance, misfortune

misinform verb MISLEAD, deceive, misdirect, misguide

misinterpret verb MISUNDERSTAND, distort, misapprehend, misconceive, misconstrue, misjudge, misread, misrepresent, mistake

misjudge verb MISCALCULATE, overestimate, overrate, underestimate, underrate

mislay verb LOSE, lose track of, misplace

mislead verb DECEIVE, delude, fool, hoodwink, misdirect, misguide, misinform, take in (informal)

misleading adjective CONFUSING, ambiguous, deceptive, disingenuous, evasive, false

mismanage verb MISHANDLE, botch, bungle, make a mess of, mess up, misconduct, misdirect, misgovern

misplace verb LOSE, lose track of, mislay

misprint noun MISTAKE, corrigendum, erratum, literal, typo (informal)

misquote verb MISREPRESENT, falsify, twist

misrepresent verb DISTORT, disguise, falsify, misinterpret

misrule noun DISORDER, anarchy, chaos, confusion, lawlessness, turmoil

miss¹ verb 1 OMIT, leave out, let go, overlook, pass over, skip
2 AVOID, escape, evade
3 LONG FOR, pine for, yearn for
▶ noun 4 MISTAKE, blunder, error, failure, omission, oversight

misshapen adjective DEFORMED, contorted, crooked, distorted, grotesque, malformed, twisted, warped

missile noun ROCKET, projectile, weapon

missing adjective ABSENT, astray, lacking, left out, lost, mislaid, misplaced, unaccounted-for

mission noun TASK, assignment, commission, duty, errand, job, quest, undertaking, vocation

missionary noun EVANGELIST, apostle, preacher

missive noun LETTER, communication, dispatch, epistle, memorandum, message, note, report

misspent adjective WASTED, dissipated, imprudent, profitless, squandered

mist noun FOG, cloud, film, haze, smog, spray, steam, vapor

mistake noun 1 ERROR, blunder, erratum, fault, faux pas, gaffe, howler (informal), miscalculation, oversight, slip
▶ verb 2 MISUNDERSTAND, misapprehend, misconstrue, misinterpret, misjudge, misread
3 CONFUSE WITH, mix up with, take for

mistaken adjective WRONG, erroneous, false, faulty, inaccurate, incorrect, misguided, unsound, wide of the mark

mistakenly *adverb* INCORRECTLY, by mistake, erroneously, fallaciously, falsely, inaccurately, misguidedly, wrongly

mistimed *adjective* INOPPORTUNE, badly timed, ill-timed, untimely

mistreat *verb* ABUSE, harm, ill-treat, injure, knock about *or* around, maltreat, manhandle, misuse, molest

mistress *noun* LOVER, concubine, girlfriend, kept woman, paramour

mistrust *verb* 1 DOUBT, be wary of, distrust, fear, suspect
▸ *noun* 2 SUSPICION, distrust, doubt, misgiving, skepticism, uncertainty, wariness

mistrustful *adjective* SUSPICIOUS, chary, cynical, distrustful, doubtful, fearful, hesitant, skeptical, uncertain, wary

misty *adjective* FOGGY, blurred, cloudy, dim, hazy, indistinct, murky, obscure, opaque, overcast

misunderstand *verb* MISINTERPRET, be at cross-purposes, get the wrong end of the stick, misapprehend, misconstrue, misjudge, misread, mistake

misunderstanding *noun* MISTAKE, error, misconception, misinterpretation, misjudgment, mix-up

misuse *noun* 1 WASTE, abuse, desecration, misapplication, squandering
▸ *verb* 2 WASTE, abuse, desecrate, misapply, prostitute, squander

mitigate *verb* EASE, extenuate, lessen, lighten, moderate, soften, subdue, temper

mitigation *noun* RELIEF, alleviation, diminution, extenuation, moderation, remission

mix *verb* 1 COMBINE, blend, cross, fuse, intermingle, interweave, join, jumble, merge, mingle
2 SOCIALIZE, associate, consort, fraternize, hang out (*informal*), hobnob, mingle
▸ *noun* 3 MIXTURE, alloy, amalgam, assortment, blend, combination, compound, fusion, medley

mixed *adjective* 1 COMBINED, amalgamated, blended, composite, compound, joint, mingled, united
2 VARIED, assorted, cosmopolitan, diverse, heterogeneous, miscellaneous, motley

mixed-up *adjective* CONFUSED, at sea, bewildered, distraught, disturbed, maladjusted, muddled, perplexed, puzzled, upset

mixture *noun* BLEND, amalgam, assortment, brew, compound, fusion, jumble, medley, mix, potpourri, variety

mix-up *noun* CONFUSION, mess, mistake, misunderstanding, muddle, tangle

mix up *verb* 1 COMBINE, blend, mix
2 CONFUSE, confound, muddle

moan *noun* 1 GROAN, lament, sigh, sob, wail, whine
2 (*informal*) GRUMBLE, complaint, gripe (*informal*), grouch (*informal*), grouse, protest, whine
▸ *verb* 3 GROAN, lament, sigh, sob, whine
4 (*informal*) GRUMBLE, bleat, carp, complain, groan, grouse, whine, whinge (*informal*)

mob *noun* 1 CROWD, drove, flock, horde, host, mass, multitude, pack, swarm, throng
2 (*slang*) GANG, crew (*informal*), group, lot, set
▸ *verb* 3 SURROUND, crowd around,

jostle, set upon, swarm around

mobile *adjective* MOVABLE, itinerant, moving, peripatetic, portable, traveling, wandering

mobilize *verb* PREPARE, activate, call to arms, call up, get *or* make ready, marshal, organize, rally, ready

mock *verb* 1 LAUGH AT, deride, jeer, make fun of, poke fun at, ridicule, scoff, scorn, sneer, taunt, tease
2 MIMIC, ape, caricature, imitate, lampoon, parody, satirize, send up (*Brit. informal*)
▶ *adjective* 3 IMITATION, artificial, dummy, fake, false, feigned, phoney *or* phony (*informal*), pretended, sham, spurious

mockery *noun* 1 DERISION, contempt, disdain, disrespect, insults, jeering, ridicule, scoffing, scorn
2 FARCE, apology (*informal*), disappointment, joke, letdown

mocking *adjective* SCORNFUL, contemptuous, derisive, disdainful, disrespectful, sarcastic, sardonic, satirical, scoffing

mode *noun* 1 METHOD, form, manner, procedure, process, style, system, technique, way
2 FASHION, craze, look, rage, style, trend, vogue

model *noun* 1 REPRESENTATION, copy, dummy, facsimile, image, imitation, miniature, mock-up, replica
2 PATTERN, archetype, example, ideal, original, paradigm, paragon, prototype, standard
3 SITTER, poser, subject
▶ *verb* 4 SHAPE, carve, design, fashion, form, mold, sculpt
5 SHOW OFF, display, sport (*informal*), wear

moderate *adjective* 1 MILD, controlled, gentle, limited, middle-of-the-road, modest, reasonable, restrained, steady
2 AVERAGE, fair, indifferent, mediocre, middling, ordinary, passable, so-so (*informal*), unexceptional
▶ *verb* 3 REGULATE, control, curb, ease, modulate, restrain, soften, subdue, temper, tone down

moderately *adverb* REASONABLY, fairly, passably, quite, rather, slightly, somewhat, tolerably

moderation *noun* RESTRAINT, fairness, reasonableness, temperance

modern *adjective* CURRENT, contemporary, fresh, new, newfangled, novel, present-day, recent, up-to-date

modernity *noun* NOVELTY, currency, freshness, innovation, newness

modernize *verb* UPDATE, make over, rejuvenate, remake, remodel, renew, renovate, revamp

modest *adjective* 1 UNPRETENTIOUS, bashful, coy, demure, diffident, reserved, reticent, retiring, self-effacing, shy
2 MODERATE, fair, limited, middling, ordinary, small, unexceptional

modesty *noun* RESERVE, bashfulness, coyness, demureness, diffidence, humility, reticence, shyness, timidity

modicum *noun* LITTLE, bit, crumb, drop, fragment, scrap, shred, touch

modification *noun* CHANGE, adjustment, alteration, qualification, refinement, revision, variation

modify *verb* 1 CHANGE, adapt,

adjust, alter, convert, reform, remodel, revise, rework
2 TONE DOWN, ease, lessen, lower, moderate, qualify, restrain, soften, temper

modish *adjective* FASHIONABLE, chic, contemporary, cool (*informal*), current, in, phat (*slang*), smart, stylish, trendy (*informal*), up-to-the-minute, voguish

modulate *verb* ADJUST, attune, balance, regulate, tune, vary

mogul *noun* TYCOON, baron, big cheese (*informal*), big noise (*informal*), big shot (*informal*), magnate, V.I.P.

moist *adjective* DAMP, clammy, dewy, humid, soggy, wet

moisten *verb* DAMPEN, damp, moisturize, soak, water, wet

moisture *noun* DAMPNESS, dew, liquid, water, wetness

mold[1] *noun* **1** CAST, pattern, shape
2 DESIGN, build, construction, fashion, form, format, kind, pattern, shape, style
3 NATURE, caliber, character, kind, quality, sort, stamp, type
▶ *verb* **4** SHAPE, construct, create, fashion, forge, form, make, model, sculpt, work
5 INFLUENCE, affect, control, direct, form, make, shape

mold[2] *noun* FUNGUS, blight, mildew, mustiness

moldy *adjective* STALE, bad, blighted, decaying, fusty, mildewed, musty, rotten

molecule *noun* PARTICLE, jot, speck

molest *verb* **1** ANNOY, badger, beset, bother, disturb, harass, persecute, pester, plague, torment, worry
2 ABUSE, attack, harm, hurt, ill-treat, interfere with, maltreat

mollify *verb* PACIFY, appease, calm, conciliate, de-stress, placate, quiet, soothe, sweeten

moment *noun* **1** INSTANT, flash, jiffy (*informal*), second, split second, trice, twinkling
2 TIME, juncture, point, stage

momentarily *adverb* BRIEFLY, for a moment, temporarily

momentary *adjective* SHORT-LIVED, brief, fleeting, passing, short, temporary, transitory

momentous *adjective* SIGNIFICANT, critical, crucial, fateful, historic, important, pivotal, vital, weighty

momentum *noun* IMPETUS, drive, energy, force, power, propulsion, push, strength, thrust

monarch *noun* RULER, emperor *or* empress, king, potentate, prince *or* princess, queen, sovereign

monarchy *noun* **1** SOVEREIGNTY, autocracy, kingship, monocracy, royalism
2 KINGDOM, empire, principality, realm

monastery *noun* ABBEY, cloister, convent, friary, nunnery, priory

monastic *adjective* MONKISH, ascetic, cloistered, contemplative, hermit-like, reclusive, secluded, sequestered, withdrawn

monetary *adjective* FINANCIAL, budgetary, capital, cash, fiscal, pecuniary

money *noun* CASH, capital, coin, currency, hard cash, legal tender, readies (*informal*), riches, silver, wealth

mongrel *noun* **1** HYBRID, cross, crossbreed, half-breed
▶ *adjective* **2** HYBRID, crossbred

monitor *noun* **1** WATCHDOG, guide, invigilator, prefect (*Brit.*), supervisor

▶ *verb* 2 CHECK, follow, keep an eye on, keep tabs on, keep track of, observe, stalk, survey, watch

monk *noun* FRIAR, brother

monkey *noun* 1 SIMIAN, primate
2 RASCAL, devil, imp, rogue, scamp
▶ *verb* 3 FOOL, meddle, mess, play, tinker

monolithic *adjective* HUGE, colossal, impenetrable, intractable, massive, monumental, solid

monologue *noun* SPEECH, harangue, lecture, sermon, soliloquy

monopolize *verb* CONTROL, corner the market in, dominate, hog (*slang*), keep to oneself, take over

monotonous *adjective* TEDIOUS, boring, dull, humdrum, mind-numbing, repetitive, tiresome, unchanging, wearisome

monotony *noun* TEDIUM, boredom, monotonousness, repetitiveness, routine, sameness, tediousness

monster *noun* 1 BRUTE, beast, demon, devil, fiend, villain
2 FREAK, monstrosity, mutant
3 GIANT, colossus, mammoth, titan
▶ *adjective* 4 HUGE, colossal, enormous, gigantic, immense, mammoth, massive, stupendous, tremendous

monstrosity *noun* EYESORE, freak, horror, monster

monstrous *adjective* 1 UNNATURAL, fiendish, freakish, frightful, grotesque, gruesome, hideous, horrible
2 OUTRAGEOUS, diabolical, disgraceful, foul, inhuman, intolerable, scandalous, shocking
3 HUGE, colossal, enormous, immense, mammoth, massive,

prodigious, stupendous, tremendous

monument *noun* MEMORIAL, cairn, cenotaph, commemoration, gravestone, headstone, marker, mausoleum, shrine, tombstone

monumental *adjective*
1 IMPORTANT, awesome, enormous, epoch-making, historic, majestic, memorable, significant, unforgettable
2 (*informal*) IMMENSE, colossal, great, massive, staggering

mood *noun* STATE OF MIND, disposition, frame of mind, humor, spirit, temper

moody *adjective* 1 SULLEN, gloomy, glum, ill-tempered, irritable, morose, sad, sulky, temperamental, touchy
2 CHANGEABLE, capricious, erratic, fickle, flighty, impulsive, mercurial, temperamental, unpredictable, volatile

moon *noun* 1 SATELLITE
▶ *verb* 2 IDLE, daydream, languish, mope, waste time

moor¹ *noun* MOORLAND, fell (*Brit.*), heath

moor² *verb* TIE UP, anchor, berth, dock, lash, make fast, secure

moot *adjective* 1 DEBATABLE, arguable, contestable, controversial, disputable, doubtful, undecided, unresolved, unsettled
▶ *verb* 2 BRING UP, broach, propose, put forward, suggest

mop *noun* 1 SQUEEGEE, sponge, swab
2 MANE, shock, tangle, thatch

mope *verb* BROOD, fret, languish, moon, pine, pout, sulk

mop up *verb* CLEAN UP, soak up, sponge, swab, wash, wipe

moral *adjective* 1 GOOD, decent,

ethical, high-minded, honorable, just, noble, principled, right, virtuous
▶ *noun* 2 LESSON, meaning, message, point, significance
morale *noun* CONFIDENCE, esprit de corps, heart, self-esteem, spirit
morality *noun* 1 INTEGRITY, decency, goodness, honesty, justice, righteousness, virtue
2 STANDARDS, conduct, ethics, manners, morals, mores, philosophy, principles
morals *plural noun* MORALITY, behavior, conduct, ethics, habits, integrity, manners, mores, principles, scruples, standards
morass *noun* 1 MARSH, bog, fen, quagmire, slough, swamp
2 MESS, confusion, mix-up, muddle, tangle
moratorium *noun* POSTPONEMENT, freeze, halt, standstill, suspension
morbid *adjective* 1 UNWHOLESOME, ghoulish, gloomy, melancholy, sick, somber, unhealthy
2 GRUESOME, dreadful, ghastly, grisly, hideous, horrid, macabre
mordant *adjective* SARCASTIC, biting, caustic, cutting, incisive, pungent, scathing, stinging, trenchant
more *adjective* 1 EXTRA, added, additional, further, new, other, supplementary
▶ *adverb* 2 TO A GREATER EXTENT, better, further, longer
moreover *adverb* FURTHERMORE, additionally, also, as well, besides, further, in addition, too
morgue *noun* MORTUARY
moribund *adjective* DECLINING, on its last legs, stagnant, waning, weak
morning *noun* DAWN, a.m., break

of day, daybreak, forenoon, morn (*poetic*), sunrise
moron *noun* FOOL, blockhead, cretin (*offensive*), dork (*slang*), dunce, dunderhead, halfwit, idiot, imbecile, oaf, schmuck (*slang*)
moronic *adjective* IDIOTIC, cretinous (*offensive*), foolish, halfwitted, imbecilic, mindless, stupid, unintelligent
morose *adjective* SULLEN, depressed, dour, gloomy, glum, ill-tempered, moody, sour, sulky, surly, taciturn
morsel *noun* PIECE, bit, bite, crumb, mouthful, part, scrap, soupçon, taste, tidbit
mortal *adjective* 1 HUMAN, ephemeral, impermanent, passing, temporal, transient, worldly
2 FATAL, deadly, death-dealing, destructive, killing, lethal, murderous, terminal
▶ *noun* 3 HUMAN BEING, being, earthling, human, individual, man, person, woman
mortality *noun* 1 HUMANITY, impermanence, transience
2 KILLING, bloodshed, carnage, death, destruction, fatality
mortification *noun*
1 HUMILIATION, annoyance, chagrin, discomfiture, embarrassment, shame, vexation
2 DISCIPLINE, abasement, chastening, control, denial, subjugation
3 (*medical*) GANGRENE, corruption, festering
mortified *adjective* HUMILIATED, ashamed, chagrined, chastened, crushed, deflated, embarrassed, humbled, shamed
mortify *verb* 1 HUMILIATE,

chagrin, chasten, crush, deflate, embarrass, humble, shame
2 DISCIPLINE, abase, chasten, control, deny, subdue
3 (of flesh) PUTREFY, deaden, die, fester

mortuary noun MORGUE, funeral parlour

mostly adverb GENERALLY, as a rule, chiefly, largely, mainly, on the whole, predominantly, primarily, principally, usually

moth-eaten adjective DECAYED, decrepit, dilapidated, ragged, shabby, tattered, threadbare, worn-out

mother noun 1 PARENT, dam, ma (informal), mama or mamma (old-fashioned informal), mater (old-fashioned informal, chiefly Brit.), mom (informal), mommy (informal), old lady (informal)
▶ adjective 2 NATIVE, inborn, innate, natural
▶ verb 3 NURTURE, care for, cherish, nurse, protect, raise, rear, tend

motherly adjective MATERNAL, affectionate, caring, comforting, loving, protective, sheltering

motif noun 1 THEME, concept, idea, leitmotif, subject
2 DESIGN, decoration, ornament, shape

motion noun 1 MOVEMENT, flow, locomotion, mobility, move, progress, travel
2 PROPOSAL, proposition, recommendation, submission, suggestion
▶ verb 3 GESTURE, beckon, direct, gesticulate, nod, signal, wave

motionless adjective STILL, fixed, frozen, immobile, paralyzed, standing, static, stationary, stock-still, transfixed, unmoving

motivate verb INSPIRE, arouse,

cause, drive, induce, move, persuade, prompt, stimulate, stir

motivation noun INCENTIVE, incitement, inducement, inspiration, motive, reason, spur, stimulus

motive noun REASON, ground(s), incentive, inducement, inspiration, object, purpose, rationale, stimulus

motley adjective 1 MISCELLANEOUS, assorted, disparate, heterogeneous, mixed, varied
2 MULTICOLORED, checkered, variegated

mottled adjective BLOTCHY, dappled, flecked, piebald, speckled, spotted, stippled, streaked

motto noun SAYING, adage, dictum, maxim, precept, proverb, rule, slogan, watchword

mound noun 1 HEAP, drift, pile, rick, stack
2 HILL, bank, dune, embankment, hillock, knoll, rise

mount verb 1 CLIMB, ascend, clamber up, go up, scale
2 BESTRIDE, climb onto, jump on
3 INCREASE, accumulate, build, escalate, grow, intensify, multiply, pile up, swell
▶ noun 4 BACKING, base, frame, setting, stand, support
5 HORSE, steed (archaic or literary)

mountain noun 1 PEAK, alp, fell (Brit.), mount
2 HEAP, abundance, mass, mound, pile, stack, ton

mountainous adjective 1 HIGH, alpine, highland, rocky, soaring, steep, towering, upland
2 HUGE, daunting, enormous, gigantic, great, immense, mammoth, mighty, monumental

mourn verb GRIEVE, bemoan,

bewail, deplore, lament, rue,
wail, weep

mournful adjective 1 SAD,
melancholy, piteous, plaintive,
sorrowful, tragic, unhappy,
woeful
2 DISMAL, disconsolate, downcast,
gloomy, grieving, heavy-hearted,
lugubrious, miserable, rueful,
somber

mourning noun 1 GRIEVING,
bereavement, grief, lamentation,
weeping, woe
2 BLACK, sackcloth and ashes,
widow's weeds

mouth noun 1 LIPS, gob (slang,
especially Brit.), jaws, maw
2 OPENING, aperture, door,
entrance, gateway, inlet, orifice

mouthful noun TASTE, bit, bite,
little, morsel, sample, spoonful,
swallow

mouthpiece noun SPOKESPERSON,
agent, delegate, representative,
spokesman or spokeswoman

movable adjective PORTABLE,
detachable, mobile, transferable,
transportable

move verb 1 GO, advance, budge,
proceed, progress, shift, stir
2 CHANGE, shift, switch, transfer,
transpose
3 LEAVE, migrate, pack one's bags
(informal), quit, relocate, remove
4 DRIVE, activate, operate, propel,
shift, start, turn
5 TOUCH, affect, excite, impress
6 INCITE, cause, induce, influence,
inspire, motivate, persuade,
prompt, rouse
7 PROPOSE, advocate, put forward,
recommend, suggest, urge
▶ noun 8 ACTION, maneuver,
measure, ploy, step, stratagem,
stroke, turn
9 TRANSFER, relocation, removal,
shift

movement noun 1 MOTION,
action, activity, change,
development, flow, maneuver,
progress, stirring
2 GROUP, campaign, crusade,
drive, faction, front, grouping,
organization, party
3 WORKINGS, action, machinery,
mechanism, works
4 (music) SECTION, division, part,
passage

movie noun FILM, feature, flick
(slang), picture

moving adjective 1 EMOTIONAL,
affecting, inspiring, pathetic,
persuasive, poignant, stirring,
touching
2 MOBILE, movable, portable,
running, unfixed

mow verb CUT, crop, scythe,
shear, trim

mow down verb MASSACRE,
butcher, cut down, cut to pieces,
shoot down, slaughter

much adjective 1 GREAT, abundant,
a lot of, ample, considerable,
copious, plenty of, sizable or
sizeable, substantial
▶ noun 2 A LOT, a good deal, a
great deal, heaps (informal), loads
(informal), lots (informal), plenty
▶ adverb 3 GREATLY, a great deal,
a lot, considerably, decidedly,
exceedingly

muck noun 1 MANURE, dung,
ordure
2 DIRT, filth, gunge (informal),
mire, mud, ooze, slime, sludge

mucky adjective DIRTY, begrimed,
filthy, grimy, messy, muddy,
scuzzy (slang)

mud noun DIRT, clay, mire, ooze,
silt, slime, sludge

muddle verb 1 JUMBLE, disarrange,
disorder, disorganize, mess,

scramble, spoil, tangle
2 CONFUSE, befuddle, bewilder, confound, daze, disorient, perplex, stupefy
▶ *noun* 3 CONFUSION, chaos, disarray, disorder, disorganization, jumble, mess, mix-up, predicament, tangle

muddy *adjective* 1 DIRTY, bespattered, grimy, mucky, mud-caked, scuzzy (*slang*), soiled
2 BOGGY, marshy, quaggy, swampy

muffle *verb* 1 WRAP UP, cloak, cover, envelop, shroud, swaddle, swathe
2 DEADEN, muzzle, quieten, silence, soften, stifle, suppress

muffled *adjective* INDISTINCT, faint, muted, stifled, strangled, subdued, suppressed

mug¹ *noun* CUP, beaker, flagon, pot, tankard

mug² *noun* FACE, countenance, features, visage 1 FOOL, chump (*informal*), dork (*slang*), easy *or* soft touch (*slang*), schmuck (*slang*), simpleton, sucker (*slang*)
▶ *verb* 2 ATTACK, assault, beat up, rob, set about *or* upon

muggy *adjective* HUMID, clammy, close, moist, oppressive, sticky, stuffy, sultry

mull *verb* PONDER, consider, contemplate, deliberate, meditate, reflect on, ruminate, think over, weigh

multifarious *adjective* DIVERSE, different, legion, manifold, many, miscellaneous, multiple, numerous, sundry, varied

multiple *adjective* MANY, manifold, multitudinous, numerous, several, sundry, various

multiply *verb* 1 INCREASE, build up, expand, extend, proliferate, spread
2 REPRODUCE, breed, propagate

multitude *noun* MASS, army, crowd, horde, host, mob, myriad, swarm, throng

munch *verb* CHEW, champ, chomp, crunch

mundane *adjective* 1 ORDINARY, banal, commonplace, day-to-day, everyday, humdrum, prosaic, routine, workaday
2 EARTHLY, mortal, secular, temporal, terrestrial, worldly

municipal *adjective* CIVIC, public, urban

municipality *noun* TOWN, borough, city, district, township

munificence *noun* GENEROSITY, beneficence, benevolence, bounty, largesse *or* largess, liberality, magnanimousness, philanthropy

munificent *adjective* GENEROUS, beneficent, benevolent, bountiful, lavish, liberal, magnanimous, open-handed, philanthropic, unstinting

murder *noun* 1 KILLING, assassination, bloodshed, butchery, carnage, homicide, manslaughter, massacre, slaying
▶ *verb* 2 KILL, assassinate, bump off (*slang*), butcher, eliminate (*slang*), massacre, slaughter, slay

murderer *noun* KILLER, assassin, butcher, cut-throat, hit man (*slang*), homicide, slaughterer, slayer

murderous *adjective* DEADLY, bloodthirsty, brutal, cruel, cut-throat, ferocious, lethal, savage

murky *adjective* DARK, cloudy, dim, dull, gloomy, gray, misty, overcast

murmur *verb* 1 MUMBLE, mutter, whisper
2 GRUMBLE, complain, moan (*informal*)
▶ *noun* 3 DRONE, buzzing, humming, purr, rumble, whisper

muscle *noun* 1 TENDON, sinew
2 STRENGTH, brawn, clout
(*informal*), forcefulness, might,
power, stamina, weight
▶ *verb* 3 ▷▷ **muscle in** (*informal*)
IMPOSE ONESELF, butt in, force
one's way in

muscular *adjective* STRONG,
athletic, powerful, robust, sinewy,
strapping, sturdy, vigorous

muse *verb* PONDER, brood,
cogitate, consider, contemplate,
deliberate, meditate, mull over,
reflect, ruminate

mushy *adjective* 1 SOFT, pulpy,
semi-solid, slushy, squashy,
squelchy, squidgy (*informal*)
2 (*informal*) SENTIMENTAL,
maudlin, mawkish, saccharine,
schmaltzy (*slang*), sloppy (*informal*),
slushy (*informal*)

musical *adjective* MELODIOUS,
dulcet, euphonious, harmonious,
lyrical, melodic, sweet-sounding,
tuneful

must[1] *noun* NECESSITY, essential,
fundamental, imperative,
prerequisite, requirement,
requisite, *sine qua non*

muster *verb* 1 ASSEMBLE, call
together, convene, gather,
marshal, mobilize, rally, summon
▶ *noun* 2 ASSEMBLY, collection,
congregation, convention,
gathering, meeting, rally,
roundup

musty *adjective* STALE, airless,
dank, funky (*slang*), fusty,
mildewed, moldy, old, smelly,
stuffy

mutability *noun* CHANGE,
alteration, evolution,
metamorphosis, transition,
variation, vicissitude

mutable *adjective* CHANGEABLE,
adaptable, alterable, fickle,

inconsistent, inconstant,
unsettled, unstable, variable,
volatile

mutation *noun* CHANGE,
alteration, evolution,
metamorphosis, modification,
transfiguration, transformation,
variation

mute *adjective* SILENT, dumb,
mum, speechless, unspoken,
voiceless, wordless

mutilate *verb* 1 MAIM, amputate,
cut up, damage, disfigure,
dismember, injure, lacerate,
mangle
2 DISTORT, adulterate, bowdlerize,
censor, cut, damage, expurgate

mutinous *adjective* REBELLIOUS,
disobedient, insubordinate,
insurgent, refractory, riotous,
subversive, unmanageable,
unruly

mutiny *noun* 1 REBELLION,
disobedience, insubordination,
insurrection, revolt, revolution,
riot, uprising
▶ *verb* 2 REBEL, disobey, resist,
revolt, rise up

mutter *verb* GRUMBLE, complain,
grouse, mumble, murmur, rumble

mutual *adjective* SHARED,
common, interchangeable, joint,
reciprocal, requited, returned

muzzle *noun* 1 JAWS, mouth, nose,
snout
2 GAG, guard
▶ *verb* 3 SUPPRESS, censor, curb,
gag, restrain, silence, stifle

myopic *adjective* SHORT-SIGHTED,
near-sighted

myriad *adjective* 1 INNUMERABLE,
countless, immeasurable,
incalculable, multitudinous,
untold
▶ *noun* 2 MULTITUDE, army, horde,
host, swarm

mysterious *adjective* STRANGE,
arcane, enigmatic, inexplicable,
inscrutable, mystifying,
perplexing, puzzling, secret,
uncanny, unfathomable, weird

mystery *noun* PUZZLE,
conundrum, enigma, problem,
question, riddle, secret, teaser

mystic, mystical *adjective*
SUPERNATURAL, inscrutable,
metaphysical, mysterious,
occult, otherworldly, paranormal,
preternatural, transcendental

mystify *verb* PUZZLE, baffle,
bewilder, confound, confuse,
flummox, nonplus, perplex,
stump

mystique *noun* FASCINATION,
awe, charisma, charm, glamour,
magic, spell

myth *noun* 1 LEGEND, allegory,
fable, fairy story, fiction, folk tale,
saga, story, urban legend *or* myth
2 ILLUSION, delusion, fancy,
fantasy, figment, imagination,
superstition, tall tale (*informal*)

mythical *adjective* 1 LEGENDARY,
fabled, fabulous, fairy-tale,
mythological
2 IMAGINARY, fabricated, fantasy,
fictitious, invented, made-up,
make-believe, nonexistent,
pretended, unreal, untrue

mythological *adjective*
LEGENDARY, fabulous, mythic,
mythical, traditional

mythology *noun* LEGEND,
folklore, lore, tradition

n

nadir *noun* BOTTOM, depths, lowest point, minimum, rock bottom

nag¹ *verb* 1 SCOLD, annoy, badger, harass, hassle (*informal*), henpeck, irritate, pester, plague, upbraid, worry
▶ *noun* 2 SCOLD, harpy, shrew, tartar, virago

nag² *noun* HORSE, hack

nagging *adjective* IRRITATING, persistent, scolding, shrewish, worrying

nail *verb* FASTEN, attach, fix, hammer, join, pin, secure, tack

naive *adjective* 1 GULLIBLE, callow, credulous, green, unsuspicious, wet behind the ears (*informal*)
2 INNOCENT, artless, guileless, ingenuous, open, simple, trusting, unsophisticated, unworldly

naivety, naÔveté *noun*
1 GULLIBILITY, callowness, credulity
2 INNOCENCE, artlessness, guilelessness, inexperience, ingenuousness, naturalness, openness, simplicity

naked *adjective* NUDE, bare, exposed, in one's birthday suit (*informal*), starkers (*informal*), stripped, unclothed, undressed, without a stitch on (*informal*)

nakedness *noun* NUDITY, bareness, undress

name *noun* 1 TITLE, designation, epithet, handle (*slang*), moniker or monicker (*slang*), nickname, sobriquet, term
2 FAME, distinction, eminence, esteem, honor, note, praise, renown, repute
▶ *verb* 3 CALL, baptize, christen, dub, entitle, label, style, term
4 NOMINATE, appoint, choose, designate, select, specify

named *adjective* 1 CALLED, baptized, christened, dubbed, entitled, known as, labeled, styled, termed
2 NOMINATED, appointed, chosen, designated, mentioned, picked, selected, singled out, specified

nameless *adjective* 1 ANONYMOUS, unnamed, untitled
2 UNKNOWN, incognito, obscure, undistinguished, unheard-of, unsung
3 HORRIBLE, abominable, indescribable, unmentionable, unspeakable, unutterable

namely *adverb* SPECIFICALLY, to wit, viz.

nap¹ *noun* 1 SLEEP, catnap, forty winks (*informal*), kip (*Brit. slang*), rest, siesta
▶ *verb* 2 SLEEP, catnap, doze, drop off (*informal*), kip (*Brit. slang*), nod off (*informal*), rest, snooze (*informal*)

nap² *noun* WEAVE, down, fiber, grain, pile

napkin *noun* CLOTH, linen, serviette (*chiefly Brit.*), wipe

narcissism *noun* EGOTISM, self-love, vanity

narcotic *noun* 1 DRUG, analgesic,

anesthetic, anodyne, opiate, painkiller, sedative, tranquilizer
▶ *adjective* 2 SEDATIVE, analgesic, calming, hypnotic, painkilling, soporific

narrate *verb* TELL, chronicle, describe, detail, recite, recount, relate, report

narration *noun* TELLING, description, explanation, reading, recital, relation

narrative *noun* STORY, account, blog (*informal*), chronicle, history, report, statement, tale, weblog

narrator *noun* STORYTELLER, author, chronicler, commentator, reporter, writer

narrow *adjective* 1 THIN, attenuated, fine, slender, slim, spare, tapering
2 LIMITED, close, confined, constricted, contracted, meager, restricted, tight
3 INSULAR, dogmatic, illiberal, intolerant, narrow-minded, partial, prejudiced, small-minded
▶ *verb* 4 TIGHTEN, constrict, limit, reduce

narrowly *adverb* JUST, barely, by the skin of one's teeth, only just, scarcely

narrow-minded *adjective* INTOLERANT, bigoted, hidebound, illiberal, opinionated, parochial, prejudiced, provincial, small-minded

nastiness *noun* UNPLEASANTNESS, malice, meanness, spitefulness

nasty *adjective* 1 OBJECTIONABLE, disagreeable, loathsome, obnoxious, offensive, unpleasant, vile
2 SPITEFUL, despicable, disagreeable, distasteful, lousy (*slang*), malicious, mean, scuzzy (*slang*), unpleasant, vicious, vile

3 PAINFUL, bad, critical, dangerous, serious, severe

nation *noun* COUNTRY, people, race, realm, society, state, tribe

national *adjective* 1 NATIONWIDE, countrywide, public, widespread
▶ *noun* 2 CITIZEN, inhabitant, native, resident, subject

nationalism *noun* PATRIOTISM, allegiance, chauvinism, jingoism, loyalty

nationality *noun* RACE, birth, nation

nationwide *adjective* NATIONAL, countrywide, general, widespread

native *adjective* 1 LOCAL, domestic, home, indigenous
2 INBORN, congenital, hereditary, inbred, ingrained, innate, instinctive, intrinsic, natural
▶ *noun* 3 INHABITANT, aborigine, citizen, countryman, dweller, national, resident

natty *adjective* SMART, dapper, elegant, fashionable, neat, phat (*slang*), snazzy (*informal*), spruce, stylish, trim

natural *adjective* 1 NORMAL, common, everyday, legitimate, logical, ordinary, regular, typical, usual
2 UNAFFECTED, genuine, ingenuous, open, real, simple, spontaneous, unpretentious, unsophisticated
3 INNATE, characteristic, essential, inborn, inherent, instinctive, intuitive, native
4 PURE, organic, plain, unrefined, whole

naturalist *noun* BIOLOGIST, botanist, ecologist, zoologist

naturalistic *adjective* REALISTIC, lifelike, true-to-life

naturally *adverb* 1 OF COURSE, certainly

2 GENUINELY, normally, simply, spontaneously, typically, unaffectedly, unpretentiously

nature noun 1 CREATION, cosmos, earth, environment, universe, world
2 MAKE-UP, character, complexion, constitution, essence
3 KIND, category, description, sort, species, style, type, variety
4 TEMPERAMENT, disposition, humor, mood, outlook, temper

naughty adjective 1 DISOBEDIENT, bad, impish, misbehaved, mischievous, refractory, wayward, wicked, worthless
2 OBSCENE, improper, lewd, ribald, risqué, smutty, vulgar

nausea noun SICKNESS, biliousness, queasiness, retching, squeamishness, vomiting

nauseate verb SICKEN, disgust, offend, repel, repulse, revolt, turn one's stomach

nauseous adjective SICKENING, abhorrent, disgusting, distasteful, nauseating, offensive, repugnant, repulsive, revolting, scuzzy (slang)

nautical adjective MARITIME, marine, naval

naval adjective NAUTICAL, marine, maritime

navigable adjective 1 PASSABLE, clear, negotiable, unobstructed
2 SAILABLE, controllable, dirigible

navigate verb SAIL, drive, guide, handle, maneuver, pilot, steer, voyage

navigation noun SAILING, helmsmanship, seamanship, voyaging

navigator noun PILOT, mariner, seaman

navy noun FLEET, armada, flotilla

near adjective 1 CLOSE, adjacent, adjoining, nearby, neighboring
2 FORTHCOMING, approaching, imminent, impending, in the offing, looming, nigh, upcoming

nearby adjective NEIGHBORING, adjacent, adjoining, convenient, handy

nearly adverb ALMOST, approximately, as good as, just about, practically, roughly, virtually, well-nigh

nearness noun CLOSENESS, accessibility, availability, handiness, proximity, vicinity

near-sighted adjective SHORT-SIGHTED, myopic

neat adjective 1 TIDY, orderly, shipshape, smart, spick-and-span, spruce, systematic, trim
2 ELEGANT, adept, adroit, deft, dexterous, efficient, graceful, nimble, skillful, stylish
3 (of alcoholic drinks) STRAIGHT, pure, undiluted, unmixed

neatly adverb 1 TIDILY, daintily, fastidiously, methodically, smartly, sprucely, systematically
2 ELEGANTLY, adeptly, adroitly, deftly, dexterously, efficiently, expertly, gracefully, nimbly, skillfully

neatness noun 1 TIDINESS, daintiness, orderliness, smartness, spruceness, trimness
2 ELEGANCE, adroitness, deftness, dexterity, efficiency, grace, nimbleness, skill, style

nebulous adjective VAGUE, confused, dim, hazy, imprecise, indefinite, indistinct, shadowy, uncertain, unclear

necessarily adverb CERTAINLY, automatically, compulsorily, incontrovertibly, inevitably, inexorably, naturally, of necessity, undoubtedly

necessary *adjective* 1 NEEDED, compulsory, essential, imperative, indispensable, mandatory, obligatory, required, requisite, vital
2 CERTAIN, fated, inescapable, inevitable, inexorable, unavoidable

necessitate *verb* COMPEL, call for, coerce, constrain, demand, force, impel, oblige, require

necessities *plural noun* ESSENTIALS, exigencies, fundamentals, needs, requirements

necessity *noun* 1 INEVITABILITY, compulsion, inexorableness, obligation
2 NEED, desideratum, essential, fundamental, prerequisite, requirement, requisite, *sine qua non*

necromancy *noun* MAGIC, black magic, divination, enchantment, sorcery, witchcraft, wizardry

necropolis *noun* CEMETERY, burial ground, churchyard, graveyard

need *verb* 1 REQUIRE, call for, demand, entail, lack, miss, necessitate, want
▶ *noun* 2 POVERTY, deprivation, destitution, inadequacy, insufficiency, lack, paucity, penury, shortage
3 REQUIREMENT, demand, desideratum, essential, requisite
4 EMERGENCY, exigency, necessity, obligation, urgency, want

needed *adjective* NECESSARY, called for, desired, lacked, required, wanted

needful *adjective* NECESSARY, essential, indispensable, needed, required, requisite, stipulated, vital

needle *verb* IRRITATE, annoy, get

on one's nerves (*informal*), goad, harass, nag, pester, provoke, rile, taunt

needless *adjective* UNNECESSARY, gratuitous, groundless, pointless, redundant, superfluous, uncalled-for, unwanted, useless

needlework *noun* EMBROIDERY, needlecraft, sewing, stitching, tailoring

needy *adjective* POOR, deprived, destitute, disadvantaged, impoverished, penniless, poverty-stricken, underprivileged

nefarious *adjective* WICKED, criminal, depraved, evil, foul, heinous, infernal, villainous

negate *verb* 1 INVALIDATE, annul, cancel, countermand, neutralize, nullify, obviate, reverse, wipe out
2 DENY, contradict, disallow, disprove, gainsay (*archaic or literary*), oppose, rebut, refute

negation *noun* 1 CANCELLATION, neutralization, nullification
2 DENIAL, contradiction, converse, disavowal, inverse, opposite, rejection, renunciation, reverse

negative *adjective*
1 CONTRADICTORY, contrary, denying, dissenting, opposing, refusing, rejecting, resisting
2 PESSIMISTIC, cynical, gloomy, jaundiced, uncooperative, unenthusiastic, unwilling
▶ *noun* 3 CONTRADICTION, denial, refusal

neglect *verb* 1 DISREGARD, blow off (*slang*), disdain, ignore, overlook, rebuff, scorn, slight, spurn
2 FORGET, be remiss, evade, omit, pass over, shirk, skimp
▶ *noun* 3 DISREGARD, disdain, inattention, indifference
4 NEGLIGENCE, carelessness, dereliction, failure, laxity,

oversight, slackness

neglected adjective 1 ABANDONED, derelict, overgrown
2 DISREGARDED, unappreciated, underestimated, undervalued

neglectful adjective CARELESS, heedless, inattentive, indifferent, lax, negligent, remiss, thoughtless, uncaring

negligence noun CARELESSNESS, dereliction, disregard, inattention, indifference, laxity, neglect, slackness, thoughtlessness

negligent adjective CARELESS, forgetful, heedless, inattentive, neglectful, remiss, slack, slapdash, thoughtless, unthinking

negligible adjective INSIGNIFICANT, imperceptible, inconsequential, minor, minute, small, trifling, trivial, unimportant

negotiable adjective DEBATABLE, variable

negotiate verb 1 DEAL, arrange, bargain, conciliate, debate, discuss, haggle, mediate, transact, work out
2 GET ROUND, clear, cross, get over, get past, pass, surmount

negotiation noun BARGAINING, arbitration, debate, diplomacy, discussion, haggling, mediation, transaction, wheeling and dealing (informal)

negotiator noun MEDIATOR, ambassador, delegate, diplomat, honest broker, intermediary, moderator

neighborhood noun DISTRICT, community, environs, locale, locality, quarter, region, vicinity

neighboring adjective NEARBY, adjacent, adjoining, bordering, connecting, near, next, surrounding

neighborly adjective HELPFUL, considerate, friendly, harmonious, hospitable, kind, obliging, sociable

nemesis noun RETRIBUTION, destiny, destruction, fate, vengeance

nepotism noun FAVORITISM, bias, partiality, patronage, preferential treatment

nerd, nurd noun BORE, anorak (informal), doofus (slang), dork (slang), drip (informal), dweeb (slang), egghead (informal), geek (slang), goober (informal), obsessive, trainspotter (informal), wonk (informal)

nerve noun 1 BRAVERY, bottle (Brit. slang), courage, daring, fearlessness, grit, guts (informal), pluck, resolution, will
2 IMPUDENCE, audacity, boldness, brazenness, cheek (informal), impertinence, insolence, temerity
▶ verb 3 ▷▷ **nerve oneself** BRACE ONESELF, fortify oneself, steel oneself

nerveless adjective CALM, composed, controlled, cool, impassive, imperturbable, self-possessed, unemotional

nerve-racking adjective TENSE, difficult, distressing, frightening, harrowing, stressful, trying, worrying

nerves plural noun TENSION, anxiety, butterflies (in one's stomach) (informal), cold feet (informal), fretfulness, nervousness, strain, stress, worry

nervous adjective APPREHENSIVE, anxious, edgy, fearful, jumpy, on edge, tense, uptight (informal), wired (slang), worried

nervousness noun ANXIETY,

agitation, disquiet, excitability, fluster, tension, touchiness, worry

nervy *adjective* ANXIOUS, agitated, fidgety, jittery (*informal*), jumpy, nervous, on edge, tense, twitchy (*informal*), wired (*slang*)

nest *noun* REFUGE, den, haunt, hideaway, retreat

nest egg *noun* RESERVE, cache, deposit, fall-back, fund(s), savings, store

nestle *verb* SNUGGLE, cuddle, curl up, huddle, nuzzle

nestling *noun* CHICK, fledgling

net¹ *noun* 1 MESH, lattice, netting, network, openwork, tracery, web
▶ *verb* 2 CATCH, bag, capture, enmesh, ensnare, entangle, trap

net², nett *adjective* 1 FINAL, after taxes, clear, take-home
▶ *verb* 2 EARN, accumulate, bring in, clear, gain, make, realize, reap

nether *adjective* LOWER, below, beneath, bottom, inferior, under, underground

nettled *adjective* IRRITATED, annoyed, exasperated, galled, harassed, incensed, peeved, put out, riled, vexed

network *noun* SYSTEM, arrangement, complex, grid, labyrinth, lattice, maze, organization, structure, web

neurosis *noun* OBSESSION, abnormality, affliction, derangement, instability, maladjustment, mental illness, phobia

neurotic *adjective* UNSTABLE, abnormal, compulsive, disturbed, maladjusted, manic, nervous, obsessive, unhealthy

neuter *verb* CASTRATE, doctor (*informal*), emasculate, fix (*informal*), geld, spay

neutral *adjective* 1 UNBIASED,

disinterested, even-handed, impartial, nonaligned, nonpartisan, uncommitted, uninvolved, unprejudiced
2 INDETERMINATE, dull, indistinct, intermediate, undefined

neutrality *noun* IMPARTIALITY, detachment, nonalignment, noninterference, noninvolvement, nonpartisanship

neutralize *verb* COUNTERACT, cancel, compensate for, counterbalance, frustrate, negate, nullify, offset, undo

never *adverb* AT NO TIME, not at all, on no account, under no circumstances

nevertheless *adverb* NONETHELESS, but, even so, (even) though, however, notwithstanding, regardless, still, yet

new *adjective* 1 MODERN, contemporary, current, fresh, ground-breaking, latest, novel, original, recent, state-of-the-art, unfamiliar, up-to-date
2 CHANGED, altered, improved, modernized, redesigned, renewed, restored
3 EXTRA, added, more, supplementary

newcomer *noun* NOVICE, arrival, beginner, Johnny-come-lately (*informal*), new kid in town (*informal*), parvenu

newfangled *adjective* NEW, contemporary, cool (*informal*), fashionable, gimmicky, modern, novel, phat (*slang*), recent, state-of-the-art

newly *adverb* RECENTLY, anew, freshly, just, lately, latterly

newness *noun* NOVELTY, freshness, innovation, oddity,

originality, strangeness, unfamiliarity, uniqueness

news *noun* INFORMATION, bulletin, communiqué, exposé, gossip, hearsay, intelligence, latest (*informal*), report, revelation, rumor, story

newsworthy *adjective* INTERESTING, important, notable, noteworthy, remarkable, significant, stimulating

next *adjective* 1 FOLLOWING, consequent, ensuing, later, subsequent, succeeding
2 NEAREST, adjacent, adjoining, closest, neighboring
► *adverb* 3 AFTERWARDS, following, later, subsequently, thereafter

nibble *verb* 1 BITE, eat, gnaw, munch, nip, peck, pick at
► *noun* 2 SNACK, bite, crumb, morsel, peck, soupçon, taste, tidbit

nice *adjective* 1 PLEASANT, agreeable, attractive, charming, delightful, good, pleasurable
2 KIND, courteous, friendly, likable *or* likeable, polite, well-mannered
3 NEAT, dainty, fine, tidy, trim
4 SUBTLE, careful, delicate, fastidious, fine, meticulous, precise, strict

nicely *adverb* 1 PLEASANTLY, acceptably, agreeably, attractively, charmingly, delightfully, pleasurably, well
2 KINDLY, amiably, commendably, courteously, politely
3 NEATLY, daintily, finely, tidily, trimly

nicety *noun* SUBTLETY, daintiness, delicacy, discrimination, distinction, nuance, refinement

niche *noun* 1 ALCOVE, corner, hollow, nook, opening, recess
2 POSITION, calling, pigeonhole (*informal*), place, slot (*informal*), vocation

nick *verb* 1 CUT, chip, dent, mark, notch, scar, score, scratch, snick
2 STEAL, pilfer, pinch (*informal*), swipe (*slang*)
► *noun* 3 CUT, chip, dent, mark, notch, scar, scratch

nickname *noun* PET NAME, diminutive, epithet, label, moniker *or* monicker (*slang*), sobriquet

nifty *adjective* NEAT, attractive, chic, deft, pleasing, smart, stylish

niggard *noun* MISER, cheapskate (*informal*), Scrooge, skinflint

niggardly *adjective* STINGY, avaricious, frugal, grudging, mean, miserly, parsimonious, tightfisted, ungenerous

niggle *verb* 1 WORRY, annoy, irritate, rankle
2 CRITICIZE, carp, cavil, find fault, fuss

niggling *adjective* 1 PERSISTENT, gnawing, irritating, troubling, worrying
2 PETTY, finicky, fussy, nit-picking (*informal*), pettifogging, picky (*informal*), quibbling

night *noun* DARKNESS, dark, night-time

nightfall *noun* EVENING, dusk, sundown, sunset, twilight

nightly *adjective* 1 NOCTURNAL, night-time
► *adverb* 2 EVERY NIGHT, each night, night after night, nights (*informal*)

nightmare *noun* 1 BAD DREAM, hallucination
2 ORDEAL, horror, torment, trial, tribulation

nil *noun* NOTHING, love, naught, none, zero

nimble *adjective* AGILE, brisk, deft, dexterous, lively, quick, sprightly, spry, swift

nimbly adverb QUICKLY, briskly, deftly, dexterously, easily, readily, smartly, spryly, swiftly

nip¹ verb PINCH, bite, squeeze, tweak

nip² noun DRAM, draft, drop, mouthful, shot (*informal*), sip, snifter (*informal*)

nippy adjective 1 CHILLY, biting, sharp, stinging
2 (*informal*) QUICK, active, agile, fast, nimble, spry

nirvana noun PARADISE, bliss, joy, peace, serenity, tranquillity

nit-picking adjective FUSSY, captious, carping, finicky, hairsplitting, pedantic, pettifogging, quibbling

nitty-gritty noun BASICS, brass tacks (*informal*), core, crux, essentials, fundamentals, gist, substance

nitwit noun (*informal*) FOOL, dimwit (*informal*), doofus (*slang*), dork (*slang*), dummy (*slang*), halfwit, nincompoop, oaf, schmuck (*slang*), simpleton

no interjection 1 NEVER, nay, not at all, no way
▶ noun 2 REFUSAL, denial, negation

nobility noun 1 INTEGRITY, honor, incorruptibility, uprightness, virtue
2 ARISTOCRACY, elite, lords, nobles, patricians, peerage, upper class

noble adjective 1 WORTHY, generous, honorable, magnanimous, upright, virtuous
2 ARISTOCRATIC, blue-blooded, highborn, lordly, patrician, titled
3 GREAT, dignified, distinguished, grand, imposing, impressive, lofty, splendid, stately
▶ noun 4 LORD, aristocrat, nobleman, peer

nobody pronoun 1 NO-ONE
▶ noun 2 NONENTITY, cipher, lightweight (*informal*), menial

nocturnal adjective NIGHTLY, night-time

nod verb 1 ACKNOWLEDGE, bow, gesture, indicate, signal
2 SLEEP, doze, drowse, nap
▶ noun 3 GESTURE, acknowledgment, greeting, indication, sign, signal

noggin noun 1 CUP, dram, mug, nip, tot
2 (*informal*) HEAD, block (*informal*), noodle (*slang*), nut (*slang*)

no go adjective IMPOSSIBLE, futile, hopeless, not on (*informal*), vain

noise noun SOUND, clamor, commotion, din, hubbub, racket, row, uproar

noiseless adjective SILENT, hushed, inaudible, mute, quiet, soundless, still

noisome adjective 1 POISONOUS, bad, harmful, pernicious, pestilential, unhealthy, unwholesome
2 OFFENSIVE, disgusting, fetid, foul, funky (*slang*), malodorous, noxious, putrid, smelly, stinking

noisy adjective LOUD, boisterous, cacophonous, clamorous, deafening, ear-splitting, strident, tumultuous, uproarious, vociferous

nomad noun WANDERER, drifter, itinerant, migrant, rambler, rover, vagabond

nomadic adjective WANDERING, itinerant, migrant, peripatetic, roaming, roving, traveling, vagrant

nom de plume noun PSEUDONYM, alias, assumed name, nom de guerre, pen name

nomenclature noun

TERMINOLOGY, classification, codification, phraseology, taxonomy, vocabulary

nominal *adjective* 1 SO-CALLED, formal, ostensible, professed, puppet, purported, supposed, theoretical, titular 2 SMALL, inconsiderable, insignificant, minimal, symbolic, token, trifling, trivial

nominate *verb* NAME, appoint, assign, choose, designate, elect, propose, recommend, select, suggest

nomination *noun* CHOICE, appointment, designation, election, proposal, recommendation, selection, suggestion

nominee *noun* CANDIDATE, aspirant, contestant, entrant, protégé, runner

nonaligned *adjective* NEUTRAL, impartial, uncommitted, undecided

nonchalance *noun* INDIFFERENCE, calm, composure, equanimity, imperturbability, sang-froid, self-possession, unconcern

nonchalant *adjective* CASUAL, blasé, calm, careless, indifferent, insouciant, laid-back (*informal*), offhand, unconcerned, unperturbed

noncombatant *noun* CIVILIAN, neutral, nonbelligerent

noncommittal *adjective* EVASIVE, cautious, circumspect, equivocal, guarded, neutral, politic, temporizing, tentative, vague, wary

non compos mentis *adjective* INSANE, crazy, deranged, mentally ill, unbalanced, unhinged

nonconformist *noun* MAVERICK, dissenter, eccentric, heretic,

iconoclast, individualist, protester, radical, rebel

nonconformity *noun* DISSENT, eccentricity, heresy, heterodoxy

nondescript *adjective* ORDINARY, commonplace, dull, featureless, run-of-the-mill, undistinguished, unexceptional, unremarkable

none *pronoun* NOT ANY, nil, nobody, no-one, nothing, not one, zero

nonentity *noun* NOBODY, cipher, lightweight (*informal*), mediocrity, small fry

nonessential *adjective* UNNECESSARY, dispensable, expendable, extraneous, inessential, peripheral, superfluous, unimportant

nonetheless *adverb* NEVERTHELESS, despite that, even so, however, in spite of that, yet

nonevent *noun* FLOP (*informal*), disappointment, dud (*informal*), failure, fiasco, washout

nonexistent *adjective* IMAGINARY, chimerical, fictional, hypothetical, illusory, legendary, mythical, unreal

nonsense *noun* RUBBISH, balderdash, claptrap (*informal*), double Dutch (*Brit. informal*), drivel, gibberish, hot air (*informal*), stupidity, tripe (*informal*), twaddle

nonsensical *adjective* SENSELESS, absurd, crazy, foolish, inane, incomprehensible, irrational, meaningless, ridiculous, silly

nonstarter *noun* DEAD LOSS, dud (*informal*), lemon (*informal*), loser, no-hoper (*informal*), turkey (*informal*), washout (*informal*)

nonstop *adjective* 1 CONTINUOUS, constant, endless, incessant, interminable, relentless, twenty-four-seven (*slang*), unbroken, uninterrupted

▶ *adverb* 2 CONTINUOUSLY, ceaselessly, constantly, endlessly, incessantly, interminably, perpetually, relentlessly, twenty-four-seven (*slang*), unremittingly

noodle *noun* (*slang*) HEAD, common sense, gumption (*Brit. informal*), gut feeling (*informal*), intuition, sense

nook *noun* NICHE, alcove, corner, cubbyhole, hideout, opening, recess, retreat

noon *noun* MIDDAY, high noon, noonday, noontide, twelve noon

norm *noun* STANDARD, average, benchmark, criterion, par, pattern, rule, yardstick

normal *adjective* 1 USUAL, average, common, conventional, natural, ordinary, regular, routine, standard, typical
2 SANE, rational, reasonable, well-adjusted

normality *noun* 1 REGULARITY, conventionality, naturalness
2 SANITY, balance, rationality, reason

normally *adverb* USUALLY, as a rule, commonly, generally, habitually, ordinarily, regularly, typically

north *adjective* 1 NORTHERN, Arctic, boreal, northerly, polar
▶ *adverb* 2 NORTHWARD(S), northerly

nose *noun* 1 SNOUT, beak, bill, hooter, honker (*slang*), proboscis
▶ *verb* 2 EASE FORWARD, nudge, nuzzle, push, shove
3 PRY, meddle, snoop (*informal*)

nosegay *noun* POSY, bouquet

nostalgia *noun* REMINISCENCE, homesickness, longing, pining, regretfulness, remembrance, wistfulness, yearning

nostalgic *adjective* SENTIMENTAL, emotional, homesick, longing, maudlin, regretful, wistful

nostrum *noun* MEDICINE, cure, drug, elixir, panacea, potion, remedy, treatment

nosy, nosey *adjective* INQUISITIVE, curious, eavesdropping, interfering, intrusive, meddlesome, prying, snooping (*informal*)

notability *noun* FAME, celebrity, distinction, eminence, esteem, renown

notable *adjective* 1 REMARKABLE, conspicuous, extraordinary, memorable, noteworthy, outstanding, rare, striking, uncommon, unusual
▶ *noun* 2 CELEBRITY, big name, dignitary, personage, V.I.P.

notably *adverb* PARTICULARLY, especially, outstandingly, strikingly

notation *noun* SIGNS, characters, code, script, symbols, system

notch *noun* 1 CUT, cleft, incision, indentation, mark, nick, score
2 (*informal*) LEVEL, degree, grade, step
▶ *verb* 3 CUT, indent, mark, nick, score, scratch

notch up *verb* REGISTER, achieve, gain, make, score

note *noun* 1 MESSAGE, comment, communication, epistle, jotting, letter, memo, memorandum, minute, remark, reminder
2 SYMBOL, indication, mark, sign, token
▶ *verb* 3 SEE, notice, observe, perceive
4 MARK, denote, designate, indicate, record, register
5 MENTION, remark

notebook *noun* JOTTER, diary, exercise book, journal, notepad

noted adjective FAMOUS, acclaimed, celebrated, distinguished, eminent, illustrious, notable, prominent, renowned, well-known

noteworthy adjective REMARKABLE, exceptional, extraordinary, important, notable, outstanding, significant, unusual

nothing noun NOUGHT, emptiness, nada (informal), nil, nothingness, nullity, void, zero

nothingness noun 1 OBLIVION, nonbeing, nonexistence, nullity
2 INSIGNIFICANCE, unimportance, worthlessness

notice noun 1 OBSERVATION, cognizance, consideration, heed, interest, note, regard
2 ATTENTION, civility, respect
3 ANNOUNCEMENT, advice, communication, instruction, intimation, news, notification, order, warning
▶ verb 4 OBSERVE, detect, discern, distinguish, mark, note, perceive, see, spot

noticeable adjective OBVIOUS, appreciable, clear, conspicuous, evident, manifest, perceptible, plain, striking

notification noun ANNOUNCEMENT, advice, declaration, information, intelligence, message, notice, statement, warning

notify verb INFORM, advise, alert, announce, declare, make known, publish, tell, warn

notion noun 1 IDEA, belief, concept, impression, inkling, opinion, sentiment, view
2 WHIM, caprice, desire, fancy, impulse, inclination, wish

notional adjective SPECULATIVE, abstract, conceptual, hypothetical, imaginary, theoretical, unreal

notoriety noun SCANDAL, dishonor, disrepute, infamy, obloquy, opprobrium

notorious adjective INFAMOUS, dishonorable, disreputable, opprobrious, scandalous

notoriously adverb INFAMOUSLY, dishonorably, disreputably, opprobriously, scandalously

notwithstanding preposition DESPITE, in spite of

nought noun ZERO, nil, nothing

nourish verb 1 FEED, nurse, nurture, supply, sustain, tend
2 ENCOURAGE, comfort, cultivate, foster, maintain, promote, support

nourishing adjective NUTRITIOUS, beneficial, nutritive, wholesome

nourishment noun FOOD, nutriment, nutrition, sustenance

novel[1] noun STORY, fiction, narrative, romance, tale

novel[2] adjective NEW, different, fresh, innovative, original, strange, uncommon, unfamiliar, unusual

novelty noun 1 NEWNESS, freshness, innovation, oddity, originality, strangeness, surprise, unfamiliarity, uniqueness
2 GIMMICK, curiosity, gadget
3 KNICK-KNACK, bauble, memento, souvenir, trifle, trinket

novice noun BEGINNER, amateur, apprentice, learner, newcomer, probationer, pupil, trainee

now adverb 1 NOWADAYS, anymore, at the moment
2 IMMEDIATELY, at once, instantly, promptly, straightaway
3 ▷▷ **now and then** or **again** OCCASIONALLY, from time to time,

infrequently, intermittently, on and off, sometimes, sporadically

nowadays *adverb* NOW, anymore, at the moment, in this day and age, today

noxious *adjective* HARMFUL, deadly, destructive, foul, hurtful, injurious, poisonous, unhealthy, unwholesome

nuance *noun* SUBTLETY, degree, distinction, gradation, nicety, refinement, shade, tinge

nubile *adjective* MARRIAGEABLE, ripe (*informal*)

nucleus *noun* CENTER, basis, core, focus, heart, kernel, nub, pivot

nude *adjective* NAKED, bare, disrobed, in one's birthday suit, stark-naked, stripped, unclad, unclothed, undressed, without a stitch on (*informal*)

nudge *verb* PUSH, bump, dig, elbow, jog, poke, prod, shove, touch

nudity *noun* NAKEDNESS, bareness, deshabille, nudism, undress

nugget *noun* LUMP, chunk, clump, hunk, mass, piece

nuisance *noun* PROBLEM, annoyance, bother, drag (*informal*), hassle (*informal*), inconvenience, irritation, pain in the neck, pest, trouble

null *adjective* ▷▷ **null and void** INVALID, inoperative, useless, valueless, void, worthless

nullify *verb* CANCEL, counteract, invalidate, negate, neutralize, obviate, render null and void, veto

nullity *noun* NONEXISTENCE, invalidity, powerlessness, uselessness, worthlessness

numb *adjective* 1 UNFEELING, benumbed, dead, deadened, frozen, immobilized, insensitive, paralyzed, torpid

▶ *verb* 2 DEADEN, benumb, dull, freeze, immobilize, paralyze

number *noun* 1 NUMERAL, character, digit, figure, integer
2 QUANTITY, aggregate, amount, collection, crowd, horde, multitude, throng
3 ISSUE, copy, edition, imprint, printing
▶ *verb* 4 COUNT, account, add, calculate, compute, enumerate, include, reckon, total

numberless *adjective* INFINITE, countless, endless, innumerable, multitudinous, myriad, unnumbered, untold

numbness *noun* DEADNESS, dullness, insensitivity, paralysis, torpor

numeral *noun* NUMBER, digit, figure, integer

numerous *adjective* MANY, abundant, copious, plentiful, profuse, several, thick on the ground

nunnery *noun* CONVENT, abbey, cloister, house

nuptial *adjective* MARITAL, bridal, conjugal, connubial, matrimonial

nuptials *plural noun* WEDDING, marriage, matrimony

nurse *verb* 1 LOOK AFTER, care for, minister to, tend, treat
2 BREAST-FEED, feed, nourish, nurture, suckle, wet-nurse
3 FOSTER, cherish, cultivate, encourage, harbor, preserve, promote, succor, support

nursery *noun* CRECHE, kindergarten, playgroup

nurture *noun* 1 DEVELOPMENT, discipline, education, instruction, rearing, training, upbringing
▶ *verb* 2 DEVELOP, bring up, discipline, educate, instruct, rear, school, train

nut *noun* **1** (*slang*) MADMAN, crank (*informal*), lunatic, maniac, nutcase (*slang*), psycho (*slang*)
2 (*slang*) HEAD, brain, mind, reason, senses

nutrition *noun* FOOD, nourishment, nutriment, sustenance

nutritious *adjective* NOURISHING, beneficial, health-giving, invigorating, nutritive, strengthening, wholesome

nuts *adjective* (*informal*) INSANE, deranged, disturbed, mad, mentally ill, psychotic, unbalanced, unstable

nuzzle *verb* SNUGGLE, burrow, cuddle, fondle, nestle, pet

nymph *noun* SYLPH, dryad, girl, maiden, naiad

O

oaf *noun* IDIOT, blockhead, clod, dolt, dork (*slang*), dunce, fool, goon, lout, moron, numbskull *or* numskull, schmuck (*slang*)

oafish *adjective* MORONIC, dense, dim-witted (*informal*), doltish, dumb (*informal*), loutish, stupid, thick

oath *noun* 1 PROMISE, affirmation, avowal, bond, pledge, vow, word 2 SWEARWORD, blasphemy, curse, expletive, profanity

obdurate *adjective* STUBBORN, dogged, hard-hearted, immovable, implacable, inflexible, obstinate, pig-headed, unyielding

obedience *noun* RESPECT, acquiescence, compliance, docility, observance, reverence, submissiveness, subservience

obedient *adjective* RESPECTFUL, acquiescent, biddable, compliant, deferential, docile, dutiful, submissive, subservient, well-trained

obelisk *noun* COLUMN, monolith, monument, needle, pillar, shaft

obese *adjective* FAT, corpulent, gross, heavy, overweight, paunchy, plump, portly, rotund, stout, tubby

obesity *noun* FATNESS, bulk, corpulence, grossness, portliness, stoutness, tubbiness

obey *verb* CARRY OUT, abide by, act upon, adhere to, comply, conform, follow, heed, keep, observe

obfuscate *verb* CONFUSE, befog, cloud, darken, muddy the waters, obscure, perplex

object¹ *noun* 1 THING, article, body, entity, item, phenomenon 2 TARGET, focus, recipient, victim 3 PURPOSE, aim, design, end, goal, idea, intention, objective, point

object² *verb* PROTEST, argue against, demur, draw the line (at something), expostulate, oppose, take exception

objection *noun* PROTEST, counter-argument, demur, doubt, opposition, remonstrance, scruple

objectionable *adjective* UNPLEASANT, deplorable, disagreeable, intolerable, obnoxious, offensive, regrettable, repugnant, unseemly

objective *noun* 1 PURPOSE, aim, ambition, end, goal, intention, mark, object, target
▶ *adjective* 2 UNBIASED, detached, disinterested, dispassionate, even-handed, fair, impartial, open-minded, unprejudiced

objectively *adverb* IMPARTIALLY, disinterestedly, dispassionately, even-handedly, with an open mind

objectivity *noun* IMPARTIALITY, detachment, disinterestedness, dispassion

obligation *noun* DUTY, accountability, burden, charge, compulsion, liability, requirement, responsibility

obligatory *adjective* COMPULSORY, binding, de rigueur, essential, imperative, mandatory, necessary, required, requisite, unavoidable

oblige *verb* 1 COMPEL, bind, constrain, force, impel, make, necessitate, require
2 INDULGE, accommodate, benefit, gratify, please

obliged *adjective* 1 GRATEFUL, appreciative, beholden, indebted, in (someone's) debt, thankful
2 BOUND, compelled, forced, required

obliging *adjective* COOPERATIVE, accommodating, agreeable, considerate, good-natured, helpful, kind, polite, willing

oblique *adjective* 1 SLANTING, angled, aslant, sloping, tilted
2 INDIRECT, backhanded, circuitous, implied, roundabout, sidelong

obliterate *verb* DESTROY, annihilate, blot out, efface, eradicate, erase, expunge, extirpate, root out, wipe out

obliteration *noun* ANNIHILATION, elimination, eradication, extirpation, wiping out

oblivion *noun* 1 NEGLECT, abeyance, disregard, forgetfulness
2 UNCONSCIOUSNESS, insensibility, obliviousness, unawareness

oblivious *adjective* UNAWARE, forgetful, heedless, ignorant, insensible, neglectful, negligent, regardless, unconcerned, unconscious, unmindful

obloquy *noun* 1 ABUSE, aspersion, attack, blame, censure, criticism, invective, reproach, slander, vilification
2 DISCREDIT, disgrace, dishonor, humiliation, ignominy, infamy, shame, stigma

obnoxious *adjective* OFFENSIVE, disagreeable, insufferable, loathsome, nasty, nauseating, objectionable, odious, repulsive, revolting, scuzzy (*slang*), unpleasant

obscene *adjective* 1 INDECENT, dirty, filthy, immoral, improper, lewd, offensive, pornographic, salacious, scuzzy (*slang*), X-rated
2 SICKENING, atrocious, disgusting, evil, heinous, loathsome, outrageous, shocking, vile, wicked

obscenity *noun* 1 INDECENCY, coarseness, dirtiness, impropriety, lewdness, licentiousness, pornography, smut
2 SWEARWORD, four-letter word, profanity, vulgarism
3 OUTRAGE, abomination, affront, atrocity, blight, evil, offense, wrong

obscure *adjective* 1 VAGUE, ambiguous, arcane, confusing, cryptic, enigmatic, esoteric, mysterious, opaque, recondite
2 INDISTINCT, blurred, cloudy, dim, faint, gloomy, murky, shadowy
3 LITTLE-KNOWN, humble, lowly, out-of-the-way, remote, undistinguished, unheard-of, unknown
▶ *verb* 4 CONCEAL, cover, disguise, hide, obfuscate, screen, veil

obscurity *noun* 1 DARKNESS, dimness, dusk, gloom, haze, shadows
2 INSIGNIFICANCE, lowliness, unimportance

obsequious *adjective* SYCOPHANTIC, cringing, deferential, fawning, flattering, grovelling, ingratiating, servile, submissive, unctuous

observable *adjective* NOTICEABLE,

apparent, detectable, discernible, evident, obvious, perceptible, recognizable, visible

observance noun HONORING, carrying out, compliance, fulfillment, performance

observant adjective ATTENTIVE, alert, eagle-eyed, perceptive, quick, sharp-eyed, vigilant, watchful, wide-awake

observation noun 1 STUDY, examination, inspection, monitoring, review, scrutiny, surveillance, watching
2 REMARK, comment, note, opinion, pronouncement, reflection, thought, utterance

observe verb 1 SEE, detect, discern, discover, note, notice, perceive, spot, witness
2 WATCH, check, keep an eye on (informal), keep track of, look at, monitor, scrutinize, study, survey, view
3 REMARK, comment, mention, note, opine, say, state
4 HONOR, abide by, adhere to, comply, conform to, follow, heed, keep, obey, respect

observer noun SPECTATOR, beholder, bystander, eyewitness, fly on the wall, looker-on, onlooker, viewer, watcher, witness

obsessed adjective PREOCCUPIED, dominated, gripped, haunted, hung up on (slang), infatuated, troubled

obsession noun PREOCCUPATION, complex, fetish, fixation, hang-up (informal), infatuation, mania, phobia, thing (informal)

obsessive adjective COMPULSIVE, besetting, consuming, gripping, haunting

obsolescent adjective WANING,

ageing, declining, dying out, on the wane, on the way out, past its prime

obsolete adjective EXTINCT, antiquated, archaic, discarded, disused, old, old-fashioned, outmoded, out of date, passé

obstacle noun DIFFICULTY, bar, barrier, block, hindrance, hitch, hurdle, impediment, obstruction, snag, stumbling block

obstinacy noun STUBBORNNESS, doggedness, inflexibility, intransigence, obduracy, persistence, pig-headedness, tenacity, willfulness

obstinate adjective STUBBORN, determined, dogged, inflexible, intractable, intransigent, pig-headed, refractory, self-willed, strong-minded, willful

obstreperous adjective UNRULY, disorderly, loud, noisy, riotous, rowdy, turbulent, unmanageable, wild

obstruct verb BLOCK, bar, barricade, check, hamper, hinder, impede, restrict, stop, thwart

obstruction noun OBSTACLE, bar, barricade, barrier, blockage, difficulty, hindrance, impediment

obstructive adjective UNCOOPERATIVE, awkward, blocking, delaying, hindering, restrictive, stalling, unhelpful

obtain verb 1 GET, achieve, acquire, attain, earn, gain, land, procure, secure
2 EXIST, be in force, be prevalent, be the case, hold, prevail

obtainable adjective AVAILABLE, achievable, attainable, on tap (informal), to be had

obtrusive adjective NOTICEABLE, blatant, obvious, prominent, protruding, protuberant, sticking out

obtuse *adjective* SLOW, dense, dull, stolid, stupid, thick, uncomprehending

obviate *verb* PRECLUDE, avert, prevent, remove

obvious *adjective* EVIDENT, apparent, clear, conspicuous, distinct, indisputable, manifest, noticeable, plain, self-evident, undeniable, unmistakable

obviously *adverb* CLEARLY, manifestly, of course, palpably, patently, plainly, undeniably, unmistakably, unquestionably, without doubt

occasion *noun* 1 TIME, chance, moment, opening, opportunity, window
2 EVENT, affair, celebration, experience, happening, occurrence
3 REASON, call, cause, excuse, ground(s), justification, motive, prompting, provocation
▶ *verb* 4 CAUSE, bring about, engender, generate, give rise to, induce, inspire, lead to, produce, prompt, provoke

occasional *adjective* INFREQUENT, incidental, intermittent, irregular, odd, rare, sporadic, uncommon

occasionally *adverb* SOMETIMES, at times, from time to time, irregularly, now and again, once in a while, periodically

occult *adjective* SUPERNATURAL, arcane, esoteric, magical, mysterious, mystical

occupancy *noun* TENURE, possession, residence, tenancy, use

occupant *noun* INHABITANT, incumbent, indweller, inmate, lessee, occupier, resident, tenant

occupation *noun* 1 PROFESSION, business, calling, employment, job, line (of work), pursuit, trade, vocation, walk of life
2 POSSESSION, control, holding, occupancy, residence, tenancy, tenure
3 INVASION, conquest, seizure, subjugation

occupied *adjective* 1 BUSY, employed, engaged, working
2 IN USE, engaged, full, taken, unavailable
3 INHABITED, lived-in, peopled, settled, tenanted

occupy *verb* 1 (often passive) TAKE UP, divert, employ, engage, engross, involve, monopolize, preoccupy, tie up
2 LIVE IN, dwell in, inhabit, own, possess, reside in
3 FILL, cover, permeate, pervade, take up
4 INVADE, capture, overrun, seize, take over

occur *verb* 1 HAPPEN, befall, come about, crop up (*informal*), take place, turn up (*informal*)
2 EXIST, appear, be found, be present, develop, manifest itself, show itself
3 ▷▷ **occur to** COME TO MIND, cross one's mind, dawn on, enter one's head, spring to mind, strike one, suggest itself

occurrence *noun* 1 INCIDENT, adventure, affair, circumstance, episode, event, happening, instance
2 EXISTENCE, appearance, development, manifestation, materialization

odd *adjective* 1 UNUSUAL, bizarre, extraordinary, freakish, irregular, peculiar, rare, remarkable, singular, strange

2 OCCASIONAL, casual, incidental, irregular, periodic, random, sundry, various

3 SPARE, leftover, remaining, solitary, surplus, unmatched, unpaired

oddity noun 1 IRREGULARITY, abnormality, anomaly, eccentricity, freak, idiosyncrasy, peculiarity, quirk

2 MISFIT, crank (informal), maverick, oddball (informal)

oddment noun LEFTOVER, bit, fag end, fragment, off cut, remnant, scrap, snippet

odds plural noun 1 PROBABILITY, chances, likelihood

2 ▷▷ **at odds** IN CONFLICT, at daggers drawn, at loggerheads, at sixes and sevens, at variance, out of line

odds and ends plural noun SCRAPS, bits, bits and pieces, debris, oddments, remnants

odious adjective OFFENSIVE, detestable, horrid, loathsome, obnoxious, repulsive, revolting, scuzzy (slang), unpleasant

odor noun SMELL, aroma, bouquet, essence, fragrance, perfume, redolence, scent, stench, stink

odyssey noun JOURNEY, crusade, pilgrimage, quest, trek, voyage

off adverb 1 AWAY, apart, aside, elsewhere, out

▶ adjective 2 UNAVAILABLE, canceled, finished, gone, postponed

3 BAD, moldy, rancid, rotten, sour, turned

offbeat adjective UNUSUAL, eccentric, left-field (informal), novel, outré, strange, unconventional, unorthodox, way-out (informal)

off color adjective ILL, out of sorts,

peaky, poorly (informal), queasy, run down, sick, under the weather (informal), unwell

offend verb INSULT, affront, annoy, displease, hurt (someone's) feelings, outrage, slight, snub, upset, wound

offended adjective RESENTFUL, affronted, disgruntled, displeased, outraged, piqued, put out (informal), smarting, stung, upset

offender noun CRIMINAL, crook, culprit, delinquent, lawbreaker, miscreant, perp (informal), sinner, transgressor, villain, wrongdoer

offense noun 1 CRIME, fault, misdeed, misdemeanor, sin, transgression, trespass, wrongdoing

2 SNUB, affront, hurt, indignity, injustice, insult, outrage, slight

3 ANNOYANCE, anger, displeasure, indignation, pique, resentment, umbrage, wrath

offensive adjective 1 INSULTING, abusive, discourteous, disrespectful, impertinent, insolent, objectionable, rude

2 DISAGREEABLE, disgusting, nauseating, obnoxious, odious, repellent, revolting, unpleasant, vile

3 AGGRESSIVE, attacking, invading

▶ noun 4 ATTACK, campaign, drive, onslaught, push (informal)

offer verb 1 BID, proffer, tender

2 PROVIDE, afford, furnish, present

3 PROPOSE, advance, submit, suggest

4 VOLUNTEER, come forward, offer one's services

▶ noun 5 BID, proposal, proposition, submission, suggestion, tender

offering noun DONATION,

contribution, gift, hand-out, present, sacrifice, subscription

offhand *adjective* 1 CASUAL, aloof, brusque, careless, curt, glib
▶ *adverb* 2 IMPROMPTU, ad lib, extempore, off the cuff (*informal*)

office *noun* POST, function, occupation, place, responsibility, role, situation

officer *noun* OFFICIAL, agent, appointee, executive, functionary, office-holder, representative

official *adjective* 1 AUTHORIZED, accredited, authentic, certified, formal, legitimate, licensed, proper, sanctioned
▶ *noun* 2 OFFICER, agent, bureaucrat, executive, functionary, office bearer, representative

officiate *verb* PRESIDE, chair, conduct, manage, oversee, serve, superintend

officious *adjective* INTERFERING, dictatorial, intrusive, meddlesome, obtrusive, overzealous, pushy (*informal*), self-important

offing *noun* ▷▷ **in the offing** IN PROSPECT, imminent, on the horizon, upcoming

offset *verb* CANCEL OUT, balance out, compensate for, counteract, counterbalance, make up for, neutralize

offshoot *noun* BY-PRODUCT, adjunct, appendage, development, spin-off

offspring *noun* 1 CHILD, descendant, heir, scion, successor
2 CHILDREN, brood, descendants, family, heirs, issue, progeny, young

often *adverb* FREQUENTLY, generally, repeatedly, time and again

ogle *verb* LEER, eye up (*informal*)

ogre *noun* MONSTER, bogeyman, bugbear, demon, devil, giant, specter

oil *verb* LUBRICATE, grease

oily *adjective* GREASY, fatty, oleaginous

ointment *noun* LOTION, balm, cream, embrocation, emollient, liniment, salve, unguent

O.K., okay *interjection* 1 ALL RIGHT, agreed, right, roger, very good, very well, yes
▶ *adjective* 2 ALL RIGHT, acceptable, adequate, fine, good, in order, permitted, satisfactory, up to scratch (*informal*)
▶ *verb* 3 APPROVE, agree to, authorize, endorse, give the green light, rubber-stamp (*informal*), sanction
▶ *noun* 4 APPROVAL, agreement, assent, authorization, consent, go-ahead (*informal*), green light, permission, sanction, say-so (*informal*), seal of approval

old *adjective* 1 SENILE, aged, ancient, decrepit, elderly, mature, venerable
2 ANTIQUE, antediluvian, antiquated, dated, obsolete, superannuated, timeworn
3 FORMER, earlier, erstwhile, one-time, previous

old-fashioned *adjective* OUT OF DATE, behind the times, dated, obsolescent, obsolete, old hat, outdated, outmoded, passé, unfashionable

omen *noun* SIGN, foreboding, indication, portent, premonition, presage, warning

ominous *adjective* SINISTER, fateful, foreboding, inauspicious, portentous, threatening, unpromising, unpropitious

omission noun EXCLUSION, failure, lack, neglect, oversight

omit verb LEAVE OUT, drop, eliminate, exclude, forget, neglect, overlook, pass over, skip

omnipotence noun SUPREMACY, invincibility, mastery

omnipotent adjective ALMIGHTY, all-powerful, supreme

omniscient adjective ALL-KNOWING, all-wise

once adverb 1 FORMERLY, at one time, long ago, once upon a time, previously
2 ▷▷ **at once: a** IMMEDIATELY, directly, forthwith, instantly, now, right away, straight away, this (very) minute **b** SIMULTANEOUSLY, at the same time, together

oncoming adjective APPROACHING, advancing, forthcoming, looming, onrushing

onerous adjective DIFFICULT, burdensome, demanding, exacting, hard, heavy, laborious, oppressive, taxing

one-sided adjective BIASED, lopsided, partial, partisan, prejudiced, unfair, unjust

ongoing adjective EVOLVING, continuous, developing, progressing, unfinished, unfolding

onlooker noun OBSERVER, bystander, eyewitness, looker-on, spectator, viewer, watcher, witness

only adjective 1 SOLE, exclusive, individual, lone, single, solitary, unique
▶ adverb 2 MERELY, barely, just, purely, simply

onset noun BEGINNING, inception, outbreak, start

onslaught noun ATTACK, assault, blitz, charge, offensive, onrush, onset

onus noun BURDEN, liability, load, obligation, responsibility, task

onward, onwards adverb AHEAD, beyond, forth, forward, in front, on

ooze¹ verb SEEP, drain, dribble, drip, escape, filter, leak

ooze² noun MUD, alluvium, mire, silt, slime, sludge

opaque adjective CLOUDY, dim, dull, filmy, hazy, impenetrable, muddy, murky

open adjective 1 UNFASTENED, agape, ajar, gaping, uncovered, unfolded, unfurled, unlocked, yawning
2 ACCESSIBLE, available, free, public, unoccupied, unrestricted, vacant
3 UNRESOLVED, arguable, debatable, moot, undecided, unsettled
4 FRANK, candid, guileless, honest, sincere, transparent
▶ verb 5 START, begin, commence, inaugurate, initiate, kick off (informal), launch, set in motion
6 UNFASTEN, unblock, uncork, uncover, undo, unlock, untie, unwrap
7 UNFOLD, expand, spread (out), unfurl, unroll

open-air adjective OUTDOOR, alfresco

open-handed adjective GENEROUS, bountiful, free, lavish, liberal, munificent, unstinting

opening noun 1 HOLE, aperture, chink, cleft, crack, fissure, gap, orifice, perforation, slot, space
2 OPPORTUNITY, chance, look-in (informal), occasion, vacancy
3 BEGINNING, commencement, dawn, inception, initiation, launch, outset, start

▶ *adjective* 4 FIRST, beginning, inaugural, initial, introductory, maiden, primary

openly *adverb* CANDIDLY, forthrightly, frankly, overtly, plainly, unhesitatingly, unreservedly

open-minded *adjective* TOLERANT, broad-minded, impartial, liberal, reasonable, receptive, unbiased, undogmatic, unprejudiced

operate *verb* 1 WORK, act, function, go, perform, run
2 HANDLE, be in charge of, manage, maneuver, use, work

operation *noun* PROCEDURE, action, course, exercise, motion, movement, performance, process

operational *adjective* WORKING, functional, going, operative, prepared, ready, up and running, usable, viable, workable

operative *adjective* 1 IN FORCE, active, effective, functioning, in operation, operational
▶ *noun* 2 WORKER, artisan, employee, laborer

operator *noun* WORKER, conductor, driver, handler, mechanic, operative, practitioner, technician

opinion *noun* BELIEF, assessment, feeling, idea, impression, judgment, point of view, sentiment, theory, view

opinionated *adjective* DOGMATIC, bigoted, cocksure, doctrinaire, overbearing, pig-headed, prejudiced, single-minded

opponent *noun* COMPETITOR, adversary, antagonist, challenger, contestant, enemy, foe, rival

opportune *adjective* TIMELY, advantageous, appropriate, apt, auspicious, convenient, favorable, fitting, suitable, well-timed

opportunism *noun* EXPEDIENCY, exploitation, pragmatism, unscrupulousness

opportunity *noun* CHANCE, moment, occasion, opening, scope, time

oppose *verb* FIGHT, block, combat, counter, defy, resist, take issue with, take on, thwart, withstand

opposed *adjective* AVERSE, antagonistic, clashing, conflicting, contrary, dissentient, hostile

opposing *adjective* HOSTILE, conflicting, contrary, enemy, incompatible, opposite, rival

opposite *adjective* 1 FACING, fronting
2 DIFFERENT, antithetical, conflicting, contrary, contrasted, reverse, unlike
▶ *noun* 3 REVERSE, antithesis, contradiction, contrary, converse, inverse

opposition *noun* 1 HOSTILITY, antagonism, competition, disapproval, obstruction, prevention, resistance, unfriendliness
2 OPPONENT, antagonist, competition, foe, other side, rival

oppress *verb* 1 DEPRESS, afflict, burden, dispirit, harass, sadden, torment, vex
2 PERSECUTE, abuse, maltreat, subdue, subjugate, suppress, wrong

oppressed *adjective* DOWNTRODDEN, abused, browbeaten, disadvantaged, harassed, maltreated, tyrannized, underprivileged

oppression *noun* PERSECUTION, abuse, brutality, cruelty, injury, injustice, maltreatment, subjection, tyranny

oppressive *adjective* 1 TYRANNICAL, brutal, cruel, despotic, harsh, inhuman, repressive, severe, unjust
2 SULTRY, airless, close, muggy, stifling, stuffy

oppressor *noun* PERSECUTOR, autocrat, bully, despot, scourge, slave-driver, tormentor, tyrant

opt *verb* (often with *for*) CHOOSE, decide (on), elect, go for, plump for, prefer

optimistic *adjective* HOPEFUL, buoyant, cheerful, confident, encouraged, expectant, positive, rosy, sanguine

optimum *adjective* IDEAL, best, highest, optimal, peak, perfect, superlative

option *noun* CHOICE, alternative, preference, selection

optional *adjective* VOLUNTARY, discretionary, elective, extra, open, possible

opulence *noun* 1 WEALTH, affluence, luxuriance, luxury, plenty, prosperity, riches
2 ABUNDANCE, copiousness, cornucopia, fullness, profusion, richness, superabundance

opulent *adjective* 1 RICH, affluent, lavish, luxurious, moneyed, prosperous, sumptuous, wealthy, well-off, well-to-do
2 ABUNDANT, copious, lavish, luxuriant, plentiful, profuse, prolific

opus *noun* WORK, brainchild, composition, creation, *oeuvre*, piece, production

oracle *noun* 1 PROPHECY, divination, prediction, prognostication, revelation
2 PUNDIT, adviser, authority, guru, mastermind, mentor, wizard

oral *adjective* SPOKEN, verbal, vocal

oration *noun* SPEECH, address, discourse, harangue, homily, lecture

orator *noun* PUBLIC SPEAKER, declaimer, lecturer, rhetorician, speaker

oratorical *adjective* RHETORICAL, bombastic, declamatory, eloquent, grandiloquent, high-flown, magniloquent, sonorous

oratory *noun* ELOQUENCE, declamation, elocution, grandiloquence, public speaking, rhetoric, speech-making

orb *noun* SPHERE, ball, circle, globe, ring

orbit *noun* 1 PATH, circle, course, cycle, revolution, rotation, trajectory
2 SPHERE OF INFLUENCE, ambit, compass, domain, influence, range, reach, scope, sweep
▶ *verb* 3 CIRCLE, circumnavigate, encircle, revolve around

orchestrate *verb* 1 SCORE, arrange
2 ORGANIZE, arrange, coordinate, put together, set up, stage-manage

ordain *verb* 1 APPOINT, anoint, consecrate, invest, nominate
2 ORDER, decree, demand, dictate, fix, lay down, legislate, prescribe, rule, will

ordeal *noun* HARDSHIP, agony, anguish, baptism of fire, nightmare, suffering, test, torture, trial, tribulation(s)

order *noun* 1 INSTRUCTION, command, decree, dictate, direction, directive, injunction, law, mandate, regulation, rule
2 SEQUENCE, arrangement, array, grouping, layout, line-up, progression, series, structure
3 TIDINESS, method, neatness, orderliness, organization, pattern,

regularity, symmetry, system
4 DISCIPLINE, calm, control, law, law and order, peace, quiet, tranquillity
5 REQUEST, application, booking, commission, requisition, reservation
6 CLASS, caste, grade, position, rank, status
7 KIND, class, family, genre, ilk, sort, type
8 SOCIETY, association, brotherhood, community, company, fraternity, guild, organization
▶ *verb* 9 INSTRUCT, bid, charge, command, decree, demand, direct, require
10 REQUEST, apply for, book, reserve, send away for
11 ARRANGE, catalog, classify, group, marshal, organize, sort out, systematize

orderly *adjective* 1 WELL-ORGANIZED, businesslike, in order, methodical, neat, regular, scientific, shipshape, systematic, tidy
2 WELL-BEHAVED, controlled, disciplined, law-abiding, peaceable, quiet, restrained

ordinarily *adverb* USUALLY, as a rule, commonly, customarily, generally, habitually, in general, normally

ordinary *adjective* 1 USUAL, common, conventional, everyday, normal, regular, routine, standard, stock, typical
2 COMMONPLACE, banal, humble, humdrum, modest, mundane, plain, run-of-the-mill, unremarkable, workaday

organ *noun* 1 PART, element, structure, unit
2 MOUTHPIECE, forum, medium,

vehicle, voice

organic *adjective* 1 NATURAL, animate, biological, live, living
2 SYSTEMATIC, integrated, methodical, ordered, organized, structured

organism *noun* CREATURE, animal, being, body, entity, structure

organization *noun* 1 GROUP, association, body, company, confederation, corporation, institution, outfit (*informal*), syndicate
2 MANAGEMENT, construction, coordination, direction, organizing, planning, running, structuring
3 ARRANGEMENT, chemistry, composition, format, make-up, pattern, structure, unity

organize *verb* ARRANGE, classify, coordinate, group, marshal, put together, run, set up, systematize, take care of

orgy *noun* 1 REVEL, bacchanalia, carousal, debauch, revelry, Saturnalia
2 SPREE, binge (*informal*), bout, excess, indulgence, overindulgence, splurge, surfeit

orient *verb* FAMILIARIZE, acclimatize, adapt, adjust, align, get one's bearings, orientate

orientation *noun* 1 POSITION, bearings, direction, location
2 FAMILIARIZATION, acclimatization, adaptation, adjustment, assimilation, introduction, settling in

orifice *noun* OPENING, aperture, cleft, hole, mouth, pore, rent, vent

origin *noun* 1 ROOT, base, basis, derivation, fount, fountainhead, source, wellspring
2 BEGINNING, birth, creation, emergence, foundation, genesis,

inception, launch, start

original *adjective* 1 FIRST, earliest, initial, introductory, opening, primary, starting
2 NEW, fresh, ground-breaking, innovative, novel, seminal, unprecedented, unusual
3 CREATIVE, fertile, imaginative, ingenious, inventive, resourceful
▶ *noun* 4 PROTOTYPE, archetype, master, model, paradigm, pattern, precedent, standard

originality *noun* NOVELTY, creativity, freshness, imagination, ingenuity, innovation, inventiveness, newness, unorthodoxy

originally *adverb* INITIALLY, at first, first, in the beginning, to begin with

originate *verb* 1 BEGIN, arise, come, derive, emerge, result, rise, spring, start, stem
2 INTRODUCE, bring about, create, formulate, generate, institute, launch, pioneer

originator *noun* CREATOR, architect, author, father *or* mother, founder, inventor, maker, pioneer

ornament *noun* 1 DECORATION, accessory, adornment, bauble, embellishment, festoon, knick-knack, trimming, trinket
▶ *verb* 2 DECORATE, adorn, beautify, embellish, festoon, grace, prettify

ornamental *adjective* DECORATIVE, attractive, beautifying, embellishing, for show, showy

ornamentation *noun* DECORATION, adornment, elaboration, embellishment, embroidery, frills, ornateness

ornate *adjective* ELABORATE, baroque, busy, decorated, fancy, florid, fussy, ornamented, overelaborate, rococo

orthodox *adjective* ESTABLISHED, accepted, approved, conventional, customary, official, received, traditional, well-established

orthodoxy *noun* CONFORMITY, authority, conventionality, received wisdom, traditionalism

oscillate *verb* FLUCTUATE, seesaw, sway, swing, vacillate, vary, vibrate, waver

oscillation *noun* SWING, fluctuation, instability, vacillation, variation, wavering

ossify *verb* HARDEN, fossilize, solidify, stiffen

ostensible *adjective* APPARENT, outward, pretended, professed, purported, seeming, so-called, superficial, supposed

ostensibly *adverb* APPARENTLY, on the face of it, professedly, seemingly, supposedly

ostentation *noun* DISPLAY, affectation, exhibitionism, flamboyance, flashiness, flaunting, parade, pomp, pretentiousness, show, showing off (*informal*)

ostentatious *adjective* PRETENTIOUS, brash, conspicuous, flamboyant, flashy, gaudy, loud, obtrusive, showy

ostracism *noun* EXCLUSION, banishment, exile, isolation, rejection

ostracize *verb* EXCLUDE, banish, cast out, cold-shoulder, exile, give (someone) the cold shoulder, reject, send to Coventry, shun

other *adjective* 1 ADDITIONAL, added, alternative, auxiliary, extra, further, more, spare, supplementary
2 DIFFERENT, contrasting, dissimilar, distinct, diverse,

separate, unrelated, variant

otherwise *conjunction* 1 OR ELSE, if not, or then
▶ *adverb* 2 DIFFERENTLY, any other way, contrarily

ounce *noun* SHRED, atom, crumb, drop, grain, scrap, speck, trace

oust *verb* EXPEL, depose, dislodge, displace, dispossess, eject, throw out, topple, turn out, unseat

out *adjective* 1 AWAY, abroad, absent, elsewhere, gone, not at home, outside
2 EXTINGUISHED, at an end, dead, ended, exhausted, expired, finished, used up

outbreak *noun* ERUPTION, burst, epidemic, explosion, flare-up, outburst, rash, upsurge

outburst *noun* OUTPOURING, eruption, explosion, flare-up, outbreak, paroxysm, spasm, surge

outcast *noun* PARIAH, castaway, exile, leper, *persona non grata*, refugee, vagabond, wretch

outclass *verb* SURPASS, eclipse, excel, leave standing (*informal*), outdo, outshine, outstrip, overshadow, run rings around (*informal*)

outcome *noun* RESULT, conclusion, consequence, end, issue, payoff (*informal*), upshot

outcry *noun* PROTEST, clamor, commotion, complaint, hue and cry, hullaballoo, outburst, uproar

outdated *adjective* OLD-FASHIONED, antiquated, archaic, obsolete, outmoded, out of date, passé, unfashionable

outdo *verb* SURPASS, beat, best, eclipse, exceed, get the better of, outclass, outmaneuver, overcome, top, transcend

outdoor *adjective* OPEN-AIR, alfresco, out-of-door(s), outside

outer *adjective* EXTERNAL, exposed, exterior, outlying, outside, outward, peripheral, surface

outfit *noun* 1 COSTUME, clothes, ensemble, garb, get-up (*informal*), kit, suit
2 GROUP, company, crew, organization, setup (*informal*), squad, team, unit

outgoing *adjective* 1 LEAVING, departing, former, retiring, withdrawing
2 SOCIABLE, approachable, communicative, expansive, extrovert, friendly, gregarious, open, warm

outgoings *plural noun* EXPENSES, costs, expenditure, outlay, overheads

outing *noun* TRIP, excursion, expedition, jaunt, spin (*informal*)

outlandish *adjective* STRANGE, bizarre, exotic, fantastic, far-out (*slang*), freakish, outré, preposterous, unheard-of, weird

outlaw *noun* 1 BANDIT, brigand, desperado, fugitive, highwayman, marauder, outcast, robber
▶ *verb* 2 FORBID, ban, bar, disallow, exclude, prohibit, proscribe

outlay *noun* EXPENDITURE, cost, expenses, investment, outgoings, spending

outlet *noun* 1 RELEASE, avenue, channel, duct, exit, opening, vent
2 SHOP, market, store

outline *noun* 1 SUMMARY, recapitulation, résumé, rundown, synopsis, thumbnail sketch
2 SHAPE, configuration, contour, delineation, figure, form, profile, silhouette
▶ *verb* 3 SUMMARIZE, adumbrate, delineate, draft, plan, rough out, sketch (in), trace

outlive *verb* SURVIVE, outlast

outlook noun 1 ATTITUDE, angle, frame of mind, perspective, point of view, slant, standpoint, viewpoint
2 PROSPECT, expectations, forecast, future

outlying adjective REMOTE, distant, far-flung, out-of-the-way, peripheral, provincial

outmoded adjective OLD-FASHIONED, anachronistic, antiquated, archaic, obsolete, out-of-date, outworn, passé, unfashionable

out-of-date adjective OLD-FASHIONED, antiquated, dated, expired, invalid, lapsed, obsolete, outmoded, outworn, passé

outpouring noun STREAM, cascade, effusion, flow, spate, spurt, torrent

output noun PRODUCTION, achievement, manufacture, productivity, yield

outrage noun 1 VIOLATION, abuse, affront, desecration, indignity, insult, offense, sacrilege, violence
2 INDIGNATION, anger, fury, hurt, resentment, shock, wrath
▶ verb 3 OFFEND, affront, incense, infuriate, madden, scandalize, shock

outrageous adjective 1 OFFENSIVE, atrocious, disgraceful, flagrant, heinous, iniquitous, nefarious, unspeakable, villainous, wicked
2 SHOCKING, exorbitant, extravagant, immoderate, preposterous, scandalous, steep (informal), unreasonable

outré adjective ECCENTRIC, bizarre, fantastic, freakish, odd, off-the-wall (slang), outlandish, unconventional, weird

outright adjective 1 ABSOLUTE, complete, out-and-out, perfect, thorough, thoroughgoing, total, unconditional, unmitigated, unqualified
2 DIRECT, definite, flat, straightforward, unequivocal, unqualified
▶ adverb 3 ABSOLUTELY, completely, openly, overtly, straightforwardly, thoroughly, to the full

outset noun BEGINNING, commencement, inauguration, inception, kickoff (informal), onset, opening, start

outshine verb OVERSHADOW, eclipse, leave or put in the shade, outclass, outdo, outstrip, surpass, transcend, upstage

outside adjective 1 EXTERNAL, exterior, extraneous, outer, outward
2 as in **an outside chance** UNLIKELY, distant, faint, marginal, remote, slight, slim, small
▶ noun 3 SURFACE, exterior, façade, face, front, skin, topside

outsider noun INTERLOPER, incomer, intruder, newcomer, odd man out, stranger

outsize adjective EXTRA-LARGE, giant, gigantic, huge, jumbo (informal), mammoth, monster, oversized, supersize

outskirts plural noun EDGE, boundary, environs, periphery, suburbia, suburbs

outspoken adjective FORTHRIGHT, abrupt, blunt, explicit, frank, open, plain-spoken, unceremonious, unequivocal

outstanding adjective 1 EXCELLENT, cool (informal), exceptional, great, important, impressive, phat (slang), special, superior, superlative
2 UNPAID, due, payable, pending,

remaining, uncollected, unsettled

outstrip verb SURPASS, better, eclipse, exceed, excel, outdistance, outdo, overtake, transcend

outward adjective APPARENT, noticeable, observable, obvious, ostensible, perceptible, surface, visible

outwardly adverb OSTENSIBLY, apparently, externally, on the face of it, on the surface, seemingly, superficially, to all intents and purposes

outweigh verb OVERRIDE, cancel (out), compensate for, eclipse, prevail over, take precedence over, tip the scales

outwit verb OUTTHINK, cheat, dupe, fool, get the better of, outfox, outmaneuver, outsmart (informal), put one over on (informal), swindle, take in (informal)

outworn adjective OUTDATED, antiquated, discredited, disused, hackneyed, obsolete, outmoded, out-of-date, threadbare, worn-out

oval adjective ELLIPTICAL, egg-shaped, ovoid

ovation noun APPLAUSE, acclaim, acclamation, big hand, cheers, clapping, plaudits, tribute

over preposition 1 ON, above, on top of, upon
2 EXCEEDING, above, in excess of, more than
▶ adverb 3 ABOVE, aloft, on high, overhead
4 EXTRA, beyond, in addition, in excess, left over
▶ adjective 5 FINISHED, bygone, closed, completed, concluded, done (with), ended, gone, past

overact verb EXAGGERATE, ham or ham up (informal), overdo, overplay

overall adjective 1 TOTAL, all-embracing, blanket, complete, comprehensive, general, global, inclusive
▶ adverb 2 IN GENERAL, on the whole

overawe verb INTIMIDATE, abash, alarm, daunt, frighten, scare, terrify

overbalance verb OVERTURN, capsize, keel over, slip, tip over, topple over, tumble, turn turtle

overbearing adjective ARROGANT, bossy (informal), dictatorial, domineering, haughty, high-handed, imperious, supercilious, superior

overblown adjective EXCESSIVE, disproportionate, immoderate, inflated, overdone, over the top, undue

overcast adjective CLOUDY, dismal, dreary, dull, gray, leaden, louring or lowering, murky

overcharge verb CHEAT, diddle (informal), fleece, rip off (slang), short-change, sting (informal), surcharge

overcome verb 1 CONQUER, beat, defeat, master, overpower, overwhelm, prevail, subdue, subjugate, surmount, triumph over, vanquish
▶ adjective 2 AFFECTED, at a loss for words, bowled over (informal), overwhelmed, speechless, swept off one's feet

overconfident adjective BRASH, cocksure, foolhardy, overweening, presumptuous

overcrowded adjective CONGESTED, bursting at the seams, choked, jam-packed, overloaded, overpopulated, packed (out), swarming

overdo verb 1 EXAGGERATE, belabor, gild the lily, go overboard (*informal*), overindulge, overreach, overstate

2 ▷▷ **overdo it** OVERWORK, bite off more than one can chew, burn the candle at both ends (*informal*), overload, strain *or* overstrain oneself, wear oneself out

overdone *adjective* 1 EXCESSIVE, exaggerated, fulsome, immoderate, inordinate, overelaborate, too much, undue, unnecessary

2 OVERCOOKED, burnt, charred, dried up, spoiled

overdue *adjective* LATE, behindhand, behind schedule, belated, owing, tardy, unpunctual

overeat *verb* OVERINDULGE, binge (*informal*), gorge, gormandize, guzzle, pig out (*slang*), stuff oneself

overemphasize *verb* OVERSTRESS, belabor, blow up out of all proportion, make a mountain out of a molehill (*informal*), overdramatize

overflow *verb* 1 SPILL, brim over, bubble over, pour over, run over, well over

▶ *noun* 2 SURPLUS, overabundance, spilling over

overhang *verb* PROJECT, extend, jut, loom, protrude, stick out

overhaul *verb* 1 REPAIR, check, do up (*informal*), examine, inspect, recondition, refurbish, restore, service

2 OVERTAKE, catch up with, get ahead of, pass

▶ *noun* 3 CHECKUP, check, examination, going-over (*informal*), inspection, reconditioning, service

overhead *adverb* 1 ABOVE, aloft, in the sky, on high, skyward, up above, upward

▶ *adjective* 2 AERIAL, overhanging,

upper

overheads *plural noun* RUNNING COSTS, operating costs

overindulgence *noun* EXCESS, immoderation, intemperance, overeating, surfeit

overjoyed *adjective* DELIGHTED, cock-a-hoop, elated, euphoric, jubilant, on cloud nine (*informal*), over the moon (*informal*), thrilled

overload *verb* OVERBURDEN, burden, encumber, oppress, overtax, saddle (with), strain, weigh down

overlook *verb* 1 FORGET, disregard, miss, neglect, omit, pass

2 IGNORE, condone, disregard, excuse, forgive, make allowances for, pardon, turn a blind eye to, wink at

3 HAVE A VIEW OF, look over *or* out on

overpower *verb* OVERWHELM, conquer, crush, defeat, master, overcome, overthrow, quell, subdue, subjugate, vanquish

overpowering *adjective* IRRESISTIBLE, forceful, invincible, irrefutable, overwhelming, powerful, strong

overrate *verb* OVERESTIMATE, exaggerate, overvalue

override *verb* OVERRULE, annul, cancel, countermand, nullify, outweigh, supersede

overriding *adjective* ULTIMATE, dominant, paramount, predominant, primary, supreme

overrule *verb* REVERSE, alter, annul, cancel, countermand, override, overturn, repeal, rescind, veto

overrun *verb* 1 INVADE, occupy, overwhelm, rout

2 INFEST, choke, inundate, permeate, ravage, spread over,

swarm over

3 EXCEED, go beyond, overshoot, run over or on

overseer noun SUPERVISOR, boss (informal), chief, foreman, master, superintendent

overshadow verb 1 OUTSHINE, dominate, dwarf, eclipse, leave or put in the shade, surpass, tower above

2 SPOIL, blight, mar, put a damper on, ruin, temper

oversight noun MISTAKE, blunder, carelessness, error, fault, lapse, neglect, omission, slip

overt adjective OPEN, blatant, manifest, observable, obvious, plain, public, unconcealed, undisguised

overtake verb 1 PASS, catch up with, get past, leave behind, outdistance, outdo, outstrip, overhaul

2 BEFALL, engulf, happen, hit, overwhelm, strike

overthrow verb 1 DEFEAT, bring down, conquer, depose, dethrone, oust, overcome, overpower, topple, unseat, vanquish

▶ noun 2 DOWNFALL, defeat, destruction, dethronement, fall, ousting, undoing, unseating

overtone noun CONNOTATION, hint, implication, innuendo, intimation, nuance, sense, suggestion, undercurrent

overture noun 1 (music) INTRODUCTION, opening, prelude

2 ▷▷ **overtures** APPROACH, advance, invitation, offer, proposal, proposition

overturn verb 1 TIP OVER, capsize, keel over, overbalance, topple, upend, upturn

2 OVERTHROW, bring down, depose, destroy, unseat

overweight adjective FAT, bulky, chubby, chunky, corpulent, heavy, hefty, obese, plump, portly, stout, tubby (informal)

overwhelm verb 1 DEVASTATE, bowl over (informal), knock (someone) for six (informal), overcome, stagger, sweep (someone) off his or her feet, take (someone's) breath away

2 DESTROY, crush, cut to pieces, massacre, overpower, overrun, rout

overwhelming adjective DEVASTATING, breathtaking, crushing, irresistible, overpowering, shattering, stunning, towering

overwork verb 1 STRAIN, burn the midnight oil, sweat (informal), work one's fingers to the bone

2 OVERUSE, exhaust, exploit, fatigue, oppress, wear out, weary

overwrought adjective AGITATED, distracted, excited, frantic, keyed up, on edge, overexcited, tense, uptight (informal), wired (slang)

owe verb BE IN DEBT, be in arrears, be obligated or indebted

owing adjective UNPAID, due, outstanding, overdue, owed, payable, unsettled

owing to preposition BECAUSE OF, as a result of, on account of

own adjective 1 PERSONAL, individual, particular, private

▶ pronoun 2 ▷▷ **hold one's own** COMPETE, keep going, keep one's end up, keep one's head above water; **on one's own** ALONE, by oneself, independently, singly, unaided, unassisted, under one's own steam

▶ verb 3 POSSESS, be in possession of, enjoy, have, hold, keep, retain

4 ACKNOWLEDGE, admit, allow,

concede, confess, grant, recognize
5 ▷▷ **own up** CONFESS, admit,
come clean, make a clean breast,
tell the truth

owner *noun* POSSESSOR, holder,
landlord *or* landlady, proprietor
ownership *noun* POSSESSION,
dominion, title

p

pace *noun* 1 STEP, gait, stride, tread, walk
2 SPEED, rate, tempo, velocity
▶ *verb* 3 STRIDE, march, patrol, pound
4 ▷▷ **pace out** MEASURE, count, mark out, step

pacifist *noun* PEACE LOVER, conscientious objector, dove

pacify *verb* CALM, allay, appease, assuage, de-stress, mollify, placate, propitiate, soothe

pack *verb* 1 PACKAGE, bundle, load, store, stow
2 CRAM, compress, crowd, fill, jam, press, ram, stuff
3 ▷▷ **pack off** SEND AWAY, dismiss, send packing (*informal*)
▶ *noun* 4 BUNDLE, back pack, burden, kitbag, knapsack, load, parcel, rucksack
5 PACKET, package
6 GROUP, band, bunch, company, crowd, flock, gang, herd, mob, troop

package *noun* 1 PARCEL, box, carton, container, packet
2 UNIT, combination, whole
▶ *verb* 3 PACK, box, parcel (up), wrap

packed *adjective* FULL, chock-a-block, chock-full, crammed, crowded, filled, jammed, jam-packed

packet *noun* 1 PACKAGE, bag, carton, container, parcel
2 (*slang*) FORTUNE, bomb (*Brit. slang*), king's ransom (*informal*), pile (*informal*), small fortune, tidy sum (*informal*)

pack it in *verb* (*informal*) STOP, cease, chuck (*informal*), give up or over, kick (*informal*)

pack up *verb* 1 PUT AWAY, store
2 (*informal*) STOP, finish, give up, pack in (*Brit. informal*), pack it in (*informal*)
3 BREAK DOWN, conk out (*informal*), fail

pact *noun* AGREEMENT, alliance, bargain, covenant, deal, treaty, understanding

pad¹ *noun* 1 CUSHION, buffer, protection, stuffing, wad
2 NOTEPAD, block, jotter, writing pad
3 PAW, foot, sole
4 (*slang, dated*) HOME, apartment, flat, place
▶ *verb* 5 PACK, cushion, fill, protect, stuff
6 ▷▷ **pad out** LENGTHEN, elaborate, fill out, flesh out, protract, spin out, stretch

pad² *verb* SNEAK, creep, go barefoot, steal

padding *noun* 1 FILLING, packing, stuffing, wadding
2 WORDINESS, waffle (*informal, chiefly Brit.*), hot air (*informal*), verbiage, verbosity

paddle¹ *noun* 1 OAR, scull
▶ *verb* 2 ROW, propel, pull, scull

paddle² *verb* 1 WADE, slop, splash (about)
2 DABBLE, stir

pagan adjective 1 HEATHEN, idolatrous, infidel, polytheistic
▶ noun 2 HEATHEN, idolater, infidel, polytheist

page¹ noun FOLIO, leaf, sheet, side

page² noun 1 ATTENDANT, pageboy, servant, squire
▶ verb 2 CALL, send for, summon

pageant noun SHOW, display, parade, procession, spectacle, tableau

pageantry noun SPECTACLE, display, grandeur, parade, pomp, show, splendor, theatricality

pain noun 1 HURT, ache, discomfort, irritation, pang, soreness, tenderness, throb, twinge
2 SUFFERING, agony, anguish, distress, heartache, misery, torment, torture
▶ verb 3 HURT, smart, sting, throb
4 DISTRESS, agonize, cut to the quick, grieve, hurt, sadden, torment, torture

pained adjective DISTRESSED, aggrieved, hurt, injured, offended, upset, wounded

painful adjective 1 DISTRESSING, disagreeable, distasteful, grievous, unpleasant
2 SORE, aching, agonizing, smarting, tender
3 DIFFICULT, arduous, hard, laborious, troublesome, trying

painfully adverb DISTRESSINGLY, clearly, dreadfully, sadly, unfortunately

painkiller noun ANALGESIC, anesthetic, anodyne, drug

painless adjective SIMPLE, easy, effortless, fast, quick

pains plural noun TROUBLE, bother, care, diligence, effort

painstaking adjective THOROUGH, assiduous, careful, conscientious, diligent, meticulous, scrupulous

paint noun 1 COLORING, color, dye, pigment, stain, tint
▶ verb 2 DEPICT, draw, picture, portray, represent, sketch
3 COAT, apply, color, cover, daub

pair noun 1 COUPLE, brace, duo, twins
▶ verb 2 COUPLE, bracket, join, match (up), team, twin

pal noun (informal) FRIEND, buddy (informal), chum (informal), companion, comrade, crony, homeboy (slang), homegirl (slang), mate (informal)

palatable adjective DELICIOUS, appetizing, luscious, mouthwatering, tasty, yummy (informal)

palate noun TASTE, appetite, stomach

palatial adjective MAGNIFICENT, grand, imposing, majestic, opulent, regal, splendid, stately

palaver noun FUSS, big deal (informal), business (informal), carry-on (informal, chiefly Brit.), pantomime (informal, chiefly Brit.), performance (informal), rigmarole, song and dance (informal), to-do

pale adjective 1 WHITE, ashen, bleached, colorless, faded, light, pallid, pasty, wan
▶ verb 2 BECOME PALE, blanch, go white, lose color, whiten

pall¹ noun 1 CLOUD, mantle, shadow, shroud, veil
2 GLOOM, check, damp, damper

pall² verb BECOME BORING, become dull, become tedious, cloy, jade, sicken, tire, weary

pallid adjective PALE, anemic, ashen, colorless, pasty, wan

pallor noun PALENESS, lack of color, pallidness, wanness, whiteness

palm off verb FOB OFF, foist off,

pass off

palpable adjective OBVIOUS, clear, conspicuous, evident, manifest, plain, unmistakable, visible

palpitate verb BEAT, flutter, pound, pulsate, throb, tremble

paltry adjective INSIGNIFICANT, contemptible, despicable, inconsiderable, lousy (slang), meager, mean, measly, minor, miserable, petty, poor, puny, scuzzy (slang), slight, small, trifling, trivial, unimportant, worthless

pamper verb SPOIL, cater to, coddle, cosset, indulge, mollycoddle, overindulge, pet

pamphlet noun BOOKLET, brochure, circular, leaflet, tract

pan¹ noun 1 POT, container, saucepan
▶ verb 2 SIFT OUT, look for, search for
3 (informal) CRITICIZE, censure, knock (informal), slam (slang), tear into (informal)

pan² verb MOVE, follow, sweep, track

panacea noun CURE-ALL, nostrum, universal cure

panache noun STYLE, dash, élan, flamboyance

pandemonium noun UPROAR, bedlam, chaos, confusion, din, hullabaloo, racket, rumpus, turmoil

pander verb ▷▷ **pander to** INDULGE, cater to, gratify, play up to (informal), please, satisfy

pang noun TWINGE, ache, pain, prick, spasm, stab, sting

panic noun 1 FEAR, alarm, fright, hysteria, scare, terror
▶ verb 2 GO TO PIECES, become hysterical, lose one's nerve
3 ALARM, scare, unnerve

panic-stricken adjective FRIGHTENED, frightened out of one's wits, hysterical, in a cold sweat (informal), panicky, scared, scared stiff, terrified

panoply noun ARRAY, attire, dress, garb, regalia, trappings

panorama noun VIEW, prospect, vista

panoramic adjective WIDE, comprehensive, extensive, overall, sweeping

pant verb PUFF, blow, breathe, gasp, heave, wheeze

pants plural noun 1 (Brit.) UNDERPANTS, boxer shorts, briefs, drawers, knickers, panties
2 (U.S.) TROUSERS, slacks

paper noun 1 NEWSPAPER, daily, gazette, journal
2 ESSAY, article, dissertation, report, treatise
3 ▷▷ **papers: a** DOCUMENTS, certificates, deeds, records
b LETTERS, archive, diaries, documents, dossier, file, records
▶ verb 4 WALLPAPER, hang

par noun AVERAGE, level, mean, norm, standard, usual

parable noun LESSON, allegory, fable, moral tale, story

parade noun 1 PROCESSION, array, cavalcade, march, pageant
2 SHOW, display, spectacle
▶ verb 3 FLAUNT, display, exhibit, show off (informal)
4 MARCH, process

paradigm noun MODEL, example, ideal, pattern

paradise noun 1 HEAVEN, Elysian fields, Happy Valley, Promised Land
2 BLISS, delight, felicity, heaven, utopia

paradox noun CONTRADICTION, anomaly, enigma, oddity, puzzle

paradoxical *adjective*
CONTRADICTORY, baffling,
confounding, enigmatic, puzzling
paragon *noun* MODEL, epitome,
exemplar, ideal, nonpareil,
pattern, quintessence
paragraph *noun* SECTION, clause,
item, part, passage, subdivision
parallel *adjective* 1 EQUIDISTANT,
alongside, side by side
2 MATCHING, analogous,
corresponding, like, resembling,
similar
▶ *noun* 3 EQUIVALENT, analogue,
counterpart, equal, match, twin
4 SIMILARITY, analogy,
comparison, likeness,
resemblance
paralysis *noun* 1 IMMOBILITY,
palsy
2 STANDSTILL, breakdown, halt,
stoppage
paralytic *adjective* PARALYZED,
challenged, crippled, disabled,
incapacitated, lame, palsied
paralyze *verb* 1 DISABLE, cripple,
incapacitate, lame
2 IMMOBILIZE, freeze, halt, numb,
petrify, stun
parameter *noun* LIMIT,
framework, limitation,
restriction, specification
paramount *adjective* PRINCIPAL,
cardinal, chief, first, foremost,
main, primary, prime, supreme
paranoid *adjective* 1 MENTALLY
ILL, deluded, disturbed, manic,
neurotic, paranoiac, psychotic
2 (*informal*) SUSPICIOUS, fearful,
nervous, wired (*slang*), worried
paraphernalia *noun* EQUIPMENT,
apparatus, baggage, belongings,
effects, gear, stuff, tackle, things,
trappings
paraphrase *noun* 1 REWORDING,
rephrasing, restatement

▶ *verb* 2 REWORD, express in
other words *or* one's own words,
rephrase, restate
parasite *noun* SPONGER (*informal*),
bloodsucker (*informal*), hanger-on,
leech, scrounger (*informal*)
parasitic, parasitical
adjective SCROUNGING (*informal*),
bloodsucking (*informal*), sponging
(*informal*)
parcel *noun* 1 PACKAGE, bundle,
pack
▶ *verb* 2 (often with *up*) WRAP, do
up, pack, package, tie up
parch *verb* DRY UP, dehydrate,
desiccate, evaporate, shrivel,
wither
parched *adjective* DRIED OUT *or* UP,
arid, dehydrated, dry, thirsty
pardon *verb* 1 FORGIVE, absolve,
acquit, excuse, exonerate, let off
(*informal*), overlook
▶ *noun* 2 FORGIVENESS, absolution,
acquittal, amnesty, exoneration
pardonable *adjective*
FORGIVABLE, excusable, minor,
understandable, venial
pare *verb* 1 PEEL, clip, cut, shave,
skin, trim
2 CUT BACK, crop, cut, decrease,
dock, reduce
parent *noun* FATHER *or* MOTHER,
procreator, progenitor, sire
parentage *noun* FAMILY, ancestry,
birth, descent, lineage, pedigree,
stock
pariah *noun* OUTCAST, exile,
undesirable, untouchable
parish *noun* COMMUNITY, church,
congregation, flock
parity *noun* EQUALITY, consistency,
equivalence, uniformity, unity
park *noun* PARKLAND, estate,
garden, grounds, woodland
parlance *noun* LANGUAGE, idiom,
jargon, phraseology, speech, talk,

tongue

parliament noun ASSEMBLY, congress, convention, council, legislature, senate

parliamentary adjective GOVERNMENTAL, law-making, legislative

parlor noun (old-fashioned) SITTING ROOM, drawing room, front room, living room, lounge

parochial adjective PROVINCIAL, insular, limited, narrow, narrow-minded, petty, small-minded

parody noun 1 TAKEOFF SATIRE (informal), burlesque, caricature, satire, send-up (Brit. informal), skit, spoof (informal)
▶ verb 2 TAKE OFF SATIRIZE (informal), burlesque, caricature, do a takeoff of (informal), satirize, send up (Brit. informal)

paroxysm noun OUTBURST, attack, convulsion, fit, seizure, spasm

parrot verb REPEAT, copy, echo, imitate, mimic

parry verb 1 WARD OFF, block, deflect, rebuff, repel, repulse
2 EVADE, avoid, dodge, sidestep

parsimonious adjective MEAN, close, frugal, miserly, niggardly, penny-pinching (informal), stingy, tightfisted

parson noun CLERGYMAN, churchman, cleric, minister, pastor, preacher, priest, vicar

part noun 1 PIECE, bit, fraction, fragment, portion, scrap, section, share
2 COMPONENT, branch, constituent, division, member, unit
3 (theatre) ROLE, character, lines
4 SIDE, behalf, cause, concern, interest
5 (often plural) REGION, area, district, neighborhood, quarter, vicinity
6 ▷▷ **in good part** GOOD-NATUREDLY, cheerfully, well, without offense; **in part** PARTLY, a little, in some measure, partially, somewhat
▶ verb 7 DIVIDE, break, come apart, detach, rend, separate, sever, split, tear
8 SEPARATE, depart, go, go away, leave, split up, withdraw

partake verb 1 ▷▷ **partake of** CONSUME, chow down (slang), eat, take; **partake in** PARTICIPATE IN, engage in, share in, take part in

partial adjective 1 INCOMPLETE, imperfect, uncompleted, unfinished
2 BIASED, discriminatory, one-sided, partisan, prejudiced, unfair, unjust

partiality noun 1 BIAS, favoritism, preference, prejudice
2 LIKING, fondness, inclination, love, penchant, predilection, taste, weakness

partially adverb PARTLY, fractionally, incompletely, in part, not wholly, somewhat

participant noun PARTICIPATOR, contributor, member, player, stakeholder

participate verb TAKE PART, be involved in, join in, partake, perform, share

participation noun TAKING PART, contribution, involvement, joining in, partaking, sharing in

particle noun BIT, grain, iota, jot, mite, piece, scrap, shred, speck

particular adjective 1 SPECIFIC, distinct, exact, peculiar, precise, special
2 SPECIAL, especial, exceptional, marked, notable, noteworthy, remarkable, singular,

uncommon, unusual

3 FUSSY, choosy (*informal*),
demanding, fastidious, finicky,
pernickety (*old-fashioned, informal*),
picky (*informal*)

▶ *noun* 4 (usually plural) DETAIL,
circumstance, fact, feature, item,
specification

5 ▷▷ **in particular** ESPECIALLY,
distinctly, exactly, particularly,
specifically

particularly *adverb* 1 ESPECIALLY,
exceptionally, notably, singularly,
uncommonly, unusually

2 SPECIFICALLY, distinctly,
especially, explicitly, expressly, in
particular

parting *noun* 1 GOING, farewell,
good-bye

2 DIVISION, breaking, rift, rupture,
separation, split

partisan *noun* 1 SUPPORTER,
adherent, devotee, upholder

2 UNDERGROUND FIGHTER,
guerrilla, resistance fighter

▶ *adjective* 3 PREJUDICED, biased,
interested, one-sided, partial,
sectarian

partition *noun* 1 SCREEN, barrier,
wall

2 DIVISION, segregation,
separation

3 ALLOTMENT, apportionment,
distribution

▶ *verb* 4 SEPARATE, divide, screen

partly *adverb* PARTIALLY, slightly,
somewhat

partner *noun* 1 SPOUSE, consort,
husband *or* wife, mate, significant
other (*informal*)

2 COMPANION, ally, associate,
colleague, comrade, helper, mate

partnership *noun* COMPANY,
alliance, cooperative, firm, house,
society, union

party *noun* 1 GET-TOGETHER

(*informal*), celebration, do (*informal*),
festivity, function, gathering,
reception, social gathering

2 GROUP, band, company, crew,
gang, squad, team, unit

3 FACTION, camp, clique, coterie,
league, set, side

4 PERSON, individual, someone

pass *verb* 1 GO BY *or* PAST, elapse, go,
lapse, move, proceed, run

2 QUALIFY, do, get through,
graduate, succeed

3 SPEND, fill, occupy, while away

4 GIVE, convey, deliver, hand,
send, transfer

5 APPROVE, accept, decree, enact,
legislate, ordain, ratify

6 EXCEED, beat, go beyond, outdo,
outstrip, surpass

7 END, blow over, cease, go

▶ *noun* 8 GAP, canyon, gorge,
ravine, route

9 LICENSE, authorization,
passport, permit, ticket, warrant

passable *adjective* ADEQUATE,
acceptable, all right, average,
fair, mediocre, so-so (*informal*),
tolerable

passage *noun* 1 WAY, alley, avenue,
channel, course, path, road, route

2 CORRIDOR, hall, lobby, vestibule

3 EXTRACT, excerpt, piece,
quotation, reading, section, text

4 JOURNEY, crossing, trek, trip,
voyage

5 SAFE-CONDUCT, freedom,
permission, right

passageway *noun* CORRIDOR,
aisle, alley, hall, hallway, lane,
passage

pass away *verb* (*euphemistic*) DIE,
expire, kick the bucket (*slang*),
pass on, pass over, shuffle off this
mortal coil, snuff it (*informal*)

passé *adjective* OUT-OF-DATE,
dated, obsolete, old-fashioned,

old hat, outdated, outmoded, unfashionable

passenger noun TRAVELER, fare, rider

passer-by noun BYSTANDER, onlooker, witness

passing adjective 1 MOMENTARY, brief, ephemeral, fleeting, short-lived, temporary, transient, transitory
2 SUPERFICIAL, casual, cursory, glancing, quick, short

passion noun 1 LOVE, ardor, desire, infatuation, lust
2 EMOTION, ardor, excitement, feeling, fervor, fire, heat, intensity, warmth, zeal
3 RAGE, anger, fit, frenzy, fury, outburst, paroxysm, storm
4 MANIA, bug (informal), craving, craze, enthusiasm, fascination, obsession

passionate adjective 1 LOVING, amorous, ardent, erotic, hot, lustful
2 EMOTIONAL, ardent, eager, fervent, fierce, heartfelt, impassioned, intense, strong

passive adjective SUBMISSIVE, compliant, docile, inactive, quiescent, receptive

pass off verb FAKE, counterfeit, make a pretense of, palm off

pass out verb FAINT, become unconscious, black out (informal), lose consciousness

pass over verb DISREGARD, ignore, overlook, take no notice of

pass up verb MISS, abstain, decline, forgo, give (something) a miss (informal), let slip, neglect

password noun SIGNAL, key word, watchword

past adjective 1 FORMER, ancient, bygone, early, olden, previous
2 OVER, done, ended, finished, gone
▶ noun 3 BACKGROUND, history, life, past life
4 ▷▷ **the past** FORMER TIMES, days gone by, long ago, olden days
▶ preposition 5 AFTER, beyond, later than
6 BEYOND, across, by, over

paste noun 1 ADHESIVE, cement, glue, gum
▶ verb 2 STICK, cement, glue, gum

pastel adjective PALE, delicate, light, muted, soft

pastiche noun MEDLEY, blend, hotchpotch, mélange, miscellany, mixture

pastime noun ACTIVITY, amusement, diversion, entertainment, game, hobby, recreation

pastor noun CLERGYMAN, churchman, ecclesiastic, minister, parson, priest, rector, vicar

pastoral adjective 1 RUSTIC, bucolic, country, rural
2 ECCLESIASTICAL, clerical, ministerial, priestly

pasture noun GRASSLAND, grass, grazing, meadow

pasty adjective PALE, anemic, pallid, sickly, wan

pat verb 1 STROKE, caress, fondle, pet, tap, touch
▶ noun 2 STROKE, clap, tap

patch noun 1 REINFORCEMENT
2 SPOT, bit, scrap, shred, small piece
3 PLOT, area, ground, land, tract
▶ verb 4 MEND, cover, reinforce, repair, sew up

patchwork noun MIXTURE, hotchpotch, jumble, medley, pastiche

patchy adjective UNEVEN, erratic, fitful, irregular, sketchy, spotty, variable

patent noun 1 COPYRIGHT, license
► adjective 2 OBVIOUS, apparent,
clear, evident, glaring, manifest

paternal adjective FATHERLY,
concerned, protective, solicitous

paternity noun 1 FATHERHOOD
2 PARENTAGE, descent, extraction,
family, lineage

path noun 1 WAY, footpath, road,
track, trail
2 COURSE, direction, road, route,
way

pathetic adjective SAD, affecting,
distressing, heart-rending,
moving, pitiable, plaintive,
poignant, tender, touching

pathos noun SADNESS, pitifulness,
plaintiveness, poignancy

patience noun 1 FORBEARANCE,
calmness, restraint, serenity,
sufferance, tolerance
2 ENDURANCE, constancy,
fortitude, long-suffering,
perseverance, resignation,
stoicism, submission

patient adjective 1 LONG-
SUFFERING, calm, enduring,
persevering, philosophical,
resigned, stoical, submissive,
uncomplaining
2 FORBEARING, even-tempered,
forgiving, indulgent, lenient,
mild, tolerant, understanding
► noun 3 SICK PERSON, case,
invalid, sufferer

patriot noun NATIONALIST,
chauvinist, loyalist

patriotic adjective NATIONALISTIC,
chauvinistic, jingoistic, loyal

patriotism noun NATIONALISM,
jingoism

patrol noun 1 POLICING, guarding,
protecting, vigilance, watching
2 GUARD, patrolman, sentinel,
watch, watchman

► verb 3 POLICE, guard, inspect,
keep guard, keep watch, safeguard

patron noun 1 SUPPORTER, backer,
benefactor, champion, friend,
helper, philanthropist, sponsor
2 CUSTOMER, buyer, client,
frequenter, habitué, shopper

patronage noun 1 SUPPORT,
aid, assistance, backing, help,
promotion, sponsorship
2 CUSTOM, business, clientele,
commerce, trade, trading, traffic

patronize verb 1 TALK DOWN TO,
look down on
2 BE A CUSTOMER OR CLIENT OF, do
business with, frequent, shop at
3 SUPPORT, back, fund, help,
maintain, promote, sponsor

patronizing adjective
CONDESCENDING, disdainful,
gracious, haughty, snobbish,
supercilious, superior

patter¹ verb 1 TAP, beat, pat,
pitter-patter
2 WALK LIGHTLY, scurry, scuttle,
skip, trip
► noun 3 TAPPING, pattering,
pitter-patter

patter² noun 1 SPIEL (informal),
line, pitch
2 CHATTER, gabble, jabber,
nattering, prattle
3 JARGON, argot, cant, lingo
(informal), patois, slang, vernacular
► verb 4 CHATTER, jabber, prate,
rattle on, spout (informal)

pattern noun 1 DESIGN,
arrangement, decoration, device,
figure, motif
2 ORDER, method, plan, sequence,
system
3 PLAN, design, diagram, guide,
original, stencil, template
► verb 4 MODEL, copy, follow, form,
imitate, mold, style

paucity noun (formal) SCARCITY,

dearth, deficiency, lack, rarity, scantiness, shortage, sparseness

paunch noun BELLY, pot, potbelly, spare tire (slang)

pauper noun DOWN-AND-OUT, bankrupt, beggar, mendicant, poor person

pause verb 1 STOP BRIEFLY, break, cease, delay, halt, have a breather (informal), interrupt, rest, take a break, wait
▶ noun 2 STOP, break, breather (informal), cessation, gap, halt, interlude, intermission, interval, lull, respite, rest, stoppage

pave verb COVER, concrete, floor, surface, tile

paw verb MANHANDLE, grab, handle roughly, maul, molest

pawn¹ verb HOCK (informal), deposit, mortgage, pledge

pawn² noun TOOL, cat's-paw, instrument, plaything, puppet, stooge (slang)

pay verb 1 REIMBURSE, compensate, give, recompense, remit, remunerate, requite, reward, settle
2 GIVE, bestow, extend, grant, hand out, present
3 BENEFIT, be worthwhile, repay
4 BE PROFITABLE, make a return, make money
5 YIELD, bring in, produce, return
▶ noun 6 WAGES, allowance, earnings, fee, income, payment, recompense, reimbursement, remuneration, reward, salary, stipend

payable adjective DUE, outstanding, owed, owing

pay back verb 1 REPAY, refund, reimburse, settle up, square
2 GET EVEN WITH (informal), get one's own back, hit back, retaliate

payment noun 1 PAYING,

discharge, remittance, settlement
2 REMITTANCE, advance, deposit, installment, premium
3 WAGE, fee, hire, remuneration, reward

pay off verb 1 SETTLE, clear, discharge, pay in full, square
2 SUCCEED, be effective, work

pay out verb SPEND, disburse, expend, fork out or over or up (slang), shell out (informal)

peace noun 1 STILLNESS, calm, calmness, hush, quiet, repose, rest, silence, tranquillity
2 SERENITY, calm, composure, contentment, repose
3 HARMONY, accord, agreement, concord
4 TRUCE, armistice, treaty

peaceable adjective PEACE-LOVING, conciliatory, friendly, gentle, mild, peaceful, unwarlike

peaceful adjective 1 AT PEACE, amicable, friendly, harmonious, nonviolent
2 CALM, placid, quiet, restful, serene, still, tranquil, undisturbed
3 PEACE-LOVING, conciliatory, peaceable, unwarlike

peacemaker noun MEDIATOR, arbitrator, conciliator, pacifier

peak noun 1 POINT, apex, brow, crest, pinnacle, summit, tip, top
2 HIGH POINT, acme, climax, crown, culmination, zenith
▶ verb 3 CULMINATE, climax, come to a head

peal noun 1 RING, blast, chime, clang, clap, crash, reverberation, roar, rumble
▶ verb 2 RING, chime, crash, resound, roar, rumble

peasant noun RUSTIC, countryman

peccadillo noun MISDEED, error, indiscretion, lapse, misdemeanor, slip

peck *verb or noun* PICK, dig, hit, jab, poke, prick, strike, tap

peculiar *adjective* 1 ODD, abnormal, bizarre, curious, eccentric, extraordinary, freakish, funny, offbeat, outlandish, outré, quaint, queer, singular, strange, uncommon, unconventional, unusual, weird
2 SPECIFIC, characteristic, distinctive, particular, special, unique

peculiarity *noun* 1 ECCENTRICITY, abnormality, foible, idiosyncrasy, mannerism, oddity, quirk
2 CHARACTERISTIC, attribute, feature, mark, particularity, property, quality, trait

pedagogue *noun* TEACHER, instructor, master *or* mistress, schoolmaster *or* schoolmistress

pedant *noun* HAIRSPLITTER, nit-picker (*informal*), quibbler

pedantic *adjective* HAIRSPLITTING, academic, bookish, donnish, formal, fussy, nit-picking (*informal*), particular, precise, punctilious

pedantry *noun* HAIRSPLITTING, punctiliousness, quibbling

peddle *verb* SELL, flog (*slang*), hawk, market, push (*informal*), trade

peddler *noun* SELLER, door-to-door salesman, hawker, huckster, vendor

pedestal *noun* SUPPORT, base, foot, mounting, plinth, stand

pedestrian *noun* 1 WALKER, foot-traveler
▶ *adjective* 2 DULL, banal, boring, commonplace, humdrum, mediocre, mundane, ordinary, prosaic, run-of-the-mill, uninspired

pedigree *noun* 1 LINEAGE, ancestry, blood, breed, descent, extraction, family, family tree, genealogy, line, race, stock
▶ *adjective* 2 PUREBRED, full-blooded, thoroughbred

peek *verb* 1 GLANCE, look, peep
▶ *noun* 2 GLANCE, glimpse, look, look-see (*slang*), peep

peel *verb* 1 SKIN, flake off, pare, scale, strip off
▶ *noun* 2 SKIN, peeling, rind

peep¹ *verb* 1 PEEK, look, sneak a look, steal a look
▶ *noun* 2 LOOK, glimpse, look-see (*slang*), peek

peep² *verb or noun* TWEET, cheep, chirp, squeak

peephole *noun* SPYHOLE, aperture, chink, crack, hole, opening

peer¹ *noun* 1 NOBLE, aristocrat, lord, nobleman
2 EQUAL, compeer, fellow, like

peer² *verb* SQUINT, gaze, inspect, peep, scan, snoop, spy

peerage *noun* ARISTOCRACY, lords and ladies, nobility, peers

peerless *adjective* UNEQUALED, beyond compare, excellent, incomparable, matchless, outstanding, unmatched, unparalleled, unrivaled

peevish *adjective* IRRITABLE, cantankerous, childish, churlish, cross, crotchety, fractious, fretful, grumpy, petulant, querulous, snappy, sulky, sullen, surly

peg *verb* FASTEN, attach, fix, join, secure

pejorative *adjective* DEROGATORY, deprecatory, depreciatory, disparaging, negative, uncomplimentary, unpleasant

pelt¹ *verb* 1 THROW, batter, bombard, cast, hurl, pepper, shower, sling, strike
2 RUSH, belt (*slang*), charge, dash,

hurry, run fast, shoot, speed, tear
3 POUR, bucket down (*informal*),
rain cats and dogs (*informal*), rain
hard, teem

pelt² *noun* COAT, fell, hide, skin

pen¹ *verb* WRITE, compose, draft,
draw up, jot down

pen² *noun* 1 ENCLOSURE, cage, coop,
fold, hutch, pound, sty
► *verb* 2 ENCLOSE, cage, confine,
coop up, fence in, hedge, shut
up *or* in

penal *adjective* DISCIPLINARY,
corrective, punitive

penalize *verb* PUNISH, discipline,
handicap, impose a penalty on

penalty *noun* PUNISHMENT, fine,
forfeit, handicap, price

penance *noun* ATONEMENT,
penalty, reparation, sackcloth
and ashes

penchant *noun* LIKING, bent, bias,
fondness, inclination, leaning,
partiality, predilection, proclivity,
propensity, taste, tendency

pending *adjective* UNDECIDED,
awaiting, imminent, impending,
in the balance, undetermined,
unsettled

penetrate *verb* 1 PIERCE, bore,
enter, go through, prick, stab
2 GRASP, comprehend, decipher,
fathom, figure out (*informal*), get
to the bottom of, suss (out) (*slang*),
work out

penetrating *adjective* 1 SHARP,
carrying, harsh, piercing, shrill
2 PERCEPTIVE, acute, astute,
incisive, intelligent, keen,
perspicacious, quick, sharp,
sharp-witted, shrewd

penetration *noun* 1 PIERCING,
entrance, entry, incision,
puncturing
2 PERCEPTION, acuteness,
astuteness, insight, keenness,

sharpness, shrewdness

penitence *noun* REPENTANCE,
compunction, contrition, regret,
remorse, shame, sorrow

penitent *adjective* REPENTANT,
abject, apologetic, conscience-
stricken, contrite, regretful,
remorseful, sorry

pen name *noun* PSEUDONYM, nom
de plume

pennant *noun* FLAG, banner,
ensign, pennon, streamer

penniless *adjective* POOR, broke
(*informal*), destitute, dirt-poor
(*informal*), down and out, down
on one's luck (*informal*), flat
broke (*informal*), impecunious,
impoverished, indigent,
penurious, poverty-stricken, skint
(*Brit. slang*), stony-broke (*Brit. slang*)

pension *noun* ALLOWANCE,
annuity, benefit, superannuation

pensive *adjective* THOUGHTFUL,
contemplative, dreamy,
meditative, musing, preoccupied,
reflective, sad, serious, solemn,
wistful

pent-up *adjective* SUPPRESSED,
bottled up, curbed, held back,
inhibited, repressed, smothered,
stifled

penury *noun* POVERTY, beggary,
destitution, indigence, need,
privation, want

people *plural noun* 1 PERSONS,
humanity, mankind, men and
women, mortals
2 NATION, citizens, community,
folk, inhabitants, population,
public
3 FAMILY, clan, race, tribe
► *verb* 4 INHABIT, colonize, occupy,
populate, settle

pepper *noun* 1 SEASONING, flavor,
spice
► *verb* 2 SPRINKLE, dot, fleck,

spatter, speck
3 PELT, bombard, shower

perceive verb 1 SEE, behold, discern, discover, espy, make out, note, notice, observe, recognize, spot
2 UNDERSTAND, comprehend, gather, grasp, learn, realize, see, suss (out) (*slang*)

perceptible adjective VISIBLE, apparent, appreciable, clear, detectable, discernible, evident, noticeable, observable, obvious, recognizable, tangible

perception noun UNDERSTANDING, awareness, conception, consciousness, feeling, grasp, idea, impression, notion, sensation, sense

perceptive adjective OBSERVANT, acute, alert, astute, aware, percipient, perspicacious, quick, sharp

perch noun 1 RESTING PLACE, branch, pole, post
▶ verb 2 SIT, alight, balance, land, rest, roost, settle

percussion noun IMPACT, blow, bump, clash, collision, crash, knock, smash, thump

peremptory adjective
1 IMPERATIVE, absolute, binding, compelling, decisive, final, obligatory
2 IMPERIOUS, authoritative, bossy (*informal*), dictatorial, dogmatic, domineering, overbearing

perennial adjective LASTING, abiding, constant, continual, enduring, incessant, persistent, recurrent, twenty-four-seven (*slang*)

perfect adjective 1 COMPLETE, absolute, consummate, entire, finished, full, sheer, unmitigated, utter, whole

2 FAULTLESS, flawless, immaculate, impeccable, pure, spotless, unblemished
3 EXCELLENT, ideal, splendid, sublime, superb, superlative, supreme
4 EXACT, accurate, correct, faithful, precise, true, unerring
▶ verb 5 IMPROVE, develop, polish, refine
6 ACCOMPLISH, achieve, carry out, complete, finish, fulfill, perform

perfection noun 1 COMPLETENESS, maturity
2 PURITY, integrity, perfectness, wholeness
3 EXCELLENCE, exquisiteness, sublimity, superiority
4 EXACTNESS, faultlessness, precision

perfectionist noun STICKLER, precisionist, purist

perfectly adverb 1 COMPLETELY, absolutely, altogether, fully, quite, thoroughly, totally, utterly, wholly
2 FLAWLESSLY, faultlessly, ideally, impeccably, superbly, supremely, wonderfully

perfidious adjective (*literary*) TREACHEROUS, disloyal, double-dealing, traitorous, two-faced, unfaithful

perforate verb PIERCE, bore, drill, penetrate, punch, puncture

perform verb 1 CARRY OUT, accomplish, achieve, complete, discharge, do, execute, fulfill, pull off, work
2 PRESENT, act, enact, play, produce, put on, represent, stage

performance noun 1 CARRYING OUT, accomplishment, achievement, act, completion, execution, fulfillment, work
2 PRESENTATION, acting, appearance, exhibition, gig

(*informal*), play, portrayal, production, show

performer *noun* ARTISTE, actor *or* actress, player, Thespian, trouper

perfume *noun* FRAGRANCE, aroma, bouquet, odor, scent, smell

perfunctory *adjective* OFFHAND, cursory, heedless, indifferent, mechanical, routine, sketchy, superficial

perhaps *adverb* MAYBE, conceivably, feasibly, it may be, perchance (*archaic*), possibly

peril *noun* DANGER, hazard, jeopardy, menace, risk, uncertainty

perilous *adjective* DANGEROUS, hazardous, precarious, risky, threatening, unsafe

perimeter *noun* BOUNDARY, ambit, border, bounds, circumference, confines, edge, limit, margin, periphery

period *noun* TIME, interval, season, space, span, spell, stretch, term, while

periodic *adjective* RECURRENT, cyclical, intermittent, occasional, regular, repeated, sporadic

periodical *noun* PUBLICATION, journal, magazine, monthly, paper, quarterly, weekly

peripheral *adjective* 1 INCIDENTAL, inessential, irrelevant, marginal, minor, secondary, unimportant 2 OUTERMOST, exterior, external, outer, outside

perish *verb* 1 DIE, be killed, expire, lose one's life, pass away 2 BE DESTROYED, collapse, decline, disappear, fall, vanish 3 ROT, decay, decompose, disintegrate, molder, waste

perishable *adjective* SHORT-LIVED, decaying, decomposable

perjure *verb* ▷▷ **perjure oneself** (*criminal law*) COMMIT PERJURY, bear false witness, forswear, give false testimony, lie under oath, swear falsely

perjury *noun* LYING UNDER OATH, bearing false witness, false statement, forswearing, giving false testimony

perk *noun* (*informal*) BONUS, benefit, extra, fringe benefit, perquisite, plus

permanence *noun* CONTINUITY, constancy, continuance, durability, endurance, finality, indestructibility, perpetuity, stability

permanent *adjective* LASTING, abiding, constant, enduring, eternal, everlasting, immutable, perpetual, persistent, stable, steadfast, twenty-four-seven (*slang*), unchanging

permeate *verb* PERVADE, charge, fill, imbue, impregnate, infiltrate, penetrate, saturate, spread through

permissible *adjective* PERMITTED, acceptable, allowable, all right, authorized, lawful, legal, legitimate, O.K. *or* okay (*informal*)

permission *noun* AUTHORIZATION, allowance, approval, assent, consent, dispensation, go-ahead (*informal*), green light, leave, liberty, license, sanction

permissive *adjective* TOLERANT, easy-going, forbearing, free, indulgent, lax, lenient, liberal

permit *verb* 1 ALLOW, authorize, consent, enable, entitle, give leave *or* permission, give the green light to, grant, let, license, sanction ▶ *noun* 2 LICENSE, authorization, pass, passport, permission, warrant

permutation *noun*

TRANSFORMATION, alteration, change, transposition

pernicious *adjective* WICKED, bad, damaging, dangerous, deadly, destructive, detrimental, evil, fatal, harmful, hurtful, malign, poisonous

perpendicular *adjective* UPRIGHT, at right angles to, on end, plumb, straight, vertical

perpetrate *verb* COMMIT, carry out, do, enact, execute, perform, wreak

perpetual *adjective* 1 EVERLASTING, endless, eternal, infinite, lasting, never-ending, perennial, permanent, unchanging, unending
2 CONTINUAL, constant, continuous, endless, incessant, interminable, never-ending, persistent, recurrent, repeated, twenty-four-seven (*slang*)

perpetuate *verb* MAINTAIN, immortalize, keep going, preserve

perplex *verb* PUZZLE, baffle, bewilder, confound, confuse, mystify, stump

✗**perplexing** *adjective* PUZZLING, baffling, bewildering, complex, complicated, confusing, difficult, enigmatic, hard, inexplicable, mystifying

✎**perplexity** *noun* 1 PUZZLEMENT, bafflement, bewilderment, confusion, incomprehension, mystification
2 PUZZLE, difficulty, fix (*informal*), mystery, paradox

perquisite *noun* (*formal*) BONUS, benefit, dividend, extra, perk (*informal*), plus

persecute *verb* 1 VICTIMIZE, afflict, ill-treat, maltreat, oppress, torment, torture
2 HARASS, annoy, badger, bother,

hassle (*informal*), pester, tease

perseverance *noun* PERSISTENCE, determination, diligence, doggedness, endurance, pertinacity, resolution, tenacity

persevere *verb* KEEP GOING, carry on, continue, go on, hang on, persist, remain, stick at *or* to

persist *verb* 1 CONTINUE, carry on, keep up, last, linger, remain
2 PERSEVERE, continue, insist, stand firm

persistence *noun* DETERMINATION, doggedness, endurance, grit, perseverance, pertinacity, resolution, tenacity, tirelessness

persistent *adjective* 1 CONTINUOUS, constant, continual, endless, incessant, never-ending, perpetual, repeated, twenty-four-seven (*slang*)
2 DETERMINED, dogged, obdurate, obstinate, persevering, pertinacious, steadfast, steady, stubborn, tenacious, tireless, unflagging

person *noun* 1 INDIVIDUAL, being, body, human, soul
2 ▷▷ **in person** PERSONALLY, bodily, in the flesh, oneself

personable *adjective* PLEASANT, agreeable, amiable, attractive, charming, good-looking, handsome, likable *or* likeable, nice

personage *noun* PERSONALITY, big shot (*informal*), celebrity, dignitary, luminary, megastar (*informal*), notable, public figure, somebody, V.I.P.

personal *adjective* 1 PRIVATE, exclusive, individual, intimate, own, particular, peculiar, special
2 OFFENSIVE, derogatory, disparaging, insulting, nasty

personality *noun* 1 NATURE,

character, disposition, identity, individuality, make-up, temperament

2 CELEBRITY, famous name, household name, megastar (*informal*), notable, personage, star

personally *adverb* 1 BY ONESELF, alone, independently, on one's own, solely

2 IN ONE'S OPINION, for one's part, from one's own viewpoint, in one's books, in one's own view

3 INDIVIDUALLY, individualistically, privately, specially, subjectively

personification *noun* EMBODIMENT, epitome, image, incarnation, portrayal, representation

personify *verb* EMBODY, epitomize, exemplify, represent, symbolize, typify

personnel *noun* EMPLOYEES, helpers, human resources, people, staff, workers, workforce

perspective *noun* 1 OUTLOOK, angle, attitude, context, frame of reference

2 OBJECTIVITY, proportion, relation, relative importance, relativity

perspicacious *adjective* PERCEPTIVE, acute, alert, astute, discerning, keen, percipient, sharp, shrewd

perspiration *noun* SWEAT, moisture, wetness

perspire *verb* SWEAT, exude, glow, pour with sweat, secrete, swelter

persuade *verb* 1 TALK INTO, bring round (*informal*), coax, entice, impel, incite, induce, influence, sway, urge, win over

2 CONVINCE, cause to believe, satisfy

persuasion *noun* 1 URGING,

cajolery, enticement, inducement, wheedling

2 PERSUASIVENESS, cogency, force, potency, power, pull (*informal*)

3 CREED, belief, conviction, credo, faith, opinion, tenet, views

4 FACTION, camp, denomination, party, school, school of thought, side

persuasive *adjective* CONVINCING, cogent, compelling, credible, effective, eloquent, forceful, influential, plausible, sound, telling, valid, weighty

pert *adjective* IMPUDENT, bold, cheeky, forward, impertinent, insolent, sassy (*informal*), saucy

pertain *verb* RELATE, apply, befit, belong, be relevant, concern, refer, regard

pertinent *adjective* RELEVANT, applicable, apposite, appropriate, apt, fit, fitting, germane, material, proper, to the point

pertness *noun* IMPUDENCE, audacity, cheek (*informal*), cheekiness, effrontery, forwardness, front, impertinence, insolence, sauciness

perturb *verb* DISTURB, agitate, bother, disconcert, faze, fluster, ruffle, trouble, unsettle, vex, worry

perturbed *adjective* DISTURBED, agitated, anxious, disconcerted, flustered, shaken, troubled, uncomfortable, uneasy, worried

peruse *verb* READ, browse, check, examine, inspect, scan, scrutinize, study

pervade *verb* SPREAD THROUGH, charge, fill, imbue, infuse, penetrate, permeate, suffuse

pervasive *adjective* WIDESPREAD, common, extensive, general, omnipresent, prevalent, rife, ubiquitous, universal

perverse *adjective* 1 ABNORMAL, contrary, deviant, disobedient, improper, rebellious, refractory, troublesome, unhealthy
2 WILLFUL, contrary, dogged, headstrong, intractable, intransigent, obdurate, wrong-headed
3 STUBBORN, contrary, cussed (*informal*), mulish, obstinate, pig-headed, stiff-necked, wayward
4 ILL-NATURED, churlish, cross, fractious, ill-tempered, peevish, stroppy (*Brit. slang*), surly

perversion *noun* 1 DEVIATION, aberration, abnormality, debauchery, depravity, immorality, kink (*informal*), kinkiness (*slang*), unnaturalness, vice
2 DISTORTION, corruption, falsification, misinterpretation, misrepresentation, twisting

perversity *noun* CONTRARINESS, contradictoriness, intransigence, obduracy, refractoriness, waywardness, wrong-headedness

pervert *verb* 1 DISTORT, abuse, falsify, garble, misrepresent, misuse, twist, warp
2 CORRUPT, debase, debauch, degrade, deprave, lead astray
▶ *noun* 3 DEVIANT, degenerate, sicko (*informal*), weirdo *or* weirdie (*informal*)

perverted *adjective* UNNATURAL, abnormal, corrupt, debased, debauched, depraved, deviant, kinky (*slang*), pervy (*slang*), sick, twisted, unhealthy, warped

pessimism *noun* GLOOMINESS, dejection, depression, despair, despondency, distrust, gloom, hopelessness, melancholy

pessimist *noun* WET BLANKET (*informal*), cynic, defeatist, killjoy, prophet of doom, worrier

pessimistic *adjective* GLOOMY, bleak, cynical, dark, dejected, depressed, despairing, despondent, glum, hopeless, morose

pest *noun* 1 NUISANCE, annoyance, bane, bother, drag (*informal*), irritation, pain (*informal*), thorn in one's flesh, trial, vexation
2 INFECTION, blight, bug, epidemic, pestilence, plague, scourge

pester *verb* ANNOY, badger, bedevil, be on one's back (*slang*), bother, bug (*informal*), harass, harry, hassle (*informal*), nag, plague, torment

pestilence *noun* PLAGUE, epidemic, visitation

pestilent *adjective* 1 ANNOYING, bothersome, irksome, irritating, tiresome, vexing
2 HARMFUL, detrimental, evil, injurious, pernicious
3 CONTAMINATED, catching, contagious, diseased, disease-ridden, infected, infectious

pestilential *adjective* DEADLY, dangerous, destructive, detrimental, harmful, hazardous, injurious, pernicious

pet¹ *noun* 1 FAVORITE, darling, idol, jewel, treasure
▶ *adjective* 2 FAVORITE, cherished, dearest, dear to one's heart
▶ *verb* 3 PAMPER, baby, coddle, cosset, mollycoddle, spoil
4 FONDLE, caress, pat, stroke
5 CUDDLE, canoodle (*slang*), kiss, make out (*informal*), neck (*informal*), smooch (*informal*), snog (*Brit. slang*)

peter out *verb* DIE OUT, dwindle, ebb, fade, fail, run out, stop, taper off, wane

petite *adjective* SMALL, dainty, delicate, elfin, little, slight

petition *noun* 1 APPEAL, entreaty, plea, prayer, request, solicitation, suit, supplication
▶ *verb* 2 APPEAL, adjure, ask, beg, beseech, entreat, plead, pray, solicit, supplicate

petrify *verb* 1 TERRIFY, horrify, immobilize, paralyze, stun, stupefy, transfix
2 FOSSILIZE, calcify, harden, turn to stone

petty *adjective* 1 TRIVIAL, contemptible, inconsiderable, insignificant, little, lousy (*slang*), measly (*informal*), negligible, paltry, slight, small, trifling, unimportant
2 SMALL-MINDED, mean, mean-minded, shabby, spiteful, ungenerous

petulance *noun* SULKINESS, bad temper, ill humor, irritability, peevishness, pique, sullenness

petulant *adjective* SULKY, bad-tempered, huffy, ill-humored, moody, peevish, sullen

phantom *noun* 1 SPECTER, apparition, ghost, phantasm, shade (*literary*), spirit, spook (*informal*), wraith
2 ILLUSION, figment of the imagination, hallucination, vision

phase *noun* STAGE, chapter, development, juncture, period, point, position, step, time

phase out *verb* WIND DOWN, close, ease off, eliminate, pull out, remove, run down, terminate, wind up, withdraw

phenomenal *adjective* EXTRAORDINARY, exceptional, fantastic, marvelous, miraculous, outstanding, prodigious, remarkable, unusual

phenomenon *noun*
1 OCCURRENCE, circumstance, episode, event, fact, happening, incident
2 WONDER, exception, marvel, miracle, prodigy, rarity, sensation

philanderer *noun* WOMANIZER (*informal*), Casanova, Don Juan, flirt, gigolo, ladies' man, lady-killer (*informal*), Lothario, playboy, stud (*slang*), wolf (*informal*)

philanthropic *adjective* HUMANITARIAN, beneficent, benevolent, charitable, humane, kind, kind-hearted, munificent, public-spirited

philanthropist *noun* HUMANITARIAN, benefactor, contributor, donor, giver, patron

philanthropy *noun* HUMANITARIANISM, almsgiving, beneficence, benevolence, brotherly love, charitableness, charity, generosity, kind-heartedness

philistine *noun* 1 BOOR, barbarian, ignoramus, lout, lowbrow, vulgarian, yahoo
▶ *adjective* 2 UNCULTURED, boorish, ignorant, lowbrow, tasteless, uncultivated, uneducated, unrefined

philosopher *noun* THINKER, logician, metaphysician, sage, theorist, wise man

philosophical, philosophic *adjective* 1 WISE, abstract, logical, rational, sagacious, theoretical, thoughtful
2 STOICAL, calm, collected, composed, cool, serene, tranquil, unruffled

philosophy *noun* 1 THOUGHT, knowledge, logic, metaphysics, rationalism, reasoning, thinking,

wisdom
2 OUTLOOK, beliefs, convictions, doctrine, ideology, principles, tenets, thinking, values, viewpoint, world view
3 STOICISM, calmness, composure, equanimity, self-possession, serenity

phlegmatic *adjective* UNEMOTIONAL, apathetic, impassive, indifferent, placid, stoical, stolid, undemonstrative, unfeeling

phobia *noun* TERROR, aversion, detestation, dread, fear, hatred, horror, loathing, repulsion, revulsion, thing (*informal*)

phone *noun* **1** TELEPHONE, blower (*informal*), cell, cell phone, horn (*informal*)
2 CALL, ring (*informal, chiefly Brit.*), tinkle (*Brit. informal*)
▶ *verb* **3** CALL, get on the blower (*informal*), get on the horn (*informal*), give someone a call, give someone a ring (*informal, chiefly Brit.*), give someone a tinkle (*Brit. informal*), make a call, ring (up) (*informal, chiefly Brit.*), telephone

phony (*informal*) *adjective* **1** FAKE, bogus, counterfeit, ersatz, false, imitation, pseudo (*informal*), sham
▶ *noun* **2** FAKE, counterfeit, forgery, fraud, impostor, pseud (*informal*), sham

photograph *noun* **1** PICTURE, photo (*informal*), print, shot, snap (*informal*), snapshot, transparency
▶ *verb* **2** TAKE A PICTURE OF, film, record, shoot, snap (*informal*), take (someone's) picture

photographic *adjective* **1** LIFELIKE, graphic, natural, pictorial, realistic, visual, vivid
2 (*of a person's memory*) ACCURATE, exact, faithful, precise, retentive

phrase *noun* **1** EXPRESSION, group of words, idiom, remark, saying
▶ *verb* **2** EXPRESS, put, put into words, say, voice, word

phraseology *noun* WORDING, choice of words, expression, idiom, language, parlance, phrase, phrasing, speech, style, syntax

physical *adjective* **1** BODILY, corporal, corporeal, earthly, fleshly, incarnate, mortal
2 MATERIAL, natural, palpable, real, solid, substantial, tangible

physician *noun* DOCTOR, doc (*informal*), doctor of medicine, general practitioner, G.P., M.D., medic (*informal*), medical practitioner

physique *noun* BUILD, body, constitution, figure, form, frame, shape, structure

pick *verb* **1** SELECT, choose, decide upon, elect, fix upon, hand-pick, opt for, settle upon, single out
2 GATHER, collect, harvest, pluck, pull
3 NIBBLE, have no appetite, peck at, play *or* toy with, push the food round the plate
4 PROVOKE, incite, instigate, start
5 OPEN, break into, break open, crack, force
▶ *noun* **6** CHOICE, decision, option, preference, selection
7 THE BEST, crème de la crème, elect, elite, the cream

picket *noun* **1** PROTESTER, demonstrator, picketer
2 LOOKOUT, guard, patrol, sentinel, sentry, watch
3 STAKE, pale, paling, post, stanchion, upright
▶ *verb* **4** BLOCKADE, boycott, demonstrate

pickle *noun* **1** (*informal*)

PREDICAMENT, bind (*informal*), difficulty, dilemma, fix (*informal*), hot water (*informal*), jam (*informal*), quandary, scrape (*informal*), tight spot

▶ *verb* 2 PRESERVE, marinade, steep

pick-me-up *noun* (*informal*) TONIC, bracer (*informal*), refreshment, restorative, shot in the arm (*informal*), stimulant

pick on *verb* TORMENT, badger, bait, bully, goad, hector, tease

pick out *verb* IDENTIFY, discriminate, distinguish, make out, perceive, recognize, tell apart

pick up *verb* 1 LIFT, gather, grasp, raise, take up, uplift

2 OBTAIN, buy, come across, find, purchase

3 RECOVER, be on the mend, get better, improve, mend, rally, take a turn for the better, turn the corner

4 LEARN, acquire, get the hang of (*informal*), master

5 COLLECT, call for, get

pick-up *noun* IMPROVEMENT, change for the better, rally, recovery, revival, rise, strengthening, upswing, upturn

picnic *noun* EXCURSION, outdoor meal, outing

pictorial *adjective* GRAPHIC, illustrated, picturesque, representational, scenic

picture *noun* 1 REPRESENTATION, drawing, engraving, illustration, image, likeness, painting, photograph, portrait, print, sketch

2 DESCRIPTION, account, depiction, image, impression, report

3 DOUBLE, carbon copy, copy, dead ringer (*slang*), duplicate, image, likeness, lookalike, replica, spitting image (*informal*), twin

4 PERSONIFICATION, embodiment, epitome, essence

5 FILM, flick (*slang*), motion picture, movie (*U.S. informal*)

▶ *verb* 6 IMAGINE, conceive of, envision, see, visualize

7 REPRESENT, depict, draw, illustrate, paint, photograph, show, sketch

picturesque *adjective* 1 PRETTY, attractive, beautiful, charming, quaint, scenic, striking

2 VIVID, colorful, graphic

piebald *adjective* PIED, black and white, brindled, dappled, flecked, mottled, speckled, spotted

piece *noun* 1 BIT, chunk, fragment, morsel, part, portion, quantity, segment, slice

2 WORK, article, composition, creation, item, study, work of art

piecemeal *adverb* BIT BY BIT, by degrees, gradually, little by little

pier *noun* 1 JETTY, landing place, promenade, quay, wharf

2 PILLAR, buttress, column, pile, post, support, upright

pierce *verb* PENETRATE, bore, drill, enter, perforate, prick, puncture, spike, stab, stick into

piercing *adjective* 1 (*usually of sound*) PENETRATING, ear-splitting, high-pitched, loud, sharp, shrill

2 KEEN, alert, penetrating, perceptive, perspicacious, quick-witted, sharp, shrewd

3 (*usually of weather*) COLD, arctic, biting, bitter, freezing, nippy, wintry

4 SHARP, acute, agonizing, excruciating, intense, painful, severe, stabbing

piety *noun* HOLINESS, faith, godliness, piousness, religion, reverence

pig noun 1 HOG, boar, porker, sow, swine

2 (informal) SLOB (slang), boor, brute, glutton, hog (informal), swine

pigeonhole noun 1 COMPARTMENT, cubbyhole, locker, niche, place, section

▶ verb 2 CLASSIFY, categorize, characterize, compartmentalize, ghettoize, label, slot (informal)

3 PUT OFF, defer, postpone, shelve

pig-headed adjective STUBBORN, contrary, inflexible, mulish, obstinate, self-willed, stiff-necked, unyielding

pigment noun COLOR, coloring, dye, paint, stain, tincture, tint

pile¹ noun 1 HEAP, accumulation, collection, hoard, mass, mound, mountain, stack

2 (often plural) (informal) A LOT, great deal, ocean, quantity, stacks

3 BUILDING, edifice, erection, structure

▶ verb 4 COLLECT, accumulate, amass, assemble, gather, heap, hoard, stack

5 CROWD, crush, flock, flood, jam, pack, rush, stream

pile² noun FOUNDATION, beam, column, pillar, post, support, upright

pile³ noun NAP, down, fiber, fur, hair, plush

pile-up noun (informal) COLLISION, accident, crash, multiple collision, smash, smash-up (informal)

pilfer verb STEAL, appropriate, embezzle, filch, knock off (slang), lift (informal), nick (slang, chiefly Brit.), pinch (informal), purloin, snaffle (Brit. informal), swipe (slang), take

pilgrim noun TRAVELER, wanderer, wayfarer

pilgrimage noun JOURNEY, excursion, expedition, mission, tour, trip

pill noun 1 TABLET, capsule, pellet

2 ▷▷ **the pill** ORAL CONTRACEPTIVE

pillage verb 1 PLUNDER, despoil, loot, maraud, raid, ransack, ravage, sack

▶ noun 2 PLUNDER, marauding, robbery, sack, spoliation

pillar noun 1 SUPPORT, column, pier, post, prop, shaft, stanchion, upright

2 SUPPORTER, follower, leader, leading light (informal), mainstay, upholder

pillory verb RIDICULE, brand, denounce, stigmatize

pilot noun 1 AIRMAN, aviator, flyer

2 HELMSMAN, navigator, steersman

▶ adjective 3 TRIAL, experimental, model, test

▶ verb 4 FLY, conduct, direct, drive, guide, handle, navigate, operate, steer

pimple noun SPOT, boil, plook (Scot.), pustule, zit (slang)

pin verb 1 FASTEN, affix, attach, fix, join, secure

2 HOLD FAST, fix, hold down, immobilize, pinion

pinch verb 1 SQUEEZE, compress, grasp, nip, press

2 HURT, cramp, crush, pain

3 (informal) STEAL, filch, knock off (slang), lift (informal), nick (slang, chiefly Brit.), pilfer, purloin, snaffle (Brit. informal), swipe (slang)

▶ noun 4 SQUEEZE, nip

5 DASH, bit, jot, mite, soupçon, speck

6 HARDSHIP, crisis, difficulty, emergency, necessity, plight, predicament, strait

pinched adjective THIN, drawn,

gaunt, haggard, peaky, worn

pin down verb 1 FORCE, compel, constrain, make, press, pressurize 2 DETERMINE, identify, locate, name, pinpoint, specify

pine verb 1 (often with for) LONG, ache, crave, desire, eat one's heart out over, hanker, hunger for, thirst for, wish for, yearn for 2 WASTE, decline, fade, languish, sicken

pinion verb IMMOBILIZE, bind, chain, fasten, fetter, manacle, shackle, tie

pink adjective ROSY, flushed, reddish, rose, roseate, salmon

pinnacle noun PEAK, apex, crest, crown, height, summit, top, vertex, zenith

pinpoint verb IDENTIFY, define, distinguish, locate

pioneer noun 1 SETTLER, colonist, explorer 2 FOUNDER, developer, innovator, leader, trailblazer ▶ verb 3 DEVELOP, create, discover, establish, initiate, instigate, institute, invent, originate, show the way, start

pious adjective RELIGIOUS, devout, God-fearing, godly, holy, reverent, righteous, saintly

pipe noun 1 TUBE, conduit, duct, hose, line, main, passage, pipeline ▶ verb 2 WHISTLE, cheep, peep, play, sing, sound, warble 3 CONVEY, channel, conduct

pipe down verb (informal) BE QUIET, hold one's tongue, hush, quieten down, shush, shut one's mouth, shut up (informal)

pipeline noun TUBE, conduit, duct, passage, pipe

piquant adjective 1 SPICY, biting, pungent, savory, sharp, tangy, tart, zesty
2 INTERESTING, lively, provocative, scintillating, sparkling, stimulating

pique noun 1 RESENTMENT, annoyance, displeasure, huff, hurt feelings, irritation, offense, umbrage, wounded pride ▶ verb 2 DISPLEASE, affront, annoy, get (informal), irk, irritate, nettle, offend, rile, sting 3 AROUSE, excite, rouse, spur, stimulate, stir, whet

piracy noun ROBBERY, buccaneering, freebooting, stealing, theft

pirate noun 1 BUCCANEER, corsair, freebooter, marauder, raider 2 PLAGIARIST, cribber (informal), infringer, plagiarizer ▶ verb 3 COPY, appropriate, crib (informal), plagiarize, poach, reproduce, steal

pit noun 1 HOLE, abyss, cavity, chasm, crater, dent, depression, hollow ▶ verb 2 SCAR, dent, indent, mark, pockmark

pitch verb 1 THROW, cast, chuck (informal), fling, heave, hurl, lob (informal), sling, toss 2 SET UP, erect, put up, raise, settle 3 FALL, dive, drop, topple, tumble 4 TOSS, lurch, plunge, roll ▶ noun 5 SPORTS FIELD, field of play, ground, park 6 LEVEL, degree, height, highest point, point, summit 7 SLOPE, angle, dip, gradient, incline, tilt 8 TONE, modulation, sound, timbre 9 SALES TALK, patter, spiel (informal)

pitch-black adjective JET-BLACK, dark, inky, pitch-dark, unlit

pitch in verb HELP, chip in (informal), contribute, cooperate, do one's bit, join in, lend a hand, participate

piteous *adjective* PATHETIC, affecting, distressing, harrowing, heartbreaking, heart-rending, moving, pitiable, pitiful, plaintive, poignant, sad

pitfall *noun* DANGER, catch, difficulty, drawback, hazard, peril, snag, trap

pith *noun* ESSENCE, core, crux, gist, heart, kernel, nub, point, quintessence, salient point

pithy *adjective* SUCCINCT, brief, cogent, concise, epigrammatic, laconic, pointed, short, terse, to the point, trenchant

pitiful *adjective* 1 PATHETIC, distressing, grievous, harrowing, heartbreaking, heart-rending, piteous, pitiable, sad, wretched
2 CONTEMPTIBLE, abject, base, lousy (*slang*), low, mean, miserable, paltry, shabby, sorry

pitiless *adjective* MERCILESS, callous, cold-blooded, cold-hearted, cruel, hardhearted, heartless, implacable, relentless, ruthless, unmerciful

pittance *noun* PEANUTS (*slang*), chicken feed (*slang*), drop, mite, slave wages, trifle

pity *noun* 1 COMPASSION, charity, clemency, fellow feeling, forbearance, kindness, mercy, sympathy
2 SHAME, bummer (*slang*), crying shame, misfortune, sin
▶ *verb* 3 FEEL SORRY FOR, bleed for, feel for, grieve for, have compassion for, sympathize with, weep for

pivot *noun* 1 AXIS, axle, fulcrum, spindle, swivel
2 HUB, center, heart, hinge, kingpin

▶ *verb* 3 TURN, revolve, rotate, spin, swivel, twirl
4 RELY, be contingent, depend, hang, hinge

pivotal *adjective* CRUCIAL, central, critical, decisive, vital

pixie *noun* ELF, brownie, fairy, sprite

placard *noun* NOTICE, advertisement, bill, poster

placate *verb* CALM, appease, assuage, conciliate, de-stress, humor, mollify, pacify, propitiate, soothe

place *noun* 1 SPOT, area, location, point, position, site, venue, whereabouts
2 REGION, district, locale, locality, neighborhood, quarter, vicinity
3 POSITION, grade, rank, station, status
4 SPACE, accommodation, room
5 HOME, abode, domicile, dwelling, house, pad (*slang, dated*), property, residence
6 DUTY, affair, charge, concern, function, prerogative, responsibility, right, role
7 JOB, appointment, employment, position, post
8 ▷▷ **take place** HAPPEN, come about, go on, occur, transpire (*informal*)
▶ *verb* 9 PUT, deposit, install, lay, locate, position, rest, set, situate, stand, station, stick (*informal*)
10 CLASSIFY, arrange, class, grade, group, order, rank, sort
11 IDENTIFY, know, put one's finger on, recognize, remember
12 ASSIGN, allocate, appoint, charge, entrust, give

placid *adjective* CALM, collected, composed, equable, even-tempered, imperturbable, serene, tranquil, unexcitable, unruffled, untroubled

plagiarism noun COPYING, borrowing, cribbing (informal), infringement, piracy, theft

plagiarize verb COPY, borrow, crib (informal), lift (informal), pirate, steal

plague noun 1 DISEASE, epidemic, infection, pestilence
2 AFFLICTION, bane, blight, curse, evil, scourge, torment
▶ verb 3 PESTER, annoy, badger, bother, harass, harry, hassle (informal), tease, torment, torture, trouble, vex

plain adjective 1 CLEAR, comprehensible, distinct, evident, manifest, obvious, overt, patent, unambiguous, understandable, unmistakable, visible
2 HONEST, blunt, candid, direct, downright, forthright, frank, open, outspoken, straightforward, upfront (informal)
3 UNADORNED, austere, bare, basic, severe, simple, Spartan, stark, unembellished, unfussy, unornamented
4 UGLY, dumpy (informal), frowzy, homely (U.S.), ill-favored, no oil painting (informal), not beautiful, unattractive, unlovely, unprepossessing
5 ORDINARY, common, commonplace, everyday, simple, unaffected, unpretentious
▶ noun 6 FLATLAND, grassland, plateau, prairie, steppe, veld

plain-spoken adjective BLUNT, candid, direct, downright, forthright, frank, outspoken

plaintive adjective SORROWFUL, heart-rending, mournful, pathetic, piteous, pitiful, sad

plan noun 1 SCHEME, design, method, plot, program, proposal, strategy, suggestion, system
2 DIAGRAM, blueprint, chart, drawing, layout, map, representation, road map, sketch
▶ verb 3 DEVISE, arrange, contrive, design, draft, formulate, organize, outline, plot, scheme, think out
4 INTEND, aim, mean, propose, purpose

plane noun 1 AIRPLANE, aircraft, jet
2 FLAT SURFACE, level surface
3 LEVEL, condition, degree, position
▶ adjective 4 LEVEL, even, flat, horizontal, regular, smooth
▶ verb 5 SKIM, glide, sail, skate

plant noun 1 VEGETABLE, bush, flower, herb, shrub, weed
2 FACTORY, foundry, mill, shop, works, yard
3 MACHINERY, apparatus, equipment, gear
▶ verb 4 SOW, put in the ground, scatter, seed, transplant
5 PLACE, establish, fix, found, insert, put, set

plaster noun 1 MORTAR, gypsum, plaster of Paris, stucco
2 BANDAGE, adhesive plaster, dressing, Elastoplast (Trademark), sticking plaster
▶ verb 3 COVER, coat, daub, overlay, smear, spread

plastic adjective 1 MANAGEABLE, docile, malleable, pliable, receptive, responsive, tractable
2 PLIANT, ductile, flexible, moldable, pliable, soft, supple

plate noun 1 PLATTER, dish, trencher (archaic)
2 HELPING, course, dish, portion, serving
3 LAYER, panel, sheet, slab
4 ILLUSTRATION, lithograph, print
▶ verb 5 COAT, cover, gild, laminate, overlay

plateau noun 1 UPLAND, highland, table, tableland
2 LEVELLING OFF, level, stability, stage

platform noun 1 STAGE, dais, podium, rostrum, stand
2 POLICY, manifesto, objective(s), party line, principle, program

platitude noun CLICHÉ, banality, commonplace, truism

platoon noun SQUAD, company, group, outfit (informal), patrol, squadron, team

platter noun PLATE, dish, salver, tray, trencher (archaic)

plaudits plural noun APPROVAL, acclaim, acclamation, applause, approbation, praise

plausible adjective 1 REASONABLE, believable, conceivable, credible, likely, persuasive, possible, probable, tenable
2 GLIB, smooth, smooth-talking, smooth-tongued, specious

play verb 1 AMUSE ONESELF, entertain oneself, fool, have fun, revel, romp, sport, trifle
2 COMPETE, challenge, contend against, participate, take on, take part
3 ACT, act the part of, perform, portray, represent
▶ noun 4 DRAMA, comedy, dramatic piece, farce, pantomime, piece, show, stage show, tragedy
5 AMUSEMENT, diversion, entertainment, fun, game, pastime, recreation, sport
6 FUN, humor, jest, joking, lark (informal), prank, sport
7 SPACE, elbowroom, latitude, leeway, margin, room, scope

playboy noun WOMANIZER, ladies' man, lady-killer (informal), philanderer, rake, roué

play down verb MINIMIZE, gloss over, make light of, make little of, soft-pedal (informal), underplay, underrate

player noun 1 SPORTSMAN or SPORTSWOMAN, competitor, contestant, participant
2 MUSICIAN, artist, instrumentalist, performer, virtuoso
3 PERFORMER, actor or actress, entertainer, Thespian, trouper

playful adjective LIVELY, frisky, impish, merry, mischievous, spirited, sportive, sprightly, vivacious

playmate noun FRIEND, chum (informal), companion, comrade, pal (informal), playfellow

play on or **upon** verb TAKE ADVANTAGE OF, abuse, capitalize on, exploit, impose on, trade on

plaything noun TOY, amusement, game, pastime, trifle

play up verb 1 EMPHASIZE, accentuate, highlight, stress, underline
2 (Brit. informal) BE AWKWARD, be disobedient, be stroppy (Brit. slang), give trouble, misbehave
3 (Brit. informal) HURT, be painful, be sore, bother, pain, trouble
4 (Brit. informal) MALFUNCTION, be on the blink (slang), not work properly

plea noun 1 APPEAL, entreaty, intercession, petition, prayer, request, suit, supplication
2 EXCUSE, defense, explanation, justification

plead verb APPEAL, ask, beg, beseech, entreat, implore, petition, request

pleasant adjective 1 PLEASING, agreeable, amusing, delightful, enjoyable, fine, lovely, nice, pleasurable

2 NICE, affable, agreeable, amiable, charming, congenial, engaging, friendly, genial, likable or likeable

pleasantry noun JOKE, badinage, banter, jest, quip, witticism

please verb DELIGHT, amuse, entertain, gladden, gratify, humor, indulge, satisfy, suit

pleased adjective HAPPY, chuffed (Brit. slang), contented, delighted, euphoric, glad, gratified, over the moon (informal), satisfied, thrilled

pleasing adjective ENJOYABLE, agreeable, charming, delightful, engaging, gratifying, likable or likeable, pleasurable, satisfying

pleasurable adjective ENJOYABLE, agreeable, delightful, fun, good, lovely, nice, pleasant

pleasure noun HAPPINESS, amusement, bliss, delectation, delight, enjoyment, gladness, gratification, joy, satisfaction

plebeian adjective **1** COMMON, base, coarse, low, lower-class, proletarian, uncultivated, unrefined, vulgar, working-class
▶ noun **2** COMMONER, common man, man in the street, pleb, prole (derogatory slang, chiefly Brit.), proletarian

pledge noun **1** PROMISE, assurance, covenant, oath, undertaking, vow, warrant, word
2 GUARANTEE, bail, collateral, deposit, pawn, security, surety
▶ verb **3** PROMISE, contract, engage, give one's oath, give one's word, swear, vow

plentiful adjective ABUNDANT, ample, bountiful, copious, generous, lavish, liberal, overflowing, plenteous, profuse

plenty noun **1** LOTS (informal), abundance, enough, great deal,

heap(s) (informal), masses, pile(s) (informal), plethora, quantity, stack(s)
2 ABUNDANCE, affluence, copiousness, fertility, fruitfulness, plenitude, profusion, prosperity, wealth

plethora noun EXCESS, glut, overabundance, profusion, superabundance, surfeit, surplus

pliable adjective **1** FLEXIBLE, bendable, bendy, malleable, plastic, pliant, supple
2 IMPRESSIONABLE, adaptable, compliant, docile, easily led, pliant, receptive, responsive, susceptible, tractable

pliant adjective **1** FLEXIBLE, bendable, bendy, plastic, pliable, supple
2 IMPRESSIONABLE, biddable, compliant, easily led, pliable, susceptible, tractable

plight[1] noun DIFFICULTY, condition, jam (informal), predicament, scrape (informal), situation, spot (informal), state, trouble

plod verb **1** TRUDGE, clump, drag, lumber, tramp, tread
2 SLOG, grind (informal), labor, persevere, plow through, plug away (informal), soldier on, toil

plot[1] noun **1** PLAN, cabal, conspiracy, intrigue, machination, scheme, stratagem
2 STORY, action, narrative, outline, scenario, story line, subject, theme
▶ verb **3** PLAN, collude, conspire, contrive, intrigue, machinate, maneuver, scheme
4 DEVISE, conceive, concoct, contrive, cook up (informal), design, hatch, lay
5 CHART, calculate, locate, map,

mark, outline

plot² noun PATCH, allotment, area, ground, lot, parcel, tract

plow verb 1 TURN OVER, cultivate, dig, till
2 (usually with *through*) FORGE, cut, drive, plunge, press, push, wade

ploy noun TACTIC, device, dodge, maneuver, move, ruse, scheme, stratagem, trick, wile

pluck verb 1 PULL OUT or OFF, collect, draw, gather, harvest, pick
2 TUG, catch, clutch, jerk, pull at, snatch, tweak, yank
3 STRUM, finger, pick, twang
▶ noun 4 COURAGE, backbone, boldness, bottle (*Brit. slang*), bravery, grit, guts (*informal*), nerve

plucky adjective COURAGEOUS, bold, brave, daring, game, gutsy (*slang*), have-a-go (*informal*), intrepid

plug noun 1 STOPPER, bung, cork, spigot
2 (*informal*) MENTION, advert (*Brit. informal*), advertisement, hype, publicity, push
▶ verb 3 SEAL, block, bung, close, cork, fill, pack, stop, stopper, stop up, stuff
4 (*informal*) MENTION, advertise, build up, hype, promote, publicize, push
5 ▷▷ **plug away** (*informal*) SLOG, grind (*informal*), labor, peg away, plod, toil

plum adjective CHOICE, best, first-class, prize

plumb verb 1 DELVE, explore, fathom, gauge, go into, penetrate, probe, unravel
▶ noun 2 WEIGHT, lead, plumb bob, plummet
▶ adverb 3 EXACTLY, bang, precisely, slap, spot-on (*Brit. informal*)

plume noun FEATHER, crest, pinion, quill

plummet verb PLUNGE, crash, descend, dive, drop down, fall, nose-dive, tumble

plump¹ adjective CHUBBY, corpulent, dumpy, fat, podgy, roly-poly, rotund, round, stout, tubby

plunder verb 1 LOOT, pillage, raid, ransack, rifle, rob, sack, strip
▶ noun 2 LOOT, booty, ill-gotten gains, pillage, prize, spoils, swag (*slang*)

plunge verb 1 THROW, cast, pitch
2 HURTLE, career, charge, dash, jump, rush, tear
3 DESCEND, dip, dive, drop, fall, nose-dive, plummet, sink, tumble
▶ noun 4 DIVE, descent, drop, fall, jump

plus preposition 1 AND, added to, coupled with, with
▶ adjective 2 ADDITIONAL, added, add-on, extra, supplementary
▶ noun 3 ADVANTAGE, asset, benefit, bonus, extra, gain, good point

plush adjective LUXURIOUS, deluxe, lavish, luxury, opulent, rich, sumptuous

ply verb 1 WORK AT, carry on, exercise, follow, practice, pursue
2 USE, employ, handle, manipulate, wield

poach verb ENCROACH, appropriate, infringe, intrude, trespass

pocket noun 1 POUCH, bag, compartment, receptacle, sack
▶ verb 2 STEAL, appropriate, filch, lift (*informal*), pilfer, purloin, take
▶ adjective 3 SMALL, abridged, compact, concise, little, miniature, portable

pod noun or verb SHELL, hull, husk, shuck

podium noun PLATFORM, dais, rostrum, stage

poem *noun* VERSE, lyric, ode, rhyme, song, sonnet

poet *noun* BARD, lyricist, rhymer, versifier

poetic *adjective* LYRICAL, elegiac, lyric, metrical

poetry *noun* VERSE, poems, rhyme, rhyming

poignancy *noun* 1 SADNESS, emotion, feeling, pathos, sentiment, tenderness
2 SHARPNESS, bitterness, intensity, keenness

poignant *adjective* MOVING, bitter, distressing, heart-rending, intense, painful, pathetic, sad, touching

point *noun* 1 ESSENCE, crux, drift, gist, heart, import, meaning, nub, pith, question, subject, thrust
2 AIM, end, goal, intent, intention, motive, object, objective, purpose, reason
3 ITEM, aspect, detail, feature, particular
4 CHARACTERISTIC, aspect, attribute, quality, respect, trait
5 PLACE, location, position, site, spot, stage
6 FULL STOP, dot, mark, period, stop
7 END, apex, prong, sharp end, spike, spur, summit, tip, top
8 HEADLAND, cape, head, promontory
9 STAGE, circumstance, condition, degree, extent, position
10 MOMENT, instant, juncture, time, very minute
11 UNIT, score, tally
▶ *verb* 12 INDICATE, call attention to, denote, designate, direct, show, signify
13 AIM, direct, level, train

point-blank *adjective* 1 DIRECT, blunt, downright, explicit, express, plain
▶ *adverb* 2 DIRECTLY, bluntly, candidly, explicitly, forthrightly, frankly, openly, plainly, straight

pointed *adjective* 1 SHARP, acute, barbed, edged
2 CUTTING, acute, biting, incisive, keen, penetrating, pertinent, sharp, telling

pointer *noun* 1 HINT, advice, caution, information, recommendation, suggestion, tip
2 INDICATOR, guide, hand, needle

pointless *adjective* SENSELESS, absurd, aimless, fruitless, futile, inane, irrelevant, meaningless, silly, stupid, useless

point out *verb* MENTION, allude to, bring up, identify, indicate, show, specify

poise *noun* COMPOSURE, aplomb, assurance, calmness, cool (*slang*), dignity, presence, sang-froid, self-possession

poised *adjective* 1 READY, all set, prepared, standing by, waiting
2 COMPOSED, calm, collected, dignified, self-confident, self-possessed, together (*informal*)

poison *noun* 1 TOXIN, bane, venom
▶ *verb* 2 MURDER, give (someone) poison, kill
3 CONTAMINATE, infect, pollute
4 CORRUPT, defile, deprave, pervert, subvert, taint, undermine, warp

poisonous *adjective* 1 TOXIC, deadly, fatal, lethal, mortal, noxious, venomous, virulent
2 EVIL, baleful, corrupting, malicious, noxious, pernicious

poke *verb* 1 JAB, dig, nudge, prod, push, shove, stab, stick, thrust
▶ *noun* 2 JAB, dig, nudge, prod, thrust

poky *adjective* SMALL, confined,

cramped, narrow, tiny

pole¹ *noun* ROD, bar, mast, post, shaft, spar, staff, stick

police *noun* 1 THE LAW (*informal*), boys in blue (*informal*), constabulary, fuzz (*slang*), police force, the Old Bill (*slang*)
▶ *verb* 2 CONTROL, guard, patrol, protect, regulate, watch

policeman *noun* COP (*slang*), bobby (*informal*), constable, copper (*slang*), fuzz (*slang*), officer

policy *noun* PROCEDURE, action, approach, code, course, custom, plan, practice, rule, scheme

polish *verb* 1 SHINE, brighten, buff, burnish, rub, smooth, wax
2 PERFECT, brush up, enhance, finish, improve, refine, touch up
▶ *noun* 3 VARNISH, wax
4 SHEEN, brightness, finish, glaze, gloss, luster
5 STYLE, breeding, class (*informal*), elegance, finesse, finish, grace, refinement

polished *adjective* 1 ACCOMPLISHED, adept, expert, fine, masterly, professional, skillful, superlative
2 SHINING, bright, burnished, gleaming, glossy, smooth
3 ELEGANT, cultivated, polite, refined, sophisticated, well-bred

polite *adjective* 1 MANNERLY, civil, complaisant, courteous, gracious, respectful, well-behaved, well-mannered
2 REFINED, civilized, cultured, elegant, genteel, polished, sophisticated, well-bred

politeness *noun* COURTESY, civility, courteousness, decency, etiquette, mannerliness

politic *adjective* WISE, advisable, diplomatic, expedient, judicious, prudent, sensible

political *adjective* GOVERNMENTAL, parliamentary, policy-making

politician *noun* STATESMAN, bureaucrat, congressman, legislator, Member of Parliament, M.P., office bearer, public servant, representative

politics *noun* STATESMANSHIP, affairs of state, civics, government, political science

poll *noun* 1 CANVASS, ballot, census, count, sampling, survey
2 VOTE, figures, returns, tally, voting
▶ *verb* 3 TALLY, register
4 QUESTION, ballot, canvass, interview, sample, survey

pollute *verb* 1 CONTAMINATE, dirty, foul, infect, poison, soil, spoil, stain, taint
2 DEFILE, corrupt, debase, debauch, deprave, desecrate, dishonor, profane, sully

pollution *noun* CONTAMINATION, corruption, defilement, dirtying, foulness, impurity, taint, uncleanness

pomp *noun* 1 CEREMONY, flourish, grandeur, magnificence, pageant, pageantry, splendor, state
2 SHOW, display, grandiosity, ostentation

pomposity *noun* SELF-IMPORTANCE, affectation, airs, grandiosity, pompousness, portentousness, pretension, pretentiousness

pompous *adjective* 1 SELF-IMPORTANT, arrogant, grandiose, ostentatious, pretentious, puffed up, showy
2 GRANDILOQUENT, boastful, bombastic, high-flown, inflated

pond *noun* POOL, duck pond, fish pond, millpond, small lake, tarn

ponder *verb* THINK, brood, cogitate, consider, contemplate, deliberate, meditate, mull over, muse, reflect, ruminate

ponderous adjective 1 DULL, heavy, long-winded, pedantic, tedious 2 UNWIELDY, bulky, cumbersome, heavy, huge, massive, weighty 3 CLUMSY, awkward, heavy-footed, lumbering

pontificate verb EXPOUND, hold forth, lay down the law, preach, pronounce, sound off

pool[1] noun 1 POND, lake, mere, puddle, tarn 2 SWIMMING POOL, swimming bath

pool[2] noun 1 SYNDICATE, collective, consortium, group, team, trust 2 KITTY, bank, funds, jackpot, pot ▶ verb 3 COMBINE, amalgamate, join forces, league, merge, put together, share

poor adjective 1 IMPOVERISHED, broke (informal), destitute, down and out, down on one's luck (informal), hard up (informal), impecunious, indigent, needy, on the breadline, penniless, penurious, poverty-stricken, short, skint (Brit. slang), stony-broke (Brit. slang) 2 INADEQUATE, deficient, incomplete, insufficient, lacking, lousy (slang), meager, measly, scant, scanty, skimpy 3 INFERIOR, below par, lousy (slang), low-grade, mediocre, no great shakes (informal), not much cop (Brit. slang), rotten (informal), rubbishy, second-rate, substandard, unsatisfactory 4 UNFORTUNATE, hapless, ill-fated, luckless, pitiable, unhappy, unlucky, wretched

poorly adverb 1 BADLY, inadequately, incompetently, inexpertly, insufficiently, unsatisfactorily, unsuccessfully ▶ adjective 2 (informal) ILL, below par, off color, rotten (informal), seedy (informal), sick, under the weather (informal), unwell

pop verb 1 BURST, bang, crack, explode, go off, snap 2 PUT, insert, push, shove, slip, stick, thrust, tuck ▶ noun 3 BANG, burst, crack, explosion, noise, report

pope noun HOLY FATHER, Bishop of Rome, pontiff, Vicar of Christ

populace noun PEOPLE, general public, hoi polloi, masses, mob, multitude

popular adjective 1 WELL-LIKED, accepted, approved, cool (informal), fashionable, favorite, in (informal), in demand, in favor, liked, phat (slang), sought-after 2 COMMON, conventional, current, general, prevailing, prevalent, universal

popularity noun FAVOR, acceptance, acclaim, approval, currency, esteem, regard, vogue

popularize verb MAKE POPULAR, disseminate, give currency to, give mass appeal, make available to all, spread, universalize

popularly adverb GENERALLY, commonly, conventionally, customarily, ordinarily, traditionally, universally, usually, widely

populate verb INHABIT, colonize, live in, occupy, settle

population noun INHABITANTS, community, denizens, folk, natives, people, residents, society

populous adjective POPULATED, crowded, heavily populated, overpopulated, packed, swarming, teeming

pore[1] verb ▷▷ **pore over** STUDY,

examine, peruse, ponder, read, scrutinize

pore² *noun* OPENING, hole, orifice, outlet

pornographic *adjective* OBSCENE, blue, dirty, filthy, indecent, lewd, salacious, scuzzy (*slang*), smutty, X-rated

pornography *noun* OBSCENITY, dirt, filth, indecency, porn (*informal*), smut

porous *adjective* PERMEABLE, absorbent, absorptive, penetrable, spongy

port *noun* HARBOR, anchorage, haven, seaport

portable *adjective* LIGHT, compact, convenient, easily carried, handy, manageable, movable

portend *verb* FORETELL, augur, betoken, bode, foreshadow, herald, indicate, predict, prognosticate, promise, warn of

portent *noun* OMEN, augury, forewarning, indication, prognostication, sign, warning

portentous *adjective*
1 SIGNIFICANT, crucial, fateful, important, menacing, momentous, ominous
2 POMPOUS, ponderous, self-important, solemn

porter¹ *noun* BAGGAGE ATTENDANT, bearer, carrier

porter² *noun* DOORMAN, caretaker, concierge, gatekeeper, janitor

portion *noun* 1 PART, bit, fragment, morsel, piece, scrap, section, segment
2 SHARE, allocation, allotment, allowance, lot, measure, quantity, quota, ration
3 HELPING, piece, serving
4 DESTINY, fate, fortune, lot, luck
▶ *verb* 5 ▷▷ **portion out** DIVIDE, allocate, allot, apportion, deal,

distribute, dole out, share out

portly *adjective* STOUT, burly, corpulent, fat, fleshy, heavy, large, plump

portrait *noun* 1 PICTURE, image, likeness, painting, photograph, representation
2 DESCRIPTION, characterization, depiction, portrayal, profile, thumbnail sketch

portray *verb* 1 REPRESENT, depict, draw, figure, illustrate, paint, picture, sketch
2 DESCRIBE, characterize, depict, put in words
3 PLAY, act the part of, represent

portrayal *noun* REPRESENTATION, characterization, depiction, interpretation, performance, picture

pose *verb* 1 POSITION, model, sit
2 PUT ON AIRS, posture, show off (*informal*)
3 ▷▷ **pose as** IMPERSONATE, masquerade as, pass oneself off as, pretend to be, profess to be
▶ *noun* 4 POSTURE, attitude, bearing, position, stance
5 ACT, affectation, air, façade, front, mannerism, posturing, pretense

poser *noun* PUZZLE, enigma, problem, question, riddle

posit *verb* PUT FORWARD, advance, assume, postulate, presume, propound, state

position *noun* 1 PLACE, area, bearings, locale, location, point, post, situation, spot, station, whereabouts
2 POSTURE, arrangement, attitude, pose, stance
3 ATTITUDE, belief, opinion, outlook, point of view, slant, stance, view, viewpoint
4 STATUS, importance, place,

prestige, rank, reputation, standing, station, stature
5 JOB, duty, employment, occupation, office, place, post, role, situation
▶ *verb* **6** PLACE, arrange, lay out, locate, put, set, stand
positive *adjective* **1** CERTAIN, assured, confident, convinced, sure
2 DEFINITE, absolute, categorical, certain, clear, conclusive, decisive, explicit, express, firm, real
3 HELPFUL, beneficial, constructive, practical, productive, progressive, useful
4 (*informal*) ABSOLUTE, complete, consummate, downright, out-and-out, perfect, thorough, utter
positively *adverb* DEFINITELY, absolutely, assuredly, categorically, certainly, emphatically, firmly, surely, unequivocally, unquestionably
possess *verb* **1** HAVE, enjoy, hold, own
2 CONTROL, acquire, dominate, hold, occupy, seize, take over
possessed *adjective* CRAZED, berserk, demented, frenzied, obsessed, raving
possession *noun* **1** OWNERSHIP, control, custody, hold, occupation, tenure, title
2 ▷▷ **possessions** PROPERTY, assets, belongings, chattels, effects, estate, things
possessive *adjective* JEALOUS, controlling, covetous, dominating, domineering, overprotective, selfish
possibility *noun* **1** FEASIBILITY, likelihood, potentiality, practicability, workableness
2 LIKELIHOOD, chance, hope, liability, odds, probability,

prospect, risk
3 (*often plural*) POTENTIAL, capabilities, potentiality, promise, prospects, talent
possible *adjective* **1** CONCEIVABLE, credible, hypothetical, imaginable, likely, potential
2 LIKELY, hopeful, potential, probable, promising
3 FEASIBLE, attainable, doable, practicable, realizable, viable, workable
possibly *adverb* PERHAPS, maybe, perchance (*archaic*)
post[1] *noun* **1** MAIL, collection, delivery, postal service
▶ *verb* **2** SEND, dispatch, mail, transmit
3 ▷▷ **keep someone posted** NOTIFY, advise, brief, fill in on (*informal*), inform, report to
post[2] *noun* **1** SUPPORT, column, picket, pillar, pole, shaft, stake, upright
▶ *verb* **2** PUT UP, affix, display, pin up
post[3] *noun* **1** JOB, appointment, assignment, employment, office, place, position, situation
2 STATION, beat, place, position
▶ *verb* **3** STATION, assign, place, position, put, situate
poster *noun* NOTICE, advertisement, announcement, bill, placard, public notice, sticker
posterity *noun* **1** FUTURE, succeeding generations
2 DESCENDANTS, children, family, heirs, issue, offspring, progeny
postpone *verb* PUT OFF, adjourn, defer, delay, put back, put on the back burner (*informal*), shelve, suspend
postponement *noun* DELAY, adjournment, deferment, deferral, stay, suspension

postscript noun P.S., addition, afterthought, supplement

postulate verb PRESUPPOSE, assume, hypothesize, posit, propose, suppose, take for granted, theorize

posture noun 1 BEARING, attitude, carriage, disposition, set, stance
▶ verb 2 SHOW OFF (informal), affect, pose, put on airs

pot noun CONTAINER, bowl, pan, vessel

potency noun POWER, effectiveness, force, influence, might, strength

potent adjective 1 POWERFUL, authoritative, commanding, dominant, dynamic, influential
2 STRONG, forceful, mighty, powerful, vigorous

potential adjective 1 POSSIBLE, dormant, future, hidden, inherent, latent, likely, promising
▶ noun 2 ABILITY, aptitude, capability, capacity, possibility, potentiality, power, wherewithal

potion noun CONCOCTION, brew, dose, draft, elixir, mixture, philtre

pottery noun CERAMICS, earthenware, stoneware, terracotta

pouch noun BAG, container, pocket, purse, sack

pounce verb 1 SPRING, attack, fall upon, jump, leap at, strike, swoop
▶ noun 2 SPRING, assault, attack, bound, jump, leap, swoop

pound[1] verb 1 BEAT, batter, belabor, clobber (slang), hammer, pummel, strike, thrash, thump
2 CRUSH, powder, pulverize
3 PULSATE, beat, palpitate, pulse, throb
4 STOMP (informal), march, thunder, tramp

pound[2] noun ENCLOSURE, compound, pen, yard

pour verb 1 FLOW, course, emit, gush, run, rush, spew, spout, stream
2 LET FLOW, decant, spill, splash
3 RAIN, bucket down (informal), pelt (down), teem
4 STREAM, crowd, swarm, teem, throng

pout verb 1 SULK, glower, look petulant, pull a long face
▶ noun 2 SULLEN LOOK, glower, long face

poverty noun 1 PENNILESSNESS, beggary, destitution, hardship, indigence, insolvency, need, penury, privation, want
2 SCARCITY, dearth, deficiency, insufficiency, lack, paucity, shortage

poverty-stricken adjective PENNILESS, broke (informal), destitute, down and out, down on one's luck (informal), flat broke (informal), impecunious, impoverished, indigent, poor

powder noun 1 DUST, fine grains, loose particles, talc
▶ verb 2 DUST, cover, dredge, scatter, sprinkle, strew

powdery adjective FINE, crumbly, dry, dusty, grainy, granular

power noun 1 ABILITY, capability, capacity, competence, competency, faculty, potential
2 CONTROL, ascendancy, authority, command, dominance, domination, dominion, influence, mastery, rule
3 AUTHORITY, authorization, license, prerogative, privilege, right, warrant
4 STRENGTH, brawn, energy, force, forcefulness, intensity, might, muscle, potency, vigor

powerful adjective 1 CONTROLLING,

authoritative, commanding,
dominant, influential, prevailing
2 STRONG, energetic, mighty,
potent, strapping, sturdy,
vigorous
3 PERSUASIVE, cogent, compelling,
convincing, effectual, forceful,
impressive, striking, telling,
weighty

powerless adjective 1 DEFENSELESS,
dependent, ineffective, subject,
tied, unarmed, vulnerable
2 HELPLESS, challenged,
debilitated, disabled, feeble,
frail, impotent, incapable,
incapacitated, ineffectual, weak

practicability noun FEASIBILITY,
advantage, possibility,
practicality, use, usefulness,
viability

practicable adjective FEASIBLE,
achievable, attainable, doable,
possible, viable

practical adjective 1 FUNCTIONAL,
applied, empirical, experimental,
factual, pragmatic, realistic,
utilitarian
2 SENSIBLE, businesslike, down-
to-earth, hard-headed, matter-of-
fact, ordinary, realistic
3 FEASIBLE, doable, practicable,
serviceable, useful, workable
4 SKILLED, accomplished,
efficient, experienced, proficient

practically adverb 1 ALMOST,
all but, basically, essentially,
fundamentally, in effect, just
about, nearly, very nearly,
virtually, well-nigh
2 SENSIBLY, clearly, matter-of-
factly, rationally, realistically,
reasonably

practice noun 1 CUSTOM, habit,
method, mode, routine, rule,
system, tradition, usage, way,
wont

2 REHEARSAL, drill, exercise,
preparation, repetition, study,
training
3 PROFESSION, business, career,
vocation, work
4 USE, action, application,
exercise, experience, operation
▶ verb 5 REHEARSE, drill, exercise,
go over, go through, prepare,
repeat, study, train
6 DO, apply, carry out, follow,
observe, perform
7 WORK AT, carry on, engage in,
pursue

practiced adjective SKILLED, able,
accomplished, experienced,
expert, proficient, seasoned,
trained, versed

pragmatic adjective PRACTICAL,
businesslike, down-to-earth,
hard-headed, realistic, sensible,
utilitarian

praise verb 1 APPROVE, acclaim,
admire, applaud, cheer,
compliment, congratulate,
eulogize, extol, honor, laud
2 GIVE THANKS TO, adore, bless,
exalt, glorify, worship
▶ noun 3 APPROVAL, acclaim,
acclamation, approbation,
commendation, compliment,
congratulation, eulogy, kudos,
plaudit, tribute
4 THANKS, adoration, glory,
homage, kudos, worship

praiseworthy adjective
CREDITABLE, admirable,
commendable, laudable,
meritorious, worthy

prance verb 1 DANCE, caper, cavort,
frisk, gambol, romp, skip
2 STRUT, parade, show off
(informal), stalk, swagger, swank
(informal)

prank noun TRICK, antic, escapade,
jape, lark (informal), practical joke

pray verb 1 SAY ONE'S PRAYERS, offer a prayer, recite the rosary
2 BEG, adjure, ask, beseech, entreat, implore, petition, plead, request, solicit

prayer noun 1 ORISON, devotion, invocation, litany, supplication
2 PLEA, appeal, entreaty, petition, request, supplication

preach verb 1 DELIVER A SERMON, address, evangelize
2 LECTURE, advocate, exhort, moralize, sermonize

preacher noun CLERGYMAN, evangelist, minister, missionary, parson

preamble noun INTRODUCTION, foreword, opening statement or remarks, preface, prelude

precarious adjective DANGEROUS, dodgy (Brit., Austral., & N.Z. informal), hazardous, insecure, perilous, risky, shaky, tricky, unreliable, unsafe, unsure

precaution noun 1 SAFEGUARD, insurance, protection, provision, safety measure
2 FORETHOUGHT, care, caution, providence, prudence, wariness

precede verb GO BEFORE, antedate, come first, head, introduce, lead, preface

precedence noun PRIORITY, antecedence, pre-eminence, primacy, rank, seniority, superiority, supremacy

precedent noun INSTANCE, antecedent, example, model, paradigm, pattern, prototype, standard

preceding adjective PREVIOUS, above, aforementioned, aforesaid, earlier, foregoing, former, past, prior

precept noun RULE, canon, command, commandment, decree, instruction, law, order, principle, regulation, statute

precinct noun 1 ENCLOSURE, confine, limit
2 AREA, district, quarter, section, sector, zone

precious adjective 1 VALUABLE, costly, dear, expensive, fine, invaluable, priceless, prized
2 LOVED, adored, beloved, cherished, darling, dear, prized, treasured
3 AFFECTED, artificial, overnice, overrefined, twee (Brit. informal)

precipice noun CLIFF, bluff, crag, height, rock face

precipitate verb 1 QUICKEN, accelerate, advance, bring on, expedite, hasten, hurry, speed up, trigger
2 THROW, cast, fling, hurl, launch, let fly
▶ adjective 3 HASTY, heedless, impetuous, impulsive, precipitous, rash, reckless
4 SWIFT, breakneck, headlong, rapid, rushing
5 SUDDEN, abrupt, brief, quick, unexpected, without warning

precipitous adjective 1 SHEER, abrupt, dizzy, high, perpendicular, steep
2 HASTY, heedless, hurried, precipitate, rash, reckless

précis noun 1 SUMMARY, abridgment, outline, résumé, synopsis
▶ verb 2 SUMMARIZE, abridge, outline, shorten, sum up

precise adjective 1 EXACT, absolute, accurate, correct, definite, explicit, express, particular, specific, strict
2 STRICT, careful, exact, fastidious, finicky, formal, meticulous, particular, punctilious, rigid,

scrupulous, stiff

precisely adverb EXACTLY, absolutely, accurately, correctly, just so, plumb (informal), smack (informal), square, squarely, strictly

precision noun EXACTNESS, accuracy, care, meticulousness, particularity, preciseness

preclude verb PREVENT, check, debar, exclude, forestall, inhibit, obviate, prohibit, rule out, stop

precocious adjective ADVANCED, ahead, bright, developed, forward, quick, smart

preconceived adjective PRESUMED, forejudged, prejudged, presupposed

preconception noun PRECONCEIVED IDEA or NOTION, bias, notion, predisposition, prejudice, presupposition

precursor noun 1 HERALD, forerunner, harbinger, vanguard 2 FORERUNNER, antecedent, forebear, predecessor

predatory adjective HUNTING, carnivorous, predacious, raptorial

predecessor noun 1 PREVIOUS JOB HOLDER, antecedent, forerunner, precursor 2 ANCESTOR, antecedent, forebear, forefather

predestination noun FATE, destiny, foreordainment, foreordination, predetermination

predestined adjective FATED, doomed, meant, preordained

predetermined adjective PREARRANGED, agreed, fixed, preplanned, set

predicament noun FIX (informal), dilemma, hole (slang), jam (informal), mess, pinch, plight, quandary, scrape (informal), situation, spot (informal)

predict verb FORETELL, augur, divine, forecast, portend, prophesy

predictable adjective LIKELY, anticipated, certain, expected, foreseeable, reliable, sure

prediction noun PROPHECY, augury, divination, forecast, prognosis, prognostication

predilection noun LIKING, bias, fondness, inclination, leaning, love, partiality, penchant, preference, propensity, taste, weakness

predispose verb INCLINE, affect, bias, dispose, influence, lead, prejudice, prompt

predisposed adjective INCLINED, given, liable, minded, ready, subject, susceptible, willing

predominant adjective MAIN, ascendant, chief, dominant, leading, paramount, prevailing, prevalent, prime, principal

predominantly adverb MAINLY, chiefly, for the most part, generally, largely, mostly, primarily, principally

predominate verb PREVAIL, be most noticeable, carry weight, hold sway, outweigh, overrule, overshadow

pre-eminence noun SUPERIORITY, distinction, excellence, predominance, prestige, prominence, renown, supremacy

pre-eminent adjective OUTSTANDING, chief, distinguished, excellent, foremost, incomparable, matchless, predominant, renowned, superior, supreme

pre-empt verb ANTICIPATE, appropriate, assume, usurp

preen verb 1 (of birds) CLEAN, plume 2 SMARTEN, dress up, spruce up, titivate

3 ▷▷ **preen oneself (on)** PRIDE ONESELF, congratulate oneself

preface noun 1 INTRODUCTION, foreword, preamble, preliminary, prelude, prologue
▶ verb 2 INTRODUCE, begin, open, prefix

prefer verb LIKE BETTER, be partial to, choose, desire, fancy, favor, go for, incline towards, opt for, pick

preferable adjective BETTER, best, chosen, favored, more desirable, superior

preferably adverb RATHER, by choice, first, in or for preference, sooner

preference noun 1 FIRST CHOICE, choice, desire, favorite, option, partiality, pick, predilection, selection
2 PRIORITY, favored treatment, favoritism, first place, precedence

preferential adjective PRIVILEGED, advantageous, better, favored, special

preferment noun PROMOTION, advancement, elevation, exaltation, rise, upgrading

pregnant adjective 1 EXPECTANT, big or heavy with child, expecting (informal), in the club (Brit. slang), with child
2 MEANINGFUL, charged, eloquent, expressive, loaded, pointed, significant, telling, weighty

prehistoric adjective EARLIEST, early, primeval, primitive, primordial

prejudge verb JUMP TO CONCLUSIONS, anticipate, presume, presuppose

prejudice noun 1 BIAS, partiality, preconceived notion, preconception, prejudgment
2 DISCRIMINATION, bigotry, chauvinism, injustice, intolerance, narrow-mindedness, unfairness
▶ verb 3 BIAS, color, distort, influence, poison, predispose, slant
4 HARM, damage, hinder, hurt, impair, injure, mar, spoil, undermine

prejudiced adjective BIASED, bigoted, influenced, intolerant, narrow-minded, one-sided, opinionated, unfair

prejudicial adjective HARMFUL, damaging, deleterious, detrimental, disadvantageous, hurtful, injurious, unfavorable

preliminary adjective 1 FIRST, initial, introductory, opening, pilot, prefatory, preparatory, prior, test, trial
▶ noun 2 INTRODUCTION, beginning, opening, overture, preamble, preface, prelude, start

prelude noun INTRODUCTION, beginning, foreword, overture, preamble, preface, prologue, start

premature adjective 1 EARLY, forward, unseasonable, untimely
2 HASTY, ill-timed, overhasty, previous (informal), rash, too soon, untimely

premeditated adjective PLANNED, calculated, conscious, considered, deliberate, intentional, willful

premeditation noun PLANNING, design, forethought, intention, plotting, prearrangement, predetermination, purpose

premier noun 1 HEAD OF GOVERNMENT, chancellor, chief minister, chief officer, P.M., prime minister
▶ adjective 2 CHIEF, alpha male, first, foremost, head, highest, leading, main, primary, prime, principal

premiere noun FIRST NIGHT, debut, opening

premise noun ASSUMPTION, argument, assertion, hypothesis, postulation, presupposition, proposition, supposition

premises plural noun BUILDING, establishment, place, property, site

premium noun 1 BONUS, bounty, fee, perk (informal), perquisite, prize, reward
2 ▷▷ **at a premium** IN GREAT DEMAND, hard to come by, in short supply, rare, scarce

premonition noun FEELING, foreboding, hunch, idea, intuition, presentiment, suspicion

preoccupation noun 1 OBSESSION, bee in one's bonnet, fixation
2 ABSORPTION, absent-mindedness, abstraction, daydreaming, engrossment, immersion, reverie, woolgathering

preoccupied adjective ABSORBED, absent-minded, distracted, engrossed, immersed, lost in, oblivious, rapt, wrapped up

preparation noun 1 GROUNDWORK, getting ready, preparing
2 (often plural) ARRANGEMENT, measure, plan, provision
3 MIXTURE, compound, concoction, medicine

preparatory adjective INTRODUCTORY, opening, prefatory, preliminary, primary

prepare verb MAKE or GET READY, adapt, adjust, arrange, practice, prime, train, warm up

prepared adjective 1 READY, arranged, in order, in readiness, primed, set
2 WILLING, disposed, inclined

preponderance noun PREDOMINANCE, dominance, domination, extensiveness, greater numbers, greater part, lion's share, mass, prevalence, supremacy

prepossessing adjective ATTRACTIVE, appealing, charming, engaging, fetching, good-looking, handsome, likable or likeable, pleasing

preposterous adjective RIDICULOUS, absurd, crazy, incredible, insane, laughable, ludicrous, nonsensical, out of the question, outrageous, unthinkable

prerequisite noun
1 REQUIREMENT, condition, essential, must, necessity, precondition, qualification, requisite, sine qua non
▶ adjective 2 REQUIRED, essential, indispensable, mandatory, necessary, obligatory, requisite, vital

prerogative noun RIGHT, advantage, due, exemption, immunity, liberty, privilege

presage verb PORTEND, augur, betoken, bode, foreshadow, foretoken, signify

prescience noun FORESIGHT, clairvoyance, foreknowledge, precognition, second sight

prescribe verb ORDER, decree, dictate, direct, lay down, ordain, recommend, rule, set, specify, stipulate

prescription noun 1 INSTRUCTION, direction, formula, recipe
2 MEDICINE, drug, mixture, preparation, remedy

presence noun 1 BEING, attendance, existence, inhabitance, occupancy, residence

2 PERSONALITY, air, appearance, aspect, aura, bearing, carriage, demeanor, poise, self-assurance

presence of mind noun LEVEL-HEADEDNESS, calmness, composure, cool (*slang*), coolness, self-possession, wits

present[1] *adjective* **1** HERE, at hand, near, nearby, ready, there

2 CURRENT, contemporary, existent, existing, immediate, present-day

▶ *noun* **3** ▷▷ **the present** NOW, here and now, the present moment, the time being, today; **at present** JUST NOW, at the moment, now, right now; **for the present** FOR NOW, for the moment, for the time being, in the meantime, temporarily

present[2] *noun* **1** GIFT, boon, donation, endowment, grant, gratuity, hand-out, offering, prezzie (*informal*)

▶ *verb* **2** INTRODUCE, acquaint with, make known

3 PUT ON, display, exhibit, give, show, stage

4 GIVE, award, bestow, confer, grant, hand out, hand over

presentable *adjective* DECENT, acceptable, becoming, fit to be seen, O.K. or okay (*informal*), passable, respectable, satisfactory, suitable

presentation *noun* **1** GIVING, award, bestowal, conferral, donation, offering

2 PRODUCTION, demonstration, display, exhibition, performance, show

presently *adverb* SOON, anon (*archaic*), before long, by and by, shortly

preservation *noun* PROTECTION, conservation, maintenance, safeguarding, safekeeping, safety, salvation, support

preserve *verb* **1** SAVE, care for, conserve, defend, keep, protect, safeguard, shelter, shield

2 MAINTAIN, continue, keep, keep up, perpetuate, sustain, uphold

▶ *noun* **3** AREA, domain, field, realm, sphere

preside *verb* RUN, administer, chair, conduct, control, direct, govern, head, lead, manage, officiate

press *verb* **1** FORCE DOWN, compress, crush, depress, jam, mash, push, squeeze

2 HUG, clasp, crush, embrace, fold in one's arms, hold close, squeeze

3 SMOOTH, flatten, iron

4 URGE, beg, entreat, exhort, implore, petition, plead, pressurize

5 CROWD, flock, gather, herd, push, seethe, surge, swarm, throng

▶ *noun* **6** ▷▷ **the press:**
a NEWSPAPERS, Fleet Street, fourth estate, news media, the papers
b JOURNALISTS, columnists, correspondents, newsmen, pressmen, reporters

pressing *adjective* URGENT, crucial, high-priority, imperative, important, importunate, serious, vital

pressure *noun* **1** FORCE, compressing, compression, crushing, squeezing, weight

2 POWER, coercion, compulsion, constraint, force, influence, sway

3 STRESS, burden, demands, hassle (*informal*), heat, load, strain, urgency

prestige *noun* STATUS, credit, distinction, eminence, fame, honor, importance, kudos, renown, reputation, standing

prestigious *adjective* CELEBRATED, eminent, esteemed, great, illustrious, important, notable, prominent, renowned, respected

presumably *adverb* IT WOULD SEEM, apparently, in all likelihood, in all probability, on the face of it, probably, seemingly

presume *verb* 1 BELIEVE, assume, conjecture, guess (*informal*), infer, postulate, suppose, surmise, take for granted, think
2 DARE, go so far, make so bold, take the liberty, venture

presumption *noun* 1 CHEEK (*informal*), audacity, boldness, effrontery, gall (*informal*), impudence, insolence, nerve (*informal*)
2 PROBABILITY, basis, chance, likelihood

presumptuous *adjective* PUSHY (*informal*), audacious, bold, forward, insolent, overconfident, too big for one's boots, uppish (*Brit.informal*)

presuppose *verb* PRESUME, assume, imply, posit, postulate, take as read, take for granted

presupposition *noun* ASSUMPTION, belief, preconception, premise, presumption, supposition

pretend *verb* 1 FEIGN, affect, allege, assume, fake, falsify, impersonate, profess, sham, simulate
2 MAKE BELIEVE, act, imagine, make up, suppose

pretended *adjective* FEIGNED, bogus, counterfeit, fake, false, phoney *or* phony (*informal*), pretend (*informal*), pseudo (*informal*), sham, so-called

pretender *noun* CLAIMANT, aspirant

pretense *noun* 1 DECEPTION, acting, charade, deceit, falsehood, feigning, sham, simulation, trickery
2 SHOW, affectation, artifice, display, façade, veneer

pretension *noun* 1 CLAIM, aspiration, assumption, demand, pretense, profession
2 AFFECTATION, airs, conceit, ostentation, pretentiousness, self-importance, show, snobbery, vanity

pretentious *adjective* AFFECTED, conceited, grandiloquent, grandiose, high-flown, inflated, mannered, ostentatious, pompous, puffed up, showy, snobbish

pretext *noun* GUISE, cloak, cover, excuse, ploy, pretense, ruse, show

pretty *adjective* 1 ATTRACTIVE, beautiful, bonny, charming, comely, fair, good-looking, lovely
▶ *adverb* 2 FAIRLY, kind of (*informal*), moderately, quite, rather, reasonably, somewhat

prevail *verb* 1 WIN, be victorious, overcome, overrule, succeed, triumph
2 BE WIDESPREAD, abound, be current, be prevalent, exist generally, predominate

prevailing *adjective* 1 WIDESPREAD, common, cool (*informal*), current, customary, established, fashionable, general, in vogue, ordinary, phat (*slang*), popular, prevalent, usual
2 PREDOMINATING, dominant, main, principal, ruling

prevalence *noun* COMMONNESS, currency, frequency, popularity, universality

prevalent *adjective* COMMON,

current, customary, established, frequent, general, popular, universal, usual, widespread

prevaricate *verb* EVADE, beat about the bush, cavil, deceive, dodge, equivocate, flannel (*Brit. informal*), hedge

prevent *verb* STOP, avert, avoid, foil, forestall, frustrate, hamper, hinder, impede, inhibit, obstruct, obviate, preclude, thwart

prevention *noun* ELIMINATION, avoidance, deterrence, precaution, safeguard, thwarting

preventive, preventative *adjective* 1 HINDERING, hampering, impeding, obstructive
2 PROTECTIVE, counteractive, deterrent, precautionary
▶ *noun* 3 HINDRANCE, block, impediment, obstacle, obstruction
4 PROTECTION, deterrent, prevention, remedy, safeguard, shield

preview *noun* ADVANCE SHOWING, foretaste, sneak preview, taster, trailer

previous *adjective* EARLIER, erstwhile, foregoing, former, past, preceding, prior

previously *adverb* BEFORE, beforehand, earlier, formerly, hitherto, in the past, once

prey *noun* 1 QUARRY, game, kill
2 VICTIM, dupe, fall guy (*informal*), mug (*Brit. slang*), target

price *noun* 1 COST, amount, charge, damage (*informal*), estimate, expense, fee, figure, rate, value, worth
2 CONSEQUENCES, cost, penalty, toll
▶ *verb* 3 EVALUATE, assess, cost, estimate, rate, value

priceless *adjective* 1 VALUABLE,

costly, dear, expensive, invaluable, precious
2 (*informal*) HILARIOUS, amusing, comic, droll, funny, rib-tickling, side-splitting

pricey, pricy *adjective* EXPENSIVE, costly, dear, high-priced, steep (*informal*)

prick *verb* 1 PIERCE, jab, lance, perforate, punch, puncture, stab
2 STING, bite, itch, prickle, smart, tingle
▶ *noun* 3 PUNCTURE, hole, perforation, pinhole, wound

prickle *noun* 1 SPIKE, barb, needle, point, spine, spur, thorn
▶ *verb* 2 TINGLE, itch, smart, sting
3 PRICK, jab, stick

prickly *adjective* 1 SPINY, barbed, bristly, thorny
2 ITCHY, crawling, scratchy, sharp, smarting, stinging, tingling

pride *noun* 1 SATISFACTION, delight, gratification, joy, pleasure
2 SELF-RESPECT, dignity, honor, self-esteem, self-worth
3 CONCEIT, arrogance, egotism, hubris, pretension, pretentiousness, self-importance, self-love, superciliousness, vanity
4 GEM, jewel, pride and joy, treasure

priest *noun* CLERGYMAN, cleric, curate, divine, ecclesiastic, father, minister, pastor, vicar

prig *noun* GOODY-GOODY (*informal*), prude, puritan, stuffed shirt (*informal*)

priggish *adjective* SELF-RIGHTEOUS, goody-goody (*informal*), holier-than-thou, prim, prudish, puritanical

prim *adjective* PRUDISH, demure, fastidious, prissy, priggish, prissy (*informal*), proper, puritanical, strait-laced

prima donna *noun* DIVA, leading lady, star

primarily *adverb* 1 CHIEFLY, above all, essentially, fundamentally, generally, largely, mainly, mostly, principally

2 AT FIRST, at *or* from the start, first and foremost, initially, in the beginning, in the first place, originally

primary *adjective* 1 CHIEF, cardinal, cutting edge, first, greatest, highest, main, paramount, prime, principal

2 ELEMENTARY, introductory, rudimentary, simple

prime *adjective* 1 MAIN, chief, leading, predominant, pre-eminent, primary, principal

2 BEST, choice, excellent, first-class, first-rate, highest, quality, select, top

▸ *noun* 3 PEAK, bloom, flower, height, heyday, zenith

▸ *verb* 4 INFORM, brief, clue in (*informal*), fill in (*informal*), notify, tell

5 PREPARE, coach, get ready, make ready, train

primeval *adjective* EARLIEST, ancient, early, first, old, prehistoric, primal, primitive, primordial

primitive *adjective* 1 EARLY, earliest, elementary, first, original, primary, primeval, primordial

2 CRUDE, rough, rudimentary, simple, unrefined

prince *noun* RULER, lord, monarch, sovereign

princely *adjective* 1 REGAL, imperial, majestic, noble, royal, sovereign

2 GENEROUS, bounteous, gracious, lavish, liberal, munificent, open-handed, rich

principal *adjective* 1 MAIN, cardinal, chief, cutting edge, essential, first, foremost, key, leading, paramount, pre-eminent, primary, prime

▸ *noun* 2 HEAD (*informal*), dean, headmaster *or* headmistress, superintendent, head teacher, master *or* mistress, rector

3 STAR, alpha male, lead, leader

4 CAPITAL, assets, money

principally *adverb* MAINLY, above all, chiefly, especially, largely, mostly, predominantly, primarily

principle *noun* 1 RULE, canon, criterion, doctrine, dogma, fundamental, law, maxim, precept, standard, truth

2 MORALS, conscience, integrity, probity, scruples, sense of honor

3 ▷▷ **in principle** IN THEORY, ideally, theoretically

print *verb* 1 PUBLISH, engrave, impress, imprint, issue, mark, stamp

▸ *noun* 2 PUBLICATION, book, magazine, newspaper, newsprint, periodical, printed matter

3 REPRODUCTION, copy, engraving, photo (*informal*), photograph, picture

prior *adjective* 1 EARLIER, foregoing, former, preceding, pre-existent, pre-existing, previous

2 ▷▷ **prior to** BEFORE, earlier than, preceding, previous to

priority *noun* PRECEDENCE, pre-eminence, preference, rank, right of way, seniority

priory *noun* MONASTERY, abbey, convent, nunnery, religious house

prison *noun* JAIL, clink (*slang*), confinement, cooler (*slang*), dungeon, jug (*slang*), lockup, nick (*Brit. slang*), penitentiary (*U.S.*),

slammer (*slang*)
prisoner *noun* 1 CONVICT, con (*slang*), jailbird, lag (*slang*)
2 CAPTIVE, detainee, hostage, internee
prissy *adjective* PRIM, old-maidish (*informal*), prim and proper, prudish, strait-laced
pristine *adjective* NEW, immaculate, pure, uncorrupted, undefiled, unspoiled, unsullied, untouched, virginal
privacy *noun* SECLUSION, isolation, retirement, retreat, solitude
private *adjective* 1 EXCLUSIVE, individual, intimate, own, personal, reserved, special
2 SECRET, clandestine, confidential, covert, hush-hush (*informal*), off the record, unofficial
3 SECLUDED, concealed, isolated, secret, separate, sequestered, solitary
privilege *noun* RIGHT, advantage, claim, concession, due, entitlement, freedom, liberty, prerogative
privileged *adjective* SPECIAL, advantaged, elite, entitled, favored, honored
privy *adjective* 1 ▷▷ **privy to** INFORMED OF, apprised of, aware of, cognizant of, in on, in the know about (*informal*), wise to (*slang*)
▶ *noun* 2 LAVATORY, latrine, outside toilet
prize¹ *noun* 1 REWARD, accolade, award, honor, trophy
2 WINNINGS, haul, jackpot, purse, stakes
▶ *adjective* 3 CHAMPION, award-winning, best, first-rate, outstanding, top, winning
prize² *verb* VALUE, cherish, esteem, hold dear, treasure

probability *noun* LIKELIHOOD, chance(s), expectation, liability, likeliness, odds, prospect
probable *adjective* LIKELY, apparent, credible, feasible, plausible, possible, presumable, reasonable
probably *adverb* LIKELY, doubtless, maybe, most likely, perchance (*archaic*), perhaps, possibly, presumably
probation *noun* TRIAL PERIOD, apprenticeship, trial
probe *verb* 1 EXAMINE, explore, go into, investigate, look into, scrutinize, search
2 EXPLORE, feel around, poke, prod
▶ *noun* 3 EXAMINATION, detection, exploration, inquiry, investigation, scrutiny, study
problem *noun* 1 DIFFICULTY, complication, dilemma, dispute, predicament, quandary, trouble
2 PUZZLE, conundrum, enigma, poser, question, riddle
problematic *adjective* TRICKY, debatable, doubtful, dubious, problematical, puzzling
procedure *noun* METHOD, action, conduct, course, custom, modus operandi, policy, practice, process, routine, strategy, system
proceed *verb* 1 GO ON, carry on, continue, go ahead, move on, press on, progress
2 ARISE, come, derive, emanate, flow, issue, originate, result, spring, stem
proceeding *noun* 1 ACTION, act, deed, measure, move, procedure, process, step
2 ▷▷ **proceedings** BUSINESS, account, affairs, archives, doings, minutes, records, report, transactions
proceeds *plural noun* INCOME,

earnings, gain, products, profit, returns, revenue, takings, yield

process noun 1 PROCEDURE, action, course, manner, means, measure, method, operation, performance, practice, system
2 DEVELOPMENT, advance, evolution, growth, movement, progress, progression
▶ verb 3 HANDLE, deal with, fulfill

procession noun PARADE, cavalcade, cortege, file, march, train

proclaim verb DECLARE, advertise, announce, circulate, herald, indicate, make known, profess, publish

proclamation noun DECLARATION, announcement, decree, edict, notice, notification, pronouncement, publication

procrastinate verb DELAY, dally, drag one's feet (informal), gain time, play for time, postpone, put off, stall, temporize

procure verb OBTAIN, acquire, buy, come by, find, gain, get, pick up, purchase, score (slang), secure, win

prod verb 1 POKE, dig, drive, jab, nudge, push, shove
2 PROMPT, egg on, goad, impel, incite, motivate, move, rouse, spur, stimulate, urge
▶ noun 3 POKE, dig, jab, nudge, push, shove
4 PROMPT, cue, reminder, signal, stimulus

prodigal adjective EXTRAVAGANT, excessive, immoderate, improvident, profligate, reckless, spendthrift, wasteful

prodigious adjective 1 HUGE, colossal, enormous, giant, gigantic, immense, massive, monstrous, vast
2 WONDERFUL, amazing,

exceptional, extraordinary, fabulous, fantastic (informal), marvelous, phenomenal, remarkable, staggering

prodigy noun 1 GENIUS, mastermind, talent, whizz (informal), wizard
2 WONDER, marvel, miracle, phenomenon, sensation

produce verb 1 CAUSE, bring about, effect, generate, give rise to
2 BRING FORTH, bear, beget, breed, deliver
3 SHOW, advance, demonstrate, exhibit, offer, present
4 MAKE, compose, construct, create, develop, fabricate, invent, manufacture
5 PRESENT, direct, do, exhibit, mount, put on, show, stage
▶ noun 6 FRUIT AND VEGETABLES, crop, greengrocery, harvest, product, yield

producer noun 1 DIRECTOR, impresario
2 MAKER, farmer, grower, manufacturer

product noun 1 GOODS, artefact, commodity, creation, invention, merchandise, produce, work
2 RESULT, consequence, effect, outcome, upshot

production noun 1 PRODUCING, construction, creation, fabrication, formation, making, manufacture, manufacturing
2 PRESENTATION, direction, management, staging

productive adjective 1 FERTILE, creative, fecund, fruitful, inventive, plentiful, prolific, rich
2 USEFUL, advantageous, beneficial, constructive, effective, profitable, rewarding, valuable, win-win (informal), worthwhile

productivity noun OUTPUT,

production, work rate, yield

profane *adjective* 1 SACRILEGIOUS, disrespectful, godless, impious, impure, irreligious, irreverent, sinful, ungodly, wicked
2 CRUDE, blasphemous, coarse, filthy, foul, obscene, vulgar
▶ *verb* 3 DESECRATE, commit sacrilege, debase, defile, violate

profanity *noun* 1 SACRILEGE, blasphemy, impiety, profaneness
2 SWEARING, curse, cursing, irreverence, obscenity

profess *verb* 1 CLAIM, allege, fake, feign, make out, pretend, purport
2 STATE, admit, affirm, announce, assert, avow, confess, declare, proclaim, vouch

professed *adjective* 1 SUPPOSED, alleged, ostensible, pretended, purported, self-styled, so-called, would-be
2 DECLARED, avowed, confessed, confirmed, proclaimed, self-acknowledged, self-confessed

profession *noun* 1 OCCUPATION, business, calling, career, employment, office, position, sphere, vocation
2 DECLARATION, affirmation, assertion, avowal, claim, confession, statement

professional *adjective* 1 EXPERT, adept, competent, efficient, experienced, masterly, proficient, qualified, skilled
▶ *noun* 2 EXPERT, adept, maestro, master, past master, pro (*slang*), specialist, virtuoso

professor *noun* TEACHER, don (*Brit.*), fellow (*Brit.*), prof (*informal*)

proficiency *noun* SKILL, ability, aptitude, competence, dexterity, expertise, knack, know-how (*informal*), mastery

proficient *adjective* SKILLED, able, accomplished, adept, capable, competent, efficient, expert, gifted, masterly, skillful

profile *noun* 1 OUTLINE, contour, drawing, figure, form, side view, silhouette, sketch
2 BIOGRAPHY, characterization, sketch, thumbnail sketch, vignette

profit *noun* 1 (*often plural*) EARNINGS, gain, proceeds, receipts, return, revenue, takings, yield
2 BENEFIT, advancement, advantage, gain, good, use, value
▶ *verb* 3 BENEFIT, be of advantage to, gain, help, improve, promote, serve
4 MAKE MONEY, earn, gain

profitable *adjective* 1 MONEY-MAKING, commercial, cost-effective, fruitful, lucrative, paying, remunerative, worthwhile
2 BENEFICIAL, advantageous, fruitful, productive, rewarding, useful, valuable, win-win (*informal*), worthwhile

profiteer *noun* 1 RACKETEER, exploiter
▶ *verb* 2 RACKETEER, exploit, make a quick buck (*slang*)

profligate *adjective*
1 EXTRAVAGANT, immoderate, improvident, prodigal, reckless, spendthrift, wasteful
2 DEPRAVED, debauched, degenerate, dissolute, immoral, licentious, shameless, wanton, wicked, wild
▶ *noun* 3 SPENDTHRIFT, squanderer, waster, wastrel
4 DEGENERATE, debauchee, libertine, rake, reprobate, roué

profound *adjective* 1 WISE, abstruse, deep, learned,

penetrating, philosophical, sagacious, sage
2 INTENSE, acute, deeply felt, extreme, great, heartfelt, keen
profuse *adjective* PLENTIFUL, abundant, ample, bountiful, copious, luxuriant, overflowing, prolific
profusion *noun* ABUNDANCE, bounty, excess, extravagance, glut, plethora, quantity, surplus, wealth
progeny *noun* CHILDREN, descendants, family, issue, lineage, offspring, posterity, race, stock, young
prognosis *noun* FORECAST, diagnosis, prediction, prognostication, projection
program *noun* 1 SCHEDULE, agenda, curriculum, line-up, list, listing, order of events, plan, syllabus, timetable
2 SHOW, broadcast, performance, presentation, production
progress *noun* 1 DEVELOPMENT, advance, breakthrough, gain, growth, headway, improvement
2 MOVEMENT, advance, course, passage, way
3 ▷▷ **in progress** GOING ON, being done, happening, occurring, proceeding, taking place, under way
▶ *verb* 4 DEVELOP, advance, gain, grow, improve
5 MOVE ON, advance, continue, go forward, make headway, proceed, travel
progression *noun* 1 PROGRESS, advance, advancement, furtherance, gain, headway, movement forward
2 SEQUENCE, chain, course, cycle, series, string, succession
progressive *adjective*

1 ENLIGHTENED, advanced, avant-garde, forward-looking, liberal, modern, radical, reformist, revolutionary
2 GROWING, advancing, continuing, developing, increasing, ongoing
prohibit *verb* 1 FORBID, ban, debar, disallow, outlaw, proscribe, veto
2 PREVENT, hamper, hinder, impede, restrict, stop
prohibition *noun* 1 PREVENTION, constraint, exclusion, obstruction, restriction
2 BAN, bar, boycott, embargo, injunction, interdict, proscription, veto
prohibitive *adjective* EXORBITANT, excessive, extortionate, steep (*informal*)
project *noun* 1 SCHEME, activity, assignment, enterprise, job, occupation, plan, task, undertaking, venture, work
▶ *verb* 2 FORECAST, calculate, estimate, extrapolate, gauge, predict, reckon
3 STICK OUT, bulge, extend, jut, overhang, protrude, stand out
projectile *noun* MISSILE, bullet, rocket, shell
projection *noun* 1 PROTRUSION, bulge, ledge, overhang, protuberance, ridge, shelf
2 FORECAST, calculation, computation, estimate, estimation, extrapolation, reckoning
proletarian *adjective* 1 WORKING-CLASS, common, plebeian
▶ *noun* 2 WORKER, commoner, man of the people, pleb, plebeian, prole (*derogatory slang, chiefly Brit.*)
proletariat *noun* WORKING CLASS, commoners, hoi polloi, laboring classes, lower classes, plebs, proles

(*derogatory slang, chiefly Brit.*), the common people, the masses

proliferate *verb* INCREASE, breed, expand, grow rapidly, multiply

proliferation *noun* MULTIPLICATION, expansion, increase, spread

prolific *adjective* PRODUCTIVE, abundant, copious, fecund, fertile, fruitful, luxuriant, profuse

prologue *noun* INTRODUCTION, foreword, preamble, preface, preliminary, prelude

prolong *verb* LENGTHEN, continue, delay, drag out, draw out, extend, perpetuate, protract, spin out, stretch

promenade *noun* 1 WALKWAY, esplanade, parade, prom
2 STROLL, constitutional, saunter, turn, walk
▶ *verb* 3 STROLL, perambulate, saunter, take a walk, walk

prominence *noun*
1 CONSPICUOUSNESS, markedness
2 FAME, celebrity, distinction, eminence, importance, name, prestige, reputation

prominent *adjective* 1 NOTICEABLE, conspicuous, eye-catching, obtrusive, obvious, outstanding, pronounced
2 FAMOUS, distinguished, eminent, foremost, important, leading, main, notable, renowned, top, well-known

promiscuity *noun*
LICENTIOUSNESS, debauchery, immorality, looseness, permissiveness, promiscuousness, wantonness

promiscuous *adjective*
LICENTIOUS, abandoned, debauched, fast, immoral, libertine, loose, wanton, wild

promise *verb* 1 GUARANTEE, assure, contract, give an undertaking, give one's word, pledge, swear, take an oath, undertake, vow, warrant
2 SEEM LIKELY, augur, betoken, indicate, look like, show signs of, suggest
▶ *noun* 3 GUARANTEE, assurance, bond, commitment, oath, pledge, undertaking, vow, word
4 POTENTIAL, ability, aptitude, capability, capacity, flair, talent

promising *adjective*
1 ENCOURAGING, auspicious, bright, favorable, hopeful, likely, propitious, reassuring, rosy
2 TALENTED, able, gifted, rising

promontory *noun* POINT, cape, foreland, head, headland

promote *verb* 1 HELP, advance, aid, assist, back, boost, encourage, forward, foster, support
2 RAISE, elevate, exalt, upgrade
3 ADVERTISE, hype, plug (*informal*), publicize, push, sell

promotion *noun* 1 RISE, advancement, elevation, exaltation, honor, move up, preferment, upgrading
2 PUBLICITY, advertising, plugging (*informal*)
3 ENCOURAGEMENT, advancement, boosting, furtherance, support

prompt *verb* 1 CAUSE, elicit, give rise to, occasion, provoke
2 REMIND, assist, cue, help out
▶ *adjective* 3 IMMEDIATE, early, instant, quick, rapid, speedy, swift, timely
▶ *adverb* 4 (*informal*) EXACTLY, on the dot, promptly, punctually, sharp

promptly *adverb* IMMEDIATELY, at once, directly, on the dot, on time, punctually, quickly, speedily, swiftly

promptness noun SWIFTNESS, briskness, eagerness, haste, punctuality, quickness, speed, willingness

promulgate verb MAKE KNOWN, broadcast, circulate, communicate, disseminate, make public, proclaim, promote, publish, spread

prone adjective 1 LIABLE, apt, bent, disposed, given, inclined, likely, predisposed, subject, susceptible, tending
2 FACE DOWN, flat, horizontal, prostrate, recumbent

prong noun POINT, spike, tine

pronounce verb 1 SAY, accent, articulate, enunciate, sound, speak
2 DECLARE, affirm, announce, decree, deliver, proclaim

pronounced adjective NOTICEABLE, conspicuous, decided, definite, distinct, evident, marked, obvious, striking

pronouncement noun ANNOUNCEMENT, declaration, decree, dictum, edict, judgment, proclamation, statement

pronunciation noun INTONATION, accent, articulation, diction, enunciation, inflection, speech, stress

proof noun 1 EVIDENCE, authentication, confirmation, corroboration, demonstration, substantiation, testimony, verification
▶ adjective 2 IMPERVIOUS, impenetrable, repellent, resistant, strong

prop verb 1 SUPPORT, bolster, brace, buttress, hold up, stay, sustain, uphold
▶ noun 2 SUPPORT, brace, buttress, mainstay, stanchion, stay

propaganda noun INFORMATION, advertising, disinformation, hype, promotion, publicity

propagate verb 1 SPREAD, broadcast, circulate, disseminate, promote, promulgate, publish, transmit
2 REPRODUCE, beget, breed, engender, generate, increase, multiply, procreate, produce

propel verb DRIVE, force, impel, launch, push, send, shoot, shove, thrust

propensity noun TENDENCY, bent, disposition, inclination, liability, penchant, predisposition, proclivity

proper adjective 1 SUITABLE, appropriate, apt, becoming, befitting, fit, fitting, right
2 CORRECT, accepted, conventional, established, formal, orthodox, precise, right
3 POLITE, decent, decorous, genteel, gentlemanly, ladylike, mannerly, respectable, seemly

properly adverb 1 SUITABLY, appropriately, aptly, fittingly, rightly
2 CORRECTLY, accurately
3 POLITELY, decently, respectably

property noun 1 POSSESSIONS, assets, belongings, capital, effects, estate, goods, holdings, riches, wealth
2 LAND, estate, freehold, holding, real estate
3 QUALITY, attribute, characteristic, feature, hallmark, trait

prophecy noun PREDICTION, augury, divination, forecast, prognostication, second sight, soothsaying

prophesy verb PREDICT, augur, divine, forecast, foresee, foretell, prognosticate

prophet noun SOOTHSAYER, diviner, forecaster, oracle, prophesier, seer, sibyl

prophetic adjective PREDICTIVE, oracular, prescient, prognostic, sibylline

propitious adjective FAVORABLE, auspicious, bright, encouraging, fortunate, happy, lucky, promising

proportion noun 1 RELATIVE AMOUNT, ratio, relationship
2 BALANCE, congruity, correspondence, harmony, symmetry
3 PART, amount, division, fraction, percentage, quota, segment, share
4 ▷▷ **proportions** DIMENSIONS, capacity, expanse, extent, size, volume

proportional, proportionate adjective BALANCED, commensurate, compatible, consistent, corresponding, equitable, even, in proportion

proposal noun SUGGESTION, bid, offer, plan, presentation, program, project, recommendation, scheme

propose verb 1 PUT FORWARD, advance, present, submit, suggest
2 NOMINATE, name, present, recommend
3 INTEND, aim, design, have in mind, mean, plan, scheme
4 OFFER MARRIAGE, ask for someone's hand (in marriage), pop the question (informal)

proposition noun 1 PROPOSAL, plan, recommendation, scheme, suggestion
▶ verb 2 MAKE A PASS AT, accost, make an improper suggestion, solicit

propound verb PUT FORWARD, advance, postulate, present, propose, submit, suggest

proprietor, proprietress noun OWNER, landlord or landlady, titleholder

propriety noun 1 CORRECTNESS, aptness, fitness, rightness, seemliness
2 DECORUM, courtesy, decency, etiquette, manners, politeness, respectability, seemliness

propulsion noun DRIVE, impetus, impulse, propelling force, push, thrust

prosaic adjective DULL, boring, everyday, humdrum, matter-of-fact, mundane, ordinary, pedestrian, routine, trite, unimaginative

proscribe verb 1 PROHIBIT, ban, embargo, forbid, interdict
2 OUTLAW, banish, deport, exclude, exile, expatriate, expel, ostracize

prosecute verb (law) PUT ON TRIAL, arraign, bring to trial, indict, litigate, sue, take to court, try

prospect noun 1 EXPECTATION, anticipation, future, hope, odds, outlook, probability, promise
2 (sometimes plural) LIKELIHOOD, chance, possibility
3 VIEW, landscape, outlook, scene, sight, spectacle, vista
▶ verb 4 LOOK FOR, search for, seek

prospective adjective FUTURE, anticipated, coming, destined, expected, forthcoming, imminent, intended, likely, possible, potential

prospectus noun CATALOG, list, outline, program, syllabus, synopsis

prosper verb SUCCEED, advance, do well, flourish, get on, progress, thrive

prosperity *noun* SUCCESS, affluence, fortune, good fortune, luxury, plenty, prosperousness, riches, wealth

prosperous *adjective* 1 WEALTHY, affluent, moneyed, rich, well-heeled (*informal*), well-off, well-to-do
2 SUCCESSFUL, booming, doing well, flourishing, fortunate, lucky, thriving

prostitute *noun* 1 WHORE, call girl, fallen woman, harlot, ho (*slang*), hooker (*slang*), loose woman, pro (*slang*), scrubber (*Brit. & Austral. slang*), streetwalker, strumpet, tart (*informal*), trollop
▶ *verb* 2 CHEAPEN, debase, degrade, demean, devalue, misapply, pervert, profane

prostrate *adjective* 1 PRONE, flat, horizontal
2 EXHAUSTED, dejected, depressed, desolate, drained, inconsolable, overcome, spent, worn out
▶ *verb* 3 EXHAUST, drain, fatigue, sap, tire, wear out, weary
4 ▷▷ **prostrate oneself** BOW DOWN TO, abase oneself, fall at (someone's) feet, grovel, kiss ass (*slang*), kneel, kowtow

protagonist *noun* 1 SUPPORTER, advocate, champion, exponent
2 LEADING CHARACTER, central character, hero *or* heroine, principal

protect *verb* KEEP SAFE, defend, guard, look after, preserve, safeguard, save, screen, shelter, shield, stick up for (*informal*), support, watch over

protection *noun* 1 SAFETY, aegis, care, custody, defense, protecting, safeguard, safekeeping, security
2 SAFEGUARD, barrier, buffer, cover, guard, screen, shelter, shield

protective *adjective* PROTECTING, defensive, fatherly, maternal, motherly, paternal, vigilant, watchful

protector *noun* DEFENDER, bodyguard, champion, guard, guardian, patron

protest *noun* 1 OBJECTION, complaint, dissent, outcry, protestation, remonstrance
▶ *verb* 2 OBJECT, complain, cry out, demonstrate, demur, disagree, disapprove, express disapproval, oppose, remonstrate
3 ASSERT, affirm, attest, avow, declare, insist, maintain, profess

protestation *noun* DECLARATION, affirmation, avowal, profession, vow

protester *noun* DEMONSTRATOR, agitator, rebel

protocol *noun* CODE OF BEHAVIOR, conventions, customs, decorum, etiquette, manners, propriety

prototype *noun* ORIGINAL, example, first, model, pattern, standard, type

protracted *adjective* EXTENDED, dragged out, drawn-out, long-drawn-out, prolonged, spun out

protrude *verb* STICK OUT, bulge, come through, extend, jut, obtrude, project, stand out

protrusion *noun* PROJECTION, bulge, bump, lump, outgrowth, protuberance

protuberance *noun* BULGE, bump, excrescence, hump, knob, lump, outgrowth, process, prominence, protrusion, swelling

proud *adjective* 1 SATISFIED, content, glad, gratified, pleased, well-pleased
2 CONCEITED, arrogant, boastful, disdainful, haughty, imperious,

lordly, overbearing, self-satisfied, snobbish, supercilious

prove *verb* 1 VERIFY, authenticate, confirm, demonstrate, determine, establish, justify, show, substantiate
2 TEST, analyze, assay, check, examine, try
3 TURN OUT, come out, end up, result

proven *adjective* ESTABLISHED, attested, confirmed, definite, proved, reliable, tested, verified

proverb *noun* SAYING, adage, dictum, maxim, saw

proverbial *adjective* CONVENTIONAL, acknowledged, axiomatic, current, famed, famous, legendary, notorious, traditional, typical, well-known

provide *verb* 1 SUPPLY, cater, equip, furnish, outfit, purvey, stock up
2 GIVE, add, afford, bring, impart, lend, present, produce, render, serve, yield
3 ▷▷ **provide for** or **against** TAKE PRECAUTIONS, anticipate, forearm, plan ahead, plan for, prepare for; **provide for** SUPPORT, care for, keep, maintain, sustain, take care of

providence *noun* FATE, destiny, fortune

provident *adjective* 1 THRIFTY, economical, frugal, prudent
2 FORESIGHTED, careful, cautious, discreet, far-seeing, forearmed, shrewd, vigilant, well-prepared, wise

providential *adjective* LUCKY, fortuitous, fortunate, happy, heaven-sent, opportune, timely

provider *noun* 1 SUPPLIER, donor, giver, source
2 BREADWINNER, earner, supporter, wage earner

providing, provided *conjunction* ON CONDITION THAT, as long as, given

province *noun* 1 REGION, colony, department, district, division, domain, patch, section, zone
2 AREA, business, capacity, concern, duty, field, function, line, responsibility, role, sphere

provincial *adjective* 1 RURAL, country, hick (*informal*), homespun, local, rustic
2 NARROW-MINDED, insular, inward-looking, limited, narrow, parochial, small-minded, small-town (*chiefly U.S.*), unsophisticated
▶ *noun* 3 YOKEL, country cousin, hayseed (*U.S. & Canad. informal*), hick (*informal*), rustic

provision *noun* 1 SUPPLYING, catering, equipping, furnishing, providing
2 CONDITION, clause, demand, proviso, requirement, rider, stipulation, term

provisional *adjective* 1 TEMPORARY, interim
2 CONDITIONAL, contingent, limited, qualified, tentative

provisions *plural noun* FOOD, comestibles, eatables, edibles, fare, foodstuff, rations, stores, supplies, victuals

proviso *noun* CONDITION, clause, qualification, requirement, rider, stipulation

provocation *noun* 1 CAUSE, grounds, incitement, motivation, reason, stimulus
2 OFFENSE, affront, annoyance, challenge, dare, grievance, indignity, injury, insult, taunt

provocative *adjective* OFFENSIVE, annoying, galling, goading, insulting, provoking, stimulating

provoke *verb* 1 ANGER, aggravate

(*informal*), annoy, enrage, hassle (*informal*), incense, infuriate, irk, irritate, madden, rile
2 CAUSE, bring about, elicit, evoke, incite, induce, occasion, produce, promote, prompt, rouse, stir

prowess noun 1 SKILL, accomplishment, adeptness, aptitude, excellence, expertise, genius, mastery, talent
2 BRAVERY, courage, daring, fearlessness, heroism, mettle, valiance, valor

prowl verb MOVE STEALTHILY, skulk, slink, sneak, stalk, steal

proximity noun NEARNESS, closeness

proxy noun REPRESENTATIVE, agent, delegate, deputy, factor, substitute

prudence noun COMMON SENSE, care, caution, discretion, good sense, judgment, vigilance, wariness, wisdom

prudent adjective 1 SENSIBLE, careful, cautious, discerning, discreet, judicious, politic, shrewd, vigilant, wary, wise
2 THRIFTY, canny, careful, economical, far-sighted, frugal, provident, sparing

prudish adjective PRIM, old-maidish (*informal*), overmodest, priggish, prissy (*informal*), proper, puritanical, starchy (*informal*), strait-laced, stuffy, Victorian

prune verb CUT, clip, dock, reduce, shape, shorten, snip, trim

pry verb BE INQUISITIVE, be nosy (*informal*), interfere, intrude, meddle, poke, snoop (*informal*)

prying adjective INQUISITIVE, curious, interfering, meddlesome, meddling, nosy (*informal*), snooping (*informal*), spying

psalm noun HYMN, chant

pseudo- adjective FALSE, artificial, fake, imitation, mock, phoney or phony (*informal*), pretended, sham, spurious

pseudonym noun FALSE NAME, alias, assumed name, incognito, nom de plume, pen name

psyche noun SOUL, anima, individuality, mind, personality, self, spirit

psychiatrist noun PSYCHOTHERAPIST, analyst, headshrinker (*slang*), psychoanalyst, psychologist, shrink (*slang*), therapist

psychic adjective 1 SUPERNATURAL, mystic, occult
2 MENTAL, psychological, spiritual

psychological adjective 1 MENTAL, cerebral, intellectual
2 IMAGINARY, all in the mind, irrational, psychosomatic, unreal

psychology noun 1 BEHAVIORISM, science of mind, study of personality
2 WAY OF THINKING, attitude, mental make-up, mental processes, thought processes, what makes one tick

psychopath noun MADMAN, headbanger (*informal*), headcase (*informal*), lunatic, maniac, nutcase (*slang*), nutter (*Brit. slang*), psychotic, sociopath

psychotic adjective MAD, certifiable, demented, deranged, insane, loony (*informal*), lunatic, mental (*slang*), non compos mentis, unbalanced

puberty noun ADOLESCENCE, pubescence, teens

public adjective 1 GENERAL, civic, common, national, popular, social, state, universal, widespread
2 COMMUNAL, accessible, open,

unrestricted
3 WELL-KNOWN, important, prominent, respected
4 PLAIN, acknowledged, known, obvious, open, overt, patent
▶ noun 5 PEOPLE, citizens, community, electorate, everyone, nation, populace, society

publication noun 1 PAMPHLET, brochure, issue, leaflet, magazine, newspaper, periodical, title
2 ANNOUNCEMENT, broadcasting, declaration, disclosure, notification, proclamation, publishing, reporting

publicity noun ADVERTISING, attention, boost, hype, plug (informal), press, promotion

publicize verb ADVERTISE, hype, make known, play up, plug (informal), promote, push

public-spirited adjective ALTRUISTIC, charitable, humanitarian, philanthropic, unselfish

publish verb 1 PUT OUT, issue, print, produce
2 ANNOUNCE, advertise, broadcast, circulate, disclose, divulge, proclaim, publicize, reveal, spread

pucker verb 1 WRINKLE, contract, crease, draw together, gather, knit, purse, screw up, tighten
▶ noun 2 WRINKLE, crease, fold

puerile adjective CHILDISH, babyish, foolish, immature, juvenile, silly, trivial

puff noun 1 BLAST, breath, draft, gust, whiff
2 SMOKE, drag (slang), pull
▶ verb 3 BLOW, breathe, exhale, gasp, gulp, pant, wheeze
4 SMOKE, drag (slang), draw, inhale, pull at or on, suck
5 (usually with up) SWELL, bloat, dilate, distend, expand, inflate

puffy adjective SWOLLEN, bloated, distended, enlarged, puffed up

pugilist noun BOXER, fighter, prizefighter

pugnacious adjective AGGRESSIVE, belligerent, combative, hot-tempered, quarrelsome

pull verb 1 DRAW, drag, haul, jerk, tow, trail, tug, yank
2 STRAIN, dislocate, rip, sprain, stretch, tear, wrench
3 EXTRACT, draw out, gather, pick, pluck, remove, take out, uproot
4 (informal) ATTRACT, draw, entice, lure, magnetize
▶ noun 5 TUG, jerk, twitch, yank
6 PUFF, drag (slang), inhalation
7 (informal) INFLUENCE, clout (informal), muscle, power, weight

pull down verb DEMOLISH, bulldoze, destroy, raze, remove

pull off verb SUCCEED, accomplish, carry out, do the trick, manage

pull out verb WITHDRAW, depart, evacuate, leave, quit, retreat

pull through verb SURVIVE, get better, rally, recover

pulp noun 1 PASTE, mash, mush
2 FLESH, soft part
▶ verb 3 CRUSH, mash, pulverize, squash
▶ adjective 4 CHEAP, lurid, rubbishy, trashy

pulsate verb THROB, beat, palpitate, pound, pulse, quiver, thump

pulse noun 1 BEAT, beating, pulsation, rhythm, throb, throbbing, vibration
▶ verb 2 BEAT, pulsate, throb, vibrate

pulverize verb 1 CRUSH, granulate, grind, mill, pound
2 DEFEAT, annihilate, crush, demolish, destroy, flatten, smash, wreck

pummel *verb* BEAT, batter, hammer, pound, punch, strike, thump

pump *verb* 1 (often with *into*) DRIVE, force, inject, pour, push, send, supply
2 INTERROGATE, cross-examine, probe, quiz

pun *noun* PLAY ON WORDS, double entendre, quip, witticism

punch¹ *verb* 1 HIT, belt (*informal*), bop (*informal*), box, pummel, smash, sock (*slang*), strike
▶ *noun* 2 BLOW, bop (*informal*), hit, jab, sock (*slang*), wallop (*informal*)
3 (*informal*) EFFECTIVENESS, bite, drive, forcefulness, impact, verve, vigor

punch² *verb* PIERCE, bore, cut, drill, perforate, prick, puncture, stamp

punctilious *adjective* PARTICULAR, exact, finicky, formal, fussy, meticulous, nice, precise, proper, strict

punctual *adjective* ON TIME, exact, on the dot, precise, prompt, timely

punctuality *noun* PROMPTNESS, promptitude, readiness

punctuate *verb* 1 INTERRUPT, break, intersperse, pepper, sprinkle
2 EMPHASIZE, accentuate, stress, underline

puncture *noun* 1 HOLE, break, cut, damage, leak, nick, opening, slit
2 FLAT TIRE, flat
▶ *verb* 3 PIERCE, bore, cut, nick, penetrate, perforate, prick, rupture

pungent *adjective* STRONG, acrid, bitter, hot, peppery, piquant, sharp, sour, spicy, tart

punish *verb* DISCIPLINE, castigate, chasten, chastise, correct, penalize, sentence

punishable *adjective* CULPABLE, blameworthy, criminal, indictable

punishing *adjective* HARD, arduous, backbreaking, exhausting, grueling, strenuous, taxing, tiring, wearing

punishment *noun* PENALTY, chastening, chastisement, correction, discipline, penance, retribution

punitive *adjective* RETALIATORY, in reprisal, retaliative

punt *verb* 1 BET, back, gamble, lay, stake, wager
▶ *noun* 2 BET, gamble, stake, wager

puny *adjective* FEEBLE, frail, little, sickly, stunted, tiny, weak

pupil *noun* LEARNER, beginner, disciple, novice, schoolboy *or* schoolgirl, student

puppet *noun* 1 MARIONETTE, doll, ventriloquist's dummy
2 PAWN, cat's-paw, instrument, mouthpiece, stooge, tool

purchase *verb* 1 BUY, acquire, come by, gain, get, obtain, pay for, pick up, score (*slang*)
▶ *noun* 2 BUY, acquisition, asset, gain, investment, possession, property
3 GRIP, foothold, hold, leverage, support

pure *adjective* 1 UNMIXED, authentic, flawless, genuine, natural, neat, real, simple, straight, unalloyed
2 CLEAN, germ-free, sanitary, spotless, squeaky-clean, sterilized, uncontaminated, unpolluted, untainted, wholesome
3 INNOCENT, blameless, chaste, impeccable, modest, uncorrupted, unsullied, virginal, virtuous
4 COMPLETE, absolute, outright, sheer, thorough, unmitigated, unqualified, utter

purely *adverb* ABSOLUTELY,

completely, entirely, exclusively, just, merely, only, simply, solely, wholly

purge verb 1 GET RID OF, do away with, eradicate, expel, exterminate, remove, wipe out
▶ noun 2 REMOVAL, ejection, elimination, eradication, expulsion

purify verb 1 CLEAN, clarify, cleanse, decontaminate, disinfect, refine, sanitize, wash
2 ABSOLVE, cleanse, redeem, sanctify

purist noun STICKLER, formalist, pedant

puritan noun 1 MORALIST, fanatic, prude, rigorist, zealot
▶ adjective 2 STRICT, ascetic, austere, moralistic, narrow-minded, prudish, severe, strait-laced

puritanical adjective STRICT, ascetic, austere, narrow-minded, proper, prudish, puritan, severe, strait-laced

purity noun 1 CLEANNESS, cleanliness, faultlessness, immaculateness, pureness, wholesomeness
2 INNOCENCE, chasteness, chastity, decency, honesty, integrity, virginity, virtue, virtuousness

purloin verb STEAL, appropriate, filch, nick (slang, chiefly Brit.), pilfer, pinch (informal), swipe (slang), thieve

purport verb 1 CLAIM, allege, assert, profess
▶ noun 2 SIGNIFICANCE, drift, gist, idea, implication, import, meaning

purpose noun 1 REASON, aim, idea, intention, object, point
2 AIM, ambition, desire, end, goal,

hope, intention, object, plan, wish
3 DETERMINATION, firmness, persistence, resolution, resolve, single-mindedness, tenacity, will
4 ▷▷ **on purpose** DELIBERATELY, designedly, intentionally, knowingly, purposely

purposeless adjective POINTLESS, aimless, empty, motiveless, needless, senseless, uncalled-for, unnecessary

purposely adverb DELIBERATELY, consciously, expressly, intentionally, knowingly, on purpose, with intent

purse noun 1 POUCH, money-bag, wallet
2 MONEY, exchequer, funds, means, resources, treasury, wealth
▶ verb 3 PUCKER, contract, pout, press together, tighten

pursue verb 1 FOLLOW, chase, dog, hound, hunt, hunt down, run after, shadow, stalk, tail (informal), track
2 TRY FOR, aim for, desire, seek, strive for, work towards
3 ENGAGE IN, carry on, conduct, perform, practice
4 CONTINUE, carry on, keep on, maintain, persevere in, persist in, proceed

pursuit noun 1 PURSUING, chase, hunt, quest, search, seeking, trailing
2 OCCUPATION, activity, hobby, interest, line, pastime, pleasure

purvey verb SUPPLY, cater, deal in, furnish, provide, sell, trade in

push verb 1 SHOVE, depress, drive, press, propel, ram, thrust
2 MAKE or FORCE ONE'S WAY, elbow, jostle, move, shoulder, shove, squeeze, thrust
3 URGE, encourage, hurry, impel,

incite, persuade, press, spur
▶ *noun* 4 SHOVE, butt, nudge, thrust
5 DRIVE, ambition, dynamism, energy, enterprise, go (*informal*), initiative, vigor, vitality
6 ▷▷ **the push** (*informal, chiefly Brit.*) DISMISSAL, discharge, one's cards (*informal*), the boot (*slang*), the sack (*informal*)

pushed *adjective* (often with *for*) SHORT OF, hurried, pressed, rushed, under pressure

pushover *noun* 1 PIECE OF CAKE (*informal*), breeze (*informal*), child's play (*informal*), cinch (*slang*), doddle (*Brit. slang*), picnic (*informal*), plain sailing, walkover (*informal*)
2 SUCKER (*slang*), easy game (*informal*), easy or soft mark (*informal*), mug (*Brit. slang*), soft touch (*informal*), walkover (*informal*)

pushy *adjective* FORCEFUL, ambitious, assertive, bold, brash, bumptious, obtrusive, presumptuous, self-assertive

pussyfoot *verb* HEDGE, beat about the bush, be noncommittal, equivocate, flannel (*Brit. informal*), hum and haw, prevaricate, sit on the fence

put *verb* 1 PLACE, deposit, lay, position, rest, set, settle, situate
2 EXPRESS, phrase, state, utter, word
3 THROW, cast, fling, heave, hurl, lob, pitch, toss

put across *or* **over** *verb* COMMUNICATE, convey, explain, get across, make clear, make oneself understood

put aside *or* **by** *verb* SAVE, deposit, lay by, stockpile, store

put away *verb* 1 SAVE, deposit, keep, put by
2 COMMIT, certify, institutionalize, lock up
3 CONSUME, devour, eat up, gobble, wolf down
4 PUT BACK, replace, tidy away

put down *verb* 1 RECORD, enter, set down, take down, write down
2 STAMP OUT, crush, quash, quell, repress, suppress
3 (usually with *to*) ATTRIBUTE, ascribe, impute, set down
4 PUT TO SLEEP, destroy, do away with, put out of its misery
5 (*slang*) HUMILIATE, disparage, mortify, shame, slight, snub

put forward *verb* 1 RECOMMEND, advance, nominate, propose, submit, suggest, tender

put off *verb* 1 POSTPONE, defer, delay, hold over, put on the back burner (*informal*), take a rain check on (*informal*)
2 DISCONCERT, confuse, discomfit, dismay, faze, nonplus, perturb, throw (*informal*), unsettle
3 DISCOURAGE, dishearten, dissuade

put on *verb* 1 DON, change into, dress, get dressed in, slip into
2 FAKE, affect, assume, feign, pretend, sham, simulate
3 PRESENT, do, mount, produce, show, stage
4 ADD, gain, increase by

put out *verb* 1 ANNOY, anger, exasperate, irk, irritate, nettle, vex
2 EXTINGUISH, blow out, douse, quench
3 INCONVENIENCE, bother, discomfit, discommode, impose upon, incommode, trouble

putrid *adjective* ROTTEN, bad, decayed, decomposed, off, putrefied, rancid, rotting, spoiled

putter *verb* MESS AROUND, dabble, dawdle, footle (*informal*), monkey around (*informal*), tinker

put up *verb* 1 ERECT, build, construct, fabricate, raise
2 ACCOMMODATE, board, house, lodge, take in
3 RECOMMEND, nominate, offer, present, propose, put forward, submit
4 ▷▷ **put up with** STAND, abide, bear, endure, stand for, swallow, take, tolerate

puzzle *verb* 1 PERPLEX, baffle, bewilder, confound, confuse, mystify, stump

▶ *noun* 2 PROBLEM, conundrum, enigma, mystery, paradox, poser, question, riddle

puzzled *adjective* PERPLEXED, at a loss, at sea, baffled, bewildered, confused, lost, mystified

puzzlement *noun* PERPLEXITY, bafflement, bewilderment, confusion, doubt, mystification

puzzling *adjective* PERPLEXING, abstruse, baffling, bewildering, enigmatic, incomprehensible, involved, mystifying

q

quack *noun* CHARLATAN, fake, fraud, humbug, impostor, mountebank, phoney *or* phony (*informal*), pretender

quaff *verb* DRINK, down, gulp, imbibe, swallow, swig (*informal*)

quagmire *noun* BOG, fen, marsh, mire, morass, quicksand, slough, swamp

quail *verb* SHRINK, blanch, blench, cower, cringe, falter, flinch, have cold feet (*informal*), recoil, shudder

quaint *adjective* 1 UNUSUAL, bizarre, curious, droll, eccentric, fanciful, odd, old-fashioned, peculiar, queer, rum (*Brit. slang*), singular, strange
2 OLD-FASHIONED, antiquated, old-world, picturesque

quake *verb* SHAKE, move, quiver, rock, shiver, shudder, tremble, vibrate

qualification *noun* 1 ATTRIBUTE, ability, aptitude, capability, eligibility, fitness, quality, skill, suitability
2 CONDITION, caveat, limitation, modification, proviso, requirement, reservation, rider, stipulation

qualified *adjective* 1 CAPABLE, able, adept, competent, efficient, experienced, expert, fit, practiced, proficient, skillful, trained
2 RESTRICTED, bounded, conditional, confined, contingent, limited, modified, provisional, reserved

qualify *verb* 1 CERTIFY, empower, equip, fit, permit, prepare, ready, train
2 MODERATE, diminish, ease, lessen, limit, reduce, regulate, restrain, restrict, soften, temper

quality *noun* 1 EXCELLENCE, caliber, distinction, grade, merit, position, rank, standing, status
2 CHARACTERISTIC, aspect, attribute, condition, feature, mark, property, trait
3 NATURE, character, kind, make, sort

qualm *noun* MISGIVING, anxiety, apprehension, compunction, disquiet, doubt, hesitation, scruple, twinge *or* pang of conscience, uneasiness

quandary *noun* DIFFICULTY, Catch-22, cleft stick, dilemma, impasse, plight, predicament, puzzle, strait

quantity *noun* 1 AMOUNT, lot, number, part, sum, total
2 SIZE, bulk, capacity, extent, length, magnitude, mass, measure, volume

quarrel *noun* 1 DISAGREEMENT, argument, brawl, breach, contention, controversy, dispute, dissension, feud, fight, row, squabble, tiff
▶ *verb* 2 DISAGREE, argue, bicker, brawl, clash, differ, dispute, fall out (*informal*), fight, row, squabble

quarrelsome *adjective* ARGUMENTATIVE, belligerent,

combative, contentious, disputatious, pugnacious

quarry noun PREY, aim, game, goal, objective, prize, victim

quarter noun 1 DISTRICT, area, locality, neighborhood, part, place, province, region, side, zone
2 MERCY, clemency, compassion, forgiveness, leniency, pity
▶ verb 3 ACCOMMODATE, billet, board, house, lodge, place, post, station

quarters plural noun LODGINGS, abode, barracks, billet, chambers, dwelling, habitation, residence, rooms

quash verb 1 ANNUL, cancel, invalidate, overrule, overthrow, rescind, reverse, revoke
2 SUPPRESS, beat, crush, overthrow, put down, quell, repress, squash, subdue

quasi- adjective PSEUDO-, apparent, seeming, semi-, so-called, would-be

quaver verb 1 TREMBLE, flicker, flutter, quake, quiver, shake, vibrate, waver
▶ noun 2 TREMBLING, quiver, shake, tremble, tremor, vibration

queasy adjective 1 SICK, bilious, green around the gills (informal), ill, nauseated, off color, squeamish, upset
2 UNEASY, anxious, fidgety, ill at ease, restless, troubled, uncertain, worried

queen noun 1 SOVEREIGN, consort, monarch, ruler
2 IDEAL, mistress, model, star

queer adjective 1 STRANGE, abnormal, curious, droll, extraordinary, funny, odd, peculiar, uncommon, unusual, weird
2 FAINT, dizzy, giddy, light-headed, queasy

quell verb 1 SUPPRESS, conquer, crush, defeat, overcome, overpower, put down, quash, subdue, vanquish
2 ASSUAGE, allay, appease, calm, mollify, pacify, quiet, soothe

quench verb 1 SATISFY, allay, appease, sate, satiate, slake
2 PUT OUT, crush, douse, extinguish, smother, stifle, suppress

querulous adjective COMPLAINING, captious, carping, critical, discontented, dissatisfied, fault-finding, grumbling, peevish, whining

query noun 1 QUESTION, doubt, inquiry, objection, problem, suspicion
▶ verb 2 DOUBT, challenge, disbelieve, dispute, distrust, mistrust, suspect
3 ASK, inquire or enquire, question

quest noun SEARCH, adventure, crusade, enterprise, expedition, hunt, journey, mission

question noun 1 ISSUE, motion, point, point at issue, proposal, proposition, subject, theme, topic
2 DIFFICULTY, argument, contention, controversy, dispute, doubt, problem, query
3 ▷▷ **in question** UNDER DISCUSSION, at issue, in doubt, open to debate; **out of the question** IMPOSSIBLE, inconceivable, unthinkable
▶ verb 4 ASK, cross-examine, examine, inquire, interrogate, interview, probe, quiz
5 DISPUTE, challenge, disbelieve, doubt, mistrust, oppose, query, suspect

questionable adjective DUBIOUS, controversial, debatable, dodgy

(Brit., Austral., & N.Z. informal), doubtful, iffy (informal), moot, suspect, suspicious

queue noun LINE, chain, file, sequence, series, string, train

quibble verb 1 SPLIT HAIRS, carp, cavil
▶ noun 2 OBJECTION, cavil, complaint, criticism, nicety, niggle

quick adjective 1 FAST, brisk, express, fleet, hasty, rapid, speedy, swift
2 BRIEF, cursory, hasty, hurried, perfunctory
3 SUDDEN, prompt
4 INTELLIGENT, acute, alert, astute, bright (informal), clever, perceptive, quick-witted, sharp, shrewd, smart
5 DEFT, adept, adroit, dexterous, skillful
6 EXCITABLE, irascible, irritable, passionate, testy, touchy

quicken verb 1 SPEED, accelerate, expedite, hasten, hurry, impel, precipitate
2 INVIGORATE, arouse, energize, excite, incite, inspire, revive, stimulate, vitalize

quickly adverb SWIFTLY, abruptly, apace, briskly, fast, hastily, hurriedly, promptly, pronto (informal), rapidly, soon, speedily

quick-tempered adjective HOT-TEMPERED, choleric, fiery, irascible, irritable, quarrelsome, ratty (Brit. & N.Z. informal), testy, tetchy

quick-witted adjective CLEVER, alert, astute, bright (informal), keen, perceptive, sharp, shrewd, smart

quiet adjective 1 SILENT, hushed, inaudible, low, noiseless, peaceful, soft, soundless
2 CALM, mild, peaceful, placid, restful, serene, smooth, tranquil
3 UNDISTURBED, isolated, private, secluded, sequestered, unfrequented
4 RESERVED, gentle, meek, mild, retiring, sedate, shy
▶ noun 5 PEACE, calmness, ease, quietness, repose, rest, serenity, silence, stillness, tranquillity

quieten verb 1 SILENCE, compose, hush, muffle, mute, quell, quiet, stifle, still, stop, subdue
2 SOOTHE, allay, appease, blunt, calm, deaden, dull

quietly adverb 1 SILENTLY, in an undertone, inaudibly, in silence, mutely, noiselessly, softly
2 CALMLY, mildly, patiently, placidly, serenely

quietness noun PEACE, calm, hush, quiet, silence, stillness, tranquillity

quilt noun BEDSPREAD, continental quilt, counterpane, coverlet, duvet, eiderdown

quintessence noun ESSENCE, distillation, soul, spirit

quintessential adjective ULTIMATE, archetypal, definitive, prototypical, typical

quip noun JOKE, gibe, jest, pleasantry, retort, riposte, sally, wisecrack (informal), witticism

quirk noun PECULIARITY, aberration, characteristic, eccentricity, foible, habit, idiosyncrasy, kink, mannerism, oddity, trait

quirky adjective ODD, eccentric, idiosyncratic, offbeat, peculiar, unusual

quit verb 1 STOP, abandon, cease, discontinue, drop, end, give up, halt

2 RESIGN, abdicate, go, leave, pull out, retire, step down (*informal*)
3 DEPART, go, leave, pull out
quite *adverb* 1 SOMEWHAT, fairly, moderately, rather, reasonably, relatively
2 ABSOLUTELY, completely, entirely, fully, perfectly, totally, wholly
3 TRULY, in fact, in reality, in truth, really
quiver *verb* 1 SHAKE, oscillate, quake, quaver, shiver, shudder, tremble, vibrate
▶ *noun* 2 SHAKE, oscillation, shiver, shudder, tremble, tremor, vibration
quixotic *adjective* UNREALISTIC, dreamy, fanciful, idealistic, impractical, romantic

quiz *noun* 1 EXAMINATION, investigation, questioning, test
▶ *verb* 2 QUESTION, ask, examine, interrogate, investigate
quizzical *adjective* MOCKING, arch, questioning, sardonic, teasing
quota *noun* SHARE, allowance, assignment, part, portion, ration, slice, whack (*informal*)
quotation *noun* 1 PASSAGE, citation, excerpt, extract, quote (*informal*), reference
2 (*commerce*) ESTIMATE, charge, cost, figure, price, quote (*informal*), rate, tender
quote *verb* REPEAT, cite, detail, instance, name, recall, recite, recollect, refer to

r

rabble *noun* MOB, canaille, crowd, herd, horde, swarm, throng

rabid *adjective* 1 FANATICAL, extreme, fervent, irrational, narrow-minded, zealous
2 MAD, hydrophobic

race¹ *noun* 1 CONTEST, chase, competition, dash, pursuit, rivalry
▶ *verb* 2 RUN, career, compete, contest, dart, dash, fly, gallop, hurry, speed, tear, zoom

race² *noun* PEOPLE, blood, folk, nation, stock, tribe, type

racial *adjective* ETHNIC, ethnological, folk, genealogical, genetic, national, tribal

rack *noun* 1 FRAME, framework, stand, structure
▶ *verb* 2 TORTURE, afflict, agonize, crucify, harrow, oppress, pain, torment

racket *noun* 1 NOISE, clamor, din, disturbance, fuss, outcry, pandemonium, row
2 FRAUD, scheme

racy *adjective* 1 RISQUÉ, bawdy, blue, naughty, near the knuckle (*informal*), smutty, suggestive
2 LIVELY, animated, energetic, entertaining, exciting, sparkling, spirited

radiance *noun* 1 HAPPINESS, delight, gaiety, joy, pleasure, rapture, warmth
2 BRIGHTNESS, brilliance, glare, gleam, glow, light, luster, shine

radiant *adjective* 1 HAPPY, blissful, delighted, ecstatic, glowing, joyful, joyous, on cloud nine (*informal*), rapturous
2 BRIGHT, brilliant, gleaming, glittering, glowing, luminous, lustrous, shining

radiate *verb* 1 SPREAD OUT, branch out, diverge, issue
2 EMIT, diffuse, give off *or* out, pour, scatter, send out, shed, spread

radical *adjective* 1 FUNDAMENTAL, basic, deep-seated, innate, natural, profound
2 EXTREME, complete, drastic, entire, extremist, fanatical, severe, sweeping, thorough
▶ *noun* 3 EXTREMIST, fanatic, militant, revolutionary

raffle *noun* DRAW, lottery, sweep, sweepstake

ragamuffin *noun* URCHIN, guttersnipe

rage *noun* 1 FURY, anger, frenzy, ire, madness, passion, rampage, wrath
2 *as in* **all the rage** CRAZE, enthusiasm, fad (*informal*), fashion, latest thing, trend, vogue
▶ *verb* 3 BE FURIOUS, blow one's top, blow up (*informal*), fly off the handle (*informal*), fume, go ballistic (*slang*), go up the wall (*slang*), lose the plot (*informal*), see red, seethe, storm, wig out (*slang*)

ragged *adjective* 1 TATTERED, in rags, in tatters, shabby, tatty, threadbare, torn, unkempt

2 ROUGH, jagged, rugged, serrated, uneven, unfinished

raging *adjective* FURIOUS, beside oneself, enraged, fuming, incensed, infuriated, mad, raving, seething

rags *plural noun* TATTERS, castoffs, old clothes, tattered clothing

raid *noun* 1 ATTACK, foray, incursion, inroad, invasion, sally, sortie
▶ *verb* 2 ATTACK, assault, foray, invade, pillage, plunder, sack

raider *noun* ATTACKER, invader, marauder, plunderer, robber, thief

railing *noun* FENCE, balustrade, barrier, paling, rails

rain *noun* 1 RAINFALL, cloudburst, deluge, downpour, drizzle, fall, raindrops, showers, torrent
▶ *verb* 2 POUR, bucket down (*informal*), come down in buckets (*informal*), drizzle, pelt (down), rain cats and dogs, teem
3 FALL, deposit, drop, shower, sprinkle

rainy *adjective* WET, damp, drizzly, showery

raise *verb* 1 LIFT, build, elevate, erect, heave, hoist, rear, uplift
2 INCREASE, advance, amplify, boost, enhance, enlarge, heighten, inflate, intensify, magnify, strengthen
3 COLLECT, assemble, form, gather, mass, obtain, rally, recruit
4 CAUSE, create, engender, occasion, originate, produce, provoke, start
5 BRING UP, develop, nurture, rear
6 SUGGEST, advance, broach, introduce, moot, put forward

rake¹ *verb* 1 GATHER, collect, remove
2 SEARCH, comb, scour, scrutinize

rake² *noun* LIBERTINE, debauchee, lecher, playboy, roué

rakish³ *adjective* DASHING, dapper, debonair, devil-may-care, jaunty, natty (*informal*), raffish, smart

rally⁴ *noun* 1 GATHERING, assembly, congress, convention, meeting
2 RECOVERY, improvement, recuperation, revival
▶ *verb* 3 REASSEMBLE, regroup, reorganize, unite
4 GATHER, assemble, collect, convene, marshal, muster, round up, unite
5 RECOVER, get better, improve, recuperate, revive

ram *verb* 1 HIT, butt, crash, dash, drive, force, impact, smash
2 CRAM, crowd, force, jam, stuff, thrust

ramble *verb* 1 WALK, range, roam, rove, saunter, stray, stroll, wander
2 BABBLE, rabbit (on) (*informal*), waffle (*informal, chiefly Brit.*), witter on (*informal*)
▶ *noun* 3 WALK, hike, roaming, roving, saunter, stroll, tour

rambler *noun* WALKER, hiker, rover, wanderer, wayfarer

rambling *adjective* LONG-WINDED, circuitous, digressive, disconnected, discursive, disjointed, incoherent, wordy

ramification *noun*
▷▷ **ramifications** CONSEQUENCES, developments, results, sequel, upshot

ramp *noun* SLOPE, gradient, incline, rise

rampage *verb* 1 GO BERSERK, rage, run amok, run riot, storm
▶ *noun* 2 ▷▷ **on the rampage** BERSERK, amok, out of control, raging, riotous, violent, wild

rampant *adjective* 1 WIDESPREAD, prevalent, profuse, rife, spreading like wildfire, unchecked,

uncontrolled, unrestrained
2 (*heraldry*) UPRIGHT, erect, rearing, standing

rampart *noun* DEFENSE, bastion, bulwark, fence, fortification, wall

ramshackle *adjective* RICKETY, crumbling, decrepit, derelict, flimsy, shaky, tumbledown, unsafe, unsteady

rancid *adjective* ROTTEN, bad, fetid, foul, off, putrid, rank, sour, stale, strong-smelling, tainted

rancor *noun* HATRED, animosity, bad blood, bitterness, hate, ill feeling, ill will

random *adjective* 1 CHANCE, accidental, adventitious, casual, fortuitous, haphazard, hit or miss, incidental
► *noun* 2 ▷▷ **at random** HAPHAZARDLY, arbitrarily, by chance, randomly, unsystematically, willy-nilly

range *noun* 1 LIMITS, area, bounds, orbit, province, radius, reach, scope, sphere
2 SERIES, assortment, collection, gamut, lot, selection, variety
► *verb* 3 VARY, extend, reach, run, stretch
4 ROAM, ramble, rove, traverse, wander

rangy *adjective* LONG-LIMBED, gangling, lanky, leggy, long-legged

rank¹ *noun* 1 STATUS, caste, class, degree, division, grade, level, order, position, sort, type
2 ROW, column, file, group, line, range, series, tier
► *verb* 3 ARRANGE, align, array, dispose, line up, order, sort

rank² *adjective* 1 ABSOLUTE, arrant, blatant, complete, downright, flagrant, gross, sheer, thorough, total, utter

2 FOUL, bad, disgusting, funky (*slang*), noisome, noxious, offensive, rancid, revolting, smelly, stinking
3 ABUNDANT, dense, lush, luxuriant, profuse

rank and file *noun* GENERAL PUBLIC, majority, mass, masses

rankle *verb* ANNOY, anger, gall, get on one's nerves (*informal*), irk, irritate, rile

ransack *verb* 1 SEARCH, comb, explore, go through, rummage, scour, turn inside out
2 PLUNDER, loot, pillage, raid, strip

ransom *noun* PAYMENT, money, payoff, price

rant *verb* SHOUT, cry, declaim, rave, roar, yell

rap *verb* 1 HIT, crack, knock, strike, tap
► *noun* 2 BLOW, clout (*informal*), crack, knock, tap
3 (*slang*) PUNISHMENT, blame, responsibility

rapacious *adjective* GREEDY, avaricious, grasping, insatiable, predatory, preying, voracious

rape *verb* 1 SEXUALLY ASSAULT, abuse, force, outrage, ravish, violate
► *noun* 2 SEXUAL ASSAULT, outrage, ravishment, violation
3 DESECRATION, abuse, defilement, violation

rapid *adjective* QUICK, brisk, express, fast, hasty, hurried, prompt, speedy, swift

rapidity *noun* SPEED, alacrity, briskness, fleetness, haste, hurry, promptness, quickness, rush, swiftness, velocity

rapidly *adverb* QUICKLY, briskly, fast, hastily, hurriedly, in haste, promptly, pronto (*informal*), speedily, swiftly

rapport noun BOND, affinity, empathy, harmony, link, relationship, sympathy, tie, understanding

rapprochement noun RECONCILIATION, detente, reunion

rapt adjective SPELLBOUND, absorbed, engrossed, enthralled, entranced, fascinated, gripped

rapture noun ECSTASY, bliss, delight, euphoria, joy, rhapsody, seventh heaven, transport

rapturous adjective ECSTATIC, blissful, euphoric, in seventh heaven, joyful, overjoyed, over the moon (informal), transported

rare¹ adjective 1 UNCOMMON, few, infrequent, scarce, singular, sparse, strange, unusual
2 SUPERB, choice, excellent, fine, great, peerless, superlative

rarefied adjective EXALTED, elevated, high, lofty, noble, spiritual, sublime

rarely adverb SELDOM, hardly, hardly ever, infrequently

raring adjective as in **raring to** EAGER, desperate, enthusiastic, impatient, keen, longing, ready

rarity noun 1 CURIO, collector's item, find, gem, treasure
2 UNCOMMONNESS, infrequency, scarcity, shortage, sparseness, strangeness, unusualness

rascal noun ROGUE, blackguard, devil, good-for-nothing, imp, ne'er-do-well, scamp, scoundrel, villain

rash¹ adjective RECKLESS, careless, foolhardy, hasty, heedless, ill-advised, impetuous, imprudent, impulsive, incautious

rash² noun 1 OUTBREAK, eruption
2 SPATE, flood, outbreak, plague, series, wave

rashness noun RECKLESSNESS, carelessness, foolhardiness, hastiness, heedlessness, indiscretion, thoughtlessness

rate¹ noun 1 SPEED, pace, tempo, velocity
2 DEGREE, proportion, ratio, scale, standard
3 CHARGE, cost, fee, figure, price
4 ▷▷ **at any rate** IN ANY CASE, anyhow, anyway, at all events
▶ verb 5 EVALUATE, consider, count, estimate, grade, measure, rank, reckon, value
6 DESERVE, be entitled to, be worthy of, merit

rather adverb 1 TO SOME EXTENT, a little, fairly, moderately, quite, relatively, somewhat, to some degree
2 PREFERABLY, more readily, more willingly, sooner

ratify verb APPROVE, affirm, authorize, confirm, endorse, establish, sanction, uphold

rating¹ noun POSITION, class, degree, grade, order, placing, rank, rate, status

ratio noun PROPORTION, fraction, percentage, rate, relation

ration noun 1 ALLOWANCE, allotment, helping, measure, part, portion, quota, share
▶ verb 2 LIMIT, budget, control, restrict

rational adjective SANE, intelligent, logical, lucid, realistic, reasonable, sensible, sound, wise

rationale noun REASON, grounds, logic, motivation, philosophy, principle, raison d'être, theory

rationalize verb JUSTIFY, account for, excuse, vindicate

rattle verb 1 CLATTER, bang, jangle
2 SHAKE, bounce, jar, jolt, vibrate
3 (informal) FLUSTER, disconcert,

disturb, faze, perturb, shake, upset

raucous adjective HARSH, grating, hoarse, loud, noisy, rough, strident

raunchy adjective (slang) SEXY, coarse, earthy, lusty, sexual, steamy (informal)

ravage verb 1 DESTROY, demolish, despoil, devastate, lay waste, ransack, ruin, spoil
▶ noun 2 ▷▷ **ravages** DAMAGE, destruction, devastation, havoc, ruin, ruination, spoliation

rave verb 1 RANT, babble, be delirious, go mad (informal), rage, roar
2 (informal) ENTHUSE, be excited about (informal), be wild about (informal), gush, praise

ravenous adjective STARVING, famished, starved

ravine noun CANYON, defile, gorge, gulch (U.S.), gully, pass

raving adjective MAD, crazed, crazy, delirious, hysterical, insane, irrational, wild

ravish verb 1 ENCHANT, captivate, charm, delight, enrapture, entrance, fascinate, spellbind
2 RAPE, abuse, force, sexually assault, violate

ravishing adjective ENCHANTING, beautiful, bewitching, charming, entrancing, gorgeous, lovely

raw adjective 1 UNCOOKED, fresh, natural
2 UNREFINED, basic, coarse, crude, natural, rough, unfinished, unprocessed
3 INEXPERIENCED, callow, green, immature, new
4 CHILLY, biting, bitter, cold, freezing, parky (Brit. informal), piercing

ray noun BEAM, bar, flash, gleam, shaft

raze verb DESTROY, demolish, flatten, knock down, level, pull down, ruin

re preposition CONCERNING, about, apropos, regarding, with reference to, with regard to

reach verb 1 ARRIVE AT, attain, get to, make
2 TOUCH, contact, extend to, grasp, stretch to
3 CONTACT, communicate with, get hold of, get in touch with, get through to
▶ noun 4 RANGE, capacity, distance, extension, extent, grasp, influence, power, scope, stretch

react verb 1 RESPOND, answer, reply
2 ACT, behave, function, operate, proceed, work

reaction noun 1 RESPONSE, answer, reply
2 RECOIL, counteraction
3 CONSERVATISM, the right

reactionary adjective
1 CONSERVATIVE, right-wing
▶ noun 2 CONSERVATIVE, die-hard, right-winger

read verb 1 LOOK AT, peruse, pore over, scan, study
2 INTERPRET, comprehend, construe, decipher, discover, see, understand
3 REGISTER, display, indicate, record, show

readable adjective 1 ENJOYABLE, entertaining, enthralling, gripping, interesting
2 LEGIBLE, clear, comprehensible, decipherable

readily adverb 1 WILLINGLY, eagerly, freely, gladly, promptly, quickly
2 EASILY, effortlessly, quickly, smoothly, speedily, unhesitatingly

readiness noun 1 WILLINGNESS, eagerness, keenness
2 EASE, adroitness, dexterity, facility, promptness

reading noun 1 PERUSAL, examination, inspection, scrutiny, study
2 RECITAL, lesson, performance, sermon
3 INTERPRETATION, grasp, impression, version
4 LEARNING, education, erudition, knowledge, scholarship

ready adjective 1 PREPARED, arranged, fit, organized, primed, ripe, set
2 WILLING, agreeable, disposed, eager, glad, happy, inclined, keen, prone
3 PROMPT, alert, bright, clever, intelligent, keen, perceptive, quick, sharp, smart
4 AVAILABLE, accessible, convenient, handy, near, present

real adjective GENUINE, actual, authentic, factual, rightful, sincere, true, unfeigned, valid

realistic adjective 1 PRACTICAL, common-sense, down-to-earth, level-headed, matter-of-fact, real, sensible
2 LIFELIKE, authentic, faithful, genuine, natural, true, true to life

reality noun TRUTH, actuality, fact, realism, validity, verity

realization noun 1 AWARENESS, cognizance, comprehension, conception, grasp, perception, recognition, understanding
2 ACHIEVEMENT, accomplishment, fulfillment

realize verb 1 BECOME AWARE OF, comprehend, get the message, grasp, take in, understand
2 ACHIEVE, accomplish, carry out or through, complete, do, effect,

fulfill, perform

really adverb TRULY, actually, certainly, genuinely, in actuality, indeed, in fact, positively, surely

realm noun 1 KINGDOM, country, domain, dominion, empire, land
2 SPHERE, area, branch, department, field, province, territory, world

reap verb 1 COLLECT, bring in, cut, garner, gather, harvest
2 OBTAIN, acquire, derive, gain, get

rear[1] noun 1 BACK, end, rearguard, stern, tail, tail end
▶ adjective 2 BACK, following, hind, last

rear[2] verb 1 BRING UP, breed, educate, foster, nurture, raise, train
2 RISE, loom, soar, tower

reason noun 1 CAUSE, aim, goal, grounds, incentive, intention, motive, object, purpose
2 SENSE(s), intellect, judgment, logic, mind, rationality, sanity, soundness, understanding
▶ verb 3 DEDUCE, conclude, infer, make out, think, work out
4 ▷▷ **reason with** PERSUADE, bring round (informal), prevail upon, talk into or out of, urge, win over

reasonable adjective 1 SENSIBLE, logical, plausible, practical, sane, sober, sound, tenable, wise
2 MODERATE, equitable, fair, fit, just, modest, O.K. or okay (informal), proper, right

reasoned adjective SENSIBLE, clear, logical, well-thought-out

reasoning noun THINKING, analysis, logic, thought

reassure verb ENCOURAGE, comfort, hearten, put or set one's mind at rest, restore confidence to

rebate noun REFUND, allowance, bonus, deduction, discount, reduction

rebel verb 1 REVOLT, mutiny, resist, rise up
2 DEFY, disobey, dissent
▶ noun 3 REVOLUTIONARY, insurgent, revolutionist, secessionist
4 NONCONFORMIST, apostate, dissenter, heretic, schismatic
▶ adjective 5 REBELLIOUS, insurgent, insurrectionary, revolutionary

rebellion noun 1 RESISTANCE, mutiny, revolt, revolution, rising, uprising
2 NONCONFORMITY, defiance, heresy, schism

rebellious adjective
1 REVOLUTIONARY, disloyal, disobedient, disorderly, insurgent, mutinous, rebel, seditious, unruly
2 DEFIANT, difficult, refractory, resistant, unmanageable

rebound verb 1 BOUNCE, recoil, ricochet
2 MISFIRE, backfire, boomerang, recoil

rebuff verb 1 REJECT, cold-shoulder, cut, knock back (slang), refuse, repulse, slight, snub, spurn, turn down
▶ noun 2 REJECTION, cold shoulder, kick in the teeth (slang), knock-back (slang), refusal, repulse, slap in the face (informal), slight, snub

rebuke verb 1 SCOLD, admonish, castigate, censure, chide, dress down (informal), give a rocket (Brit. & N.Z. informal), haul (someone) over the coals (informal), reprimand, reprove, tear (someone) off a strip (informal), tell off (informal)
▶ noun 2 SCOLDING, admonition, censure, dressing-down (informal), reprimand, row, telling-off (informal)

rebut verb DISPROVE, confute, invalidate, negate, overturn, prove wrong, refute

rebuttal noun DISPROOF, confutation, invalidation, negation, refutation

recalcitrant adjective DISOBEDIENT, defiant, insubordinate, refractory, unmanageable, unruly, wayward, willful

recall verb 1 RECOLLECT, bring or call to mind, evoke, remember
2 ANNUL, cancel, countermand, repeal, retract, revoke, withdraw
▶ noun 3 RECOLLECTION, memory, remembrance
4 ANNULMENT, cancellation, repeal, rescindment, retraction, withdrawal

recant verb WITHDRAW, disclaim, forswear, renege, repudiate, retract, revoke, take back

recapitulate verb REPEAT, outline, recap (informal), recount, restate, summarize

recede verb FALL BACK, abate, ebb, regress, retire, retreat, return, subside, withdraw

receipt noun 1 SALES SLIP, counterfoil, proof of purchase
2 RECEIVING, acceptance, delivery, reception

receive verb 1 GET, accept, acquire, be given, collect, obtain, pick up, take
2 EXPERIENCE, bear, encounter, suffer, sustain, undergo
3 GREET, accommodate, admit, entertain, meet, welcome

recent adjective 1 NEW, current, fresh, late, modern, novel, present-day, up-to-date

recently adverb NEWLY, currently,

freshly, lately, latterly, not long ago, of late

receptacle noun CONTAINER, holder, repository

reception noun 1 PARTY, function, levee, soirée
2 WELCOME, acknowledgment, greeting, reaction, response, treatment

receptive adjective OPEN, amenable, interested, open-minded, open to suggestions, susceptible, sympathetic

recess noun 1 ALCOVE, bay, corner, hollow, niche, nook
2 BREAK, holiday, intermission, interval, respite, rest, vacation

recession noun DEPRESSION, decline, drop, slump

recipe noun 1 DIRECTIONS, ingredients, instructions
2 METHOD, formula, prescription, procedure, process, technique

reciprocal adjective MUTUAL, alternate, complementary, correlative, corresponding, equivalent, exchanged, interchangeable

reciprocate verb RETURN, exchange, reply, requite, respond, swap, trade

recital noun 1 PERFORMANCE, rehearsal, rendering
2 RECITATION, account, narrative, reading, relation, statement, telling

recitation noun RECITAL, lecture, passage, performance, piece, reading

recite verb REPEAT, declaim, deliver, narrate, perform, speak

reckless adjective CARELESS, hasty, headlong, heedless, imprudent, mindless, precipitate, rash, thoughtless, wild

reckon verb 1 THINK, assume,

believe, guess (*informal*), imagine, suppose
2 CONSIDER, account, count, deem, esteem, judge, rate, regard
3 COUNT, add up, calculate, compute, figure, number, tally, total

reckoning noun 1 COUNT, addition, calculation, estimate
2 BILL, account, charge, due, score

reclaim verb REGAIN, recapture, recover, redeem, reform, retrieve, salvage

recline verb LEAN, lie (down), loll, lounge, repose, rest, sprawl

recluse noun HERMIT, anchoress, anchorite, monk, solitary

reclusive adjective SOLITARY, hermit-like, isolated, retiring, withdrawn

recognition noun
1 IDENTIFICATION, discovery, recollection, remembrance
2 ACCEPTANCE, admission, allowance, confession
3 APPRECIATION, notice, respect

recognize verb 1 IDENTIFY, know, notice, place, recall, recollect, remember, spot
2 ACCEPT, acknowledge, admit, allow, concede, grant
3 APPRECIATE, notice, respect

recoil verb 1 JERK BACK, kick, react, rebound, spring back
2 DRAW BACK, falter, quail, shrink
3 BACKFIRE, boomerang, misfire, rebound
▶ noun 4 REACTION, backlash, kick, rebound, repercussion

recollect verb REMEMBER, place, recall, summon up

recollection noun MEMORY, impression, recall, remembrance, reminiscence

recommend verb 1 ADVISE, advance, advocate, counsel,

prescribe, propose, put forward, suggest

2 PRAISE, approve, commend, endorse

recommendation noun 1 ADVICE, counsel, proposal, suggestion

2 PRAISE, advocacy, approval, commendation, endorsement, reference, sanction, testimonial

recompense verb 1 REWARD, pay, remunerate

2 COMPENSATE, make up for, pay for, redress, reimburse, repay, requite

▶ noun 3 COMPENSATION, amends, damages, payment, remuneration, reparation, repayment, requital, restitution

4 REWARD, payment, return, wages

reconcile verb 1 RESOLVE, adjust, compose, put to rights, rectify, settle, square

2 REUNITE, appease, conciliate, make peace between, propitiate

3 ACCEPT, put up with (informal), resign oneself, submit, yield

reconciliation noun REUNION, conciliation, pacification, reconcilement

recondite adjective OBSCURE, arcane, concealed, dark, deep, difficult, hidden, mysterious, occult, profound, secret

recondition verb RESTORE, do up (informal), overhaul, remodel, renew, renovate, repair, revamp

reconnaissance noun INSPECTION, exploration, investigation, observation, recce (slang), scan, survey

reconnoiter verb INSPECT, case (slang), explore, investigate, observe, scan, spy out, survey

reconsider verb RETHINK, reassess, review, revise, think

again

reconstruct verb 1 REBUILD, recreate, regenerate, remake, remodel, renovate, restore

2 DEDUCE, build up, piece together

record noun 1 DOCUMENT, account, blog (informal), chronicle, diary, entry, file, journal, log, register, report, weblog

2 EVIDENCE, documentation, testimony, trace, witness

3 DISC, album, LP, single, vinyl

4 BACKGROUND, career, history, performance

5 ▷▷ **off the record** CONFIDENTIAL, not for publication, private, unofficial

▶ verb 6 WRITE DOWN, chronicle, document, enter, log, minute, note, register, set down, take down

7 TAPE, make a recording of, tape-record, video, video-tape

8 REGISTER, give evidence of, indicate, say, show

recorder noun CHRONICLER, archivist, clerk, diarist, historian, scribe

recording noun RECORD, disc, tape, video

recount verb TELL, depict, describe, narrate, recite, relate, repeat, report

recoup verb 1 REGAIN, recover, retrieve, win back

2 COMPENSATE, make up for, refund, reimburse, remunerate, repay, requite

recourse noun OPTION, alternative, choice, expedient, remedy, resort, resource, way out

recover verb 1 GET BETTER, convalesce, get well, heal, improve, mend, rally, recuperate, revive

2 REGAIN, get back, recapture,

reclaim, redeem, repossess, restore, retrieve

recovery noun 1 IMPROVEMENT, convalescence, healing, mending, recuperation, revival

2 RETRIEVAL, reclamation, repossession, restoration

recreation noun PASTIME, amusement, diversion, enjoyment, entertainment, fun, hobby, leisure activity, play, relaxation, sport

recrimination noun BICKERING, counterattack, mutual accusation, quarrel, squabbling

recruit verb 1 ENLIST, draft, enroll, levy, mobilize, muster, raise

2 WIN (OVER), engage, obtain, procure

▶ noun 3 BEGINNER, apprentice, convert, helper, initiate, learner, novice, trainee

rectify verb CORRECT, adjust, emend, fix, improve, redress, remedy, repair, right

rectitude noun MORALITY, decency, goodness, honesty, honor, integrity, principle, probity, virtue

recuperate verb RECOVER, convalesce, get better, improve, mend

recur verb HAPPEN AGAIN, come again, persist, reappear, repeat, return, revert

recurrent adjective PERIODIC, continued, frequent, habitual, recurring

recycle verb REPROCESS, reclaim, reuse, salvage, save

red adjective 1 CRIMSON, carmine, cherry, coral, ruby, scarlet, vermilion

2 (of hair) CHESTNUT, carroty, flame-colored, reddish, sandy, titian

3 FLUSHED, blushing, embarrassed, florid, shamefaced

▶ noun 4 ▷▷ **in the red** (informal) IN DEBT, in arrears, insolvent, overdrawn; **see red** (informal) LOSE ONE'S TEMPER, blow one's top, crack up (informal), fly off the handle (informal), go ballistic (slang), go mad (informal)

red-blooded adjective (informal) VIGOROUS, lusty, robust, strong, virile

redden verb FLUSH, blush, color (up), crimson, go red

redeem verb 1 MAKE UP FOR, atone for, compensate for, make amends for

2 REINSTATE, absolve, restore to favor

3 SAVE, deliver, emancipate, free, liberate, ransom

4 BUY BACK, reclaim, recover, regain, repurchase, retrieve

redemption noun 1 COMPENSATION, amends, atonement, reparation

2 SALVATION, deliverance, emancipation, liberation, release, rescue

3 REPURCHASE, reclamation, recovery, repossession, retrieval

red-handed adjective IN THE ACT, bang to rights (slang), (in) flagrante delicto

redolent adjective 1 REMINISCENT, evocative, suggestive

2 SCENTED, aromatic, fragrant, odorous, perfumed, sweet-smelling

redoubtable adjective FORMIDABLE, fearful, fearsome, mighty, powerful, strong

redress verb 1 MAKE AMENDS FOR, compensate for, make up for

2 PUT RIGHT, adjust, balance, correct, even up, rectify, regulate

▶ noun 3 AMENDS, atonement, compensation, payment, recompense, reparation

reduce verb 1 LESSEN, abate, curtail, cut down, decrease, diminish, lower, moderate, shorten, weaken
2 DEGRADE, break, bring low, downgrade, humble

redundant adjective SUPERFLUOUS, extra, inessential, supernumerary, surplus, unnecessary, unwanted

reek verb 1 STINK, pong (Brit. informal), smell
▶ noun 2 STINK, fetor, odor, pong (Brit. informal), smell, stench

reel verb 1 STAGGER, lurch, pitch, rock, roll, sway
2 WHIRL, revolve, spin, swirl

refer verb 1 ALLUDE, bring up, cite, mention, speak of
2 RELATE, apply, belong, be relevant to, concern, pertain
3 CONSULT, apply, go, look up, turn to
4 DIRECT, guide, point, send

referee noun 1 UMPIRE, adjudicator, arbiter, arbitrator, judge, ref (informal)
▶ verb 2 UMPIRE, adjudicate, arbitrate, judge, mediate

reference noun 1 CITATION, allusion, mention, note, quotation
2 TESTIMONIAL, character, credentials, endorsement, recommendation
3 RELEVANCE, applicability, bearing, connection, relation

referendum noun PUBLIC VOTE, plebiscite, popular vote

refine verb 1 PURIFY, clarify, cleanse, distill, filter, process
2 IMPROVE, hone, perfect, polish

refined adjective 1 CULTURED, civilized, cultivated, elegant, polished, polite, well-bred
2 PURE, clarified, clean, distilled, filtered, processed, purified
3 DISCERNING, delicate, discriminating, fastidious, fine, precise, sensitive

refinement noun
1 SOPHISTICATION, breeding, civility, courtesy, cultivation, culture, discrimination, gentility, good breeding, polish, taste
2 SUBTLETY, fine point, nicety, nuance
3 PURIFICATION, clarification, cleansing, distillation, filtering, processing

reflect verb 1 THROW BACK, echo, mirror, reproduce, return
2 SHOW, demonstrate, display, indicate, manifest, reveal
3 THINK, cogitate, consider, meditate, muse, ponder, ruminate, wonder

reflection noun 1 IMAGE, echo, mirror image
2 THOUGHT, cogitation, consideration, contemplation, idea, meditation, musing, observation, opinion, thinking

reflective adjective THOUGHTFUL, contemplative, meditative, pensive

reform noun 1 IMPROVEMENT, amendment, betterment, rehabilitation
▶ verb 2 IMPROVE, amend, correct, mend, rectify, restore
3 MEND ONE'S WAYS, clean up one's act (informal), go straight (informal), pull one's socks up (Brit. informal), shape up (informal), turn over a new leaf

refractory adjective UNMANAGEABLE, difficult, disobedient, headstrong, high-maintenance, intractable, uncontrollable, unruly, willful

refrain¹ verb STOP, abstain, avoid, cease, desist, forbear, leave off, renounce

refrain² noun CHORUS, melody, tune

refresh verb 1 REVIVE, brace, enliven, freshen, reinvigorate, revitalize, stimulate
2 STIMULATE, jog, prompt, renew

refreshing adjective
1 STIMULATING, bracing, fresh, invigorating
2 NEW, novel, original

refreshment noun
▷▷ **refreshments** FOOD AND DRINK, drinks, snacks, tidbits

refrigerate verb COOL, chill, freeze, keep cold

refuge noun SHELTER, asylum, haven, hideout, protection, retreat, sanctuary

refugee noun EXILE, displaced person, émigré, escapee

refund verb 1 REPAY, pay back, reimburse, restore, return
▶ noun 2 REPAYMENT, reimbursement, return

refurbish verb RENOVATE, clean up, do up (informal), mend, overhaul, repair, restore, revamp

refusal noun DENIAL, knock-back (slang), rebuff, rejection

refuse¹ verb REJECT, decline, deny, say no, spurn, turn down, withhold

refuse² noun RUBBISH, garbage, junk (informal), litter, trash, waste

refute verb DISPROVE, discredit, negate, overthrow, prove false, rebut

regain verb 1 RECOVER, get back, recapture, recoup, retrieve, take back, win back
2 GET BACK TO, reach again, return to

regal adjective ROYAL, kingly or queenly, magnificent, majestic, noble, princely

regale verb ENTERTAIN, amuse, delight, divert

regalia plural noun EMBLEMS, accouterments, decorations, finery, paraphernalia, trappings

regard verb 1 CONSIDER, believe, deem, esteem, judge, rate, see, suppose, think, view
2 LOOK AT, behold, check out (informal), clock (Brit. slang), eye, gaze at, observe, scrutinize, view, watch
3 HEED, attend, listen to, mind, pay attention to, take notice of
4 ▷▷ **as regards** CONCERNING, pertaining to, regarding, relating to
▶ noun 5 HEED, attention, interest, mind, notice
6 RESPECT, care, concern, consideration, esteem, thought
7 LOOK, gaze, glance, scrutiny, stare

regarding preposition CONCERNING, about, as regards, in or with regard to, on the subject of, re, respecting, with reference to

regardless adjective 1 HEEDLESS, inconsiderate, indifferent, neglectful, negligent, rash, reckless, unmindful
▶ adverb 2 ANYWAY, in any case, in spite of everything, nevertheless

regards plural noun GOOD WISHES, best wishes, compliments, greetings, respects

regenerate verb RENEW, breathe new life into, invigorate, reawaken, reinvigorate, rejuvenate, restore, revive

regime noun GOVERNMENT, leadership, management, reign,

rule, system

regimented *adjective*
CONTROLLED, disciplined,
ordered, organized, regulated,
systematized

region *noun* AREA, district, locality,
part, place, quarter, section,
sector, territory, tract, zone

regional *adjective* LOCAL, district,
parochial, provincial, zonal

register *noun* 1 LIST, archives,
catalog, chronicle, diary, file, log,
record, roll, roster
▸ *verb* 2 RECORD, catalog,
chronicle, enlist, enroll, enter,
list, note
3 SHOW, display, exhibit, express,
indicate, manifest, mark, reveal

regress *verb* REVERT, backslide,
degenerate, deteriorate, fall away
or off, go back, lapse, relapse,
return

regret *verb* 1 FEEL SORRY ABOUT,
bemoan, bewail, deplore, grieve,
lament, miss, mourn, repent, rue
▸ *noun* 2 SORROW, bitterness,
compunction, contrition,
penitence, remorse, repentance,
ruefulness

regretful *adjective* SORRY,
apologetic, contrite, penitent,
remorseful, repentant, rueful,
sad, sorrowful

regrettable *adjective*
UNFORTUNATE, disappointing,
distressing, lamentable, sad,
shameful

regular *adjective* 1 NORMAL,
common, customary, habitual,
ordinary, routine, typical, usual
2 EVEN, balanced, flat, level,
smooth, straight, symmetrical,
uniform
3 SYSTEMATIC, consistent,
constant, even, fixed, ordered, set,
stated, steady, uniform

regulate *verb* 1 CONTROL, direct,
govern, guide, handle, manage,
rule, run, supervise
2 ADJUST, balance, fit, moderate,
modulate, tune

regulation *noun* 1 RULE, decree,
dictate, edict, law, order, precept,
statute
2 CONTROL, direction,
government, management,
supervision
3 ADJUSTMENT, modulation,
tuning

regurgitate *verb* VOMIT, barf
(*slang*), disgorge, puke (*slang*), sick
up (*informal*), spew (out *or* up),
throw up (*informal*)

rehabilitate *verb* 1 REINTEGRATE,
adjust
2 REDEEM, clear, reform, restore,
save

rehash *verb* 1 REWORK, refashion,
rejig (*informal*), reuse, rewrite
▸ *noun* 2 REWORKING, new version,
rearrangement, rewrite

rehearsal *noun* PRACTICE, drill,
preparation, rehearsing, run-
through

rehearse *verb* PRACTICE, drill, go
over, prepare, recite, repeat, run
through, train

reign *noun* 1 RULE, command,
control, dominion, monarchy,
power
▸ *verb* 2 RULE, be in power,
command, govern, influence
3 BE SUPREME, hold sway,
predominate, prevail

reimburse *verb* PAY BACK,
compensate, recompense, refund,
remunerate, repay, return

rein *verb* 1 CONTROL, check, curb,
halt, hold back, limit, restrain,
restrict
▸ *noun* 2 CONTROL, brake, bridle,
check, curb, harness, hold,

restraint

reincarnation *noun* REBIRTH, transmigration of souls

reinforce *verb* SUPPORT, bolster, emphasize, fortify, prop, strengthen, stress, supplement, toughen

reinforcement *noun*
1 STRENGTHENING, augmentation, fortification, increase
2 SUPPORT, brace, buttress, prop, stay
3 ▷▷ **reinforcements** RESERVES, additional *or* fresh troops, auxiliaries, support

reinstate *verb* RESTORE, recall, re-establish, replace, return

reiterate *verb* REPEAT, do again, restate, say again

reject *verb* 1 DENY, decline, disallow, exclude, renounce, repudiate, veto
2 REBUFF, jilt, refuse, repulse, say no to, spurn, turn down
3 DISCARD, eliminate, jettison, scrap, throw away *or* out
▶ *noun* 4 CASTOFF, discard, failure, second

rejection *noun* 1 DENIAL, dismissal, exclusion, renunciation, repudiation, thumbs down, veto
2 REBUFF, brushoff (*slang*), kick in the teeth (*slang*), knock-back (*slang*), refusal

rejig *verb* REARRANGE, alter, juggle, manipulate, reorganize, tweak

rejoice *verb* BE GLAD, be happy, be overjoyed, celebrate, exult, glory

rejoicing *noun* HAPPINESS, celebration, elation, exultation, gladness, joy, jubilation, merrymaking

rejoin *verb* REPLY, answer, respond, retort, riposte

rejoinder *noun* REPLY, answer,

comeback (*informal*), response, retort, riposte

rejuvenate *verb* REVITALIZE, breathe new life into, refresh, regenerate, reinvigorate, renew, restore

relapse *verb* 1 LAPSE, backslide, degenerate, fail, regress, revert, slip back
2 WORSEN, deteriorate, fade, fail, sicken, sink, weaken
▶ *noun* 3 LAPSE, backsliding, regression, retrogression
4 WORSENING, deterioration, turn for the worse, weakening

relate *verb* 1 CONNECT, associate, correlate, couple, join, link
2 CONCERN, apply, be relevant to, have to do with, pertain, refer
3 TELL, describe, detail, narrate, recite, recount, report

related *adjective* 1 AKIN, kindred
2 ASSOCIATED, affiliated, akin, connected, interconnected, joint, linked

relation *noun* 1 CONNECTION, bearing, bond, comparison, correlation, link
2 RELATIVE, kin, kinsman *or* kinswoman
3 KINSHIP, affinity, kindred

relations *plural noun* 1 DEALINGS, affairs, connections, contact, interaction, intercourse, relationship
2 FAMILY, clan, kin, kindred, kinsfolk, kinsmen, relatives, tribe

relationship *noun* 1 ASSOCIATION, affinity, bond, connection, kinship, rapport
2 AFFAIR, liaison
3 CONNECTION, correlation, link, parallel, similarity, tie-up

relative *adjective* 1 DEPENDENT, allied, associated, comparative, contingent, corresponding,

proportionate, related
2 RELEVANT, applicable, apposite, appropriate, apropos, germane, pertinent
▶ *noun* 3 RELATION, kinsman *or* kinswoman, member of one's *or* the family

relatively *adverb* COMPARATIVELY, rather, somewhat

relax *verb* 1 BE *or* FEEL AT EASE, calm, chill out (*slang*), de-stress, lighten up (*slang*), rest, take it easy, unwind
2 LESSEN, abate, ease, ebb, let up, loosen, lower, moderate, reduce, relieve, slacken, weaken

relaxation *noun* LEISURE, enjoyment, fun, pleasure, recreation, rest

relaxed *adjective* EASY-GOING, casual, comfortable, easy, free and easy, homey, informal, laid-back (*informal*), leisurely

relay *noun* 1 SHIFT, relief, turn
2 MESSAGE, dispatch, transmission
▶ *verb* 3 PASS ON, broadcast, carry, communicate, send, spread, transmit

release *verb* 1 SET FREE, discharge, drop, extricate, free, liberate, loose, unbridle, undo, unfasten
2 ACQUIT, absolve, exonerate, let go, let off
3 ISSUE, circulate, distribute, launch, make known, make public, publish, put out
▶ *noun* 4 LIBERATION, deliverance, discharge, emancipation, freedom, liberty
5 ACQUITTAL, absolution, exemption, exoneration
6 ISSUE, proclamation, publication

relegate *verb* DEMOTE, downgrade

relent *verb* BE MERCIFUL,

capitulate, change one's mind, come round, have pity, show mercy, soften, yield

relentless *adjective*
1 UNREMITTING, incessant, nonstop, persistent, unrelenting, unrelieved
2 MERCILESS, cruel, fierce, implacable, pitiless, remorseless, ruthless, unrelenting

relevant *adjective* SIGNIFICANT, apposite, appropriate, apt, fitting, germane, pertinent, related, to the point

reliable *adjective* DEPENDABLE, faithful, safe, sound, staunch, sure, true, trustworthy

reliance *noun* TRUST, belief, confidence, dependence, faith

relic *noun* REMNANT, fragment, keepsake, memento, souvenir, trace, vestige

relief *noun* 1 EASE, comfort, cure, deliverance, mitigation, release, remedy, solace
2 REST, break, breather (*informal*), relaxation, respite
3 AID, assistance, help, succor, support

relieve *verb* 1 EASE, alleviate, assuage, calm, comfort, console, cure, mitigate, relax, soften, soothe
2 HELP, aid, assist, succor, support, sustain

religious *adjective* 1 DEVOUT, devotional, faithful, godly, holy, pious, sacred, spiritual
2 CONSCIENTIOUS, faithful, meticulous, punctilious, rigid, scrupulous

relinquish *verb* GIVE UP, abandon, abdicate, cede, drop, forsake, leave, let go, renounce, surrender

relish *verb* 1 ENJOY, delight in, fancy, like, revel in, savor

▶ *noun* 2 ENJOYMENT, fancy, fondness, gusto, liking, love, partiality, penchant, predilection, taste

3 CONDIMENT, sauce, seasoning

4 FLAVOR, piquancy, smack, spice, tang, taste, trace

reluctance *noun* UNWILLINGNESS, aversion, disinclination, dislike, distaste, loathing, repugnance

reluctant *adjective* UNWILLING, disinclined, hesitant, loath, unenthusiastic

rely *verb* DEPEND, bank, bet, count, trust

remain *verb* 1 CONTINUE, abide, dwell, endure, go on, last, persist, stand, stay, survive

2 STAY BEHIND, be left, delay, linger, wait

remainder *noun* REST, balance, excess, leavings, remains, remnant, residue, surplus

remaining *adjective* LEFT-OVER, lingering, outstanding, persisting, surviving, unfinished

remains *plural noun* 1 REMNANTS, debris, dregs, leavings, leftovers, relics, residue, rest

2 BODY, cadaver, carcass, corpse

remark *verb* 1 COMMENT, declare, mention, observe, pass comment, reflect, say, state

2 NOTICE, espy, make out, mark, note, observe, perceive, see

▶ *noun* 3 COMMENT, observation, reflection, statement, utterance

remarkable *adjective* EXTRAORDINARY, notable, outstanding, rare, singular, striking, surprising, uncommon, unusual, wonderful

remedy *noun* 1 CURE, medicine, nostrum, treatment

▶ *verb* 2 PUT RIGHT, correct, fix, rectify, set to rights

remember *verb* 1 RECALL, call to mind, commemorate, look back (on), recollect, reminisce, think back

2 BEAR IN MIND, keep in mind

remembrance *noun* 1 MEMORY, recall, recollection, reminiscence, thought

2 SOUVENIR, commemoration, keepsake, memento, memorial, monument, reminder, token

remind *verb* CALL TO MIND, jog one's memory, make (someone) remember, prompt

reminisce *verb* RECALL, hark back, look back, recollect, remember, think back

reminiscence *noun* RECOLLECTION, anecdote, memoir, memory, recall, remembrance

reminiscent *adjective* SUGGESTIVE, evocative, similar

remiss *adjective* CARELESS, forgetful, heedless, lax, neglectful, negligent, thoughtless

remission *noun* 1 PARDON, absolution, amnesty, discharge, exemption, release, reprieve

2 LESSENING, abatement, alleviation, ebb, lull, relaxation, respite

remit *verb* 1 SEND, dispatch, forward, mail, post, transmit

2 CANCEL, halt, repeal, rescind, stop

3 POSTPONE, defer, delay, put off, shelve, suspend

▶ *noun* 4 INSTRUCTIONS, brief, guidelines, orders

remittance *noun* PAYMENT, allowance, fee

remnant *noun* REMAINDER, end, fragment, leftovers, remains, residue, rest, trace, vestige

remonstrate *verb* ARGUE, dispute, dissent, object, protest, take issue

remorse *noun* REGRET, anguish, compunction, contrition, grief, guilt, penitence, repentance, shame, sorrow

remorseful *adjective* REGRETFUL, apologetic, ashamed, conscience-stricken, contrite, guilty, penitent, repentant, sorry

remorseless *adjective* 1 PITILESS, callous, cruel, inhumane, merciless, ruthless
2 RELENTLESS, inexorable

remote *adjective* 1 DISTANT, far, inaccessible, in the middle of nowhere, isolated, out-of-the-way, secluded
2 ALOOF, abstracted, cold, detached, distant, reserved, standoffish, uncommunicative, withdrawn
3 SLIGHT, doubtful, dubious, faint, outside, slender, slim, small, unlikely

removal *noun* 1 TAKING AWAY or OFF or OUT, dislodgment, ejection, elimination, eradication, extraction, uprooting, withdrawal
2 DISMISSAL, expulsion
3 MOVE, departure, flitting (*Scot. & Northern English dialect*), relocation, transfer

remove *verb* 1 TAKE AWAY or OFF or OUT, abolish, delete, detach, displace, eject, eliminate, erase, excise, extract, get rid of, wipe from the face of the earth, withdraw
2 DISMISS, depose, dethrone, discharge, expel, oust, throw out
3 MOVE, depart, flit (*Scot. & Northern English dialect*), relocate

remunerate *verb* PAY, compensate, recompense, reimburse, repay, requite, reward

remuneration *noun* PAYMENT, earnings, fee, income, pay, return, reward, salary, stipend, wages

remunerative *adjective* PROFITABLE, economic, lucrative, moneymaking, paying, rewarding, worthwhile

renaissance, renascence *noun* REBIRTH, reappearance, reawakening, renewal, restoration, resurgence, revival

rend *verb* TEAR, rip, rupture, separate, wrench

render *verb* 1 MAKE, cause to become, leave
2 PROVIDE, furnish, give, hand out, pay, present, submit, supply, tender
3 PORTRAY, act, depict, do, give, perform, play, represent

rendezvous *noun* 1 APPOINTMENT, assignation, date, engagement, meeting, tryst
2 MEETING PLACE, gathering point, venue
▶ *verb* 3 MEET, assemble, come together, gather, join up

rendition *noun* 1 PERFORMANCE, arrangement, interpretation, portrayal, presentation, reading, rendering, version
2 TRANSLATION, interpretation, reading, transcription, version

renegade *noun* 1 DESERTER, apostate, defector, traitor, turncoat
▶ *adjective* 2 REBELLIOUS, apostate, disloyal, traitorous, unfaithful

renege *verb* BREAK ONE'S WORD, back out, break a promise, default, go back

renew *verb* 1 RECOMMENCE, continue, extend, reaffirm, recreate, reopen, repeat, resume
2 RESTORE, mend, modernize, overhaul, refit, refurbish, renovate, repair

3 REPLACE, refresh, replenish, restock

renounce verb GIVE UP, abjure, deny, disown, forsake, forswear, quit, recant, relinquish, waive

renovate verb RESTORE, do up (*informal*), modernize, overhaul, recondition, refit, refurbish, renew, repair

renown noun FAME, distinction, eminence, note, reputation, repute

renowned adjective FAMOUS, celebrated, distinguished, eminent, esteemed, notable, noted, well-known

rent¹ verb 1 HIRE, charter, lease, let
▶ noun 2 HIRE, fee, lease, payment, rental

rent² noun TEAR, gash, hole, opening, rip, slash, slit, split

renunciation noun GIVING UP, abandonment, abdication, abjuration, denial, disavowal, forswearing, rejection, relinquishment, repudiation

reorganize verb REARRANGE, reshuffle, restructure

repair¹ verb 1 MEND, fix, heal, patch, patch up, renovate, restore
▶ noun 2 MEND, darn, overhaul, patch, restoration
3 CONDITION, form, shape (*informal*), state

reparation noun COMPENSATION, atonement, damages, recompense, restitution, satisfaction

repartee noun WIT, badinage, banter, riposte, wittiness, wordplay

repast noun MEAL, food

repay verb 1 PAY BACK, compensate, recompense, refund, reimburse, requite, return, square
2 GET EVEN WITH (*informal*), avenge,

get one's own back on (*informal*), hit back, reciprocate, retaliate, revenge

repeal verb 1 ABOLISH, annul, cancel, invalidate, nullify, recall, reverse, revoke
▶ noun 2 ABOLITION, annulment, cancellation, invalidation, rescindment

repeat verb 1 REITERATE, echo, replay, reproduce, rerun, reshow, restate, retell
▶ noun 2 REPETITION, echo, reiteration, replay, rerun, reshowing

repeatedly adverb OVER AND OVER, frequently, many times, often

repel verb 1 DISGUST, gross out (*slang*), nauseate, offend, revolt, sicken
2 DRIVE OFF, fight, hold off, parry, rebuff, repulse, resist, ward off

repellent adjective 1 DISGUSTING, abhorrent, hateful, horrid, loathsome, nauseating, noxious, offensive, repugnant, repulsive, revolting, scuzzy (*slang*), sickening
2 PROOF, impermeable, repelling, resistant

repent verb REGRET, be sorry, feel remorse, rue

repentance noun REGRET, compunction, contrition, grief, guilt, penitence, remorse

repentant adjective REGRETFUL, contrite, penitent, remorseful, rueful, sorry

repercussion noun
▷▷ **repercussions** CONSEQUENCES, backlash, result, sequel, side effects

repertoire noun RANGE, collection, list, repertory, stock, store, supply

repetition noun REPEATING, echo, recurrence, reiteration, renewal, replication, restatement, tautology

repetitious adjective LONG-WINDED, prolix, tautological, tedious, verbose, wordy

repetitive adjective MONOTONOUS, boring, dull, mechanical, recurrent, tedious, unchanging, unvaried

rephrase verb REWORD, paraphrase, put differently

repine verb COMPLAIN, fret, grumble, moan

replace verb TAKE THE PLACE OF, follow, oust, substitute, succeed, supersede, supplant, take over from

replacement noun SUCCESSOR, double, proxy, stand-in, substitute, surrogate, understudy

replenish verb REFILL, fill, provide, reload, replace, restore, top up

replete adjective FULL, crammed, filled, full up, glutted, gorged, stuffed

replica noun DUPLICATE, carbon copy (informal), copy, facsimile, imitation, model, reproduction

replicate verb COPY, duplicate, mimic, recreate, reduplicate, reproduce

reply verb 1 ANSWER, counter, reciprocate, rejoin, respond, retaliate, retort
▶ noun 2 ANSWER, counter, counterattack, reaction, rejoinder, response, retaliation, retort, riposte

report verb 1 COMMUNICATE, broadcast, cover, describe, detail, inform of, narrate, pass on, recount, relate, state, tell
2 PRESENT ONESELF, appear, arrive, come, turn up
▶ noun 3 ACCOUNT, communication, description,

narrative, news, record, statement, word
4 ARTICLE, piece, story, write-up
5 RUMOR, buzz, gossip, hearsay, talk
6 BANG, blast, boom, crack, detonation, discharge, explosion, noise, sound

reporter noun JOURNALIST, correspondent, hack (derogatory), journo (slang), pressman, writer

repose¹ noun 1 PEACE, ease, quietness, relaxation, respite, rest, stillness, tranquillity
2 COMPOSURE, calmness, poise, self-possession
3 SLEEP, slumber
▶ verb 4 REST, lie, lie down, recline, rest upon

repository noun STORE, depository, storehouse, treasury, vault

reprehensible adjective BLAMEWORTHY, bad, culpable, disgraceful, shameful, unworthy

represent verb 1 STAND FOR, act for, betoken, mean, serve as, speak for, symbolize
2 SYMBOLIZE, embody, epitomize, exemplify, personify, typify
3 PORTRAY, denote, depict, describe, illustrate, outline, picture, show

representation noun PORTRAYAL, account, depiction, description, illustration, image, likeness, model, picture, portrait

representative noun 1 DELEGATE, agent, deputy, member, proxy, spokesman or spokeswoman
2 SALESMAN, agent, commercial traveler, rep
▶ adjective 3 TYPICAL, archetypal, characteristic, exemplary, symbolic

repress verb 1 INHIBIT, bottle up,

check, control, curb, hold back, restrain, stifle, suppress
2 SUBDUE, quell, subjugate
repression noun SUBJUGATION, constraint, control, despotism, domination, restraint, suppression, tyranny
repressive adjective OPPRESSIVE, absolute, authoritarian, despotic, dictatorial, tyrannical
reprieve verb 1 GRANT A STAY OF EXECUTION TO, let off the hook (slang), pardon
2 RELIEVE, abate, allay, alleviate, mitigate, palliate
▶ noun 3 STAY OF EXECUTION, amnesty, deferment, pardon, postponement, remission
4 RELIEF, alleviation, mitigation, palliation, respite
reprimand verb 1 BLAME, censure, dress down (informal), haul over the coals (informal), rap over the knuckles, rebuke, scold, tear (someone) off a strip (Brit. informal)
▶ noun 2 BLAME, censure, dressing-down (informal), rebuke, reproach, reproof, talking-to (informal)
reprisal noun RETALIATION, retribution, revenge, vengeance
reproach noun 1 BLAME, censure, condemnation, disapproval, opprobrium, rebuke
▶ verb 2 BLAME, censure, condemn, criticize, lambast(e), read the riot act, rebuke, reprimand, scold, upbraid
reproachful adjective CRITICAL, censorious, condemnatory, disapproving, fault-finding, reproving
reprobate noun 1 SCOUNDREL, bad egg (old-fashioned informal), blackguard, degenerate, evildoer, miscreant, ne'er-do-well, profligate, rake, rascal, villain

▶ adjective 2 DEPRAVED, abandoned, bad, base, corrupt, degenerate, dissolute, immoral, sinful, wicked
reproduce verb 1 COPY, duplicate, echo, imitate, match, mirror, recreate, repeat, replicate
2 BREED, multiply, procreate, propagate, spawn
reproduction noun 1 BREEDING, generation, increase, multiplication
2 COPY, duplicate, facsimile, imitation, picture, print, replica
reproof noun REBUKE, blame, censure, condemnation, criticism, reprimand, scolding
reprove verb REBUKE, berate, blame, censure, condemn, read the riot act, reprimand, scold, tear into (informal), tear (someone) off a strip (Brit. informal), tell off (informal)
repudiate verb REJECT, deny, disavow, disclaim, disown, renounce
repugnance noun DISTASTE, abhorrence, aversion, disgust, dislike, hatred, loathing
repugnant adjective DISTASTEFUL, abhorrent, disgusting, loathsome, nauseating, offensive, repellent, revolting, sickening, vile
repulse verb 1 DRIVE BACK, beat off, fight off, rebuff, repel, ward off
2 REBUFF, refuse, reject, snub, spurn, turn down
repulsion noun DISTASTE, abhorrence, aversion, detestation, disgust, hatred, loathing, repugnance, revulsion
repulsive adjective DISGUSTING, abhorrent, foul, loathsome, nauseating, repellent, revolting, scuzzy (slang), sickening, vile
reputable adjective RESPECTABLE,

creditable, excellent, good, honorable, reliable, trustworthy, well-thought-of, worthy

reputation noun ESTIMATION, character, esteem, name, renown, repute, standing, stature

repute noun REPUTATION, celebrity, distinction, eminence, fame, name, renown, standing, stature

reputed adjective SUPPOSED, alleged, believed, considered, deemed, estimated, held, reckoned, regarded

reputedly adverb SUPPOSEDLY, allegedly, apparently, seemingly

request verb 1 ASK (FOR), appeal for, demand, desire, entreat, invite, seek, solicit
▶ noun 2 ASKING, appeal, call, demand, desire, entreaty, suit

require verb 1 NEED, crave, desire, lack, miss, want, wish
2 DEMAND, ask, bid, call upon, command, compel, exact, insist upon, oblige, order

required adjective NEEDED, called for, essential, necessary, obligatory, requisite

requirement noun NECESSITY, demand, essential, lack, must, need, prerequisite, stipulation, want

requisite adjective 1 NECESSARY, called for, essential, indispensable, needed, needful, obligatory, required
▶ noun 2 NECESSITY, condition, essential, must, need, prerequisite, requirement

requisition verb 1 DEMAND, call for, request
▶ noun 2 DEMAND, call, request, summons

requital noun RETURN, repayment

requite verb RETURN, get even, give in return, pay (someone) back in his or her own coin, reciprocate, repay, respond, retaliate

rescind verb ANNUL, cancel, countermand, declare null and void, invalidate, repeal, set aside

rescue verb 1 SAVE, deliver, get out, liberate, recover, redeem, release, salvage
▶ noun 2 LIBERATION, deliverance, recovery, redemption, release, salvage, salvation, saving

research noun 1 INVESTIGATION, analysis, examination, exploration, probe, study
▶ verb 2 INVESTIGATE, analyze, examine, explore, probe, study

resemblance noun SIMILARITY, correspondence, kinship, likeness, parallel, sameness, similitude

resemble verb BE LIKE, bear a resemblance to, be similar to, look like, mirror, parallel

resent verb BE BITTER ABOUT, begrudge, grudge, object to, take exception to, take offense at

resentful adjective BITTER, angry, embittered, grudging, indignant, miffed (informal), offended, piqued, ticked off (informal)

resentment noun BITTERNESS, animosity, bad blood, grudge, ill feeling, ill will, indignation, pique, rancor, umbrage

reservation noun 1 DOUBT, hesitancy, scruple
2 CONDITION, proviso, qualification, rider, stipulation
3 RESERVE, preserve, sanctuary, territory

reserve verb 1 KEEP, hoard, hold, put by, retain, save, set aside, stockpile, store
2 BOOK, engage, prearrange, secure

▶ *noun* 3 STORE, cache, fund, hoard, reservoir, savings, stock, supply
4 RESERVATION, park, preserve, sanctuary, tract
5 SHYNESS, constraint, reservation, restraint, reticence, secretiveness, silence, taciturnity
▶ *adjective* 6 SUBSTITUTE, auxiliary, extra, fall-back, secondary, spare

reserved *adjective*
1 UNCOMMUNICATIVE, restrained, reticent, retiring, secretive, shy, silent, standoffish, taciturn, undemonstrative
2 SET ASIDE, booked, engaged, held, kept, restricted, retained, spoken for, taken

reservoir *noun* 1 LAKE, basin, pond, tank
2 STORE, pool, reserves, source, stock, supply

reshuffle *noun* 1 REORGANIZATION, change, rearrangement, redistribution, regrouping, restructuring, revision
▶ *verb* 2 REORGANIZE, change around, rearrange, redistribute, regroup, restructure, revise

reside *verb* LIVE, abide, dwell, inhabit, lodge, stay

residence *noun* HOME, abode, domicile, dwelling, flat, habitation, house, lodging, place

resident *noun* INHABITANT, citizen, local, lodger, occupant, occupier, tenant

residual *adjective* REMAINING, leftover, unconsumed, unused, vestigial

residue *noun* REMAINDER, dregs, excess, extra, leftovers, remains, remnant, rest, surplus

resign *verb* 1 QUIT, abdicate, give in one's notice, leave, step down (*informal*), vacate

2 GIVE UP, abandon, forgo, forsake, relinquish, renounce, surrender, yield
3 ▷▷ **resign oneself** ACCEPT, acquiesce, give in, submit, succumb, yield

resignation *noun* 1 LEAVING, abandonment, abdication, departure
2 ENDURANCE, acceptance, acquiescence, compliance, nonresistance, passivity, patience, submission, sufferance

resigned *adjective* STOICAL, compliant, long-suffering, patient, subdued, unresisting

resilient *adjective* 1 TOUGH, buoyant, hardy, irrepressible, strong
2 FLEXIBLE, elastic, plastic, pliable, rubbery, springy, supple

resist *verb* 1 OPPOSE, battle, combat, defy, hinder, stand up to
2 REFRAIN FROM, abstain from, avoid, forbear, forgo, keep from
3 WITHSTAND, be proof against

resistance *noun* FIGHTING, battle, defiance, fight, hindrance, impediment, obstruction, opposition, struggle

resistant *adjective* 1 IMPERVIOUS, hard, proof against, strong, tough, unaffected by
2 OPPOSED, antagonistic, hostile, intractable, intransigent, unwilling

resolute *adjective* DETERMINED, dogged, firm, fixed, immovable, inflexible, set, steadfast, strong-willed, tenacious, unshakable, unwavering

resolution *noun*
1 DETERMINATION, doggedness, firmness, perseverance, purpose, resoluteness, resolve, steadfastness, tenacity, willpower

2 DECISION, aim, declaration, determination, intent, intention, purpose, resolve

resolve *verb* **1** DECIDE, agree, conclude, determine, fix, intend, purpose
2 BREAK DOWN, analyze, reduce, separate
3 WORK OUT, answer, clear up, crack, fathom
▶ *noun* **4** DETERMINATION, firmness, resoluteness, resolution, steadfastness, willpower
5 DECISION, intention, objective, purpose, resolution

resonant *adjective* ECHOING, booming, resounding, reverberating, ringing, sonorous

resort *verb* **1** ▷▷ **resort to** USE, employ, fall back on, have recourse to, turn to, utilize
▶ *noun* **2** HOLIDAY CENTER, haunt, retreat, spot, tourist center
3 RECOURSE, reference

resound *verb* ECHO, re-echo, resonate, reverberate, ring

resounding *adjective* ECHOING, booming, full, powerful, resonant, reverberating, ringing, sonorous

resource *noun* **1** INGENUITY, ability, capability, cleverness, initiative, inventiveness
2 MEANS, course, device, expedient, resort

resourceful *adjective* INGENIOUS, able, bright, capable, clever, creative, inventive

resources *plural noun* RESERVES, assets, capital, funds, holdings, money, riches, supplies, wealth

respect *noun* **1** REGARD, admiration, consideration, deference, esteem, estimation, honor, recognition

2 POINT, aspect, characteristic, detail, feature, matter, particular, sense, way
3 RELATION, bearing, connection, reference, regard
▶ *verb* **4** THINK HIGHLY OF, admire, defer to, esteem, have a good *or* high opinion of, honor, look up to, value
5 SHOW CONSIDERATION FOR, abide by, adhere to, comply with, follow, heed, honor, obey, observe

respectable *adjective*
1 HONORABLE, decent, estimable, good, honest, reputable, upright, worthy
2 REASONABLE, ample, appreciable, considerable, decent, fair, sizable *or* sizeable, substantial

respectful *adjective* POLITE, civil, courteous, deferential, mannerly, reverent, well-mannered

respective *adjective* SPECIFIC, individual, own, particular, relevant

respite *noun* PAUSE, break, cessation, halt, interval, lull, recess, relief, rest

resplendent *adjective* BRILLIANT, bright, dazzling, glorious, radiant, shining, splendid

respond *verb* ANSWER, counter, react, reciprocate, rejoin, reply, retort, return

response *noun* ANSWER, counterattack, feedback, reaction, rejoinder, reply, retort, return

responsibility *noun* **1** AUTHORITY, importance, power
2 FAULT, blame, culpability, guilt
3 DUTY, care, charge, liability, obligation, onus
4 LEVEL-HEADEDNESS, conscientiousness, dependability, rationality, sensibleness,

trustworthiness
responsible adjective 1 IN CHARGE, in authority, in control
2 TO BLAME, at fault, culpable, guilty
3 ACCOUNTABLE, answerable, liable
4 SENSIBLE, dependable, level-headed, rational, reliable, trustworthy
responsive adjective SENSITIVE, alive, impressionable, open, reactive, receptive, susceptible
rest¹ noun 1 REPOSE, calm, inactivity, leisure, relaxation, relief, stillness, tranquillity
2 PAUSE, break, cessation, halt, interlude, intermission, interval, lull, respite, stop
3 SUPPORT, base, holder, prop, stand
▶ verb 4 RELAX, be at ease, de-stress, put one's feet up, sit down, take it easy
5 BE SUPPORTED, lean, lie, prop, recline, repose, sit
rest² noun REMAINDER, balance, excess, others, remains, remnants, residue, surplus
restaurant noun BISTRO, café, cafeteria, diner (chiefly U.S. & Canad.), eatery, tearoom
restful adjective RELAXING, calm, calming, peaceful, quiet, relaxed, serene, soothing, tranquil
restitution noun COMPENSATION, amends, recompense, reparation, requital
restive adjective RESTLESS, edgy, fidgety, impatient, jumpy, nervous, on edge, wired (slang)
restless adjective 1 MOVING, nomadic, roving, transient, unsettled, unstable, wandering
2 UNSETTLED, antsy (slang), edgy, fidgeting, fidgety, jumpy, nervous, on edge, restive, wired (slang)

restlessness noun 1 MOVEMENT, activity, bustle, unrest, unsettledness
2 RESTIVENESS, edginess, jitters (informal), jumpiness, nervousness
restoration noun 1 REPAIR, reconstruction, renewal, renovation, revitalization, revival
2 REINSTATEMENT, re-establishment, replacement, restitution, return
restore verb 1 REPAIR, fix, mend, rebuild, recondition, reconstruct, refurbish, renew, renovate
2 REVIVE, build up, refresh, revitalize, strengthen
3 RETURN, bring back, give back, hand back, recover, reinstate, replace, send back
4 REINSTATE, reintroduce
restrain verb HOLD BACK, check, constrain, contain, control, curb, curtail, hamper, hinder, inhibit, restrict
restrained adjective CONTROLLED, calm, mild, moderate, self-controlled, undemonstrative
restraint noun 1 SELF-CONTROL, control, inhibition, moderation, self-discipline, self-possession, self-restraint
2 LIMITATION, ban, check, curb, embargo, interdict, limit, rein
restrict verb LIMIT, bound, confine, contain, hamper, handicap, inhibit, regulate, restrain
restriction noun LIMITATION, confinement, control, curb, handicap, inhibition, regulation, restraint, rule
result noun 1 CONSEQUENCE, effect, end, end result, outcome, product, sequel, upshot
▶ verb 2 HAPPEN, appear, arise, derive, develop, ensue, follow,

issue, spring

3 ▷▷ **result in** END IN, culminate in, finish with

resume verb BEGIN AGAIN, carry on, continue, go on, proceed, reopen, restart

résumé noun SUMMARY, précis, recapitulation, rundown, synopsis

resumption noun CONTINUATION, carrying on, re-establishment, renewal, reopening, restart, resurgence

resurgence noun REVIVAL, rebirth, re-emergence, renaissance, resumption, resurrection, return

resurrect verb REVIVE, bring back, reintroduce, renew

resurrection noun REVIVAL, reappearance, rebirth, renaissance, renewal, restoration, resurgence, return

resuscitate verb REVIVE, bring round, resurrect, revitalize, save

retain verb 1 KEEP, hold, hold back, maintain, preserve, reserve, save
2 HIRE, commission, employ, engage, pay, reserve

retainer noun 1 FEE, advance, deposit
2 SERVANT, attendant, domestic

retaliate verb PAY (SOMEONE) BACK, get even with (informal), get one's own back (informal), hit back, reciprocate, strike back, take revenge

retaliation noun REVENGE, an eye for an eye, counterblow, reciprocation, repayment, reprisal, requital, vengeance

retard verb SLOW DOWN, arrest, check, delay, handicap, hinder, hold back or up, impede, set back

retch verb GAG, barf (slang), be sick, heave, puke (slang), regurgitate, spew, throw up (informal), vomit

reticence noun SILENCE, quietness, reserve, taciturnity

reticent adjective UNCOMMUNICATIVE, close-lipped, quiet, reserved, silent, taciturn, tight-lipped, unforthcoming

retinue noun ATTENDANTS, aides, entourage, escort, followers, servants

retire verb 1 STOP WORKING, give up work
2 WITHDRAW, depart, exit, go away, leave
3 GO TO BED, hit the hay (slang), hit the sack (slang), turn in (informal)

retirement noun WITHDRAWAL, privacy, retreat, seclusion, solitude

retiring adjective SHY, bashful, quiet, reserved, self-effacing, timid, unassertive, unassuming

retort verb 1 REPLY, answer, come back with, counter, respond, return, riposte
▶ noun 2 REPLY, answer, comeback (informal), rejoinder, response, riposte

retract verb 1 WITHDRAW, deny, disavow, disclaim, eat one's words, recant, renege, renounce, revoke, take back
2 DRAW IN, pull back, pull in, sheathe

retreat verb 1 WITHDRAW, back away, back off, depart, draw back, fall back, go back, leave, pull back
▶ noun 2 WITHDRAWAL, departure, evacuation, flight, retirement
3 REFUGE, haven, hideaway, sanctuary, seclusion, shelter

retrench verb CUT BACK, economize, make economies, save, tighten one's belt

retrenchment noun CUTBACK, cost-cutting, cut, economy, tightening one's belt

retribution noun PUNISHMENT, justice, Nemesis, reckoning, reprisal, retaliation, revenge, vengeance

retrieve verb GET BACK, recapture, recoup, recover, redeem, regain, restore, save, win back

retrograde adjective DECLINING, backward, degenerative, deteriorating, downward, regressive, retrogressive, worsening

retrogress verb DECLINE, backslide, deteriorate, go back, go downhill (informal), regress, relapse, worsen

retrospect noun HINDSIGHT, re-examination, review

return verb 1 COME BACK, go back, reappear, rebound, recur, retreat, revert, turn back
2 PUT BACK, re-establish, reinstate, replace, restore
3 GIVE BACK, pay back, recompense, refund, reimburse, repay
4 REPLY, answer, respond, retort
5 ELECT, choose, vote in
▶ noun 6 RESTORATION, re-establishment, reinstatement
7 REAPPEARANCE, recurrence
8 RETREAT, rebound, recoil
9 PROFIT, gain, income, interest, proceeds, revenue, takings, yield
10 REPORT, account, form, list, statement, summary
11 REPLY, answer, comeback (informal), rejoinder, response, retort

revamp verb RENOVATE, do up (informal), overhaul, recondition, refurbish, restore

reveal verb 1 MAKE KNOWN, announce, disclose, divulge, give away, impart, let out, let slip, make public, proclaim, tell
2 SHOW, display, exhibit, manifest, uncover, unearth, unmask, unveil

revel verb 1 CELEBRATE, carouse, live it up (informal), make merry
2 ▷▷ **revel in** ENJOY, delight in, indulge in, lap up, luxuriate in, relish, take pleasure in, thrive on
▶ noun 3 (often plural) MERRYMAKING, carousal, celebration, festivity, party, spree

revelation noun DISCLOSURE, exhibition, exposé, exposure, news, proclamation, publication, uncovering, unearthing, unveiling

reveller noun CAROUSER, merrymaker, partygoer

revelry noun FESTIVITY, carousal, celebration, fun, jollity, merrymaking, party, spree

revenge noun 1 RETALIATION, an eye for an eye, reprisal, retribution, vengeance
▶ verb 2 AVENGE, get even, get one's own back for (informal), hit back, repay, retaliate, take revenge for

revenue noun INCOME, gain, proceeds, profits, receipts, returns, takings, yield

reverberate verb ECHO, re-echo, resound, ring, vibrate

revere verb BE IN AWE OF, exalt, honor, look up to, respect, reverence, venerate, worship

reverence noun AWE, admiration, high esteem, honor, respect, veneration, worship

reverent adjective RESPECTFUL, awed, deferential, humble, reverential

reverie noun DAYDREAM, abstraction, brown study, woolgathering

reverse verb 1 TURN ROUND, invert, transpose, turn back, turn over,

turn upside down, upend
2 CHANGE, annul, cancel, countermand, invalidate, overrule, overthrow, overturn, quash, repeal, rescind, revoke, undo
3 GO BACKWARDS, back, back up, move backwards, retreat
▶ *noun* **4** OPPOSITE, contrary, converse, inverse
5 BACK, other side, rear, underside, wrong side
6 MISFORTUNE, adversity, affliction, blow, disappointment, failure, hardship, misadventure, mishap, reversal, setback
▶ *adjective* **7** OPPOSITE, contrary, converse

revert *verb* RETURN, come back, go back, resume

review *noun* **1** CRITIQUE, commentary, criticism, evaluation, judgment, notice
2 MAGAZINE, journal, periodical
3 SURVEY, analysis, examination, scrutiny, study
4 (*military*) INSPECTION, march past, parade
▶ *verb* **5** ASSESS, criticize, evaluate, judge, study
6 RECONSIDER, reassess, re-evaluate, re-examine, rethink, revise, think over
7 LOOK BACK ON, recall, recollect, reflect on, remember
8 INSPECT, examine
9 STUDY, cram (*informal*), revise (*chiefly Brit.*)

reviewer *noun* CRITIC, commentator, judge

revile *verb* MALIGN, abuse, bad-mouth (*slang*), denigrate, knock (*informal*), reproach, run down, slag (off) (*slang*), vilify

revise *verb* **1** CHANGE, alter, amend, correct, edit, emend, redo, review,

rework, update
2 STUDY, go over, run through, swot up (*Brit. informal*)

revision *noun* **1** CHANGE, amendment, correction, emendation, updating
2 STUDYING, homework, swotting (*Brit. informal*)

revival *noun* RENEWAL, reawakening, rebirth, renaissance, resurgence, resurrection, revitalization

revive *verb* REVITALIZE, awaken, bring round, come round, invigorate, reanimate, recover, refresh, rekindle, renew, restore

revoke *verb* CANCEL, annul, countermand, disclaim, invalidate, negate, nullify, obviate, quash, repeal, rescind, retract, reverse, set aside, withdraw

revolt *noun* **1** UPRISING, insurgency, insurrection, mutiny, rebellion, revolution, rising
▶ *verb* **2** REBEL, mutiny, resist, rise
3 DISGUST, gross out (*slang*), make one's flesh creep, nauseate, repel, repulse, sicken, turn one's stomach

revolting *adjective* DISGUSTING, foul, horrible, horrid, nauseating, repellent, repugnant, repulsive, scuzzy (*slang*), sickening, yucky or yukky (*slang*)

revolution *noun* **1** REVOLT, coup, insurgency, mutiny, rebellion, rising, uprising
2 TRANSFORMATION, innovation, reformation, sea change, shift, upheaval
3 ROTATION, circle, circuit, cycle, lap, orbit, spin, turn

revolutionary *adjective* **1** REBEL, extremist, insurgent, radical, subversive

2 NEW, different, drastic, groundbreaking, innovative, novel, progressive, radical
▶ noun 3 REBEL, insurgent, revolutionist

revolutionize verb TRANSFORM, modernize, reform

revolve verb ROTATE, circle, go round, orbit, spin, turn, twist, wheel, whirl

revulsion noun DISGUST, abhorrence, detestation, loathing, repugnance, repulsion

reward noun 1 PAYMENT, bonus, bounty, premium, prize, recompense, repayment, return, wages
2 PUNISHMENT, comeuppance (informal), just deserts, retribution
▶ verb 3 PAY, compensate, recompense, remunerate, repay

rewarding adjective WORTHWHILE, beneficial, enriching, fruitful, fulfilling, productive, profitable, satisfying, valuable

rhapsodize verb ENTHUSE, go into ecstasies, gush, rave (informal)

rhetoric noun 1 ORATORY, eloquence
2 HYPERBOLE, bombast, grandiloquence, magniloquence, verbosity, wordiness

rhetorical adjective ORATORICAL, bombastic, declamatory, grandiloquent, high-flown, magniloquent, verbose

rhyme noun 1 POETRY, ode, poem, song, verse
▶ verb 2 SOUND LIKE, harmonize

rhythm noun BEAT, accent, cadence, lilt, meter, pulse, swing, tempo, time

rhythmic, rhythmical adjective CADENCED, lilting, metrical, musical, periodic, pulsating, throbbing

ribald adjective RUDE, bawdy, blue, broad, coarse, earthy, naughty, near the knuckle (informal), obscene, racy, smutty, vulgar

rich adjective 1 WEALTHY, affluent, loaded (slang), moneyed, prosperous, well-heeled (informal), well-off, well-to-do
2 WELL-STOCKED, full, productive, well-supplied
3 ABUNDANT, abounding, ample, copious, fertile, fruitful, lush, luxurious, plentiful, productive, prolific
4 FULL-BODIED, creamy, fatty, luscious, succulent, sweet, tasty

riches plural noun WEALTH, affluence, assets, fortune, plenty, resources, substance, treasure

richly adverb 1 ELABORATELY, elegantly, expensively, exquisitely, gorgeously, lavishly, luxuriously, opulently, splendidly, sumptuously
2 FULLY, amply, appropriately, properly, suitably, thoroughly, well

rickety adjective SHAKY, insecure, precarious, ramshackle, tottering, unsound, unsteady, wobbly

rid verb 1 FREE, clear, deliver, disburden, disencumber, make free, purge, relieve, unburden
2 ▷▷ **get rid of** DISPOSE OF, dump, eject, eliminate, expel, remove, throw away or out

riddle noun PUZZLE, conundrum, enigma, mystery, poser, problem

riddled adjective FILLED, damaged, infested, permeated, pervaded, spoilt

ride verb 1 CONTROL, handle, manage
2 TRAVEL, be carried, go, move
▶ noun 3 TRIP, drive, jaunt, journey, lift, outing

ridicule noun 1 MOCKERY, chaff, derision, gibe, jeer, laughter, raillery, scorn
▶ verb 2 LAUGH AT, chaff, deride, jeer, make fun of, mock, poke fun at, sneer

ridiculous adjective LAUGHABLE, absurd, comical, farcical, funny, ludicrous, risible, silly, stupid

rife adjective WIDESPREAD, common, frequent, general, prevalent, rampant, ubiquitous, universal

riffraff noun RABBLE, dregs of society (slang), hoi polloi, ragtag and bobtail, scum of the earth (slang)

rifle verb RANSACK, burgle, go through, loot, pillage, plunder, rob, sack, strip

rift noun 1 BREACH, disagreement, division, falling out (informal), quarrel, separation, split
2 SPLIT, break, cleft, crack, crevice, fault, fissure, flaw, gap, opening

rig verb 1 FIX (informal), arrange, engineer, gerrymander, manipulate, tamper with
2 EQUIP, fit out, furnish, kit out, outfit, supply
▶ noun 3 APPARATUS, equipment, fittings, fixtures, gear, tackle

right adjective 1 JUST, equitable, ethical, fair, good, honest, lawful, moral, proper
2 CORRECT, accurate, exact, factual, genuine, precise, true, valid
3 PROPER, appropriate, becoming, desirable, done, fit, fitting, seemly, suitable
▶ adverb 4 CORRECTLY, accurately, exactly, genuinely, precisely, truly
5 PROPERLY, appropriately, aptly, fittingly, suitably
6 STRAIGHT, directly, promptly, quickly, straightaway
7 EXACTLY, precisely, squarely
▶ noun 8 CLAIM, authority, business, due, freedom, liberty, license, permission, power, prerogative, privilege
▶ verb 9 RECTIFY, correct, fix, put right, redress, settle, sort out, straighten

right away adverb IMMEDIATELY, at once, directly, forthwith, instantly, now, pronto (informal), straightaway

righteous adjective VIRTUOUS, ethical, fair, good, honest, honorable, just, moral, pure, upright

righteousness noun VIRTUE, goodness, honesty, honor, integrity, justice, morality, probity, purity, rectitude, uprightness

rightful adjective LAWFUL, due, just, legal, legitimate, proper, real, true, valid

rigid adjective 1 STRICT, exact, fixed, inflexible, rigorous, set, stringent, unbending, uncompromising
2 STIFF, inflexible, unyielding

rigmarole noun PROCEDURE, bother, carry-on (informal, chiefly Brit.), fuss, hassle (informal), nonsense, palaver, pantomime (informal), performance (informal)

rigor noun 1 STRICTNESS, harshness, inflexibility, rigidity, sternness, stringency
2 HARDSHIP, ordeal, privation, suffering, trial

rigorous adjective STRICT, demanding, exacting, hard, harsh, inflexible, severe, stern, stringent, tough

rig-out noun OUTFIT, costume, dress, garb, gear (informal), get-up (informal), togs

rig out *verb* 1 DRESS, array, attire, clothe, costume, kit out
2 EQUIP, fit, furnish, kit out, outfit

rig up *verb* SET UP, arrange, assemble, build, construct, erect, fix up, improvise, put together, put up

rile *verb* ANGER, aggravate (*informal*), annoy, get *or* put one's back up, irk, irritate

rim *noun* EDGE, border, brim, brink, lip, margin, verge

rind *noun* SKIN, crust, husk, outer layer, peel

ring[1] *verb* 1 CHIME, clang, peal, reverberate, sound, toll
2 PHONE, buzz (*informal*), call, telephone
▶ *noun* 3 CHIME, knell, peal
4 CALL, buzz (*informal*), phone call

ring[2] *noun* 1 CIRCLE, band, circuit, halo, hoop, loop, round
2 ARENA, circus, enclosure, rink
3 GANG, association, band, cartel, circle, group, mob, syndicate
▶ *verb* 4 ENCIRCLE, enclose, gird, girdle, surround

rinse *verb* 1 WASH, bathe, clean, cleanse, dip, splash
▶ *noun* 2 WASH, bath, dip, splash

riot *noun* 1 DISTURBANCE, anarchy, confusion, disorder, lawlessness, strife, tumult, turbulence, turmoil, upheaval
2 REVELRY, carousal, festivity, frolic, high jinks, merrymaking
3 PROFUSION, display, extravaganza, show, splash
4 ▷▷ **run riot: a** RAMPAGE, be out of control, go wild **b** GROW PROFUSELY, spread like wildfire
▶ *verb* 5 RAMPAGE, go on the rampage, run riot

riotous *adjective* 1 UNRESTRAINED, boisterous, loud, noisy, uproarious, wild

2 UNRULY, anarchic, disorderly, lawless, rebellious, rowdy, ungovernable, violent

rip *verb* 1 TEAR, burst, claw, cut, gash, lacerate, rend, slash, slit, split
▶ *noun* 2 TEAR, cut, gash, hole, laceration, rent, slash, slit, split

ripe *adjective* 1 MATURE, mellow, ready, ripened, seasoned
2 SUITABLE, auspicious, favorable, ideal, opportune, right, timely

ripen *verb* MATURE, burgeon, develop, grow ripe, season

rip-off *noun* SWINDLE, cheat, con (*informal*), con trick (*informal*), fraud, scam (*slang*), theft

rip off *verb* (*slang*) SWINDLE, cheat, con (*informal*), defraud, fleece, rob, skin (*slang*)

riposte *noun* 1 RETORT, answer, comeback (*informal*), rejoinder, reply, response, sally
▶ *verb* 2 RETORT, answer, come back, reply, respond

rise *verb* 1 GET UP, arise, get to one's feet, stand up
2 GO UP, ascend, climb
3 ADVANCE, get on, progress, prosper
4 GET STEEPER, ascend, go uphill, slope upwards
5 INCREASE, go up, grow, intensify, mount
6 REBEL, mutiny, revolt
7 ORIGINATE, happen, issue, occur, spring
▶ *noun* 8 INCREASE, upsurge, upswing, upturn
9 ADVANCEMENT, climb, progress, promotion
10 UPWARD SLOPE, ascent, elevation, incline
11 PAY INCREASE, increment, raise (*U.S.*)
12 ▷▷ **give rise to** CAUSE, bring

about, effect, produce, result in

risk noun 1 DANGER, chance, gamble, hazard, jeopardy, peril, pitfall, possibility
▶ verb 2 DARE, chance, endanger, gamble, hazard, imperil, jeopardize, venture

risky adjective DANGEROUS, chancy (*informal*), dicey (*informal, chiefly Brit.*), dodgy (*Brit., Austral., & N.Z. informal*), hazardous, perilous, uncertain, unsafe

risqué adjective SUGGESTIVE, bawdy, blue, improper, indelicate, naughty, near the knuckle (*informal*), racy, ribald

rite noun CEREMONY, custom, observance, practice, procedure, ritual

ritual noun 1 CEREMONY, observance, rite
2 CUSTOM, convention, habit, practice, procedure, protocol, routine, tradition
▶ adjective 3 CEREMONIAL, conventional, customary, habitual, routine

rival noun 1 OPPONENT, adversary, competitor, contender, contestant
▶ adjective 2 COMPETING, conflicting, opposing
▶ verb 3 EQUAL, be a match for, come up to, compare with, compete, match

rivalry noun COMPETITION, conflict, contention, contest, opposition

river noun 1 STREAM, brook, burn (*Scot.*), creek, tributary, waterway
2 FLOW, flood, rush, spate, torrent

riveting adjective ENTHRALLING, absorbing, captivating, engrossing, fascinating, gripping, hypnotic, spellbinding

road noun WAY, course, highway, lane, motorway, path, pathway, roadway, route, track

roam verb WANDER, prowl, ramble, range, rove, stray, travel, walk

roar verb 1 CRY, bawl, bay, bellow, howl, shout, yell
2 GUFFAW, hoot, laugh heartily, split one's sides (*informal*)
▶ noun 3 CRY, bellow, howl, outcry, shout, yell
4 GUFFAW, hoot

rob verb STEAL FROM, burgle, cheat, con (*informal*), defraud, deprive, dispossess, do out of (*informal*), hold up, loot, mug (*informal*), pillage, plunder, raid

robber noun THIEF, bandit, brigand, burglar, cheat, con man (*informal*), fraud, looter, mugger (*informal*), plunderer, raider, stealer

robbery noun THEFT, burglary, hold-up, larceny, mugging (*informal*), pillage, plunder, raid, rip-off (*slang*), stealing, stick-up (*slang*), swindle

robe noun 1 GOWN, costume, habit
▶ verb 2 CLOTHE, dress, garb

robot noun MACHINE, android, automaton, mechanical man

robust adjective STRONG, fit, hale, hardy, healthy, muscular, powerful, stout, strapping, sturdy, tough, vigorous

rock¹ noun STONE, boulder

rock² verb 1 SWAY, lurch, pitch, reel, roll, swing, toss
2 SHOCK, astonish, astound, shake, stagger, stun, surprise

rocky³ adjective ROUGH, craggy, rugged, stony

rocky⁴ adjective UNSTABLE, rickety, shaky, unsteady, wobbly

rod noun STICK, bar, baton, cane, pole, shaft, staff, wand

rogue noun SCOUNDREL, blackguard, crook (*informal*), fraud, rascal, scally (*Northwest English* *dialect*), scamp, villain

role *noun* 1 JOB, capacity, duty, function, part, position, post, task
2 PART, character, portrayal, representation

roll *verb* 1 TURN, go round, revolve, rotate, spin, swivel, trundle, twirl, wheel, whirl
2 WIND, bind, enfold, envelop, furl, swathe, wrap
3 FLOW, run, undulate
4 LEVEL, even, flatten, press, smooth
5 TUMBLE, lurch, reel, rock, sway, toss
▶ *noun* 6 TURN, cycle, reel, revolution, rotation, spin, twirl, wheel, whirl
7 REGISTER, census, index, list, record
8 RUMBLE, boom, reverberation, roar, thunder

rollicking *adjective* BOISTEROUS, carefree, devil-may-care, exuberant, hearty, jaunty, lively, playful

roly-poly *adjective* PLUMP, buxom, chubby, fat, podgy, rounded, tubby

romance *noun* 1 LOVE AFFAIR, affair, amour, attachment, liaison, relationship
2 EXCITEMENT, charm, color, fascination, glamour, mystery
3 STORY, fairy tale, fantasy, legend, love story, melodrama, tale

romantic *adjective* 1 LOVING, amorous, fond, passionate, sentimental, tender
2 IDEALISTIC, dreamy, impractical, starry-eyed, unrealistic
3 EXCITING, colorful, fascinating, glamorous, mysterious
▶ *noun* 4 IDEALIST, dreamer, sentimentalist

romp *verb* 1 FROLIC, caper, cavort, frisk, gambol, have fun, sport

2 WIN EASILY, walk it (*informal*), win by a mile (*informal*), win hands down
▶ *noun* 3 FROLIC, caper, lark (*informal*)

room *noun* 1 CHAMBER, apartment, office
2 SPACE, area, capacity, expanse, extent, leeway, margin, range, scope
3 OPPORTUNITY, chance, occasion, scope

roomy *adjective* SPACIOUS, ample, broad, capacious, commodious, extensive, generous, large, sizable or sizeable, wide

root[1] *noun* 1 STEM, rhizome, tuber
2 SOURCE, base, bottom, cause, core, foundation, heart, nucleus, origin, seat, seed
3 ▷▷ **roots** SENSE OF BELONGING, birthplace, cradle, family, heritage, home, origins
▶ *verb* 4 ESTABLISH, anchor, fasten, fix, ground, implant, moor, set, stick

root[2] *verb* DIG, burrow, ferret

rooted *adjective* DEEP-SEATED, confirmed, deep, deeply felt, entrenched, established, firm, fixed, ingrained

root out *verb* GET RID OF, abolish, do away with, eliminate, eradicate, exterminate, extirpate, remove, weed out

rope *noun* 1 CORD, cable, hawser, line, strand
2 ▷▷ **know the ropes** BE EXPERIENCED, be an old hand, be knowledgeable

rope in *verb* PERSUADE, engage, enlist, inveigle, involve, talk into

roster *noun* ROTA, agenda, catalog, list, register, roll, schedule, table

rostrum *noun* STAGE, dais, platform, podium, stand

rosy *adjective* 1 PINK, red
2 GLOWING, blooming, healthy-looking, radiant, ruddy
3 PROMISING, auspicious, bright, cheerful, encouraging, favorable, hopeful, optimistic

rot *verb* 1 DECAY, crumble, decompose, deteriorate, go bad, molder, perish, putrefy, spoil
2 DETERIORATE, decline, waste away
▶ *noun* 3 DECAY, blight, canker, corruption, decomposition, mold, putrefaction
4 (*informal*) NONSENSE, claptrap (*informal*), codswallop (*Brit. slang*), drivel, garbage (*chiefly U.S.*), hogwash, poppycock (*informal*), rubbish, stuff and nonsense, trash, tripe (*informal*), twaddle

rotary *adjective* REVOLVING, rotating, spinning, turning

rotate *verb* 1 REVOLVE, go round, gyrate, pivot, reel, spin, swivel, turn, wheel
2 TAKE TURNS, alternate, switch

rotation *noun* 1 REVOLUTION, orbit, reel, spin, spinning, turn, turning, wheel
2 SEQUENCE, alternation, cycle, succession, switching

rotten *adjective* 1 DECAYING, bad, corrupt, crumbling, decomposing, festering, funky (*slang*), moldy, perished, putrescent, rank, smelly, sour, stinking
2 CORRUPT, crooked (*informal*), dishonest, dishonorable, immoral, perfidious
3 (*informal*) DESPICABLE, base, contemptible, dirty, lousy (*slang*), mean, nasty, scuzzy (*slang*)
4 (*informal*) INFERIOR, crummy (*slang*), duff (*Brit. informal*), inadequate, lousy (*slang*), poor, substandard, unsatisfactory

rotund *adjective* 1 ROUND, globular, rounded, spherical
2 PLUMP, chubby, corpulent, fat, fleshy, podgy, portly, stout, tubby

rough *adjective* 1 UNEVEN, broken, bumpy, craggy, irregular, jagged, rocky, stony
2 UNGRACIOUS, blunt, brusque, coarse, impolite, rude, unceremonious, uncivil, uncouth, unmannerly
3 APPROXIMATE, estimated, general, imprecise, inexact, sketchy, vague
4 STORMY, choppy, squally, turbulent, wild
5 NASTY, cruel, hard, harsh, tough, unfeeling, unpleasant, violent
6 BASIC, crude, imperfect, incomplete, rudimentary, sketchy, unfinished, unpolished, unrefined
7 UNPLEASANT, arduous, hard, tough, uncomfortable
▶ *verb* 8 ▷▷ **rough out** OUTLINE, draft, plan, sketch
▶ *noun* 9 OUTLINE, draft, mock-up, preliminary sketch

rough-and-ready *adjective* MAKESHIFT, crude, improvised, provisional, sketchy, stopgap, unpolished, unrefined

round *adjective* 1 SPHERICAL, circular, curved, cylindrical, globular, rotund, rounded
2 PLUMP, ample, fleshy, full, full-fleshed, rotund
▶ *verb* 3 GO ROUND, bypass, circle, encircle, flank, skirt, turn
▶ *noun* 4 SPHERE, ball, band, circle, disc, globe, orb, ring
5 STAGE, division, lap, level, period, session, turn
6 SERIES, cycle, sequence, session, succession
7 COURSE, beat, circuit, routine,

schedule, series, tour
roundabout *adjective* INDIRECT,
circuitous, devious, discursive,
evasive, oblique, tortuous
round off *verb* COMPLETE, close,
conclude, finish off
roundup *noun* GATHERING,
assembly, collection, herding,
marshalling, muster, rally
round up *verb* GATHER, collect,
drive, group, herd, marshal,
muster, rally
rouse *verb* 1 WAKE UP, awaken, call,
rise, wake
2 EXCITE, agitate, anger, animate,
incite, inflame, move, provoke,
stimulate, stir
rousing *adjective* LIVELY, exciting,
inspiring, moving, spirited,
stimulating, stirring
rout *noun* 1 DEFEAT, beating,
debacle, drubbing, overthrow,
pasting (*slang*), thrashing
▶ *verb* 2 DEFEAT, beat, conquer,
crush, destroy, drub, overthrow,
thrash, trounce, wipe the floor
with (*informal*)
route *noun* WAY, beat, circuit,
course, direction, itinerary,
journey, path, road
routine *noun* 1 PROCEDURE,
custom, method, order, pattern,
practice, program
▶ *adjective* 2 USUAL, customary,
everyday, habitual, normal,
ordinary, standard, typical
3 BORING, dull, humdrum,
predictable, tedious, tiresome
rove *verb* WANDER, drift, ramble,
range, roam, stray, traipse
(*informal*)
row¹ *noun* LINE, bank, column, file,
range, series, string
row² *noun* 1 DISPUTE, brawl,
quarrel, squabble, tiff, trouble
2 DISTURBANCE, commotion,

noise, racket, rumpus, tumult,
uproar
▶ *verb* 3 QUARREL, argue, dispute,
fight, squabble, wrangle
rowdy *adjective* 1 DISORDERLY,
loud, noisy, rough, unruly, wild
▶ *noun* 2 HOOLIGAN, lout, ruffian,
tearaway (*Brit.*), yob or yobbo
(*Brit. slang*)
royal *adjective* 1 REGAL, imperial,
kingly, princely, queenly,
sovereign
2 SPLENDID, grand, impressive,
magnificent, majestic, stately
rub *verb* 1 POLISH, clean, scour,
shine, wipe
2 CHAFE, abrade, fray, grate, scrape
▶ *noun* 3 POLISH, shine, stroke,
wipe
4 MASSAGE, caress, kneading
rubbish *noun* 1 WASTE, garbage
(*chiefly U.S.*), junk (*informal*), litter,
lumber, refuse, scrap, trash
2 NONSENSE, claptrap (*informal*),
codswallop (*Brit. slang*), garbage
(*chiefly U.S.*), hogwash, hot air
(*informal*), rot, tommyrot, trash,
tripe (*informal*), twaddle
rub out *verb* ERASE, cancel,
delete, efface, obliterate, remove,
wipe out
ruckus *noun* (*informal*) UPROAR,
commotion, disturbance, fracas,
fuss, hoopla, trouble
ruddy *adjective* ROSY, blooming,
fresh, glowing, healthy, radiant,
red, reddish, rosy-cheeked
rude *adjective* 1 IMPOLITE,
abusive, cheeky, discourteous,
disrespectful, ill-mannered,
impertinent, impudent, insolent,
insulting, uncivil, unmannerly
2 VULGAR, boorish, brutish, coarse,
graceless, loutish, oafish, rough,
uncivilized, uncouth, uncultured
3 UNPLEASANT, abrupt, harsh,

sharp, startling, sudden
4 ROUGHLY-MADE, artless, crude, inartistic, inelegant, makeshift, primitive, raw, rough, simple

rudimentary adjective BASIC, early, elementary, fundamental, initial, primitive, undeveloped

rudiments plural noun BASICS, beginnings, elements, essentials, foundation, fundamentals

rue verb REGRET, be sorry for, kick oneself for, lament, mourn, repent

rueful adjective REGRETFUL, contrite, mournful, penitent, remorseful, repentant, sorrowful, sorry

ruffian noun THUG, brute, bully, heavy (slang), hoodlum, hooligan, rough (informal), tough

ruffle verb 1 DISARRANGE, dishevel, disorder, mess up, rumple, tousle
2 ANNOY, agitate, fluster, irritate, nettle, peeve (informal), tick off, upset

rugged adjective 1 ROUGH, broken, bumpy, craggy, difficult, irregular, jagged, ragged, rocky, uneven
2 STRONG-FEATURED, rough-hewn, weather-beaten
3 TOUGH, brawny, burly, husky (informal), muscular, robust, strong, sturdy, well-built

ruin verb 1 DESTROY, crush, defeat, demolish, devastate, lay waste, smash, wreck
2 BANKRUPT, impoverish, pauperize
3 SPOIL, blow (slang), botch, damage, make a mess of, mess up, screw up (informal)
▶ noun 4 DESTRUCTION, breakdown, collapse, defeat, devastation, downfall, fall, undoing, wreck
5 DISREPAIR, decay, disintegration, ruination, wreckage

6 BANKRUPTCY, destitution, insolvency

ruinous adjective 1 DEVASTATING, calamitous, catastrophic, destructive, dire, disastrous, shattering
2 EXTRAVAGANT, crippling, immoderate, wasteful

rule noun 1 REGULATION, axiom, canon, decree, direction, guideline, law, maxim, precept, principle, tenet
2 CUSTOM, convention, habit, practice, procedure, routine, tradition
3 GOVERNMENT, authority, command, control, dominion, jurisdiction, mastery, power, regime, reign
4 ▷▷ **as a rule** USUALLY, generally, mainly, normally, on the whole, ordinarily
▶ verb 5 GOVERN, be in authority, be in power, command, control, direct, reign
6 BE PREVALENT, be customary, predominate, preponderate, prevail
7 DECREE, decide, judge, pronounce, settle

rule out verb EXCLUDE, ban, debar, dismiss, disqualify, eliminate, leave out, preclude, prohibit, reject

ruler noun 1 GOVERNOR, alpha male, commander, controller, head of state, king or queen, leader, lord, monarch, potentate, sovereign
2 MEASURE, rule, yardstick

ruling noun 1 DECISION, adjudication, decree, judgment, pronouncement, verdict
▶ adjective 2 GOVERNING, commanding, controlling, reigning

3 PREDOMINANT, chief, dominant, main, pre-eminent, preponderant, prevailing, principal

ruminate *verb* PONDER, cogitate, consider, contemplate, deliberate, mull over, muse, reflect, think, turn over in one's mind

rummage *verb* SEARCH, delve, forage, hunt, ransack, root

rumor *noun* STORY, buzz, dirt (*slang*), gossip, hearsay, news, report, talk, whisper, word

rump *noun* BUTTOCKS, backside (*informal*), bottom, bum (*Brit. slang*), buns (*slang*), butt (*informal*), derrière (*euphemistic*), hindquarters, posterior, rear, rear end, seat

rumpus *noun* COMMOTION, disturbance, furor, fuss, hue and cry, noise, row, uproar

run *verb* 1 RACE, bolt, dash, gallop, hare (*Brit. informal*), hurry, jog, leg it (*informal*), lope, rush, scurry, sprint

2 FLEE, beat a retreat, beat it (*slang*), bolt, do a runner (*slang*), escape, leg it (*informal*), make a run for it, take flight, take off (*informal*), take to one's heels

3 MOVE, course, glide, go, pass, roll, skim

4 WORK, function, go, operate, perform

5 MANAGE, administer, be in charge of, control, direct, handle, head, lead, operate

6 CONTINUE, extend, go, proceed, reach, stretch

7 FLOW, discharge, go, gush, leak, pour, spill, spout, stream

8 MELT, dissolve, go soft, liquefy

9 PUBLISH, display, feature, print

10 COMPETE, be a candidate, contend, put oneself up for, stand, take part

11 SMUGGLE, bootleg, traffic in

▶ *noun* 12 RACE, dash, gallop, jog, rush, sprint, spurt

13 RIDE, drive, excursion, jaunt, outing, spin (*informal*), trip

14 SEQUENCE, course, period, season, series, spell, stretch, string

15 ENCLOSURE, coop, pen

16 ▷▷ **in the long run** EVENTUALLY, in the end, ultimately

run across *verb* MEET, bump into, come across, encounter, run into

runaway *noun* 1 FUGITIVE, deserter, escapee, refugee, truant

▶ *adjective* 2 ESCAPED, fleeing, fugitive, loose, wild

run away *verb* FLEE, abscond, bolt, do a runner (*slang*), escape, fly the coop (*informal*), make a run for it, scram (*informal*), take to one's heels

run-down *adjective* 1 EXHAUSTED, below par, debilitated, drained, enervated, unhealthy, weak, weary, worn-out

2 DILAPIDATED, broken-down, decrepit, ramshackle, seedy, shabby, worn-out

run down *verb* 1 CRITICIZE, bad-mouth (*slang, chiefly U.S. & Canad.*), belittle, decry, denigrate, disparage, knock (*informal*), rubbish (*informal*), slag (off) (*slang*)

2 REDUCE, curtail, cut, cut back, decrease, downsize, trim

3 KNOCK DOWN, hit, knock over, run into, run over

4 WEAKEN, debilitate, exhaust

run into *verb* 1 MEET, bump into, come across *or* upon, encounter, run across

2 HIT, collide with, strike

runner *noun* 1 ATHLETE, jogger, sprinter

2 MESSENGER, courier, dispatch

bearer, errand boy

running *adjective* 1 CONTINUOUS, constant, incessant, perpetual, twenty-four-seven (*slang*), unbroken, uninterrupted
2 FLOWING, moving, streaming
▶ *noun* 3 MANAGEMENT, administration, control, direction, leadership, organization, supervision
4 WORKING, functioning, maintenance, operation, performance

runny *adjective* FLOWING, fluid, liquefied, liquid, melted, watery

run off *verb* FLEE, bolt, do a runner (*slang*), escape, fly the coop (*informal*), make off, run away, take flight, take to one's heels

run out *verb* BE USED UP, be exhausted, dry up, end, fail, finish, give out

run over *verb* 1 KNOCK DOWN, hit, knock over, run down
2 GO THROUGH, check, go over, rehearse, run through

run through *verb* REHEARSE, go over, practise, read, run over

rupture *noun* 1 BREAK, breach, burst, crack, fissure, rent, split, tear
▶ *verb* 2 BREAK, burst, crack, separate, sever, split, tear

rural *adjective* RUSTIC, agricultural, country, pastoral, sylvan

ruse *noun* TRICK, device, dodge, hoax, maneuver, ploy, stratagem, subterfuge

rush *verb* 1 HURRY, bolt, career, dash, fly, hasten, race, run, shoot, speed, tear
2 PUSH, hurry, hustle, press

3 ATTACK, charge, storm
▶ *noun* 4 HURRY, charge, dash, haste, race, scramble, stampede, surge
5 ATTACK, assault, charge, onslaught
▶ *adjective* 6 HASTY, fast, hurried, quick, rapid, swift, urgent

rust *noun* 1 CORROSION, oxidation
2 MILDEW, blight, mold, must, rot
▶ *verb* 3 CORRODE, oxidize

rustic *adjective* 1 RURAL, country, pastoral, sylvan
2 UNCOUTH, awkward, coarse, crude, rough
▶ *noun* 3 YOKEL, boor, bumpkin, clod, clodhopper (*informal*), hick (*informal*), hillbilly, peasant, redneck (*slang*)

rustle *verb* 1 CRACKLE, crinkle, whisper
▶ *noun* 2 CRACKLE, crinkling, rustling, whisper

rusty *adjective* 1 CORRODED, oxidized, rust-covered, rusted
2 REDDISH, chestnut, coppery, reddish-brown, russet, rust-colored
3 OUT OF PRACTICE, stale, unpracticed, weak

rut *noun* 1 GROOVE, furrow, indentation, track, trough, wheel mark
2 HABIT, dead end, pattern, routine, system

ruthless *adjective* MERCILESS, brutal, callous, cruel, harsh, heartless, pitiless, relentless, remorseless

rutted *adjective* GROOVED, cut, furrowed, gouged, holed, indented, marked, scored

S

sabotage *noun* 1 DAMAGE, destruction, disruption, subversion, wrecking
▶ *verb* 2 DAMAGE, destroy, disable, disrupt, incapacitate, subvert, vandalize, wreck

saccharine *adjective* OVERSWEET, cloying, honeyed, nauseating, sickly, sugary, syrupy

sack¹ *noun* 1 ▷▷ **the sack** DISMISSAL, discharge, the ax (*informal*), the boot (*slang*), the push (*slang*)
▶ *verb* 2 DISMISS, ax (*informal*), discharge, fire (*informal*), give (someone) the push (*informal*)

sack² *noun* 1 PLUNDERING, looting, pillage
▶ *verb* 2 PLUNDER, loot, pillage, raid, rob, ruin, strip

sacred *adjective* 1 HOLY, blessed, divine, hallowed, revered, sanctified
2 RELIGIOUS, ecclesiastical, holy
3 INVIOLABLE, protected, sacrosanct

sacrifice *noun* 1 SURRENDER, loss, renunciation
2 OFFERING, oblation
▶ *verb* 3 GIVE UP, forego, forfeit, let go, lose, say good-bye to, surrender
4 OFFER, immolate, offer up

sacrilege *noun* DESECRATION, blasphemy, heresy, impiety, irreverence, profanation, violation

sacrilegious *adjective* PROFANE, blasphemous, desecrating, impious, irreligious, irreverent

sacrosanct *adjective* INVIOLABLE, hallowed, inviolate, sacred, sanctified, set apart, untouchable

sad *adjective* 1 UNHAPPY, blue, dejected, depressed, doleful, down, low, low-spirited, melancholy, mournful, woebegone
2 TRAGIC, depressing, dismal, grievous, harrowing, heart-rending, moving, pathetic, pitiful, poignant, upsetting
3 DEPLORABLE, bad, lamentable, sorry, wretched

sadden *verb* UPSET, deject, depress, distress, grieve, make sad

saddle *verb* BURDEN, encumber, load, lumber (*informal*)

sadistic *adjective* CRUEL, barbarous, brutal, ruthless, vicious

sadness *noun* UNHAPPINESS, dejection, depression, despondency, grief, melancholy, misery, poignancy, sorrow, the blues

safe *adjective* 1 SECURE, impregnable, in safe hands, out of danger, out of harm's way, protected, safe and sound
2 UNHARMED, all right, intact, O.K. or okay (*informal*), undamaged, unhurt, unscathed
3 RISK-FREE, certain, impregnable, secure, sound
▶ *noun* 4 STRONGBOX, coffer, deposit box, repository, safe-

deposit box, vault

safeguard verb 1 PROTECT, defend, guard, look after, preserve
▶ noun 2 PROTECTION, defense, guard, security

safely adverb IN SAFETY, in one piece, safe and sound, with impunity, without risk

safety noun 1 SECURITY, impregnability, protection
2 SHELTER, cover, refuge, sanctuary

sag verb 1 SINK, bag, dip, droop, fall, give way, hang loosely, slump
2 TIRE, droop, flag, wane, weaken, wilt

saga noun TALE, epic, legend, narrative, story, yarn

sage noun 1 WISE MAN, elder, guru, master, philosopher
▶ adjective 2 WISE, judicious, sagacious, sapient, sensible

sail verb 1 EMBARK, set sail
2 GLIDE, drift, float, fly, skim, soar, sweep, wing
3 PILOT, steer

sailor noun MARINER, marine, sea dog, seafarer, seaman

saintly adjective VIRTUOUS, godly, holy, pious, religious, righteous, saintlike

sake noun 1 BENEFIT, account, behalf, good, interest, welfare
2 PURPOSE, aim, end, motive, objective, reason

salacious adjective LASCIVIOUS, carnal, erotic, lecherous, lewd, libidinous, lustful

salary noun PAY, earnings, income, wage, wages

sale noun 1 SELLING, deal, disposal, marketing, transaction
2 ▷▷ **for sale** AVAILABLE, obtainable, on the market

salient adjective PROMINENT, conspicuous, important, noticeable, outstanding, pronounced, striking

sallow adjective WAN, anemic, pale, pallid, pasty, sickly, unhealthy, yellowish

salt noun 1 SEASONING, flavor, relish, savor, taste
2 ▷▷ **with a grain or pinch of salt** SKEPTICALLY, cynically, disbelievingly, suspiciously, with reservations
▶ adjective 3 SALTY, brackish, briny, saline

salty adjective SALT, brackish, briny, saline

salubrious adjective HEALTHY, beneficial, good for one, health-giving, wholesome

salutary adjective BENEFICIAL, advantageous, good for one, profitable, useful, valuable

salute noun 1 GREETING, address, recognition, salutation
▶ verb 2 GREET, acknowledge, address, hail, welcome
3 HONOR, acknowledge, pay tribute or homage to, recognize

salvage verb SAVE, recover, redeem, rescue, retrieve

salvation noun SAVING, deliverance, escape, preservation, redemption, rescue

salve noun OINTMENT, balm, cream, emollient, lotion

same adjective 1 AFOREMENTIONED, aforesaid
2 IDENTICAL, alike, corresponding, duplicate, equal, twin
3 UNCHANGED, changeless, consistent, constant, invariable, unaltered, unvarying

sample noun 1 SPECIMEN, example, instance, model, pattern
▶ verb 2 TEST, experience, inspect, taste, try
▶ adjective 3 TEST, representative,

specimen, trial

sanctify *verb* CONSECRATE, cleanse, hallow

sanctimonious *adjective* HOLIER-THAN-THOU, hypocritical, pious, self-righteous, smug

sanction *noun* **1** PERMISSION, approval, authority, authorization, backing, O.K. *or* okay (*informal*), stamp *or* seal of approval
2 (*often plural*) BAN, boycott, coercive measures, embargo, penalty
▶ *verb* **3** PERMIT, allow, approve, authorize, endorse

sanctity *noun* **1** SACREDNESS, inviolability
2 HOLINESS, godliness, goodness, grace, piety, righteousness

sanctuary *noun* **1** SHRINE, altar, church, temple
2 PROTECTION, asylum, haven, refuge, retreat, shelter
3 RESERVE, conservation area, national park, nature reserve

sane *adjective* **1** RATIONAL, all there (*informal*), *compos mentis*, in one's right mind, mentally sound, of sound mind
2 SENSIBLE, balanced, judicious, level-headed, reasonable, sound

sanguine *adjective* CHEERFUL, buoyant, confident, hopeful, optimistic

sanitary *adjective* HYGIENIC, clean, germ-free, healthy, wholesome

sanity *noun* **1** MENTAL HEALTH, normality, rationality, reason, saneness
2 GOOD SENSE, common sense, level-headedness, rationality, sense

sap¹ *noun* **1** VITAL FLUID, essence, lifeblood
2 (*informal*) (*slang*) FOOL, dork,

(*slang*), idiot, jerk (*slang*), ninny, schmuck (*slang*), simpleton, twit (*informal, chiefly Brit.*), wally (*slang*)

sap² *verb* WEAKEN, deplete, drain, exhaust, undermine

sarcasm *noun* IRONY, bitterness, cynicism, derision, mockery, satire

sarcastic *adjective* IRONIC, acid, biting, caustic, cutting, cynical, mocking, sardonic, sarky (*Brit. informal*), satirical

sardonic *adjective* MOCKING, cynical, derisive, dry, ironic, sarcastic, sneering, wry

Satan *noun* THE DEVIL, Beelzebub, Lord of the Flies, Lucifer, Mephistopheles, Old Nick (*informal*), Prince of Darkness, The Evil One

satanic *adjective* EVIL, black, demonic, devilish, diabolic, fiendish, hellish, infernal, wicked

satiate *verb* **1** GLUT, cloy, gorge, jade, nauseate, overfill, stuff, surfeit
2 SATISFY, sate, slake

satire *noun* MOCKERY, burlesque, caricature, irony, lampoon, parody, ridicule, spoof (*informal*)

satirical, satiric *adjective* MOCKING, biting, caustic, cutting, incisive, ironic

satirize *verb* RIDICULE, burlesque, deride, lampoon, parody, pillory

satisfaction *noun*
1 CONTENTMENT, comfort, content, enjoyment, happiness, pleasure, pride, repletion, satiety
2 FULFILLMENT, achievement, assuaging, gratification

satisfactory *adjective* ADEQUATE, acceptable, all right, average, fair, good enough, passable, sufficient

satisfy *verb* **1** CONTENT, assuage, gratify, indulge, pacify, pander to, please, quench, sate, slake

2 FULFILL, answer, do, meet, serve, suffice

3 PERSUADE, assure, convince, reassure

saturate verb SOAK, drench, imbue, souse, steep, suffuse, waterlog, wet through

saturated adjective SOAKED, drenched, dripping, soaking (wet), sodden, sopping (wet), waterlogged, wet through

saturnine adjective GLOOMY, dour, glum, grave, morose, somber

saucy adjective 1 IMPUDENT, cheeky (informal), forward, impertinent, insolent, pert, presumptuous, rude

2 JAUNTY, dashing, gay, natty (informal), perky

saunter verb 1 STROLL, amble, meander, mosey (informal), ramble, roam, wander

▶ noun 2 STROLL, airing, amble, ramble, turn, walk

savage adjective 1 WILD, feral, undomesticated, untamed

2 UNCULTIVATED, rough, rugged, uncivilized

3 CRUEL, barbarous, bestial, bloodthirsty, brutal, ferocious, fierce, harsh, ruthless, sadistic, vicious

4 PRIMITIVE, rude, unspoilt

▶ noun 5 LOUT, boor, yahoo, yob or yobbo (Brit. slang)

▶ verb 6 ATTACK, lacerate, mangle, maul

savagery noun CRUELTY, barbarity, brutality, ferocity, ruthlessness, viciousness

save verb 1 RESCUE, deliver, free, liberate, recover, redeem, salvage

2 PROTECT, conserve, guard, keep safe, look after, preserve, safeguard

3 KEEP, collect, gather, hoard, hold, husband, lay by, put by, reserve, set aside, store

saving noun 1 ECONOMY, bargain, discount, reduction

▶ adjective 2 REDEEMING, compensatory, extenuating

savings plural noun NEST EGG, fund, reserves, resources, store

savior noun RESCUER, defender, deliverer, liberator, preserver, protector, redeemer

Savior noun CHRIST, Jesus, Messiah, Redeemer

savoir-faire noun SOCIAL KNOW-HOW (informal), diplomacy, discretion, finesse, poise, social graces, tact, urbanity, worldliness

savor verb 1 ENJOY, appreciate, delight in, luxuriate in, relish, revel in

2 (often with of) SUGGEST, be suggestive, show signs, smack

▶ noun 3 FLAVOR, piquancy, relish, smack, smell, tang, taste

savory adjective SPICY, appetizing, full-flavored, luscious, mouthwatering, palatable, piquant, rich, tasty

say verb 1 SPEAK, affirm, announce, assert, declare, maintain, mention, pronounce, remark, state, utter, voice

2 SUPPOSE, assume, conjecture, estimate, guess, imagine, presume, surmise

3 EXPRESS, communicate, convey, imply

▶ noun 4 CHANCE TO SPEAK, voice, vote

5 INFLUENCE, authority, clout (informal), power, weight

saying noun PROVERB, adage, aphorism, axiom, dictum, maxim

scale[1] noun FLAKE, lamina, layer, plate

scale² noun 1 GRADUATION, gradation, hierarchy, ladder, progression, ranking, sequence, series, steps
2 RATIO, proportion
3 DEGREE, extent, range, reach, scope
▶ verb 4 CLIMB, ascend, clamber, escalade, mount, surmount
5 ADJUST, proportion, regulate

scam verb (slang) 1 CHEAT, cook the books (informal), diddle (informal), fix, swindle, wangle (informal)
▶ noun 2 (slang) FRAUD, fix, racket (slang), swindle

scamp noun RASCAL, devil, imp, monkey, rogue, scallywag (informal)

scamper verb RUN, dart, dash, hasten, hurry, romp, scoot, scurry, scuttle

scan verb 1 GLANCE OVER, check, check out (informal), examine, eye, look through, run one's eye over, run over, skim
2 SCRUTINIZE, investigate, scour, search, survey, sweep

scandal noun 1 CRIME, disgrace, embarrassment, offense, sin, wrongdoing
2 SHAME, defamation, discredit, disgrace, dishonor, ignominy, infamy, opprobrium, stigma
3 GOSSIP, aspersion, dirt, rumors, slander, talk, tattle

scandalize verb SHOCK, affront, appall, horrify, offend, outrage

scandalous adjective 1 SHOCKING, disgraceful, disreputable, infamous, outrageous, shameful, unseemly
2 SLANDEROUS, defamatory, libelous, scurrilous, untrue

scant adjective MEAGER, barely sufficient, little, minimal, sparse

scanty adjective MEAGER, bare, deficient, inadequate, insufficient, lousy (slang), poor, scant, short, skimpy, sparse, thin

scapegoat noun WHIPPING BOY, fall guy (informal)

scar noun 1 MARK, blemish, injury, wound
▶ verb 2 MARK, damage, disfigure

scarce adjective RARE, few, few and far between, infrequent, in short supply, uncommon

scarcely adverb 1 HARDLY, barely
2 DEFINITELY NOT, hardly

scarcity noun SHORTAGE, dearth, deficiency, insufficiency, lack, paucity, rareness, want

scare verb 1 FRIGHTEN, alarm, dismay, intimidate, panic, shock, startle, terrify
▶ noun 2 FRIGHT, panic, shock, start, terror

scared adjective FRIGHTENED, fearful, panicky, panic-stricken, petrified, shaken, startled, terrified

scary adjective FRIGHTENING, alarming, chilling, creepy (informal), horrifying, spine-chilling, spooky (informal), terrifying

scathing adjective CRITICAL, biting, caustic, cutting, harsh, sarcastic, scornful, trenchant, withering

scatter verb 1 THROW ABOUT, diffuse, disseminate, fling, shower, spread, sprinkle, strew
2 DISPERSE, disband, dispel, dissipate

scatterbrain noun FEATHERBRAIN, butterfly, flibbertigibbet

scenario noun STORY LINE, outline, résumé, summary, synopsis

scene noun 1 SITE, area, locality, place, position, setting, spot
2 SETTING, backdrop, background, location, set

3 SHOW, display, drama,
exhibition, pageant, picture,
sight, spectacle
4 ACT, division, episode, part
5 VIEW, landscape, panorama,
prospect, vista
6 FUSS, carry-on (informal, chiefly
Brit.), commotion, exhibition,
performance, row, tantrum, to-do
7 (informal) WORLD, arena,
business, environment
scenery noun 1 LANDSCAPE,
surroundings, terrain, view, vista
2 (theatre) SET, backdrop, flats,
setting, stage set
scenic adjective PICTURESQUE,
beautiful, panoramic, spectacular,
striking
scent noun 1 FRAGRANCE, aroma,
bouquet, odor, perfume, smell
2 TRAIL, spoor, track
▶ verb 3 DETECT, discern, nose out,
sense, smell, sniff
scented adjective FRAGRANT,
aromatic, odoriferous, perfumed,
sweet-smelling
schedule noun 1 PLAN, agenda,
calendar, catalog, inventory, list,
program, timetable
▶ verb 2 PLAN, appoint, arrange,
book, organize, program
scheme noun 1 PLAN, program,
project, proposal, road map,
strategy, system, tactics
2 DIAGRAM, blueprint, chart, draft,
layout, outline, pattern
3 PLOT, conspiracy, intrigue,
maneuver, ploy, ruse, stratagem,
subterfuge
▶ verb 4 PLAN, lay plans, project,
work out
5 PLOT, collude, conspire, intrigue,
machinate, maneuver
scheming adjective CALCULATING,
artful, conniving, cunning, sly,
tricky, underhand, wily

schism noun DIVISION, breach,
break, rift, rupture, separation,
split
scholar noun 1 INTELLECTUAL,
academic, savant
2 STUDENT, disciple, learner, pupil,
schoolboy or schoolgirl
scholarly adjective LEARNED,
academic, bookish, erudite,
intellectual, lettered, scholastic
scholarship noun 1 LEARNING,
book-learning, education,
erudition, knowledge
2 BURSARY, fellowship
scholastic adjective LEARNED,
academic, lettered, scholarly
school noun 1 ACADEMY, college,
faculty, institute, institution,
seminary
2 GROUP, adherents, circle,
denomination, devotees,
disciples, faction, followers, set
▶ verb 3 TRAIN, coach, discipline,
drill, educate, instruct, tutor
schooling noun 1 TEACHING,
education, tuition
2 TRAINING, coaching, drill,
instruction
science noun 1 DISCIPLINE, body of
knowledge, branch of knowledge
2 SKILL, art, technique
scientific adjective SYSTEMATIC,
accurate, controlled, exact,
mathematical, precise
scientist noun INVENTOR, boffin
(informal), technophile
scintillating adjective BRILLIANT,
animated, bright, dazzling,
exciting, glittering, lively,
sparkling, stimulating
scoff[1] verb SCORN, belittle, deride,
despise, jeer, knock (informal),
laugh at, mock, pooh-pooh,
ridicule, sneer
scoff[2] verb GOBBLE (UP), bolt,
devour, gorge oneself on, gulp

down, guzzle, wolf

scold verb 1 REPRIMAND, berate, castigate, censure, chew out (slang), find fault with, give (someone) a dressing-down (informal), lecture, rebuke, reproach, reprove, tell off (informal), tick off (informal), upbraid
▶ noun 2 NAG, shrew, termagant (rare)

scolding noun REBUKE, dressing-down (informal), lecture, row, telling-off (informal), ticking-off (informal)

scoop noun 1 LADLE, dipper, spoon
2 EXCLUSIVE, exposé, revelation, sensation
▶ verb 3 (often with up) LIFT, gather up, pick up, take up
4 (often with out) HOLLOW, bail, dig, empty, excavate, gouge, shovel

scope noun 1 OPPORTUNITY, freedom, latitude, liberty, room, space
2 RANGE, area, capacity, orbit, outlook, reach, span, sphere

scorch verb BURN, parch, roast, sear, shrivel, singe, wither

scorching adjective BURNING, baking, boiling, fiery, flaming, red-hot, roasting, searing

score noun 1 POINTS, grade, mark, outcome, record, result, total
2 GROUNDS, basis, cause, ground, reason
3 GRIEVANCE, grudge, injury, injustice, wrong
4 ▷▷ **scores** LOTS, hundreds, masses, millions, multitudes, myriads, swarms
▶ verb 5 GAIN, achieve, chalk up (informal), make, notch up (informal), win
6 KEEP COUNT, count, record,

register, tally
7 CUT, deface, gouge, graze, mark, scrape, scratch, slash
8 (with out or through) CROSS OUT, cancel, delete, obliterate, strike out
9 (music) ARRANGE, adapt, orchestrate, set

scorn noun 1 CONTEMPT, derision, disdain, disparagement, mockery, sarcasm
▶ verb 2 DESPISE, be above, deride, disdain, flout, reject, scoff at, slight, spurn

scornful adjective CONTEMPTUOUS, derisive, disdainful, haughty, jeering, mocking, sarcastic, sardonic, scathing, scoffing, sneering

scoundrel noun ROGUE, bastard (offensive), blackguard, good-for-nothing, heel (slang), miscreant, ne'er-do-well, rascal, reprobate, rotter (slang, chiefly Brit.), scally (Northwest English dialect), scamp, swine, villain

scour¹ verb RUB, abrade, buff, clean, polish, scrub, wash

scour² verb SEARCH, beat, comb, hunt, ransack

scourge noun 1 AFFLICTION, bane, curse, infliction, misfortune, pest, plague, terror, torment
2 WHIP, cat, lash, strap, switch, thong
▶ verb 3 AFFLICT, curse, plague, terrorize, torment
4 WHIP, beat, cane, flog, horsewhip, lash, thrash

scout noun 1 VANGUARD, advance guard, lookout, outrider, precursor, reconnoiterer
▶ verb 2 RECONNOITER, investigate, observe, probe, recce (slang), spy, survey, watch

scowl verb 1 GLOWER, frown, lour

or lower

▶ *noun* 2 GLOWER, black look, dirty look, frown

scrabble *verb* SCRAPE, claw, scramble, scratch

scraggy *adjective* SCRAWNY, angular, bony, lean, skinny

scram *verb* GO AWAY, abscond, beat it (*slang*), clear off (*informal*), get lost (*informal*), leave, make oneself scarce (*informal*), make tracks, scarper (*Brit. slang*), vamoose (*slang*)

scramble *verb* 1 STRUGGLE, climb, crawl, scrabble, swarm
2 STRIVE, contend, jostle, push, run, rush, vie

▶ *noun* 3 CLIMB, trek
4 STRUGGLE, commotion, competition, confusion, melee *or* mêlée, race, rush, tussle

scrap¹ *noun* 1 PIECE, bit, crumb, fragment, grain, morsel, part, particle, portion, sliver, snippet
2 WASTE, junk, off cuts
3 ▷▷ **scraps** LEFTOVERS, bits, leavings, remains

▶ *verb* 4 DISCARD, abandon, ditch (*slang*), drop, jettison, throw away *or* out, write off

scrap² (*informal*) *noun* 1 FIGHT, argument, battle, disagreement, dispute, quarrel, row, squabble, wrangle

▶ *verb* 2 FIGHT, argue, row, squabble, wrangle

scrape *verb* 1 GRAZE, bark, rub, scratch, scuff, skin
2 RUB, clean, erase, remove, scour
3 GRATE, grind, rasp, scratch, squeak
4 SCRIMP, pinch, save, skimp, stint
5 ▷▷ **scrape through** GET BY (*informal*), just make it, struggle

noun (*informal*) PREDICAMENT, awkward situation, difficulty, dilemma, fix (*informal*), mess,

plight, tight spot

scrapheap *noun* ▷▷ **on the scrapheap** DISCARDED, ditched (*slang*), jettisoned, put out to grass, put out to pasture (*informal*), redundant, written off

scrappy *adjective* FRAGMENTARY, bitty, disjointed, incomplete, piecemeal, sketchy, thrown together

scratch *verb* 1 MARK, claw, cut, damage, etch, grate, graze, lacerate, score, scrape
2 WITHDRAW, abolish, call off, cancel, delete, eliminate, erase, pull out

▶ *noun* 3 MARK, blemish, claw mark, gash, graze, laceration, scrape
4 ▷▷ **up to scratch** ADEQUATE, acceptable, satisfactory, sufficient, up to standard

▶ *adjective* 5 IMPROVISED, impromptu, rough-and-ready

scrawl *verb* SCRIBBLE, doodle, squiggle, writing

scrawny *adjective* THIN, bony, gaunt, lean, scraggy, skin-and-bones (*informal*), skinny, undernourished

scream *verb* 1 CRY, bawl, screech, shriek, yell

▶ *noun* 2 CRY, howl, screech, shriek, yell, yelp

screech *noun or verb* CRY, scream, shriek

screen *noun* 1 COVER, awning, canopy, cloak, guard, partition, room divider, shade, shelter, shield
2 MESH, net

▶ *verb* 3 COVER, cloak, conceal, hide, mask, shade, veil
4 PROTECT, defend, guard, shelter, shield
5 VET, evaluate, examine, filter,

gauge, scan, sift, sort
6 BROADCAST, present, put on, show

screw verb 1 TURN, tighten, twist
2 (*informal*) (often with *out of*) EXTORT, extract, wrest, wring

screw up verb 1 (*informal*) BUNGLE, botch, make a hash of (*informal*), make a mess of (*slang*), mess up, mishandle, spoil
2 DISTORT, contort, pucker, wrinkle

screwy adjective CRAZY, crackpot (*informal*), eccentric, loopy (*informal*), nutty (*slang*), odd, off-the-wall (*slang*), out to lunch (*informal*), round the bend (*Brit. slang*), weird

scribble verb SCRAWL, dash off, jot, write

scribe noun COPYIST, amanuensis, writer

scrimp verb ECONOMIZE, be frugal, save, scrape, skimp, stint, tighten one's belt

script noun 1 TEXT, book, copy, dialogue, libretto, lines, words
2 HANDWRITING, calligraphy, penmanship, writing

Scripture noun THE BIBLE, Holy Bible, Holy Scripture, Holy Writ, The Good Book, The Gospels, The Scriptures

scrounge verb (*informal*) CADGE, beg, blag (*slang*), bum (*informal*), freeload (*slang*), sponge (*informal*)

scrounger adjective CADGER, freeloader (*slang*), parasite, sponger (*informal*)

scrub verb 1 SCOUR, clean, cleanse, rub
2 (*informal*) CANCEL, abolish, call off, delete, drop, forget about, give up

scruple noun 1 MISGIVING, compunction, doubt, hesitation,

qualm, reluctance, second thoughts, uneasiness
▶ verb 2 HAVE MISGIVINGS ABOUT, demur, doubt, have qualms about, hesitate, think twice about

scrupulous adjective 1 MORAL, conscientious, honorable, principled, upright
2 CAREFUL, exact, fastidious, meticulous, precise, punctilious, rigorous, strict

scrutinize verb EXAMINE, explore, inspect, investigate, peruse, pore over, probe, scan, search, study

scrutiny noun EXAMINATION, analysis, exploration, inspection, investigation, perusal, search, study

scuffle verb 1 FIGHT, clash, grapple, jostle, struggle, tussle
▶ noun 2 FIGHT, brawl, commotion, disturbance, fray, scrimmage, skirmish, tussle

sculpture verb SCULPT, carve, chisel, fashion, form, hew, model, mold, shape

scum noun 1 IMPURITIES, dross, film, froth
2 RABBLE, dregs of society, riffraff, trash (*chiefly U.S. & Canad.*)

scurrilous adjective SLANDEROUS, abusive, defamatory, insulting, scandalous, vituperative

scurry verb 1 HURRY, dart, dash, race, scamper, scoot, scuttle, sprint
▶ noun 2 FLURRY, scampering, whirl

scuttle verb RUN, bustle, hasten, hurry, rush, scamper, scoot, scurry

sea noun 1 OCEAN, main, the deep, the waves
2 EXPANSE, abundance, mass, multitude, plethora, profusion
3 ▷▷ at sea BEWILDERED, baffled, confused, lost, mystified, puzzled

seafaring adjective NAUTICAL, marine, maritime, naval

seal noun 1 AUTHENTICATION, confirmation, imprimatur, insignia, ratification, stamp
▶ verb 2 CLOSE, bung, enclose, fasten, plug, shut, stop, stopper, stop up
3 AUTHENTICATE, confirm, ratify, stamp, validate
4 SETTLE, clinch, conclude, consummate, finalize
5 ▷▷ **seal off** ISOLATE, put out of bounds, quarantine, segregate

seam noun 1 JOINT, closure
2 LAYER, lode, stratum, vein
3 RIDGE, furrow, line, wrinkle

sear verb SCORCH, burn, sizzle

search verb 1 LOOK, comb, examine, explore, hunt, inspect, investigate, ransack, scour, scrutinize
▶ noun 2 LOOK, examination, exploration, hunt, inspection, investigation, pursuit, quest

searching adjective KEEN, close, intent, penetrating, piercing, probing, quizzical, sharp

season noun 1 PERIOD, spell, term, time
▶ verb 2 FLAVOR, enliven, pep up, salt, spice

seasonable adjective APPROPRIATE, convenient, fit, opportune, providential, suitable, timely, well-timed

seasoned adjective EXPERIENCED, hardened, practiced, time-served, veteran

seasoning noun FLAVORING, condiment, dressing, relish, salt and pepper, sauce, spice

seat noun 1 CHAIR, bench, pew, settle, stall, stool
2 CENTER, capital, heart, hub, place, site, situation, source
3 RESIDENCE, abode, ancestral hall, house, mansion
4 MEMBERSHIP, chair, constituency, incumbency, place
▶ verb 5 SIT, fix, install, locate, place, set, settle
6 HOLD, accommodate, cater for, contain, sit, take

seating noun ACCOMMODATION, chairs, places, room, seats

secede verb WITHDRAW, break with, leave, pull out, quit, resign, split from

secluded adjective PRIVATE, cloistered, cut off, isolated, lonely, out-of-the-way, sheltered, solitary

seclusion noun PRIVACY, isolation, shelter, solitude

second[1] adjective 1 NEXT, following, subsequent, succeeding
2 ADDITIONAL, alternative, extra, further, other
3 INFERIOR, lesser, lower, secondary, subordinate
▶ noun 4 SUPPORTER, assistant, backer, helper
▶ verb 5 SUPPORT, approve, assist, back, endorse, go along with

second[2] noun MOMENT, flash, instant, jiffy (informal), minute, sec (informal), trice

secondary adjective 1 SUBORDINATE, inferior, lesser, lower, minor, unimportant
2 RESULTANT, contingent, derived, indirect
3 BACKUP, auxiliary, fall-back, reserve, subsidiary, supporting

second-class adjective INFERIOR, indifferent, mediocre, second-best, second-rate, undistinguished, uninspiring

second-hand adjective 1 USED, hand-me-down (informal), nearly new

▶ *adverb* 2 INDIRECTLY

second in command *noun*
DEPUTY, number two, right-hand
man

secondly *adverb* NEXT, in the
second place, second

second-rate *adjective* INFERIOR,
low-grade, low-quality,
mediocre, poor, rubbishy, shoddy,
substandard, tacky (*informal*),
tawdry, two-bit (*slang*)

secrecy *noun* 1 MYSTERY,
concealment, confidentiality,
privacy, silence
2 SECRETIVENESS, clandestineness,
covertness, furtiveness, stealth

secret *adjective* 1 CONCEALED,
close, disguised, furtive, hidden,
undercover, underground,
undisclosed, unknown,
unrevealed
2 STEALTHY, secretive, sly,
underhand
3 MYSTERIOUS, abstruse, arcane,
clandestine, cryptic, occult
▶ *noun* 4 MYSTERY, code, enigma,
key
5 ▷▷ **in secret** SECRETLY, slyly,
surreptitiously

secrete[1] *verb* GIVE OFF, emanate,
emit, exude

secrete[2] *verb* HIDE, cache, conceal,
harbor, stash (*informal*), stow

secretive *adjective* RETICENT,
close, deep, reserved, tight-lipped,
uncommunicative

secretly *adverb* IN SECRET,
clandestinely, covertly, furtively,
privately, quietly, stealthily,
surreptitiously

sect *noun* GROUP, camp,
denomination, division, faction,
party, schism

sectarian *adjective* 1 NARROW-
MINDED, bigoted, doctrinaire,
dogmatic, factional, fanatical,

limited, parochial, partisan
▶ *noun* 2 BIGOT, dogmatist,
extremist, fanatic, partisan,
zealot

section *noun* 1 PART, division,
fraction, installment, passage,
piece, portion, segment, slice
2 (*chiefly U.S.*) DISTRICT, area,
region, sector, zone

sector *noun* PART, area, district,
division, quarter, region, zone

secular *adjective* WORLDLY,
civil, earthly, lay, nonspiritual,
temporal

secure *adjective* 1 SAFE, immune,
protected, unassailable
2 SURE, assured, certain,
confident, easy, reassured
3 FIXED, fast, fastened, firm,
immovable, stable, steady
▶ *verb* 4 OBTAIN, acquire, gain, get,
procure, score (*slang*)
5 FASTEN, attach, bolt, chain, fix,
lock, make fast, tie up

security *noun* 1 PRECAUTIONS,
defense, protection, safeguards,
safety measures
2 SAFETY, care, custody, refuge,
safekeeping, sanctuary
3 SURENESS, assurance, certainty,
confidence, conviction,
positiveness, reliance
4 PLEDGE, collateral, gage,
guarantee, hostage, insurance,
pawn, surety

sedate *adjective* CALM, collected,
composed, cool, dignified, serene,
tranquil

sedative *adjective* 1 CALMING,
anodyne, relaxing, soothing,
tranquilizing
▶ *noun* 2 TRANQUILIZER, anodyne,
downer *or* down (*slang*)

sedentary *adjective* INACTIVE,
desk, desk-bound, seated, sitting

sediment *noun* DREGS, deposit,

grounds, lees, residue

sedition noun RABBLE-ROUSING, agitation, incitement to riot, subversion

seditious adjective REVOLUTIONARY, dissident, mutinous, rebellious, refractory, subversive

seduce verb 1 CORRUPT, debauch, deflower, deprave, dishonor
2 TEMPT, beguile, deceive, entice, inveigle, lead astray, lure, mislead

seduction noun 1 CORRUPTION
2 TEMPTATION, enticement, lure, snare

seductive adjective ALLURING, attractive, bewitching, enticing, inviting, provocative, tempting

seductress noun TEMPTRESS, enchantress, *femme fatale*, siren, succubus, vamp (*informal*)

see¹ verb 1 PERCEIVE, behold, catch sight of, discern, distinguish, espy, glimpse, look, make out, notice, observe, sight, spot, witness
2 UNDERSTAND, appreciate, comprehend, fathom, feel, follow, get, grasp, realize
3 FIND OUT, ascertain, determine, discover, learn
4 MAKE SURE, ensure, guarantee, make certain, see to it
5 CONSIDER, decide, deliberate, reflect, think over
6 VISIT, confer with, consult, interview, receive, speak to
7 GO OUT WITH, court, date (*informal*), go steady with (*informal*)
8 ACCOMPANY, escort, lead, show, usher, walk

seed noun 1 GRAIN, egg, embryo, germ, kernel, ovum, pip, spore
2 ORIGIN, beginning, germ, nucleus, source, start
3 OFFSPRING, children,

descendants, issue, progeny
4 ▷▷ **go** or **run to seed** DECLINE, decay, degenerate, deteriorate, go downhill (*informal*), go to pot, let oneself go

seedy (*informal*) adjective 1 SHABBY, dilapidated, dirty, grotty (*slang*), grubby, mangy, run-down, scruffy, scuzzy (*slang*), sleazy, squalid, tatty
2 (*informal*) UNWELL, ill, off color, out of sorts, poorly (*informal*), under the weather (*informal*)

seeing conjunction SINCE, as, inasmuch as, in view of the fact that

seek verb 1 LOOK FOR, be after, follow, hunt, pursue, search for, stalk
2 TRY, aim, aspire to, attempt, endeavor, essay, strive

seem verb APPEAR, assume, give the impression, look

seemly adjective FITTING, appropriate, becoming, correct, decent, decorous, fit, proper, suitable

seep verb OOZE, exude, leak, permeate, soak, trickle, well

seer noun PROPHET, sibyl, soothsayer

seesaw verb ALTERNATE, fluctuate, oscillate, swing

seethe verb 1 BE FURIOUS, be livid, fume, go ballistic (*slang*), rage, see red (*informal*), simmer
2 BOIL, bubble, fizz, foam, froth

see through verb 1 BE UNDECEIVED BY, be wise to (*informal*), fathom, not fall for, penetrate
2 ▷▷ **see (something) through** PERSEVERE (WITH), keep at, persist, stick out (*informal*); **see (someone) through** HELP OUT, stick by, support

segment noun SECTION, bit, division, part, piece, portion, slice, wedge

segregate *verb* SET APART,
discriminate against, dissociate,
isolate, separate

segregation *noun* SEPARATION,
apartheid, discrimination,
isolation

seize *verb* **1** GRAB, catch up, clutch,
grasp, grip, lay hands on, snatch,
take
2 CONFISCATE, appropriate,
commandeer, impound, take
possession of
3 CAPTURE, apprehend, arrest,
catch, take captive

seizure *noun* **1** ATTACK, convulsion,
fit, paroxysm, spasm
2 CAPTURE, apprehension, arrest
3 TAKING, annexation,
commandeering, confiscation,
grabbing

seldom *adverb* RARELY, hardly ever,
infrequently, not often

select *verb* **1** CHOOSE, opt for, pick,
single out
▶ *adjective* **2** CHOICE, excellent,
first-class, hand-picked, special,
superior, top-notch (*informal*)
3 EXCLUSIVE, cliquish, elite,
privileged

selection *noun* **1** CHOICE,
choosing, option, pick, preference
2 RANGE, assortment, choice,
collection, medley, variety

selective *adjective* PARTICULAR,
careful, discerning,
discriminating

self-assurance *noun*
CONFIDENCE, assertiveness,
positiveness, self-confidence,
self-possession

self-centered *adjective* SELFISH,
egotistic, narcissistic, self-seeking

self-confidence *noun* SELF-
ASSURANCE, aplomb, confidence,
nerve, poise

self-confident *adjective* SELF-
ASSURED, assured, confident,
poised, sure of oneself

self-conscious *adjective*
EMBARRASSED, awkward, bashful,
diffident, ill at ease, insecure,
nervous, uncomfortable, wired
(*slang*)

self-control *noun* WILLPOWER,
restraint, self-discipline, self-
restraint

self-esteem *noun* SELF-RESPECT,
confidence, faith in oneself, pride,
self-assurance, self-regard

self-evident *adjective* OBVIOUS,
clear, incontrovertible,
inescapable, undeniable

self-important *adjective*
CONCEITED, bigheaded, cocky, full
of oneself, pompous, swollen-
headed

self-indulgence *noun*
INTEMPERANCE, excess,
extravagance

selfish *adjective* SELF-CENTERED,
egoistic, egoistical, egotistic,
egotistical, greedy, self-interested,
ungenerous

selfless *adjective* UNSELFISH,
altruistic, generous, self-denying,
self-sacrificing

self-possessed *adjective* SELF-
ASSURED, collected, confident,
cool, poised, unruffled

self-reliant *adjective*
INDEPENDENT, self-sufficient,
self-supporting

self-respect *noun* PRIDE, dignity,
morale, self-esteem

self-restraint *noun* SELF-
CONTROL, self-command, self-
discipline, willpower

self-righteous *adjective*
SANCTIMONIOUS, complacent,
holier-than-thou, priggish, self-
satisfied, smug, superior

self-sacrifice noun SELFLESSNESS, altruism, generosity, self-denial

self-satisfied adjective SMUG, complacent, pleased with oneself, self-congratulatory

self-seeking adjective SELFISH, careerist, looking out for number one (informal), out for what one can get, self-interested, self-serving

sell verb 1 TRADE, barter, exchange 2 DEAL IN, handle, market, peddle, retail, stock, trade in, traffic in

seller noun DEALER, agent, merchant, purveyor, retailer, salesman or saleswoman, supplier, vendor

selling noun DEALING, business, trading, traffic

sell out verb 1 DISPOSE OF, be out of stock of, get rid of, run out of 2 (informal) BETRAY, double-cross (informal), sell down the river (informal), stab in the back

semblance noun APPEARANCE, aspect, façade, mask, pretense, resemblance, show, veneer

seminal adjective INFLUENTIAL, formative, ground-breaking, important, innovative, original

send verb 1 CONVEY, direct, dispatch, forward, remit, transmit 2 PROPEL, cast, fire, fling, hurl, let fly, shoot

send for verb SUMMON, call for, order, request

sendoff noun FAREWELL, departure, leave-taking, start, valediction

senile adjective DODDERING, decrepit, doting, in one's dotage

senility noun DOTAGE, decrepitude, infirmity, loss of one's faculties, senile dementia

senior adjective 1 HIGHER RANKING, superior

2 OLDER, elder, major (Brit.)

senior citizen noun PENSIONER, O.A.P., old age pensioner, old fogey (slang), old or elderly person, retired person

seniority noun SUPERIORITY, precedence, priority, rank

sensation noun 1 FEELING, awareness, consciousness, impression, perception, sense 2 EXCITEMENT, commotion, furor, stir, thrill

sensational adjective 1 DRAMATIC, amazing, astounding, awesome, exciting, melodramatic, shock-horror (facetious), shocking, thrilling
2 EXCELLENT, awesome (informal), cool (informal), fabulous (informal), impressive, marvelous, mean (slang), mind-blowing (informal), out of this world (informal), phat (slang), smashing (informal), superb

sense noun 1 FACULTY, feeling, sensation
2 FEELING, atmosphere, aura, awareness, consciousness, impression, perception
3 (sometimes plural) INTELLIGENCE, brains (informal), cleverness, common sense, judgment, reason, sagacity, sanity, sharpness, understanding, wisdom, wit(s)
4 MEANING, drift, gist, implication, import, significance
▶ verb 5 PERCEIVE, be aware of, discern, feel, get the impression, pick up, realize, understand

senseless adjective 1 STUPID, asinine, bonkers (informal), crazy, daft (informal), foolish, idiotic, illogical, inane, irrational, mad, mindless, nonsensical, pointless, ridiculous, silly
2 UNCONSCIOUS, insensible, out,

out cold, stunned

sensibility noun 1 (often plural) FEELINGS, emotions, moral sense, sentiments, susceptibilities
2 SENSITIVITY, responsiveness, sensitiveness, susceptibility

sensible adjective 1 WISE, canny, down-to-earth, intelligent, judicious, practical, prudent, rational, realistic, sage, sane, shrewd, sound
2 (usually with of) AWARE, conscious, mindful, sensitive to

sensitive adjective 1 EASILY HURT, delicate, tender
2 SUSCEPTIBLE, easily affected, impressionable, responsive, touchy-feely (informal)
3 TOUCHY, easily offended, easily upset, thin-skinned
4 RESPONSIVE, acute, fine, keen, precise

sensitivity noun SENSITIVENESS, delicacy, receptiveness, responsiveness, susceptibility

sensual adjective 1 PHYSICAL, animal, bodily, carnal, fleshly, luxurious, voluptuous
2 EROTIC, lascivious, lecherous, lewd, lustful, raunchy (slang), sexual

sensuality noun EROTICISM, carnality, lasciviousness, lecherousness, lewdness, sexiness (informal), voluptuousness

sensuous adjective PLEASURABLE, gratifying, hedonistic, sybaritic

sentence noun 1 PUNISHMENT, condemnation, decision, decree, judgment, order, ruling, verdict
▶ verb 2 CONDEMN, doom, penalize

sententious adjective POMPOUS, canting, judgmental, moralistic, preachifying (informal), sanctimonious

sentient adjective FEELING, conscious, living, sensitive

sentiment noun 1 EMOTION, sensibility, tenderness
2 (often plural) FEELING, attitude, belief, idea, judgment, opinion, view
3 SENTIMENTALITY, emotionalism, mawkishness, romanticism

sentimental adjective ROMANTIC, emotional, maudlin, nostalgic, overemotional, schmaltzy (slang), slushy (informal), soft-hearted, touching, weepy (informal)

sentimentality noun ROMANTICISM, corniness (slang), emotionalism, mawkishness, nostalgia, schmaltz (slang)

sentinel noun GUARD, lookout, sentry, watch, watchman

separable adjective DISTINGUISHABLE, detachable, divisible

separate verb 1 DIVIDE, come apart, come away, detach, disconnect, disjoin, remove, sever, split, sunder
2 PART, break up, disunite, diverge, divorce, estrange, part company, split up
3 ISOLATE, segregate, single out
▶ adjective 4 UNCONNECTED, detached, disconnected, divided, divorced, isolated, unattached
5 INDIVIDUAL, alone, apart, distinct, particular, single, solitary

separated adjective DISCONNECTED, apart, disassociated, disunited, divided, parted, separate, sundered

separately adverb INDIVIDUALLY, alone, apart, severally, singly

separation noun 1 DIVISION, break, disconnection, dissociation, disunion, gap
2 SPLIT-UP, break-up, divorce,

parting, rift, split

septic *adjective* INFECTED, festering, poisoned, putrefying, putrid, suppurating

sepulcher *noun* TOMB, burial place, grave, mausoleum, vault

sequel *noun* 1 FOLLOW-UP, continuation, development
2 CONSEQUENCE, conclusion, end, outcome, result, upshot

sequence *noun* SUCCESSION, arrangement, chain, course, cycle, order, progression, series

serene *adjective* CALM, composed, peaceful, tranquil, unruffled, untroubled

serenity *noun* CALMNESS, calm, composure, peace, peacefulness, quietness, stillness, tranquillity

series *noun* SEQUENCE, chain, course, order, progression, run, set, string, succession, train

serious *adjective* 1 SEVERE, acute, critical, dangerous
2 IMPORTANT, crucial, fateful, grim, momentous, no laughing matter, pressing, significant, urgent, worrying
3 SOLEMN, grave, humorless, sober, unsmiling
4 SINCERE, earnest, genuine, honest, in earnest

seriously *adverb* 1 GRAVELY, acutely, badly, critically, dangerously, severely
2 SINCERELY, gravely, in earnest

seriousness *noun* 1 IMPORTANCE, gravity, significance, urgency
2 SOLEMNITY, earnestness, gravitas, gravity

sermon *noun* 1 HOMILY, address
2 LECTURE, harangue, talking-to (*informal*)

servant *noun* ATTENDANT, domestic, help, maid, retainer, skivvy (*chiefly Brit.*), slave

serve *verb* 1 WORK FOR, aid, assist, attend to, help, minister to, wait on
2 PERFORM, act, complete, discharge, do, fulfill
3 PROVIDE, deliver, dish up, present, set out, supply
4 BE ADEQUATE, answer the purpose, be acceptable, do, function as, satisfy, suffice, suit

service *noun* 1 HELP, assistance, avail, benefit, use, usefulness
2 WORK, business, duty, employment, labor, office
3 OVERHAUL, check, maintenance
4 CEREMONY, observance, rite, worship
▶ *verb* 5 OVERHAUL, check, fine tune, go over, maintain, tune (up)

serviceable *adjective* USEFUL, beneficial, functional, helpful, operative, practical, profitable, usable, utilitarian

servile *adjective* SUBSERVIENT, abject, fawning, grovelling, obsequious, sycophantic, toadying

serving *noun* PORTION, helping

session *noun* MEETING, assembly, conference, congress, discussion, hearing, period, sitting

set¹ *verb* 1 PUT, deposit, lay, locate, place, plant, position, rest, seat, situate, station, stick
2 PREPARE, arrange, lay, make ready, spread
3 HARDEN, cake, congeal, crystallize, solidify, stiffen, thicken
4 ARRANGE, appoint, decide (upon), determine, establish, fix, fix up, resolve, schedule, settle, specify
5 ASSIGN, allot, decree, impose, ordain, prescribe, specify
6 GO DOWN, decline, dip,

disappear, sink, subside, vanish
► *noun* **7** POSITION, attitude, bearing, carriage, posture
8 SCENERY, scene, setting, stage set
► *adjective* **9** FIXED, agreed, appointed, arranged, decided, definite, established, prearranged, predetermined, scheduled, settled
10 INFLEXIBLE, hard and fast, immovable, rigid, stubborn
11 CONVENTIONAL, stereotyped, stock, traditional, unspontaneous
12 ▷▷ **set on** *or* **upon** DETERMINED, bent, intent, resolute
set² *noun* **1** SERIES, assortment, batch, collection, compendium
2 GROUP, band, circle, clique, company, coterie, crowd, faction, gang
setback *noun* HOLD-UP, blow, check, defeat, disappointment, hitch, misfortune, reverse
set back *verb* HOLD UP, delay, hinder, impede, retard, slow
set off *verb* **1** LEAVE, depart, embark, start out
2 DETONATE, explode, ignite
setting *noun* BACKGROUND, backdrop, context, location, scene, scenery, set, site, surroundings
settle *verb* **1** PUT IN ORDER, adjust, order, regulate, straighten out, work out
2 LAND, alight, come to rest, descend, light
3 MOVE TO, dwell, inhabit, live, make one's home, put down roots, reside, set up home, take up residence
4 COLONIZE, people, pioneer, populate
5 CALM, lull, pacify, quell, quiet, quieten, reassure, relax, relieve, soothe

6 PAY, clear, discharge, square (up)
7 (often with *on* or *upon*) DECIDE, agree, confirm, determine, establish, fix
8 RESOLVE, clear up, decide, put an end to, reconcile
settlement *noun* **1** AGREEMENT, arrangement, conclusion, confirmation, establishment, working out
2 PAYMENT, clearing, discharge
3 COLONY, community, encampment, outpost
settler *noun* COLONIST, colonizer, frontiersman, immigrant, pioneer
setup *noun* ARRANGEMENT, conditions, organization, regime, structure, system
set up *verb* **1** BUILD, assemble, construct, erect, put together, put up, raise
2 ESTABLISH, arrange, begin, found, initiate, institute, organize, prearrange, prepare
sever *verb* **1** CUT, cut in two, detach, disconnect, disjoin, divide, part, separate, split
2 BREAK OFF, dissociate, put an end to, terminate
several *adjective* SOME, different, diverse, manifold, many, sundry, various
severe *adjective* **1** STRICT, austere, cruel, drastic, hard, harsh, oppressive, rigid, unbending
2 GRIM, forbidding, grave, serious, stern, tight-lipped, unsmiling
3 INTENSE, acute, extreme, fierce
4 PLAIN, austere, classic, homely, restrained, simple, Spartan, unadorned, unembellished, unfussy
severely *adverb* **1** STRICTLY, harshly, sharply, sternly
2 SERIOUSLY, acutely, badly,

extremely, gravely

severity noun STRICTNESS, hardness, harshness, severeness, sternness, toughness

sex noun 1 GENDER

2 (SEXUAL) INTERCOURSE, coition, coitus, copulation, fornication, lovemaking, sexual relations

sexual adjective 1 CARNAL, erotic, intimate, sensual, sexy

2 REPRODUCTIVE, genital, procreative, sex

sexual intercourse noun COPULATION, bonking (informal), carnal knowledge, coition, coitus, sex, union

sexuality noun DESIRE, carnality, eroticism, lust, sensuality, sexiness (informal)

sexy adjective EROTIC, arousing, naughty, provocative, seductive, sensual, sensuous, suggestive, titillating

shabby adjective 1 TATTY, dilapidated, mean, ragged, run-down, scruffy, seedy, tattered, threadbare, worn

2 MEAN, cheap, contemptible, despicable, dirty, dishonorable, lousy (slang), low, rotten (informal), scurvy, scuzzy (slang)

shack noun HUT, cabin, shanty

shackle noun 1 (often plural) FETTER, bond, chain, iron, leg-iron, manacle

▶ verb 2 FETTER, bind, chain, manacle, put in irons

shade noun 1 DIMNESS, dusk, gloom, gloominess, semidarkness, shadow

2 SCREEN, blind, canopy, cover, covering, curtain, shield, veil

3 COLOR, hue, tinge, tint, tone

4 DASH, hint, suggestion, trace

5 (literary) GHOST, apparition, phantom, specter, spirit

6 ▷▷ **put into the shade** OUTSHINE, eclipse, outclass, overshadow

▶ verb 7 COVER, conceal, hide, obscure, protect, screen, shield, veil

8 DARKEN, cloud, dim, shadow

shadow noun 1 DIMNESS, cover, darkness, dusk, gloom, shade

2 TRACE, hint, suggestion, suspicion

3 CLOUD, blight, gloom, sadness

▶ verb 4 SHADE, darken, overhang, screen, shield

5 FOLLOW, stalk, tail (informal), trail

shadowy adjective 1 DARK, dim, dusky, gloomy, murky, shaded, shady

2 VAGUE, dim, dreamlike, faint, ghostly, nebulous, phantom, spectral, unsubstantial

shady adjective 1 SHADED, cool, dim

2 (informal) CROOKED, disreputable, dodgy (Brit., Austral., & N.Z. informal), dubious, questionable, shifty, suspect, suspicious, unethical

shaft noun 1 HANDLE, pole, rod, shank, stem

2 RAY, beam, gleam

shaggy adjective UNKEMPT, hairy, hirsute, long-haired, rough, tousled, unshorn

shake verb 1 VIBRATE, bump, jar, jolt, quake, rock, shiver, totter, tremble

2 WAVE, brandish, flourish

3 UPSET, distress, disturb, frighten, rattle (informal), shock, unnerve

▶ noun 4 VIBRATION, agitation, convulsion, jerk, jolt, quaking, shiver, shudder, trembling, tremor

shake up verb 1 STIR (UP), agitate, churn (up), mix

2 UPSET, disturb, shock, unsettle

shaky adjective 1 UNSTEADY,

faltering, precarious, quivery, rickety, trembling, unstable, weak
2 UNCERTAIN, dubious, iffy (*informal*), questionable, suspect

shallow *adjective* 1 SUPERFICIAL, empty, slight, surface, trivial
2 UNINTELLIGENT, foolish, frivolous, ignorant, puerile, simple

sham *noun* 1 PHONEY *or* PHONY (*informal*), counterfeit, forgery, fraud, hoax, humbug, imitation, impostor, pretense
▶ *adjective* FALSE, artificial, bogus, counterfeit, feigned, imitation, mock, phoney *or* phony (*informal*), pretended, simulated
▶ *verb* 3 FAKE, affect, assume, feign, pretend, put on, simulate

shambles *noun* CHAOS, confusion, disarray, disorder, havoc, madhouse, mess, muddle

shame *noun* 1 EMBARRASSMENT, abashment, humiliation, ignominy, mortification
2 DISGRACE, blot, discredit, dishonor, disrepute, infamy, reproach, scandal, smear
▶ *verb* 3 EMBARRASS, abash, disgrace, humble, humiliate, mortify
4 DISHONOR, blot, debase, defile, degrade, smear, stain

shamefaced *adjective* EMBARRASSED, abashed, ashamed, humiliated, mortified, red-faced, sheepish

shameful *adjective*
1 EMBARRASSING, cringe-making (*Brit. informal*), humiliating, mortifying
2 DISGRACEFUL, base, dishonorable, low, mean, outrageous, scandalous, wicked

shameless *adjective* BRAZEN, audacious, barefaced, flagrant, hardened, insolent, unabashed, unashamed

shanty *noun* SHACK, cabin, hut, shed

shape *noun* 1 FORM, build, configuration, contours, figure, lines, outline, profile, silhouette
2 PATTERN, frame, model, mold
3 CONDITION, fettle, health, state, trim
▶ *verb* 4 FORM, create, fashion, make, model, mold, produce
5 DEVELOP, adapt, devise, frame, modify, plan

shapeless *adjective* FORMLESS, amorphous, irregular, misshapen, unstructured

shapely *adjective* WELL-FORMED, curvaceous, elegant, graceful, neat, trim, well-proportioned

share *noun* 1 PART, allotment, allowance, contribution, due, lot, portion, quota, ration, whack (*informal*)
▶ *verb* 2 DIVIDE, assign, distribute, partake, participate, receive, split

sharp *adjective* 1 KEEN, acute, jagged, pointed, serrated, spiky
2 SUDDEN, abrupt, distinct, extreme, marked
3 CLEAR, crisp, distinct, well-defined
4 QUICK-WITTED, alert, astute, bright, clever, discerning, knowing, penetrating, perceptive, quick
5 DISHONEST, artful, crafty, cunning, sly, unscrupulous, wily
6 CUTTING, barbed, biting, bitter, caustic, harsh, hurtful
7 SOUR, acid, acrid, hot, piquant, pungent, tart
8 ACUTE, intense, painful, piercing, severe, shooting, stabbing
▶ *adverb* 9 PROMPTLY, exactly,

on the dot, on time, precisely, punctually

sharpen verb WHET, edge, grind, hone

shatter verb 1 SMASH, break, burst, crack, crush, pulverize
2 DESTROY, demolish, ruin, torpedo, wreck

shattered adjective (informal)
1 EXHAUSTED, all in (slang), dead beat (informal), done in (informal), drained, knackered (slang), ready to drop, tired out, worn out
2 DEVASTATED, blown away, crushed

shave verb TRIM, crop, pare, shear

shed¹ noun HUT, outhouse, shack

shed² verb 1 GIVE OUT, cast, drop, emit, give, radiate, scatter, shower, spill
2 CAST OFF, discard, moult, slough

sheen noun SHINE, brightness, gleam, gloss, luster, polish

sheepish adjective EMBARRASSED, abashed, ashamed, mortified, self-conscious, shamefaced

sheer adjective 1 TOTAL, absolute, complete, downright, out-and-out, pure, unmitigated, utter
2 STEEP, abrupt, precipitous
3 FINE, diaphanous, gauzy, gossamer, see-through, thin, transparent

sheet noun 1 COAT, film, lamina, layer, overlay, stratum, surface, veneer
2 PIECE, panel, plate, slab
3 EXPANSE, area, blanket, covering, stretch, sweep

shell noun 1 CASE, husk, pod
2 FRAME, framework, hull, structure
▶ verb 3 BOMB, attack, blitz, bombard, strafe

shell out verb PAY OUT, fork out (slang), give, hand over

shelter noun 1 PROTECTION, cover, defense, guard, screen
2 SAFETY, asylum, haven, refuge, retreat, sanctuary, security
▶ verb 3 PROTECT, cover, defend, guard, harbor, hide, safeguard, shield
4 TAKE SHELTER, hide, seek refuge

sheltered adjective PROTECTED, cloistered, isolated, quiet, screened, secluded, shaded, shielded

shelve verb POSTPONE, defer, freeze, put aside, put on ice, put on the back burner (informal), suspend, take a rain check on (informal)

shepherd verb GUIDE, conduct, herd, steer, usher

shield noun 1 PROTECTION, cover, defense, guard, safeguard, screen, shelter
▶ verb 2 PROTECT, cover, defend, guard, safeguard, screen, shelter

shift verb 1 MOVE, budge, displace, move around, rearrange, relocate, reposition
▶ noun 2 MOVE, displacement, rearrangement, shifting

shiftless adjective LAZY, aimless, good-for-nothing, idle, lackadaisical, slothful, unambitious, unenterprising

shifty adjective UNTRUSTWORTHY, deceitful, devious, evasive, furtive, slippery, sly, tricky, underhand

shimmer verb 1 GLEAM, glisten, scintillate, twinkle
▶ noun 2 GLEAM, iridescence

shine verb 1 GLEAM, beam, flash, glare, glisten, glitter, glow, radiate, sparkle, twinkle
2 POLISH, brush, buff, burnish
3 STAND OUT, be conspicuous, excel

▶ *noun* **4** BRIGHTNESS, glare, gleam, light, radiance, shimmer, sparkle

5 POLISH, gloss, luster, sheen

shining *adjective* BRIGHT, beaming, brilliant, gleaming, glistening, luminous, radiant, shimmering, sparkling

shiny *adjective* BRIGHT, gleaming, glistening, glossy, lustrous, polished

ship *noun* VESSEL, boat, craft

shipshape *adjective* TIDY, neat, orderly, spick-and-span, trim, well-ordered, well-organized

shirk *verb* DODGE, avoid, evade, get out of, skive (*Brit. slang*), slack

shirker *noun* SLACKER, clock-watcher, dodger, idler, skiver (*Brit. slang*)

shiver¹ *verb* **1** TREMBLE, quake, quiver, shake, shudder

▶ *noun* **2** TREMBLING, flutter, quiver, shudder, tremor

shiver² *verb* SPLINTER, break, crack, fragment, shatter, smash, smash to smithereens

shivery *adjective* SHAKING, chilled, chilly, cold, quaking, quivery, shaky

shock *verb* **1** HORRIFY, appall, disgust, nauseate, revolt, scandalize, sicken

2 ASTOUND, jolt, shake, stagger, stun, stupefy

▶ *noun* **3** IMPACT, blow, clash, collision

4 UPSET, blow, bombshell, distress, disturbance, stupefaction, stupor, trauma, turn (*informal*)

shocking *adjective* DREADFUL, appalling, atrocious, disgraceful, disgusting, ghastly, horrifying, nauseating, outrageous, revolting, scandalous, sickening

shoddy *adjective* INFERIOR, poor, rubbishy, second-rate, slipshod, tawdry, trashy

shoot *verb* **1** HIT, blast (*slang*), bring down, kill, open fire, plug (*slang*)

2 FIRE, discharge, emit, fling, hurl, launch, project, propel

3 SPEED, bolt, charge, dart, dash, fly, hurtle, race, rush, streak, tear

▶ *noun* **4** BRANCH, bud, offshoot, sprig, sprout

shop *noun* STORE, boutique, emporium, hypermarket, supermarket

shore *noun* BEACH, coast, sands, seashore, strand (*poetic*)

shore up *verb* SUPPORT, brace, buttress, hold, prop, reinforce, strengthen, underpin

short *adjective* **1** CONCISE, brief, compressed, laconic, pithy, succinct, summary, terse

2 SMALL, diminutive, dumpy, little, petite, squat

3 BRIEF, fleeting, momentary

4 (*often with of*) LACKING, deficient, limited, low (on), scant, scarce, wanting

5 ABRUPT, brusque, curt, discourteous, impolite, sharp, terse, uncivil

▶ *adverb* **6** ABRUPTLY, suddenly, without warning

shortage *noun* DEFICIENCY, dearth, insufficiency, lack, paucity, scarcity, want

shortcoming *noun* FAILING, defect, fault, flaw, imperfection, weakness

shorten *verb* CUT, abbreviate, abridge, curtail, decrease, diminish, lessen, reduce

shortly *adverb* SOON, before long, in a little while, presently

short-sighted *adjective* **1** NEAR-SIGHTED, myopic

2 UNTHINKING, ill-advised,

ill-considered, impolitic,
impractical, improvident,
imprudent, injudicious

short-tempered *adjective*
QUICK-TEMPERED, hot-tempered,
impatient, irascible, ratty (*Brit. &
N.Z. informal*), testy

shot¹ *noun* 1 THROW, discharge,
lob, pot shot
2 PELLET, ball, bullet, lead,
projectile, slug
3 MARKSMAN, shooter
4 (*slang*) ATTEMPT, effort, endeavor,
go (*informal*), stab (*informal*), try,
turn

shoulder *verb* 1 BEAR, accept,
assume, be responsible for, carry,
take on
2 PUSH, elbow, jostle, press, shove

shout *noun* 1 CRY, bellow, call, roar,
scream, yell
▶ *verb* 2 CRY (OUT), bawl, bellow,
call (out), holler (*informal*), roar,
scream, yell

shout down *verb* SILENCE, drown,
drown out, overwhelm

shove *verb* PUSH, drive, elbow,
impel, jostle, press, propel, thrust

shovel *verb* MOVE, dredge, heap,
ladle, load, scoop, toss

shove off *verb* GO AWAY, clear off
(*informal*), depart, leave, push off
(*informal*), scram (*informal*)

show *verb* 1 BE VISIBLE, appear
2 DISPLAY, exhibit, present
3 PROVE, clarify, demonstrate,
elucidate, point out
4 INSTRUCT, demonstrate, explain,
teach
5 DISPLAY, indicate, manifest,
register, reveal
6 GUIDE, accompany, attend,
conduct, escort, lead
▶ *noun* 7 ENTERTAINMENT,
presentation, production
8 EXHIBITION, array, display, fair,

pageant, parade, sight, spectacle
9 PRETENSE, affectation, air,
appearance, display, illusion,
parade, pose

showdown *noun* CONFRONTATION,
clash, face-off (*slang*)

shower *noun* 1 DELUGE, barrage,
stream, torrent, volley
▶ *verb* 2 INUNDATE, deluge, heap,
lavish, pour, rain

showman *noun* PERFORMER,
entertainer

show-off *noun* EXHIBITIONIST,
boaster, braggart, poseur

show off *verb* 1 EXHIBIT,
demonstrate, display, flaunt,
parade
2 BOAST, blow one's own trumpet,
brag, swagger

show up *verb* 1 STAND OUT, appear,
be conspicuous, be visible
2 REVEAL, expose, highlight,
lay bare
3 (*informal*) EMBARRASS, let down,
mortify, put to shame
4 ARRIVE, appear, come, turn up

showy *adjective* 1 OSTENTATIOUS,
brash, flamboyant, flash (*informal*),
flashy, over the top (*informal*)
2 GAUDY, garish, loud

shred *noun* 1 STRIP, bit, fragment,
piece, scrap, sliver, tatter
2 PARTICLE, atom, grain, iota, jot,
scrap, trace

shrew *noun* NAG, harpy, harridan,
scold, spitfire, vixen

shrewd *adjective* CLEVER, astute,
calculating, canny, crafty,
cunning, intelligent, keen,
perceptive, perspicacious, sharp,
smart

shrewdness *noun* ASTUTENESS,
canniness, discernment,
judgment, perspicacity, quick
wits, sharpness, smartness

shriek *verb or noun* CRY, scream,

screech, squeal, yell

shrill *adjective* PIERCING, high, penetrating, sharp

shrink *verb* 1 DECREASE, contract, diminish, dwindle, grow smaller, lessen, narrow, shorten

2 RECOIL, cower, cringe, draw back, flinch, quail

shrivel *verb* WITHER, dehydrate, desiccate, shrink, wilt, wizen

shroud *noun* 1 WINDING SHEET, grave clothes

2 COVERING, mantle, pall, screen, veil

▶ *verb* 3 CONCEAL, blanket, cloak, cover, envelop, hide, screen, veil

shudder *verb* 1 SHIVER, convulse, quake, quiver, shake, tremble

▶ *noun* 2 SHIVER, quiver, spasm, tremor

shuffle *verb* 1 SCUFFLE, drag, scrape, shamble

2 REARRANGE, disarrange, disorder, jumble, mix

shun *verb* AVOID, keep away from, steer clear of

shut *verb* CLOSE, fasten, seal, secure, slam

shut down *verb* 1 STOP, halt, switch off

2 CLOSE, shut up

shut out *verb* EXCLUDE, bar, debar, keep out, lock out

shuttle *verb* GO BACK AND FORTH, alternate, commute, go to and fro

shut up *verb* 1 (*informal*) BE QUIET, fall silent, gag, hold one's tongue, hush, silence

2 CONFINE, cage, coop up, immure, imprison, incarcerate

shy¹ *adjective* 1 TIMID, bashful, coy, diffident, retiring, self-conscious, self-effacing, shrinking

2 CAUTIOUS, chary, distrustful, hesitant, suspicious, wary

▶ *verb* 3 (sometimes with *off* or

away) RECOIL, balk, draw back, flinch, start

shy² *verb* THROW, cast, fling, hurl, pitch, sling, toss

shyness *noun* TIMIDNESS, bashfulness, diffidence, lack of confidence, self-consciousness, timidity, timorousness

sick *adjective* 1 NAUSEOUS, ill, nauseated, queasy

2 UNWELL, ailing, diseased, indisposed, poorly (*informal*), under the weather (*informal*)

3 (*informal*) MORBID, black, ghoulish, macabre, sadistic

4 ▷▷ **sick of** TIRED, bored, fed up, jaded, weary

sicken *verb* 1 DISGUST, gross out (*slang*), nauseate, repel, revolt, turn one's stomach

2 FALL ILL, ail, take sick

sickening *adjective* DISGUSTING, distasteful, foul, gross (*slang*), loathsome, nauseating, noisome, offensive, repulsive, revolting, scuzzy (*slang*), stomach-turning (*informal*), vile, yucky *or* yukky (*slang*)

sickly *adjective* 1 UNHEALTHY, ailing, delicate, faint, feeble, infirm, pallid, peaky, wan, weak

2 NAUSEATING, cloying, mawkish

sickness *noun* 1 ILLNESS, affliction, ailment, bug (*informal*), complaint, disease, disorder, malady

2 NAUSEA, queasiness, vomiting

side *noun* 1 BORDER, boundary, division, edge, limit, margin, perimeter, rim, sector, verge

2 PART, aspect, face, facet, flank, hand, surface, view

3 PARTY, camp, cause, faction, sect, team

4 POINT OF VIEW, angle, opinion, position, slant, stand, standpoint, viewpoint

5 (*Brit. slang*) CONCEIT, airs, arrogance
▶ *adjective* **6** SUBORDINATE, ancillary, incidental, lesser, marginal, minor, secondary, subsidiary
▶ *verb* **7** (usually with *with*) SUPPORT, ally with, favor, go along with, take the part of

sidelong *adjective* SIDEWAYS, covert, indirect, oblique

sidestep *verb* AVOID, circumvent, dodge, duck (*informal*), evade, skirt

sidetrack *verb* DIVERT, deflect, distract

sideways *adverb* **1** OBLIQUELY, edgeways, laterally, sidelong, to the side
▶ *adjective* **2** OBLIQUE, sidelong

sidle *verb* EDGE, creep, inch, slink, sneak, steal

siesta *noun* NAP, catnap, doze, forty winks (*informal*), sleep, snooze (*informal*)

sieve *noun* **1** STRAINER, colander
▶ *verb* **2** SIFT, separate, strain

sift *verb* **1** SIEVE, filter, separate
2 EXAMINE, analyze, go through, investigate, research, scrutinize, work over

sight *noun* **1** VISION, eye, eyes, eyesight, seeing
2 VIEW, appearance, perception, range of vision, visibility
3 SPECTACLE, display, exhibition, pageant, scene, show, vista
4 EYESORE, mess, monstrosity
5 ▷▷ **catch sight of** SPOT, espy, glimpse
▶ *verb* **6** SPOT, behold, discern, distinguish, make out, observe, perceive, see

sign *noun* **1** INDICATION, clue, evidence, hint, mark, proof, signal, symptom, token
2 NOTICE, board, placard, warning

3 SYMBOL, badge, device, emblem, logo, mark
4 OMEN, augury, auspice, foreboding, portent, warning
▶ *verb* **5** AUTOGRAPH, endorse, initial, inscribe
6 GESTURE, beckon, gesticulate, indicate, signal

signal *noun* **1** SIGN, beacon, cue, gesture, indication, mark, token
▶ *verb* **2** GESTURE, beckon, gesticulate, indicate, motion, sign, wave

significance *noun* **1** IMPORTANCE, consequence, moment, relevance, weight
2 MEANING, force, implication(s), import, message, point, purport, sense

significant *adjective* **1** IMPORTANT, critical, material, momentous, noteworthy, serious, vital, weighty
2 MEANINGFUL, eloquent, expressive, indicative, suggestive

signify *verb* **1** INDICATE, be a sign of, betoken, connote, denote, imply, intimate, mean, portend, suggest
2 MATTER, be important, carry weight, count

silence *noun* **1** QUIET, calm, hush, lull, peace, stillness
2 MUTENESS, dumbness, reticence, taciturnity
▶ *verb* **3** QUIETEN, cut off, cut short, deaden, gag, muffle, quiet, stifle, still, suppress

silent *adjective* **1** QUIET, hushed, muted, noiseless, soundless, still
2 MUTE, dumb, speechless, taciturn, voiceless, wordless

silently *adjective* QUIETLY, inaudibly, in silence, mutely, noiselessly, soundlessly, without a sound, wordlessly

silhouette noun 1 OUTLINE, form, profile, shape
► verb 2 OUTLINE, etch, stand out
silky adjective SMOOTH, silken, sleek, velvety
silly adjective FOOLISH, absurd, asinine, fatuous, idiotic, inane, ridiculous, senseless, stupid, unwise
silt noun 1 SEDIMENT, alluvium, deposit, ooze, sludge
► verb 2 ▷▷ **silt up** CLOG, choke, congest
similar adjective ALIKE, analogous, close, comparable, like, resembling
similarity noun RESEMBLANCE, affinity, agreement, analogy, closeness, comparability, correspondence, likeness, sameness
simmer verb FUME, be angry, rage, seethe, smolder
simmer down verb CALM DOWN, control oneself, cool off or down, de-stress
simper verb SMILE COYLY, smile affectedly, smirk
simple adjective 1 EASY, clear, intelligible, lucid, plain, straightforward, uncomplicated, understandable, uninvolved
2 PLAIN, classic, natural, unembellished, unfussy
3 PURE, elementary, unalloyed, uncombined, unmixed
4 ARTLESS, childlike, guileless, ingenuous, innocent, naive, natural, sincere, unaffected, unsophisticated
5 HONEST, bald, basic, direct, frank, naked, plain, sincere, stark
6 HUMBLE, dumpy (informal), homely, modest, unpretentious
7 FEEBLE-MINDED, foolish, half-witted, moronic, slow, stupid

simple-minded adjective FEEBLE-MINDED, backward, dim-witted, foolish, idiot, idiotic, moronic, retarded, simple, stupid
simpleton noun HALFWIT, doofus (slang), dork (slang), dullard, fool, idiot, imbecile (informal), moron, numbskull or numskull, schmuck (slang)
simplicity noun 1 EASE, clarity, clearness, straightforwardness
2 PLAINNESS, lack of adornment, purity, restraint
3 ARTLESSNESS, candor, directness, innocence, naivety, openness
simplify verb MAKE SIMPLER, abridge, disentangle, dumb down, reduce to essentials, streamline
simply adverb 1 PLAINLY, clearly, directly, easily, intelligibly, naturally, straightforwardly, unpretentiously
2 JUST, merely, only, purely, solely
3 TOTALLY, absolutely, completely, really, utterly, wholly
simulate verb PRETEND, act, affect, feign, put on, sham
simultaneous adjective COINCIDING, at the same time, coincident, concurrent, contemporaneous, synchronous
simultaneously adverb AT THE SAME TIME, concurrently, together
sin noun 1 WRONGDOING, crime, error, evil, guilt, iniquity, misdeed, offense, transgression
► verb 2 TRANSGRESS, err, fall, go astray, lapse, offend
sincere adjective HONEST, candid, earnest, frank, genuine, guileless, heartfelt, real, serious, true, unaffected
sincerely adverb HONESTLY, earnestly, genuinely, in earnest, seriously, truly, wholeheartedly
sincerity noun HONESTY, candor,

frankness, genuineness, seriousness, truth

sinecure noun SOFT JOB (informal), cushy number (informal), gravy train (slang), money for jam or old rope (informal), soft option

sinful adjective GUILTY, bad, corrupt, criminal, erring, immoral, iniquitous, wicked

sing verb 1 WARBLE, carol, chant, chirp, croon, pipe, trill, yodel
2 HUM, buzz, purr, whine

singe verb BURN, char, scorch, sear

singer noun VOCALIST, balladeer, cantor, chorister, crooner, minstrel, soloist

single adjective 1 ONE, distinct, individual, lone, only, separate, sole, solitary
2 INDIVIDUAL, exclusive, separate, undivided, unshared
3 SIMPLE, unblended, unmixed
4 UNMARRIED, free, unattached, unwed
▶ verb 5 (usually with out) PICK, choose, distinguish, fix on, pick on or out, select, separate, set apart

single-handed adverb UNAIDED, alone, by oneself, independently, on one's own, solo, unassisted, without help

single-minded adjective DETERMINED, dedicated, dogged, fixed, unswerving

singly adverb ONE BY ONE, individually, one at a time, separately

singular adjective 1 SINGLE, individual, separate, sole
2 REMARKABLE, eminent, exceptional, notable, noteworthy, outstanding
3 UNUSUAL, curious, eccentric, extraordinary, odd, peculiar, queer, strange

singularly adverb REMARKABLY,

especially, exceptionally, notably, outstandingly, particularly, uncommonly, unusually

sinister adjective THREATENING, dire, disquieting, evil, malign, menacing, ominous

sink verb 1 DESCEND, dip, drop, fall, founder, go down, go under, lower, plunge, submerge, subside
2 FALL, abate, collapse, drop, lapse, slip, subside
3 DECLINE, decay, deteriorate, diminish, dwindle, fade, fail, flag, lessen, weaken, worsen
4 DIG, bore, drill, drive, excavate
5 STOOP, be reduced to, lower oneself

sink in verb BE UNDERSTOOD, get through to, penetrate, register (informal)

sinner noun WRONGDOER, evildoer, malefactor, miscreant, offender, transgressor

sip verb 1 DRINK, sample, sup, taste
▶ noun 2 SWALLOW, drop, taste, thimbleful

sissy noun 1 WIMP (informal), coward, jessie (Scot. slang), milksop, mama's boy, mummy's boy, namby-pamby, softie (informal), weakling, wet (Brit. informal)
▶ adjective 2 WIMPISH or WIMPY (informal), cowardly, effeminate, feeble, namby-pamby, soft (informal), unmanly, weak, wet (Brit. informal)

sit verb 1 REST, perch, settle
2 CONVENE, assemble, deliberate, meet, officiate, preside

site noun 1 LOCATION, place, plot, position, setting, spot
▶ verb 2 LOCATE, install, place, position, set, situate

situation noun 1 STATE OF AFFAIRS, case, circumstances, condition, plight, state

2 LOCATION, place, position, setting, site, spot

3 STATUS, rank, station

4 JOB, employment, office, place, position, post

sizable, sizeable *adjective* LARGE, considerable, decent, goodly, largish, respectable, substantial, supersize

size *noun* DIMENSIONS, amount, bulk, extent, immensity, magnitude, mass, proportions, range, volume

size up *verb* ASSESS, appraise, evaluate, take stock of

sizzle *verb* HISS, crackle, frizzle, fry, spit

skedaddle *verb* (*slang*) RUN AWAY, abscond, beat it (*slang*), clear off (*informal*), disappear, flee, run for it, scram (*informal*), take to one's heels

skeleton *noun* FRAMEWORK, bare bones, draft, frame, outline, sketch, structure

skeptic *noun* DOUBTER, cynic, disbeliever, doubting Thomas

skeptical *adjective* DOUBTFUL, cynical, disbelieving, dubious, incredulous, mistrustful, unconvinced

skepticism *noun* DOUBT, cynicism, disbelief, incredulity, unbelief

sketch *noun* 1 DRAWING, delineation, design, draft, outline, plan

▶ *verb* 2 DRAW, delineate, depict, draft, outline, represent, rough out

sketchy *adjective* INCOMPLETE, cursory, inadequate, perfunctory, rough, scrappy, skimpy, superficial

skill *noun* EXPERTISE, ability,

art, cleverness, competence, craft, dexterity, facility, knack, proficiency, skillfulness, talent, technique

skilled *adjective* EXPERT, able, masterly, professional, proficient, skillful

skillful *adjective* EXPERT, able, adept, adroit, clever, competent, dexterous, masterly, practiced, professional, proficient, skilled

skim *verb* 1 SEPARATE, cream

2 GLIDE, coast, float, fly, sail, soar

3 (usually with *through*) SCAN, glance, run one's eye over

skimp *verb* STINT, be mean with, be sparing with, cut corners, scamp, scrimp

skin *noun* 1 HIDE, fell, pelt

2 COATING, casing, crust, film, husk, outside, peel, rind

▶ *verb* 3 PEEL, flay, scrape

skin alive *verb* (*informal*) ATTACK, assail, assault, let have it (*informal*), let loose on (*informal*)

skinflint *noun* MISER, meanie or meany (*informal, chiefly Brit.*), niggard, penny-pincher (*informal*), Scrooge

skinny *adjective* THIN, emaciated, lean, scrawny, undernourished

skip *verb* 1 HOP, bob, bounce, caper, dance, flit, frisk, gambol, prance, trip

2 PASS OVER, eschew, give (something) a miss, leave out, miss out, omit

skirmish *noun* 1 FIGHT, battle, brush, clash, conflict, encounter, fracas, scrap (*informal*)

▶ *verb* 2 FIGHT, clash, collide

skirt *verb* 1 BORDER, edge, flank

2 (often with *around* or *round*) AVOID, circumvent, evade, steer clear of

skit *noun* 1 PARODY, burlesque,

sketch, spoof (*informal*), takeoff (*informal*)

2 PLAY, comedy, drama, performance

skittish *adjective* LIVELY, excitable, fidgety, highly strung, jumpy, nervous, restive, wired (*slang*)

skulk *verb* LURK, creep, prowl, slink, sneak

sky *noun* HEAVENS, firmament

slab *noun* PIECE, chunk, lump, portion, slice, wedge

slack *adjective* 1 LOOSE, baggy, lax, limp, relaxed

2 NEGLIGENT, idle, inactive, lax, lazy, neglectful, remiss, slapdash, slipshod

3 SLOW, dull, inactive, quiet, slow-moving, sluggish

▶ *noun* 4 ROOM, excess, give (*informal*), leeway

▶ *verb* 5 SHIRK, dodge, idle, skive (*Brit. slang*)

slacken *verb* (often with *off*) LESSEN, abate, decrease, diminish, drop off, moderate, reduce, relax

slacker *noun* LAYABOUT IDLER, couch potato (*slang*), dodger, loafer, shirker, skiver (*Brit. slang*)

slake *verb* SATISFY, assuage, quench, sate

slam *verb* BANG, crash, dash, fling, hurl, smash, throw

slander *noun* 1 DEFAMATION, calumny, libel, scandal, smear

▶ *verb* 2 DEFAME, blacken (someone's) name, libel, malign, smear

slanderous *adjective* DEFAMATORY, damaging, libelous, malicious

slant *verb* 1 SLOPE, bend, bevel, cant, heel, incline, lean, list, tilt

2 BIAS, angle, color, distort, twist

▶ *noun* 3 SLOPE, camber, gradient, incline, tilt

4 BIAS, angle, emphasis, one-sidedness, point of view, prejudice

slanting *adjective* SLOPING, angled, at an angle, bent, diagonal, inclined, oblique, tilted, tilting

slap *noun* 1 SMACK, blow, cuff, spank

▶ *verb* 2 SMACK, clap, cuff, paddle (*U.S. & Canad.*), spank

slapdash *adjective* CARELESS, clumsy, hasty, hurried, messy, slipshod, sloppy (*informal*)

slash *verb* 1 CUT, gash, hack, lacerate, rend, rip, score, slit

2 REDUCE, cut, drop, lower

▶ *noun* 3 CUT, gash, incision, laceration, rent, rip, slit

slaughter *verb* 1 MURDER, butcher, kill, massacre, slay

▶ *noun* 2 MURDER, bloodshed, butchery, carnage, killing, massacre, slaying

slaughterhouse *noun* ABATTOIR

slave *noun* 1 SERVANT, drudge, serf, skivvy (*chiefly Brit.*), vassal

▶ *verb* 2 TOIL, drudge, slog

slavery *noun* ENSLAVEMENT, bondage, captivity, servitude, subjugation

slavish *adjective* 1 SERVILE, abject, base, cringing, fawning, grovelling, obsequious, submissive, sycophantic

2 IMITATIVE, second-hand, unimaginative, unoriginal

slay *verb* KILL, butcher, massacre, mow down, murder, slaughter

sleaze *noun* CORRUPTION, bribery, dishonesty, extortion, fraud, unscrupulousness, venality

sleazy *adjective* SORDID, disreputable, low, run-down, scuzzy (*slang*), seedy, squalid

sleek *adjective* GLOSSY, lustrous, shiny, smooth

sleep *noun* 1 SLUMBER(S), doze, forty winks (*informal*), hibernation,

nap, siesta, snooze (*informal*), zizz
(*Brit. informal*)
▶ *verb* 2 SLUMBER, catnap, doze,
drowse, hibernate, snooze
(*informal*), take a nap

sleepless *adjective* WAKEFUL,
insomniac, restless

sleepy *adjective* DROWSY, dull,
heavy, inactive, lethargic,
sluggish

slender *adjective* 1 SLIM, lean,
narrow, slight, willowy
2 FAINT, poor, remote, slight, slim,
tenuous, thin
3 MEAGER, little, scant, scanty,
small

sleuth *noun* DETECTIVE, gumshoe
(*slang*), private eye (*informal*),
(private) investigator

slice *noun* 1 SHARE, cut, helping,
portion, segment, sliver, wedge
▶ *verb* 2 CUT, carve, divide, sever

slick *adjective* 1 GLIB, plausible,
polished, smooth, specious
2 SKILLFUL, adroit, deft, dexterous,
polished, professional
▶ *verb* 3 SMOOTH, plaster down,
sleek

slide *verb* SLIP, coast, glide, skim,
slither

slight *adjective* 1 SMALL, feeble,
insignificant, meager, measly,
minor, paltry, scanty, trifling,
trivial, unimportant
2 SLIM, delicate, feeble, fragile,
lightly-built, small, spare
▶ *verb* 3 SNUB, affront, blow off
(*slang*), disdain, ignore, insult,
scorn
▶ *noun* 4 SNUB, affront, insult,
neglect, rebuff, slap in the face
(*informal*), (the) cold shoulder

slightly *adverb* A LITTLE, somewhat

slim *adjective* 1 SLENDER, lean,
narrow, slight, svelte, thin, trim
2 SLIGHT, faint, poor, remote,

slender
▶ *verb* 3 LOSE WEIGHT, diet, reduce

slimy *adjective* 1 VISCOUS, clammy,
glutinous, oozy
2 OBSEQUIOUS, creeping,
grovelling, oily, servile, smarmy
(*Brit. informal*), unctuous

sling *verb* 1 THROW, cast, chuck
(*informal*), fling, heave, hurl, lob
(*informal*), shy, toss
2 HANG, dangle, suspend

slink *verb* CREEP, prowl, skulk, slip,
sneak, steal

slinky *adjective* FIGURE-HUGGING,
clinging, close-fitting, skintight

slip¹ *verb* 1 FALL, skid
2 SLIDE, glide, skate, slither
3 SNEAK, conceal, creep, hide, steal
4 (sometimes with *up*) MAKE
A MISTAKE, blunder, err,
miscalculate
5 ▷▷ **let slip** GIVE AWAY, disclose,
divulge, leak, reveal
▶ *noun* 6 MISTAKE, blunder, error,
failure, fault, lapse, omission,
oversight
7 ▷▷ **give (someone) the slip**
ESCAPE FROM, dodge, elude, evade,
get away from, lose (someone)

slippery *adjective* 1 SMOOTH, glassy,
greasy, icy, slippy (*informal or
dialect*), unsafe
2 DEVIOUS, crafty, cunning,
dishonest, evasive, shifty, tricky,
untrustworthy

slipshod *adjective* CARELESS,
casual, slapdash, sloppy (*informal*),
slovenly, untidy

slit *noun* 1 CUT, gash, incision,
opening, rent, split, tear
▶ *verb* 2 CUT (OPEN), gash, knife,
lance, pierce, rip, slash

slither *verb* SLIDE, glide, slink, slip,
snake, undulate

sliver *noun* SHRED, fragment,
paring, shaving, splinter

slobber verb DROOL, dribble, drivel, salivate, slaver

slobbish adjective MESSY, slovenly, unclean, unkempt, untidy

slog verb 1 WORK, labor, plod, plow through, slave, toil
2 TRUDGE, tramp, trek
3 HIT, punch, slug, sock (slang), strike, thump, wallop (informal)
▶ noun 4 LABOR, effort, exertion, struggle
5 TRUDGE, hike, tramp, trek

slogan noun CATCH PHRASE, catchword, motto

slop verb 1 SPILL, overflow, slosh (informal), splash
▶ noun 2 (informal) FOOD, grub (slang), mess (slang), nosh (slang)

slope noun 1 INCLINATION, gradient, incline, ramp, rise, slant, tilt
▶ verb 2 SLANT, drop away, fall, incline, lean, rise, tilt
3 ▷▷ **slope off** SLINK AWAY, creep away, slip away

sloping adjective SLANTING, inclined, leaning, oblique

sloppy adjective 1 CARELESS, messy, slipshod, slovenly, untidy
2 SENTIMENTAL, gushing, mawkish, slushy (informal), soppy (Brit. informal)

slot noun 1 OPENING, aperture, groove, hole, slit, vent
2 (informal) PLACE, opening, position, space, time, vacancy
▶ verb 3 FIT IN, fit, insert

sloth noun LAZINESS, idleness, inactivity, inertia, slackness, sluggishness, torpor

slothful adjective LAZY, idle, inactive, indolent, skiving (Brit. slang), workshy

slouch verb SLUMP, droop, loll, stoop

slovenly adjective CARELESS, disorderly, negligent, slack, slapdash, slipshod, sloppy (informal), untidy

slow adjective 1 PROLONGED, gradual, lingering, long-drawn-out, protracted
2 UNHURRIED, dawdling, lackadaisical, laggard, lazy, leisurely, ponderous, sluggish
3 LATE, backward, behind, delayed, tardy
4 STUPID, braindead (informal), dense, dim, dozy (Brit. informal), dull-witted, obtuse, retarded, thick
▶ verb 5 (often with up or down) REDUCE SPEED, brake, decelerate, handicap, hold up, retard, slacken (off)

slowly adverb GRADUALLY, leisurely, unhurriedly

sludge noun SEDIMENT, mire, muck, mud, ooze, residue, silt, slime

sluggish adjective INACTIVE, dull, heavy, indolent, inert, lethargic, slothful, slow, torpid

slum noun HOVEL, ghetto

slumber verb SLEEP, doze, drowse, nap, snooze (informal), zizz (Brit. informal)

slump verb 1 FALL, collapse, crash, plunge, sink, slip
2 SAG, droop, hunch, loll, slouch
▶ noun 3 FALL, collapse, crash, decline, downturn, drop, reverse, trough
4 RECESSION, depression

slur noun INSULT, affront, aspersion, calumny, innuendo, insinuation, smear, stain

slut noun (offensive) TART, ho (slang), scrubber (Brit. & Austral. slang), slag (Brit. slang), slapper (Brit. slang), trollop, whore

sly adjective 1 CUNNING, artful,

clever, crafty, devious, scheming, secret, shifty, stealthy, subtle, underhand, wily

2 ROGUISH, arch, impish, knowing, mischievous

▶ noun 3 ▷▷ **on the sly** SECRETLY, covertly, on the quiet, privately, surreptitiously

smack verb 1 SLAP, clap, cuff, hit, paddle (U.S. & Canad.), spank, strike

▶ noun 2 SLAP, blow

▶ adverb 3 (informal) DIRECTLY, exactly, precisely, right, slap (informal), squarely, straight

small adjective 1 LITTLE, diminutive, mini, miniature, minute, petite, pygmy or pigmy, teeny, teeny-weeny, tiny, undersized, wee

2 UNIMPORTANT, insignificant, minor, negligible, paltry, petty, trifling, trivial

3 PETTY, base, mean, narrow

4 MODEST, humble, unpretentious

small-minded adjective PETTY, bigoted, intolerant, mean, narrow-minded, ungenerous

small-time adjective MINOR, insignificant, of no account, petty, unimportant

smarmy adjective (Brit. informal) OBSEQUIOUS, crawling, ingratiating, servile, smooth, suave, sycophantic, toadying, unctuous

smart adjective 1 NEAT, chic, elegant, natty (informal), snappy, spruce, stylish, trim

2 CLEVER, acute, astute, bright, canny, ingenious, intelligent, keen, quick, sharp, shrewd

3 BRISK, lively, quick, vigorous

▶ verb 4 STING, burn, hurt

▶ noun 5 STING, pain, soreness

smart aleck noun (informal) KNOW-ALL (informal), clever-clogs

(informal), smarty pants (informal), wise guy (informal)

smarten verb TIDY, groom, put in order, put to rights, spruce up

smash verb 1 BREAK, crush, demolish, pulverize, shatter

2 COLLIDE, crash

3 DESTROY, lay waste, ruin, trash (slang), wreck

▶ noun 4 DESTRUCTION, collapse, downfall, failure, ruin

5 COLLISION, accident, crash

smattering noun MODICUM, bit, rudiments

smear verb 1 SPREAD OVER, bedaub, coat, cover, daub, rub on

2 DIRTY, smudge, soil, stain, sully

3 SLANDER, besmirch, blacken, malign

▶ noun 4 SMUDGE, blot, blotch, daub, splotch, streak

5 SLANDER, calumny, defamation, libel

smell verb 1 SNIFF, scent

2 STINK, pong (Brit. informal), reek

▶ noun 3 ODOR, aroma, bouquet, fragrance, perfume, scent

4 STINK, fetor, pong (Brit. informal), stench

smelly adjective STINKING, fetid, foul, foul-smelling, funky (slang), malodorous, noisome, reeking

smirk noun SMUG LOOK, simper

smitten adjective 1 AFFLICTED, laid low, plagued, struck

2 INFATUATED, beguiled, bewitched, captivated, charmed, enamored

smolder verb SEETHE, boil, fume, rage, simmer

smooth adjective 1 EVEN, flat, flush, horizontal, level, plane

2 SLEEK, glossy, polished, shiny, silky, soft, velvety

3 EASY, effortless, well-ordered

4 FLOWING, regular, rhythmic,

steady, uniform

5 SUAVE, facile, glib, persuasive, slick, smarmy (*Brit. informal*), unctuous, urbane

6 MELLOW, agreeable, mild, pleasant

▶ *verb* **7** FLATTEN, iron, level, plane, press

8 CALM, appease, assuage, ease, mitigate, mollify, soften

smother *verb* **1** SUFFOCATE, choke, stifle, strangle

2 SUPPRESS, conceal, hide, muffle, repress, stifle

smudge *noun* **1** SMEAR, daub, dirty, mark, smirch

▶ *noun* **2** SMEAR, blemish, blot

smug *adjective* SELF-SATISFIED, complacent, conceited, superior

smuggler *noun* TRAFFICKER, bootlegger, runner

smutty *adjective* OBSCENE, bawdy, blue, coarse, crude, dirty, indecent, indelicate, suggestive, vulgar

snack *noun* LIGHT MEAL, bite, refreshment(s)

snag *noun* **1** DIFFICULTY, catch, complication, disadvantage, downside, drawback, hitch, obstacle, problem

▶ *verb* **2** CATCH, rip, tear

snap *verb* **1** BREAK, crack, separate

2 CRACKLE, click, pop

3 BITE AT, bite, nip, snatch

4 SPEAK SHARPLY, bark, jump down (someone's) throat (*informal*), lash out at

▶ *noun* **5** CRACKLE, pop

6 BITE, grab, nip

▶ *adjective* **7** INSTANT, immediate, spur-of-the-moment, sudden

snappy *adjective* **1** IRRITABLE, cross, edgy, ratty (*Brit. & N.Z. informal*), testy, tetchy, touchy

2 SMART, chic, cool (*informal*),

dapper, fashionable, natty (*informal*), phat (*slang*), stylish

snap up *verb* SEIZE, grab, pounce upon, take advantage of

snare *noun* **1** TRAP, gin, net, noose, wire

▶ *verb* **2** TRAP, catch, entrap, net, seize, wire

snarl¹ *verb* (often with *up*) TANGLE, entangle, entwine, muddle, ravel

snarl-up *noun* TANGLE, confusion, entanglement, muddle

snatch *verb* **1** SEIZE, clutch, grab, grasp, grip

▶ *noun* **2** BIT, fragment, part, piece, snippet

sneak *verb* **1** SLINK, lurk, pad, skulk, slip, steal

2 SLIP, smuggle, spirit

3 (*informal*) INFORM ON, grass on (*Brit. slang*), shop (*slang, chiefly Brit.*), tell on (*informal*), tell tales

▶ *noun* **4** INFORMER, telltale

sneaking *adjective* **1** NAGGING, persistent, uncomfortable, worrying

2 SECRET, hidden, private, undivulged, unexpressed, unvoiced

sneaky *adjective* SLY, deceitful, devious, dishonest, double-dealing, down and dirty (*informal*), furtive, low, mean, shifty, untrustworthy

sneer *noun* **1** SCORN, derision, gibe, jeer, mockery, ridicule

▶ *verb* **2** SCORN, deride, disdain, jeer, laugh, mock, ridicule

snide *adjective* NASTY, cynical, disparaging, hurtful, ill-natured, malicious, sarcastic, scornful, sneering, spiteful

sniff *verb* INHALE, breathe, smell

snigger *noun or verb* LAUGH, giggle, snicker, titter

snip *verb* **1** CUT, clip, crop, dock,

shave, trim
► *noun* **2** (*informal*) BARGAIN,
giveaway, good buy, steal (*informal*)
3 BIT, clipping, fragment, piece,
scrap, shred
snipe *verb* CRITICIZE, carp,
denigrate, disparage, jeer, knock
(*informal*), put down
snippet *noun* PIECE, fragment,
part, scrap, shred
snitch *verb* **1** (*informal*) INFORM ON,
grass on (*Brit. slang*), tattle on, tell
on (*informal*), tell tales
► *noun* **2** INFORMER, tattletale,
telltale
snivel *verb* WHINE, cry, grizzle
(*informal, chiefly Brit.*), moan, sniffle,
whimper, whinge (*informal*)
snob *noun* ELITIST, highbrow, prig
snobbery *noun* ARROGANCE, airs,
pretension, pride, snobbishness
snobbish *adjective* SUPERIOR,
arrogant, patronizing,
pretentious, snooty (*informal*),
stuck-up (*informal*)
snoop *verb* PRY, interfere, poke
one's nose in (*informal*), spy
snooper *noun* NOSY ROSY (*U.S.
informal*), nosy parker (*informal*),
busybody, meddler, snoop
(*informal*)
snooze *verb* **1** DOZE, catnap, nap,
take forty winks (*informal*)
► *noun* **2** DOZE, catnap, forty winks
(*informal*), nap, siesta
snub *verb* **1** PUT DOWN, avoid,
blow off (*slang*), cold-shoulder,
cut (*informal*), humiliate, ignore,
rebuff, slight
► *noun* **2** INSULT, affront, put-
down, slap in the face
snug *adjective* COZY, comfortable,
comfy (*informal*), homey, warm
snuggle *verb* NESTLE, cuddle,
nuzzle
soak *verb* **1** WET, bathe, damp,

drench, immerse, moisten,
saturate, steep
2 PENETRATE, permeate, seep
3 ▷▷ **soak up** ABSORB, assimilate
soaking *adjective* SOAKED,
drenched, dripping, saturated,
sodden, sopping, streaming, wet
through, wringing wet
soar *verb* **1** ASCEND, fly, mount,
rise, wing
2 RISE, climb, escalate, rocket,
shoot up
sob *verb* CRY, howl, shed tears,
weep
sober *adjective* **1** ABSTINENT,
abstemious, moderate, temperate
2 SERIOUS, composed, cool,
grave, level-headed, rational,
reasonable, sedate, solemn, staid,
steady
3 PLAIN, dark, drab, dumpy
(*informal*), frowzy, homely (*U.S.*),
quiet, somber, subdued
sobriety *noun* **1** ABSTINENCE,
abstemiousness, moderation,
nonindulgence, soberness,
temperance
2 SERIOUSNESS, gravity, level-
headedness, solemnity, staidness,
steadiness
so-called *adjective* ALLEGED,
pretended, professed, self-styled,
supposed
sociable *adjective* FRIENDLY,
affable, companionable,
convivial, cordial, genial,
gregarious, outgoing, social,
warm
social *adjective* **1** COMMUNAL,
collective, common, community,
general, group, public
► *noun* **2** GET-TOGETHER (*informal*),
gathering, party
socialize *verb* MIX, fraternize, get
about *or* around, go out
society *noun* **1** MANKIND,

civilization, humanity, people, the community, the public
2 ORGANIZATION, association, circle, club, fellowship, group, guild, institute, league, order, union
3 UPPER CLASSES, beau monde, elite, gentry, high society
4 COMPANIONSHIP, company, fellowship, friendship

sodden *adjective* SOAKED, drenched, saturated, soggy, sopping, waterlogged

sofa *noun* COUCH, chaise longue, divan, settee

soft *adjective* **1** PLIABLE, bendable, elastic, flexible, malleable, moldable, plastic, supple
2 YIELDING, elastic, gelatinous, pulpy, spongy, squashy
3 VELVETY, downy, feathery, fleecy, silky, smooth
4 QUIET, dulcet, gentle, murmured, muted, soft-toned
5 PALE, bland, light, mellow, pastel, subdued
6 DIM, dimmed, faint, restful
7 MILD, balmy, temperate
8 LENIENT, easy-going, indulgent, lax, overindulgent, permissive, spineless
9 OUT OF CONDITION, effeminate, flabby, flaccid, limp, weak
10 (*informal*) EASY, comfortable, cushy (*informal*), undemanding
11 KIND, compassionate, gentle, sensitive, sentimental, tenderhearted, touchy-feely (*informal*)

soften *verb* LESSEN, allay, appease, cushion, ease, mitigate, moderate, mollify, still, subdue, temper

softhearted *adjective* KIND, charitable, compassionate, sentimental, sympathetic, tender, tenderhearted, warm-hearted

soggy *adjective* SODDEN, dripping, moist, saturated, soaked, sopping, waterlogged

soil[1] *noun* **1** EARTH, clay, dirt, dust, ground
2 LAND, country

soil[2] *verb* DIRTY, befoul, besmirch, defile, foul, pollute, spot, stain, sully, tarnish

solace *noun* **1** COMFORT, consolation, relief
▶ *verb* **2** COMFORT, console

soldier *noun* FIGHTER, man-at-arms, serviceman, squaddie *or* squaddy (*Brit. slang*), trooper, warrior

sole *adjective* ONLY, alone, exclusive, individual, one, single, solitary

solely *adverb* ONLY, alone, completely, entirely, exclusively, merely

solemn *adjective* **1** FORMAL, ceremonial, dignified, grand, grave, momentous, stately
2 SERIOUS, earnest, grave, sedate, sober, staid

solemnity *noun* **1** SERIOUSNESS, earnestness, gravity
2 FORMALITY, grandeur, impressiveness, momentousness

solicitous *adjective* CONCERNED, anxious, attentive, careful

solicitude *noun* CONCERN, anxiety, attentiveness, care, consideration, regard

solid *adjective* **1** FIRM, compact, concrete, dense, hard
2 STRONG, stable, sturdy, substantial, unshakable
3 SOUND, genuine, good, pure, real, reliable
4 RELIABLE, dependable, trusty, upright, upstanding, worthy

solidarity *noun* UNITY, accord, cohesion, concordance,

like-mindedness, team spirit, unanimity, unification

solidify *verb* HARDEN, cake, coagulate, cohere, congeal, jell, set

solitary *adjective* 1 UNSOCIABLE, cloistered, isolated, reclusive, unsocial

2 SINGLE, alone, lone, sole

3 LONELY, companionless, friendless, lonesome

4 ISOLATED, hidden, out-of-the-way, remote, unfrequented

solitude *noun* ISOLATION, loneliness, privacy, retirement, seclusion

solution *noun* 1 ANSWER, explanation, key, result

2 (*chemistry*) MIXTURE, blend, compound, mix, solvent

solve *verb* ANSWER, clear up, crack, decipher, disentangle, get to the bottom of, resolve, suss (out) (*slang*), unravel, work out

somber *adjective* 1 DARK, dim, drab, dull, gloomy, sober

2 GLOOMY, dismal, doleful, grave, joyless, lugubrious, mournful, sad, sober

somebody *noun* CELEBRITY, dignitary, household name, luminary, megastar (*informal*), name, notable, personage, star

someday *adverb* EVENTUALLY, one day, one of these (fine) days, sooner or later

somehow *adverb* ONE WAY OR ANOTHER, by fair means or foul, by hook or (by) crook, by some means or other, come hell or high water (*informal*), come what may

sometimes *adverb* OCCASIONALLY, at times, now and then

song *noun* BALLAD, air, anthem, carol, chant, chorus, ditty, hymn, number, psalm, tune

soon *adverb* BEFORE LONG, in the near future, shortly

soothe *verb* 1 CALM, allay, appease, de-stress, hush, lull, mollify, pacify, quiet, still

2 RELIEVE, alleviate, assuage, ease

soothing *adjective* CALMING, emollient, palliative, relaxing, restful

soothsayer *noun* PROPHET, diviner, fortune-teller, seer, sibyl

sophisticated *adjective* 1 CULTURED, cosmopolitan, cultivated, refined, urbane, worldly

2 COMPLEX, advanced, complicated, delicate, elaborate, intricate, refined, subtle

sophistication *noun* SAVOIR-FAIRE, finesse, poise, urbanity, worldliness, worldly wisdom

soporific *adjective* 1 SLEEP-INDUCING, sedative, somnolent, tranquilizing

▶ *noun* 2 SEDATIVE, narcotic, opiate, tranquilizer

sorcerer *noun* MAGICIAN, enchanter, necromancer, warlock, witch, wizard

sorcery *noun* BLACK MAGIC, black art, enchantment, magic, necromancy, witchcraft, wizardry

sordid *adjective* 1 DIRTY, filthy, foul, mean, scuzzy (*slang*), seedy, sleazy, squalid, unclean

2 BASE, debauched, degenerate, low, shabby, shameful, vicious, vile

3 MERCENARY, avaricious, covetous, grasping, selfish

sore *adjective* 1 PAINFUL, angry, burning, inflamed, irritated, raw, sensitive, smarting, tender

2 ANNOYING, severe, sharp, troublesome

3 ANNOYED, aggrieved, angry, cross, hurt, irked, irritated,

pained, resentful, stung, upset
4 URGENT, acute, critical,
desperate, dire, extreme, pressing
sorrow noun 1 GRIEF, anguish,
distress, heartache, heartbreak,
misery, mourning, regret,
sadness, unhappiness, woe
2 AFFLICTION, hardship,
misfortune, trial, tribulation,
trouble, woe
▶ verb 3 GRIEVE, agonize, bemoan,
be sad, bewail, lament, mourn
sorrowful adjective SAD, dejected,
dismal, doleful, grieving,
miserable, mournful, sorry,
unhappy, woebegone, woeful,
wretched
sorry adjective 1 REGRETFUL,
apologetic, conscience-stricken,
contrite, penitent, remorseful,
repentant, shamefaced
2 SYMPATHETIC, commiserative,
compassionate, full of pity, moved
3 WRETCHED, deplorable, mean,
miserable, pathetic, pitiful,
poor, sad
sort noun 1 KIND, brand, category,
class, ilk, make, nature, order,
quality, style, type, variety
▶ verb 2 ARRANGE, categorize,
classify, divide, grade, group,
order, put in order, rank
sort out verb 1 RESOLVE, clarify,
clear up
2 ORGANIZE, tidy up
soul noun 1 SPIRIT, essence, life,
vital force
2 PERSONIFICATION, embodiment,
epitome, essence, quintessence,
type
3 PERSON, being, body, creature,
individual, man or woman
sound¹ noun 1 NOISE, din, report,
reverberation, tone
2 IMPRESSION, drift, idea, look
▶ verb 3 RESOUND, echo,

reverberate
4 SEEM, appear, look
5 PRONOUNCE, announce,
articulate, declare, express, utter
sound² adjective 1 PERFECT, fit,
healthy, intact, solid, unhurt,
unimpaired, uninjured, whole
2 SENSIBLE, correct, logical, proper,
prudent, rational, reasonable,
right, trustworthy, valid, well-
founded, wise
3 DEEP, unbroken, undisturbed,
untroubled
sound³ verb FATHOM, plumb, probe
sound out verb PROBE, canvass,
pump, question, see how the
land lies
sour adjective 1 SHARP, acetic, acid,
bitter, pungent, tart
2 GONE OFF, curdled, gone bad,
turned
3 ILL-NATURED, acrimonious,
disagreeable, embittered,
ill-tempered, peevish, tart,
ungenerous, waspish
source noun 1 ORIGIN, author,
beginning, cause, derivation,
fount, originator
2 INFORMANT, authority
souvenir noun KEEPSAKE,
memento, reminder
sovereign noun 1 MONARCH, chief,
emperor or empress, king or queen,
potentate, prince, ruler
▶ adjective 2 SUPREME, absolute,
imperial, kingly or queenly,
principal, royal, ruling
3 EXCELLENT, effectual,
efficacious, efficient
sovereignty noun SUPREME
POWER, domination, kingship,
primacy, supremacy
sow verb SCATTER, implant,
plant, seed
space noun 1 ROOM, capacity,
elbowroom, expanse, extent,

leeway, margin, play, scope

2 GAP, blank, distance, interval, omission

3 TIME, duration, interval, period, span, while

spacious *adjective* ROOMY, ample, broad, capacious, commodious, expansive, extensive, huge, large, sizable *or* sizeable

spadework *noun* PREPARATION, donkey-work, groundwork, labor

span *noun* **1** EXTENT, amount, distance, length, reach, spread, stretch

2 PERIOD, duration, spell, term

▶ *verb* **3** EXTEND ACROSS, bridge, cover, cross, link, traverse

spank *verb* SMACK, cuff, paddle (*U.S. & Canad.*), slap

spar *verb* ARGUE, bicker, row, scrap (*informal*), squabble, wrangle

spare *adjective* **1** EXTRA, additional, free, leftover, odd, over, superfluous, surplus, unoccupied, unused, unwanted

2 THIN, gaunt, lean, meager, wiry

▶ *verb* **3** HAVE MERCY ON, be merciful to, go easy on (*informal*), leave, let off (*informal*), pardon, save from

4 AFFORD, do without, give, grant, let (someone) have, manage without, part with

spare time *noun* LEISURE, free time, odd moments

sparing *adjective* ECONOMICAL, careful, frugal, prudent, saving, thrifty

spark *noun* **1** FLICKER, flare, flash, gleam, glint

2 TRACE, atom, hint, jot, scrap, vestige

▶ *verb* **3** (often with *off*) START, inspire, precipitate, provoke, set off, stimulate, trigger (off)

sparkle *verb* **1** GLITTER, dance,

flash, gleam, glint, glisten, scintillate, shimmer, shine, twinkle

▶ *noun* **2** GLITTER, brilliance, flash, flicker, gleam, glint, twinkle

3 VIVACITY, dash, élan, life, spirit, vitality

sparse *adjective* SCATTERED, few and far between, meager, scanty, scarce

spartan *adjective* AUSTERE, ascetic, disciplined, frugal, plain, rigorous, self-denying, severe, strict

spasm *noun* **1** CONVULSION, contraction, paroxysm, twitch

2 BURST, eruption, fit, frenzy, outburst, seizure

spasmodic *adjective* SPORADIC, convulsive, erratic, fitful, intermittent, irregular, jerky

spate *noun* FLOOD, deluge, flow, outpouring, rush, torrent

speak *verb* **1** TALK, articulate, converse, express, pronounce, say, state, tell, utter

2 LECTURE, address, declaim, discourse, hold forth

speaker *noun* LECTURER, orator, public speaker, spokesman *or* spokeswoman, spokesperson

speak out *or* **up** *verb* SPEAK ONE'S MIND, have one's say, make one's position plain, voice one's opinions

spearhead *verb* LEAD, head, initiate, launch, pioneer, set in motion, set off

special *adjective* **1** EXCEPTIONAL, extraordinary, important, memorable, significant, uncommon, unique, unusual

2 PARTICULAR, appropriate, distinctive, individual, precise, specific

specialist *noun* EXPERT, authority,

buff (*informal*), connoisseur, consultant, master, professional

speciality *noun* FORTE, bag (*slang, dated*), métier, pièce de résistance, specialty

species *noun* KIND, breed, category, class, group, sort, type, variety

specific *adjective* 1 PARTICULAR, characteristic, distinguishing, special
2 DEFINITE, clear-cut, exact, explicit, express, precise, unequivocal

specification *noun* REQUIREMENT, condition, detail, particular, qualification, stipulation

specify *verb* STATE, define, designate, detail, indicate, mention, name, stipulate

specimen *noun* SAMPLE, example, exemplification, instance, model, pattern, representative, type

speck *noun* 1 MARK, blemish, dot, fleck, mote, speckle, spot, stain
2 PARTICLE, atom, bit, grain, iota, jot, mite, shred

speckled *adjective* FLECKED, dappled, dotted, mottled, spotted, sprinkled

spectacle *noun* 1 SIGHT, curiosity, marvel, phenomenon, scene, wonder
2 SHOW, display, event, exhibition, extravaganza, pageant, performance

spectacular *adjective*
1 IMPRESSIVE, cool (*informal*), dazzling, dramatic, grand, magnificent, phat (*slang*), sensational, splendid, striking, stunning (*informal*)
▶ *noun* 2 SHOW, display, spectacle

spectator *noun* ONLOOKER, bystander, looker-on, observer, viewer, watcher

specter *noun* GHOST, apparition, phantom, spirit, vision, wraith

speculate *verb* 1 CONJECTURE, consider, guess, hypothesize, suppose, surmise, theorize, wonder
2 GAMBLE, hazard, risk, venture

speculation *noun* 1 GUESSWORK, conjecture, hypothesis, opinion, supposition, surmise, theory
2 GAMBLE, hazard, risk

speculative *adjective* HYPOTHETICAL, academic, conjectural, notional, suppositional, theoretical

speech *noun* 1 COMMUNICATION, conversation, dialogue, discussion, talk
2 TALK, address, discourse, homily, lecture, oration, spiel (*informal*)
3 LANGUAGE, articulation, dialect, diction, enunciation, idiom, jargon, parlance, tongue

speechless *adjective* 1 MUTE, dumb, inarticulate, silent, wordless
2 ASTOUNDED, aghast, amazed, dazed, shocked

speed *noun* 1 SWIFTNESS, haste, hurry, pace, quickness, rapidity, rush, velocity
▶ *verb* 2 RACE, career, gallop, hasten, hurry, make haste, rush, tear, zoom
3 HELP, advance, aid, assist, boost, expedite, facilitate

speed up *verb* ACCELERATE, gather momentum, increase the tempo

speedy *adjective* QUICK, express, fast, hasty, headlong, hurried, immediate, precipitate, prompt, rapid, swift

spell[1] *verb* INDICATE, augur, imply, mean, point to, portend, signify

spell[2] *noun* 1 INCANTATION, charm
2 FASCINATION, allure,

bewitchment, enchantment, glamour, magic

spell³ noun PERIOD, bout, course, interval, season, stretch, term, time

spellbound adjective ENTRANCED, bewitched, captivated, charmed, enthralled, fascinated, gripped, mesmerized, rapt

spend verb 1 PAY OUT, disburse, expend, fork out (slang)
2 PASS, fill, occupy, while away
3 USE UP, consume, dissipate, drain, empty, exhaust, run through, squander, waste

spendthrift noun 1 SQUANDERER, big spender, profligate, spender, waster
▶ adjective 2 WASTEFUL, extravagant, improvident, prodigal, profligate

spew verb VOMIT, barf (slang), disgorge, puke (slang), regurgitate, throw up (informal)

sphere noun 1 BALL, circle, globe, globule, orb
2 FIELD, capacity, department, domain, function, patch, province, realm, scope, territory, turf (slang)

spherical adjective ROUND, globe-shaped, globular, rotund

spice noun 1 SEASONING, relish, savor
2 EXCITEMENT, color, pep, piquancy, zest, zing (informal)

spicy adjective 1 HOT, aromatic, piquant, savory, seasoned
2 (informal) SCANDALOUS, hot (informal), indelicate, racy, ribald, risqué, suggestive, titillating

spike noun 1 POINT, barb, prong, spine
▶ verb 2 IMPALE, spear, spit, stick

spill verb 1 POUR, discharge, disgorge, overflow, slop over

▶ noun 2 FALL, tumble

spin verb 1 REVOLVE, gyrate, pirouette, reel, rotate, turn, twirl, whirl
2 REEL, swim, whirl
▶ noun 3 REVOLUTION, gyration, roll, whirl
4 (informal) DRIVE, joy ride (informal), ride

spine noun 1 BACKBONE, spinal column, vertebrae, vertebral column
2 BARB, needle, quill, ray, spike, spur

spine-chilling adjective FRIGHTENING, bloodcurdling, eerie, horrifying, scary (informal), spooky (informal), terrifying

spineless adjective WEAK, cowardly, faint-hearted, feeble, gutless (informal), lily-livered, soft, weak-kneed (informal)

spin out verb PROLONG, amplify, delay, drag out, draw out, extend, lengthen

spiral noun 1 COIL, corkscrew, helix, whorl
▶ adjective 2 COILED, helical, whorled, winding

spirit noun 1 LIFE FORCE, life, soul, vital spark
2 FEELING, atmosphere, gist, tenor, tone
3 TEMPERAMENT, attitude, character, disposition, outlook, temper
4 LIVELINESS, animation, brio, energy, enthusiasm, fire, force, life, mettle, vigor, zest
5 COURAGE, backbone, gameness, grit, guts (informal), spunk (informal)
6 ESSENCE, intention, meaning, purport, purpose, sense, substance
7 GHOST, apparition, phantom,

specter

8 ▷▷ **spirits** MOOD, feelings, frame of mind, morale

▶ *verb* 9 (with *away* or *off*) REMOVE, abduct, abstract, carry, purloin, seize, steal, whisk

spirited *adjective* LIVELY, active, animated, energetic, feisty (*informal*), mettlesome, vivacious

spiritual *adjective* SACRED, devotional, divine, holy, religious

spit *verb* 1 EJECT, expectorate, splutter, throw out

▶ *noun* 2 SALIVA, dribble, drool, slaver, spittle

spite *noun* 1 MALICE, animosity, hatred, ill will, malevolence, spitefulness, spleen, venom

2 ▷▷ **in spite of** DESPITE, (even) though, notwithstanding, regardless of

▶ *verb* 3 HURT, annoy, harm, injure, vex

spiteful *adjective* MALICIOUS, bitchy (*informal*), ill-natured, malevolent, nasty, vindictive

splash *verb* 1 SCATTER, shower, slop, spatter, spray, sprinkle, wet

2 PUBLICIZE, broadcast, tout, trumpet

▶ *noun* 3 DASH, burst, patch, spattering, touch

4 (*informal*) DISPLAY, effect, impact, sensation, stir

splash out *verb* (*informal*) SPEND, be extravagant, push the boat out (*Brit. informal*), spare no expense, splurge

splendid *adjective* 1 excellent, cracking (*Brit. informal*), fantastic (*informal*), first-class, glorious, great (*informal*) MARVELOUS, wonderful

2 MAGNIFICENT, cool (*informal*), costly, gorgeous, impressive, lavish, luxurious, ornate,

phat (*slang*), resplendent, rich, sumptuous, superb

splendor *noun* MAGNIFICENCE, brightness, brilliance, display, glory, grandeur, pomp, richness, show, spectacle, sumptuousness

splinter *noun* 1 SLIVER, chip, flake, fragment

▶ *verb* 2 SHATTER, disintegrate, fracture, split

split *verb* 1 BREAK, burst, come apart, come undone, crack, give way, open, rend, rip

2 SEPARATE, branch, cleave, disband, disunite, diverge, fork, part

3 SHARE OUT, allocate, allot, apportion, distribute, divide, halve, partition

▶ *noun* 4 CRACK, breach, division, fissure, gap, rent, rip, separation, slit, tear

5 DIVISION, breach, break-up, discord, dissension, estrangement, rift, rupture, schism

▶ *adjective* 6 DIVIDED, broken, cleft, cracked, fractured, ruptured

split up *verb* SEPARATE, break up, divorce, part

spoil *verb* 1 RUIN, damage, destroy, disfigure, harm, impair, injure, mar, mess up, trash (*slang*), wreck

2 OVERINDULGE, coddle, cosset, indulge, mollycoddle, pamper

3 GO BAD, addle, curdle, decay, decompose, go off (*Brit. informal*), rot, turn

spoils *plural noun* BOOTY, loot, plunder, prey, swag (*slang*), treasure

spoilsport *noun* KILLJOY, damper, dog in the manger, misery (*informal*), sourpuss, wet blanket (*informal*)

spoken *adjective* SAID, expressed,

oral, told, unwritten, uttered, verbal, viva voce, voiced

spokesperson noun SPEAKER, mouthpiece, official, spin doctor (informal), spokesman or spokeswoman, voice

spongy adjective POROUS, absorbent

sponsor noun 1 BACKER, patron, promoter
▶ verb 2 BACK, finance, fund, patronize, promote, subsidize

spontaneous adjective UNPLANNED, impromptu, impulsive, instinctive, natural, unprompted, voluntary, willing

spoof noun (informal) PARODY, burlesque, caricature, mockery, satire, send-up (Brit. informal), take-off (informal)

spooky adjective EERIE, chilling, creepy (informal), frightening, scary (informal), spine-chilling, uncanny, unearthly, weird

sporadic adjective INTERMITTENT, irregular, occasional, scattered, spasmodic

sport noun 1 GAME, amusement, diversion, exercise, pastime, play, recreation
2 FUN, badinage, banter, jest, joking, teasing
▶ verb 3 (old-fashioned, informal) WEAR, display, exhibit, show off

sporting adjective FAIR, game (informal), sportsmanlike

sporty adjective ATHLETIC, energetic, outdoor

spot noun 1 MARK, blemish, blot, blotch, scar, smudge, speck, speckle, stain
2 PIMPLE, pustule, zit (slang)
3 PLACE, location, point, position, scene, site
4 (informal) PREDICAMENT, difficulty, hot water (informal),

mess, plight, quandary, tight spot, trouble
▶ verb 5 SEE, catch a glimpse of, catch sight of, detect, discern, espy, make out, observe, recognize, sight
6 MARK, dirty, fleck, mottle, smirch, soil, spatter, speckle, splodge, splotch, stain

spotless adjective CLEAN, flawless, gleaming, immaculate, impeccable, pure, shining, unblemished, unstained, unsullied, untarnished

spotlight noun 1 ATTENTION, fame, limelight, public eye
▶ verb 2 HIGHLIGHT, accentuate, draw attention to

spotted adjective SPECKLED, dappled, dotted, flecked, mottled

spouse noun PARTNER, consort, husband or wife, mate, significant other (informal)

spout verb STREAM, discharge, gush, shoot, spray, spurt, surge

sprawl verb LOLL, flop, lounge, slouch, slump

spray¹ noun 1 DROPLETS, drizzle, fine mist
2 AEROSOL, atomizer, sprinkler
▶ verb 3 SCATTER, diffuse, shower, sprinkle

spray² noun SPRIG, branch, corsage, floral arrangement

spread verb 1 OPEN (OUT), broaden, dilate, expand, extend, sprawl, stretch, unfold, unroll, widen
2 PROLIFERATE, escalate, multiply
3 CIRCULATE, broadcast, disseminate, make known, propagate
▶ noun 4 INCREASE, advance, development, dispersal, dissemination, expansion, proliferation
5 EXTENT, span, stretch, sweep

spree noun BINGE (informal), bacchanalia, bender (informal), carousal, fling, orgy, revel

sprightly adjective LIVELY, active, agile, brisk, energetic, nimble, spirited, spry, vivacious

spring verb 1 JUMP, bounce, bound, leap, vault
2 (often with from) ORIGINATE, arise, come, derive, descend, issue, proceed, start, stem
3 (often with up) APPEAR, develop, mushroom, shoot up
▶ noun 4 JUMP, bound, leap, vault
5 ELASTICITY, bounce, buoyancy, flexibility, resilience

springy adjective ELASTIC, bouncy, buoyant, flexible, resilient, rubbery

sprinkle verb SCATTER, dredge, dust, pepper, powder, shower, spray, strew

sprinkling noun SCATTERING, dash, dusting, few, handful, sprinkle

sprint verb RACE, dart, dash, hare (Brit. informal), shoot, tear

sprite noun SPIRIT, brownie, elf, fairy, goblin, imp, pixie

sprout verb GROW, bud, develop, shoot, spring

spruce adjective SMART, dapper, natty (informal), neat, trim, well-groomed, well turned out

spruce up verb SMARTEN UP, tidy, titivate

spry adjective ACTIVE, agile, nimble, sprightly, supple

spur noun 1 STIMULUS, impetus, impulse, incentive, incitement, inducement, motive
2 GOAD, prick
3 ▷▷ **on the spur of the moment** ON IMPULSE, impromptu, impulsively, on the spot, without planning
▶ verb 4 INCITE, animate, drive, goad, impel, prick, prod, prompt, stimulate, urge

spurious adjective FALSE, artificial, bogus, fake, phoney or phony (informal), pretended or sham, specious, unauthentic

spurn verb REJECT, despise, disdain, rebuff, repulse, scorn, slight, snub

spurt verb 1 GUSH, burst, erupt, shoot, squirt, surge
▶ noun 2 BURST, fit, rush, spate, surge

spy noun 1 UNDERCOVER AGENT, mole, nark (Brit., Austral., & N.Z. slang)
▶ verb 2 CATCH SIGHT OF, espy, glimpse, notice, observe, spot

squabble verb 1 QUARREL, argue, bicker, dispute, fight, row, wrangle
▶ noun 2 QUARREL, argument, disagreement, dispute, fight, row, tiff

squad noun TEAM, band, company, crew, force, gang, group, troop

squalid adjective DIRTY, filthy, scuzzy (slang), seedy, sleazy, slummy, sordid, unclean

squalor noun FILTH, foulness, sleaziness, squalidness

squander verb WASTE, blow (slang), expend, fritter away, misspend, misuse, spend

square adjective 1 HONEST, above board, ethical, fair, genuine, kosher (informal), on the level (informal), straight
2 (informal) UNCOOL, dorky (slang), nerdy, unhip
▶ verb 3 EVEN UP, adjust, align, level
4 (sometimes with up) PAY OFF, settle
5 (often with with) AGREE, correspond, fit, match, reconcile,

tally

squash verb 1 CRUSH, compress, distort, flatten, mash, press, pulp, smash

2 SUPPRESS, annihilate, crush, humiliate, quell, silence

squashy adjective SOFT, mushy, pulpy, spongy, yielding

squawk verb CRY, hoot, screech

squeak verb PEEP, pipe, squeal

squeal noun or verb SCREAM, screech, shriek, wail, yell

squeamish adjective 1 DELICATE, fastidious, prudish, strait-laced

2 SICK, nauseous, queasy

squeeze verb 1 PRESS, clutch, compress, crush, grip, pinch, squash, wring

2 CRAM, crowd, force, jam, pack, press, ram, stuff

3 HUG, clasp, cuddle, embrace, enfold

4 EXTORT, milk, pressurize, wrest

▶ noun 5 HUG, clasp, embrace

6 CRUSH, congestion, crowd, jam, press, squash

squirm verb WRIGGLE, twist, writhe

squirt noun (informal) CHILD, baby, boy, girl, infant, kid (informal), minor, toddler, tot, whippersnapper (old-fashioned), youngster

stab verb 1 PIERCE, impale, jab, knife, spear, stick, thrust, transfix, wound

▶ noun 2 WOUND, gash, incision, jab, puncture, thrust

3 TWINGE, ache, pang, prick

4 ▷▷ **make** or **have a stab at** (informal) ATTEMPT, endeavor, have a go, try

stability noun FIRMNESS, solidity, soundness, steadiness, strength

stable adjective 1 FIRM, constant, established, fast, fixed,

immovable, lasting, permanent, secure, sound, strong

2 STEADY, reliable, staunch, steadfast, sure

stack noun 1 PILE, heap, load, mass, mound, mountain

▶ verb 2 PILE, accumulate, amass, assemble, heap up, load

staff noun 1 WORKERS, employees, personnel, team, workforce

2 STICK, cane, crook, pole, rod, scepter, stave, wand

stage noun POINT, division, juncture, lap, leg, level, period, phase, step

stagger verb 1 TOTTER, lurch, reel, sway, wobble

2 ASTOUND, amaze, astonish, confound, overwhelm, shake, shock, stun, stupefy

3 OVERLAP, alternate, step

stagnant adjective STALE, quiet, sluggish, still

stagnate verb VEGETATE, decay, decline, idle, languish, rot, rust

staid adjective SEDATE, calm, composed, grave, serious, sober, solemn, steady

stain verb 1 MARK, blemish, blot, dirty, discolor, smirch, soil, spot, tinge

▶ noun 2 MARK, blemish, blot, discoloration, smirch, spot

3 STIGMA, disgrace, dishonor, shame, slur

stake¹ noun POLE, pale, paling, palisade, picket, post, stick

stake² noun 1 BET, ante, pledge, wager

2 INTEREST, concern, investment, involvement, share

▶ verb 3 BET, chance, gamble, hazard, risk, venture, wager

stale adjective 1 OLD, decayed, dry, flat, fusty, hard, musty, sour

2 UNORIGINAL, banal, hackneyed,

overused, stereotyped, threadbare, trite, worn-out

stalk verb PURSUE, follow, haunt, hunt, shadow, track

stall verb PLAY FOR TIME, hedge, temporize

stalwart adjective STRONG, staunch, stout, strapping, sturdy

stamina noun STAYING POWER, endurance, energy, force, power, resilience, strength

stammer verb STUTTER, falter, hesitate, pause, stumble

stamp noun 1 IMPRINT, brand, earmark, hallmark, mark, signature
▶ verb 2 TRAMPLE, crush
3 IDENTIFY, brand, categorize, label, mark, reveal, show to be
4 IMPRINT, impress, mark, print

stampede noun RUSH, charge, flight, rout

stamp out verb ELIMINATE, crush, destroy, eradicate, put down, quell, scotch, suppress

stance noun 1 ATTITUDE, position, stand, standpoint, viewpoint
2 POSTURE, bearing, carriage, deportment

stand verb 1 BE UPRIGHT, be erect, be vertical, rise
2 PUT, mount, place, position, set
3 EXIST, be valid, continue, hold, obtain, prevail, remain
4 TOLERATE, abide, allow, bear, brook, countenance, deal with (slang), endure, handle, put up with (informal), stomach, take
▶ noun 5 STALL, booth, table
6 POSITION, attitude, determination, opinion, stance
7 SUPPORT, base, bracket, dais, platform, rack, stage, tripod

standard noun 1 BENCHMARK, average, criterion, gauge, grade, guideline, measure, model, norm, yardstick
2 (often plural) PRINCIPLES, ethics, ideals, morals
3 FLAG, banner, ensign
▶ adjective 4 USUAL, average, basic, customary, normal, orthodox, regular, typical
5 ACCEPTED, approved, authoritative, definitive, established, official, recognized

standardize verb BRING INTO LINE, institutionalize, regiment

stand by verb 1 BE PREPARED, wait
2 SUPPORT, back, be loyal to, champion, take (someone's) part

stand for verb 1 REPRESENT, betoken, denote, indicate, mean, signify, symbolize
2 (informal) TOLERATE, bear, brook, endure, put up with

stand-in noun SUBSTITUTE, deputy, locum, replacement, reserve, stopgap, surrogate, understudy

stand in for verb BE A SUBSTITUTE FOR, cover for, deputize for, represent, take the place of

standing adjective 1 PERMANENT, fixed, lasting, regular
2 UPRIGHT, erect, vertical
▶ noun 3 STATUS, eminence, footing, position, rank, reputation, repute
4 DURATION, continuance, existence

standoffish adjective RESERVED, aloof, cold, distant, haughty, remote, unapproachable, unsociable

stand out verb BE CONSPICUOUS, be distinct, be obvious, be prominent

standpoint noun POINT OF VIEW, angle, position, stance, viewpoint

stand up for verb SUPPORT, champion, defend, stick up for (informal), uphold

staple adjective PRINCIPAL, basic,

chief, fundamental, key, main, predominant

star *noun* 1 HEAVENLY BODY
2 CELEBRITY, big name, luminary, main attraction, megastar (*informal*), name, superstar (*informal*)
▶ *adjective* 3 LEADING, brilliant, celebrated, major, prominent, well-known

stare *verb* GAZE, eyeball (*slang*), gape, gawk, gawp (*Brit. slang*), goggle, look, watch

stark *adjective* 1 HARSH, austere, bare, barren, bleak, grim, hard, homely, plain, severe
2 ABSOLUTE, blunt, downright, out-and-out, pure, sheer, unmitigated, utter
▶ *adverb* 3 ABSOLUTELY, altogether, completely, entirely, quite, utterly, wholly

start *verb* 1 BEGIN, appear, arise, commence, issue, originate
2 SET ABOUT, embark upon, make a beginning, take the first step
3 SET IN MOTION, activate, get going, initiate, instigate, kick-start, open, originate, trigger
4 JUMP, flinch, jerk, recoil, shy
5 ESTABLISH, begin, create, found, inaugurate, initiate, institute, launch, pioneer, set up
▶ *noun* 6 BEGINNING, birth, dawn, foundation, inception, initiation, onset, opening, outset
7 ADVANTAGE, edge, head start, lead
8 JUMP, convulsion, spasm

startle *verb* SURPRISE, frighten, make (someone) jump, scare, shock

starving *adjective* HUNGRY, famished, ravenous, starved

state *noun* 1 CONDITION, circumstances, position,

predicament, shape, situation
2 FRAME OF MIND, attitude, humor, mood, spirits
3 COUNTRY, commonwealth, federation, government, kingdom, land, nation, republic, territory
4 CEREMONY, display, glory, grandeur, majesty, pomp, splendor, style
▶ *verb* 5 EXPRESS, affirm, articulate, assert, declare, expound, present, say, specify, utter, voice

stately *adjective* GRAND, august, dignified, lofty, majestic, noble, regal, royal

statement *noun* ACCOUNT, announcement, communication, communiqué, declaration, proclamation, report

state-of-the-art *adjective* LATEST, newest, up-to-date, up-to-the-minute

static *adjective* STATIONARY, fixed, immobile, motionless, still, unmoving

station *noun* 1 HEADQUARTERS, base, depot
2 PLACE, location, position, post, seat, situation
3 POSITION, post, rank, situation, standing, status
▶ *verb* 4 ASSIGN, establish, install, locate, post, set

stationary *adjective* MOTIONLESS, fixed, parked, standing, static, stock-still, unmoving

statuesque *adjective* WELL-PROPORTIONED, imposing, Junoesque

stature *noun* IMPORTANCE, eminence, prestige, prominence, rank, standing

status *noun* POSITION, condition, consequence, eminence, grade, prestige, rank, standing

staunch¹ adjective LOYAL, faithful, firm, sound, stalwart, steadfast, true, trusty

staunch² verb STOP, check, dam, halt, stay, stem

stay³ verb 1 REMAIN, abide, continue, halt, linger, loiter, pause, stop, tarry, wait
  ▶ noun 2 VISIT, holiday, sojourn, stop, stopover
  3 POSTPONEMENT, deferment, delay, halt, stopping, suspension

steadfast adjective FIRM, faithful, fast, fixed, intent, loyal, resolute, stalwart, staunch, steady, unswerving, unwavering

steady adjective 1 FIRM, fixed, safe, stable
  2 SENSIBLE, balanced, calm, dependable, equable, level-headed, reliable, sober
  3 CONTINUOUS, ceaseless, consistent, constant, incessant, nonstop, persistent, regular, twenty-four-seven (slang), unbroken, uninterrupted
  ▶ verb 4 STABILIZE, balance, brace, secure, support

steal verb 1 TAKE, appropriate, embezzle, filch, lift (informal), misappropriate, nick (slang, chiefly Brit.), pilfer, pinch (informal), purloin, thieve
  2 SNEAK, creep, slink, slip, tiptoe

stealth noun SECRECY, furtiveness, slyness, sneakiness, stealthiness, surreptitiousness, unobtrusiveness

stealthy adjective SECRET, furtive, secretive, sneaking, surreptitious

steep¹ adjective 1 SHEER, abrupt, precipitous
  2 HIGH, exorbitant, extortionate, extreme, overpriced, unreasonable

steep² verb 1 SOAK, drench, immerse, macerate, marinate (Cookery), moisten, souse, submerge
  2 SATURATE, fill, imbue, infuse, permeate, pervade, suffuse

steer verb DIRECT, conduct, control, guide, handle, pilot

stem¹ noun 1 STALK, axis, branch, shoot, trunk
  ▶ verb 2 ▷▷ **stem from** ORIGINATE IN, arise from, be caused by, derive from

stem² verb STOP, check, curb, dam, hold back, staunch

stench noun STINK, foul smell, pong (Brit. informal), reek, whiff

step noun 1 FOOTSTEP, footfall, footprint, pace, print, stride, track
  2 STAGE, move, phase, point
  3 ACTION, act, deed, expedient, means, measure, move
  4 DEGREE, level, rank
  ▶ verb 5 WALK, move, pace, tread

step in verb INTERVENE, become involved, take action

step up verb INCREASE, intensify, raise

stereotype noun 1 FORMULA, pattern
  ▶ verb 2 CATEGORIZE, pigeonhole, standardize, typecast

sterile adjective 1 GERM-FREE, aseptic, disinfected, sterilized
  2 BARREN, bare, dry, empty, fruitless, unfruitful, unproductive

sterilize verb DISINFECT, fumigate, purify

sterling adjective EXCELLENT, fine, genuine, sound, superlative, true

stern adjective SEVERE, austere, forbidding, grim, hard, harsh, inflexible, rigid, serious, strict

stick¹ noun 1 CANE, baton, crook, pole, rod, staff, twig

2 (*brit. slang*) ABUSE, criticism, flak (*informal*)

stick² *verb* 1 POKE, dig, jab, penetrate, pierce, prod, puncture, spear, stab, thrust, transfix

2 FASTEN, adhere, affix, attach, bind, bond, cling, fix, glue, hold, join, paste, weld

3 (with *out, up,* etc.) PROTRUDE, bulge, extend, jut, obtrude, poke, project, show

4 (*informal*) PUT, deposit, lay, place, set

5 STAY, linger, persist, remain

6 (*slang*) TOLERATE, abide, stand, stomach, take

7 ▷▷ **stick up for** DEFEND, champion, stand up for, support

stickler *noun* PERFECTIONIST, fanatic, fusspot (*informal*), purist

sticky *adjective* 1 TACKY, adhesive, clinging, gluey, glutinous, gooey (*informal*), gummy, viscid, viscous

2 (*informal*) DIFFICULT, awkward, delicate, embarrassing, nasty, tricky, unpleasant

3 HUMID, clammy, close, muggy, oppressive, sultry, sweltering

stiff *adjective* 1 INFLEXIBLE, firm, hard, inelastic, rigid, solid, taut, tense, tight, unbending, unyielding

2 AWKWARD, clumsy, graceless, inelegant, jerky (*informal*), ungainly, ungraceful

3 DIFFICULT, arduous, exacting, hard, tough

4 SEVERE, drastic, extreme, hard, harsh, heavy, strict

5 UNRELAXED, artifical, constrained, forced, formal, stilted, unnatural

stiffen *verb* 1 BRACE, reinforce, tauten, tense

2 SET, congeal, crystallize, harden, jell, solidify, thicken

stifle *verb* 1 SUPPRESS, check, hush, repress, restrain, silence, smother, stop

2 SUFFOCATE, asphyxiate, choke, smother, strangle

stigma *noun* DISGRACE, dishonor, shame, slur, smirch, stain

still *adjective* 1 MOTIONLESS, calm, peaceful, restful, serene, stationary, tranquil, undisturbed

2 SILENT, hushed, quiet

▶ *verb* 3 QUIETEN, allay, calm, hush, lull, pacify, quiet, settle, silence, soothe

▶ *conjunction* 4 HOWEVER, but, nevertheless, notwithstanding, yet

stilted *adjective* STIFF, constrained, forced, unnatural, wooden

stimulant *noun* PICK-ME-UP (*informal*), restorative, tonic, upper (*slang*)

stimulate *verb* AROUSE, encourage, fire, impel, incite, prompt, provoke, rouse, spur

stimulating *adjective* EXCITING, exhilarating, inspiring, provocative, rousing, stirring

stimulus *noun* INCENTIVE, encouragement, fillip, goad, impetus, incitement, inducement, spur

sting *verb* 1 HURT, burn, pain, smart, tingle, wound

2 (*informal*) CHEAT, defraud, do (*slang*), fleece, overcharge, rip off (*slang*), swindle

stingy *adjective* MEAN, miserly, niggardly, parsimonious, penny-pinching (*informal*), tightfisted, ungenerous

stink *noun* 1 STENCH, fetor, foul smell, pong (*Brit. informal*)

▶ *verb* 2 REEK, pong (*Brit. informal*)

stint *verb* 1 BE MEAN, be frugal, be sparing, hold back, skimp on

▶ *noun* 2 SHARE, period, quota, shift, spell, stretch, term, time, turn

stipulate *verb* SPECIFY, agree, contract, covenant, insist upon, require, settle

stipulation *noun* SPECIFICATION, agreement, clause, condition, precondition, proviso, qualification, requirement

stir *verb* 1 MIX, agitate, beat, shake
2 STIMULATE, arouse, awaken, excite, incite, provoke, rouse, spur
▶ *noun* 3 COMMOTION, activity, bustle, disorder, disturbance, excitement, flurry, fuss

stock *noun* 1 GOODS, array, choice, commodities, merchandise, range, selection, variety, wares
2 SUPPLY, fund, hoard, reserve, stockpile, store
3 PROPERTY, assets, capital, funds, investment
4 LIVESTOCK, beasts, cattle, domestic animals
▶ *adjective* 5 STANDARD, conventional, customary, ordinary, regular, routine, usual
6 HACKNEYED, banal, overused, trite
▶ *verb* 7 SELL, deal in, handle, keep, supply, trade in
8 PROVIDE WITH, equip, fit out, furnish, supply
9 ▷▷ **stock up** STORE (UP), accumulate, amass, gather, hoard, lay in, put away, save

stocky *adjective* THICKSET, chunky, dumpy, solid, stubby, sturdy

stodgy *adjective* 1 HEAVY, filling, leaden, starchy
2 DULL, boring, fuddy-duddy (*informal*), heavy going, staid, stuffy, tedious, unexciting

stoical *adjective* RESIGNED, dispassionate, impassive, long-suffering, philosophical, phlegmatic, stoic, stolid

stoicism *noun* RESIGNATION, acceptance, forbearance, fortitude, impassivity, long-suffering, patience, stolidity

stolid *adjective* APATHETIC, dull, lumpish, unemotional, wooden

stomach *noun* 1 BELLY, abdomen, gut (*informal*), pot, tummy (*informal*)
2 INCLINATION, appetite, desire, relish, taste
▶ *verb* 3 BEAR, abide, endure, swallow, take, tolerate

stony *adjective* COLD, blank, chilly, expressionless, hard, hostile, icy, unresponsive

stoop *verb* 1 BEND, bow, crouch, duck, hunch, lean
2 ▷▷ **stoop to** SINK TO, descend to, lower oneself by, resort to
▶ *noun* 3 SLOUCH, bad posture, round-shoulderedness

stop *verb* 1 HALT, cease, conclude, cut short, desist, discontinue, end, finish, pause, put an end to, quit, refrain, shut down, terminate
2 PREVENT, arrest, forestall, hinder, hold back, impede, repress, restrain
3 PLUG, block, obstruct, seal, staunch, stem
4 STAY, lodge, rest
▶ *noun* 5 END, cessation, finish, halt, standstill
6 STAY, break, rest
7 STATION, depot, terminus

stopgap *noun* MAKESHIFT, improvisation, resort, substitute

stoppage *noun* STOPPING, arrest, close, closure, cutoff, halt, hindrance, shutdown, standstill

store *verb* 1 PUT BY, deposit, garner, hoard, keep, put aside, reserve, save, stockpile
▶ *noun* 2 SHOP, market, mart,

outlet
3 SUPPLY, accumulation, cache,
fund, hoard, quantity, reserve,
stock, stockpile
4 REPOSITORY, depository,
storeroom, warehouse
storm noun 1 TEMPEST, blizzard,
gale, hurricane, squall
2 OUTBURST, agitation,
commotion, disturbance, furor,
outbreak, outcry, row, rumpus,
strife, tumult, turmoil
▶ verb 3 ATTACK, assail, assault,
charge, rush
4 RAGE, bluster, rant, rave,
thunder
5 RUSH, flounce, fly, stamp
stormy adjective WILD, blustery,
inclement, raging, rough, squally,
turbulent, windy
story noun 1 TALE, account,
anecdote, history, legend,
narrative, romance, yarn
2 REPORT, article, feature, news,
news item, scoop
stout adjective 1 FAT, big, bulky,
burly, corpulent, fleshy, heavy,
overweight, plump, portly,
rotund, tubby
2 STRONG, able-bodied, brawny,
muscular, robust, stalwart,
strapping, sturdy
3 BRAVE, bold, courageous,
fearless, gallant, intrepid, plucky,
resolute, valiant
stow verb PACK, bundle, load, put
away, stash (informal), store
straight adjective 1 DIRECT, near,
short
2 LEVEL, aligned, even, horizontal,
right, smooth, square, true
3 UPRIGHT, erect, plumb, vertical
4 HONEST, above board, accurate,
fair, honorable, just, law-abiding,
trustworthy, upright
5 FRANK, blunt, bold, candid,

forthright, honest, outright,
plain, straightforward
6 SUCCESSIVE, consecutive,
continuous, nonstop, running,
solid
7 UNDILUTED, neat, pure,
unadulterated, unmixed
8 ORDERLY, arranged, in order,
neat, organized, shipshape, tidy
9 (slang) CONVENTIONAL,
bourgeois, conservative
▶ adverb 10 DIRECTLY, at once,
immediately, instantly
straight away adverb
IMMEDIATELY, at once, directly,
instantly, now, right away
straighten verb NEATEN, arrange,
order, put in order, tidy (up)
straightforward adjective
1 HONEST, candid, direct,
forthright, genuine, open,
sincere, truthful, upfront
(informal)
2 EASY, easy-peasy (slang),
elementary, routine, simple,
uncomplicated
strain¹ verb 1 STRETCH, distend,
draw tight, tauten, tighten
2 OVEREXERT, injure, overtax,
overwork, pull, sprain, tax, tear,
twist, wrench
3 STRIVE, bend over backwards
(informal), endeavor, give it
one's best shot (informal), go for
it (informal), knock oneself out
(informal), labor, struggle
4 SIEVE, filter, purify, sift
▶ noun 5 STRESS, anxiety, burden,
pressure, tension
6 EXERTION, effort, force, struggle
7 INJURY, pull, sprain, wrench
strain² noun 1 BREED, ancestry,
blood, descent, extraction, family,
lineage, race
2 TRACE, streak, suggestion,
tendency

strained *adjective* 1 FORCED, artificial, false, put on, unnatural
2 TENSE, awkward, difficult, embarrassed, stiff, uneasy

strait *noun* 1 (often plural) CHANNEL, narrows, sound
2 ▷▷ **straits** DIFFICULTY, dilemma, extremity, hardship, plight, predicament

strait-laced *adjective* STRICT, moralistic, narrow-minded, prim, proper, prudish, puritanical

strand *noun* FILAMENT, fiber, string, thread

stranded *adjective* 1 BEACHED, aground, ashore, grounded, marooned, shipwrecked
2 HELPLESS, abandoned, high and dry

strange *adjective* 1 ODD, abnormal, bizarre, curious, extraordinary, peculiar, queer, uncommon, weird, wonderful
2 UNFAMILIAR, alien, exotic, foreign, new, novel, unknown, untried

stranger *noun* NEWCOMER, alien, foreigner, guest, incomer, outlander, visitor

strangle *verb* 1 THROTTLE, asphyxiate, choke, strangulate
2 SUPPRESS, inhibit, repress, stifle

strap *noun* 1 BELT, thong, tie
▶ *verb* 2 FASTEN, bind, buckle, lash, secure, tie

strapping *adjective* WELL-BUILT, big, brawny, husky (*informal*), powerful, robust, sturdy

stratagem *noun* TRICK, device, dodge, maneuver, plan, ploy, ruse, scheme, subterfuge

strategic *adjective* 1 TACTICAL, calculated, deliberate, diplomatic, planned, politic
2 CRUCIAL, cardinal, critical, decisive, important, key, vital

strategy *noun* PLAN, approach, policy, procedure, scheme

stray *verb* 1 WANDER, drift, err, go astray
2 DIGRESS, deviate, diverge, get off the point
▶ *adjective* 3 LOST, abandoned, homeless, roaming, vagrant
4 RANDOM, accidental, chance

streak *noun* 1 BAND, layer, line, slash, strip, stripe, stroke, vein
2 TRACE, dash, element, strain, touch, vein
▶ *verb* 3 SPEED, dart, flash, fly, hurtle, sprint, tear, whizz (*informal*), zoom

stream *noun* 1 RIVER, bayou, beck, brook, burn (*Scot.*), rivulet, tributary
2 FLOW, course, current, drift, run, rush, surge, tide, torrent
▶ *verb* 3 FLOW, cascade, course, flood, gush, issue, pour, run, spill, spout

streamlined *adjective* EFFICIENT, organized, rationalized, slick, smooth-running

street *noun* ROAD, avenue, boulevard, lane, parkway, roadway, row, terrace

strength *noun* 1 MIGHT, brawn, courage, fortitude, muscle, robustness, stamina, sturdiness, toughness
2 INTENSITY, effectiveness, efficacy, force, potency, power, vigor
3 ADVANTAGE, asset, strong point

strengthen *verb* 1 FORTIFY, brace up, consolidate, harden, invigorate, restore, stiffen, toughen
2 REINFORCE, augment, bolster, brace, build up, buttress, harden, intensify, support

strenuous *adjective* DEMANDING,

arduous, hard, laborious, taxing, tough, uphill

stress noun 1 STRAIN, anxiety, burden, pressure, tension, trauma, worry
2 EMPHASIS, force, significance, weight
3 ACCENT, accentuation, beat, emphasis
▶ verb 4 EMPHASIZE, accentuate, dwell on, underline

stretch verb 1 EXTEND, cover, put forth, reach, spread, unroll
2 PULL, distend, draw out, elongate, expand, strain, tighten
▶ noun 3 EXPANSE, area, distance, extent, spread, tract
4 PERIOD, space, spell, stint, term, time

strict adjective 1 SEVERE, authoritarian, firm, harsh, stern, stringent
2 EXACT, accurate, close, faithful, meticulous, precise, scrupulous, true
3 ABSOLUTE, total, utter

strident adjective HARSH, discordant, grating, jarring, raucous, screeching, shrill

strife noun CONFLICT, battle, clash, discord, dissension, friction, quarrel

strike verb 1 WALK OUT, down tools, mutiny, revolt
2 HIT, beat, clobber (slang), clout (informal), cuff, hammer, knock, punch, slap, smack, thump, wallop (informal)
3 COLLIDE WITH, bump into, hit, run into
4 ATTACK, assail, assault, hit
5 OCCUR TO, come to, dawn on or upon, hit, register (informal)

striking adjective IMPRESSIVE, conspicuous, cool (informal), dramatic, noticeable, outstanding, phat (slang)

string noun 1 CORD, fiber, twine
2 SERIES, chain, file, line, procession, row, sequence, succession

stringent adjective STRICT, inflexible, rigid, rigorous, severe, tight, tough

stringy adjective FIBROUS, gristly, sinewy, tough

strip[1] verb 1 UNDRESS, disrobe, unclothe
2 PLUNDER, despoil, divest, empty, loot, pillage, ransack, rob, sack

strip[2] noun PIECE, band, belt, shred

strive verb TRY, attempt, bend over backwards (informal), break one's neck (informal), do one's best, give it one's best shot (informal), go all out (informal), knock oneself out (informal), labor, make an all-out effort (informal), struggle, toil

stroke verb 1 CARESS, fondle, pet, rub
▶ noun 2 APOPLEXY, attack, collapse, fit, seizure
3 BLOW, hit, knock, pat, rap, thump

stroll verb 1 WALK, amble, promenade, ramble, saunter
▶ noun 2 WALK, breath of air, constitutional, promenade, ramble, turn

strong adjective 1 POWERFUL, athletic, brawny, burly, hardy, lusty, muscular, robust, strapping, sturdy, tough
2 DURABLE, hard-wearing, heavy-duty, sturdy, substantial, well-built
3 PERSUASIVE, compelling, convincing, effective, potent, sound, telling, weighty, well-founded
4 INTENSE, acute, deep, fervent, fervid, fierce, firm, keen,

vehement, violent, zealous

5 EXTREME, drastic, forceful, severe

6 BRIGHT, bold, brilliant, dazzling

stronghold noun FORTRESS, bastion, bulwark, castle, citadel, fort

structure noun 1 BUILDING, construction, edifice, erection

2 ARRANGEMENT, configuration, construction, design, form, formation, make-up, organization

▶ verb 3 ARRANGE, assemble, build up, design, organize, shape

struggle verb 1 STRIVE, exert oneself, give it one's best shot (informal), go all out (informal), knock oneself out (informal), labor, make an all-out effort (informal), strain, toil, work

2 FIGHT, battle, compete, contend, grapple, wrestle

▶ noun 3 EFFORT, exertion, labor, pains, scramble, toil, work

4 FIGHT, battle, brush, clash, combat, conflict, contest, tussle

strut verb SWAGGER, parade, peacock, prance

stub noun 1 BUTT, dog-end (informal), end, remainder, remnant, stump, tail, tail end

2 COUNTERFOIL

stubborn adjective OBSTINATE, dogged, headstrong, inflexible, intractable, obdurate, persistent, pig-headed, recalcitrant, tenacious, unyielding

stubby adjective STOCKY, chunky, dumpy, short, squat, thickset

stuck adjective 1 FASTENED, cemented, fast, fixed, glued, joined

2 (informal) BAFFLED, beaten, stumped

stuck-up adjective SNOBBISH, arrogant, bigheaded (informal), conceited, haughty, proud, snooty (informal), toffee-nosed (slang, chiefly Brit.)

stud verb ORNAMENT, bejewel, dot, spangle, spot

student noun LEARNER, apprentice, disciple, pupil, scholar, trainee, undergraduate

studied adjective PLANNED, conscious, deliberate, intentional, premeditated

studio noun WORKSHOP, atelier

studious adjective SCHOLARLY, academic, assiduous, bookish, diligent, hard-working, intellectual

study verb 1 CONTEMPLATE, consider, examine, go into, ponder, pore over, read

2 LEARN, cram (informal), mug up (Brit. slang), read up, review, swot (up) (Brit. informal)

3 EXAMINE, analyze, investigate, look into, research, scrutinize, survey

▶ noun 4 LEARNING, application, lessons, reading, research, school work, swotting (Brit. informal)

5 EXAMINATION, analysis, consideration, contemplation, inquiry, inspection, investigation, review, scrutiny, survey

stuff noun 1 THINGS, belongings, effects, equipment, gear, kit, objects, paraphernalia, possessions, tackle

2 SUBSTANCE, essence, matter

3 MATERIAL, cloth, fabric, textile

▶ verb 4 CRAM, crowd, fill, force, jam, pack, push, ram, shove, squeeze

stuffing noun FILLING, packing, wadding

stuffy adjective 1 AIRLESS, close, frowsty, heavy, muggy, oppressive, stale, stifling, sultry, unventilated

2 (*informal*) STAID, dreary, dull, pompous, priggish, prim, stodgy

stumble *verb* **1** TRIP, fall, falter, lurch, reel, slip, stagger

2 (with *across, on* or *upon*) DISCOVER, chance upon, come across, find

stump *verb* BAFFLE, bewilder, confuse, flummox, mystify, nonplus, perplex, puzzle

stumpy *adjective* STOCKY, dumpy, short, squat, stubby, thickset

stun *verb* OVERCOME, astonish, astound, bewilder, confound, confuse, overpower, shock, stagger, stupefy

stunning *adjective* WONDERFUL, beautiful, cool (*informal*), dazzling, gorgeous, impressive, lovely, marvelous, phat (*slang*), sensational (*informal*), spectacular, striking

stunt *noun* FEAT, act, deed, exploit, trick

stunted *adjective* UNDERSIZED, diminutive, little, small, tiny

stupefy *verb* ASTOUND, amaze, daze, dumbfound, shock, stagger, stun

stupendous *adjective*
1 WONDERFUL, amazing, astounding, breathtaking, marvelous, overwhelming, sensational (*informal*), staggering, superb

2 HUGE, colossal, enormous, gigantic, mega (*slang*), vast

stupid *adjective* **1** UNINTELLIGENT, brainless, dense, dim, dumb (*informal*), half-witted, moronic, obtuse, simple, simple-minded, slow, slow-witted, thick

2 FOOLISH, asinine, bonkers (*informal*), daft (*informal*), idiotic, imbecilic, inane, nonsensical, pointless, rash, senseless, unintelligent

3 DAZED, groggy, insensate, semiconscious, stunned, stupefied

stupidity *noun* **1** LACK OF INTELLIGENCE, brainlessness, denseness, dimness, dullness, imbecility, obtuseness, slowness, thickness

2 FOOLISHNESS, absurdity, fatuousness, folly, idiocy, inanity, lunacy, madness, silliness

stupor *noun* DAZE, coma, insensibility, stupefaction, unconsciousness

sturdy *adjective* **1** ROBUST, athletic, brawny, hardy, lusty, muscular, powerful

2 WELL-BUILT, durable, solid, substantial, well-made

stutter *verb* STAMMER, falter, hesitate, stumble

style *noun* **1** DESIGN, cut, form, manner

2 MANNER, approach, method, mode, technique, way

3 ELEGANCE, chic, élan, flair, panache, polish, smartness, sophistication, taste

4 TYPE, category, genre, kind, sort, variety

5 FASHION, mode, rage, trend, vogue

6 LUXURY, affluence, comfort, ease, elegance, grandeur

▶ *verb* **7** DESIGN, adapt, arrange, cut, fashion, shape, tailor

8 CALL, designate, dub, entitle, label, name, term

stylish *adjective* SMART, chic, cool (*informal*), dressy (*informal*), fashionable, modish, phat (*slang*), trendy (*informal*), voguish

suave *adjective* SMOOTH, charming, courteous, debonair, polite, sophisticated, urbane

subconscious *adjective* HIDDEN,

inner, intuitive, latent, repressed, subliminal

subdue verb 1 OVERCOME, break, conquer, control, crush, defeat, master, overpower, quell, tame, vanquish

2 MODERATE, mellow, quieten down, soften, suppress, tone down

subdued adjective 1 QUIET, chastened, crestfallen, dejected, downcast, down in the mouth, sad, serious

2 SOFT, dim, hushed, muted, quiet, subtle, toned down, unobtrusive

subject noun 1 TOPIC, affair, business, issue, matter, object, point, question, substance, theme

2 CITIZEN, national, subordinate

▶ adjective 3 SUBORDINATE, dependent, inferior, obedient, satellite

4 ▷▷ **subject to: a** LIABLE TO, exposed to, in danger of, open to, prone to, susceptible to, vulnerable to **b** CONDITIONAL ON, contingent on, dependent on

▶ verb 5 PUT THROUGH, expose, lay open, submit, treat

subjective adjective PERSONAL, biased, nonobjective, prejudiced

subjugate verb CONQUER, enslave, master, overcome, overpower, quell, subdue, suppress, vanquish

sublime adjective NOBLE, elevated, exalted, glorious, grand, great, high, lofty

submerge verb IMMERSE, deluge, dip, duck, engulf, flood, inundate, overflow, overwhelm, plunge, sink, swamp

submission noun 1 SURRENDER, assent, capitulation, giving in, yielding

2 PRESENTATION, entry, handing

in, tendering

3 MEEKNESS, compliance, deference, docility, obedience, passivity, resignation

submissive adjective MEEK, accommodating, acquiescent, amenable, compliant, docile, obedient, passive, pliant, tractable, unresisting, yielding

submit verb 1 SURRENDER, accede, agree, capitulate, comply, endure, give in, succumb, tolerate, yield

2 PUT FORWARD, hand in, present, proffer, table, tender

subordinate adjective 1 LESSER, dependent, inferior, junior, lower, minor, secondary, subject

▶ noun 2 INFERIOR, aide, assistant, attendant, junior, second

subordination noun INFERIORITY, inferior or secondary status, servitude, subjection

subscribe verb 1 DONATE, contribute, give

2 SUPPORT, advocate, endorse

subscription noun 1 MEMBERSHIP FEE, annual payment, dues

2 DONATION, contribution, gift

subsequent adjective FOLLOWING, after, ensuing, later, succeeding, successive

subsequently adverb LATER, afterwards

subservient adjective SERVILE, abject, deferential, obsequious, slavish, submissive, sycophantic

subside verb 1 DECREASE, abate, diminish, ease, ebb, lessen, quieten, slacken, wane

2 SINK, cave in, collapse, drop, lower, settle

subsidence noun 1 SINKING, settling

2 DECREASE, abatement, easing off, lessening, slackening

subsidiary adjective LESSER,

ancillary, auxiliary, minor, secondary, subordinate, supplementary

subsidize verb FUND, finance, promote, sponsor, support

subsidy noun AID, allowance, assistance, grant, help, support

substance noun 1 MATERIAL, body, fabric, stuff
2 MEANING, essence, gist, import, main point, significance
3 REALITY, actuality, concreteness
4 WEALTH, assets, estate, means, property, resources

substantial adjective BIG, ample, considerable, important, large, significant, sizable or sizeable, supersize

substantiate verb SUPPORT, authenticate, confirm, establish, prove, verify

substitute verb 1 REPLACE, change, exchange, interchange, swap, switch
▶ noun 2 REPLACEMENT, agent, deputy, locum, proxy, reserve, sub, surrogate
▶ adjective 3 REPLACEMENT, alternative, fall-back, proxy, reserve, second, surrogate

substitution noun REPLACEMENT, change, exchange, swap, switch

subterfuge noun TRICK, deception, dodge, maneuver, ploy, ruse, stratagem

subtle adjective 1 SOPHISTICATED, delicate, refined
2 FAINT, delicate, implied, slight, understated
3 CRAFTY, artful, cunning, devious, ingenious, shrewd, sly, wily

subtlety noun 1 SOPHISTICATION, delicacy, refinement
2 CUNNING, artfulness, cleverness, craftiness, deviousness,

ingenuity, slyness, wiliness

subtract verb TAKE AWAY, deduct, diminish, remove, take from, take off

subversive adjective 1 SEDITIOUS, riotous, treasonous
▶ noun 2 DISSIDENT, fifth columnist, saboteur, terrorist, traitor

subvert verb OVERTURN, sabotage, undermine

succeed verb 1 MAKE IT (informal), be successful, crack it (informal), flourish, make good, make the grade (informal), prosper, thrive, triumph, work
2 FOLLOW, come next, ensue, result

success noun 1 LUCK, fame, fortune, happiness, prosperity, triumph
2 HIT (informal), celebrity, megastar (informal), sensation, smash (informal), star, superstar, winner

successful adjective THRIVING, booming, flourishing, fortunate, fruitful, lucky, profitable, prosperous, rewarding, top, victorious

successfully adverb WELL, favorably, victoriously, with flying colors

succession noun 1 SERIES, chain, course, cycle, order, progression, run, sequence, train
2 TAKING OVER, accession, assumption, inheritance

successive adjective CONSECUTIVE, following, in succession

succinct adjective BRIEF, compact, concise, laconic, pithy, terse

succor noun 1 HELP, aid, assistance
▶ verb 2 HELP, aid, assist

succulent adjective JUICY, luscious, lush, moist

succumb verb 1 SURRENDER,

capitulate, give in, submit, yield
2 DIE, fall

sucker noun (slang) FOOL, dork
(slang), dupe, mug (Brit. slang),
pushover (slang), schmuck (slang),
victim

sudden adjective QUICK, abrupt,
hasty, hurried, rapid, rash, swift,
unexpected

suddenly adverb ABRUPTLY, all of a
sudden, unexpectedly

sue verb (law) TAKE (SOMEONE) TO
COURT, charge, indict, prosecute,
summon

suffer verb 1 UNDERGO, bear,
endure, experience, go through,
sustain
2 TOLERATE, put up with (informal)

suffering noun PAIN, agony,
anguish, discomfort, distress,
hardship, misery, ordeal, torment

suffice verb BE ENOUGH, be
adequate, be sufficient, do, meet
requirements, serve

sufficient adjective ADEQUATE,
enough, satisfactory

suffocate verb CHOKE, asphyxiate,
smother, stifle

suggest verb 1 RECOMMEND,
advise, advocate, prescribe,
propose
2 BRING TO MIND, evoke
3 HINT, imply, indicate, intimate

suggestion noun
1 RECOMMENDATION, motion, plan,
proposal, proposition
2 HINT, breath, indication,
intimation, trace, whisper

suggestive adjective SMUTTY,
bawdy, blue, indelicate,
provocative, racy, ribald, risqué,
rude

suit noun 1 OUTFIT, clothing,
costume, dress, ensemble, habit
2 LAWSUIT, action, case, cause,
proceeding, prosecution, trial

▶ verb 3 BE ACCEPTABLE TO, do,
gratify, please, satisfy
4 BEFIT, agree, become, go with,
harmonize, match, tally

suitability noun
APPROPRIATENESS, aptness,
fitness, rightness

suitable adjective APPROPRIATE,
apt, becoming, befitting, fit,
fitting, proper, right, satisfactory

suite noun ROOMS, apartment

suitor noun (old-fashioned)
ADMIRER, beau (old-fashioned),
young man

sulk verb BE SULLEN, be in a huff,
pout

sulky adjective HUFFY, cross,
disgruntled, in the sulks, moody,
petulant, querulous, resentful,
sullen

sullen adjective MOROSE, cross,
dour, glowering, moody, sour,
surly, unsociable

sully verb DEFILE, besmirch,
disgrace, dishonor, smirch, stain,
tarnish

sultry adjective 1 HUMID, close, hot,
muggy, oppressive, sticky, stifling
2 SEDUCTIVE, provocative, sensual,
sexy (informal)

sum noun TOTAL, aggregate,
amount, tally, whole

summarize verb SUM UP, abridge,
condense, encapsulate, epitomize,
précis

summary noun SYNOPSIS,
abridgment, outline, précis,
résumé, review, rundown

summit noun PEAK, acme, apex,
head, height, pinnacle, top,
zenith

summon verb 1 SEND FOR, bid,
call, invite
2 (often with up) GATHER, draw
on, muster

sumptuous adjective LUXURIOUS,

gorgeous, grand, lavish, opulent, splendid, superb

sum up *verb* SUMMARIZE, put in a nutshell, recapitulate, review

sunburned *adjective* TANNED, bronzed, brown, burnt, peeling, red

sundry *adjective* VARIOUS, assorted, different, miscellaneous, several, some

sunken *adjective* 1 HOLLOW, drawn, haggard
2 LOWER, buried, recessed, submerged

sunny *adjective* 1 BRIGHT, clear, fine, radiant, summery, sunlit, unclouded
2 CHEERFUL, buoyant, cheery, happy, joyful, light-hearted

sunrise *noun* DAWN, break of day, cockcrow, daybreak

sunset *noun* NIGHTFALL, close of (the) day, dusk, eventide

super *adjective* (*informal*) EXCELLENT, cracking (*Brit. informal*), glorious, magnificent, marvelous, outstanding, sensational (*informal*), smashing (*informal*), superb, terrific (*informal*), wonderful

superb *adjective* SPLENDID, excellent, exquisite, fine, first-rate, grand, magnificent, marvelous, superior, superlative, world-class

supercilious *adjective* SCORNFUL, arrogant, contemptuous, disdainful, haughty, lofty, snooty (*informal*), stuck-up (*informal*)

superficial *adjective* 1 HASTY, casual, cursory, desultory, hurried, perfunctory, sketchy, slapdash
2 SHALLOW, empty-headed, frivolous, silly, trivial
3 SURFACE, exterior, external, on the surface, slight

superfluous *adjective* EXCESS, extra, left over, redundant, remaining, spare, supernumerary, surplus

superhuman *adjective* 1 HEROIC, phenomenal, prodigious
2 SUPERNATURAL, paranormal

superintendence *noun* SUPERVISION, charge, control, direction, government, management

superintendent *noun* SUPERVISOR, chief, controller, director, governor, inspector, manager, overseer

superior *adjective* 1 BETTER, grander, greater, higher, surpassing, unrivaled
2 SUPERCILIOUS, condescending, disdainful, haughty, lofty, lordly, patronizing, pretentious, snobbish
3 FIRST-CLASS, choice, deluxe, excellent, exceptional, exclusive, first-rate
▶ *noun* 4 BOSS (*informal*), chief, director, manager, principal, senior, supervisor

superiority *noun* SUPREMACY, advantage, ascendancy, excellence, lead, predominance

superlative *adjective* OUTSTANDING, excellent, supreme, unparalleled, unrivaled, unsurpassed

supernatural *adjective* PARANORMAL, ghostly, hidden, miraculous, mystic, occult, psychic, spectral, uncanny, unearthly

supersede *verb* REPLACE, displace, oust, supplant, take the place of, usurp

supervise *verb* OVERSEE, control, direct, handle, look after, manage, run, superintend

supervision noun
SUPERINTENDENCE, care, charge,
control, direction, guidance,
management

supervisor noun BOSS (informal),
administrator, chief, foreman,
inspector, manager, overseer

supplant verb REPLACE, displace,
oust, supersede, take the place of

supple adjective FLEXIBLE, limber,
lissom(e), lithe, pliable, pliant

supplement noun 1 ADDITION,
add-on, appendix, extra, insert,
postscript, pull-out
▶ verb 2 ADD, augment,
complement, extend, reinforce

supplementary adjective
ADDITIONAL, add-on, ancillary,
auxiliary, extra, secondary

supplication noun PLEA, appeal,
entreaty, petition, prayer, request

supply verb 1 PROVIDE, contribute,
endow, equip, furnish, give, grant,
produce, stock, yield
▶ noun 2 STORE, cache, fund,
hoard, quantity, reserve, source,
stock
3 (usually plural) PROVISIONS,
equipment, food, materials,
necessities, rations, stores

support verb 1 BEAR, brace,
buttress, carry, hold, prop,
reinforce, sustain
2 PROVIDE FOR, finance, fund,
keep, look after, maintain, sustain
3 HELP, aid, assist, back,
champion, defend, second, side
with
4 BEAR OUT, confirm, corroborate,
substantiate, verify
▶ noun 5 HELP, aid, assistance,
backing, encouragement, loyalty
6 PROP, brace, foundation, pillar,
post
7 SUPPORTER, backer, mainstay,
prop, second, tower of strength

8 UPKEEP, keep, maintenance,
subsistence, sustenance

supporter noun FOLLOWER,
adherent, advocate, champion,
fan, friend, helper, patron,
sponsor, well-wisher

supportive adjective HELPFUL,
encouraging, sympathetic,
understanding

suppose verb 1 PRESUME, assume,
conjecture, expect, guess
(informal), imagine, think
2 IMAGINE, conjecture, consider,
hypothesize, postulate, pretend

supposed adjective 1 PRESUMED,
accepted, alleged, assumed,
professed
2 (usually with to) MEANT,
expected, obliged, required

supposedly adverb ALLEGEDLY,
hypothetically, ostensibly,
presumably, theoretically

supposition noun GUESS,
conjecture, hypothesis,
presumption, speculation,
surmise, theory

suppress verb 1 STOP, check,
conquer, crush, overpower, put an
end to, quash, quell, subdue
2 RESTRAIN, conceal, contain,
curb, hold in or back, repress,
silence, smother, stifle

suppression noun ELIMINATION,
check, crushing, quashing,
smothering

supremacy noun DOMINATION,
mastery, predominance, primacy,
sovereignty, supreme power, sway

supreme adjective HIGHEST, chief,
foremost, greatest, head, leading,
paramount, pre-eminent, prime,
principal, top, ultimate

sure adjective 1 CERTAIN, assured,
confident, convinced, decided,
definite, positive
2 RELIABLE, accurate, dependable,

foolproof, infallible, undeniable, undoubted, unerring, unfailing
3 INEVITABLE, assured, bound, guaranteed, inescapable

surely adverb UNDOUBTEDLY, certainly, definitely, doubtlessly, indubitably, unquestionably, without doubt

surface noun 1 OUTSIDE, covering, exterior, face, side, top, veneer
▶ verb 2 APPEAR, arise, come to light, come up, crop up (informal), emerge, materialize, transpire

surfeit noun EXCESS, glut, plethora, superfluity

surge noun 1 RUSH, flood, flow, gush, outpouring
2 WAVE, billow, roller, swell
▶ verb 3 RUSH, gush, heave, rise, roll

surly adjective ILL-TEMPERED, churlish, cross, grouchy (informal), morose, sulky, sullen, uncivil, ungracious

surmise verb 1 GUESS, conjecture, imagine, presume, speculate, suppose
▶ noun 2 GUESS, assumption, conjecture, presumption, speculation, supposition

surpass verb OUTDO, beat, eclipse, exceed, excel, outshine, outstrip, transcend

surpassing adjective SUPREME, exceptional, extraordinary, incomparable, matchless, outstanding, unrivaled

surplus noun 1 EXCESS, balance, remainder, residue, surfeit
▶ adjective 2 EXCESS, extra, odd, remaining, spare, superfluous

surprise noun 1 SHOCK, bombshell, eye-opener (informal), jolt, revelation
2 AMAZEMENT, astonishment, incredulity, wonder

▶ verb 3 AMAZE, astonish, stagger, stun, take aback
4 CATCH UNAWARES or OFF-GUARD, discover, spring upon, startle

surprised adjective AMAZED, astonished, speechless, taken by surprise, thunderstruck

surprising adjective AMAZING, astonishing, extraordinary, incredible, remarkable, staggering, unexpected, unusual

surrender verb 1 GIVE IN, capitulate, give way, submit, succumb, yield
2 GIVE UP, abandon, cede, concede, part with, relinquish, renounce, waive, yield
▶ noun 3 SUBMISSION, capitulation, relinquishment, renunciation, resignation

surreptitious adjective SECRET, covert, furtive, sly, stealthy, underhand

surrogate noun SUBSTITUTE, proxy, representative, stand-in

surround verb ENCLOSE, encircle, encompass, envelop, hem in, ring

surroundings plural noun ENVIRONMENT, background, location, milieu, setting

surveillance noun OBSERVATION, inspection, scrutiny, supervision, watch

survey verb 1 LOOK OVER, contemplate, examine, inspect, observe, scan, scrutinize, view
2 ESTIMATE, appraise, assess, measure, plan, plot, size up
▶ noun 3 EXAMINATION, inspection, scrutiny
4 STUDY, inquiry, review

survive verb REMAIN ALIVE, endure, last, live on, outlast, outlive

susceptible adjective 1 (usually with to) LIABLE, disposed, given, inclined, prone, subject, vulnerable

2 IMPRESSIONABLE, receptive, responsive, sensitive, suggestible

suspect verb 1 BELIEVE, consider, feel, guess, speculate, suppose

2 DISTRUST, doubt, mistrust

▶ adjective 3 DUBIOUS, doubtful, iffy (informal), questionable

suspend verb 1 HANG, attach, dangle

2 POSTPONE, cease, cut short, defer, discontinue, interrupt, put off, shelve

suspense noun UNCERTAINTY, anxiety, apprehension, doubt, expectation, insecurity, irresolution, tension

suspension noun POSTPONEMENT, abeyance, break, breaking off, deferment, discontinuation, interruption

suspicion noun 1 DISTRUST, doubt, dubiety, misgiving, mistrust, qualm, skepticism, wariness

2 IDEA, guess, hunch, impression, notion

3 TRACE, hint, shade, soupçon, streak, suggestion, tinge, touch

suspicious adjective 1 DISTRUSTFUL, doubtful, skeptical, unbelieving, wary

2 SUSPECT, dodgy (Brit., Austral., & N.Z. informal), doubtful, dubious, fishy (informal), questionable

sustain verb 1 MAINTAIN, continue, keep up, prolong, protract

2 KEEP ALIVE, aid, assist, help, nourish

3 WITHSTAND, bear, endure, experience, feel, suffer, undergo

4 SUPPORT, bear, uphold

sustained adjective CONTINUOUS, constant, nonstop, perpetual, prolonged, steady, twenty-four-seven (slang), unremitting

swagger verb SHOW OFF (informal), boast, brag, parade

swallow verb GULP, chow down (slang), consume, devour, drink, eat, swig (informal)

swamp noun 1 BOG, fen, marsh, mire, morass, quagmire, slough

▶ verb 2 FLOOD, capsize, engulf, inundate, sink, submerge

3 OVERWHELM, flood, inundate, overload

swarm noun 1 MULTITUDE, army, crowd, flock, herd, horde, host, mass, throng

▶ verb 2 CROWD, flock, mass, stream, throng

3 TEEM, abound, bristle, crawl

swarthy adjective DARK-SKINNED, black, brown, dark, dark-complexioned, dusky

swashbuckling adjective DASHING, bold, daredevil, flamboyant

swathe verb WRAP, bundle up, cloak, drape, envelop, shroud

sway verb 1 LEAN, bend, rock, roll, swing

2 INFLUENCE, affect, guide, induce, persuade

▶ noun 3 POWER, authority, clout (informal), control, influence

swear verb 1 CURSE, be foul-mouthed, blaspheme

2 DECLARE, affirm, assert, attest, promise, testify, vow

swearing noun BAD LANGUAGE, blasphemy, cursing, foul language, profanity

swearword noun OATH, curse, expletive, four-letter word, obscenity, profanity

sweat noun 1 PERSPIRATION

2 (informal) LABOR, chore, drudgery, toil

3 (informal) WORRY, agitation, anxiety, distress, panic, strain

▶ *verb* **4** PERSPIRE, glow

5 (*informal*) WORRY, agonize, fret, suffer, torture oneself

sweaty *adjective* PERSPIRING, clammy, sticky

sweep *verb* **1** CLEAR, brush, clean, remove

2 SAIL, fly, glide, pass, skim, tear, zoom

▶ *noun* **3** ARC, bend, curve, move, stroke, swing

4 EXTENT, range, scope, stretch

sweeping *adjective* **1** WIDE-RANGING, all-embracing, all-inclusive, broad, comprehensive, extensive, global, wide

2 INDISCRIMINATE, blanket, exaggerated, overstated, unqualified, wholesale

sweet *adjective* **1** SUGARY, cloying, saccharine

2 CHARMING, agreeable, appealing, cute, delightful, engaging, kind, likable *or* likeable, lovable, winning

3 MELODIOUS, dulcet, harmonious, mellow, musical

4 FRAGRANT, aromatic, clean, fresh, pure

▶ *noun* **5** (*usually plural*) CONFECTIONERY, bonbon, candy (*U.S.*)

6 dessert, pudding

sweeten *verb* **1** SUGAR

2 MOLLIFY, appease, pacify, soothe

sweetheart *noun* LOVER, beloved, boyfriend *or* girlfriend, darling, dear, love

swell *verb* **1** EXPAND, balloon, bloat, bulge, dilate, distend, enlarge, grow, increase, rise

▶ *noun* **2** WAVE, billow, surge

swelling *noun* ENLARGEMENT, bulge, bump, distension, inflammation, lump, protuberance

sweltering *adjective* HOT, boiling, burning, oppressive, scorching, stifling

swerve *verb* VEER, bend, deflect, deviate, diverge, stray, swing, turn, turn aside

swift *adjective* QUICK, fast, hurried, prompt, rapid, speedy

swiftly *adverb* QUICKLY, fast, hurriedly, promptly, rapidly, speedily

swiftness *noun* SPEED, promptness, quickness, rapidity, speediness, velocity

swindle *verb* **1** CHEAT, con, defraud, do (*slang*), fleece, rip (someone) off (*slang*), skin (*slang*), sting (*informal*), trick

▶ *noun* **2** FRAUD, con trick (*informal*), deception, fiddle (*Brit. informal*), racket, rip-off (*slang*), scam (*slang*)

swindler *noun* CHEAT, con man (*informal*), fraud, rogue, shark, trickster

swing *verb* **1** SWAY, oscillate, rock, veer, wave

2 (*usually with* round) TURN, curve, pivot, rotate, swivel

3 HANG, dangle, suspend

▶ *noun* **4** SWAYING, oscillation

swipe *verb* **1** HIT, lash out at, slap, strike, wallop (*informal*)

2 (*slang*) STEAL, appropriate, filch, lift (*informal*), nick (*slang, chiefly Brit.*), pinch (*informal*), purloin

▶ *noun* **3** BLOW, clout (*informal*), cuff, slap, smack, wallop (*informal*)

swirl *verb* WHIRL, churn, eddy, spin, twist

switch *noun* **1** CHANGE, reversal, shift

2 EXCHANGE, substitution, swap

▶ *verb* **3** CHANGE, deflect, deviate, divert, shift

4 EXCHANGE, substitute, swap

swivel *verb* TURN, pivot, revolve,

rotate, spin

swollen *adjective* ENLARGED, bloated, distended, inflamed, puffed up

swoop *verb* 1 POUNCE, descend, dive, rush, stoop, sweep
▶ *noun* 2 POUNCE, descent, drop, lunge, plunge, rush, stoop, sweep

swop, swap *verb* EXCHANGE, barter, interchange, switch, trade

sycophant *noun* CRAWLER, bootlicker (*informal*), brown-noser (*slang*), fawner, flatterer, toady, yes man

sycophantic *adjective* OBSEQUIOUS, crawling, fawning, flattering, grovelling, ingratiating, servile, slimy, smarmy (*Brit. informal*), toadying, unctuous

syllabus *noun* COURSE OF STUDY, curriculum

symbol *noun* SIGN, badge, emblem, figure, icon, image, logo, mark, representation, token

symbolic *adjective* REPRESENTATIVE, allegorical, emblematic, figurative

symbolize *verb* REPRESENT, denote, mean, personify, signify, stand for, typify

symmetrical *adjective* BALANCED, in proportion, regular

symmetry *noun* BALANCE, evenness, order, proportion, regularity

sympathetic *adjective* 1 CARING, compassionate, concerned, interested, kind, pitying, supportive, understanding, warm
2 LIKE-MINDED, agreeable, companionable, compatible, congenial, friendly

sympathize *verb* 1 FEEL FOR, commiserate, condole, pity
2 AGREE, side with, understand

sympathizer *noun* SUPPORTER, partisan, well-wisher

sympathy *noun* 1 COMPASSION, commiseration, pity, understanding
2 AGREEMENT, affinity, fellow feeling, rapport

symptom *noun* SIGN, expression, indication, mark, token, warning

symptomatic *adjective* INDICATIVE, characteristic, suggestive

synthetic *adjective* ARTIFICIAL, fake, man-made

system *noun* 1 METHOD, practice, procedure, routine, technique
2 ARRANGEMENT, classification, organization, scheme, structure

systematic *adjective* METHODICAL, efficient, orderly, organized

table *noun* 1 COUNTER, bench, board, stand
2 LIST, catalog, chart, diagram, record, register, roll, schedule, tabulation
▸ *verb* 3 SUBMIT, enter, move, propose, put forward, suggest

tableau *noun* PICTURE, representation, scene, spectacle

taboo *noun* 1 PROHIBITION, anathema, ban, interdict, proscription, restriction
▸ *adjective* 2 FORBIDDEN, anathema, banned, outlawed, prohibited, proscribed, unacceptable, unmentionable

tacit *adjective* IMPLIED, implicit, inferred, undeclared, understood, unexpressed, unspoken, unstated

taciturn *adjective* UNCOMMUNICATIVE, quiet, reserved, reticent, silent, tight-lipped, unforthcoming, withdrawn

tack¹ *noun* 1 NAIL, drawing pin, pin
▸ *verb* 2 FASTEN, affix, attach, fix, nail, pin
3 STITCH, baste
4 ▷▷ **tack on** APPEND, add, attach, tag

tack² *noun* COURSE, approach, direction, heading, line, method, path, plan, procedure, way

tackle *verb* 1 DEAL WITH, attempt, come *or* get to grips with, embark upon, get stuck into (*informal*), have a go at (*informal*), set about, undertake
2 CONFRONT, challenge, grab, grasp, halt, intercept, seize, stop
▸ *noun* 3 CHALLENGE, block
4 EQUIPMENT, accouterments, apparatus, gear, paraphernalia, tools, trappings

tacky¹ *adjective* STICKY, adhesive, gluey, gummy, wet

tacky² *adjective* (*informal*) VULGAR, cheap, naff (*Brit. slang*), off-color, scuzzy (*slang*), seedy, shabby, shoddy, sleazy, tasteless, tatty

tact *noun* DIPLOMACY, consideration, delicacy, discretion, sensitivity, thoughtfulness, understanding

tactful *adjective* DIPLOMATIC, considerate, delicate, discreet, polite, politic, sensitive, thoughtful, understanding

tactic *noun* 1 POLICY, approach, maneuver, method, move, ploy, scheme, stratagem
2 ▷▷ **tactics** STRATEGY, campaigning, generalship, maneuvers, plans

tactical *adjective* STRATEGIC, cunning, diplomatic, shrewd, smart

tactician *noun* STRATEGIST, general, mastermind, planner

tactless *adjective* INSENSITIVE, impolite, impolitic, inconsiderate, indelicate, indiscreet, thoughtless, undiplomatic, unsubtle

tag *noun* 1 LABEL, flap, identification, mark, marker,

note, slip, tab, ticket
▶ *verb* 2 LABEL, mark
3 (with *along* or *on*) ACCOMPANY, attend, follow, shadow, stalk, tail (*informal*), trail

tail *noun* 1 EXTREMITY, appendage, end, rear end, tailpiece
2 ▷▷ **turn tail** RUN AWAY, cut and run, flee, retreat, run off, take to one's heels
▶ *verb* 3 (*informal*) FOLLOW, shadow, stalk, track, trail

tailor *noun* 1 OUTFITTER, clothier, costumier, couturier, dressmaker, seamstress
▶ *verb* 2 ADAPT, adjust, alter, customize, fashion, modify, mold, shape, style

taint *verb* 1 SPOIL, blemish, contaminate, corrupt, damage, defile, pollute, ruin, stain, sully, tarnish
▶ *noun* 2 STAIN, black mark, blemish, blot, defect, demerit, fault, flaw, spot

take *verb* 1 CAPTURE, acquire, catch, get, grasp, grip, obtain, secure, seize
2 ACCOMPANY, bring, conduct, convoy, escort, guide, lead, usher
3 CARRY, bear, bring, convey, ferry, fetch, haul, transport
4 STEAL, appropriate, misappropriate, pinch (*informal*), pocket, purloin
5 REQUIRE, call for, demand, necessitate, need
6 TOLERATE, abide, bear, endure, put up with (*informal*), stand, stomach, withstand
7 HAVE ROOM FOR, accept, accommodate, contain, hold
8 SUBTRACT, deduct, eliminate, remove
9 ASSUME, believe, consider, perceive, presume, regard, understand

take in *verb* 1 UNDERSTAND, absorb, assimilate, comprehend, digest, get the hang of (*informal*), grasp
2 DECEIVE, cheat, con (*informal*), dupe, fool, hoodwink, mislead, swindle, trick

takeoff *noun* 1 DEPARTURE, launch, liftoff
2 (*informal*) PARODY, caricature, imitation, lampoon, satire, send-up (*Brit. informal*), spoof (*informal*)

take off *verb* 1 REMOVE, discard, peel off, strip off
2 LIFT OFF, take to the air
3 (*informal*) DEPART, abscond, decamp, disappear, go, leave, slope off
4 (*informal*) PARODY, caricature, imitate, lampoon, mimic, mock, satirize, send up (*Brit. informal*)

takeover *noun* MERGER, coup, incorporation

take up *verb* 1 OCCUPY, absorb, consume, cover, extend over, fill, use up
2 START, adopt, become involved in, engage in

taking *adjective* 1 CHARMING, attractive, beguiling, captivating, enchanting, engaging, fetching (*informal*), likable *or* likeable, prepossessing
▶ *noun* 2 ▷▷ **takings** REVENUE, earnings, income, proceeds, profits, receipts, returns, take

tale *noun* STORY, account, anecdote, fable, legend, narrative, saga, yarn (*informal*)

talent *noun* ABILITY, aptitude, capacity, flair, genius, gift, knack

talented *adjective* GIFTED, able, brilliant

talisman *noun* CHARM, amulet, fetish, lucky charm, mascot

talk *verb* 1 SPEAK, chat, chatter,

chew the fat (*slang*), communicate, converse, gossip, natter, utter
2 NEGOTIATE, confabulate, confer, parley
3 INFORM, blab, give the game away, grass (*Brit. slang*), let the cat out of the bag, nark (*Brit., Austral., & N.Z. slang*), tell all
▶ *noun* **4** SPEECH, address, discourse, disquisition, lecture, oration, sermon

talkative *adjective* LOQUACIOUS, chatty, effusive, garrulous, gossipy, long-winded, mouthy, verbose, voluble, wordy

talker *noun* SPEAKER, chatterbox, conversationalist, lecturer, orator

talking-to *noun* REPRIMAND, criticism, dressing-down (*informal*), lecture, rebuke, reproach, reproof, scolding, telling-off (*informal*), ticking-off (*informal*)

tall *adjective* **1** HIGH, big, elevated, giant, lanky, lofty, soaring, towering
2 *as in* **tall tale** (*informal*) IMPLAUSIBLE, absurd, cock-and-bull (*informal*), exaggerated, far-fetched, incredible, preposterous, unbelievable
3 *as in* **tall order** DIFFICULT, demanding, hard, unreasonable, well-nigh impossible

tally *verb* **1** CORRESPOND, accord, agree, coincide, concur, conform, fit, harmonize, match, square
▶ *noun* **2** RECORD, count, mark, reckoning, running total, score, total

tame *adjective* **1** DOMESTICATED, amenable, broken, disciplined, docile, gentle, obedient, tractable
2 SUBMISSIVE, compliant, docile, manageable, meek, obedient, subdued, unresisting

3 UNINTERESTING, bland, boring, dull, humdrum, insipid, unexciting, uninspiring, vapid
▶ *verb* **4** DOMESTICATE, break in, house-train, train
5 DISCIPLINE, bring to heel, conquer, humble, master, subdue, subjugate, suppress

tamper *verb* INTERFERE, alter, fiddle (*informal*), fool about (*informal*), meddle, mess about, tinker

tangible *adjective* DEFINITE, actual, concrete, material, palpable, perceptible, positive, real

tangle *noun* **1** KNOT, coil, entanglement, jungle, twist, web
2 CONFUSION, complication, entanglement, fix (*informal*), imbroglio, jam, mess, mix-up
▶ *verb* **3** TWIST, coil, entangle, interweave, knot, mat, mesh, ravel
4 (*often with* **with**) COME INTO CONFLICT, come up against, contend, contest, cross swords, dispute, lock horns

tangled *adjective* **1** TWISTED, entangled, jumbled, knotted, matted, messy, snarled, tousled
2 COMPLICATED, complex, confused, convoluted, involved, knotty, messy, mixed-up

tangy *adjective* SHARP, piquant, pungent, spicy, tart

tantalize *verb* TORMENT, frustrate, lead on, taunt, tease, torture

tantamount *adjective* EQUIVALENT, commensurate, equal, synonymous

tantrum *noun* OUTBURST, fit, flare-up, hysterics, temper

tap¹ *verb* **1** KNOCK, beat, drum, pat, rap, strike, touch
▶ *noun* **2** KNOCK, pat, rap, touch

tap² *noun* **1** VALVE, stopcock

2 ▷▷ **on tap: a** (*informal*) AVAILABLE, at hand, in reserve, on hand, ready **b** ON DRAFT

▶ *verb* **3** LISTEN IN ON, bug (*informal*), eavesdrop on

4 DRAW OFF, bleed, drain, siphon off

tape *noun* **1** STRIP, band, ribbon

▶ *verb* **2** RECORD, tape-record, video

3 BIND, seal, secure, stick, wrap

taper *verb* **1** NARROW, come to a point, thin

2 ▷▷ **taper off** LESSEN, decrease, die away, dwindle, fade, reduce, subside, wane, wind down

target *noun* **1** GOAL, aim, ambition, end, intention, mark, object, objective

2 VICTIM, butt, scapegoat

tariff *noun* **1** TAX, duty, excise, levy, toll

2 SCHEDULE, menu

tarnish *verb* **1** STAIN, blacken, blemish, blot, darken, discolor, sully, taint

▶ *noun* **2** STAIN, blemish, blot, discoloration, spot, taint

tart¹ *noun* PIE, pastry, tartlet

tart² *adjective* SHARP, acid, bitter, piquant, pungent, sour, tangy, vinegary

tart³ *noun* SLUT, call girl, floozy (*slang*), ho (*slang*), prostitute, trollop, whore

task *noun* **1** JOB, assignment, chore, duty, enterprise, exercise, mission, undertaking

2 ▷▷ **take to task** CRITICIZE, blame, censure, reprimand, reproach, reprove, scold, tell off (*informal*), upbraid

taste *noun* **1** FLAVOR, relish, savor, smack, tang

2 BIT, bite, dash, morsel, mouthful, sample, *soupçon*, spoonful, tidbit

3 LIKING, appetite, fancy, fondness, inclination, partiality, penchant, predilection, preference

4 REFINEMENT, appreciation, discernment, discrimination, elegance, judgment, sophistication, style

▶ *verb* **5** DISTINGUISH, differentiate, discern, perceive

6 SAMPLE, savor, sip, test, try

7 HAVE A FLAVOR OF, savor of, smack of

8 EXPERIENCE, encounter, know, meet with, partake of, undergo

tasteful *adjective* REFINED, artistic, cultivated, cultured, discriminating, elegant, exquisite, in good taste, polished, stylish

tasteless *adjective* **1** INSIPID, bland, boring, dull, flat, flavorless, mild, thin, weak

2 VULGAR, crass, crude, gaudy, gross, inelegant, naff (*Brit. slang*), off-color, tacky (*informal*), tawdry

tasty *adjective* DELICIOUS, appetizing, delectable, full-flavored, luscious, palatable, savory, scrumptious (*informal*), toothsome, yummy (*informal*)

tatters *noun* ▷▷ **in tatters** RAGGED, down at heel, in rags, in shreds, ripped, tattered, threadbare, torn

tatty *adjective* RAGGED, bedraggled, dilapidated, down at heel, neglected, run-down, scruffy, shabby, threadbare, worn

taunt *verb* **1** TEASE, deride, insult, jeer, mock, provoke, ridicule, torment

▶ *noun* **2** JEER, derision, dig, gibe, insult, provocation, ridicule, sarcasm, teasing

taut *adjective* TIGHT, flexed, rigid, strained, stressed, stretched, tense

tavern noun INN, alehouse (archaic), bar, hostelry, pub (informal), public house

tawdry adjective VULGAR, cheap, flashy, gaudy, gimcrack, naff (Brit. slang), tacky (informal), tasteless, tatty, tinselly

tax noun 1 CHARGE, duty, excise, levy, tariff, tithe, toll
▶ verb 2 CHARGE, assess, rate 3 STRAIN, burden, exhaust, load, stretch, test, try, weaken, weary

taxing adjective DEMANDING, exacting, exhausting, onerous, punishing, sapping, stressful, tiring, tough, trying

teach verb INSTRUCT, coach, drill, educate, enlighten, guide, inform, show, train, tutor

teacher noun INSTRUCTOR, coach, educator, guide, lecturer, master or mistress, mentor, schoolteacher, trainer, tutor

team noun 1 GROUP, band, body, bunch, company, gang, line-up, set, side, squad
▶ verb 2 (often with up) JOIN, band together, cooperate, couple, get together, link, unite, work together

teamwork noun COOPERATION, collaboration, coordination, esprit de corps, fellowship, harmony, unity

tear verb 1 RIP, claw, lacerate, mangle, mutilate, pull apart, rend, rupture, scratch, shred, split 2 RUSH, bolt, charge, dash, fly, hurry, race, run, speed, sprint, zoom
▶ noun 3 HOLE, laceration, rent, rip, rupture, scratch, split

tearful adjective WEEPING, blubbering, crying, in tears, lachrymose, sobbing, weepy

(informal), whimpering

tears plural noun 1 CRYING, blubbering, sobbing, wailing, weeping
2 ▷▷ **in tears** CRYING, blubbering, distressed, sobbing, weeping

tease verb MOCK, goad, lead on, provoke, pull someone's leg (informal), tantalize, taunt, torment

technical adjective SCIENTIFIC, hi-tech or high-tech, skilled, specialist, specialized, technological

technique noun 1 METHOD, approach, manner, means, mode, procedure, style, system, way 2 SKILL, artistry, craft, craftsmanship, execution, performance, proficiency, touch

tedious adjective BORING, drab, dreary, dull, humdrum, irksome, laborious, mind-numbing, monotonous, tiresome, wearisome

tedium noun BOREDOM, drabness, dreariness, dullness, monotony, routine, sameness, tediousness

teeming[1] adjective FULL, abundant, alive, brimming, bristling, bursting, crawling, overflowing, swarming, thick

teeming[2] adjective POURING, bucketing down (informal), pelting, raining cats and dogs (informal)

teenager noun YOUTH, adolescent, boy, girl, juvenile, minor

teeter verb WOBBLE, rock, seesaw, stagger, sway, totter, waver

teetotaler noun ABSTAINER, nondrinker

telepathy noun MIND-READING, E.S.P., sixth sense

telephone noun 1 PHONE, cell, cell phone, handset, line
▶ verb 2 CALL, dial, phone, ring

(*chiefly Brit.*)

telescope noun 1 GLASS, spyglass
► *verb* 2 SHORTEN, abbreviate,
abridge, compress, condense,
contract, shrink

television noun TV, small screen
(*informal*), telly (*Brit. informal*), the
box (*Brit. informal*), the tube (*slang*)

tell verb 1 INFORM, announce,
communicate, disclose, divulge,
express, make known, notify,
proclaim, reveal, state
2 INSTRUCT, bid, call upon,
command, direct, order, require,
summon
3 DESCRIBE, chronicle, depict,
narrate, portray, recount, relate,
report
4 DISTINGUISH, differentiate,
discern, discriminate, identify
5 CARRY WEIGHT, count, have *or*
take effect, make its presence felt,
register, take its toll, weigh

telling adjective EFFECTIVE,
considerable, decisive, forceful,
impressive, influential, marked,
powerful, significant, striking

telling-off noun REPRIMAND,
criticism, dressing-down
(*informal*), lecture, rebuke,
reproach, reproof, scolding,
talking-to, ticking-off (*informal*)

tell off verb REPRIMAND, berate,
censure, chide, haul over the coals
(*informal*), lecture, read the riot act,
rebuke, reproach, scold

temerity noun BOLDNESS,
audacity, chutzpah (*informal*),
effrontery, front, impudence,
nerve (*informal*), rashness,
recklessness

temper noun 1 RAGE, bad mood,
fury, passion, tantrum
2 IRRITABILITY, hot-headedness,
irascibility, passion, petulance,
resentment, surliness

3 SELF-CONTROL, calmness,
composure, cool (*slang*),
equanimity
4 FRAME OF MIND, constitution,
disposition, humor, mind, mood,
nature, temperament
► *verb* 5 MODERATE, assuage,
lessen, mitigate, mollify, restrain,
soften, soothe, tone down
6 STRENGTHEN, anneal, harden,
toughen

temperament noun 1 NATURE,
bent, character, constitution,
disposition, humor, make-up,
outlook, personality, temper
2 EXCITABILITY, anger, hot-
headedness, moodiness,
petulance, volatility

temperamental adjective
1 MOODY, capricious, emotional,
excitable, highly strung,
hypersensitive, irritable,
sensitive, touchy, volatile
2 UNRELIABLE, erratic,
inconsistent, inconstant,
unpredictable

temperance noun 1 MODERATION,
continence, discretion,
forbearance, restraint, self-
control, self-discipline, self-
restraint
2 TEETOTALISM, abstemiousness,
abstinence, sobriety

temperate adjective 1 MILD,
calm, cool, fair, gentle, moderate,
pleasant
2 SELF-RESTRAINED, calm,
composed, dispassionate,
even-tempered, mild, moderate,
reasonable, self-controlled,
sensible

tempest noun GALE, cyclone,
hurricane, squall, storm, tornado,
typhoon

tempestuous adjective 1 STORMY,
blustery, gusty, inclement, raging,

squally, turbulent, windy
2 VIOLENT, boisterous, emotional, furious, heated, intense, passionate, stormy, turbulent, wild

temple noun SHRINE, church, place of worship, sanctuary

temporarily adverb BRIEFLY, fleetingly, for the time being, momentarily, pro tem

temporary adjective IMPERMANENT, brief, ephemeral, fleeting, interim, momentary, provisional, short-lived, transitory

tempt verb ENTICE, allure, attract, coax, invite, lead on, lure, seduce, tantalize

temptation noun ENTICEMENT, allurement, inducement, lure, pull, seduction, tantalization

tempting adjective ENTICING, alluring, appetizing, attractive, inviting, mouthwatering, seductive, tantalizing

tenable adjective SOUND, arguable, believable, defensible, justifiable, plausible, rational, reasonable, viable

tenacious adjective 1 FIRM, clinging, forceful, immovable, iron, strong, tight, unshakable
2 STUBBORN, adamant, determined, dogged, obdurate, obstinate, persistent, resolute, steadfast, unswerving, unyielding

tenacity noun PERSEVERANCE, application, determination, doggedness, obduracy, persistence, resolve, steadfastness, stubbornness

tenancy noun LEASE, occupancy, possession, renting, residence

tenant noun LEASEHOLDER, inhabitant, lessee, occupant, occupier, renter, resident

tend[1] verb 1 BE INCLINED, be apt, be liable, gravitate, have a tendency, incline, lean
2 GO, aim, bear, head, lead, make for, point

tend[2] verb TAKE CARE OF, attend, cultivate, keep, look after, maintain, manage, nurture, watch over

tendency noun INCLINATION, disposition, leaning, liability, proclivity, proneness, propensity, susceptibility

tender[1] adjective 1 GENTLE, affectionate, caring, compassionate, considerate, kind, loving, sympathetic, tenderhearted, warm-hearted
2 VULNERABLE, immature, impressionable, inexperienced, raw, sensitive, young, youthful
3 SENSITIVE, bruised, inflamed, painful, raw, sore

tender[2] verb 1 OFFER, give, hand in, present, proffer, propose, put forward, submit, volunteer
▶ noun 2 OFFER, bid, estimate, proposal, submission
3 as in **legal tender** CURRENCY, money, payment

tenderness noun 1 GENTLENESS, affection, care, compassion, consideration, kindness, love, sentimentality, sympathy, warmth
2 SORENESS, inflammation, pain, sensitivity

tense adjective 1 NERVOUS, anxious, apprehensive, edgy, jumpy, keyed up, on edge, on tenterhooks, strained, uptight (informal), wired (slang)
2 STRESSFUL, exciting, nerve-racking, worrying
3 TIGHT, rigid, strained, stretched,

taut
▶ *verb* **4** TIGHTEN, brace, flex, strain, stretch

tension *noun* **1** SUSPENSE, anxiety, apprehension, hostility, nervousness, pressure, strain, stress, unease
2 TIGHTNESS, pressure, rigidity, stiffness, stress, stretching, tautness

tentative *adjective*
1 EXPERIMENTAL, conjectural, indefinite, provisional, speculative, unconfirmed, unsettled
2 HESITANT, cautious, diffident, doubtful, faltering, timid, uncertain, undecided, unsure

tenuous *adjective* SLIGHT, doubtful, dubious, flimsy, insubstantial, nebulous, shaky, sketchy, weak

tepid *adjective* **1** LUKEWARM, warmish
2 HALF-HEARTED, apathetic, cool, indifferent, lukewarm, unenthusiastic

term *noun* **1** WORD, expression, name, phrase, title
2 PERIOD, duration, interval, season, span, spell, time, while
▶ *verb* **3** CALL, designate, dub, entitle, label, name, style

terminal *adjective* **1** DEADLY, fatal, incurable, killing, lethal, mortal
2 FINAL, concluding, extreme, last, ultimate, utmost
▶ *noun* **3** TERMINUS, depot, end of the line, station

terminate *verb* END, abort, cease, close, complete, conclude, discontinue, finish, stop

termination *noun* ENDING, abortion, cessation, completion, conclusion, discontinuation, end, finish

terminology *noun* LANGUAGE, jargon, nomenclature, phraseology, terms, vocabulary

terminus *noun* END OF THE LINE, depot, garage, last stop, station

terms *plural noun* **1** CONDITIONS, particulars, provisions, provisos, qualifications, specifications, stipulations
2 RELATIONSHIP, footing, relations, standing, status

terrain *noun* GROUND, country, going, land, landscape, topography

terrestrial *adjective* EARTHLY, global, worldly

terrible *adjective* **1** SERIOUS, dangerous, desperate, extreme, severe
2 BAD, abysmal, awful, dire, dreadful, poor, rotten (*informal*)
3 FEARFUL, dreadful, frightful, horrendous, horrible, horrifying, monstrous, shocking, terrifying

terribly *adverb* EXTREMELY, awfully (*informal*), decidedly, desperately, exceedingly, seriously, thoroughly, very

terrific *adjective* **1** GREAT, enormous, fearful, gigantic, huge, intense, tremendous
2 (*informal*) EXCELLENT, amazing, brilliant, fantastic (*informal*), magnificent, marvelous, outstanding, sensational (*informal*), stupendous, superb, wonderful

terrified *adjective* FRIGHTENED, alarmed, appalled, horrified, horror-struck, panic-stricken, petrified, scared

terrify *verb* FRIGHTEN, alarm, appall, horrify, make one's hair stand on end, scare, shock, terrorize

territory *noun* DISTRICT, area,

country, domain, land, patch, province, region, zone

terror noun 1 FEAR, alarm, anxiety, dread, fright, horror, panic, shock
2 SCOURGE, bogeyman, bugbear, devil, fiend, monster

terrorize verb OPPRESS, browbeat, bully, coerce, intimidate, menace, threaten

terse adjective 1 CONCISE, brief, condensed, laconic, monosyllabic, pithy, short, succinct
2 CURT, abrupt, brusque, short, snappy

test verb 1 CHECK, analyze, assess, examine, experiment, investigate, put to the test, research, try out
▶ noun 2 EXAMINATION, acid test, analysis, assessment, check, evaluation, investigation, research, trial

testament noun 1 PROOF, demonstration, evidence, testimony, tribute, witness
2 WILL, last wishes

testify verb BEAR WITNESS, affirm, assert, attest, certify, corroborate, state, swear, vouch

testimonial noun TRIBUTE, commendation, endorsement, recommendation, reference

testimony noun 1 EVIDENCE, affidavit, deposition, statement, submission
2 PROOF, corroboration, demonstration, evidence, indication, manifestation, support, verification

testing adjective DIFFICULT, arduous, challenging, demanding, exacting, rigorous, searching, strenuous, taxing, tough

tether noun 1 ROPE, chain, fetter, halter, lead, leash
2 ▷▷ **at the end of one's tether**

EXASPERATED, at one's wits' end, exhausted
▶ verb 3 TIE, bind, chain, fasten, fetter, secure

text noun 1 CONTENTS, body
2 WORDS, wording

texture noun FEEL, consistency, grain, structure, surface, tissue

thank verb SAY THANK YOU, show one's appreciation

thankful adjective GRATEFUL, appreciative, beholden, indebted, obliged, pleased, relieved

thankless adjective UNREWARDING, fruitless, unappreciated, unprofitable, unrequited

thanks plural noun 1 GRATITUDE, acknowledgment, appreciation, credit, gratefulness, kudos, recognition
2 ▷▷ **thanks to** BECAUSE OF, as a result of, due to, owing to, through

thaw verb MELT, defrost, dissolve, liquefy, soften, unfreeze, warm

theatrical adjective 1 DRAMATIC, Thespian
2 EXAGGERATED, affected, dramatic, histrionic, mannered, melodramatic, ostentatious, showy, stagy

theft noun STEALING, embezzlement, fraud, larceny, pilfering, purloining, robbery, thieving

theme noun 1 SUBJECT, idea, keynote, subject matter, topic
2 MOTIF, leitmotif

theological adjective RELIGIOUS, doctrinal, ecclesiastical

theoretical adjective ABSTRACT, academic, conjectural, hypothetical, notional, speculative

theorize verb SPECULATE, conjecture, formulate, guess,

hypothesize, project, propound, suppose

theory noun SUPPOSITION, assumption, conjecture, hypothesis, presumption, speculation, surmise, thesis

therapeutic adjective BENEFICIAL, corrective, curative, good, healing, remedial, restorative, salutary

therapist noun HEALER, physician

therapy noun REMEDY, cure, healing, treatment

therefore adverb CONSEQUENTLY, accordingly, as a result, ergo, hence, so, then, thence, thus

thesis noun 1 DISSERTATION, essay, monograph, paper, treatise
2 PROPOSITION, contention, hypothesis, idea, opinion, proposal, theory, view

thick adjective 1 WIDE, broad, bulky, fat, solid, substantial
2 DENSE, close, compact, concentrated, condensed, heavy, impenetrable, opaque
3 (informal) STUPID, brainless, dense, dopey (informal), moronic, obtuse, slow, thickheaded
4 (informal) FRIENDLY, close, devoted, familiar, inseparable, intimate, pally (informal)
5 FULL, brimming, bristling, bursting, covered, crawling, packed, swarming, teeming
6 ▷▷ **a bit thick** UNFAIR, unjust, unreasonable

thicken verb SET, clot, coagulate, condense, congeal, jell

thicket noun WOOD, brake, coppice, copse, covert, grove

thickset adjective WELL-BUILT, bulky, burly, heavy, muscular, stocky, strong, sturdy

thief noun ROBBER, burglar, embezzler, housebreaker, pickpocket, pilferer, plunderer, shoplifter, stealer

thieve verb STEAL, filch, nick (slang, chiefly Brit.), pilfer, pinch (informal), purloin, rob, swipe (slang)

thin adjective 1 NARROW, attenuated, fine
2 SLIM, bony, emaciated, lean, scrawny, skeletal, skinny, slender, slight, spare, spindly
3 MEAGER, deficient, scanty, scarce, scattered, skimpy, sparse, wispy
4 DELICATE, diaphanous, filmy, fine, flimsy, gossamer, sheer, unsubstantial
5 UNCONVINCING, feeble, flimsy, inadequate, lame, lousy (slang), poor, superficial, weak

thing noun 1 OBJECT, article, being, body, entity, something, substance
2 (informal) OBSESSION, bee in one's bonnet, fetish, fixation, hang-up (informal), mania, phobia, preoccupation
3 ▷▷ **things** POSSESSIONS, belongings, clobber (Brit. slang), effects, equipment, gear, luggage, stuff

think verb 1 BELIEVE, consider, deem, estimate, imagine, judge, reckon, regard, suppose
2 PONDER, cerebrate, cogitate, contemplate, deliberate, meditate, muse, reason, reflect, ruminate

thinker noun PHILOSOPHER, brain (informal), intellect (informal), mastermind, sage, theorist, wise man

thinking noun 1 REASONING, conjecture, idea, judgment, opinion, position, theory, view
▶ adjective 2 THOUGHTFUL, contemplative, intelligent, meditative, philosophical,

rational, reasoning, reflective

think up verb DEVISE, come up with, concoct, contrive, create, dream up, invent, visualize

thirst noun 1 THIRSTINESS, drought, dryness
2 CRAVING, appetite, desire, hankering, keenness, longing, passion, yearning

thirsty adjective 1 PARCHED, arid, dehydrated, dry
2 EAGER, avid, craving, desirous, greedy, hungry, itching, longing, yearning

thorn noun PRICKLE, barb, spike, spine

thorny adjective PRICKLY, barbed, bristly, pointed, sharp, spiky, spiny

thorough adjective 1 CAREFUL, assiduous, conscientious, efficient, exhaustive, full, in-depth, intensive, meticulous, painstaking, sweeping
2 COMPLETE, absolute, out-and-out, outright, perfect, total, unmitigated, unqualified, utter

thoroughbred adjective PUREBRED, pedigree

thoroughfare noun ROAD, avenue, highway, passage, passageway, street, way

thoroughly adverb 1 CAREFULLY, assiduously, conscientiously, efficiently, exhaustively, from top to bottom, fully, intensively, meticulously, painstakingly, scrupulously
2 COMPLETELY, absolutely, downright, perfectly, quite, totally, to the hilt, utterly

though conjunction 1 ALTHOUGH, even if, even though, notwithstanding, while
▶ adverb 2 NEVERTHELESS, for all that, however, nonetheless, notwithstanding, still, yet

thought noun 1 THINKING, brainwork, cogitation, consideration, deliberation, meditation, musing, reflection, rumination
2 IDEA, concept, judgment, notion, opinion, view
3 CONSIDERATION, attention, heed, regard, scrutiny, study
4 INTENTION, aim, design, idea, notion, object, plan, purpose
5 EXPECTATION, anticipation, aspiration, hope, prospect

thoughtful adjective
1 CONSIDERATE, attentive, caring, helpful, kind, kindly, solicitous, unselfish
2 WELL-THOUGHT-OUT, astute, canny, prudent
3 REFLECTIVE, contemplative, deliberative, meditative, pensive, ruminative, serious, studious

thoughtless adjective
INCONSIDERATE, impolite, insensitive, rude, selfish, tactless, uncaring, undiplomatic, unkind

thrash verb 1 BEAT, belt (informal), cane, flog, give (someone) a (good) hiding (informal), paddle (U.S. & Canad.), scourge, spank, whip
2 DEFEAT, beat, crush, drub, rout, run rings around (informal), slaughter (informal), trounce, wipe the floor with (informal)
3 THRESH, flail, jerk, toss and turn, writhe

thrashing noun 1 BEATING, belting (informal), flogging, hiding (informal), punishment, whipping
2 DEFEAT, beating, drubbing, hammering (informal), hiding (informal), rout, trouncing

thrash out verb SETTLE, argue out, debate, discuss, have out, resolve, solve, talk over

thread noun 1 STRAND, fiber, filament, line, string, yarn
2 THEME, direction, drift, plot, story line, train of thought
▶ verb 3 PASS, ease, pick (one's way), squeeze through

threadbare adjective 1 SHABBY, down at heel, frayed, old, ragged, scruffy, tattered, tatty, worn
2 HACKNEYED, commonplace, conventional, familiar, overused, stale, stereotyped, tired, trite, well-worn

threat noun 1 WARNING, foreboding, foreshadowing, omen, portent, presage, writing on the wall
2 DANGER, hazard, menace, peril, risk

threaten verb 1 INTIMIDATE, browbeat, bully, lean on (slang), menace, pressurize, terrorize
2 ENDANGER, imperil, jeopardize, put at risk, put in jeopardy, put on the line
3 FORESHADOW, forebode, impend, portend, presage

threatening adjective 1 MENACING, bullying, intimidatory
2 OMINOUS, forbidding, grim, inauspicious, sinister

threshold noun 1 ENTRANCE, door, doorstep, doorway
2 START, beginning, brink, dawn, inception, opening, outset, verge
3 MINIMUM, lower limit

thrift noun FRUGALITY, carefulness, economy, parsimony, prudence, saving, thriftiness

thrifty adjective ECONOMICAL, careful, frugal, parsimonious, provident, prudent, saving, sparing

thrill noun 1 PLEASURE, buzz (slang), kick (informal), stimulation, tingle, titillation
▶ verb 2 EXCITE, arouse, electrify, move, stimulate, stir, titillate

thrilling adjective EXCITING, electrifying, gripping, riveting, rousing, sensational, stimulating, stirring

thrive verb PROSPER, boom, develop, do well, flourish, get on, grow, increase, succeed

thriving adjective PROSPEROUS, blooming, booming, burgeoning, flourishing, healthy, successful, well

throb verb 1 PULSATE, beat, palpitate, pound, pulse, thump, vibrate
▶ noun 2 PULSE, beat, palpitation, pounding, pulsating, thump, thumping, vibration

throng noun 1 CROWD, crush, horde, host, mass, mob, multitude, pack, swarm
▶ verb 2 CROWD, congregate, converge, flock, mill around, pack, swarm around

throttle verb STRANGLE, choke, garrotte, strangulate

through preposition 1 BETWEEN, by, past
2 BECAUSE OF, by means of, by way of, using, via
3 DURING, in, throughout
▶ adjective 4 FINISHED, completed, done, ended
▶ adverb 5 ▷▷ **through and through** COMPLETELY, altogether, entirely, fully, thoroughly, totally, utterly, wholly

throughout adverb EVERYWHERE, all over, from start to finish, right through

throw verb 1 HURL, cast, chuck (informal), fling, launch, lob (informal), pitch, send, sling, toss
2 (informal) CONFUSE, astonish, baffle, confound, disconcert,

dumbfound, faze
▶ *noun* 3 TOSS, fling, heave, lob (*informal*), pitch, sling

throwaway *adjective* CASUAL, careless, offhand, passing, understated

throw away *verb* DISCARD, dispense with, dispose of, ditch (*slang*), dump (*informal*), get rid of, jettison, reject, scrap, throw out

thrust *verb* 1 PUSH, drive, force, jam, plunge, propel, ram, shove
▶ *noun* 2 PUSH, drive, lunge, poke, prod, shove, stab
3 MOMENTUM, impetus

thud *noun or verb* THUMP, clunk, crash, knock, smack

thug *noun* RUFFIAN, bruiser (*informal*), bully boy, gangster, heavy (*slang*), hooligan, tough

thump *noun* 1 CRASH, bang, clunk, thud, thwack
2 BLOW, clout (*informal*), knock, punch, rap, smack, wallop (*informal*), whack
▶ *verb* 3 STRIKE, beat, clobber (*slang*), clout (*informal*), hit, knock, pound, punch, smack, wallop (*informal*), whack

thunder *noun* 1 RUMBLE, boom, crash, explosion
▶ *verb* 2 RUMBLE, boom, crash, peal, resound, reverberate, roar
3 SHOUT, bark, bellow, roar, yell

thunderous *adjective* LOUD, booming, deafening, ear-splitting, noisy, resounding, roaring, tumultuous

thunderstruck *adjective* AMAZED, astonished, astounded, dumbfounded, flabbergasted (*informal*), open-mouthed, shocked, staggered, stunned, taken aback

thus *adverb* 1 THEREFORE, accordingly, consequently, ergo,

for this reason, hence, on that account, so, then
2 IN THIS WAY, as follows, like this, so

thwart *verb* FRUSTRATE, foil, hinder, obstruct, outwit, prevent, snooker, stymie

tick[1] *noun* 1 MARK, dash, stroke
2 MITE, bug, insect
3 TAPPING, clicking, ticktock
4 (*brit. informal*) MOMENT, flash, instant, minute, second, split second, trice, twinkling
▶ *verb* 5 MARK, check off, indicate
6 TAP, click, ticktock

tick[2] *noun* CREDIT, account, the slate (*Brit. informal*)

ticket *noun* 1 VOUCHER, card, certificate, coupon, pass, slip, token
2 LABEL, card, docket, marker, slip, sticker, tab, tag

tidbit *noun* DELICACY, dainty, morsel, snack, treat

tide *noun* 1 CURRENT, ebb, flow, stream, tideway, undertow
2 TENDENCY, direction, drift, movement, trend

tidy *adjective* 1 NEAT, clean, methodical, orderly, shipshape, spruce, well-kept, well-ordered
2 (*informal*) CONSIDERABLE, ample, generous, goodly, handsome, healthy, large, sizable *or* sizeable, substantial
▶ *verb* 3 NEATEN, clean, groom, order, spruce up, straighten

tie *verb* 1 FASTEN, attach, bind, connect, join, knot, link, secure, tether
2 RESTRICT, bind, confine, hamper, hinder, limit, restrain
3 DRAW, equal, match
▶ *noun* 4 BOND, affiliation, allegiance, commitment, connection, liaison, relationship

5 FASTENING, bond, cord, fetter, knot, ligature, link
6 DRAW, dead heat, deadlock, gridlock, stalemate

tier noun ROW, bank, layer, level, line, rank, story, stratum

tight adjective 1 STRETCHED, close, constricted, cramped, narrow, rigid, snug, taut
2 (informal) MISERLY, grasping, mean, niggardly, parsimonious, stingy, tightfisted
3 CLOSE, even, evenly-balanced, well-matched
4 (informal) DRUNK, inebriated, intoxicated, paralytic (informal), plastered (slang), tipsy, under the influence (informal)

tighten verb SQUEEZE, close, constrict, narrow

till¹ verb CULTIVATE, dig, plow, work

till² noun CASH REGISTER, cash box

tilt verb 1 SLANT, heel, incline, lean, list, slope, tip
▶ noun 2 SLOPE, angle, inclination, incline, list, pitch, slant
3 (medieval history) JOUST, combat, duel, fight, lists, tournament
4 ▷▷ (at) full tilt FULL SPEED, for dear life, headlong

timber noun WOOD, beams, boards, logs, planks, trees

timbre noun TONE, color, resonance, ring

time noun 1 PERIOD, duration, interval, season, space, span, spell, stretch, term
2 OCCASION, instance, juncture, point, stage
3 (music) TEMPO, beat, measure, rhythm
▶ verb 4 SCHEDULE, set

timeless adjective ETERNAL, ageless, changeless, enduring, everlasting, immortal, lasting, permanent

timely adjective OPPORTUNE, appropriate, convenient, judicious, propitious, seasonable, suitable, well-timed

timetable noun SCHEDULE, agenda, calendar, curriculum, diary, list, program

timid adjective FEARFUL, apprehensive, bashful, coy, diffident, faint-hearted, shrinking, shy, timorous

timorous adjective TIMID, apprehensive, bashful, coy, diffident, faint-hearted, fearful, shrinking, shy

tinge noun 1 TINT, color, shade
2 BIT, dash, drop, smattering, sprinkling, suggestion, touch, trace
▶ verb 3 TINT, color, imbue, suffuse

tingle verb 1 PRICKLE, have goose pimples, itch, sting, tickle
▶ noun 2 QUIVER, goose pimples, itch, pins and needles (informal), prickling, shiver, thrill

tinker verb MEDDLE, dabble, fiddle (informal), mess about, play, potter

tint noun 1 SHADE, color, hue, tone
2 DYE, rinse, tincture, tinge, wash
▶ verb 3 DYE, color

tiny adjective SMALL, diminutive, infinitesimal, little, microscopic, miniature, minute, negligible, petite, slight

tip¹ noun 1 END, extremity, head, peak, pinnacle, point, summit, top
▶ verb 2 CAP, crown, finish, surmount, top

tip² noun 1 GRATUITY, gift
2 HINT, clue, pointer, suggestion, warning
▶ verb 3 REWARD, remunerate
4 ADVISE, caution, forewarn, suggest, warn

tip³ verb 1 TILT, incline, lean,

list, slant
2 DUMP, empty, pour out, unload
▶ noun 3 DUMP, refuse heap,
rubbish heap

tipple verb 1 DRINK, imbibe,
indulge (*informal*), quaff, swig, tope
▶ noun 2 ALCOHOL, booze (*informal*),
drink, liquor

tipsy adjective DRUNK, fuzzy, happy,
mellow, three sheets to the wind

tirade noun OUTBURST, diatribe,
fulmination, harangue, invective,
lecture

tire verb 1 FATIGUE, drain, exhaust,
wear out, weary
2 BORE, exasperate, irk, irritate,
weary

tired adjective 1 EXHAUSTED,
drained, drowsy, fatigued,
flagging, jaded, sleepy, weary,
worn out
2 BORED, fed up, sick, weary
3 HACKNEYED, clichéd, corny
(*slang*), old, outworn, stale,
threadbare, trite, well-worn

tireless adjective ENERGETIC,
indefatigable, industrious,
resolute, unflagging, untiring,
vigorous

tiresome adjective BORING, dull,
irksome, irritating, tedious,
trying, vexatious, wearing,
wearisome

tiring adjective EXHAUSTING,
arduous, demanding, exacting,
laborious, strenuous, tough,
wearing

titillate verb EXCITE, arouse,
interest, stimulate, tantalize,
tease, thrill

titillating adjective EXCITING,
arousing, interesting, lurid,
provocative, stimulating,
suggestive, teasing

title noun 1 NAME, designation,
handle (*slang*), moniker or

monicker (*slang*), term
2 CHAMPIONSHIP, crown
3 OWNERSHIP, claim, entitlement,
prerogative, privilege, right

titter verb LAUGH, chortle (*informal*),
chuckle, giggle, snigger

tizzy noun (*informal*) PANIC,
agitation, commotion, fluster,
state (*informal*), sweat (*informal*)

toady noun 1 SYCOPHANT,
bootlicker (*informal*), brown-noser
(*slang*), crawler (*slang*), creep (*slang*),
flatterer, flunkey, hanger-on,
lackey, minion, scuzzbucket
(*slang*), yes man
▶ verb 2 FLATTER, brown-nose
(*slang*), crawl, creep, cringe, fawn
on, grovel, kiss ass (*slang*), kowtow
to, pander to, suck up to (*informal*)

toast¹ verb WARM, brown, grill,
heat, roast

toast² noun 1 TRIBUTE,
compliment, health, pledge,
salutation, salute
2 FAVORITE, darling, hero or
heroine
▶ verb 3 DRINK TO, drink (to) the
health of, salute

together adverb 1 COLLECTIVELY,
as one, hand in glove, in concert,
in unison, jointly, mutually,
shoulder to shoulder, side by side
2 AT THE SAME TIME, at one
fell swoop, concurrently,
contemporaneously,
simultaneously
▶ adjective 3 (*informal*) WELL-
ORGANIZED, composed, well-
adjusted, well-balanced

toil noun 1 HARD WORK, application,
drudgery, effort, elbow grease
(*informal*), exertion, graft (*informal*),
slog, sweat
▶ verb 2 WORK, drudge, graft
(*informal*), labor, slave, slog, strive,
struggle, sweat (*informal*), work

one's fingers to the bone

toilet noun LAVATORY, bathroom, convenience, gents (*Brit. informal*), ladies' room, latrine, loo (*Brit. informal*), privy, urinal, water closet, W.C.

token noun 1 SYMBOL, badge, expression, indication, mark, note, representation, sign
▶ *adjective* 2 NOMINAL, hollow, minimal, perfunctory, superficial, symbolic

tolerable *adjective* 1 BEARABLE, acceptable, allowable, endurable, sufferable, supportable
2 FAIR, acceptable, adequate, all right, average, O.K. *or* okay (*informal*), passable

tolerance noun 1 BROAD-MINDEDNESS, forbearance, indulgence, open-mindedness, permissiveness
2 ENDURANCE, fortitude, hardiness, resilience, resistance, stamina, staying power, toughness

tolerant *adjective* BROAD-MINDED, catholic, forbearing, liberal, long-suffering, open-minded, understanding, unprejudiced

tolerate *verb* ALLOW, accept, brook, condone, endure, permit, put up with (*informal*), stand, stomach, take

toleration noun ACCEPTANCE, allowance, endurance, indulgence, permissiveness, sanction

toll¹ *verb* 1 RING, chime, clang, knell, peal, sound, strike
▶ *noun* 2 RINGING, chime, clang, knell, peal

toll² noun 1 CHARGE, duty, fee, levy, payment, tariff, tax
2 DAMAGE, cost, loss, penalty

tomb noun GRAVE, catacomb, crypt, mausoleum, sarcophagus, sepulcher, vault

tombstone noun GRAVESTONE, headstone, marker, memorial, monument

tomfoolery noun FOOLISHNESS, buffoonery, clowning, fooling around (*informal*), horseplay, shenanigans (*informal*), silliness, skylarking (*informal*), stupidity

ton noun (often plural) (*informal*) A LOT, great deal, ocean, quantity, stacks

tone noun 1 PITCH, inflection, intonation, modulation, timbre
2 CHARACTER, air, attitude, feel, manner, mood, spirit, style, temper
3 COLOR, hue, shade, tinge, tint
▶ *verb* 4 HARMONIZE, blend, go well with, match, suit

tone down *verb* MODERATE, play down, reduce, restrain, soften, subdue, temper

tongue noun LANGUAGE, dialect, parlance, speech

tonic noun STIMULANT, boost, fillip, pick-me-up (*informal*), restorative, shot in the arm (*informal*)

too *adverb* 1 ALSO, as well, besides, further, in addition, likewise, moreover, to boot
2 EXCESSIVELY, extremely, immoderately, inordinately, overly, unduly, unreasonably, very

tool noun 1 IMPLEMENT, appliance, contraption, contrivance, device, gadget, instrument, machine, utensil
2 PUPPET, cat's-paw, creature, flunkey, hireling, lackey, minion, pawn, stooge (*slang*)

top noun 1 PEAK, apex, crest, crown, culmination, head, height, pinnacle, summit, zenith
2 FIRST PLACE, head, lead

3 LID, cap, cover, stopper
▶ *adjective* 4 LEADING, alpha male, best, chief, elite, finest, first, foremost, head, highest, pre-eminent, principal, uppermost
▶ *verb* 5 COVER, cap, crown, finish, garnish
6 LEAD, be first, head
7 SURPASS, beat, best, better, eclipse, exceed, excel, outstrip, transcend

topic *noun* SUBJECT, issue, matter, point, question, subject matter, theme

topical *adjective* CURRENT, contemporary, newsworthy, popular, up-to-date, up-to-the-minute

topmost *adjective* HIGHEST, dominant, foremost, leading, paramount, principal, supreme, top, uppermost

topple *verb* 1 FALL OVER, collapse, fall, keel over, overbalance, overturn, totter, tumble
2 OVERTHROW, bring down, bring low, oust, overturn, unseat

topsy-turvy *adjective* CONFUSED, chaotic, disorderly, disorganized, inside-out, jumbled, messy, mixed-up, upside-down

torment *verb* 1 TORTURE, crucify, distress, rack
2 TEASE, annoy, bother, harass, hassle (*informal*), irritate, nag, pester, vex
▶ *noun* 3 SUFFERING, agony, anguish, distress, hell, misery, pain, torture

torn *adjective* 1 CUT, lacerated, ragged, rent, ripped, slit, split
2 UNDECIDED, in two minds (*informal*), irresolute, uncertain, unsure, vacillating, wavering

tornado *noun* WHIRLWIND, cyclone, gale, hurricane, squall, storm, tempest, typhoon

torpor *noun* INACTIVITY, apathy, drowsiness, indolence, laziness, lethargy, listlessness, sloth, sluggishness

torrent *noun* STREAM, cascade, deluge, downpour, flood, flow, rush, spate, tide

torrid *adjective* 1 ARID, dried, parched, scorched
2 PASSIONATE, ardent, fervent, intense, steamy (*informal*)

tortuous *adjective* 1 WINDING, circuitous, convoluted, indirect, mazy, meandering, serpentine, sinuous, twisting, twisty
2 COMPLICATED, ambiguous, convoluted, devious, indirect, involved, roundabout, tricky

torture *verb* 1 TORMENT, afflict, crucify, distress, persecute, put on the rack, rack
▶ *noun* 2 AGONY, anguish, distress, pain, persecution, suffering, torment

toss *verb* 1 THROW, cast, fling, flip, hurl, launch, lob (*informal*), pitch, sling
2 THRASH, rock, roll, shake, wriggle, writhe
▶ *noun* 3 THROW, lob (*informal*), pitch

tot¹ *noun* 1 INFANT, baby, child, mite, toddler
2 MEASURE, dram, finger, nip, shot (*informal*), slug, snifter (*informal*)

total *noun* 1 WHOLE, aggregate, entirety, full amount, sum, totality
▶ *adjective* 2 COMPLETE, absolute, comprehensive, entire, full, gross, thoroughgoing, undivided, utter, whole
▶ *verb* 3 AMOUNT TO, come to, mount up to, reach
4 ADD UP, reckon, tot up

totalitarian *adjective* DICTATORIAL, authoritarian, despotic, oppressive, tyrannous, undemocratic

totality *noun* WHOLE, aggregate, entirety, sum, total

totally *adverb* COMPLETELY, absolutely, comprehensively, entirely, fully, one hundred per cent, thoroughly, utterly, wholly

totter *verb* STAGGER, falter, lurch, reel, stumble, sway

touch *verb* 1 HANDLE, brush, caress, contact, feel, finger, fondle, stroke, tap
2 MEET, abut, adjoin, be in contact, border, contact, graze, impinge upon
3 AFFECT, disturb, impress, influence, inspire, move, stir
4 EAT, chow down (*slang*), consume, drink, partake of
5 MATCH, compare with, equal, hold a candle to (*informal*), parallel, rival
6 ▷▷ **touch on** REFER TO, allude to, bring in, cover, deal with, mention, speak of
▶ *noun* 7 FEELING, handling, physical contact
8 TAP, brush, contact, pat, stroke
9 BIT, dash, drop, jot, small amount, smattering, *soupçon*, spot, trace
10 STYLE, manner, method, technique, trademark, way

touch and go *adjective* RISKY, close, critical, near, nerve-racking, precarious

touching *adjective* MOVING, affecting, emotive, pathetic, pitiable, poignant, sad, stirring

touchstone *noun* STANDARD, criterion, gauge, measure, norm, par, yardstick

touchy *adjective* OVERSENSITIVE, irascible, irritable, querulous, quick-tempered, testy, tetchy, thin-skinned

tough *adjective* 1 RESILIENT, durable, hard, inflexible, leathery, resistant, rugged, solid, strong, sturdy
2 STRONG, hardy, seasoned, stout, strapping, sturdy, vigorous
3 ROUGH, hard-bitten, hard-boiled, pugnacious, ruthless, violent
4 STRICT, firm, hard, merciless, resolute, severe, stern, unbending
5 DIFFICULT, arduous, exacting, hard, laborious, strenuous, troublesome, uphill
6 (*informal*) UNLUCKY, lamentable, regrettable, unfortunate
▶ *noun* 7 RUFFIAN, bruiser (*informal*), bully, hooligan, roughneck (*slang*), thug

tour *noun* 1 JOURNEY, excursion, expedition, jaunt, outing, trip
▶ *verb* 2 VISIT, explore, go round, journey, sightsee, travel through

tourist *noun* TRAVELER, excursionist, globetrotter, holiday-maker, sightseer, tripper, voyager

tournament *noun* COMPETITION, contest, event, meeting, series

tow *verb* DRAG, draw, haul, lug, pull, tug

towards *preposition* 1 IN THE DIRECTION OF, en route for, for, on the way to, to
2 REGARDING, about, concerning, for, with regard to, with respect to

tower *noun* COLUMN, belfry, obelisk, pillar, skyscraper, steeple, turret

towering *adjective* HIGH, colossal, elevated, imposing, impressive, lofty, magnificent, soaring, tall

toxic *adjective* POISONOUS, deadly,

harmful, lethal, noxious, pernicious, pestiential, septic

toy noun 1 PLAYTHING, doll, game
▶ verb 2 PLAY, amuse oneself, dally, fiddle (informal), fool (about or around), trifle

trace verb 1 FIND, detect, discover, ferret out, hunt down, track, unearth

2 COPY, draw, outline, sketch
▶ noun 3 TRACK, footmark, footprint, footstep, path, spoor, trail

4 BIT, drop, hint, shadow, suggestion, suspicion, tinge, touch, whiff

5 INDICATION, evidence, mark, record, remnant, sign, survival, vestige

track noun 1 PATH, course, line, orbit, pathway, road, trajectory, way

2 TRAIL, footmark, footprint, footstep, mark, path, spoor, trace, wake

3 LINE, permanent way, rails
▶ verb 4 FOLLOW, chase, hunt down, pursue, shadow, stalk, tail (informal), trace, trail

track down verb FIND, dig up, discover, hunt down, run to earth or ground, sniff out, trace, unearth

tract¹ noun AREA, district, expanse, extent, plot, region, stretch, territory

tract² noun TREATISE, booklet, dissertation, essay, homily, monograph, pamphlet

tractable adjective MANAGEABLE, amenable, biddable, compliant, docile, obedient, submissive, tame, willing, yielding

traction noun GRIP, friction, pull, purchase, resistance

trade noun 1 COMMERCE, barter, business, dealing, exchange, traffic, transactions, truck

2 JOB, business, craft, employment, line of work, métier, occupation, profession
▶ verb 3 DEAL, bargain, do business, have dealings, peddle, traffic, transact, truck

4 EXCHANGE, barter, swap, switch

trader noun DEALER, merchant, purveyor, seller, supplier

tradesman noun 1 CRAFTSMAN, artisan, journeyman, workman

2 SHOPKEEPER, dealer, merchant, purveyor, retailer, seller, supplier, vendor

tradition noun CUSTOM, convention, folklore, habit, institution, lore, ritual

traditional adjective CUSTOMARY, accustomed, conventional, established, old, time-honored, usual

traffic noun 1 TRANSPORT, freight, transportation, vehicles

2 TRADE, business, commerce, dealings, exchange, peddling, truck
▶ verb 3 TRADE, bargain, deal, do business, exchange, have dealings, peddle

tragedy noun DISASTER, adversity, calamity, catastrophe, misfortune

tragic adjective DISASTROUS, appalling, calamitous, catastrophic, deadly, dire, dreadful, miserable, pathetic, sad, unfortunate

trail noun 1 PATH, footpath, road, route, track, way

2 TRACKS, footprints, marks, path, scent, spoor, trace, wake
▶ verb 3 DRAG, dangle, draw, haul, pull, tow

4 LAG, dawdle, follow, hang back, linger, loiter, straggle, traipse (informal)

5 FOLLOW, chase, hunt, pursue, shadow, stalk, tail (*informal*), trace, track

train *verb* **1** INSTRUCT, coach, drill, educate, guide, prepare, school, teach, tutor
2 EXERCISE, prepare, work out
3 AIM, direct, focus, level, point
▶ *noun* **4** SEQUENCE, chain, progression, series, set, string, succession

trainer *noun* COACH, handler

training *noun* **1** INSTRUCTION, coaching, discipline, education, grounding, schooling, teaching, tuition
2 EXERCISE, practice, preparation, working out

traipse *verb* TRUDGE, drag oneself, footslog, slouch, trail, tramp

trait *noun* CHARACTERISTIC, attribute, feature, idiosyncrasy, mannerism, peculiarity, quality, quirk

traitor *noun* BETRAYER, apostate, back-stabber, defector, deserter, Judas, quisling, rebel, renegade, turncoat

trajectory *noun* PATH, course, flight path, line, route, track

tramp *verb* **1** HIKE, footslog, march, ramble, roam, rove, slog, trek, walk
2 TRUDGE, plod, stump, toil, traipse (*informal*)
▶ *noun* **3** VAGRANT, derelict, down-and-out, drifter
4 HIKE, march, ramble, slog, trek
5 TREAD, footfall, footstep, stamp

trample *verb* CRUSH, flatten, run over, squash, stamp, tread, walk over

trance *noun* DAZE, abstraction, dream, rapture, reverie, stupor, unconsciousness

tranquil *adjective* CALM, peaceful, placid, quiet, restful, sedate, serene, still, undisturbed

tranquilize *verb* CALM, lull, pacify, quell, quiet, relax, sedate, settle one's nerves, soothe

tranquilizer *noun* SEDATIVE, barbiturate, bromide, downer (*slang*), opiate

tranquillity *noun* CALM, hush, peace, placidity, quiet, repose, rest, serenity, stillness

transaction *noun* DEAL, bargain, business, enterprise, negotiation, undertaking

transcend *verb* SURPASS, eclipse, exceed, excel, go beyond, outdo, outstrip, rise above

transcendent *adjective* UNPARALLELED, consummate, incomparable, matchless, pre-eminent, sublime, unequaled, unrivaled

transcribe *verb* WRITE OUT, copy out, reproduce, take down, transfer

transcript *noun* COPY, duplicate, manuscript, record, reproduction, transcription

transfer *verb* **1** MOVE, change, convey, hand over, pass on, relocate, shift, transplant, transport, transpose
▶ *noun* **2** MOVE, change, handover, relocation, shift, transference, translation, transmission, transposition

transfix *verb* **1** STUN, engross, fascinate, hold, hypnotize, mesmerize, paralyze
2 PIERCE, impale, puncture, run through, skewer, spear

transform *verb* CHANGE, alter, convert, remodel, revolutionize, transmute

transformation *noun* CHANGE, alteration, conversion,

metamorphosis, revolution, sea change, transmutation

transgress *verb* OFFEND, break the law, contravene, disobey, encroach, infringe, sin, trespass, violate

transgression *noun* OFFENSE, contravention, crime, encroachment, infraction, infringement, misdeed, misdemeanor, sin, trespass, violation, wrongdoing

transgressor *noun* OFFENDER, criminal, culprit, lawbreaker, miscreant, sinner, perp (*informal*), trespasser, villain, wrongdoer

transient *adjective* TEMPORARY, brief, ephemeral, fleeting, impermanent, momentary, passing, short-lived, transitory

transit *noun* MOVEMENT, carriage, conveyance, crossing, passage, transfer, transport, transportation

transition *noun* CHANGE, alteration, conversion, development, metamorphosis, passing, progression, shift, transmutation

transitional *adjective* CHANGING, developmental, fluid, intermediate, passing, provisional, temporary, unsettled

transitory *adjective* SHORT-LIVED, brief, ephemeral, fleeting, impermanent, momentary, passing, short, temporary, transient

translate *verb* INTERPRET, construe, convert, decipher, decode, paraphrase, render

translation *noun* INTERPRETATION, decoding, paraphrase, rendering, rendition, version

transmission *noun* 1 TRANSFER, conveyance, dissemination, sending, shipment, spread, transference
2 BROADCASTING, dissemination, putting out, relaying, sending, showing
3 PROGRAM, broadcast, show

transmit *verb* 1 PASS ON, bear, carry, convey, disseminate, hand on, impart, send, spread, transfer
2 BROADCAST, disseminate, radio, relay, send out

transparency *noun* 1 CLARITY, clearness, limpidity, pellucidness, translucence
2 PHOTOGRAPH, slide

transparent *adjective* 1 CLEAR, crystalline, diaphanous, limpid, lucid, see-through, sheer, translucent
2 PLAIN, evident, explicit, manifest, obvious, patent, recognizable, unambiguous, undisguised

transpire *verb* 1 EMERGE, become known, come out, come to light
2 (*informal*) HAPPEN, arise, befall, chance, come about, occur, take place

transplant *verb* TRANSFER, displace, relocate, remove, resettle, shift, uproot

transport *verb* 1 CONVEY, bear, bring, carry, haul, move, take, transfer
2 EXILE, banish, deport
3 ENRAPTURE, captivate, delight, enchant, entrance, move, ravish
▶ *noun* 4 VEHICLE, conveyance, transportation
5 TRANSFERENCE, conveyance, shipment, transportation
6 ECSTASY, bliss, delight, enchantment, euphoria, heaven, rapture, ravishment

transpose *verb* INTERCHANGE, alter, change, exchange, move, reorder, shift, substitute, swap, switch, transfer

trap *noun* 1 SNARE, ambush, gin, net, noose, pitfall

2 TRICK, ambush, deception, ruse, stratagem, subterfuge, wile

▶ *verb* 3 CATCH, corner, enmesh, ensnare, entrap, snare, take

4 TRICK, ambush, beguile, deceive, dupe, ensnare, inveigle

trappings *plural noun* ACCESSORIES, accouterments, equipment, finery, furnishings, gear, panoply, paraphernalia, things, trimmings

trash *noun* 1 NONSENSE, drivel, hogwash, moonshine, poppycock (*informal*), rot, rubbish, tripe (*informal*), twaddle

2 LITTER, dross, garbage, junk (*informal*), refuse, rubbish, waste

▶ *verb* 3 DESTROY, defeat, demolish, put paid to, ruin, torpedo, trounce, wreck

trashy *adjective* WORTHLESS, cheap, inferior, rubbishy, shabby, shoddy, tawdry

trauma *noun* SUFFERING, agony, anguish, hurt, ordeal, pain, shock, torture

traumatic *adjective* SHOCKING, agonizing, damaging, disturbing, hurtful, injurious, painful, scarring, upsetting, wounding

travel *verb* 1 GO, journey, move, progress, roam, tour, trek, voyage, wander

▶ *noun* 2 (usually plural) WANDERING, excursion, expedition, globetrotting, journey, tour, trip, voyage

traveler *noun* WANDERER, explorer, globetrotter, gypsy, holiday-maker, tourist, voyager, wayfarer

traveling *adjective* MOBILE, itinerant, migrant, nomadic, peripatetic, roaming, roving, touring, wandering, wayfaring

traverse *verb* CROSS, go over, span, travel over

travesty *noun* 1 MOCKERY, burlesque, caricature, distortion, lampoon, parody, perversion

▶ *verb* 2 MOCK, burlesque, caricature, distort, lampoon, make a mockery of, parody, ridicule

treacherous *adjective* 1 DISLOYAL, deceitful, double-dealing, duplicitous, faithless, false, perfidious, traitorous, unfaithful, untrustworthy

2 DANGEROUS, deceptive, hazardous, icy, perilous, precarious, risky, slippery, unreliable, unsafe, unstable

treachery *noun* BETRAYAL, back-stabbing (*informal*), disloyalty, double-dealing, duplicity, faithlessness, infidelity, perfidy, treason

tread *verb* 1 STEP, hike, march, pace, stamp, stride, walk

2 TRAMPLE, crush underfoot, squash

▶ *noun* 3 STEP, footfall, footstep, gait, pace, stride, walk

treason *noun* DISLOYALTY, back-stabbing (*informal*), duplicity, lese-majesty, mutiny, perfidy, sedition, traitorousness, treachery

treasonable *adjective* DISLOYAL, mutinous, perfidious, seditious, subversive, traitorous, treacherous

treasure *noun* 1 RICHES, cash, fortune, gold, jewels, money, valuables, wealth

2 DARLING, apple of one's eye, gem, jewel, nonpareil, paragon, pride and joy

▶ *verb* 3 PRIZE, adore, cherish,

esteem, hold dear, idolize, love, revere, value

treasury noun STOREHOUSE, bank, cache, hoard, repository, store, vault

treat verb 1 HANDLE, act towards, behave towards, consider, deal with, look upon, manage, regard, use
2 ATTEND TO, care for, nurse
3 ENTERTAIN, lay on, provide, regale, stand (informal)
▶ noun 4 ENTERTAINMENT, banquet, celebration, feast, gift, party, refreshment
5 PLEASURE, delight, enjoyment, fun, joy, satisfaction, surprise, thrill

treatise noun ESSAY, dissertation, monograph, pamphlet, paper, study, thesis, tract, work

treatment noun 1 CARE, cure, healing, medication, medicine, remedy, surgery, therapy
2 HANDLING, action, behavior, conduct, dealing, management, manipulation

treaty noun PACT, agreement, alliance, compact, concordat, contract, convention, covenant, entente

trek noun 1 JOURNEY, expedition, hike, march, odyssey, safari, slog, tramp
▶ verb 2 JOURNEY, footslog, hike, march, rove, slog, traipse (informal), tramp, trudge

tremble verb 1 SHAKE, quake, quiver, shiver, shudder, totter, vibrate, wobble
▶ noun 2 SHAKE, quake, quiver, shiver, shudder, tremor, vibration, wobble

tremendous adjective 1 HUGE, colossal, enormous, formidable, gigantic, great, immense,

stupendous, terrific
2 (informal) EXCELLENT, amazing, brilliant, exceptional, extraordinary, fantastic (informal), great, marvelous, sensational (informal), wonderful

tremor noun 1 SHAKE, quaking, quaver, quiver, shiver, trembling, wobble
2 EARTHQUAKE, quake (informal), shock

trench noun DITCH, channel, drain, excavation, furrow, gutter, trough

trenchant adjective 1 INCISIVE, acerbic, caustic, cutting, penetrating, pointed, pungent, scathing
2 EFFECTIVE, energetic, forceful, potent, powerful, strong, vigorous

trend noun 1 TENDENCY, bias, current, direction, drift, flow, inclination, leaning
2 FASHION, craze, fad (informal), mode, rage, style, thing, vogue

trendy adjective (informal) FASHIONABLE, cool (informal), in fashion, in vogue, modish, phat (slang), stylish, voguish, with it (informal)

trepidation noun ANXIETY, alarm, apprehension, consternation, disquiet, dread, fear, nervousness, uneasiness, worry

trespass verb 1 INTRUDE, encroach, infringe, invade, obtrude
▶ noun 2 INTRUSION, encroachment, infringement, invasion, unlawful entry

trespasser noun INTRUDER, interloper, invader, poacher

trial noun 1 HEARING, litigation, tribunal
2 TEST, audition, dry run (informal), experiment, probation, test-run
3 HARDSHIP, adversity, affliction,

distress, ordeal, suffering, tribulation, trouble

tribe noun RACE, clan, family, people

tribunal noun HEARING, court, trial

tribute noun **1** ACCOLADE, commendation, compliment, eulogy, panegyric, recognition, testimonial
2 TAX, charge, homage, payment, ransom

trick noun **1** DECEPTION, fraud, hoax, maneuver, ploy, ruse, stratagem, subterfuge, swindle, trap, wile
2 JOKE, antic, jape, leg-pull (*Brit. informal*), practical joke, prank, stunt
3 SECRET, hang (*informal*), knack, know-how (*informal*), skill, technique
4 MANNERISM, characteristic, foible, habit, idiosyncrasy, peculiarity, practice, quirk, trait
► *verb* **5** DECEIVE, cheat, con (*informal*), dupe, fool, hoodwink, kid (*informal*), mislead, swindle, take in (*informal*), trap

trickery noun DECEPTION, cheating, chicanery, deceit, dishonesty, guile, jiggery-pokery (*informal, chiefly Brit.*), monkey business (*informal*)

trickle *verb* **1** DRIBBLE, drip, drop, exude, ooze, run, seep, stream
► *noun* **2** DRIBBLE, drip, seepage

tricky adjective **1** DIFFICULT, complicated, delicate, knotty, problematic, risky, thorny, ticklish
2 CRAFTY, artful, cunning, deceitful, devious, scheming, slippery, sly, wily

trifle noun **1** KNICK-KNACK, bagatelle, bauble, plaything, toy
► *verb* **2** TOY, dally, mess about, play

trifling adjective INSIGNIFICANT, measly, negligible, paltry, trivial, unimportant, worthless

trigger *verb* SET OFF, activate, cause, generate, produce, prompt, provoke, set in motion, spark off, start

trim adjective **1** NEAT, dapper, natty (*informal*), shipshape, smart, spruce, tidy, well-groomed
2 SLENDER, fit, shapely, sleek, slim, streamlined, svelte, willowy
► *verb* **3** CUT, clip, crop, even up, pare, prune, shave, tidy
4 DECORATE, adorn, array, beautify, deck out, dress, embellish, ornament
► *noun* **5** DECORATION, adornment, border, edging, embellishment, frill, ornamentation, piping, trimming
6 CONDITION, fettle, fitness, health, shape (*informal*), state
7 CUT, clipping, crop, pruning, shave, shearing, tidying up

trimming noun **1** DECORATION, adornment, border, edging, embellishment, frill, ornamentation, piping
2 ▷▷ **trimmings** EXTRAS, accessories, accompaniments, frills, ornaments, paraphernalia, trappings

trinity noun THREESOME, triad, trio, triumvirate

trinket noun ORNAMENT, bagatelle, bauble, knick-knack, toy, trifle

trio noun THREESOME, triad, trilogy, trinity, triumvirate

trip noun **1** JOURNEY, errand, excursion, expedition, foray, jaunt, outing, run, tour, voyage
2 STUMBLE, fall, misstep, slip
► *verb* **3** STUMBLE, fall, lose one's footing, misstep, slip, tumble
4 CATCH OUT, trap

5 SKIP, dance, gambol, hop

triple adjective 1 THREEFOLD, three-way, tripartite
▶ verb 2 TREBLE, increase threefold

trite adjective UNORIGINAL, banal, clichéd, commonplace, hackneyed, stale, stereotyped, threadbare, tired

triumph noun 1 JOY, elation, exultation, happiness, jubilation, pride, rejoicing
2 SUCCESS, accomplishment, achievement, attainment, conquest, coup, feat, victory
▶ verb 3 (often with over) WIN, overcome, prevail, prosper, succeed, vanquish
4 REJOICE, celebrate, crow, exult, gloat, glory, revel

triumphant adjective VICTORIOUS, celebratory, cock-a-hoop, conquering, elated, exultant, jubilant, proud, successful, winning

trivia plural noun MINUTIAE, details, trifles, trivialities

trivial adjective UNIMPORTANT, incidental, inconsequential, insignificant, meaningless, minor, petty, small, trifling, worthless

triviality noun INSIGNIFICANCE, meaninglessness, pettiness, unimportance, worthlessness

trivialize verb UNDERVALUE, belittle, laugh off, make light of, minimize, play down, scoff at, underestimate, underplay

troop noun 1 GROUP, band, body, company, crowd, horde, multitude, squad, team, unit
2 ▷▷ **troops** SOLDIERS, armed forces, army, men, servicemen, soldiery
▶ verb 3 FLOCK, march, stream, swarm, throng, traipse (informal)

trophy noun PRIZE, award, booty, cup, laurels, memento, souvenir, spoils

tropical adjective HOT, steamy, stifling, sultry, sweltering, torrid

trot verb 1 RUN, canter, jog, lope, scamper
▶ noun 2 RUN, canter, jog, lope

trouble noun 1 DISTRESS, anxiety, disquiet, grief, misfortune, pain, sorrow, torment, woe, worry
2 DISEASE, ailment, complaint, defect, disorder, failure, illness, malfunction
3 DISORDER, agitation, bother (informal), commotion, discord, disturbance, strife, tumult, unrest
4 EFFORT, care, exertion, inconvenience, labor, pains, thought, work
▶ verb 5 WORRY, bother, disconcert, distress, disturb, pain, perturb, plague, sadden, upset
6 TAKE PAINS, exert oneself, make an effort, take the time
7 INCONVENIENCE, bother, burden, disturb, impose upon, incommode, put out

troublesome adjective
1 WORRYING, annoying, demanding, difficult, inconvenient, irksome, high-maintenance, taxing, tricky, trying, vexatious
2 DISORDERLY, rebellious, rowdy, turbulent, uncooperative, undisciplined, unruly, violent

trough noun 1 MANGER, water trough
2 CHANNEL, canal, depression, ditch, duct, furrow, gully, gutter, trench

trounce verb THRASH, beat, crush, drub, give a hiding (informal), hammer (informal), rout, slaughter (informal), wipe the floor with

(*informal*)

troupe noun COMPANY, band, cast

truancy noun ABSENCE, absence without leave, malingering, shirking, skiving (*Brit. slang*)

truant noun ABSENTEE, malingerer, runaway, shirker, skiver (*Brit. slang*)

truce noun CEASEFIRE, armistice, cessation, let-up (*informal*), lull, moratorium, peace, respite

truculent adjective HOSTILE, aggressive, bellicose, belligerent, defiant, ill-tempered, obstreperous, pugnacious

trudge verb 1 PLOD, footslog, lumber, slog, stump, traipse (*informal*), tramp, trek
▶ noun 2 HIKE, footslog, march, slog, traipse (*informal*), tramp, trek

true adjective 1 CORRECT, accurate, authentic, factual, genuine, precise, real, right, truthful, veracious
2 FAITHFUL, dedicated, devoted, dutiful, loyal, reliable, staunch, steady, trustworthy
3 EXACT, accurate, on target, perfect, precise, spot-on (*Brit. informal*), unerring

truism noun CLICHÉ, axiom, bromide, commonplace, platitude

truly adverb 1 CORRECTLY, authentically, exactly, factually, genuinely, legitimately, precisely, rightly, truthfully
2 FAITHFULLY, devotedly, dutifully, loyally, sincerely, staunchly, steadily
3 REALLY, extremely, greatly, indeed, of course, very

trumpet noun 1 HORN, bugle, clarion
▶ verb 2 PROCLAIM, advertise, announce, broadcast, shout from the rooftops, tout (*informal*)

trump up verb FABRICATE, concoct, contrive, cook up (*informal*), create, fake, invent, make up

truncate verb SHORTEN, abbreviate, curtail, cut short, dock, lop, pare, prune, trim

truncheon noun CLUB, baton, cudgel, staff

trunk noun 1 STEM, bole, stalk
2 CHEST, box, case, casket, coffer, crate
3 BODY, torso
4 SNOUT, proboscis

truss verb 1 TIE, bind, fasten, make fast, secure, strap, tether
▶ noun 2 (*medical*) SUPPORT, bandage
3 JOIST, beam, brace, buttress, prop, stanchion, stay, strut, support

trust verb 1 BELIEVE IN, bank on, count on, depend on, have faith in, rely upon
2 CONSIGN, assign, commit, confide, delegate, entrust, give
3 EXPECT, assume, hope, presume, suppose, surmise
▶ noun 4 CONFIDENCE, assurance, belief, certainty, conviction, credence, credit, expectation, faith, reliance

trustful, trusting adjective UNWARY, credulous, gullible, naive, unsuspecting, unsuspicious

trustworthy adjective HONEST, dependable, honorable, principled, reliable, reputable, responsible, staunch, steadfast, trusty

trusty adjective FAITHFUL, dependable, reliable, solid, staunch, steady, strong, trustworthy

truth noun TRUTHFULNESS, accuracy, exactness, fact,

genuineness, legitimacy, precision, reality, validity, veracity

truthful adjective HONEST, candid, frank, precise, sincere, straight, true, trustworthy

try verb 1 ATTEMPT, aim, endeavor, have a go, make an effort, seek, strive, struggle
2 TEST, appraise, check out, evaluate, examine, investigate, put to the test, sample, taste
▶ noun 3 ATTEMPT, crack (informal), effort, go (informal), shot (informal), stab (informal), whack (informal)

trying adjective ANNOYING, bothersome, difficult, exasperating, hard, high-maintenance, stressful, taxing, tiresome, tough, wearisome

tubby adjective FAT, chubby, corpulent, obese, overweight, plump, portly, stout

tuck verb 1 PUSH, fold, gather, insert
▶ noun 2 FOLD, gather, pinch, pleat
3 (informal) FOOD, grub (slang), nosh (slang)

tuft noun CLUMP, bunch, cluster, collection, knot, tussock

tug verb 1 PULL, jerk, wrench, yank
▶ noun 2 PULL, jerk, yank

tuition noun TRAINING, education, instruction, lessons, schooling, teaching, tutelage, tutoring

tumble verb 1 FALL, drop, flop, plummet, stumble, topple
▶ noun 2 FALL, drop, plunge, spill, stumble, trip

tumbledown adjective DILAPIDATED, crumbling, decrepit, ramshackle, rickety, ruined

tumor noun GROWTH, cancer, carcinoma (pathology), lump, sarcoma (medical), swelling

tumult noun COMMOTION, clamor, din, hubbub, pandemonium, riot, row, turmoil, upheaval, uproar

tumultuous adjective WILD, boisterous, excited, noisy, riotous, rowdy, turbulent, unruly, uproarious, wired (slang)

tune noun 1 MELODY, air, song, strain, theme
2 PITCH, concord, consonance, euphony, harmony
▶ verb 3 ADJUST, adapt, attune, harmonize, pitch, regulate

tuneful adjective MELODIOUS, catchy, euphonious, harmonious, mellifluous, melodic, musical, pleasant

tuneless adjective DISCORDANT, atonal, cacophonous, dissonant, harsh, unmusical

tunnel noun 1 PASSAGE, burrow, channel, hole, passageway, shaft, subway, underpass
▶ verb 2 DIG, burrow, excavate, mine, scoop out

turbulence noun CONFUSION, agitation, commotion, disorder, instability, tumult, turmoil, unrest, upheaval

turbulent adjective AGITATED, blustery, choppy, foaming, furious, raging, rough, tempestuous, tumultuous

turf noun 1 GRASS, sod, sward
2 ▷▷ **the turf** HORSE-RACING, racing, the flat

turmoil noun CONFUSION, agitation, chaos, commotion, disarray, disorder, tumult, upheaval, uproar

turn verb 1 CHANGE COURSE, move, shift, swerve, switch, veer, wheel
2 ROTATE, circle, go round, gyrate, pivot, revolve, roll, spin, twist, whirl
3 CHANGE, alter, convert, mold, mutate, remodel, shape, transform

4 SHAPE, fashion, frame, make, mold

5 GO BAD, curdle, go off (*Brit. informal*), sour, spoil, taint

▶ *noun* 6 ROTATION, circle, cycle, gyration, revolution, spin, twist, whirl

7 SHIFT, departure, deviation

8 OPPORTUNITY, chance, crack (*informal*), go, stint, time, try

9 DIRECTION, drift, heading, tendency, trend

10 *as in* **good turn** ACT, action, deed, favor, gesture, service

turncoat *noun* TRAITOR, apostate, backslider, defector, deserter, renegade

turn down *verb* 1 LOWER, lessen, muffle, mute, quieten, soften

2 REFUSE, decline, rebuff, reject, repudiate, spurn

turn in *verb* 1 GO TO BED, go to sleep, hit the sack (*slang*)

2 HAND IN, deliver, give up, hand over, return, submit, surrender, tender

turning *noun* JUNCTION, bend, crossroads, curve, side road, turn, turn-off

turning point *noun* CROSSROADS, change, crisis, crux, moment of truth

turn off *verb* STOP, cut out, put out, shut down, switch off, turn out, unplug

turn on *verb* 1 START, activate, ignite, kick-start, start up, switch on

2 ATTACK, assail, assault, fall on, round on

3 (*informal*) EXCITE, arouse, attract, please, stimulate, thrill, titillate

turnout *noun* ATTENDANCE, assembly, audience, congregation, crowd, gate, number, throng

turnover *noun* 1 OUTPUT, business, productivity

2 MOVEMENT, change, coming and going

turn up *verb* 1 ARRIVE, appear, attend, come, put in an appearance, show one's face, show up (*informal*)

2 FIND, dig up, disclose, discover, expose, reveal, unearth

3 COME TO LIGHT, crop up (*informal*), pop up

4 INCREASE, amplify, boost, enhance, intensify, raise

tussle *noun* 1 FIGHT, battle, brawl, conflict, contest, scrap (*informal*), scuffle, struggle

▶ *verb* 2 FIGHT, battle, grapple, scrap (*informal*), scuffle, struggle, vie, wrestle

tutor *noun* 1 TEACHER, coach, educator, guardian, guide, guru, instructor, lecturer, mentor

▶ *verb* 2 TEACH, coach, drill, educate, guide, instruct, school, train

twaddle *noun* NONSENSE, claptrap (*informal*), drivel, garbage (*informal*), gobbledegook (*informal*), poppycock (*informal*), rubbish, waffle (*informal, chiefly Brit.*)

tweak *verb or noun* TWIST, jerk, pinch, pull, squeeze

twig[1] *noun* BRANCH, shoot, spray, sprig, stick

twilight *noun* DUSK, dimness, evening, gloaming (*Scot. or poetic*), gloom, half-light, sundown, sunset

twin *noun* 1 DOUBLE, clone, counterpart, duplicate, fellow, likeness, lookalike, match, mate

▶ *verb* 2 PAIR, couple, join, link, match, yoke

twine *noun* 1 STRING, cord, yarn

▶ *verb* 2 COIL, bend, curl, encircle, loop, spiral, twist, wind

twinge *noun* PAIN, pang, prick, spasm, stab, stitch

twinkle *verb* 1 SPARKLE, blink, flash, flicker, gleam, glint, glisten, glitter, shimmer, shine
► *noun* 2 FLICKER, flash, gleam, glimmer, shimmer, spark, sparkle

twirl *verb* 1 TURN, pirouette, pivot, revolve, rotate, spin, twist, wheel, whirl, wind
► *noun* 2 TURN, pirouette, revolution, rotation, spin, twist, wheel, whirl

twist *verb* 1 WIND, coil, curl, screw, spin, swivel, wrap, wring
2 DISTORT, contort, screw up
► *noun* 3 WIND, coil, curl, spin, swivel
4 DEVELOPMENT, change, revelation, slant, surprise, turn, variation
5 CURVE, arc, bend, meander, turn, undulation, zigzag
6 DISTORTION, defect, deformation, flaw, imperfection, kink, warp

twitch *verb* 1 JERK, flutter, jump, squirm
► *noun* 2 SPASM, flutter, jerk, jump, tic

two-faced *adjective* HYPOCRITICAL, deceitful, dissembling, duplicitous, false, insincere, treacherous, untrustworthy

tycoon *noun* MAGNATE, baron, capitalist, fat cat (*slang*), financier, industrialist, mogul, plutocrat

type *noun* CATEGORY, class, genre, group, kind, order, sort, species, style, variety

typhoon *noun* STORM, cyclone, squall, tempest, tornado

typical *adjective* CHARACTERISTIC, archetypal, average, classic, model, normal, orthodox, representative, standard, stock, usual

typify *verb* SYMBOLIZE, characterize, embody, epitomize, exemplify, illustrate, personify, represent, sum up

tyrannical *adjective* OPPRESSIVE, authoritarian, autocratic, cruel, despotic, dictatorial, domineering, high-handed, imperious, overbearing, tyrannous

tyranny *noun* OPPRESSION, absolutism, authoritarianism, autocracy, cruelty, despotism, dictatorship, high-handedness, imperiousness

tyrant *noun* DICTATOR, absolutist, authoritarian, autocrat, bully, despot, martinet, oppressor, slave-driver

ubiquitous *adjective* EVERYWHERE, ever-present, omnipresent, pervasive, universal

ugly *adjective* 1 UNATTRACTIVE, dumpy (*informal*), frowzy, hideous, homely (*U.S.*), ill-favored, plain, unlovely, unprepossessing, unsightly
2 UNPLEASANT, disagreeable, distasteful, horrid, objectionable, shocking, terrible
3 OMINOUS, baleful, dangerous, menacing, sinister

ulcer *noun* SORE, abscess, boil, gumboil, peptic ulcer, pustule

ulterior *adjective* HIDDEN, concealed, covert, secret, undisclosed

ultimate *adjective* 1 FINAL, end, last
2 SUPREME, extreme, greatest, highest, paramount, superlative, utmost

ultimately *adverb* FINALLY, after all, at last, eventually, in due time, in the end, sooner or later

umpire *noun* 1 REFEREE, arbiter, arbitrator, judge
▶ *verb* 2 REFEREE, adjudicate, arbitrate, judge

unabashed *adjective* UNEMBARRASSED, blatant, bold, brazen

unable *adjective* INCAPABLE, impotent, ineffectual, powerless, unfit, unqualified

unabridged *adjective* UNCUT, complete, full-length, unexpurgated, whole

unacceptable *adjective* UNSATISFACTORY, displeasing, objectionable

unaccompanied *adjective* 1 ALONE, by oneself, lone, on one's own, solo, unescorted
2 (*music*) A CAPPELLA

unaccountable *adjective* 1 INEXPLICABLE, baffling, mysterious, odd, puzzling, unexplainable, unfathomable
2 NOT ANSWERABLE, exempt, not responsible

unaccustomed *adjective* 1 UNFAMILIAR, new, strange, unwonted
2 ▷▷ **unaccustomed to** NOT USED TO, inexperienced at, unfamiliar with, unused to

unaffected¹ *adjective* NATURAL, artless, genuine, plain, simple, sincere, unpretentious

unaffected² *adjective* IMPERVIOUS, proof, unmoved, unresponsive, untouched

unafraid *adjective* FEARLESS, daring, dauntless, intrepid

unalterable *adjective* UNCHANGEABLE, fixed, immutable, permanent

unanimity *noun* AGREEMENT, accord, assent, concord, concurrence, consensus, harmony, like-mindedness, unison

unanimous *adjective* AGREED, common, concerted, harmonious, in agreement, like-minded, united

unanimously *adverb* WITHOUT EXCEPTION, as one, in concert, of one mind, nem. con., with one accord

unanswerable *adjective* CONCLUSIVE, absolute, incontestable, incontrovertible, indisputable

unanswered *adjective* UNRESOLVED, disputed, open, undecided

unappetizing *adjective* UNPLEASANT, distasteful, off-putting (*Brit. informal*), repulsive, scuzzy (*slang*), unappealing, unattractive, unpalatable

unapproachable *adjective*
1 UNFRIENDLY, aloof, chilly, cool, distant, remote, reserved, standoffish
2 INACCESSIBLE, out of reach, remote

unarmed *adjective* DEFENSELESS, exposed, helpless, open, unprotected, weak

unassailable *adjective* IMPREGNABLE, invincible, invulnerable, secure

unassuming *adjective* MODEST, humble, quiet, reserved, retiring, self-effacing, unassertive, unobtrusive, unpretentious

unattached *adjective* 1 FREE, independent
2 SINGLE, available, not spoken for, unengaged, unmarried

unattended *adjective*
1 ABANDONED, unguarded, unwatched
2 ALONE, on one's own, unaccompanied

unauthorized *adjective* ILLEGAL, unlawful, unofficial, unsanctioned

unavoidable *adjective* INEVITABLE, certain, fated, inescapable

unaware *adjective* IGNORANT, oblivious, unconscious, uninformed, unknowing

unawares *adverb* 1 BY SURPRISE, off guard, suddenly, unexpectedly
2 UNKNOWINGLY, accidentally, by accident, inadvertently, unwittingly

unbalanced *adjective* 1 BIASED, one-sided, partial, partisan, prejudiced, unfair
2 SHAKY, lopsided, uneven, unstable, wobbly
3 DERANGED, crazy, demented, disturbed, eccentric, insane, irrational, mad, *non compos mentis*, not all there, unhinged, unstable

unbearable *adjective* INTOLERABLE, insufferable, too much (*informal*), unacceptable

unbeatable *adjective* INVINCIBLE, indomitable

unbeaten *adjective* UNDEFEATED, triumphant, victorious

unbecoming *adjective*
1 UNSIGHTLY, unattractive, unbefitting, unflattering, unsuitable
2 UNSEEMLY, discreditable, improper, offensive

unbelievable *adjective* INCREDIBLE, astonishing, far-fetched, implausible, impossible, improbable, inconceivable, preposterous, unconvincing, unimaginable

unbending *adjective* INFLEXIBLE, firm, intractable, resolute, rigid, severe, strict, stubborn, tough, uncompromising

unbiased *adjective* FAIR, disinterested, equitable, impartial, just, neutral, objective, unprejudiced

unblemished *adjective*

SPOTLESS, flawless, immaculate, impeccable, perfect, pure, untarnished

unborn *adjective* EXPECTED, awaited, embryonic, fetal

unbreakable *adjective* INDESTRUCTIBLE, durable, lasting, rugged, strong

unbridled *adjective* UNRESTRAINED, excessive, intemperate, licentious, riotous, unchecked, unruly, wanton

unbroken *adjective* 1 INTACT, complete, entire, whole
2 CONTINUOUS, constant, incessant, twenty-four-seven (*slang*), uninterrupted

unburden *verb* CONFESS, confide, disclose, get (something) off one's chest (*informal*), reveal

uncalled-for *adjective* UNJUSTIFIED, gratuitous, needless, undeserved, unnecessary, unwarranted

uncanny *adjective* 1 WEIRD, mysterious, strange, supernatural, unearthly, unnatural
2 EXTRAORDINARY, astounding, exceptional, incredible, miraculous, remarkable, unusual

unceasing *adjective* CONTINUAL, constant, continuous, endless, incessant, nonstop, perpetual, twenty-four-seven (*slang*)

uncertain *adjective*
1 UNPREDICTABLE, doubtful, indefinite, questionable, risky, speculative
2 UNSURE, dubious, hazy, irresolute, unclear, unconfirmed, undecided, vague

uncertainty *noun* DOUBT, ambiguity, confusion, dubiety, hesitancy, indecision, unpredictability

unchangeable *adjective* UNALTERABLE, constant, fixed, immutable, invariable, irreversible, permanent, stable

unchanging *adjective* CONSTANT, continuing, enduring, eternal, immutable, lasting, permanent, perpetual, twenty-four-seven (*slang*), unvarying

uncharitable *adjective* UNKIND, cruel, hardhearted, unfeeling, ungenerous

uncharted *adjective* UNEXPLORED, strange, undiscovered, unfamiliar, unknown

uncivil *adjective* IMPOLITE, bad-mannered, discourteous, ill-mannered, rude, unmannerly

uncivilized *adjective* 1 PRIMITIVE, barbarian, savage, wild
2 UNCOUTH, boorish, coarse, philistine, uncultivated, uneducated

unclean *adjective* DIRTY, corrupt, defiled, evil, filthy, foul, impure, polluted, scuzzy (*slang*), soiled, stained

unclear *adjective* 1 INDISTINCT, blurred, dim, faint, fuzzy, hazy, obscure, shadowy, undefined, vague
2 DOUBTFUL, ambiguous, indefinite, indeterminate, vague

uncomfortable *adjective*
1 AWKWARD, cramped, painful, rough
2 UNEASY, awkward, discomfited, disturbed, embarrassed, troubled

uncommitted *adjective* UNINVOLVED, floating, free, neutral, nonaligned, not involved, unattached

uncommon *adjective* 1 RARE, infrequent, novel, odd, peculiar, queer, scarce, strange, unusual
2 EXTRAORDINARY, distinctive,

exceptional, notable, outstanding, remarkable, special

uncommonly *adverb* 1 RARELY, hardly ever, infrequently, occasionally, seldom
2 EXCEPTIONALLY, particularly, very

uncommunicative *adjective* RETICENT, close, reserved, secretive, silent, taciturn, tight-lipped, unforthcoming

uncompromising *adjective* INFLEXIBLE, firm, inexorable, intransigent, rigid, strict, tough, unbending

unconcern *noun* INDIFFERENCE, aloofness, apathy, detachment, lack of interest, nonchalance

unconcerned *adjective* INDIFFERENT, aloof, apathetic, cool, detached, dispassionate, distant, uninterested, unmoved

unconditional *adjective* ABSOLUTE, complete, entire, full, outright, positive, total, unlimited, unqualified, unreserved

unconnected *adjective*
1 SEPARATE, detached, divided
2 MEANINGLESS, disjointed, illogical, incoherent, irrelevant

unconscious *adjective*
1 SENSELESS, insensible, knocked out, out cold, stunned
2 UNAWARE, ignorant, oblivious, unknowing
3 UNINTENTIONAL, accidental, inadvertent, unwitting

uncontrollable *adjective* WILD, frantic, furious, mad, strong, unruly, violent

uncontrolled *adjective* UNRESTRAINED, rampant, riotous, unbridled, unchecked, undisciplined

unconventional *adjective*

UNUSUAL, eccentric, individual, irregular, nonconformist, odd, offbeat, original, outré, unorthodox

unconvincing *adjective* IMPLAUSIBLE, dubious, feeble, flimsy, improbable, lame, questionable, suspect, thin, unlikely, weak

uncooperative *adjective* UNHELPFUL, awkward, difficult, disobliging, high-maintenance, obstructive

uncoordinated *adjective* CLUMSY, awkward, bungling, graceless, lumbering, maladroit, ungainly, ungraceful

uncouth *adjective* COARSE, boorish, crude, graceless, ill-mannered, loutish, oafish, rough, rude, vulgar

uncover *verb* 1 REVEAL, disclose, divulge, expose, make known
2 OPEN, bare, show, strip, unwrap

uncritical *adjective* UNDISCRIMINATING, indiscriminate, undiscerning

undecided *adjective* 1 UNSURE, dithering, hesitant, in two minds, irresolute, torn, uncertain
2 UNSETTLED, debatable, iffy (*informal*), indefinite, moot, open, unconcluded, undetermined

undefined *adjective* 1 UNSPECIFIED, imprecise, inexact, unclear
2 INDISTINCT, formless, indefinite, vague

undeniable *adjective* CERTAIN, clear, incontrovertible, indisputable, obvious, sure, unquestionable

under *preposition* 1 BELOW, beneath, underneath
2 SUBJECT TO, governed by, secondary to, subordinate to
▶ *adverb* 3 BELOW, beneath, down,

lower
underclothes *plural noun*
UNDERWEAR, lingerie,
undergarments, undies (*informal*)
undercover *adjective* SECRET,
concealed, covert, hidden, private
undercurrent *noun* 1 UNDERTOW,
riptide
2 UNDERTONE, atmosphere,
feeling, hint, overtone, sense,
suggestion, tendency, tinge,
vibes (*slang*)
underdog *noun* OUTSIDER, little
fellow (*informal*)
underestimate *verb* UNDERRATE,
belittle, minimize, miscalculate,
undervalue
undergo *verb* EXPERIENCE, bear,
endure, go through, stand, suffer,
sustain
underground *adjective*
1 SUBTERRANEAN, buried, covered
2 SECRET, clandestine, covert,
hidden
▶ *noun* 3 ▷▷ **the underground**
a THE RESISTANCE, partisans **b** THE
TUBE (*Brit.*), the metro, the subway
undergrowth *noun* SCRUB,
bracken, briars, brush,
underbrush
underhand, underhanded
adjective SLY, crafty, deceitful,
devious, dishonest, down and
dirty (*informal*), furtive, secret,
sneaky, stealthy
underline *verb* 1 UNDERSCORE,
mark
2 EMPHASIZE, accentuate,
highlight, stress
underlying *adjective*
FUNDAMENTAL, basic, elementary,
intrinsic, primary, prime
undermine *verb* WEAKEN, disable,
sabotage, sap, subvert
underprivileged *adjective*
DISADVANTAGED, deprived,

destitute, impoverished, needy,
poor
underrate *verb* UNDERESTIMATE,
belittle, discount, undervalue
undersized *adjective* STUNTED,
dwarfish, miniature, pygmy or
pigmy, small
understand *verb* 1 COMPREHEND,
conceive, fathom, follow, get,
grasp, perceive, realize, see,
take in
2 BELIEVE, assume, gather,
presume, suppose, think
understandable *adjective*
REASONABLE, justifiable,
legitimate, natural, to be expected
understanding *noun*
1 PERCEPTION, appreciation,
awareness, comprehension,
discernment, grasp, insight,
judgment, knowledge, sense
2 INTERPRETATION, belief, idea,
judgment, notion, opinion,
perception, view
3 AGREEMENT, accord, pact
▶ *adjective* 4 SYMPATHETIC,
compassionate, considerate, kind,
patient, sensitive, tolerant
understood *adjective* 1 IMPLIED,
implicit, inferred, tacit,
unspoken, unstated
2 ASSUMED, accepted, taken for
granted
understudy *noun* STAND-IN,
replacement, reserve, substitute
undertake *verb* AGREE, bargain,
contract, engage, guarantee,
pledge, promise
undertaking *noun* 1 TASK,
affair, attempt, business, effort,
endeavor, enterprise, operation,
project, venture
2 PROMISE, assurance,
commitment, pledge, vow, word
undertone *noun* 1 MURMUR,
whisper

2 UNDERCURRENT, hint, suggestion, tinge, touch, trace

undervalue verb UNDERRATE, depreciate, hold cheap, minimize, misjudge, underestimate

underwater adjective SUBMERGED, submarine, sunken

under way adjective BEGUN, going on, in progress, started

underwear noun UNDERCLOTHES, lingerie, undergarments, underthings, undies (informal)

underweight adjective SKINNY, emaciated, half-starved, puny, skin and bone (informal), undernourished, undersized

underworld noun 1 CRIMINALS, gangland (informal), gangsters, organized crime

2 NETHER WORLD, Hades, nether regions

underwrite verb 1 FINANCE, back, fund, guarantee, insure, sponsor, subsidize

2 SIGN, endorse, initial

undesirable adjective OBJECTIONABLE, disagreeable, distasteful, unacceptable, unattractive, unsuitable, unwanted, unwelcome

undeveloped adjective POTENTIAL, immature, latent

undignified adjective UNSEEMLY, improper, indecorous, inelegant, unbecoming, unsuitable

undisciplined adjective UNCONTROLLED, obstreperous, unrestrained, unruly, wayward, wild, willful

undisguised adjective OBVIOUS, blatant, evident, explicit, open, overt, patent, unconcealed

undisputed adjective ACKNOWLEDGED, accepted, certain, indisputable, recognized, unchallenged, undeniable, undoubted

undistinguished adjective ORDINARY, everyday, mediocre, run-of-the-mill, unexceptional, unimpressive, unremarkable

undisturbed adjective 1 QUIET, tranquil

2 CALM, collected, composed, placid, sedate, serene, tranquil, unfazed (informal), unperturbed, untroubled

undivided adjective COMPLETE, entire, exclusive, full, solid, thorough, undistracted, united, whole

undo verb 1 OPEN, disentangle, loose, unbutton, unfasten, untie

2 REVERSE, annul, cancel, invalidate, neutralize, offset

3 RUIN, defeat, destroy, overturn, quash, shatter, subvert, undermine, upset, wreck

undoing noun DOWNFALL, collapse, defeat, disgrace, overthrow, reversal, ruin, shame

undone¹ adjective UNFINISHED, left, neglected, omitted, unfulfilled, unperformed

undoubted adjective CERTAIN, acknowledged, definite, indisputable, indubitable, sure, undisputed, unquestioned

undoubtedly adverb CERTAINLY, assuredly, definitely, doubtless, surely, without doubt

undress verb 1 STRIP, disrobe, shed, take off one's clothes
▶ noun 2 NAKEDNESS, nudity

undue adjective EXCESSIVE, extreme, improper, needless, uncalled-for, unnecessary, unwarranted

unduly adverb EXCESSIVELY, overly, unnecessarily, unreasonably

undying adjective ETERNAL, constant, deathless, everlasting, infinite, permanent, perpetual, twenty-four-seven (*slang*), unending

unearth *verb* **1** DISCOVER, expose, find, reveal, uncover
2 DIG UP, dredge up, excavate, exhume

unearthly *adjective* EERIE, ghostly, phantom, spectral, spooky (*informal*), strange, supernatural, uncanny, weird

uneasiness *noun* ANXIETY, disquiet, doubt, misgiving, qualms, trepidation, worry

uneasy *adjective* **1** ANXIOUS, disturbed, edgy, nervous, on edge, perturbed, troubled, twitchy (*informal*), uncomfortable, wired (*slang*), worried
2 AWKWARD, insecure, precarious, shaky, strained, tense, uncomfortable

uneconomic *adjective* UNPROFITABLE, loss-making, nonpaying

uneducated *adjective* **1** IGNORANT, illiterate, unlettered, unschooled, untaught
2 LOWBROW, uncultivated, uncultured

unemotional *adjective* IMPASSIVE, apathetic, cold, cool, phlegmatic, reserved, undemonstrative, unexcitable

unemployed *adjective* OUT OF WORK, idle, jobless, laid off, redundant

unending *adjective* PERPETUAL, continual, endless, eternal, everlasting, interminable, unceasing

unendurable *adjective* UNBEARABLE, insufferable, insupportable, intolerable

unenthusiastic *adjective* INDIFFERENT, apathetic, half-hearted, nonchalant

unenviable *adjective* UNPLEASANT, disagreeable, uncomfortable, undesirable

unequal *adjective* **1** DIFFERENT, differing, disparate, dissimilar, unlike, unmatched, varying
2 DISPROPORTIONATE, asymmetrical, ill-matched, irregular, unbalanced, uneven

unequaled *adjective* INCOMPARABLE, matchless, paramount, peerless, supreme, unparalleled, unrivaled

unequivocal *adjective* CLEAR, absolute, certain, definite, explicit, incontrovertible, indubitable, manifest, plain, unambiguous

unerring *adjective* ACCURATE, exact, infallible, perfect, sure, unfailing

unethical *adjective* DISHONEST, disreputable, illegal, immoral, improper, shady (*informal*), unprincipled, unscrupulous, wrong

uneven *adjective* **1** ROUGH, bumpy
2 VARIABLE, broken, fitful, irregular, jerky, patchy, spasmodic
3 UNBALANCED, lopsided, odd
4 UNEQUAL, ill-matched, unfair

uneventful *adjective* HUMDRUM, boring, dull, ho-hum (*informal*), monotonous, routine, tedious, unexciting

unexceptional *adjective* ORDINARY, commonplace, conventional, mediocre, normal, pedestrian, run-of-the-mill, undistinguished, unremarkable

unexpected *adjective* UNFORESEEN, abrupt, chance, fortuitous, sudden, surprising, unanticipated, unlooked-for, unpredictable

unfailing *adjective* 1 CONTINUOUS, boundless, endless, persistent, unflagging

2 RELIABLE, certain, dependable, faithful, loyal, staunch, sure, true

unfair *adjective* 1 BIASED, bigoted, one-sided, partial, partisan, prejudiced, unjust

2 UNSCRUPULOUS, dishonest, unethical, unsporting, wrongful

unfaithful *adjective* 1 FAITHLESS, adulterous, two-timing (*informal*), untrue

2 DISLOYAL, deceitful, faithless, false, traitorous, treacherous, untrustworthy

unfamiliar *adjective* STRANGE, alien, different, new, novel, unknown, unusual

unfashionable *adjective* PASSÉ, antiquated, dated, dumpy (*informal*), frowzy, homely (U.S.), obsolete, old-fashioned, old hat

unfasten *verb* UNDO, detach, let go, loosen, open, separate, unlace, untie

unfathomable *adjective* 1 BAFFLING, deep, impenetrable, incomprehensible, indecipherable, inexplicable, profound

2 IMMEASURABLE, bottomless, unmeasured

unfavorable *adjective* 1 ADVERSE, contrary, inauspicious, unfortunate, unlucky, unpropitious

2 HOSTILE, inimical, negative, unfriendly

unfeeling *adjective* 1 HARDHEARTED, apathetic, callous, cold, cruel, heartless, insensitive, pitiless, uncaring

2 NUMB, insensate, insensible

unfinished *adjective* 1 INCOMPLETE, half-done, uncompleted, undone

2 ROUGH, bare, crude, natural, raw, unrefined

unfit *adjective* 1 INCAPABLE, inadequate, incompetent, lousy (*slang*), no good, unqualified, useless

2 UNSUITABLE, inadequate, ineffective, unsuited, useless

3 OUT OF SHAPE, feeble, flabby, in poor condition, unhealthy

unflappable *adjective* IMPERTURBABLE, calm, collected, composed, cool, impassive, level-headed, self-possessed

unflattering *adjective* 1 BLUNT, candid, critical, honest

2 UNATTRACTIVE, dumpy (*informal*), frowzy, homely (U.S.), plain, unbecoming

unflinching *adjective* DETERMINED, firm, immovable, resolute, staunch, steadfast, steady, unfaltering

unfold *verb* 1 OPEN, expand, spread out, undo, unfurl, unravel, unroll, unwrap

2 REVEAL, disclose, divulge, make known, present, show, uncover

unforeseen *adjective* UNEXPECTED, accidental, sudden, surprising, unanticipated, unpredicted

unforgettable *adjective* MEMORABLE, exceptional, impressive, notable

unforgivable *adjective* INEXCUSABLE, deplorable, disgraceful, shameful, unpardonable

unfortunate *adjective* 1 DISASTROUS, adverse, calamitous, ill-fated

2 UNLUCKY, cursed, doomed, hapless, unhappy, unsuccessful, wretched

3 REGRETTABLE, deplorable, lamentable, unsuitable

unfounded *adjective* GROUNDLESS, baseless, false, idle, spurious, unjustified

unfriendly *adjective* 1 HOSTILE, aloof, chilly, cold, distant, uncongenial, unsociable
2 UNFAVORABLE, alien, hostile, inhospitable

ungainly *adjective* AWKWARD, clumsy, inelegant, lumbering, ungraceful

ungodly *adjective* 1 UNREASONABLE, dreadful, intolerable, outrageous, unearthly
2 WICKED, corrupt, depraved, godless, immoral, impious, irreligious, profane, sinful

ungracious *adjective* BAD-MANNERED, churlish, discourteous, impolite, rude, uncivil, unmannerly

ungrateful *adjective* UNAPPRECIATIVE, unmindful, unthankful

unguarded *adjective*
1 UNPROTECTED, defenseless, undefended, vulnerable
2 CARELESS, heedless, ill-considered, imprudent, incautious, rash, thoughtless, unthinking, unwary

unhappiness *noun* SADNESS, blues, dejection, depression, despondency, gloom, heartache, low spirits, melancholy, misery, sorrow, wretchedness

unhappy *adjective* 1 SAD, blue, dejected, depressed, despondent, downcast, melancholy, miserable, mournful, sorrowful
2 UNLUCKY, cursed, hapless, ill-fated, unfortunate, wretched

unharmed *adjective* UNHURT, intact, safe, sound, undamaged, unscathed, whole

unhealthy *adjective* 1 HARMFUL, detrimental, insalubrious, insanitary, unwholesome
2 SICK, ailing, delicate, feeble, frail, infirm, invalid, sickly, unwell

unheard-of *adjective*
1 UNPRECEDENTED, inconceivable, new, novel, singular, unique
2 SHOCKING, disgraceful, outrageous, preposterous
3 OBSCURE, unfamiliar, unknown

unhesitating *adjective* 1 INSTANT, immediate, prompt, ready
2 WHOLEHEARTED, resolute, unfaltering, unquestioning, unreserved

unholy *adjective* EVIL, corrupt, profane, sinful, ungodly, wicked

unhurried *adjective* LEISURELY, easy, sedate, slow

unidentified *adjective* UNNAMED, anonymous, nameless, unfamiliar, unrecognized

unification *noun* UNION, alliance, amalgamation, coalescence, coalition, confederation, federation, uniting

uniform *noun* 1 OUTFIT, costume, dress, garb, habit, livery, regalia, suit
▸ *adjective* 2 UNVARYING, consistent, constant, even, regular, smooth, unchanging
3 ALIKE, equal, like, on a level playing field (*informal*), same, similar

uniformity *noun* 1 REGULARITY, constancy, evenness, invariability, sameness, similarity
2 MONOTONY, dullness, flatness, sameness, tedium

unify *verb* UNITE, amalgamate, combine, confederate, consolidate, join, merge

unimaginable *adjective* INCONCEIVABLE, fantastic,

impossible, incredible, unbelievable

unimaginative adjective
UNORIGINAL, banal, derivative, dull, hackneyed, ordinary, pedestrian, predictable, prosaic, uncreative, uninspired

unimportant adjective
INSIGNIFICANT, inconsequential, irrelevant, minor, paltry, petty, trifling, trivial, worthless

uninhabited adjective DESERTED, barren, desolate, empty, unpopulated, vacant

uninhibited adjective
1 UNSELFCONSCIOUS, free, liberated, natural, open, relaxed, spontaneous, unrepressed, unreserved
2 UNRESTRAINED, free, unbridled, unchecked, unconstrained, uncontrolled, unrestricted

uninspired adjective
UNIMAGINATIVE, banal, dull, humdrum, ordinary, prosaic, unexciting, unoriginal

unintelligent adjective STUPID, braindead (*informal*), brainless, dense, dull, foolish, gormless (*Brit. informal*), obtuse, slow, thick

unintelligible adjective
INCOMPREHENSIBLE, inarticulate, incoherent, indistinct, jumbled, meaningless, muddled

unintentional adjective
ACCIDENTAL, casual, inadvertent, involuntary, unconscious, unintended

uninterested adjective
INDIFFERENT, apathetic, blasé, bored, listless, unconcerned

uninteresting adjective BORING, drab, dreary, dry, dull, flat, humdrum, monotonous, tedious, unexciting

uninterrupted adjective
CONTINUOUS, constant, nonstop, steady, sustained, unbroken

union noun 1 JOINING, amalgamation, blend, combination, conjunction, fusion, mixture, uniting
2 ALLIANCE, association, coalition, confederacy, federation, league
3 AGREEMENT, accord, concord, harmony, unanimity, unison, unity

unique adjective 1 SINGLE, lone, only, solitary
2 UNPARALLELED, incomparable, inimitable, matchless, unequaled, unmatched, unrivaled

unison noun AGREEMENT, accord, accordance, concert, concord, harmony, unity

unit noun 1 ITEM, entity, whole
2 PART, component, constituent, element, member, section, segment
3 SECTION, detachment, group
4 MEASURE, measurement, quantity

unite verb 1 JOIN, amalgamate, blend, combine, couple, fuse, link, merge, unify
2 COOPERATE, ally, band, join forces, pool

united adjective 1 COMBINED, affiliated, allied, banded together, collective, concerted, pooled, unified
2 IN AGREEMENT, agreed, of one mind, of the same opinion, unanimous

unity noun 1 WHOLENESS, entity, integrity, oneness, singleness, union
2 AGREEMENT, accord, assent, concord, consensus, harmony, solidarity, unison

universal adjective WIDESPREAD, common, general, total,

unlimited, whole, worldwide

universally *adverb* EVERYWHERE, always, invariably, without exception

universe *noun* COSMOS, creation, macrocosm, nature

unjust *adjective* UNFAIR, biased, one-sided, partial, partisan, prejudiced, wrong, wrongful

unjustifiable *adjective* INEXCUSABLE, indefensible, outrageous, unacceptable, unforgivable, unpardonable, wrong

unkempt *adjective* 1 UNCOMBED, shaggy, tousled
2 UNTIDY, disheveled, disordered, messy, scruffy, slovenly, ungroomed

unkind *adjective* CRUEL, harsh, malicious, mean, nasty, spiteful, uncharitable, unfeeling, unfriendly, unsympathetic

unknown *adjective* 1 HIDDEN, concealed, dark, mysterious, secret, unrevealed
2 STRANGE, alien, new
3 UNIDENTIFIED, anonymous, nameless, uncharted, undiscovered, unexplored, unnamed
4 OBSCURE, humble, unfamiliar

unlawful *adjective* ILLEGAL, banned, criminal, forbidden, illicit, outlawed, prohibited

unleash *verb* RELEASE, free, let go, let loose

unlike *adjective* DIFFERENT, dissimilar, distinct, diverse, not alike, opposite, unequal

unlikely *adjective* 1 IMPROBABLE, doubtful, faint, remote, slight
2 UNBELIEVABLE, implausible, incredible, questionable

unlimited *adjective* 1 INFINITE, boundless, countless, endless,

extensive, great, immense, limitless, unbounded, vast
2 COMPLETE, absolute, full, total, unqualified, unrestricted

unload *verb* EMPTY, discharge, dump, lighten, relieve, unpack

unlock *verb* OPEN, release, undo, unfasten, unlatch

unlooked-for *adjective* UNEXPECTED, chance, fortuitous, surprising, unanticipated, unforeseen, unpredicted

unloved *adjective* NEGLECTED, forsaken, loveless, rejected, spurned, unpopular, unwanted

unlucky *adjective* 1 UNFORTUNATE, cursed, hapless, luckless, miserable, unhappy, wretched
2 ILL-FATED, doomed, inauspicious, ominous, unfavorable

unmarried *adjective* SINGLE, bachelor, maiden, unattached, unwed

unmask *verb* REVEAL, disclose, discover, expose, lay bare, uncover

unmentionable *adjective* TABOO, forbidden, indecent, obscene, scandalous, shameful, shocking, unspeakable

unmerciful *adjective* MERCILESS, brutal, cruel, hard, implacable, pitiless, remorseless, ruthless

unmistakable *adjective* CLEAR, certain, distinct, evident, manifest, obvious, plain, sure, unambiguous

unmitigated *adjective*
1 UNRELIEVED, intense, persistent, unalleviated, unbroken, undiminished
2 COMPLETE, absolute, arrant, downright, outright, sheer, thorough, utter

unmoved *adjective* UNAFFECTED, cold, impassive, indifferent,

unimpressed, unresponsive,
untouched

unnatural *adjective* 1 STRANGE,
extraordinary, freakish,
outlandish, queer
2 ABNORMAL, anomalous,
irregular, odd, perverse, perverted,
unusual
3 FALSE, affected, artificial,
feigned, forced, insincere, phoney
or phony (*informal*), stiff, stilted

unnecessary *adjective* NEEDLESS,
expendable, inessential,
redundant, superfluous,
unneeded, unrequired

unnerve *verb* INTIMIDATE,
demoralize, discourage,
dishearten, dismay, faze, fluster,
frighten, psych out (*informal*),
rattle (*informal*), shake, upset

unnoticed *adjective* UNOBSERVED,
disregarded, ignored, neglected,
overlooked, unheeded,
unperceived, unrecognized,
unseen

unobtrusive *adjective*
INCONSPICUOUS, low-key, modest,
quiet, restrained, retiring, self-
effacing, unassuming

unoccupied *adjective* EMPTY,
uninhabited, vacant

unofficial *adjective*
UNAUTHORIZED, informal, private,
unconfirmed

unorthodox *adjective*
UNCONVENTIONAL, abnormal,
irregular, off-the-wall (*slang*),
unusual

unpaid *adjective* 1 VOLUNTARY,
honorary, unsalaried
2 OWING, due, outstanding,
overdue, payable, unsettled

unpalatable *adjective*
UNPLEASANT, disagreeable,
distasteful, horrid, offensive,
repugnant, unappetizing,

unsavory

unparalleled *adjective*
UNEQUALED, incomparable,
matchless, superlative, unique,
unmatched, unprecedented,
unsurpassed

unpardonable *adjective*
UNFORGIVABLE, deplorable,
disgraceful, indefensible,
inexcusable

unperturbed *adjective* CALM, as
cool as a cucumber, composed,
cool, placid, unfazed (*informal*),
unruffled, untroubled, unworried

unpleasant *adjective* NASTY,
bad, disagreeable, displeasing,
distasteful, horrid, objectionable

unpopular *adjective* DISLIKED,
rejected, shunned, unwanted,
unwelcome

unprecedented *adjective*
EXTRAORDINARY, abnormal, new,
novel, original, remarkable,
singular, unheard-of

unpredictable *adjective*
INCONSTANT, chance, changeable,
doubtful, erratic, random,
unforeseeable, unreliable,
variable

unprejudiced *adjective* IMPARTIAL,
balanced, fair, just, objective,
open-minded, unbiased

unprepared *adjective* 1 TAKEN
OFF GUARD, surprised, unaware,
unready
2 IMPROVISED, ad-lib, off the cuff
(*informal*), spontaneous

unpretentious *adjective* MODEST,
dumpy (*informal*), homely, humble,
plain, simple, straightforward,
unaffected, unassuming,
unostentatious

unprincipled *adjective* DISHONEST,
amoral, crooked, devious,
immoral, underhand, unethical,
unscrupulous

unproductive adjective 1 USELESS, fruitless, futile, idle, ineffective, unprofitable, unrewarding, vain
2 BARREN, fruitless, sterile

unprofessional adjective
1 UNETHICAL, improper, lax, negligent, unprincipled
2 AMATEURISH, cowboy (informal), incompetent, inefficient, inexpert

unprotected adjective
VULNERABLE, defenseless, helpless, open, undefended

unqualified adjective 1 UNFIT, ill-equipped, incapable, incompetent, ineligible, unprepared
2 TOTAL, absolute, complete, downright, outright, thorough, utter

unquestionable adjective
CERTAIN, absolute, clear, conclusive, definite, incontrovertible, indisputable, sure, undeniable, unequivocal, unmistakable

unravel verb 1 UNDO, disentangle, free, separate, untangle, unwind
2 SOLVE, explain, figure out (informal), resolve, work out

unreal adjective 1 IMAGINARY, dreamlike, fabulous, fanciful, illusory, make-believe, visionary
2 INSUBSTANTIAL, immaterial, intangible, nebulous
3 FAKE, artificial, false, insincere, mock, pretended, sham

unrealistic adjective IMPRACTICAL, impracticable, improbable, romantic, unworkable

unreasonable adjective
1 EXCESSIVE, extortionate, immoderate, undue, unfair, unjust, unwarranted
2 BIASED, blinkered, opinionated

unrelated adjective 1 DIFFERENT, unconnected, unlike
2 IRRELEVANT, extraneous, inapplicable, inappropriate, unconnected

unreliable adjective
1 UNDEPENDABLE, irresponsible, treacherous, untrustworthy
2 UNCERTAIN, deceptive, fallible, false, implausible, inaccurate, unsound

unrepentant adjective
IMPENITENT, abandoned, callous, hardened, incorrigible, shameless, unremorseful

unreserved adjective 1 TOTAL, absolute, complete, entire, full, unlimited, wholehearted
2 OPEN, demonstrative, extrovert, free, outgoing, uninhibited, unrestrained

unresolved adjective UNDECIDED, doubtful, moot, unanswered, undetermined, unsettled, unsolved, vague

unrest noun DISCONTENT, agitation, discord, dissension, protest, rebellion, sedition, strife

unrestrained adjective
UNCONTROLLED, abandoned, free, immoderate, intemperate, unbounded, unbridled, unchecked, uninhibited

unrestricted adjective
1 UNLIMITED, absolute, free, open, unbounded, unregulated
2 OPEN, public

unrivaled adjective UNPARALLELED, beyond compare, incomparable, matchless, supreme, unequaled, unmatched, unsurpassed

unruly adjective UNCONTROLLABLE, disobedient, mutinous, rebellious, wayward, wild, willful

unsafe adjective DANGEROUS, hazardous, insecure, perilous, risky, unreliable

unsatisfactory adjective

UNACCEPTABLE, deficient,
disappointing, inadequate,
insufficient, lousy (*slang*), not
good enough, not up to scratch
(*informal*), poor

unsavory *adjective* 1 UNPLEASANT,
distasteful, nasty, obnoxious,
offensive, repellent, repulsive,
revolting, scuzzy (*slang*)

2 UNAPPETIZING, nauseating,
sickening, unpalatable

unscathed *adjective* UNHARMED,
safe, unhurt, uninjured,
unmarked, whole

unscrupulous *adjective*
UNPRINCIPLED, corrupt, dishonest,
dishonorable, immoral, improper,
unethical

unseat *verb* 1 THROW, unhorse,
unsaddle

2 DEPOSE, dethrone, displace,
oust, overthrow, remove

unseemly *adjective* IMPROPER,
inappropriate, indecorous,
unbecoming, undignified,
unsuitable

unseen *adjective* UNOBSERVED,
concealed, hidden, invisible,
obscure, undetected, unnoticed

unselfish *adjective* GENEROUS,
altruistic, kind, magnanimous,
noble, selfless, self-sacrificing

unsettle *verb* DISTURB, agitate,
bother, confuse, disconcert, faze,
fluster, perturb, ruffle, trouble,
upset

unsettled *adjective* 1 UNSTABLE,
disorderly, insecure, shaky,
unsteady

2 RESTLESS, agitated, anxious,
confused, disturbed, flustered,
restive, shaken, tense, wired
(*slang*)

3 CHANGING, inconstant,
uncertain, variable

unshakable *adjective* FIRM,

absolute, fixed, immovable,
staunch, steadfast, sure,
unswerving, unwavering

unsightly *adjective* UGLY,
disagreeable, dumpy (*informal*),
hideous, homely (*U.S.*), horrid,
repulsive, scuzzy (*slang*),
unattractive

unskilled *adjective*
UNPROFESSIONAL, amateurish,
cowboy (*informal*), inexperienced,
unqualified, untrained

unsociable *adjective* UNFRIENDLY,
chilly, cold, distant, hostile,
retiring, unforthcoming,
withdrawn

unsolicited *adjective*
UNREQUESTED, gratuitous,
unasked for, uncalled-for,
uninvited, unsought

unsophisticated *adjective*
1 NATURAL, artless, childlike,
guileless, ingenuous, unaffected

2 SIMPLE, dumpy (*informal*),
frowzy, homely (*U.S.*), plain,
uncomplicated, unrefined,
unspecialized

unsound *adjective* 1 UNHEALTHY,
ailing, defective, diseased, ill,
unbalanced, unstable, unwell,
weak

2 UNRELIABLE, defective,
fallacious, false, flawed, illogical,
shaky, specious, weak

unspeakable *adjective*
1 INDESCRIBABLE, inconceivable,
unbelievable, unimaginable

2 DREADFUL, abominable,
appalling, awful, heinous,
horrible, monstrous, shocking

unspoiled, unspoilt *adjective*
1 PERFECT, intact, preserved,
unchanged, undamaged,
untouched

2 NATURAL, artless, innocent,
unaffected

unspoken *adjective* TACIT, implicit, implied, understood, unexpressed, unstated

unstable *adjective* 1 INSECURE, precarious, shaky, tottering, unsettled, unsteady, wobbly
2 CHANGEABLE, fitful, fluctuating, inconstant, unpredictable, variable, volatile
3 UNPREDICTABLE, capricious, changeable, erratic, inconsistent, irrational, temperamental

unsteady *adjective* 1 UNSTABLE, infirm, insecure, precarious, shaky, unsafe, wobbly
2 CHANGEABLE, erratic, inconstant, temperamental, unsettled, volatile

unsuccessful *adjective* 1 USELESS, failed, fruitless, futile, unavailing, unproductive, vain
2 UNLUCKY, hapless, luckless, unfortunate

unsuitable *adjective* INAPPROPRIATE, improper, inapposite, inapt, ineligible, unacceptable, unbecoming, unfit, unfitting, unseemly

unsure *adjective* 1 UNCONFIDENT, insecure, unassured
2 DOUBTFUL, distrustful, dubious, hesitant, mistrustful, skeptical, suspicious, unconvinced

unsuspecting *adjective* TRUSTING, credulous, gullible, trustful, unwary

unswerving *adjective* CONSTANT, firm, resolute, single-minded, staunch, steadfast, steady, true, unwavering

unsympathetic *adjective* HARD, callous, cold, cruel, harsh, heartless, insensitive, unfeeling, unkind, unmoved

untangle *verb* DISENTANGLE, extricate, unravel, unsnarl

untenable *adjective* UNSUSTAINABLE, groundless, illogical, indefensible, insupportable, shaky, unsound, weak

unthinkable *adjective* 1 IMPOSSIBLE, absurd, out of the question, unreasonable
2 INCONCEIVABLE, implausible, incredible, unimaginable

untidy *adjective* MESSY, chaotic, cluttered, disarrayed, disordered, jumbled, littered, muddled, shambolic, unkempt

untie *verb* UNDO, free, loosen, release, unbind, unfasten, unknot, unlace

untimely *adjective* 1 EARLY, premature
2 ILL-TIMED, awkward, inappropriate, inconvenient, inopportune, mistimed

untiring *adjective* TIRELESS, constant, determined, dogged, persevering, steady, unflagging, unremitting

untold *adjective* 1 INDESCRIBABLE, inexpressible, undreamed of, unimaginable, unthinkable, unutterable
2 COUNTLESS, incalculable, innumerable, myriad, numberless, uncountable

untouched *adjective* UNHARMED, intact, undamaged, unhurt, uninjured, unscathed

untoward *adjective* 1 ANNOYING, awkward, inconvenient, irritating, troublesome, unfortunate
2 UNLUCKY, adverse, inauspicious, inopportune, unfavorable

untrained *adjective* AMATEUR, green, inexperienced, raw, uneducated, unqualified, unschooled, unskilled, untaught

untroubled *adjective*
UNDISTURBED, calm, cool,
peaceful, placid, tranquil, unfazed
(*informal*), unperturbed, unworried

untrue *adjective* 1 FALSE, deceptive,
dishonest, erroneous, inaccurate,
incorrect, lying, mistaken, wrong
2 UNFAITHFUL, deceitful, disloyal,
faithless, false, inconstant,
treacherous, untrustworthy

untrustworthy *adjective*
UNRELIABLE, deceitful, devious,
dishonest, disloyal, false, slippery,
treacherous, tricky

untruth *noun* LIE, deceit,
falsehood, fib, pork pie (*Brit. slang*),
porky (*Brit. slang*), story, white lie

untruthful *adjective* DISHONEST,
deceitful, deceptive, false, lying,
mendacious

unusual *adjective* EXTRAORDINARY,
curious, different, exceptional,
odd, queer, rare, remarkable,
singular, strange, uncommon,
unconventional

unveil *verb* REVEAL, disclose,
divulge, expose, make known,
uncover

unwanted *adjective* UNDESIRED,
outcast, rejected, uninvited,
unneeded, unsolicited,
unwelcome

unwarranted *adjective*
UNNECESSARY, gratuitous,
groundless, indefensible,
inexcusable, uncalled-for,
unjustified, unprovoked

unwavering *adjective* STEADY,
consistent, determined,
immovable, resolute, staunch,
steadfast, unshakable,
unswerving

unwelcome *adjective* 1 UNWANTED,
excluded, rejected, unacceptable,
undesirable
2 DISAGREEABLE, displeasing,

distasteful, undesirable,
unpleasant

unwell *adjective* ILL, ailing,
sick, sickly, under the weather
(*informal*), unhealthy

unwholesome *adjective*
1 HARMFUL, deleterious, noxious,
poisonous, unhealthy
2 WICKED, bad, corrupting,
degrading, demoralizing, evil,
immoral

unwieldy *adjective* 1 AWKWARD,
cumbersome, inconvenient,
unmanageable
2 BULKY, clumsy, hefty, massive,
ponderous

unwilling *adjective* RELUCTANT,
averse, disinclined, grudging,
indisposed, loath, resistant,
unenthusiastic

unwind *verb* 1 UNRAVEL, slacken,
uncoil, undo, unroll, untwine,
untwist
2 RELAX, de-stress, loosen up, take
it easy, wind down

unwise *adjective* FOOLISH,
foolhardy, improvident,
imprudent, inadvisable,
injudicious, rash, reckless,
senseless, silly, stupid

unwitting *adjective*
1 UNINTENTIONAL, accidental,
chance, inadvertent, involuntary,
unplanned
2 UNKNOWING, ignorant,
innocent, unaware, unconscious,
unsuspecting

unworldly *adjective* 1 SPIRITUAL,
metaphysical, nonmaterialistic
2 NAIVE, idealistic, innocent,
unsophisticated

unworthy *adjective*
1 UNDESERVING, not fit for, not
good enough
2 DISHONORABLE, base,
contemptible, degrading,

discreditable, disgraceful, disreputable, ignoble, lousy (*slang*), shameful

3 ▷▷ **unworthy of** UNBEFITTING, beneath, inappropriate, unbecoming, unfitting, unseemly, unsuitable

unwritten *adjective* 1 ORAL, vocal
2 CUSTOMARY, accepted, tacit, understood

unyielding *adjective* FIRM, adamant, immovable, inflexible, obdurate, obstinate, resolute, rigid, stiff-necked, stubborn, tough, uncompromising

upbeat *adjective* CHEERFUL, cheery, encouraging, hopeful, optimistic, positive

upbraid *verb* SCOLD, admonish, berate, rebuke, reprimand, reproach, reprove

upbringing *noun* EDUCATION, breeding, raising, rearing, training

update *verb* REVISE, amend, bring up to date, modernize, renew

upgrade *verb* PROMOTE, advance, better, elevate, enhance, improve, raise

upheaval *noun* DISTURBANCE, disorder, disruption, revolution, turmoil

uphill *adjective* 1 ASCENDING, climbing, mounting, rising
2 ARDUOUS, difficult, exhausting, grueling, hard, laborious, strenuous, taxing, tough

uphold *verb* SUPPORT, advocate, aid, back, champion, defend, endorse, maintain, promote, sustain

upkeep *noun* 1 MAINTENANCE, keep, repair, running, subsistence
2 OVERHEADS, expenditure, expenses, running costs

uplift *verb* 1 RAISE, elevate, hoist, lift up
2 IMPROVE, advance, better, edify, inspire, raise, refine
▶ *noun* 3 IMPROVEMENT, advancement, edification, enhancement, enlightenment, enrichment, refinement

upmarket *adjective* (*informal*) UPPER-CLASS, classy (*informal*), grand, high-class, luxurious, posh (*informal, chiefly Brit.*), ritzy (*slang*), smart, stylish, swanky (*informal*), swish (*informal, chiefly Brit.*)

upper *adjective* 1 HIGHER, high, loftier, top, topmost
2 SUPERIOR, eminent, greater, important

upper-class *adjective* ARISTOCRATIC, blue-blooded, highborn, high-class, noble, patrician

upper hand *noun* CONTROL, advantage, ascendancy, edge, mastery, supremacy

uppermost *adjective* 1 TOP, highest, loftiest, topmost
2 SUPREME, chief, dominant, foremost, greatest, leading, main, principal

uppity *adjective* (*informal*) CONCEITED, bumptious, cocky, full of oneself, impertinent, self-important, uppish (*Brit. informal*)

upright *adjective* 1 VERTICAL, erect, perpendicular, straight
2 HONEST, conscientious, ethical, good, honorable, just, principled, righteous, virtuous

uprising *noun* REBELLION, disturbance, insurgence, insurrection, mutiny, revolt, revolution, rising

uproar *noun* COMMOTION, din, furor, mayhem, noise, outcry, pandemonium, racket, riot, turmoil

uproarious adjective 1 HILARIOUS, hysterical, killing (*informal*), rib-tickling, rip-roaring (*informal*), side-splitting, very funny
2 LOUD, boisterous, rollicking, unrestrained

uproot verb 1 PULL UP, dig up, rip up, root out, weed out
2 DISPLACE, exile

upset adjective 1 SICK, ill, queasy
2 DISTRESSED, agitated, bothered, dismayed, disturbed, grieved, hurt, put out, troubled, worried
3 DISORDERED, chaotic, confused, disarrayed, in disarray, muddled
4 OVERTURNED, capsized, spilled, upside down
▶ verb 5 TIP OVER, capsize, knock over, overturn, spill
6 MESS UP, change, disorder, disorganize, disturb, spoil
7 DISTRESS, agitate, bother, disconcert, disturb, faze, fluster, grieve, perturb, ruffle, trouble
▶ noun 8 REVERSAL, defeat, shake-up (*informal*)
9 ILLNESS, bug (*informal*), complaint, disorder, malady, sickness
10 DISTRESS, agitation, bother, disturbance, shock, trouble, worry

upshot noun RESULT, culmination, end, end result, finale, outcome, sequel

upside down adjective 1 INVERTED, backward, overturned, upturned
2 CONFUSED, chaotic, disordered, higgledy-piggledy (*informal*), muddled, topsy-turvy

upstanding adjective HONEST, ethical, good, honorable, incorruptible, moral, principled, upright

upstart noun SOCIAL CLIMBER, arriviste, *nouveau riche*, parvenu

uptight adjective (*informal*) TENSE, anxious, edgy, on edge, uneasy, wired (*slang*)

up-to-date adjective MODERN, cool (*informal*), current, fashionable, in vogue, phat (*slang*), stylish, trendy (*informal*), up-to-the-minute

upturn noun RISE, advancement, improvement, increase, recovery, revival, upsurge, upswing

urban adjective CIVIC, city, metropolitan, municipal, town

urbane adjective SOPHISTICATED, courteous, cultivated, cultured, debonair, polished, refined, smooth, suave, well-bred

urchin noun RAGAMUFFIN, brat, gamin, waif

urge noun 1 IMPULSE, compulsion, desire, drive, itch, longing, thirst, wish, yearning
▶ verb 2 BEG, beseech, entreat, exhort, implore, plead
3 ADVOCATE, advise, counsel, recommend, support
4 DRIVE, compel, force, goad, impel, incite, induce, press, push, spur

urgency noun IMPORTANCE, extremity, gravity, hurry, necessity, need, pressure, seriousness

urgent adjective CRUCIAL, compelling, critical, immediate, imperative, important, pressing

usable adjective SERVICEABLE, available, current, functional, practical, utilizable, valid, working

usage noun 1 USE, control, employment, handling, management, operation, running
2 PRACTICE, convention, custom, habit, method, mode, procedure, regime, routine

use verb 1 EMPLOY, apply, exercise, exert, operate, practice, utilize, work

2 TAKE ADVANTAGE OF, exploit, manipulate

3 CONSUME, exhaust, expend, run through, spend

▶ *noun* **4** USAGE, application, employment, exercise, handling, operation, practice, service

5 GOOD, advantage, avail, benefit, help, point, profit, service, usefulness, value

6 PURPOSE, end, object, reason

used *adjective* SECOND-HAND, cast-off, nearly new, shopsoiled

used to *adjective* ACCUSTOMED TO, familiar with

useful *adjective* HELPFUL, advantageous, beneficial, effective, fruitful, practical, profitable, serviceable, valuable, win-win (*informal*), worthwhile

usefulness *noun* HELPFULNESS, benefit, convenience, effectiveness, efficacy, practicality, use, utility, value, worth

useless *adjective* **1** WORTHLESS, fruitless, futile, impractical, ineffectual, pointless, unproductive, vain, valueless

2 (*informal*) INEPT, hopeless, incompetent, ineffectual, no good

use up *verb* CONSUME, absorb, drain, exhaust, finish, run through

usher *noun* **1** ATTENDANT, doorkeeper, doorman, escort, guide

▶ *verb* **2** ESCORT, conduct, direct, guide, lead

usual *adjective* NORMAL, common, customary, everyday, general, habitual, ordinary, regular, routine, standard, typical

usually *adverb* NORMALLY, as a rule, commonly, generally, habitually, mainly, mostly, on the whole

usurp *verb* SEIZE, appropriate, assume, commandeer, take, take over, wrest

utility *noun* USEFULNESS, benefit, convenience, efficacy, practicality, serviceableness

utilize *verb* USE, avail oneself of, employ, make use of, put to use, take advantage of, turn to account

utmost *adjective* **1** GREATEST, chief, highest, maximum, paramount, pre-eminent, supreme

2 FARTHEST, extreme, final, last

▶ *noun* **3** GREATEST, best, hardest, highest

Utopia *noun* PARADISE, bliss, Eden, Garden of Eden, heaven, Shangri-la

Utopian *adjective* PERFECT, dream, fantasy, ideal, idealistic, imaginary, romantic, visionary

utter[1] *verb* EXPRESS, articulate, pronounce, say, speak, voice

utter[2] *adjective* ABSOLUTE, complete, downright, outright, sheer, thorough, total, unmitigated

utterance *noun* SPEECH, announcement, declaration, expression, remark, statement, words

utterly *adverb* TOTALLY, absolutely, completely, entirely, extremely, fully, perfectly, thoroughly

vacancy *noun* JOB, opening, opportunity, position, post, situation

vacant *adjective* 1 UNOCCUPIED, available, empty, free, idle, unfilled, untenanted, void
2 VAGUE, absent-minded, abstracted, blank, dreamy, idle, inane, vacuous

vacate *verb* LEAVE, evacuate, quit

vacuous *adjective* UNINTELLIGENT, blank, inane, stupid, uncomprehending, vacant

vacuum *noun* EMPTINESS, gap, nothingness, space, vacuity, void

vagabond *noun* BEGGAR, down-and-out, itinerant, rover, tramp, vagrant

vagrant *noun* 1 TRAMP, drifter, hobo (U.S.), itinerant, rolling stone, wanderer
► *adjective* 2 ITINERANT, nomadic, roaming, rootless, roving, unsettled, vagabond

vague *adjective* UNCLEAR, equivocal, hazy, ill-defined, imprecise, indefinite, indeterminate, indistinct, loose, nebulous, uncertain, unspecified

vain *adjective* 1 PROUD, arrogant, conceited, egotistical, narcissistic, self-important, swaggering
2 FUTILE, abortive, fruitless, idle, pointless, senseless, unavailing, unprofitable, useless, worthless
► *noun* 3 ▷▷ **in vain** TO NO AVAIL, fruitless(ly), ineffectual(ly), unsuccessful(ly), useless(ly), vain(ly)

valiant *adjective* BRAVE, bold, courageous, fearless, gallant, heroic, intrepid, lion-hearted

valid *adjective* 1 LOGICAL, cogent, convincing, good, sound, telling, well-founded, well-grounded
2 LEGAL, authentic, bona fide, genuine, lawful, legitimate, official

validate *verb* CONFIRM, authenticate, authorize, certify, corroborate, endorse, ratify, substantiate

validity *noun* 1 SOUNDNESS, cogency, force, power, strength, weight
2 LEGALITY, authority, lawfulness, legitimacy, right

valley *noun* HOLLOW, dale, dell, depression, glen, vale

valor *noun* BRAVERY, boldness, courage, fearlessness, gallantry, heroism, intrepidity, spirit

valuable *adjective* 1 PRECIOUS, costly, dear, expensive, high-priced
2 USEFUL, beneficial, helpful, important, prized, profitable, worthwhile
► *noun* 3 ▷▷ **valuables** TREASURES, heirlooms

value *noun* 1 IMPORTANCE, advantage, benefit, desirability, merit, profit, usefulness, utility, worth
2 COST, market price, rate
3 ▷▷ **values** PRINCIPLES, ethics,

(moral) standards
▶ *verb* 4 EVALUATE, appraise,
assess, estimate, price, rate, set at
5 RESPECT, appreciate, cherish,
esteem, hold dear, prize, regard
highly, treasure

vandal *noun* HOOLIGAN,
delinquent, rowdy, yob *or* yobbo
(*Brit. slang*)

vanguard *noun* FORERUNNERS,
cutting edge, forefront, front line,
leaders, spearhead, trailblazers,
trendsetters, van

vanish *verb* DISAPPEAR, dissolve,
evanesce, evaporate, fade (away),
melt (away)

vanity *noun* PRIDE, arrogance,
conceit, conceitedness, egotism,
narcissism

vanquish *verb* (*literary*) DEFEAT,
beat, conquer, crush, master,
overcome, overpower, overwhelm,
triumph over

vapid *adjective* DULL, bland, boring,
flat, insipid, tame, uninspiring,
uninteresting, weak, wishy-
washy (*informal*)

vapor *noun* MIST, exhalation, fog,
haze, steam

variable *adjective* CHANGEABLE,
flexible, fluctuating,
inconstant, mutable, shifting,
temperamental, uneven,
unstable, unsteady

variance *noun* ▷▷ **at variance** IN
DISAGREEMENT, at loggerheads, at
odds, at sixes and sevens (*informal*),
conflicting, out of line

variant *adjective* 1 DIFFERENT,
alternative, divergent, modified
▶ *noun* 2 VARIATION, alternative,
development, modification

variation *noun* DIFFERENCE,
change, departure, deviation,
diversity, innovation,
modification, novelty, variety

varied *adjective* DIFFERENT,
assorted, diverse, heterogeneous,
miscellaneous, mixed, motley,
sundry, various

variety *noun* 1 DIVERSITY,
change, difference, discrepancy,
diversification, multifariousness,
variation
2 RANGE, array, assortment,
collection, cross section, medley,
miscellany, mixture
3 TYPE, brand, breed, category,
class, kind, sort, species, strain

various *adjective* DIFFERENT,
assorted, disparate, distinct,
diverse, miscellaneous, several,
sundry, varied

varnish *noun or verb* POLISH, glaze,
gloss, lacquer

vary *verb* CHANGE, alter, differ,
disagree, diverge, fluctuate

vast *adjective* HUGE, boundless,
colossal, enormous, gigantic,
great, immense, massive,
monumental, wide

vault¹ *noun* 1 STRONGROOM,
depository, repository
2 CRYPT, catacomb, cellar, charnel
house, mausoleum, tomb,
undercroft

vault² *verb* JUMP, bound, clear,
hurdle, leap, spring

vaulted *adjective* ARCHED,
cavernous, domed

veer *verb* SWERVE, change course,
change direction, sheer, shift,
turn

vegetate *verb* STAGNATE,
deteriorate, go to seed, idle,
languish, loaf

vehemence *noun* FORCEFULNESS,
ardor, emphasis, energy, fervor,
force, intensity, passion, vigor

vehement *adjective* STRONG,
ardent, emphatic, fervent, fierce,
forceful, impassioned, intense,

passionate, powerful

vehicle *noun* 1 TRANSPORT, conveyance, transportation
2 MEDIUM, apparatus, channel, means, mechanism, organ

veil *noun* 1 COVER, blind, cloak, curtain, disguise, film, mask, screen, shroud
▶ *verb* 2 COVER, cloak, conceal, disguise, hide, mask, obscure, screen, shield

veiled *adjective* DISGUISED, concealed, covert, hinted at, implied, masked, suppressed

vein *noun* 1 BLOOD VESSEL
2 SEAM, course, current, lode, stratum, streak, stripe
3 MOOD, mode, note, style, temper, tenor, tone

velocity *noun* SPEED, pace, quickness, rapidity, swiftness

velvety *adjective* SMOOTH, delicate, downy, soft

vendetta *noun* FEUD, bad blood, quarrel

veneer *noun* MASK, appearance, façade, front, guise, pretense, semblance, show

venerable *adjective* RESPECTED, august, esteemed, honored, revered, sage, wise, worshipped

venerate *verb* RESPECT, adore, esteem, honor, look up to, revere, reverence, worship

vengeance *noun* REVENGE, reprisal, requital, retaliation, retribution

venom *noun* 1 MALICE, acrimony, bitterness, hate, rancor, spite, spleen, virulence
2 POISON, bane, toxin

venomous *adjective* 1 MALICIOUS, hostile, malignant, rancorous, savage, spiteful, vicious, vindictive
2 POISONOUS, mephitic, noxious,

toxic, virulent

vent *noun* 1 OUTLET, aperture, duct, opening, orifice
▶ *verb* 2 EXPRESS, air, discharge, emit, give vent to, pour out, release, utter, voice

venture *noun* 1 UNDERTAKING, adventure, endeavor, enterprise, gamble, hazard, project, risk
▶ *verb* 2 RISK, chance, hazard, speculate, stake, wager
3 DARE, hazard, make bold, presume, take the liberty, volunteer
4 GO, embark on, plunge into, set out

verbal *adjective* SPOKEN, oral, unwritten, word-of-mouth

verbatim *adverb* EXACTLY, precisely, to the letter, word for word

verbose *adjective* LONG-WINDED, circumlocutory, diffuse, periphrastic, prolix, tautological, windy, wordy

verbosity *noun* LONG-WINDEDNESS, loquaciousness, prolixity, verboseness, wordiness

verdant *adjective* GREEN, flourishing, fresh, grassy, leafy, lush

verdict *noun* DECISION, adjudication, conclusion, finding, judgment, opinion, sentence

verge *noun* 1 BORDER, boundary, brim, brink, edge, limit, margin, threshold
▶ *verb* 2 ▷▷ **verge on** BORDER, approach, come near

verification *noun* PROOF, authentication, confirmation, corroboration, substantiation, validation

verify *verb* CHECK, authenticate, bear out, confirm, corroborate, prove, substantiate, support, validate

vernacular *noun* DIALECT, idiom, parlance, patois, speech

versatile *adjective* ADAPTABLE, adjustable, all-purpose, all-round, flexible, multifaceted, resourceful, variable

versed *adjective* KNOWLEDGEABLE, acquainted, conversant, experienced, familiar, practiced, proficient, seasoned, well informed

version *noun* 1 FORM, design, model, style, variant
2 ACCOUNT, adaptation, interpretation, portrayal, rendering

vertical *adjective* UPRIGHT, erect, on end, perpendicular

vertigo *noun* DIZZINESS, giddiness, light-headedness

verve *noun* ENTHUSIASM, animation, energy, gusto, liveliness, sparkle, spirit, vitality

very *adverb* 1 EXTREMELY, acutely, decidedly, deeply, exceedingly, greatly, highly, profoundly, uncommonly, unusually
▶ *adjective* 2 EXACT, precise, selfsame

vessel *noun* 1 SHIP, boat, craft
2 CONTAINER, pot, receptacle, utensil

vest *verb* (with *in* or *with*) PLACE, bestow, confer, consign, endow, entrust, invest, settle

vestibule *noun* HALL, anteroom, foyer, lobby, porch, portico

vestige *noun* TRACE, glimmer, indication, remnant, scrap, suspicion

vet *verb* CHECK, appraise, examine, investigate, review, scrutinize

veteran *noun* 1 OLD HAND, old stager, past master, warhorse (*informal*)
▶ *adjective* 2 LONG-SERVING, battle-scarred, old, seasoned

veto *noun* 1 BAN, boycott, embargo, interdict, prohibition
▶ *verb* 2 BAN, boycott, disallow, forbid, prohibit, reject, rule out, turn down

vex *verb* ANNOY, bother, distress, exasperate, irritate, plague, trouble, upset, worry

vexation *noun* 1 ANNOYANCE, chagrin, displeasure, dissatisfaction, exasperation, frustration, irritation, pique
2 PROBLEM, bother, difficulty, hassle (*informal*), headache (*informal*), nuisance, trouble, worry

viable *adjective* WORKABLE, applicable, feasible, operable, practicable, usable

vibrant *adjective* ENERGETIC, alive, animated, dynamic, sparkling, spirited, vigorous, vivacious, vivid

vibrate *verb* SHAKE, fluctuate, judder (*informal*), oscillate, pulsate, quiver, reverberate, shudder, sway, throb, tremble

vibration *noun* TREMOR, judder (*informal*), oscillation, pulsation, quiver, reverberation, shake, shudder, throbbing, trembling

vicarious *adjective* INDIRECT, delegated, substituted, surrogate

vice *noun* 1 WICKEDNESS, corruption, depravity, evil, immorality, iniquity, sin, turpitude
2 FAULT, blemish, defect, failing, imperfection, shortcoming, weakness

vice versa *adverb* CONVERSELY, contrariwise, in reverse, the other way round

vicinity *noun* NEIGHBORHOOD, area, district, environs, locality, neck of the woods (*informal*), proximity

vicious *adjective* 1 VIOLENT,
barbarous, cruel, ferocious,
savage, wicked
2 MALICIOUS, cruel, mean, spiteful,
venomous, vindictive

victim *noun* CASUALTY, fatality,
martyr, sacrifice, scapegoat,
sufferer

victimize *verb* PERSECUTE,
discriminate against, have it in
for (someone) (*informal*), pick on

victor *noun* WINNER, champion,
conqueror, prizewinner,
vanquisher

victorious *adjective* WINNING,
champion, conquering, first,
prizewinning, successful,
triumphant, vanquishing

victory *noun* WIN, conquest,
success, triumph

vie *verb* COMPETE, contend, strive,
struggle

view *noun* 1 (sometimes plural)
OPINION, attitude, belief,
conviction, feeling, impression,
point of view, sentiment
2 SCENE, landscape, outlook,
panorama, perspective, picture,
prospect, spectacle, vista
3 VISION, sight
▶ *verb* 4 REGARD, consider, deem,
look on

viewer *noun* WATCHER, observer,
onlooker, spectator

vigilance *noun* WATCHFULNESS,
alertness, attentiveness,
carefulness, caution,
circumspection, observance

vigilant *adjective* WATCHFUL, alert,
attentive, careful, cautious,
circumspect, on one's guard, on
the lookout, wakeful

vigor *noun* ENERGY, animation,
dynamism, forcefulness, gusto,
liveliness, power, spirit, strength,

verve, vitality

vigorous *adjective* ENERGETIC,
active, dynamic, forceful,
lively, lusty, powerful, spirited,
strenuous, strong

vigorously *adverb* ENERGETICALLY,
forcefully, hard, lustily,
strenuously, strongly

vile *adjective* 1 WICKED, corrupt,
degenerate, depraved, evil,
nefarious, perverted
2 DISGUSTING, foul, horrid, nasty,
nauseating, offensive, repugnant,
repulsive, revolting, scuzzy (*slang*),
sickening

vilify *verb* MALIGN, abuse, berate,
denigrate, disparage, revile,
slander, smear

villain *noun* 1 EVILDOER,
blackguard, criminal, miscreant,
reprobate, rogue, scoundrel,
wretch
2 ANTIHERO, baddy (*informal*)

villainous *adjective* WICKED, bad,
cruel, degenerate, depraved, evil,
fiendish, nefarious, vicious, vile

villainy *noun* WICKEDNESS,
delinquency, depravity, devilry,
iniquity, turpitude, vice

vindicate *verb* 1 CLEAR, absolve,
acquit, exculpate, exonerate,
rehabilitate
2 JUSTIFY, defend, excuse

vindication *noun* 1 EXONERATION,
exculpation, rehabilitation
2 JUSTIFICATION, defense, excuse

vindictive *adjective* VENGEFUL,
implacable, malicious, resentful,
revengeful, spiteful, unforgiving,
unrelenting

vintage *adjective* BEST, choice,
classic, prime, select, superior

violate *verb* 1 BREAK, contravene,
disobey, disregard, encroach
upon, infringe, transgress
2 DESECRATE, abuse, befoul, defile,

dishonor, pollute, profane
3 RAPE, abuse, assault, debauch, ravish

violation noun 1 INFRINGEMENT, abuse, breach, contravention, encroachment, infraction, transgression, trespass
2 DESECRATION, defilement, profanation, sacrilege, spoliation

violence noun 1 FORCE, bloodshed, brutality, cruelty, ferocity, fighting, savagery, terrorism
2 INTENSITY, abandon, fervor, force, severity, vehemence

violent adjective DESTRUCTIVE, brutal, cruel, hot-headed, murderous, riotous, savage, uncontrollable, unrestrained, vicious

V.I.P. noun CELEBRITY, big name, luminary, somebody, star

virgin noun 1 MAIDEN, girl
▶ adjective 2 PURE, chaste, immaculate, uncorrupted, undefiled, vestal, virginal

virginity noun CHASTITY, maidenhood

virile adjective MANLY, lusty, macho, manlike, masculine, red-blooded, strong, vigorous

virility noun MASCULINITY, machismo, manhood, vigor

virtual adjective PRACTICAL, essential, in all but name

virtually adverb PRACTICALLY, almost, as good as, in all but name, in effect, in essence, nearly

virtue noun 1 GOODNESS, incorruptibility, integrity, morality, probity, rectitude, righteousness, uprightness, worth
2 MERIT, advantage, asset, attribute, credit, good point, plus (informal), strength

virtuosity noun MASTERY,

brilliance, craft, expertise, flair, panache, polish, skill

virtuoso noun MASTER, artist, genius, maestro, magician

virtuous adjective GOOD, ethical, honorable, incorruptible, moral, praiseworthy, righteous, upright, worthy

virulent adjective POISONOUS, deadly, lethal, pernicious, toxic, venomous

viscous adjective THICK, gelatinous, sticky, syrupy

visible adjective APPARENT, clear, discernible, evident, in view, manifest, observable, perceptible, unconcealed

vision noun 1 SIGHT, eyesight, perception, seeing, view
2 IMAGE, concept, conception, daydream, dream, fantasy, idea, ideal
3 HALLUCINATION, apparition, chimera, delusion, illusion, mirage, revelation
4 FORESIGHT, discernment, farsightedness, imagination, insight, intuition, penetration, prescience

visionary adjective 1 PROPHETIC, mystical
2 IMPRACTICAL, idealistic, quixotic, romantic, speculative, starry-eyed, unrealistic, unworkable, utopian
▶ noun 3 PROPHET, mystic, seer

visit verb 1 CALL ON, drop in on (informal), look (someone) up, stay with, stop by
▶ noun 2 CALL, sojourn, stay, stop

visitation noun 1 INSPECTION, examination, visit
2 CATASTROPHE, blight, calamity, cataclysm, disaster, ordeal, punishment, scourge

visitor noun GUEST, caller,

company

vista *noun* VIEW, panorama, perspective, prospect

visual *adjective* 1 OPTICAL, ocular, optic

2 OBSERVABLE, discernible, perceptible, visible

visualize *verb* PICTURE, conceive of, envisage, imagine

vital *adjective* 1 ESSENTIAL, basic, fundamental, imperative, indispensable, necessary, requisite

2 IMPORTANT, critical, crucial, decisive, key, life-or-death, significant, urgent

3 LIVELY, animated, dynamic, energetic, spirited, vibrant, vigorous, vivacious, zestful

vitality *noun* ENERGY, animation, exuberance, life, liveliness, strength, vigor, vivacity

vitriolic *adjective* BITTER, acerbic, caustic, envenomed, sardonic, scathing, venomous, virulent, withering

vivacious *adjective* LIVELY, bubbling, ebullient, high-spirited, sparkling, spirited, sprightly, upbeat (*informal*), vital

vivacity *noun* LIVELINESS, animation, ebullience, energy, gaiety, high spirits, sparkle, spirit, sprightliness

vivid *adjective* 1 BRIGHT, brilliant, clear, colorful, glowing, intense, rich

2 LIFELIKE, dramatic, graphic, memorable, powerful, realistic, stirring, telling, true to life

vocabulary *noun* WORDS, dictionary, glossary, language, lexicon

vocal *adjective* 1 SPOKEN, oral, said, uttered, voiced

2 OUTSPOKEN, articulate, eloquent, expressive, forthright, frank, plain-spoken, strident, vociferous

vocation *noun* PROFESSION, calling, career, job, mission, pursuit, trade

vociferous *adjective* NOISY, clamorous, loud, outspoken, strident, uproarious, vehement, vocal

vogue *noun* 1 FASHION, craze, custom, mode, style, trend, way

2 *as in* **in vogue** POPULARITY, acceptance, currency, favor, prevalence, usage, use

voice *noun* 1 SOUND, articulation, tone, utterance

2 SAY, view, vote, will, wish

▶ *verb* 3 EXPRESS, air, articulate, declare, enunciate, utter

void *noun* 1 EMPTINESS, blankness, gap, lack, space, vacuity, vacuum

▶ *adjective* 2 INVALID, ineffective, inoperative, null and void, useless, vain, worthless

3 EMPTY, bare, free, tenantless, unfilled, unoccupied, vacant

▶ *verb* 4 INVALIDATE, cancel, nullify, rescind

5 EMPTY, drain, evacuate

volatile *adjective* 1 CHANGEABLE, explosive, inconstant, unsettled, unstable, unsteady, variable

2 TEMPERAMENTAL, erratic, fickle, mercurial, up and down (*informal*)

volition *noun* FREE WILL, choice, choosing, discretion, preference, will

volley *noun* BARRAGE, blast, bombardment, burst, cannonade, fusillade, hail, salvo, shower

voluble *adjective* TALKATIVE, articulate, fluent, forthcoming, glib, loquacious

volume *noun* 1 CAPACITY, compass, dimensions

2 AMOUNT, aggregate, body, bulk, mass, quantity, total

3 BOOK, publication, title, tome, treatise

voluminous adjective LARGE, ample, capacious, cavernous, roomy, vast

voluntarily adverb WILLINGLY, by choice, freely, off one's own bat, of one's own accord

voluntary adjective UNFORCED, discretionary, free, optional, spontaneous, willing

volunteer verb OFFER, step forward

voluptuous adjective 1 BUXOM, ample, curvaceous (informal), enticing, seductive, shapely

2 SENSUAL, epicurean, hedonistic, licentious, luxurious, self-indulgent, sybaritic

vomit verb BE SICK RETCH, barf (slang), disgorge, emit, heave, regurgitate, spew out or up, throw up (informal)

voracious adjective 1 GLUTTONOUS, greedy, hungry, insatiable, omnivorous, ravenous

2 AVID, hungry, insatiable, rapacious, uncontrolled, unquenchable

vortex noun WHIRLPOOL, eddy, maelstrom

vote noun 1 POLL, ballot, franchise, plebiscite, referendum, show of hands

▶ verb 2 ELECT, cast one's vote, opt

voucher noun TICKET, coupon, token

vouch for verb 1 GUARANTEE, answer for, certify, give assurance of, stand witness, swear to

2 CONFIRM, affirm, assert, attest to, support, uphold

vow noun 1 PROMISE, oath, pledge

▶ verb 2 PROMISE, affirm, pledge, swear

voyage noun JOURNEY, crossing, cruise, passage, trip

vulgar adjective CRUDE, coarse, common, impolite, indecent, off-color, ribald, risqué, rude, tasteless, uncouth, unrefined

vulgarity noun CRUDENESS, bad taste, coarseness, indelicacy, ribaldry, rudeness, tastelessness

vulnerable adjective 1 WEAK, sensitive, susceptible, tender, thin-skinned

2 EXPOSED, accessible, assailable, defenseless, unprotected, wide open

wacky *adjective* (*informal*) FOOLISH, absurd, asinine, crackpot (*informal*), crazy, idiotic, silly, stupid, witless

wad *noun* MASS, bundle, hunk, roll

waddle *verb* SHUFFLE, sway, toddle, totter, wobble

wade *verb* 1 WALK THROUGH, ford, paddle, splash
2 ▷▷ **wade through** PLOW THROUGH, drudge at, labor at, peg away at, toil at, work one's way through

waft *verb* CARRY, bear, convey, drift, float, transport

wag¹ *verb* 1 WAVE, bob, nod, quiver, shake, stir, vibrate, waggle, wiggle
▶ *noun* 2 WAVE, bob, nod, quiver, shake, vibration, waggle, wiggle

wage *noun* 1 *or* **wages** PAYMENT, allowance, emolument, fee, pay, recompense, remuneration, reward, stipend
▶ *verb* 2 ENGAGE IN, carry on, conduct, practice, proceed with, prosecute, pursue, undertake

wager *noun* 1 BET, flutter (*Brit. informal*), gamble, punt (*chiefly Brit.*)
▶ *verb* 2 BET, chance, gamble, lay,

pledge, risk, speculate, stake, venture

waif *noun* STRAY, foundling, orphan

wail *verb* 1 CRY, bawl, grieve, howl, lament, weep, yowl
▶ *noun* 2 CRY, complaint, howl, lament, moan, weeping, yowl

wait *verb* 1 REMAIN, hang fire, hold back, linger, pause, rest, stay, tarry
▶ *noun* 2 DELAY, halt, hold-up, interval, pause, rest, stay

waiter, waitress *noun* ATTENDANT, server, steward *or* stewardess

wait on *or* **upon** *verb* SERVE, attend, minister to, tend

waive *verb* SET ASIDE, abandon, dispense with, forgo, give up, relinquish, remit, renounce

wake¹ *verb* 1 AWAKEN, arise, awake, bestir, come to, get up, rouse, stir
2 ACTIVATE, animate, arouse, excite, fire, galvanize, kindle, provoke, stimulate, stir up
▶ *noun* 3 VIGIL, deathwatch, funeral, watch

wake² *noun* SLIPSTREAM, aftermath, backwash, path, track, trail, train, wash, waves

wakeful *adjective* 1 SLEEPLESS, insomniac, restless
2 WATCHFUL, alert, alive, attentive, observant, on guard, vigilant, wary

waken *verb* AWAKEN, activate, arouse, awake, rouse, stir

walk *verb* 1 GO, amble, hike, march, move, pace, step, stride, stroll
2 ESCORT, accompany, convoy, take
▶ *noun* 3 STROLL, hike, march, promenade, ramble, saunter, trek, trudge
4 GAIT, carriage, step
5 PATH, alley, avenue, esplanade, footpath, lane, promenade, trail

6 ▷▷ **walk of life** PROFESSION, calling, career, field, line, trade, vocation

walker noun PEDESTRIAN, hiker, rambler, wayfarer

walkout noun STRIKE, industrial action, protest, stoppage

walkover noun PUSHOVER (*slang*), breeze (*informal*), cakewalk (*informal*), child's play (*informal*), doddle (*Brit. slang*), picnic (*informal*), piece of cake (*informal*)

wall noun 1 PARTITION, enclosure, screen
2 BARRIER, fence, hedge, impediment, obstacle, obstruction

wallet noun HOLDER, case, pocketbook, pouch, purse

wallop verb 1 HIT, batter, beat, clobber (*slang*), pound, pummel, strike, thrash, thump, whack
▶ noun 2 BLOW, bash, punch, slug, smack, thump, thwack, whack

wallow verb 1 REVEL, bask, delight, glory, luxuriate, relish, take pleasure
2 ROLL ABOUT, splash around

wan adjective PALE, anemic, ashen, pallid, pasty, sickly, washed out, white

wand noun STICK, baton, rod

wander verb 1 ROAM, drift, meander, ramble, range, rove, stray, stroll
2 DEVIATE, depart, digress, diverge, err, go astray, swerve, veer
▶ noun 3 EXCURSION, cruise, meander, ramble

wanderer noun TRAVELER, drifter, gypsy, nomad, rambler, rover, vagabond, voyager

wandering adjective NOMADIC, itinerant, migratory, peripatetic, rootless, roving, traveling, vagrant, wayfaring

wane verb 1 DECLINE, decrease, diminish, dwindle, ebb, fade, fail, lessen, subside, taper off, weaken
▶ noun 2 ▷▷ **on the wane**
DECLINING, dwindling, ebbing, fading, obsolescent, on the decline, tapering off, weakening

wangle verb CONTRIVE, arrange, engineer, fiddle (*informal*), fix (*informal*), maneuver, manipulate, pull off

want verb 1 DESIRE, covet, crave, hanker after, hope for, hunger for, long for, thirst for, wish, yearn for
2 NEED, call for, demand, lack, miss, require
▶ noun 3 WISH, appetite, craving, desire, longing, need, requirement, yearning
4 LACK, absence, dearth, deficiency, famine, insufficiency, paucity, scarcity, shortage
5 POVERTY, destitution, neediness, penury, privation

wanting adjective 1 LACKING, absent, incomplete, missing, short, shy
2 INADEQUATE, defective, deficient, faulty, imperfect, lousy (*slang*), poor, substandard, unsound

wanton adjective 1 UNPROVOKED, arbitrary, gratuitous, groundless, motiveless, needless, senseless, uncalled-for, unjustifiable, willful
2 PROMISCUOUS, dissipated, dissolute, immoral, lecherous, libidinous, loose, lustful, shameless, unchaste

war noun 1 FIGHTING, battle, combat, conflict, enmity, hostilities, struggle, warfare
▶ verb 2 FIGHT, battle, campaign against, clash, combat, take up arms, wage war

warble verb SING, chirp, trill, twitter

ward noun 1 ROOM, apartment, cubicle
2 DISTRICT, area, division, precinct, quarter, zone
3 DEPENDANT, charge, minor, protégé, pupil

warden noun KEEPER, administrator, caretaker, curator, custodian, guardian, ranger, superintendent

ward off verb REPEL, avert, avoid, deflect, fend off, parry, stave off

wardrobe noun 1 CLOTHES CUPBOARD, closet
2 CLOTHES, apparel, attire

warehouse noun STORE, depository, depot, stockroom, storehouse

wares plural noun GOODS, commodities, merchandise, produce, products, stock, stuff

warfare noun WAR, arms, battle, combat, conflict, fighting, hostilities

warily adverb CAUTIOUSLY, carefully, charily, circumspectly, distrustfully, gingerly, suspiciously, vigilantly, watchfully, with care

warlike adjective BELLIGERENT, aggressive, bellicose, bloodthirsty, hawkish, hostile, martial, warmongering

warlock noun MAGICIAN, conjurer, enchanter, sorcerer, wizard

warm adjective 1 HEATED, balmy, lukewarm, pleasant, sunny, tepid, thermal
2 AFFECTIONATE, amorous, cordial, friendly, hospitable, kindly, loving, tender
▶ verb 3 HEAT, heat up, melt, thaw, warm up

warmonger noun HAWK, belligerent, militarist, saber-rattler

warmth noun 1 HEAT, hotness, warmness
2 AFFECTION, amorousness, cordiality, heartiness, kindliness, love, tenderness

warn verb NOTIFY, advise, alert, apprise, caution, forewarn, give notice, inform, make (someone) aware, tip off

warning noun CAUTION, advice, alarm, alert, notification, omen, sign, tip-off

warp verb 1 TWIST, bend, contort, deform, distort
▶ noun 2 TWIST, bend, contortion, distortion, kink

warrant noun 1 AUTHORIZATION, authority, license, permission, permit, sanction
▶ verb 2 CALL FOR, demand, deserve, excuse, justify, license, necessitate, permit, require, sanction
3 GUARANTEE, affirm, attest, certify, declare, pledge, vouch for

warranty noun GUARANTEE, assurance, bond, certificate, contract, covenant, pledge

warrior noun SOLDIER, combatant, fighter, gladiator, man-at-arms

wary adjective CAUTIOUS, alert, careful, chary, circumspect, distrustful, guarded, suspicious, vigilant, watchful

wash verb 1 CLEAN, bathe, cleanse, launder, rinse, scrub
2 SWEEP AWAY, bear away, carry off, move
3 (informal) BE PLAUSIBLE, bear scrutiny, be convincing, carry weight, hold up, hold water, stand up, stick
▶ noun 4 CLEANING, cleansing, laundering, rinse, scrub

5 COAT, coating, film, layer, overlay
6 SWELL, surge, wave

washout noun FAILURE, disappointment, disaster, dud (*informal*), fiasco, flop (*informal*)

waste verb **1** MISUSE, blow (*slang*), dissipate, fritter away, lavish, squander, throw away
2 ▷▷ **waste away** DECLINE, atrophy, crumble, decay, dwindle, fade, wane, wear out, wither
► noun **3** MISUSE, dissipation, extravagance, frittering away, prodigality, squandering, wastefulness
4 RUBBISH, debris, dross, garbage, leftovers, litter, refuse, scrap, trash
5 ▷▷ **wastes** DESERT, wasteland, wilderness
► adjective **6** UNWANTED, leftover, superfluous, supernumerary, unused, useless, worthless
7 UNCULTIVATED, bare, barren, desolate, empty, uninhabited, unproductive, wild

wasteful adjective EXTRAVAGANT, lavish, prodigal, profligate, spendthrift, thriftless, uneconomical

waster noun LAYABOUT IDLER, couch potato (*slang*), good-for-nothing, loafer, ne'er-do-well, shirker, skiver (*Brit. slang*), wastrel

watch verb **1** LOOK AT, contemplate, eye, observe, regard, see, view
2 GUARD, keep, look after, mind, protect, superintend, take care of, tend
► noun **3** WRISTWATCH, chronometer, timepiece
4 LOOKOUT, observation, surveillance, vigil

watchdog noun **1** GUARD DOG

2 GUARDIAN, custodian, monitor, protector, scrutineer

watchful adjective ALERT, attentive, observant, on the lookout, suspicious, vigilant, wary, wide awake

watchman noun GUARD, caretaker, custodian, security guard

watchword noun MOTTO, battle cry, byword, catch phrase, catchword, maxim, rallying cry, slogan

water noun **1** LIQUID, Hxx2xxO
► verb **2** MOISTEN, dampen, douse, drench, hose, irrigate, soak, spray

water down verb DILUTE, thin, water, weaken

waterfall noun CASCADE, cataract, fall

watertight adjective
1 WATERPROOF
2 FOOLPROOF, airtight, flawless, impregnable, sound, unassailable

watery adjective **1** WET, aqueous, damp, fluid, liquid, moist, soggy
2 DILUTED, runny, thin, washy, watered-down, weak

wave verb **1** SIGNAL, beckon, direct, gesticulate, gesture, indicate, sign
2 FLAP, brandish, flourish, flutter, oscillate, shake, stir, swing, wag
► noun **3** RIPPLE, billow, breaker, ridge, roller, swell, undulation
4 OUTBREAK, flood, rash, rush, stream, surge, upsurge

waver verb **1** HESITATE, dither, falter, fluctuate, hum and haw, seesaw, vacillate
2 TREMBLE, flicker, quiver, shake, totter, wobble

wax verb INCREASE, develop, enlarge, expand, grow, magnify, swell

way noun **1** METHOD, fashion, manner, means, mode, procedure,

process, system, technique
2 STYLE, custom, habit, manner, nature, personality, practice, wont
3 ROUTE, channel, course, direction, path, pathway, road, track, trail
4 JOURNEY, approach, march, passage
5 DISTANCE, length, stretch

wayfarer noun TRAVELER, gypsy, itinerant, nomad, rover, voyager, wanderer

wayward adjective ERRATIC, capricious, inconstant, ungovernable, unmanageable, unpredictable, unruly

weak adjective 1 FEEBLE, debilitated, effete, fragile, frail, infirm, puny, sickly, unsteady
2 UNSAFE, defenseless, exposed, helpless, unguarded, unprotected, vulnerable
3 UNCONVINCING, feeble, flimsy, hollow, lame, pathetic, unsatisfactory
4 TASTELESS, diluted, insipid, runny, thin, watery

weaken verb 1 LESSEN, diminish, dwindle, fade, flag, lower, moderate, reduce, sap, undermine, wane
2 DILUTE, thin out, water down

weakling noun SISSY, baby (informal), drip (informal), wet (Brit. informal), wimp (informal)

weakness noun 1 FRAILTY, decrepitude, feebleness, fragility, infirmity, powerlessness, vulnerability
2 FAILING, blemish, defect, deficiency, fault, flaw, imperfection, lack, shortcoming
3 LIKING, fondness, inclination, partiality, passion, penchant, soft spot

wealth noun 1 RICHES, affluence, capital, fortune, money, opulence, prosperity
2 PLENTY, abundance, copiousness, cornucopia, fullness, profusion, richness

wealthy adjective RICH, affluent, flush (informal), moneyed, opulent, prosperous, well-heeled (informal), well-off, well-to-do

wear verb 1 BE DRESSED IN, don, have on, put on, sport (informal)
2 SHOW, display, exhibit
3 DETERIORATE, abrade, corrode, erode, fray, grind, rub
▶ noun 4 CLOTHES, apparel, attire, costume, dress, garb, garments, gear (informal), things
5 DAMAGE, abrasion, attrition, corrosion, deterioration, erosion, wear and tear

weariness noun TIREDNESS, drowsiness, exhaustion, fatigue, languor, lassitude, lethargy, listlessness

wearing adjective TIRESOME, exasperating, fatiguing, irksome, oppressive, trying, wearisome

wearisome adjective TEDIOUS, annoying, boring, exhausting, fatiguing, irksome, oppressive, tiresome, troublesome, trying, wearing

wear off verb SUBSIDE, decrease, diminish, disappear, dwindle, fade, peter out, wane

weary adjective 1 TIRED, done in (informal), drained, drowsy, exhausted, fatigued, flagging, jaded, sleepy, worn out
2 TIRING, arduous, laborious, tiresome, wearisome
▶ verb 3 TIRE, drain, enervate, fatigue, sap, take it out of (informal), tax, tire out, wear out

weather noun 1 CLIMATE, conditions

▶ *verb* 2 WITHSTAND, brave, come through, endure, overcome, resist, ride out, stand, survive

weave *verb* 1 KNIT, braid, entwine, interlace, intertwine, plait
2 CREATE, build, construct, contrive, fabricate, make up, put together, spin
3 ZIGZAG, crisscross, wind

web *noun* 1 SPIDER'S WEB, cobweb
2 NETWORK, lattice, tangle

wed *verb* 1 MARRY, get married, take the plunge (*informal*), tie the knot (*informal*)
2 UNITE, ally, blend, combine, interweave, join, link, merge

wedding *noun* MARRIAGE, nuptials, wedlock

wedge *noun* 1 BLOCK, chunk, lump
▶ *verb* 2 SQUEEZE, cram, crowd, force, jam, lodge, pack, ram, stuff, thrust

wedlock *noun* MARRIAGE, matrimony

weed out *verb* ELIMINATE, dispense with, eradicate, get rid of, remove, root out, uproot

weedy *adjective* WEAK, feeble, frail, ineffectual, namby-pamby, puny, skinny, thin

weep *verb* CRY, blubber, lament, mourn, shed tears, snivel, sob, whimper

weepy *adjective* (*informal*) SENTIMENTAL, overemotional, schmaltzy (*slang*), slushy (*informal*), soppy (*informal*)

weigh *verb* 1 HAVE A WEIGHT OF, tip the scales at (*informal*)
2 CONSIDER, contemplate, deliberate upon, evaluate, examine, meditate upon, ponder, reflect upon, think over
3 MATTER, carry weight, count

weight *noun* 1 HEAVINESS, load, mass, poundage, tonnage

2 IMPORTANCE, authority, consequence, impact, import, influence, power, value
▶ *verb* 3 LOAD, freight
4 BIAS, load, slant, unbalance

weighty *adjective* 1 IMPORTANT, consequential, crucial, grave, momentous, portentous, serious, significant, solemn
2 HEAVY, burdensome, cumbersome, hefty (*informal*), massive, ponderous

weird *adjective* STRANGE, bizarre, creepy (*informal*), eerie, freakish, mysterious, odd, queer, spooky (*informal*), unnatural

welcome *verb* 1 GREET, embrace, hail, meet, receive
▶ *noun* 2 GREETING, acceptance, hospitality, reception, salutation
▶ *adjective* 3 ACCEPTABLE, agreeable, appreciated, delightful, desirable, gratifying, pleasant, refreshing
4 FREE, under no obligation

weld *verb* JOIN, bind, bond, connect, fuse, link, solder, unite

welfare *noun* 1 WELLBEING, advantage, benefit, good, happiness, health, interest, prosperity
2 BENEFIT, allowance, gift, grant, handout

well¹ *adverb* 1 SATISFACTORILY, agreeably, nicely, pleasantly, smoothly, splendidly, successfully
2 SKILLFULLY, ably, adeptly, adequately, admirably, correctly, efficiently, expertly, proficiently, properly
3 PROSPEROUSLY, comfortably
4 SUITABLY, fairly, fittingly, justly, properly, rightly
5 INTIMATELY, deeply, fully, profoundly, thoroughly
6 FAVORABLY, approvingly,

glowingly, highly, kindly, warmly
7 CONSIDERABLY, abundantly,
amply, fully, greatly, heartily,
highly, substantially, thoroughly,
very much
▶ *adjective* 8 HEALTHY, fit, in fine
fettle, sound
9 SATISFACTORY, agreeable, fine,
pleasing, proper, right, thriving
well² *noun* 1 HOLE, bore, pit, shaft
▶ *verb* 2 FLOW, gush, jet, pour,
spout, spring, spurt, surge
well-known *adjective* FAMOUS,
celebrated, familiar, noted,
popular, renowned
well-off *adjective* RICH, affluent,
comfortable (*informal*), moneyed,
prosperous, wealthy, well-heeled
(*informal*), well-to-do
well-to-do *adjective* RICH,
affluent, comfortable (*informal*),
moneyed, prosperous, wealthy,
well-heeled (*informal*), well-off
well-worn *adjective* STALE, banal,
commonplace, hackneyed,
overused, stereotyped, trite
welt *noun* MARK, contusion, streak,
stripe, wale, weal
welter *noun* JUMBLE, confusion,
hotchpotch, mess, muddle,
tangle, web
wet *adjective* 1 DAMP, dank, moist,
saturated, soaking, sodden, soggy,
sopping, waterlogged, watery
2 RAINY, drizzling, pouring,
raining, showery, teeming
3 (*informal*) FEEBLE, effete,
ineffectual, namby-pamby, soft,
spineless, timorous, weak, weedy
(*informal*)
▶ *noun* 4 RAIN, drizzle
5 (*informal*) WEAKLING, drip
(*informal*), weed (*informal*), wimp
(*informal*)
6 MOISTURE, condensation, damp,
dampness, humidity, liquid,

water, wetness
▶ *verb* 7 MOISTEN, dampen, douse,
irrigate, saturate, soak, spray,
water
whack *verb* 1 STRIKE, bang, belt
(*informal*), clobber (*slang*), hit,
smack, thrash, thump, thwack,
wallop (*informal*)
▶ *noun* 2 BLOW, bang, belt
(*informal*), hit, smack, stroke,
thump, thwack, wallop (*informal*)
3 (*informal*) SHARE, bit, cut
(*informal*), part, portion, quota
4 *as in* **have a whack** ATTEMPT,
bash (*informal*), crack (*informal*),
go (*informal*), shot (*informal*), stab
(*informal*), try, turn
wharf *noun* DOCK, jetty, landing
stage, pier, quay
wheedle *verb* COAX, cajole, entice,
inveigle, persuade
wheel *noun* 1 CIRCLE, gyration,
pivot, revolution, rotation, spin,
turn
▶ *verb* 2 TURN, gyrate, pirouette,
revolve, rotate, spin, swing,
swivel, twirl, whirl
wheeze *verb* 1 GASP, cough, hiss,
rasp, whistle
▶ *noun* 2 GASP, cough, hiss, rasp,
whistle
3 (*Brit. slang*) TRICK, idea, plan,
ploy, ruse, scheme, stunt
whereabouts *noun* POSITION,
location, site, situation
wherewithal *noun* RESOURCES,
capital, funds, means, money,
supplies
whet *verb* 1 *as in* **whet someone's
appetite** STIMULATE, arouse,
awaken, enhance, excite, kindle,
quicken, rouse, stir
2 SHARPEN, hone
whiff *noun* SMELL, aroma, hint,
odor, scent, sniff
whim *noun* IMPULSE, caprice,

fancy, notion, urge

whimper *verb* 1 CRY, moan, snivel, sob, weep, whine, whinge (*informal*)

▶ *noun* 2 SOB, moan, snivel, whine

whimsical *adjective* FANCIFUL, curious, eccentric, freakish, funny, odd, playful, quaint, unusual

whine *noun* 1 CRY, moan, sob, wail, whimper

2 COMPLAINT, gripe (*informal*), grouch (*informal*), grouse, grumble, moan

whip *noun* 1 LASH, birch, cane, cat-o'-nine-tails, crop, scourge

▶ *verb* 2 LASH, beat, birch, cane, flagellate, flog, paddle (*U.S. & Canad.*), scourge, spank, strap, thrash

3 (*informal*) DASH, dart, dive, fly, rush, shoot, tear, whisk

4 BEAT, whisk

5 INCITE, agitate, drive, foment, goad, spur, stir, work up

whirl *verb* 1 SPIN, pirouette, revolve, roll, rotate, swirl, turn, twirl, twist

2 FEEL DIZZY, reel, spin

▶ *noun* 3 REVOLUTION, pirouette, roll, rotation, spin, swirl, turn, twirl, twist

4 BUSTLE, flurry, merry-go-round, round, series, succession

5 CONFUSION, daze, dither, giddiness, spin

whirlwind *noun* 1 TORNADO, waterspout

▶ *adjective* 2 RAPID, hasty, quick, short, speedy, swift

whisk *verb* 1 FLICK, brush, sweep, whip

2 BEAT, fluff up, whip

▶ *noun* 3 FLICK, brush, sweep, whip

4 BEATER

whisper *verb* 1 MURMUR, breathe

2 RUSTLE, hiss, sigh, swish

▶ *noun* 3 MURMUR, undertone

4 (*informal*) RUMOR, gossip, innuendo, insinuation, report

5 RUSTLE, hiss, sigh, swish

white *adjective* PALE, ashen, pallid, pasty, wan

white-collar *adjective* CLERICAL, nonmanual, professional, salaried

whiten *verb* PALE, blanch, bleach, fade

whitewash *noun* 1 COVER-UP, camouflage, concealment, deception

▶ *verb* 2 COVER UP, camouflage, conceal, gloss over, suppress

whittle *verb* 1 CARVE, cut, hew, pare, shape, shave, trim

2 ▷▷ **whittle down** *or* **away** REDUCE, consume, eat away, erode, wear away

whole *adjective* 1 COMPLETE, entire, full, total, unabridged, uncut, undivided

2 UNDAMAGED, in one piece, intact, unbroken, unharmed, unscathed, untouched

▶ *noun* 3 TOTALITY, ensemble, entirety

4 ▷▷ **on the whole: a** ALL IN ALL, all things considered, by and large **b** GENERALLY, as a rule, in general, in the main, mostly, predominantly

wholehearted *adjective* SINCERE, committed, dedicated, determined, devoted, enthusiastic, unstinting, zealous

wholesale *adjective* 1 EXTENSIVE, broad, comprehensive, far-reaching, indiscriminate, mass, sweeping, wide-ranging

▶ *adverb* 2 EXTENSIVELY, comprehensively, indiscriminately

wholesome *adjective* 1 BENEFICIAL, good, healthy, nourishing, nutritious, salubrious
2 MORAL, decent, edifying, improving, respectable

wholly *adverb* COMPLETELY, altogether, entirely, fully, in every respect, perfectly, thoroughly, totally, utterly

whopper *noun* 1 GIANT, colossus, crackerjack (*informal*), jumbo (*informal*), leviathan, mammoth, monster
2 BIG LIE, fabrication, falsehood, tall tale (*informal*), untruth

whopping *adjective* GIGANTIC, big, enormous, giant, great, huge, mammoth, massive

whore *noun* PROSTITUTE, call girl, ho (*slang*), streetwalker, tart (*informal*)

wicked *adjective* 1 BAD, corrupt, depraved, devilish, evil, fiendish, immoral, sinful, vicious, villainous
2 MISCHIEVOUS, impish, incorrigible, naughty, rascally, roguish

wide *adjective* 1 BROAD, expansive, extensive, far-reaching, immense, large, sweeping, vast
2 SPACIOUS, baggy, capacious, commodious, full, loose, roomy
3 EXPANDED, dilated, distended, outspread, outstretched
4 DISTANT, off course, off target, remote
▶ *adverb* 5 FULLY, completely
6 OFF TARGET, astray, off course, off the mark, out

widen *verb* BROADEN, dilate, enlarge, expand, extend, spread, stretch

widespread *adjective* COMMON, broad, extensive, far-reaching, general, pervasive, popular, universal

width *noun* BREADTH, compass, diameter, extent, girth, scope, span, thickness

wield *verb* 1 BRANDISH, employ, flourish, handle, manage, manipulate, ply, swing, use
2 *as in* **wield power** EXERT, exercise, have, maintain, possess

wife *noun* SPOUSE, better half (*humorous*), bride, mate, partner

wiggle *verb or noun* JERK, flutter, jiggle, oscillate, shake, shimmy, squirm, twitch, wag, waggle, wave, writhe

wild *adjective* 1 UNTAMED, feral, ferocious, fierce, savage, unbroken, undomesticated
2 UNCULTIVATED, free, natural
3 UNCIVILIZED, barbaric, barbarous, brutish, ferocious, fierce, primitive, savage
4 UNCONTROLLED, disorderly, riotous, rowdy, turbulent, undisciplined, unfettered, unmanageable, unrestrained, unruly, wayward
5 STORMY, blustery, choppy, raging, rough, tempestuous, violent
6 EXCITED, crazy (*informal*), enthusiastic, hysterical, raving, wired (*slang*)
▶ *noun* 7 ▷▷ **wilds** WILDERNESS, back of beyond (*informal*), desert, middle of nowhere (*informal*), wasteland

wilderness *noun* DESERT, jungle, wasteland, wilds

wiles *plural noun* TRICKERY, artfulness, chicanery, craftiness, cunning, guile, slyness

will *noun* 1 DETERMINATION, purpose, resolution, resolve, willpower
2 WISH, desire, fancy, inclination,

mind, preference, volition
3 TESTAMENT, last wishes
▶ *verb* 4 WISH, desire, prefer, see fit, want
5 BEQUEATH, confer, give, leave, pass on, transfer

willful *adjective* 1 OBSTINATE, determined, headstrong, inflexible, intransigent, obdurate, perverse, pig-headed, stubborn, uncompromising
2 INTENTIONAL, conscious, deliberate, intended, purposeful, voluntary

willing *adjective* READY, agreeable, amenable, compliant, consenting, game (*informal*), inclined, prepared

willingly *adverb* READILY, by choice, cheerfully, eagerly, freely, gladly, happily, of one's own accord, voluntarily

willingness *noun* INCLINATION, agreement, consent, volition, will, wish

willowy *adjective* SLENDER, graceful, lithe, slim, supple, svelte, sylphlike

willpower *noun* SELF-CONTROL, determination, drive, grit, resolution, resolve, self-discipline, single-mindedness

wilt *verb* 1 DROOP, sag, shrivel, wither
2 WEAKEN, fade, flag, languish, wane

wily *adjective* CUNNING, artful, astute, crafty, guileful, sharp, shrewd, sly, tricky

wimp *noun* (*informal*) WEAKLING, coward, drip (*informal*), loser (*slang*), mouse, sissy, softy *or* softie

wimpy *adjective* (*informal*) FEEBLE, effete, ineffectual, namby-pamby, soft, spineless, timorous, weak, weedy (*informal*)

win *verb* 1 TRIUMPH, come first, conquer, overcome, prevail, succeed, sweep the board
2 GAIN, achieve, acquire, attain, earn, get, land, obtain, procure, secure
▶ *noun* 3 VICTORY, conquest, success, triumph

wince *verb* 1 FLINCH, blench, cower, cringe, draw back, quail, recoil, shrink, start
▶ *noun* 2 FLINCH, cringe, start

wind¹ *noun* 1 AIR, blast, breeze, draft, gust, zephyr
2 BREATH, puff, respiration
3 FLATULENCE, gas
4 TALK, babble, blather, bluster, boasting, hot air, humbug
5 *as in* **get wind of** HINT, inkling, notice, report, rumor, suggestion, warning, whisper

wind² *verb* 1 COIL, curl, encircle, loop, reel, roll, spiral, twist
2 MEANDER, bend, curve, ramble, snake, turn, twist, zigzag

windfall *noun* GODSEND, bonanza, find, jackpot, manna from heaven

wind up *verb* 1 END, close, conclude, finalize, finish, settle, terminate, wrap up
2 END UP, be left, finish up
3 (*informal*) EXCITE, put on edge, work up

windy *adjective* BREEZY, blowy, blustery, gusty, squally, stormy, wild, windswept

wing *noun* 1 FACTION, arm, branch, group, section
▶ *verb* 2 FLY, glide, soar
3 WOUND, clip, hit

wink *verb* 1 BLINK, bat, flutter
2 TWINKLE, flash, gleam, glimmer, sparkle
▶ *noun* 3 BLINK, flutter

winner *noun* VICTOR, champ (*informal*), champion, conqueror, master

winning *adjective* 1 VICTORIOUS, conquering, successful, triumphant
2 CHARMING, alluring, attractive, cute, disarming, enchanting, endearing, engaging, likable *or* likeable, pleasing

winnings *plural noun* SPOILS, gains, prize, proceeds, profits, takings

winnow *verb* SEPARATE, divide, select, sift, sort out

win over *verb* CONVINCE, bring *or* talk round, convert, influence, persuade, prevail upon, sway

wintry *adjective* COLD, chilly, freezing, frosty, frozen, icy, snowy

wipe *verb* 1 CLEAN, brush, mop, rub, sponge, swab
2 ERASE, remove
▶ *noun* 3 RUB, brush

wipe out *verb* DESTROY, annihilate, eradicate, erase, expunge, exterminate, massacre, obliterate

wiry *adjective* LEAN, sinewy, strong, tough

wisdom *noun* UNDERSTANDING, discernment, enlightenment, erudition, insight, intelligence, judgment, knowledge, learning, sense

wise *adjective* SENSIBLE, clever, discerning, enlightened, erudite, intelligent, judicious, perceptive, prudent, sage

wisecrack *noun* (*informal*) 1 JOKE, jest, jibe, quip, witticism
▶ *verb* 2 JOKE, jest, jibe, quip

wish *verb* 1 WANT, aspire, crave, desire, hanker, hope, long, yearn
▶ *noun* 2 DESIRE, aspiration, hope, intention, urge, want, whim, will

wispy *adjective* THIN, attenuated, delicate, fine, flimsy, fragile, frail

wistful *adjective* MELANCHOLY, contemplative, dreamy, longing, meditative, pensive, reflective, thoughtful

wit *noun* 1 HUMOR, badinage, banter, drollery, jocularity, raillery, repartee, wordplay
2 HUMORIST, card (*informal*), comedian, joker, wag
3 CLEVERNESS, acumen, brains, common sense, ingenuity, intellect, sense, wisdom

witch *noun* ENCHANTRESS, crone, hag, magician, sorceress

witchcraft *noun* MAGIC, enchantment, necromancy, occultism, sorcery, the black art, voodoo, wizardry

withdraw *verb* REMOVE, draw back, extract, pull out, take away, take off

withdrawal *noun* REMOVAL, extraction

withdrawn *adjective* UNCOMMUNICATIVE, distant, introverted, reserved, retiring, shy, taciturn, unforthcoming

wither *verb* WILT, decay, decline, disintegrate, fade, perish, shrivel, waste

withering *adjective* SCORNFUL, devastating, humiliating, hurtful, mortifying, snubbing

withhold *verb* KEEP BACK, conceal, hide, hold back, refuse, reserve, retain, suppress

withstand *verb* RESIST, bear, cope with, endure, hold off, oppose, stand up to, suffer, tolerate

witless *adjective* FOOLISH, halfwitted, idiotic, inane, moronic, senseless, silly, stupid

witness *noun* 1 OBSERVER, beholder, bystander, eyewitness, looker-on, onlooker, spectator, viewer, watcher
2 TESTIFIER, corroborator
▶ *verb* 3 SEE, note, notice, observe,

perceive, view, watch
4 SIGN, countersign, endorse

wits plural noun INTELLIGENCE,
acumen, brains (informal),
cleverness, comprehension,
faculties, ingenuity, reason,
sense, understanding

witticism noun QUIP, bon mot,
one-liner (slang), pun, riposte

witty adjective HUMOROUS,
amusing, clever, droll, funny,
piquant, sparkling, waggish,
whimsical

wizard noun MAGICIAN, conjurer,
magus, necromancer, occultist,
shaman, sorcerer, warlock, witch

wizardry noun MAGIC, sorcery,
voodoo, witchcraft

wizened adjective WRINKLED, dried
up, gnarled, lined, shriveled,
shrunken, withered

wobble verb 1 SHAKE, rock, sway,
teeter, totter, tremble
▶ noun 2 UNSTEADINESS, shake,
tremble, tremor

wobbly adjective UNSTEADY,
rickety, shaky, teetering,
tottering, uneven

woe noun GRIEF, agony, anguish,
distress, gloom, misery,
sadness, sorrow, unhappiness,
wretchedness

woeful adjective 1 SAD, deplorable,
dismal, distressing, grievous,
lamentable, miserable, pathetic,
tragic, wretched
2 PITIFUL, abysmal, appalling,
bad, deplorable, dreadful, feeble,
pathetic, poor, sorry

woman noun LADY, female, girl

womanizer noun PHILANDERER,
Casanova, Don Juan, lady-killer
(informal), lecher, seducer

womanly adjective FEMININE,
female, ladylike, matronly,
motherly, tender, warm

wonder verb 1 THINK, conjecture,
meditate, ponder, puzzle, query,
question, speculate
2 BE AMAZED, be astonished, gape,
marvel, stare
▶ noun 3 PHENOMENON, curiosity,
marvel, miracle, prodigy, rarity,
sight, spectacle
4 AMAZEMENT, admiration,
astonishment, awe,
bewilderment, fascination,
surprise, wonderment

wonderful adjective 1 EXCELLENT,
brilliant, fabulous (informal),
fantastic (informal), great (informal),
magnificent, marvelous,
outstanding, superb, terrific
(informal), tremendous
2 REMARKABLE, amazing,
astonishing, extraordinary,
incredible, miraculous,
phenomenal, staggering,
startling, unheard-of

woo verb COURT, cultivate, pursue

wood noun 1 TIMBER
2 WOODLAND, coppice, copse,
forest, grove, thicket

wooded adjective TREE-COVERED,
forested, sylvan (poetic), timbered,
tree-clad

wooden adjective 1 WOODY,
ligneous, timber
2 EXPRESSIONLESS, deadpan,
lifeless, unresponsive

wool noun FLEECE, hair, yarn

woolly adjective 1 FLEECY, hairy,
shaggy, woollen
2 VAGUE, confused, hazy, ill-
defined, indefinite, indistinct,
muddled, unclear

word noun 1 TERM, expression,
name
2 CHAT, confab (informal),
consultation, discussion, talk,
tête-à-tête
3 REMARK, comment, utterance

4 MESSAGE, communiqué, dispatch, information, intelligence, news, notice, report
5 PROMISE, assurance, guarantee, oath, pledge, vow
6 COMMAND, bidding, decree, mandate, order
▶ verb 7 EXPRESS, couch, phrase, put, say, state, utter

wording noun PHRASEOLOGY, language, phrasing, terminology, words

wordy adjective LONG-WINDED, diffuse, prolix, rambling, verbose, windy

work noun 1 EFFORT, drudgery, elbow grease (facetious), exertion, industry, labor, sweat, toil
2 EMPLOYMENT, business, duty, job, livelihood, occupation, profession, trade
3 TASK, assignment, chore, commission, duty, job, stint, undertaking
4 CREATION, achievement, composition, handiwork, opus, piece, production
▶ verb 5 LABOR, drudge, exert oneself, peg away, slave, slog (away), sweat, toil
6 BE EMPLOYED, be in work
7 OPERATE, control, drive, handle, manage, manipulate, move, use
8 FUNCTION, go, operate, run
9 CULTIVATE, dig, farm, till
10 MANIPULATE, fashion, form, knead, mold, shape

workable adjective VIABLE, doable, feasible, possible, practicable, practical

worker noun EMPLOYEE, artisan, craftsman, hand, laborer, tradesman, workman

working adjective 1 EMPLOYED, active, in work
2 FUNCTIONING, going, operative, running

workman noun LABORER, artisan, craftsman, employee, hand, journeyman, mechanic, operative, tradesman, worker

workmanship noun SKILL, artistry, craftsmanship, expertise, handiwork, technique

work out verb 1 SOLVE, calculate, figure out, find out
2 HAPPEN, develop, evolve, result, turn out
3 EXERCISE, practice, train, warm up

works plural noun 1 FACTORY, mill, plant, workshop
2 WRITINGS, canon, oeuvre, output
3 MECHANISM, action, machinery, movement, parts, workings

workshop noun STUDIO, factory, mill, plant, workroom

world noun 1 EARTH, globe
2 MANKIND, everybody, everyone, humanity, humankind, man, the public
3 SPHERE, area, domain, environment, field, realm

worldly adjective 1 EARTHLY, physical, profane, secular, temporal, terrestrial
2 MATERIALISTIC, grasping, greedy, selfish
3 WORLDLY-WISE, blasé, cosmopolitan, experienced, knowing, sophisticated, urbane

worldwide adjective GLOBAL, general, international, omnipresent, pandemic, ubiquitous, universal

worn adjective RAGGED, frayed, shabby, tattered, tatty, the worse for wear, threadbare

worn-out adjective 1 RUN-DOWN, on its last legs, ragged, shabby, threadbare, used-up, useless, worn

2 EXHAUSTED, all in (*slang*), dead-tired, done in (*informal*), fatigued, ready to drop, fit to drop, spent, tired out, weary

worried *adjective* ANXIOUS, afraid, apprehensive, concerned, fearful, frightened, nervous, perturbed, tense, troubled, uneasy, wired (*slang*)

worry *verb* 1 BE ANXIOUS, agonize, brood, fret
2 TROUBLE, annoy, bother, disturb, perturb, pester, unsettle, upset, vex
▶ *noun* 3 ANXIETY, apprehension, concern, fear, misgiving, trepidation, trouble, unease
4 PROBLEM, bother, care, hassle (*informal*), trouble

worsen *verb* 1 AGGRAVATE, damage, exacerbate
2 DETERIORATE, decay, decline, degenerate, get worse, go downhill (*informal*), sink

worship *verb* 1 PRAISE, adore, exalt, glorify, honor, pray to, revere, venerate
2 LOVE, adore, idolize, put on a pedestal
▶ *noun* 3 PRAISE, adoration, adulation, devotion, glory, honor, kudos, regard, respect, reverence

worth *noun* 1 VALUE, cost, price, rate, valuation
2 EXCELLENCE, goodness, importance, merit, quality, usefulness, value, worthiness

worthless *adjective* 1 USELESS, ineffectual, rubbishy, unimportant, valueless
2 GOOD-FOR-NOTHING, contemptible, despicable, lousy (*slang*), scuzzy (*slang*), vile

worthwhile *adjective* USEFUL, beneficial, constructive, expedient, helpful, productive, profitable, valuable

worthy *adjective* PRAISEWORTHY, admirable, creditable, deserving, laudable, meritorious, valuable, virtuous, worthwhile

would-be *adjective* BUDDING, self-appointed, self-styled, unfulfilled, wannabe (*informal*)

wound *noun* 1 INJURY, cut, gash, hurt, laceration, lesion, trauma (*Pathology*)
2 INSULT, offense, slight
▶ *verb* 3 INJURE, cut, gash, hurt, lacerate, pierce, wing
4 OFFEND, annoy, cut (someone) to the quick, hurt, mortify, sting

wrangle *verb* 1 ARGUE, bicker, contend, disagree, dispute, fight, quarrel, row, squabble
▶ *noun* 2 ARGUMENT, altercation, bickering, dispute, quarrel, row, squabble, tiff

wrap *verb* 1 COVER, bind, bundle up, encase, enclose, enfold, pack, package, shroud, swathe
▶ *noun* 2 CLOAK, cape, mantle, shawl, stole

wrapper *noun* COVER, case, envelope, jacket, packaging, wrapping

wrap up *verb* 1 GIFTWRAP, bundle up, pack, package
2 (*informal*) END, conclude, finish off, polish off, round off, terminate, wind up

wrath *noun* ANGER, displeasure, fury, indignation, ire, rage, resentment, temper

wreath *noun* GARLAND, band, chaplet, crown, festoon, ring

wreck *verb* 1 DESTROY, break, demolish, devastate, ruin, shatter, smash, spoil
▶ *noun* 2 SHIPWRECK, hulk

wreckage *noun* REMAINS, debris, fragments, pieces, rubble, ruin

wrench verb 1 TWIST, force, jerk, pull, rip, tear, tug, yank
2 SPRAIN, rick, strain
▶ noun 3 TWIST, jerk, pull, rip, tug, yank
4 SPRAIN, strain, twist
5 BLOW, pang, shock, upheaval
6 SPANNER, adjustable spanner

wrest verb SEIZE, extract, force, take, win, wrench

wrestle verb FIGHT, battle, combat, grapple, scuffle, struggle, tussle

wretch noun SCOUNDREL, good-for-nothing, miscreant, rascal, rogue, swine, worm

wretched adjective 1 UNHAPPY, dejected, depressed, disconsolate, downcast, forlorn, hapless, miserable, woebegone
2 WORTHLESS, inferior, miserable, paltry, pathetic, poor, sorry

wriggle verb 1 TWIST, jerk, jiggle, squirm, turn, waggle, wiggle, writhe
2 CRAWL, slink, snake, worm, zigzag
3 as in **wriggle out of** MANEUVER, dodge, extricate oneself
▶ verb 4 TWIST, jerk, jiggle, squirm, turn, waggle, wiggle

wring verb TWIST, extract, force, screw, squeeze

wrinkle¹ noun 1 CREASE, corrugation, crinkle, crow's-foot, crumple, fold, furrow, line
▶ verb 2 CREASE, corrugate, crumple, fold, furrow, gather, pucker, rumple

writ noun SUMMONS, court order, decree, document

write verb RECORD, draft, draw up, inscribe, jot down, pen, scribble, set down

writer noun AUTHOR, hack, novelist, penpusher, scribbler, scribe, wordsmith

writhe verb SQUIRM, jerk, struggle, thrash, thresh, toss, twist, wiggle, wriggle

writing noun 1 SCRIPT, calligraphy, hand, handwriting, penmanship, scrawl, scribble
2 DOCUMENT, book, composition, opus, publication, work

wrong adjective 1 INCORRECT, erroneous, fallacious, false, inaccurate, mistaken, untrue, wide of the mark
2 BAD, criminal, dishonest, evil, illegal, immoral, sinful, unjust, unlawful, wicked, wrongful
3 INAPPROPRIATE, incongruous, incorrect, unacceptable, unbecoming, undesirable, unseemly, unsuitable
4 DEFECTIVE, amiss, askew, awry, faulty
▶ adverb 5 INCORRECTLY, badly, erroneously, inaccurately, mistakenly, wrongly
6 AMISS, askew, astray, awry
▶ noun 7 OFFENSE, crime, error, injury, injustice, misdeed, sin, transgression, wickedness
▶ verb 8 MISTREAT, abuse, cheat, dishonor, harm, hurt, malign, oppress, take advantage of

wrongdoer noun OFFENDER, criminal, culprit, delinquent, evildoer, lawbreaker, miscreant, perp (informal), sinner, villain

wrongful adjective IMPROPER, criminal, evil, illegal, illegitimate, immoral, unethical, unjust, unlawful, wicked

wry adjective 1 IRONIC, droll, dry, mocking, sarcastic, sardonic
2 CONTORTED, crooked, twisted, uneven

Xmas noun CHRISTMAS, festive season, Noel, Yule, Yuletide
X-rated adjective PORNOGRAPHIC, adult, dirty, graphic, hardcore (slang), obscene, scuzzy (slang)
X rays plural noun RÖNTGEN RAYS (old name)

...k verb or noun PULL, hitch, jerk, ...tch, tug, wrench
...dstick noun STANDARD, ...chmark, criterion, gauge, ...asure, par, touchstone
...n noun 1 THREAD, fiber

2 (old-fashioned, informal) STORY, anecdote, cock and bull story (informal), fable, tale, tall tale (informal)
yawning adjective GAPING, cavernous, vast, wide
yearly adjective 1 ANNUAL
▶ adverb 2 ANNUALLY, every year, once a year, per annum
yearn verb LONG, ache, covet, crave, desire, hanker, hunger, itch
yell verb 1 SCREAM, bawl, holler (informal), howl, screech, shout, shriek, squeal
▶ noun 2 SCREAM, cry, howl, screech, shriek, whoop
yell at verb (informal) CRITICIZE, censure, rebuke, scold, tear into (informal)
yelp verb CRY, yap, yowl
yen noun LONGING, ache, craving, desire, hankering, hunger, itch, passion, thirst, yearning
yes man noun SYCOPHANT, bootlicker (informal), brown-noser (slang), crawler (slang), minion, timeserver, toady
yet conjunction 1 NEVERTHELESS, however, notwithstanding, still
▶ adverb 2 SO FAR, as yet, thus far, until now, up to now
3 STILL, besides, in addition, into the bargain, to boot
4 NOW, just now, right now, so soon
yield verb 1 PRODUCE, bear, bring forth, earn, generate, give, net, provide, return, supply
2 SURRENDER, bow, capitulate, give in, relinquish, resign, submit, succumb
▶ noun 3 PROFIT, crop, earnings, harvest, income, output, produce, return, revenue, takings
yielding adjective 1 SUBMISSIVE, accommodating, acquiescent, biddable, compliant, docile,

flexible, obedient, pliant
2 SOFT, elastic, pliable, spongy,
springy, supple, unresisting
yoke *verb* BURDEN, encumber,
land, load, saddle
yokel *noun* PEASANT, (country)
bumpkin, countryman, hick
(*informal, chiefly U.S. & Canad.*),
hillbilly, redneck (*slang*), rustic
young *adjective* 1 IMMATURE,
adolescent, callow, green, infant,
junior, juvenile, little, youthful
2 NEW, early, fledgling, recent,
undeveloped
▶ *plural noun* 3 OFFSPRING, babies,
brood, family, issue, litter,
progeny
youngster *noun* YOUTH, boy, girl,
juvenile, kid (*informal*), lad, lass,
teenager
youth *noun* 1 IMMATURITY,
adolescence, boyhood, girlhood,
salad days
2 BOY, adolescent, kid (*informal*),
lad, stripling, teenager, young
man, youngster
youthful *adjective* YOUNG, boyish,
childish, fresh-faced, girlish,
immature, inexperienced,
juvenile, rosy-cheeked

Z

zany *adjective* COMICAL, clownish,
crazy, eccentric, goofy (*informal*),
madcap, wacky (*slang*)
zeal *noun* ENTHUSIASM, ardor,
eagerness, fanaticism, fervor, gusto,
keenness, passion, spirit, verve, zest
zealot *noun* FANATIC, bigot,
enthusiast, extremist,
militant
zealous *adjective* ENTHUSIASTIC,
ardent, devoted, eager, fanatical,
fervent, impassioned, keen,
passionate
zenith *noun* HEIGHT, acme, apex,
apogee, climax, crest, high point,
peak, pinnacle, summit, top
zero *noun* 1 NOTHING, nada
(*informal*), nil, nought, zilch (*informal*)
2 BOTTOM, nadir, rock bottom
zest *noun* 1 ENJOYMENT, appetite,
gusto, keenness, relish, zeal
2 FLAVOR, charm, interest,
piquancy, pungency, relish, spi
tang, taste
zip *noun* 1 (*informal*) ENERGY, driv
gusto, liveliness, verve, vigor, ze
▶ *verb* 2 SPEED, flash, fly, shoot,
whizz (*informal*), zoom
zone *noun* AREA, belt, district,
region, section, sector, sphere
zoom *verb* SPEED, dash, flash, f
hurtle, pelt, rush, shoot, whizz
(*informal*)